# AP® Psychology Science Practices

CA = Cultural Awareness buckets
RM Tip = Research buckets
DI = Data buckets and Data Interpretation features
DA = Developing Arguments feature

| | Science Practice* | Selected examples of coverage in *Myers' Psychology for the AP® Course, 4e*** |
|---|---|---|
| 1. Concept Application | 1A. Apply psychological perspectives, theories, concepts, and research findings to a scenario. | Check Your Understanding, AP® Practice Multiple Choice Questions throughout the text |
| | 1B. Explain how cultural norms, expectations, and circumstances, as well as cognitive biases apply to behavior and mental processes. | CA M3.2b, CA M4.1, RM Tip M5.3 |
| 2. Research Methods & Design | 2A. Determine the type of research design(s) used in a given study. | RM Tip M1.3b, RM Tip M2.8a, RM Tip M4.1 |
| | 2B. Evaluate the appropriate use of research design elements in experimental methodology. | RM Tip M1.3a, RM Tip M3.2a, RM Tip M5.1a |
| | 2C. Evaluate the appropriate use of research design elements in non-experimental methodologies. | RM Tip M1.4b, RM Tip M3.6b, RM Tip M5.1a |
| | 2D. Evaluate whether a psychological research scenario followed appropriate ethical procedures. | RM Tip 3.2a, RM Tip M4.7c, RM Tip M5.1b |
| 3. Data Interpretation | 3A. Identify psychology-related concepts in descriptions or representations of data. | RM Tip M2.4, DI M3.2b, DI M4.8b |
| | 3B. Calculate and interpret measures of central tendency, variation, and percentile rank in a given data set. | DI M2.8b, DI M4.6a, DI M5.4a |
| | 3C. Interpret quantitative or qualitative inferential data from a given table, graph, chart, figure, or diagram. | DI M2.8a, DI M3.3a, DI M4.6c |
| 4. Argumentation | 4A. Propose a defensible claim. | DA M2.2b, DA M3.7b, DA M4.8a |
| | 4B. Provide reasoning that is grounded in scientifically derived evidence to support, refute, or modify an established or provided claim, policy, or norm. | DA M2.7, DA M3.1, DA M4.7c |

*Following is the wording of the Science Practices at the time this book was printed.

**Note that all examples of coverage of the Science Practices will appear in the Teacher's Edition.

Please check the BFW AP® Updates page at bfwpub.com/ap-updates to get the latest course updates.

# Myers' Psychology
# for the AP® Course

**FOURTH EDITION**

## David G. Myers
Hope College
Holland, Michigan

## C. Nathan DeWall
University of Kentucky
Lexington, Kentucky

## Elizabeth Yost Hammer
Xavier University of Louisiana
New Orleans, Louisiana

bedford, freeman & worth
publishers
New York | Boston

*High School Program Director:* Yolanda Cossio

*Program Managers:* Heidi Bamatter, Anna Olcott

*Development Editors:* Christine Brune, Danielle Slevens, Karen Misler

*Editorial Assistant:* Calyn Clare Liss

*Director of High School Marketing:* Janie Pierce-Bratcher

*Assistant Marketing Manager:* Tiffani Tang

*Marketing Assistant:* Brianna DiGeronimo

*Executive Development Editor for High School Media:* Lisa Samols

*Senior Media Editor:* Justin Perry

*Associate Media Editor:* Michael Emig

*Senior Director, Content Management Enhancement:* Tracey Kuehn

*Executive Managing Editor:* Michael Granger

*Manager, Publishing Services:* Ryan Sullivan

*Senior Lead Content Project Manager:* Won McIntosh

*Senior Workflow Project Manager:* Paul Rohloff

*Production Supervisor:* Robert Cherry

*Director of Design, Content Management:* Diana Blume

*Senior Design Services Manager:* Natasha A. S. Wolfe

*Interior Designer:* Dirk Kaufman

*Senior Cover Design Manager:* John Callahan

*Art Manager:* Matthew McAdams

*Illustrations:* Evelyn Pence

*Senior Director, Rights and Permissions:* Hilary Newman

*Executive Permissions Editor:* Robin Fadool

*Photo Researcher:* Cheryl DuBois, Lumina Datamatics, Inc.

*Senior Director of Digital Production:* Keri deManigold

*Executive Media Project Manager:* Eve Conte

*Composition:* Lumina Datamatics, Inc.

*Printing and Binding:* Transcontinental

ISBN 978-1-319-28116-8 (Student Edition)
ISBN 978-1-319-49018-8 (Review Copy)

Library of Congress Control Number: 2023940132

Printed in Canada

2   3   4   5   6        29   28   27   26   25   24

David Myers' royalties from the sale of this book are assigned to the David and Carol Myers Foundation, which exists to receive and distribute funds to other charitable organizations.

Bedford, Freeman & Worth Publishers
120 Broadway, New York, NY 10271
highschool.bfwpub.com/apmyers4e

# Dedication

To the many past AP® Psych students who have, with such kindness, shared their feedback and encouragement.

DM

To Steve James: Wonderful high school coach, counselor, and role model.

ND

To every AP® Psychology teacher who has crossed my path and enriched my life.

EYH

# About the Authors

Hope College Public Relations

**David Myers** received his B.A. in chemistry from Whitworth University, and his psychology Ph.D. from the University of Iowa. He has spent his career at Michigan's Hope College, where he has taught dozens of introductory psychology sections. Hope College students have invited him to be their commencement speaker and voted him "outstanding professor." His research and writings have been recognized by the Gordon Allport Intergroup Relations Prize, an Honored Scientist award from the Federation of Associations in Behavioral & Brain Sciences, an Award for Distinguished Service on Behalf of Social-Personality Psychology, a Presidential Citation from APA Division 2, election as an American Association for the Advancement of Science Fellow, and three honorary doctorates.

With support from National Science Foundation grants, David's scientific articles have appeared in three dozen scientific periodicals, including *Science, American Scientist, Psychological Science*, and *American Psychologist*. In addition to his scholarly and textbook writing, he digests psychological science for the general public. His writings have appeared in four dozen magazines, from *Today's Education* to *Scientific American*. He also has authored five general-audience books, including *How Do We Know Ourselves: Curiosities and Marvels of the Human Mind* (2022). And he blogs about psychology and life at TalkPsych.com.

David has chaired his city's Human Relations Commission, helped found a thriving assistance center for families in poverty, and spoken to hundreds of college, community, and professional groups worldwide. He has also spoken to many high school groups, including AP® Psychology conferences, an AP® Psychology reading, Teachers of Psychology in Secondary Schools, the National Council for Social Studies Psychology Community, and the 2017 APA Summit on High School Psychology Education. David has twice offered AP® Psychology workshops in China, and he served on the APA's working group that created the 2010 revision of the *National Standards for High School Psychology Curricula.*

Drawing on his experience, David has written articles and a book (*A Quiet World*) about hearing loss, and he is advocating a transformation in American assistive listening technology (see HearingLoop.org). For his leadership, he has received awards from the American Academy of Audiology, the hearing industry, and the Hearing Loss Association of America.

David and Carol Myers met and married while undergraduates, and have raised sons Peter and Andrew, and a daughter, Laura. They have one grandchild, Allie (seen on page 351).

**Nathan DeWall** is professor of psychology at the University of Kentucky. He received his bachelor's degree from St. Olaf College, a master's degree in social science from the University of Chicago, and a master's degree and Ph.D. in social psychology from Florida State University. Nathan received the College of Arts and Sciences Outstanding Teaching Award, which recognizes excellence in undergraduate and graduate teaching. The Association for Psychological Science identified Nathan as a "Rising Star" early in his career for "making significant contributions to the field of psychological science." He is in the top 1 percent of all cited scientists in psychology and psychiatry on the Institute for Scientific Information list, according to the Web of Science.

Nathan researches close relationships, self-control, and aggression. With funding from the National Institutes of Health, the National Science Foundation, and the John Templeton Foundation he has published more than 220 scientific articles and chapters. His research awards include the SAGE Young Scholars Award from the Foundation for Personality and Social Psychology, the Young Investigator Award from the International Society for Research on Aggression, and the Early Career Award from the International Society for Self and Identity. His research has been covered by numerous media outlets, including *Good Morning America*, *The Wall Street Journal*, *Newsweek*, *The Atlantic Monthly*, *The New York Times*, *The Los Angeles Times*, *Harvard Business Review*, *USA Today*, National Public Radio, the BBC, and *The Guardian*. He has lectured nationally and internationally, including in Hong Kong, China, the Netherlands, England, Greece, Hungary, Sweden, Australia, and France.

Nathan is happily married to Alice DeWall and is the proud father of Beverly "Bevy" and Ellis. As an ultramarathon runner, he completed numerous races, including the Badwater 135 in 2017 (dubbed "the world's toughest foot race"). In his spare time now, he reads, writes novels, takes care of his aquariums, watches sports, and plays guitar and sings in local rock bands.

**Elizabeth (Liz) Yost Hammer** is the director of the Center for the Advancement of Teaching and Faculty Development and a Kellogg professor in teaching at Xavier University of Louisiana. Her work includes organizing pedagogical workshops and faculty development initiatives for instructors, both new and seasoned, though her favorite part of her job is trying out teaching innovations in her own classroom. She is a recipient of the College of Arts & Sciences Excellence in Teaching Award, and received an XU Girls Rock! Award from Xavier students. She is also the 2021 recipient of the American Psychological Foundation Charles L. Brewer Distinguished Teaching of Psychology Award.

Liz received her Ph.D. in social psychology from Tulane University. Her research interests focus on the scholarship of teaching and learning, and she has contributed to books intended to enhance teaching preparation, including *The Oxford Handbook of Psychology Education* and *Effective College and University Teaching: Strategies and Tactics for the New Professoriate*. In addition, Liz has published in *Teaching of Psychology*, for which she has served as consulting editor, and in a special teaching-related issue of the *Journal of Social and Clinical Psychology*. She is also a co-author (along with Weiten and Dunn) of the textbook *Psychology Applied to Modern Life* and is the author of the *Teacher's Edition* for Myers' Psychology for the AP® Course.

In 2005, Liz was named a Fellow of the American Psychological Association. She is a past president of Psi Chi (the international honor society in psychology) and a past treasurer of the Society for the Teaching of Psychology. She was a member of the Introductory Psychology Initiative, focusing on teacher training. AP® Psychology has had an influential role in Liz's professional development. She began attending the AP® Psychology reading in 1998, where she developed a national network of dedicated high school teachers who have informed both her own teaching and her faculty development work. Liz served as Chief Reader for AP® Psychology from 2012 to 2016 and was a co-strand leader (along with Randy Ernst) at the 2017 APA Summit on High School Psychology Education.

Liz is married to Elliott Hammer, also a social psychologist and the John LaFarge Professor in Social Justice. He is also involved in the AP® Psychology reading. They and their two rescue dogs work and play, and self-isolate when necessary, in New Orleans, Louisiana.

# Content Advisory & Resources Team

Creating this book is a team sport. Like so many human achievements, it is the product of a collective intelligence. For this edition, we were fortunate to collaborate closely with an expert Content Advisory and Resources Team throughout the development process. The Content Advisory and Resources Team understands the needs of the AP® Psychology teacher and student. They provided sage guidance on key content, organizational, and pedagogical issues and ensured that the assessments provide the practice students need for the AP® exam. We extend our gratitude and admiration to each of these talented educators for their enduring contributions to the teaching of psychology.

### TINA ATHANASOPOULOS
#### Prospect High School, IL
Tina has taught AP® Psychology since 1997 and has implemented the AP® Psychology program for District 214 in Illinois. She has been involved with the AP® Psychology reading since 2000 as a reader, table leader, exam leader, and assistant chief reader. Tina has also been a College Board Consultant since 2001, and has presented at College Board workshops across the country. She was on the Test Development Committee for the AP® Psychology Exam from 2005 through 2009, was awarded the Mary Margaret Moffett Memorial Teaching Award in 2015, and was awarded a Presidential Citation for her leadership as Chair of the APA National Standards for High School Psychology Curricula Working Group and for her dedication to teaching psychology as a science in 2022.

### WYNDOLYN LUDWIKOWSKI
#### Spring Hill College, AL
Wyndi has participated in the AP® Psychology reading since 2014, serving as a reader and as a table leader. A counseling psychologist with a certificate in quantitative psychology, she regularly teaches introductory psychology, research methods, psychological statistics, abnormal psychology, and measurement. Wyndi has also served as an item writer for the AP® Psychology Exam. In addition to working at Spring Hill College, she conducts psychological assessments in Mobile, Alabama.

### JENNIFER OGOZALEK
#### Sachem North High School, NY
Jennifer has taught AP® Psychology for 22 years at Sachem North High School, one of the largest New York State school districts. She has served as an AP® Psychology Exam reader for the past three years and in 2005. Jennifer has conducted new teacher AP® Psychology presentations for Long Island Council for the Social Studies, which serves all Long Island social studies teachers. She has also mentored new teachers in the teaching of AP® Psychology.

### SEJAL SCHULLO
#### Glenbrook South High School, IL
Sejal is a co-chair of the National Council for the Social Studies Psychology Community and has helped to plan many national conferences and provide psychology teachers with quality professional development. Sejal is also a member of APA Teachers of Psychology in Secondary Schools, has helped host webinars, and worked on the Skills strand at the APA Summit for High School Psychology in 2017. She has hosted CHITOPSS, a regional conference in the Chicagoland area, and attended both the Clark University and Oregon State University psychology teachers workshops. Sejal has been teaching for 26 years and currently teaches AP® Psychology and Introduction to Psychology courses.

### KRISTIN WHITLOCK
#### Davis High School, UT
Kristin has been teaching AP® Psychology since 1992 and has taught at Davis High School since 2014. She has been a part of the annual AP® Psychology reading since 2001 and has served as the assistant chief reader, exam leader, question leader, table leader, and reader. Kristin is also a College Board Consultant and served as the College Board Advisor to the Test Development Committee. She served on the Steering Committee of the APA's Introductory Psychology Initiative and as co-leader for the Student Learning Outcomes and Assessment working group. Kristin co-authored Barron's *AP® Q&A Psychology 600 Questions*.

### JESSICA FLITTER
#### West Bend East High School, WI

Jessica teaches AP® Psychology at West Bend East High School in West Bend, Wisconsin. She has taught the course since 2004 and has participated in the AP® Reading since 2014 as a reader, table leader, and question leader. She has also served as an item writer for the AP® Psychology Exam. Jessica is a College Board Consultant and has presented nationally. She has also co-authored REA AP® Psychology All Access and writes for the Books for Psychology Class blog.

### SHAWN STARCHER
#### La Plata High School, MD

Shawn has taught for Charles County Public Schools since 1998 and has been teaching AP® Psychology since 2007. She has participated in the AP® Psychology Reading since 2013, serving as a reader and as a table leader. Shawn has been a frequent participant in the annual Mid-Atlantic Teaching of Psychology Conference and created psychology curricula for both AP® Psychology and Introduction to Psychology courses for Charles County Public Schools. She also serves as a teaching mentor and student-teaching intern coordinator for La Plata High School. Shawn was previously awarded a Maryland Governor's Citation in Mathematics and Science, and more recently, was the SMECO STEM Teacher of the Year for Charles County in 2021.

### REBECCA MILLER
#### Lincoln Land Community College, IL

Rebecca has participated in the AP® Psychology reading since 2006, serving as a reader, table leader, question leader, and currently as the assistant chief reader. As a professor at Lincoln Land Community College, she regularly teaches multiple sections of Introduction to Psychology each semester, along with Personality and Human Adjustment, Human Development, and Educational Psychology courses. She also mentors LLCC adjunct faculty teaching Introduction to Psychology and served in other capacities, which earned her the 2023 Faculty Distinguished Service award.

*For this edition, we would like to thank the following students for lending their voices and expertise to creating the answer videos for the Research Methods & Design and Data Interpretation boxes in the book: Chandler McRae Whitlock (University of Utah), Sydney Morris (Palo Alto University), and Alia Wells (Xavier University of Louisiana, '23).*

# In Appreciation

Aided by input from thousands of teachers and students over the years, this has become a better, more effective, more accurate book than three authors alone (these authors at least) could write. Our indebtedness continues to the innumerable researchers who have been so willing to share their time and talent to help us accurately report their research, and to the hundreds of educators who have taken the time to offer feedback.

Our gratitude extends to the colleagues who contributed criticism, corrections, and creative ideas related to the content, pedagogy, and format of the thirteenth edition of our college text *Psychology*, and to prior editions of *Myers' Psychology for the AP® Course.* For their expertise and encouragement, and the gift of their time to the teaching of psychology, we thank the reviewers and consultants listed here.

**Michael Bailey**
*Northwestern University*

**Charles Blair-Broeker**
*Hawkeye Community College*

**Laura Brandt**
*Collège du Léman*

**Andrea Brown**
*College of Southern Nevada*

**Christia Brown**
*University of Kentucky*

**Michelle Butler**
*United States Air Force Academy*

**Ann Coker**
*University of Kentucky*

**Gary Creasey**
*Old Dominion University*

**Kimberly Cruz**
*Cypress Bay High School*

**Brian Day**
*Clemson University*

**Jane Dickie**
*Hope College*

**Douglas Dinero**
*Onondaga Community College*

**Sara Dorer**
*Hope College*

**Angela B. Dortch**
*Ivy Tech Community College*

**Joseph Eastwood**
*University of Ontario Institute of Technology*

**Randal Ernst**
*Nebraska Wesleyan University*

**Nancy Fenton**
*Adlai E. Stevenson High School*

**Vivian Ferry**
*Mount Saint Charles Academy*

**Amy Fineburg**
*Jefferson County Schools*

**Timothy Flemming**
*Georgia State University*

**Jessica Flitter**
*West Bend East High School*

**Perry Fuchs**
*The University of Texas at Arlington*

**Heather V. Ganginis Del Pino**
*Montgomery College*

**Joe Geiger**
*Carl Sandburg High School*

**Jerry Green**
*Tarrant County College*

**Ruth Hallongren**
*Triton College*

**Dann Hazel**
*Polk State College*

**Antonia Henderson**
*Langara College*

**Allison Herzig**
*Langley High School*

**Regina M. Hughes**
*Collin College*

**Carrie Kobelsky**
*University of Victoria*

**Kent Korek**
*Germantown High School*

**Erin Lea**
*Langara College*

**Valerie L. Lloyd**
*Langara College*

**Kellie McCants-Price**
*Anne Arundel Community College*

**Robert McEntarffer**
*University of Nebraska*

**Michelle Merwin**
*The University of Tennessee at Martin*

**Beth Morling**
*University of Delaware*

**Robin Musselman**
*Lehigh Carbon Community College*

**Nathaniel Naughton**
*Arlington Catholic High School*

**Hayley Kleitz Nelson**
*Delaware County Community College*

**Thelisa E. Nutt**
*Tarrant County College District—Southeast Campus*

**John M. O'Brien**
*University of Maine at Augusta*

**Levente Orban**
*Kwantlen Polytechnic University*

**Elaine M. O'Reilly**
*University of North Carolina at Charlotte*

**Debra Park**
*Rutgers University*

**L. Alison Phillips**
*Iowa State University*

**Claire Renzetti**
*University of Kentucky*

**Alan Roberts**
*Indiana University*

**David L. Roby**
*Texas Southmost College*

**Hilary Rosenthal**
*Glenbrook South High School*

**Edie Sample**
*Metropolitan Community College*

**Jon Sigurjonsson**
*Caldwell University*

**Joseph Swope**
*Northwest High School*

**Kamara Taylor**
*Michigan Technological University*

**Melissa S. Terlecki**
*Cabrini University*

**Elizabeth Veinott**
*Michigan Technological University*

**Jeanne Viviani**
*LaGuardia Community College*

**Virginia Welle**
*Chippewa Falls Senior High School*

**Kimberly Wood**
*Samford University*

**Carol Wilkinson**
*Whatcom Community College*

# Brief Contents

## Unit 4   SOCIAL PSYCHOLOGY AND PERSONALITY   453

## Unit 5   MENTAL AND PHYSICAL HEALTH   637

## Enrichment Modules   798

*All References can be found online.*

# Contents

## Unit 2 COGNITION     165

# Unit 4 SOCIAL PSYCHOLOGY AND PERSONALITY 453

## Enrichment Modules 798

*All References can be found online.*

# To the Student

## How to Get the Most From Your Psychology Text for the AP® Course

The AP® Psychology course represents a wonderful opportunity for you to be challenged by the rigor of a college-level course, while learning life-relevant, mind-expanding concepts from the humanly significant discipline of psychology. Our unwavering vision for this text has been to *merge rigorous science with a broad human perspective that engages both mind and heart.* We aim to offer a state-of-the-art introduction to psychological science that speaks to your needs and interests. We aspire to help you understand and appreciate the wonders of your everyday life. And we seek to convey the inquisitive spirit with which psychologists *do* psychology.

This fourth edition continues to build on our trademark: a readable, relatable text-book that effectively prepares students for the AP® Psychology Exam by keeping true to the College Board® Curriculum Framework, with new research and student-relevant discoveries throughout. We aim for clear and concise explanations and a conversational tone that—we hope—will encourage you to read, and enjoy, the content. The fourth edition is organized by units and modules. The units mirror the major content areas in the College Board's Curriculum Framework that are supported by Personal Project Check assessments. The units are divided into short, manageable **modules** that provide bite-sized chunks of content to study. Each module is organized by clear and measurable **Learning Targets** that orient you to the material you are about to read and allow you to "check off" each objective as you master it.

Be sure to take advantage of all that this text has to offer. You can learn a lot by simply reading the text, but you will develop a deeper understanding by completing the many review questions and self-assessment activities along the way. The walk-through guide on pages xxv–xxxi gives you an inside look at the important features of the text.

In Unit 2, we discuss the importance of "retrieving" what you've read and then "reviewing" what you've learned by testing yourself. Researchers have found that self-testing, and regularly engaging with "desirable difficulties" are great ways to learn and remember. This book offers many different types of self-tests and learning opportunities for you:

- **Check Your Understanding** boxes, found at the end of major sections of text, include **Examine the Concept** questions (with answers in Appendix C) that assess mastery, and **Apply the Concept** questions, which encourage you to apply new concepts to your own experiences (thus making them more meaningful and memorable).

- **Try This** features sprinkled throughout the margins allow you to connect more deeply with the concepts you're learning by putting them into real-life practice.

- **AP® Practice Multiple Choice Questions** appear at the end of each module. Try the multiple choice questions to assess your understanding of the module content.

- **AP® Practice Evidence-Based Questions and Article Analysis questions** for each unit appear in Appendix D at the end of the book.

- **Unit Review Questions** offer a cumulative assessment on concepts learned from reading all modules within the unit.
- **The Practice AP®-Style Exam** in Appendix A covers material learned throughout the entire course and simulates the real AP® Psychology Exam.

## AP®-Focused Elements and Science Practice Development

In addition to providing you with a rich introduction to the field of psychology, *Myers' Psychology for the AP® Course* is designed to help you prepare for the AP® Psychology Exam. That is why we have expanded on the following AP®-specific tips and science practice skill development features:

- **Unit 0** offers an introduction to the foundations of your AP® Psychology course. This unit emphasizes the fallacies of our everyday "common sense" thinking and, therefore, the need for psychological science. The Statistical Reasoning discussion encourages you to focus on thinking smarter by applying simple statistical principles to everyday reasoning. This unit, which is referenced throughout the textbook, offers many opportunities for you to learn critical thinking skills and to better understand research and design principles—both of which are essential to success on the AP® exam and will also be invaluable skills to have in your college courses.

- **Science Practice 1: Concept Application** is assessed through the Check Your Understanding checkpoints located at the end of each major section in the text. These boxes allow you to test yourself on the material you've just learned and make connections with the material. "Cultural Awareness" margin tips are found throughout the book, and will help you navigate how cultural norms and cognitive biases apply to our behavior and beliefs—another key aspect of Science Practice 1.

- **Science Practice 2: Research Methods & Design,** one of the most important skills to learn in AP® Psychology, is highlighted throughout several features in the fourth edition. All-new "Exploring Research Methods & Design" features allow you to practice evaluating quantitative and qualitative research methods and to study designs relevant to the material you're learning in the module. Each feature is paired with an instructional video. You'll also see helpful "Research" tips placed throughout the margins at the best point of use to remind you of important concepts you'll need to know for the exam.

- **Science Practice 3: Data Interpretation,** another crucial skill and one that students sometimes struggle with, is highlighted through all-new "Data Interpretation" features. These boxed features ask you to evaluate psychological concepts as depicted in graphs, tables, charts, and more. Each feature is paired with an instructional video. You can get additional practice with this skill by analyzing the data found in the stunning visuals throughout the textbook.

- **Science Practice 4: Argumentation** offers interactive infographics found in each unit. This tool helps you learn the importance of using scientifically derived evidence to support or refute a claim in psychology. Each feature is paired with assessment questions to help you develop your critical thinking skills.

- **AP® Exam Tips,** found in the margin throughout the text, provide invaluable advice on where to focus and how to avoid pitfalls so that you may be successful in the course and on the exam.

- A **Key Terms and Contributors List** appears at the end of each unit to remind you of the important terms and contributors to psychology that were bolded and defined in the marginal glossary throughout the modules. These terms highlight the vocabulary you'll need to know for the AP® exam. These terms are also defined in the English and Spanish **Glossary/Glosario** at the end of the book.

\* \* \*

What an amazing success story AP® Psychology has become since 1992, when 3,916 students took the first exam. In 2023, approximately 323,000 students sat for the AP® Psychology Exam! It has been an honor for us to support the teaching of our humanly significant discipline to so many of those students, and a great pleasure to have met or corresponded with so many AP® Psychology teachers and their students. It is also a keenly felt responsibility. So, please do feel free to be in touch with your feedback and suggestions. With every good wish,

Hope College
Holland, Michigan 49422-9000 USA
DavidMyers.org
@DavidGMyers

University of Kentucky
Lexington, Kentucky 40506-0044 USA
NathanDeWall.com
@cndewall

Xavier University of Louisiana
New Orleans, Louisiana 70125-1056 USA
@eyhammer

# Get the most from your book's organization and pacing

Your AP® Psychology adventure begins here! This book has been created with you in mind. It is packed with features to help you learn effectively and to prepare for the AP® Psychology Exam.

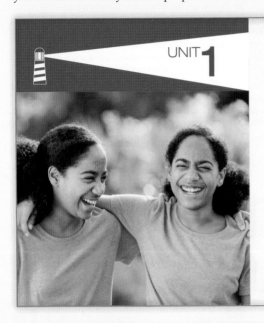

**Unit Introduction.** Units start with real-world examples and engaging stories that illustrate important psychological concepts to be introduced in the modules that follow.

**Overview Videos.** Look for the video icons throughout the text. There will be one at the beginning of each unit, which directs you to watch a Unit Overview Video.

## Module 1.6b Sensation: Vision

**LEARNING TARGETS**

**1.6-4** Explain the characteristics of the energy that we see as visible light, and describe the structures in the eye that help focus that energy.

**1.6-5** Describe how the rods and cones process information, and explain the path information travels from the eye to the brain.

**1.6-6** Explain how we perceive color in the world around us.

**1.6-7** Describe the location and explain the function of feature detectors.

**1.6-8** Explain how the brain uses parallel processing to construct visual perceptions.

### AP® Exam Tip

There's a lot of vocabulary here. Make sure you understand the name and the function of each part of the eye. To learn how all the parts fit together, it may help to make rough sketches (you don't need to be an artist to try this!) and then compare your sketches with Figures 1.6-7 and 1.6-9. You'll be better off making several quick, rough sketches than one time-consuming, nicely drawn one.

### Light Energy and Eye Structures

**1.6-4** What are the characteristics of the energy that we see as visible light? What structures in the eye help focus that energy?

Our eyes receive light energy and *transduce* (transform) it into neural messages. Our brain—in one of life's greatest wonders—then creates what we consciously see. How does such a taken-for-granted yet extraordinary thing happen?

### The Stimulus Input: Light Energy

When you look at a bright red tulip, the stimuli striking your eyes are not particles of the color red but rather pulses of electromagnetic energy that your visual system *perceives* as red. What we see as visible light is but a thin slice of the wide spectrum of electromagnetic energy, ranging from imperceptibly short gamma waves to the long waves of radio transmission (Figure 1.6-6). Other portions are visible to other animals. Bees, for instance, cannot see what we perceive as red but can see ultraviolet light.

**wavelength** the distance from the peak of one light wave or sound wave to the peak of the next. Electromagnetic wavelengths vary from the short gamma waves to the long pulses of radio transmission.

**hue** the dimension of color that is determined by the wavelength of light; what we know as the color names *blue*, *green*, and so forth.

**intensity** the amount of energy in a light wave or sound

**Module Format.** Each unit is divided into brief modules that will help pace your learning so you can tackle difficult topics in manageable chunks and assess your knowledge at appropriate midpoints.

**Learning Targets.** A list of critical concepts appears at the beginning of each module, keeping you focused as you read and guiding your comprehension. These Learning Targets are revisited in the Module Reviews.

**Running Glossary.** Knowing and understanding the language of psychology is critical for success on the AP® Psychology Exam. Key terms appear in bold type in the text, and are defined in the purple margin boxes on the page. All terms can also be found in the Glossary/Glosario at the end of the book.

## Module 1.6b REVIEW

**1.6-4** What are the characteristics of the energy that we see as visible light? What structures in the eye help focus that energy?

- What we see as light is only a thin slice of the broad spectrum of electromagnetic energy. The portion visible to humans extends from the shorter blue-violet *wavelengths* to the longer red wavelengths.
- After entering the eye through the *cornea*, passing through the *pupil* and *iris*, and being focused by the *lens*, light energy particles (from a thin slice of the broad spectrum of electromagnetic energy) strike the eye's inner surface, the *retina*.
- Wavelength determines *hue*, the color we perceive; amplitude determines *intensity*, the brightness we perceive.

**1.6-5** How do the rods and cones process information, and what is the path information travels from the eye to the brain?

- Light entering the eye triggers chemical changes that convert light energy into neural impulses.
- Photoreceptors called *cones* and *rods* at the back of the retina provide differing sensitivities—cones to detail and color, rods to faint light and peripheral motion.
- After processing by bipolar and ganglion cells, neural impulses travel from the retina through the *optic nerve* to the thalamus, and on to the visual cortex.

Contemporary research has found three types of cones, each most sensitive to the wavelengths of one of the three primary colors of light (red, green, or blue).

- Hering's *opponent-process theory* proposed three additional sets of opposing retinal processes (red-green, blue-yellow, white-black). Research has confirmed that, en route to the brain, neurons in the retina and the thalamus code the color-related information from the cones into pairs of opponent colors.
- These two theories, and the research supporting them, show that color processing occurs in two stages.

**1.6-7** Where are feature detectors located, and what do they do?

- *Feature detectors*, specialized nerve cells in the visual cortex, respond to specific features of the visual stimulus, such as shape, angle, or movement.
- Feature detectors pass information on to other cortical areas, where supercell clusters respond to more complex patterns.

**1.6-8** How does the brain use parallel processing to construct visual perceptions?

- Through *parallel processing*, the brain handles many aspects of vision (color, movement, form, and depth) simultaneously. Other neural teams integrate the results, comparing them with stored information and enabling perceptions.

# Build essential skills with the Science Practices

Use these features spiraled throughout the text to help you hone the skills that are central to the study of psychology.

**Check Your Understanding.** Test yourself on the material you've just learned with the Check Your Understanding features at the end of main sections. Apply the Concept questions help you make connections with the material, and address **Science Practice 1: Concept Application,** while Examine the Concept questions assess your mastery of the content you've just read.

Answers to Examine the Concept questions are available in Appendix C at the back of the book.

---

**AP® Science Practice**    **Check Your Understanding**

**Examine the Concept**
▶ Explain the differences among the stages of sleep.
▶ Explain the role of the suprachiasmatic nucleus in sleep.
▶ Explain how REM sleep relates to dreaming.

**Apply the Concept**
▶ Would you consider yourself a night owl or a morning lark? Explain how this relates to your circadian rhythm.

*Answers to the Examine the Concept questions can be found in Appendix C at the end of the book.*

---

**Cultural Awareness.** Margin tips help drive home how our cognitive biases and cultural norms can apply to behaviors and beliefs. These tips address **Science Practice 1.B.**

## CULTURAL AWARENESS

Pay close attention to the difference between sensation and perception. Many people mistakenly believe that the brain perceives situations in an objective, calculating way. In fact, the brain implements a number of biases and filters that influence our experience in the world, and those applied are often influenced by our culture.

---

**Developing Arguments.** These infographics, found in each unit, assess **Science Practice 4: Argumentation.** This tool helps you learn the importance of citing scientifically derived evidence to support or refute a claim in psychology, a skill you will continue to develop throughout your studies and your life. Each feature is paired with assessment questions to help you develop your critical thinking skills.

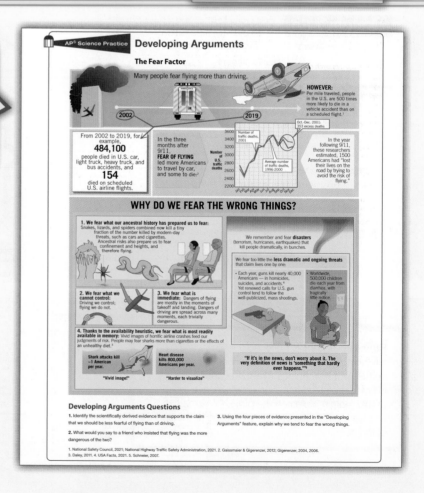

# Infuse research methods and data interpretation throughout the course

Developing your study of research methods and data interpretation throughout the course is key to understanding psychology as a science!

> **Unit 0.** A new introductory Unit 0 builds the foundation of the course by offering context into **Science Practice 2: Research Methods & Design** and **Science Practice 3: Data Interpretation.** This crucial introductory unit is often referred back to at key points throughout your studies.

> In-text features offer you plenty of practice with Science Practices 2 and 3. **Exploring Research Methods & Design** allows you to practice evaluating quantitative and qualitative research methods and study designs. **Data Interpretation** asks you to evaluate psychological concepts as depicted in graphs, tables, charts, and more. Notice that each of these features is paired with a helpful video, guiding you through the information presented and walking you through the answers to each of the questions in the boxes.

---

**AP® Science Practice**

### Exploring Research Methods & Design

As a result of research on traumatic brain injuries, the NFL implemented new procedures to protect players who experience concussions, including neuropsychological tests for players before they can return to play after sustaining a head injury. Research shows that repeated concussions are associated w depression, impaired judgment, memory loss, and, in later life, dementia.

Researchers autopsied the brains of former players and found neuro at a much higher rate than in the general population: A study of 111 decea players found that 99 percent had neurodegeneration (Mez et al., 2017).

- Determine which research design was employed in the 2017 study — c experimental.
- Explain the difference between the sample and the population in this st
- Explain what conclusions you can and cannot draw from this study.
- What ethical guidelines, if any, would prevent you from using random a when studying this topic?

*Remember, you can always revisit Unit 0 to review information related to psychological*

---

**AP® Science Practice**

### Data Interpretation

| | Number of Presses | |
|---|---|---|
| | Rats receiving reward center activation | Rats not receiving reward center activation |
| Trial 1 | 204 | 202 |
| Trial 2 | 813 | 250 |
| Trial 3 | 857 | 300 |
| Trial 4 | 900 | 156 |
| Trial 5 | 1001 | 158 |

This module describes research on rats that led to the identification of the hypothalamus as a reward center in the brain. Consider the data set above.

- Describe the general difference in number of presses *between* the groups represented in this table.
- Describe the trends in the data *within* each group.
- Calculate the mean for each group.
- Is the variable "number of presses" qualitative or quantitative? Explain.

*Remember, you can always revisit Unit 0 to review information related to psychological research.*

---

**Data and Research Margin Tips** also remind you of important concepts you'll need to know in the context of the exam.

**AP® Science Practice**

#### Research

The idea that expectations *influence* perceptions implies a cause (expectations) and an effect (changes in perceptions). Studies such as the ones presented here allow for such conclusions, because they used experimental methods — for example, randomly assigning how the french fries were served. Module 0.5 provides more details on how random assignment allows for causal conclusions.

ment, by a 6-to-1
red in a McDonald's
experiment invited campus bar patrons at the Massachusetts Institute of Technology to sample free beer (Lee et al., 2006). When researchers added a few drops of vinegar to a brand-name beer and called it "MIT Brew," the tasters preferred it—unless they had been told they were drinking vinegar-laced beer. In that case, they expected, and usually experienced, a worse taste.

What determines our perceptual set? As Module 3.4 will explain, through experience we form concepts, or *schemas*, that organize and interpret unfamiliar information. Our pre-existing schemas for monsters and tree limbs influence how we apply top-down processing to interpret ambiguous sensations.

In everyday life, stereotypes—about culture, ethnicity, gender, sexual orientation, income, age, abilities, and more—can color perception. People (especially children) have, for example, perceived new baby "David" as bigger and stronger than when the same infant was called "Diana" (Stern & Karraker, 1989). Some differences, it seems, exist merely in the eyes of their beholders.

# Practice for the AP® exam all year long

This book is your ultimate study tool. Use all the AP® Psychology practice opportunities at the module, unit, and book level to give you the confidence you need on exam day.

## AP® Exam Tip

There is a ton of vocabulary in this unit, and in psychology. Learning vocabulary is really not so hard: The secret is to work on it every day. Try flash cards or an online quizzing memory game. Work with a study buddy. Impress your friends with your new vocabulary. Just don't leave it until the night before the test. If you rehearse the vocabulary throughout the unit, you will do better on the unit test. Don't just reread the flash cards, but rather quiz yourself on them or paraphrase them in your own words. The big bonus is that you will also retain far more information for the AP® exam.

**AP® Exam Tips.** These tips help you focus on key content that you should know for the exam, as well as avoid common misconceptions.

## AP® Exam Tip

Note the important shift here. So far, you have been learning about how just one neuron operates. The action potential is the mechanism for communication within a single neuron. Now you are moving on to a discussion of two neurons and how communication occurs between them — very different, but equally important. Both ideas are important for the AP® exam.

## AP® Practice Multiple Choice Questions

1. Andriy has not been getting enough sleep the last few months. He has gained weight and has been getting sick often. What other effect of sleep deprivation will Andriy likely experience?

   a. Increased productivity
   b. Depression
   c. Increased feeling of well-being
   d. Sleep apnea

2. Shortly after falling asleep, and hundreds of times during the night, Paola wakes up after a loud gasp because she has stopped breathing. With which sleep disorder would she most likely be diagnosed?

   a. Narcolepsy
   b. Insomnia
   c. Sleep apnea
   d. REM sleep behavior disorder

**Module AP® Practice Multiple Choice Questions.** At the end of each module, AP® Practice Multiple Choice Questions, which are structured like the questions you'll see on the actual exam, help you build confidence as you sharpen your test-taking skills.

3. Bohdana believes that she dreams to help her remember what happened during the day. Which dream theory aligns with her view?

   a. Information processing
   b. Cognitive development
   c. Physiological function
   d. Neural activation

4. After two nights without sleep, which of the following can be expected?

   a. Insomnia
   b. Sleep apnea
   c. Narcolepsy
   d. REM rebound

**Use the following data to answer questions 5 and 6:**

Dr. Truman conducted a study where she drew numbers out of a hat to determine which half of the participants slept only 4 hours per night for 4 weeks (Group A) and which half of the

participants slept 8 to 9 hours per night for 4 weeks (Group B). She ensured that the participants' living quarters were the same for the duration of the study, changing only the amount of time each group slept. Using the graphs and information in the prompt, address the following questions:

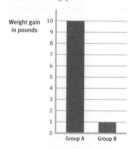

5. Based on the data in the graph, which of the following statements best describes the results of Dr. Truman's study?

   a. A lack of sleep causes weight loss.
   b. Participants' living quarters impact weight.
   c. A lack of sleep causes weight gain.
   d. Participants' living quarters impact sleep.

6. Which of the following aspects of Dr. Truman's study allows her to draw a cause-effect conclusion about the impact of sleep on hormones?

   a. Random selection
   b. Experimental control
   c. Confounding variables
   d. Qualitative methodology

## Unit 1 AP® Practice Multiple Choice Questions

1. Jay is an evolutionary psychologist. He seeks to understand how traits and behavioral tendencies have been shaped by
   a. natural selection.
   b. psychophysics.
   c. prenatal nutrition.
   d. parallel processing.
2. Torin believes in nature's influence on behavior, while Kyla believes in nurture's influence. Which aligns with Torin's view and Kyla's view, respectively?
   a. Genetic factors; environmental factors
   b. Heredity; genetic factors
   c. Epigenetics; environmental factors
   d. Environmental factors; heredity
3. Rather than acting as blueprints that lead to the same result no matter the context, genes react to the environment. The gene–environment interaction is the basic tenet of which of the following?
   a. Evolutionary psychology
   b. Epigenetics
   c. Heredity
   d. Parallel processing
4. Why do researchers find the study of fraternal twins important?
   a. They share similar environments and the same genetic code.
   b. Their environments differ based on their individual traits.
   c. They are usually raised in similar environments, but they do not have the same genetic code.
   d. They are typically raised in less similar environments than nontwin siblings.
5. Why do researchers use adoption studies in an effort to reveal genetic influences on personality?
   a. To compare adopted children with nonadopted children
   b. To study the effect of prior neglect on adopted children
   c. To study the effect of a child's age at adoption
   d. To evaluate whether adopted children more closely resemble their adoptive parents or their biological parents
6. What should Ezra say if he was asked to describe the main function of the peripheral nervous system?
   a. It connects the brain and spinal cord to the rest of the body.
   b. It calms the body after an emergency.
   c. It prepares the body for action.
   d. It focuses on thinking and feeling.
7. To accurately identify the two parts of the central nervous system in an oral exam, what should Kitab say?
   a. Sensory and motor neurons
   b. The somatic and autonomic nervous systems
   c. The brain and the spinal cord
   d. The sympathetic and parasympathetic nervous systems
8. What does the figure below illustrate?

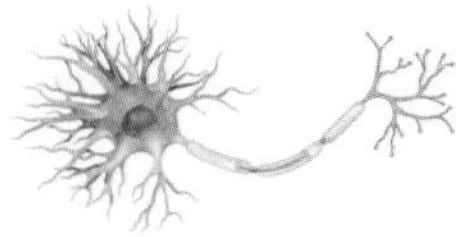

   a. A glial cell
   b. A hormone
   c. A neuron
   d. A neurotransmitter
9. What is the purpose of the myelin sheath?
   a. To make the transfer of information across a synapse more efficient
   b. To increase the amount of neurotransmitter available in the synapse
   c. To reduce the antagonistic effect of certain drugs
   d. To speed up the transmission of information within a neuron
10. When Janice's finger touches a candle flame, her hand jerks away *before* her brain receives and responds to the information that causes her to feel pain. This is due to which of the following?
    a. The reflex arc
    b. The all-or-none process
    c. Reuptake
    d. Endorphins
11. Jessika wants to do research that examines the electrical impulses that travel down axons to better understand
    a. the refractory period.
    b. the action potential.
    c. the threshold.
    d. the all-or-none process.
12. Lei has been diagnosed with schizophrenia. Which of the following neurotransmitters most likely contributed to this disorder?
    a. Acetylcholine c. Glutamate
    b. Dopamine d. GABA
13. Calvin takes a drug that acts as both a stimulant and a hallucinogen. It could cause him to become dangerously dehydrated in the short term and disrupt his serotonin in the long term. What drug did Calvin most likely take?
    a. LSD c. Alcohol
    b. Ecstasy d. Cocaine
14. After taking a drug, Carmen is experiencing slowed reactions, slurred speech, and decreased skill performance. Which drug did she most likely take?
    a. Nicotine c. Alcohol
    b. Caffeine d. Ecstasy
15. Thomas, who drinks alcohol regularly, now finds that he requires a larger dose to experience the same effect. Which term best describes his experience?
    a. Withdrawal
    b. Tolerance
    c. Addiction
    d. Substance use disorder
16. When Honque ingested an opioid drug, what neurotransmitter(s) did the opioid mimic in his brain?
    a. Serotonin c. Norepinephrine
    b. Endorphins d. Acetylcholine
17. A researcher interested in determining the size of a particular area of the brain would be most likely to use which of the following techniques?
    a. EEG c. fMRI
    b. MRI d. PET scan
18. Sara is about to take her driver's test. Which region of the brain plays the most significant role in her sense of alertness and arousal?
    a. Medulla c. Hippocampus
    b. Parietal lobe d. Reticular formation
19. Ray has a damaged hippocampus. Which of the following would he most likely experience as a result?
    a. Difficulties with balance and coordination
    b. Difficulty in creating new memories
    c. A false sensation of burning in parts of the body
    d. Inability to regulate body temperature and hunger
20. Surgical stimulation of the somatosensory cortex might result in the false sensation of what?
    a. Flashes of colored light
    b. Someone whispering your name
    c. Someone tickling you
    d. A bad odor
21. During which task might the right hemisphere of the brain be most active?
    a. Solving a mathematical equation
    b. Enduring a long run
    c. Making a brief oral presentation to a class
    d. Imagining what a dress would look like on a friend
22. When researchers surgically lesioned the amygdala of a rhesus monkey's brain, what was the impact on the monkey's behavior?
    a. Lost its ability to coordinate movement
    b. Became less aggressive
    c. Lost its memory of where food was stored
    d. Sank into an irreversible coma
23. Which of the following scenarios best illustrates neuroplasticity?
    a. Aaron has healthy human brain tissue.
    b. Khadija's brain is able to transfer information from one hemisphere to the other.
    c. Alycia's brain gets larger as she grows.
    d. Pham's brain tissue has the ability to take on new functions.
24. Jazmine experiences brain damage that results in an inability to make plans about the future. Which lobe of her brain was most likely damaged?
    a. Parietal lobe
    b. Frontal lobe
    c. Occipital lobe
    d. Temporal lobe
25. When Elliott is sleep deprived, he is more likely to catch a cold. Why is this the case?
    a. Sleep helps restore the immune system.
    b. Sleep suppresses the immune system.
    c. Sleep strengthens neural connections that build muscle memory.
    d. Sleep enhances the production of growth hormones.
26. As part of a sleep study, researchers notice bursts of rapid, rhythmic brain-wave activity and determine that Jane is in Stage 2 sleep. This type of brain activity is referred to as
    a. circadian rhythms. c. sleep spindles.
    b. alpha waves. d. delta waves.





**Unit AP® Practice Exams.** At the end of each unit, a comprehensive set of AP® Practice Questions address content across the unit. These multiple-choice questions, Evidence-Based Questions, and Article Analysis Questions match the style and scope you can expect to see on the exam in May. The Evidence-Based Questions and Article Analysis Questions for each unit can be found in Appendix D.

## Appendix A PRACTICE AP®-STYLE EXAM

### Section I
MULTIPLE CHOICE

1. A job advertisement for a salesperson position stated that the company was looking for extraverted, conscientious, agreeable employees who are open to trying new things and who can manage their emotional reactions well. What personality theory does this job advertisement illustrate?
   a. Trait theories c. Psychoanalytic theories
   b. Psychodynamic theories d. Humanistic theories
2. Warren has a bacterial infection that has affected the ability of the rods in his eyes to function correctly. This issue should have the greatest impact on which of the following?
   a. Visual clarity c. Color vision
   b. Peripheral vision d. Shape constancy
3. Ethan believes in recycling. He often reads books about the benefits of recycling; however, he found himself skipping over a magazine article about the problems associated with recycling. In this example, Ethan demonstrated
   a. a heuristic. c. a mental set.
   b. overconfidence. d. confirmation bias.
4. Joe is taking a new job on the night shift next week. His supervisors have informed him that he may have some problems with his level of alertness and his memory as he adjusts to his new overnight work schedule. Joe's supervisors are sharing with Joe their knowledge of
   a. circadian rhythms. c. sleep spindles.
   b. REM sleep. d. NREM sleep.
5. A researcher who is trying to determine how sociocultural changes might be correlated with the incidence of bipolar disorder would be most interested in which of the following?
   a. The brain changes in a person with bipolar disorder as measured by a PET scan
   b. The association between rates of poverty and cases of bipolar disorder
   c. Neurotransmitter levels in patients diagnosed with bipolar disorder
   d. The number of close biological relatives who also suffer from bipolar disorder
6. Zeina cocked her head to the side immediately when she heard the fire truck's siren. Turning her head enabled each ear to detect a slightly different intensity of sound, thereby enabling her to determine the siren's
   a. pitch. c. location.
   b. frequency. d. tone.
7. How many phonemes are in the word charity?
   a. Four c. Two
   b. Three d. One
8. People diagnosed with obsessive-compulsive disorder experience compulsions. Which of the following is a compulsion?
   a. Eric frequently worries that there may be germs on his hands.
   b. Brianna has an ongoing fear that she might have left the oven on at home.
   c. Stefan often feels great anxiety if things are not in exact order in his room.
   d. Tyrik flips the light switch seven times every evening when he gets home.
9. Darla's family has a pet dog. When Darla sees a cat for the first time, she points and says "dog." Darla is demonstrating
   a. accommodation. c. assimilation.
   b. fixation. d. dual processing.
10. Persephone wants to borrow her friend's car for the weekend. She starts by asking her friend if she can borrow the car for an entire month. Her friend declines, stating it would be too long. Persephone then follows up by asking if she can borrow the car for just the weekend. In this scenario, Persephone's initial request for borrowing the car for a month is an example of which persuasion technique?
    a. Central route c. Foot-in-the-door
    b. Peripheral route d. Door-in-the-face
11. A rat jumps each time it sees a green light flash because the green light has always appeared just before an electric shock. In classical conditioning, the initial learning of the connection between the light and the shock is referred to as
    a. spontaneous recovery. c. generalization.
    b. extinction. d. acquisition.
12. Which of the following examples is the best illustration of cognitive dissonance?
    a. The cult member who admires the leader of his group and follows the leader without doubt
    b. The teacher who reprimands a student because she feels the student could do much better academically despite past poor performance
    c. The librarian who dreams of returning to graduate school to become a professor and who begins to submit applications
    d. The student who loves math but after failing a calculus test says he doesn't like calculus that much anyway



**Cumulative AP® Practice Exam.** A complete practice exam at the end of the book matches the structure of the actual AP® Psychology Exam. This comprehensive test ensures that you get enough practice so you can strive for a 5 on the day of the exam.

# Use the stunning visuals and engaging features to bring psychology to life

The figures, photographs, graphs, and infographics will help you understand and remember the key themes and important concepts that will be covered on the exam.

**Photos, Illustrations, and Graphs.** The visuals in this text have been carefully chosen and drawn to help clarify and support key concepts from the narrative and give you practice in analyzing data that are presented in a variety of formats. That's a key skill needed for the AP® Psychology Exam.

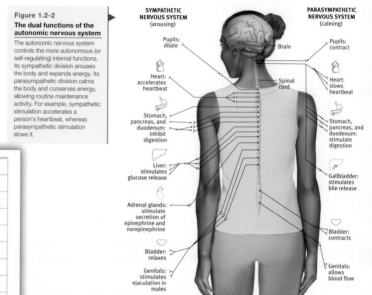

Figure 1.2-2

**The dual functions of the autonomic nervous system**

The autonomic nervous system controls the more autonomous (or self-regulating) internal functions. Its sympathetic division arouses the body and expends energy. Its parasympathetic division calms the body and conserves energy, allowing routine maintenance activity. For example, sympathetic stimulation accelerates a person's heartbeat, whereas parasympathetic stimulation slows it.

**SYMPATHETIC NERVOUS SYSTEM** (arousing)

Pupils: dilate
Heart: accelerates heartbeat
Stomach, pancreas, and duodenum: inhibit digestion
Liver: stimulates glucose release
Adrenal glands: stimulate secretion of epinephrine and norepinephrine
Bladder: relaxes
Genitals: stimulates ejaculation in males

Brain
Spinal cord

**PARASYMPATHETIC NERVOUS SYSTEM** (calming)

Pupils: contract
Heart: slows heartbeat
Stomach, pancreas, and duodenum: stimulate digestion
Gallbladder: stimulates bile release
Bladder: contracts
Genitals: allows blood flow

Positive words in tweets

Sun
Sat
Thurs
Mon
Fri
Wed
Tues

Positive tweets were highest late Saturday night

Positive tweets were lowest on Tuesday afternoon

Midnight — 6 A.M. — Noon — 6 P.M. — 11 P.M.

Time of day

Figure 0.3-2

**Twitter message moods, by time and by day**

This graph illustrates how, without knowing anyone's identity, researchers can use big data to study human behavior on a massive scale. It is now possible to associate people's moods with, for example, their locations or the weather, and to study the spread of ideas through social networks. (Data from Golder & Macy, 2011.)

**Cartoons.** Lighthearted cartoons are sprinkled throughout the text to show real-world connections to psychology in a humorous and fun way.

THE MIND-BODY PROBLEM

Get up.

No.

Roz Chast/The New Yorker Collection/The Cartoon Bank

## TRY THIS

Try out this old riddle on a couple of friends. "You're driving a bus with 12 passengers. At your first stop, 6 passengers get off. At the second stop, 3 get off. At the third stop, 2 more get off but 3 new people get on. What color are the bus driver's eyes?" Do your friends detect the signal — who is the bus driver? — amid the accompanying noise?

**SPOTLIGHT ON:**
Linda Bartoshuk

*From a tongue-in-cheek Twitter feed:*
❝ *The problem with quotes on the internet is that you never know if they're true.* ❞

*Abraham Lincoln*

**Try This, Spotlight On, and Margin Quotes.** Engaging margin features help you connect with psychology by suggesting fun activities to try with your friends, offering opportunities to learn more about influential psychologists, and providing humorous quotes that help you appreciate the module's key concepts.

# Access everything you need for this course
## in  Achieve

Our **Achieve** digital platform includes all of the resources you need in one convenient place.

**E-book.** The interactive, mobile-ready e-book allows you to read and reference the text whether you are online or offline. All offline highlights and notes sync when you connect to the internet.

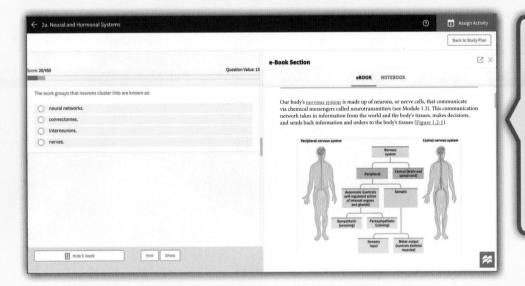

**Achieve Homework System.** Created and supported by educators, Achieve includes a multitude of homework questions and supporting resources. Videos, animations, and simulations teach key concepts in an interesting and engaging way, while the integrated LearningCurve adaptive quizzes offer formative feedback, even when you get the answer wrong. Achieve for Myers' Psychology for the AP® Course, 4th Edition is the ultimate tool for AP® Exam preparation.

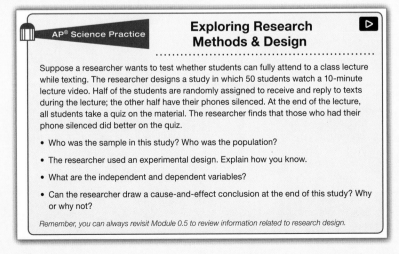

### Exploring Research Methods & Design
**AP® Science Practice**

Suppose a researcher wants to test whether students can fully attend to a class lecture while texting. The researcher designs a study in which 50 students watch a 10-minute lecture video. Half of the students are randomly assigned to receive and reply to texts during the lecture; the other half have their phones silenced. At the end of the lecture, all students take a quiz on the material. The researcher finds that those who had their phone silenced did better on the quiz.

- Who was the sample in this study? Who was the population?

- The researcher used an experimental design. Explain how you know.

- What are the independent and dependent variables?

- Can the researcher draw a cause-and-effect conclusion at the end of this study? Why or why not?

*Remember, you can always revisit Module 0.5 to review information related to research design.*

**Science Practice Videos** paired with each of the Exploring Research Methods & Design and Data Interpretation features walk you through the answers to the questions posed in each boxed feature, and help you develop the skills you need for the AP® Psychology Exam.

# UNIT 0

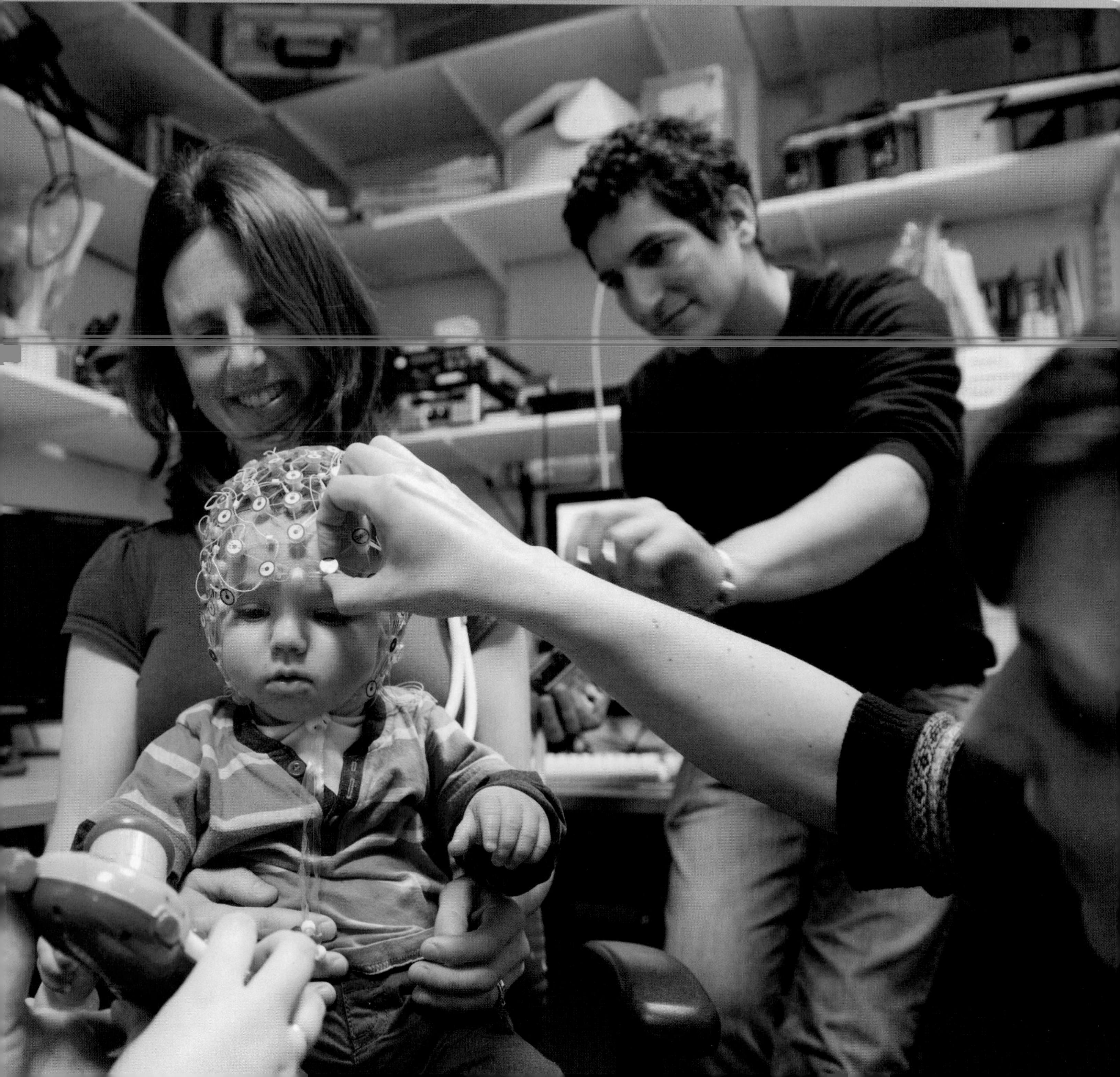

# An Introduction to Psychological Science Practices: Research Methods and Data Interpretation

As you will learn through this course, psychology is the *science* of behavior and mental processes. What do psychologists do? You might think that they offer counseling, analyze personality, give out child-raising advice, examine crime scenes, and testify in court. Do they? *Yes*—and much more. Consider some of psychology's questions that you may wonder about:

- Have you ever awakened from a nightmare and wondered why you had such a crazy dream? ***Why do we dream?***

- Have you ever played peekaboo with a 6-month-old and wondered why the baby finds your disappearing/reappearing act so delightful? ***What do babies perceive and think?***

- Have you ever wondered what fosters school and work success? ***Does inborn intelligence explain why some people get richer, think more creatively, or relate more sensitively? Or does gritty effort and a belief in the power of persistence matter more?***

- Have you ever become depressed or anxious and wondered whether you'll ever feel "normal"? ***What triggers our bad moods—and our good ones? What's the line between a routine mood swing and a psychological disorder?***

Psychology seeks to answer such questions about us all—how and why we think, feel, and act as we do. But as a *science*, psychology does more than speculate: It uses research and interpretation of the resulting data to separate uninformed opinions from examined conclusions.

UNIT **0**
Overview Video
▷

Oli Scarff/Getty Images

◀ Leo, aged 9 months, wears a Geodesic Sensor Net as he prepares to take part in an experiment at the Birkbeck Babylab Centre for Brain and Cognitive Development in London, England. The experiment uses an electroencephalogram (EEG) to study brain activity while the baby examines different objects of varying complexity. The scientists use various experiments to test the babies' physical or cognitive responses with sensors including: eye-tracking, brain activation, and motion capture.

# The Scientific Attitude, Critical Thinking, and Developing Arguments

## AP® Science Practice

### Research

Because the scientific approach is so foundational to psychology, we will provide research tips (such as this one) throughout the modules in this text. This will allow you to learn about and understand research terminology in the context of psychological theories and concepts. Research methods and design will be an important part of the AP® exam!

## LEARNING TARGETS

**0.1-1** Explain how psychology is a science.

**0.1-2** Describe the three key elements of the scientific attitude and how they support scientific inquiry.

**0.1-3** Explain how critical thinking feeds a scientific attitude, and smarter thinking for everyday life.

## Psychology Is a Science

**0.1-1 How is psychology a science?**

Underlying all science is, first, a passion for exploring and understanding without misleading or being misled. Some questions (*Is there life after death?*) are beyond science. Answering them in any way requires a leap of faith. With many other ideas (*Can some people demonstrate extrasensory perception [ESP]?*), the proof is in the pudding. Let the facts speak for themselves. In other words, look for *scientifically derived* evidence.

Magician James Randi (1928–2020) used an evidence-based approach that drew on observation and experimentation when testing those claiming to see glowing auras around people's bodies:

> **Randi:** *Do you see an aura around my head?*
>
> **Aura seer:** *Yes, indeed.*
>
> **Randi:** *Can you still see the aura if I put this magazine in front of my face?*
>
> **Aura seer:** *Of course.*
>
> **Randi:** *Then if I were to step behind a wall barely taller than I am, you could determine my location from the aura visible above my head, right?*

Randi once told me [DM] that no aura seer agreed to take this simple test.

## Key Elements of the Scientific Attitude

**0.1-2 What are the three key elements of the scientific attitude and how do they support scientific inquiry?**

No matter how sensible-seeming or how wild an idea is, the smart thinker asks: *Does it work?* When put to the test, do the data support its predictions? When subjected to scrutiny, crazy-sounding ideas sometimes find support. More often, science is self-cleansing. Right ideas stick around. Wrong ideas head to the waste heap, where they're discarded atop previous claims of miracle cancer cures and out-of-body travels into centuries past. To sift reality from fantasy and fact from fiction requires a scientific attitude: being skeptical but not cynical, open-minded but not gullible.

Alan Diaz/AP Photo

**The Amazing Randi** The late magician James Randi was an enthusiastic skeptic. During his life, he tested and debunked supposed psychic phenomena.

Putting a scientific attitude into practice requires not only curiosity and skepticism but also humility—awareness of our vulnerability to error and openness to surprises and new perspectives. What matters is not our opinion or yours, but rather the truths revealed by our questioning and testing. If people or other animals don't behave as our ideas predict, then so much the worse for our inaccurate ideas—and so much the better for scientific progress. One of psychology's early mottos expressed this humble attitude: "The rat is always right." See Developing Arguments: The Scientific Attitude.

**AP® Science Practice** Developing Arguments

### The Scientific Attitude

**1 CURIOSITY:**

**Does it work?**

**When put to the test, can its predictions be confirmed?**

Can some people read minds? •

Are stress levels related to health and well-being? ○

• No one has yet been able to demonstrate extrasensory mind-reading.

○ Many studies have found that higher stress relates to poorer health.

**2 SKEPTICISM:**

**What do you mean?**

**How do you know?**

Sifting reality from fantasy requires a healthy skepticism — an attitude that is not cynical (doubting everything), but also not gullible (believing everything).

Do our facial expressions and body postures affect how we actually feel? ○

Do parental behaviors determine children's sexual orientation? ○

○ Our facial expressions and body postures can affect how we feel.

○ Module 3.3 explains that there is not a relationship between parental behaviors and children's sexual orientation.

**3 HUMILITY:**

**That was unexpected! Let's explore further.**

Researchers must be willing to be surprised and follow new ideas. People and other animals don't always behave as our ideas and beliefs would predict.

*The rat is always right.*

### Developing Arguments Questions

By addressing these critical thinking questions, you will enhance your ability to develop arguments based on scientifically derived evidence. This is one of the skills that will be emphasized on the AP® exam.

**1.** Identify the reasoning against extrasensory mind-reading.

**2.** Using scientifically derived evidence, explain why skepticism is important in science.

# Critical Thinking

**0.1-3** How does critical thinking feed a scientific attitude, and smarter thinking for everyday life?

The scientific attitude—curiosity + skepticism + humility—prepares us to think harder and smarter. This smart thinking, called **critical thinking**, examines assumptions, appraises the source, discerns hidden biases, evaluates evidence, and assesses conclusions. When reading a research report, an online opinion, or a news story, critical thinkers ask questions: *How do they know that? What is this person's agenda? Is the conclusion based on an anecdote, or scientifically derived evidence? Does the evidence justify a cause-effect conclusion? What alternative explanations are possible?*

Critical thinkers wince when people make factual claims based on their gut: "I *feel like* climate change is [or isn't] happening." "I *feel like* self-driving cars are more [or less] dangerous." Such beliefs (commonly mislabeled as feelings) may or may not be true. Critical thinkers realize that they might be wrong. Sometimes, the best evidence confirms our beliefs. At other times, it beckons us to a different way of thinking. Cynics sometimes seem smart, yet most demonstrate less cognitive ability and academic competence than average (Stavrova & Ehlebracht, 2019).

Critical inquiry can surprise us. Here are some examples from psychological science: Massive losses of brain tissue early in life may have minimal long-term effects (see Module 1.4). People of differing age, gender, and wealth report roughly comparable levels of personal happiness (see Module 5.2). Depression touches many people, but most recover (see Module 5.4). Critical inquiry also sometimes debunks popular presumptions, by checking intuitive fiction with scientific fact: Sleepwalkers are *not* acting out their dreams (see Module 1.5). With brain stimulation or hypnosis, someone *cannot* immediately replay and relive long-buried or repressed memories (see Module 2.7). In these instances, and many others, what psychological scientists have learned is not what is widely believed. Psychology rests on a strong foundation of scientific inquiry.

**critical thinking** thinking that does not automatically accept arguments and conclusions. Rather, it examines assumptions, appraises the source, discerns hidden biases, evaluates evidence, and assesses conclusions.

THE IRRESISTIBLE FORCE MEETS THE IMMOVABLE OBJECT

THE FACTS AS THEY ARE

THE TRUTH AS I SEE IT

WILEY 5-16

---

 **AP® Science Practice**

## Check Your Understanding

**Examine the Concept**

▶ Explain what's involved in critical thinking.

**Apply the Concept**

▶ Were you surprised to learn that psychology is a science? How would you defend the point that psychology is a science if someone asked you about this?

*Answers to the Examine the Concept questions can be found in Appendix C at the end of the book.*

# Module 0.1 REVIEW

**0.1-1** How is psychology a science?

- Psychology's findings are the result of a scientific approach—based on careful observation and testing. Sifting reality from fantasy requires a scientific attitude.

**0.1-2** What are the three key elements of the scientific attitude, and how do they support scientific inquiry?

- The scientific attitude equips us to be curious, skeptical, and humble in scrutinizing competing ideas or our own observations.

**0.1-3** How does critical thinking feed a scientific attitude, and smarter thinking for everyday life?

- Critical thinking puts ideas to the test by examining assumptions, appraising the source, discerning hidden biases, evaluating evidence, and assessing conclusions.

## AP® Practice Multiple Choice Questions

**Use the following text to answer questions 1 and 2:**

Harrison observed that people who read fiction novels were also artists. Whenever Harrison shared this observation with his friends, they said that teenagers only do those activities to meet school requirements. Harrison disagreed, instead believing that personality explained an association between reading novels and being artistic. Even when Harrison learned that having access to books and art was the biggest predictor of participating in these activities, he continued to believe that his original idea was correct.

**1.** Which element of the scientific attitude should Harrison improve if he wants to engage in scientific inquiry more effectively?

   a. Curiosity
   b. Skepticism
   c. Humility
   d. Questioning

**2.** If Harrison wanted to increase his use of critical thinking, which of the following questions might he ask?

   a. How can I share my results with more people?
   b. How can I sell my ideas to make a profit?
   c. How can I interpret this result?
   d. How can I minimize the impact of this result?

**3.** What is the name of the approach that uses observation and testing to draw conclusions?

   a. Qualitative
   b. Quantitative
   c. Scientific
   d. Critical

**4.** Which of the following best illustrates a skeptical attitude?

   a. Evelyn believes that all animals turn into balloons at night because her older brother told her that he saw their dog floating around the house at night.
   b. After Matsuo's mother told him that chewing on his fingernails might make him sick, Matsuo asked her to provide an explanation of how he might get sick from chewing his nails.
   c. Hayden argues with all her teachers when they lecture because she doubts how they can possibly remember all the information from the textbooks they have read.
   d. After reading a blog post online about the dangers of walking near busy streets, Beck decided to avoid walking near busy streets for the next five years.

**5.** Which of the elements of a scientific attitude is most associated with the question, "Does it work?"

a. Humility
b. Skepticism
c. Argumentation
d. Curiosity

**6.** Why is psychology considered a science?

a. Psychological researchers rely on observation and experimentation when testing claims.
b. Psychological researchers ask questions about behavior and mental processes.
c. Psychological researchers speculate about how and why people act as they do.
d. Psychological researchers utilize critical thinking.

# Module 0.2 The Need for Psychological Science

## LEARNING TARGETS

**0.2-1** Explain how cognitive biases, such as hindsight bias, overconfidence, and the tendency to perceive order in random events illustrate why science-based answers are more valid than those based on common sense.

**0.2-1** How do cognitive biases, such as hindsight bias, overconfidence, and the tendency to perceive order in random events illustrate why science-based answers are more valid than those based on common sense?

Some people suppose that psychology is mere common sense—documenting and dressing in jargon what people already know: "You get paid for using fancy methods to prove what everyone knows?" Indeed, our intuition is often right. As the baseball great Yogi Berra (1925–2015) once said, "You can observe a lot by watching." (We have Berra to thank for other gems, such as "Nobody ever goes there any more—it's too crowded," and "If the people don't want to come out to the ballpark, nobody's gonna stop 'em.") Because we're all behavior watchers, it would be surprising if many of psychology's findings had *not* been foreseen. Many people believe that love breeds happiness, for example, and they are right (we have what Module 4.7 calls a deep "need to belong").

But sometimes what seems like common sense, informed by countless casual observations, is wrong. In many other modules in this text, we will see how research has overturned popular ideas—that familiarity breeds contempt, that dreams predict the future, and that most of us use only 10 percent of our brain. We will also see how research has surprised us with discoveries about how the brain's chemical messengers control our moods and memories, about other animals' abilities, and about the relationship between social media use and depression.

Other things seem like commonsense truth only because we so often hear them repeated. Mere repetition of statements—whether true or false—makes them easier to

### MYTH: GOING OUTSIDE IN COLD WEATHER WILL MAKE YOU SICK

#### THE FACTS:
- Colds and the flu are caused by viruses.
- Viruses spread more in the winter because people are indoors more, humidity is lower, and having a lower body temperature weakens the immune system.
- You can get hypothermia or frostbite from the cold.

#### THE BOTTOM-LINE:
Cold weather can make you more susceptible to viruses, but going outside while it's cold will not make you sick.

**Critical thinking beats common sense** Psychological scientists use critical thinking to determine whether scientifically derived evidence supports their assumptions. Critical thinking helps us discard myths and seek the truth.

process and remember, and thus more true-seeming (Dechêne at al., 2010; Fazio et al., 2015). Easy-to-remember misconceptions ("Bundle up before you go outside, or you will catch a cold!") can therefore overwhelm hard truths.

Three roadblocks to critical thinking—*hindsight bias, overconfidence,* and *perceiving patterns in random events*—help illustrate why we cannot rely solely on common sense.

## Did We Know It All Along? Hindsight Bias

Consider how easy it is to draw the bull's-eye *after* the arrow strikes. After a couple breaks up, their friends say, "They weren't a good match." After the game, we credit the coach if a "gutsy play" wins the game, and criticize the same "stupid play" if it doesn't. After a war or an election, its outcome usually seems obvious. Although history may therefore seem like a series of inevitable events, the actual future is seldom foreseen. No one's diary recorded, "Today the Hundred Years War began."

This **hindsight bias** (also known as the *I-knew-it-all-along phenomenon*) is easy to demonstrate by giving half the members of a group some purported psychological finding and giving the other half an opposite result. Tell the first group, for example, "Psychologists have found that separation weakens romantic attraction. As the saying goes, 'Out of sight, out of mind.'" Ask them to imagine why this might be true. Most people can, and after hearing an explanation, nearly all will then view this true finding as unsurprising.

Tell the second group the opposite: "Psychologists have found that separation strengthens romantic attraction. As the saying goes, 'Absence makes the heart grow fonder.'" People given this untrue result can also easily imagine it, and most will also see it as unsurprising. When opposite findings both seem like common sense, there is a problem.

Such errors in people's recollections and explanations show why we need psychological research. It's not that common sense is usually wrong. Rather, common sense describes, after the fact, what *has* happened better than it predicts what *will* happen.

**Hindsight bias** When drilling its Deepwater Horizon oil well in 2010, BP employees took shortcuts and ignored warning signs, without intending to harm the environment, their employees, or their company's reputation. After the resulting oil spill in the Gulf of Mexico, with the benefit of 20/20 hindsight, the foolishness of those judgments became obvious.

Everett Collection/Newscom

More than 800 scholarly papers have shown hindsight bias in people young and old from around the world (Roese & Vohs, 2012). As physicist Niels Bohr reportedly jested, "Prediction is very difficult, especially if it's about the future."

# Overconfidence

We humans tend to think we know more than we do. Asked how sure we are of our answers to factual questions (*Is Boston north or south of Paris?*), we tend to be more confident than correct.[1] And our confidence often drives us to quick—rather than correct—thinking (Rahnev et al., 2020). Consider these three anagrams, shown beside their solutions (from Goranson, 1978):

WREAT → WATER

ETRYN → ENTRY

GRABE → BARGE

How many seconds do you think it would have taken you to unscramble each of these? Knowing the answer tends to make us overconfident. (Surely, the solution would take only 10 seconds or so?) In reality, the average problem solver spends 3 minutes, as you also might, given a similar anagram without the solution: OCHSA.[2]

Are we any better at predicting social behavior? Psychologist Philip Tetlock (1998, 2005) collected more than 27,000 expert predictions of world events, such as whether Quebec would separate from Canada. His repeated finding: These predictions, which experts made with 80 percent confidence on average, were right less than 40 percent of the time. It turns out that only about 2 percent of people excel at predicting social behavior. Tetlock (with Gardner, 2016) calls them "superforecasters." Superforecasters avoid overconfidence. Faced with a difficult prediction, a superforecaster "gathers facts, balances clashing arguments, and settles on an answer."

# Perceiving Order in Random Events

We're born with an eagerness to make sense of our world. People see a face on the Moon, or believe their watch shows some number groups more than others. Even in random

*Bizarre-looking, perhaps. But actually no more unlikely than any other number sequence.*

1. Boston is south of Paris.
2. The anagram solution: CHAOS.

data, we often find patterns, because—here's a curious fact of life—*random sequences often don't look random* (Falk et al., 2009; Nickerson, 2002, 2005). Flip a coin 50 times and you may be surprised at the streaks of heads and tails—much like supposed "hot" and "cold" streaks in basketball shooting and baseball hitting. In actual random sequences, patterns and streaks (such as repeating digits) occur more often than people expect (Oskarsson et al., 2009). That also makes it hard for people to generate random-like sequences. When embezzlers try to simulate random digits when specifying how much to steal, their nonrandom patterns can alert fraud experts (Poundstone, 2014).

Why are we so prone to pattern-seeking? For most people, a random, unpredictable world is unsettling (Tullett et al., 2015). Making sense of our world relieves stress and helps us get on with daily living (Ma et al., 2017).

*The point to remember:* Our commonsense thinking is flawed due to three powerful tendencies: hindsight bias, overconfidence, and our tendency to perceive patterns in random events. But scientific inquiry can help us sift reality from illusion.

---

### AP® Science Practice

## Check Your Understanding

**Examine the Concept**

▶ Explain the difference between hindsight bias and overconfidence.

**Apply the Concept**

▶ Do you have a hard time believing you may be overconfident? Could overconfidence be at work in that self-assessment? How might reading this section about overconfidence help reduce your tendency to be overconfident?

▶ Explain why, after friends start dating, we often feel that we *knew* they were meant to be together.

*Answers to the Examine the Concept questions can be found in Appendix C at the end of the book.*

---

# Module 0.2 REVIEW

**0.2-1 How do cognitive biases, such as hindsight bias, overconfidence, and the tendency to perceive order in random events illustrate why science-based answers are more valid than those based on common sense?**

- *Hindsight bias* (also called the "I-knew-it-all-along phenomenon") is the tendency to believe, after learning an outcome, that we would have foreseen it.

- Overconfidence in our judgments results partly from our bias to seek information that confirms them.

- These tendencies, along with our eagerness to perceive patterns in random events, lead us to overestimate the importance of commonsense thinking. Although limited by the testable questions it can address, scientific inquiry can help us overcome such biases and shortcomings.

# AP® Practice Multiple Choice Questions

**1.** The tendency to exaggerate the correctness or accuracy of our beliefs and predictions is called

a. hindsight bias.
b. overconfidence.
c. critical thinking.
d. skepticism.

**2.** While sitting at a stoplight, Nancy believes that the next car she sees will be blue because the previous three cars have been blue. Which psychological concept best explains her belief?

a. Hindsight bias
b. Critical thinking
c. Perceiving order in random events
d. Overconfidence

**3.** After the student council election, a friend tells you he could have guessed who would be elected president. Which psychological phenomenon might this scenario best illustrate?

a. Common sense
b. Hindsight bias
c. Overconfidence
d. Perceiving order in random events

**4.** While taking a standardized test with randomly scrambled answers, you notice that your last four answers have been "c." Which of the following is true concerning the probability of the next answer being "c"?

a. It is higher because previous answers have been "c." Once a streak begins, it is likely to last for a while.
b. It is lower since prior answers have been "c." Since answers are distributed randomly, "c" answers become less common.
c. It is unaffected by previous answers. It is as likely to be "c" as any other answer.
d. It is higher based on previous answers being "c." Test constructors' default answer choice is "c."

**5.** Which of the following is an example of hindsight bias?

a. Armend is certain that electric cars will represent 80 percent of vehicles in 20 years and only reads research studies that support his hypothesis.
b. Liza underestimates how much time it will take her to finish writing her college application essays and fails to meet an important deadline.
c. Alliyah, after reading a definition on one of her flashcards, turns the card over to see the term and then tells herself she knew what the answer was all along.
d. Dr. Grace overestimates the effectiveness of her new treatment method because she fails to seek out any evidence refuting her theory.

# Module 0.3 The Scientific Method

## The Scientific Method

Psychological scientists use the *scientific method*—a self-correcting process for evaluating ideas with observation and analysis. Psychological science welcomes hunches and plausible-sounding theories. And it puts them to the test. If a theory works—if the data support its predictions—so much the better for that theory. If the predictions fail, the theory gets revised or rejected. When researchers submit their work to a scientific journal, **peer reviewers**—other scientists who are experts—evaluate a study's theory, originality, and accuracy. The journal editor then uses the peer reviews to decide whether the research deserves publication.

## Constructing Theories

**0.3-1** How do theories advance psychological science?

**peer reviewers** scientific experts who evaluate a research article's theory, originality, and accuracy.

**theory** an explanation using an integrated set of principles that organizes observations and predicts behaviors or events.

**hypothesis** a testable prediction, often implied by a theory.

**falsifiable** the possibility that an idea, hypothesis, or theory can be disproven by observation or experiment.

In everyday conversation, we often use *theory* to mean "mere hunch." In science, a **theory** *explains* behaviors or events by offering ideas that *organize* observations. By using deeper principles to organize isolated facts, a theory summarizes and simplifies. As we connect the observed dots, a coherent picture emerges. A theory of how sleep affects memory, for example, helps us organize countless sleep-related observations into a short list of principles. Imagine that we observe over and over that people with good sleep habits tend to answer questions correctly in class and do well at test time. We might therefore theorize that sleep improves memory. So far, so good: Our principle neatly summarizes a list of observations about the effects of a good night's sleep.

Yet no matter how reasonable a theory may sound—and it does seem reasonable to suggest that sleep boosts memory—we must put it to the test. A good theory produces testable *predictions*, called **hypotheses**. Such predictions specify which results would support the theory and which results would disconfirm it. The **falsifiability** of a hypothesis is a mark of its scientific strength. (Can it be proven false?) To test our theory about sleep effects on memory, we might hypothesize that when sleep deprived, people will remember less from the day before. To test that hypothesis, we might assess how well people remember class materials they studied either before a good night's sleep or before

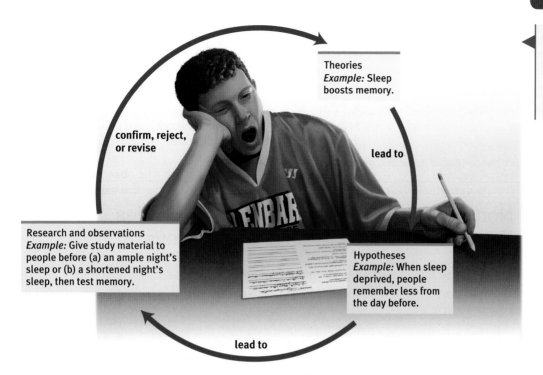

Figure 0.3-1
**The scientific method**
This self-correcting process asks questions and observes nature's answers.

Theories
*Example:* Sleep boosts memory.

confirm, reject, or revise

lead to

Research and observations
*Example:* Give study material to people before (a) an ample night's sleep or (b) a shortened night's sleep, then test memory.

Hypotheses
*Example:* When sleep deprived, people remember less from the day before.

lead to

a shortened night's sleep (**Figure 0.3-1**). The results will either support our theory or lead us to revise or reject it.

Our theories can bias our observations. Having theorized that better memory springs from more sleep, we may see what we expect: Sleep-deprived people's answers are less accurate. The urge to see what we expect is strong, both inside and outside the laboratory, as when people's views of climate change influence their interpretation of local weather events.

In the end, our theory will be useful if it (1) *organizes* observations and (2) implies *predictions* that anyone can use to check the theory or to derive practical applications. (Does people's sleep predict their retention?) Eventually, our research may (3) stimulate further research that leads to a revised theory that better organizes and predicts.

As a check on their own biases, psychologists report their research with precise, measurable **operational definitions** of research procedures and concepts. *Sleep deprived*, for example, may be defined as "at least 2 hours less than a person's natural sleep"; a study of *aggression* may observe how many pins a person stabs into a doll representing a lab partner; and a study of *helping* may record the number of dollars a person donates. By using carefully worded statements, others can **replicate** (repeat) the original observations with different participants, materials, and circumstances. If they get similar results, confidence in the finding's reliability grows. The first study of sleep deprivation aroused psychologists' curiosity. Now, after many successful replications with different people and questions, we feel sure of the phenomenon's power. Replication is confirmation.

We can test our hypotheses and refine our theories using *non-experimental* methods or *experimental* methods. Some non-experimental methods describe behaviors via *case studies, surveys,* or *naturalistic observations;* others compute *correlations* that assess associations among different factors. Experimental methods manipulate variables to see their effects. (As we will see in Module 0.6, *meta-analyses* may be used to analyze the results of multiple studies to reach an overall conclusion.)

**operational definition** a carefully worded statement of the exact procedures (operations) used in a research study. For example, *human intelligence* may be operationally defined as what an intelligence test measures. (Also known as *operationalization*.)

**replication** repeating the essence of a research study, usually with different participants in different situations, to see whether the basic finding can be reproduced.

# Check Your Understanding

**Examine the Concept**

▶ Explain the role of peer review in the scientific process.

▶ Explain why replication is important.

**Apply the Concept**

▶ What are two operational definitions of academic success?

▶ Will what you've learned about theories and replication change the way you read about research results, such as in your news feed?

*Answers to Examine the Concept questions can be found in Appendix C at the end of the book.*

# Non-Experimental Methods: Case Studies, Naturalistic Observations, and Surveys

**0.3-2** How do psychologists use case studies, naturalistic observations, and surveys to observe and describe behavior, and why is random sampling important?

In everyday life, we all observe and describe people, often drawing conclusions about why they think, feel, and act as they do. Professional psychologists do much the same, though more objectively and systematically, using *non-experimental methods*, such as:

- *case studies* (in-depth analyses of individuals or groups),
- *naturalistic observations* (recording the natural behavior of many individuals), and
- *surveys* and interviews (asking people questions).

## The Case Study

Among the oldest research methods, the **case study** examines one individual or group in depth in the hope of revealing things true of us all. Some examples:

- *Brain damage.* Much of our early knowledge about the brain came from case studies of individuals who suffered a particular impairment after damage to a certain brain region.

- *Children's minds.* Developmental psychologist Jean Piaget taught us about children's thinking after carefully observing and questioning only a few children.

- *Animal intelligence.* Studies of various animals, including only a few chimpanzees, have revealed their capacity for understanding and language.

Intensive case studies are sometimes very revealing, and they often suggest directions for further study. But atypical individual cases may mislead us. Both in our everyday lives and in science, unrepresentative information can lead to mistaken conclusions. Indeed, anytime a researcher mentions a finding (*Smokers die younger: 95 percent of men over 85 are nonsmokers*) someone is sure to offer a contradictory anecdote (*Well, I have an uncle who smoked two packs a day and lived to be 89!*).

Dramatic stories and personal experiences (even psychological case examples) command our attention and are easily remembered. Journalists understand this point, so they often begin their articles with compelling stories. Stories move us, but stories can also mislead. Which of the following do you find more memorable? (1) "In one study of 1300 dream reports concerning a kidnapped child, only 5 percent correctly envisioned the child as dead" (Murray & Wheeler,

**Freud and Little Hans** Sigmund Freud's case study of 5-year-old Hans' extreme fear of horses led Freud to his theory of childhood sexuality. He conjectured that Hans felt unconscious desire for his mother, feared castration by his rival father, and then transferred this fear into his phobia about being bitten by a horse. As Module 4.5 will explain, today's psychological science discounts Freud's theory of childhood sexuality but does agree that much of the human mind operates outside our conscious awareness.

**case study** a non-experimental technique in which one individual or group is studied in depth in the hope of revealing universal principles.

1937) or (2) "I know a man who dreamed his sister was in a car accident, and two days later she died in a head-on collision!" Numbers can be numbing, but *the plural of anecdote is not evidence.* As psychologist Gordon Allport (1954, p. 9) said, "Given a thimbleful of [dramatic] facts we rush to make generalizations as large as a tub."

*The point to remember:* Individual cases can suggest fruitful ideas. What's true of all of us can be glimpsed in any one of us. But to find those general truths, we must employ other research methods.

## Naturalistic Observation

A second non-experimental method involves recording responses in natural environments. These **naturalistic observations** have traditionally ranged from watching chimpanzee societies in the jungle, to videotaping and analyzing parent–child interactions in different cultures, to recording racial differences in students' self-seating patterns in a school lunchroom. Until recently, such naturalistic observation was mostly "small science"—possible to do with pen and paper rather than fancy equipment and a big budget (Provine, 2012). But today's digital technologies—thanks to "big data" harvested from phone apps, social media, online searches, and more—have transformed naturalistic observations into big science. Anonymously tapping into 15 million cell phones' GPS (global positioning system) data allowed scientists to track how often people in different geological regions obeyed stay-at-home orders and social distancing recommendations during the Covid pandemic (Glanz et al., 2020). New technologies—wearable cameras and fitness sensors, and internet-connected smart-home sensors—offer increasing possibilities for people to allow accurate recording of their activity, relationships, sleep, and stress (Nelson & Allen, 2018; Yokum et al., 2019).

The billions of people entering personal information online have also enabled big-data observations (without disclosing anyone's identity). One research team studied the ups and downs of human moods by counting positive and negative words in 504 million tweets from 84 countries (Golder & Macy, 2011). As **Figure 0.3-2** shows, people seemed happier on weekends, shortly after waking, and in the evenings. (Are late Saturday

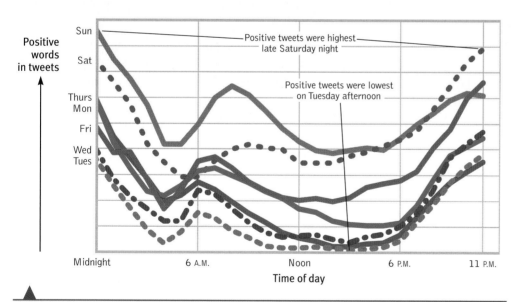

**Figure 0.3-2**

**Twitter message moods, by time and by day**

This graph illustrates how, without knowing anyone's identity, researchers can use big data to study human behavior on a massive scale. It is now possible to associate people's moods with, for example, their locations or the weather, and to study the spread of ideas through social networks. (Data from Golder & Macy, 2011.)

**naturalistic observation** a non-experimental technique of observing and recording behavior in naturally occurring situations without trying to manipulate and control the situation.

**A natural observer** "Observations, made in the natural habitat," noted chimpanzee observer Jane Goodall (1998), "helped to show that the societies and behavior of animals are far more complex than previously supposed."

evenings often a happy time for you, too?) Another study found that negative emotion (especially anger-related) words in 148 million tweets from 1347 U.S. counties predicted the counties' heart disease rates better than other predictors such as smoking and obesity rates (Eichstaedt et al., 2015). Google enables us to learn about the world, and people's Google use enables us to learn about them. For example, the words people search and the questions they ask can gauge a region's level of racism and depression. But Google searches also reveal our universal human likeness—as illustrated by the word "pregnant" being searched in conjunction with the same food cravings worldwide (Stephens-Davidowitz, 2017). Across the globe, we are kin beneath the skin.

Like the case study, naturalistic observation does not *explain* behavior: It *describes* it. Nevertheless, descriptions can be revealing. We once thought, for example, that only humans use tools. Then naturalistic observation revealed that chimpanzees sometimes insert a stick in a termite mound and withdraw it, eating the stick's load of termites. Such unobtrusive naturalistic observations paved the way for later studies of animal thinking, language, and emotion, which further expanded our understanding of our fellow animals.

Naturalistic observations also illuminate human behavior. Here are two findings you might enjoy:

- *A funny finding.* We humans laugh 30 times more often in social situations than in solitary situations (Provine, 2001). (Have you noticed how seldom you laugh when alone?)
- *Culture and the pace of life.* Naturalistic observation also enabled Robert Levine and Ara Norenzayan (1999) to compare the pace of life—walking speed, the accuracy of public clocks, and so forth—in 31 countries. Their conclusion: Life is fastest paced in Japan and Western Europe and slower-paced in economically less-developed countries.

Naturalistic observation offers interesting snapshots of everyday life, but it does so without controlling for all the factors that may influence behavior. It's one thing to observe the pace of life in various places, but another to understand what makes some people walk faster than others. Nevertheless, descriptions can be revealing: The starting point of any science is description.

---

**AP® Science Practice**

## Research

Can you explain how surveys differ from case studies or naturalistic observation? Case studies examine one individual or group in depth, while surveys look at many cases. Naturalistic observation records behavior in naturally occurring situations, as distinguished from the self-report nature of surveys. Being able to explain the differences among the various research methods and designs is an important skill in psychology.

**survey** a non-experimental technique for obtaining the self-reported attitudes or behaviors of a particular group, usually by questioning a representative, *random sample* of the group.

## The Survey

A **survey** looks at many cases in less depth, asking people to report their behavior or opinions. Questions about everything from social media use to political opinions are put to the public. Here are some recent survey findings:

- 1 in 2 people across 24 countries reported believing in the "existence of intelligent alien civilizations in the universe" (Lampert, 2017).
- 54 percent of all humans—some 4.1 billion people—say that religion is very important in their lives (Pew, 2019).

But asking questions is tricky. People may shade their answers in a socially desirable direction, such as by underreporting their cigarette consumption or overreporting their voting. And the answers often depend on how questions are worded and how respondents are chosen.

## Wording Effects

Even small changes in the order or wording of questions can make a big difference (Table 0.3-1). Researchers attempt to phrase questions in a way that reduces **social desirability bias** (people answering in a way they think will please the researcher). To counter **self-report bias** (when people don't accurately report or remember their behaviors), researchers may pair surveys with other means of measuring behaviors.

## Random Sampling

In everyday thinking, we tend to generalize from samples we observe, especially vivid cases. Given (1) a statistical summary of auto owners' evaluations of their car model and (2) the vivid comments of two frustrated owners, our impression may be influenced as much by the two unhappy owners as by the many more summarized evaluations. The temptation to succumb to **sampling bias**—to generalize from a few vivid but unrepresentative cases—is nearly irresistible. *Convenience sampling* is also tempting—collecting research from a group that is readily available, such as your friends at school, rather than a sample that would represent *all* the students at your school.

So how do you obtain a *representative sample?* Say you want to learn how students at your high school feel about online instruction. How could you choose a group that would represent the total student body? Typically, you would seek a **random sample**, in which every person in the entire **population** has an equal chance of being included in the sample group. You might number the names in the school directory and use a random-number generator to pick your survey participants. (Sending each student a questionnaire wouldn't work, because the conscientious people who returned it would not be a random sample.) Large representative samples are better than small ones, but a smaller representative sample of 100 is better than a larger unrepresentative sample of 500. You cannot compensate for an unrepresentative sample by simply adding more people.

Political pollsters sample voters in national election surveys just this way. Without random sampling, large samples—such as from "opt-in" website polls—often give misleading results. But by using some 1500 randomly sampled people, drawn from all areas of a country, they can provide a reasonably accurate snapshot of the nation's opinions. In today's world, however, with so many people not answering phones, door knocks, and emails, getting a random sample is a challenge.

*The point to remember:* Before accepting survey findings, think critically. Consider the sample. The best basis for generalizing is from a representative, random sample.

**social desirability bias** bias from people's responding in ways they presume a researcher expects or wishes.

**self-report bias** bias when people report their behavior inaccurately.

**sampling bias** a flawed sampling process that produces an unrepresentative sample.

**random sample** a sample that fairly represents a population because each member has an equal chance of inclusion.

**population** all those in a group being studied, from which random samples may be drawn. (*Note:* Except for national studies, this does not refer to a country's whole population.)

| TABLE 0.3-1 Survey Wording Effects | |
| --- | --- |
| **Garners More Approval** | **Garners Less Approval** |
| "aid to those in need" | "welfare" |
| "undocumented workers" | "illegal aliens" |
| "gun safety laws" | "gun control laws" |
| "revenue enhancers" | "taxes" |
| "enhanced interrogation" | "torture" |
| "pre-owned" | "used" |

### Examine the Concept

▶ Explain why we cannot assume that case studies always reveal general principles that apply to all of us.

▶ Explain how the wording can change the results of a survey.

▶ Explain the differences among case studies, naturalistic observation, and surveys.

*Answers to the Examine the Concept questions can be found in Appendix C at the end of the book.*

### Apply the Concept

▶ From your observations of people, can you think of a "case study" that has taught you something about people in general?

▶ Can you recall a misleading survey you have experienced or read about?

## Module 0.3 REVIEW

**0.3-1 How do theories advance psychological science?**

- Psychological *theories* are explanations that apply an integrated set of principles to organize observations and generate *hypotheses*—predictions that are falsifiable and can be used to check the theory or produce practical applications of it. By testing their hypotheses, researchers can confirm, reject, or revise their theories.

- To enable other researchers to *replicate* their studies, researchers report them using precise *operational definitions* of their procedures and concepts. If others achieve similar results, confidence in the conclusion will be greater.

**0.3-2 How do psychologists use case studies, naturalistic observations, and surveys to observe and describe behavior, and why is random sampling important?**

- Non-experimental methods, which include *case studies, naturalistic observations*, and *surveys*, show us what can happen, and they may offer ideas for further study.

- The best basis for generalizing about a *population* is a representative sample; in a *random sample*, every person in the entire population being studied has an equal chance of participating.

- Non-experimental methods describe but do not *explain* behavior, because these methods do not control for the many variables that can affect behavior.

## AP® Practice Multiple Choice Questions

**1.** Why is an operational definition necessary when reporting research findings?

a. An operational definition allows others to replicate the study.

b. An operational definition provides many examples of the concept.

c. An operational definition uses more scientific language than a dictionary definition.

d. An operational definition considers contextual elements that may affect the study's results.

**2.** Which of the following questions is best investigated by means of a survey?

a. Are people more likely to vote Republican or Democrat in the next U.S. election?

b. Does extra sleep improve memory?

c. What is the most effective study technique for AP® exams?

d. What role does exercise play in heart health?

**3.** A testable prediction that drives research is known as a(n)

a. theory.

b. hypothesis.

c. operational definition.

d. random sample.

4. Researchers are interested in finding out if voters are more likely to vote for candidates who have more pleasant facial expressions. The researchers contact every hundredth person on the voter list to ask about candidate facial expressions. Which method are the researchers using in choosing the people they will call?

   a. Random sample
   b. Biased sample
   c. Survey
   d. Population

5. An individual with an exceptional memory is identified. For any given date, she is capable of recalling major events, the weather, and what she did that day. Which research method is being used if a psychologist conducts an in-depth investigation of this individual using questionnaires, brain scans, and memory tests?

   a. Naturalistic observation
   b. Survey
   c. Interview
   d. Case study

6. Dr. Tazurphase asked 100 people who were in line to ride the largest roller coaster in the world if they would be willing to purchase and drive a flying car. He also gave each person a survey asking questions about their personalities. Based on his results, he claimed that people who are efficient and open to new things were the most willing to purchase and drive a flying car. Which of the following describes one issue with Dr. Tazurphase's study?

   a. Dr. Tazurphase did not choose a representative sample, so he is unable to make claims about the larger population's willingness to purchase a flying car.
   b. Dr. Tazurphase did not choose a large enough sample, so he is unable to make claims about the larger population's willingness to buy a flying car.

   c. Dr. Tazurphase did not include a control group to compare his results against, so he cannot determine the cause of someone's willingness to purchase a flying car.
   d. Dr. Tazurphase did not randomly assign participants to groups, so he cannot determine the cause of someone's willingness to purchase a flying car.

7. Town City is considering installing new street lamps. Which question might Town City officials ask to ensure that they do not bias respondents?

   a. "How much do you want to replace the broken, old lamps with working, new lamps?"
   b. "Are you in favor of the inflated taxes associated with the installation of the existing street lamps?"
   c. "To what extent are you in favor of installing street lamps throughout Town City?"
   d. "When should we replace the street lamps?"

8. Dr. Buzz wanted to understand the impact of stressful life events on irritability. He asked college students to reflect on three major stressors in their lives, and then he asked the students how many times in a week they yelled at other people. Which of the following captures how Dr. Buzz operationally defined irritability?

   a. Reflecting on three major stressors
   b. Irritability
   c. The number of times the students yelled in a week
   d. Stressful life events

# Correlation and Experimentation

**correlation** a measure of the extent to which two factors vary together, and thus of how well either factor predicts the other.

**correlation coefficient** a statistical index of the relationship between two variables (from −1.00 to +1.00).

**variable** anything that can vary and is feasible and ethical to measure.

**scatterplot** a graphed cluster of dots, each of which represents the values of two variables. The slope of the points suggests the direction of the relationship between the two variables. The amount of scatter suggests the strength of the correlation (little scatter indicates high correlation).

Psychologists use different methods to describe, predict, and explain how we think, feel, and act. Correlational research (a *non-experimental* method) describes the relationship between two or more variables. *Experiments* attempt to establish a cause-and-effect connection.

## Correlation

**0.4-1** What does it mean when we say two things are correlated, and what are positive and negative correlations?

Describing behavior is a first step toward predicting it. Naturalistic observations and surveys often show us that one trait or behavior tends to coincide with another. In such cases, we say the two **correlate**. A statistical measure (the **correlation coefficient**) helps us figure out how closely two things vary together, and thus how well either one *predicts* the other. Knowing how much aptitude test scores *correlate* with school success tells us how well the scores *predict* school success.

Throughout this book, we often ask how strongly two **variables** are related: How closely related are the personality test scores for identical twins? How well do intelligence test scores predict career achievement? In such cases, **scatterplots** can be very revealing.

Each dot in a scatterplot represents the values of two variables. The three scatterplots in **Figure 0.4-1** illustrate the range of possible correlations from a perfect positive to a

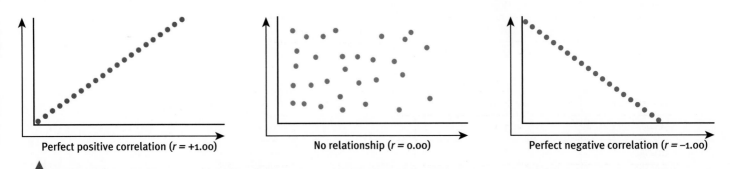

Perfect positive correlation (*r* = +1.00)　　　No relationship (*r* = 0.00)　　　Perfect negative correlation (*r* = −1.00)

**Figure 0.4-1**

**Scatterplots, showing patterns of correlation**

Correlations — abbreviated *r* — can range from +1.00 (scores for one variable increase in direct proportion to scores for another variable) to 0.00 (no relationship) to −1.00 (scores for one variable decrease precisely as scores for the other variable rise).

perfect negative. (Perfect correlations rarely occur in the real world.) A correlation is positive if two sets of scores, such as for height and weight, tend to rise or fall together.

Saying that a correlation is "negative" says nothing about its strength. A negative correlation isn't "bad." It simply means two sets of scores relate inversely, one set going up as the other goes down. The correlation between people's height and the distance from their head to the ceiling is strongly (perfectly, in fact) negative.

Statistics can reveal what we might miss with casual observation. To demonstrate, consider the responses of 2291 Czech and Slovakian volunteers who were asked to rate, on a 1 to 7 scale, their *fear* and *disgust* related to each of 24 animals (Polák et al., 2020). With all the relevant data right in front of you (Table 0.4-1), can you tell whether the correlation between participants' fear and their disgust is positive, negative, or close to zero?

### TABLE 0.4-1 People's Fear and Disgust Responses to Various Animals

| Animal | Average Fear | Average Disgust |
|---|---|---|
| Ant | 2.12 | 2.26 |
| Bat | 2.11 | 2.01 |
| Bull | 3.84 | 1.62 |
| Cat | 1.24 | 1.17 |
| Cockroach | 3.10 | 4.16 |
| Dog | 2.25 | 1.20 |
| Fish | 1.15 | 1.38 |
| Frog | 1.84 | 2.48 |
| Grass snake | 3.32 | 2.47 |
| Horse | 1.82 | 1.11 |
| Lizard | 1.46 | 1.46 |
| Louse | 3.58 | 4.83 |
| Maggot | 2.90 | 4.49 |
| Mouse | 1.62 | 1.78 |
| Panda | 1.57 | 1.17 |
| Pigeon | 1.48 | 2.01 |
| Rat | 2.11 | 2.25 |
| Rooster | 1.78 | 1.34 |
| Roundworm | 3.49 | 4.79 |
| Snail | 1.15 | 1.69 |
| Spider | 4.39 | 4.47 |
| Tapeworm | 3.60 | 4.83 |
| Viper | 4.34 | 2.83 |
| Wasp | 3.42 | 2.84 |

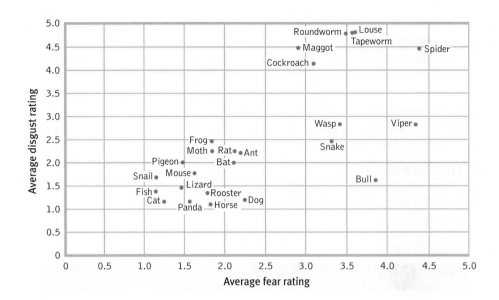

**Figure 0.4-2**

**Scatterplot for fear and disgust felt toward 24 animals**

This display of average self-reported fear and disgust (each represented by a data point) reveals an upward slope, indicating a positive correlation. The considerable scatter of the data indicates the correlation is much lower than +1.00.

When comparing the columns in Table 0.4-1, you might not detect much of a relationship between fear and disgust. In fact, the correlation in this example is positive ($r = +.72$), as we can see if we display the data as a scatterplot (**Figure 0.4-2**).

If we fail to see a relationship when data are presented as systematically as in Table 0.4-1, how much less likely are we to notice them in everyday life? To see what is right in front of us, we sometimes need statistical illumination. We can easily see evidence of gender discrimination when given statistically summarized information about job level, seniority, performance, gender, and salary. But we often see no discrimination when the same information dribbles in, case by case (Twiss et al., 1989). Single events or individuals catch our attention, especially if we want to see (or deny) bias. In contrast, statistics calculate patterns by counting every case equally. See **Table 0.4-2** to test your understanding further.

Correlations can help us see the world more clearly by revealing the extent to which two things relate. However, correlational research has a *directionality problem*—it cannot tell us which variable is the cause, and which one is the effect. If teen social media use correlates with (predicts) teen risk of depression, that may—or may not—indicate that social media use causes an increased risk of depression. The research may also have a *third variable problem* (see Developing Arguments: Correlation and Causation).

---

**TABLE 0.4-2  Test Your Understanding of Correlation**

Which of the following news reports are examples of a *positive* correlation, and which are examples of a *negative* correlation? (Check your answers below.)

1. The more college students sleep, the better their academic performance (Okano et al., 2019). _____

2. The more time teen girls spend absorbed with online social media, the more at risk they are for depression and suicidal thoughts (Kelly et al., 2019; Twenge & Campbell, 2019). _____

3. The longer children were breast-fed, the greater their later academic achievement (Horwood & Fergusson, 1998). _____

4. The more leafy vegetables older adults eat, the less their mental decline over the ensuing 5 years (Morris et al., 2018). _____

ANSWERS: 1. positive; 2. positive; 3. positive; 4. negative.

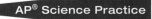 **AP® Science Practice** # Developing Arguments

## Correlation and Causation

Mental illness *correlates* with smoking—meaning that those who experience mental illness are also more likely to be smokers.[1] Does this tell us anything about what *causes* mental illness or smoking? **NO.**

There is a *directionality problem*: There may be something about smoking that leads to mental illness...

Or those with mental illness may be more likely to smoke.

**OR**

There may be some *third variable*, such as a stressful home life, for example, that triggers *both* smoking and mental illness.

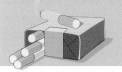

So, then, how would you interpret these recent findings: a) sexual hook-ups correlate with college women's experiencing depression, and b) *delaying* sexual intimacy correlates with positive outcomes such as greater relationship satisfaction and stability?[2]

**Possible explanations:**

| | |
|---|---|
| 1. Sexual restraint → | Better mental health and stronger relationships |
| 2. Depression → | People being more likely to hook up |
| 3. Some third variable, such as lower impulsivity → | Sexual restraint, psychological well-being, and better relationships |

Correlations do help us predict. Consider: Self-esteem correlates negatively with (and therefore predicts) depression. The lower people's self-esteem, the greater their risk for depression.

**Possible interpretations:**

| | | |
|---|---|---|
| 1. Low self-esteem → | Depression | Directionality problem |
| 2. Depression → | Low self-esteem | |
| 3. Some third variable, such as distressing events or biological predispostion → | Both low self-esteem and depression | |

**You try it!**
A survey of over 12,000 adolescents found that the more teens feel loved by their parents, the less likely they are to behave in unhealthy ways—having early sex, smoking, abusing alcohol and drugs, exhibiting violence.[3] What are three possible ways we could interpret that finding?

---

*The point to remember:* **Correlation does not equal causation.**
Correlation suggests a possible cause-effect relationship but does not prove it. Remember this principle and you will be wiser as you read and hear news of scientific studies.

---

## Developing Arguments Questions

**1.** What were your responses to the "You Try It" question? Were you able to identify three possible ways to interpret that finding?

**2.** Using scientifically derived evidence presented above, explain why correlation does not equal causation.

1. Belluck, 2013. 2. Fielder et al., 2013; Willoughby et al., 2014. 3. Resnick et al., 1997.

## Illusory Correlations and Regression Toward the Mean

**0.4-2** What are illusory correlations, and what is regression toward the mean?

Nancy Brown/The Image Bank/Getty Images

**Correlation need not mean causation** Length of marriage positively correlates with hair loss in men. Does this mean that marriage causes men to lose their hair (or that balding men make better husbands)?[3]

❝ *Once you become sensitized to it, you see regression everywhere.* ❞

*Psychologist Daniel Kahneman (1985)*

Correlations make clear the relationships we might otherwise miss; they also keep us from falsely assuming a relationship exists where there really is none. When we believe there is a relationship between two things, we are likely to notice and recall instances that confirm our belief. If we believe that dreams forecast actual events, we may notice and recall confirming instances more than disconfirming instances. The result is an **illusory correlation**.

Illusory correlations can feed an illusion of control—that we can personally influence chance events. Gamblers, remembering past lucky rolls, may come to believe they influenced the roll of the dice by throwing gently for low numbers and hard for high numbers. The illusion that uncontrollable events correlate with our actions is also fed by a statistical phenomenon called **regression toward the mean**. Extreme results, such as a lower-than-expected test score, are caused by unfortunate combinations—test topic, question difficulty, our sleep (or lack thereof), the weather. The same combination may not happen again, so our next test score should be higher. Simply said, extraordinary happenings tend to be followed by more ordinary ones. Outlier grades will usually regress toward students' average grades. And a team's unusually poor performance in one game will usually improve the next.

Failure to recognize regression can cause superstitious thinking. After berating a team for poorer-than-usual performance, a coach may—when the team regresses to normal—think the scolding actually worked. After lavishing praise for an exceptionally fine performance, the coach may be disappointed when a team's behavior migrates back toward its average. In an unexpected twist, then, regression toward the average can mislead us into feeling rewarded after criticizing others ("That criticism really made them work harder!") and feeling punished after praising them ("All those compliments made them slack off!") (Tversky & Kahneman, 1974).

*The point to remember:* When a fluctuating behavior returns to normal, fancy explanations for why it does so are often wrong. Regression toward the mean is probably at work.

---

### AP® Science Practice

## Check Your Understanding

**Examine the Concept**

▶ How would you interpret a *correlation coefficient* of –0.87?

▶ Describe a scatterplot.

**Apply the Concept**

▶ Can you think of a popular media report you've read that confused correlation with causation?

▶ You hear the school basketball coach telling her friend that she rescued her team's winning streak by yelling at the players after an unusually bad first half. What is another explanation of why the team's performance improved?

*Answers to the Examine the Concept questions can be found in Appendix C at the end of the book.*

---

## Experimentation

**0.4-3** What are the characteristics of experimentation that make it possible to isolate cause and effect?

**illusory correlation** perceiving a relationship where none exists, or perceiving a stronger-than-actual relationship.

**regression toward the mean** the tendency for extreme or unusual scores or events to fall back (regress) toward the average.

Happy are they, remarked the Roman poet Virgil, "who have been able to perceive the causes of things." How might psychologists sleuth out the causes in correlational studies, such as the correlation between teen girls' social media use and their risk of depression and self-harm (Odgers & Jensen, 2020)? To establish cause and effect, psychologists use experimentation.

3. In this case, as in many others, a third variable can explain the correlation: Golden anniversaries and baldness both accompany aging.

## Experimental Manipulation

Our sleuthing starts with two plain facts:

1. Beginning in 2010, worldwide smartphone and social media use swelled.

2. Simultaneously, Canadian, American, and British teen girls' rates of depression, anxiety, self-harm, and suicide also mushroomed (Mercado et al., 2017; Morgan et al., 2017; Statistics Canada, 2016).

What do such findings mean? Is there a cause-effect connection, perhaps above a certain amount of screen time? Should parents limit their children's screen time? Even big correlational data from a million teens couldn't tell us. Moving beyond the simple correlation, in seven of nine *longitudinal* (over time) studies, teens' current social media use predicted future mental health issues (Haidt & Twenge, 2019; Zhou et al., 2020). Even so, to identify cause and effect, researchers must **experiment**. Experiments enable researchers to isolate the effects of one or more factors by (1) *manipulating the factors of interest* and (2) *holding constant ("controlling") other factors*. To do so, they often create an **experimental group**, in which people receive the treatment (such as reduced screen time), and a contrasting **control group**, in which they do not.

To minimize any preexisting differences between the two groups, experimenters **randomly assign** people to each condition. Random assignment—whether with a random numbers table or the flip of a coin—effectively equalizes the two groups. If one-third of the volunteers for an experiment can wiggle their ears, then about one-third of the people in each group will be ear wigglers. So, too, with age, attitudes, and other characteristics, which will be similar in the experimental and control groups. Thus, if the groups differ at the experiment's end, we can surmise that the treatment had an effect. (Note the difference between random *sampling*, which creates a representative survey sample, and random *assignment*, which equalizes the experimental and control groups.)

So, what do *experiments* reveal about the relationship between girls' social media use and their risk of depression and self-harm? One experiment identified nearly 1700 people who agreed to deactivate their Facebook account for 4 weeks (Allcott et al., 2020). Compared with people in the control group, those randomly assigned to the deactivation group spent more time watching TV and socializing with friends and family—and they reported lower depression, and greater happiness and satisfaction with their lives (and less post-experiment Facebook use). Less Facebook time meant a happier life.

The debate over the effects of prolonged social media use is ongoing. For now, most researchers agree that unlimited teen social media use poses a modest mental health risk. With more large correlational and longitudinal studies, and more experiments, researchers will refine this tentative conclusion.

*The point to remember:* Correlational studies, which uncover naturally occurring relationships, are complemented by experiments, which manipulate a factor to determine its effect.

**experiment** a research method in which an investigator manipulates one or more factors (independent variables) to observe the effect on some behavior or mental process (the dependent variable). By *random assignment* of participants, the experimenter aims to control other relevant factors.

**experimental group** in an experiment, the group exposed to the treatment—that is, to one version of the independent variable.

**control group** in an experiment, the group *not* exposed to the treatment; contrasts with the experimental group and serves as a comparison for evaluating the effect of the treatment.

**random assignment** assigning participants to experimental and control groups by chance, thus minimizing preexisting differences between the different groups.

## Procedures and the Placebo Effect

Consider, then, how we might assess therapeutic interventions. Our tendency to seek new remedies when we are ill or emotionally down can produce misleading testimonies. If three days into a cold we start taking zinc tablets and find our cold symptoms lessening, we may credit the pills rather than the cold naturally subsiding. In the 1700s, bloodletting *seemed* effective. When the patient actually survived, this "treatment" was credited for the recovery. When patients didn't survive, the practitioner inferred the disease was too advanced to be reversed. So, whether or not a remedy is truly effective, enthusiastic users will probably endorse it. To determine a treatment's effect, we must control for other factors.

And that is precisely how new drugs and new methods of psychological therapy are evaluated (Module 5.5). Investigators randomly assign participants in these

*"If I don't think it's going to work, will it still work?"*

**single-blind procedure** an experimental procedure in which the research participants are ignorant (blind) about whether they have received the treatment or a placebo.

**double-blind procedure** an experimental procedure in which both the research participants and the research staff are ignorant (blind) about whether the research participants have received the treatment or a placebo. Commonly used in drug-evaluation studies.

**placebo** [pluh-SEE-bo; Latin for "I shall please"] **effect** experimental results caused by expectations alone; any effect on behavior caused by the administration of an inert substance or condition, which the recipient assumes is an active agent.

**independent variable** in an experiment, the factor that is manipulated; the variable whose effect is being studied.

**confounding variable** in an experiment, a factor other than the factor being studied that might influence a study's results.

**experimenter bias** bias caused when researchers may unintentionally influence results to confirm their own beliefs.

**dependent variable** in an experiment, the outcome that is measured; the variable that may change when the independent variable is manipulated.

studies to research groups. One group receives a pseudotreatment—an inert *placebo* (perhaps a pill with no drug in it). The other group receives a treatment, such as an antidepressant medication. The participants are often *blind* (uninformed) about what treatment, if any, they are receiving, which is considered a **single-blind procedure**. If the study is using a **double-blind procedure**, neither the participants nor those who administer the drug and collect the data will know which group is receiving the treatment.

In double-blind studies, researchers check a treatment's actual effects apart from the participants' and the staff's belief in its healing powers. Just *thinking* you are getting a treatment can boost your spirits, relax your body, and relieve your symptoms. This **placebo effect** is well documented in reducing pain, depression, anxiety, and even auditory hallucinations in schizophrenia (Dollfus et al., 2016; Kirsch, 2010). Athletes have run faster when given a supposed performance-enhancing drug (McClung & Collins, 2007). Decaf-coffee drinkers have reported increased vigor and alertness when they thought their brew had caffeine in it (Dawkins et al., 2011). And the more expensive the placebo, the more "real" it seems to us—a fake pill that costs $2.50 works better than one costing 10 cents (Waber et al., 2008). To know how effective a therapy really is, researchers must control for a possible placebo effect.

## Independent and Dependent Variables

Here is a practical experiment: Victor Benassi and his colleagues gave college psychology students frequent in-class quizzes. Some items served merely as review—students were given questions with answers. Other self-testing items required students to actively produce the answers. When tested weeks later on a final exam, students did far better on material on which they had been tested (75 percent correct) rather than merely reviewed (51 percent correct). By a wide margin, testing beat restudy.

This simple experiment manipulated just one factor: the study procedure (reading answers versus self-testing). We call this experimental factor the **independent variable** because we can vary it *independently* of other factors, such as the students' memories, intelligence, and age. Other factors that can potentially influence a study's results are called **confounding variables**. Single-blind procedures help control for the *social desirability bias* (participants affecting results by trying to please the researchers). Double-blind procedures reduce **experimenter bias** (when researchers may unintentionally influence results to confirm their own beliefs). In experiments, random assignment ensures that confounding variables have an equal chance of appearing in the experimental and control conditions. Therefore, random assignment controls for possible confounding variables.

Experiments examine the effect of one or more independent variables on some measurable behavior, called the **dependent variable** because it can vary *depending* on what takes place during the experiment. Both variables are given precise *operational definitions*, which specify the procedures that manipulate the independent variable (the review versus self-testing study method in this experiment) and measure the dependent variable (final exam performance). These definitions offer a level of precision that enables others to replicate the study. (**Figure 0.4-3** depicts the previously mentioned Facebook experiment design.)

### Figure 0.4-3
### Experimentation

To establish causation, psychologists control for confounding variables by randomly assigning some participants to an experimental group and others to a control group. Measuring the dependent variable (depression score) will determine the effect of the independent variable (social media exposure).

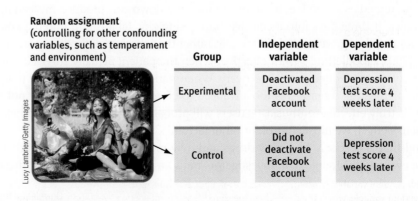

Random assignment (controlling for other confounding variables, such as temperament and environment)

| Group | Independent variable | Dependent variable |
|---|---|---|
| Experimental | Deactivated Facebook account | Depression test score 4 weeks later |
| Control | Did not deactivate Facebook account | Depression test score 4 weeks later |

Let's pause to check your understanding using a simple psychology experiment: To test the effect of perceived ethnicity on the availability of rental housing, researchers sent identically worded email inquiries to 1115 Los Angeles–area landlords (Carpusor & Loges, 2006). The researchers varied the ethnic connotation of the sender's name and tracked the percentage of positive replies (invitations to view the apartment in person). "Patrick McDougall," "Said Al-Rahman," and "Tyrell Jackson" received, respectively, 89 percent, 66 percent, and 56 percent invitations. In this experiment, what was the independent variable? What was the dependent variable?[4]

A key goal of experimental design is **validity**, which means the experiment tests what it is supposed to test. In the rental housing experiment, we might ask, "Did the email inquiries test the effect of perceived ethnicity? Did the landlords' responses actually vary with the ethnicity of the name?"

Let's recap. A *variable* is anything that can vary (social media exposure, test performance, landlord responses—anything within the bounds of what is feasible and ethical). Experiments aim to *manipulate* an *independent* variable, *measure* a *dependent* variable, and *control confounding* variables. An experiment has at least two different conditions: an *experimental condition* and a *comparison* or *control condition*. *Random assignment* works to minimize preexisting differences between the groups before any treatment effects occur. In this way, an experiment tests the effect of at least one independent variable (what we manipulate) on at least one dependent variable (the outcome we measure).

**AP® Science Practice**

**Research**

Independent and dependent variables are only relevant to experimental methods in which an investigator manipulates one or more factors (the independent variable) to observe the effect on some behavior or mental process (the dependent variable).

**AP® Science Practice**

**Research**

Researchers strive for both validity (the extent to which a test or experiment measures what it is supposed to measure) *and* reliability (the extent to which findings can be replicated, as described in Module 0.3).

---

**AP® Science Practice** · **Check Your Understanding**

**Examine the Concept**

▶ By using *random assignment*, researchers are able to control for _____ _____, which are other factors besides the independent variable(s) that may influence research results.

▶ Match the term on the left (i through iii) with the description on the right (a through c).

| | |
|---|---|
| i. Double-blind procedure | a. in an experiment, the outcome that is measured; the variable that may change when the independent variable is manipulated |
| ii. Dependent variable | b. helps minimize preexisting differences between experimental and control groups |
| iii. Random assignment | c. controls for the placebo effect; neither researchers nor participants know who receives the real treatment |

▶ Explain the difference between random assignment and random sampling.

**Apply the Concept**

▶ Explain why, when testing a new drug to control blood pressure, we would learn more about its effectiveness by giving it to half the participants in a group of 1000 rather than to all 1000 participants.

▶ If you became a research psychologist, which questions would you like to explore with experiments?

▶ Can you think of a time when you may have been fooled by the placebo effect?

*Answers to the Examine the Concept questions can be found in Appendix C at the end of the book.*

---

**❝** *[We must guard] against not just racial slurs, but . . . against the subtle impulse to call Johnny back for a job interview, but not Jamal.* **❞**

*U.S. President Barack Obama, Eulogy for Clementa Pinckney, June 26, 2015*

**AP® Exam Tip**

The identification of independent and dependent variables will likely be tested on the AP® exam. Experiments are critical to psychology, and independent and dependent variables are critical to experiments.

**validity** the extent to which a test or experiment measures or predicts what it is supposed to.

---

4. The independent variable, which the researchers manipulated, was the implied ethnicity of the applicants' names. The dependent variable, which the researchers measured, was the rate of positive responses from the landlords.

 **AP® Science Practice**

## Exploring Research Methods & Design

This feature, which shows up throughout the modules in this text, allows you to apply your knowledge of research methods in the context of psychological content.

Imagine you are a researcher interested in stress and the immune system. You want to answer this question: Does stress cause a decrease in immune functioning?

• Explain why you would need to use the experimental method to address this question.

• What would be your independent variable? What would be your dependent variable?

# Module 0.4 REVIEW

**0.4-1** What does it mean when we say two things are correlated, and what are positive and negative correlations?

• *Correlation* is the degree to which two variables are related, and how well one predicts the other.

• In a positive correlation, two factors increase or decrease together. In a negative correlation, one variable increases as the other decreases.

• A *correlation coefficient* describes the strength and direction of a relationship between two variables, from +1.00 (a perfect positive correlation) through zero (no correlation at all) to −1.00 (a perfect negative correlation).

• Data on a relationship may be displayed in a *scatterplot*, in which each dot represents a value for the two variables.

• Correlational research is a non-experimental method. Correlations enable prediction because they show how two factors are related—either positively or negatively. A correlation can indicate the possibility of a cause-effect relationship, but it does not prove the direction of the influence, or whether an underlying third variable may explain the correlation.

**0.4-2** What are illusory correlations, and what is regression toward the mean?

• *Illusory correlations* are random events that we notice and falsely assume are related.

• *Regression toward the mean* is the tendency for extreme or unusual scores to fall back toward their average.

**0.4-3** What are the characteristics of experimentation that make it possible to isolate cause and effect?

• To discover cause-effect relationships, psychologists conduct *experiments*, manipulating one or more variables of interest and controlling other variables.

• Using *random assignment*, they can minimize *confounding variables*, such as preexisting differences between the *experimental group* (exposed to the treatment) and the *control group* (given a placebo or different version of the treatment).

• The *independent variable* is the factor that the experimenter manipulates to study its effect; the *dependent variable* is the factor that the experimenter measures to discover any changes occurring in response to the manipulation of the independent variable.

• Studies may use a *single-blind procedure* to control for the social desirability bias, and they may use a *double-blind procedure* to avoid the *placebo effect* and experimenter bias.

• An experiment has *validity* if it tests what it is supposed to test.

# AP® Practice Multiple Choice Questions

**1.** Which of the following is an example of negative correlation?

   a. People who spend more time exercising tend to experience less depression.

   b. Students with lower IQ scores tend to have lower grades.

   c. As hours studying for a test decrease, so do grades on that test.

   d. Students' shoe sizes are not related to their grades.

**2.** In an experiment to test the effects of room temperature on test performance, the independent variable is

   a. the scores on the test before the experiment begins.

   b. the scores on the test at the end of the experiment.

   c. the role of the teacher.

   d. the temperature of the room.

**3.** Researchers have discovered that individuals with lower income levels report having fewer hours of total sleep. Therefore,

   a. income and sleep levels are positively correlated.

   b. income and sleep levels are negatively correlated.

   c. income and sleep levels are not correlated.

   d. lower income levels cause individuals to have fewer hours of sleep.

**4.** Which of the following correlation coefficients represents the strongest relationship between two variables?

   a. +0.75

   b. +1.3

   c. −0.85

   d. −0.05

**5.** The purpose of random assignment is to

   a. give every member of the population an equal chance to participate in the research.

   b. eliminate the placebo effect.

   c. reduce potential confounding variables.

   d. generate operational definitions for the independent and dependent variables.

**6.** In a drug study, neither the participants nor the person distributing the pills knows who is receiving the new drug and who is receiving the placebo. This type of research design is said to be a(n) _____ study.

   a. correlational

   b. confounding

   c. double-blind

   d. single-blind

**7.** Which of the following best describes the purpose of a control group in an experimental design?

   a. Having a control group allows researchers to reduce the effect of confounding variables on the dynamic between the independent variable and the dependent variable.

   b. Having a control group allows researchers to determine a cause-and-effect relation between the independent variable and dependent variable.

   c. Having a control group allows researchers to better generalize their results to the population of interest.

   d. Having a control group allows researchers to replicate the results from past research.

# Module 0.5 Research Design and Ethics in Psychology

## LEARNING TARGETS

**0.5-1** Explain the process of determining which research design to use.

**0.5-2** Explain the value of simplified laboratory conditions in illuminating everyday life.

**0.5-3** Explain why psychologists study animals, and explain the ethical research guidelines that safeguard human and animal welfare.

**0.5-4** Describe how psychologists' values influence what they study and how they apply their results.

Psychologists use research to ask questions about how we think, feel, and act. Before doing their research, psychologists need to consider which research design to use. They need to reflect on whether their laboratory findings may generalize across different populations, time periods, and cultures. And they need to carefully think through how their research will follow ethical research guidelines.

## Research Design

### AP® Exam Tip

Table 0.5-1 summarizes over 13 pages of coverage. Spend some time with it, as it is information you will likely encounter on the AP® exam.

**0.5-1** How would you know which research design to use?

Throughout this book, you will read about amazing psychological science discoveries. How do psychological scientists choose research methods and design their studies in ways that provide meaningful results? Understanding how research is done—how testable questions are developed and studied—is key to appreciating all of psychology. **Table 0.5-1**

### TABLE 0.5-1 Comparing Research Methods

| Research Method | Basic Purpose | How Conducted | What Is Manipulated | Weaknesses |
|---|---|---|---|---|
| *Non-experimental: Case Studies, Naturalistic Observations, Surveys* | To observe and record behavior | Do case studies, naturalistic observations, or surveys | Nothing | No control of variables; single cases may be misleading |
| *Non-experimental: Correlational Studies* | To detect naturally occurring relationships; to assess how well one variable predicts another | Collect data on two or more variables; no manipulation | Nothing | Cannot specify cause and effect |
| *Experimental* | To explore cause and effect | Manipulate one or more factors; use random assignment | The independent variable(s) | Sometimes not feasible; results may not generalize to other contexts; not ethical to manipulate certain variables |

compares the features of psychology's main research methods. In later modules, you will read about other research designs, including *twin studies* (Module 1.1) and *cross-sectional* and *longitudinal research* (Module 2.8).

In psychological research, no questions are off limits, except untestable (or unethical) ones: Does free will exist? Are people born evil? Is there an afterlife? Psychologists can't test those questions. But they *can* test whether free-will beliefs, aggressive personalities, and a belief in life after death influence how people think, feel, and act (Dechesne et al., 2003; Shariff et al., 2014; Webster et al., 2014).

Having chosen their question, psychologists then select the most appropriate research design—*experimental, correlational, case study, naturalistic observation, twin study, longitudinal,* or *cross-sectional*—and determine how to set it up most effectively. They consider the amount of money and time available, ethical issues, and other limitations. For example, it wouldn't be ethical for a researcher studying child development to use the experimental method and randomly assign children to loving versus punishing homes.

Next, psychological scientists decide how to measure the behavior or mental process being studied, using either quantitative or qualitative methods. **Quantitative research** methods use numerical data to represent degrees of a variable, for example using a *Likert scale*, where questionnaire responses fall on a continuum (such as from "strongly disagree" to "strongly agree"). **Qualitative research** methods rely on in-depth, narrative data. For example, psychologists may conduct *structured interviews* to understand the causes and consequences of individuals' aggression. Both quantitative and qualitative methods provide valuable information about human behavior and often complement each other.

Regardless of the methods and measures they choose, researchers want to have confidence in their findings. Therefore, they carefully consider confounding variables—factors other than those being studied that may affect their interpretation of results.

Finally, researchers should strive to plan and conduct their studies with diversity, equity, and inclusion in mind—considering potential biases and working to represent marginalized groups.

**AP® Science Practice**

## Research

How researchers choose to measure their variables reflects their operational definitions. Recall from Module 0.3 that an operational definition is a carefully worded statement of the exact procedures (operations) used in a research study. Researchers create operational definitions in a way that ensures broad groups are represented, and equitable procedures are followed.

## Predicting Everyday Behavior

**0.5-2** How can simplified laboratory conditions illuminate everyday life?

When you see or hear about psychological research, do you ever wonder whether people's behavior in the lab will predict their behavior in real life? For example, does detecting the blink of a faint red light in a dark room say anything useful about flying a plane at night? Or imagine that, after playing violent video games in the lab, teens become more willing to push buttons that they think blast someone with unpleasant noise. Would this behavior indicate that playing shooter games makes someone more likely to commit violence in everyday life?

Before you answer, consider this: The experimenter *intends* the laboratory environment to be a simplified reality—one that simulates and controls important features of everyday life. Just as a wind tunnel lets airplane designers re-create airflow forces under controlled conditions, a laboratory experiment lets psychologists re-create psychological forces under controlled conditions. An experiment's purpose is not to re-create the exact behaviors of everyday life, but rather to test *theoretical principles* (Mook, 1983). In aggression studies, deciding whether to push a button that delivers a noise blast may not be the same as slapping someone in the face, but the principle is the same. It is *the resulting principles—not the specific findings—that help explain everyday behaviors.*

**quantitative research** a research method that relies on quantifiable, numerical data.

**qualitative research** a research method that relies on in-depth, narrative data that are not translated into numbers.

When psychologists apply laboratory research on aggression to actual violence, they are applying theoretical principles of aggressive behavior, principles refined through many experiments. Similarly, it is the principles of the visual system, developed from experiments in artificial settings (such as looking at red lights in the dark), that researchers apply to more complex behaviors such as night flying. And many investigations show that principles derived in the laboratory typically generalize to the everyday world (Mitchell, 2012).

*The point to remember:* Psychological science focuses less on specific behaviors than on revealing general principles that help explain many behaviors.

# Psychology's Research Ethics

**0.5-3** Why do psychologists study animals, and what ethical research guidelines safeguard human and animal welfare?

We have reflected on how using a scientific approach can restrain biases. We have seen how case studies, naturalistic observations, and surveys help us describe behavior. We have also noted that correlational studies assess the association between two factors, showing how well one predicts another. We have examined the logic that underlies experiments, which use control conditions and random assignment of participants to isolate the causal effects of an independent variable on a dependent variable.

Yet even knowing this much, you may still be approaching psychology with a mixture of curiosity and apprehension. So, before we plunge in, let's entertain some common questions about psychology's ethics and values.

## Protecting Research Participants

### Studying and Protecting Animals

Many psychologists study nonhuman animals because they find them fascinating. They want to understand how different species learn, think, and behave. Psychologists also study animals to learn about people. We humans are not *like* animals; we *are* animals, sharing a common biology. Animal experiments have, therefore, led to treatments for human diseases—insulin for diabetes, vaccines to prevent polio and rabies, transplants to replace defective organs.

Humans are complex. But some of the same processes by which we learn are present in other animals, even sea slugs and honeybees. The simplicity of the sea slug's nervous system is precisely what makes it so revealing of the neural mechanisms of learning. Ditto for the honeybee, which resembles us humans in how it learns to cope with stress (Dinges et al., 2017).

Sharing such similarities, should we not respect our animal relatives? The animal protection movement protests the use of animals in psychological, biological, and medical research. "We cannot defend our scientific work with animals on the basis of the similarities between them and ourselves and then defend it morally on the basis of differences," noted Roger Ulrich (1991).

Out of this heated debate, two issues emerge. The basic one is whether it is right to place the well-being of humans above that of other animals. In experiments on stress and cancer, is it right that mice get tumors in the hope that people might not? Was it right that researchers exposed monkeys to a coronavirus in the search for a Covid vaccine (Shandrashekar et al., 2020)? Humans raise and slaughter 56 billion animals each year (Thornton, 2019). Is our use and consumption of other animals as natural as the behavior of carnivorous hawks, cats, and whales?

*❝ Rats are very similar to humans except that they are not stupid enough to purchase lottery tickets. ❞*

*Dave Barry, 2002*

*❝ Please do not forget those of us who suffer from incurable diseases or disabilities who hope for a cure through research that requires the use of animals. ❞*

*Psychologist Dennis Feeney (1987)*

For those who give human life top priority, a second question emerges: What safeguards should protect the well-being of animals in research? One survey of animal researchers gave an answer. Some 98 percent supported government regulations protecting primates, dogs, and cats, and 74 percent also supported regulations providing humane care for rats and mice (Plous & Herzog, 2000). Many professional associations and funding agencies already have such guidelines. British Psychological Society (BPS) guidelines call for housing animals under reasonably natural living conditions, with companions for social animals (Lea, 2000). American Psychological Association (APA) guidelines state that researchers must provide "humane care and healthful conditions" and that testing should "minimize discomfort" (APA, 2012). The European Parliament also mandates standards for animal care and housing (Vogel, 2010). Most universities screen research proposals, often through an animal care ethics committee or *Institutional Review Board* (more on this below), and laboratories are regulated and inspected.

Animals have themselves benefited from animal research. One team of research psychologists measured stress hormone levels in samples of millions of dogs brought each year to animal shelters. They devised handling and stroking methods to reduce stress and ease the dogs' transition to adoptive homes (Tuber et al., 1999). Other studies have helped improve care and management in animals' natural habitats. By revealing our behavioral kinship with animals and the remarkable intelligence of chimpanzees, gorillas, and other animals, experiments have also led to increased empathy and protection for them. At its best, a psychology concerned for humans and sensitive to animals serves the welfare of both.

## Studying and Protecting Humans

What about human participants? Does the image of white-coated scientists seeming to deliver electric shocks trouble you? Actually, most psychological studies are free of such stress. Blinking lights, flashing words, and pleasant social interactions are more common.

Occasionally, though, researchers do temporarily stress or deceive people (sometimes with the help of *confederates*, who pretend to be fellow participants but are actually part of the experiment), but only when they believe it is essential to a justifiable end, such as understanding and controlling violent behavior or studying mood swings. Many experiments won't work if participants know everything beforehand. (Wanting to be helpful, the participants might try to confirm the researcher's predictions, thus causing the *social desirability bias*.)

Some of psychology's famous early experiments used stressful and deceptive methods that are considered unacceptable today. These psychologists deprived baby monkeys of their mothers, conditioned human babies to burst into tears, and semi-starved men who refused to perform military service during World War II. More to come on each of these in later modules.

Today's ethics codes, from the APA and Britain's BPS, urge researchers to (1) obtain potential participants' **informed consent** (called *informed assent* in the case of minors) to take part, (2) protect participants from greater-than-usual harm and discomfort, (3) keep information about individual participants confidential, and (4) fully **debrief** people (explain the research afterward, including any temporary deception). To enforce these ethical standards, universities and research organizations have established *Institutional Review Boards* (IRBs) comprised of at least five people, which must include one scientist, one non-scientist, and one community representative. IRBs screen research proposals and safeguard "the rights, welfare, and well-being of human research participants" (NIEHS, 2019).

**AP® Science Practice**

## Research

You will come across examples of animal research throughout the modules in this text. When you do, remember that contemporary psychologists conduct this research according to ethical guidelines.

" *The greatness of a nation can be judged by the way its animals are treated.* "

*Mahatma Gandhi, 1869–1948*

MARY ALTAFFER/AP Photo

**Animal research benefiting animals** Psychologists have helped zoos enrich animal environments — for example, by giving animals more choices to reduce the learned helplessness of captivity (Kurtycz, 2015; Weir, 2013). Thanks partly to research on the benefits of novelty, control, and stimulation, these gorillas are enjoying an improved quality of life in New York's Bronx Zoo.

**informed consent** giving potential participants enough information about a study to enable them to choose whether they wish to participate.

**debriefing** the postexperimental explanation of a study, including its purpose and any deceptions, to its participants.

## Ensuring Scientific Integrity

### AP® Exam Tip

The ability to explain the differences among similar concepts is an important skill that will be tested on the AP® exam. Can you explain the difference between informed consent and debriefing? Informed consent happens *before* the study and allows participants to make an informed choice about whether to participate. Debriefing occurs *after* the study and aims to educate participants about the true nature of the study.

In science, as in everyday life, mistakes happen. When data get accidentally miscomputed or misreported, that's forgivable and correctable. What's not acceptable—and will get a scientist banished from the profession—is fraud. Leading scientists cite honesty as the most important scientific value, followed by curiosity and perseverance (*Nature*, 2016). Community members rate scientists as the most trusted professionals, followed by doctors, judges, and members of the armed forces (Ipsos, 2019). To seek career advancement by plagiarizing another's words or ideas, or to make up data, is to risk a swift end to one's career.

Fake science also has the potential to cause great harm. This happened in 1998 when a now-disbarred British physician published an article in the prestigious journal *The Lancet*, reporting a dozen cases in which British children given the measles, mumps, and rubella (MMR) vaccine supposedly developed autism afterward. Other studies failed to reproduce the finding (replication matters!) (Hviid et al., 2019). An investigation revealed a fraud—with falsified data—and the journal retracted the report (Godlee, 2011). Alas, by then the widely publicized finding—"the most damaging medical hoax of the last 100 years" (Flaherty, 2011)—had produced declining vaccination rates. Instead of following the typical path toward disease elimination, U.S. measles rates in 2019 rose to their highest levels in 25 years (CDC, 2019; Graham et al., 2019). Though the science was self-correcting, the damage lingers on. Nevertheless, the good news is that scientific scrutiny, complete with replication, can inform and protect us.

## Values in Psychology

**0.5-4** How do psychologists' values influence what they study and how they apply their results?

Values affect what we study, how we study it, and how we interpret results. Researchers' values influence their choice of topics. Should we study worker productivity or worker morale? Cultural differences or social injustice? Conformity or independence? Values can also color "the facts"—our observations and interpretations. Sometimes we see what we want or expect to see (**Figure 0.5-1**).

**Figure 0.5-1**

**What do you see?**

Our expectations influence what we perceive in (a). Did you see a duck or a rabbit? Show some friends this image with the rabbit photo (b) covered up and see if they are more likely to perceive a duck. (Inspired by Shepard, 1990.)

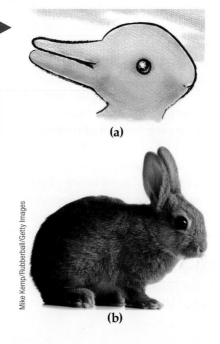

"There can be no peace until they renounce their Rabbit God and accept our Duck God."

Even the words we use to describe traits and tendencies can reflect our values. In psychology and in everyday speech, labels describe and labels evaluate: One person's *rigidity* is another's *consistency*. One person's *faith* is another's *fanaticism*. Our labeling someone as *firm* or *stubborn, careful* or *picky, discreet* or *secretive* reveals our own attitudes.

So, values inform psychological science—and psychological science has the power to persuade. This may lead some to feel distrustful: Is psychology dangerously powerful? Might it be used to manipulate people? Knowledge, like all power, can be used for good or evil. Nuclear power has been used to light up cities—and to demolish them. Persuasive power has been used to educate people—and to deceive them. Although psychology does have the power to deceive, its purpose is to enlighten. Every day, psychologists explore ways to enhance learning, creativity, and compassion. Psychology speaks to many of our world's great problems—extremist terrorism, political corruption, economic inequality, climate change, prejudice, refugee crises—all of which involve attitudes and behaviors. Psychology also speaks to our deepest longings—for love, for happiness, for meaning. Psychology cannot address all of life's great questions, but it speaks to some mighty important ones.

**Psychology speaks** In making its historic 1954 school desegregation decision, the U.S. Supreme Court cited the expert testimony and research of psychologists Kenneth Clark and Mamie Phipps Clark (1947). The Clarks reported that, when given a choice between Black and White dolls, most African American children chose the White doll, which indicated that they had likely absorbed and internalized anti-Black prejudice.

---

**AP® Science Practice**

## Check Your Understanding

### Examine the Concept

▶ Explain the difference between quantitative and qualitative research methods.

▶ Describe informed consent and debriefing, and explain their importance to research.

*Answers to the Examine the Concept questions can be found in Appendix C at the end of the book.*

### Apply the Concept

▶ In what ways do values affect researchers? Does this surprise you?

▶ What other questions do you have about psychological research?

# Module 0.5 REVIEW

**0.5-1** How would you know which research design to use?

- Psychological scientists design studies and choose research methods that will best provide meaningful results.

- Researchers generate *testable questions,* and then carefully consider the best *design* to use in studying those questions (experimental, correlational, case study, naturalistic observation, twin study, longitudinal, or cross-sectional).

- Researchers next *measure* the variables they are studying, and finally they *interpret* their results, keeping possible confounding variables in mind.

**0.5-2** How can simplified laboratory conditions illuminate everyday life?

- Researchers intentionally create a controlled, artificial environment in the laboratory so as to test general theoretical principles. These general principles help explain everyday behaviors.

**0.5-3** Why do psychologists study animals, and what ethical research guidelines safeguard human and animal welfare?

- Some psychologists are primarily interested in animal behavior; others want to better understand the physiological and psychological processes shared by humans and other species.

- Government agencies have established standards for animal care and housing. Professional associations and funding agencies also have guidelines for protecting animals' well-being.

- The APA ethics code outlines standards for safeguarding human participants' well-being, including obtaining their *informed consent* and *debriefing* them later.

**0.5-4** How do psychologists' values influence what they study and how they apply their results?

- Psychologists' values influence their choice of research topics, their theories and observations, their labels for behavior, and their professional advice.

- Applications of psychology's principles have been used mainly in the service of humanity.

## AP® Practice Multiple Choice Questions

**1.** What must a researcher do to fulfill the ethical principle of informed consent?

  a. Keep information about participants confidential.

  b. Protect participants from potential harm and compensate them for participation in a study.

  c. Provide participants with enough information about a study to enable them to make a rational decision about whether to participate.

  d. Explain the purpose of study and any deception in the study to participants after they participate.

**2.** Which ethical principle requires that participants be told about the true purpose of the research at the end of the study?

  a. Informed consent

  b. Informed assent

  c. Debriefing

  d. Protection from physical harm

3. The laboratory environment is designed to
   a. exactly re-create the events of everyday life.
   b. re-create psychological forces under controlled conditions.
   c. re-create psychological forces under random conditions.
   d. provide the opportunity to do case study research.

4. Which of the following animal studies is most likely to meet ethical principles and receive Institutional Review Board approval?
   a. Do monkeys that smoke get cancer?
   b. Will rats deprived of food for one week survive?
   c. What are the effects of raising kittens in isolation?
   d. Can dolphins learn simple language?

5. Which of the following accurately illustrates the correct order of the scientific process in psychological research?
   a. First, researchers interpret their results, and then they measure their variables, after which they identify hypotheses that align with their research design.
   b. First, researchers choose the best design, and then they interpret their results, after which they measure their variables.
   c. First, researchers measure their variables, and then they identify their hypotheses, after which they choose the best design for their study.
   d. First, researchers create hypotheses, and then they design their study to measure their variables, after which they interpret their results.

# Module 0.6 Statistical Reasoning in Everyday Life

> ## LEARNING TARGETS
>
> **0.6-1**  Describe descriptive statistics.
>
> **0.6-2**  Explain how we describe data using three measures of central tendency, and percentile rank.
>
> **0.6-3**  Explain the relative usefulness of the two measures of variation.
>
> **0.6-4**  Describe inferential statistics.
>
> **0.6-5**  Explain how we determine whether an observed difference can be generalized to other populations.

Statistics are important tools for psychological scientists. But statistics also benefit us all, by helping us see what the unaided eye might miss. To be an educated person today is to be able to apply simple statistical principles to everyday reasoning. We needn't memorize complicated formulas to think more clearly and critically about data.

Off-the-top-of-the-head estimates often misread reality and mislead the public. Someone throws out a big, round number. Others echo it, and before long the big, round number becomes public misinformation. Two examples:

- *We ordinarily use only 10 percent of our brain.* Or is it closer to 100 percent (Module 1.4)?
- *To be healthy, walk 10,000 steps a day.* Or will 8500 or 13,000 steps do the trick, or how about swimming or jogging (Mull, 2019)?

If you see an attention-grabbing headline presented without scientifically derived evidence—that nationally there are 1 million teen pregnancies, 2 million homeless seniors, or 3 million alcohol-related motor vehicle accidents each year—you can be pretty sure that someone is estimating. If they want to emphasize the problem, they will be motivated to estimate high. If they want to minimize the problem, they will estimate low. *The point to remember:* Use critical thinking when presented with big, round, undocumented numbers.

Statistical illiteracy also feeds needless health scares (Gigerenzer, 2010). In the 1990s, the British press reported a study showing that women taking a particular contraceptive pill had a 100 percent increased risk of blood clots that could produce strokes. The story went viral, causing thousands of women to stop taking the pill. What happened as a result? A wave of unwanted pregnancies and an estimated 13,000 additional abortions (which, like other medical procedures, also are associated with increased blood clot risk). Distracted by big, round numbers, few people focused on the study's actual findings: A 100 percent increased risk, indeed—but only from 1 in 7000 to 2 in 7000. Such false alarms underscore the need to think critically, to learn statistical reasoning, and to present statistical information more transparently.

More recently, statistical confusion about health information also infected people's understanding of Covid vaccine effectiveness. If a vaccine is "95 percent effective," does that mean a recipient has a 5 percent chance of contracting the virus? As a *New York Times* story explained, Pfizer/BioNTech's clinical trial enrolled nearly 44,000 people, half of whom received its vaccine and half of whom received a placebo (Thomas, 2020). "Out of 170 cases of Covid, 162 were in the placebo group, and eight were in the vaccine group." So, there was a 162 to 8 (95 percent to 5 percent) ratio—which defined the vaccine as 95 percent effective. Of those vaccinated, only 8 of nearly 22,000 people—less than 1/10th of 1 percent (not 5 percent)—contracted the virus during the study period. And of the 32,000 people who received either the Moderna or Pfizer vaccine, how many during the study contracted a *severe* case of Covid? The grand total, noted a follow-up *New York Times* report, was *one* (Leonhardt, 2021).

# Descriptive Statistics

### 0.6-1 What are descriptive statistics?

Once researchers have gathered their data, they may use **descriptive statistics** to measure and describe characteristics of the group under study—similar to the way teachers use descriptive statistics to assess how their students have performed. One way to do this is to show the data in a simple *bar graph*, called a **histogram**. Figure 0.6-1 is a histogram that displays a distribution of different brands of trucks still on the road after a decade. When reading statistical graphs such as this one, take care. It's easy to design a graph to make a difference look big (Figure 0.6-1a) or small (Figure 0.6-1b). The secret lies in how you label the vertical scale (the *y-axis*).

*The point to remember:* Think smart. When interpreting graphs, consider the scale labels and note their *range*.

**Figure 0.6-1**
**Read the scale labels**

A truck manufacturer offered graph (a) — with actual brand names included — to suggest the much greater durability of its trucks. Note, however, how the *y*-axis of each graph is labeled. The range for the *y*-axis label in graph (a) is only from 95 to 100. The range for graph (b) is from 0 to 100. All the trucks rank as 95 percent and up, so almost all are still functioning after 10 years, which graph (b) makes clear.

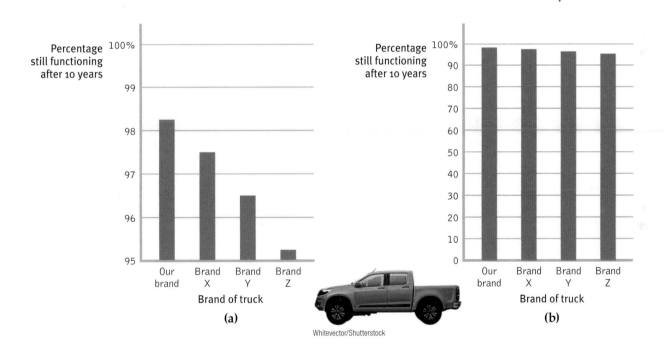

Whitevector/Shutterstock

**AP® Science Practice**   ▷   **Data Interpretation**

The ability to evaluate graphical representations of data is important in psychology, and it will show up in the AP® exam. Study the histograms in Figure 0.6-1 and answer the following questions.

- Identify the two variables represented in these graphs.

- Are these data quantitative or qualitative?

- What conclusions can you draw from the data depicted in these graphs?

**descriptive statistics** numerical data used to measure and describe characteristics of groups; include measures of central tendency and measures of variation.

**histogram** a bar graph depicting a frequency distribution.

## Measures of Central Tendency

### 0.6-2 How do we describe data using three measures of central tendency, and percentile rank?

**mode** the most frequently occurring score(s) in a distribution.

**mean** the arithmetic average of a distribution, obtained by adding the scores and then dividing by the number of scores.

**median** the middle score in a distribution; half the scores are above it and half are below it.

**percentile rank** the percentage of scores that are lower than a given score.

**skewed distribution** a representation of scores that lack symmetry around their average value.

After organizing and describing their data, researchers' next step is to summarize the data using some *measure of central tendency*, a single score that represents a whole set of scores. The simplest measure is the **mode**, the most frequently occurring score or scores. (A *bimodal distribution* occurs when there are two frequently occurring scores.) The most familiar measure of central tendency is the **mean**, or arithmetic average—the total sum of all the scores divided by the number of scores. The midpoint of a data distribution—the 50th percentile—is the **median**. If you arrange all the scores in order from the highest to the lowest, half will be above the median and half will be below it. **Percentile rank** is the percentage of scores that are less than a given score. So, if you are in the 79th percentile in a math competition in your state, your score is higher than 79 percent of your peers.

Measures of central tendency neatly summarize data. But consider what happens to the mean when a distribution is lopsided, when it's **skewed** by a few way-out scores. With income data, for example, the mode, median, and mean often tell very different stories (**Figure 0.6-2**). This happens because the mean is biased by a few extreme incomes. When SpaceX and Tesla CEO Elon Musk sits down in a small café, its average (mean) customer instantly becomes a billionaire. But median customer wealth remains unchanged. Understanding this, you can see why, according to the 2020 U.S. Census, nearly 60 percent of U.S. households have "below average" income. The bottom half of earners receive much less than half of the total national income. So, most Americans make less than average (the mean). Mean and median tell different true stories.

*The point to remember:* Always note which measure of central tendency is reported. If it is a mean, consider whether a few atypical scores could be distorting it.

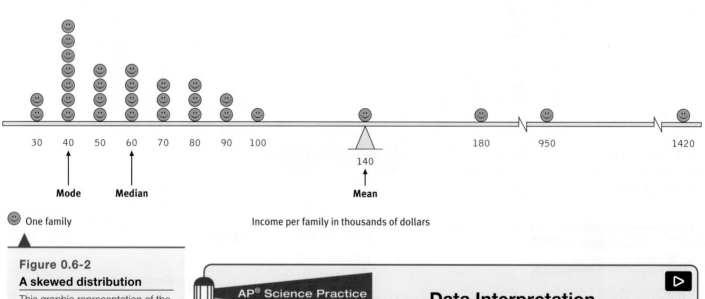

😊 One family

Income per family in thousands of dollars

**Figure 0.6-2**

**A skewed distribution**

This graphic representation of the distribution of a village's incomes illustrates the three measures of central tendency: mode, median, and mean. Note how just a few high incomes make the mean — the fulcrum point that balances the incomes above and below — deceptively high.

---

**AP® Science Practice**

### Data Interpretation

Consider the following data set representing scores on an exam:

24  87  27  89  80  92  85  94  87  99

• Calculate the mean, median, and mode for this set of data.

• Explain why the mean might be misleading in interpreting this data set.

# Measures of Variation

**0.6-3** What is the relative usefulness of the two measures of variation?

Knowing the value of an appropriate measure of central tendency can tell us a great deal. But the single number omits other information. It helps to know something about the amount of *variation* in the data—how similar or diverse the scores are. Averages derived from scores with low variability are more reliable than averages based on scores with high variability. Consider a basketball player who scored between 13 and 17 points in each of the season's first 10 games. Knowing this, we would be more confident that she would score near 15 points in her next game than if her scores had varied from 5 to 25 points.

The **range** of scores—the gap between the lowest and highest—provides only a crude estimate of variation. In an otherwise similar group, a couple of extreme scores, such as the $950,000 and $1,420,000 incomes in Figure 0.6-2, will create a deceptively large range.

A more useful standard for measuring how much scores deviate (differ) from one another is the **standard deviation**. It better gauges whether scores are packed together or dispersed, because it incorporates information from each score. The computation[5] assembles information about how much individual scores differ from the mean, which can be very telling. Let's say test scores from Class A and Class B both have the same mean (75 percent correct), but very different standard deviations (5.0 for Class A and 15.0 for Class B). Have you ever had test experiences like that—where two-thirds of your classmates in one class score in the 70 to 80 percent range, but scores in another class are more spread out (two-thirds between 60 and 90 percent)? The standard deviation, as well as the mean score, tell us about how each class is faring.

You can grasp the meaning of the standard deviation if you consider how scores naturally tend to be distributed. Large numbers of data—such as heights, intelligence scores, and life expectancy (though not incomes)—often form a symmetrical, *bell-shaped* distribution. Most cases fall near the mean, and fewer cases fall near either extreme. This bell-shaped distribution is so typical that we call the curve it forms the **normal curve**.

As **Figure 0.6-3** shows, a useful property of the normal curve is that roughly 68 percent of the cases fall within one standard deviation on either side of the mean. About 95 percent of cases fall within two standard deviations. Thus, as Module 2.8 notes, about 68 percent of people taking an intelligence test will score within ±15 points of 100. About 95 percent will score within ±30 points.

**range** the difference between the highest and lowest scores in a distribution.

**standard deviation** a computed measure of how much scores vary around the mean score.

**normal curve** a symmetrical, bell-shaped curve that describes the distribution of many types of data; most scores fall near the mean (about 68 percent fall within one standard deviation of it) and fewer and fewer scores lie near the extremes. (Also called a *normal distribution*.)

**Figure 0.6-3**
**The normal curve**

Scores on aptitude tests tend to form a normal, or bell-shaped, curve. The most commonly used intelligence test, the Wechsler Adult Intelligence Scale, calls the average score 100.

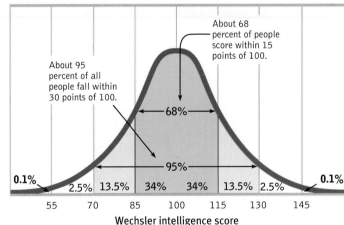

---

![AP® Science Practice] **Check Your Understanding**

**Examine the Concept**

▶ Explain what is meant by mean, mode, median, and percentile rank.

▶ We determine how much scores vary around the average in a way that includes information about the _____ of scores (difference between highest and lowest) by using the _____ _____ formula.

*Answers to the Examine the Concept questions can be found in Appendix C at the end of the book.*

**Apply the Concept**

▶ Find a graph in an online or print magazine, newspaper, or advertisement. How does the advertiser use (or misuse) statistics to make a point?

---

5. The actual standard deviation formula is: $\sqrt{\dfrac{\text{Sum of (deviations)}^2}{\text{Number of scores} - 1\ (n-1)}}$

# Inferential Statistics

**AP® Science Practice**

## Data

Inferential statistics help researchers draw conclusions about the population based on the sample in their study. They are quite different from descriptive statistics, which are used to simply describe a sample's characteristics.

> **0.6-4** What are inferential statistics?

Data are noisy. The average score from an experimental group (such as those who deactivated their Facebook account, in the experiment we mentioned in Module 0.4) could conceivably differ from the average score from the control group (those who didn't) not because of any real difference, but merely because of chance fluctuations in the people sampled. How confidently, then, can we *infer* that an observed difference is not just a fluke—a chance result from the research sample? For guidance, we can ask how reliable and statistically significant the differences are. These **inferential statistics** help us determine if results can be generalized to a larger population (all those in a group being studied).

## When Is an Observed Difference Reliable?

> **0.6-5** How do we determine whether an observed difference can be generalized to other populations?

**inferential statistics** numerical data that allow one to generalize—to infer from sample data the probability of something being true of a population.

**meta-analysis** a statistical procedure for analyzing the results of multiple studies to reach an overall conclusion.

Imagine an eager high school senior who visits two university campuses, each for a day. At the first school, the student randomly samples two classes and finds that both instructors are witty and engaging. At the second school, the two sampled instructors seem dull and uninspiring. Should the student conclude that the first school's teachers are "great" and the second school's teachers are "bores"?

You might respond that the student should sample more classes—and you'd be right. It's possible that the populations of teachers at the two universities are equal. Just by chance, the student could have sampled two great (and two boring) teachers.

When deciding whether it is safe to infer a population difference from a sample difference, we should keep three principles in mind:

1. *Representative samples are better than biased (unrepresentative) samples.* The best basis for generalizing is from a representative sample of cases, not from the exceptional and memorable cases one finds at the extremes. Research never randomly samples the whole human population. Thus, it pays to remember which population a study has sampled.

2. *Bigger samples are better than smaller ones.* We know it but we ignore it: Averages based on many cases are more precise than averages based on a few. More (randomly sampled) cases make the sample's estimate more precise. Larger samples also make for a more *replicable* study—one that will find a similar estimate the next time.

3. *More estimates are better than fewer estimates.* A study gives one brief peek at what's going on in the population. But the best thing to do is conduct multiple studies and combine all the estimates, using **meta-analysis**. Better to consider an entire forest of findings rather than focusing on a single study.

*The point to remember:* Smart thinkers are not overly impressed by a few anecdotes. Estimates based on only a few unrepresentative cases are imprecise.

*"The poor are getting poorer, but with the rich getting richer it all averages out in the long run."*

# When Is an Observed Difference Significant?

Suppose you sampled men's and women's scores on a laboratory test of aggression and found a gender difference. But samples can vary. So, how likely is it that your observed gender difference was just a fluke?

Researchers use statistical testing to estimate the probability of the result occurring by chance. They begin with the assumption that no difference exists between groups, an assumption called the *null hypothesis*. Then, using statistics, they evaluate whether the observed gender difference is so rare that it's unlikely to fit the null hypothesis. If so, they reject the null hypothesis of no differences, and they say that the result is **statistically significant**. Such a large difference would support an *alternative hypothesis*—that the populations of men and women really do differ in aggression.

What factors determine statistical significance? When averages from two samples are precise estimates of their respective populations (as when each is based on many observations that have low variability), then any *difference* between the two samples is more likely to be statistically significant. (For our example: The less the variability in women's and in men's aggression scores, and the more scores we observe, the more precisely we will estimate that the observed gender difference is real.) When the difference we estimate is *large, it's also more likely to reflect* a real difference in the population.

In short, when estimates are precise and when the difference between them is relatively large, we're more likely to find that the difference is statistically significant. This means that the observed difference in the sample is probably more than just chance variation, so we reject the original null hypothesis of no existing differences.

In judging statistical significance, psychologists are conservative. They are like juries who must presume innocence until guilt is proven. Many psychological tests provide *p*-values, which indicate the probability of the result, given the null hypothesis. For most psychologists, strong evidence that we can reject the null (no-difference) hypothesis occurs when the probability (*p*-value) of that result is very low. "Very low" is usually set at less than 5 percent ($p < .05$). When a sample's result would occur less than 5 percent of the time assuming the null hypothesis, we say it is significant.

When learning about research, you should remember that a "statistically significant" result may have little *practical significance*. Especially when a sample is very large, a result might be statistically significant but have a tiny **effect size**. One large study tested the intelligence of first-born and later-born individuals. Researchers revealed a statistically significant tendency for first-born individuals to have higher average scores than their later-born siblings (Rohrer et al., 2015; Zajonc & Markus, 1975). But the difference was only about 1.5 IQ points, so the vast majority of IQ is determined by factors other than birth order. There were 20,000 people in the study, so this difference was "significant," but it had little practical importance.

To interpret results, researchers also use the *confidence interval*—a range of values that likely includes the population's true mean value. If one high school class has a mean score of 80 on an academic achievement test, we would not assume that 80 is the true mean value of all

**AP® Exam Tip**

Sometimes a phrase that is frequently used in the media has a more specific meaning when used in psychology. That's the case with the phrase "statistically significant." Make sure you know the precise meaning of this. It has been on the AP® exam in the past.

**statistical significance** a statistical statement of how likely it is that a result (such as a difference between samples) occurred by chance, assuming there is no difference between the populations being studied.

**effect size** the strength of the relationship between two variables. The larger the effect size, the more one variable can be explained by the other.

**PEANUTS**

Reprinted by permission of Andrews McMeel Syndicate, Inc.

high school test-takers (the population). But statistical analyses can provide a range of values—for example, between 70 and 90—that gives researchers a degree of "confidence" that the population's true mean falls in this interval. Thus, a confidence interval helps researchers estimate whether a sample's range of scores likely includes the population's true mean value.

*The point to remember:* Statistical significance indicates the likelihood that the result would have happened by chance if the null hypothesis (of no difference) were true. But statistically significant is not the same as *important* or *strong*.

---

### AP® Science Practice

## Check Your Understanding

#### Examine the Concept

▶ _____ statistics summarize data, while _____ statistics determine whether data can be generalized to other populations.

▶ Explain the three principles we should keep in mind when deciding if it is safe to infer a population difference from a sample difference.

#### Apply the Concept

▶ Can you think of a situation where you were fooled by writers or speakers attempting to persuade you with statistics? What have you learned in this module that will be most helpful in the future to avoid being misled? Explain what is meant by a skewed distribution.

*Answers to the Examine the Concept questions can be found in Appendix C at the end of the book.*

---

# Module 0.6 REVIEW

### 0.6-1 What are descriptive statistics?

- Researchers use descriptive statistics to measure and describe characteristics of groups under study, often using a histogram to display their data.

- Descriptive statistics include measures of central tendency, percentile rank, and measures of variation.

### 0.6-2 How do we describe data using three measures of central tendency, and percentile rank?

- A measure of central tendency is a single score that represents a whole set of scores. Three such measures are the *mode* (the most frequently occurring score), the *mean* (the arithmetic average), and the *median* (the middle score in a group of data). *Percentile rank* indicates what percentage of scores falls beneath a given score.

### 0.6-3 What is the relative usefulness of the two measures of variation?

- Measures of variation tell us how diverse data are. Two measures of variation are the *range* (which describes the gap between the highest and lowest scores) and the *standard deviation* (which states how much scores vary around the mean, or average, score).

- The range offers only a crude measure of how much the data vary; the standard deviation is far better at giving researchers a clear understanding of variation.

- Scores often form a *normal* (or bell-shaped) *curve*.

### 0.6-4 What are inferential statistics?

- Researchers use *inferential statistics* to determine the probability of their findings being also true of the larger population.

- Inferential statistics include ways of determining the reliability and significance of an observed difference between the results for different groups.

### 0.6-5 How do we determine whether an observed difference can be generalized to other populations?

- To feel confident about generalizing an observed difference to other populations, we would need to know that the difference is both reliable and significant. Reliable differences are based on samples that:
  - are representative of the larger population being studied,
  - demonstrate low variability, on average; and
  - consist of many cases.

- We can say that an observed difference has *statistical significance* if the sample averages are reliable and the difference between them is large.

# AP® Practice Multiple Choice Questions

**For questions 1–3, use the following data: 33, 40, 12, 25, 80.**

**1.** What is the mean of the data?

   a. 68
   b. 98
   c. 33
   d. 38

**2.** What is the median of the data?

   a. 33
   b. 68
   c. 38
   d. 80

**3.** What is the mode of the data?

   a. 33
   b. 25
   c. 12
   d. There is no mode.

**4.** Which measure of central tendency is most influenced by skewed data or extreme scores in a distribution?

   a. Mean
   b. Median
   c. Mode
   d. Percentile rank

**5.** A researcher calculates statistical significance for her study and finds a 5 percent possibility that the results are due to chance. Which of the following is an accurate interpretation of this finding?

   a. This result is highly statistically significant.
   b. This result reflects the minimum standard typically considered statistically significant.
   c. This result is not statistically significant.
   d. This result cannot be evaluated on statistical significance without replication of the study.

**6.** Descriptive statistics _____, while inferential statistics _____.

   a. describe data from experiments; describe data from surveys and case studies
   b. are measures of central tendency; are measures of variance
   c. determine whether data can be generalized to other populations; summarize data
   d. summarize data; assess if data can be generalized

**7.** In a normal distribution, what percentage of the scores in the distribution falls within one standard deviation on either side of the mean?

   a. 34 percent
   b. 50 percent
   c. 68 percent
   d. 95 percent

## KEY TERMS AND CONTRIBUTORS TO REMEMBER

critical thinking, p. 0-6

hindsight bias, p. 0-10

peer reviewers, p. 0-14

theory, p. 0-14

hypothesis, p. 0-14

falsifiable, p. 0-14

operational definition, p. 0-15

replication, p. 0-15

case study, p. 0-16

naturalistic observation, p. 0-17

survey, p. 0-18

social desirability bias, p. 0-19

self-report bias, p. 0-19

sampling bias, p. 0-19

random sample, p. 0-19

population, p. 0-19

correlation, p. 0-22

correlation coefficient, p. 0-22

variable, p. 0-22

scatterplot, p. 0-22

illusory correlation, p. 0-26

regression toward the mean, p. 0-26

experiment, p. 0-27

experimental group, p. 0-27

control group, p. 0-27

random assignment, p. 0-27

single-blind procedure, p. 0-28

double-blind procedure, p. 0-28

placebo effect, p. 0-28

independent variable, p. 0-28

confounding variable, p. 0-28

experimenter bias, p. 0-28

dependent variable, p. 0-28

validity, p. 0-29

quantitative research, p. 0-33

qualitative research, p. 0-33

informed consent, p. 0-35

debriefing, p. 0-35

descriptive statistics, p. 0-41

histogram, p. 0-41

mode, p. 0-42

mean, p. 0-42

median, p. 0-42

percentile rank, p. 0-42

skewed distribution, p. 0-42

range, p. 0-43

standard deviation, p. 0-43

normal curve, p. 0-43

inferential statistics, p. 0-44

meta-analysis, p. 0-44

statistical significance, p. 0-45

effect size, p. 0-45

# Unit 0 AP® Practice Multiple Choice Questions

1. A student is interested in knowing how widely the academic aptitude of college-bound students varies at her school. Which of the following statistical methods should she use to determine how much students' SAT scores vary from the school's average SAT score?

   a. Correlation coefficient
   b. Mean
   c. Percentile rank
   d. Standard deviation

2. Which method should a psychology researcher use if she is interested in testing whether a specific reward in a classroom situation causes students to behave better?

   a. Case study
   b. Experiment
   c. Survey
   d. Correlation

3. In a perfectly normal distribution of scores, which of the following statements is true?

   a. The mean, median, and mode are all the same number.
   b. The mode is equal to the standard deviation.
   c. The scores are positively correlated.
   d. There is a positive skew to the distribution of data.

4. Which of the following describes the placebo effect?

   a. Students in art class are not told that their work will be evaluated for a scholarship so they do not submit their best work.
   b. Participants in an experiment do not know if they are in the experimental or control group so their attitudes about the study are unaffected.
   c. Participants in a drug study are given an inert pill instead of the drug and behave as though they were given the drug.
   d. Only women are chosen for a study, even though the population included men.

5. Which of the following represents naturalistic observation?

   a. Researchers go to the mall and distribute surveys about the stores in the mall.
   b. Researchers bring participants into a laboratory to see how they respond to a puzzle with no solution.
   c. A principal looks at the relationship between the number of student absences and their grades.
   d. Researchers observe students' seating patterns in the cafeteria.

6. "Monday morning quarterbacks" rarely act surprised about the outcome of weekend football games. This tendency to believe they knew how the game would turn out is best explained by which psychological principle?

   a. Overconfidence
   b. Hindsight bias
   c. Illusory correlation
   d. Random sampling

7. Which of the following statements best describes the graph below?

   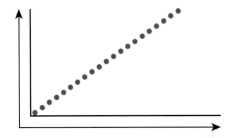

   a. This is a scatterplot of a perfect positive correlation.
   b. This is a scatterplot of a weak negative correlation.
   c. This is a histogram of a weak positive correlation.
   d. This is a histogram of a perfect positive correlation.

8. A journalism student is writing an article about her school's new cell-phone policy, and she'd like to interview a random sample of students. Which of the following is the best example of a random sample?

   a. The writer arrives at school early and interviews the first five students who come through the main entrance.
   b. The writer pulls the names of five students from a hat that contains all students' names. She interviews the five selected students.
   c. The writer asks her teacher if she can distribute a brief survey to the students in her AP® Psychology class.
   d. The writer passes out brief surveys to 50 students in the hall and uses the 18 surveys returned to her as the basis of her article.

9. Which of the following is a positive correlation?

   a. As study time increases, students achieve lower grades.
   b. As levels of self-esteem decline, levels of depression increase.
   c. The more people exercise, the better they sleep.
   d. Gas mileage decreases as vehicle weight increases.

**10.** Why is random assignment of participants to groups an important aspect of a properly designed experiment?

    a. If the participants are randomly assigned, the researcher can assume that each group is similar to each other at the beginning of the study.

    b. By randomly assigning participants, the researcher knows that whatever is learned from the experiment will also be true for the population from which the participants were selected.

    c. If participants are not randomly assigned, it is impossible to replicate the experiment.

    d. Statistical analysis cannot be performed on an experiment if random assignment is not used.

**11.** A social psychology researcher operationally defines aggression as loudness of a noise blast (ranging from 0 to 105 decibels) supposedly delivered to a stranger. This research method is best described as

    a. inferential.

    b. qualitative.

    c. quantitative.

    d. replication.

**12.** Which of the following is a potential problem with case studies?

    a. They provide too much detail, and the researcher is likely to lose track of the most important facts.

    b. They are generally too expensive to be feasible.

    c. The information learned may not apply to the wider population.

    d. The dependent variable is difficult to operationally define in a case study.

**13.** Which of the following is an ethical principle regarding experimental research on humans?

    a. Researchers must protect participants from needless harm and discomfort.

    b. Regardless of the research design, all participants sign an informed consent form.

    c. Personal information about individual participants can only be revealed in peer-reviewed journals.

    d. Participants should always be informed of the hypothesis of the study before they agree to participate.

**14.** There is a negative correlation between TV watching and grades. What can we conclude from this research finding?

    a. We can conclude that this is an illusory correlation.

    b. We can conclude that TV watching leads to lower grades.

    c. We can conclude that TV watching leads to higher grades.

    d. We can conclude that a student who watches a lot of TV is likely to have lower grades.

**15.** Which of the following groups of scores would have the smallest standard deviation?

    a. 20, 40, 60, 80, 100

    b. 5, 15, 25, 35, 45

    c. 2, 4, 6, 8, 10

    d. 100, 200, 300, 400, 500

**Use this scenario to answer questions 16–20:**

Researchers wanted to find out if eating sugary foods would increase a person's ability to remember the names of U.S. presidents. The experiment involved 30 female and 30 male participants. A third of the participants (Group A) were given cookies while studying the names. Another third (Group B) were given nothing while studying the names. The final third (Group C) were given mint-flavored candy while studying the names. They were tested on the names a day later. The researchers found that Group A did substantially better than Group B, but about the same as Group C.

**16.** The dependent variable in this study is

    a. the mint candy.

    b. the test scores.

    c. the cookies.

    d. the list of presidents.

**17.** The independent variable in this study is

    a. the list of presidents.

    b. the test scores.

    c. food given.

    d. gender.

**18.** Which of the following is/are the experimental group(s) of this study?

    a. Group B

    b. Group C

    c. Groups A & C

    d. Groups B & C

**19.** Which of the following is/are the control group(s) of this study?

    a. Group A

    b. Group B

    c. Groups A & B

    d. Groups B & C

**20.** Which of the following is the best conclusion for this study?

    a. Only eating cookies tends to improve memory recall.

    b. Eating cookies or mint candy tends to improve memory recall.

    c. Eating nothing tends to improve memory recall.

    d. Only eating mint-flavored candy tends to improve memory recall.

**21.** Kai scored in the 90th percentile in a math competition in her state. Which of the following statements is true of Kai's score?

a. Her score is higher than 10 percent of others in the competition.
b. Her score is lower than 89 percent of others in the competition.
c. Her score is higher than 90 percent of others in the competition.
d. Her score is an outlier in this competition.

**22.** Paulette is taking a survey. Instead of being honest, she is answering it in a way that she thinks will please the researchers. Paulette is showing a(n)

a. hindsight bias.
b. sampling bias.
c. experimenter bias.
d. social desirability bias.

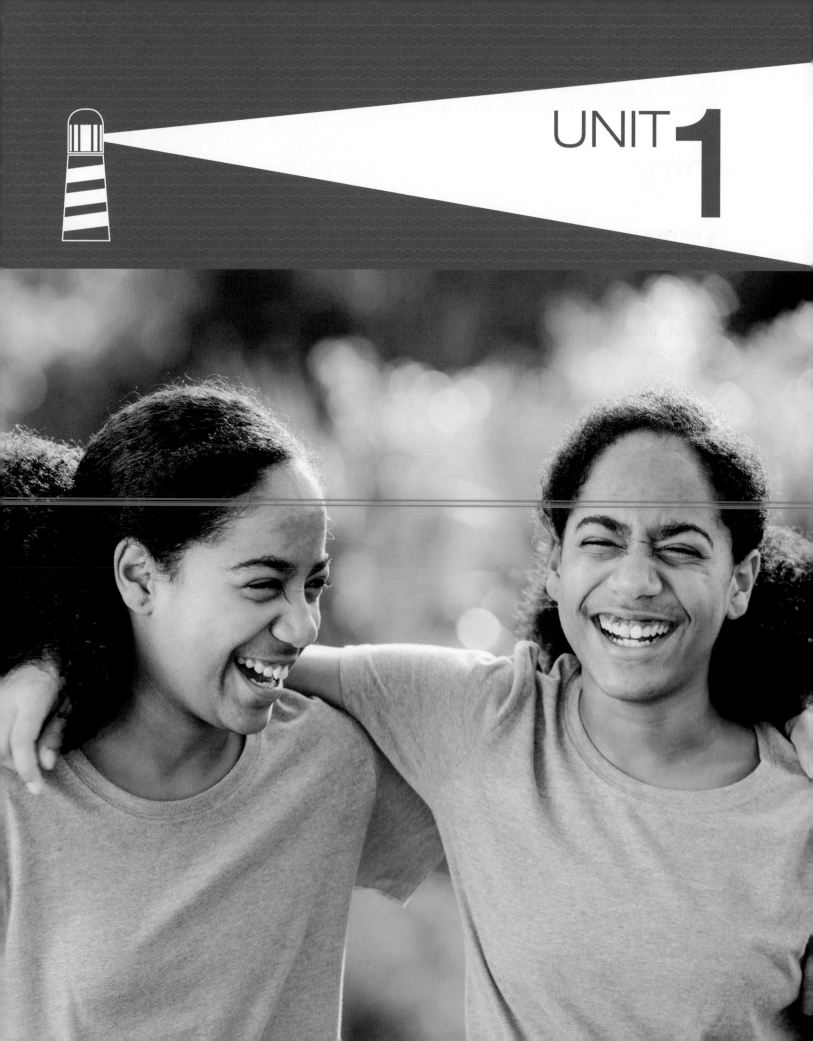

UNIT**1**

# Biological Bases of Behavior

Once upon a time, on a planet in our neighborhood of the universe, there came to be people. Soon thereafter, these creatures became intensely interested in themselves and in one another: "Who are we? What produces our thoughts? Our feelings? Our actions? And how are we to understand and manage those around us?" Psychological science seeks to answer such questions about how and why we think, feel, and act as we do.

Unit 0 introduced us to **psychology**—the *science of behavior and mental processes.* Let's unpack this definition. Behavior is anything an organism does—any action we can observe and record. Yelling, smiling, blinking, sweating, talking, tweeting, and questionnaire marking are all observable behaviors. Mental processes are our internal, subjective experiences—our sensations, perceptions, dreams, thoughts, beliefs, and feelings. You have seen in Unit 0 that scientific inquiry requires *curiosity*, *skepticism*, and *humility*—attitudes that can also help us discern truth amid a sea of misinformation. You have begun to understand the appropriate use of *surveys* (using random sampling), of *correlational* studies (that reveal associations without indicating causation), and of *experiments* (which randomly assign participants to different conditions). You have appreciated the ethical constraints that guide researchers.

This scientific attitude—curiosity + skepticism + humility—helps us to think harder and smarter. To do well in this course, on the AP® Psychology exam, and in your college courses and life beyond, you will want to thoroughly internalize this scientific way of thinking. And throughout this text, you will be actively applying these concepts to the content in each unit with our "AP® Science Practice" features.

Perhaps you didn't expect this scientific focus in psychology. And maybe you're wondering why a "biological" unit is the first thing you're encountering in this psychology course. No principle is more central to today's psychology, or to this book, than this: *Everything psychological is simultaneously biological.* Your every idea, every mood, every urge is a biological happening. You love, laugh, and cry with your body. Without your body—your genes, your nervous system, your hormones, your appearance—you truly would be nobody. Moreover, your body and your brain both influence and are influenced by your experiences.

Consider a daring medical venture proposed by two transplant surgeons and their international team—a head transplant (Kean, 2016; Ren & Canavero, 2017; Ren et al., 2019). Wang Huanming, who is paralyzed from the neck down, volunteered to have his fully functioning head transferred to a brain-dead person's still-functioning body.

Ignore for the moment the ethical issues of such an experiment, which some have called "reckless and ghastly" and part of the scientists' "ghoulish fantasies"

UNIT **1**
**Overview Video**
▶

**psychology** the science of behavior and mental processes.

*kall9/E+/Getty Images*

3

(Illes & McDonald, 2017; Wolpe, 2018). Ignore the procedure's cost, estimated at as much as $100 million (Hjelmgaard, 2019). And ignore the seeming impossibility of precisely connecting the head-to-spinal-cord nerves. Imagine, just imagine, that the procedure could work. With the same brain and a new body, would Wang still be Wang? To whose home should he return? If the old Wang was a skilled musician, would the new Wang conceivably retain that skill—or would that depend on the muscle memories stored in the new body? And if he (assuming the new body was male) later fathered a child, whom should the birth certificate list as the father?

Most of us twenty-first-century people (you, too?) presume that, even with a new body, Wang would still be Wang. We presume that our brain, designed by our genes and sculpted by our experiences, provides our identity and enables our mind. No brain, no mind.

In this unit, we examine the mind's biology and its relationship to our behavior, our consciousness, and how we sense the world around us. We discuss the interaction of our genes and our experiences. We consider *epigenetics* (how experience can influence genetic expression) and see that our species has been graced with the tremendous biological gift of brain *plasticity* (our enormous capacity to learn and adapt). We examine our biology from the bottom up—from nerve cells up to the brain—and from the top down, considering how behavior and environment can influence our biology. We explore our nightly loss of consciousness—sleep—and the fascinating world of dreams. Finally, we examine how our brain helps us sense and make sense of our world.

## Module 1.1 Interaction of Heredity and Environment

**nature–nurture issue** the longstanding controversy over the relative contributions that genes and experience make to the development of psychological traits and behaviors. Today's science views traits and behaviors as arising from the interaction of nature and nurture.

### LEARNING TARGETS

1.1-1    Describe evolutionary psychologists' use of natural selection to explain behavior tendencies.

1.1-2    Describe how behavior geneticists explain our individual differences.

1.1-3    Explain how twin and adoption studies help us understand the effects and interactions of nature and nurture.

1.1-4    Explain how heredity and environment work together.

## The Nature–Nurture Issue

Consider psychology's biggest and most persistent issue: Are our human traits present at birth, or do they develop through experience? The debate over this big **nature–nurture issue** is ancient. The Greek philosopher Plato (428–348 B.C.E.) assumed that we inherit character and intelligence and that certain ideas are inborn. Aristotle (384–322 B.C.E.)

**A nature-made nature–nurture experiment** Identical twins have the same genes. This makes them ideal participants in studies designed to shed light on hereditary and environmental influences on personality, intelligence, and other traits. Fraternal twins have different genes but often share a similar environment. Twin studies provide a wealth of findings — described in later modules — showing the importance of both nature and nurture.

countered that there is nothing in the mind that does not first come in from the external world through the senses.

Insight into how our species' history sways our behavior arose after 22-year-old Charles Darwin embarked on a seafaring voyage. During his adventure, Darwin pondered the incredible species variation he encountered, including tortoises on one island that differed from those on nearby islands. Darwin's *On the Origin of Species* (1859) explained this diversity by proposing the evolutionary process of **natural selection**: From among chance variations, nature selects those traits that best enable an organism to survive and reproduce in a specific environment. Darwin's principle of natural selection is still with us 160+ years later as biology's organizing principle. While some theorists used evolutionary principles in discriminatory or racist ways (such as the discredited idea of *eugenics,* or selectively breeding humans to promote certain characteristics), evolution also has become an important principle for twenty-first-century psychology. This would surely have pleased Darwin, who believed his theory explained not only animal structures but also animal behaviors.

The nature–nurture issue recurs throughout this text, as today's psychologists continue to explore the relative contributions of biology and experience. They ask, for example: How are we humans *alike* because of our shared biology and evolutionary history? That's the focus of **evolutionary psychology**. And how do we individually *differ* because of our differing genes and environments? That's the focus of **behavior genetics**.

We can, for example, ask: Are gender differences biologically predisposed or socially constructed? Is children's grammar mostly innate or formed by experience? How are intelligence and personality differences influenced by heredity and by environment? Should we treat psychological disorders—depression, for example—as disorders of the brain, disorders of thought, or both?

Again and again, we will see that in contemporary science, the nature–nurture tension dissolves: *Nurture works on what nature provides.* Moreover, every psychological event (every thought, every emotion) is simultaneously a biological event. Thus, depression can be both a brain disorder *and* a thought disorder.

**Charles Darwin (1809–1882)** Darwin argued that natural selection shapes behaviors as well as bodies.

**AP® Exam Tip**

Pay close attention to what your authors emphasize as they tell the story of psychology. When they say the nature–nurture issue is the *biggest* issue in psychology, that's a sign that it's likely to appear on the AP® exam.

**AP® Exam Tip**

There is a ton of vocabulary in this unit, and in psychology. Learning vocabulary is really not so hard: The secret is to work on it every day. Try flash cards or an online quizzing memory game. Work with a study buddy. Impress your friends with your new vocabulary. Just don't leave it until the night before the test. If you rehearse the vocabulary throughout the unit, you will do better on the unit test. Don't just reread the flash cards, but rather quiz yourself on them or paraphrase them in your own words. The big bonus is that you will also retain far more information for the AP® exam.

**natural selection** the principle that the inherited traits enabling an organism to survive and reproduce in a particular environment will (in competition with other trait variations) most likely be passed on to succeeding generations.

**evolutionary psychology** the study of the evolution of behavior and the mind, using principles of natural selection.

**behavior genetics** the study of the relative power and limits of genetic and environmental influences on behavior.

# Check Your Understanding

**Examine the Concept**

▶ Explain contemporary psychology's position on the nature–nurture issue.

**Apply the Concept**

▶ Think of one of your own traits. (For example, are you a planner or a procrastinator — do you usually complete assignments on time or late? Are you more of an extravert or an introvert — do you become energized by social interactions or do you recharge by spending time alone?) How do you think that trait was influenced by nature and nurture?

*Answers to the Examine the Concept questions can be found in Appendix C at the end of the book.*

**AP® Exam Tip**

To assist your active learning of psychology, Learning Targets are grouped together at the start of each module and then framed as questions that appear at the beginning of the pertinent section of reading. It helps to keep the question in mind as you read through a section to make sure that you are following the main point of the discussion.

# Evolutionary Psychology: Understanding Human Nature

**1.1-1** How do evolutionary psychologists use natural selection to explain behavior tendencies?

*Evolutionary psychologists* focus mostly on what makes us so much alike as humans. They use Charles Darwin's principle of *natural selection* to understand the roots of behavior and mental processes. The idea, simplified, is this:

- Organisms' varied offspring compete for survival.
- Certain biological and behavioral variations increase organisms' reproductive and survival chances in their particular environment.
- Offspring that survive are more likely to pass their genes to ensuing generations.
- In this way, over time, population characteristics may change.

To see these principles at work, let's consider a straightforward example in foxes.

## Natural Selection and Adaptation

A fox is a wild and wary animal. If you capture a fox and try to befriend it, be careful: If the timid fox cannot flee, it may snack on your fingers. In the early 1950s, Russian scientist Dmitry Belyaev wondered how our human ancestors had domesticated dogs from their wild wolf forebears. Might he, within a comparatively short stretch of time, accomplish a similar feat by transforming the fearful fox into a friendly fox?

To find out, Belyaev set to work with 100 female and 30 male foxes selected from fox farms (where some domestication would have already occurred [Gorman, 2019]). From their offspring he selected and mated the tamest 20 percent of females and 5 percent of males. (He measured tameness based on the foxes' responses to attempts to feed, handle, and stroke them.) Over 57 generations of foxes, Belyaev and his successor, Lyudmila Trut, repeated that simple procedure (Dugatkin & Trut, 2017). After 40 years and 45,000 foxes, they had a new breed of foxes that, in Trut's (1999) words, were "docile, eager to please, and unmistakably domesticated . . . Before our eyes, 'the Beast' has turned into 'beauty,' as the aggressive behavior of our herd's wild [ancestors] entirely disappeared." So friendly and eager for human contact were these animals, so inclined to whimper to attract attention and to lick people like affectionate dogs, that the researchers' cash-strapped institute seized on a way to raise funds — by marketing its friendly foxes as house pets.

**How to tame a fox** Over six decades, geneticist Lyudmila Trut has genetically bred silver foxes to become friendly human companions.

Does the same process work with naturally occurring selection? Does natural selection explain our human tendencies? Nature has indeed selected advantageous variations from the new gene combinations produced at each human conception plus occasional **mutations** (random errors in gene replication that become nature's preliminary tests of alternative possibilities). But the tight genetic leash that predisposes a dog's retrieving, a cat's pouncing, or a bird's nesting is looser on humans. The genes selected during our ancestral history provide more than a long leash; they give us a great capacity to learn and therefore to *adapt* to life in varied environments, from the tundra to the jungle. Genes and experience together wire the brain. Our adaptive flexibility in responding to different environments contributes to our *fitness*—our ability to survive and reproduce.

## Evolutionary Success Helps Explain Similarities

Human differences grab our attention. The Guinness World Records, for example, entertain us by highlighting the tallest, oldest, longest-haired, and most-tattooed humans. But our deep similarities also demand explanation. At the Amsterdam Airport's international arrivals area, one sees the same delighted joy on the faces of Indonesian grandmothers, Chinese children, and homecoming Dutch. In our genes and our behaviors, we humans are more alike than different. "Your DNA and mine are 99.9 percent the same," observed Francis Collins (2007), who led the human genome's decoding. "At the DNA level, we are clearly all part of one big worldwide family."

### Our Genetic Legacy

Our similarities reflect our shared human *genome*—our common set of genes. No more than 5 percent of the genetic differences among humans arise from population group differences. Some 95 percent of genetic variation exists *within* populations (Rosenberg et al., 2002). Thus, the typical genetic difference between two South Africans or between two Singaporeans is much greater than the *average* difference between the two groups (Lewontin, 1982).

And how did we develop this shared human genome? At the dawn of human history, our ancestors faced certain questions: Who is my ally, who is my foe? With whom should I mate? What food should I eat? Some individuals answered those questions more successfully than others. For example, women who experienced nausea in the critical first 3 months of pregnancy were genetically predisposed to avoid certain bitter, strongly flavored, and novel foods. Avoiding such foods had survival value, since they are the very foods most often toxic to prenatal development (Profet, 1992; Schmitt & Pilcher, 2004). Early humans disposed to eat nourishing rather than poisonous foods survived to contribute their genes to later generations. Those who deemed leopards "nice to pet" often did not.

Similarly successful were those whose mating helped them produce and nurture offspring. Over generations, the genes of individuals not disposed to mate or nurture tended to be lost from the human gene pool. As success-enhancing genes continued to be selected, behavioral tendencies and learning capacities emerged that prepared our Stone Age ancestors to survive, reproduce, and send their genes into the future, and into you. For all such universal human tendencies, from our intense need to give parental care to our shared fears and lusts, evolutionary theory proposes a single, all-encompassing explanation (Schloss, 2009).

As heirs to this prehistoric legacy, we were not born as unprogrammed "blank slates." Instead, we are genetically predisposed to think and act in ways that promoted our biological ancestors' survival and reproduction. But in some ways, we are biologically prepared for a world that no longer exists. We love the taste of sweets and fats, nutrients that prepared our physically active ancestors to survive food shortages. Few of us now hunt and gather for our food; instead, we too readily find sweets and fats in fast-food outlets and vending machines. Our deeply rooted natural dispositions are mismatched with today's proliferation

**AP® Science Practice**

**Research**

In research terminology, a *population* refers to all those in a group being studied, say in a survey or experiment, from which a sample can be drawn. You can review this and other terms related to research methods in Unit 0.

**AP® Science Practice**

**Research**

The text refers to *average* differences here. Recall from Unit 0 that the average is determined by calculating the mean, which is a measure of central tendency.

**mutation** a random error in gene replication that leads to a change.

of junk foods and often inactive lifestyles. The stress response that helped our ancestors escape temporary, mortal threats *(That's a tiger in the grass!)* now threatens our health, as we experience the long-term stressors of modern living *(That exam is tomorrow! The traffic is making me late!).*

## Evolutionary Psychology Today

Darwin's theory of evolution has become one of biology's fundamental organizing principles and lives on in the *second Darwinian revolution:* the application of evolutionary principles to psychology. In concluding *On the Origin of Species,* Darwin (1859, p. 346) anticipated this development, foreseeing "open fields for far more important researches. Psychology will be based on a new foundation."

In modules to come, we address questions that intrigue evolutionary psychologists: Why do infants start to fear strangers about the time they become mobile? Why do more people develop a *specific phobia* in response to spiders, snakes, and heights than to modern threats, such as guns? And why do women tend to be choosier than men when selecting sexual partners?

---

### AP® Science Practice

## Check Your Understanding

**Examine the Concept**

▶ Explain the principle of natural selection.

**Apply the Concept**

▶ Imagine that a futuristic scientist wanted to breed humans to favor particular behavioral traits. How would the scientist go about it? Why might this prove a greater challenge than breeding less complex mammals?

*Answers to the Examine the Concept questions can be found in Appendix C at the end of the book.*

---

# Behavior Genetics: Predicting Individual Differences

**1.1-2** How do behavior geneticists explain our individual differences?

**The nurture of nature** Parents everywhere wonder: Will my baby grow up to be agreeable or aggressive? Cautious or courageous? Successful or struggling? What comes built in, and what is nurtured — and how? Research reveals that nature and nurture together shape our development — every step of the way.

While evolutionary psychologists tend to focus on human similarities, behavior geneticists explore the genetic and environmental roots of human differences. Our shared brain architecture predisposes all of us humans to some common behavioral tendencies. Whether we live in the Arctic or in the tropics, we sense the world, develop language, and feel hunger through identical mechanisms. We prefer sweet tastes to sour. We divide the color spectrum into similar colors. And we feel drawn to behaviors that produce and protect offspring.

Our human family shares not only a common biological heritage — cut us and we bleed — but also common social behaviors. Whether we're named Gonzales, Nkomo, Smith, or Wong, we start fearing strangers at about 8 months, and as adults we prefer the company of people with attitudes and attributes similar to our own. As members of one species, we affiliate, conform, return favors, punish offenses, organize hierarchies of status, and grieve a child's death. A visitor from outer space could drop in anywhere and find humans dancing and feasting, singing and worshiping, playing sports and games, laughing and crying, living in families and forming groups. We are the leaves of one tree.

But in important ways, we also are each unique. We are each a one-of-a-kind package of looks, language, personality, interests, and cultural background. What causes our striking diversity? How much is our individuality shaped by our differing genes, and how much by our **environment**—by every external influence, from maternal nutrition while in the womb to social support while nearing the tomb? How does our **heredity** interact with our experiences to create both our universal human nature and our individual and social diversity? Such questions intrigue *behavior geneticists.*

## Genes: Our Codes for Life

Barely more than a century ago, few would have guessed that every cell nucleus in your body contains the genetic master code for your entire body. It's as if every room in Dubai's Burj Khalifa (the world's tallest structure) contained a book detailing the architect's plans for the entire structure. The plans for your own book of life run to 46 chapters—23 donated by your mother's egg and 23 by your father's sperm. Each of these 46 chapters, called a *chromosome,* is composed of a coiled chain of the molecule *DNA (deoxyribonucleic acid).* **Genes**, small segments of the giant DNA molecules, form the words of those chapters (**Figure 1.1-1**). Altogether, you have some 20,000 genes, which are either active (*expressed*) or inactive. Environmental events "turn on" genes, rather like hot water enabling a tea bag to express its flavor. When turned on, genes provide the code for creating *protein molecules,* our body's building blocks.

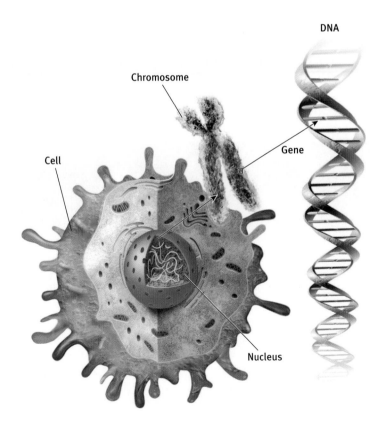

DNA

Chromosome

Gene

Cell

Nucleus

**Figure 1.1-1**
**The life code**

The nucleus of every human cell contains chromosomes, each of which is made up of two strands of DNA connected in a double helix. Genes are DNA segments that, when expressed (turned on), direct the development of proteins that influence a person's individual development.

**environment** every nongenetic influence, from prenatal nutrition to our experiences of the people and things around us.

**heredity** the genetic transfer of characteristics from parents to offspring.

**genes** the biochemical units of heredity.

**genome** the complete instructions for making an organism.

Genetically speaking, every other human is nearly your identical twin. Researchers exploring the human **genome** have discovered the common sequence within human DNA. This shared genetic profile is what makes us humans, rather than tulips, bananas, or chimpanzees.

Yet we aren't really all that different from our chimpanzee cousins. At a genetic level, humans and chimpanzees are 96 percent identical (Mikkelsen et al., 2005). At "functionally important" DNA sites, this proportion reaches 99.4 percent (Wildman et al., 2003)! Yet that wee 0.6 percent difference matters. It took a human, Shakespeare, to do what a chimpanzee cannot—weave 17,677 words into literary masterpieces.

Small differences matter among other species, too. Common chimpanzees and bonobos resemble each other in many ways. They should—their genomes differ by much less than 1 percent. But they display markedly differing behaviors. Chimpanzees are aggressive and their family groups are male dominated; bonobos are peaceable and live in female-led groups.

The occasional variations found at particular gene sites in human DNA fascinate geneticists and psychologists. Slight person-to-person variations from the common pattern give clues to our uniqueness—why one person is more susceptible than another to Covid, why one is tall and another short, why one is anxious and another calm (Ellinghaus et al., 2020). Taking advantage of these distinctions, some scientists are now developing *gene therapies,* which use gene-editing technology to prevent or treat diseases with a genetic basis (Coller, 2019).

Most of our traits have complex genetic roots. How tall you are, for example, reflects the size of your face, vertebrae, leg bones, and so forth—each of which may be influenced by different genes interacting with your specific environment. Traits such as intelligence, happiness, and aggressiveness are similarly influenced by a whole orchestra of genes (Holden, 2008). Indeed, one of the big take-home findings of today's behavior genetics is that there is no single gene that predicts your smarts, sexual orientation, or personality. Gene analyses of more than 800,000 people have, for example, identified 269 genes associated with depression (Howard et al., 2019). Another study of 1.1 million people identified 1271 gene variations that together predicted about 12 percent of the differences in people's years of schooling (Lee et al., 2018). *The bottom line:* Our differing traits are *polygenetic*—they are influenced by "many genes of small effect" (Lee et al., 2018; Matoba et al., 2019; Plomin, 2018a).

**Nature or nurture or both?** When talent runs in families, as with Wynton Marsalis, Branford Marsalis, and Delfeayo Marsalis, how do heredity and environment together do their work?

So, our many genes help explain both our shared human nature and our human diversity. But—here's another take-home finding—knowing our heredity tells only part of our story. To form us, environmental influences interact with our genetic predispositions.

To better understand these interactions, behavior geneticists conduct studies of genetically related and unrelated people. *Family studies* search for traits and diseases that tend to be shared by family members—for example, among biological siblings, or by a parent and a child. *Twin studies* and *adoption studies,* to which we will now turn, assess in more detail the effects of shared genes and shared environments.

 **AP® Science Practice**

## Check Your Understanding

### Examine the Concept

▶ Explain the difference between heredity and environment.

▶ Explain some effects of small genetic variations within and between species.

### Apply the Concept

▶ Were you surprised to learn how genetically similar we are to our chimpanzee cousins? What was your impression before reading this section?

▶ Come up with one unique research question or topic that would be of interest to a behavioral geneticist.

*Answers to the Examine the Concept questions can be found in Appendix C at the end of the book.*

## Twin and Adoption Studies

**1.1-3** How do twin and adoption studies help us understand the effects and interactions of nature and nurture?

To scientifically tease apart the influences of environment and heredity, behavior geneticists could wish for two types of studies. The first would control heredity while varying the home environment. The second would control the home environment while varying heredity. Such studies with human infants would be unethical, but nature has done this work for us.

### Identical Versus Fraternal Twins

**Identical (monozygotic) twins** develop from a single fertilized egg that splits. Thus, they are *genetically* identical—nature's own human clones (**Figure 1.1-2**). Indeed, they are clones who share not only the same genes but also the same conception and uterus, and usually the same birth date and cultural history. Two slight qualifications:

- Although identical twins have the same genes, they don't always have the same *number of copies* of those genes repeated within their genome, and they sometimes differ in their brain's tiny wiring structures. These variations help explain why one twin may have a greater risk for certain illnesses and disorders, including schizophrenia (Lee et al., 2018; Maiti et al., 2011).

- During prenatal development, most identical twins share a *placenta* (the structure that transfers nutrients and oxygen from mother to embryo), but one of every three sets has separate placentas. One twin's placenta may provide slightly better nourishment, which may contribute to a few identical twin differences (Marceau et al., 2016; van Beijsterveldt et al., 2016).

**AP® Science Practice**

### Research

Dramatically manipulating an infant's home environment, which has the potential to cause harm, would be unethical. Unit 0 has a full discussion of psychology's ethical guidelines for research.

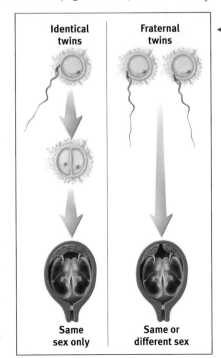

**Figure 1.1-2**

**Same fertilized egg, same genes; different eggs, different genes**

Identical twins develop from a single fertilized egg, fraternal twins from two.

Identical twins / Fraternal twins

Same sex only / Same or different sex

**identical (monozygotic) twins** individuals who developed from a single fertilized egg that split in two, creating two genetically identical organisms.

**Fraternal (dizygotic) twins** develop from two separate fertilized eggs. Although they were wombmates, they are genetically no more similar than ordinary siblings.

Shared genes can translate into shared experiences. A person whose identical twin has *autism spectrum disorder,* for example, has about a 3 in 4 risk of being similarly diagnosed. If the affected twin is fraternal, the co-twin has about a 1 in 3 risk (Tick et al., 2016). To study the effects of genes and environments, several thousand medical and psychological researchers have studied nearly 15 million identical and fraternal twin pairs (Polderman et al., 2015).

Are genetically identical twins also *behaviorally* more similar than fraternal twins? Compared with fraternal twins, identical twins are much more alike in their personality, their politics, and even the age when they begin using marijuana, if they do so (Hufer et al., 2020; Minică et al., 2018).

Identical twins, more than fraternal twins, look alike—so much so that most have difficulty distinguishing a flashed photo of their own face from their co-twin's face (Martini et al., 2015). Does that mean people's responses to their looks account for their similarities? *No.* In a clever approach, researcher (and fraternal twin) Nancy Segal (2013) compared personality similarity between identical twins and unrelated look-alike pairs. Only the identical twins reported similar personalities.

Other studies have shown that identical twins whose parents treated them alike (for example, dressing them identically) are *not* psychologically more alike than other identical twins (Kendler et al., 1994; Loehlin & Nichols, 1976). In explaining individual differences, identical genes matter more than identical jeans.

Charlie Riedel/AP Photo

Icon Sportswire/Getty Images

**Do look-alikes act alike?** Genetically unrelated look-alikes, called doppelgangers, tend not to have notably similar personalities (Segal, 2013). Amazingly, these two bearded, red-haired, 6 foot 4 inch tall, minor league baseball pitchers also share the same unusual name — Brady Feigl — but are unrelated and grew up unaware of each other.

## Separated Twins

Imagine the following science fiction experiment: A mad scientist, given two pairs of identical twins, swaps one in each pair. The resulting pairs are then raised in separate environments as if they were fraternal twins. Better yet, consider a *true* story (Dominus, 2015; Segal & Montoya, 2018).

In 2015, William Velasco was working as a butcher in Bogotá, Colombia. One day, customer Laura Vega Garzón mistook him for her colleague, Jorge, who looked the same — same

**fraternal (dizygotic) twins**
individuals who developed from separate fertilized eggs. They are genetically no closer than ordinary siblings, but they shared a prenatal environment.

high cheekbones, same smile, same walking style. Was it Jorge, pretending to be someone else? Confused, she returned to the butcher shop to show William a picture of his look-alike, Jorge. William laughed and didn't take it seriously, but Laura later showed Jorge a photograph of William. "That's me!" Jorge exclaimed. Scrolling through William's social media photos, Jorge found another surprise: his look-alike, William, sitting next to a mirror image of Jorge's fraternal twin brother.

Until then, William and Jorge had lived utterly separate lives. William grew up in a rural village, while Jorge was city-raised. William and Jorge both—thanks to a colossal hospital mistake—believed they had fraternal twin brothers, Wilber and Carlos, respectively. In reality, Wilber and Carlos, like William and Jorge, were identical twins. The hospital had sent William home with Wilber, and Carlos home with Jorge.

Although they were raised apart, William and Jorge both were jokesters, physically strong, and supportive. Wilber and Carlos were moody and serious, always organized, and prone to crying, and they had the same speech impediment. Each of them had wondered why he felt so different from his supposed fraternal twin. Meeting their identical twin revealed the power of genetics.

Genes matter, but so does environment. Urban-dwellers Jorge and Carlos had better nutrition, and were taller than rural-raised William and Wilber. Wilber didn't have access to the speech therapy that Carlos did, which meant that only Wilber struggled with speaking as an adult.

The remarkable story of the "Bogotá brothers" resembles that of many separated twin pairs. When tested by psychologists Thomas Bouchard and Nancy Segal, separated identical twins exhibited similarities in not only tastes and physical attributes but also personality, abilities, attitudes, interests, and fears.

**Bogotá brothers** Due to a medical error, two sets of identical twins born in Bogotá, Colombia, were separated at birth. The identical twin brothers were later reunited and noticed that they shared many of their twins' physical and personality traits. Yet the identical twins were raised in different environments, which led to differences in their access to quality education and nutrition. The Bogotá brothers illustrate how nature and nurture interact.

Stories of startling twin similarities have not impressed critics, who remind us that "the plural of *anecdote* is not *data*." They note that if any two strangers of similar age, sex, and ethnicity were to spend hours comparing their behaviors and life histories, they would probably discover many coincidental similarities (Joseph, 2001). Twin researchers reply that separated fraternal twins do not, however, exhibit similarities comparable to those of separated identical twins.

### AP® Science Practice

#### Research

To draw conclusions, psychological scientists rely on data gathered from studies — not anecdotes, hearsay, or common sense. This is why it is so important to understand the information about research methods in Unit 0.

Even the impressive data from personality assessments are clouded by the reunion of many of the separated twins some years before they were tested. Moreover, when adoption agencies are involved, separated twins tend to be placed in similar homes. Despite these criticisms, the striking twin-study results helped shift scientific thinking toward a greater appreciation of genetic influences.

## Biological Versus Adoptive Relatives

For behavior geneticists, nature's second real-life study—adoption—creates two groups: *genetic relatives* (biological parents and siblings) and *environmental relatives* (adoptive parents and siblings). For personality or any other given trait, we can therefore ask whether adopted children are more like their biological parents, who contributed their genes, or their adoptive parents, who contributed their home environment. And while sharing that home environment, do adopted siblings come to share traits?

The stunning finding from studies of hundreds of adoptive families is that, apart from identical twins, people who grow up together—whether biologically related or not—do not much resemble one another in personality (McGue & Bouchard, 1998; Plomin, 2011; Rowe, 1990). On personality traits such as extraversion and agreeableness, for example, people who have been adopted are more similar to their *biological* parents than to their caregiving adoptive parents.

The finding is important enough to bear repeating: *The normal range of environments shared by a family's children has little discernible impact on their personalities.* Two adopted children raised in the same home are no more likely to share personality traits with each other than with the child down the block.

Heredity shapes other primates' personalities, too. For example, macaque monkeys raised by foster mothers exhibit social behaviors that resemble those of their biological, rather than foster, mothers (Maestripieri, 2003).

*Why are children in the same family so different?* Why does a shared family environment have so little effect on children's personalities? Is it because each sibling experiences unique peer influences and life events? Because sibling relationships ricochet off each other, amplifying their differences? Because siblings—despite sharing half their genes—have very different combinations of genes and may evoke very different kinds of parenting? Such questions fuel behavior geneticists' curiosity.

**Adoption matters** Olympic gold medal gymnast Simone Biles benefited from one of the biggest gifts of love: adoption.

The genetic leash may limit the family environment's influence on personality, but it does not mean that adoptive parenting is a fruitless venture. One study followed more than 3000 Swedish children with at least one biological parent who had depression. Compared to their not-adopted siblings, those raised by an adoptive family were about 20 percent less likely to develop depression (Kendler et al., 2020a). As an adoptive parent, I [ND] especially find it heartening to know that parents do influence their children's attitudes, values, manners, politics, education, and faith (Gould et al., 2019; Kandler & Riemann, 2013). This was dramatically illustrated during World War II by separated identical twins Jack Yufe, a Jew, and Oskar Stöhr, a member of Germany's Hitler Youth. After later reuniting, Oskar mused to Jack: "If we had been switched, I would have been the Jew, and you would have been the Nazi" (Segal, 2005, p. 70). Parenting—and the cultural environments in which parents raise their children—matters!

Moreover, child neglect and abuse and even parental divorce are rare in adoptive homes. (Adoptive parents are carefully screened; biological parents are not.) One study looked at the parenting of siblings being raised apart—some with their biological mother, some with an adoptive mother (Natsuaki et al., 2019). Compared with the biological mothers, the adoptive mothers used gentler parenting, gave more guidance, and experienced less depression. It is not surprising, then, that studies have shown that, despite a slightly greater risk of psychological disorder, most adopted children thrive, especially when adopted as infants (Loehlin et al., 2007; van IJzendoorn & Juffer, 2006; Wierzbicki, 1993). Seven in eight adopted children have reported feeling strongly attached to one or both adoptive parents. As children of self-giving parents, they grow up to be more self-giving and unselfish than average (Sharma et al., 1998). Many score higher than their biological parents and raised-apart biological siblings on intelligence tests, and most grow into happier and more stable adults (Kendler et al., 2015b; van IJzendoorn et al., 2005). In one Swedish study, children adopted as infants grew up with fewer problems than were experienced by children whose biological mothers initially registered them for adoption but then decided to raise the children themselves (Bohman & Sigvardsson, 1990). *The bottom line:* Most adopted children benefit from adoption.

## AP® Science Practice

### Research

Results such as "seven in eight adopted children have reported feeling strongly attached to one or both adoptive parents" indicate the descriptive research method. The purpose of the descriptive method is to observe and record behavior. You can revisit Unit 0 to review basic research methods.

---

## AP® Science Practice

## Check Your Understanding

**Examine the Concept**

▶ Explain how researchers use twin and adoption studies to learn about psychological principles.

**Apply the Concept**

▶ Do you know biological siblings who, despite having been raised together, have very different personalities? (Are *you* one of these siblings, perhaps?) Knowing what you do of their lives and upbringing, what do you think contributed to these differences?

*Answers to the Examine the Concept questions can be found in Appendix C at the end of the book.*

*"The title of my science project is 'My Little Brother: Nature or Nurture.'"*

# Gene–Environment Interaction

### 1.1-4 How do heredity and environment work together?

Among our similarities, the most important—the behavioral hallmark of our species—is our enormous adaptive capacity. Some human traits develop the same way in virtually every environment. But other traits are expressed only in particular environments. Go barefoot for a summer and you will develop toughened, callused feet—a biological adaptation to friction. Meanwhile, your neighbor who wears shoes will remain a tenderfoot. The difference between the two of you is an effect of environment. But it is the product of a biological mechanism—*adaptation*. To say that genes and experience are *both* important is true. But more precisely, they **interact**.

Just *how* our genes and our experiences interact to form us as unique individuals is one of the hottest topics in psychology today. Gene–environment interaction studies are revealing, for example, who is most at risk of permanent harm from stress or abuse and who is most likely to benefit from interventions (Byrd et al., 2019; Manuck & McCaffery, 2014). The National Institutes of Health's (NIH's) *All of Us* research program is now studying 1 million people to pinpoint precisely how their genes and environment together predict physical and mental health (NIH, 2019).

**interaction** the interplay that occurs when the effect of one factor (such as environment) depends on another factor (such as heredity).

**An out-of-this-world study of genes and environments** In 2015, Scott Kelly (left) spent 340 days orbiting the planet in the International Space Station. His identical twin, Mark Kelly (right), remained on Earth. Both twins underwent the same physical and psychological testing (Garrett-Bakelman et al., 2019). Only Scott Kelly's immune system temporarily went into overdrive, possibly due to the stresses of living in space and exposure to greater-than-average levels of radiation.

Derek Storm/Splash News/Newscom

# Epigenetics: Triggers That Switch Genes On and Off

Recall that genes can be either active (expressed, as the hot water activates a tea bag) or inactive. **Epigenetics** studies the molecular mechanisms by which environments can trigger or block genetic expression. Genes are *self-regulating.* Rather than acting as blueprints that lead to the same result no matter what the context, genes react. An African butterfly that is green in summer turns brown in fall, thanks to a temperature-controlled genetic switch. The same genes that produce green in one situation produce brown in another.

Our experiences create *epigenetic marks,* which are often organic methyl molecules attached to part of a DNA strand (**Figure 1.1-3**). If a mark instructs the cell to ignore any gene present in that DNA segment, those genes will be "turned off"—they will prevent the DNA from producing the proteins normally coded by that gene. As one geneticist explained, "Things written in pen you can't change. That's DNA. But things written in pencil you can. That's epigenetics" (Reed, 2012).

Environmental factors such as diet, drugs, and stress can affect the epigenetic molecules that regulate gene expression. Mother rats normally lick their infants. In experiments, infant rats deprived of this licking had more epigenetic molecules blocking access to their brain's "on" switch for developing stress hormone receptors. When stressed, animals that had above-average levels of free-floating stress hormones displayed more stress (Champagne et al., 2003; Champagne & Mashoodh, 2009).

Epigenetics provides a possible mechanism by which the effects of childhood trauma, poverty, or malnutrition may last a lifetime (Neves et al., 2019). Such experiences may leave fingerprints in a person's genome. Some epigenetic changes may even get passed down to future generations. Holocaust survivors and former prisoners of war have shared epigenetic alterations with their offspring (Costa et al., 2018; Yehuda et al., 2016). Such findings have led some evolutionary biologists to theorize that inheritance occurs not only through gene transmission, but also through environmental influences (Uller & Laland, 2019). Evolution, they argue, shapes human culture and experience, which influence evolution. Other scientists dispute the idea that children can inherit their parents' epigenetic changes (Horsthemke, 2018; Ryan & Kuzawa, 2020). Stay tuned: This scientific story is still being written.

## Figure 1.1-3
### Epigenetic expression

Beginning in the womb, life experiences lay down *epigenetic marks* — often organic methyl molecules — that can influence the expression of any gene in the DNA segment they affect. (Research from Champagne, 2010.)

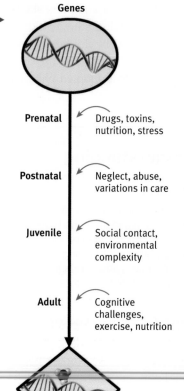

Genes

Prenatal — Drugs, toxins, nutrition, stress

Postnatal — Neglect, abuse, variations in care

Juvenile — Social contact, environmental complexity

Adult — Cognitive challenges, exercise, nutrition

**Gene expression affected by epigenetic molecules**

## AP® Science Practice

### Research

The environmental factors mentioned here — diet, drugs, and stress — could be variables in an epigenetic study. If the research *manipulates* the amount of stress the rats experience, it would be the independent variable.

**epigenetics** "above" or "in addition to" (*epi*) genetics; the study of the molecular mechanisms by which environments can influence genetic expression (without a DNA change).

**Lasting effects** Canadian Senator Murray Sinclair received a humanitarian award from the Canadian Psychological Association for an in-depth report on the devastating effects of Canada's long-running residential school program that removed Indigenous children from their families. Psychologist Susan Pinker (2015) observed that the epigenetic effects of forced family separation "can play out, not only in the survivors of residential schools but in subsequent generations."

Adrian Wyld/The Canadian Press/AP Photo

Epigenetics research may solve some scientific mysteries, such as why only one member of an identical twin pair may develop a genetically influenced mental disorder (Spector, 2012). Epigenetics can also help explain why identical twins may look slightly different. Researchers studying mice have found that in utero exposure to certain chemicals can cause genetically identical twins to have different-colored fur (Dolinoy et al., 2007).

So, if Beyoncé and JAY-Z's eldest daughter, Blue Ivy, grows up to be a popular recording artist, should we attribute her musical talent to her "superstar genes"? To her childhood in a musically rich environment? To high expectations? The best answer seems to be "All of the above." From conception onward, we are the product of a cascade of interactions between our genetic predispositions and our surrounding environments (McGue, 2010). Our genes affect how people react to and influence us. Forget nature *versus* nurture; think nature *via* nurture.

\* \* \*

We know from our correspondence and from surveys that some readers are troubled by the naturalism and evolutionism of contemporary science. "The idea that human minds are the product of evolution is . . . unassailable fact," declared a 2007 editorial in *Nature,* a leading science journal. In *The Language of God,* Human Genome Project director Francis Collins (2006, pp. 141, 146), a self-described evangelical Christian, compiled the "utterly compelling" evidence that led him to conclude that Darwin's big idea is "unquestionably correct." Yet Gallup pollsters report that 40 percent of U.S. adults believe that humans were created "pretty much in their present form" within the last 10,000 years (Brenan, 2019). Many people who dispute the scientific story worry that a science of behavior (and evolutionary science in particular) will destroy our sense of the beauty, mystery, and spiritual significance of the human creature. For those concerned, we offer some reassuring thoughts.

When Isaac Newton explained the rainbow in terms of light of differing wavelengths, the British poet John Keats feared that Newton had destroyed the rainbow's mysterious beauty. Yet, as evolutionary biologist Richard Dawkins (1998) noted in *Unweaving the Rainbow,* Newton's analysis led to an even deeper mystery — Einstein's theory of special relativity. Nothing about Newton's optics need diminish our appreciation for the dramatic elegance of a rainbow arching across a brightening sky.

When Galileo assembled evidence that Earth revolved around the Sun, not vice versa, he did not offer irrefutable proof for his theory. Rather, he offered a coherent explanation for a variety of observations, such as the changing shadows cast by the Moon's mountains. His explanation eventually won the day because it described and explained things in a way that made sense, that hung together. Darwin's theory of evolution likewise is a coherent view of natural history. It offers an organizing principle that unifies various observations.

Many people of faith find the scientific idea of human origins congenial with their spirituality. In the fifth century, St. Augustine (quoted by Wilford, 1999) wrote, "The universe was brought into being in a less than fully formed state, but was gifted with the capacity to transform itself from unformed matter into a truly marvelous array of structures and life forms." In the fourteenth century, Muslim historian Ibn Khaldun (1377) wrote, "One should then look at the world of creation. It started out from the minerals and progressed, in an ingenious, gradual manner to plants and animals." Some 800 years later, Pope Francis in 2015 welcomed a science–religion dialogue, saying, "Evolution in nature is not inconsistent with the notion of creation, because evolution requires the creation of beings that evolve."

Meanwhile, many people of science are awestruck at the emerging understanding of the universe and the human creature. It boggles the mind — the entire universe popping out of a point some 14 billion years ago, and instantly inflating to cosmological size. Had the energy of this Big Bang been the tiniest bit less, the universe would have collapsed back on itself. Had it been the tiniest bit more, the result would have been a soup too thin to support life. Astronomer Sir Martin Rees has described *Just Six Numbers* (1999), any one of which, if changed ever so slightly, would produce a cosmos in which life could not exist. Had gravity been a tad stronger or weaker, or had the weight of a carbon proton been a wee bit different, our universe just wouldn't have worked.

What caused this almost-too-good-to-be-true, finely tuned universe? Why is there something rather than nothing? How did it come to be, in the words of Harvard-Smithsonian astrophysicist Owen Gingerich (1999), "so extraordinarily right, that it seemed the universe had been expressly designed to produce intelligent, sentient beings"? On such matters, a humble, awed, scientific silence is appropriate, suggested philosopher Ludwig Wittgenstein: "Whereof one cannot speak, thereof one must be silent" (1922, p. 189).

Rather than fearing science, we can welcome its enlarging our understanding and awakening our sense of awe. In *The Fragile Species,* Lewis Thomas (1992) described his utter amazement that Earth in time gave rise to bacteria and eventually to Bach's Mass in B Minor. In a short 4 billion years, life on Earth has come from nothing to structures as complex as a 6-billion-unit strand of DNA and the incomprehensible intricacy of the human brain. Atoms no different from those in a rock somehow formed dynamic entities that produce extraordinary, self-replicating, information-processing systems—us (Davies, 2007). Although we appear to have been created from dust, over eons of time, the end result is a priceless creature, one rich with potential beyond our imagining.

## AP® Science Practice

# Check Your Understanding

### Examine the Concept

▶ Match the following terms (i–iii) to the correct definition (a–c).

**Term:**
i.   Epigenetics
ii.  Heredity
iii. Behavior genetics

**Definition:**
a.   Study of the relative effects of our genes and our environment on our behavior.
b.   The genetic transfer of characteristics from parents to offspring.
c.   Study of the environmental factors that affect how our genes are *expressed.*

### Apply the Concept

▶ Imagine that prenatal genetic testing could eventually predict the likelihood of certain complex traits, such as extraversion. What would be the benefits and drawbacks of such testing? If such tests had been available when you were in the womb, would you want them to have been conducted?

*Answers to the Examine the Concept questions can be found in Appendix C at the end of the book.*

# Module 1.1 REVIEW

**1.1-1 How do evolutionary psychologists use natural selection to explain behavior tendencies?**

- *Evolutionary psychologists* seek to understand how our traits and behavior tendencies are shaped by *natural selection.* Genetic variations that increase the odds of reproducing and surviving in a particular environment are most likely to be passed on to future generations.

- Some genetic variations arise from *mutations,* others from new gene combinations forged at conception.

- Humans share a genetic legacy and are predisposed to behave in ways that promoted our ancestors' surviving and reproducing.

- Charles Darwin's theory of evolution is one of biology's fundamental organizing principles. He anticipated today's application of evolutionary principles in psychology.

**1.1-2** How do behavior geneticists explain our individual differences?

- *Behavior geneticists* study the relative power and limits of genetic and *environmental* influences on behavior.

- Most of our differing traits are polygenetic, and are influenced by the interaction of our individual environments with these genetic predispositions.

**1.1-3** How do twin and adoption studies help us understand the effects and interactions of nature and nurture?

- Studies of *identical (monozygotic) twins* versus *fraternal (dizygotic) twins,* separated twins, and biological versus adoptive relatives allow researchers to consider the effects of shared environment and shared genes, which sheds light on how nature and nurture influence our traits.

- Shared family environments have little effect on personality, although parenting does influence other factors.

**1.1-4** How do heredity and environment work together?

- Our genetic predispositions and our surrounding environments *interact.* Environments can trigger genetic expression, and genetically influenced traits can influence the experiences we seek and the responses we evoke from others.

- The field of *epigenetics* studies the molecular mechanisms by which environments can trigger or block genetic expression.

# AP® Practice Multiple Choice Questions

**1.** Dr. Grant conducted a study examining the extent to which humans share genes with each other and with other animals. She is also interested in understanding how genes contribute to behavior. Which conclusion would Dr. Grant most likely reach based on her research and the results of previous research?

  a. Chimpanzees share very few genes with humans.
  b. Complex behaviors are determined by specific individual genes.
  c. Human genes are mostly the same across all people.
  d. Genetic predispositions do not explain our shared human nature.

**2.** Dr. Koulianos conducted a study on 1000 sets of identical and fraternal twin pairs being raised in the same household versus in different households to determine which twin pairs were most similar in their athletic abilities. Based on previous research, who should Dr. Koulianos expect to be most alike?

  a. Fraternal twins raised in the same households
  b. Identical twins raised in different households
  c. Fraternal twins raised in different households
  d. Identical twins raised in the same households

**3.** Dr. Yondu believes that having good social skills improves emotional stability. He conducts an experiment in which 100 children are randomly assigned to one of two conditions. One group of children receives a social skills intervention, while the other group of children listens to an instructional talk about how to whistle. Both groups complete an emotional stability questionnaire four weeks later. What does Dr. Yondu's independent variable measure?

  a. The impact of nature
  b. The impact of epigenetics
  c. The impact of nurture
  d. The impact of evolution

**4.** Dr. Quill wants to conduct a study on how heredity may influence musical ability. Which of the following would be the best operational definition for his dependent variable?

  a. Compare the genes of master musicians to the genes of individuals without musical aptitude.
  b. Rate the quality of musical performance from 1 (indicating poor performance) to 5 (indicating superior performance).
  c. Provide musical instruments to one group of children and provide no musical instruments to a second group of children.
  d. Assign one group of pregnant women to listen to music daily and assign a second group of pregnant women to avoid music.

**5.** Which of the following illustrates how a researcher might examine the influence of nature on behavior?

    a.  Dr. Hayakawa examined the influence of parenting on eating choices in children.

    b.  Dr. Rojas examined the influence of genes on academic performance in teenagers.

    c.  Dr. Williams examined the influence of media exposure on occupational choice in college students.

    d.  Dr. Olofsson examined the influence of exercise on attention in middle schoolers.

**6.** Dr. Frances conducted a study on the impact of prenatal exposure to cocaine on hyperactivity in rats. Which is an accurate statement about this research study?

    a.  The independent variable is hyperactivity, which reflects the impact of nurture.

    b.  The independent variable is exposure to cocaine, which reflects the impact of nature.

    c.  The independent variable is hyperactivity, which reflects the impact of nature.

    d.  The independent variable is exposure to cocaine, which reflects the impact of nurture.

**7.** Which of the following is an example of gene–environment interaction?

    a.  Yeh Lin experiences flushing syndrome, which often occurs in people of Asian heritage.

    b.  Alfonso gets food poisoning from eating undercooked meat.

    c.  Ted develops high cholesterol, which runs in his family, because his diet contains too much saturated fat.

    d.  Jordan has an autoimmune disorder that causes him to lose hair.

**Use the following text to answer questions 8 and 9:**

Dr. Freedia conducted a study in which she randomly assigned mice to one of two conditions. One group of mice was moved to a new cage every week for 8 weeks, while the other group of mice was allowed to remain in the same cage during this period. Dr. Freedia measured the levels of stress hormones in the mice's bloodstream at the beginning and at the end of the experiment. She also measured the level of stress hormones in the mice's offspring, and she found that the offspring of the mice that were exposed to frequent housing changes had higher levels than did the offspring of the mice that were not exposed to frequent housing changes.

**8.** Which of the following statements about this study is most accurate?

    a.  By randomly choosing mice from the entire population of mice, Dr. Freedia can ensure that her results regarding the effects of natural selection apply to all mice.

    b.  By randomly placing mice into the two groups of the study, Dr. Freedia can explain her results based on the effects of epigenetics rather than other factors.

    c.  By randomly choosing mice from the entire population of mice, Dr. Freedia can explain her results based on the effects of epigenetics rather than other factors.

    d.  By randomly placing mice into the two groups of the study, Dr. Freedia can explain her results based on evolution.

**9.** Based on the results of this study, a journalist wrote an article encouraging parents to avoid moving so as not to increase their children's and future grandchildren's stress hormone levels. What is the biggest problem with this reasoning?

    a.  Dr. Freedia did not employ random assignment, so the journalist cannot make claims about the impact of the independent variable on the dependent variable.

    b.  Dr. Freedia did not employ random selection, so the journalist cannot generalize the results to the larger population.

    c.  Dr. Freedia employed a nonexperimental design in her study, so the journalist is unable to infer a cause-effect relationship between the variables.

    d.  Dr. Freedia conducted her study on mice, so the results may not generalize to the population of humans.

**10.** Which of the following concepts is an example of using evolutionary principles in a discriminatory way?

a. Eugenics
b. Epigenetics
c. Natural selection
d. Mutations

**11.** Dr. Vaughn studies how population characteristics change over time based on how surviving members of a species pass on their genes to future generations. Dr. Vaughn studies

a. eugenics.
b. heredity.
c. epigenetics.
d. natural selection.

**12.** Dr. Privit examines how nongenetic factors impact behavior to better understand the role of

a. nature.
b. heredity.
c. environment.
d. epigenetics.

# Module 1.2 Overview of the Nervous System

## The Nervous System

**1.2-1** What are the functions of the nervous system's main divisions, and what are the three main types of neurons?

**nervous system** the body's speedy, electrochemical communication network, consisting of all the nerve cells of the peripheral and central nervous systems.

**central nervous system (CNS)** the brain and spinal cord.

**peripheral nervous system (PNS)** the sensory and motor neurons that connect the central nervous system (CNS) to the rest of the body.

**nerves** bundled axons that form neural cables connecting the central nervous system with muscles, glands, and sensory organs.

**sensory (afferent) neurons** neurons that carry incoming information from the body's tissues and sensory receptors to the brain and spinal cord.

**motor (efferent) neurons** neurons that carry outgoing information from the brain and spinal cord to the muscles and glands.

**interneurons** neurons within the brain and spinal cord; they communicate internally and process information between the sensory inputs and motor outputs.

My [DM's] nervous system recently gave me an emotional roller-coaster ride. Before sending me into a magnetic resonance imaging (MRI) machine for a shoulder scan, the technician asked if I had issues with claustrophobia (fear of enclosed spaces). "No, I'm fine," I assured her, with perhaps a hint of macho swagger. Moments later, as I found myself on my back, stuck deep inside a coffin-sized box and unable to move, my nervous system had a different idea. Claustrophobia overtook me. My heart began pounding, and I felt a desperate urge to escape. Just as I was about to cry out for release, I suddenly felt my nervous system having a reverse calming influence. My heart rate slowed and my body relaxed, though my arousal surged again before the 20-minute confinement ended. "You did well!" the technician said, unaware of my emotional roller-coaster ride. What happens inside our brain and body to produce such surging and subsiding emotions? Is the nervous system that stirs us the same nervous system that soothes us?

Our body's **nervous system** is made up of *neurons,* or nerve cells, that communicate via chemical messengers called *neurotransmitters* (see Module 1.3). This communication network takes in information from the world and the body's tissues, makes decisions, and sends back information and orders to the body's tissues (**Figure 1.2-1**).

A quick overview: The brain and spinal cord form the **central nervous system (CNS)**, the body's decision maker. The **peripheral nervous system (PNS)** is responsible for gathering information and for transmitting CNS decisions to other body parts. **Nerves** are electrical cables formed from bundles of *axons* (the neuron extension that passes messages to other neurons or to muscles or glands; see Module 1.3). Nerves link the CNS with the body's sensory receptors, muscles, and glands. The optic nerve, for example, bundles a million axons into a single cable carrying the messages from the eye to the brain (Mason & Kandel, 1991).

Information travels in the nervous system through three types of neurons. **Sensory neurons** carry messages from the body's tissues and sensory receptors inward (which biologists term *afferent*) to the brain and spinal cord for processing. **Motor neurons** (which are *efferent*) carry instructions from the CNS outward to the body's muscles and glands. Between the sensory input and motor output, information is processed via **interneurons**. Our complexity resides mostly in these interneurons. Our nervous system has a few million sensory neurons, a few million motor neurons, and billions and billions of interneurons.

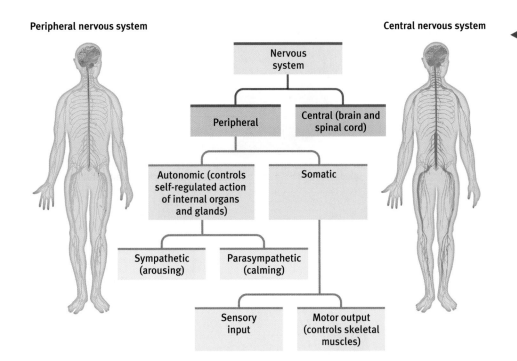

**Peripheral nervous system**

**Central nervous system**

**Figure 1.2-1**
**The functional divisions of the human nervous system**

## The Peripheral Nervous System

Our peripheral nervous system has two components—somatic and autonomic. Our **somatic nervous system** enables voluntary control of our skeletal muscles. When a friend taps your shoulder, your somatic nervous system reports to your brain the current state of your skeletal muscles and carries instructions back, triggering your head to turn.

Our **autonomic nervous system (ANS)** controls our glands and our internal organ muscles. The ANS influences functions such as glandular activity, heartbeat, and digestion. (*Autonomic* means "self-regulating.") As with a self-driving car, we may consciously override this system, but usually it operates on its own (autonomously).

The autonomic nervous system's subdivisions serve two important functions (Figure 1.2-2). The **sympathetic nervous system** arouses and expends energy (think "fight or flight"). Imagine an activity that alarms or challenges you (such as taking the AP® Psychology exam or being stuffed in an MRI machine). Your sympathetic nervous system accelerates your heartbeat, raises your blood pressure, slows your digestion, raises your blood sugar, and cools you with sweat, making you alert and ready for action. When the stress subsides (the AP® exam or MRI is over), your **parasympathetic nervous system** will produce the opposite effects, conserving energy as it calms you (think "rest and digest"). The sympathetic and parasympathetic nervous systems work together to keep our bodies in a steady internal state called *homeostasis*.

**somatic nervous system** the division of the peripheral nervous system that controls the body's skeletal muscles. Also called the *skeletal nervous system*.

**autonomic** [aw-tuh-NAHM-ik] **nervous system (ANS)** the part of the peripheral nervous system that controls the glands and the muscles of the internal organs (such as the heart). Its sympathetic division arouses; its parasympathetic division calms.

**sympathetic nervous system** the division of the autonomic nervous system that arouses the body, mobilizing its energy.

**parasympathetic nervous system** the division of the autonomic nervous system that calms the body, conserving its energy.

## Figure 1.2-2

### The dual functions of the autonomic nervous system

The autonomic nervous system controls the more autonomous (or self-regulating) internal functions. Its sympathetic division arouses the body and expends energy. Its parasympathetic division calms the body and conserves energy, allowing routine maintenance activity. For example, sympathetic stimulation accelerates a person's heartbeat, whereas parasympathetic stimulation slows it.

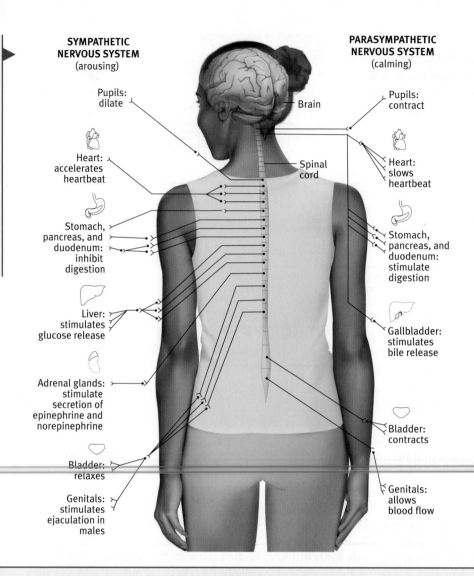

**SYMPATHETIC NERVOUS SYSTEM** (arousing)

**PARASYMPATHETIC NERVOUS SYSTEM** (calming)

Pupils: dilate

Brain

Pupils: contract

Heart: accelerates heartbeat

Spinal cord

Heart: slows heartbeat

Stomach, pancreas, and duodenum: inhibit digestion

Stomach, pancreas, and duodenum: stimulate digestion

Liver: stimulates glucose release

Gallbladder: stimulates bile release

Adrenal glands: stimulate secretion of epinephrine and norepinephrine

Bladder: contracts

Bladder: relaxes

Genitals: stimulates ejaculation in males

Genitals: allows blood flow

---

**AP® Science Practice**

## Check Your Understanding

### Examine the Concept

▶ Match the type of neuron (i–iii) to its description (a–c).

**Type:**
i.   Motor neurons
ii.  Sensory neurons
iii. Interneurons

**Description:**
a.  Carry incoming messages from sensory receptors to the CNS.
b.  Communicate within the CNS and process information between incoming and outgoing messages.
c.  Carry outgoing messages from the CNS to muscles and glands.

**Ballistic stress** In 2018, Hawaiians received this terrifying alert, amid concerns about the launch of North Korean nuclear warheads. "We fully felt we were about to die," reported one panicked mother (Nagourney et al., 2018). Thirty-eight minutes later, the alert was declared a false alarm.

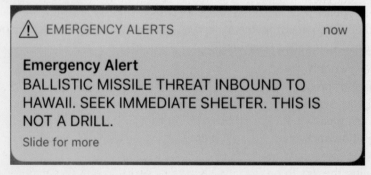

⚠ EMERGENCY ALERTS                     now

**Emergency Alert**
BALLISTIC MISSILE THREAT INBOUND TO HAWAII. SEEK IMMEDIATE SHELTER. THIS IS NOT A DRILL.

Slide for more

▶ Explain how the ANS was involved in Hawaiians' terrified responses, and in calming their bodies once they realized it was a false alarm.

*(continued)*

## The Central Nervous System

From the process of neurons "talking" to other neurons arises the complexity of the central nervous system's brain and spinal cord.

It is the brain that enables our humanity—our thinking, feeling, and acting. Tens of billions of neurons, each communicating with thousands of other neurons, yield an ever-changing wiring web. By one estimate—projecting from neuron counts in small brain samples—our brain contains some 128 billion neurons (Barrett, 2020).

Just as individual pixels combine to form a picture, the brain's individual neurons cluster into work groups called *neural networks.* To understand why, Stephen Kosslyn and Olivier Koenig (1992, p. 12) have invited us to "think about why cities exist; why don't people distribute themselves more evenly across the countryside?" Like people networking with people, neurons network with nearby neurons with which they can have short, fast connections; each layer's cells connect with various cells in the neural network's next layer. Learning—to play the violin, speak a foreign language, or solve a math problem—occurs as experience strengthens connections. To paraphrase one neuropsychologist, neurons that fire together, wire together (Hebb, 1949).

*"The body is made up of millions and millions of crumbs."*

The other part of the CNS, the *spinal cord,* is a two-way information highway connecting the peripheral nervous system and the brain. Ascending neural fibers send up sensory information, and descending fibers send back motor-control information. The neural pathways governing our **reflexes**, our automatic responses to stimuli, illustrate the spinal cord's work. A simple spinal reflex pathway—the *reflex arc*—is composed of a single sensory neuron and a single motor neuron. These often communicate through a spinal cord interneuron. The knee-jerk reflex, for example, involves one such simple pathway (from the peripheral nervous system to the central nervous system's spinal cord, and back out through the peripheral nervous system). A headless warm body could do it.

Another neural circuit enables the pain reflex (**Figure 1.2-3**). When your finger touches a flame, neural activity (excited by the heat) travels via sensory neurons to interneurons in your spinal cord. These interneurons respond by activating motor neurons leading to the muscles in your arm. Because the simple pain-reflex pathway runs through the spinal cord and right back out, your hand jerks away from the candle's flame *before* your brain receives and responds to the information that causes you to feel pain. That's why it feels as if your hand jerks away not by your choice, but on its own.

Information travels to and from the brain by way of the spinal cord. Were the top of your spinal cord severed, you would not feel pain from your paralyzed body below. Nor would you feel pleasure. With your brain literally out of touch with your body, you would lose all sensation and voluntary movement in body regions with sensory and motor connections to the spinal cord below its point of injury. You would exhibit the knee-jerk reflex without feeling the tap. To produce bodily pain or pleasure, the sensory information must reach the brain.

**reflex** a simple, automatic response to a sensory stimulus, such as the knee-jerk reflex.

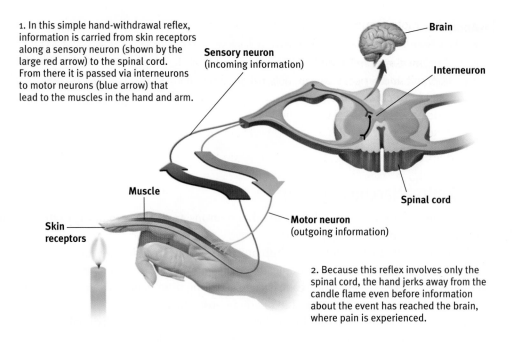

**Figure 1.2-3**
**A simple reflex**

1. In this simple hand-withdrawal reflex, information is carried from skin receptors along a sensory neuron (shown by the large red arrow) to the spinal cord. From there it is passed via interneurons to motor neurons (blue arrow) that lead to the muscles in the hand and arm.

Brain

Sensory neuron
(incoming information)

Interneuron

Spinal cord

Motor neuron
(outgoing information)

Muscle

Skin receptors

2. Because this reflex involves only the spinal cord, the hand jerks away from the candle flame even before information about the event has reached the brain, where pain is experienced.

# Module 1.2 REVIEW

**1.2-1 What are the functions of the nervous system's main divisions, and what are the three main types of neurons?**

- The *central nervous system (CNS)*—the brain and the spinal cord—is the *nervous system's* decision maker.

- The *peripheral nervous system (PNS)*, which connects the CNS to the rest of the body by means of *nerves*, gathers information and transmits CNS decisions to the rest of the body.

- The two main PNS divisions are the *somatic nervous system* (which enables voluntary control of the skeletal muscles) and the *autonomic nervous system* (which controls involuntary muscles and glands by means of its *sympathetic* and *parasympathetic* divisions).

- The three types of neurons cluster into working networks:
  (1) *Sensory (afferent) neurons* carry incoming information from sense receptors to the brain and spinal cord.
  (2) *Motor (efferent) neurons* carry information from the brain and spinal cord out to the muscles and glands.
  (3) *Interneurons* communicate within the brain and spinal cord and process information between the sensory inputs and motor outputs.

## AP® Practice Multiple Choice Questions

**1.** Which division of the nervous system calms a person down once a stressful event has passed?

a. Parasympathetic
b. Central
c. Somatic
d. Sympathetic

**2.** Thomas is walking down his favorite street in town. Which division of the nervous system enables him to move the muscles necessary to do this?

a. Central
b. Sympathetic
c. Parasympathetic
d. Somatic

**3.** If Drew's motor neurons were impaired, he would experience a disruption in the ability to

a. send messages from specific body parts to the brain.
b. transmit and process information within the brain and spinal cord.
c. process neurotransmiters in the brain.
d. send messages from the brain to body parts.

**4.** Maddox correctly defined *autonomic* as meaning

a. calming.
b. voluntary.
c. self-regulating.
d. arousing.

**5.** Dr. Veloso wants to conduct a study on how the central nervous system affects emotional expression in young children. Which of the following is an appropriate independent variable for her study?

a. Motor neuron activity
b. Brain activity
c. Sensory neuron activity
d. Somatic nervous system activity

**The Neuron and Neural Firing: Neural Communication and the Endocrine System**

---

**LEARNING TARGETS**

**1.3-1**  Describe *neurons*, and explain how they transmit information.

**1.3-2**  Explain how nerve cells communicate with other nerve cells.

**1.3-3**  Explain how neurotransmitters influence behavior, and explain how drugs and other chemicals affect neurotransmission.

**1.3-4**  Explain how the endocrine system transmits information and interacts with the nervous system.

---

## Neural Communication

For scientists, it is a happy fact of nature that the information systems of humans and other animals operate similarly. This similarity allows researchers to study relatively simple animals to discover how our own neural systems operate. Cars differ, but all have engines, accelerators, steering wheels, and brakes. A space alien could study any one of them and grasp the operating principles. Likewise, animals differ, yet their nervous systems operate similarly.

### Neurons

**1.3-1** What are *neurons*, and how do they transmit information?

Our body's neural information system comprises a complexity built from simplicity. Its building blocks are **neurons**, or nerve cells. Throughout life, new neurons are born and unused neurons wither away (O'Leary et al., 2014; Shors, 2014). To fathom our thoughts and actions, our memories and moods, we must first understand how neurons work and communicate.

Neurons differ, but all are variations on the same theme (**Figure 1.3-1**). Each consists of a **cell body** and its branching fibers. The often bushy **dendrite** fibers receive and integrate

**neuron** a nerve cell; the basic building block of the nervous system.

**cell body** the part of a neuron that contains the nucleus; the cell's life-support center.

**dendrites** a neuron's often bushy, branching extensions that receive and integrate messages, conducting impulses toward the cell body.

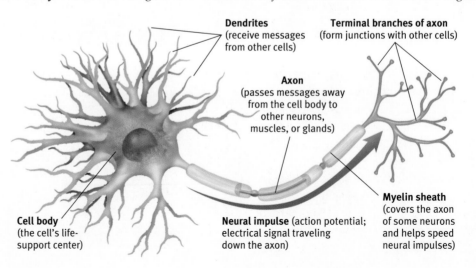

**Figure 1.3-1**
**A motor neuron**

**Dendrites** (receive messages from other cells)

**Terminal branches of axon** (form junctions with other cells)

**Axon** (passes messages away from the cell body to other neurons, muscles, or glands)

**Cell body** (the cell's life-support center)

**Neural impulse** (action potential; electrical signal traveling down the axon)

**Myelin sheath** (covers the axon of some neurons and helps speed neural impulses)

information, conducting it toward the cell body (Poirazi & Papoutsi, 2020). From there, the cell's single lengthy **axon** fiber passes the message through its terminal branches to other neurons or to muscles or glands (**Figure 1.3-2**). Dendrites listen; axons speak.

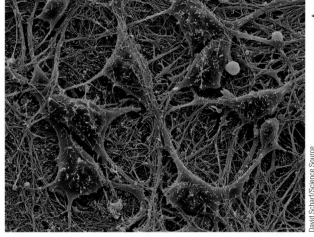

**Figure 1.3-2**
**Neurons communicating**
Our billions of neurons exist in a vast and densely interconnected web. As part of a fascinating electrochemical communication process, one neuron's terminal branches send messages to neighboring dendrites.

David Scharf/Science Source

Unlike the short dendrites, axons may be very long, projecting several feet through the body. A human neuron carrying orders from the brain to a leg muscle, for example, has a cell body and axon roughly on the scale of a basketball attached to a rope that's 4 miles (6.4 kilometers) long. Much as home electrical wire is insulated, some axons are encased in a **myelin sheath**, a layer of fatty tissue that insulates them and speeds their impulses. As myelin is laid down up to about age 25, neural efficiency, judgment, and self-control grow (Nakamura et al., 2018; Van Munster et al., 2015). If the myelin sheath degenerates, this deterioration leads to diminished control and slower reaction time. In extreme cases, it results in the disease known as *multiple sclerosis.* Communication to muscles and brain regions slows. The result: diminished muscle control and sometimes impaired cognition.

Supporting our billions of nerve cells are spidery **glial cells** ("glue cells"). Neurons are like queen bees; on their own, they cannot feed or sheathe themselves. Glial cells are the worker bees. They provide nutrients and insulating myelin, guide neural connections, and clean up waste after neurons send messages to one another. Glia also play a role in learning, thinking, and memory. By "chatting" with neurons, they participate in information transmission and memory (Fields, 2013; Martín et al., 2015).

In more complex animal brains, the proportion of glia to neurons increases. A postmortem analysis of Albert Einstein's brain did not find more or larger-than-usual neurons. However, it did reveal a much greater concentration of glial cells than found in the average Albert's head (Fields, 2004). Einstein's glial cells likely kept his brain abuzz with activity.

## The Neural Impulse

Neurons transmit messages when stimulated by our senses or by neighboring neurons. A neuron sends a message by firing an impulse, called the **action potential**—a brief electrical charge that travels down its axon.

Depending on the type of fiber, a neural impulse travels at speeds ranging from a sluggish 2 miles (3 kilometers) per hour to more than 200 miles (320 kilometers) per hour. But even its

**axon** the segmented neuron extension that passes messages through its branches to other neurons or to muscles or glands.

**myelin** [MY-uh-lin] **sheath** a fatty tissue layer segmentally encasing the axons of some neurons; it enables vastly greater transmission speed as neural impulses hop from one node to the next.

**glial cells (glia)** cells in the nervous system that support, nourish, and protect neurons; they may also play a role in learning, thinking, and memory.

**action potential** a neural impulse; a brief electrical charge that travels down an axon.

**Managing multiple sclerosis**
Actor Selma Blair's multiple sclerosis results from a loss of the myelin sheath that insulates her motor axons and speeds their neural impulses. She has discussed her challenges openly, including difficulty speaking and walking. In 2018, Blair attended a Hollywood event using a cane.

John Sheerer/Getty Images

top speed is 3 million times slower than that of electricity flowing through a wire. We measure brain activity in milliseconds (thousandths of a second) and computer activity in nanoseconds (billionths of a second). Unlike a computer's nearly instantaneous reaction, your response to a sudden event, such as a book slipping off your desk during class, may take a quarter-second or more. Your brain is vastly more complex than a computer but slower at executing simple responses.

Like batteries, neurons generate electricity from chemical events. In the neuron's chemistry-to-electricity process, *ions* (electrically charged atoms) are exchanged. The fluid outside an axon's membrane has mostly positively charged ions; a resting axon's fluid interior has a mostly negative charge. This positive-outside/negative-inside state is called the *resting potential.* When a neuron fires, the first section of the axon opens its gates, rather like a storm sewer cover flipping open, and positively charged ions (attracted to the negative interior) flood in through the now-open channels. The loss of the inside/outside charge difference, called *depolarization,* causes the next section of axon channels to open, and then the next, like a line of falling dominos. This temporary inflow of positive ions is the neural impulse—the action potential.

Each neuron is itself a miniature decision-making device performing complex calculations as it receives signals from hundreds, even thousands, of other neurons. The mind boggles when imagining this electrochemical process repeating up to 100 or even 1000 times a second. But this is just the first of many astonishments.

"What one neuron tells another neuron," noted Nobel laureate Francis Crick (1994), "is simply how much it is excited." Indeed, most neural signals are *excitatory,* somewhat like pushing a neuron's accelerator. Others are *inhibitory,* more like pushing its brake. If excitatory signals exceed the inhibitory signals by a minimum intensity, or **threshold**, the combined signals trigger an action potential. (Think of it as a class vote: If the excitatory people with their hands up outvote the inhibitory people with their hands down, then the vote passes.) The action potential then travels down the axon, which branches into junctions with hundreds or thousands of other neurons or with the body's muscles and glands.

Neurons need short breaks (a tiny fraction of an eyeblink). During a resting pause called the **refractory period**, subsequent action potentials cannot occur until the axon recharges and returns to its resting state. Then the neuron can fire again.

Increasing the level of stimulation above the threshold will not increase the neural impulse's intensity. Instead, the neuron's reaction is an **all-or-none response** (also known as the *all-or-nothing principle*): Like mechanical mousetraps, neurons either fire or they don't. How, then, do we detect the intensity of a stimulus? How do we distinguish a gentle touch from a big hug? A strong stimulus can trigger *more* neurons to fire, and to fire more often. But it does not affect the action potential's strength or speed. Triggering a mousetrap with a firmer push won't make it snap harder or faster.

**threshold** the level of stimulation required to trigger a neural impulse.

**refractory period** in neural processing, a brief resting pause that occurs after a neuron has fired; subsequent action potentials cannot occur until the axon returns to its resting state.

**all-or-none response** a neuron's reaction of either firing (with a full-strength response) or not firing.

---

### AP® Science Practice

## Check Your Understanding

#### Examine the Concept

▶ Explain the functions of the dendrites, the axon, and the cell body.

▶ Explain the *refractory period*.

*Answers to the Examine the Concept questions can be found in Appendix C at the end of the book.*

#### Apply the Concept

▶ Explain how our nervous system allows us to experience the difference between a slap and a tap on the back.

▶ Explain how the all-or-none response is like a mousetrap.

# How Neurons Communicate

**1.3-2** How do nerve cells communicate with other nerve cells?

Neurons are interweaved so intricately that even with a microscope, you would struggle to see where one neuron ends and another begins. Scientists once believed that the axon of one cell fused with the dendrites of another in an uninterrupted fabric. Then British physiologist Sir Charles Sherrington (1857–1952) noticed that neural impulses were taking an unexpectedly long time to travel a neural pathway. Inferring that there must be a brief interruption in the transmission, Sherrington called the meeting point between neurons a **synapse**.

We now know that the axon terminal of one neuron is, in fact, separated from the receiving neuron by a tiny *synaptic gap* (or *synaptic cleft*). Spanish anatomist Santiago Ramón y Cajal (1852–1934) marveled at these near-unions of neurons, calling them "protoplasmic kisses." "Like elegant ladies air-kissing so as not to muss their makeup, dendrites and axons don't quite touch," noted poet Diane Ackerman (2004, p. 37). How do the neurons execute this protoplasmic kiss, sending information across the synaptic gap? The answer is one of the important scientific discoveries of our age.

Neuroscientist Solomon Snyder (1984) captured your brain's information processing in simple words: It's "neurons 'talking to' each other at synapses." When an action potential reaches the button-like terminals at an axon's end, it triggers the release of chemical messengers, called **neurotransmitters** (Figure 1.3-3). Within 1/10,000th of a second, the neurotransmitter molecules cross the synaptic gap and bind to receptor sites on the receiving

**synapse** [SIN-aps] the junction between the axon tip of the sending neuron and the dendrite or cell body of the receiving neuron. The tiny gap at this junction is called the *synaptic gap* or *synaptic cleft*.

**neurotransmitters** chemical messengers that cross the synaptic gap between neurons. When released by the sending neuron, neurotransmitters travel across the synapse and bind to receptor sites on the receiving neuron, thereby influencing whether that neuron will generate a neural impulse.

**Figure 1.3-3
How neurons communicate**

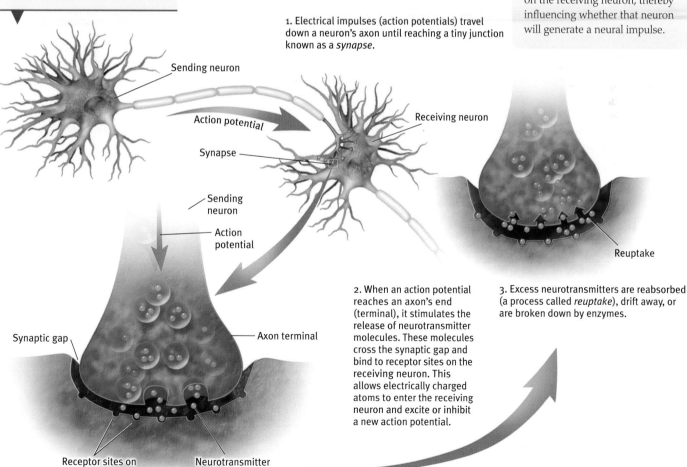

1. Electrical impulses (action potentials) travel down a neuron's axon until reaching a tiny junction known as a *synapse*.

Sending neuron

Action potential

Receiving neuron

Synapse

Sending neuron

Action potential

Reuptake

Synaptic gap

Axon terminal

2. When an action potential reaches an axon's end (terminal), it stimulates the release of neurotransmitter molecules. These molecules cross the synaptic gap and bind to receptor sites on the receiving neuron. This allows electrically charged atoms to enter the receiving neuron and excite or inhibit a new action potential.

3. Excess neurotransmitters are reabsorbed (a process called *reuptake*), drift away, or are broken down by enzymes.

Receptor sites on receiving neuron

Neurotransmitter

**reuptake** a neurotransmitter's reabsorption by the sending neuron.

neuron—as precisely as a key fits a lock. For an instant, the neurotransmitter unlocks tiny channels at the receiving site, and electrically charged atoms flow in, exciting or inhibiting the receiving neuron's readiness to fire. The excess neurotransmitters finally drift away, to be either broken down by enzymes or reabsorbed by the sending neuron—a process called **reuptake**. Some antidepressant medications partially block the reuptake of mood-enhancing neurotransmitters (**Figure 1.3-4**).

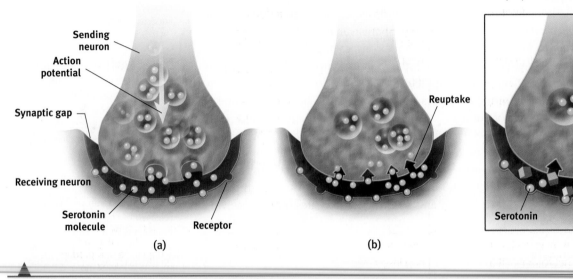

Message is sent across synaptic gap.

Message is received; excess serotonin molecules are reabsorbed by sending neuron.

Prozac partially blocks normal reuptake of the neurotransmitter serotonin; excess serotonin in synapse enhances its mood-lifting effect.

Sending neuron
Action potential
Synaptic gap
Receiving neuron
Serotonin molecule
Receptor
Reuptake
Serotonin
Prozac

(a)　　　　(b)　　　　(c)

**Figure 1.3-4**
**Biology of antidepressants**
Selective serotonin reuptake inhibitors (SSRIs) are popularly prescribed antidepressants. They relieve depression by partially blocking the reuptake of the neurotransmitter serotonin. Shown here is the action of the SSRI fluoxetine, which is marketed under the brand name Prozac.

---

**AP® Science Practice**

## Check Your Understanding

### Examine the Concept

▶ Explain *reuptake*. What two other things can happen to excess neurotransmitters after a neuron reacts?

▶ Explain what happens in the synaptic gap.

*Answers to the Examine the Concept questions can be found in Appendix C at the end of the book.*

### Apply the Concept

▶ How would you explain neural communication to a friend? Why was the discovery of neurons' communication mechanism so important?

---

## How Neurotransmitters Influence Us

**1.3-3** How do neurotransmitters influence behavior, and how do drugs and other chemicals affect neurotransmission?

In their quest to understand neural communication, researchers have discovered several dozen neurotransmitters and almost as many new questions: Are certain neurotransmitters found only in specific places? How do neurotransmitters affect our moods, memories, and mental abilities? Can we boost or diminish these effects through drugs or diet?

Other modules explore neurotransmitter influences on hunger and thinking, depression and euphoria, and addictions and therapy. For now, let's see how neurotransmitters influence our motions and emotions. A particular brain pathway may use only one or two neurotransmitters, such as serotonin and dopamine, and particular neurotransmitters (depending on their brain locations) affect specific behaviors and emotions (**Table 1.3-1**). But neurotransmitter systems don't operate in isolation; they interact, and their effects vary with the receptors they stimulate (**Figure 1.3-5**).

**AP® Exam Tip**

As the text indicates, there are dozens of different neurotransmitters. Though there's no way to predict exactly which ones you'll need to know on the AP® exam, it's quite likely you will be asked about the neurotransmitters in Table 1.3-1.

**TABLE 1.3-1 Commonly Studied Neurotransmitters and Their Functions**

| Neurotransmitter | Function | Examples of Malfunctions |
|---|---|---|
| Acetylcholine (ACh) | Enables muscle action, learning, and memory | With Alzheimer's disease, ACh-producing neurons deteriorate. |
| Dopamine | Influences movement, learning, attention, and emotion | Oversupply linked to schizophrenia. Undersupply linked to tremors and decreased mobility in Parkinson's disease. |
| Serotonin | Affects mood, hunger, sleep, and arousal | Undersupply linked to depression. Some drugs that raise serotonin levels are used to treat depression. |
| Norepinephrine | Helps control alertness and arousal | Undersupply can depress mood. |
| GABA (gamma-aminobutyric acid) | A major inhibitory neurotransmitter | Undersupply linked to seizures, tremors, and insomnia. |
| Glutamate | A major excitatory neurotransmitter; involved in memory | Oversupply can overstimulate the brain, producing migraines or seizures. |
| Endorphins | Neurotransmitters that influence the perception of pain or pleasure | Oversupply with opioid drugs can suppress the body's natural endorphin supply. |
| Substance P | Involved in pain perception and immune response | Oversupply can lead to chronic pain. |

**Dependent upon dopamine** The neurotransmitter dopamine helps us move, think, and feel. Too little dopamine may produce the tremors and loss of motor control of Parkinson's disease (National Institute on Aging [NIA], 2019; Weinstein et al., 2018). More than 10 million people worldwide have Parkinson's disease, including actor Michael J. Fox and the late boxing legend Muhammad Ali (Parkinson's Foundation, 2018).

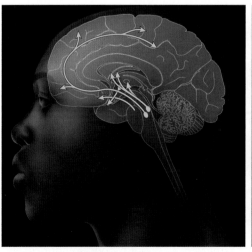

Dopamine pathway                    Serotonin pathway

**Figure 1.3-5**
**Neurotransmitter pathways**

Each of the brain's differing chemical messengers has designated pathways where it operates, as shown here for serotonin and dopamine (Carter, 1998).

One of the best-understood neurotransmitters, *acetylcholine (ACh)*, plays a role in learning and memory. ACh also enables muscle action, by acting as the messenger at every junction between motor neurons (which carry information from the brain and spinal cord to the body's tissues) and skeletal muscles. When ACh is released to our muscle cell receptors, the targeted muscle contracts. If ACh transmission is blocked, as happens during some kinds of anesthesia, with some poisons, and with the neuromuscular disease *myasthenia gravis,* the muscles cannot contract. The result is weakness, difficulties with muscle control, or paralysis.

Candace Pert and Solomon Snyder (1973) made an exciting discovery about neurotransmitters when they attached a harmless radioactive tracer to morphine, an opioid drug that elevates mood and eases pain. As the researchers tracked the morphine in an animal's brain, they noticed it was binding to receptors in areas linked with mood and pain sensations. But why would the brain have these "opioid receptors"? Why would it have a chemical lock, unless it also had a key—a natural painkiller—to open it?

Researchers soon confirmed that the brain does, indeed, produce its own naturally occurring opioids. Our body releases several types of neurotransmitter molecules similar to morphine in response to pain and vigorous exercise. These **endorphins** (short for *endogenous* [produced within] *morphine*) help explain good feelings such as the "runner's high," the painkilling effects of acupuncture, and the indifference to pain in some severely injured people (Boecker et al., 2008; Fuss et al., 2015). Physician Lewis Thomas (1983) called the endorphins "a biologically universal act of mercy. I cannot explain it, except to say that I would have put it in had I been around at the very beginning, sitting as a member of a planning committee."

## How Drugs and Other Chemicals Alter Neurotransmission

If natural endorphins lessen pain and boost mood, why shouldn't we increase this effect by flooding the brain with artificial opioids, thereby intensifying the brain's own "feel-good" chemistry? The answer: Because that would disrupt the brain's chemical balancing act. When flooded with opioid drugs such as heroin, morphine, and fentanyl, the brain—to maintain its chemical balance—may stop producing its own natural opioids. When the drug is withdrawn, the brain may then be deprived of any form of opioid, causing intense discomfort. For suppressing the body's own neurotransmitter production, nature charges a price.

Drugs and other chemicals affect brain chemistry, often by either exciting or inhibiting neurons' firing. **Agonist** molecules increase a neurotransmitter's action. Some agonists increase the production or release of neurotransmitters, or block synaptic reuptake. Other agonists may be similar enough to a neurotransmitter to bind to its receptor and mimic its excitatory or inhibitory effects. Some opioid drugs are agonists and produce a temporary "high" by amplifying normal sensations of arousal or pleasure (**Figure 1.3-6**).

**Antagonists** decrease a neurotransmitter's action by blocking production or release. Botulin, a poison that can grow in improperly canned food, causes paralysis by blocking ACh release. (Small injections of botulin—known by the brand name Botox™—smooth wrinkles by paralyzing the underlying facial muscles.) These antagonists are enough like the natural neurotransmitter to occupy its receptor site and block its effect, but are not similar enough to stimulate the receptor (rather like foreign coins that fit into, but won't operate, a vending machine). Curare, a poison that some South American Indigenous people have applied to hunting-dart tips, occupies and blocks ACh receptor sites on muscles, producing paralysis in their prey.

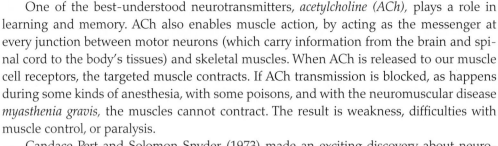

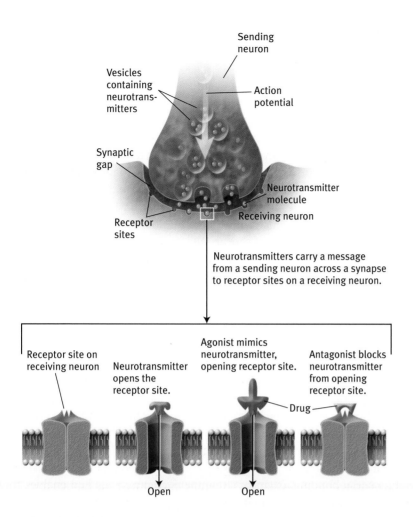

Sending neuron

Vesicles containing neurotrans-mitters

Action potential

Synaptic gap

Neurotransmitter molecule

Receptor sites

Receiving neuron

Neurotransmitters carry a message from a sending neuron across a synapse to receptor sites on a receiving neuron.

Receptor site on receiving neuron

Neurotransmitter opens the receptor site.

Agonist mimics neurotransmitter, opening receptor site.

Antagonist blocks neurotransmitter from opening receptor site.

Drug

Open          Open

**Figure 1.3-6**
**Agonists and antagonists**
Curare poisoning paralyzes its victims by blocking ACh receptors involved in muscle movements. Morphine mimics endorphin actions. Which is an agonist, and which is an antagonist? (Information from Higgins & George, 2007.)

---

**AP® Science Practice**

## Check Your Understanding

**Examine the Concept**

▶ Serotonin, dopamine, and endorphins are all chemical messengers called _____ .

**Apply the Concept**

▶ Can you recall a time, perhaps after a workout, when you felt the effects of endorphins? How would you explain those feelings?

▶ Curare poisoning paralyzes animals by blocking ACh receptors involved in muscle movements. Morphine mimics the actions of endorphins. Which is an agonist, and which is an antagonist?

*Answers to the Examine the Concept questions can be found in Appendix C at the end of the book.*

---

# The Endocrine System

**1.3-4** How does the endocrine system transmit information and interact with the nervous system?

So far, we have focused on the body's speedy electrochemical information system. Inter-connected with your nervous system is a second communication system, the **endocrine system**. The endocrine system's glands and fat tissue secrete another form of chemical

**endocrine** [EN-duh-krin] **system** the body's "slow" chemical communication system; a set of glands and fat tissue that secrete hormones into the bloodstream.

messengers, **hormones**, which travel through the bloodstream and affect other tissues, including the brain. When hormones act on the brain, they influence our interest in sex, food, and aggression.

Some hormones are chemically identical to neurotransmitters (the chemical messengers that diffuse across a synapse and excite or inhibit an adjacent neuron). The endocrine system and nervous system are therefore close relatives: Both produce molecules that act on receptors elsewhere. But like many family members, they also differ. The speedier nervous system zips messages from eyes to brain to hand in a fraction of a second. Meanwhile, endocrine messages trudge along in the bloodstream, taking several seconds or more to travel from the gland to the target tissue. If the nervous system transmits information with text-message speed, the endocrine system delivers an old-fashioned letter.

But slow and steady sometimes wins the race. Endocrine messages tend to outlast the effects of neural messages. Have you ever felt angry long after the cause of your angry feelings was resolved (say, your friend apologized for their rudeness)? You may have experienced an "endocrine hangover" from lingering emotion-related hormones.

In a moment of danger, the ANS orders the *adrenal glands* on top of the kidneys to release *epinephrine* and *norepinephrine* (also called *adrenaline* and *noradrenaline*). These hormones increase heart rate, blood pressure, and blood sugar, providing a surge of energy to power our *fight-or-flight* response. When the emergency passes, the hormones—and the feelings—linger a while.

The most influential endocrine gland is the *pituitary gland,* a pea-sized structure located in the core of the brain, where it is controlled by an adjacent brain area, the *hypothalamus* (more on that shortly). Among the hormones released by the pituitary is a growth hormone that stimulates physical development. Another is *oxytocin,* which enables orgasm and, in women, labor contractions and milk flow while nursing. Oxytocin also aids social support. While grooming their children, male baboons' oxytocin levels surge (Rincon et al., 2020). By promoting social bonding, oxytocin strengthens communities and enables them to act cooperatively against threats (Quintana & Guastella, 2020; Zhang et al., 2019).

Pituitary secretions also direct other endocrine glands to release their hormones. The pituitary, then, is a maestro gland (whose own director is the hypothalamus). For example, under the brain's influence, the pituitary triggers your sex glands to release sex hormones. These hormones, in turn, influence your brain and behavior (Goetz et al., 2014). So, too, with stress. A stressful event triggers your hypothalamus to instruct your pituitary to release a hormone that causes your adrenal glands to flood your body with cortisol, a stress hormone that increases blood sugar.

**Prejudice causes stress** Research demonstrates that an experience of prejudice may trigger release of the stress hormone cortisol (Deer et al., 2018).

**hormones** chemical messengers that are manufactured by the endocrine glands, travel through the bloodstream, and affect other tissues.

fizkes/Getty Images

This feedback system (brain → pituitary → other glands → hormones → body and brain) reveals the intimate connections between the nervous and endocrine systems. The nervous system directs endocrine secretions, which then affect the nervous system. Conducting and coordinating this whole electrochemical orchestra is that flexible maestro we call the brain.

---

**AP® Science Practice**

## Check Your Understanding

### Examine the Concept

► Explain the relationship between the nervous and endocrine systems.

### Apply the Concept

► Compare and contrast the nervous and endocrine systems.

► Do you remember feeling the lingering effects of a hormonal response, such as anger, after some particularly aggravating event? Describe how it felt. How long did it last?

*Answers to the Examine the Concept questions can be found in Appendix C at the end of the book.*

---

# Module 1.3a REVIEW

### 1.3-1 What are *neurons,* and how do they transmit information?

- *Neurons* are the elementary components of the nervous system, the body's speedy electrochemical information system.

- A neuron consists of a *cell body* and its branching fibers. It receives signals through its often bushy, branching *dendrites* and sends signals through its *axons.*

- Some axons are encased in a *myelin sheath,* which enables faster transmission.

- *Glial cells* support, nourish, and protect neurons and also play a role in learning, thinking, and memory.

- If the combined signals received by a neuron exceed a minimum *threshold,* the neuron fires, transmitting an electrical impulse (the *action potential*) down its axon by means of a chemistry-to-electricity process.

- Neurons need a short rest called the *refractory period,* after which they can fire again. The neuron's reaction is an *all-or-none response.*

### 1.3-2 How do nerve cells communicate with other nerve cells?

- When action potentials reach the end of an axon (the button-like axon terminals), they stimulate the release of *neurotransmitters.* These chemical messengers carry a message from the sending neuron across a *synapse* to receptor sites on a receiving neuron.

- The sending neuron, in a process called *reuptake,* then normally reabsorbs the excess neurotransmitter molecules in the synaptic gap.

- If incoming signals are strong enough, the receiving neuron generates its own action potential and relays the message to other cells.

### 1.3-3 How do neurotransmitters influence behavior, and how do drugs and other chemicals affect neurotransmission?

- Neurotransmitters travel along designated pathways in the brain and may influence specific behaviors and emotions.

- Acetylcholine (ACh) affects muscle action, learning, and memory.

- *Endorphins* are natural opioids released by the body in response to pain and exercise.

- Drugs and other chemicals affect brain chemistry at synapses.

- *Agonists* increase a neurotransmitter's action, and may do so in various ways.

- *Antagonists* decrease a neurotransmitter's action by blocking its production or release.

### 1.3-4 How does the endocrine system transmit information and interact with the nervous system?

- The *endocrine system* secretes *hormones* into the bloodstream, where they travel throughout the body, enabling them to affect other tissues, including the brain.

- In an intricate feedback system, the brain's hypothalamus influences the endocrine system's pituitary gland, which influences other glands, which release hormones, which in turn influence the brain.

# AP® Practice Multiple Choice Questions

1. For a neuron to generate an action potential, which of the following must be true?

   a. The neuron must be in the refractory period.
   b. Glial cells must release neurotransmitters into the axon.
   c. Excitatory impulses must outnumber inhibitory impulses.
   d. Dopamine and serotonin must be present in equal amounts.

2. Dr. Hansel studies the speed of neurotransmitters crossing the space between neurons. Which of the following does Dr. Hansel study?

   a. Synaptic gap
   b. Axon
   c. Myelin sheath
   d. Dendrites

3. Dr. Gretel asked her students to identify what happens after neurotransmitters are released and trigger an action potential in a neighboring neuron. Which student response is accurate?

   a. The synaptic cleft closes temporarily to terminate the action potential.
   b. The myelin sheath absorbs the excess neurotransmitters.
   c. The receiving neuron absorbs the neurotransmitter to send to the next neuron.
   d. The sending neuron reabsorbs the neurotransmitter for reuse.

4. Hollinger was recently diagnosed with major depressive disorder. Which neurotransmitters are most likely in undersupply in Hollinger's brain?

   a. Oxytocin and gamma-aminobutyric acid (GABA)
   b. Acetylcholine (ACh) and histamine
   c. Dopamine and acetylcholine (ACh)
   d. Serotonin and norepinephrine

5. Dr. Shill conducted a study in which she administered morphine, which mimics the action of naturally occurring endorphins, to volunteers in hopes of determining whether morphine boosts mood. In this instance, the independent variable is a(n)

   a. antagonist.
   b. synapse.
   c. ion.
   d. agonist.

6. In this image of a neuron, which letter corresponds with the neuron's axon?

   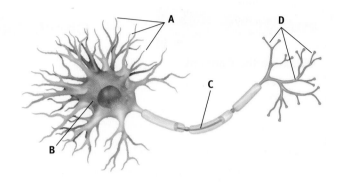

   a. A
   b. B
   c. C
   d. D

7. Imagine you are the teacher of an AP® Psychology course, and one of your students declares, "Hormones are the same thing as neurotransmitters." Which statement best modifies this student's claim to make it more accurate?

   a. "While neurotransmitters and hormones are both electrical messages within the nervous system, neurotransmitters travel much more slowly than hormones do, and their effects last longer."
   b. "While neurotransmitters and hormones are both chemical messages within the nervous system, hormones travel much more slowly than neurotransmitters do, and their effects last longer."
   c. "While neurotransmitters and hormones are both electrical messages within the nervous system, neurotransmitters travel much more quickly than hormones do, and their effects last longer."
   d. "While neurotransmitters and hormones are both chemical messages within the nervous system, hormones travel much more quickly than neurotransmitters do, and their effects last longer."

**8.** Axel woke up feeling alert. Which neurotransmitter impacted his alertness?

   a. Acetylcholine

   b. Norepinephrine

   c. Substance P

   d. Dopamine

**9.** Which statement should Prim say to accurately discuss myelin sheath?

   a. It supports, nourishes, and protects neurons.

   b. It contains the cell's life-support center.

   c. It blocks a neurotransmitter's action.

   d. It enables vastly greater transmission speed as neural impulses hop from one node to the next.

# Module 1.3b The Neuron and Neural Firing: Substance Use Disorders and Psychoactive Drugs

## LEARNING TARGETS

**1.3-5** Explain *substance use disorders*.

**1.3-6** Describe the *depressants*, and explain their effects.

**1.3-7** Describe the *stimulants*, and explain their effects.

**1.3-8** Describe the *hallucinogens*, and explain their effects.

As we have seen, your brain's information processing occurs as neurons talk to other neurons, by sending chemical messengers across the tiny synaptic gaps. When these neurotransmitter chemicals are supplemented or replaced by drugs, strange things can happen.

# Tolerance and Addiction in Substance Use Disorders

**1.3-5** What are *substance use disorders?*

Let's imagine a day in the life of a legal-drug-using adult. The day begins with a couple shots of espresso to feel alert, then an Adderall pill to help focus on a morning meeting. At midday, an energy drink offsets post-lunch drowsiness, and vaping calms anxiety before a presentation. Later, a friend suggests meeting for after-work drinks. It used to take only a drink or two to feel relaxed, but now it's three or four. Back home, two Advil PMs before bed help induce sleep. The alarm beeps just a few hours later. Then the daily cycle of drug use resumes. Over time, our imagined person—and many actual people—may struggle to keep up with work and family responsibilities, experience strained relationships, and have difficulty limiting their substance use. How do we know when substance use becomes a problem?

The substances our imaginary person uses are **psychoactive drugs**—chemicals that alter the brain, producing changes in perceptions and moods. Most of us manage to use some psychoactive drugs in moderation and without disrupting our lives. But sometimes, drug use crosses the line between moderation and **substance use disorder** (Table 1.3-2).

| TABLE 1.3-2 **When Is Drug Use a Disorder?** |
| --- |
| According to the American Psychiatric Association (2013), a person may be diagnosed with *substance use disorder* when drug use continues despite significant life disruptions. The resulting brain changes may persist after quitting use of the substance (thus leading to strong cravings when exposed to people and situations that trigger memories of drug use). The severity of substance use disorder varies from *mild* (two to three of the indicators listed below) to *moderate* (four to five indicators) to *severe* (six or more indicators). If you are concerned about your substance use or that of a loved one, contact your school counselor, health clinic, or physician. |
| **Diminished Control** |
| 1. Uses more substance, or for longer than intended. |
| 2. Tries unsuccessfully to regulate use of substance. |
| 3. Spends much time acquiring, using, or recovering from effects of substance. |
| 4. Craves the substance. |
| **Diminished Social Functioning** |
| 5. Use disrupts commitments at work, school, or home. |
| 6. Continues use despite social problems. |
| 7. Causes reduced social, recreational, and work activities. |
| **Hazardous Use** |
| 8. Continues use despite hazards. |
| 9. Continues use despite worsening physical or psychological problems. |
| **Drug Action** |
| 10. Experiences tolerance (needing more substance for the desired effect). |
| 11. Experiences withdrawal (unpleasant mental or physical reactions) when attempting to end use. |

**psychoactive drug** a chemical substance that alters the brain, causing changes in perceptions and moods.

**substance use disorder** a disorder characterized by continued substance use despite resulting life disruption.

A drug's overall effect depends not only on its biological effects but also on the user's expectations, which vary with social and cultural contexts (Gu et al., 2015; Ward, 1994). If one culture assumes that a particular drug produces euphoria (or aggression or sexual arousal) and another does not, each culture may find its expectations fulfilled. We'll take a closer look at these interacting forces in the use and potential abuse of particular psychoactive drugs. But first, to consider what contributes to the disordered use of various substances, see the Developing Arguments feature: Tolerance and Addiction.

---

**AP® Science Practice**

## Check Your Understanding

**Examine the Concept**

▶ Explain *substance use disorder*. What determines whether someone has a substance use disorder?

**Apply the Concept**

▶ Explain the process that generally leads to drug tolerance.

▶ Compare and contrast tolerance and addiction.

*Answers to the Examine the Concept questions can be found in Appendix C at the end of the book.*

---

# Types of Psychoactive Drugs

The three major categories of psychoactive drugs are *depressants, stimulants,* and *hallucinogens.* All do their work at the brain's synapses, stimulating, inhibiting, or mimicking the activity of the brain's own chemical messengers, the neurotransmitters.

## Depressants

**1.3-6** What are *depressants,* and what are their effects?

**Depressants** are drugs such as alcohol, barbiturates (tranquilizers), and opioids that calm neural activity and slow body functions.

## Alcohol

True or false? Alcohol is a depressant in large amounts but a stimulant in small amounts. *False.* In any amount, alcohol is a depressant. Low doses of alcohol may enliven a drinker, but they do so by acting as a *disinhibitor.* Alcohol slows brain activity that controls judgment and inhibitions—causing 3 million yearly deaths worldwide (WHO, 2018b).

Alcohol is an equal-opportunity drug: It increases (disinhibits) helpful tendencies, as when tipsy restaurant patrons leave extravagant tips and social drinkers bond in groups (Fairbairn & Sayette, 2014; Lynn, 1988). And it increases harmful tendencies, as when sexually aroused men become more disposed to sexual aggression. One University of Illinois campus survey showed that before sexual assaults, 80 percent of the male assailants and 70 percent of the female victims had been drinking (Camper, 1990). Another survey of 89,874 American collegians found alcohol or other drugs involved in 79 percent of unwanted sexual intercourse experiences (Presley et al., 1997). Drinking increases men's and women's desire for casual sex and perception of attractiveness in others (Bowdring & Sayette, 2018; Johnson & Chen, 2015). *The bottom line:* The urges you would feel if sober are the ones you will be more likely to act upon when intoxicated.

The prolonged and excessive drinking that characterizes *alcohol use disorder* contributes to more than 200 diseases, and can even shrink the brain and contribute to premature

---

**AP® Exam Tip**

These three categories — depressants, stimulants, and hallucinogens — are important. There are likely to be questions on the AP® exam that will require you to know what effect the drugs within these categories have on the body.

**AP® Science Practice**

### Research

Surveys, such as the one used by the University of Illinois, are a non-experimental technique for obtaining the self-reported attitudes or behaviors of a particular group. Wording is very important in surveys; even small changes in the phrasing of questions can make a big difference in the results. For example, how might the results be different if the respondents were asked if they were "drinking" versus if they were "drunk"?

**depressants** drugs that reduce neural activity and slow body functions.

---

# Developing Arguments
## Tolerance and Addiction

## Tolerance

With continued use of alcohol and some other drugs (but not marijuana), users develop **tolerance** as their brain chemistry adapts to offset the drug effect (*neuroadaptation*). To experience the same effect, users require larger and larger doses, which increase the risk of becoming **addicted** and developing a *substance use disorder*.

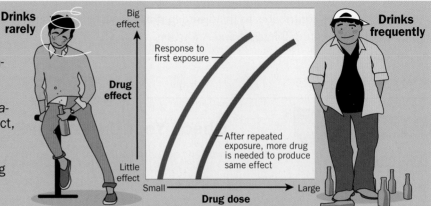

**Drinks rarely**

**Drinks frequently**

Big effect

Response to first exposure

**Drug effect**

After repeated exposure, more drug is needed to produce same effect

Little effect

Small — **Drug dose** — Large

## Addiction

Caused by ever-increasing doses of most psychoactive drugs (including prescription painkillers). Prompts user to crave the drug, to continue use despite adverse consequences, and to struggle when attempting to **withdraw** from it. These behaviors suggest a substance use disorder. Once in the grip of addiction, people *want* the drug more than they *like* the drug.[1]

**4%**

4% of the world's people have an alcohol use disorder.[2]

The lifetime odds of getting hooked after using various drugs:

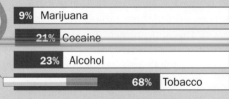

| 9% | Marijuana |
| 21% | Cocaine |
| 23% | Alcohol |
| 68% | Tobacco |

Data from National Epidemiologic Survey on Alcohol and Related Conditions[3]

Therapy or group support, such as from Alcoholics Anonymous, may help. It also helps to believe that addictions are controllable and that people can change. Many people do voluntarily stop using addictive drugs without any treatment. "Most people who successfully quit smoking kicked the habit on their own.[4]"

## Behavior Addictions

Psychologists try to avoid using "addiction" to label driven, excessive behaviors such as eating, work, sex, and accumulating wealth.

I'm ADDICTED to cheeseburgers!

Yet some behaviors can become compulsive and dysfunctional — similar to problematic alcohol and drug use.[5] Behavior addictions include *gambling disorder*. *Internet gaming disorder* is also now a diagnosable condition.[6] Such gamers display a consistent inability to resist logging on and staying on, even when this excessive use impairs their work and relationships. One international study of 19,000 gamers found that 1 in 3 had at least one symptom of the disorder. But fewer than 1 percent met criteria for a diagnosis.[7]

Psychological and drug therapies may be "highly effective" for problematic internet use.[8]

## Developing Arguments Questions

**1.** Explain the difference between tolerance and withdrawal.

**2.** Using the scientifically derived evidence cited here, explain how tolerance and withdrawal relate to substance use disorders.

**3.** Identify one piece of scientifically derived evidence that supports the concept of behavioral addictions.

1. Berridge et al., 2009; Robinson & Berridge, 2003. 2. WHO, 2014b. 3. Lopez-Quintero et al., 2011. 4. Newport, 2013. 5. Gentile, 2009; Griffiths, 2001; Hoeft et al., 2008. 6. WHO, 2018b. 7. Przybylski et al., 2017. 8. Winkler et al., 2013.

death (Kendler et al., 2016; Mackey et al., 2019; WHO, 2018b; **Figure 1.3-7**). Girls and young women (who have less of a stomach enzyme that digests alcohol) can become addicted to alcohol more quickly than boys and young men do, and they are at risk for lung, brain, and liver damage at lower consumption levels (CASA, 2003). With increased heavy drinking among women, these gender differences can have life-or-death consequences: Between 2001 and 2017, Canadian women's risk for alcohol-related death increased at five times the rate for men (Tam, 2018).

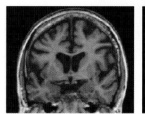
Scan of woman with alcohol use disorder
**(a)**

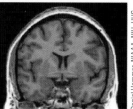
Scan of woman without alcohol use disorder
**(b)**

Daniel Hommer, NIAAA, NIH, HHS

**Figure 1.3-7**

**Disordered drinking shrinks the brain**

MRI scans show brain shrinkage in women with alcohol use disorder (a) compared with women in a control group (b).

**Slowed Neural Processing** Alcohol slows sympathetic nervous system activity. Larger doses cause reactions to slow, speech to slur, and skilled performance to deteriorate. Alcohol is a potent sedative, especially when paired with sleep deprivation. Add these physical effects to lowered inhibitions, and the result can be deadly. As blood-alcohol levels rise and judgment falters, people's qualms about drinking and driving lessen. When drunk, people aren't aware of *how* drunk they are (Moore et al., 2016). Almost all drinkers insist when sober that they would not drive under the influence later. Yet, in experiments, the majority of intoxicated participants decided to drink and drive (MacDonald et al., 1995; Ouimet et al., 2020). Unaware of their intoxication, people may think they can drive safely even when they can't.

Alcohol can also be life threatening when heavy drinking suppresses the gag reflex. Usually, vomiting releases toxins. When people drink heavily, however, they may inadvertently poison themselves with an overdose that their body would normally throw up.

Lon Clark Diehl

**Drinking disaster demo**
Firefighters reenacted the trauma of an alcohol-related car accident, providing a memorable demonstration for these high school students. Alcohol consumption leads to feelings of invincibility, which become especially dangerous behind the wheel of a car.

**Memory Disruption** Alcohol can disrupt memory formation, and heavy drinking can have long-term effects on the brain and cognition. In rats, at a developmental period corresponding to human adolescence, binge drinking contributes to nerve cell death and reduces the birth of new nerve cells. It also impairs the growth of synaptic connections (Crews et al., 2006, 2007). In humans, heavy drinking may lead to blackouts, in which drinkers continue to interact but are unable to later recall people they met or what they said or did while intoxicated. These blackouts result partly from the way alcohol suppresses rapid eye movement (REM) sleep, which helps store the day's experiences into permanent memories.

**Reduced Self-Awareness** In one experiment, those who consumed alcohol (rather than a placebo beverage) were doubly likely to be caught mind-wandering during a reading task, yet were *less* likely to notice that they zoned out (Sayette et al., 2009).

**tolerance** the diminishing effect with regular use of the same dose of a drug, requiring the user to take larger and larger doses before experiencing the drug's effect.

**addiction** an everyday term for compulsive substance use (and sometimes for dysfunctional behavior patterns, such as out-of-control gambling) that continue despite harmful consequences. (See also *substance use disorder.*)

**withdrawal** the discomfort and distress that follow discontinuing an addictive drug or behavior.

Sometimes we mind-wander to give our brains a break, but unintentional zoning out—while driving, for example—can cause later regret (Seli et al., 2016). Alcohol also focuses attention on an immediate arousing situation (say, provocation) and distracts it from normal inhibitions and future consequences (Giancola et al., 2010; Steele & Josephs, 1990).

Reduced self-awareness may help explain why people who want to suppress their awareness of failures or shortcomings often drink more than do those who feel good about themselves. Losing a business deal, a game, or a romantic partner sometimes elicits binge drinking.

**Expectancy Effects** Expectations influence behavior. Adolescents—presuming that alcohol will lift their spirits—sometimes drink when they're upset and alone (Bresin et al., 2018). But solitary drinking boosts their chance of developing a substance use disorder (Creswell et al., 2014; Fairbairn & Sayette, 2014).

Simply *believing* we're consuming alcohol can cause us to act out alcohol's presumed influence (Christiansen et al., 2016; Moss & Albery, 2009). In a classic experiment, researchers gave Rutgers University men (who had volunteered for a study on "alcohol and sexual stimulation") either an alcoholic or a nonalcoholic drink (Abrams & Wilson, 1983). (Both had strong tastes that masked any alcohol.) After watching an erotic movie clip, the men who *thought* they had consumed alcohol were more likely to report having strong sexual fantasies and feeling guilt free. Being able to *attribute* their sexual responses to alcohol released their inhibitions—whether or not they had actually consumed any alcohol. *The point to remember:* Alcohol's effect lies partly in that powerful sex organ, the mind.

## Barbiturates

Like alcohol, the **barbiturate** drugs, which are *tranquilizers*, depress nervous system activity. Barbiturates such as Nembutal, Seconal, and Amytal are sometimes prescribed to induce sleep or reduce anxiety. In larger doses, they can impair memory and judgment. If combined with alcohol—say, a sleeping pill after an evening of heavy drinking—the total depressive effect on body functions can be lethal.

## Opioids

The **opioids**—opium and its derivatives—also depress neural functioning. Opioids include *heroin* and its medically prescribed synthetic substitute, *methadone.* They also include pain-relief *narcotics* such as codeine, OxyContin, Vicodin, and morphine (and morphine's dangerously powerful synthetic counterpart, fentanyl). As blissful pleasure replaces pain and anxiety, the user's pupils constrict and breathing slows; lethargy sets in. People who become addicted to this short-term pleasure may pay a long-term price: a gnawing craving for another fix, a need for progressively larger doses (as tolerance develops), and the extreme discomfort of withdrawal. When repeatedly flooded with a synthetic opioid, the brain eventually stops producing *endorphins,* its own natural opioids. If the artificial opioid is then withdrawn, the brain will lack the normal level of these painkilling neurotransmitters.

An alarming number of Americans have become unable or unwilling to tolerate this state and have paid an ultimate price—death by overdose. Between 2013 and 2016, the U.S. rate of opioid overdose deaths increased almost *10 times* to 43,036 (NIDA, 2018; NSC, 2019). "For the first time in U.S. history, a person is more likely to die from an accidental opioid overdose than from a motor vehicle crash," reported the National Safety Council in 2019. The Covid pandemic increased stress, uncertainty, and social isolation that may have contributed to even more U.S. and Canadian opioid-related deaths in 2020 (Katz et al., 2020; Schmunk, 2020).

**barbiturates** drugs that depress central nervous system activity, reducing anxiety but impairing memory and judgment.

**opioids** opium and its derivatives; they depress neural activity, temporarily lessening pain and anxiety.

**Lives lost to opioids** Actor Angus Cloud and musician Juice WRLD are among those who have died of opioid overdoses.

---

**AP® Science Practice**

## Check Your Understanding

**Examine the Concept**

▶ Which category of psychoactive drugs is known to calm neural activity and slow body functions?

**Apply the Concept**

▶ Explain how alcohol's effects can be influenced by our expectations.

*Answers to the Examine the Concept questions can be found in Appendix C at the end of the book.*

---

## Stimulants

**1.3-7** What are *stimulants,* and what are their effects?

**Stimulants** excite neural activity and speed up body functions. Pupils dilate, heart and breathing rates increase, and blood sugar levels rise, reducing appetite. Energy and self-confidence also rise.

Stimulants include caffeine, nicotine, and the more powerful cocaine, amphetamines, methamphetamine (also known as "speed"), and Ecstasy. People may use stimulants to feel alert, lose weight, or boost mood or athletic performance. Some students resort to stronger stimulant drugs in hopes of boosting their academic performance, despite these drugs offering little or no benefit (Ilieva et al., 2015; Teter et al., 2018). Stimulants can be addictive, as many know from the fatigue, headaches, irritability, and depression that result from missing their usual caffeine dose (Silverman et al., 1992). A mild dose typically lasts 3 or 4 hours, so—if taken in the evening—a stimulant may impair sleep.

### Nicotine

Tobacco products deliver highly addictive *nicotine.* Imagine that cigarettes and vaping were harmless—except, once in every 25,000 packs, an occasional innocent-looking one was filled with dynamite instead of tobacco. Not such a bad risk of having your head blown off. But with 250 million packs a day consumed worldwide, we could expect more than 10,000 gruesome daily deaths—surely enough to have cigarettes banned everywhere.[1]

**stimulants** drugs that excite neural activity and speed up body functions.

---

[1]This analogy, adapted here with world-based numbers, was suggested by mathematician Sam Saunders, as reported by K. C. Cole (1998).

The lost lives from these dynamite-loaded cigarettes approximate those from today's actual cigarettes. A teen-to-the-grave smoker has a 50 percent chance of dying from the habit, and each year, tobacco kills nearly 7 million people worldwide, with another 1.2 million people killed due to exposure to second-hand smoke (WHO, 2020b). By 2030, annual tobacco deaths are expected to increase to 8 million. That means that *1 billion* people this century may be killed by tobacco (WHO, 2012a).

Tobacco products include cigarettes, cigars, chewing tobacco, pipe tobacco, snuff, and—most recently—e-cigarettes. Inhaling e-cigarette vapor (vaping) gives users a jolt of nicotine without cigarettes' cancer-causing tar. Thanks to vaping's rapid increase—the fastest drug use increase on record—U.S. high school students in 2021 daily used e-cigarettes at 2.7 times the rate of traditional cigarettes (Johnston et al., 2021).

In one survey of regular e-cigarette users from the United States, England, Canada, and Australia, 85 percent reported they vaped because they believed it would help them cut down on smoking traditional cigarettes (Yong et al., 2019). Experts debate whether e-cigarettes can really help smokers quit smoking (Hajek et al., 2019; HHS, 2020a). But they agree that cigarettes are addictive nicotine dispensers that introduce nonsmokers to smoking (Prochaska, 2019). In a British study, nonsmoking teens who started vaping became four times more likely to move on to cigarette smoking (Miech et al., 2017).

Teen use has prompted legal restrictions as well as investigations, including one by the U.S. Food and Drug Administration on whether e-cigarette companies target teenage users (Richtel & Kaplan, 2018). Fruity flavors, for example, increase teen use (Buckell & Sindelar, 2019; O'Connor et al., 2019). These troubling trends prompted U.S. Surgeon General Jerome Adams to "officially declar[e] e-cigarette use among youth an epidemic" (Stein, 2018).

**Nic-a-teen** Seeing celebrities, such as singer Lily Allen, vaping or smoking may tempt young people in the vulnerable teen and early-adult years to imitate. In 2017, more than one-third of youth-rated (G, PG, PG-13) American movies showed smoking (CDC, 2020b).

Smoke a cigarette and nature will charge you 12 minutes—ironically, just about the length of time you spend smoking it (*Discover*, 1996). (Researchers don't yet know how e-cigarette use affects life expectancy.) Compared with nonsmokers, smokers' life expectancy is "at least 10 years shorter" (CDC, 2013). Eliminating smoking would increase life expectancy more than any other preventive measure. Why, then, do so many people smoke?

Tobacco products are as powerfully and quickly addictive as heroin and cocaine. Attempts to quit tobacco use even within the first weeks often fail (DiFranza, 2008). And, as with other addictions, smokers develop *tolerance.* Those who attempt to quit will experience nicotine withdrawal symptoms—craving, insomnia, anxiety, irritability, and distractibility. When trying to focus on a task, their mind wanders at three times the normal rate (Sayette et al., 2010). When not craving a cigarette, they tend to underestimate the power of such cravings (Sayette et al., 2008).

All it takes to relieve this aversive state is a single drag from a cigarette. With that inhalation, a rush of nicotine will signal the central nervous system to release a flood of neurotransmitters (**Figure 1.3-8**). Epinephrine and norepinephrine will diminish appetite and boost alertness and mental efficiency. Dopamine and opioids will temporarily calm anxiety and reduce sensitivity to pain (Ditre et al., 2011; Gavin, 2004). No wonder some ex-users, under stress, resume their habit—as did some 1 million Americans after the 9/11 terrorist attacks (Pesko, 2014). Ditto for people with major depressive disorder, who are more likely than others to see their efforts to quit go up in smoke (Zvolensky et al., 2015).

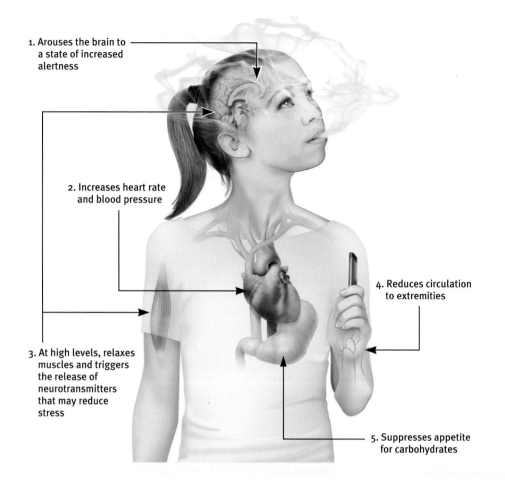

1. Arouses the brain to a state of increased alertness

2. Increases heart rate and blood pressure

3. At high levels, relaxes muscles and triggers the release of neurotransmitters that may reduce stress

4. Reduces circulation to extremities

5. Suppresses appetite for carbohydrates

**FIGURE 1.3-8**

**Physiological effects of nicotine**

Nicotine reaches the brain within 7 seconds, twice as fast as intravenous heroin. Within minutes, the amount in the blood soars.

Cigarette smoking is the leading cause of preventable death in the United States, killing 480,000 people each year (CDC, 2020b). Although 3 in 4 smokers wish they could stop, each year fewer than 1 in 7 will be successful (Newport, 2013). Even those who know they are speeding up their own death may be unable to stop (Saad, 2002).

Nevertheless, repeated attempts seem to pay off. The worldwide smoking rate— 25 percent among men and 5 percent among women—is down about 30 percent since 1990 (GBD, 2017). The U.S. smoking rate has plummeted from 45 percent in 1955 to 15 percent in 2019 (Saad, 2019b). Half of all Americans who have ever smoked have quit, sometimes aided by a nicotine replacement drug and with encouragement from a counselor or support group. Some researchers argue that it is best to quit abruptly—to go "cold turkey" (Lindson-Hawley et al., 2016). Others suggest that success is equally likely whether smokers quit abruptly or gradually (Fiore et al., 2008; Lichtenstein et al., 2010). *The point to remember:* If you want to quit using tobacco, there is hope regardless of how you choose to quit.

For those who endure, the acute craving and withdrawal symptoms slowly dissipate over the following 6 months (Ward et al., 1997). After a year's abstinence, only 10 percent will relapse in the next year (Hughes, 2010). These nonsmokers may live not only healthier but also happier lives. Smoking correlates with higher rates of depression, chronic disabilities, and divorce (Doherty & Doherty, 1998; Edwards & Kendler, 2012; Vita et al., 1998). Healthy living seems to add both years to life and life to years. Awareness of nonsmokers' better health and happiness has contributed to 87 percent of U.S. twelfth graders disapproving of smoking a pack or more a day, as well as to a plunge in their daily smoking rate, from 25 percent in 1997 to 2 percent in 2021 (Johnston et al., 2021).

## Cocaine

*Cocaine* is a powerfully addictive stimulant derived from the coca plant. The recipe for Coca-Cola originally included a coca extract, creating a mild cocaine tonic intended for tired elderly people. Between 1896 and 1905, Coke was indeed "the real thing." Today, cocaine is snorted, injected, or smoked (sometimes as *crack cocaine,* a faster-working crystallized form that produces a briefer but more intense high, followed by a more intense crash). Cocaine enters the bloodstream quickly, producing a rush of euphoria that depletes the brain's supply of the neurotransmitters dopamine, serotonin, and norepinephrine (**Figure 1.3-9**). Within the hour, a crash of agitated depression follows as the drug's effect wears off. After several hours, the craving for more wanes, only to return several days later (Gawin, 1991).

In situations that trigger aggression, ingesting cocaine may heighten reactions. Caged rats fight when given foot shocks, and they fight even more when given cocaine *and* foot

**Figure 1.3-9**

**Cocaine euphoria and crash**

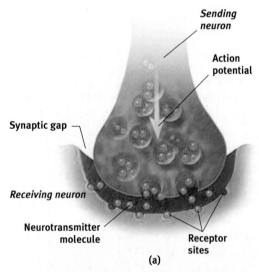

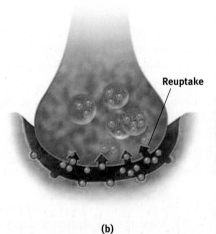

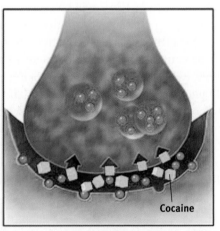

**(a)** Neurotransmitters carry a message from a sending neuron across a synapse to receptor sites on a receiving neuron.

**(b)** The sending neuron normally reabsorbs excess neurotransmitter molecules, a process called *reuptake.*

**(c)** By binding to the sites that normally reabsorb neurotransmitter molecules, cocaine blocks reuptake of dopamine, norepinephrine, and serotonin (Ray & Ksir, 1990). The extra neurotransmitter molecules therefore remain in the synapse, intensifying their normal mood-altering effects and producing a euphoric rush. When the cocaine level drops, the absence of these neurotransmitters produces a crash.

shocks. Likewise, humans who voluntarily ingest high doses of cocaine in laboratory experiments impose higher shock levels on a presumed opponent than do those receiving a placebo (Licata et al., 1993). Cocaine use may also lead to emotional disturbances, suspiciousness, convulsions, cardiac arrest, or respiratory failure.

Cocaine powerfully stimulates the brain's reward pathways (Keramati et al., 2017; Walker et al., 2018). Its psychological effects vary with the dosage and form consumed, but the situation and the user's expectations and personality also play a role. Given a placebo, cocaine users who *thought* they were taking cocaine often had a cocaine-like experience (Van Dyke & Byck, 1982).

In national surveys, 1 percent of American twelfth graders and 6 percent of British 18- to 24-year-olds reported having tried cocaine during the past year (ACMD, 2009; Johnston et al., 2021).

### Methamphetamine

*Amphetamines* stimulate neural activity. As body functions speed up, the user's energy rises and mood soars. Amphetamines are the parent drug for the highly addictive *methamphetamine*, which is chemically similar but has stronger effects (NIDA, 2002, 2005). Methamphetamine triggers the release of the neurotransmitter dopamine, which stimulates brain cells that enhance energy and mood, leading to 8 hours or so of heightened energy and euphoria. Its aftereffects may include irritability, insomnia, hypertension, seizures, social isolation, depression, and occasional violent outbursts (Homer et al., 2008). Over time, methamphetamine reduces baseline dopamine levels, leaving the user with depressed functioning.

### Ecstasy

*Ecstasy,* a street name for *MDMA* (*methylenedioxymethamphetamine,* also known in its powder form as *Molly*), is both a stimulant and a mild hallucinogen. As an amphetamine derivative, Ecstasy triggers dopamine release, but its major effect is releasing stored serotonin and blocking its reuptake, thereby prolonging serotonin's feel-good flood (Braun, 2001). Users feel the effect about a half-hour after taking an Ecstasy pill.

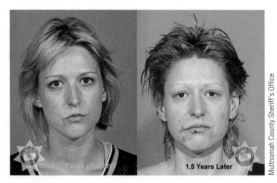

Multnomah County Sheriff's Office

1.5 Years Later

**Dramatic drug-induced decline** In the 18 months between these two mug shots, this woman's methamphetamine addiction led to obvious physical changes.

PYMCA/UIG/AGE Fotostock

**The hug drug** MDMA, known as Ecstasy and often taken at clubs, produces a euphoric high and feelings of intimacy. But repeated use can destroy serotonin-producing neurons, impair memory, and permanently deflate mood.

For 3 or 4 hours, they experience high energy, emotional elevation, and (given a social context) connectedness with those around them ("I love everyone"). Octopuses became similarly sociable when researchers gave them MDMA (Edsinger et al., 2018). Eight arms and MDMA = a lot of reaching out.

Ecstasy's popularity first soared globally in the late 1990s as a "club drug" taken at nightclubs and all-night dance parties (Landry, 2002). But there are good reasons not to be ecstatic about Ecstasy. One is its dehydrating effect, which—when combined with prolonged dancing—can lead to severe overheating, increased blood pressure, and death. Another is that repeated leaching of brain serotonin can damage serotonin-producing neurons, leading to decreased output and increased risk of permanently depressed mood (Croft et al., 2001; McCann et al., 2001; Roiser et al., 2005). Ecstasy also suppresses the immune system, impairs memory, slows thought, and disrupts sleep by interfering with serotonin's control of the circadian clock (Laws & Kokkalis, 2007; Schilt et al., 2007; Wagner et al., 2012). Ecstasy delights for the night but dispirits the morrow.

## Hallucinogens

> **1.3-8** What are *hallucinogens,* and what are their effects?

**Hallucinogens** distort perceptions and evoke sensory images in the absence of sensory input (which is why these drugs are also called *psychedelics,* meaning "mind-manifesting"). Some, such as LSD and MDMA (Ecstasy), are synthetic. Others, including psilocybin, ayahuasca, and the mild hallucinogen marijuana, are natural substances.

Whether provoked to hallucinate by drugs, loss of oxygen, or extreme sensory deprivation, the brain hallucinates in basically the same way (Martial et al., 2019; Siegel, 1982). The experience typically begins with simple geometric forms, such as a spiral. Then come more meaningful images, which may be superimposed on a tunnel; others may be replays of past emotional experiences. Brain scans of people on an LSD trip reveal that their visual cortex becomes hypersensitive and strongly connected to their brain's emotion centers (Carhart-Harris et al., 2016). As the hallucination peaks, people frequently feel separated from their body and experience dreamlike scenes. Their sense of self dissolves, as does the border between themselves and the external world (Lebedev et al., 2015).

These sensations are strikingly similar to the **near-death experience**, an altered state of consciousness reported by 10 to 23 percent of people revived from cardiac arrest (Martial et al., 2020). Many describe visions of tunnels (**Figure 1.3-10**), bright lights, a replay of old memories, and out-of-body sensations (Siegel, 1980). These experiences can later enhance spirituality and promote feelings of personal growth (Khanna & Greyson, 2014, 2015). Given that oxygen deprivation and other insults to the brain are known to produce hallucinations, we may wonder: Does a brain under stress manufacture the near-death experience? During epileptic seizures and migraines, people may experience similar hallucinations of geometric patterns (Billock & Tsou, 2012). So have solitary sailors and polar

---

**hallucinogens** psychedelic ("mind-manifesting") drugs that distort perceptions and evoke sensory images in the absence of sensory input.

**near-death experience** an altered state of consciousness reported after a close brush with death (such as cardiac arrest); often similar to drug-induced hallucinations.

---

**Figure 1.3-10**

**Near-death vision or hallucination?**

Psychologist Ronald Siegel (1977) reported that people under the influence of hallucinogenic drugs often see "a bright light in the center of the field of vision. . . . The location of this point of light create[s] a tunnel-like perspective." This is very similar to others' near-death experiences.

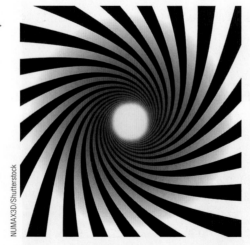

NUMAX3D/Shutterstock

explorers while enduring monotony, isolation, and cold (Suedfeld & Mocellin, 1987). The philosopher-neuroscientist Patricia Churchland (2013, p. 70) has called such experiences "neural funny business."

## LSD

Chemist Albert Hofmann created—and on one Friday afternoon in April 1943 accidentally ingested—*LSD (lysergic acid diethylamide)*. The result—"an uninterrupted stream of fantastic pictures, extraordinary shapes with intense, kaleidoscopic play of colors"—reminded him of a childhood mystical experience that had left him longing for another glimpse of "a miraculous, powerful, unfathomable reality" (Siegel, 1984; Smith, 2006).

The emotions experienced during an LSD (or *acid*) trip range from euphoria to detachment to panic. Users' mood and expectations (their "high hopes") color the emotional experience, but the perceptual distortions and hallucinations have some commonalities.

## Marijuana

The straight dope on marijuana: Marijuana leaves and flowers contain *THC (delta-9-tetrahydrocannabinol)*. Whether inhaled (getting to the brain quickly) or consumed (traveling through the body slowly), THC produces a mix of effects. An analysis of 15 studies showed that the THC in a single joint may induce psychiatric symptoms such as hallucinations, delusions, and anxiety (Hindley et al., 2020). Synthetic cannabinoids (also known as *synthetic marijuana, Spice,* or *K2*) mimic THC.

**AP® Science Practice**

### Research

Statistically analyzing the results of multiple studies to reach an overall conclusion, as Hindley did here, is referred to as a *meta-analysis*.

Marijuana amplifies sensitivity to colors, sounds, tastes, and smells. But like the depressant alcohol, it relaxes, disinhibits, and may produce a euphoric high. As is the case with alcohol, people sometimes consume marijuana to help them sleep or improve their mood (Buckner et al., 2019; Wong et al., 2019). Both alcohol and marijuana impair the motor coordination, perceptual skills, and reaction time necessary for safely operating a vehicle or other machine. "THC causes animals to misjudge events," reported Ronald Siegel (1990, p. 163). "Pigeons wait too long to respond to buzzers or lights that tell them food is available for brief periods; and rats turn the wrong way in mazes."

Like people who repeatedly consume alcohol, marijuana users develop tolerance—a lesser high with the same single dose. But marijuana and alcohol also differ. The body eliminates alcohol within hours, while THC and its by-products linger in the body for more than a week; so with repeated use marijuana accumulates in the body's tissues (Volkow et al., 2014).

After considering more than 10,000 scientific reports, the U.S. National Academies of Sciences, Engineering, and Medicine (2017) concluded that marijuana use

- alleviates chronic pain, chemotherapy-related nausea, and muscle soreness among people with multiple sclerosis;

- may offer short-term sleep improvements;

- does not increase risk for tobacco-related diseases such as lung cancer;

- predicts increased risk of traffic accidents, chronic bronchitis, psychosis, social anxiety disorder, and suicidal thoughts; and

- likely contributes to impaired attention, learning, and memory, and possibly to academic underachievement.

The more often the person uses marijuana, especially during adolescence, the greater the risk of anxiety, depression, psychosis, and suicidal behavior (Gage, 2019; Gobbi et al., 2019; Huckins, 2017). One study of nearly 4000 Canadian seventh graders concluded that marijuana use at that early age was "neurotoxic"; it predicted long-term cognitive impairment (Harvey, 2019). "Nearly 1 in 5 people who begin marijuana use during adolescence become addicted," warned U.S. Surgeon General Jerome Adams (Aubrey, 2019).

Attitudes toward marijuana use have changed remarkably—from 12 percent support for legalizing marijuana in 1969 to 66 percent in 2019 (De Pinto, 2019; McCarthy, 2018). Some countries and U.S. states have legalized marijuana possession. Greater legal acceptance may explain why rates of Americans who have tried marijuana rose dramatically between 1969 and 2019, from 4 to 45 percent, with 12 percent saying they now smoke marijuana (Gallup, 2019b).

\* \* \*

Despite their differences, the psychoactive drugs summarized in **Table 1.3-3** share a common feature: They trigger changes to the brain and body that grow stronger with repetition. This helps explain both tolerance and withdrawal.

| TABLE 1.3-3 | **A Guide to Selected Psychoactive Drugs** | | |
|---|---|---|---|
| **Drug** | **Type** | **Pleasurable Effects** | **Possible Negative Effects** |
| Alcohol | Depressant | Initial high followed by relaxation and disinhibition | Depression, memory loss, organ damage, impaired reactions |
| Heroin | Depressant | Rush of euphoria, relief from pain | Depressed physiology, loss of natural endorphin function |
| Caffeine | Stimulant | Increased alertness and wakefulness | Anxiety, restlessness, and insomnia in high doses |
| Nicotine | Stimulant | Arousal and relaxation, sense of well-being | Heart disease, cancer |
| Cocaine | Stimulant | Rush of euphoria, confidence, energy | Cardiovascular stress, suspiciousness, depressive crash |
| Methamphetamine | Stimulant | Euphoria, alertness, energy | Irritability, insomnia, hypertension, seizures |
| Ecstasy (methylenedioxy-methamphetamine, MDMA) | Stimulant; mild hallucinogen | Emotional elevation, disinhibition | Dehydration, overheating, depressed mood, impaired cognitive and immune functioning |
| LSD (lysergic acid diethylamide) | Hallucinogen | Visual "trip" | Risk of panic |
| Marijuana (delta-9-tetrahydrocannabinol, THC) | Mild hallucinogen | Enhanced sensation, relief of pain, distortion of time, relaxation | Impaired learning and memory, increased risk of psychological disorders |

**AP® Science Practice**

## Check Your Understanding

**Examine the Concept**

▶ How would you explain each category of psychoactive drugs to a classmate?

**Apply the Concept**

▶ "How curiously [pleasure] is related to what is thought to be its opposite, pain! . . . Wherever the one is found, the other follows up behind" (Plato, *Phaedo*, fourth century B.C.E.). How does this pleasure–pain description apply to the repeated use of psychoactive drugs?

*Answers to the Examine the Concept questions can be found in Appendix C at the end of the book.*

# Module 1.3b REVIEW

**1.3-5** What are *substance use disorders?*

- People with a *substance use disorder* engage in continued substance use despite its significant life disruption.
- *Psychoactive drugs* alter perceptions and moods.

**1.3-6** What are *depressants,* and what are their effects?

- *Depressants* dampen neural activity and slow body functions.

**1.3-7** What are *stimulants,* and what are their effects?

- *Stimulants* excite neural activity and speed up body functions, triggering energy and mood changes. Stimulants can be highly addictive.

**1.3-8** What are *hallucinogens,* and what are their effects?

- *Hallucinogens* distort perceptions and evoke *hallucinations* (sensory images in the absence of sensory input), some of which resemble the altered consciousness of *near-death experiences.*

---

## AP® Practice Multiple Choice Questions

1. Which of the following represents drug tolerance?

   a. Hans has grown to accept the fact that his partner likes to have a beer with dinner, even though he personally does not approve of the use of alcohol.

   b. José often wakes up with a headache that lasts until he has his morning cup of coffee.

   c. Pierre enjoys the effect of marijuana and is now using the drug several times a week.

   d. Jacob had to increase the dosage of his pain medication when the old dosage no longer effectively controlled the pain from his chronic back condition.

2. One hundred people reported the most impactful effect of a substance they recently ingested. Which classification of drug is most likely represented in the bar graph?

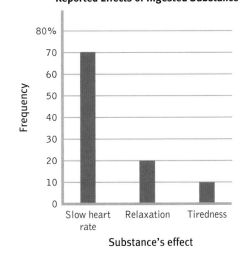

**Reported Effects of Ingested Substance**

   a. Stimulant
   b. Depressant
   c. Hallucinogen
   d. Tolerance

3. Fifty people were asked to participate in a study on the effects of substances that speed up bodily systems with the hope that the research findings could help people in the United States stop using substances that excite neural and bodily activity. What is the researchers' likely target population to which they want to generalize their results?

   a. All 50 people in the study who used hallucinogens
   b. All individuals in the United States who use depressants
   c. All individuals in the United States who use stimulants
   d. All 50 people in the study who used stimulants

4. Dr. Bannion conducted a study on how depressants produce their effects in the body. Which of the following is the operational definition that Dr. Bannion most likely used?

   a. Participants' positive mood ratings on a scale from 1 to 10
   b. The number of hours participants sleep
   c. The level of endorphins in the brain
   d. The amount of time spent trying to obtain depressant drugs

5. After ingesting a substance, Yi began to see geometric shapes moving in her field of vision, and she felt as if she was separated from her body. Which of the following classifications of psychoactive drugs did Yi likely ingest?

   a. Depressant
   b. Stimulant
   c. Hallucinogen
   d. Withdrawal

# Module 1.4a The Brain: Neuroplasticity and Tools of Discovery

## LEARNING TARGETS

**1.4-1** Explain why psychologists are concerned with human biology.

**1.4-2** Explain how biology and experience together enable neuroplasticity.

**1.4-3** Compare and contrast several techniques for studying the brain's connections to behavior and mind.

### 1.4-1 Why are psychologists concerned with human biology?

Our understanding of how the brain gives birth to the mind has come a long way. The ancient Greek physician Hippocrates correctly located the mind in the brain. His contemporary, the philosopher Aristotle, believed the mind was sited in the heart, which pumps warmth and vitality to the body. The heart remains our symbol for love, but science has long since overtaken philosophy on this issue: It's your brain, not your heart, that falls in love.

In the early 1800s, German physician Franz Gall proposed that *phrenology,* studying bumps on the skull, could reveal a person's mental abilities and character traits (**Figure 1.4-1**). At one point, Britain was home to 29 phrenological societies. Phrenologists also traveled North America to give skull readings (Dean, 2012; Hunt, 1993). Using a false name, humorist Mark Twain put one famous phrenologist to the test. "He found a cavity [and] startled me by saying that that cavity represented the total absence of the sense of humor!" Three months later, Twain sat for a second reading, this time identifying himself. Now "the cavity was gone, and in its place was . . . the loftiest bump of humor he had ever encountered in his life-long experience!" (Lopez, 2002). Today, the "science" of phrenology reminds us of our need to engage in critical thinking and scientific analysis. Phrenology did at least succeed in focusing attention on the *localization of function*—the idea that various brain regions have particular functions.

Today, we are living in a time Gall could only dream about. **Biological psychologists** use advanced technologies to study the links between biological (genetic, neural, hormonal)

**AP® Science Practice**

### Research

Unlike phrenologists, psychological scientists take an empirical, or scientifically derived approach to studying the brain. As Unit 0 explained, they use an evidence-based method that draws on observation and experimentation.

**biological psychology** the scientific study of the links between biological (genetic, neural, hormonal) and psychological processes. Some biological psychologists call themselves *behavioral neuroscientists, neuropsychologists, behavior geneticists, physiological psychologists,* or *biopsychologists.*

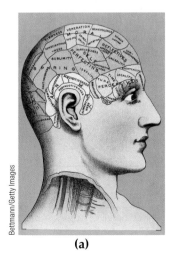

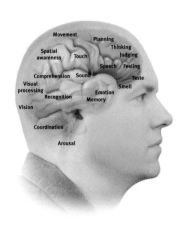

(a)                              (b)

**Figure 1.4-1**
**A wrongheaded theory**

(a) Despite scientists' initial acceptance of Franz Gall's speculations, bumps on the skull tell us nothing about the brain's underlying functions. Nevertheless, some of his assumptions have held true. Though they are not the functions Gall proposed, different parts of the brain do control different aspects of behavior, as suggested in (b) (from *The Human Brain Book*), and as you will see throughout this unit.

**biopsychosocial approach** an integrated approach that incorporates biological, psychological, and social-cultural levels of analysis.

**levels of analysis** the differing complementary views, from biological to psychological to social-cultural, for analyzing any given phenomenon.

and psychological processes. They and other researchers working from a biological perspective are announcing discoveries about the interplay of our biology and our behavior and mind at an exhilarating pace. Within little more than the past century, researchers seeking to understand the biology of the mind have discovered that:

- Among the body's cells are neurons that conduct electricity and "talk" to one another by sending chemical messages across a synapse (see Module 1.3).
- Our experiences wire our adaptive brain.
- Specific brain systems serve specific functions (though not the functions Gall supposed).
- We integrate information processed in these different brain systems to construct our experiences of sights and sounds, meanings and memories, pain and passion.

We have also realized that we are each a system composed of subsystems that are in turn composed of even smaller subsystems. Tiny cells organize to form body organs. These organs form larger systems for digestion, circulation, and information processing. And those systems are part of an even larger system — the individual, who in turn is a part of a family, a community, and a culture. Thus, we are *biopsychosocial* systems. To understand our behavior, we need to study how these biological, psychological, and social-cultural systems work and interact, and how they shape us over time. The **biopsychosocial approach** integrates these three **levels of analysis**—the biological, psychological, and social-cultural (**Figure 1.4-2**).

As we've seen, we are formed by both ancient evolution and our fluctuating hormones—but we are also shaped by our enduring cultures, by our daily experiences, and by our immediate neural activity (Sapolsky, 2017). Consider, for example, the brain's ability to rewire itself as it adapts to experience.

**Biological influences:**
- genetic *predispositions* (genetically influenced traits)
- genetic *mutations* (random errors in gene replication)
- natural selection of adaptive traits and behaviors passed down through generations
- genes responding to the environment

**Psychological influences:**
- learned fears and other learned expectations
- emotional responses
- cognitive processing and perceptual interpretations

**Behavior or mental process**

**Social-cultural influences:**
- presence of others
- cultural, societal, and family expectations
- peer and other group influences
- compelling models (such as in the media)

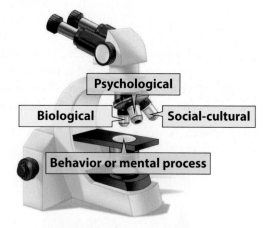

### Figure 1.4-2
### Biopsychosocial approach

This integrated viewpoint incorporates various levels of analysis and offers a more complete picture of any given behavior or mental process.

# The Power of Neuroplasticity

**1.4-2** How do biology and experience together enable neuroplasticity?

Your brain is sculpted not only by your genes but also by your life. Under the surface of your awareness, your brain is constantly changing, building new pathways as it adjusts to little mishaps and new experiences. This change is called **neuroplasticity**. Neuroplasticity is greatest in childhood, but it persists throughout life (Lindenberger & Lövdén, 2019).

To see neuroplasticity at work, consider London's taxi driver trainees. They spend years learning and remembering the city's 25,000 street locations and connections. For the half who pass the difficult final test, big rewards are in store: not only a better income but also an enlarged hippocampus, one of the brain's memory centers that processes spatial memories. London's bus drivers, who navigate a smaller set of roads, gain no similar neural rewards (Maguire et al., 2000, 2006; Woollett & Maguire, 2012).

We also see neuroplasticity in well-practiced pianists, who have a larger-than-usual auditory cortex area, a sound-processing region (Bavelier et al., 2000; Pantev et al., 1998). Practice likewise sculpts the brains of ballerinas, jugglers, and unicyclists (Draganski et al., 2004; Hänggi et al., 2010; Weber et al., 2019).

Your brain is a work in progress. The brain you were born with is not the brain you will die with. Even limited practice times may produce neural benefits. If you spend 45 minutes learning how to play the piano, as did non-piano-playing participants in one study, you may grow your motor learning–related brain areas (Tavor et al., 2020). Even an hour of learning produces subtle brain changes (Brodt et al., 2018). Remember that the next time you attend class!

Neuroplasticity is part of what makes humans exceptional (Gómez-Robles et al., 2015). Think of how much the world has changed over the past 50 years, and how much more it will change in the next 50. Our neuroplasticity enables us, more than other species, to adapt to our changing world (Roberts & Stewart, 2018).

**neuroplasticity** the brain's ability to change, especially during childhood, by reorganizing after damage or by building new pathways based on experience.

**The mind's eye** Daniel Kish, who is completely blind, enjoys going for walks in the woods. To stay safe, he uses echolocation — the same navigation method used by bats and dolphins. Blind echolocation experts such as Kish engage the brain's visual centers to navigate their surroundings (Thaler et al., 2011, 2014). Although Kish is blind, his flexible brain helps him "see."

**Marian Diamond (1926–2017)** This ground-breaking neuroscientist explored how experience changes the brain.

---

**AP® Science Practice**

## Check Your Understanding

**Examine the Concept**

▶ Explain *neuroplasticity*.

▶ Explain how learning a new skill affects the structure of our brain.

**Apply the Concept**

▶ Which skills did you practice the most as a child — sports, music, cooking, video gaming? Explain how this affected your brain development and how your brain will continue to develop with new learning and new skills.

*Answers to the Examine the Concept questions can be found in Appendix C at the end of the book.*

# Tools of Discovery: Having Our Head Examined

**1.4-3** How do neuroscientists study the brain's connections to behavior and mind?

The mind seeking to understand the brain—that is among the ultimate scientific challenges. And so it will always be. To paraphrase cosmologist John Barrow, a brain simple enough to be fully understood is too simple to produce a mind able to understand it.

When you think *about* your brain, you're thinking *with* your brain—by releasing billions of neurotransmitter molecules across trillions of synapses. Indeed, say neuroscientists, *the mind is what the brain does.* In "The Adventure of the Mazarin Stone," Sherlock Holmes declared: "I am a brain, Watson. The rest of me is a mere appendix." Would you agree?

For most of human history, scientists had no tools high-powered yet gentle enough to reveal a living brain's activity. Early case studies helped localize some brain functions. Damage to one side of the brain often caused numbness or paralysis on the opposite side, suggesting that the body's right side is wired to the brain's left side, and vice versa. Damage to the back of the brain disrupted vision, and damage to the left-front part of the brain produced speech difficulties. Gradually, these early explorers were mapping the brain.

Now, a new generation of neural mapmakers is charting the known universe's most amazing organ. Scientists can selectively **lesion** (destroy) tiny clusters of normal or defective brain cells, observing any effect on brain function. In the laboratory, such studies have revealed, for example, that damage to one area of a rat's hypothalamus reduces eating to the point of starvation, whereas damage to another area produces overeating.

Today's neuroscientists can also stimulate various brain parts—electrically, chemically, or magnetically—and note the effect. Depending on the stimulated brain part, people may—to name a few examples—giggle, hear voices, turn their head, feel themselves falling, or have an out-of-body experience (Selimbeyoglu & Parvizi, 2010).

Scientists can even snoop on the messages transmitted by individual neurons. With tips small enough to detect the electrical pulse in a single neuron, modern electrodes can, for example, now detect exactly where the information goes in a rat's brain when someone tickles its belly (Ishiyama & Brecht, 2017). They can also eavesdrop on the chatter of billions of neurons and see color representations of the brain's energy-consuming activity. Promising new tools include *optogenetics,* a technique that allows neuroscientists to control the activity of individual neurons (Boyden, 2014). By programming neurons to become receptive to light, researchers can examine the biological bases of sensations, fear, depression, and substance use disorders (Dygalo & Shishkina, 2019; Firsov, 2019; Juarez et al., 2019; Nikitin et al., 2019).

Right now, your mental activity is emitting telltale electrical, metabolic, and magnetic signals that would enable neuroscientists to observe your brain at work. Electrical activity in your brain's billions of neurons sweeps in regular waves across its surface. An **EEG (electroencephalogram)** is an amplified readout of such waves. Researchers record the brain waves through a shower-cap-like hat that is filled with electrodes covered with a conductive gel. Studying an EEG of the brain's activity is like studying a blender's motor by listening to its hum. Researchers may lack direct access to the brain, but they can present a stimulus repeatedly and have a computer filter out brain activity unrelated to the stimulus. What remains is the electrical wave evoked by the stimulus.

A related technique, **MEG (magnetoencephalography)**, measures magnetic fields from the brain's natural electrical activity. To isolate the brain's magnetic fields, researchers create special rooms that cancel out other magnetic signals, such as the Earth's magnetic field. Participants sit underneath a head coil that resembles a salon hair dryer. While participants complete activities, tens of thousands of neurons generate electrical pulses, which in turn create magnetic fields. The speed and strength of the magnetic fields enable researchers to understand how certain tasks influence brain activity (Samuelsson et al., 2020).

**lesion** [LEE-zhuhn] tissue destruction. Brain lesions may occur naturally (from disease or trauma), during surgery, or experimentally (using electrodes to destroy brain cells).

**EEG (electroencephalogram)** an amplified recording of the waves of electrical activity sweeping across the brain's surface. These waves are measured by electrodes placed on the scalp.

**MEG (magnetoencephalography)** a brain-imaging technique that measures magnetic fields from the brain's natural electrical activity.

Newer neuroimaging techniques give us a superhero-like ability to see inside the living brain. For example, the **CT (computed tomography) scan** examines the brain by taking X-ray photographs that can reveal brain damage. Another such tool, **PET (positron emission tomography)** (Figure 1.4-3), depicts brain activity by showing each brain area's consumption of its chemical fuel, the sugar glucose. Active neurons gobble glucose. Our brain, though only about 2 percent of our body weight, consumes 20 percent of our calorie intake. After a person receives temporarily radioactive glucose, the PET scan can track the gamma rays released by this "food for thought" as a task is performed. Rather like weather radar showing rain activity, PET-scan "hot spots" show the most active brain areas as the person does mathematical calculations, looks at images of faces, or daydreams.

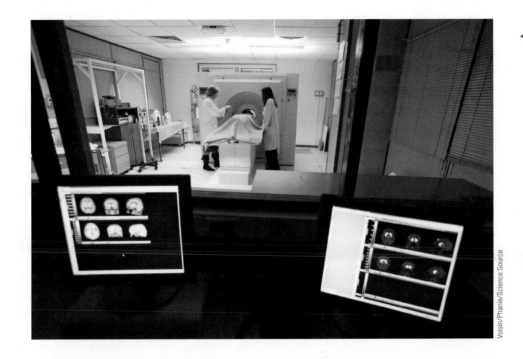

Voisin/Phanie/Science Source

**Figure 1.4-3**
**The PET scan**

**CT (computed tomography) scan** a series of X-ray photographs taken from different angles and combined by computer into a composite representation of a slice of the brain's structure.

**PET (positron emission tomography)** a technique for detecting brain activity that displays where a radioactive form of glucose goes while the brain performs a given task.

**MRI (magnetic resonance imaging)** a technique that uses magnetic fields and radio waves to produce computer-generated images of soft tissue. MRI scans show brain anatomy.

**fMRI (functional MRI)** a technique for revealing blood flow and, therefore, brain activity by comparing successive MRI scans. fMRI scans show brain function as well as structure.

In **MRI (magnetic resonance imaging)** brain scans, the person's head is put in a strong magnetic field, which aligns the spinning atoms in brain molecules. Then, a radio-wave pulse momentarily disorients the atoms. When the atoms return to their normal spin, they emit signals that provide a detailed picture of soft tissues, including the brain. MRI scans have revealed a larger-than-average neural area in the left hemisphere of musicians who display perfect pitch (Yuskaitis et al., 2015). They have also revealed enlarged *ventricles*—fluid-filled brain areas (marked by the red arrows in Figure 1.4-4)—in some people with schizophrenia.

A special application of MRI— **fMRI (functional MRI)**—can reveal the brain's functioning as well as its structure. Where the brain is especially active, blood goes. By comparing successive MRI scans, researchers can watch as specific brain areas activate, showing increased oxygen-laden blood flow. As a person looks at a scene, for example, the fMRI machine detects

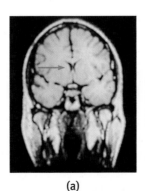

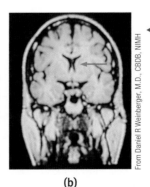

From Daniel R Weinberger, M.D., CBDB, NIMH

**(a)**    **(b)**

**Figure 1.4-4**

**MRI scans of individuals without schizophrenia (a) and with schizophrenia (b)**

Note the enlarged ventricle — the fluid-filled brain region at the tip of the arrow in the image — in the brain of the person with schizophrenia (b).

blood rushing to the back of the brain, which processes visual information. Another tool, *functional near-infrared spectroscopy (fNIRS)*, shines infrared light on blood molecules to identify brain activity. The fNIRS equipment can fit in a large backpack, enabling researchers to study the biology of mind in difficult-to-reach populations (Burns et al., 2019; Perdue et al., 2019). **Table 1.4-1** compares imaging techniques.

Such snapshots of the brain's activity provide new insights into how the brain divides its labor and reacts to changing needs. A mountain of recent fMRI studies has revealed which brain areas are most active when people feel pain or rejection, listen to angry voices, think about scary things, feel happy, or become sexually aroused. The technology enables a very basic sort of mind reading.

**Understanding the non-WEIRD brain** Most neuroscience research studies people from Western, Educated, Industrialized, Rich, and Democratic (WEIRD) populations (Falk et al., 2013). Using functional near-infrared spectroscopy (fNIRS), the researchers shown here were able to identify brain areas involved in persuasion among a Jordanian sample (Burns et al., 2019).

| TABLE 1.4-1 | Common Types of Neural Measures | |
|---|---|---|
| **Name** | **How Does It Work?** | **Sample Finding** |
| *Electroencephalography (EEG)* | Electrodes placed on the scalp measure electrical activity in neurons. | Symptoms of depression and anxiety correlate with increased activity in the right frontal lobe, a brain area associated with behavioral withdrawal and negative emotion (Thibodeau et al., 2006). |
| *Magnetoencephalography (MEG)* | A head coil records magnetic fields from the brain's natural electrical currents. | Soldiers with posttraumatic stress disorder (PTSD), compared with soldiers who do not have PTSD, show stronger magnetic fields in the visual cortex when they view trauma-related images (Todd et al., 2015). |
| *Computed tomography (CT)* | X-rays of the head generate images that may locate brain damage. | Children's brain injuries, shown in CT scans, predict impairments in their intelligence and memory processing (Königs et al., 2017). |
| *Positron emission tomography (PET)* | Tracks where in the brain a temporarily radioactive form of glucose goes while the person given it performs a task. | Monkeys with an anxious temperament have brains that use more glucose in regions related to fear, memory, and expectations of reward and punishment (Fox et al., 2015). |
| *Magnetic resonance imaging (MRI)* | People sit or lie down in a chamber that uses magnetic fields and radio waves to provide a map of brain structure. | People with a history of violence tend to have smaller frontal lobes, especially in regions that aid moral judgment and self-control (Glenn & Raine, 2014). |
| *Functional magnetic resonance imaging (fMRI)* | Measures blood flow to brain regions by comparing continuous MRI scans. | Years after surviving a near plane crash, passengers who viewed material related to their trauma showed greater activation in the brain's fear, memory, and visual centers than when they watched footage related to the 9/11 terrorist attacks (Palombo et al., 2015). |

One neuroscience team scanned 129 people's brains as they did eight different mental tasks (such as reading, gambling, or rhyming). Later, they were able, with 80 percent accuracy, to identify which of these mental activities the study participants had been doing (Poldrack et al., 2018).

You've undoubtedly seen pictures of colorful "lit-up" brain regions with accompanying headlines, such as "your brain on music." Although brain areas don't actually light up, vivid brain scan images seem impressive. In fact, people have rated scientific explanations as more believable and interesting when they contain neuroscience (Fernandez-Duque et al., 2015; Im et al., 2017). But "neuroskeptics" caution against overblown claims about any ability to predict customer preferences, to detect lies, and to foretell crime based on neuroscience (Schwartz et al., 2016). Neuromarketing, neuroleadership, neurolaw, and neuropolitics are often neurohype. Imaging techniques illuminate brain structure and activity, and sometimes they can help us test different theories of behavior (Mather et al., 2013). But given that all human experience is brain based, it's no surprise that different brain areas become active when one listens to a lecture or lusts for a lover.

Today's techniques for peering into the thinking, feeling brain are doing for psychology what the microscope did for biology and the telescope did for astronomy. European researchers have undertaken a $1 billion Human Brain Project (Salles et al., 2019). Another project is exploring brain aging from age 3 to 96 (Pomponio et al., 2020). These massive undertakings harness the collective power of hundreds of scientists from dozens of countries (Thompson et al., 2020) (**Figure 1.4-5**). "Individually, we contribute little or nothing to the truth," said Aristotle. "By the union of all a considerable amount is amassed."

To learn about the neurosciences now is like studying world geography when Magellan explored the seas. This truly is the golden age of brain science.

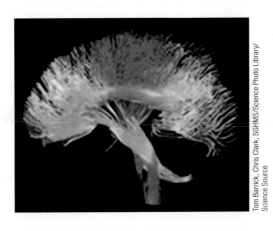

*Tom Barrick, Chris Clark, SGHMS/Science Photo Library/ Science Source*

**Figure 1.4-5**
**Beautiful brain connections**
The Human Connectome Project is using cutting-edge *diffusion tensor imaging* MRI methods to map the brain's interconnected network of neurons (Glasser et al., 2016; Wang & Olson, 2018). Such efforts have led to the creation of a new brain map with 100 neural centers not previously described (Glasser et al., 2016). Scientists created this multicolored "symphony" of neural fibers transporting water through different brain regions.

---

### AP® Science Practice

## Check Your Understanding

**Examine the Concept**
Match the scanning technique (i–iii) with the correct description (a–c).

**Technique:**
i.   fMRI scan
ii.  PET scan
iii. MRI scan

**Description:**
a. Tracks radioactive glucose to reveal brain *activity*.
b. Tracks successive images of brain tissue to show brain *function*.
c. Uses magnetic fields and radio waves to show brain *anatomy*.

**Apply the Concept**

▶ Compare and contrast each of the common types of neural measures.

▶ Were you surprised to learn that there are so many technologies to study the brain's structures and functions? Which techniques do you find most interesting? Why?

*Answers to the Examine the Concept questions can be found in Appendix C at the end of the book.*

**1.4-1 Why are psychologists concerned with human biology?**

- Researchers working from a *biological* perspective study the links between our biology and our behavior.

- We are *biopsychosocial* systems: biological, psychological, and social-cultural factors interact to influence behavior.

**1.4-2 How do biology and experience together enable neuroplasticity?**

- Our brain's neuroplasticity allows us to build new neural pathways as we adjust to new experiences. Our brain is a work in progress, changing with the focus and practice we devote to new ventures.

- Neural plasticity is strongest in childhood, but it continues throughout life.

**1.4-3 How do neuroscientists study the brain's connections to behavior and mind?**

- Case studies and *lesioning* first revealed the general effects of brain damage.

- Modern electrical, chemical, or magnetic stimulation also reveals aspects of information processing in the brain.

- *CT* and *MRI* scans show anatomy. *EEG, MEG, PET,* and *fMRI (functional MRI)* recordings reveal brain function.

## AP® Practice Multiple Choice Questions

1. Researchers wanted to determine the brain waves present when individuals were sleeping. They placed electrodes on the scalps of 100 volunteers, and then asked the volunteers to sleep in the laboratory each night for one week. The researchers obtained recordings of the electrical activity across the volunteers' brain surfaces. Which of the following represents the operational definition of the dependent variable in this study?

    a. MRI readings
    b. CT readings
    c. MEG readings
    d. EEG readings

2. Dr. Ultrone uses a technique to measure glucose consumption as an indicator of brain activity. What is the name of this technique?

    a. MRI
    b. fMRI
    c. PET
    d. EEG

3. Zoey did a report on the brain's ability to change in response to both experience and damage. What was her report about?

    a. Neurostimulation
    b. Neuroplasticity
    c. Neurobiology
    d. Neuropsychology

4. When Amita is in a car accident, her neurologist, Dr. Lang, suspects she has sustained an injury to the back of her brain. "Can you check with an EEG?" asks Amita's brother. Dr. Lang explains that an EEG is not the best method for assessing this injury, because

    a. an EEG only provides images of how the brain consumes glucose.
    b. an EEG only provides images of brain-wave activity.
    c. an EEG only provides still images of the brain.
    d. an EEG only provides stimulation to one region of the brain.

5. Dr. Translucent measures the brain's electrical activity via magnetic fields, using a(n)

    a. CT.
    b. EEG.
    c. MEG.
    d. PET.

**Use the following text to answer questions 6 and 7:**

Dr. Ludwikowski was interested in studying effects of stress on the brain. She randomly assigned 10 middle-aged participants to experience stress by placing them in a room with a loud, unpleasant noise. The other 10 middle-aged participants were placed in a room with no noise. She then used an fMRI to compare participants' brain activity.

6. In this study, what was Dr. Ludwikowski's operational definition of her dependent variable?

   a. fMRI results
   b. Noise
   c. Stress
   d. Age

7. In Dr. Ludwikowski's study, the participants in the room with no noise served as the

   a. independent variable.
   b. confederates.
   c. control group.
   d. placebo group.

# Module 1.4b The Brain: Brain Regions and Structures

## LEARNING TARGETS

**1.4-4** Explain how the *hindbrain, midbrain,* and *forebrain* apply to behavior and mental processes.

**1.4-5** Describe the structures of the brainstem, and explain the functions of the brainstem, thalamus, reticular formation, and cerebellum.

**1.4-6** Explain the limbic system's structures and functions.

**1.4-7** Describe the four lobes that make up the cerebral cortex and explain the functions of the motor cortex, somatosensory cortex, and association areas.

**1.4-4** What are the *hindbrain, midbrain,* and *forebrain*?

Vertebrate brains have three main divisions. The **hindbrain** contains brainstem structures that direct essential survival functions, such as breathing, sleeping, arousal, coordination, and balance. The **midbrain**, atop the brainstem, connects the hindbrain with

**hindbrain** consists of the medulla, pons, and cerebellum; directs essential survival functions, such as breathing, sleeping, and wakefulness, as well as coordination and balance.

**midbrain** found atop the brainstem; connects the *hindbrain* with the *forebrain,* controls some motor movement, and transmits auditory and visual information.

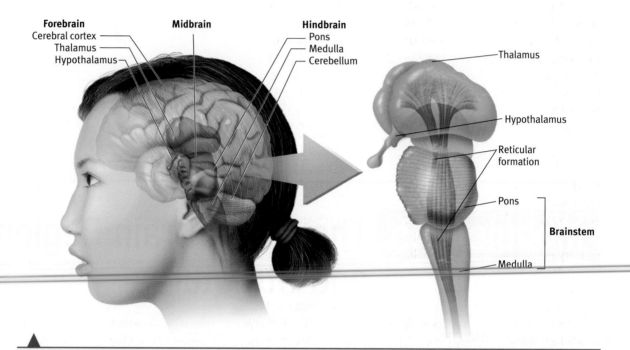

the forebrain; it also controls some movement and transmits information that enables our seeing and hearing. The **forebrain** manages complex cognitive activities, sensory and associative functions, and voluntary motor activities (**Figure 1.4-6**). Individual organisms' brains have evolved to best suit their environment (Cesario et al., 2020). We humans, for example, have extremely well-developed forebrains, allowing us an unparalleled ability to make complex decisions and judgments. Predatory sharks have complex hindbrains, supporting their impressive ability to chase down prey (Yopak et al., 2010).

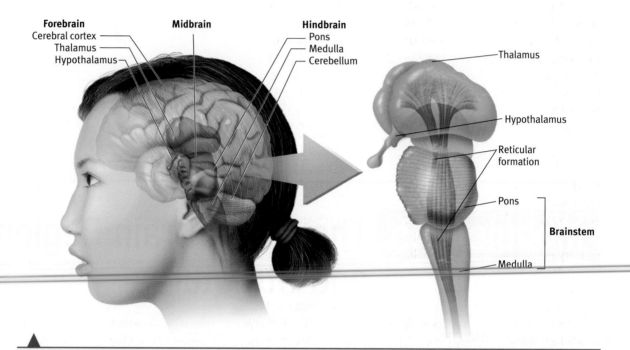

**Figure 1.4-6**

**Brain divisions: forebrain, midbrain, hindbrain**

In the hindbrain, the brainstem (including the pons and medulla) is an extension of the spinal cord. The thalamus is attached to the top of the brainstem. The reticular formation passes through both structures.

## The Brainstem

> **1.4-5** Which structures make up the brainstem, and what are the functions of the brainstem, thalamus, reticular formation, and cerebellum?

The **brainstem** is the brain's innermost region. Its base is the **medulla**, the slight swelling in the spinal cord just after it enters the skull (see Figure 1.4-6). Here lie the controls for your heartbeat and breathing. As some brain-damaged patients in a vegetative state illustrate, we do not need a conscious mind to orchestrate our heart's pumping and lungs' breathing. The brainstem handles those tasks. Just above the medulla sits the *pons,* which helps coordinate movements and control sleep.

If a researcher severs a cat's brainstem from the rest of its brain, the animal will still breathe and live—and even run, climb, and groom (Klemm, 1990). But cut off from its midbrain and forebrain, the cat won't *purposefully* run or climb to get food.

The brainstem is also a crossover point, where most nerves to and from each side of the brain connect with the body's opposite side (**Figure 1.4-7**). This peculiar cross-wiring—the brain's *contralateral* hemispheric organization—is but one of the brain's many surprises.

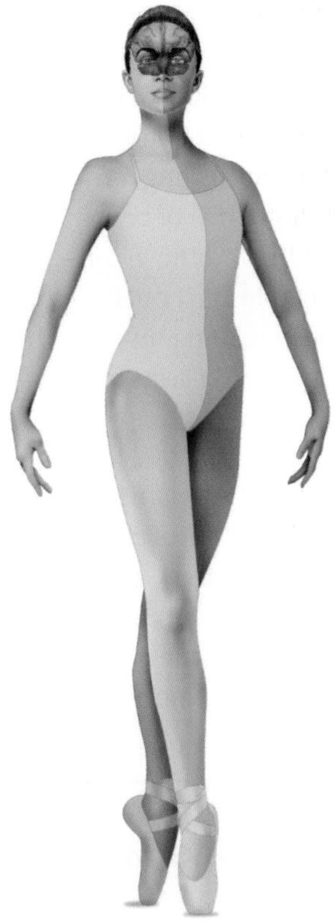

## The Thalamus

Sitting atop the brainstem is the forebrain's **thalamus**, a pair of egg-shaped structures that act as the brain's sensory control center (see Figure 1.4-6). The thalamus receives information from all the senses except smell, and routes that information to the brain regions that deal with seeing, hearing, tasting, and touching. The thalamus also receives some of the replies from those regions, which it then directs to the medulla and to the hindbrain's *cerebellum.* Think of the thalamus as being to sensory information what Seoul is to South Korea's trains: a hub through which traffic passes en route to various destinations.

## The Reticular Formation

Inside the brainstem, between your ears, lies the **reticular** ("netlike") **formation**. This nerve network, which is governed by the *reticular activating system*, extends from the spinal cord right up through the thalamus. As the spinal cord's sensory input flows up to the thalamus, some of it travels through the reticular formation, which filters incoming stimuli and relays important information to other brain areas.

The reticular formation also controls arousal—our state of alertness—as Giuseppe Moruzzi and Horace Magoun discovered in 1949. When they electrically stimulated a sleeping cat's reticular formation, it almost instantly produced an awake, alert animal. When Magoun *severed* a cat's reticular formation without damaging nearby sensory pathways, the effect was equally dramatic: The cat lapsed into a coma from which it never awakened.

## The Cerebellum

Extending from the rear of the brainstem is the hindbrain's baseball-sized **cerebellum**; its name means "little brain," which is what its two wrinkled halves resemble (**Figure 1.4-8**). The cerebellum (along with the *basal ganglia*—deep brain structures involved in motor

◀ **FIGURE 1.4-7**
**The body's wiring**

**forebrain** consists of the cerebral cortex, thalamus, and hypothalamus; manages complex cognitive activities, sensory and associative functions, and voluntary motor activities.

**brainstem** the central core of the brain, beginning where the spinal cord swells as it enters the skull; the brainstem is responsible for automatic survival functions.

**medulla** [muh-DUL-uh] the hindbrain structure that is the brainstem's base; controls heartbeat and breathing.

**thalamus** [THAL-uh-muss] the forebrain's sensory control center, located on top of the brainstem; it directs messages to the sensory receiving areas in the cortex and transmits replies to the cerebellum and medulla.

**reticular formation** a nerve network that travels through the brainstem into the thalamus; it filters information and plays an important role in controlling arousal.

**cerebellum** [sehr-uh-BELL-um] the hindbrain's "little brain" at the rear of the brainstem; its functions include processing sensory input, coordinating movement output and balance, and enabling nonverbal learning and memory.

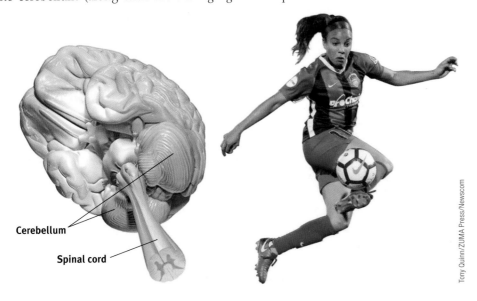

Cerebellum

Spinal cord

Tony Quinn/ZUMA Press/Newscom

◀ **Figure 1.4-8**
**The brain's organ of agility**

Hanging at the back of the brain, the cerebellum coordinates our voluntary movements, as when soccer player Mallory Pugh controls the ball.

movement) enables nonverbal and skill (or *procedural*) learning. With assistance from the pons, it also coordinates voluntary movement. When a soccer player masterfully controls the ball, give their cerebellum some credit. Under alcohol's influence, coordination suffers. And if you injured your cerebellum, you would have difficulty walking, keeping your balance, or texting a friend. Your movements would be jerky and exaggerated. Gone would be any dreams of being a dancer or guitarist.

This little brain—which actually contains more than half your brain's neurons—operates just outside your awareness. Quickly answer these questions: How long have you been reading this text? Do your clothes feel loose or tight? How's your mood? You probably answered easily, thanks to your cerebellum.

\* \* \*

*Note:* The brain functions we've discussed so far all occur without any conscious effort. This illustrates another of our recurring themes: *Our brain processes most information outside of our awareness.* We are aware of the *results* of our brain's labor—say, our current visual experience—but not *how* we construct the visual image. Likewise, whether we are asleep or awake, our brainstem manages its life-sustaining functions, freeing our conscious brain regions to think, talk, dream, or savor a memory.

---

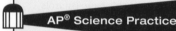

**AP® Science Practice**

# Check Your Understanding

## Examine the Concept

▶ Explain some brain functions that happen without any conscious effort.

▶ The _____ is a crossover point where nerves from the left side of the brain are mostly linked to the right side of the body, and vice versa.

## Apply the Concept

▶ Are you surprised to learn about all the information processing that happens automatically, without your knowledge? Why or why not?

▶ In which brain region would damage be most likely to (a) disrupt your ability to jump rope? (b) disrupt your ability to hear? (c) leave you in a coma? (d) cut off the very breath and heartbeat of life?

*Answers to the Examine the Concept questions can be found in Appendix C at the end of the book.*

---

**limbic system** neural system located mostly in the forebrain—below the cerebral hemispheres—that includes the *amygdala, hypothalamus, hippocampus, thalamus,* and *pituitary gland;* associated with emotions and drives.

**amygdala** [uh-MIG-duh-la] two lima-bean–sized neural clusters in the limbic system; linked to emotion.

### Figure 1.4-9

### The limbic system

This neural system is located mostly in the forebrain. The limbic system's hypothalamus controls the nearby pituitary gland.

# The Limbic System

**1.4-6** What are the limbic system's structures and functions?

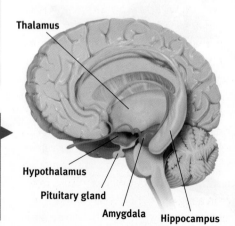

Thalamus

Hypothalamus

Pituitary gland

Amygdala    Hippocampus

A skeleton walks into a café. "What would you like?" asks the barista. The skeleton replies, "I'll take a latte and a mop."

We can thank our **limbic system** for that wonderful emotion when we enjoy a joke. This system, which is associated with emotions, drives, and memory formation, contains the *amygdala, hypothalamus, hippocampus, thalamus,* and *pituitary gland* (Figure 1.4-9).

## The Amygdala

The **amygdala**—two lima-bean–sized neural clusters—enables aggression and fear. In 1939, psychologist Heinrich Klüver and neurosurgeon

Paul Bucy surgically removed a rhesus monkey's amygdala, turning the normally ill-tempered animal into the mellowest of creatures. So, too, with humans. People with amygdala lesions often display reduced arousal to fear- and anger-arousing stimuli (Berntson et al., 2011). One woman with an amygdala lesion, patient S. M., has been called "the woman with no fear," even if being threatened with a gun (Feinstein et al., 2013).

What, then, might happen if we electrically stimulated the amygdala of a normally placid domestic animal, such as a cat? Do so in one spot and the cat prepares to attack, hissing with its back arched, its pupils dilated, its hair on end. Move the electrode only slightly within the amygdala, cage the cat with a small mouse, and now it cowers in terror.

These and other experiments have confirmed the amygdala's role in fear and rage. Monkeys and humans with amygdala damage become less fearful of strangers (Harrison et al., 2015). Other studies link criminal behavior with amygdala dysfunction (Dotterer et al., 2017; Ermer et al., 2012a).

But we must be careful. The brain is not neatly organized into structures that correspond to our behavior categories. The amygdala is engaged with other mental phenomena as well. And when we feel afraid or act aggressively, neural activity occurs in many areas of our brain—not just the amygdala. If you destroy a car's battery, the car won't run. But the battery is merely one link in an integrated system.

GK Hart/Vikki Hart/Getty Images

## The Hypothalamus

Just below (*hypo*) the thalamus is the **hypothalamus** (Figure 1.4-10), an important link in the command chain governing bodily maintenance. Some neural clusters in the hypothalamus influence hunger; others regulate thirst, body temperature, and sexual behavior. Together, they help maintain a steady (*homeostatic*) internal state.

To monitor your body state, the hypothalamus tunes into your blood chemistry and any incoming orders from other brain parts. For example, if it picks up signals from your brain's cerebral cortex that you are thinking about sex, your hypothalamus will secrete hormones. These hormones will, in turn, trigger the pituitary, which controls your endocrine system (Figure 1.4-9) to influence your sex glands to release *their* hormones. These hormones will intensify the thoughts of sex in your cerebral cortex. (Note the interplay between the nervous and endocrine systems: The brain influences the endocrine system, which in turn influences the brain.)

A remarkable discovery about the hypothalamus illustrates how progress in science often occurs—when curious, open-minded investigators make an unexpected observation. Two young McGill University neuropsychologists, James Olds and Peter Milner (1954), were trying to implant an electrode in a rat's reticular formation when they made a magnificent mistake: They placed the electrode incorrectly (Olds, 1975). Strangely, as if seeking more stimulation, the rat kept returning to the location where it had been stimulated by this misplaced electrode. On discovering that they had actually placed the device in a region of the hypothalamus, Olds and Milner realized they had stumbled upon a brain center that provides pleasurable rewards.

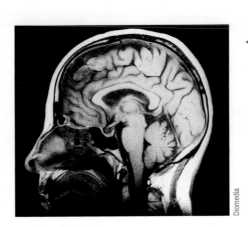

Diomedia

**Figure 1.4-10**

**The hypothalamus**

This small but important structure, colored yellow/orange in this MRI scan, helps keep the body's internal environment in a steady state.

**hypothalamus** [hi-po-THAL-uh-muss] a limbic system neural structure lying below (*hypo*) the thalamus; it directs several maintenance activities (eating, drinking, body temperature), helps govern the endocrine system, and is linked to emotion and reward.

Later experiments located other "pleasure centers" (Olds, 1958). (What the rats actually experience only they know, and they aren't telling. Rather than attribute human feelings to rats, today's scientists refer to *reward centers*.) Just how rewarding are these reward centers? Enough to cause rats to self-stimulate these brain regions more than 1000 times per hour. In other species, including dolphins and monkeys, researchers later discovered other limbic system reward centers, such as the *nucleus accumbens* in front of the hypothalamus (Hamid et al., 2016).

Animal research has also revealed both a general dopamine-related reward system and specific centers associated with the pleasures of eating, drinking, and sex. Animals, it seems, come equipped with built-in systems that reward activities essential to survival. As neuroscientist Candice Pert (1986) observed, "If you were designing a robot vehicle to walk into the future and survive, . . . you'd wire it up so that behavior that ensured the survival of the self or the species—like sex and eating—would be naturally reinforcing."

---

**AP® Science Practice**

## Data Interpretation

| | Number of Presses | |
| --- | --- | --- |
| | **Rats receiving reward center activation** | **Rats not receiving reward center activation** |
| Trial 1 | 204 | 202 |
| Trial 2 | 813 | 250 |
| Trial 3 | 857 | 300 |
| Trial 4 | 900 | 156 |
| Trial 5 | 1001 | 158 |

This module describes research on rats that led to the identification of the hypothalamus as a reward center in the brain. Consider the data set above.

- Describe the general difference in number of presses *between* the groups represented in this table.

- Describe the trends in the data *within* each group.

- Calculate the mean for each group.

- Is the variable "number of presses" qualitative or quantitative? Explain.

*Remember, you can always revisit Unit 0 to review information related to psychological research.*

---

Do humans have limbic centers for pleasure? Some evidence indicates we do. When we meet likable people or read affirming messages from friends, our brain bursts with reward center activity (Inagaki et al., 2019; Zerubavel et al., 2018). But when one neurosurgeon implanted electrodes in violent patients' reward center areas, the patients reported only mild pleasure. Unlike Olds and Milner's rats, the patients were not driven to a frenzy (Deutsch, 1972; Hooper & Teresi, 1986). Stimulating the brain's "hedonic hot spots" (its reward circuits) produces more *desire* than pure enjoyment (Kringelbach & Berridge, 2012).

Experiments have also revealed the effects of a dopamine-related reward system in people. For example, experimentally boosting dopamine levels increases the pleasurable "chills" response to a favorite piece of music, whereas reducing dopamine levels decreases musical-related pleasure (Ferreri et al., 2019). Some researchers believe that many disordered behaviors may stem from malfunctions in the natural brain systems for pleasure and well-being. People genetically predisposed to this *reward deficiency syndrome* may crave whatever provides that missing pleasure or relieves negative feelings, such as aggression, rich food, or drugs and alcohol (Blum et al., 1996, 2014; Chester et al., 2016).

**hippocampus** a neural center in the limbic system that helps process explicit (conscious) memories—of facts and events—for storage.

## The Hippocampus

The **hippocampus** is a curved brain structure that processes conscious, explicit memories. Humans who lose their hippocampus to surgery or injury also lose their ability to form new memories of facts and events (Clark & Maguire, 2016). Those who survive a hippocampal brain tumor in childhood struggle to remember new information in adulthood (Jayakar et al., 2015). National Football League (NFL) players who experience one or more loss-of-consciousness concussions may later have a shrunken hippocampus and poor memory (Strain et al., 2015; Tharmaratnam et al., 2018). Hippocampus size and function decrease as we grow older, which furthers cognitive decline (O'Callaghan et al., 2019; see Module 3.2). Modules 2.5 and 2.7 explain how our two-track mind uses the hippocampus to process our memories.

\* \* \*

Figure 1.4-11 locates the brain areas we've discussed, as well as the *cerebral cortex*—the body's ultimate control and information-processing center, to which we will turn next—and the *corpus callosum,* which connects the two brain hemispheres (see Module 1.4c).

**Are football players' brains protected?** When researchers analyzed the brains of 111 deceased National Football League players, 99 percent showed signs of degeneration related to frequent head trauma (Mez et al., 2017). In 2017, NFL player Aaron Hernandez (#81) died by suicide while imprisoned for murder. An autopsy revealed that his brain, at age 27, was already showing advanced degeneration (Kilgore, 2017). In hopes of protecting players, some teams use more protective gear and portable brain-imaging tools (Canadian Press, 2018).

**Figure 1.4-11**
**Brain structures and their functions**

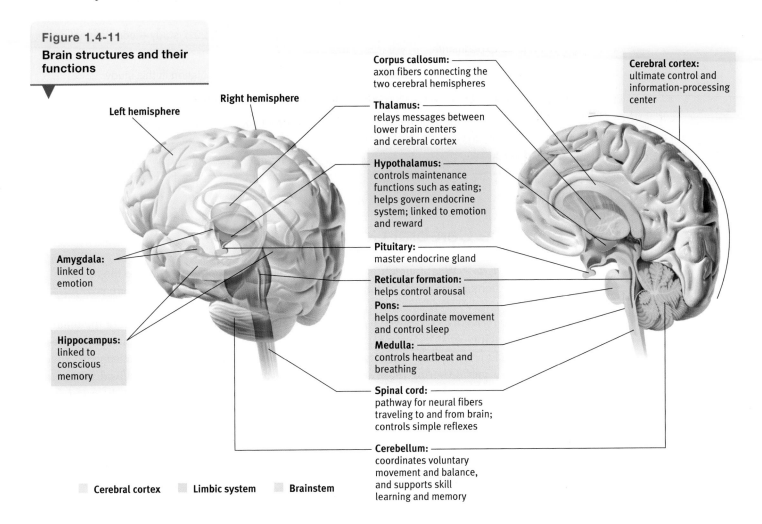

**Right hemisphere**

**Left hemisphere**

**Corpus callosum:** axon fibers connecting the two cerebral hemispheres

**Cerebral cortex:** ultimate control and information-processing center

**Thalamus:** relays messages between lower brain centers and cerebral cortex

**Hypothalamus:** controls maintenance functions such as eating; helps govern endocrine system; linked to emotion and reward

**Amygdala:** linked to emotion

**Pituitary:** master endocrine gland

**Reticular formation:** helps control arousal

**Pons:** helps coordinate movement and control sleep

**Medulla:** controls heartbeat and breathing

**Hippocampus:** linked to conscious memory

**Spinal cord:** pathway for neural fibers traveling to and from brain; controls simple reflexes

**Cerebellum:** coordinates voluntary movement and balance, and supports skill learning and memory

Cerebral cortex    Limbic system    Brainstem

Elise Amendola/AP Images

## The Cerebral Cortex

**1.4-7** What four lobes make up the cerebral cortex, and what are the functions of the motor cortex, somatosensory cortex, and association areas?

The *cerebrum*—the two cerebral hemispheres that contribute 85 percent of the brain's weight—enables our perceiving, thinking, and speaking. Like other brain structures, including the thalamus, hippocampus, and amygdala, the cerebral hemispheres come as a pair. Covering those hemispheres, like bark on a tree, is the **cerebral cortex**, a thin surface layer of interconnected neural cells. (The scholars who first dissected and labeled the brain used Latin and Greek words as graphic descriptions. For example, *cortex* means "bark.")

Mammals' complex cerebral cortex offers high capacity for learning and thinking, enabling them to adapt to ever-changing environments. What makes humans distinct is the size and interconnectivity of our cerebral cortex (Donahue et al., 2018). Let's take a look at its structure and function.

**cerebral** [seh-REE-bruhl] **cortex** the intricate fabric of interconnected neural cells covering the forebrain's cerebral hemispheres; the body's ultimate control and information-processing center.

## Structure of the Cortex

If you opened a human skull, exposing the brain, you would see a wrinkled organ, shaped somewhat like an oversized walnut. Without these wrinkles, a flattened cerebral cortex would require triple the area—roughly that of a large pizza. The brain's left and right hemispheres are filled mainly with axons connecting the cortex to the brain's other regions. The cerebral cortex—that thin surface layer—contains some 20 to 23 billion of the brain's nerve cells and 300 trillion synaptic connections (de Courten-Myers, 2005). Being human takes a lot of nerve.

Each hemisphere's cortex is subdivided into four *lobes,* separated by prominent *fissures,* or folds (**Figure 1.4-12**). Starting at the front of your brain and moving over the top, there are the **frontal lobes** (behind your forehead), the **parietal lobes** (at the top and to the rear), and the **occipital lobes** (at the back of your head). Reversing direction and moving forward, just above your ears, you find the **temporal lobes**. Each of the four lobes carries out many functions, and many functions require the interplay of several lobes.

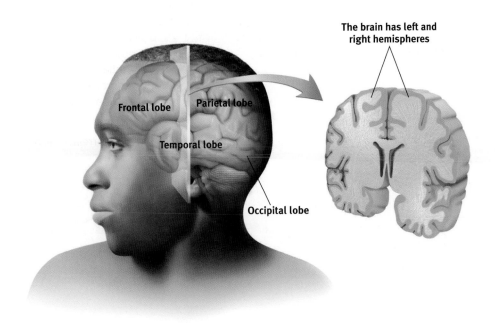

The brain has left and right hemispheres

Frontal lobe
Parietal lobe
Temporal lobe
Occipital lobe

**Figure 1.4-12**
**The cortex and its basic subdivisions**

**frontal lobes** the portion of the cerebral cortex lying just behind the forehead. They enable linguistic processing, muscle movements, higher-order thinking, and executive functioning (such as making plans and judgments).

**parietal** [puh-RYE-uh-tuhl] **lobes** the portion of the cerebral cortex lying at the top of the head and toward the rear; it receives sensory input for touch and body position.

**occipital** [ahk-SIP-uh-tuhl] **lobes** the portion of the cerebral cortex lying at the back of the head; it includes areas that receive information from the visual fields.

**temporal lobes** the portion of the cerebral cortex lying roughly above the ears; it includes the auditory areas, each of which receives information primarily from the opposite ear. They also enable language processing.

## Functions of the Cortex

More than a century ago, surgeons found damaged cortical areas during autopsies of people who had been partially paralyzed or speechless. This rather crude evidence did not prove that specific parts of the cortex control complex functions like movement or speech. A laptop with a broken power cord might go dead, but we would be fooling ourselves if we thought we had "localized" the internet in the cord.

### Motor Functions

Scientists had better luck in localizing simpler brain functions. For example, in 1870, German physicians Gustav Fritsch and Eduard Hitzig made an important discovery: Mild electrical stimulation to parts of an animal's cortex made parts of its body move. The effects were selective: Stimulation caused movement only when applied to an arch-shaped region at the back of the frontal lobe, running roughly ear-to-ear across the top of the brain. Moreover, stimulating parts of this region in the left or right hemisphere caused movements of specific body parts on the *opposite* side of the body. Fritsch and Hitzig had discovered what is now called the **motor cortex**.

**Mapping the Motor Cortex**  Luckily for brain surgeons and their patients, the brain has no sensory receptors. Knowing this, in the 1930s, Otfrid Foerster and Wilder Penfield were able to map the motor cortex in hundreds of wide-awake patients by stimulating different cortical areas and observing the body's responses. They discovered that body areas requiring precise control, such as the fingers and mouth, occupy the greatest amount of cortical space (**Figure 1.4-13**). In one of his many demonstrations of motor behavior mechanics, Spanish neuroscientist José Delgado stimulated a spot on a patient's left motor cortex, triggering the right hand to make a fist. Asked to keep the fingers open during the next stimulation, the patient, whose fingers closed despite his best efforts, remarked, "I guess, Doctor, that your electricity is stronger than my will" (Delgado, 1969, p. 114).

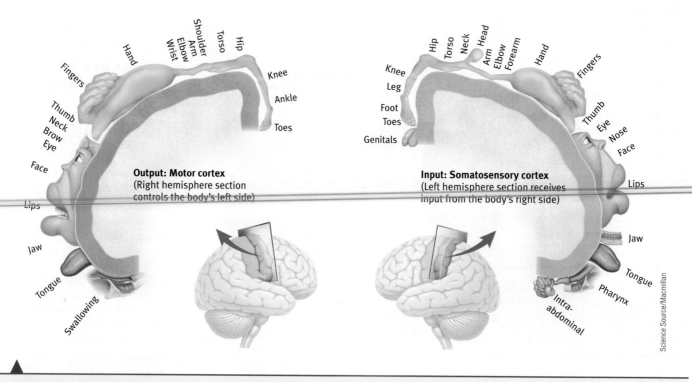

**FIGURE 1.4-13**

**Motor cortex and somatosensory cortex tissue devoted to each body part**

As you can see from this classic though inexact representation, the amount of cortex devoted to a body part in the motor cortex (in the frontal lobes) or in the somatosensory cortex (in the parietal lobes) is not proportional to that body part's size. Rather, the brain devotes more tissue to sensitive areas and to areas requiring precise control. So, your fingers have a greater representation in the cortex than does your upper arm.

Scientists can now predict a monkey's arm motion *just before* it moves — by repeatedly measuring motor cortex activity preceding specific arm movements (Livi et al., 2019). Such findings have opened the door to research on brain-controlled computer technology.

**Brain–Machine Interfaces**  Researchers wondered: By stimulating the brain, could we enable a person with paralysis to move a robotic limb? Could a brain–machine interface help someone with paralysis learn to command a cursor to write an email? To find out, researchers implanted 100 tiny recording electrodes in the motor cortexes of three monkeys (Nicolelis, 2011; Serruya et al., 2002). As the monkeys gained rewards by using a joystick to follow a

**motor cortex** a cerebral cortex area at the rear of the frontal lobes that controls voluntary movements.

moving red target, the researchers matched the brain signals with the arm movements. Then they programmed a computer to monitor the signals and operate the joystick. When a monkey merely thought about a move, the mind-reading computer moved the cursor with nearly the same proficiency as had the reward-seeking monkey. Monkey think, computer do.

Clinical trials of such *cognitive neural prosthetics* have been under way with people who have severe paralysis or have lost a limb (Andersen et al., 2010; Rajangam et al., 2016). The first patient, a 25-year-old man with paralysis, was able to mentally control a TV, draw shapes on a computer screen, and play video games—all thanks to an aspirin-sized chip with 100 microelectrodes recording activity in his motor cortex (Hochberg et al., 2006). Other people with paralysis who have received implants have learned to direct robotic arms with their thoughts (Clausen et al., 2017).

And then there is Ian Burkhart, who lost the use of his arms and legs at age 19. Ohio State University brain researchers implanted recording electrodes in his motor cortex (Schwemmer et al., 2018). Imagine the process: Researchers instruct Burkhart to stare at a screen that shows a moving hand. Next, Burkhart imagines moving his own hand. Brain signals from his motor cortex feed into a computer, which gets the message that he wants to move his arm and thus stimulates those muscles. The result? Burkhart, with his very own paralyzed arm, grasps a bottle, dumps out its contents, and picks up a stick. He can even play the video game *Guitar Hero.* By learning Burkhart's unique brain response patterns, the computer can predict his brain activity to help him make these movements. "It's really restored a lot of the hope I have for the future to know that a device like this will be possible to use in everyday life," Burkhart says, "for me and for many other people" (Wood, 2018). (See tinyurl .com/ControlMotorCortex.)

*Andrew Spear/Redux Pictures*

If everything psychological is also biological—if, for example, every thought is also a neural event—could microelectrodes someday detect thoughts well enough to enable people to control their environment with ever-greater precision (see **Figure 1.4-14**)? Scientists have even created a prosthetic voice, which creates (mostly) understandable speech by reading the brain's motor commands that direct vocal movement (Anumanchipalli et al., 2019).

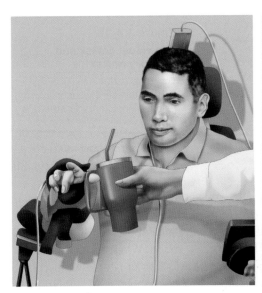
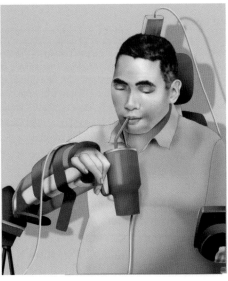

**Figure 1.4-14**
**Brain–machine interaction**

Electrodes planted in the hand area of the motor cortex, and in the hand, elbow, and shoulder muscles, helped a man with paralysis in all four limbs use his paralyzed arm to take a drink of coffee (Ajiboye et al., 2017). Such research advances are paving the way for restored movement in daily life, outside the controlled laboratory environment (Andersen, 2019; Andersen et al., 2010).

## Sensory Functions

If the motor cortex sends messages out to the body, where does the cortex receive incoming messages? Penfield identified a cortical area—at the front of the parietal lobes, parallel to and just behind the motor cortex—that specializes in receiving information from the skin senses, such as touch and temperature, and from the movement of body parts. We now call this area the **somatosensory cortex**. Stimulate a point on the top of this band of tissue and a person may report being touched on the shoulder; stimulate some point on the side and the person may feel something on the face.

The more sensitive the body region, the larger the somatosensory cortex area devoted to it (see Figure 1.4-13). Your supersensitive lips project to a larger brain area than do your toes, which is one reason we kiss rather than touch toes. Rats have a large area of the brain devoted to their whisker sensations, and owls to their hearing sensations.

Scientists have identified additional areas where the cortex receives input from senses other than touch. Any visual information you are receiving now is going to the visual cortex in your occipital lobes, at the back of your brain (**Figures 1.4-15** and **1.4-16**). If you have normal vision, you might see flashes of light or dashes of color if stimulated in your occipital lobes. (In a sense, we *do* have eyes in the back of our head!) Having lost much of his right occipital lobe in a tumor removal, a friend of mine [DM's] was blind to the left half of his field of vision. Visual information travels from the occipital lobes to other areas that specialize in tasks such as identifying words, detecting emotions, and recognizing faces.

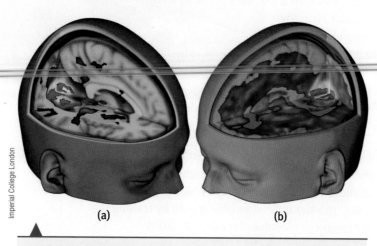

Imperial College London

(a)                                                (b)

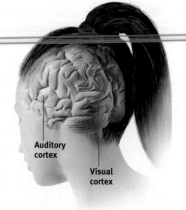

Auditory cortex

Visual cortex

### Figure 1.4-15

### Seeing without eyes

The psychoactive drug LSD often produces vivid *hallucinations*. Why? Because it dramatically increases communication between the visual cortex (in the occipital lobe) and other brain regions. These fMRI scans show (a) a research participant with closed eyes who has been given a placebo and (b) the same person under the influence of LSD. Color represents increased blood flow (Carhart-Harris et al., 2016). Other researchers have confirmed that LSD increases communication between brain regions (Preller et al., 2019; Timmermann et al., 2018).

### Figure 1.4-16

### The visual cortex and auditory cortex

The visual cortex in the occipital lobes at the rear of your brain receives input from your eyes. The auditory cortex in your temporal lobes — above your ears — receives information from your ears.

**somatosensory cortex**
a cerebral cortex area at the front of the parietal lobes that registers and processes body touch and movement sensations.

Any sound you now hear is processed by your auditory cortex in your temporal lobes (just above your ears; see Figure 1.4-16). Most of this auditory information travels a circuitous route from one ear to the auditory receiving area above your opposite ear. If stimulated in your auditory cortex, you might hear a sound. When taken during the false sensory experience of auditory hallucinations, fMRI scans of people with schizophrenia reveal active auditory areas in the temporal lobes (Lennox et al., 1999). Even the phantom ringing ("tinnitus") sound experienced by people with hearing loss is—if heard in one ear—associated with activity in the temporal lobe on the brain's opposite side (Muhlnickel, 1998).

## Association Areas

So far, we have pointed out small cortical areas that either receive sensory input or direct muscular output. Together, these occupy about one-fourth of the human brain's thin, wrinkled cover. What, then, goes on in the remaining vast regions of the cortex? In these **association areas**, neurons are busy with higher mental functions—many of the tasks that make us human.

Electrically probing an association area won't trigger any observable response. So, unlike the somatosensory and motor areas, association area functions cannot be neatly mapped. Does this mean we don't use them—or that, as some 4 in 10 people agreed in two surveys, "We use only 10 percent of our brains" (Furnham, 2018; Macdonald et al., 2017)? (See the Developing Arguments feature: Do We Use Only 10 Percent of Our Brain?)

**association areas** areas of the cerebral cortex that are not involved in primary motor or sensory functions, but rather are involved in higher mental functions such as learning, remembering, thinking, and speaking.

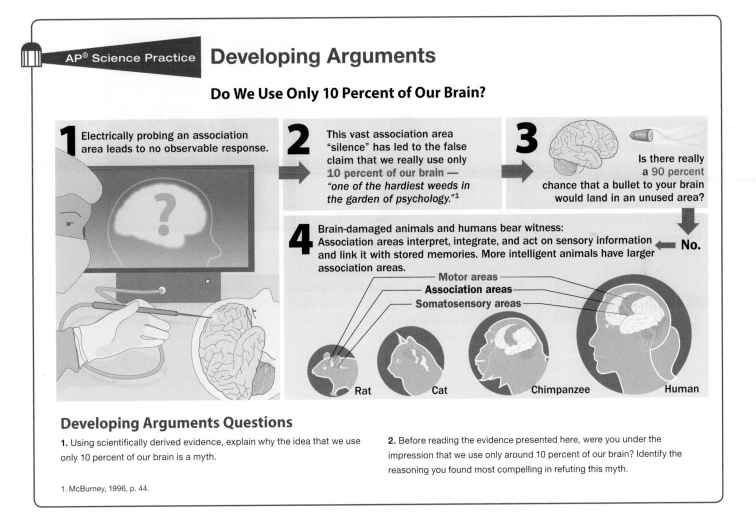

### AP® Science Practice
# Developing Arguments

## Do We Use Only 10 Percent of Our Brain?

**1** Electrically probing an association area leads to no observable response.

**2** This vast association area "silence" has led to the false claim that we really use only **10 percent of our brain**— *"one of the hardiest weeds in the garden of psychology."*[1]

**3** Is there really a 90 percent chance that a bullet to your brain would land in an unused area?

**No.**

**4** Brain-damaged animals and humans bear witness: Association areas interpret, integrate, and act on sensory information and link it with stored memories. More intelligent animals have larger association areas.

Motor areas
Association areas
Somatosensory areas

Rat  Cat  Chimpanzee  Human

### Developing Arguments Questions

**1.** Using scientifically derived evidence, explain why the idea that we use only 10 percent of our brain is a myth.

**2.** Before reading the evidence presented here, were you under the impression that we use only around 10 percent of our brain? Identify the reasoning you found most compelling in refuting this myth.

1. McBurney, 1996, p. 44.

Association areas are found in all four brain lobes. The *prefrontal cortex* in the forward part of the frontal lobes enables judgment, planning, social interactions, and processing of new memories. People with damage to this area may have high intelligence test scores and great cake-baking skills. Yet they would not be able to plan ahead to *begin* baking a cake for a birthday party (Huey et al., 2006). If they did begin to bake, they might forget the recipe

(MacPherson et al., 2016). And if responsible for the absence of birthday cake, they may feel no regret (Bault et al., 2019).

Frontal lobe damage also can alter personality and remove a person's inhibitions. Consider the classic case of railroad worker Phineas Gage. One afternoon in 1848, Gage, then 25 years old, was using a tamping iron to pack gunpowder into a rock. A spark ignited the gunpowder, shooting the rod up through his left cheek and out the top of his skull, leaving his frontal lobes damaged (**Figure 1.4-17**). To everyone's amazement, Gage was immediately able to sit up and speak, and after the wound healed, he returned to work. But the blast damaged connections between his frontal lobes and the brain regions that control emotion and decision making (Thiebaut de Schotten et al., 2015; Van Horn et al., 2012). The previously friendly, soft-spoken man was now irritable, profane, and dishonest. This person, said his friends, was "no longer Gage." Most of his mental abilities and memories were intact, but for the next few years his personality was not. (Gage later lost his railroad job, but over time he adapted to his disability and found work as a stagecoach driver [Macmillan & Lena, 2010].)

### Figure 1.4-17

#### A blast from the past

(a) Phineas Gage's skull was kept as a medical record. Using measurements and modern neuroimaging techniques, researchers have reconstructed the probable path of the rod through Gage's brain (Van Horn et al., 2012). (b) This photo shows Gage after his accident. (The image has been reversed to show the features correctly. Early photos, including this one, were actually mirror images.)

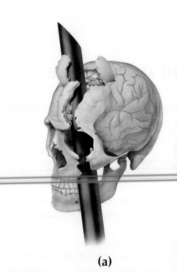

(a)        (b)

Warren Anatomical Museum in the Francis A. Countway Library of Medicine. Gift of Jack and Beverly Wigus.

Studies of other people with damaged frontal lobes have revealed similar impairments. Not only do they become less inhibited (without the frontal lobe brakes on their impulses), but their moral judgments also seem unrestrained. Cecil Clayton lost 20 percent of his left frontal lobe in a 1972 sawmill accident. Thereafter, his intelligence test score dropped to an elementary school level and he displayed increased impulsivity. In 1996, he fatally shot a deputy sheriff. In 2015, when he was 74, the State of Missouri executed him (Williams, 2015).

The frontal lobes help steer us toward kindness and away from violence (Achterberg et al., 2020; Lieberman et al., 2019). With their frontal lobes ruptured, people's moral compass seems separated from their actions. They know right from wrong but often don't care.

Association areas also perform other mental functions. The parietal lobes, parts of which were large and unusually shaped in Einstein's normal-weight brain, enable mathematical and spatial reasoning (Amalric & Dehaene, 2019; Wilkey et al., 2018). Stimulation of one parietal lobe area in patients undergoing brain surgery produced a feeling of wanting to move an upper limb, the lips, or the tongue, but without any actual movement. With increased stimulation, patients falsely believed they *had* moved. Curiously, when surgeons stimulated a different association area near the motor cortex in the frontal lobes, the patients did move but had no awareness of doing so (Desmurget et al., 2009). These head-scratching findings suggest that our perception of moving flows not from the movement itself, but rather from our intention.

On the underside of the right temporal lobe, another association area enables us to instantly recognize faces (Retter et al., 2020). If a stroke or head injury destroyed this area of your brain, you would still be able to describe facial features and to recognize someone's gender and approximate age, yet be strangely unable to identify the person as, say, Ariana Grande or even your grandmother.

Nevertheless, complex mental functions don't reside in any single place. During a complex task, a brain scan shows many islands of brain activity working together—some running automatically in the background, and others under conscious control (Chein & Schneider, 2012). Your memory, language, attention, and social skills result from *functional connectivity*—communication among distinct brain areas and neural networks (Bassett et al., 2018; Silston et al., 2018). What happens when brain areas struggle to communicate with each other? People are at increased risk for mental disorders (Baker et al., 2019; Zhang et al., 2019). *The point to remember:* Our mental experiences—and our psychological health—rely on coordinated brain activity.

---

**AP® Science Practice**

## Check Your Understanding

**Examine the Concept**

▶ Which part of the human brain distinguishes us most from other animals?

▶ Explain the differences among the brain's four lobes in terms of their location and function.

**Apply the Concept**

▶ If you are able, try moving your right hand in a circular motion, as if cleaning a table. Then start your right foot doing the same motion, synchronized with your hand. Now reverse the right foot's motion, but not the hand's. Finally, try moving the *left* foot opposite to the right hand.

a. Why is reversing the right foot's motion so hard?

b. Why is it easier to move the left foot opposite to the right hand?

▶ Explain why association areas are important using specific examples from your own experience.

*Answers to the Examine the Concept questions can be found in Appendix C at the end of the book.*

---

## Module 1.4b REVIEW

**1.4-4** What are the *hindbrain*, *midbrain*, and *forebrain*?

- Vertebrate brains have three main divisions.

- The *hindbrain* contains brainstem structures that direct essential survival functions, such as breathing, sleeping, arousal, coordination, and balance.

- The *midbrain* connects the hindbrain with the forebrain; it controls some movement and transmits information that enables seeing and hearing.

- The *forebrain* manages complex cognitive activities, sensory and associative functions, and voluntary motor activities.

**1.4-5** Which structures make up the brainstem, and what are the functions of the brainstem, thalamus, reticular formation, and cerebellum?

- The *brainstem* is responsible for automatic survival functions. Its components are the *medulla* (which controls heartbeat and breathing), the pons (which helps coordinate movements and control sleep), and the *reticular formation* (which filters incoming stimuli, relays information to other brain areas, and affects arousal).

- The *thalamus*, sitting above the brainstem, acts as the brain's sensory control center.

- The *cerebellum*, attached to the rear of the brainstem, coordinates voluntary movement and balance and enables nonverbal learning and memory.

> **1.4-6** What are the limbic system's structures and functions?

- The *limbic system* is linked to emotions, memory, and drives.
- Its neural centers include the *amygdala* (involved in behavior and emotional responses, such as aggression and fear), the *hypothalamus* (directs various bodily maintenance functions, helps govern the endocrine system, and is linked to emotion and reward), the *hippocampus* (helps process explicit, conscious memories), the *thalamus,* and the *pituitary gland.*
- The hypothalamus controls the pituitary by stimulating it to trigger the release of hormones.

> **1.4-7** What four lobes make up the cerebral cortex, and what are the functions of the motor cortex, somatosensory cortex, and association areas?

- The *cerebral cortex* has two hemispheres, and each hemisphere has four lobes: *frontal, parietal, occipital,* and *temporal.* Each lobe performs many functions and interacts with other areas of the cortex.
- The *motor cortex,* at the rear of the frontal lobes, controls voluntary movements.
- The *somatosensory cortex,* at the front of the parietal lobes, registers and processes body touch and movement sensations.
- Body parts requiring precise control (in the motor cortex) or those that are especially sensitive (in the somatosensory cortex) occupy the greatest amount of space.
- Most of the brain's cortex—the major portion of each of the four lobes—is devoted to uncommitted *association areas,* which integrate information involved in higher mental functions such as learning, remembering, thinking, and speaking.
- Our mental experiences arise from coordinated brain activity.

# AP® Practice Multiple Choice Questions

1. Damage to which of the following puts a person's life in the most danger because it may cause breathing to stop?
   a. Amygdala
   b. Thalamus
   c. Medulla
   d. Hypothalamus

2. A gymnast falls and hits her head on the floor. She attempts to continue practicing but has trouble maintaining balance. What part of her brain has probably been affected?
   a. Reticular formation
   b. Cerebellum
   c. Amygdala
   d. Medulla

3. Stimulation of the amygdala is most likely to have which of the following effects?
   a. Happiness
   b. Aggression
   c. Hunger
   d. Loss of balance

4. Brennan feels hungry. Which brain area is most responsible for his hunger?
   a. Amygdala
   b. Hypothalamus
   c. Hippocampus
   d. Brainstem

**5.** Damage to which of the following brain structures would affect the processing of new explicit memories?

 a. Cerebral cortex
 b. Medulla
 c. Hippocampus
 d. Hypothalamus

**6.** After being late to work for the fifth time, Hester declared, "My occipital lobes must not be working optimally! I have a hard time planning my day to be here on time!" If you were Hester's boss, what might you say to her to modify her claim to make it more accurate?

 a. "Hester, it's your frontal lobes that are not working optimally."
 b. "Hester, it's your temporal lobes that are not working optimally."
 c. "Hester, it's your parietal lobes that are not working optimally."
 d. "Hester, it's your somatosensory cortex that is not working optimally."

**7.** Stimulation of which of the following may cause a person to involuntarily move their arm?

 a. Somatosensory cortex
 b. Motor cortex
 c. Glial cells
 d. Visual cortex

**8.** Which lobe of the brain is the arrow pointing to?

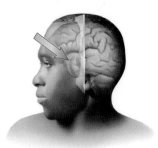

 a. Occipital
 b. Parietal
 c. Frontal
 d. Temporal

# Module 1.4c The Brain: Damage Response and Brain Hemispheres

## Responses to Damage

**1.4-8** To what extent can a damaged brain reorganize itself, and what is *neurogenesis*?

Earlier, we learned about *neuroplasticity*—how our brain adapts to new situations. What happens when we experience mishaps, large and small? Let's explore the brain's ability to modify itself after damage.

Most brain-damage effects described earlier can be traced to two hard facts: (1) Severed brain and spinal cord neurons, unlike cut skin, usually do not regenerate. (If your spinal cord were severed, you would probably be permanently paralyzed.) And (2) some brain functions seem preassigned to specific areas. One newborn who suffered damage to a temporal lobe area responsible for facial recognition was never able to recognize faces (Farah et al., 2000). But there is good news: Some neural tissue can *reorganize* in response to damage.

Neuroplasticity may also occur after serious damage, especially in young children whose undamaged hemisphere develops extra connections (Lindenberger & Lövdén, 2019; see also **Figure 1.4-18**). The brain's plasticity is good news for those with vision or hearing

**Figure 1.4-18**

**Brain work is child's play**

This 6-year-old child had surgery to end her life-threatening seizures. Although most of her right hemisphere was removed (see the MRI of a similar hemispherectomy), her remaining hemisphere compensated by putting other areas to work. Reflecting on their child hemispherectomies, one Johns Hopkins team reported being "awed" by how well the children had retained their memory, personality, and humor (Vining et al., 1997). The younger the child, the greater the chance that the remaining hemisphere can take over the functions of the one that was surgically removed.

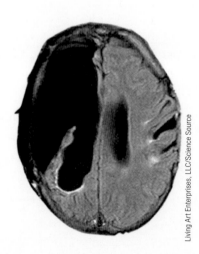

Living Art Enterprises, LLC/Science Source

Joe McNally/Hulton Archive/Getty Images

loss. Blindness or deafness makes unused brain areas available for other uses, such as sound and smell (Amedi et al., 2005; Bauer et al., 2017). If a blind person uses one finger to read Braille, the brain area dedicated to that finger expands as the sense of touch invades the visual cortex that normally helps people see (Barinaga, 1992; Sadato et al., 1996). In sighted people, Braille-reading training produces similar brain changes (Debowska et al., 2016).

Neuroplasticity also helps explain why some studies have found that deaf people who learned sign language before another language may have enhanced peripheral and motion-detection vision (Brooks et al., 2020). In deaf people whose native language is sign, the temporal lobe area dedicated to hearing waits in vain for stimulation. Finally, it looks for other signals to process, such as those from the visual system used to see and interpret signs.

Similar reassignment may occur when disease or damage frees up other brain areas normally dedicated to specific functions. If a slow-growing left hemisphere tumor disrupts language (which resides mostly in the left hemisphere), the right hemisphere may compensate (Thiel et al., 2006). If a finger is amputated, the somatosensory cortex that received its input will begin to receive input from the adjacent fingers, which then become more sensitive (Oelschläger et al., 2014).

Although the brain often attempts self-repair by reorganizing existing tissue, researchers are debating whether it can also mend itself through **neurogenesis**—producing new neurons (Kempermann et al., 2018). Researchers have found baby neurons deep in the brains of adult mice, birds, monkeys, and humans (He & Jin, 2016; Jessberger et al., 2008). These neurons may then form connections with neighboring neurons (Gould, 2007; Luna et al., 2019).

*Stem cells,* which can develop into any type of brain cell, have also been discovered in the human embryo. If mass-produced in a lab and injected into a damaged brain, might neural stem cells turn themselves into replacements for lost brain cells? Might surgeons someday be able to rebuild damaged brains, much as we reseed the grass on damaged sports fields? Stay tuned. In the meantime, we can all benefit from natural promoters of neurogenesis, such as exercise, sleep, and nonstressful but stimulating environments (Liu & Nusslock, 2018; Monteiro et al., 2014; Nollet et al., 2019).

## The Divided Brain

**1.4-9** What do split brains reveal about the functions of our two brain hemispheres?

Our brain's look-alike left and right hemispheres serve differing functions. This *lateralization* becomes apparent after brain damage. Research spanning more than a century has shown that left-hemisphere accidents, strokes, and tumors can impair reading, writing, speaking, arithmetic reasoning, and understanding. Similar right-hemisphere damage has less visibly dramatic effects. Does this mean that the right hemisphere is just along for the ride? Many believed this was the case until the 1960s, when a fascinating chapter in psychology's history began to unfold: Researchers found that the "minor" right hemisphere was not so limited after all.

### Splitting the Brain

In the early 1960s, two neurosurgeons speculated that major epileptic seizures were caused by an amplification of abnormal brain activity bouncing back and forth between the two cerebral hemispheres, which work together as an integrated system (Bogen & Vogel, 1962). They wondered if they could end this biological tennis match by severing the **corpus callosum**, the wide band of axon fibers connecting the two hemispheres and carrying

**neurogenesis** the formation of new neurons.

**corpus callosum** [KOR-pus kah-LOW-sum] the large band of neural fibers connecting the two brain hemispheres and carrying messages between them.

**Figure 1.4-19**

**The corpus callosum**

**Figure 1.4-19**

**The corpus callosum**

This large band of neural fibers connects the two brain hemispheres. (a) To photograph this half-brain, a surgeon separated the hemispheres by cutting through the corpus callosum (see the blue arrow) and lower brain regions. (b) This high-resolution diffusion spectrum image, showing a top-facing brain from above, reveals the brain neural networks within the two hemispheres, and the corpus callosum neural bridge between them.

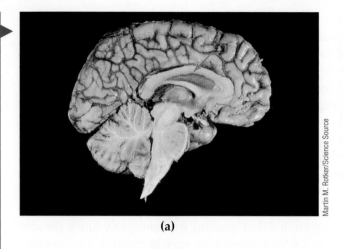
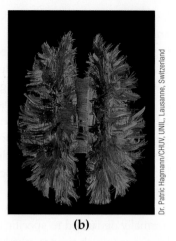

Martin M. Rotker/Science Source

Dr. Patric Hagmann/CHUV, UNIL, Lausanne, Switzerland

**(a)**  **(b)**

messages between them (**Figure 1.4-19**). The neurosurgeons knew that psychologists Roger Sperry, Ronald Myers, and Michael Gazzaniga had divided cats' and monkeys' brains in this manner, with no serious ill effects.

So, the surgeons operated. The result? The seizures all but disappeared. The patients with these **split brains** were surprisingly healthy, with their personality and intellect hardly affected. Waking from surgery, one even joked that he had a "splitting headache" (Gazzaniga, 1967). By sharing their experiences, these patients have greatly expanded our understanding of interactions between the intact brain's two hemispheres.

**Figure 1.4-20**

**The information highway from eye to brain**

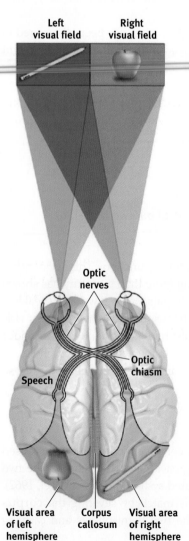

Left visual field

Right visual field

Optic nerves

Speech

Optic chiasm

Visual area of left hemisphere

Corpus callosum

Visual area of right hemisphere

**split brain** a condition resulting from surgery that separates the brain's two hemispheres by cutting the fibers (mainly those of the corpus callosum) connecting them.

To appreciate these findings, we need to focus for a minute on the peculiar nature of our visual wiring, illustrated in **Figure 1.4-20**. Note that each eye receives sensory information from the entire visual field. But in each eye, information from the left half of your field of vision goes to your right hemisphere, and information from the right half of your visual field goes to your left hemisphere, which usually controls speech. Information received by either hemisphere is quickly transmitted to the other across the corpus callosum. In a person with a severed corpus callosum, this information sharing does not take place.

Knowing these facts, Sperry and Gazzaniga could send information to a patient's left or right hemisphere. As the person stared at a spot, the researchers flashed a stimulus to its right or left. They could do this with you, too, but in your intact brain, the hemisphere receiving the information would instantly pass the news to the other side. Because the split-brain surgery had cut the communication lines between the hemispheres, the researchers could, with these patients, quiz each hemisphere separately.

In an early experiment, Gazzaniga (1967) asked split-brain patients to stare at a dot as he flashed HE•ART on a screen (**Figure 1.4-21**). Thus, HE appeared in their left visual field (which transmits to the right hemisphere) and ART in the right field (which transmits to the left hemisphere). When he then asked them to *say* what they had seen, the patients reported that they had seen ART. But when asked to *point* with

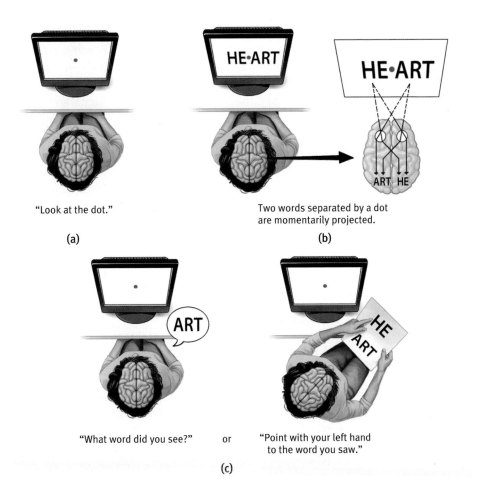

Figure 1.4-21
**One skull, two minds**

When an experimenter flashes HE•ART across the visual field, a woman with a split brain verbally reports seeing the word transmitted to her left hemisphere. However, if asked to indicate with her left hand what she saw, she points to the word transmitted to her right hemisphere (Gazzaniga, 1983).

"Look at the dot."

(a)

Two words separated by a dot are momentarily projected.

(b)

"What word did you see?" or "Point with your left hand to the word you saw."

(c)

their left hand to what they had seen, they were startled when their hand (controlled by the right hemisphere) pointed to HE. Given an opportunity to express itself, each hemisphere indicated what it had seen. The right hemisphere (controlling the left hand) intuitively knew what it could not verbally report.

When a picture of a spoon was flashed to their right hemisphere, the patients could not *say* what they had viewed. But when asked to *identify* what they had viewed by feeling an assortment of hidden objects with their left hand, they readily selected the spoon. If the experimenter said, "Correct!" the patient might reply, "What? Correct? How could I possibly pick out the correct object when I don't know what I saw?" It is, of course, the left hemisphere doing the talking here, bewildered by what the nonverbal right hemisphere knows.

A few people who have undergone split-brain surgery have been for a time bothered by the unruly independence of their left hand. It was as if the left hand truly didn't know what the right hand was doing. The left hand might unbutton a shirt while the right hand buttoned it, or put grocery store items back on the shelf after the right hand put them in the cart. It was as if each hemisphere was thinking, "I've half a mind to wear my green (blue) shirt today." Indeed, said Sperry (1964), split-brain surgery leaves people "with two separate minds." With a split brain, both hemispheres can comprehend and follow an instruction to copy—*simultaneously*—different figures with the left and right hands (Franz et al., 2000; see also **Figure 1.4-22**). Today's researchers

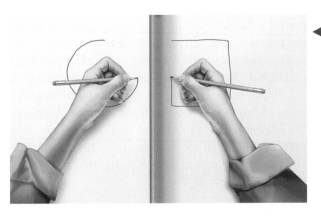

**Figure 1.4-22
Try this!**

People who have had split-brain surgery can simultaneously draw two different shapes.

believe that a split-brain patient's mind resembles a river that has branched into separate streams, each unaware of its influence on the other (Pinto et al., 2017). (Reading these reports, can you imagine a patient enjoying a solitary game of "rock, paper, scissors"—left versus right hand?)

When the "two minds" are at odds, the left hemisphere does mental gymnastics to rationalize reactions it does not understand. If a patient follows an order ("Walk") sent to the right hemisphere, a strange thing happens. The left hemisphere, unaware of the order, doesn't know why the patient begins walking. But if asked, the patient doesn't reply, "I don't know." Instead, the left hemisphere improvises—"I'm going into the house to get a Coke." Gazzaniga (2006), who described these patients as "the most fascinating people on earth," realized that the conscious left hemisphere resembles an "interpreter" that instantly constructs explanations. The brain, he concluded, often runs on autopilot; it acts first and then explains itself.

 **AP® Science Practice**

## Check Your Understanding

### Examine the Concept

▶ Explain what is meant by *split brain*.

▶ Explain the classic split-brain studies.

### Apply the Concept

▶ (a) If we flash a red light to the right hemisphere of a person with a split brain, and flash a green light to the left hemisphere, will each hemisphere observe its own color? (b) Will the person be aware that the colors differ? (c) What will the person verbally report seeing?

▶ Can you put yourself in the shoes of a patient with a split brain? What would it be like to have knowledge which you were unaware of and couldn't verbally report but were nevertheless able to act on?

*Answers to the Examine the Concept questions can be found in Appendix C at the end of the book.*

## Right–Left Differences in the Intact Brain

So, what about the 99.99+ percent of us with undivided brains? Does each of *our* hemispheres also perform distinct functions? The short answer is *Yes*. When a person performs a *perceptual* task, a brain scan often reveals increased activity (brain waves, blood flow, and glucose consumption) in the *right* hemisphere. When the person speaks or does a math calculation, activity usually increases in the *left* hemisphere.

A dramatic demonstration of hemispheric specialization happens before some types of brain surgery. To locate the patient's language centers, the surgeon injects a sedative into the neck artery feeding blood to the left hemisphere, which usually controls speech. Before the injection, the patient is lying down, arms in the air, chatting with the doctor. Can you predict what happens when the drug puts the left hemisphere to sleep? Within seconds, the person's right arm falls limp. If the left hemisphere is controlling language, the patient will be speechless until the drug wears off. If the drug is injected into the artery to the right hemisphere, the *left* arm will fall limp, but the person will still be able to speak.

To the brain, language is language, whether spoken or signed. (See Module 3.5 for more on how and where the brain processes language.) Just as hearing people usually use the left hemisphere to process spoken language, deaf people use the left hemisphere to process sign language (Corina et al., 1992; Hickok et al., 2001). Thus, a left hemisphere stroke disrupts a deaf person's signing, much as it would disrupt a hearing person's speaking (Corina, 1998).

Although the left hemisphere is skilled at making quick, literal interpretations of language, the right hemisphere

- *excels at making inferences* (Beeman & Chiarello, 1998; Bowden & Beeman, 1998; Mason & Just, 2004). When given an insight-like problem—"Which word goes with *boot, summer,* and *ground?*"—the right hemisphere more quickly comes to a reasoned conclusion and recognizes the solution: *camp.* As one patient explained after a right hemisphere stroke, "I understand words, but I'm missing the subtleties."

- *helps us modulate our speech* to make meaning clear—as when we say, "Let's eat, Grandpa!" instead of "Let's eat Grandpa!" (Heller, 1990).

- *helps orchestrate our self-awareness.* People who suffer partial paralysis will sometimes stubbornly deny their impairment—constantly claiming they can move a paralyzed limb—if the damage occurs to the right hemisphere (Berti et al., 2005).

Simply looking at the two hemispheres, so alike to the naked eye, who would suppose they each contribute uniquely to the harmony of the whole? Yet a variety of observations—of people with split brains, of people with healthy brains, and even of other species' brains—converge beautifully, leaving little doubt that we have unified brains with specialized parts (Hopkins & Cantalupo, 2008; MacNeilage et al., 2009).

> **AP® Exam Tip**
>
> Notice that your authors never refer to your left brain or your right brain. You have two brain hemispheres, each with its own responsibilities, but you have only one brain. It's very misleading when the popular press refers to the left brain and the right brain. When studying for the AP® exam, avoid psychology myths.

## Module 1.4c REVIEW

**1.4-8 To what extent can a damaged brain reorganize itself, and what is *neurogenesis*?**

- While brain and spinal cord neurons usually do not regenerate, some neural tissue can *reorganize* in response to damage.

- The damaged brain may demonstrate neuroplasticity, especially in young children, as new pathways are built and functions migrate to other brain regions.

- Reassignment of functions to different areas of the brain may also occur in blindness and deafness, or as a result of damage and disease.

- Some research suggests that the brain may sometimes mend itself by forming new neurons, a process known as *neurogenesis.*

**1.4-9 What do split brains reveal about the functions of our two brain hemispheres?**

- *Split-brain* research (experiments on people with a severed *corpus callosum*) has confirmed that in most people, the left hemisphere is the more verbal. The right hemisphere excels in visual perception and making inferences, and helps us modulate our speech and orchestrate our self-awareness.

- Studies of the intact brain in healthy people confirm that each hemisphere makes unique contributions to the integrated functioning of the whole brain.

## AP® Practice Multiple Choice Questions

**1.** Nan was in a car accident, which resulted in brain damage. However, some of her brain areas took over the function of the damaged area, thanks to the role of

   a. lesioning.

   b. positron emission training.

   c. neuroplasticity.

   d. the split brain.

**2.** Dr. Cantor studies neurogenesis, to understand how

   a. one brain structure takes on the functions of an adjacent structure.

   b. the brain creates new neurons.

   c. association areas expand as new material is learned.

   d. the brain adapts to new learning.

**Use the following text to answer questions 3 and 4:**

A patient who has undergone split-brain surgery has a picture of a dog flashed to his right hemisphere and a cat to his left hemisphere.

3. In this example, the patient will be able to identify the
   a. cat using his right hand.
   b. dog using his right hand.
   c. dog using either hand.
   d. cat using his left hand.

4. In this example, which of the following will the patient be able to verbalize?
   a. That he saw a dog
   b. That he saw a cat
   c. That he saw both a dog and a cat
   d. That he did not see anything at all

5. One of your friends received the following results after she took an online quiz: "You are left-brained! Your left brain is exceptionally strong, which makes you very good with language." Which of the following statements explains nuances associated with this claim?
   a. "People have only one brain, which has left and right hemispheres."
   b. "The left brain controls speech and self-awareness."
   c. "The right brain controls speech."
   d. "The left hemisphere is used for making inferences."

6. Doctors in the 1960s severed a brain region to attempt to stop epileptic seizures. Which of the following was the independent variable in their investigations?
   a. The thalamus
   b. The corpus callosum
   c. The pons
   d. The cerebral cortex

# Module 1.5a Sleep: Consciousness

## LEARNING TARGETS

**1.5-1** Explain the place of *consciousness* in psychology's history.

**1.5-2** Explain the *dual processing* being revealed by today's cognitive neuroscience.

Consciousness is a funny thing. It offers us weird experiences, as when entering sleep or leaving a dream. And sometimes, it leaves us wondering who is really in control. After zoning me [DM] out with nitrous oxide, my dentist tells me to turn my head to the left. My conscious mind resists: "No way," I silently say. "You can't boss me around!" Whereupon my robotic head, ignoring my conscious mind, turns obligingly under the dentist's control.

What do such experiences tell us? And how do our states of consciousness play out in our sleep and dreams?

## Defining Consciousness

**1.5-1** What is the place of *consciousness* in psychology's history?

Every science has concepts so fundamental that they are nearly impossible to define. Biologists agree on what is alive but not on precisely what *life* is. In physics, *matter* and *energy* elude simple definition. To psychologists, *consciousness* is similarly a fundamental yet slippery concept.

At its beginning, *psychology* was "the description and explanation of states of consciousness" (Ladd, 1887). But during the first half of the twentieth century, the difficulty of scientifically studying consciousness led many psychologists—including those in the emerging school of *behaviorism*—to turn to direct observations of behavior. By 1960, psychology had nearly lost consciousness, defining itself as "the science of behavior." Like a car's speedometer, consciousness "just reflects what's happening" (Seligman, 1991, p. 24).

But in the 1960s, psychology began regaining consciousness. Neuroscience advances linked brain activity to sleeping, dreaming, and other mental states. Researchers began studying consciousness altered by drugs, hypnosis, and meditation. Psychologists of all persuasions were affirming the importance of *cognition*, or mental processes. Most psychologists today define **consciousness** as our subjective awareness of ourselves and our environment (Feinberg & Mallatt, 2016).

- Conscious awareness helps us make sense of our life, including our sensations, emotions, and choices (Weisman et al., 2017). It allows us to set and achieve goals as we reflect on our past, adapt to our present, and plan for our future. Most conscious thoughts focus on the present and the future (Baumeister et al., 2020).

- When learning a behavior, conscious awareness focuses our attention (Logan, 2018; Servant et al., 2018). Over time, our mind tends to run on autopilot (Logan, 2018; Rand et al., 2017). When learning to ride a bike, we focus on obstacles that we have to steer around and on how to use the brakes. With practice, riding a bike becomes semi-automatic.

- Over time, we flit between different *states of consciousness,* including normal waking awareness and various altered states (**Figure 1.5-1**).

### AP® Exam Tip

Our modern-day understanding of the unconscious differs from Sigmund Freud's theory of the unconscious (Module 4.5). Freud believed the unconscious was a hiding place for our most anxiety-provoking ideas and emotions, and that uncovering those hidden thoughts could lead to healing. Now, most psychologists simply view the unconscious track as information processing without awareness. Make sure you keep these two ideas of the unconscious straight. Both interpretations could be seen on the AP® exam.

**consciousness** our subjective awareness of ourselves and our environment.

| Some states occur spontaneously | Daydreaming and drowsiness | Flow | Dreaming |
| Some are physio-logically induced | Hallucinations | Orgasm | Food or oxygen starvation |
| Some are psycho-logically induced | Sensory deprivation | Hypnosis | Meditation |

INSADCO Photography/Alamy Stock Photo

**Figure 1.5-1**

**Altered states of consciousness**

In addition to normal, waking awareness, consciousness comes to us in altered states, including daydreaming, sleeping, drug-induced hallucinating, meditating, and hypnosis. (More on meditating in Module 5.1 and hypnosis in Module 5.5.)

**AP® Science Practice**

# Check Your Understanding

**Examine the Concept**

▶ Explain *consciousness*.

**Apply the Concept**

▶ Compare and contrast the different states of consciousness.

▶ What are some examples of things you do on "autopilot"? What behaviors require your conscious attention?

*Answers to the Examine the Concept questions can be found in Appendix C at the end of the book.*

# Cognitive Neuroscience

How does the brain make the mind? Researchers call this the "hard problem": How do brain cells jabbering to one another create our awareness of the taste of toast, the idea of infinity, the feeling of fright? The question of how consciousness arises from the material brain is one of life's deepest mysteries. Such questions lie at the heart of **cognitive neuroscience**—the interdisciplinary study of the brain activity linked with our mental processes.

If you just *think* about kicking a soccer ball, an fMRI scan could detect increased blood flow to the brain region that plans such action. In one study, researchers asked skilled soccer players to imagine they were making either creative moves (complex bicycle kicks) or ordinary moves (simply kicking the ball from foot to foot). Scans showed that thinking about creative moves produced the most coordinated brain activity across different brain regions (Fink et al., 2019).

If brain activity can reveal conscious thinking, could brain scans allow us to discern mental activity in unresponsive patients? *Yes.* A stunning demonstration of consciousness appeared in brain scans of a noncommunicative patient—a 23-year-old woman who had been in a car accident and showed no outward signs of conscious awareness (Owen, 2017a; Owen et al., 2006). When researchers asked her to *imagine* playing tennis, fMRI scans revealed activity in a brain area that normally controls arm and leg movements (**Figure 1.5-2**). Even in a motionless, noncommunicative body, researchers concluded, the brain—and the mind—may still be active. Follow-up studies of brain activity in dozens of unresponsive patients suggest that 15 to 30 percent may be experiencing meaningful conscious awareness (Claassen et al., 2019; Owen, 2017b).

**cognitive neuroscience**
the interdisciplinary study of the brain activity linked with cognition (thinking, knowing, remembering, and communicating).

Many cognitive neuroscientists are exploring and mapping the conscious functions of the cortex. Based on your cortical activation patterns, they can now, in limited ways, read your mind (Bor, 2010). They could, for example, tell which of 10 similar objects (hammer, drill, and so forth) you were viewing (Shinkareva et al., 2008).

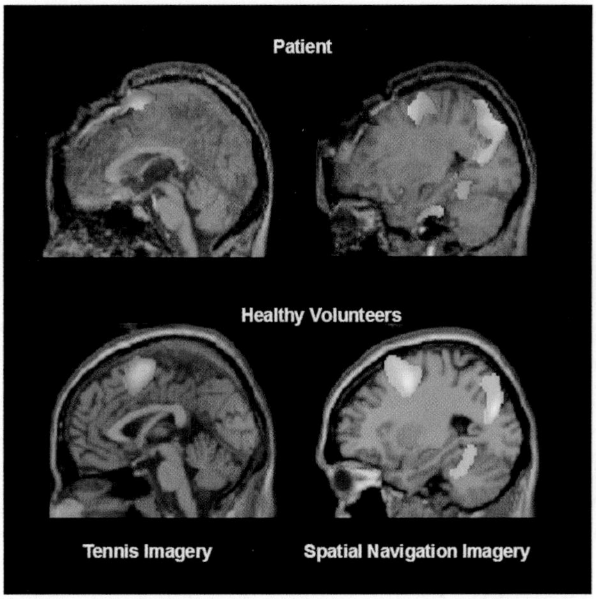

Conscious experience arises from synchronized activity across the brain (Mashour, 2018; Vaz et al., 2019). If a stimulus activates enough brain-wide coordinated neural activity—with strong signals in one brain area triggering activity elsewhere—it crosses a threshold for consciousness. A weaker stimulus—perhaps a word flashed too briefly to be consciously perceived—may trigger localized visual cortex activity that quickly fades. A stronger visual stimulus will engage other brain areas, such as those involved with language, attention, and memory. Such reverberating activity, detected by brain scans, is a telltale sign of conscious awareness (Boly et al., 2011; Silverstein et al., 2015). Coordinated activity across brain areas can therefore provide another indication of awareness in unresponsive patients (Demertzi et al., 2019). How the synchronized activity produces awareness—how matter makes mind—remains a mystery.

**Figure 1.5-2**

**Evidence of awareness**

When a noncommunicative patient was asked to imagine playing tennis or walking, her brain (top) exhibited activity similar to a healthy person's brain (bottom). Such fMRI scans enable a "conversation" with some unresponsive patients, by instructing them, for example, to answer *yes* to a question by imagining playing tennis (top and bottom left), and *no* by imagining walking (top and bottom right).

Courtesy of Adrian M. Owen, the Brain and Mind Institute, Western University

**AP® Science Practice**

**Research**

Neuroscientists could never do a true experiment on unresponsive patients because it would be unethical to randomly assign some participants to be nonresponsive and others to be responsive. That's the value of case studies, a non-experimental approach, in brain research.

**AP® Science Practice** | **Check Your Understanding**

**Examine the Concept**

▶ Explain what a cognitive neuroscientist does.

**Apply the Concept**

▶ Explain how brain scans provide evidence of awareness.

*Answers to the Examine the Concept questions can be found in Appendix C at the end of the book.*

## Dual Processing: The Two-Track Mind

**1.5-2** What is the *dual processing* being revealed by today's cognitive neuroscience?

Discovering which brain regions become active with a particular conscious experience strikes many people as interesting, but not mind blowing. If everything psychological is simultaneously biological, then our ideas, emotions, and spirituality must all, somehow, be embodied. What *is* mind blowing to many of us is evidence that we have, so to speak, two minds, each supported by its own neural equipment.

At any moment, we are aware of little more than what's on the screen of our consciousness. But beneath the surface, unconscious information processing occurs simultaneously on many parallel tracks. When we look at a bird flying, we are consciously aware of the result of our cognitive processing (*It's a hummingbird!*) but not of our subprocessing of the

**AP® Exam Tip**

Dual processing is another one of those big ideas that shows up in several units. Pay attention for the AP® exam!

bird's color, form, movement, and distance. One of the grand ideas of today's cognitive neuroscience is that much of our brain work occurs off stage, out of sight. Thinking, knowing, remembering, and communicating all operate on two independent levels—a conscious, deliberate "high road" and an unconscious, automatic "low road." The high road is reflective, the low road intuitive—together creating what researchers call **dual processing** (Kahneman, 2011; Pennycook et al., 2018). We know more than we know we know.

If you are a driver, consider how you move into the right lane. Drivers know this unconsciously but cannot accurately explain it (Eagleman, 2011). Most say they would bank to the right, then straighten out—a procedure that would actually steer them off the road. In reality, an experienced driver, after moving right, automatically reverses the steering wheel just as far to the left of center, only then returning to center. The lesson: The human brain is a device for converting conscious into unconscious knowledge.

Or consider this story, which illustrates how science can be stranger than science fiction. During my sojourns at Scotland's University of St Andrews, I [DM] came to know cognitive neuroscientists David Milner and Melvyn Goodale (2008). They studied a local woman, D. F., who suffered brain damage when overcome by carbon monoxide, leaving her unable to recognize and discriminate objects visually. Consciously, D. F. could see nothing. Yet she exhibited **blindsight**—she acted *as though* she could see. Asked to slip a postcard into a vertical or horizontal mail slot, she could do so without error. Asked the width of a block in front of her, she was at a loss, but she could grasp it with just the right finger–thumb distance. Likewise, if your right and left eyes view different scenes, you will be consciously aware of only one at a time—yet you will display some blindsight awareness of the other (Baker & Cass, 2013).

**Figure 1.5-3**
**When the blind can "see"**

In this compelling demonstration of blindsight and the two-track mind, researcher Lawrence Weiskrantz trailed a blindsight patient down a cluttered hallway. Although told the hallway was empty, the patient meandered around all the obstacles without any awareness of them.

How could this be? Don't we have one visual system? Goodale and Milner knew from animal research that the eye sends information simultaneously to different brain areas, which support different tasks (Weiskrantz, 2009, 2010). Sure enough, a scan of D. F.'s brain activity revealed normal activity in the area concerned with reaching for, grasping, and navigating objects, but damage in the area concerned with consciously recognizing objects. (See another example in **Figure 1.5-3**.)

How strangely intricate is this thing we call vision, conclude Goodale and Milner in their aptly titled book, *Sight Unseen* (2004). We may think of our vision as a single system that controls our visually guided actions. Actually, it is a dual-processing system (Foley et al., 2015). A *visual perception track* enables us "to think about the world"—to recognize things and to plan future actions. A *visual action track* guides our moment-to-moment movements.

The dual-track mind also appeared in a patient who lost all of his left visual cortex, leaving him blind to objects and faces presented on the right side of his field of vision. He nevertheless could sense the emotion expressed in faces that he did not consciously perceive (de Gelder, 2010). The same is true of normally sighted people whose visual cortex has been disabled with magnetic stimulation. Such findings suggest that brain areas below the cortex process emotion-related information.

Much of our everyday thinking, feeling, and acting operates outside our conscious awareness (Bargh & Chartrand, 1999). Some "80 to 90 percent of what we do is unconscious," says Nobel laureate and memory expert Eric Kandel (2008). Sometimes our unconscious biases (discomfort around someone of a different race or sexual orientation) do not

**dual processing** the principle that information is often simultaneously processed on separate conscious and unconscious tracks.

**blindsight** a condition in which a person can respond to a visual stimulus without consciously experiencing it.

match our conscious beliefs *(I am not prejudiced)* (Greenwald & Lai, 2020). At other times, we're motivated to avoid thinking, especially when careful thought *(How much sugar is in that dessert?)* conflicts with temptations *(I want that piece of cake!)* (Woolley & Risen, 2018). Yet most people, most of the time, mistakenly believe that their intentions and deliberate choices rule their lives. They don't.

Although consciousness enables us to exert voluntary control and to communicate our mental states to others, it is but the tip of the information-processing iceberg. Just ask the volunteers who chose a card after watching a magician shuffle through the deck (Olson et al., 2015). In nearly every case, the magician swayed participants' decisions by subtly allowing one card to show for longer—but 91 percent of participants believed they had made the choice on their own. Being intensely focused on an activity (such as reading about consciousness, we hope) increases your total brain activity no more than 5 percent above its baseline rate. Even when you rest, activity whirls inside your head (Raichle, 2010).

This unconscious parallel processing is faster than conscious sequential processing, but both are essential. **Parallel processing** enables your mind to take care of routine business. **Sequential processing** is best for solving new problems, which requires your focused attention on one thing at a time. Try this: If you are right-handed, move your right foot in a smooth counterclockwise circle and write the number 3 repeatedly with your right hand—at the same time. Try something equally difficult: Tap a steady beat three times with your left hand while tapping four times with your right hand. Both tasks require conscious attention, which can be in only one place at a time. If time is nature's way of keeping everything from happening at once, then consciousness is nature's way of keeping us from thinking and doing everything at once.

> **parallel processing** processing multiple aspects of a stimulus or problem simultaneously.
>
> **sequential processing** processing one aspect of a stimulus or problem at a time; generally used to process new information or to solve difficult problems.

---

### AP® Science Practice

## Check Your Understanding

**Examine the Concept**

▶ What is *dual processing*?

▶ Explain blindsight.

**Apply the Concept**

▶ Explain the concept of the two-track mind.

▶ Compare and contrast parallel and sequential processing.

*Answers to the Examine the Concept questions can be found in Appendix C at the end of the book.*

---

# Module 1.5a REVIEW

**1.5-1** What is the place of *consciousness* in psychology's history?

- After initially claiming consciousness as their area of study in the nineteenth century, psychologists abandoned it in the first half of the twentieth century, turning instead to the study of observable behavior because they believed consciousness was too difficult to study scientifically.

- Since the 1960s, our awareness of ourselves and our environment—our *consciousness*—has reclaimed its place as an important area of research, such as in the interdisciplinary field of *cognitive neuroscience*.

**1.5-2** What is the *dual processing* being revealed by today's cognitive neuroscience?

- Scientists studying the brain mechanisms underlying consciousness and cognition have discovered that the mind processes information on two separate tracks, one operating at a conscious level *(sequential processing)* and the other at an implicit, unconscious level *(parallel processing)*. Parallel processing takes care of routine business, while sequential processing is best for solving new problems that require our attention.

- Together, this *dual processing*—conscious and unconscious—affects our perception, memory, attitudes, and other cognitions.

# AP® Practice Multiple Choice Questions

**1.** As Doreen is reading her Psychology textbook, which statement is she most likely to encounter about consciousness?

a. It was studied only by Sigmund Freud.
b. It has been discredited in favor of studying behaviors.
c. It has been discredited in light of research showing the significant role of the unconscious.
d. It is an important way of studying our two-track minds.

**2.** Which statement should Mason say to his friend to discuss the dual-processing model most accurately?

a. The right and left hemispheres of the brain both process incoming messages.
b. Incoming information is processed by both conscious and unconscious tracks.
c. Each lobe of the brain processes incoming information.
d. The brain first processes emotional information and then processes analytical information.

**3.** In chemistry class, Teresa was aware that she was writing down her teacher's words. Which psychological concept best describes Teresa's experience?

a. Teresa was consciously aware of her experience.
b. Teresa was unconscious during her experience.
c. Teresa was experiencing blindsight during her experience.
d. Teresa was biased during her experience.

**4.** What do hallucinating, dreaming, and meditating have in common?

a. They are all states of sequential processing.
b. They are all states of blindsight.
c. They are all states of consciousness.
d. They are all states of neurogenesis.

**5.** Dr. James collected EEG data on 100 participants as they were daydreaming to determine which brain-wave patterns were present during this activity. Which of the following best depicts the independent variable in this example?

a. The 100 participants
b. Daydreaming, a state of consciousness
c. The EEG data measuring brain-wave patterns
d. The effect of daydreaming on EEG data

# Module 1.5b Sleep: Sleep Stages and Theories

## LEARNING TARGETS

**1.5-3** Explain *sleep* as a state of consciousness.

**1.5-4** Explain how our biological rhythms influence our daily functioning.

**1.5-5** Explain the biological rhythm of our sleeping and dreaming stages.

**1.5-6** Explain how biology and environment interact in our sleep patterns.

**1.5-7** Explain sleep's functions.

### 1.5-3 What is *sleep?*

We humans have about a 16-hour battery life before we lie down on our comfy wireless charging pad and slip into **sleep**. While sleeping, we may feel "dead to the world," but we are not. Although the roar of my [ND's] neighborhood garbage truck leaves me undisturbed, my child's cry will shatter my sleep. Even when you are deeply asleep, your perceptual window is open a crack. You move around on your bed, but you manage not to fall out. You maintain a sense of time, perhaps even awakening when you wish without an alarm. And when you sleep, as when awake, you process most information outside your conscious awareness.

By recording the brain waves and muscle movements of sleeping participants, and by observing and occasionally waking them, researchers are solving some of sleep's deepest mysteries. Perhaps you can anticipate some of their discoveries. Are the following statements true or false?

1. When people dream of performing some activity, their limbs often move in concert with the dream.

2. Older adults sleep more than young adults.

3. Sleepwalkers are acting out their dreams.

4. Sleep experts recommend treating insomnia with an occasional sleeping pill.

5. Some people dream every night; others seldom dream.

All these statements (adapted from Palladino & Carducci, 1983) are *false*. To see why, read on.

Angel Boligan/Cagle Cartoons

**sleep** a periodic, natural loss of consciousness—as distinct from unconsciousness resulting from a coma, general anesthesia, or hibernation. (Adapted from Dement, 1999.)

## Research

These studies on circadian rhythms were correlational: Researchers measured whether participants were larks or owls, and then measured variables such as creativity and punctuality. As a result, they can't conclude that being a lark or an owl *causes* the reported differences. Drawing causal inferences would require random assignment.

**circadian** [ser-KAY-dee-an] **rhythm** our biological clock; regular bodily rhythms (for example, of temperature and wakefulness) that occur on a 24-hour cycle.

**REM sleep** rapid eye movement sleep; a recurring sleep stage during which vivid dreams commonly occur. Also known as *paradoxical sleep,* because the muscles are relaxed (except for minor twitches) but other body systems are active. (Sometimes called *R sleep.*)

# Biological Rhythms and Sleep

Like the ocean, life has its rhythmic tides. Over varying time periods, our bodies fluctuate, and with them, our minds. Let's look more closely at two of those biological rhythms—our 24-hour biological clock and our 90-minute sleep cycle.

## Circadian Rhythm

**1.5-4** How do our biological rhythms influence our daily functioning?

The rhythm of the day parallels the rhythm of life—from our waking at a new day's birth to our nightly return to what Shakespeare called "death's counterfeit." Our bodies roughly synchronize with the 24-hour cycle of day and night thanks to an internal biological clock called the **circadian rhythm** (from the Latin *circa,* "about," and *diem,* "day"). As morning nears, body temperature rises; it then peaks during the day, dips for a time in the early afternoon (when many people take siestas), and begins to drop again in the evening. Thinking is sharpest and memory most accurate as we approach our daily peak in circadian arousal. Have you ever pulled an all-nighter? You might remember feeling groggiest in the middle of the night, but gaining a sense of new alertness with the arrival of your normal wake-up time.

Age and experience can alter our circadian rhythm. Most 20-year-olds are evening-energized "owls," with performance improving across the day (May & Hasher, 1998). Most older adults experience more fragile sleep and are morning-loving "larks." For our ancestors (and for today's hunter-gatherers), a grandparent who awakened easily and early helped protect the family from predators (Samson et al., 2017). By mid-evening, when the night has hardly begun for many young adults, retirement homes are typically quiet. After about age 20 (slightly earlier for women), we gradually shift from being owls to being larks (Roenneberg et al., 2004). Night owls tend to be smart and creative (Giampietro & Cavallera, 2007). Morning types tend to do better in school, take more initiative, be more punctual, and be less vulnerable to depression (Preckel et al., 2013; Randler, 2008, 2009; Werner et al., 2015).

## Sleep Stages

**1.5-5** What is the biological rhythm of our sleeping and dreaming stages?

Seeking sleep, we crawl into bed and fake it until we make it. Eventually, sleep overtakes us, and consciousness fades as different parts of our brain's cortex stop communicating (Massimini et al., 2005). Sleep may feel like time-traveling a few hours into the future. Yet the sleeping brain remains active and has its own biological rhythm.

About every 90 minutes, you cycle through distinct sleep stages. This fact came to light when 8-year-old Armond Aserinsky went to bed one night in 1952. His father, Eugene, a University of Chicago graduate student, needed to test an electroencephalograph he had repaired that day (Aserinsky, 1988; Seligman & Yellen, 1987). Placing electrodes near Armond's eyes to record the rolling eye movements then believed to occur during sleep, Aserinsky watched the machine go wild, tracing deep zigzags on the graph paper. Could the machine still be broken? As the night proceeded and the activity recurred, Aserinsky realized that the periods of fast, jerky eye movements were accompanied by energetic brain activity. Awakened during one such episode, Armond reported having a dream, Aserinsky recalled 65 years later, of "a chicken walking through a barnyard" (Nichols, 2018). Aserinsky had discovered what we now know as **REM sleep** (rapid *e*ye *m*ovement sleep; sometimes called *R sleep*).

Similar procedures used with thousands of volunteers showed the cycles were a normal part of sleep (Kleitman, 1960). To appreciate these studies, imagine yourself as a participant. As the hour grows late, you feel sleepy and yawn in response to reduced brain metabolism. (Yawning, which is also socially contagious, stretches your neck muscles and increases your heart rate, which increases your alertness [Moorcroft, 2003].) When you are ready for bed, a researcher comes in and tapes electrodes to your scalp (to detect your brain waves), on your chin (to detect muscle tension), and just outside the corners of your eyes (to detect eye movements) (**Figure 1.5-4**). Other devices may record your heart rate, respiration rate, and genital arousal.

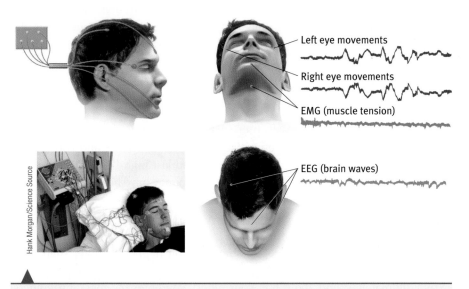

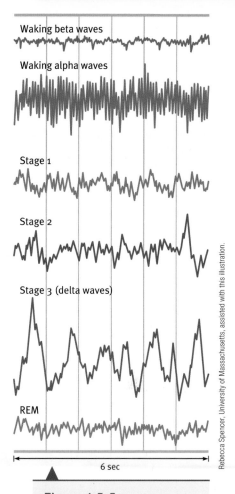

### Figure 1.5-4
#### Measuring sleep activity

Sleep researchers measure brain-wave activity, eye movements, and muscle tension with electrodes that pick up weak electrical signals from the brain, eyes, and facial muscles (Dement, 1978).

When you are in bed with your eyes closed, the researcher in the next room sees on the EEG the relatively slow **alpha waves** of your awake but relaxed state (**Figure 1.5-5**). As time wears on, you adapt to all this equipment, grow tired and, in an unremembered moment, slip into sleep (**Figure 1.5-6**). This transition is marked by the slowed breathing and the irregular brain waves of *Stage 1* sleep. (Sleep stages 1, 2, and 3 are now called N1, N2, and N3—indicating that they occur during **NREM** sleep.)

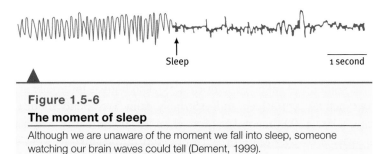

### Figure 1.5-6
#### The moment of sleep

Although we are unaware of the moment we fall into sleep, someone watching our brain waves could tell (Dement, 1999).

In one of his 15,000 research participants, William Dement (1999) observed the moment the brain's perceptual window to the outside world slammed shut. Dement asked this sleep-deprived young man with eyelids taped open to press a button every time a strobe light flashed in his eyes (about every 6 seconds). After a few minutes, the young man missed one. Asked why, he said, "Because there was no flash." But there was a flash. He had missed it because (as his brain activity revealed) he had fallen asleep for 2 seconds, missing not only the flash 6 inches from his nose but also the awareness of the abrupt moment of entry into sleep.

### Figure 1.5-5
#### Brain waves and sleep stages

The beta waves of an alert, waking state and the regular alpha waves of an awake, relaxed state differ from the slower, larger delta waves of deep Stage 3 sleep. Although the rapid REM sleep waves resemble the near-waking Stage 1 sleep waves, the body is more internally aroused during REM sleep than during NREM sleep (Stages 1, 2, and 3).

**alpha waves** the relatively slow brain waves of a relaxed, awake state.

**NREM sleep** non-rapid eye movement sleep; encompasses all sleep stages except for REM sleep.

During this brief Stage 1 sleep, you may experience fantastic images resembling **hallucinations**—sensory experiences that occur without a sensory stimulus. You may have a sensation of falling (when your body may suddenly jerk) or of floating weightlessly. These **hypnagogic sensations** (also called *hypnic sensations*) may later be incorporated into your memories. People who claim aliens abducted them—often shortly after getting into bed—commonly recall being floated off (or pinned down on) their beds (Clancy, 2005; McNally, 2012). To catch your own hypnagogic experiences, you might use your alarm's snooze function.

You then relax more deeply and begin about 20 minutes of *Stage 2* sleep, with its periodic *sleep spindles*—bursts of rapid, rhythmic brain-wave activity that aid memory processing (Studte et al., 2017). Although you could still be awakened without too much difficulty, you are now clearly asleep.

Then you transition to the deep sleep of *Stage 3*. During this slow-wave sleep, which lasts for about 30 minutes, your brain emits large, slow **delta waves** and you are hard to awaken. Have you ever said, "That thunder was so loud last night!" only to have a friend respond, "What thunder?" Those who missed the storm may have been in delta sleep. (It is at the end of this stage that children may wet the bed.)

## REM Sleep

About an hour after you first fall asleep, a strange thing happens. Rather than continuing in deep slumber, you ascend from your initial sleep dive. Returning through Stage 2 (where you'll ultimately spend about half your night), you enter the most intriguing sleep phase—REM (R) sleep. For about 10 minutes, your brain waves become rapid and sawtoothed, more like those of the nearly awake Stage 1 sleep. But unlike in Stage 1, during REM sleep your heart rate rises, your breathing becomes rapid and irregular, and every half-minute or so your eyes dart around in momentary bursts of activity behind closed lids. These eye movements announce the beginning of a dream—often emotional, usually story-like, and richly hallucinatory. Dreams aren't real, but REM sleep tricks your brain into responding as if they were (Andrillon et al., 2015). Because anyone watching a sleeper's eyes can notice these REM bursts, it is amazing that science was ignorant of REM sleep until 1952.

Except during very scary dreams, your genitals become aroused during REM sleep. You may have an erection or increased vaginal lubrication, regardless of whether the dream's content is sexual (Karacan et al., 1966). Men's common "morning erection" stems from the night's last REM period, often just before waking.

During REM sleep, your brain's motor cortex is active, but your brainstem blocks its messages. This leaves your muscles relaxed—so much so that except for an occasional finger, toe, or facial twitch, you are essentially paralyzed. (This immobility may occasionally linger as you awaken from REM sleep, producing the disturbing experience of *sleep paralysis* [Santomauro & French, 2009].) Moreover, you cannot easily be awakened. REM sleep is thus sometimes called *paradoxical sleep:* The body is internally aroused, with waking-like brain activity, yet asleep and externally calm. We spend about 600 hours a year experiencing some 1500 dreams, or more than 100,000 dreams over a typical lifetime—dreams swallowed by the night but not acted out, thanks to REM's protective paralysis.

The sleep cycle repeats itself about every 90 minutes for younger adults (with shorter, more frequent cycles for older adults). As the night wears on, deep Stage 3 sleep grows shorter and disappears. The REM and Stage 2 sleep periods get longer (**Figure 1.5-7**). By morning, we have spent 20 to 25 percent of an average night's sleep—some 100 minutes—in REM sleep. In sleep lab studies, 37 percent of participants have reported rarely or never having dreams that they "can remember the next morning" (Moore, 2004). Yet even they, more than 80 percent of the time, could recall a dream after being awakened

**hallucinations** false sensory experiences, such as seeing something in the absence of an external visual stimulus.

**hypnagogic sensations** bizarre experiences, such as jerking or a feeling of falling or floating weightlessly, while transitioning to sleep. (Also called *hypnic sensations*.)

**delta waves** the large, slow brain waves associated with deep sleep.

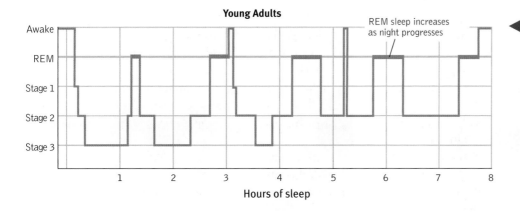

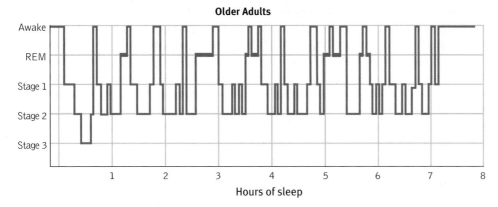

► **Figure 1.5-7**

**The stages in a typical night's sleep**

People pass through a multistage sleep cycle several times each night. As the night goes on, periods of deep sleep diminish and, for younger adults, REM sleep increases. As people age, sleep becomes more fragile, with awakenings being more common among older adults (Kamel & Gammack, 2006; Neubauer, 1999).

**AP® Exam Tip**

Study this cycle of sleep carefully. One common mistake that students make is to believe that REM sleep comes directly after deep Stage 3 sleep. As you can see, it does not. Generally, Stage 2 follows Stage 3; then comes REM. This clarification will help for the AP® exam.

during REM sleep. Neuroscientists have also identified brain regions that are active during dreaming, which enables them to detect when dreaming occurs (Siclari et al., 2017).

## What Affects Our Sleep Patterns?

**1.5-6** How do biology and environment interact in our sleep patterns?

True or false? "Everyone needs 8 hours of sleep." *False.* Newborns often sleep two-thirds of their day, most adults no more than one-third (with some thriving on fewer than 6 hours nightly, while others slumber 9 or more hours). But there is more to our sleep differences than age. Some people are awake between nightly sleep periods—sometimes called "first sleep" and "second sleep" (Randall, 2012). And some find that a 15-minute midday nap is as effective as another hour of nighttime sleep (Horne, 2011).

Sleep patterns are genetically influenced (Hayashi et al., 2015; Mackenzie et al., 2015). One analysis of 1.3 million people identified 956 genes related to sleep patterns such as *insomnia* (Jansen et al., 2019). Another identified genes associated with being a morning person (Jones et al., 2019).

Sleep patterns are also culturally, socially, and economically influenced. In Britain, Canada, Germany, Japan, and the United States, adults average 7 hours of sleep on workdays and 7 to 8 hours on other days (NSF, 2013). Earlier school start times, more extracurricular activities, and fewer parent-set bedtimes lead American adolescents to get less sleep than their Australian counterparts (Short et al., 2013). Stress, including the experience of discrimination or poverty, can also disturb sleep (Johnson et al., 2018; Mai et al., 2019; Vancampfort et al., 2018; Yip et al., 2020).

 **AP® Science Practice**

**Research**

Having a huge sample size, such as 1.3 million people, allows researchers to easily generalize their findings to the intended population—in this case, all people.

**CULTURAL AWARENESS**

While the function and purpose of sleep (which we will discuss later in this unit) transcend culture, you can see here that our beliefs and values about sleep are heavily influenced by our culture.

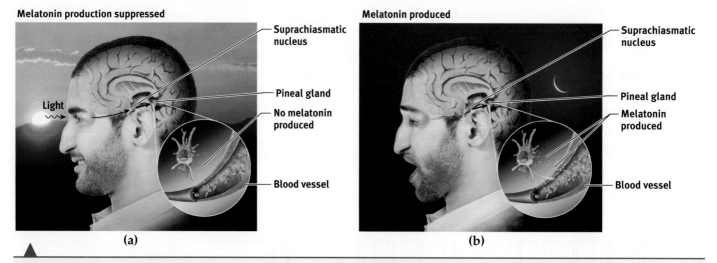

**Melatonin production suppressed**

- Suprachiasmatic nucleus
- Pineal gland
- No melatonin produced
- Blood vessel

Light

**(a)**

**Melatonin produced**

- Suprachiasmatic nucleus
- Pineal gland
- Melatonin produced
- Blood vessel

**(b)**

**Figure 1.5-8**

**The biological clock**

(a) Light striking the retina signals the suprachiasmatic nucleus (SCN) to suppress the pineal gland's production of the sleep hormone melatonin.
(b) At night, the SCN quiets down, allowing the pineal gland to release melatonin into the bloodstream.

With sleep, as with waking behavior, biology and environment interact. Thanks to modern lighting, shift work, and social media diversions, many people who might have gone to bed at 9:00 P.M. in days past are now up until 11:00 P.M. or later. Whether for work or play, bright light affects our sleepiness by activating light-sensitive retinal proteins. This signals the brain's **suprachiasmatic nucleus (SCN)** to decrease production of *melatonin*, a sleep-inducing hormone found in the hypothalamus (Chang et al., 2015; Gandhi et al., 2015) (**Figure 1.5-8**). (A 2017 Nobel Prize was awarded for research on the molecular biology that runs our biological clock.)

Being bathed in (or deprived of) light disrupts our 24-hour biological clock (Czeisler et al., 1999; Dement, 1999). Imposed stay-at-home orders during the Covid pandemic led people in many countries to experience lower-than-normal levels of light (María et al., 2020). Night-shift workers may experience a chronic state of *desynchronization*. As a result, they become more likely to develop fatigue, stomach problems, heart disease, and, for women, breast cancer (Knutsson & Bøggild, 2010; Lin et al., 2015; Puttonen et al., 2009).

Our ancestors' body clocks were attuned to the rising and setting Sun of the 24-hour day, leading them to get more sleep during the dark winter months and less during the sunny summer months (van Egmond et al., 2019). Today's young adults adopt something closer to a 25-hour day, by staying up too late to get 8 hours of sleep. Approximately 90 percent of Americans report using a light-emitting electronic device one hour before going to sleep (Chang et al., 2015). Such artificial light delays sleep and affects sleep quality. This phenomenon was seen in first-year college students who stayed up late for entertainment viewing, which interfered with the onset, quality, and duration of their sleep (Exelmans & Van den Bulck, 2018). Streaming disrupts dreaming.

Sleep often eludes those who stay up late and sleep in on weekends, then go to bed earlier on Sunday to prepare for the new school week (Oren & Terman, 1998). Like New Yorkers readjusting after a trip to California, they experience a kind of jet lag. For North Americans who fly to Europe and need to be up when their circadian rhythm cries "*SLEEP*," bright light (spending the next day outdoors) helps reset the biological clock (Czeisler et al., 1986, 1989; Eastman et al., 1995).

**suprachiasmatic nucleus (SCN)** a pair of cell clusters in the hypothalamus that controls circadian rhythm. In response to light, the SCN adjusts melatonin production, thus modifying our feelings of sleepiness.

## Check Your Understanding

**Examine the Concept**

▶ Explain the differences among the stages of sleep.

▶ Explain the role of the suprachiasmatic nucleus in sleep.

▶ Explain how REM sleep relates to dreaming.

*Answers to the Examine the Concept questions can be found in Appendix C at the end of the book.*

**Apply the Concept**

▶ Would you consider yourself a night owl or a morning lark? Explain how this relates to your circadian rhythm.

# Why Do We Sleep?

**1.5-7** What are sleep's functions?

As we've just seen, our sleep patterns differ from person to person and from culture to culture. But why do we have this need for sleep? Psychologists offer six possible reasons:

1. ***Sleep protects.*** When darkness shut down the day's hunting, gathering, and travel, our distant ancestors were better off asleep in a cave, out of harm's way. Those who didn't wander around dark cliffs were more likely to leave descendants. This fits a broader principle: A species' sleep pattern tends to suit its ecological niche (Siegel, 2009). Animals with the greatest need to graze and the least ability to hide tend to sleep less. Animals also sleep less, with no ill effects, during times of mating and migration (Siegel, 2012). (For a sampling of animal sleep times, see **Figure 1.5-9**.)

| | | | | | | |
|---|---|---|---|---|---|---|
| **20 hours** | **16 hours** | **12 hours** | **10 hours** | **8 hours** | **4 hours** | **2 hours** |

2. ***Sleep restores.*** Sleep gives your body and brain the chance to repair, rewire, and reorganize. It helps the body heal from infection and restores the immune system (Dimitrov et al., 2019). Sleep gives resting neurons time to repair themselves, while pruning or weakening unused connections (Ascády & Harris, 2017; Ding et al., 2016; Li et al., 2017). Bats and other animals with high waking metabolism burn a lot of calories, producing *free radicals,* molecules that are toxic to neurons. Sleep sweeps away this toxic waste, along with protein fragments that for humans can cause Alzheimer's disease (Beil, 2018; Xie et al., 2013). Imagine that when consciousness leaves your house, cleaners come in and say, "Good night. Sleep tidy."

3. ***Sleep aids memory consolidation.*** Sleep helps restore and rebuild our fading memories of the day's experiences. Our memories are *consolidated* during slow-wave deep sleep, by replaying recent learning and strengthening neural connections (Paller & Oudiette, 2018; Todorva & Zugaro, 2019). Sleep reactivates recent experiences stored in the hippocampus and moves them to permanent storage elsewhere in the cortex (Racsmány et al., 2010; Urbain et al., 2016). In consequence, adults and children trained to perform tasks recall them better after a night's sleep, or even after a short nap, than after several hours awake (He et al., 2020; Seehagen et al., 2015). Older adults' more frequently disrupted sleep also disrupts their memory consolidation (Boyce et al., 2016; Pace-Schott & Spencer, 2011).

**Figure 1.5-9**

**Animal sleep time**

Would you rather be a brown bat that sleeps 20 hours a day or a giraffe that sleeps 2 hours a day? (Data from National Institutes of Health [NIH], 2010.)

**4. Sleep feeds creative thinking.** Dreams can inspire noteworthy artistic and scientific achievements, such as the dreams that inspired novelist Stephanie Meyer to write the first book in the *Twilight* series (CNN, 2009) and medical researcher Carl Alving (2011) to invent the vaccine patch. More commonplace is the boost that a complete night's sleep gives to our thinking and learning. After working on a task, then sleeping on it, people solve difficult problems more insightfully than do those who stay awake (Barrett, 2011; Sio et al., 2013). They also are better at spotting connections among novel pieces of information (Ellenbogen et al., 2007; Whitehurst et al., 2016). To think smart and see connections, it often pays to ponder a problem just before bed and then sleep on it.

**5. Sleep supports growth.** During slow-wave sleep, the pituitary gland releases human growth hormone, which is necessary for muscle development.

**6. Sleep conserves energy.** By making us inactive during the night, when food gathering and other activity would be inefficient, sleep preserves our energy for waking times.

A regular full night's sleep can also "*dramatically* improve your athletic ability," report James Maas and Rebecca Robbins (2010). REM sleep and Stage 2 sleep—which occur mostly in the final hours of a long night's sleep—help strengthen the neural connections that build enduring memories, including the "muscle memories" learned while practicing tennis or shooting baskets. Sleep scientist Cheri Mah and her colleagues (2011) advise athletes on how to build sleep into their training. Mah helped transform professional basketball player Andre Igoudala from an afternoon-napping, late-night videogamer into someone with healthy sleep habits (Gonzalez, 2018). The result? Igoudala played more minutes, shot more effectively, and received the 2015 National Basketball Association Finals Most Valuable Player award. Given all the benefits of sleep, it's no wonder that sleep loss hits us so hard.

**Ample sleep supports skill learning and high performance** Figure skater Sarah Hughes was advised to cut her early-morning practices as part of a recommended sleep regimen. This led to improved performances, better scores, and finally a 2002 Olympic gold medal.

---

### AP® Science Practice

## Check Your Understanding

**Examine the Concept**

▶ Explain how sleep aids in memory consolidation.

**Apply the Concept**

▶ Compare and contrast the proposed functions of sleep.

▶ Have you ever experienced enhanced creativity or problem-solving abilities after getting a good night's sleep? Explain.

*Answers to the Examine the Concept questions can be found in Appendix C at the end of the book.*

---

## Module 1.5b REVIEW

### 1.5-3 What is *sleep?*

● *Sleep* is the periodic, natural loss of normal consciousness—as distinct from unconsciousness resulting from a coma, general anesthesia, or hibernation.

### 1.5-4 How do our biological rhythms influence our daily functioning?

● Our bodies have an internal biological clock, which is roughly synchronized with the 24-hour cycle of night and day.

● This *circadian rhythm* appears in our daily patterns of body temperature, arousal, sleeping, and waking. Age and experiences can alter these patterns, resetting our biological clock.

### 1.5-5 What is the biological rhythm of our sleeping and dreaming stages?

● Younger adults cycle through four distinct sleep stages about every 90 minutes (the sleep cycle repeats more frequently for older adults):

- Leaving the *alpha waves* of the awake, relaxed stage, we descend into the irregular brain waves of Stage 1 sleep, the first non-REM (NREM) sleep stage, which is often associated with *hallucinations*.
- Stage 2 sleep (in which we spend about half our sleep time) follows, with its characteristic sleep spindles.
- We then enter Stage 3 sleep, lasting about 30 minutes, with large, slow *delta waves*.
- About an hour after falling asleep, we ascend from our initial sleep dive and begin periods of *REM* (rapid eye movement or *R*) *sleep*. REM sleep, which includes most dreaming, is described as a paradoxical sleep stage because it features internal arousal but external calm (near paralysis).

- During a normal night's sleep, Stage 3 sleep shortens and REM and Stage 2 sleep lengthens.

### 1.5-6 How do biology and environment interact in our sleep patterns?

- Biology—our circadian rhythm as well as our age and our body's production of melatonin (influenced by the brain's *suprachiasmatic nucleus*)—interacts with social, cultural, and economic influences and individual behaviors to determine our sleeping and waking patterns.

- Being bathed in (or deprived of) light disrupts our 24-hour biological clock. People who are chronically deprived of natural sunlight, such as night-shift workers, may experience desynchronization.
- Artificial light, including that from light-emitting electronic devices, delays sleep and affects sleep quality.

### 1.5-7 What are sleep's functions?

- Sleep may have played a protective role in human evolution by keeping people safe during potentially dangerous periods.
- Sleep helps restore the immune system and repair damaged neurons.
- Sleep consolidates our memories by replaying recent learning and strengthening neural connections.
- Sleep promotes creative problem solving the next day.
- During slow-wave sleep, the pituitary gland secretes human growth hormone, which is necessary for muscle development.
- Sleep conserves energy, helping us preserve it for when we need it most.

## AP® Practice Multiple Choice Questions

1. Which of the following psychological concepts refers to a student's biological clock's sleep–wake pattern that follows a 24-hour cycle?

   a. Melatonin
   b. Circadian rhythm
   c. Suprachiasmatic nucleus
   d. Rapid eye movement sleep

**Use the following text to answer questions 2–5:**

Dr. Liza conducted a sleep study in which half of the volunteers were randomly assigned to scroll through their friends' photos on social media right before bedtime. The other half of the volunteers were told to avoid screens at bedtime. Dr. Liza measured the length of time it took for the volunteers to fall asleep once they got into their beds.

2. Which brain area is the likely focus of Dr. Liza's research?

   a. Hippocampus
   b. Cerebellum
   c. Suprachiasmatic nucleus
   d. Motor cortex

3. Which body chemical is most implicated in Dr. Liza's research?

   a. Dopamine
   b. Melatonin
   c. Norepinephrine
   d. Epinephrine

4. If Dr. Liza finds that the group who scrolled through their friends' photos on social media took longer to fall asleep than the other group, what conclusion can she draw?

   a. Scrolling through friends' photos on social media caused the volunteers to take longer to fall asleep.
   b. There is a positive correlation between scrolling through friends' photos on social media and the length of time it took the volunteers to fall asleep.
   c. The effect of social media usage prior to bedtime can be applied to the general population.
   d. Dr. Liza cannot draw any conclusions about this research given its qualitative nature.

**5.** Based on Dr. Liza's study, a journalist writes a magazine article claiming that everyone should avoid scrolling through friends' photos on social media prior to bedtime, because it will then take them longer to fall asleep. Which of the following describes the journalist's error?

a. The journalist cannot generalize these research findings to the general population, because Dr. Liza did not use random assignment.

b. The journalist cannot generalize these research findings to the general population, because Dr. Liza did not use random selection.

c. The journalist cannot infer causality from Dr. Liza's study, as it was a nonexperimental design.

d. Providing general advice based on the results of one study is unethical.

**6.** Dr. Hedge replicated past EEG research by showing that alpha waves were present

a. when people are in REM sleep.

b. when people are in Stage 2 sleep.

c. when people are in Stage 3 sleep.

d. when people are awake.

# Module 1.5c Sleep: Sleep Loss, Sleep Disorders, and Dreams

## LEARNING TARGETS

**1.5-8** Explain the effects of sleep loss.

**1.5-9** Explain the major sleep disorders.

**1.5-10** Describe the most common content of dreams, and explain the functions theorists have proposed for dreams.

## Sleep Deprivation

**1.5-8** How does sleep loss affect us?

When our body yearns for sleep but does not get it, we begin to feel terrible. Trying to stay awake, we will eventually lose. In the tiredness battle, sleep always wins. In 1989, Michael Doucette was named America's Safest Driving Teen. In 1990, while driving home from college, he fell asleep at the wheel and collided with an oncoming car, killing both himself and the other driver. Michael's driving instructor later acknowledged never having mentioned sleep deprivation and drowsy driving (Dement, 1999).

### Effects of Sleep Loss

Modern sleep patterns—the "Great Sleep Recession"—leave us not only sleepy but also drained of energy and our sense of well-being (Keyes et al., 2015; Thorarinsdottir et al., 2019). After several nights in which we obtain only 5 hours of sleep, we accumulate a sleep debt that cannot be satisfied by one long sleep. "The brain keeps an accurate count of sleep debt for at least two weeks," reported sleep researcher William Dement (1999, p. 64).

Obviously, then, we need sleep. Sleep commands roughly one-third of our lives—some 25 years, on average. Allowed to sleep unhindered, most adults paying off a sleep debt will sleep at least 9 hours a night (Coren, 1996). One study demonstrated the benefits of unrestricted sleep by having volunteers spend 14 hours daily in bed for at least a week. For the first few days, the volunteers averaged 12 hours of sleep or more per day, apparently paying off a sleep debt that averaged 25 to 30 hours. That accomplished, they then settled back to 7.5 to 9 hours nightly and felt energized and happier (Dement, 1999).

Seventy-five percent of U.S. high school students report getting fewer than 8 hours of sleep nightly, with 28 percent admitting they fall asleep in class at least once a week (CDC, 2019b; NSF, 2006). College and university students are also sleep deprived; 69 percent in one U.S. survey reported "feeling tired" or "having little energy" on at least several days during the previous two weeks (Associated Press [AP], 2009). One in four Chinese university students has serious sleep problems (Li et al., 2018). The going needn't get boring before students start snoring.

### AP® Science Practice

#### Research

The results from the CDC and NSF studies discussed here represent non-experimental, descriptive methods, which simply describe behaviors. The researchers likely used surveys to obtain data on the students' self-reported sleep behaviors.

I WOKE UP IN THE MIDDLE OF THE NIGHT AND QUICKLY CHECKED INSTAGRAM, TWITTER, FACEBOOK, GMAIL, MY WEATHER APP, AND MY TEXTS, AND NOW I'M A TAD TOO STIMULATED TO CLOSE MY EYES AGAIN.

Phil McAndrew/The Cartoonbank/The New Yorker

Sleep loss affects our mood. Tiredness triggers testiness—more anger and conflicts (Keller et al., 2019; Krizan & Hisler, 2019). Sleep loss also predicts depressive disorders (Palagini et al., 2019). In two large studies, adolescents who slept 5 or fewer hours nightly had 70 percent and 80 percent higher risks of depression and suicidal thinking, respectively, than peers who slept 8 hours or more (Gangwisch et al., 2010; Whitmore et al., 2018). Among a half million people from China, those who slept 5 or fewer hours a night had a more than doubled rate of depression (Sun et al., 2018). This correlation appears to be one-way: When children and youth are followed through time, sleep loss predicts depression, rather than vice versa (Gregory et al., 2009). (To assess whether you are one of the many sleep-deprived students, see **Table 1.5-1**.)

REM sleep's processing of emotional experiences helps protect against depression (Walker & van der Helm, 2009). This may help to explain why parentally enforced bedtimes predict less depression. Later secondary school start times consistently produce more sleep, better and more on-time attendance, improved alertness, and fewer car accidents among students (Bowers & Moyer, 2017; Foss et al., 2019; Morgenthaler et al., 2016). Thus, the American Academy of Pediatrics (2014) advocates delaying adolescents' school start times to "allow students the opportunity to achieve optimal levels of sleep (8.5–9.5 hours)." As psychologist Roxanne Prichard notes, "Nothing gets worse with better sleep, and a lot of things get better" (Brody, 2018).

When one psychology professor challenged students to sleep at least 8 hours each night during final exams week, those who completed the challenge earned higher final exam grades (Scullin, 2019). *The bottom line:* Sleep better to perform better.

Lack of sleep can also make you gain weight. Sleep deprivation messes with our hormones, our metabolism, and our brain's responses to food by

- increasing *ghrelin*, a hunger-arousing hormone, and decreasing its hunger-suppressing partner, *leptin* (Shilsky et al., 2012).

- increasing *cortisol*, a stress hormone that stimulates the body to make fat, and decreasing metabolic rate (Potter et al., 2017; Schmid et al., 2015).

- disrupting gene expression, which increases risk for heart disease and other negative health outcomes (Möller-Levet et al., 2013; Mure et al., 2018).

**TABLE 1.5-1**

Cornell University psychologist James Maas reported that most students suffer the consequences of sleeping less than they should. To see if you are in that group, answer the following true-false questions:

| True | False | |
|------|-------|---|
| | | 1. I need an alarm to wake up at the appropriate time. |
| | | 2. It's a struggle for me to get out of bed in the morning. |
| | | 3. On weekday mornings, I hit the snooze button several times to get more sleep. |
| | | 4. I feel tired, irritable, and stressed out during the week. |
| | | 5. I have trouble concentrating and remembering. |
| | | 6. I feel slow with critical thinking, problem solving, and being creative. |
| | | 7. I often fall asleep watching TV. |
| | | 8. I often fall asleep in boring meetings or lectures or in warm rooms. |
| | | 9. I often fall asleep after heavy meals. |
| | | 10. I often fall asleep while relaxing after dinner. |
| | | 11. I often fall asleep within five minutes of getting into bed. |
| | | 12. I often feel drowsy while driving. |
| | | 13. I often sleep extra hours on weekend mornings. |
| | | 14. I often need a nap to get through the day. |
| | | 15. I have dark circles around my eyes. |

If you answered "true" to three or more items, you probably are not getting enough sleep. To determine your sleep needs, Maas recommends that you "go to bed 15 minutes earlier than usual every night for the next week — and continue this practice by adding 15 more minutes each week — until you wake without an alarm and feel alert all day." [Sleep Quiz reprinted with permission from James B. Maas. (2013). *Sleep to win!* AuthorHouse.]

- enhancing limbic brain responses to the mere sight of food and decreasing cortical responses that help us resist temptation (Benedict et al., 2012; Greer et al., 2013; St-Onge et al., 2012).

Thus, children and adults who sleep less are heavier than average, and in recent decades people have been sleeping less and weighing more (Hall et al., 2018; Miller et al., 2018). Moreover, experimental sleep deprivation increases appetite and consumption of junk foods; our tired brain finds fatty foods more enticing (Fang et al., 2015; Rihm, 2019). So, sleep loss helps explain the weight gain common among sleep-deprived students (Hull et al., 2007).

When we get sick, we typically sleep more, boosting our immune cells. Sleep deprivation can suppress the immune cells that battle both viral infections and cancer (Opp & Krueger, 2015). In one study, when researchers exposed volunteers to a cold virus, those who had averaged less than 5 hours sleep a night were 4.5 times more likely to develop a cold than those who slept more than 7 hours a night (Prather et al., 2015). Sleep's protective effect may help explain why people who sleep 7 to 8 hours a night tend to outlive those who are chronically sleep deprived (Dew et al., 2003; Parthasarathy et al., 2015; Scullin & Bliwise, 2015).

Sleep deprivation slows reactions and increases errors on visual attention tasks similar to those involved in screening airport baggage, performing surgery, and reading X-rays (Caldwell, 2012; Lim & Dinges, 2010). When especially drowsy, we may unknowingly experience a 1- to 6-second *microsleep* (Koch, 2016). Consider the engineer of a New York–area commuter train, whose fatigue from *sleep apnea* caused him to crash the train, injuring more than 100 people and killing a bystander (McGeehan, 2018). When sleepy frontal lobes confront an unexpected situation, misfortune often results.

For many North Americans, a semi-annual sleep-manipulation experiment is the "spring forward" to daylight saving time and "fall back" to standard time. Millions of Canadian and American records have revealed that accidents increase immediately after the spring-forward time change, which shortens sleep (Figure 1.5-10).

**Figure 1.5-10**

**Less sleep = more accidents**

(a) On the Monday after the spring time change, when people lose one hour of sleep, accidents increased, as compared with the Monday before. (b) In the fall, traffic accidents normally increase because of greater snow, ice, and darkness, but they diminished after the time change. (Data from Coren, 1996.)

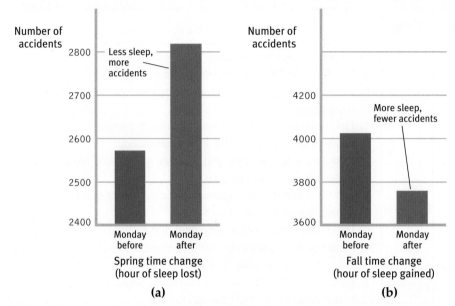

Figure 1.5-11 summarizes the effects of sleep deprivation. But there is good news! Psychologists have discovered a treatment that strengthens memory, increases concentration, boosts mood, moderates hunger, reduces obesity, fortifies the immune system, improves school performance, and lessens the risk of fatal accidents. Even better news: The treatment feels good, it can be self-administered, and it's free! If you are a typical high school student, you might feel trapped in a cycle of sleeplessness. Stress—from school and life generally—might make adequate sleep seem like a luxury. But one night this week, try to add 15 minutes to your sleep. Until you feel more rested and less like a zombie, try adding more sleep as often as you can. For some additional tips on getting better-quality sleep, see **Table 1.5-2**.

**Figure 1.5-11**

**How sleep deprivation affects us**

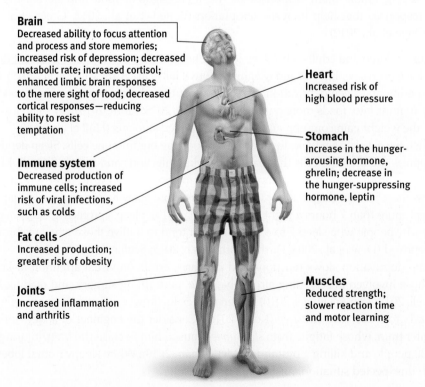

### TABLE 1.5-2 How to Improve Your Sleep Hygiene

- Exercise regularly but not in the late evening (Lowe et al., 2019). (Late afternoon is best.)

- Avoid caffeine after early afternoon, and avoid food and drink near bedtime. The exception would be a glass of milk, which provides raw materials for the manufacture of serotonin, a neurotransmitter that facilitates sleep.

- Relax before bedtime, using dimmer light.

- Set an alarm for when you intend to get ready for bed each night — a reminder of your plan.

- Sleep on a consistent schedule (rise at the same time even after a restless night) and avoid long naps (Jansson-Fröjmark et al., 2019).

- Hide time displays so you aren't tempted to check repeatedly.

- Reassure yourself that temporary sleep loss happens, and it's normal to struggle to sleep sometimes. Try not to overthink your sleep, and just try to do your best each day (Baron et al., 2017).

- Focus your mind on nonarousing, engaging thoughts, such as song lyrics or vacation travel (Gellis et al., 2013). (Thinking about falling asleep may keep you awake.)

- Manage stress. Realize that for any stressed organism, being vigilant is natural and adaptive. Less stress = better sleep.

---

**AP® Science Practice**

## Check Your Understanding

**Examine the Concept**

▶ A well-rested person would be more likely to have _____ (trouble concentrating/quick reaction times) and a sleep-deprived person would be more likely to _____ (gain weight/fight off a cold).

*Answers to the Examine the Concept questions can be found in Appendix C at the end of the book.*

**Apply the Concept**

▶ Explain some of the effects sleep loss has on you.

▶ What have you learned about sleep hygiene that you could apply to yourself?

---

# Major Sleep Disorders

**1.5-9 What are the major sleep disorders?**

An occasional loss of sleep is nothing to worry about. But for those who have a major sleep disorder—**insomnia**, **narcolepsy**, **sleep apnea**, sleepwalking (*somnambulism*), or **REM sleep behavior disorder**—trying to sleep can be a nightmare. (**Table 1.5-3** summarizes these disorders.)

Approximately 1 in every 5 adults has insomnia—persistent problems in either falling or staying asleep (Irwin et al., 2006; Sivertsen et al., 2020). The result is tiredness and increased risk of depression (Baglioni et al., 2016). Sleep researcher Wilse Webb (1992) likened sleep to love or happiness: "If you pursue it too ardently, it will elude you." But from middle age on, awakening occasionally during the night becomes the norm, not something to fret over or treat with medication (Vitiello, 2009). Ironically, insomnia becomes worse when we fret about it. In laboratory studies, people with insomnia do sleep less than others. But even they typically overestimate how long it takes them to fall asleep and underestimate how long they actually have slept (te Lindert et al., 2020). Even if we have been awake for only an hour or two, we may *think* we have had very little sleep because it's the waking part we remember.

**insomnia** recurring problems in falling or staying asleep.

**narcolepsy** a sleep disorder characterized by uncontrollable sleep attacks. The affected person may lapse directly into REM sleep, often at inopportune times.

**sleep apnea** a sleep disorder characterized by temporary cessations of breathing during sleep and repeated momentary awakenings.

**REM sleep behavior disorder** a sleep disorder in which normal REM paralysis does not occur; instead, twitching, talking, or even kicking or punching may occur, often acting out one's dream.

## TABLE 1.5-3  Sleep Disorders

| Disorder | Rate | Description | Effects |
|---|---|---|---|
| *Insomnia* | 1 in 5 adults (based on past year's symptoms) | Ongoing difficulty falling or staying asleep. | Chronic tiredness, increased risk of depression, obesity, hypertension, and arthritic and fibromyalgia pain (Olfson et al., 2018). |
| *Narcolepsy* | 1 in 2000 adults | Sudden attacks of overwhelming sleepiness. | Risk of falling asleep at a dangerous moment. Narcolepsy attacks usually last less than 5 minutes, but they can happen at the worst and most emotional times. Everyday activities, such as driving, require extra caution. |
| *Sleep apnea* | 1 in 20 adults | Stopping breathing repeatedly while sleeping. | Fatigue and depression (as a result of slow-wave sleep deprivation). Associated with obesity (especially among men). |
| *Sleepwalking* | 1–15 in 100 in the general population (NSF, 2020) | Repeated episodes of complex motor behavior, such as walking, while asleep. Sleepwalking happens in Stage 3 sleep. | Few serious concerns. Sleepwalkers return to their beds on their own or with the help of a family member, rarely remembering their trip the next morning. |
| *REM sleep behavior disorder* | 1 in 100 adults for the general population; 1 in 50 adults for those over age 50 | Acting out the content of dreams while asleep, including vocalizing or motor behaviors such as kicking or punching. | Risk of accidental injury to the sleeping person or to a bed partner. |

### AP® Exam Tip

The AP® exam could have you identify and explain the differences among the sleep disorders. For example, you might be asked to explain the difference between sleep apnea and narcolepsy.

The most common quick fixes for true insomnia—sleeping pills and alcohol—typically aggravate the problem by reducing REM sleep, causing concentration and memory problems, and leaving the person with next-day blahs. Such aids can also lead to *tolerance*—a state in which increasing doses are needed to produce an effect. Better to visit a sleep specialist to obtain a healthy long-term treatment plan.

### AP® Science Practice

## Check Your Understanding

**Examine the Concept**

▶ Explain each of the sleep disorders presented in Table 1.5-3.

**Apply the Concept**

▶ Imagine a friend tells you that they are having trouble sleeping and are considering taking sleeping pills. How would you respond?

*Answers to the Examine the Concept questions can be found in Appendix C at the end of the book.*

# Dreams

**1.5-10** What do we dream, and what functions have theorists proposed for dreams?

Now playing at an inner theater near you: the premiere of a sleeping person's vivid dream. This never-before-seen mental movie features captivating characters wrapped in a plot so original and unlikely, yet so intricate and so seemingly real, that the viewer later marvels at its creation.

REM **dreams** are vivid, emotional, and often bizarre (Loftus & Ketchum, 1994). Waking from one, we may wonder how our brain can so creatively, colorfully, and completely construct this alternative world. In the shadowland between our dreaming and waking consciousness, we may even wonder for a moment which is real. Awakening from a nightmare, a 4-year-old may be sure there is a bear in the house.

Discovering the link between REM sleep and dreaming began a new era in dream research. Instead of relying on someone's hazy recall hours later, researchers could catch dreams as they happened, awakening people during or shortly after a REM sleep period to hear a vivid account.

> **dream** a sequence of images, emotions, and thoughts passing through a sleeping person's mind.

## What We Dream

Many of our dreams are anything but sweet. For women and men, 8 in 10 dreams are marked by at least one negative event or emotion (Domhoff, 2007). Common themes include repeatedly failing in an attempt to do something; being attacked, pursued, or rejected; or experiencing misfortune (Hall et al., 1982). Dreams with sexual imagery occur less often than you might think (though more often after consuming sexual media [Van den Bulck et al., 2016]). In one study, only 1 in 10 dreams among young men and 1 in 30 among young women had sexual content (Domhoff, 1996).

More commonly, a dream's storyline incorporates traces of recent experiences and preoccupations (Nikles et al., 2017):

- **Trauma and dreams.** After suffering a trauma, people commonly report nightmares, which help extinguish daytime fears (Petrov & Robinson, 2020). Survivors of the Auschwitz concentration camp, Palestinian children living amid conflict, and Americans after the 9/11 terrorist attacks all have experienced frequent trauma-related dreams (Owczarski, 2018; Propper et al., 2007; Punamäki & Joustie, 1998).

- **Music and dreams.** Compared with nonmusicians, musicians report twice as many dreams of music (Uga et al., 2006).

- **Vision loss and dreams.** Studies in four countries have found people who are blind mostly dreaming of using their nonvisual senses (Buquet, 1988; Taha, 1972; Vekassy, 1977). But even people born blind sometimes "see" in their dreams (Bértolo, 2005). Likewise, people born paralyzed below the waist sometimes dream of walking, standing, running, or cycling (Saurat et al., 2011; Voss et al., 2011).

- **Media experiences and dreams.** In a study of 1287 Turkish people, "participants who consumed violent media tended to have violent dreams, and participants who consumed sexual media tended to have sexual dreams" (Van den Bulck et al., 2016).

> **AP® Science Practice**
>
> **Research**
>
> By conducting studies on blindness and dreaming in multiple countries, the researchers ensure that their results are more generalizable to all individuals who are blind and not just a select group.

In the experiment in which researchers sprayed water on the faces of sleeping individuals, the *independent* variable (the factor that is manipulated by the investigator) was the cold-water treatment. Can you identify the *dependent* variable (the outcome that is measured)?

Our two-track mind continues to monitor our environment while we sleep. A sensory stimulus—a particular odor or a phone's ringing—may be instantly and ingeniously woven into the dream story. In a classic experiment, researchers lightly sprayed cold water on dreamers' faces (Dement & Wolpert, 1958). Compared with sleepers who did not get the cold-water treatment, these people were more likely to dream about a waterfall, a leaky roof, or even about being sprayed by someone.

So, could we learn a foreign language by hearing it played while we sleep? If only. While sleeping, we can learn to associate a sound with a mild electric shock (and to react to the sound accordingly). We can also learn to associate a particular sound with a pleasant or unpleasant odor (Arzi et al., 2012). But we do not remember recorded information played while we are soundly asleep (Eich, 1990; Wyatt & Bootzin, 1994). In fact, anything that happens during the 5 minutes just before sleep is typically lost from memory (Roth et al., 1988). This explains why people with sleep apnea, who repeatedly awaken with a gasp and then immediately fall back to sleep, do not recall these episodes. Ditto for someone who awakens momentarily, sends a text message, and the next day can't remember doing so. It also explains why dreams that momentarily awaken us are mostly forgotten by morning. To remember a dream, get up and stay awake for a few minutes.

*"I'd like to extend a special welcome to those of you who are joining us for the first time, as part of a nightmare you're having."*

## Why We Dream

In his landmark book *The Interpretation of Dreams*, Sigmund Freud offered what he thought was "the most valuable of all the discoveries it has been my good fortune to make." He proposed that dreams provide a psychic safety valve that discharges otherwise unacceptable feelings. Freud viewed a dream's *manifest content* (the apparent and remembered story line) as a censored, symbolic version of its *latent content*, the unconscious drives and wishes (often erotic) that would be threatening if expressed directly. Thus, a gun might be a disguised representation of a penis.

Freud considered dreams the key to understanding our inner conflicts. However, his critics say it is time to wake up from Freud's dream theory, which they regard as a scientific nightmare. Legend has it that even Freud, who loved to smoke cigars, acknowledged that "sometimes, a cigar is just a cigar." Freud's wish-fulfillment theory of dreams has largely given way to other theories. "There is no reason to believe any of Freud's specific claims about dreams and their purposes," observed dream researcher William Domhoff (2003).

*To file away memories.* The *information-processing* perspective proposes that dreams help sift, sort, and fix (consolidate) the day's experiences in our memory. Some research supports this view. When tested the day after learning a task, people who were deprived of both slow-wave and REM sleep did not do as well as those who had slept undisturbed (Stickgold, 2012). Other studies have shown similar memory lapses for new material among people awakened every time they began REM sleep (Empson & Clarke, 1970; Karni & Sagi, 1994).

Brain scans confirm the link between REM sleep and memory. The brain regions that were active as rats learned to navigate a maze, or as people learned to perform a visual-discrimination task, became active again later during REM sleep (Louie & Wilson, 2001;

Maquet, 2001). So precise were these activity patterns that scientists could tell where in the maze the rat would be if awake. To sleep, perchance to remember.

This is important news for students, many of whom are sleep deprived on weekdays and binge sleep on the weekend (Stickgold, 2000). High school students with high grades slept about 25 minutes longer each night than their lower-achieving classmates (Wolfson & Carskadon, 1998; see **Figure 1.5-12**). Sacrificing sleep time to study actually *worsens* academic performance, by making it harder the next day to understand class material or do well on a test (Gillen-O'Neel et al., 2013).

 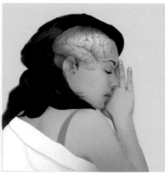 

**Figure 1.5-12**

**A sleeping brain is a working brain**

**(a)** Learning.

**(b)** Sleep consolidates our learning into long-term memory.

**(c)** Learning is retained.

***To develop and preserve neural pathways.*** Perhaps dreams, or the brain activity associated with REM sleep, serve a *physiological* function, providing the sleeping brain with periodic stimulation. This theory makes developmental sense. As you will see in Module 3.2, stimulating experiences preserve and expand the brain's neural pathways. Infants, whose neural networks are developing quickly, spend much of their abundant sleep time in REM sleep (**Figure 1.5-13**).

**Figure 1.5-13**

**Sleep across the lifespan**

As we age, our sleep patterns change. During infancy and our first 2 years, we spend progressively less time in REM sleep. During our first 20 years, we spend progressively less time asleep. (Data from Snyder & Scott, 1972.)

***To make sense of neural static.*** Other researchers propose that dreams erupt from *neural activation* spreading upward from the brainstem (Antrobus, 1991; Hobson, 2009). According to the *activation-synthesis theory,* dreams are the brain's attempt to synthesize random neural activity. Much as a neurosurgeon can produce hallucinations by stimulating different parts of a patient's cortex, so can stimulation originating within the brain. As Freud might have expected, PET scans of sleeping people also reveal increased activity in the emotion-related limbic system (in the amygdala) during emotional dreams (Schwartz, 2012). In contrast, the frontal lobe regions responsible for inhibition and logical thinking seem to idle, which may explain why we are less inhibited when dreaming than when awake (Maquet et al., 1996). Add the limbic system's emotional tone to the brain's visual bursts and—voila!—we dream. Damage either the limbic system or the visual centers active during dreaming, and dreaming itself may be impaired (Domhoff, 2003).

***To reflect cognitive development.*** Some dream researchers focus on dreams as part of brain maturation and cognitive development (Domhoff, 2010, 2011; Foulkes, 1999). For example, prior to age 9, children's dreams seem more like a slide show and less like an active story in which the dreamer is an actor. Dreams overlap with waking cognition and feature coherent speech. They *simulate reality* by drawing on our concepts and knowledge. They engage brain networks that also are active during daydreaming—and so may be viewed as intensified mind-wandering, enhanced by visual imagery (Fox et al., 2013). Unlike the idea that dreams arise from bottom-up brain activation, the cognitive perspective emphasizes our mind's top-down control of our dream content (Nir & Tononi, 2010). Dreams, says Domhoff (2014), "dramatize our wishes, fears, concerns, and interests in striking scenarios that we experience as real events."

**Table 1.5-4** compares these major dream theories. Although today's sleep researchers debate dreams' functions—and some are skeptical that dreams serve any function—they do agree on one thing: We need REM sleep. Deprived of it by repeated awakenings, people return more and more quickly to the REM stage after falling back to sleep. When finally allowed to sleep undisturbed, they literally sleep like babies—with increased REM sleep, a phenomenon called **REM rebound**. Most other mammals also experience REM rebound, suggesting that the causes and functions of REM sleep are deeply biological. (That REM sleep occurs in mammals—and not in animals such as fish, whose behavior is less influenced by learning—fits the information-processing, or *consolidation,* theory of dreams.)

**REM rebound** the tendency for REM sleep to increase following REM sleep deprivation.

### TABLE 1.5-4 Dream Theories

| Theory | Explanation | Critical Considerations |
|---|---|---|
| *Information processing/ consolidation* | Dreams help us sort out the day's events and consolidate our memories. | But why do we sometimes dream about things we have not experienced and about past events? |
| *Physiological function* | Regular brain stimulation from REM sleep may help develop and preserve neural pathways. | This does not explain why we experience *meaningful* dreams. |
| *Activation synthesis* | REM sleep triggers neural activity that evokes random visual memories, which our sleeping brain weaves into stories. | The individual's brain is weaving the stories, which still tells us something about the dreamer. |
| *Cognitive development* | Dream content reflects dreamers' level of cognitive development — their knowledge and understanding. Dreams simulate our lives, including worst-case scenarios. | Does not propose an adaptive function of dreams. |

So, does this mean that because dreams serve physiological functions and extend normal cognition, they are psychologically meaningless? Not necessarily. Every psychologically meaningful experience involves an active brain. We are once again reminded of a basic principle: *Biological and psychological explanations of behavior are partners, not competitors.*

---

 **AP® Science Practice**

## Check Your Understanding

**Examine the Concept**

▶ Explain the theories that propose explanations for why we dream.

**Apply the Concept**

▶ Which explanation for why we dream makes the most sense to you? Explain how this theory would account for your own dreams.

*Answers to the Examine the Concept questions can be found in Appendix C at the end of the book.*

---

## Module 1.5c REVIEW

### 1.5-8 How does sleep loss affect us?

- Sleep deprivation causes fatigue and irritability, and it impairs concentration and memory consolidation. It can also lead to depression, obesity, joint inflammation, a suppressed immune system, and slowed performance (with greater vulnerability to accidents).

### 1.5-9 What are the major sleep disorders?

- Sleep disorders include *insomnia* (recurring problems in falling or staying asleep), *narcolepsy* (sudden uncontrollable sleepiness, sometimes lapsing directly into REM sleep), *sleep apnea* (the repeated stopping of breathing while asleep; associated with obesity, especially in men), and sleepwalking.

### 1.5-10 What do we dream, and what functions have theorists proposed for dreams?

- We usually *dream* of ordinary events and everyday experiences, with most dreams involving some anxiety or misfortune.

- Fewer than 10 percent of dreams among men, and fewer still among women, have any sexual content.

- There are four major contemporary views of the function of dreams:
  - Information processing/consolidation: Dreams help us sort out the day's events and consolidate them in memory.
  - Physiological function: Regular brain stimulation may help develop and preserve neural pathways in the brain.
  - Neural activation: The brain attempts to make sense of neural "static" by weaving it into a storyline.
  - Cognitive development: Dreams reflect the dreamers' level of development—their knowledge and understanding.

- Most sleep theorists agree that REM sleep and its associated dreams serve an important function, as shown by the *REM rebound* that occurs following REM deprivation in humans and other mammals.

# AP® Practice Multiple Choice Questions

1. Andriy has not been getting enough sleep the last few months. He has gained weight and has been getting sick often. What other effect of sleep deprivation will Andriy likely experience?

   a. Increased productivity
   b. Depression
   c. Increased feeling of well-being
   d. Sleep apnea

2. Shortly after falling asleep, and hundreds of times during the night, Paola wakes up after a loud gasp because she has stopped breathing. With which sleep disorder would she most likely be diagnosed?

   a. Narcolepsy
   b. Insomnia
   c. Sleep apnea
   d. REM sleep behavior disorder

3. Bohdana believes that she dreams to help her remember what happened during the day. Which dream theory aligns with her view?

   a. Information processing
   b. Cognitive development
   c. Physiological function
   d. Neural activation

4. After two nights without sleep, which of the following can be expected?

   a. Insomnia
   b. Sleep apnea
   c. Narcolepsy
   d. REM rebound

**Use the following data to answer questions 5 and 6:**

Dr. Truman conducted a study where she drew numbers out of a hat to determine which half of the participants slept only 4 hours per night for 4 weeks (Group A) and which half of the participants slept 8 to 9 hours per night for 4 weeks (Group B). She ensured that the participants' living quarters were the same for the duration of the study, changing only the amount of time each group slept. Using the graphs and information in the prompt, address the following questions:

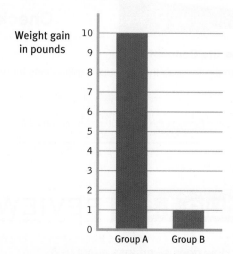

5. Based on the data in the graph, which of the following statements best describes the results of Dr. Truman's study?

   a. A lack of sleep causes weight loss.
   b. Participants' living quarters impact weight.
   c. A lack of sleep causes weight gain.
   d. Participants' living quarters impact sleep.

6. Which of the following aspects of Dr. Truman's study allows her to draw a cause-effect conclusion about the impact of sleep on hormones?

   a. Random selection
   b. Experimental control
   c. Confounding variables
   d. Qualitative methodology

# Module 1.6a Sensation: Basic Concepts

When Indiana Adams awoke on New Year's Day in 2020, she decided to buy her husband exercise equipment. As she scrolled through the social media marketplace, a used psychology textbook cover caught her attention. Adams' vision is perfect, but her perception is not. A former model and actor, Adams noted that the woman on the textbook cover wore clothes that evoked memories of one of her photoshoots. But Adams has *prosopagnosia*—face blindness—which means she can't even recognize her own face.

She went into her bedroom and showed her husband the picture. "That's you!" he said. And we [DM and ND] were that textbook's authors.

People with face blindness sometimes struggle socially. On one occasion, Adams was shopping and complimented another woman on her cute clothes. When the woman didn't respond, Adams realized she was actually looking at herself in the mirror—and talking to her own reflection! Other people with face blindness report being aloof or experiencing distress when they confuse coworkers and strangers with loved ones. Face-blind people sometimes pretend to recognize people, just in case they turn out to be someone they know. One woman found a way to use her face blindness to build friendships (Dingfelder, 2019). "When I was walking to class, if someone seemed to look my way, I smiled. If they smiled, I stopped to chat," she said. "Before long, the whole campus was brimming with close, personal friends of mine."

Unlike Adams, most of us have a functioning area on the underside of our brain's right hemisphere that helps us recognize a familiar human face, including our own, as soon as we detect it—in only one-seventh of a second (Jacques & Rossion, 2006). Our remarkable ability illustrates a broader principle: *Nature's sensory gifts enable each animal to obtain essential information.* Other examples:

- Human ears are most sensitive to sound frequencies that include human voices, especially a baby's cry.

- Frogs, which feed on flying insects, have cells in their eyes that fire only in response to small, dark, moving objects. A frog could starve to death knee-deep in

David G. Myers   C. Nathan DeWall
PSYCHOLOGY
12th edition

Red Chopsticks/Getty Images

Could that be me?

motionless flies. But let one zoom by and the frog's "bug detector" cells snap awake. (As Kermit the Frog said, "Time's fun when you're having flies.")

- Male silkworm moths' odor receptors can detect one-billionth of an ounce of chemical sex attractant per second, released by a female one mile away (Sagan, 1977). That is why there continue to be silkworms.

In Module 1.6, we'll look at what psychologists have learned about how we *sense* our world; in Module 2.1, we'll explore how we *perceive* our world. Let's begin by considering some basic principles of both sensation and perception.

# Basic Concepts of Sensation and Perception

How do we create meaning from the blizzard of sensory stimuli that bombards our body 24 hours a day? In its silent, cushioned, inner world, our brain floats in utter darkness. By itself, it sees nothing. It hears nothing. It feels nothing. *So, how does the world out there get in?* To phrase the question scientifically: How do we construct our representations of the external world? How do a campfire's flicker, crackle, heat, and smoky scent activate neural connections? And how, from this living neurochemistry, do we create our conscious experience of the fire's motion and temperature, its aroma and beauty?

## Processing Sensations and Perceptions

Indiana Adams' curious mix of perfect vision and face blindness illustrates the distinction between *sensation* and *perception*. When she looks at a friend, her **sensation** is normal: Her **sensory receptors** detect the same information any sighted person's would, and her nervous system transmits that information to her brain. Her **perception**—the processes by which her brain organizes and interprets sensory input—is *almost* normal (see Module 2.1). Thus, she may recognize people from their hair, gait, voice, or particular physique, just not from their face. Her experience is much like the struggle any human would have trying to recognize a specific penguin.

Under normal circumstances, sensation and perception blend into one continuous process. In this module and Module 2.1, we slow down that process to study its parts; in real life, your sensory and perceptual processes work together to help you decipher the world around you. As your brain absorbs the information in **Figure 1.6-1**, **bottom-up processing** enables your sensory systems to detect the lines, angles, and colors that form the images. Using **top-down processing**, you interpret what your senses detect. We miss our own typos because we know what we intended, which (top-down) controls what we read.

**sensation** the process by which our sensory receptors and nervous system receive and represent stimulus energies from our environment.

**sensory receptors** sensory nerve endings that respond to stimuli.

**perception** the process by which our brain organizes and interprets sensory information, enabling us to recognize objects and events as meaningful.

**bottom-up processing** information processing that begins with the sensory receptors and works up to the brain's integration of sensory information.

**top-down processing** information processing guided by higher-level mental processes, as when we construct perceptions drawing on our experience and expectations.

**Figure 1.6-1**
**What's going on here?**

Our sensory and perceptual processes work together to help us sort out complex images, including the hidden donkey rider in Sandro Del-Prete's drawing, *Homage to Leonardo de Vinci*.

© Sandro Del-Prete

# Transduction

**1.6-1** Which three steps are basic to all of our sensory systems?

Our sensory systems perform the amazing feat of **transduction**: They convert outside energy into a form our brain can use. Vision processes light energy. Hearing processes sound waves. All of our senses

- *receive* sensory stimulation, often using specialized receptor cells,
- *transform* that stimulation into neural impulses, and
- *deliver* the neural information to our brain.

Transduction is rather like translation — in this case, of a physical energy such as light waves into the brain's electrochemical language. **Psychophysics** studies the relationships between the physical energy we can detect and its effects on our psychological experiences.

Later in this module, we'll focus on specific sensory systems. How do we see? Hear? Feel pain? Taste? Smell? Keep our balance? In each case, a sensory system receives, transforms, and delivers the information to our brain. And our senses work together.

Let's first explore some strengths and weaknesses in our ability to detect and interpret stimuli in the vast sea of energy around us.

# Thresholds

**1.6-2** How do *absolute thresholds* and *difference thresholds* differ?

At this moment, each of us is being struck by X-rays and radio waves, ultraviolet and infrared light, and sound waves of very high and very low frequencies. To all of these we are blind and deaf. In contrast, other animals with differing needs detect a world that lies beyond our experience. Migrating birds stay on course aided by an internal magnetic compass. Bats and dolphins locate their prey using sonar, bouncing echoing sound off objects. Bees navigate on cloudy days by detecting invisible (to us) polarized light.

Our senses open the shades just a crack, allowing us a restricted awareness of this vast sea of energy. But for our needs, this is enough.

## Absolute Thresholds

To some kinds of stimuli we are exquisitely sensitive. Standing atop a mountain on an utterly dark, clear night, most of us could see a candle flame atop another mountain 30 miles (nearly 50 kilometers) away. We could feel the wing of a bee falling on our cheek. We could smell a single drop of perfume in a three-room apartment (Galanter, 1962).

German scientist and philosopher Gustav Fechner (1801–1887) studied the edge of our awareness of these faint stimuli, which he called an **absolute threshold**. To test your absolute threshold for sounds, a hearing specialist would send tones, at varying levels, into each of your ears and record whether you could hear each tone (**Figure 1.6-2**). The test results would show the point where, for any sound frequency, half the time you could detect the sound and half the time you could not. That 50-50 point would define your absolute threshold.

Detecting a weak stimulus, or signal (such as a hearing-test tone), depends not only on its strength but also on our psychological state — our experience, expectations, motivation, and alertness. **Signal detection theory** predicts when we will detect weak signals (measured as our ratio of "hits" to "false alarms"). Signal detection theorists seek to understand why people respond differently to the same stimuli, and why the same person's reactions vary as circumstances change.

**transduction** conversion of one form of energy into another. In sensation, the transforming of physical energy, such as sights, sounds, and smells, into neural impulses the brain can interpret.

**psychophysics** the study of relationships between the physical characteristics of stimuli, such as their intensity, and our psychological experience of them.

**absolute threshold** the minimum stimulus energy needed to detect a particular stimulus 50 percent of the time.

**signal detection theory** a theory predicting how and when we detect the presence of a faint stimulus (*signal*) amid background stimulation (*noise*); assumes there is no single absolute threshold and that detection depends partly on a person's experience, expectations, motivation, and alertness.

**SPOTLIGHT ON:**
Gustav Fechner

## AP® Science Practice

## Research

Depending on their research question, signal detection theorists might use non-experimental or experimental methods. Could you identify the difference? These methods are described in Unit 0.

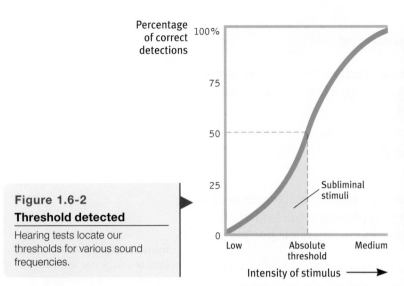

**Figure 1.6-2**
**Threshold detected**

Hearing tests locate our thresholds for various sound frequencies.

Percentage of correct detections

100%

75

50

25

0

Low      Absolute threshold      Medium

Subliminal stimuli

Intensity of stimulus ⟶

**Signal success** When reading mammograms, health professionals seek to detect the presence of a faint cancer stimulus (*signal*) amid background stimulation (*noise*), and without raising false alarms. New 3-D ultrasound breast-imaging technologies aim to clarify the signal and reduce the rate of false-positive results.

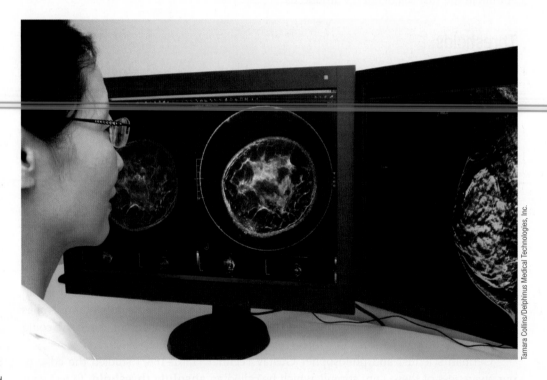

**TRY THIS**

Try out this old riddle on a couple of friends. "You're driving a bus with 12 passengers. At your first stop, 6 passengers get off. At the second stop, 3 get off. At the third stop, 2 more get off but 3 new people get on. What color are the bus driver's eyes?" Do your friends detect the signal — who is the bus driver? — amid the accompanying noise?

**subliminal** below one's absolute threshold for conscious awareness.

Stimuli you cannot consciously detect 50 percent of the time are **subliminal**—below your absolute threshold (Figure 1.6-2). The unconscious mind is like the wind: We don't see it, but we see its effects. When your face appears on a screen faster than you can perceive it consciously, researchers can nevertheless detect your brain's response (Wójcik et al., 2019). The brain knows what the conscious mind doesn't. So, can we be *controlled* by subliminal messages? (See the Developing Arguments feature: Subliminal Sensation and Subliminal Persuasion.)

 **AP® Science Practice**

# Developing Arguments

## Subliminal Sensation and Subliminal Persuasion

**We can be affected by *subliminal* sensations** — stimuli so weak that we don't consciously notice them.

Researchers use **priming** to activate unconscious associations.

Participant views slides of people and offers either favorable or unfavorable ratings of each person.

**BUT**

an instant before each slide appears, the trickster researcher subliminally flashes another image — either pleasant (for example, kittens), or unpleasant (for example, a werewolf).

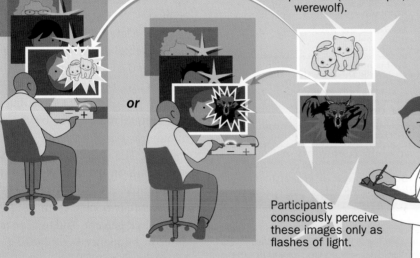

*or*

Participants consciously perceive these images only as flashes of light.

### Will participants' ratings of the faces be affected?

**Yes!**[1]

More **favorable** ratings of people

More **unfavorable** ratings of people

Our two-track mind: Priming happens even though the viewer's brain does not have time to consciously perceive the flashed images. We may evaluate a stimulus even when we are not consciously aware of it.[2]

**So, we can be *primed*, but can we be *persuaded* by subliminal stimuli,** for example to lose weight, stop smoking, or improve our memory?

Quiz 100%

Audio and video messages subliminally (without recipients' conscious awareness) announce:

"I am thin,"
"Cigarette smoke tastes bad," and
"I do well on tests. I have total recall of information."

Results from 16 experiments[3] showed no powerful, enduring influence on behavior. Not one of the recordings helped more than a placebo, which works only because we believe it will.

## Developing Arguments Questions

**1.** Describe the empirical approach that utilizes scientifically derived evidence. (Need a review? Consult Unit 0.)

**2.** Explain how the scientifically derived evidence presented here either supports or refutes subliminal priming.

**3.** Use the scientifically derived evidence presented here to explain why subliminal persuasion is ineffective.

**priming** the activation, often unconsciously, of certain associations, thus predisposing one's perception, memory, or response.

1. Krosnick et al., 1992. 2. Ferguson & Zayas, 2009. 3. Greenwald et al., 1991, 1992.

## Difference Thresholds

To function effectively, we need absolute thresholds low enough to allow us to detect important sights, sounds, textures, tastes, and smells. We also need to detect small differences among stimuli. A musician must detect minute discrepancies when tuning an instrument. Students in the hallway will detect the sound of their friends' voices amid all the other voices. Even after 2 years living in Scotland, all lamb *baas* sounded alike to my [DM's] ears—but not to the lambs' mothers. After shearing, I observed, each ewe would streak directly to the *baa* of *her* lamb amid the chorus of other distressed lambs.

The **difference threshold** (or the *just noticeable difference [jnd]*) is the minimum stimulus difference a person can detect half the time. That detectable difference increases with the size of the stimulus. If we listen to our music at 40 decibels, we might barely detect an added 5 decibels (the jnd). But if we increase the volume to 110 decibels, we probably won't detect an additional 5-decibel change.

In the late 1800s, German physician Ernst Weber described a principle so simple and so widely applicable that we still refer to it as **Weber's law**: For an average person to perceive a difference, two stimuli must differ by a constant minimum *percentage* (not a constant *amount*). The exact percentage varies, depending on the stimulus. Two lights, for example, must differ in intensity by 8 percent. Two objects must differ in weight by 2 percent. And two tones must differ in frequency by only 0.3 percent (Teghtsoonian, 1971).

**difference threshold** the minimum difference between two stimuli required for detection 50 percent of the time. We experience the difference threshold as a *just noticeable difference (jnd)*.

**Weber's law** the principle that, to be perceived as different, two stimuli must differ by a constant minimum percentage (rather than a constant amount).

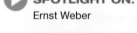

The LORD is my shepherd;
    I shall not want.
He maketh me to lie down
        in green pastures:
    he leadeth me
        beside the still waters.
He restoreth my soul:
    he leadeth me
        in the paths of righteousness
            for his name's sake.
Yea, though I walk through the valley
        of the shadow of death,
    I will fear no evil:
for thou art with me;
    thy rod and thy staff
    they comfort me.
Thou preparest a table before me
    in the presence of mine enemies:
    thou anointest my head with oil,
        my cup runneth over.
Surely goodness and mercy
        shall follow me
    all the days of my life:
and I will dwell
    in the house of the LORD
        for ever.

**The difference threshold** In this copy of the Twenty-Third Psalm, each line of the typeface increases in size slightly. How many lines are required for you to experience a just noticeable difference?

▶ **SPOTLIGHT ON:**
Ernst Weber

---

**AP® Science Practice**

# Check Your Understanding

**Examine the Concept**

▶ Explain the difference between bottom-up and top-down processing.

▶ Explain the basic steps of transduction.

*Answers to the Examine the Concept questions can be found in Appendix C at the end of the book.*

**Apply the Concept**

▶ Using sound as your example, explain how these concepts differ: *absolute threshold*, *subliminal stimulation*, and *difference threshold*.

## Sensory Adaptation

**1.6-3** What is the function of sensory adaptation?

It's one of life's little curiosities: You may not notice a fan's noise until it's turned off. The same is true for odors. Sitting down on the bus, you are struck by your seatmate's heavy perfume. You wonder how she endures it, but within minutes you no longer notice. **Sensory adaptation** has come to your rescue. When constantly exposed to an unchanging stimulus, we become less aware of it because our nerve cells fire less frequently. (To experience sensory adaptation, put a rubber band on your wrist. You will feel it—but only for a few moments.)

**sensory adaptation** diminished sensitivity as a consequence of constant stimulation.

Why, then, if we stare at an object without flinching, does it *not* vanish from sight? Because, unnoticed by us, our eyes are always moving. This continual flitting from one spot to another ensures that stimulation of the eyes' receptors continually changes (**Figure 1.6-3**).

### Figure 1.6-3
**The jumpy eye**

Our gaze jumps from one spot to another every one-third of a second or so. Eye-tracking equipment recorded a person's eye jumps while looking at this photograph of Edinburgh's Princes Street Gardens (Henderson, 2007). The circles represent visual fixations, and the numbers indicate the time of fixation in milliseconds (300 milliseconds = 3/10ths of a second).

What if we actually could stop our eyes from moving? Would sights seem to vanish, as odors do? To find out, psychologists have devised ingenious instruments that maintain a constant image on the eye's inner surface. Imagine that we have fitted a volunteer, Mary, with such an instrument—a miniature projector mounted on a contact lens. When Mary's eye moves, the image from the projector moves as well. So everywhere that Mary looks, the scene is sure to go. Can you guess the weird result? (See **Figure 1.6-4**.)

**AP® Science Practice**

### Research

The ability to track and measure eye movements helped advance the field of visual sensation. Investigators are now able to obtain concrete evidence of the way our eyes naturally avoid sensory adaptation. It is often advances in technology or equipment that help theories evolve.

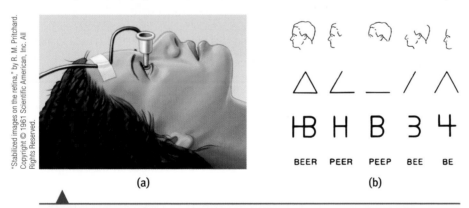

(a)

(b)

BEER   PEER   PEEP   BEE   BE

### Figure 1.6-4
**Sensory adaptation: Now you see it, now you don't!**

(a) A projector mounted on a contact lens makes the projected image move with the eye. (b) Initially, the person sees the stabilized image. But thanks to sensory adaptation, her eye soon becomes accustomed to the unchanging stimulus. Rather than the full image, she begins to see fragments fading and reappearing.

**AP® Science Practice**

### Research

Remember that there are strict guidelines for the ethical treatment of human participants. So while the study presented here might seem uncomfortable, the volunteers provide informed consent.

Although sensory adaptation reduces our sensitivity, it offers an important benefit: freedom to focus on informative changes in our environment. Technology companies understand the attention-grabbing power of changing stimulation: Our phone's notifications are hard to ignore. If we're performing other tasks, these intrusions can harm our performance (Stothart et al., 2015).

Sensory adaptation even influences how we perceive emotions. By creating a 50-50 morphed blend of an angry face and a scared face, researchers showed that our visual system adapts to a static facial expression by becoming less responsive to it (Butler et al., 2008; **Figure 1.6-5**). The effect is created by our brain, not by our retinas. We know this because the illusion also works when we view either side image with one eye, and the center image with the other eye.

**Figure 1.6-5**
**Emotion adaptation**

Gaze at the angry face on the left for 20 to 30 seconds, then look at the center face (looks scared, yes?). Then gaze at the scared face on the right for 20 to 30 seconds, before returning to the center face (now looks angry, yes?). (From Butler et al., 2008.)

Factors contributing to the adaptation after effects of facial expression, Andrea Butler, Ipek Oruc, Christopher J. Fox, Jason J.S. Barton, Brain Research, 29 January 2008.

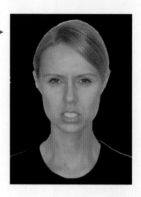  

*The point to remember:* Our sensory system is alert to novelty. Bore it with repetition and it frees our attention for more important things. *We perceive the world not exactly as it is, but as it is useful for us to perceive it.*

Next up, let's consider some marvels that enable our seeing, hearing, and in other ways experiencing our worlds.

---

**AP® Science Practice**

## Check Your Understanding

**Examine the Concept**

▶ Explain sensory adaptation.

**Apply the Concept**

▶ In the last day, what types of sensory adaptation have you experienced?

▶ Why is it that after wearing shoes for a while, you cease to notice them (until questions like this draw your attention back to them)?

*Answers to the Examine the Concept questions can be found in Appendix C at the end of the book.*

---

# Module 1.6a REVIEW

**1.6-1** Which three steps are basic to all of our sensory systems?

● Our senses (1) receive sensory stimulation (often using specialized receptor cells), (2) transform that stimulation into neural impulses, and (3) deliver the neural information to the brain. *Transduction* is the process of converting one form of energy into another.

**1.6-2** How do *absolute thresholds* and *difference thresholds* differ?

● Our *absolute threshold* for any stimulus is the minimum stimulation necessary for us to detect it 50 percent of the time. *Signal detection theory* predicts how and when

we will detect a faint stimulus amid background noise. Individual absolute thresholds vary, depending on the strength of the signal as well as on our experience, expectations, motivation, and alertness.

● Our *difference threshold* (also called the *just noticeable difference [jnd]*) is the minimum stimulus difference we can discern between two stimuli 50 percent of the time. *Weber's law* states that two stimuli must differ by a constant minimum percentage (not by a constant amount) to be perceived as different.

**1.6-3** What is the function of sensory adaptation?

● *Sensory adaptation* (our diminished sensitivity to routine odors, sights, sounds, and touches) focuses our attention on informative changes in our environment.

# AP® Practice Multiple Choice Questions

1. When she sees a photo of a face, Juana is able to recognize it as the face of her mother. Which of the following explains why?

   a. Weber's law
   b. Bottom-up processing
   c. Top-down processing
   d. Signal detection theory

2. As Jeff reads his psychology textbook, he is able to convert the light waves into signals that his brain can interpret due to

   a. transduction.
   b. perception.
   c. priming.
   d. sensory adaptation.

3. Natalia is washing her hands, and she adjusts the faucet handle until the water feels just slightly hotter than it did before. Natalia's adjustment until she feels the change in temperature is an example of

   a. a subliminal stimulus.
   b. an absolute threshold.
   c. a difference threshold.
   d. signal detection.

4. Tyshane went swimming with friends who did not want to get into the pool because the water felt cold. Tyshane jumped in and after a few minutes declared, "It was cold when I first got in, but now it's fine. Come on in!" Tyshane's body became accustomed to the water temperature due to

   a. priming.
   b. absolute threshold.
   c. difference threshold.
   d. sensory adaptation.

**Use the following graph to answer questions 5 and 6:**

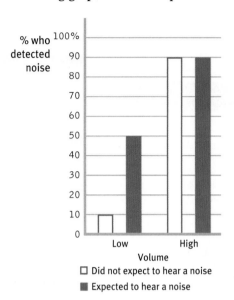

5. What type of data does the graph represent?

   a. Qualitative data
   b. Quantitative data
   c. Median data
   d. Range data

6. Which of the following is depicted in the graph?

   a. Absolute threshold
   b. Transduction
   c. Signal detection theory
   d. Weber's law

# Module 1.6b Sensation: Vision

## AP® Exam Tip

There's a lot of vocabulary here. Make sure you understand the name and the function of each part of the eye. To learn how all the parts fit together, it may help to make rough sketches (you don't need to be an artist to try this!) and then compare your sketches with Figures 1.6-7 and 1.6-9. You'll be better off making several quick, rough sketches than one time-consuming, nicely drawn one.

**wavelength** the distance from the peak of one light wave or sound wave to the peak of the next. Electromagnetic wavelengths vary from the short gamma waves to the long pulses of radio transmission.

**hue** the dimension of color that is determined by the wavelength of light; what we know as the color names *blue, green,* and so forth.

**intensity** the amount of energy in a light wave or sound wave, which influences what we perceive as brightness or loudness. Intensity is determined by the wave's amplitude (height).

**cornea** the eye's clear, protective outer layer, covering the pupil and iris.

**pupil** the adjustable opening in the center of the eye through which light enters.

**iris** a ring of muscle tissue that forms the colored portion of the eye around the pupil and controls the size of the pupil opening.

## Light Energy and Eye Structures

**1.6-4 What are the characteristics of the energy that we see as visible light? What structures in the eye help focus that energy?**

Our eyes receive light energy and *transduce* (transform) it into neural messages. Our brain—in one of life's greatest wonders—then creates what we consciously see. How does such a taken-for-granted yet extraordinary thing happen?

### The Stimulus Input: Light Energy

When you look at a bright red tulip, the stimuli striking your eyes are not particles of the color red but rather pulses of electromagnetic energy that your visual system *perceives* as red. What we see as visible light is but a thin slice of the wide spectrum of electromagnetic energy, ranging from imperceptibly short gamma waves to the long waves of radio transmission (**Figure 1.6-6**). Other portions are visible to other animals. Bees, for instance, cannot see what we perceive as red but can see ultraviolet light.

Light travels in waves, and the shape of those waves influences what we see. Light's **wavelength** is the distance from one wave peak to the next (**Figure 1.6-7**). Wavelength determines **hue**, the color we experience, such as a tulip's red petals or green leaves. A light wave's *amplitude,* or height, determines its **intensity**, the amount of energy the wave contains. Intensity influences *brightness* (Figure 1.6-7b).

To understand *how* we transform physical energy into color and meaning, we need to know more about vision's window—the eye.

### The Eye

Light enters the eye through the **cornea**, which bends light to help provide focus. The light then passes through the **pupil**, a small adjustable opening. Surrounding the pupil and controlling its size is the **iris**, a colored muscle that dilates or constricts in response to light intensity. Each iris is so distinctive that iris-scanning technology can often confirm your identity.

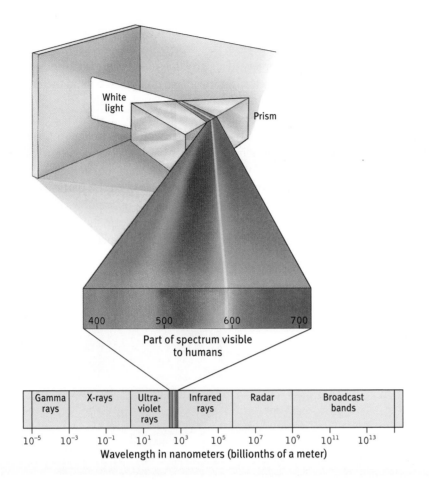

Figure 1.6-6
**The wavelengths we see**

The wide spectrum of electromagnetic energy ranges from gamma rays as short as the diameter of an atom to radio waves as long as 62 miles (100 kilometers). The wavelengths visible to the human eye (shown enlarged) extend from the shorter blue-violet light waves to the longer waves of red light.

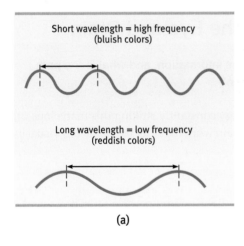

(a)

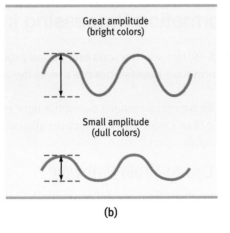

(b)

**Figure 1.6-7**
**The physical properties of waves**

(a) Waves vary in *wavelength* (the distance between successive peaks). *Frequency,* the number of complete wavelengths that can pass a point in a given amount of time, depends on the wavelength. The shorter the wavelength, the higher the frequency. Wavelength determines the perceived *color* of light. (b) Waves also vary in *amplitude* (the height from peak to trough). Wave *amplitude* influences the perceived *brightness* of colors.

The iris responds to your cognitive and emotional states. If you have vision, imagine a sunny sky and your iris will constrict; imagine a dark room and it will dilate (Laeng & Sulutvedt, 2014). The iris also constricts when you feel disgust or you are about to answer *No* to a question (de Gee et al., 2014; Goldinger & Papesh, 2012). And when you're feeling amorous or trusting, your telltale dilated pupils subtly signal your feelings (Attard-Johnson et al., 2016, 2017; Kret & De Dreu, 2017; Prochanzkova et al., 2018).

After passing through your pupil, light hits the transparent **lens** in your eye. The lens then focuses the light rays into an image on your **retina**, the multilayered tissue lining the back inner surface of the eyeball. To focus the rays, the lens changes its curvature and thickness in a process

**lens** the transparent structure behind the pupil that changes shape to help focus images on the retina.

**retina** the light-sensitive back inner surface of the eye, containing the receptor rods and cones plus layers of neurons that begin the processing of visual information.

called **accommodation**. If the lens focuses the image on a point in front of the retina, you see near objects clearly but not distant objects. This nearsightedness—*myopia*—can be remedied with glasses, contact lenses, or surgery. (Farsightedness—seeing distant objects better than near objects—occurs when the lens focuses the image on a point behind the retina.)

For centuries, scientists knew that an image of a candle passing through a small opening will cast an inverted mirror image on a dark wall behind. If the image passing through the pupil casts this sort of upside-down image on the retina, as in **Figure 1.6-8**, how can we see the world right-side up? Eventually, the answer became clear: The retina doesn't "see" a whole image. Consider the four-tenths of a second a baseball batter takes to respond to a pitcher's fastball. The retina's millions of receptor cells convert the particles of light energy into neural impulses and forward those to the brain, which reassembles them, right-side up, into what the batter perceives—incoming fastball! Visual information processing percolates through progressively more abstract levels, all at astonishing speed.

**Figure 1.6-8**
**The eye**
Light rays reflected from a candle pass through the cornea, pupil, and lens. The curvature and thickness of the lens change to bring nearby or distant objects into focus on the retina. Rays from the top of the candle strike the bottom of the retina, and those from the left side of the candle strike the right side of the retina. The candle's image on the retina thus appears upside down and reversed.

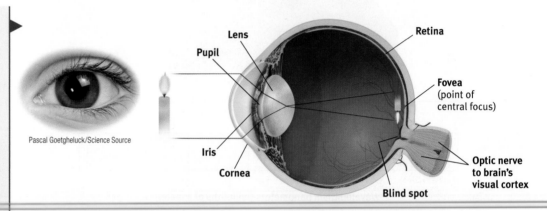

Pascal Goetgheluck/Science Source

Lens
Pupil
Retina
Fovea (point of central focus)
Iris
Cornea
Blind spot
Optic nerve to brain's visual cortex

## Information Processing in the Eye and Brain

**1.6-5** How do the rods and cones process information, and what is the path information travels from the eye to the brain?

How do we make *meaning* out of the light energy constantly striking this marvelous organ, the eye? Let's examine how our eyes and our brain work together to enable our visual experience of the world.

### The Eye-to-Brain Pathway

Imagine that you could follow behind a single light-energy particle after it reached your retina. First, you would thread your way through the retina's sparse outer layer of cells. Then, reaching the very back of your eye, you would encounter the retina's buried photoreceptor cells, the **rods** and **cones** (Figure 1.6-9). There, you would see the light energy trigger chemical changes. That chemical reaction would spark neural signals in nearby *bipolar cells.* You could then watch the bipolar cells activate neighboring *ganglion cells,* whose axons twine together like the strands of a rope to form the **optic nerve**. After a momentary stopover at the thalamus, the information would fly on to its final destination, your visual cortex, in the occipital lobe at the back of your brain.

The optic nerve is an information highway from the eye to the brain. This nerve can send nearly 1 million messages at once through its nearly 1 million ganglion fibers. (The auditory nerve, which enables hearing, carries much less information through its mere 30,000 fibers.) We pay a price for this high-speed connection. Your eye has a **blind spot**, with no receptor cells, where the optic nerve leaves the eye (Figure 1.6-10). Close one eye. Do you see a black hole? *No*—because without seeking your approval, your brain fills in the hole.

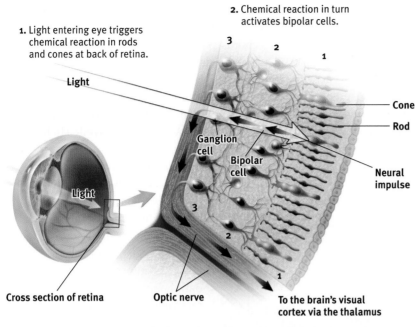

**1.** Light entering eye triggers chemical reaction in rods and cones at back of retina.

**2.** Chemical reaction in turn activates bipolar cells.

Figure 1.6-9
**The retina's reaction to light**

Light

Cone

Rod

Ganglion cell

Bipolar cell

Neural impulse

Light

Cross section of retina

Optic nerve

To the brain's visual cortex via the thalamus

**3.** Bipolar cells then activate the ganglion cells, whose combined axons form the optic nerve. This nerve transmits information (via the thalamus) to the brain's visual cortex.

---

**Figure 1.6-10**

**The blind spot**

There are no receptor cells where the optic nerve leaves the eye. This creates a blind spot in your vision. To demonstrate, close your left eye, look at the black dot, and move your face away until one of the cars disappears. (Which one do you predict it will be?) Repeat with your right eye closed — and note that now the other car disappears. Can you explain why?

---

Rods and cones are our eyes' light-sensitive *photoreceptors*. They differ in where they're found and what they do (**Table 1.6-1**). *Cones* cluster in and around the **fovea**, the retina's area of central focus (Figure 1.6-8). Many cones have their own hotline to the brain: One cone transmits its message to a single bipolar cell, which relays the message to the visual cortex (where a large area receives input from the fovea). These direct connections preserve the cones' precise information, making them better able to detect fine detail. Cones can detect white and enable you to perceive color — but not in the dark (Sabesan et al., 2016).

**fovea** the central focal point in the retina, around which the eye's cones cluster.

| TABLE 1.6-1 Receptors in the Human Eye: Rod-Shaped Rods and Cone-Shaped Cones | Cones | Rods |
| --- | --- | --- |
| *Number* | 6 million | 120 million |
| *Location in retina* | Center | Periphery |
| *Sensitivity in dim light* | Low | High |
| *Color sensitivity* | High | Low |
| *Detail sensitivity* | High | Low |

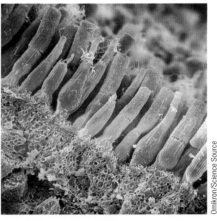

Omikron/Science Source

Unlike cones, rods congregate in the retina's outer regions. Rods remain sensitive in dim light, and they enable black-and-white vision. Rods have no hotline to the brain. If cones are soloists, rods perform as a chorus. Several rods pool their faint energy output and funnel it onto a single bipolar cell, which sends the combined message to your brain.

Cones and rods each provide a special sensitivity—cones to detail and color, and rods to faint light and peripheral motion. Stop for a minute and experience this rod–cone difference. Pick a word in this sentence and stare directly at it, focusing its image on the cones in your fovea. Notice that words distant from it appear blurred? Their image is striking your retina's outer regions, where rods predominate. Thus, when you drive or bike, rods help you detect a car in your peripheral vision well before you perceive its details. How many of the black dots can you see at once in **Figure 1.6-11**?

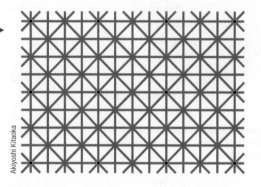

**Figure 1.6-11**

**Disappearing dots**

Look at or near any of the 12 black dots and you can see them, but not in your peripheral vision (Kitaoka, 2016, adapting Ninio & Stevens, 2000).

Akiyoshi Kitaoka

When you enter a darkened theater or turn off the light at night, your pupils dilate to allow more light to reach your retina. Your eyes adapt, but fully adapting typically takes 20 minutes or more. This period of dark adaptation matches the average natural twilight transition between the Sun's setting and darkness. How wonderfully made we are.

At the entry level, the retina's neural layers don't just pass along electrical impulses; they also help to encode and analyze sensory information. (The third neural layer in a frog's eye, for example, contains those "bug detector" cells that fire only in response to moving fly-like stimuli.) In human eyes, any given retinal area relays its information to a corresponding location in the visual cortex, in the occipital lobe. The brain's peculiar wiring means that half of each eye's sensory information arrives in the opposite side of the brain, by crossing the X-shaped *optic chiasm* (**Figure 1.6-12**).

The same sensitivity that enables retinal cells to fire messages can lead them to misfire, as you can demonstrate. Turn your eyes to the left, close them, and then gently rub the right side of your right eyelid with your fingertip. Note the patch of light to the left, moving as

**Figure 1.6-12**

**Pathway from the eyes to the visual cortex**

The retina's ganglion axons form the optic nerve. It runs to the thalamus, where the axons synapse with neurons that run to the visual cortex.

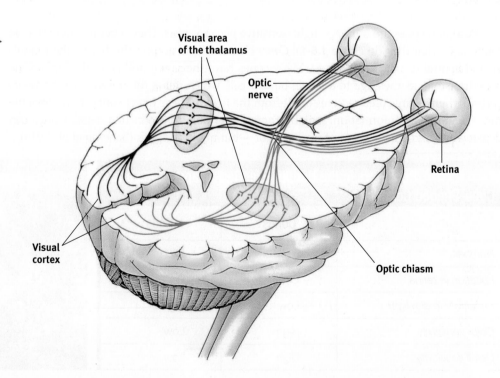

Visual area of the thalamus

Optic nerve

Retina

Visual cortex

Optic chiasm

your finger moves. Why do you see light? Why at the left? This happens because your retinal cells are so responsive that even pressure triggers them. But your brain interprets their firing as light. Moreover, it interprets the light as coming from the left—the normal direction of light that activates the right side of the retina.

## Color Processing

**1.6-6 How do we perceive color in the world around us?**

We talk as though objects possess color: "A tomato is red." Recall the old question, "If a tree falls in the forest and no one hears it, does it make a sound?" We can ask the same of color: If no one sees the tomato, is it red?

The answer is *No.* First, the tomato is everything *but* red, because it *rejects* (reflects) the long wavelengths of red. Second, the tomato's color is our mental construction. As Sir Isaac Newton (1704) noted, "The [light] rays are not colored." Like all aspects of vision, our perception of color resides not in the object itself but in the theater of our brain; even while dreaming, we usually perceive things in color. Likewise, air molecules striking the eardrum are silent and scent molecules have no smell. Our brain creates experiences of sight, sound, and smell.

One of vision's most basic and intriguing mysteries is how we see the world in color. How, from the light energy striking the retina, does our brain construct our experience of such a multitude of colors?

Modern detective work on the mystery of color vision began in the nineteenth century, when German scientist Hermann von Helmholtz built on the insights of an English physicist, Thomas Young. Both knew that any color can be created by combining the light waves of three primary colors—red, green, and blue. So Young and von Helmholtz's research led to a hypothesis: The eye must have three corresponding types of color receptors.

Researchers later confirmed the **Young–Helmholtz trichromatic (three-color) theory** by measuring the responses of various cones to different color stimuli. The retina does indeed have three types of color receptors, each especially sensitive to the wavelengths of red, green, and blue. When light stimulates combinations of these cones, we see other colors. For example, the retina has no separate receptors especially sensitive to yellow. But when red and green wavelengths stimulate both red-sensitive and green-sensitive cones, we see yellow. Said differently, when your eyes see red and green without blue, your brain says *yellow.*

Worldwide, about 1 in 12 males and 1 in 200 females have the genetically sex-linked condition of *color-deficient vision.* Most with color vision deficiency are not entirely "colorblind": They simply lack functioning red- or green-sensitive cones, or sometimes both. Their vision—perhaps unknown to them, because their lifelong vision *seems* normal—is monochromatic (one-color) or dichromatic (two-color) instead of trichromatic, making it impossible to distinguish the red and green in **Figure 1.6-13** (Boynton, 1979). Dogs, too, lack receptors for the wavelengths of red, giving them only limited, dichromatic color vision (Neitz et al., 1989).

**Young–Helmholtz trichromatic (three-color) theory** the theory that the retina contains three different types of color receptors—one most sensitive to red, one to green, one to blue—which, when stimulated in combination, can produce the perception of any color.

### AP® Science Practice

**Research**

Recall from Unit 0 that a hypothesis is a falsifiable prediction that can be used to check the theory or produce practical applications of it. By testing Young and Helmholtz's hypothesis, researchers supported their theory of color vision.

**Figure 1.6-13**
**Color-deficient vision**

The photo in image (a) shows how people with red-green deficiency perceived a 2015 Buffalo Bills versus New York Jets football game. "For the 8 percent of Americans like me that are red-green colorblind, this game is a nightmare to watch," tweeted one fan. "Everyone looks like they're on the same team," said another. The photo in image (b) shows how the game looked for those viewers with normal color vision.

(a)

(b)

Ben Solomon/The New York Times/Redux Pictures

**Figure 1.6-14**

**Afterimage effect**

**AP® Science Practice**

### Research

Notice how these two theories build on each other to give us a more complete understanding of color vision. This is the way science works — theories evolve via the scientific process. As a result, some theories described in this textbook might look different in years to come.

**opponent-process theory** the theory that opposing retinal processes (red-green, blue-yellow, white-black) enable color vision. For example, some cells are stimulated by green and inhibited by red; others are stimulated by red and inhibited by green.

**feature detectors** nerve cells in the brain's visual cortex that respond to specific features of the stimulus, such as shape, angle, or movement.

But why do people blind to red and green often still see yellow? And why does yellow appear to be a pure color and not a mixture of red and green, the way purple combines red and blue? As physiologist Ewald Hering—a contemporary of von Helmholtz—noted, trichromatic theory leaves some parts of the color vision mystery unsolved.

Hering found a clue in *afterimages.* If you stare at a green shape for a while and then look at a white sheet of paper, you will see red, green's *opponent color.* Stare at a yellow square and its opponent color, blue, will appear on the white paper. (To experience this, try the flag demonstration in **Figure 1.6-14.**) Hering formed another hypothesis: Color vision must involve two *additional* color processes, one responsible for red-versus-green perception and one responsible for blue-versus-yellow perception.

A century later, researchers confirmed Hering's hypothesis, now called the **opponent-process theory.** This concept is tricky, but here's the gist: Color vision depends on three sets of opposing retinal processes—*red-green, blue-yellow,* and *white-black.* As impulses travel to the visual cortex, some neurons in both the retina and the thalamus are turned "on" by red but turned "off" by green. Others are turned on by green but off by red (DeValois & DeValois, 1975). Like red and green marbles sent down a narrow tube, "red" and "green" messages cannot both travel at once. We see either red or green, not a reddish-green mixture. But red and blue travel in separate channels, so we *can* see a reddish-blue magenta.

So how does opponent-process theory help us understand negative afterimages, as in the flag demonstration? Here's the answer (for the green changing to red): First, you stared at green bars, which tired your green response. Then you stared at a white area. White contains all colors, including red. Because you had tired your green response, only the red part of the green-red pairing fired normally.

The present solution to the mystery of color vision is therefore roughly this: *Color processing occurs in two stages.*

1. The retina's red-, green-, and blue-sensitive cones respond in varying degrees to different color stimuli, as the Young–Helmholtz trichromatic theory suggested.

2. The cones' responses are then processed by opponent-process cells, as Hering's theory proposed.

## Feature Detection

**1.6-7** Where are feature detectors located, and what do they do?

Scientists once likened the brain to a movie screen on which the eye projected images. Then along came David Hubel and Torsten Wiesel (1979), who showed that our visual processing deconstructs visual images and then reassembles them. Hubel and Wiesel received a Nobel Prize for their work on **feature detectors**, nerve cells in the occipital lobe's visual cortex that respond to a scene's specific visual features—to particular edges, lines, angles, and movements.

Using microelectrodes, Hubel and Wiesel discovered that some neurons fired actively when cats were shown lines at one angle, while other neurons responded to lines at a different angle. They surmised that these specialized neurons, now known as feature detectors, receive information from individual ganglion cells in the retina. Feature detectors pass this specific information to other cortical areas, where teams of cells (*supercell clusters*) respond to more complex patterns.

For biologically important objects and events, monkey brains (and surely ours as well) have a "vast visual encyclopedia" distributed in the form of specialized cells (Perrett et al., 1990, 1992, 1994). These cells respond to one type of stimulus, such as a specific gaze, head angle, posture, or body movement. Other supercell clusters integrate this information and fire only when the cues collectively indicate the direction of someone's attention and approach. This instant analysis, which aided our ancestors' survival, also helps a hockey player anticipate where to shoot the puck, and a driver to anticipate a pedestrian's next movement.

As we noted in Module 1.4, one temporal lobe area by your right ear (**Figure 1.6-15**) enables you to perceive faces and, thanks to a specialized neural network, to recognize them from varied viewpoints (Connor, 2010). This *fusiform face area* helps us recognize friends (Wiese et al., 2019). If your fusiform face area were stimulated, you might spontaneously see faces. One study participant reported to an experimenter, "You just turned into someone else. Your face metamorphosed" (Koch, 2015).

When researchers temporarily disrupt the brain's face-processing areas with magnetic pulses, people cannot recognize faces. But they can still recognize other objects, such as houses, because the brain's face perception occurs separately from its object perception (McKone et al., 2007; Pitcher et al., 2007). Thus, fMRI scans have shown different brain areas becoming activated when people view varied objects (Downing et al., 2001). Brain activity is so specific that, with the help of brain scans, researchers can tell whether people are "looking at a shoe, a chair, or a face, based on the pattern of their brain activity" (Haxby, 2001).

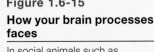

**Face recognition area (fusiform face area)**

### Figure 1.6-15
### How your brain processes faces

In social animals such as humans, a large right temporal lobe area (shown here in a right-facing brain) is dedicated to the crucial task of face recognition. Viewing famous people's faces, compared with famous buildings, increases activation in this fusiform face area (Gorno-Tempini & Price, 2001).

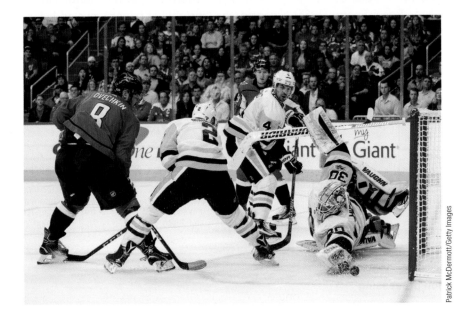

Patrick McDermott/Getty Images

**AP® Science Practice**

## Research

An fMRI is often used as an operational definition of brain activity in neuroscience research. Operational definitions are the exact procedures (or operations) used in a research study. Without them, researchers couldn't replicate studies to ensure the results are valid.

**Supercells score** In this 2017 National Hockey League game, Alex Ovechkin (in red) instantly processed visual information about the positions and movements of three opponents. By using his pattern-detecting supercells, Ovechkin somehow managed to get the puck into the net.

## Parallel Processing

**1.6-8** How does the brain use parallel processing to construct visual perceptions?

Our brain achieves these and other remarkable feats by **parallel processing**: doing many things at once. To analyze a visual scene, the brain processes its subdimensions—motion, form, depth, color—simultaneously.

To recognize a face, your brain integrates information projected by your retinas to several visual cortex areas and compares it with stored information, thus enabling your fusiform face area to recognize the face: *Grandma!* Scientists have debated whether this stored information is contained in a single cell or, as now seems more likely, distributed over a network of cells that build a facial image bit by bit (Tsao, 2019). But some supercells—actually nicknamed "grandmother cells"—do appear to respond very selectively to 1 or 2 faces in 100 (Bowers, 2009; Quiroga et al., 2013). The whole face recognition process involves connections between visual, memory, social, and auditory networks (Ramot et al., 2019). Supercells require supersized brain power.

Destroy or disable a neural workstation for a visual subtask, and something peculiar occurs, as happened to "Mrs. M." (Hoffman, 1998). After a stroke damaged areas near the rear of both sides of her brain, she could not perceive motion. People in a room seemed "suddenly here or there but I [had] not seen them moving." Pouring tea into a cup was a challenge because the fluid appeared frozen—she could not perceive it rising in the cup.

After a stroke or surgery has damaged their brain's visual cortex, some people have experienced prosopagnosia (face blindness). Others have experienced *blindsight* (see Module 1.5a). Shown a series of sticks, they report seeing nothing. Yet when asked to guess whether the sticks are vertical or horizontal, their visual intuition typically offers the correct response. When told, "You got them all right," they are astounded. There is, it seems, a second "mind"—a parallel processing system—operating unseen. These separate visual systems for perceiving and for acting illustrate once again the astonishing dual processing of our two-track mind.

\* \* \*

Think about the wonders of visual processing. As you read these words, the letters reflect light rays onto your retina, which triggers a process that sends formless nerve impulses to several areas of your brain, integrating the information and decoding meaning. The amazing result: We have transferred information across time and space, from our minds to yours (**Figure 1.6-16**). That all of this happens instantly, effortlessly, and continuously is indeed awesome. As Roger Sperry (1985) observed, the "insights of science give added, not lessened, reasons for awe, respect, and reverence."

**parallel processing** processing multiple aspects of a stimulus or problem simultaneously.

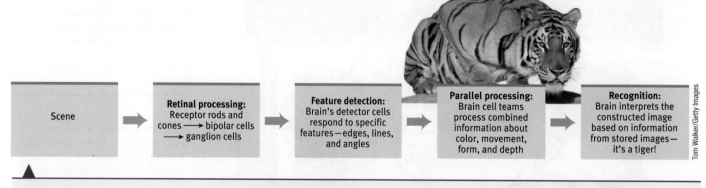

| Scene | → | Retinal processing: Receptor rods and cones → bipolar cells → ganglion cells | → | Feature detection: Brain's detector cells respond to specific features—edges, lines, and angles | → | Parallel processing: Brain cell teams process combined information about color, movement, form, and depth | → | Recognition: Brain interprets the constructed image based on information from stored images—it's a tiger! |

Tom Walker/Getty Images

**Figure 1.6-16**

**A simplified summary of visual information processing**

## Check Your Understanding

### Examine the Concept

▶ Some nocturnal animals, such as toads, mice, rats, and bats, have impressive night vision thanks to having many more _____ (rods/cones) than _____ (rods/cones) in their retinas. These creatures probably have very poor _____ (color/black-and-white) vision.

▶ Cats are able to open their _____ much wider than we can, which allows more light into their eyes so they can see better at night.

▶ Explain the difference between the two key theories of color vision. Are they contradictory or complementary? Explain.

Kruglov_Orda/Shutterstock

### Apply the Concept

▶ If someone had asked you "Is grass green?" before you read this section, how would you have responded? Explain why your response might be different now.

▶ Consider your activities in the last day. Which of them relied on your rods? Which relied on your cones? Explain why these activities would be different — or impossible — without these cells' different abilities.

▶ Explain the rapid sequence of events that occurs when you see and recognize a friend.

*Answers to the Examine the Concept questions can be found in Appendix C at the end of the book.*

## Module 1.6b REVIEW

**1.6-4 What are the characteristics of the energy that we see as visible light? What structures in the eye help focus that energy?**

- What we see as light is only a thin slice of the broad spectrum of electromagnetic energy. The portion visible to humans extends from the shorter blue-violet *wavelengths* to the longer red wavelengths.

- After entering the eye through the *cornea,* passing through the *pupil* and *iris,* and being focused by the *lens,* light energy particles (from a thin slice of the broad spectrum of electromagnetic energy) strike the eye's inner surface, the *retina.*

- Wavelength determines *hue,* the color we perceive; amplitude determines *intensity,* the brightness we perceive.

**1.6-5 How do the rods and cones process information, and what is the path information travels from the eye to the brain?**

- Light entering the eye triggers chemical changes that convert light energy into neural impulses.

- Photoreceptors called *cones* and *rods* at the back of the retina provide differing sensitivities — cones to detail and color, rods to faint light and peripheral motion.

- After processing by bipolar and ganglion cells, neural impulses travel from the retina through the *optic nerve* to the thalamus, and on to the visual cortex.

**1.6-6 How do we perceive color in the world around us?**

- The *Young–Helmholtz trichromatic (three-color) theory* proposed that the retina contains three types of color receptors.

Contemporary research has found three types of cones, each most sensitive to the wavelengths of one of the three primary colors of light (red, green, or blue).

- Hering's *opponent-process theory* proposed three additional sets of opposing retinal processes (red-green, blue-yellow, white-black). Research has confirmed that, en route to the brain, neurons in the retina and the thalamus code the color-related information from the cones into pairs of opponent colors.

- These two theories, and the research supporting them, show that color processing occurs in two stages.

**1.6-7 Where are feature detectors located, and what do they do?**

- *Feature detectors,* specialized nerve cells in the visual cortex, respond to specific features of the visual stimulus, such as shape, angle, or movement.

- Feature detectors pass information on to other cortical areas, where supercell clusters respond to more complex patterns.

**1.6-8 How does the brain use parallel processing to construct visual perceptions?**

- Through *parallel processing,* the brain handles many aspects of vision (color, movement, form, and depth) simultaneously. Other neural teams integrate the results, comparing them with stored information and enabling perceptions.

# AP® Practice Multiple Choice Questions

**Refer to the image below to answer questions 1 and 2.**

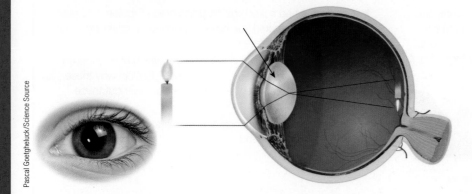

1. To which eye structure does the arrow point in the image?

   a. Iris
   b. Cornea
   c. Lens
   d. Retina

2. What function is most associated with the eye structure identified in question #1?

   a. Color vision
   b. Accommodation
   c. Feature detection
   d. Peripheral vision

3. Which of the following structures helps you *most* in detecting the color of your friend's shirt?

   a. Rods
   b. Cones
   c. Fovea
   d. Lens

4. Your best friend decides to paint her room an extremely bright electric blue. Which of the following best describes the physical properties of the color's light waves?

   a. No wavelength; large amplitude
   b. Short wavelength; large amplitude
   c. Short wavelength; small amplitude
   d. Long wavelength; large amplitude

5. If you scratch your eye, which structure are you most likely to damage?

   a. Pupil
   b. Iris
   c. Cornea
   d. Lens

# Module 1.6c Sensation: Hearing

Like our other senses, our hearing—**audition**—helps us adapt and survive. Hearing provides information and enables relationships. Hearing humanizes: People seem more thoughtful, competent, and likable when we hear, not just read, their words (Schroeder & Epley, 2015, 2016). And hearing is pretty spectacular. It lets us communicate invisibly—by shooting unseen air waves across space and receiving the same from others. Hearing loss is the great invisible disability. To not catch someone's name, to not grasp what someone is asking, and to miss the hilarious joke is to be deprived of what others know, and sometimes to feel excluded. As a person with inherited hearing loss, I [DM] know the feeling, and can understand why adults with significant hearing loss experience increased risk of depression and anxiety (Blazer & Tucci, 2019; Scinicariello et al., 2019).

Most of us, however, can hear a wide range of sounds, and the ones we hear best are those in the range of the human voice. With normal hearing, we are remarkably sensitive to faint sounds, such as a phone ping. (If our ears were only slightly more sensitive, we would hear a constant hiss from the movement of air molecules.) Our distant ancestors' survival depended on this keen hearing when hunting or being hunted.

We are also remarkably attuned to sound variations. Among thousands of possible voices, we easily recognize an unseen friend's voice. Moreover, hearing is fast. "It might take you a full second to notice something out of the corner of your eye, turn your head toward it, recognize it, and respond to it," notes auditory neuroscientist Seth Horowitz (2012). "The same reaction to a new or sudden sound happens at least 10 times as fast." A fraction of a second after such events stimulate your ear's receptors, millions of neurons have simultaneously coordinated in extracting the essential features, comparing them with past experience, and identifying the stimulus (Freeman, 1991). For hearing, as for our other senses, we wonder: How do we do it?

## Sound Waves and the Ear

Draw a bow across a violin, and you will unleash the energy of sound waves. Each bumping into the next, air molecules create waves of compressed and expanded air, like the ripples on a pond circling out from a tossed stone. As we swim in our ocean of moving air molecules, our ears detect these brief air pressure changes.

**audition** the sense or act of hearing.

## The Stimulus Input: Sound Waves

**1.6-9** What are the characteristics of air pressure waves that we hear as sound?

Like light waves, sound waves vary in shape (**Figure 1.6-17**). The height, or *amplitude,* of sound waves determines their perceived *loudness.* Their **frequency** (measured in *hertz*) determines the **pitch** we experience. Long waves have low frequency—and low pitch. Short waves have high frequency—and high pitch. The sound waves produced by a violin are much shorter and faster than those produced by a cello or a bass guitar.

We measure sound intensity in *decibels,* with zero decibels representing the absolute threshold for hearing. Every 10 decibels correspond to a tenfold increase in sound intensity. Thus, normal conversation (60 decibels) is 10,000 times more intense than a 20-decibel whisper. And a temporarily tolerable 100-decibel passing subway train is 10 billion times more intense than the faintest detectable sound. If prolonged, exposure to sounds above 85 decibels can produce hearing loss. Tell that to basketball fans at the University of Kentucky who, in 2017, broke the Guinness World Record for the noisiest indoor stadium at 126 decibels (WKYT, 2017). Hear today, gone tomorrow.

**frequency** the number of complete wavelengths that pass a point in a given time (for example, per second).

**pitch** a tone's experienced highness or lowness; depends on frequency.

**Figure 1.6-17**

**The physical properties of waves**

(a) Waves vary in *wavelength* (the distance between successive peaks). *Frequency,* the number of complete wavelengths that can pass a point in a given time, depends on the wavelength. The shorter the wavelength, the higher the frequency. Wavelength determines the *pitch* of sound. (b) Waves also vary in *amplitude* (the height from peak to trough). Wave amplitude influences sound *intensity.*

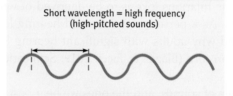

Short wavelength = high frequency (high-pitched sounds)

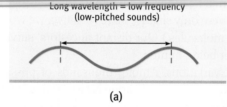

Long wavelength = low frequency (low-pitched sounds)

**(a)**

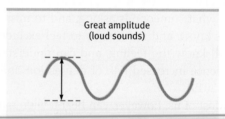

Great amplitude (loud sounds)

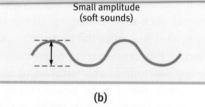

Small amplitude (soft sounds)

**(b)**

**The sounds of music** A violin's short, fast waves create a high pitch. The longer, slower waves of Chi-chi Nwanoku OBE's double bass create a lower pitch. Differences in the waves' height, or amplitude, also create differing degrees of loudness.

Vereshchagin Dmitry/Shutterstock

Courtesy of Eric Richmond/The Chineke! Foundation

# The Ear

**1.6-10** How does the ear transform sound energy into neural messages?

How does vibrating air trigger nerve impulses that your brain can decode as sounds? The process begins when sound waves strike your *eardrum,* causing this tight membrane to vibrate (**Figure 1.6-18**).

In your **middle ear**, a piston made of three tiny bones—the *hammer* (malleus), *anvil* (incus), and *stirrup* (stapes)—picks up the vibrations and transmits them to the **cochlea**, a snail-shaped tube in your **inner ear**.

The incoming vibrations then cause the cochlea's membrane-covered opening (the *oval window*) to vibrate, jostling the fluid inside the cochlea. This motion causes ripples in the *basilar membrane,* bending the *hair cells* lining its surface, rather like grass blades bending in the wind.

The hair cell movements in turn trigger impulses in the adjacent nerve cells, whose axons converge to form the *auditory nerve.* The auditory nerve carries the neural messages to your thalamus and then on to the *auditory cortex* in your brain's temporal lobe. From vibrating air, to tiny moving bones, to fluid waves, to electrical impulses to the brain: Voila! You hear!

**middle ear** the chamber between the eardrum and the cochlea containing three tiny bones that concentrate the vibrations of the eardrum on the cochlea's oval window.

**cochlea** [KOHK-lee-uh] a coiled, bony, fluid-filled tube in the inner ear; sound waves traveling through the cochlear fluid trigger nerve impulses.

**inner ear** the innermost part of the ear, containing the cochlea, semicircular canals, and vestibular sacs.

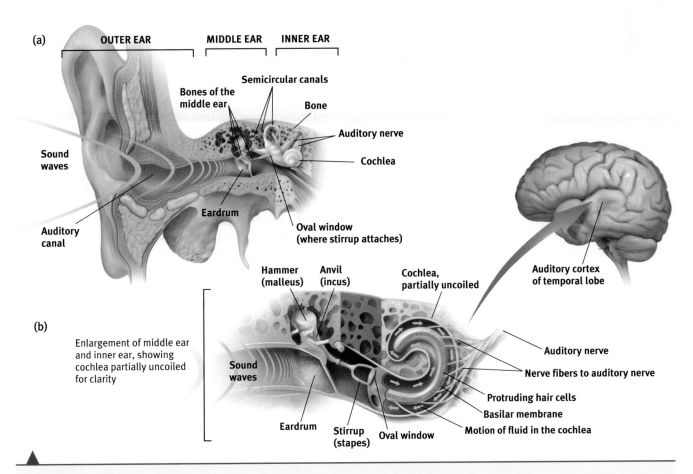

**Figure 1.6-18**

**Hear here: How we transform sound waves into nerve impulses that our brain interprets**

(a) The outer ear funnels sound waves to the eardrum. The bones of the middle ear amplify and relay the eardrum's vibrations through the oval window into the fluid-filled cochlea. (b) As shown in this detail of the middle ear and inner ear, the cochlear fluid's resulting pressure changes cause the basilar membrane to ripple, bending the hair cells on its surface. Hair cell movements trigger impulses at the nerve cells' base, whose fibers converge to form the auditory nerve. That nerve sends neural messages to the thalamus and on to the auditory cortex.

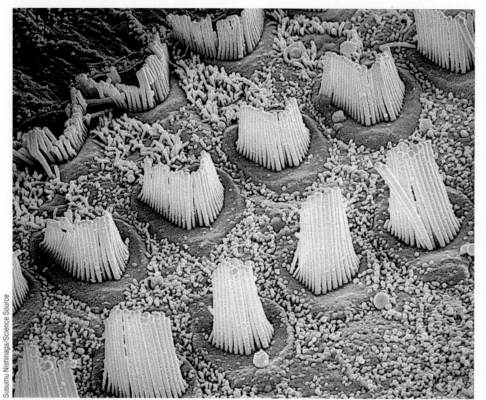

**Be kind to your inner ear's hair cells** When vibrating in response to sound, the hair cells (shown here lining the cochlea) produce an electrical signal.

Perhaps the most intriguing part of the hearing process is the hair cells—"quivering bundles that let us hear" thanks to their "extreme sensitivity and extreme speed" (Goldberg, 2007). A cochlea has 16,000 of them, which sounds like a lot until we compare that number with the eye's 130 million or so photoreceptors. But consider a hair cell's responsiveness. Deflect the tiny bundles of *cilia* on its tip by only the width of an atom (!), and the alert hair cell, thanks to a special protein, will trigger a neural response (Corey et al., 2004).

Worldwide, 1.23 billion people are challenged by hearing loss and an estimated half a billion have a disabling hearing loss (GBD, 2015; Wilson et al., 2017). Damage to the cochlea's hair cell receptors or the auditory nerve can cause **sensorineural hearing loss** (or nerve deafness). With auditory nerve damage, people may hear sound but have trouble discerning what someone is saying (Liberman, 2015). Sensorineural hearing loss is more common than **conduction hearing loss** from damage to the mechanical system—the eardrum and middle ear bones—that conducts sound waves to the cochlea. Occasionally, disease damages hair cell receptors, but more often the culprit is biological changes linked with heredity and aging. I [DM] understand—as one who lives with severe hearing loss passed down from my grandmother and mother, thanks to a single genetic mutation.

Toxic noise, such as prolonged exposure to ear-splitting music, is another culprit. The cochlea's hair cells have been likened to carpet fibers. Walk around on them and they will spring back. But leave a heavy piece of furniture on them and they may never rebound. As a general rule, any noise we cannot talk over (loud machinery, fans screaming at a concert or sports event, our favorite playlist blasting at maximum volume) may be harmful, especially if prolonged and repeated (Roesser, 1998) **(Figure 1.6-19)**. And if our ears ring after such exposures, we have been bad to our unhappy hair cells. Just as pain alerts us to possible bodily harm, ringing of the ears alerts us to possible hearing damage. It is hearing's equivalent of bleeding.

Since the early 1990s, the prevalence of teen hearing loss has increased by one-third, to the point that this condition now affects 1 in 6 teens (Shargorodsky et al., 2010; Weichbold et al., 2012). After 3 hours at a rock concert averaging 99 decibels, 54 percent of teens reported temporarily not hearing as well, and 1 in 4 had ringing in their ears (Derebery et al., 2012). Teen boys more than teen girls or adults blast themselves with loud volumes for long periods (Widén et al., 2017; Zogby, 2006). Greater noise exposure may help explain why men's hearing tends to be less acute than women's. Anyone who spends many hours in a loud nightclub, behind a power mower, or above a jackhammer should wear earplugs, or they risk needing a hearing aid later.

Nerve deafness cannot, as yet, be reversed. One way to restore hearing is with a sort of bionic ear—a **cochlear implant**. Such implants, which had been placed in 737,000 people as of the end of 2019, translate sounds into electrical signals that, when wired into

**sensorineural hearing loss** the most common form of hearing loss, caused by damage to the cochlea's receptor cells or to the auditory nerve; also called *nerve deafness*.

**conduction hearing loss** a less common form of hearing loss, caused by damage to the mechanical system that conducts sound waves to the cochlea.

**cochlear implant** a device for converting sounds into electrical signals and stimulating the auditory nerve through electrodes threaded into the cochlea.

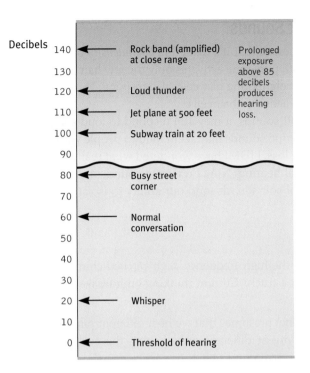

Decibels

| | |
|---|---|
| 140 | Rock band (amplified) at close range |
| 130 | |
| 120 | Loud thunder |
| 110 | Jet plane at 500 feet |
| 100 | Subway train at 20 feet |
| 90 | |
| 80 | Busy street corner |
| 70 | |
| 60 | Normal conversation |
| 50 | |
| 40 | |
| 30 | |
| 20 | Whisper |
| 10 | |
| 0 | Threshold of hearing |

Prolonged exposure above 85 decibels produces hearing loss.

sebra/Shutterstock

**Figure 1.6-19**

**The intensity of some common sounds**

One study found 3 million professional musicians had almost four times the normal rate of noise-induced hearing loss (Schink et al., 2014). Noise-blocking earpieces and headphones reduce the need to blast the music at dangerous volumes.

the cochlea's nerves, convey sound information to the brain (National Institute on Deafness and Other Communication Disorders [NIDCD], 2021; **Figure 1.6-20**). When given to deaf kittens and human infants, cochlear implants have seemed to trigger an "awakening" of the pertinent brain area (Klinke et al., 1999; Sireteanu, 1999). These devices can help children become proficient in oral communication, especially if they receive them as preschoolers or ideally before age 1 (Dettman et al., 2007; Schorr et al., 2005). Hearing, like vision, has a *critical period*. Cochlear implants can help restore hearing for most adults, but only if their brain learned to process sound during childhood. The restored hearing can also reduce social isolation and the risk of depression (Mosnier et al., 2015).

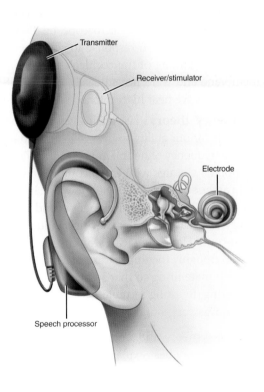

Transmitter

Receiver/stimulator

Electrode

Speech processor

**Figure 1.6-20**

**Hardware for hearing**

Cochlear implants work by translating sounds into electrical signals that are transmitted to the cochlea and then, via the auditory nerve, relayed to the brain.

## Perceiving Loudness, Pitch, and Location

**1.6-11** How do we detect loudness, discriminate pitch, and locate sounds?

We've discussed the mechanics of hearing. But how do we experience the *variety* of sounds—loud and soft, high and low—that help us navigate our world? And how do we know where these sounds are coming from?

## Responding to Loud and Soft Sounds

How do we detect loudness? If you guessed that it's related to the *intensity* of a hair cell's response, you'd be wrong. Rather, a soft, pure tone activates only the few hair cells attuned to its frequency. Given louder sounds, neighboring hair cells also respond. Thus, your brain interprets loudness from the *number* of activated hair cells.

If a hair cell loses sensitivity to soft sounds, it may still respond to loud sounds. This helps explain another surprise: Really loud sounds may seem loud to people with or without normal hearing. Given my hearing loss, I [DM] have wondered what really loud music must sound like to people with normal hearing. Now I realize it sounds much the same; where we differ is in our perception of soft sounds (and our ability to isolate one sound amid noise).

## Hearing Different Pitches

How do we know whether a sound is the high-frequency, high-pitched chirp of a bird or the low-frequency, low-pitched roar of a truck? Current thinking on how we discriminate pitch combines two theories.

- **Place theory** (also called *place coding*) presumes that we hear different pitches because different sound waves trigger activity at different places along the cochlea's basilar membrane. Thus, the brain determines a sound's pitch by recognizing the specific place (on the membrane) that is generating the neural signal. When Nobel laureate-to-be Georg von Békésy (1957) cut holes in the cochleas of guinea pigs and human cadavers and looked inside with a microscope, he discovered that the cochlea vibrated, rather like a shaken bedsheet, in response to sound. High frequencies produced large vibrations near the beginning of the cochlea's membrane. Low frequencies vibrated more of the membrane and were not so easily localized. So, there is a problem: Place theory can explain how we hear high-pitched sounds but not low-pitched sounds.

- **Frequency theory** (also called *temporal coding*) suggests another explanation that accounts for our ability to hear low-pitched sounds: The brain reads pitch by monitoring the frequency of neural impulses traveling up the auditory nerve. The whole basilar membrane vibrates with the incoming sound wave, triggering neural impulses to the brain at the same rate as the sound wave. If the sound wave has a frequency of 100 waves per second, then 100 pulses per second travel up the auditory nerve. But frequency theory also has a problem: An individual neuron cannot fire faster than 1000 times per second. How, then, can we sense sounds with frequencies above 1000 waves per second (roughly the upper third of a piano keyboard)? Enter *volley theory:* Like soldiers who alternate firing so that some can shoot while others reload, neural cells can alternate firing. By firing in rapid succession, they can achieve a *combined frequency* above 1000 waves per second.

So, place theory and frequency theory work together to enable our perception of pitch. Place theory best explains how we sense *high pitches*. Frequency theory, extended by volley theory, also explains how we sense *low pitches*. Finally, some combination of the place and frequency theories likely explains how we sense *pitches in the intermediate range*.

## Localizing Sounds

Why don't we have one big ear—perhaps above our one nose? "All the better to hear you with," as the wolf said to Little Red Riding Hood. Thanks to the placement of our two ears, we enjoy stereophonic ("three-dimensional") hearing. Two ears are better than one for at least two reasons (**Figure 1.6-21**). If a car to your right honks, your right ear will receive a more *intense* sound, and it will receive the sound slightly *sooner* than your left ear.

**place theory** in hearing, the theory that links the pitch we hear with the place where the cochlea's membrane is stimulated. (Also called *place coding*.)

**frequency theory** in hearing, the theory that the rate of nerve impulses traveling up the auditory nerve matches the frequency of a tone, thus enabling us to sense its pitch. (Also called *temporal coding*.)

Because sound travels fast and human ears are not very far apart, the intensity difference and the time lag are extremely small. A *just noticeable difference* in the direction of two sound sources corresponds to a time difference of just 0.000027 second! Luckily for us, our supersensitive auditory system can detect such minute differences and locate the sound (Brown & Deffenbacher, 1979; Middlebrooks & Green, 1991).

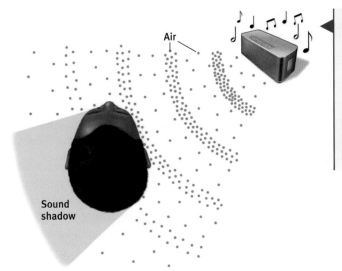

Air

Sound shadow

**Figure 1.6-21**

**How we locate sounds**

Sound waves strike one ear sooner and more intensely than the other. From this information, our nimble brain can compute the sound's location. As you might expect, people who lose all hearing in one ear often have difficulty locating sounds.

---

**AP® Science Practice**

## Check Your Understanding

**Examine the Concept**

▶ The amplitude of a sound wave determines our perception of _____ (loudness/pitch).

▶ The longer the sound waves are, the _____ (lower/higher) their frequency and the _____ (higher/lower) their pitch.

*Answers to the Examine the Concept questions can be found in Appendix C at the end of the book.*

**Apply the Concept**

▶ Imagine you are attending a symphonic concert. Explain the theories of pitch perception that best help you enjoy the sounds of (1) a high-pitched piccolo and (2) a low-pitched cello.

---

# Module 1.6c REVIEW

**1.6-9 What are the characteristics of air pressure waves that we hear as sound?**

● Sound waves are bands of compressed and expanded air. Our ears detect these brief changes in air pressure.

● Sound waves vary in amplitude, which we perceive as differing loudness (with sound intensity measured in decibels), and in *frequency* (measured in hertz), which we experience as differing *pitch*.

**1.6-10 How does the ear transform sound energy into neural messages?**

● The *middle ear* is the chamber between the eardrum and the *cochlea*.

● The *inner ear* consists of the cochlea, semicircular canals, and vestibular sacs.

● Sound waves traveling through the auditory canal cause tiny vibrations in the eardrum. The bones of the middle ear amplify these vibrations and relay them to the fluid-filled cochlea. Rippling of the basilar membrane, caused by pressure changes in the cochlear fluid, causes movement of the tiny hair cells, triggering neural messages to be sent (via the thalamus) to the auditory cortex in the brain.

● *Sensorineural hearing loss* (or nerve deafness) results from damage to the cochlea's hair cells or the auditory nerve. *Conduction hearing loss* results from damage to the mechanical system that transmits sound waves to the cochlea. *Cochlear implants* can restore hearing for some people.

**1.6-11 How do we detect loudness, discriminate pitch, and locate sounds?**

● Loudness is not related to the intensity of a hair cell's response, but rather to the number of activated hair cells.

● *Place theory* (place coding) explains how we hear high-pitched sounds, and *frequency theory* (temporal coding), extended by volley theory, explains how we hear low-pitched sounds. A combination of the two theories explains how we hear pitches in the middle range.

● Sound waves strike one ear sooner and more intensely than the other. The brain analyzes the minute differences in the sounds received by the two ears and computes the sound's source.

# AP® Practice Multiple Choice Questions

1. Your friend is playing the low notes on her tuba quite loudly. Which of the following best explains the physical properties of the sound waves?

   a. No wavelength; large amplitude
   b. Short wavelength; large amplitude
   c. Short wavelength; small amplitude
   d. Long wavelength; large amplitude

2. After being exposed to loud music for many years, which of the following types of hearing loss is more likely in a musician?

   a. Conduction
   b. Accommodation
   c. Sensorineural
   d. Frequency

3. Nicholas can tell the difference between different pitches because his cochlea's basilar membrane is stimulated in different areas. Nicholas' experience aligns with which theory?

   a. Place theory
   b. Frequency theory
   c. Volley theory
   d. Sound localization

4. When Yaroslav listens to music, the sound waves cause which of the following to vibrate first?

   a. cochlea
   b. hammer, anvil, and stirrup
   c. eardrum
   d. oval window

5. Dr. Seesmay wants to conduct a study in which she examines sensorineural hearing loss. Which of the following would be an appropriate operational definition for her variable of interest?

   a. The number of hair cells damaged in the cochlea among individuals with hearing loss
   b. The functioning of the hammer, anvil, and stirrup among individuals with hearing loss
   c. The rate of firing in the occipital lobe among individuals with hearing loss
   d. The subjective experience of pitch among individuals with hearing loss

# Module 1.6d Sensation: Skin, Chemical, and Body Senses and Sensory Interaction

## LEARNING TARGETS

**1.6-12** Explain the four basic touch sensations, and explain how we sense touch.

**1.6-13** Compare and contrast the biological, psychological, and social-cultural influences that affect our experience of pain, and explain how placebos and distraction help control pain.

**1.6-14** Explain our senses of taste and smell.

**1.6-15** Explain how we sense our body's position and movement.

**1.6-16** Explain how *sensory interaction* influences our perceptions, and explain the concept of *embodied cognition*.

Sharks and dogs rely on their outstanding sense of smell, aided by their large smell-related brain areas. By comparison, our human brain allocates more of its real estate to seeing and hearing. But extraordinary happenings also occur as part of our skin (touch and pain), chemical (taste and smell), and body (position and movement) senses. Without these other senses, we humans would be seriously hampered, and our capacity for enjoying the world would be greatly diminished.

## Touch

**1.6-12** What are the four basic touch sensations, and how do we sense touch?

*Touch,* our tactile sense, is vital. From infancy to adulthood, affectionate touches promote our well-being (Jakubiak & Feeney, 2017). Right from the start, touch aids our development. Infant rats deprived of their mother's grooming produce less growth hormone and have a lower metabolic rate—a good way to keep alive until the mother returns, but a reaction that stunts growth if prolonged. Infant monkeys that are allowed to see, hear, and smell—but not touch—their mother become desperately unhappy (Suomi et al., 1976). Premature human babies gain weight faster and go home sooner if they are stimulated by hand massage (Field et al., 2006). When coping with disaster or grieving a death, we may find comfort in a hug. As adults, we still yearn to touch—to kiss, to stroke, to snuggle.

Humorist Dave Barry (1985) was perhaps right to jest that your skin "keeps people from seeing the inside of your body, which is repulsive, and it prevents your organs from falling onto the ground." But skin does much more. Touching various spots on the skin with a soft hair, a warm or cool wire, and the point of a pin reveals that some spots are especially sensitive to *pressure,* others to *warmth,* others to *cold,* and still others to *pain.* Our "sense of touch" is actually a mix of these four basic and distinct skin senses, and our other skin sensations are variations of pressure, warmth, cold, and pain. For example, stroking adjacent pressure spots creates a tickle. Repeated gentle stroking of a pain spot creates an itching

**The precious sense of touch** As William James wrote in his *Principles of Psychology* (1890), "Touch is both the alpha and omega of affection."

"Pain is a gift." So said a doctor studying Ashlyn Blocker, who has a rare genetic mutation that prevents her from feeling pain. At birth, she didn't cry. As a child, she ran around for 2 days on a broken ankle. She has put her hands on a hot machine and burned the flesh off. And she has reached into boiling water to retrieve a dropped spoon. "Everyone in my class asks me about it, and I say, 'I can feel pressure, but I can't feel pain.' Pain! I cannot feel it!" (Heckert, 2012).

sensation. Touching adjacent cold and pressure spots triggers a sense of wetness (which you can experience by touching dry, cold metal). Activating receptors for cold and warmth produces a hot sensation.

Touch sensations involve more than tactile stimulation, however. A self-administered tickle produces less somatosensory cortex activation than does the same tickle from something or someone else (Blakemore et al., 1998). Likewise, a leg caress evokes a different somatosensory cortex response when a straight man believes it comes from an attractive woman rather than a man (Gazzola et al., 2012). Such responses reveal how quickly cognition influences our brain's sensory response.

## Pain

> **1.6-13** What biological, psychological, and social-cultural influences affect our experience of pain? How do placebos and distraction help control pain?

Be thankful for occasional pain. Pain is your body's way of telling you something has gone wrong. By drawing your attention to a burn, a break, or a sprain, pain orders you to change your behavior—"Stay off that ankle!" Pain also serves a psychological purpose, enhancing our self-awareness, arousing others' empathy, and promoting social connections (Bastian et al., 2014).

The rare people born without the ability to feel pain are at risk of severe injury or even early death (Habib et al., 2019). Without the discomfort that makes the rest of us shift position, their joints can fail from excess strain. Without the warnings of pain, infections can run wild and injuries can accumulate (Neese, 1991).

More numerous are the people who live with chronic pain, which is rather like an alarm that won't shut off. Persistent backaches, arthritis, headaches, and cancer-related pain prompt two questions: What is pain? How might we control it?

## Understanding Pain

Our experience of pain reflects both *bottom-up* sensations and *top-down* cognition. Pain is a biopsychosocial phenomenon (Hadjistavropoulos et al., 2011). As such, pain experiences vary widely, both from group to group and from person to person. Viewing pain from many perspectives can help us better understand how to cope with it and treat it (**Figure 1.6-22**).

### Figure 1.6-22

**Biopsychosocial approach to pain**

Our experience of pain is much more than the neural messages sent to our brain.

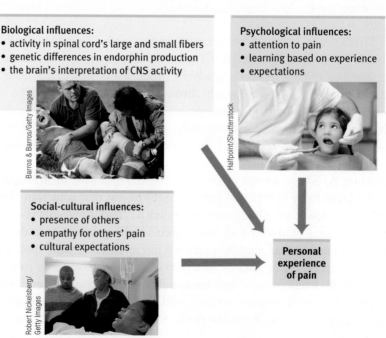

Biological influences:
- activity in spinal cord's large and small fibers
- genetic differences in endorphin production
- the brain's interpretation of CNS activity

Psychological influences:
- attention to pain
- learning based on experience
- expectations

Social-cultural influences:
- presence of others
- empathy for others' pain
- cultural expectations

Personal experience of pain

## Biological Influences

Pain is a physical event produced by your senses. But pain differs from some of your other sensations. No one type of stimulus triggers pain the way that light triggers vision. And no specialized receptors process pain signals the way that your retina receptors react to light rays. Instead, sensory receptors called *nociceptors*—mostly in your skin, but also in your muscles and organs—detect harmful temperatures, pressure, or chemicals (Figure 1.6-23).

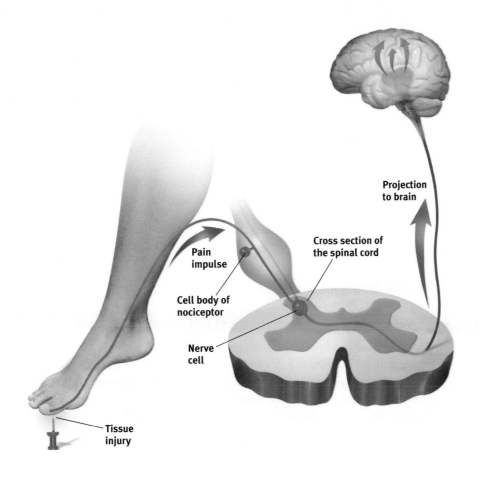

**Figure 1.6-23**
**The pain circuit**

Sensory receptors (*nociceptors*) respond to potentially damaging stimuli by sending an impulse to the spinal cord, which passes the message to the brain, which interprets the signal as pain.

Projection to brain

Pain impulse

Cross section of the spinal cord

Cell body of nociceptor

Nerve cell

Tissue injury

Your pain experience depends in part on the genes you inherited and on your physical characteristics (Gatchel et al., 2007; Reimann et al., 2010). Women are more sensitive to pain than men are (their senses of hearing and smell also tend to be more sensitive) (Ruau et al., 2012; Wickelgren, 2009).

No pain theory can explain all findings from research on pain. One useful model, **gate-control theory**, suggests that the spinal cord contains a neurological "gate" that controls the transmission of pain messages to the brain (Melzack & Katz, 2013; Melzack & Wall, 1965, 1983).

Small spinal cord nerve fibers conduct most pain signals. An injury activates the small fibers and opens the gate. The pain signals can then travel to your brain, and you feel pain. But large-fiber activity (stimulated by massage, electrical stimulation, or acupuncture) can close the pain gate by blocking pain signals. Brain-to-spinal-cord messages can also close the gate. Thus, chronic pain can be treated both by gate-closing stimulation, such as massage, and by mental activity, such as distraction (Wall, 2000).

We also benefit from our own natural painkillers, *endorphins*, which are released in response to severe pain or vigorous exercise. People who carry a gene that boosts the availability of endorphins are less bothered by pain, and their brain is less responsive to pain

**gate-control theory** the theory that the spinal cord contains a neurological "gate" that blocks pain signals or allows them to pass on to the brain. The "gate" is opened by the activity of pain signals traveling up small nerve fibers, and is closed by activity in larger fibers or by information coming from the brain.

**Distracted from the pain** After a tackle in the first half of a competitive game, Mohammed Ali Khan (here playing for BK Häcken in white) said he "had a bit of pain" but thought it was "just a bruise." With his attention focused on the game, he played on. In the second half, he was surprised to learn that his leg was broken.

(Zubieta et al., 2003). Others, who carry a mutated gene that disrupts pain circuit neurotransmission, may not experience pain (Cox et al., 2006). Such discoveries point the way toward future pain medications that can mimic these genetic effects.

Pain is not merely a physical phenomenon of injured nerves sending impulses to a definable brain or spinal cord area—like pulling on a rope to ring a bell. The brain can also create pain, as it does in *phantom limb sensations.* When it lacks the normal sensory input from a missing limb, the brain may misinterpret and amplify spontaneous but irrelevant central nervous system activity. As the dreamer sees with eyes closed, so 7 in 10 people who have undergone limb amputation feel pain or movement in their nonexistent limbs (Melzack, 1992, 2005). Some may even try to lift a cup with a phantom hand, or step off a bed onto a phantom leg. Even those born without a limb sometimes perceive sensations from the absent arm or leg; the brain comes prepared to anticipate "that it will be getting information from a body that has limbs" (Melzack, 1998).

Phantoms may haunt other senses, too. People with hearing loss often experience the sound of silence. *Tinnitus,* the phantom sound of ringing in the ears, is not produced by vibrating air molecules but is accompanied by auditory brain activity (Sedley et al., 2015). People who lose vision to glaucoma, cataracts, diabetes, or macular degeneration may experience phantom sights—nonthreatening hallucinations (Painter et al., 2018). Others who have nerve damage in the tasting and smelling systems have experienced phantom tastes or smells, such as ice water that seems sickeningly sweet or fresh air that reeks of rotten food (Goode, 1999). *The point to remember:* We feel, see, hear, taste, and smell with our brain.

## Psychological Influences

One powerful influence on our perception of pain is the attention we focus on it. Athletes, focused on winning, may perceive pain differently and play through it. Injured soldiers, caught up in battle, may feel little or no pain until they reach safety.

We also seem to edit our *memories* of pain, which often differ from the pain we actually experienced. In experiments, and after painful medical procedures or childbirth, people overlook a pain's duration. Instead, their memory snapshots record two factors: their pain's *peak* moment (which can lead them to recall variable pain, with peaks, as worse [Chajut et al., 2014; Stone et al., 2005]) and how much pain they felt at the *end.* In one experiment, people immersed one hand in painfully cold water for 60 seconds, and then the other hand in the same painfully cold water for 60 seconds followed by a slightly less painful 30 seconds more (Kahneman et al., 1993). Which experience would you expect they recalled as most painful?

Curiously, when asked which trial they would prefer to repeat, most preferred the 90-second trial, with more net pain—but less pain at the end. Physicians have used this principle with patients undergoing sedation-free colon exams—lengthening the discomfort by a minute but lessening its intensity at the end (Kahneman, 1999). Imagine undergoing a painful procedure and having the doctor ask if you'd rather go home now or bear a few more minutes of milder discomfort. There's a case to be made for prolonging a tapered hurt.

The end of an experience can color our memory of pleasures, too. In one simple experiment, some people, on receiving a fifth and last piece of chocolate, were told it was their "next" one. Others, told it was their "last" piece, liked it better and rated the whole experiment as more enjoyable (O'Brien & Ellsworth, 2012). Endings matter.

## Social-Cultural Influences

Pain is a product of our attention, our expectations, and also our culture (Gatchel et al., 2007; Reimann et al., 2010). Not surprisingly, then, our perception of pain varies with our social situation and our cultural traditions. We tend to perceive more pain when others

**CULTURAL AWARENESS**

Our cultural beliefs and traditions influence our experience of pain. Had you ever thought about social-cultural influences on pain? What are some ways your culture might play a role in your experience of pain?

also seem to be experiencing pain (Symbaluk et al., 1997). This may help explain the apparent social aspects of pain, as when groups of Australian keyboard operators during the mid-1980s suffered outbreaks of severe pain while typing or performing other repetitive work—without any discernible physical abnormalities (Gawande, 1998). Sometimes, the pain in a sprain is mainly in the brain—literally. When people feel empathy for another's pain, their own brain activity partly mirrors the activity of the actual brain in pain (Singer et al., 2004).

## Controlling Pain

If pain is where body meets mind—if it is both a physical and a psychological phenomenon—then it should be treatable both physically and psychologically. Depending on the symptoms, pain control therapies may include drugs, surgery, acupuncture, electrical stimulation, massage, exercise, hypnosis (see Module 5.5), relaxation training, meditation, and thought distraction.

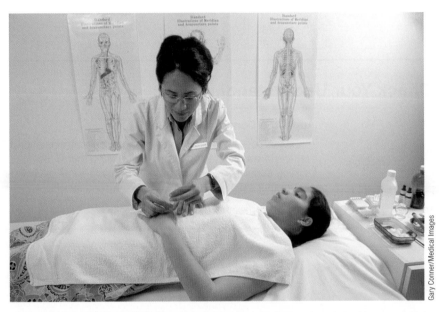

**Acupuncture: A jab well done** This acupuncturist is attempting to help this woman gain relief from back pain by using needles on points of the patient's hand.

## Placebos

Even *placebos* can help, by dampening the central nervous system's attention and responses to painful experiences—mimicking painkilling drugs (Eippert et al., 2009; Wager & Atlas, 2013). After being injected in the jaw with a stinging saltwater solution, men in one experiment received a placebo they had been told would relieve the pain. It did—they immediately felt better. "Nothing" worked. The men's belief in the fake painkiller triggered their brain to respond by dispensing endorphins, as revealed by activity in an area that releases natural painkilling opioids (Scott et al., 2007; Zubieta et al., 2005).

Another experiment pitted two placebos—fake pills and pretend acupuncture—against each other (Kaptchuk et al., 2006). People with persistent arm pain received either sham acupuncture (with trick needles that retracted without puncturing the skin) or blue cornstarch pills that looked like a medication often prescribed for strain injury. After two months, both groups were reporting less pain, with the fake acupuncture group reporting the greater pain drop. One-fourth of those receiving the nonexistent needle pricks and 31 percent of those receiving the fake pills even complained of side effects, such as painful skin or dry mouth and fatigue.

**AP® Science Practice**

### Research

Placebos play an important role in medical research. The experimental method typically includes an experimental group (exposed to the treatment) and a control group (given a placebo or different version of the treatment).

*"It's like I'm actually walking."*

Ellis Rosen/Cartoon Stock

## Distraction

Have you ever had a health care professional suggest that you focus on a pleasant image (*"Think of a warm, comfortable environment"*) or perform some task (*"Count backward by 3s"*)? Drawing attention away from the painful stimulation is an effective way to activate brain pathways that inhibit pain and increase pain tolerance (Edwards et al., 2009). For patients who have experienced burns and are receiving excruciating wound care, an even more effective distraction is escaping into virtual reality. As shown by fMRI scans, playing in a computer-generated 3-D world reduces the brain's pain-related activity (Hoffman, 2004). Being "fully immersed in a virtual environment [is] like a 'brain hack,'" said one doctor who uses virtual reality to treat pain. "You can't be engaged in anything else" (Brody, 2019).

---

**AP® Science Practice**

## Check Your Understanding

### Examine the Concept

► Explain the gate-control theory of pain.

► Explain the differences among the biological, psychological, and social-cultural influences on pain.

### Apply the Concept

► Explain some ways to control pain. Which methods of pain control do you usually turn to when you need them? Has learning about ways to control pain given you some new ideas about other strategies to try?

*Answers to the Examine the Concept questions can be found in Appendix C at the end of the book.*

---

# Taste

**1.6-14** In what ways are our senses of taste and smell similar, and how do they differ?

Like touch, **gustation**—our sense of taste—involves several basic sensations. Taste's sensations were once thought to be *sweet, sour, salty,* and *bitter,* with all others stemming from mixtures of these four (McBurney & Gent, 1979). Then, as investigators searched for specialized nerve fibers for taste, they encountered a receptor for a fifth taste sensation—the savory, meaty taste of *umami,* best experienced as the flavor enhancer monosodium glutamate (MSG). Other researchers then identified a sixth sensation: *oleogustus,* or the unique taste of fat.

Tastes exist for more than our pleasure (see **Table 1.6-2**). Pleasureful tastes attracted our ancestors to energy- or protein-rich foods that enabled their survival. Aversive tastes deterred them from new foods that might be toxic. We see the inheritance of this biological wisdom in today's 2- to 6-year-olds, who are typically fussy eaters, especially when offered new meats or bitter-tasting vegetables, such as spinach and brussels sprouts (Cooke et al., 2003). Meat and plant toxins were both potentially dangerous sources of food poisoning for our ancestors, especially children. Given repeated small tastes of disliked but safe new foods, however, most children begin to accept them (Wardle et al., 2003). We come to like what we eat. Compared with breast-fed babies, German babies bottle-fed vanilla-flavored milk grew up to be adults with a striking preference

**gustation** our sense of taste.

for vanilla flavoring (Haller et al., 1999). The taste-exposure phenomenon even extends to the womb. In one experiment, babies whose mothers drank carrot juice late in their pregnancy and during the early weeks of nursing developed a liking for carrot-flavored cereal (Mennella et al., 2001). (Module 4.7 explores cultural influences on our taste preferences.)

**CULTURAL AWARENESS**

Developing taste preferences for foods we are used to eating is a good example of how culture influences our beliefs and behaviors. We might decide we don't like an unfamiliar dish before we even try it.

| TABLE 1.6-2 | The Survival Functions of Basic Tastes |
|---|---|
| **Taste** | **Indicates** |
| Sweet | Energy source |
| Salty | Sodium essential to physiological processes |
| Sour | Potentially toxic acid |
| Bitter | Potential poisons |
| Umami | Proteins to grow and repair tissue |
| Oleogustus | Fats for energy, insulation, and cell growth |

Lauren Burke/Getty Images

Macmillan Learning

Taste is a chemical sense. Inside each little bump on the top and sides of your tongue are 200 or more taste buds, each containing a pore that catches food chemicals and releases neurotransmitters (Roper & Chaudhari, 2017). In each pore, 50 to 100 taste receptor cells project antenna-like hairs that sense food molecules. Some receptors respond mostly to sweet-tasting molecules, others to the other flavors' molecules. Each receptor transmits its message to a matching partner cell in your brain's temporal lobe (Barretto et al., 2015). Some people have more taste buds than others, enabling them to experience more intense tastes. Psychologist Linda Bartoshuk (2000) has researched these *supertasters*. Other researchers have investigated average-ability *medium tasters* and lower-than-average *nontasters*.

For most people, it doesn't take much to trigger a taste response. If a stream of water is pumped across your tongue, the addition of a concentrated salty or sweet taste for but one-tenth of a second will get your attention (Kelling & Halpern, 1983). When a friend asks for "just a taste" of your smoothie, you can squeeze off the straw after a mere instant.

Taste receptors reproduce themselves every week or two, so if you burn your tongue it hardly matters. However, as you grow older, the number of taste buds decreases, as does taste sensitivity (Cowart, 1981). (No wonder adults enjoy strong-tasting foods that children resist.) Smoking and alcohol use accelerate these declines. People who have lost their sense of taste have reported that food tastes like "straw" and is hard to swallow (Cowart, 2005).

There's more to taste than meets the tongue. Wear a blindfold when eating a meal and you will attend more to (and savor) its taste (O'Brien & Smith, 2019). Expectations also influence taste. When told a sausage roll was "vegetarian," nonvegetarian people judged it decidedly inferior to its identical partner labeled "meat" (Allen et al., 2008). In another experiment, hearing that a wine cost $90 rather than its real $10 price made it taste better and triggered more activity in a brain area that responds to pleasant experiences (Plassmann et al., 2008). Contrary to Shakespeare's presumption (in *Romeo and Juliet*) that "a rose by any other name would smell as sweet," labels matter. And speaking of smell . . .

**Linda Bartoshuk (born 1938)**
As a student in the late 1950s era of gender discrimination, Bartoshuk (2010) abandoned her interest in astronomy when she learned that "women weren't allowed to use the big telescopes." This led her to *psychophysics* — the study of how physical stimuli, such as substances on the tongue, create our subjective experience. While studying taste experiences, she discovered *supertasters*, who can taste some things the rest of us cannot.

 **SPOTLIGHT ON:**
Linda Bartoshuk

 **AP® Science Practice**

**Research**

There is an important difference between random assignment and random sampling. In this taste study, researchers might randomly assign participants to get the "vegetarian" or "meat" sausage roll, while also using random sampling, in which every person in the population being studied has an equal chance of participating. Random assignment allows us to draw cause-effect conclusions. Random sampling allows us to generalize our findings.

# Smell

Inhale, exhale. Between birth's first inhale and death's last exhale, an average 500 million breaths of life-sustaining air bathe human nostrils in a stream of scent-laden molecules. The resulting experience of smell—**olfaction**—is strikingly intimate. With every breath, you inhale something of whatever or whoever it is you smell.

**olfaction** our sense of smell.

Smell, like taste, is a chemical sense. We smell something when molecules of a substance carried in the air reach a tiny cluster of receptor cells at the top of each nasal cavity (Figure 1.6-24). By sniffing, you swirl air up to those receptors, enhancing the aroma. These 20 million olfactory receptors, waving like sea anemones on a reef, respond selectively—to the aroma of a cake baking, to a wisp of smoke, to a friend's fragrance. Instantly, they alert the brain through their axon fibers.

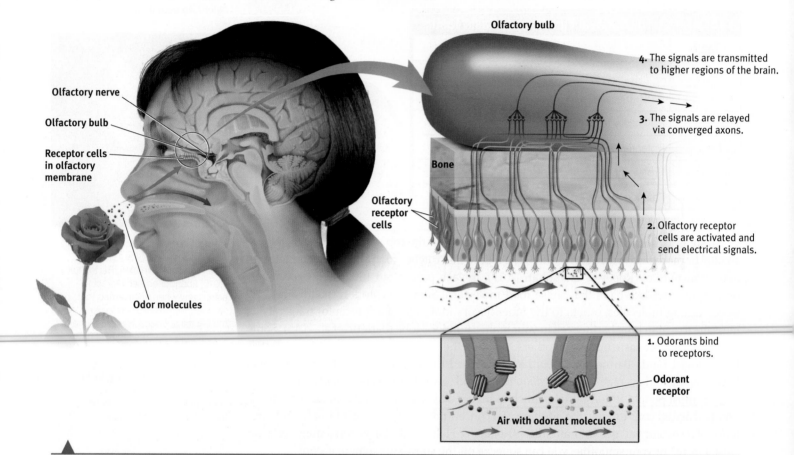

**Figure 1.6-24**
**The sense of smell**

Olfactory receptor cells send messages to the brain's olfactory bulb, and then onward to the temporal lobe's primary smell cortex and to the parts of the limbic system involved in memory and emotion.

### TRY THIS

Impress your friends with your new word for the day: People unable to see are said to experience blindness. People unable to hear experience deafness. People unable to smell experience *anosmia*. The 1 in 7500 people born with anosmia not only have trouble cooking and eating, but also are somewhat more prone to depression, accidents, and relationship insecurity (Croy et al., 2012, 2013). Loss of smell and taste have been commonly reported symptoms of Covid.

Being part of an old, primitive sense, olfactory neurons bypass the brain's sensory control center, the thalamus. Eons before our cerebral cortex had fully evolved, our mammalian ancestors sniffed for food—and for predators. They also smelled molecules called *pheromones*—olfactory chemical messages—especially those secreted by other members of their species. Some pheromones serve as sexual attractants. When straight men smelled ovulating women's T-shirts, the men became more sexually interested and experienced increased testosterone (Miller & Maner, 2010, 2011).

Odor molecules come in many shapes and sizes—so many, in fact, that it takes many different receptors to detect them. A large family of genes designs the 350 or so receptor proteins that recognize particular odor molecules (Miller, 2004). Linda Buck and Richard Axel (1991) discovered (in work for which they received a Nobel Prize in 2004) that these receptor proteins are embedded on the surface of nasal cavity neurons. Just as a key slips into a lock, odor molecules slip into these receptors. Yet we don't seem to have a distinct receptor for each detectable odor. Odors trigger combinations of receptors, in patterns that are interpreted by the olfactory cortex. Just as the English alphabet's 26 letters can combine to form many words, so odor molecules bind to different receptor arrays, producing as many as 1 trillion odors that we could potentially discriminate (Bushdid et al., 2014). Neuroscientists have identified complex combinations of olfactory receptors that trigger different neural networks, allowing us to distinguish between delightful and disagreeable odors (Zou et al., 2016).

Animals that have many times more olfactory receptors than we do also use their sense of smell to survive, to communicate, and to navigate. Elephants can smell the difference between small and large amounts of food—letting them know whether they have enough to feed themselves or their herd (Plotnik et al., 2019). And long before a shark can see its prey, or a moth its mate, olfactory cues direct them on their way to their target, just as they do for migrating salmon returning to their home stream. After being exposed in a hatchery to one of two odorant chemicals, returning salmon will later seek whichever stream was spiked with the familiar smell (Barinaga, 1999).

Aided by smell, a mother fur seal returning to a beach crowded with pups will find her own. Human mothers and nursing infants also quickly learn to recognize each other's scents (McCarthy, 1986). When people in relationships catch a whiff of their romantic partner's scent, their stress levels drop (Granqvist et al., 2019; Hofer et al., 2018). As any dog or cat with a good nose could tell us, we each have our own identifiable chemical signature. (One noteworthy exception: A dog will follow the tracks of one identical twin as though they had been made by the other person [Thomas, 1974].)

The brain knows what the nose knows (Cook et al., 2017; Zou et al., 2016). When mice sniff a predator's scent, their brain instinctively sends signals to stress-related neurons (Kondoh et al., 2016). But smell expert Rachel Herz (2001) notes that a smell's appeal—or lack of it—also depends on learned associations. In North America, people associate the smell of wintergreen with candy and gum, and they tend to like it. In Britain, wintergreen often is associated with medicine, and people find it less appealing. Odors also evoked unpleasant emotions when researchers frustrated Brown University students with a rigged computer game in a scented room (Herz et al., 2004). Later, if exposed to the same odor while working on a verbal task, the students' frustration was rekindled and they gave up sooner than others exposed to a different odor or no odor.

**The nose knows** Humans have some 20 million olfactory receptors. A bloodhound has 220 million (Herz, 2007).

Although important, our sense of smell is less acute than our senses of seeing and hearing. Looking out across a garden, we see its forms and colors in exquisite detail and hear a variety of birds singing, yet we miss some of a garden's scents unless we stick our nose into the blossoms. We can learn to identify subtle smell differences, but it isn't easy (Al Aïn et al., 2019). Compared with how we experience and remember sights and sounds, smells are harder to describe and recall (Richardson & Zucco, 1989; Zucco, 2003). Test it yourself: Which is easier, describing the *sound* of coffee brewing or the *aroma* of coffee? For most people in Western cultures, it's the sound.

We might struggle to recall odors by name, but we have a remarkable capacity to recognize long-forgotten odors and their associated memories (Engen, 1987; Schab, 1991). Our brain's circuitry helps explain why the smell of the sea, the scent of a perfume, or an aroma of a favorite relative's kitchen can bring to mind a happy time. Other odors remind us of traumatic events, activating brain regions related to fear (Kadohisa, 2013). Indeed, a hotline runs between the brain area receiving information from the nose and the brain's limbic centers associated with memory and emotion (**Figure 1.6-25**). Thus, when put in a foul-smelling room, people have expressed harsher judgments of immoral acts (such as lying or keeping a found wallet) (Inbar et al., 2012; Schnall et al., 2008). Exposed to a fishy smell, people became more suspicious (Lee et al., 2015; Lee & Schwarz, 2012). And when riding in a train car with the citrus scent of a cleaning product, people have left behind less trash (de Lange et al., 2012).

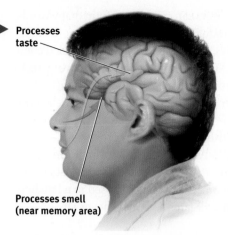

Processes taste

Processes smell
(near memory area)

Gender, age, and experience influence our ability to identify and remember scents. Women tend to have a better sense of smell, but for all of us, the sense of smell peaks in early adulthood and gradually declines thereafter (Doty, 2001; Wickelgren, 2009; Wysocki & Gilbert, 1989). Physical condition also matters: Smokers and people with Alzheimer's disease, Parkinson's disease, or alcohol use disorder typically have a diminished sense of smell (Doty, 2001). Moreover, the smells we detect and the ways we experience them differ, thanks to our individual genes (Trimmer et al., 2019). The scent of a flower may be different for you than for a friend.

## Body Position and Movement

**1.6-15** How do we sense our body's position and movement?

If you did not sense your body's position and movement, you could not put food in your mouth, stand up, or reach out and touch someone. Nor could you perform the "simple" act of taking one step forward. That act requires feedback from, and instructions to, some 200 muscles, and it engages brain power that exceeds the mental activity involved in reasoning. Millions of position and motion sensors in muscles, tendons, and joints all over your body, called *proprioceptors,* provide constant feedback to your brain. This enables your sense of **kinesthesis**, which keeps you aware of your body parts' position and movement. Twist your wrist one degree and your brain receives an immediate update.

If you are able to experience sight and sound, you can momentarily imagine being blind and deaf by closing your eyes and plugging your ears to experience the dark silence. But what would it be like to live without touch or kinesthesis—without being able to sense the positions of your limbs when you wake during the night? Ian Waterman of Hampshire, England, knows. At age 19, Waterman contracted a rare viral infection that destroyed the nerves enabling his senses of light touch *and* of body position and movement. People with this condition report feeling disembodied, as though their body is dead, not real, not theirs (Sacks, 1985). With prolonged practice, Waterman learned to walk and eat—by visually focusing on his limbs and directing them accordingly. But if the lights went out, he would crumple to the floor (Azar, 1998).

Vision interacts with kinesthesis for you, too. If you are able, stand with your right heel in front of your left toes. Easy. Now close your eyes and try again. Did you wobble?

A companion **vestibular sense** monitors your head's (and thus your body's) position and movement. The biological gyroscopes for this sense of equilibrium are two structures in your inner ear. The first, your fluid-filled *semicircular canals,* look like a three-dimensional pretzel (Figure 1.6-18a). The second structure is the pair of calcium-crystal–filled *vestibular sacs.* When your head rotates or tilts, the movement of these organs stimulates hair-like receptors, which send nerve signals to your cerebellum at the back of your brain, enabling you to sense your body position and maintain your balance.

If you twirl around and then come to an abrupt halt, neither the fluid in your semicircular canals nor your kinesthetic receptors will immediately return to their neutral state. The dizzy aftereffect fools your brain with the sensation that you're still spinning. This illustrates a principle that underlies perceptual illusions: *Mechanisms that normally give*

**kinesthesis** [kin-ehs-THEE-sis] our movement sense; our system for sensing the position and movement of individual body parts.

**vestibular sense** our balance sense; our sense of body movement and position that enables our sense of balance.

*us an accurate experience of the world can, under certain conditions, fool us.* Understanding how we get fooled provides clues to how our perceptual system works.

Your vestibular sense is super speedy. If you slip, your vestibular sensors automatically and instantly order your skeletal response, well before you have consciously decided how to right yourself. You might try this: Hold one of your thumbs in front of your face, then move it rapidly right to left and back. Notice how your thumb blurs (your vision isn't fast enough to track it). Now hold your thumb still and swivel your *head* from left to right—just as fast. Voila! Your thumb stays clear—because your vestibular system, which is monitoring your head position, speedily moves the eyes. Head moves right, eyes move left. Vision is fast, but the vestibular sense is faster.

\* \* \*

For a summary of our sensory systems, see **Table 1.6-3**.

Tony Quinn/Icon Sportswire/Getty Images

**Body in space** By using information from her inner ears, this college cheerleader's brain expertly monitors her body position.

| TABLE 1.6-3 **Summarizing the Senses** | | | |
|---|---|---|---|
| **Sensory System** | **Source** | **Receptors** | **Key Brain Areas** |
| *Vision* | Light waves striking the eye | Rods and cones in the retina | Occipital lobes |
| *Hearing* | Sound waves striking the outer ear | Cochlear hair cells (*cilia*) in the inner ear | Temporal lobes |
| *Touch* | Pressure, warmth, cold, harmful chemicals | Receptors (including pain-sensitive *nociceptors*), mostly in the skin, which detect pressure, warmth, cold, and pain | Somatosensory cortex |
| *Taste* | Chemical molecules in the mouth | Basic taste receptors for sweet, sour, salty, bitter, umami, and oleogustus | Frontal/temporal lobe border |
| *Smell* | Chemical molecules breathed in through the nose | Millions of receptors at the top of the nasal cavities | Olfactory bulb |
| *Kinesthesis — position and movement* | Any change in position of a body part, interacting with vision | Kinesthetic sensors in the joints, tendons, and muscles (*proprioceptors*) | Cerebellum |
| *Vestibular sense — balance and movement* | Movement of fluids in the inner ear caused by head/body movement | Hair-like receptors (*cilia*) in the ears' semicircular canals and vestibular sacs | Cerebellum |

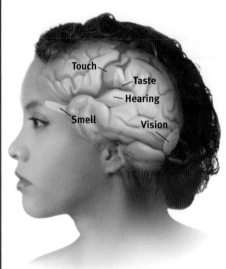

# Sensory Interaction

**1.6-16** How does *sensory interaction* influence our perceptions, and what is *embodied cognition*?

We have seen that vision and kinesthesis interact. Actually, none of our senses acts alone. All of them—seeing, hearing, tasting, smelling, touching—eavesdrop on one another, and our brain blends their inputs to interpret the world (Rosenblum, 2013). This is **sensory interaction** at work. One sense can influence another.

Consider how smell sticks its nose into the business of taste. Hold your nose, close your eyes, and have someone feed you various foods. A slice of apple may be indistinguishable from a chunk of raw potato. A cracker may taste like cardboard. Without their smells, a cup of cold coffee may be hard to distinguish from a glass of Gatorade. A big part of taste is right under your nose.

Contrary to Aristotle's presumption that taste sensors were found only on the tongue, you also inhale the aroma through your nose—a scientific fact not understood until 1812 (Bartoshuk et al., 2019). Like smoke rising in a chimney, food molecules released by chewing rise into your nasal cavity. This is why food tastes bland when you have a bad cold. Smell can also change our perception of taste: A drink's strawberry odor enhances our perception of its sweetness. Even touch can influence taste. Depending on its texture, a potato chip "tastes" fresh or stale (Smith, 2011). Smell + texture + taste = flavor. Yet perhaps you have noticed: Flavor *feels* located in the mouth (Stevenson, 2014).

Vision and hearing may similarly interact. Baseball umpires' vision informs their hearing of when the ball hits a player's glove, influencing their judgments of whether baserunners are safe or out (Krynen & McBeath, 2019). Likewise, a weak flicker of light becomes more visible when accompanied by a short burst of sound (Kayser, 2007). The reverse is also true: Soft sounds are more easily heard when paired with a visual cue. If I [DM], as a person with hearing loss, watch a video with on-screen captions, I have no trouble hearing the words I am seeing. But if I then decide I don't need the captions and turn them off, I quickly realize I do need them. The eyes guide the ears (**Figure 1.6-26**).

So, our senses interact. But what happens if they disagree? What if our eyes *see* a speaker form one sound but our ears *hear* another sound? Surprise: Our brain may perceive a third sound that blends both inputs. Seeing mouth movements for *ga* while hearing *ba,* we may perceive *da.* This phenomenon is known as the *McGurk effect,* after Scottish psychologist Harry McGurk, who, with his assistant John MacDonald, discovered the effect (McGurk & MacDonald, 1976). For most of us, lip reading is part of hearing, which is why mask wearing during the Covid pandemic has made communication more challenging.

We have seen that our perceptions have two main ingredients: our bottom-up sensations and our top-down cognitions (such as expectations, attitudes, thoughts, and memories). In everyday

**sensory interaction** the principle that one sense can influence another, as when the smell of food influences its taste.

**Figure 1.6-26**
**Sensory interaction**

Seeing the speaker forming the words in video chats makes those words easier to understand for hard-of-hearing people (Knight, 2004).

© Albrecht Weisser/Westend61/Corbis

life, sensation and perception are two points on a continuum. It's not surprising, then, that the brain circuits processing our physical sensations sometimes interact with the brain circuits responsible for cognition. The result is **embodied cognition**. We think from within a body. Two examples:

- *Judgments may mimic body sensations.* Sitting at a wobbly desk and chair may make relationships seem less stable (Forest et al., 2015: Kille et al., 2013).

- *Hard chair, hard on crime.* People who sat in a hard chair, compared with a soft chair, gave harsher punishments to criminals, and to college students who cheated on a final paper (Schaefer et al., 2018).

As we attempt to decipher our world, our brain blends inputs from multiple channels. But in a few select individuals, the brain circuits for two or more senses become joined in a phenomenon called *synesthesia,* in which the stimulation of one sense triggers an experience of another (**Figure 1.6-27**). Early in life, "exuberant neural connectivity" produces some arbitrary associations among the senses, which later are normally—but not always—pruned (Wagner & Dobkins, 2011). In a brain that blends sensations, hearing music may activate color-sensitive cortex regions and trigger a sensation of color (Brang et al., 2008; Hubbard et al., 2005). Seeing a number may evoke a taste or color sensation (Newell & Mitchell, 2016; Ranzini & Girelli, 2019). People with synesthesia experience these kinds of sensory shifts.

**embodied cognition** the influence of bodily sensations, gestures, and other states on cognitive preferences and judgments.

Person without synesthesia

Person with synesthesia

**Figure 1.6-27**
**Synesthesia's symphony**

A person with *synesthesia* experiences blended sensations. For example, hearing numbers may evoke an experience of specific colors or smells or musical notes.

---

**AP® Science Practice**

## Check Your Understanding

### Examine the Concept

▶ Explain the difference between our systems for sensing smell, touch, and taste.

▶ Where are the kinesthetic receptors and the vestibular sense receptors located?

### Apply the Concept

▶ Before reading this module, had you ever considered the importance of your vestibular sense? Explain how it has influenced your behavior today.

▶ Have you ever experienced a feeling that you think could be explained by embodied cognition?

*Answers to the Examine the Concept questions can be found in Appendix C at the end of the book.*

# Exploring Research Methods & Design

Earlier in this module, we explored the positive effects of touch. Development psychologists report that touch enhances the development of premature infants. To test the effects of touch therapy on physical development, researchers randomly assigned hospitalized premature infants to one of two groups. The experimental group had their limbs massaged for 15 minutes, 3 times a day, for 10 days. The control group did not receive massages. On average, the massaged preemies gained 47 percent more weight and went home 6 days sooner than did the control group preemies. As a result of this and other studies, many neonatal intensive care units now provide touch therapy to premature infants.

- Explain which research design is being employed in the study described here (correlational or experimental).

- Explain how the use of random assignment strengthened this study.

- Can you draw a cause-and-effect conclusion from this study? Explain.

- Imagine that you are on an institutional review board. Which questions would you ask the researchers to ensure that the study follows ethical guidelines?

*Remember, you can always revisit Unit 0 to review information related to psychological research.*

# Module 1.6d REVIEW

### 1.6-12 What are the four basic touch sensations, and how do we sense touch?

- Our sense of touch consists of four basic sensations—pressure, warmth, cold, and pain—that combine to produce other sensations, such as "itchy" or "wet."

### 1.6-13 What biological, psychological, and social-cultural influences affect our experience of pain? How do placebos and distraction help control pain?

- The biopsychosocial perspective views our perception of pain as the sum of biological, psychological, and social-cultural influences.

- Pain reflects bottom-up sensations and top-down cognition.

- The *gate-control theory* of pain suggests that a "gate" in the spinal cord either opens to permit pain signals traveling up small nerve fibers to reach the brain, or closes to prevent their passage.

- Pain treatments often combine physical and psychological elements. Placebos can diminish the central nervous system's attention and responses to painful experiences. Distraction can activate neural pathways that inhibit pain and increase pain tolerance.

### 1.6-14 In what ways are our senses of taste and smell similar, and how do they differ?

- Taste and smell are both chemical senses.

- Taste (*gustation*) is a composite of six basic sensations—sweet, sour, salty, bitter, umami, and oleogustus—and of

the aromas that interact with information from the taste receptor cells of the taste buds.

- There are no basic sensations for smell (*olfaction*). From the top of each nasal cavity, some 20 million olfactory receptor cells for smell send messages to the brain's olfactory bulb, and then onward to the temporal lobe's primary smell cortex and to the parts of the limbic system involved in memory and emotion.

### 1.6-15 How do we sense our body's position and movement?

- Position and motion sensors in muscles, tendons, and joints called proprioceptors enable *kinesthesis*, our sense of the position and movement of our body parts.

- We monitor our head's (and thus our body's) position and movement, and maintain our balance, with our *vestibular sense*, which relies on the semicircular canals and vestibular sacs to sense the tilt or rotation of our head.

### 1.6-16 How does *sensory interaction* influence our perceptions, and what is *embodied cognition?*

- Our senses influence one another. This *sensory interaction* occurs, for example, when the smell of a favorite food amplifies its taste.

- *Embodied cognition* is the influence of bodily sensations, gestures, and other states on cognitive preferences and judgments.

# AP® Practice Multiple Choice Questions

1. Dr. Hessler asked a group of participants with damage to their sensory systems to touch their noses with their eyes closed 10 times. He asked a group of participants without sensory system damage to engage in the same action. The median number of times the group with sensory system damage touched their noses was 5, while the median number of times the group without sensory system damage touched their noses was 10. Which of the following is the likely variable of interest in Dr. Hessler's study?

   a. Kinesthesis
   b. Olfaction
   c. Gustation
   d. Chemical sensation

2. Jaymie felt intense pain when she broke her finger. According to gate-control theory, where are the "gates" located to enable Jaymie's brain to receive pain messages from her finger?

   a. Thalamus
   b. Semicircular canals
   c. Amygdala
   d. Spinal cord

3. Which of the following is the best example of sensory interaction?

   a. Finding that food tastes bland when you have a bad cold
   b. Finding it difficult to maintain your balance when you have an ear infection
   c. Finding that the cold pool water doesn't feel so cold after a while
   d. Finding that the hot peppers get hotter as you consume more of them

4. Austin damaged the hair-like receptors in his semicircular canals. Which sensation will be most impacted?

   a. Balance           c. Hearing
   b. Smell             d. Pain

5. Which research method might be best for conducting research on phantom limb sensations?

   a. Experiment
   b. Surveys
   c. Naturalistic observation
   d. Case study

## KEY TERMS AND CONTRIBUTORS TO REMEMBER

nature–nurture issue, p. 4

Charles Darwin, p. 5

natural selection, p. 5

evolutionary psychology, p. 5

behavior genetics, p. 5

mutation, p. 7

environment, p. 9

heredity, p. 9

genes, p. 9

genome, p. 9

identical (monozygotic) twins, p. 11

fraternal (dizygotic) twins, p. 12

interaction, p. 15

epigenetics, p. 16

nervous system, p. 22

central nervous system (CNS), p. 22

peripheral nervous system (PNS), p. 22

nerves, p. 22

sensory (afferent) neurons, p. 22

motor (efferent) neurons, p. 22

interneurons, p. 22

somatic nervous system, p. 23

autonomic [aw-tuh-NAHM-ik]
  nervous system (ANS), p. 23

sympathetic nervous system, p. 23

parasympathetic nervous system,
  p. 23

reflex, p. 25

neuron, p. 28

cell body, p. 28

dendrites, p. 28

axon, p. 29

myelin [MY-uh-lin] sheath, p. 29

glial cells (glia), p. 29

action potential, p. 29

threshold, p. 30

refractory period, p. 30

all-or-none response, p. 30

synapse [SIN-aps], p. 31

neurotransmitters, p. 31

reuptake, p. 32

endorphins [en-DOR-fins], p. 34

agonist, p. 34

antagonist, p. 34

endocrine [EN-duh-krin] system,
  p. 35

hormones, p. 36

psychoactive drug, p. 40

substance use disorder, p. 40

depressants, p. 41

tolerance, p. 43

addiction, p. 43

withdrawal, p. 43

barbiturates, p. 44

opioids, p. 44

stimulants, p. 45

hallucinogens, p. 50

near-death experience, p. 50

biological psychology, p. 55

biopsychosocial approach, p. 56

levels of analysis, p. 56

neuroplasticity, p. 57

lesion [LEE-zhuhn], p. 58

EEG (electroencephalogram), p. 58

MEG (magnetoencephalography),
  p. 58

CT (computed tomography) scan,
  p. 59

PET (positron emission tomography),
  p. 59

MRI (magnetic resonance imaging),
  p. 59

fMRI (functional MRI), p. 59

hindbrain, p. 63

midbrain, p. 63

forebrain, p. 65

brainstem, p. 65

medulla [muh-DUL-uh], p. 65

thalamus [THAL-uh-muss], p. 65

reticular formation, p. 65

cerebellum [sehr-uh-BELL-um], p. 65

limbic system, p. 66

amygdala [uh-MIG-duh-la], p. 66

hypothalamus [hi-po-THAL-uh-muss],
  p. 67

hippocampus, p. 69

cerebral [seh-REE-bruhl] cortex, p. 70

frontal lobes, p. 71

parietal [puh-RYE-uh-tuhl] lobes,
  p. 71

occipital [ahk-SIP-uh-tuhl] lobes,
  p. 71

temporal lobes, p. 71

motor cortex, p. 72

somatosensory cortex, p. 74

association areas, p. 75

neurogenesis, p. 81

corpus callosum, p. 81

Roger Sperry, p. 82

Michael Gazzaniga, p. 82

# Unit 1 AP® Practice Multiple Choice Questions

1. Jay is an evolutionary psychologist. He seeks to understand how traits and behavioral tendencies have been shaped by

   a. natural selection.
   b. psychophysics.
   c. prenatal nutrition.
   d. parallel processing.

2. Torin believes in nature's influence on behavior, while Kyla believes in nurture's influence. Which aligns with Torin's view and Kyla's view, respectively?

   a. Genetic factors; environmental factors
   b. Heredity; genetic factors
   c. Epigenetics; environmental factors
   d. Environmental factors; heredity

3. Rather than acting as blueprints that lead to the same result no matter the context, genes react to the environment. The gene–environment interaction is the basic tenet of which of the following?

   a. Evolutionary psychology
   b. Epigenetics
   c. Heredity
   d. Parallel processing

4. Why do researchers find the study of fraternal twins important?

   a. They share similar environments and the same genetic code.
   b. Their environments differ based on their individual traits.
   c. They are usually raised in similar environments, but they do not have the same genetic code.
   d. They are typically raised in less similar environments than nontwin siblings.

5. Why do researchers use adoption studies in an effort to reveal genetic influences on personality?

   a. To compare adopted children with nonadopted children
   b. To study the effect of prior neglect on adopted children
   c. To study the effect of a child's age at adoption
   d. To evaluate whether adopted children more closely resemble their adoptive parents or their biological parents

6. What should Ezra say if he was asked to describe the main function of the peripheral nervous system?

   a. It connects the brain and spinal cord to the rest of the body.
   b. It calms the body after an emergency.
   c. It prepares the body for action.
   d. It focuses on thinking and feeling.

7. To accurately identify the two parts of the central nervous system in an oral exam, what should Kitab say?

   a. Sensory and motor neurons
   b. The somatic and autonomic nervous systems
   c. The brain and the spinal cord
   d. The sympathetic and parasympathetic nervous systems

8. What does the figure below illustrate?

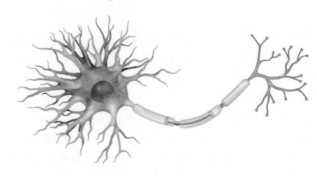

   a. A glial cell
   b. A hormone
   c. A neuron
   d. A neurotransmitter

9. What is the purpose of the myelin sheath?

   a. To make the transfer of information across a synapse more efficient
   b. To increase the amount of neurotransmitter available in the synapse
   c. To reduce the antagonistic effect of certain drugs
   d. To speed up the transmission of information within a neuron

10. When Janice's finger touches a candle flame, her hand jerks away *before* her brain receives and responds to the information that causes her to feel pain. This is due to which of the following?

    a. The reflex arc
    b. The all-or-none process
    c. Reuptake
    d. Endorphins

11. Jessika wants to do research that examines the electrical impulses that travel down axons to better understand

    a. the refractory period.
    b. the action potential.
    c. the threshold.
    d. the all-or-none process.

**12.** Lei has been diagnosed with schizophrenia. Which of the following neurotransmitters most likely contributed to this disorder?

a. Acetylcholine      c. Glutamate
b. Dopamine      d. GABA

**13.** Calvin takes a drug that acts as both a stimulant and a hallucinogen. It could cause him to become dangerously dehydrated in the short term and disrupt his serotonin in the long term. What drug did Calvin most likely take?

a. LSD      c. Alcohol
b. Ecstasy      d. Cocaine

**14.** After taking a drug, Carmen is experiencing slowed re-actions, slurred speech, and decreased skill performance. Which drug did she most likely take?

a. Nicotine      c. Alcohol
b. Caffeine      d. Ecstasy

**15.** Thomas, who drinks alcohol regularly, now finds that he requires a larger dose to experience the same effect. Which term best describes his experience?

a. Withdrawal
b. Tolerance
c. Addiction
d. Substance use disorder

**16.** When Honque ingested an opioid drug, what neuro-transmitter(s) did the opioid mimic in his brain?

a. Serotonin      c. Norepinephrine
b. Endorphins      d. Acetylcholine

**17.** A researcher interested in determining the size of a particular area of the brain would be most likely to use which of the following techniques?

a. EEG      c. fMRI
b. MRI      d. PET scan

**18.** Sara is about to take her driver's test. Which region of the brain plays the most significant role in her sense of alertness and arousal?

a. Medulla      c. Hippocampus
b. Parietal lobe      d. Reticular formation

**19.** Ray has a damaged hippocampus. Which of the following would he most likely experience as a result?

a. Difficulties with balance and coordination
b. Difficulty in creating new memories
c. A false sensation of burning in parts of the body
d. Inability to regulate body temperature and hunger

**20.** Surgical stimulation of the somatosensory cortex might result in the false sensation of what?

a. Flashes of colored light
b. Someone whispering your name
c. Someone tickling you
d. A bad odor

**21.** During which task might the right hemisphere of the brain be most active?

a. Solving a mathematical equation
b. Enduring a long run
c. Making a brief oral presentation to a class
d. Imagining what a dress would look like on a friend

**22.** When researchers surgically lesioned the amygdala of a rhesus monkey's brain, what was the impact on the monkey's behavior?

a. Lost its ability to coordinate movement
b. Became less aggressive
c. Lost its memory of where food was stored
d. Sank into an irreversible coma

**23.** Which of the following scenarios best illustrates neuroplasticity?

a. Aaron has healthy human brain tissue.
b. Khadija's brain is able to transfer information from one hemisphere to the other.
c. Alycia's brain gets larger as she grows.
d. Pham's brain tissue has the ability to take on new functions.

**24.** Jazmine experiences brain damage that results in an inability to make plans about the future. Which lobe of her brain was most likely damaged?

a. Parietal lobe
b. Frontal lobe
c. Occipital lobe
d. Temporal lobe

**25.** When Elliott is sleep deprived, he is more likely to catch a cold. Why is this the case?

a. Sleep helps restore the immune system.
b. Sleep suppresses the immune system.
c. Sleep strengthens neural connections that build muscle memory.
d. Sleep enhances the production of growth hormones.

**26.** As part of a sleep study, researchers notice bursts of rapid, rhythmic brain-wave activity and determine that Jane is in Stage 2 sleep. This type of brain activity is referred to as

a. circadian rhythms.      c. sleep spindles.
b. alpha waves.      d. delta waves.

27. Taylor has been deprived of sleep for several nights. She is now showing increasing amounts of paradoxical sleep. This increase indicates that she is experiencing which of the following?

    a. Circadian rhythms
    b. Narcolepsy
    c. Sleep apnea
    d. REM rebound

28. While engaged in an argument with his brother, a man suddenly falls asleep. With which sleep disorder is he most likely to be diagnosed?

    a. Sleep apnea
    b. REM sleep behavior disorder
    c. Sleepwalking
    d. Narcolepsy

29. Ama's physician has encouraged her to relax before bed-time, using dimmer light. Her physician is advising her to

    a. manage her stress better.
    b. improve her sleep hygiene.
    c. improve her coping skills.
    d. enhance her cognitive skills.

30. After reading the textbook, Gerard excitedly told his mother that the iris' primary function is to

    a. focus light on the retina.
    b. process color.
    c. allow light into the eye.
    d. enable night vision.

31. In explaining signal detection theory to his class, Dr. Neufeld should say which of the following?

    a. Difference thresholds are based on a ratio.
    b. Various factors determine whether a person will detect a faint stimulus.
    c. A person's absolute threshold is stable across situations.
    d. Detection of all stimuli runs through the thalamus.

32. Which of the following is most likely to influence your memory of a physically painful event?

    a. The overall length of the event
    b. The intensity of pain at the end of the event
    c. The amount of rest you've had in the 24 hours preceding the event
    d. The specific part of the body that experiences the pain

33. Nena's research project is based on the theory that the rate of nerve impulses traveling up the auditory nerve matches the frequency of a tone, thus enabling us to sense its pitch. Which theory is her project based on?

    a. Frequency theory
    b. Place theory
    c. Sound localization
    d. Gate-control theory

34. Which of the following best represents an absolute threshold?

    a. A guitar player knows that his D string has just gone out of tune.
    b. A photographer can tell that the natural light available for a photograph has just faded slightly.
    c. Your friend amazes you by correctly identifying unlabeled glasses of Coke and Pepsi.
    d. A cook can just barely taste the small amount of salt she has added to her soup.

35. Jude's hammer, anvil, and stirrup were activated. Which sensory process were they involved in?

    a. Processing information related to his sense of balance
    b. Transmitting light energy to ganglion cells
    c. Transmitting sound waves to the cochlea
    d. Smelling the foul odors of a locker room

36. Which of the following might result from a disruption of your vestibular sense?

    a. Inability to detect the position of your arm without looking at it
    b. Loss of the ability to detect bitter tastes
    c. Dizziness and a loss of balance
    d. An inability to detect pain

37. Because of the repeated exposure to loud noise they experience daily, airport ground workers are most susceptible to damage to which of the following?

    a. Olfactory nerve
    b. Cochlea
    c. Ganglion cells
    d. Bipolar cells

38. Which of the following is the best example of sensory interaction?

    a. Simultaneous exposure to warm and cold produces the skin sensation of hot.
    b. Some cones have the ability to detect red and green, or blue and yellow, light.
    c. You notice a slight flicker of a light when a sound accompanies it.
    d. Pitch perception is explained by the frequency and place theories.

39. After looking at a yellow, black, and green American flag for a minute, you shift your gaze to a white wall. Which of the following theories best explains why you "see" a red, white, and blue flag when looking at the white wall?

    a. Frequency theory
    b. Young–Helmholtz theory
    c. Opponent-process theory
    d. Ganglion-bipolar theory

**40.** Bart can easily reach out and pet his dog because he is aware of his body parts' position and movement. This awareness is due to which of the following?

a. Kinesthesis
b. Vestibular sense
c. Association areas
d. Sequential processing

Go to Appendix D to complete the **AP® Practice** Evidence-Based Question and Article Analysis Question for this unit.

# Cognition

As authors privileged to share psychological science with so many AP® students, two aims thread through our writing: to assist you, as you swim in a sea of misinformation, **(1) to *think smarter* about your life and (2) to *savor the wonders* of** your life. These two aims weave through this unit on *cognition*. As we will see, our perceptions of the world, our solving problems and making decisions, our memories, and our intelligence all are vulnerable to errors. Yet each also manifests marvels that we can savor. To be an educated person is to be mindful of potential pitfalls that can distort our thinking and direct ill-fated decisions, and also to appreciate how wonderfully made we are. So read on, alert to fresh ways in which you might think smarter, while more deeply appreciating the wonders of your humanity.

UNIT **2**
Overview
Video
▶

FatCamera/Getty Images

# Module 2.1a Perception: Influences on Perception

How do we *perceive* the world around us? In some ways, we may not perceive things as they are, but rather as *we* are. Internal factors—our attention, expectations, motivations, and emotions—interact with external sensory information and context to affect our perceptions. When our perceptual system gets tricked, we may find ourselves experiencing illusions.

## Selective Attention

**2.1-1** How does *selective attention* direct our perceptions?

Through **selective attention**, our awareness focuses, like a flashlight beam, on a minute aspect of all that we experience. We may think we can fully attend to a conversation or a class lecture while checking and returning text messages. Actually, our consciousness focuses on but one thing at a time.

 **AP® Science Practice**

## Exploring Research Methods & Design

Suppose a researcher wants to test whether students can fully attend to a class lecture while texting. The researcher designs a study in which 50 students watch a 10-minute lecture video. Half of the students are randomly assigned to receive and reply to texts during the lecture; the other half have their phones silenced. At the end of the lecture, all students take a quiz on the material. The researcher finds that those who had their phone silenced did better on the quiz.

- Who was the sample in this study? Who was the population?

- The researcher used an experimental design. Explain how you know.

- What are the independent and dependent variables?

- Can the researcher draw a cause-and-effect conclusion at the end of this study? Why or why not?

*Remember, you can always revisit Module 0.5 to review information related to research design.*

**selective attention** focusing conscious awareness on a particular stimulus.

By one estimate, our five senses take in 11,000,000 bits of information per second, of which we consciously process about 40 (Wilson, 2002). Yet our mind's unconscious track intuitively makes great use of the other 10,999,960 bits.

What captures our limited attention? Things we deem important. A classic example of selective attention is the *cocktail party effect*—your ability to attend to only one voice within a sea of many as you chat with a party guest. But what happens when another voice speaks your name? Your cognitive radar, operating on your mind's other track, instantly brings that unattended voice into consciousness. This effect might have prevented an embarrassing and dangerous situation in 2009, when two Northwest Airlines pilots "lost track of time." Focused on their laptops and in conversation, they ignored alarmed air traffic controllers' attempts to reach them and overflew their Minneapolis destination by 150 miles. If only the controllers had known and spoken the pilots' names.

## Selective Attention and Accidents

In the last month, 60 percent of American drivers have read or sent a text message or viewed a phone map while driving (Gliklich et al., 2016). These distracted drivers may have thought—wrongly—that they could simultaneously attend to the road. Such digital distractions can have tragic consequences, as our selective attention shifts more than we realize (Stavrinos et al., 2017). One study left people in a room for 28 minutes with both internet and television access. On average, they guessed their attention switched 15 times. But they were not even close. Eye-tracking revealed eight times that many attentional switches—120 on average (Brasel & Gips, 2011).

Rapid toggling between activities is today's great enemy of sustained, focused attention. When we switch attentional gears, especially when we shift to and from complex tasks like noticing and avoiding cars around us, we pay a toll—a slight and sometimes fatal delay in coping (Rubenstein et al., 2001). When a driver attends to a conversation, activity in brain areas vital to driving decreases by an average of 37 percent (Just et al., 2008).

Just how dangerous is distracted driving? Each day, distracted driving kills about 9 Americans (CDC, 2018a). One video camera–based study of teen drivers found that driver distraction from passengers or phones occurred right before 58 percent of their crashes (AAA, 2015). Talking with passengers makes the risk of an accident 1.6 times higher than normal. Using a phone (even hands-free) makes the risk 4 times higher than normal— equal to the risk of drunk driving (McEvoy et al., 2005, 2007). And while talking is distracting, texting wins the danger game. One 18-month video camera–based study tracked the driving habits of long-haul truckers. When they were texting, their risk of a collision increased 23 times (Olson et al., 2009)! So, the

Reprinted with permission of Bill Whitehead

next time you're behind the wheel, put the brakes on your texts. Your passengers and fellow drivers will thank you.

## Inattentional Blindness

At the level of conscious awareness, we are "blind" to all but a tiny sliver of visual stimuli. Ulric Neisser (1979) and Robert Becklen and Daniel Cervone (1983) demonstrated this **inattentional blindness** dramatically by showing people a 1-minute video of basketball players, three in black shirts and three in white shirts, tossing a ball. Researchers told the viewers to press a key every time they saw a black-shirted player pass the ball. Most viewers were so intent on their task that they failed to notice a young woman carrying an umbrella

**AP® Science Practice**

### Research

In the study described here, researchers were interested in attentional shifts, which they operationally defined as shifts in eye-tracking. Can you think of other ways they could have operationally defined attentional shifts?

**AP® Exam Tip**

You may wish to think about how the information on selective attention relates to studying. The same principles apply. The more time you spend texting, tweeting, and social networking, the less focused you'll be on the material you're trying to master. A better strategy is to spend 25 minutes doing schoolwork and schoolwork alone, without dividing your attention. Then you can reward yourself with a few minutes online. Studying this way will help you master the material for the AP® exam.

**inattentional blindness**
failing to see visible objects when our attention is directed elsewhere.

## Figure 2.1-1
### Inattentional blindness

Viewers who attended to basketball tosses among the black-shirted players usually failed to spot the umbrella-toting woman sauntering across the screen (Neisser, 1979).

saunter across the screen midway through the video (**Figure 2.1-1**). Watching a later replay, viewers were astonished to see her (Mack & Rock, 2000). This inattentional blindness is a by-product of what we are really good at: focusing attention on some part of our environment.

In a repeat of the experiment, smart-aleck researchers sent a gorilla-suited assistant through a swirl of players (Simons & Chabris, 1999). During its 5- to 9-second cameo appearance, the gorilla paused and thumped its chest. But the gorilla did not steal the show: Half of the conscientious pass-counting viewers failed to see it. Psychologists like to have fun, and have continued to do so with the help of "invisible" gorillas. When 24 radiologists were looking for cancer nodules in lung scans, 20 of them missed a tiny gorilla superimposed in the upper right—though, to their credit, their focus enabled them to discover the much tinier cancer tissue (Drew et al., 2013). The point of these purposeful pranks: Our attention is a wonderful gift, given to one thing at a time.

Knowing that most people miss someone in a gorilla suit while their attention is riveted elsewhere, imagine the fun magicians can have by manipulating our selective attention. Misdirect people's attention and they will miss the hand slipping into the pocket. "Every time you perform a magic trick, you're engaging in experimental psychology," says magician Teller (2009), a master of mind-messing methods. Clever thieves know this, too. One Swedish psychologist was surprised in Stockholm by a woman suddenly exposing herself; only later did he realize that he had been pickpocketed, outwitted by thieves who understood the limits of our selective attention (Gallace, 2012).

In other studies, people exhibited a form of inattentional blindness called **change blindness**. Viewers have failed to notice that, after a brief visual interruption, a big Coke bottle had disappeared, a railing had risen, clothing had changed color—and someone they'd been talking to had been replaced by a different person (**Figure 2.1-2**) (Chabris & Simons, 2010; Resnick et al., 1997). Out of sight, out of mind.

(a)　　　　　　　(b)　　　　　　　(c)

## Figure 2.1-2
### Change blindness

While a man (in red) provides directions to another (a), two experimenters rudely pass between them carrying a door (b). During this interruption, the original direction seeker switches places with another person wearing different-colored clothing (c). Most people, focused on their direction giving, do not notice the switch (Simons & Levin, 1998).

**change blindness** failing to notice changes in the environment; a form of *inattentional blindness*.

## Check Your Understanding

**AP® Science Practice**

**Examine the Concept**

▶ Explain an attentional principle that magicians may use to fool us.

**Apply the Concept**

▶ Can you recall a recent time when, as your attention focused on one thing, you were oblivious to something else (perhaps to pain, to someone's approach, or to music lyrics)? Explain what happened. (If you're reading this while listening to exciting music, you may have struggled to understand the question 😊 [Vasilev et al., 2018].)

*Answers to the Examine the Concept questions can be found in Appendix C at the end of the book.*

# Expectations, Context, Motivation, and Emotion

**2.1-2** How do our expectations, contexts, motivation, and emotions influence our perceptions?

To see is to believe. As we less fully appreciate, to believe is to see. As we learned in Module 1.6a, information processing occurs both from the bottom up (beginning with the sensory receptors, and working up to the brain's integration of sensory information) and from the top down (as we draw from our experience and expectations when constructing perceptions). Our perceived world is our brain's explanation of incoming sensations.

## Perceptual Set

Through experience, we come to expect certain results. Those expectations may give us a **perceptual set**—a set of mental tendencies and assumptions that affects, *top-down*, what we hear, taste, feel, and see. Consider **Figure 2.1-3**.

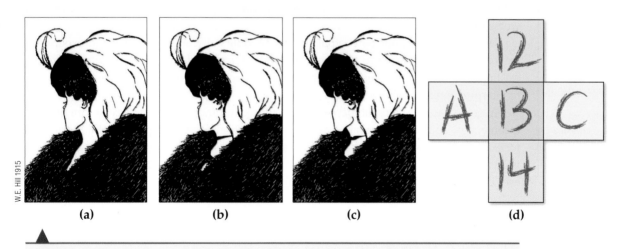

W.E. Hill 1915

(a)       (b)       (c)       (d)

**Figure 2.1-3**

**Two examples of perceptual set**

Show a friend *either* image (a) or image (c). Then show image (b) and ask, "What do you see?" Whether your friend reports seeing an old woman's face or a young woman's profile may depend on which of the other two drawings was viewed first. In images (a) and (c), the meaning is clear, and it will establish perceptual expectations (Boring, 1930). In image (d), do you perceive a number or letter in the middle? If you read from left to right, you likely perceive a letter. But if you read from top to bottom, you may perceive the same center image as a number.

**perceptual set** a mental predisposition to perceive one thing and not another.

*"Can I see your I.D? Wait, never mind. Wait — yeah, I need to see your I.D? Wait —"*

**Figure 2.1-4**

**Believing is seeing**

What do you perceive? Is this Nessie, the Loch Ness monster, or a log?

Everyday examples abound of perceptual set—of "mind over mind." In 1972, a British newspaper published unretouched photographs of a "monster" in Scotland's Loch Ness, proclaiming them "the most amazing pictures ever taken." If this information creates in you the same expectations it did in most of the paper's readers, you, too, will see the monster in a similar photo in **Figure 2.1-4**. But when a skeptical researcher approached the original photos with different expectations, he saw a curved tree limb—as had others the day that photo was shot (Campbell, 1986). What a difference a new perceptual set makes.

Perceptual set also affects what we hear—"stuffy nose" or "stuff he knows"? Consider the kindly airline pilot who, on a takeoff run, looked over at his sad co-pilot and said, "Cheer up." Expecting to hear the usual "Gear up," the co-pilot promptly raised the wheels—before

they left the ground (Reason & Mycielska, 1982). Or ask the little boy who loved the prelude to Major League Baseball games when people rose to sing to him: "José, can you see?" Music lovers have recorded thousands of these mishearings at KissThisGuy.com (named for Jimi Hendrix's oft-misheard "kiss the sky").

Our expectations can influence our taste perceptions, too. In one experiment, by a 6-to-1 margin, preschool children thought french fries tasted better when served in a McDonald's bag rather than a plain white bag (Robinson et al., 2007). Another experiment invited campus bar patrons at the Massachusetts Institute of Technology to sample free beer (Lee et al., 2006). When researchers added a few drops of vinegar to a brand-name beer and called it "MIT Brew," the tasters preferred it—unless they had been told they were drinking vinegar-laced beer. In that case, they expected, and usually experienced, a worse taste.

What determines our perceptual set? As Module 3.4 will explain, through experience we form concepts, or *schemas*, that organize and interpret unfamiliar information. Our pre-existing schemas for monsters and tree limbs influence how we apply top-down processing to interpret ambiguous sensations.

In everyday life, stereotypes—about culture, ethnicity, gender, sexual orientation, income, age, abilities, and more—can color perception. People (especially children) have, for example, perceived new baby "David" as bigger and stronger than when the same infant was called "Diana" (Stern & Karraker, 1989). Some differences, it seems, exist merely in the eyes of their beholders.

---

**AP® Science Practice**

**Research**

The idea that expectations *influence* perceptions implies a cause (expectations) and an effect (changes in perceptions). Studies such as the ones presented here allow for such conclusions, because they used experimental methods — for example, randomly assigning how the french fries were served. Module 0.5 provides more details on how random assignment allows for causal conclusions.

---

**AP® Science Practice**    **Check Your Understanding**

**Examine the Concept**

▶ Explain bottom-up and top-down processing. Which of these does perceptual set involve?

**Apply the Concept**

▶ Have you ever had an experience where your expectations influenced your perspective? Explain how this happened.

*Answers to the Examine the Concept questions can be found in Appendix C at the end of the book.*

## Context, Motivation, and Emotion

Perceptual set influences how we interpret stimuli. But our immediate context, and the motivation and emotion we bring to a situation, also affect our interpretations.

### Context

Social psychologist Lee Ross invited us to recall our own perceptions in different contexts: "Ever notice that when you're driving you hate . . . the way [pedestrians] saunter through the crosswalk, almost daring you to hit them, but when you're walking you hate drivers?" (Jaffe, 2004).

Some other examples of the power of context:

- Imagine hearing a noise interrupted by the words "eel is on the wagon." Likely, you would actually perceive the first word as *wheel*. Given "eel is on the orange," you would more likely hear *peel*. In each case, the context creates an expectation that, top-down, influences our perception of a previously heard phrase (Grossberg, 1995).

- Cultural context helps inform our perceptions, so it's not surprising that people's varying cultures may cause them to view things differently, as in **Figure 2.1-5**.

- How is the woman in **Figure 2.1-6** feeling? The context provided in **Figure 2.1-7** will leave no doubt.

**Hearing hype** Why do people pay millions of dollars for old Italian violins? Many people believe the sound quality is unmatched. But a recent study showed that, under blind conditions, expert violin soloists generally preferred the sound of less expensive, modern violins over expensive, old Italian violins (Fritz et al., 2017).

Inti St. Clair/Getty Images

**Figure 2.1-5**

**Culture and context effects**

What is above the woman's head? In one classic study, most rural East Africans questioned said the woman was balancing a metal box or can on her head (a typical way to carry water at that time). They also perceived the family as sitting under a tree. Westerners, used to tap water and box-like homes with corners, were more likely to perceive the family as being indoors, with the woman sitting under a window (Gregory & Gombrich, 1973).

Craig Klomparens/Hope College

**Figure 2.1-6**

**What emotion is this?**

(See Figure 2.1-7.)

**Figure 2.1-7**

**Context makes clearer**

The Hope College volleyball team celebrates its national championship-winning moment.

## Motivation

Motives give us energy as we work toward a goal. Like context, they can bias our interpretations of neutral stimuli:

- Desirable objects, such as a water bottle viewed by a thirsty person, seem closer than they really are (Balcetis & Dunning, 2010). And closeness can increase desire itself. Heterosexual men, for example, find women who are physically closer more desirable (Shin et al., 2019).

- A to-be-climbed hill can seem steeper when we are carrying a heavy backpack, and a walking destination farther away when we are feeling tired (Burrow et al., 2016; Philbeck & Witt, 2015; Proffitt, 2006a,b). When heavy people lose weight, hills and stairs no longer seem so steep (Taylor-Covill & Eves, 2016).

- A softball appears bigger when you're hitting well, as researchers observed after asking players to choose a circle the size of the ball they had just hit well or poorly (Witt & Proffitt, 2005). There's also a reciprocal phenomenon: Seeing a target as bigger—as happens when athletes focus directly on a target—improves performance (Witt et al., 2012).

## Emotion

Other clever experiments have demonstrated that emotions can shove our perceptions in one direction or another:

- Hearing sad music can predispose people to perceive a sad meaning in spoken homophonic words—*mourning* rather than *morning, die* rather than *dye, pain* rather than *pane* (Halberstadt et al., 1995).

- Hearing cheerful music, such as Beyoncé's "Single Ladies," speeds up identification of happy emotion words (Tay & Ng, 2019).

- When angry, people more often perceive neutral objects as guns (Baumann & DeSteno, 2010). When hungry, they find larger bodies more attractive (Saxton et al., 2020).

- When made to feel mildly upset by subliminal exposure to a scowling face, people perceive a neutral face as less attractive and less likable (Anderson et al., 2012).

*The point to remember*: Much of what we perceive comes not just from what's "out there," but also from what's behind our eyes and between our ears. Our experiences, assumptions, expectations—and even our context, motivation, and emotions—can shape and color our views of reality through top-down processing.

**AP® Science Practice**

## Research

By randomly assigning participants to conditions, these *experiments* control for possible confounding variables. A confounding variable is a factor other than the factor being studied that might influence a study's results. If you need a review of confounding variables, you can revisit the concept in Module 0.4.

**AP® Science Practice**

## Check Your Understanding

### Examine the Concept

▶ Explain how emotions can influence our perceptions. Provide a piece of evidence to support your point.

### Apply the Concept

▶ Can you think of a time when your expectations caused you to misperceive the intentions of a person or group? Explain how your awareness of *context effects* might help you modify your expectations next time.

▶ What are some ways your culture might influence your perceptions?

*Answers to the Examine the Concept questions can be found in Appendix C at the end of the book.*

## Module 2.1a REVIEW

**2.1-1 How does *selective attention* direct our perceptions?**

- We *selectively attend* to, and process, a very limited portion of incoming information, blocking out much and often shifting the spotlight of our attention from one thing to another.

- Focused intently on one task, we often display *inattentional blindness* to other events, including *change blindness* to changes around us.

**2.1-2 How do our expectations, contexts, motivation, and emotions influence our perceptions?**

- *Perceptual set* is a mental predisposition that functions as a lens through which we perceive the world.

- Our learned concepts (schemas) prime us to organize and interpret ambiguous stimuli in certain ways.

- Our expectations, contexts, motivation, and emotion can color our interpretation of events and behaviors.

## AP® Practice Multiple Choice Questions

**1.** A pair of friends at a noisy baseball game are able to have a conversation with each other in spite of all the noise around them. Which principle best explains this scenario?

  a. Bottom-up processing
  b. The cocktail party effect
  c. Top-down processing
  d. Change blindness

**2.** Tonya's psychology teacher played some backwards music to the class, and they were not able to make out any words or phrases in the selection. Then the teacher told them to listen for the words "The rat ate the cat" and played it again. Now most of the class heard the words. Which principle explains this experience?

  a. Bottom-up processing
  b. Perceptual set
  c. Extrasensory perception
  d. Top-down processing

**3.** On a warm summer day, Kimberly tells her brother to put on a suit. Kimberly's brother knows to put on a swimsuit instead of a business suit because of

  a. context.
  b. priming.
  c. bottom-up processing.
  d. clairvoyance.

**4.** Dr. Jasper conducted a study in which he asked participants to view a video of a cat playing with yarn and told them to count the number of times the cat rolls the yarn. Halfway through the video, two bulldogs walk behind the cat. After the study, Dr. Jasper asks participants to indicate whether they saw the bulldogs in the video, but few participants reported seeing the bulldogs. What is the dependent variable in this study?

  a. The cocktail party effect
  b. Perceptual set
  c. Inattentional blindness
  d. Bottom-up processing

**5.** While teaching his students about perceptual sets, what topic would Dr. Kravstov most want his students to learn?

  a. Bottom-up processing
  b. Top-down processing
  c. Clairvoyance
  d. Selective attention

**6.** After moving to Alabama from Minnesota, Darnesha visited the eye doctor. While sitting in the waiting room, she overheard the receptionist making a call and mistakenly believed that the receptionist said "Sweetie, extra eyes," rather than "Sweet tea, extra ice." Which statement is true about this scenario?

a. Darnesha was influenced by context effects.
b. Darnesha was influenced by the cocktail party effect.
c. Darnesha demonstrated inattentional blindness.
d. Darnesha demonstrated selective attention.

**7.** After 13 weeks, Tran finally noticed the pink clock in the classroom where she took a challenging chemistry class. What concept best explains Tran's failure to notice the clock?

a. Context effects
b. Selective attention
c. Culture effect
d. Schemas

# Module 2.1b Perception: Perceptual Organization and Interpretation

## LEARNING TARGETS

**2.1-3** Explain the Gestalt psychologists' understanding of perceptual organization, and explain how figure-ground and grouping principles contribute to our perceptions.

**2.1-4** Explain how we use binocular and monocular cues to see in three dimensions, and discuss how we perceive motion.

**2.1-5** Explain how perceptual constancies help us construct meaningful perceptions.

**2.1-6** Explain what research on restored vision, sensory restriction, and perceptual adaptation reveals about the effects of experience on perception.

## Perceptual Organization

**2.1-3 How did the Gestalt psychologists understand perceptual organization, and how do figure-ground and grouping principles contribute to our perceptions?**

**gestalt** an organized whole. Gestalt psychologists emphasized our tendency to integrate pieces of information into meaningful wholes.

How do we organize and interpret sensory input so that it becomes *meaningful* perceptions—a rose in bloom, a familiar face, a sunset? Early in the twentieth century, some German psychologists noticed that people tend to organize visual sensations into a **gestalt**, a German

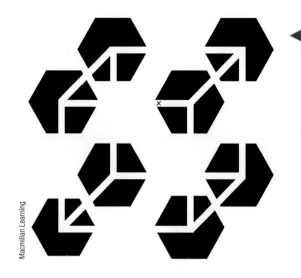

**Figure 2.1-8**
**A Necker cube**

What do you see: hexagons with white lines, or a cube? If you stare at the cube, you may notice that it reverses location, moving the tiny X from the front edge to the back. At times, the cube may seem to float forward, with hexagons behind it. At other times, the hexagons may become holes through which the cube appears, as though it were floating behind them. There is far more to perception than meets the eye. (Information from Bradley et al., 1976.)

Macmillan Learning

word meaning a "form" or a "whole." As we look straight ahead, we cannot separate the perceived scene into our left and right fields of view. Our conscious perception is, at every moment, a seamless scene — an integrated whole.

Consider **Figure 2.1-8**: The individual elements of this figure are really nothing but eight hexagons, each containing three converging white lines. What happens when we view these elements together? The resulting *Necker cube* nicely illustrates a favorite saying of Gestalt psychologists: *In perception, the whole may exceed the sum of its parts*.

Over the years, the Gestalt psychologists demonstrated many principles we use to organize our sensations into perceptions (Wagemans et al., 2012a,b). Underlying all of them is a fundamental truth: *Our brain does more than register information about the world*. Perception is not a picture printing itself on the brain. We filter incoming information and *construct* perceptions. Mind matters.

## Form Perception

Imagine designing an artificial intelligence (AI) system that, like your eye-brain system, recognizes faces at a glance. Which abilities would it need?

### Figure and Ground

To start with, the system needs to perceive **figure-ground** — to separate faces from their backgrounds. In our eye-brain system, this is our first perceptual task — perceiving any object (the *figure*) as distinct from its surroundings (the *ground*). As you read, the words are the figure; the white space is the ground. This perception applies to our hearing, too. As you hear voices at a party, the one you attend to becomes the figure; all others are part of the ground. Sometimes the same stimulus can trigger more than one perception. In **Figure 2.1-9**, the figure-ground relationship continually reverses. First we see the vase (or the faces), then the faces (or the vase), but we always organize the stimulus into a figure seen against a ground.

### Grouping

Having discriminated figure from ground, we (and our AI system) must also organize the figure into a *meaningful* form. Some basic features of a scene — such as color, movement, and light-dark contrast — we process instantly and automatically (Treisman, 1987). Our mind brings order and form to other stimuli by following certain rules for **grouping**, also identified by the Gestalt psychologists. These rules, which we apply even as infants and

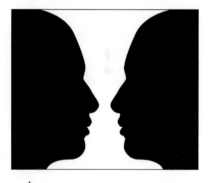

**Figure 2.1-9**
**Reversible figure and ground**

**figure-ground** the organization of the visual field into objects (the *figures*) that stand out from their surroundings (the *ground*).

**grouping** the perceptual tendency to organize stimuli into coherent groups.

**depth perception** the ability to see objects in three dimensions, although the images that strike the retina are two-dimensional; allows us to judge distance.

**visual cliff** a laboratory device for testing depth perception in infants and young animals.

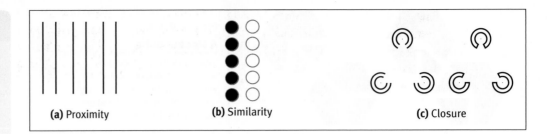

**(a)** Proximity     **(b)** Similarity     **(c)** Closure

### Figure 2.1-10
### Three principles of grouping

(a) Thanks to *proximity*, we group nearby figures together. We see not six separate lines, but three sets of two lines. (b) Through *similarity*, we group objects according to how similar they are to each other. This pattern could be a series of circles, but we perceive it as two groups — one with color, one without color. (c) Using *closure*, we fill in gaps to create a complete, whole object. Thus, we assume that the circles on the left are complete but partially blocked by the (illusory) triangle. Add nothing more than little line segments to close off the circles and your brain may stop constructing a triangle.

### Figure 2.1-11
### Great gestalt!

What's the secret to this impossible doghouse? You probably perceive this doghouse as a gestalt — a whole (though impossible) structure. Actually, your brain imposes this sense of wholeness on the picture. As **Figure 2.1-16** shows, Gestalt grouping principles such as closure and proximity are at work here.

even in our touch perceptions, illustrate how the perceived whole differs from the sum of its parts (Gallace & Spence, 2011; Quinn et al., 2002; Rock & Palmer, 1990). See **Figure 2.1-10** for three examples.

Such principles usually help us construct reality. Sometimes, however, they lead us astray, as when we look at the doghouse in **Figure 2.1-11**.

## Depth Perception

> **2.1-4** How do we use binocular and monocular cues to see in three dimensions, and how do we perceive motion?

Our eye-brain system performs many remarkable feats, among which is **depth perception**. From the two-dimensional images falling on our retinas, we somehow organize three-dimensional perceptions that, for example, let us estimate the distance of an oncoming car. How do we acquire this ability? Are we born with it? Do we learn it?

As psychologist Eleanor Gibson picnicked on the rim of the Grand Canyon, her scientific curiosity kicked in. She wondered: *Would a toddler peering over the rim perceive the dangerous drop-off and draw back?* To answer that question and others, Gibson and Richard Walk (1960) designed a series of experiments in their Cornell University laboratory using a **visual cliff** — a model of a cliff with a "drop-off" area that was actually covered by sturdy glass. They placed 6- to 14-month-old infants on the edge of the "cliff" and had one of the parents coax the infants to lean over the glass or crawl out onto it (**Figure 2.1-12**). Most infants refused to do so, indicating that they could perceive depth.

Had the infants *learned* to perceive depth? Learning appears also to be part of the human story. Years after Gibson and Walk's classic visual cliff studies, psychologist Karen Adolph continued to study infant motor development (Adolph & Hoch, 2019). Adolph and others showed that crawling, no matter when it begins, seems to increase an infant's wariness of heights (Adolph et al., 2014; Campos et al., 1992). Crawling infants tend to gaze downward, making it more likely that they will stare at possible hazards they are approaching (Kretch et al., 2014). They likely evolved this tendency because learning to avoid cliffs helped them survive. Mobile newborn animals—even those with no visual experience (including young kittens, a day-old goat, and newly hatched chicks)—also refuse to venture across the visual cliff. Thus, biology prepares us to be wary of heights, and experience amplifies that fear.

If we were to build the ability to perceive depth into our AI system, what rules might enable it to convert two-dimensional images into a single three-dimensional perception? A good place to start would be the depth cues our brain receives from information supplied by one or both eyes.

## Binocular Cues

People who see with two eyes perceive depth thanks partly to **binocular cues**. Here's a demonstration you might try: With both eyes open, hold two pens or pencils in front of you and touch their tips together. Now do so with one eye closed. A more difficult task, yes?

We use binocular cues to judge the distance of nearby objects. One such cue is **convergence**, in which retinal images are combined by the brain. Another is **retinal disparity**: Because there is space between your eyes, each retina receives a slightly different image of the world. By comparing these two images, your brain can judge how close an object is to you. The greater the disparity (difference) between the two retinal images, the closer the object. Try it. Hold your two index fingers about 5 inches (12 centimeters) in front of your eyes, with their tips half an inch (1 centimeter) apart. Your retinas will receive quite different views. If you close one eye and then the other, you can see the difference. Now look beyond your fingers and note the weird result. Move your fingers out farther and the retinal disparity—and the finger sausage—will shrink (**Figure 2.1-13**).

We could easily include retinal disparity in our AI system. Moviemakers sometimes film a scene through two lenses placed a bit apart. Viewers then watch the film through glasses that allow the left eye to see only the image from the left camera, and the right eye to see only the image from the right camera. As 3-D movie fans know, the resulting effect mimics or exaggerates normal retinal disparity, giving the perception of depth.

**Figure 2.1-12**
**Gibson and Walk's visual cliff**

### AP® Science Practice

#### Research

The visual cliff provides a clever operational definition of depth perception. Operational definitions represent the exact procedures (or operations) used in a research study, and they allow for replication. In this case the variable, depth perception, is operationalized by whether or not infants will crawl across the visual cliff.

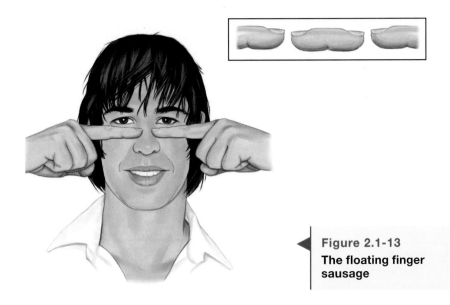

**Figure 2.1-13**
**The floating finger sausage**

**binocular cue** a depth cue, such as retinal disparity, that depends on the use of two eyes.

**convergence** a cue to nearby objects' distance, enabled by the brain combining retinal images.

**retinal disparity** a binocular cue for perceiving depth. By comparing retinal images from the two eyes, the brain computes distance—the greater the disparity (difference) between the two images, the closer the object.

Monika Skolimowska//picture-alliance/dpa/AP Photo

**Creating three-dimensional perceptions from two dimensions** Several of the world's cities slow traffic with illusory 3-D crosswalk paintings, thanks to artists Saumya Pandya Thakkar and Shakuntala Pandyaand, who created the first of these in India.

## Monocular Cues

**Figure 2.1-14**
**Monocular depth cues**

How do we judge whether a person is 10 or 100 meters away? Retinal disparity won't help us here, because there won't be much difference between the images cast on our right and left retinas. At such distances, we depend on **monocular cues** (depth cues available to each eye separately). **Figure 2.1-14** provides some examples.

stockers asia/Shutterstock

**Relative clarity** Because more light passes through objects that are farther away, we perceive these objects as hazy, blurry, or unclear. Nearby objects, by contrast, appear sharp and clear.

I have no depth perception. Is there a cop standing on the corner, or do you have a tiny person in your hair?

BIZARRO © 2014 Dan Piraro, Dist. by King Features

**Relative size** If we assume two objects are similar in size, *most* people perceive the one that casts the smaller retinal image as farther away.

Christopher Harriot/500px/Getty Images

**Texture gradient** Moving toward or away from an object changes our perception of its smoothness or texture. When a wall is viewed from a distance, we will perceive it as smooth. Viewing the same wall up close will reveal greater texture and detail. The same can be seen in the close-up and distant views of these sand dunes.

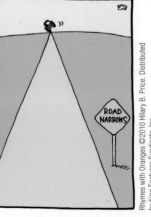

Rhymes with Oranges ©2010 Hilary B. Price. Distributed by King Features Syndicate, Inc.

**Linear perspective** Parallel lines appear to meet in the distance. The sharper the angle of convergence, the greater the perceived distance is.

Philip Mugridge/Alamy Stock Photo

**Interposition** If one object partially blocks our view of another, we perceive it as closer.

# Check Your Understanding

### Examine the Concept

▶ What do we mean when we say that, in perception, "the whole may exceed the sum of its parts"?

▶ Explain how convergence and retinal disparity relate to depth perception.

### Apply the Concept

▶ Explain why, in terms of perception, a band's lead singer would be considered the figure and the other musicians would be considered the ground.

▶ Try drawing a realistic depiction of the scene from your window. Which monocular cues will you use in your drawing?

*Answers to the Examine the Concept questions can be found in Appendix C at the end of the book.*

## Motion Perception

Imagine that, like Mrs. M. described in Module 1.6b, you could perceive the world as having color, form, and depth but you could not see motion. Not only would you be unable to bike or drive, you would have trouble writing, eating, and walking.

Normally your brain computes motion based partly on its assumption that shrinking objects are retreating (not getting smaller) and enlarging objects are approaching. In young children, this ability to correctly perceive approaching (and enlarging) vehicles is not yet fully developed, which puts them at risk for pedestrian accidents (Wann et al., 2011). But it's not just children who have occasional difficulties with motion perception. An adolescent or adult brain is sometimes tricked into believing what it is not seeing. When large and small objects move at the same speed, the large objects appear to move more slowly. Thus, trains seem to move more slowly than cars, and jumbo jets seem to land more slowly than little jets. **Figure 2.1-15** depicts another perceptual phenomenon related to motion.

Have you noticed how often you interrupt your vision with a 0.1-second blink—about 15 times per minute, or 15,000 unnoticed missing time slices per day (Grossman et al., 2019)? Probably not. Our brain perceives a rapid series of slightly varying still images as continuous movement—a phenomenon called **stroboscopic movement**. As film animators know well, a superfast slide show of 24 still images a second will create an illusion of movement. We construct that motion in our head, just as we construct movement in blinking marquees and holiday lights. We perceive two adjacent stationary lights blinking on and off quickly as one single light jumping back and forth. Lighted signs exploit this **phi phenomenon** with a succession of lights that creates the impression of, say, a moving arrow. When we stare at a stationary light in a dark room, our natural eye movement makes the light seem to move. This illusory movement is called the **autokinetic effect**.

**Figure 2.1-15**
**Apparent movement**

As we move, stable objects may also appear to move. If, while riding on a bus, you fix your gaze on some point — say, a house — the objects beyond the fixation point will appear to move with you. Objects in front of the point will appear to move backward.

**monocular cue** a depth cue, such as interposition or linear perspective, available to either eye alone.

**stroboscopic movement** an illusion of continuous movement (as in a motion picture) experienced when viewing a rapid series of slightly varying still images.

**phi phenomenon** an illusion of movement created when two or more adjacent lights blink on and off in quick succession.

**autokinetic effect** the illusory movement of a still spot of light in a dark room.

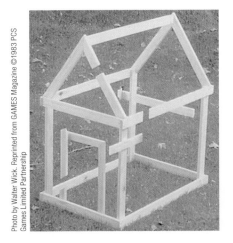

**Figure 2.1-16**
**The solution**

Another view of the impossible doghouse in Figure 2.1-11 reveals the secrets of this illusion. From the photo angle, the grouping principles of closure and proximity lead us to perceive the boards as continuous.

Photo by Walter Wick. Reprinted from GAMES Magazine ©1983 PCS Games Limited Partnership

# Perceptual Constancy

**2.1-5** How do perceptual constancies help us construct meaningful perceptions?

**perceptual constancy** perceiving objects as unchanging (having consistent color, brightness, shape, and size) even as illumination and retinal images change.

**color constancy** perceiving familiar objects as having consistent color, even if changing illumination alters the wavelengths reflected by the object.

So far, we have noted that our AI system must perceive objects as we do—as having a distinct form and location. Its next task is to recognize objects without being deceived by changes in their color, brightness, shape, or size—a *top-down* process called **perceptual constancy**. Regardless of the viewing angle, distance, and illumination, we can identify people and things in less time than it takes to draw a breath. This feat is a huge challenge for an AI system.

## Color and Brightness Constancies

James Gibson (1979) argued for an ecological approach to perception, in which our perceptions depend on an object's context. Consider how you experience the color of a tomato—and how it would change if you viewed it through a paper tube over the course of a day. As the light—and thus the tomato's reflected wavelengths—changed, the tomato's color would also seem to change. But if you discarded the paper tube and viewed the tomato as one item in a salad bowl, its perceived color would remain essentially constant, a consistent perception we call **color constancy**.

Though we take color constancy for granted, this ability is truly remarkable. Under indoor lighting, a blue poker chip reflects wavelengths that match those reflected by a sunlit gold chip (Jameson, 1985). Yet bring a goldfinch indoors and it won't look like a bluebird. The color is not in the bird's feathers. We see color thanks to our brain's computations of the light reflected by an object *relative to the objects surrounding it*. **Figure 2.1-17** dramatically

**Figure 2.1-17**

**Color depends on context**

(a) Believe it or not, these three blue disks are identical in color. (b) Remove the surrounding context and see what results.

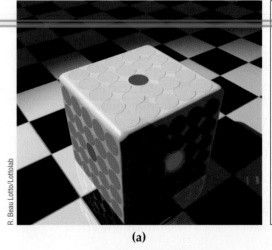

R. Beau Lotto/Lottolab

**(a)**

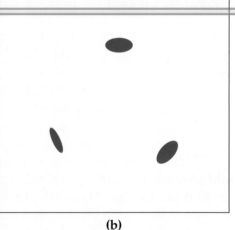

**(b)**

Photo by Manuel Schmalsteig/Color illusory color remix by Øyvind Kolås

**Seeing color?** Surprise! This is actually a black-and-white photo. Did the colorful overlaid grid lines trick your eyes, too?

illustrates the ability of a blue object to appear very different in three different contexts. Knowing the truth—that these disks are identically colored—does not diminish our perception that they are quite different. Because we construct our perceptions, we can simultaneously accept alternative objective and subjective realities.

*Brightness constancy* (also called *lightness constancy*) similarly depends on context. We perceive an object as having a constant brightness even as its illumination varies. This perception of constancy depends on *relative luminance*—the amount of light an object reflects *relative to its surroundings* (**Figure 2.1-18**). White paper reflects 90 percent of the light falling on it; black paper, only 10 percent. Although a black paper viewed in sunlight may reflect 100 times more light than does a white paper viewed indoors, it will still look black (McBurney & Collings, 1984). But try viewing sunlit black paper through a narrow tube that has been moved just slightly away from the paper, but close enough so nothing else is visible. Now the paper may look gray, because in bright sunshine it reflects a fair amount of light. View it without the tube and it is again black, because it reflects much less light than the objects around it.

This principle—that we perceive objects not in isolation but in their environmental context—matters to artists, interior decorators, and clothing designers. Our perception of the color and brightness of a wall or of a streak of paint on a canvas is determined not just by the paint itself but by the surrounding colors. The take-home lesson: *Context governs our perceptions.*

## Shape and Size Constancies

Thanks to *shape constancy*, we perceive the form of familiar objects, such as the door in **Figure 2.1-19**, as constant even while our retinas receive changing images of them. Our brain manages this feat because visual cortex neurons rapidly learn to associate different views of an object (Li & DiCarlo, 2008).

Thanks to *size constancy*, we perceive an object as having an unchanging size, even while our distance from it varies. We assume a bus is large enough to carry people, even when we see its tiny image from two blocks away. This assumption also illustrates the close connection between perceived *distance* and perceived *size*. Perceiving an object's distance gives us cues about its size. Likewise, knowing its general size—that the object is a bus—provides us with cues about its distance. To our long-ago ancestors, the similar-sized sun and moon likely seemed equally distant.

Even when making size-distance judgments, however, we consider an object's context. This interplay between perceived size and perceived distance helps explain several well-known illusions, including the *Moon illusion*: The Moon looks up to 50 percent larger when near the horizon than when high in the sky. Can you imagine why?

For at least 22 centuries, scholars have wondered (Hershenson, 1989). One reason is that monocular cues about objects' distance make the horizon Moon appear farther away. If it's farther away, our brain assumes, it must be larger than the Moon high in the night sky (Kaufman & Kaufman, 2000). But again, if you use a paper tube to take away the distance cue, the horizon Moon will immediately seem smaller.

Perceptual illusions reinforce a fundamental lesson: Perception is not merely a projection of the world onto our brain. Rather, our sensations are disassembled into information bits that our brain then reassembles to create its own functional model of the external world. During this reassembly process, our assumptions—such as the usual relationship between distance and size—can lead us astray. *Our brain constructs our perceptions.*

\* \* \*

Form perception, depth perception, motion perception, and perceptual constancies illuminate how we organize our visual experiences. Perceptual organization applies to our other

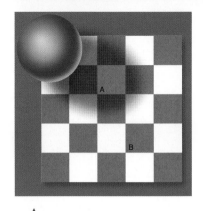

**Figure 2.1-18**
**Relative luminance**

Because of its surrounding context, we perceive Square A as lighter than Square B. But believe it or not, they are identical. To channel comedian Richard Pryor, "Who you gonna believe: me, or your lying eyes?" If you believe your lying eyes—actually, your lying brain—you can photocopy (or screen-capture and print) the illustration, then cut out the squares and compare them. (Information from Edward Adelson.) Such human mistakes are so reliable that computer systems use them to identify human website users—knowing that computer spam robots answer *correctly*.

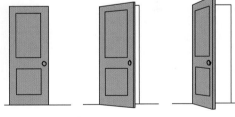

**Figure 2.1-19**
**Shape constancy**

A door casts an increasingly trapezoidal image on our retinas as it opens. Yet we still perceive it as rectangular.

❝ *Sometimes I wonder: Why is that Frisbee getting bigger? And then it hits me.* ❞
*Anonymous*

senses, too. When listening to an unfamiliar language, we have trouble hearing where one word stops and the next one begins. When listening to our own language, we automatically hear distinct words. This, too, reflects perceptual organization. But it is more, for we even organize a string of letters—THEDOGATEMEAT—into words that make an intelligible phrase; it's more likely "The dog ate meat" than "The do gate me at" (McBurney & Collings, 1984). This process involves not only the organization we've been discussing, but also interpretation—discerning meaning in what we perceive.

# Perceptual Interpretation

Philosophers have debated whether our perceptual abilities should be credited to our nature or our nurture. To what extent do we *learn* to perceive? German philosopher Immanuel Kant (1724–1804) maintained that knowledge comes from our *inborn* ways of organizing sensory experiences. Indeed, we come equipped to process sensory information. But British philosopher John Locke (1632–1704) argued that through our experiences we also *learn* to perceive the world. Indeed, we learn to link an object's distance with its size. So, just how important is experience? How radically does it shape our perceptual interpretations?

## Experience and Visual Perception

> **2.1-6** What does research on restored vision, sensory restriction, and perceptual adaptation reveal about the effects of experience on perception?

### Restored Vision and Sensory Restriction

Writing to his friend John Locke, William Molyneux wondered whether "a man *born* blind, and now adult, taught by his *touch* to distinguish between a cube and a sphere" could, if made to see, visually distinguish the two. Locke's answer was *No*, because the man would never have *learned* to see the difference. How does the human mind come "to be furnished?" asked Locke (1690). "To this I answer, in one word, from EXPERIENCE."

**Learning to see** At age 3, Mike May lost his vision in an explosion. Decades later, after a new cornea restored vision to his right eye, he got his first look at his wife and children. Although signals were now reaching his visual cortex, it lacked the experience to interpret them. May could not recognize expressions or faces, apart from features such as hair. Yet he can see an object in motion and has learned to navigate his world and to marvel at such things as dust floating in sunlight (Abrams, 2002; Gorlick, 2010; Huber et al., 2015).

Marcio Jose Sanchez/AP Photo

Molyneux's hypothetical case has since been put to the test with people who, though blind from birth, later gained sight (Gandhi et al., 2017; Gregory, 1978; von Senden, 1932). Most were born with cataracts—clouded lenses that allowed them to see only diffused light, rather as a sighted person might see a foggy image through a table-tennis ball sliced in half. After cataract surgery, the patients could distinguish figure from ground, differentiate colors, and distinguish faces from nonfaces—suggesting that these aspects of perception are innate. But much as Locke supposed, they often could not visually recognize objects that were familiar by touch.

Seeking to gain more control than is provided by clinical cases, researchers have outfitted infant kittens and monkeys with goggles through which they could see only diffuse, unpatterned light (Hubel & Wiesel, 1963). After infancy, when their vision was restored, these animals behaved much like the humans born with cataracts. They could distinguish color and brightness, but not a circle from a square. Their eyes had not degenerated; their retinas still relayed signals to their visual cortex. But lacking early stimulation, their brain's cortical cells had not developed normal connections. Thus, the animals remained functionally blind to shape.

Surgery on children in India has revealed that those who are blind from birth can benefit from removal of cataracts, and the younger they are, the more they benefit. But their visual acuity (sharpness) may never be normal (Chatterjee, 2015; Gandhi et al., 2014). For normal sensory and perceptual development, there is a *critical period*—an optimal period when exposure to certain stimuli or experiences is required. (We'll explore critical periods further in Module 3.2.)

Once this critical period has passed, sensory restrictions later in life do no permanent harm. When researchers cover an adult animal's eye for several months, its vision will be unaffected after the eye patch is removed. When surgeons remove cataracts that develop during late adulthood, most people are thrilled at the return to normal vision.

## Perceptual Adaptation

Given a new pair of glasses, we may feel slightly disoriented, even dizzy. Within a day or two, we adjust. Our **perceptual adaptation** to changed visual input makes the world seem normal again. But imagine wearing a far more dramatic new pair of glasses—one that shifts the apparent location of objects 40 degrees to the left. When you first toss a ball to a friend, it sails off to the left. Walking forward to shake hands with someone, you veer to the left.

Could you adapt to this distorted world? Not if you were a baby chicken. When fitted with such lenses, baby chicks continue to peck where food grains *seem* to be (Hess, 1956; Rossi, 1968). But we humans adapt to distorting lenses quickly. Within a few minutes your throws would again be accurate, your stride on target. Remove the lenses and you would experience an aftereffect: At first your throws would err in the *opposite* direction, sailing off to the right; but again, within minutes you would readapt.

Indeed, given an even more radical pair of glasses—one that literally turns the world upside down—you could still adapt. Psychologist George Stratton (1896) experienced this. He invented, and for 8 days wore, optical headgear that flipped left to right *and* up to down, making him the first person to experience a right-side-up retinal image while standing upright. The ground was up, the sky was down.

At first, when Stratton wanted to walk, he found himself searching for his feet, which were now "up." Eating was nearly impossible. He became nauseated and depressed. But he persisted, and by the eighth day he could comfortably reach for an object and, if his hands were in view, could walk without bumping into things. When Stratton finally removed the headgear, he readapted quickly. So did research participants who later wore such gear—while riding a motorcycle, skiing the Alps, or flying an airplane (Dolezal, 1982; Kohler, 1962). By actively moving about in their topsy-turvy world, they adapted to their new context and learned to coordinate their movements.

Courtesy of Hubert Dolezal

**Perceptual adaptation** "Oops, missed," thought researcher Hubert Dolezal as he attempted a handshake while viewing the world through inverting goggles. Yet, believe it or not, kittens, monkeys, and humans can adapt to an inverted world.

**perceptual adaptation** the ability to adjust to changed sensory input, including an artificially displaced or even inverted visual field.

So, do we learn to perceive the world? In part we do, as we constantly adjust to changed sensory input. Research on critical periods teaches us that early nurture sculpts what nature has provided. In less dramatic ways, nurture continues to do so throughout our lives. Radiologists, who spend their careers inspecting complex visual patterns, outperform novices in detecting unfamiliar visual information (Hussain, 2020). Experience guides, sustains, and maintains the brain pathways that enable our perception.

---

 **Check Your Understanding**

**Examine the Concept**

▶ Explain perceptual adaptation.

**Apply the Concept**

▶ Compare and contrast color constancy and shape constancy.

▶ Provide an example of perceptual constancy from your own experience.

*Answers to the Examine the Concept questions can be found in Appendix C at the end of the book.*

---

\* \* \*

To feel awe, mystery, and a deep reverence for life, we need look no further than our own perceptual system and its capacity for organizing formless nerve impulses into colorful sights, vivid sounds, and evocative smells. As Shakespeare's Hamlet recognized, "There are more things in Heaven and Earth, Horatio, than are dreamt of in your philosophy." Within our ordinary sensory and perceptual experiences lies much that is truly extraordinary—surely much more than has so far been dreamt of in our psychology.

# Module 2.1b REVIEW

**2.1-3** How did the Gestalt psychologists understand perceptual organization, and how do figure-ground and grouping principles contribute to our perceptions?

- Gestalt psychologists searched for rules by which the brain organizes fragments of sensory data into *gestalts*, or meaningful forms. In pointing out that the whole may exceed the sum of its parts, they noted that we filter sensory information and construct our perceptions.

- To recognize an object, we must first perceive it (see it as a *figure*) as distinct from its surroundings (the *ground*). We bring order and form to stimuli by organizing them into meaningful *groups*, following such rules as proximity, similarity, and closure.

**2.1-4** How do we use binocular and monocular cues to see in three dimensions, and how do we perceive motion?

- *Depth perception* is our ability to see objects in three dimensions and judge distance. The *visual cliff* and other research demonstrate that many species perceive the world in three dimensions at, or very soon after, birth.

- *Binocular cues*, such as *convergence* and *retinal disparity*, are depth cues that rely on information from both eyes.

- *Monocular cues* (such as relative clarity, relative size, texture gradient, linear perspective, and interposition) let us judge depth using information transmitted by only one eye.

- The brain computes motion imperfectly, based partly on its assumption that shrinking objects are retreating and enlarging objects are approaching.

- A quick succession of images on the retina can create an illusion of movement, as in *stroboscopic movement* or the *phi phenomenon*. We may also perceive illusory movement in a still spot of light in a dark room—the *autokinetic effect*.

**2.1-5** How do perceptual constancies help us construct meaningful perceptions?

- *Perceptual constancies*, such as in color, brightness (or lightness), shape, or size, enable us to perceive objects as stable despite the changing image they cast on our retinas.

- Our brain constructs our experience of an object's color or brightness through comparisons with other surrounding objects.

- Knowing an object's size gives us clues to its distance; knowing its distance gives clues about its size, but we sometimes misread monocular distance cues and reach the wrong conclusions, as in the Moon illusion.

**2.1-6** What does research on restored vision, sensory restriction, and perceptual adaptation reveal about the effects of experience on perception?

- Experience guides our perceptual interpretations. People who are blind from birth and then gain sight after surgery lack the experience to visually recognize shapes and forms.

- Sensory restriction research indicates that there is a critical period for some aspects of sensory and perceptual development. Without early stimulation, the brain's neural organization does not develop normally.

- People given glasses that shift the world slightly to the left or right, or even upside down, experience *perceptual adaptation*. They are initially disoriented, but they manage to adapt to their new context.

---

# AP® Practice Multiple Choice Questions

1. After purchasing a new color printer, Sheila was annoyed that the pink bulldog she printed on gray paper was much brighter than the image of the pink bulldog she saw against the backdrop of her white computer screen. She called a printer expert, claiming that her printer was broken. Which of the following statements should the printer expert make to explain to Sheila why her belief is incorrect?

    a. "Because of shape constancy, you should perceive the same pink bulldog on the computer and on the paper."
    b. "Because of relative luminance, you may perceive the pink bulldog to be brighter against a darker background."
    c. "Because of color constancy, you may perceive the colors shifting from a computer screen to a piece of paper."
    d. "Because of size constancy, you should perceive the pink bulldog in roughly the same manner on the computer and on the paper."

2. Amber experienced the illusion of movement when looking at three stationary, adjacent, blinking lights. What is this effect called?

    a. Phi phenomenon
    b. Binocular cues
    c. Retinal disparity
    d. Stroboscopic movement

3. Bryanna and Charles are participating in a dance competition. It is easy for spectators to see them against the dance floor because of

    a. texture gradient.
    b. the phi phenomenon.
    c. color constancy.
    d. figure-ground relationships.

4. Narmeen is viewing the board in the classroom. She knows that the board is located far away, because the view from her left eye is only slightly different than the view from her right eye. Her ability to judge the distance of the board is due to which depth cue?

    a. Retinal disparity
    b. Relative size
    c. Linear perspective
    d. Convergence

5. Which of the following statements is best explained by research on depth perception using the visual cliff?

    a. Based on research with newborn animals that refuse to cross the visual cliff, it can be inferred that monocular depth cues develop before binocular depth cues.
    b. Based on research with mobile newborn animals that refuse to cross the visual cliff, it can be inferred that newborn human infants are also born with an innate sense of depth.
    c. Based on research with newborn animals that willingly cross the visual cliff, it can be inferred that human infants must learn to perceive depth.
    d. Based on research with newborn animals that do not willingly cross the visual cliff, it can be inferred that humans do not develop the perception of depth until 24 months of age.

6. Even though the banana seemed to change color as the lighting in the room changed, Jane knew that the color of the banana was not actually changing. This perception is due to

    a. relative clarity.
    b. color constancy.
    c. interposition.
    d. relative luminance.

**7.** Students in a marching band stand close together in tight lines in order to form the initials of their high school. Which Gestalt principle is the marching band using to form the initials?

a. Convergence
b. Linear perspective
c. Proximity
d. Interposition

**8.** What should Mischa say in a speech to describe relative size most accurately?

a. If we assume two objects are similar in size, most people perceive objects lower in their field of vision as farther away.
b. If we assume two objects are similar in size, most people perceive objects higher in their field of vision as farther away.
c. If we assume two objects are similar in size, most people perceive the one that casts the larger retinal image as farther away.
d. If we assume two objects are similar in size, most people perceive the one that casts the smaller retinal image as farther away.

# Module 2.2a Thinking, Problem Solving, Judgments, and Decision Making: Concepts and Creativity

### LEARNING TARGETS

**2.2-1** Define *cognition*, and explain the functions of concepts.

**2.2-2** Explain the factors associated with *creativity*, and describe some ways of fostering creativity.

In some ways, we display remarkable mental powers. Indeed, our ability to think creatively—to consider many different options and produce novel and valuable ideas—is a *Homo sapiens* hallmark.

## Concepts

**2.2-1** What are *cognition* and *metacognition*, and what are the functions of concepts?

Psychologists who study **cognition** focus on the mental activities associated with thinking, knowing, remembering, and communicating information. One of these activities is **metacognition** (literally "beyond cognition"), or thinking about our thinking. Metacognition refers to our thinking when planning and assessing our understanding and performance. Students who use metacognition—who monitor and evaluate their learning—perform better academically (de Boer et al., 2018).

At a basic level, we form **concepts**—mental groupings of similar objects, events, ideas, or people. The concept *chair* includes many items—a baby's high chair, a reclining chair, a dentist's chair—all for sitting. Concepts simplify our thinking. Imagine life without them. We could not ask a child to "throw the ball" because there would be no concept of *throw* or *ball*. We could not say, "I want to earn money" because people aren't born with a concept of *earn* or *money*. Concepts such as *ball* and *money* give us much information with little cognitive effort.

We often form our concepts by developing a **prototype**—a mental image or best example of a category (Rosch, 1978). People more quickly agree that "a crow is a bird" than that "a penguin is a bird." For most of us, the crow is the birdier bird; it more closely resembles our *bird* prototype. When something closely matches our prototype of a concept, we more readily recognize it as an example of the concept.

When we categorize people, we mentally shift them toward our category prototypes. Such was the experience of Belgian students who viewed ethnically blended faces. When viewing a blended face in which 70 percent of the features were prototypically White and 30 percent Asian, the students categorized the

**cognition** all the mental activities associated with thinking, knowing, remembering, and communicating.

**metacognition** cognition about our cognition; keeping track of and evaluating our mental processes.

**concept** a mental grouping of similar objects, events, ideas, or people.

**prototype** a mental image or best example of a category. Matching new items to a prototype provides a quick and easy method for sorting items into categories (as when comparing feathered creatures to a prototypical bird, such as a crow).

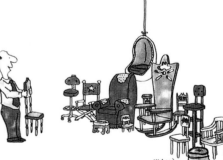

*"Attention, everyone! I'd like to introduce the newest member of our family."*

Jeff Kaufman The New Yorker Collection/The Cartoon Bank

90% WH    80% WH    70% WH    60% WH    50%/50%    60% AS    70% AS    80% AS    90% AS

FaceGen TM

### Figure 2.2-1
### Categorizing faces influences recollection

Shown a face that was 70 percent White, people tended to classify the person as White and to recollect the face as more White than it was. (Re-creation of experiment courtesy of Olivier Corneille.)

**CULTURAL AWARENESS**

Our schemas are quite useful in helping us organize and interpret information from the world around us. However, schemas for groups of people or social categories can lead to bias if we are not careful. For example, if we have in our woman schema that women aren't good at science, we might discount the important accomplishments of women scientists.

face as White (**Figure 2.2-1**). Later, as their memory shifted toward the White prototype, they were more likely to remember an 80 percent White face than the 70 percent White face they had actually seen (Corneille et al., 2004). Likewise, if shown a 70 percent Asian face, they later remembered a more prototypically Asian face. So, too, with sex: People who viewed 70 percent male faces later misremembered them as even more prototypically male (Huart et al., 2005).

Move away from our prototypes, and category boundaries may blur. Is a tomato a fruit? Is a 17-year-old female a girl or a woman? Is a whale a fish or a mammal? Because a whale fails to match our *mammal* prototype, we are slower to recognize it as a mammal. Similarly, when symptoms don't fit one of our disease prototypes, we are slow to perceive an illness (Bishop, 1991). People whose heart attack symptoms (shortness of breath, exhaustion, a dull weight in the chest) don't match their *heart attack* prototype (sharp chest pain) may not seek help. And when behaviors don't fit our *discrimination* prototypes, of White against Black, male against female, young against old, we often fail to notice prejudice. People more easily detect male prejudice against females than female prejudice against males or female prejudice against females (Cunningham et al., 2009; Inman & Baron, 1996). Although concepts speed and guide our thinking, they don't always make us wise.

Developmental psychologist Jean Piaget [pee-ah-ZHAY], who studied the development of cognition in children, argued that our intellectual progression reflects an unceasing struggle to make sense of our experiences. To this end, the maturing brain builds **schemas**—concepts or mental molds into which we pour our experiences (**Figure 2.2-2**).

Image Ideas/Getty Images

Christian L Birmele

### Figure 2.2-2
### A changing marriage schema

Most people once had a marriage schema as a union between a man and a woman. By 2023, more than two dozen countries had legalized same-sex marriage. These new laws are both informed by and inform a culture's changing marriage schema.

**schema** a concept or framework that organizes and interprets information.

To explain how we use and adjust our schemas, Piaget proposed two more concepts. First, we **assimilate** new experiences—we interpret them according to our current schemas (understandings). Having a simple schema for dog, for example, a toddler may call all four-legged animals dogs. But as we interact with the world, we also adjust, or **accommodate**, our schemas to incorporate information provided by new experiences. Thus, the child soon learns that the original dog schema is too broad and accommodates by refining the category.

---

**AP® Science Practice**

## Check Your Understanding

### Examine the Concept

▶ Describe *prototypes* and explain how they might feed discrimination.

▶ Explain cognition and metacognition.

### Apply the Concept

▶ Imagine patiently waiting your turn at a store, and then having some later-arriving adults attended to before you. The clerk also wants to check inside your bag before you leave the store. What might all this say about the "teenager" prototype the clerk seems to have?

▶ Compare and contrast assimilation and accommodation. Can you think of an example of each from your own experience?

*Answers to the Examine the Concept questions can be found in Appendix C at the end of the book.*

---

# Thinking Creatively

**2.2-2** What is *creativity*, and what fosters it?

**Creativity** is the ability to produce novel and valuable ideas (Hennessey & Amabile, 2010). Consider mathematician Andrew Wiles' incredible, creative moment. *Fermat's last theorem* (dreamed up by seventeenth-century mischievous genius Pierre de Fermat) had baffled the greatest mathematical minds for centuries—even after a $2 million prize (in today's dollars) for the first proof was offered in 1908.

Wiles had pondered Fermat's theorem for more than 30 years. One morning, out of the blue, the final "incredible revelation" struck him. "It was so indescribably beautiful; it was so simple and so elegant. I couldn't understand how I'd missed it. . . . It was the most important moment of my working life" (Singh, 1997, p. 25). Creative writers and physicists likewise experience many significant ideas, unbidden, during mind wandering (Gable et al., 2019). (Perhaps you can recall such an experience?)

Creativity is supported by a certain level of *aptitude* (ability to learn). Those who score exceptionally high in quantitative aptitude as 13-year-olds, for example, are later more likely to create published or patented work (Bernstein et al., 2019; Lubinski et al., 2014). Yet there is more to creativity than aptitude, or what intelligence tests reveal.

Aptitude tests (such as the SAT) require **convergent thinking**—an ability to provide a single correct answer. Creativity tests (*How many uses can you think of for a brick?*) require **divergent thinking**—the ability to consider many different options and to think in novel ways. *Functional fixedness* occurs when our prior experiences inhibit our ability to find creative solutions (Chrysikou et al., 2016). Bricklayers may only see a brick as part of a home rather than as a possible doorstop.

**assimilation** interpreting our new experiences in terms of our existing schemas.

**accommodation** adapting our current schemas (understandings) to incorporate new information.

**creativity** the ability to produce new and valuable ideas.

**convergent thinking** narrowing the available problem solutions to determine the single best solution.

**divergent thinking** expanding the number of possible problem solutions; creative thinking that diverges in different directions.

**Creative women** Researcher Sally Reis (2001) found that notably creative women, such as Nobel laureate geneticist Barbara McClintock, were typically "intelligent, hardworking, imaginative, and strong willed" as girls. In her 2013 Nobel Prize for Literature acceptance speech, author Alice Munro, shown here, described the creative process as hard work: "The part that's hardest is when you go over the story and realize how bad it is. You know, the first part, excitement, the second, pretty good, but then you pick it up one morning and you think, 'what nonsense,' and that is when you really have to get to work."

PETER MUHLY/Getty Images

"For the love of God, is there a doctor in the house?"

WELL, I TOLD YOU TO ADD YEAST TO YOUR SHAMPOO.

**Imaginative thinking** Cartoonists often display creativity as they see things in new ways or make unusual connections.

Robert Sternberg and his colleagues believe creativity has five components (Sternberg, 1988, 2003; Sternberg & Lubart, 1991, 1992):

1. **Expertise**—well-developed knowledge—furnishes the ideas, images, and phrases we use as mental building blocks. "Chance favors only the prepared mind," observed Louis Pasteur. The more blocks we have, the more chances we have to combine them in novel ways. And the longer we work on a problem, the more creative are our solutions (Lucas & Nordgren, 2020).

2. **Imaginative thinking skills** provide the ability to see things in novel ways, to recognize patterns, and to make connections. Having mastered a problem's basic elements, we can redefine or explore it in a new way.

3. **A venturesome personality** seeks new experiences, tolerates ambiguity and risk, and perseveres in overcoming obstacles.

4. **Intrinsic motivation** is the quality of being driven more by interest, satisfaction, and challenge than by external pressures (Amabile & Hennessey, 1992). Creative people focus less on extrinsic motivators—meeting deadlines, impressing people, or making money—than on the pleasure and stimulation of the work itself.

5. **A creative environment** sparks, supports, and refines creative ideas. Wiles stood on the shoulders of others and collaborated with a former student. A study of the careers of 2026 prominent scientists and inventors revealed that the most eminent were mentored, challenged, and supported by their colleagues (Simonton, 1992). Creativity-fostering environments support innovation, team building, and communication (Hülsheger et al., 2009). They also minimize anxiety and foster contemplation (Byron & Khazanchi, 2011).

For those seeking to boost the creative process, research offers some ideas:

A creative environment

- **Develop your expertise.** Ask yourself what you care about and most enjoy. Follow your passion by broadening your knowledge base and becoming an expert at something.

- **Allow time for incubation.** Think hard on a problem, but then set it aside and come back to it later. Periods of inattention to a problem ("sleeping on it") allow for automatic processing to form associations (Zhong et al., 2008).

- **Set aside time for the mind to roam freely.** Creativity springs from "defocused attention" (Simonton, 2012a,b). So, detach from attention-grabbing TV shows, social media, and video gaming. Jog, go for a long walk, or meditate. Serenity seeds spontaneity. "Time alone is . . . the font of creativity," says playwright and musician Lin-Manuel Miranda (Hainey, 2016).

● *Experience other cultures and ways of thinking.* Viewing life from a different perspective sometimes sets the creative juices flowing. Students who spend time in other cultures learn how to blend new norms with those from their home culture, which increases creativity (Godart et al., 2015; Lu et al., 2018). Even getting out of your neighborhood or embracing intercultural friendships fosters flexible thinking (Kim et al., 2013; Ritter et al., 2012).

---

 **AP® Science Practice**

## Check Your Understanding

**Examine the Concept**

▶ Explain convergent and divergent thinking. When might each be most helpful?

▶ Explain the five components of creativity identified by Robert Sternberg.

*Answers to the Examine the Concept questions can be found in Appendix C at the end of the book.*

**Apply the Concept**

▶ Using the four suggestions provided in this section, explain what you might do to boost your creativity.

---

## Module 2.2a REVIEW

**2.2-1 What are *cognition* and *metacognition*, and what are the functions of concepts?**

● *Cognition* refers to all the mental activities associated with thinking, knowing, remembering, and communicating.

● *Metacognition* is cognition about our cognition, or keeping track of and evaluating our mental processes.

● We use *concepts*, mental groupings of similar objects, events, ideas, or people, to simplify and order the world around us.

● We form most concepts around *prototypes*, or best examples of a category.

**2.2-2 What is *creativity*, and what fosters it?**

● *Creativity*, the ability to produce novel and valuable ideas, is supported by a certain level of aptitude, but is more than what intelligence tests reveal. Aptitude tests require *convergent thinking*, but creativity requires *divergent thinking*.

● Robert Sternberg has proposed that creativity involves expertise; imaginative thinking skills; a venturesome personality; intrinsic motivation; and a creative environment that sparks, supports, and refines creative ideas.

---

## AP® Practice Multiple Choice Questions

**1.** To find the best route to work, Vlad identified all routes and eliminated options one-by-one. Which of the following did Vlad use?

a. Incubation
b. Divergent thinking
c. Expertise
d. Convergent thinking

**2.** When asked to think of a ball, Carlos quickly thought of images of baseballs, basketballs, and footballs. Which psychological concept best applies to this scenario?

a. Prototypes
b. Convergent thinking
c. Creativity
d. Venturesome personality

**3.** Dr. Yamlak discovered that there was only a 3 percent chance of error in his finding that people who produce new and valuable ideas also tend to earn more money. Which of the following statements provides the most accurate interpretation of these results?

a. Dr. Yamlak's result that creativity relates to income is statistically significant.
b. Dr. Yamlak's result that convergent thinking relates to income is statistically significant.
c. Dr. Yamlak's result that creativity relates to income is not statistically significant.
d. Dr. Yamlak's result that accommodation relates to income is not statistically significant.

**4.** Your teacher asks how many uses you can think of for a pencil. She is testing your

    a. convergent thinking.
    b. intrinsic motivation.
    c. divergent thinking.
    d. prototypes.

**Use the following text to answer questions 5 and 6:**

Dr. Jablonski conducted a study in which she measured the amount of time it took for participants to categorize one of two actions as discrimination: (1) failing to hire someone who appeared to be White or (2) failing to hire someone who appeared to be Black. The median amount of time it took participants to categorize action 1 as discrimination was 3 seconds, and the median amount of time it took participants to categorize action 2 as discrimination was 1 second.

**5.** Which psychological concept is Dr. Jablonski most likely interested in measuring in this scenario?

    a. Creativity
    b. Prototypes
    c. Divergent thinking
    d. Convergent thinking

**6.** Which of the following provides the most accurate interpretation of the medians in the scenario?

    a. The average amount of time it took participants to identify action 1 as discrimination was longer than the average amount of time it took participants to identify action 2 as discrimination.
    b. The middle number in a list of times for identifying action 1 as discrimination was larger than the middle number in a list of times for identifying action 2 as discrimination.
    c. Three seconds was the most common time it took for participants to identify action 1 as discrimination, while 1 second was the most common time it took participants to identify action 2 as discrimination.
    d. There were 3 seconds of spread in the data for identifying action 1 as discrimination, while there was 1 second of spread in the data for identifying action 2 as discrimination.

# Module 2.2b Thinking, Problem Solving, Judgments, and Decision Making: Solving Problems and Making Decisions

## LEARNING TARGETS

**2.2-3** Explain the cognitive strategies that assist our problem solving and the obstacles that hinder it.

**2.2-4** Explain the meaning of *intuition*, and explain how the availability and representativeness heuristics influence our decisions and judgments.

**2.2-5** Explain how our decisions and judgments are affected by overconfidence, belief perseverance, and framing.

**2.2-6** Explain how smart thinkers use intuition.

In some ways we are not, as we will see, the "wise humans" our species name suggests. We fear the wrong things. We allow the day's local hot or cold weather to color our judgments of global climate change. We tend to be overconfident in our judgments and to persevere in clinging to discredited beliefs. Clearly, we are often in need of improving our **executive functions**—the high-level cognitive abilities that collectively allow us to solve problems and make decisions effectively.

## Problem Solving: Strategies and Obstacles

**2.2-3** Which cognitive strategies assist our problem solving, and which obstacles hinder it?

One tribute to our rationality is our problem-solving skill. What's the best route around this traffic jam? How should we handle a friend's criticism? How, without our keys, can we get into the house?

Some problems we solve through *trial and error*. Thomas Edison tried thousands of light bulb filaments before stumbling upon one that worked. For other problems, we use **algorithms**, step-by-step procedures that guarantee a solution. But step-by-step algorithms can be laborious and exasperating. To find a word using the 10 letters in *SPLOYOCHYG*, for example, you could try each letter in each of the 10 positions—907,200 permutations in all. Rather than give you a computing brain the size of a beach ball, nature resorts to **heuristics**, simpler thinking strategies. Thus, you might reduce the number of options in the *SPLOYOCHYG* example by grouping letters that often appear together (*CH* and *GY*) and excluding rare letter combinations (such as *YY*). By using heuristics and then applying trial and error, you may hit on the answer. Have you guessed it?[1]

**executive functions**
cognitive skills that work together, enabling us to generate, organize, plan, and implement goal-directed behavior.

**algorithm** a methodical, logical rule or procedure that guarantees solving a particular problem. Contrasts with the usually speedier—but also more error-prone—use of *heuristics*.

**heuristic** a simple thinking strategy—a mental shortcut— that often allows us to make judgments and solve problems efficiently; usually speedier but also more error-prone than an *algorithm*.

[1]Answer to SPLOYOCHYG anagram: PSYCHOLOGY.

**Figure 2.2-3**

**The Aha! moment**

A burst of right temporal lobe activity accompanied insight solutions to word problems (Jung-Beeman et al., 2004). The red dots designate EEG electrodes. The light gray lines show the distribution of high-frequency activity accompanying insight. The insight-related activity is centered in the right temporal lobe (yellow area).

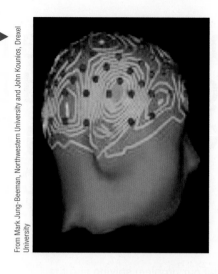

Sometimes no problem-solving strategy seems to be at work at all, and we arrive at a solution to a problem through **insight**. Brain scans show bursts of activity associated with sudden flashes of insight (Kounios & Beeman, 2014). In one study, researchers asked people to think of a word that forms a compound word or phrase with each of three other words in a set (such as *cream, skate,* and *water*) and to press a button to sound a bell when they knew the answer.[2] A sudden Aha! insight led to about half the solutions. Before the Aha! moment, the problem solvers' frontal lobes (involved in focusing attention) were active. At the instant of discovery, there was a burst of activity in the right temporal lobe, just above the ear (Figure 2.2-3).

Psychologist Wolfgang Köhler (1925) showed that humans are not the only creatures to display insight. He placed a piece of fruit and a long stick outside the cage of a chimpanzee named Sultan, beyond his reach. Inside the cage, Köhler placed a short stick, which Sultan grabbed, using it to try to reach the fruit. After several failed attempts, the chimpanzee dropped the stick and seemed to survey the situation. Then suddenly (as if thinking "Aha!"), Sultan jumped up and seized the short stick again. This time, he used it to pull in the longer stick—which he then used to reach the fruit. (For one example of a chimpanzee's use of foresight, see Figure EM.3-1a.)

Birds, too, have displayed insight. One experiment, by Christopher Bird (yes, really) and Nathan Emery (2009), brought to life an Aesop fable in which a thirsty crow is unable to reach the water in a partly filled pitcher. See the crow's solution in Figure EM.3-1b. Other crows have fashioned wire or sticks for extracting food, such as insects in rotting logs (Jelbert et al., 2018; Rutz et al., 2016). One African grey parrot has equaled or bettered the performance of Harvard students at a complex shell game testing visual memory (Pailian et al., 2020).

Insight often strikes suddenly, creating a happy sense of satisfaction (Knoblich & Oellinger, 2006; Metcalfe, 1986). The joy of a joke may similarly lie in our sudden comprehension of an unexpected ending or a double meaning: "You don't need a parachute to skydive. You only need a parachute to skydive twice."

Insightful as we are, other cognitive tendencies may lead us astray. We seek news that not only informs us, but also affirms us. **Confirmation bias**, for example, leads us to seek evidence *for* our ideas more eagerly than we hunt for evidence *against* them (Klayman & Ha, 1987; Skov & Sherman, 1986). In a classic study, Peter Wason (1960) gave British university students a set of three numbers *(2-4-6)* and told them the series was based on a rule. Their task was to guess the rule. (It was simple: any three ascending numbers.) Before submitting their answers, students generated their own three-number sets, and Wason told them whether their sets conformed to his rule. Once they were *certain* they had the rule, the students could announce it. The result? Most students formed a wrong idea (*"Maybe it's counting by twos"*) and then searched *only* for confirming evidence (by testing *6-8-10, 100-102-104,* and so forth). Seldom right but never in doubt.

In real life, having formed a belief—that people can (or cannot) change their sexual orientation, that gun control laws fail (or do not fail) to save lives—we prefer information that supports our belief. And once we get hung up on an incorrect view of a problem, it's hard

**insight** a sudden realization of a problem's solution; contrasts with strategy-based solutions.

**confirmation bias** a tendency to search for information that supports our preconceptions and to ignore or distort contradictory evidence.

shchambers.com©

[2]The word is *ice.*

to approach it from a different angle. This obstacle to problem solving is called **fixation**, an inability to come to a fresh perspective. See if fixation prevents you from solving the matchstick problem in **Figure 2.2-4**. (For the solution, see **Figure 2.2-5** on page 196.)

A prime example of fixation is **mental set**, our tendency to approach a problem with the mindset of what has worked for us previously. Indeed, solutions that worked in the past often do work on new problems. Consider:

Given the sequence *O-T-T-F-?-?-?*, what are the final three letters?

Most people have difficulty recognizing that the three final letters are *F*(ive), *S*(ix), and *S*(even). But solving this problem may make the next one easier:

Given the sequence *J-F-M-A-?-?-?*, what are the final three letters? (If you don't get this one, ask yourself what month it is.)

Just as a *perceptual set* predisposes us to what we perceive, a mental set predisposes us to how we think. Sometimes this can be an obstacle to problem solving, as when our mental set from our past experiences with matchsticks predisposes us to arrange them in two dimensions.

**Figure 2.2-4**
**The matchstick problem**
How would you arrange six matches to form four equilateral triangles?

---

 **AP® Science Practice**

## Check Your Understanding

### Examine the Concept
▶ Explain the difference between algorithms and heuristics.
▶ Explain *fixation*. Provide a specific example.

### Apply the Concept
▶ Describe a time when you had trouble solving a problem. Explain how your mental set might have played a role.

*Answers to the Examine the Concept questions can be found in Appendix C at the end of the book.*

---

# Forming Good (and Bad) Decisions and Judgments

**2.2-4** What is *intuition*, and how can the representativeness and availability heuristics influence our decisions and judgments?

When making each day's hundreds of judgments and decisions (*Should I take a jacket? Can I trust this person? Is that a friendly dog?*), we seldom take the time and effort to reason systematically. Instead, we more often follow our **intuition**, our fast, automatic, unreasoned feelings and thoughts. After interviewing policy makers in government, business, and education, social psychologist Irving Janis (1986) concluded that they "often do not use a reflective problem-solving approach. How do they usually arrive at their decisions? If you ask, they are likely to tell you . . . they do it mostly *by the seat of their pants.*"

## Two Quick But Risky Shortcuts

When we need to make snap judgments, heuristics enable quick thinking that often serves us well (Gigerenzer, 2015). But as cognitive psychologists Amos Tversky and Daniel Kahneman (1974) showed, some intuitive mental shortcuts—the *representativeness* and *availability heuristics*—can lead even the smartest people to make dumb decisions.[3]

**fixation** in cognition, the inability to see a problem from a new perspective; an obstacle to problem solving.

**mental set** a tendency to approach a problem in one particular way, often a way that has been successful in the past.

**intuition** an effortless, immediate, automatic feeling or thought, as contrasted with explicit, conscious reasoning.

[3]Tversky and Kahneman's joint work on decision making received a 2002 Nobel Prize; sadly, only Kahneman was alive to receive the honor. As Kahneman wrote in a vignette for my [DM's] *Social Psychology* text, "Amos and I shared the wonder of together owning a goose that could lay golden eggs—a joint mind that was better than our separate minds."

 **SPOTLIGHT ON:**
Tversky and Kahneman

"In creating these problems, we didn't set out to fool people. All our problems fooled us, too."
— Amos Tversky (1985)

"Intuitive thinking [is] fine most of the time. . . . But sometimes that habit of mind gets us in trouble."
— Daniel Kahneman (2005)

**Figure 2.2-5**

**Solution to the matchstick problem**

To solve this problem, you must view it from a new perspective, breaking the fixation of limiting solutions to two dimensions.

**representativeness heuristic** judging the likelihood of events in terms of how well they seem to represent, or match, particular prototypes; may lead us to ignore other relevant information.

**availability heuristic** judging the likelihood of events based on their availability in memory; if instances come readily to mind (perhaps because of their vividness), we presume such events are common.

## The Representativeness Heuristic

To judge the likelihood of something by intuitively comparing it to particular prototypes is to use the **representativeness heuristic**. Imagine someone who is short and slim, and likes to read poetry. Is this person more likely to be an Ivy League university English professor or a truck driver (Nisbett & Ross, 1980)?

Many people guess English professor—because this description better fits their prototype of a nerdy professor than of a truck driver. In doing so, they fail to consider the *base rate* number of Ivy League English professors (fewer than 400) and truck drivers (3.5 million in the United States alone). Instead, they recall situations that confirm their nerdy professor prototype (Bordalo et al., 2021). Thus, even if the description is 50 times more typical of English professors than of truck drivers, the fact that there are about 7000 times more truck drivers means that the poetry reader is many times more likely to be a truck driver.

Some prototypes have social and economic consequences. If people have a prototype—a *stereotype*—of members of certain racial groups, they may unconsciously use the representativeness heuristic when judging individuals. The result is racial bias. If people observe random events happening repeatedly (flipping a coin and having it land on heads eight times in a row), they may unconsciously use the representativeness heuristic when judging the likelihood of future events (assuming the coin will surely land on tails the next time). The result is what is known as the *gambler's fallacy*.

## The Availability Heuristic

The **availability heuristic** operates when we evaluate the commonality of an event *based on its mental availability*. Anything that makes information pop into mind—its vividness, recency, or distinctiveness—can make it seem commonplace. Watching a horrific terrorist beheading implants a fear of global terrorism that lingers for 2 years (Redmond et al., 2019). Sometimes photos—say, of terrified children separated from their parents at the U.S. border, or of a working mother being appointed to the U.S. Supreme Court—can change thinking for years. As climate change has become more vividly associated with extreme weather—fires, floods, hurricanes—public concern has risen.

The availability heuristic distorts our judgments of risks. After one celebrity's vaccinated child later developed autism spectrum disorder, thousands found her gripping story more persuasive than widely replicated scientific data disproving any vaccine–autism link (Hoffman, 2019). *The bottom* line: We often fear the wrong things (see Developing Arguments: The Fear Factor).

 AP® Science Practice

# Developing Arguments

## The Fear Factor

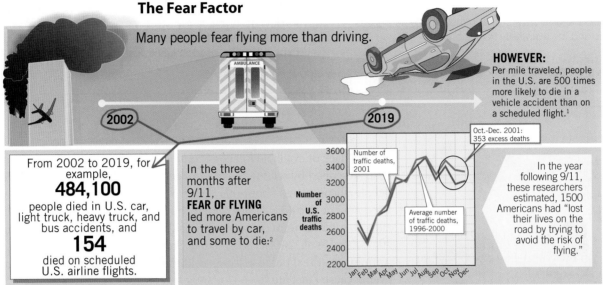

Many people fear flying more than driving.

**HOWEVER:** Per mile traveled, people in the U.S. are 500 times more likely to die in a vehicle accident than on a scheduled flight.[1]

2002 · 2019

From 2002 to 2019, for example, **484,100** people died in U.S. car, light truck, heavy truck, and bus accidents, and **154** died on scheduled U.S. airline flights.

In the three months after 9/11, **FEAR OF FLYING** led more Americans to travel by car, and some to die:[2]

Oct.-Dec. 2001: 353 excess deaths

Number of traffic deaths, 2001

Average number of traffic deaths, 1996-2000

Number of U.S. traffic deaths

3600 3400 3200 3000 2800 2600 2400 2200

Jan Feb Mar Apr May Jun Jul Aug Sep Oct Nov Dec

In the year following 9/11, these researchers estimated, 1500 Americans had "lost their lives on the road by trying to avoid the risk of flying."

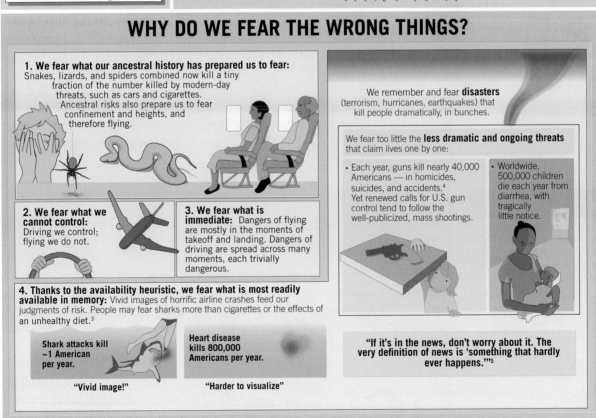

# WHY DO WE FEAR THE WRONG THINGS?

**1. We fear what our ancestral history has prepared us to fear:** Snakes, lizards, and spiders combined now kill a tiny fraction of the number killed by modern-day threats, such as cars and cigarettes. Ancestral risks also prepare us to fear confinement and heights, and therefore flying.

**2. We fear what we cannot control:** Driving we control; flying we do not.

**3. We fear what is immediate:** Dangers of flying are mostly in the moments of takeoff and landing. Dangers of driving are spread across many moments, each trivially dangerous.

**4. Thanks to the availability heuristic, we fear what is most readily available in memory:** Vivid images of horrific airline crashes feed our judgments of risk. People may fear sharks more than cigarettes or the effects of an unhealthy diet.[3]

Shark attacks kill ~1 American per year.
"Vivid image!"

Heart disease kills 800,000 Americans per year.
"Harder to visualize"

We remember and fear **disasters** (terrorism, hurricanes, earthquakes) that kill people dramatically, in bunches.

We fear too little the **less dramatic and ongoing threats** that claim lives one by one:

- Each year, guns kill nearly 40,000 Americans — in homicides, suicides, and accidents.[4] Yet renewed calls for U.S. gun control tend to follow the well-publicized, mass shootings.

- Worldwide, 500,000 children die each year from diarrhea, with tragically little notice.

**"If it's in the news, don't worry about it. The very definition of news is 'something that hardly ever happens.'"[5]**

## Developing Arguments Questions

**1.** Identify the scientifically derived evidence that supports the claim that we should be less fearful of flying than of driving.

**2.** What would you say to a friend who insisted that flying was the more dangerous of the two?

**3.** Using the four pieces of evidence presented in the "Developing Arguments" feature, explain why we tend to fear the wrong things.

1. National Safety Council, 2021; National Highway Traffic Safety Administration, 2021. 2. Gaissmaier & Gigerenzer, 2012; Gigerenzer, 2004, 2006. 3. Daley, 2011. 4. USA Facts, 2021. 5. Schneier, 2007.

**Examine the Concept**

▶ Explain the difference between the representativeness heuristic and the availability heuristic.

**Apply the Concept**

▶ How does your family typically manage risk in a time of crisis? Are some of your fears excessive, or do you not fear enough? Explain how heuristics might influence your thinking.

*Answers to the Examine the Concept questions can be found in Appendix C at the end of the book.*

*"Don't let this beautiful weather fool you into thinking everything's fine."*

The lack of available images of a *future* climate change disaster—a climate crisis described by scientists as "Armageddon in slow motion"—has left some people unconcerned about this threat. Moreover, climate beliefs can shift with the day's hot or cold weather, which, though more cognitively available, tells us zilch about long-term planetary trends (Egan & Mullin, 2012; Kaufmann et al., 2017; Zaval et al., 2014). As comedian Stephen Colbert (2014) tweeted, "Global warming isn't real because it was cold today! Also great news: World hunger is over because I just ate."

More than 40 nations have sought to harness the positive power of vivid, memorable images by putting eye-catching warnings and graphic photos on cigarette packages (Riordan, 2013). This campaign has worked because we reason emotionally (Huang et al., 2013). In 2015, a viral photo of a Syrian child lying dead on a beach had massive impact on public opinion. Red Cross donations to Syrian refugees were 55 times greater in response to that photo than in response to statistics describing the hundreds of thousands of other refugee deaths (Slovic et al., 2017). Dramatic incidents make us gasp; probabilities we barely grasp.

## Overconfidence

**2.2-5 How are our decisions and judgments affected by overconfidence, belief perseverance, and framing?**

Sometimes we are more confident than correct. When answering factual questions, such as "Is absinthe a liqueur or a precious stone?" only 60 percent of people in one study answered correctly. (It's a licorice-flavored liqueur.) Yet those answering felt, on average, 75 percent confident (Fischhoff et al., 1977). This tendency to overestimate the accuracy of our knowledge and judgments is termed **overconfidence**.

**overconfidence** the tendency to be more confident than correct—to overestimate the accuracy of our beliefs and judgments.

*"Let me interrupt your expertise with my confidence."*

It is overconfidence that so often leads us to succumb to a *planning fallacy*—overestimating our future leisure time and income (Zauberman & Lynch, 2005). Students and others often expect to finish assignments ahead of schedule (Buehler et al., 1994, 2002). In fact, such projects generally take about twice the predicted time. Overconfidence can also fuel the *sunk-cost fallacy*, in which we stick to our original plan because we've invested our time, even when switching to a new approach could save us time.

Overconfidence—the bias that Kahneman (2015), if given a magic wand, would most like to eliminate—affects life-or-death decisions. In politics, overconfidence feeds extreme political views. In medicine, overconfidence can lead to incorrect diagnoses (Saposnik et al., 2016). One research team tested 743 U.S. federal intelligence analysts' ability to predict future events—predictions that typically are overconfident. Those whose predictions most often failed tended to be inflexible and closed-minded (Mellers et al., 2015).

Nevertheless, overconfidence can have adaptive value. Believing that their decisions are right and they have time to spare, self-confident people tend to live more happily. They make tough decisions more easily, and they seem competent (Anderson et al., 2012). Given prompt and clear feedback, we can also learn to be more realistic about our judgments' accuracy (Fischhoff, 1982). The wisdom to know when we know a thing and when we do not is born of experience.

### AP® Science Practice

#### Research

This finding—that those analysts whose predictions most often failed tended to be inflexible and closed-minded—comes from a correlational study. The researchers were attempting to see how two variables (accuracy of predictions and personality) were associated.

**Predict your own behavior** When will you finish reading this module?

## Belief Perseverance

Our overconfidence is startling. Equally so is our **belief perseverance**—our tendency to cling to our beliefs in the face of contrary evidence (sometimes aided by *confirmation bias*). A classic study of belief perseverance engaged people with opposing views of capital punishment (Lord et al., 1979). After studying two supposedly new research findings, one supporting and the other refuting the claim that the death penalty deters crime, each side was more impressed by the study supporting its own beliefs. And each readily disputed the other study. Thus, showing the pro- and anti-capital-punishment groups the *same* mixed evidence actually *increased* their disagreement. Rather than using evidence to draw conclusions, they used their conclusions to assess the evidence—a phenomenon also known as *motivated reasoning*.

In other studies and in everyday life, people have similarly welcomed belief-supporting logic and evidence—about climate change, same-sex marriage, or politics—while discounting challenging evidence (Friesen et al., 2015; Gampe et al., 2019; Sunstein et al., 2016). Often, prejudice persists. Beliefs persevere. It's hard to teach old dogma new tricks.

### AP® Exam Tip

We're all human—and vulnerable to confirmation bias, overconfidence, and belief perseverance. Can you explain the differences among these?

**belief perseverance** the persistence of one's initial conceptions even after the basis on which they were formed has been discredited.

Ellis Rosen/Cartoon Stock

*"And in this corner, still undefeated, Frank's long-held beliefs!"*

**framing** the way an issue is posed; how an issue is framed can significantly affect decisions and judgments.

**nudge** framing choices in a way that encourages people to make beneficial decisions.

To rein in belief perseverance, a simple remedy exists: *Consider the opposite.* When the same researchers repeated the capital-punishment study, they asked some participants to be "as *objective* and *unbiased* as possible" (Lord et al., 1984). The plea did nothing to reduce biased evaluations of evidence. They also asked another group to consider "whether you would have made the same high or low evaluations had exactly the same study produced results on the *other* side of the issue." Having imagined and pondered the *opposite* findings, these people became much less biased. Newer studies confirm the point: Considering opposing arguments reduces bias (Catapano et al., 2019; Van Boven et al., 2019).

Once beliefs take root, it takes more compelling evidence to change them than it did to create them. We often label belief-contradicting evidence as "weak" (Anglin, 2019). Climate change skeptics, for example, tend to view evidence of the climate crisis as inaccurate or untrustworthy (Druckman & McGrath, 2019). As an old Chinese proverb says, "Two-thirds of what we see is behind our eyes."

## The Effects of Framing

**Framing**—the way we present an issue—can be a powerful tool of persuasion for good or ill, as psychologists and economists have together learned. Long before the Covid pandemic occurred, Amos Tversky and Daniel Kahneman (1981) asked people to consider a scenario: How should the United States prepare for the outbreak of an unusual disease that could kill 600 people? Participants strongly preferred solutions framed as *gains* ("200 people will be saved") rather than *losses* ("400 people will die").

As a young scholar, working closely with Tversky and Kahneman, behavioral economist Richard Thaler and his colleagues showed how the framing of options can **nudge** people toward beneficial decisions (Benartzi et al., 2017; Daniels & Zlatev, 2019; Thaler & Sunstein, 2008).

- *Healthier eating.* Knowing that many people prefer tasty to healthy foods, researchers have nudged healthy choices with tasty-sounding food labels. The university dining hall turnips get chosen more when they're labeled "Herb n' Honey Balsamic Glazed Turnips" (Turnwald et al., 2019).

- *Saving for retirement.* U.S. companies once required employees who wanted to contribute to a retirement plan to choose a lower take-home pay, which few people did. Today, companies can automatically enroll their employees in the plan but allow them to opt out. Either way, the decision is the employee's. But under the new opt-out arrangement, enrollments in one analysis of 3.4 million workers soared from 59 percent to 86 percent (Rosenberg, 2010).

- *Making moral decisions.* Imagine an experimenter gives you $5.00 and asks how much (if any) you want to donate to charity, then asks, "What do you personally think is the morally right thing to do in this situation?" Nudging people to take a moral mindset made them more generous, increasing donations by 44 percent (Capraro et al., 2019).

- *Becoming an organ donor.* In many countries, people renewing their driver's license can decide whether to be organ donors. Sometimes the default option is *Yes*, but people can opt out. Nearly 100 percent of the people in opt-out countries have agreed to be donors. In countries where the default option is *No*, most do *not* agree to be donors (Hajhosseini et al., 2013; Johnson & Goldstein, 2003).

*The point to remember*: Framing can nudge our attitudes and decisions.

# The Perils and Powers of Intuition

### 2.2-6 How do smart thinkers use intuition?

It's clear that very smart people can make intuitive but not-so-smart judgments. So, are our heads indeed "filled with straw," as T. S. Eliot suggested? Good news: Cognitive scientists are also revealing intuition's powers:

- *Intuition is recognition born of experience.* It is implicit (unconscious) knowledge— what we've recorded in our brains but can't fully explain (Chassy & Gobet, 2011; Gore & Sadler-Smith, 2011). We see it in the smart and quick judgments of experienced nurses, firefighters, art critics, car mechanics, and athletes who react *without thinking*. And we would see this instant intuition in you, too, for anything in which you have developed knowledge based on experience.

- *Intuition is usually adaptive.* Our fast and frugal heuristics let us intuitively rely on learned associations that surface as gut feelings, right or wrong: Seeing a stranger who resembles someone who has harmed or threatened us previously, we may automatically react with distrust. Our intuition aids our survival, and it can also steer us toward satisfying relationship partners: Newlyweds' implicit, gut-level attitudes toward their new spouse predict their future marital happiness (McNulty et al., 2017). Smart thinking often means having smart intuitions (Raoelison et al., 2020).

- *Intuition is huge.* Recall from Module 2.1a that through *selective attention*, we can focus our conscious awareness on a particular aspect of all we experience. Our mind's unconscious track, however, makes good use intuitively of what we are not consciously processing. Unconscious, automatic influences constantly affect our judgments (Custers & Aarts, 2010; Kihlstrom, 2019). Consider this: Most people guess that the more complex the choice, the smarter it is to make decisions rationally rather than intuitively (Inbar et al., 2010). Actually, in making complex decisions, we sometimes benefit by letting our brain work on a problem without consciously thinking about it (Strick et al., 2010, 2011). In one series of experiments, three groups of people read complex information (for example, about apartments or European football matches). Those in the first group stated their preference immediately after reading information about four possible options. The second group, given several minutes to analyze the information, made slightly smarter decisions. But wisest of all, in several studies, were those in the third group, whose attention was distracted for a time, enabling their minds to engage in automatic, unconscious processing of the complex information. The practical lesson: Letting a problem incubate while we attend to other things can pay dividends (Dijksterhuis & Strick, 2016). Facing a difficult decision involving lots of facts, we're wise to gather all the information we can, and then say, "Give me some time to *not* think about this." Even sleeping on it can help. Thanks to our ever-active brain, nonconscious thinking (reasoning, problem solving, decision making, planning) can be surprisingly astute (Creswell et al., 2013; Hassin, 2013; Lin & Murray, 2015).

Critics note that some studies have not found the supposed power of unconscious thought, and they remind us that deliberate, conscious thought also furthers smart thinking (Newell, 2015; Nieuwenstein et al., 2015; Phillips et al., 2016). In challenging situations— making the best chess move, distinguishing between false and real news headlines— deliberate thinking beats instant intuition (Bago et al., 2020; Moxley et al., 2012). Consider:

1. A bat and a ball together cost 110 cents. The bat costs 100 cents more than the ball. How much does the ball cost?

2. Emily's father has three daughters. The first two are named April and May. What is the third daughter's name?

Most people's intuitive responses—10 cents and June—are wrong, and a few moments of deliberate thinking reveals why.[4]

*The bottom line*: Our two-track mind makes sweet harmony as smart, critical thinking listens to the creative whispers of our vast unseen mind and then evaluates evidence, tests conclusions, and plans for the future.

For a summary of some key ideas from this module, see **Table 2.2-1**.

### TABLE 2.2-1 Comparing Cognitive Processes and Strategies

| Process or Strategy | Description | Powers | Perils |
|---|---|---|---|
| Algorithm | Methodical rule or procedure | Guarantees solution | Requires time and effort |
| Heuristic | Simple thinking shortcut, such as the availability heuristic (which estimates likelihood based on how easily events come to mind) | Lets us act quickly and efficiently | Puts us at risk for errors |
| Insight | Sudden Aha! reaction | Provides instant realization of solution | May not happen |
| Confirmation bias | Tendency to search for support for our own views and ignore contradictory evidence | Lets us quickly recognize supporting evidence | Hinders recognition of contradictory evidence |
| Fixation | Inability to view problems from a new angle | Focuses thinking | Hinders creative problem solving |
| Intuition | Fast, automatic feelings and thoughts | Is based on our experience; huge and adaptive | Can lead us to overfeel and underthink |
| Overconfidence | Overestimating the accuracy of our beliefs and judgments | Allows us to live more happily and to make decisions easily | Puts us at risk for errors |
| Belief perseverance | Ignoring evidence that contradicts our beliefs | Supports our enduring beliefs | Closes our mind to new ideas |
| Framing | Wording a question or statement so that it evokes a desired response | Can influence others' decisions | Can produce a misleading result |
| Creativity | Ability to innovate valuable ideas | Produces new insights and products | May distract from structured, routine work |

[4]The first answer is 5 cents. The bat would then cost $1.05, for a $1.10 total. If the ball cost the *intuitive* answer of 10 cents, the bat would then have to cost $1.10 (for a bat-and-ball total of $1.20, not $1.10). The second answer is Emily. If you answered incorrectly, don't fret—so do many others (Frederick, 2005; Thomson & Oppenheimer, 2016).

AP® Science Practice

# Check Your Understanding

## Examine the Concept

▶ Match each process or strategy (i–x) with its description (a–j).

| | | | |
|---|---|---|---|
| i. | Algorithm | a. | Inability to view problems from a new angle; focuses thinking but hinders creative problem solving |
| ii. | Intuition | b. | Methodological rule or procedure that guarantees a solution but requires time and effort |
| iii. | Insight | c. | Your fast, automatic, effortless feelings and thoughts based on your experience; huge and adaptive but can lead you to overfeel and underthink |
| iv. | Heuristic | d. | Simple thinking shortcut that lets you act quickly and efficiently but puts you at risk for errors |
| v. | Fixation | e. | Sudden Aha! reaction that instantly reveals the solution |
| vi. | Confirmation bias | f. | Tendency to search for support for your own views and to ignore contradictory evidence |
| vii. | Overconfidence | g. | Holding on to your beliefs even after they are proven wrong; closing your mind to new ideas |
| viii. | Creativity | h. | Overestimating the accuracy of your beliefs and judgments; allows you to be happier and to make decisions more easily, but puts you at risk for errors |
| ix. | Framing | i. | Wording a question or statement so that it evokes a desired response; can mislead people and influence their decisions |
| x. | Belief perseverance | j. | The ability to produce novel and valuable ideas |

## Apply the Concept

▶ Can you recall a time when contradictory information challenged one of your views? Was it hard for you to consider the opposite view? Explain how this relates to belief perseverance.

*Answers to the Examine the Concept questions can be found in Appendix C at the end of the book.*

# Module 2.2b REVIEW

## 2.2-3 What cognitive strategies assist our problem solving, and what obstacles hinder it?

- An *algorithm* is a methodical, logical rule or procedure (such as a step-by-step description for evacuating a building during a fire) that guarantees a solution to a problem.

- A *heuristic* is a simpler strategy—a mental shortcut (such as running for an exit if you smell smoke)—that is usually speedier than an algorithm but is also more error-prone.

- *Insight* is not a strategy-based solution, but rather a sudden flash of inspiration that solves a problem.

- Obstacles to problem solving include *confirmation bias*, which predisposes us to verify rather than challenge our preconceptions, and *fixation*, which may prevent us from taking the fresh perspective that would lead to a solution.

## 2.2-4 What is *intuition*, and how can the representativeness and availability heuristics influence our decisions and judgments?

- *Intuition* is the effortless, immediate, automatic feeling or thoughts we often use instead of systematic reasoning.

- Heuristics enable snap judgments. *Using the representativeness heuristic*, we judge the likelihood of events based on how well they seem to represent particular prototypes. Using the *availability heuristic*, we judge the likelihood of things based on how readily they come to mind.

## 2.2-5 How are our decisions and judgments affected by overconfidence, belief perseverance, and framing?

- *Overconfidence* can lead us to overestimate the accuracy of our beliefs, which can fuel the planning and sunk-cost fallacies.

- When a belief we have formed and explained has been discredited, *belief perseverance* may cause us to cling to that belief. A remedy for belief perseverance is to consider how we might have explained the opposite result.

- *Framing* is the way an issue is posed. Subtle differences in presentation can dramatically alter our responses and *nudge* us toward beneficial decisions.

## 2.2-6 How do smart thinkers use intuition?

- Smart thinkers welcome their intuitions (which are usually adaptive), but also know when to override them.

- When making complex decisions, we may benefit from gathering as much information as possible and then taking time to let our two-track mind process it.

# AP® Practice Multiple Choice Questions

1. To solve calculus problems, Ridge always uses the same logical and methodical rule that guarantees a solution. Ridge uses a(n)
   a. heuristic.
   b. algorithm.
   c. insight.
   d. mental set.

**Use the following text to answer questions 2 and 3:**

Thom believes that his congresswoman is an honest woman. He looks for examples of her giving to charity and ignores her ethics violations, which have recently been in the news. Even after she is arrested and sent to jail, Thom still believes that the congresswoman is an honest person.

2. When Thom looks for examples of his congresswoman giving to charity, while ignoring her ethics violations, he is being affected by
   a. confirmation bias.
   b. intuition.
   c. the sunk-cost fallacy.
   d. the availability heuristic.

3. When Thom continues to believe that his congresswoman is an honest person even after she is sent to jail, Thom is experiencing
   a. framing.
   b. intuition.
   c. belief perseverance.
   d. confirmation bias.

4. Jarvis has found himself purchasing meat labeled as "80 percent lean" more often than meat labeled as "20 percent fat," even though the meat is the same. Which psychological concept best applies to this scenario?
   a. Intuition
   b. Insight
   c. Framing
   d. Overconfidence

5. After seeing a news story about a kidnapping, Odessa felt more afraid that her children would be kidnapped, even though it is a very rare occurrence. Which of the following psychological concepts best applies to this scenario?
   a. Intuition
   b. Belief perseverance
   c. Mental set
   d. Availability heuristic

6. Bre generates, organizes, plans, and implements goal-directed behavior to complete her homework on time. What are these cognitive skills called?
   a. Heuristics
   b. Intuition
   c. Executive functions
   d. Stereotypes

7. What psychological concept is being represented in this graph?

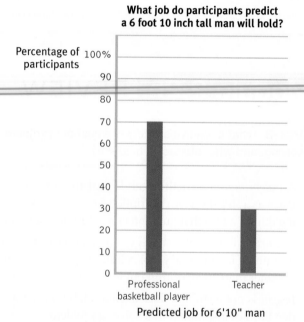

**What job do participants predict a 6 foot 10 inch tall man will hold?**

Percentage of participants

Predicted job for 6'10" man

   a. Gambler's fallacy
   b. Confirmation bias
   c. Representativeness heuristic
   d. Motivated reasoning

8. Janelle had been working on a chemistry problem for some time when all of a sudden the answer came to her in a single moment. What cognitive process did Janelle experience?

   a. Insight
   b. Fixation
   c. Framing
   d. Creativity

9. Many students underestimate the time it will take to complete an assignment because they succumb to the planning fallacy. This fallacy is rooted in which cognitive bias?

   a. Fixation
   b. Overconfidence
   c. Mental set
   d. Belief perseverance

# Module 2.3 Introduction to Memory

Be thankful for your memory. We often take memory for granted, except when it malfunctions. But it is our memory that accounts for time and defines our life. It is our memory that enables us to recognize family members, speak our language, and find our way home. It is our memory that enables us to enjoy an experience and then mentally replay it to enjoy again. It is our memory that enables us to build histories with those we love. And it is our shared memories that bind us together as Irish or Iranian, Somalian or Samoan—and occasionally pit us against others whose offenses we cannot forget.

In large part, we are what we remember. Without memory—our archive of accumulated learning—there would be no savoring of past joys, no guilt or anger over painful recollections. We would instead live in an enduring present, each moment fresh. Each person would be a stranger, every language foreign, every task—dressing, cooking, biking—a new challenge. You would even be a stranger to yourself, lacking that continuous sense of self that extends from your distant past to your momentary present.

Researchers study memory from many perspectives. In this module, we'll begin by looking at the measuring and modeling of memories. In Module 2.4, we'll explore the encoding of memories; in Modules 2.5 and 2.6, we'll examine how memories are stored and retrieved. And in Module 2.7, we'll consider what happens when our memories fail us and look at ways to improve memory.

## Studying Memory

### 2.3-1 What is *memory*, and how is it measured?

**Memory** is learning that persists over time; it is information that has been acquired and stored and can be retrieved. Research on memory's extremes has helped us understand how memory works. At age 92, my [DM's] father suffered a small stroke-like brain event that had but one peculiar effect. His genial personality was intact. He knew us and enjoyed poring over family photo albums and reminiscing about his past. But he had lost most of his ability to form new memories of conversations and everyday episodes. He could not tell me what day of the week it was, or what he had eaten for lunch. Told repeatedly of his brother-in-law's recent death, he was surprised and saddened each time he heard the news.

Some disorders slowly strip away memory. *Alzheimer's disease* begins as difficulty remembering new information, progressing to an inability to do everyday tasks. Complex speech becomes simple sentences; family members and close friends become strangers; the brain's memory centers, once strong, become weak and wither away (Desikan et al., 2009). Over several years, individuals with Alzheimer's disease may become unknowing and unknowable. Their sense of self weakens, leaving them wondering, "Who am I?" (Ben Malek et al., 2019). Lost memory strikes at the core of their humanity, robbing them of their joy, meaning, and companionship.

---

**AP® Exam Tip**

The next five modules deal with memory. Not only is this a significant topic on the AP® exam, but it is also, for students, one of psychology's most practical topics! As you read, think about how you can apply what you're learning about encoding, storing, and retrieving information — and become a better student.

---

**memory** the persistence of learning over time through the encoding, storage, and retrieval of information.

At the other extreme are people who win gold medals in memory competitions. When two-time World Memory Champion Feng Wang was a 21-year-old college student, he didn't need help from his phone to remember his friends' numbers. The average person can parrot back a string of about 7—maybe even 9—digits. If numbers were read about 1 per second, Feng could reliably repeat up to 200 (Ericsson et al., 2017). In 2015, Rajveer Meena of India broke the world record by reciting 70,000 digits of pi (*Guinness World Records*, 2019).

Amazing? Yes, but consider your own impressive memory. You remember countless faces, places, and happenings; tastes, smells, and textures; voices, sounds, and songs. One study asked students to listen to snippets—a mere four-tenths of a second—from popular songs. How often did they recognize the artist and song? More than 25 percent of the time (Krumhansl, 2010). We often recognize songs as quickly as we recognize a familiar voice.

So, too, with faces and places. Imagine viewing more than 2500 slides of faces and places for 10 seconds each. Later, you see 280 of these slides, paired with others you've never seen. Actual participants recognized 90 percent of the slides they had viewed in the first round (Haber, 1970). In a follow-up study, people who viewed 2800 images for only 3 seconds each spotted the repeats with 82 percent accuracy (Konkle et al., 2010). Look for a target face in a sea of faces and you later will recognize other faces from the scene as well (Kaunitz et al., 2016).

The average person permanently stores and recognizes about 5000 faces (Jenkins et al., 2018). But some *super-recognizers* display an extraordinary face-recognition ability. By watching street footage, super-recognizers have helped British, Asian, and German police to solve difficult cases (Keefe, 2016; NPR, 2018). Eighteen months after viewing a video of an armed robbery, one super-recognizer police officer spotted and arrested the robber walking on a busy street (Davis et al., 2013). And it's not just humans who have shown remarkable memory for faces. Sheep remember faces, too (**Figure 2.3-1**). And so has at least one fish species—as demonstrated by their spitting at familiar faces to trigger a food reward (Newport et al., 2016).

How do we humans accomplish such memory feats? How does our brain pluck information from the world around us and tuck it away for later use? How can we remember things we have not thought about for years, yet forget the name of someone we just met? How are memories stored in our brain? Why will you be likely, later in this unit, to misrecall this sentence: "*The angry rioter threw the rock at the window*"?

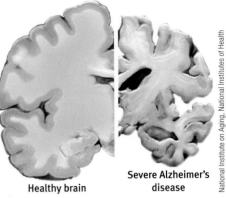

**Severe Alzheimer's disease**

**Healthy brain**

National Institute on Aging, National Institutes of Health

**Extreme forgetting** Alzheimer's disease severely damages the brain, and in the process strips away memory.

A. Jennifer Morton/University of Cambridge

**Figure 2.3-1**

**Other animals also display face smarts**

After food rewards are repeatedly associated with some sheep and human faces, but not with others, sheep remember food-associated faces for 2 years (Kendrick & Feng, 2011; Knolle et al., 2017).

## Measuring Retention

To a psychologist, evidence that learning persists includes these three *retention measures*:

- **Recall**—*retrieving* information that is not currently in your conscious awareness but that was learned at an earlier time. A fill-in-the-blank question tests your recall.

**recall** a measure of memory in which the person must retrieve information learned earlier, as on a fill-in-the-blank test.

**Remembering Faces**
Even if Taylor Swift and Denzel Washington had not become famous, their high school classmates would most likely still recognize them in these photos.

SPOTLIGHT ON:
Hermann Ebbinghaus

- **Recognition**—*identifying* items previously learned. A multiple-choice question tests your recognition.

- **Relearning**—*learning something more quickly* when you learn it a second or later time. When you review the first weeks of course work to prepare for your final exam, or speak a language used in early childhood, it will be easier to relearn the material than it was to learn it initially.

Long after you cannot recall most of the people in your high school graduating class, you may still be able to recognize their yearbook pictures and spot their names in a list of names. In one study, people who had graduated 25 years earlier could not recall many of their old classmates. But they could *recognize* 90 percent of their pictures and names (Bahrick et al., 1975). If you are like most students, you, too, could probably recognize more names of Snow White's seven dwarfs than you could recall (Miserandino, 1991).

Our recognition memory is impressively quick and vast. "Is your friend wearing a new or old outfit?" *Old.* "Have you read this textbook material before?" *No.* "Have you ever seen this person before?" *No.* Before the mouth can form our answer to any of millions of such questions, the mind knows, and knows that it knows.

Our response speed when recalling or recognizing information indicates memory strength, as does our speed at *relearning*. Pioneering memory researcher Hermann Ebbinghaus (1850–1909) showed this in the nineteenth century using nonsense syllables. He randomly selected a sample of syllables, practiced them, and tested himself. To get a feel for his experiments, rapidly read aloud, eight times over, the following list of syllables (from Baddeley, 1982). Then, look away and try to recall the items:

JIH, BAZ, FUB, YOX, SUJ, XIR, DAX, LEQ, VUM, PID, KEL, WAV, TUV, ZOF, GEK, HIW.

**Figure 2.3-2**

**Ebbinghaus' retention curve**

(Data from Baddeley, 1982.)

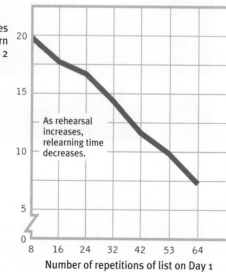

Time in minutes taken to relearn list on Day 2

As rehearsal increases, relearning time decreases.

Number of repetitions of list on Day 1

**recognition** a measure of memory in which the person identifies items previously learned, as on a multiple-choice test.

**relearning** a measure of memory that assesses the amount of time saved when learning material again.

The day after learning such a list, Ebbinghaus could recall few of the syllables. But they weren't entirely forgotten. As **Figure 2.3-2** portrays, the more frequently he repeated the list aloud on Day 1, the less time he required to relearn the list on Day 2. Additional rehearsal (*overlearning*) of verbal information increases retention—especially when practice is distributed over time. For students, this means that it helps to rehearse course material over time, even after you know it. Better to rehearse and overlearn than to relax and remember too little.

*The point to remember:* Tests of recognition and of time spent relearning demonstrate that we remember more than we can recall.

---

**AP® Science Practice**

# Check Your Understanding

## Examine the Concept

▶ Explain each of the three retention measures. Provide examples of each.

## Apply the Concept

▶ Imagine having an injury that significantly impairs your ability to form new memories. Now imagine having a record-setting ability to remember, like Feng Wang. How would each condition affect your daily routine?

▶ If you want to be sure to remember what you're learning for an upcoming test, would it be better to use *recall* or *recognition* to check your memory? Explain your choice.

*Answers to the Examine the Concept questions can be found in Appendix C at the end of the book.*

---

## Memory Models

**2.3-2** How do memory models help us study memory, and how has later research updated the three-stage multi-store model?

Architects create virtual models to help clients imagine their future homes. Similarly, psychologists create memory models. Such models aren't perfect, but they help us think about how our brain forms and retrieves memories. History has offered varied memory models: a wax tablet (Aristotle); a "mystic writing pad" (Freud); a house, a library, a telephone switchboard, a videotape (Roediger, 1980). Today's *information-processing model* likens human memory to computer operations. Thus, to remember, we must

- **encode**—get information into our brain.
- **store**—retain the information.
- **retrieve**—later get the information back out of our brain.

Like all analogies, computer models have their limits. Our memories are less literal and more fragile than a computer's. Most computers also process information *sequentially*, even while alternating between tasks. Our agile brain processes many things *simultaneously* (some of them unconsciously) using **parallel processing** (see Module 1.5a). To focus on this multitrack processing, one information-processing model, known as *connectionism*, views memories as products of interconnected neural networks. Specific memories arise from particular activation patterns within these networks. Every time you learn something new, your brain's neural connections change—an example of *neuroplasticity* (see Module 1.4a)—forming and strengthening pathways that allow you to interact with and learn from your constantly changing environment.

To explain our memory-forming process, Richard Atkinson and Richard Shiffrin (1968, 2016) proposed the three-stage *multi-store model*:

1. We first record to-be-remembered information as a fleeting **sensory memory**.
2. From there, we process information into **short-term memory**, where we encode it through *rehearsal*.
3. Finally, information moves into **long-term memory** for later retrieval.

**encoding** the process of getting information into the memory system—for example, by extracting meaning.

**storage** the process of retaining encoded information over time.

**retrieval** the process of getting information out of memory storage.

**parallel processing** processing multiple aspects of a stimulus or problem simultaneously.

**sensory memory** the immediate, very brief recording of sensory information in the memory system.

**short-term memory** briefly activated memory of a few items (such as digits of a phone number while calling) that is later stored or forgotten.

**long-term memory** the relatively permanent and limitless archive of the memory system. Includes knowledge, skills, and experiences.

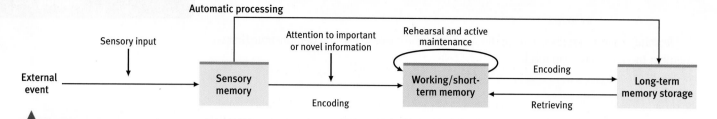

**Figure 2.3-3**

**A modified three-stage model of memory**

Atkinson and Shiffrin's classic three-stage multi-store model is shown updated here with the modern concepts of *automatic processing* and *working memory*.

**working memory** a newer understanding of short-term memory; conscious, active processing of both (1) incoming sensory information and (2) information retrieved from long-term memory.

**central executive** a memory component that coordinates the activities of the *phonological loop* and *visuospatial sketchpad*.

**phonological loop** a memory component that briefly holds auditory information.

**visuospatial sketchpad** a memory component that briefly holds information about objects' appearance and location in space.

This model has since been updated (**Figure 2.3-3**) with important newer concepts, including *working memory* and *automatic processing*.

## Working Memory

Atkinson and Shiffrin saw short-term memory merely as a space for briefly storing recent thoughts and experiences. Alan Baddeley and others (Baddeley, 2002; Barrouillet et al., 2011; Engle, 2002) extended our understanding of this memory storage process. They began calling this stage **working memory**, a stage where short-term and long-term memories combine. Baddeley likened working memory to an active "scratch pad" where our brain actively processes important information by linking our new experiences with our long-term memories. This "system for holding information in mind and working on it" (Oberauer et al., 2018) helps us prolong memory storage through rehearsal over time (*maintenance rehearsal*) and through rehearsing information in ways that promote meaning (*elaborative rehearsal*).

As you integrate new information with your existing long-term memory, your attention is focused (recall from Module 2.1a the mental spotlight we call *selective attention*). In Baddeley's (2002) model, a **central executive** coordinates this focused processing. Without focused attention, information typically fades. The **phonological loop** holds auditory information in short-term memory, such as when you repeat a friend's phone number before entering it into your contact list. To remember information about objects and their relation in space—where you parked your car, or the route from school to home—you would use the **visuospatial sketchpad**.

Right now, your working memory is actively linking what you're reading with what you already know (Cowan, 2010, 2016; deBettencourt et al., 2019). If you hear "eye-screem," you may encode it as *ice cream* or *I scream*, depending on both your experiences and the context (snack shop or horror film).

For most of you, what you are reading enters working memory through vision. You might also use the phonological loop to repeat the information using auditory rehearsal. Some groups, such as the Inuit people in northern Canada, use repeated oral histories to help younger group members remember important information. In one dramatic case, repeated information passed down through many generations was crucial to the archeological discovery of the doomed ships of the 1845 Franklin Expedition, which sank near where local Inuit lived (Neatby & Mercer, 2018). Whether we soak up information with our eyes or our ears, working memory helps us integrate our previous experiences to make smart decisions.

---

**AP® Science Practice**

## Check Your Understanding

### Examine the Concept

▶ Explain how the *working memory* concept updated the classic Atkinson-Shiffrin three-stage multi-store model.

▶ Explain the two basic functions of working memory.

*Answers to the Examine the Concept questions can be found in Appendix C at the end of the book.*

### Apply the Concept

▶ Explain how your memory system has used encoding, storage, and retrieval today.

# Biological Processes of Memory

**2.3-3** How do changes at the synapse level affect our memory processing?

As you now think and learn about memory processes, your flexible brain is changing. Given increased activity in particular pathways, neural interconnections are forming and strengthening. And **neurogenesis** is occurring. As we saw in Module 1.4c, new neurons may form in response to exercise, sleep, and nonstressful but stimulating environments (Liu & Nusslock, 2018; Monteiro et al., 2014; Nollet et al., 2019).

The quest to understand the physical basis of memory—how information becomes embedded in brain matter—has sparked research into the synaptic meeting places where neurons communicate with one another via their neurotransmitter messengers. Eric Kandel and James Schwartz (1982) recruited a seemingly unlikely candidate for this research: the California sea slug, a simple animal with a mere 20,000 or so unusually large and accessible nerve cells. It learns to reflexively withdraw its gills when squirted with water, much as a soldier traumatized by combat might jump at the sound of a firecracker. When learning occurs, the researchers discovered, the slug releases more of the neurotransmitter *serotonin* into certain neurons. These cells' synapses then become more efficient at transmitting signals. Experience and learning can increase—even double—the number of synapses, even in slugs (Kandel, 2012).

In experiments with people, rapidly stimulating certain memory-circuit connections has increased their sensitivity for hours or even weeks to come. The sending neuron now needs less prompting to release its neurotransmitter, and more connections exist between neurons. This increased efficiency of potential neural firing, called **long-term potentiation (LTP)**, provides a neural basis for learning and remembering associations (Lynch, 2002; Whitlock et al., 2006) **(Figure 2.3-4)**. (To *potentiate* something is to increase its power or likelihood, so long-term potentiation refers to a long-lasting increase in a nerve cell's firing power.) Several lines of evidence confirm that LTP is a physical basis for memory. For example, drugs that block LTP interfere with learning (Lynch & Staubli, 1991). Drugs that mimic what happens during learning increase LTP (Harward et al., 2016). And rats given a drug that enhances LTP learn a maze with half the usual number of mistakes (Service, 1994).

**Not-so-sluggish synapses** The California sea slug, which neuroscientist Eric Kandel studied for 45 years, has increased our understanding of the neural basis of learning and memory.

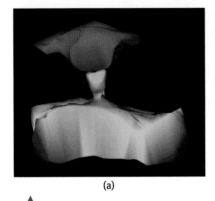
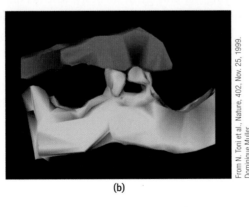

(a)        (b)

From N. Toni et al., Nature, 402, Nov. 25, 1999. Dominique Muller

**Figure 2.3-4**

**Doubled receptor sites**

An electron microscope image (a) shows just one receptor site (gray) reaching toward a sending neuron before long-term potentiation. Image (b) shows that, after LTP, the receptor sites have doubled. This means the receiving neuron has increased sensitivity for detecting the presence of the neurotransmitter molecules that may be released by the sending neuron (Toni et al., 1999).

**neurogenesis** the formation of new neurons.

**long-term potentiation (LTP)** an increase in a nerve cell's firing potential after brief, rapid stimulation; a neural basis for learning and memory.

After LTP has occurred, passing an electric current through the brain won't disrupt old memories—but the current will wipe out very recent memories. Such is the experience both of laboratory animals and of severely depressed people given *electroconvulsive therapy (ECT)*. A blow to the head can do the same. Football players and boxers momentarily knocked unconscious typically have no memory of events just before the knockout (Yarnell & Lynch, 1970). Their working memory had no time to *consolidate* the information—that is, to shift it into long-term memory storage—before the lights went out. (See Module 2.5 for more on memory consolidation.)

Recently, I [DM] did a little test of memory consolidation. While on an operating table for a basketball-related tendon repair, I was given a face mask and soon could smell the anesthesia gas. "So how much longer will I be with you?" I asked the anesthesiologist (knowing that our last seconds before falling asleep go unremembered). My last moment of memory was her answer: "About 10 seconds." My brain spent that 10 seconds consolidating a memory for her 2-second answer, but could not tuck any further memory away before I was out cold.

Some memory-biology explorers have helped found companies that are competing to develop memory-altering drugs. The target market for memory-boosting drugs is massive: people with Alzheimer's disease or the *mild cognitive impairment* that often evolves into Alzheimer's disease, people with more typical age-related memory decline, and anyone who simply wants a better memory.

One approach to improving memory focuses on drugs that boost levels of glutamate, an LTP-enhancing neurotransmitter (Lynch et al., 2011). Another approach involves developing drugs that boost production of CREB, a protein that also enhances the LTP process (Fields, 2005). Boosting CREB production might trigger increased production of other proteins that help reshape synapses and transfer short-term memories into long-term memories.

### AP® Science Practice

#### Research

Placebos are often used in drug studies because these studies run the risk of creating *placebo effects*—experimental results caused by expectations alone.

Some of us may wish for memory-*blocking* drugs that could blunt intrusive memories when they're taken after a traumatic experience (Adler, 2012; Kearns et al., 2012). In experiments, victims of events such as car accidents and sexual assault received, afterward, several doses of one such drug (propranolol) or a placebo. Later testing revealed greater stress reduction in the drug-treated group (Brunet et al., 2018; Pitman et al., 2002).

In studying the biology of memory, researchers have also learned that our memories are not stored intact—like photos in an album—in single spots in our brain. Rather, many brain structures interact to enable the encoding, storage, and retrieval of our memories. The frontal lobes and hippocampus aid in the formation of *explicit memories*—the facts, events, and experiences that we consciously know. The cerebellum and basal ganglia are part of the brain network dedicated to the formation of *implicit memories*—our learned skills and learned associations. (We will explore how our brain handles these different types of memories in Module 2.4.)

---

### AP® Science Practice  Check Your Understanding

**Examine the Concept**

▶ Explain *long-term potentiation*.

**Apply the Concept**

▶ Do you know someone with *cognitive impairment*? How would you explain to them the way memory-enhancing drugs affect the brain?

*Answers to the Examine the Concept questions can be found in Appendix C at the end of the book.*

# Module 2.3 REVIEW

### 2.3-1 What is *memory*, and how is it measured?

- *Memory* is learning that persists over time, through the encoding, storage, and retrieval of information.

- Evidence of memory may be seen in an ability to *recall* information, *recognize* it, or *relearn* it more easily on a later attempt. Psychologists can measure these different forms of memory separately.

### 2.3-2 How do memory models help us study memory, and how has later research updated the three-stage multi-store model?

- Psychologists use memory models to think about and explain how our brain forms and retrieves memories.

- Information-processing models, like the multi-store model, involve three processes: *encoding, storage,* and *retrieval.*

- Our agile brain processes many things simultaneously by means of *parallel processing.*

- The connectionism information-processing model focuses on this multitrack processing, viewing memories as products of interconnected neural networks.

- The three processing stages in the Atkinson-Shiffrin model are *sensory memory, short-term memory,* and *long-term memory.* This model has since been updated to include important newer concepts, such as *working memory* (the active "scratch pad" processing that occurs at the stage when our short-term memories combine with our long-term memories) and *automatic processing* (which occurs behind the scenes to allow information to slip into long-term memory without the need to consciously attend to it).

- The *central executive* coordinates the activity of the *phonological loop* (which briefly holds auditory information) and the *visuospatial sketchpad* (which briefly holds information about objects' appearance and location).

### 2.3-3 How do changes at the synapse level affect our memory processing?

- *Long-term potentiation (LTP)* is the neural basis for learning and memory. In LTP, neurons become more efficient at releasing and sensing the presence of neurotransmitters, and more connections develop between neurons.

## AP® Practice Multiple Choice Questions

1. Caitlin, a fifth grader, is asked to remember her second-grade teacher's name. What measure of retention will Caitlin use to answer this question?

    a. Storage
    b. Recognition
    c. Relearning
    d. Recall

2. In history class, James is effortfully and actively thinking about how various events connect with one another, connecting the new material to what he has learned in the past. This making of connections in the moment best describes James'

    a. sensory memory.
    b. working memory.
    c. relearning information.
    d. long-term memory.

3. Which of the following is a logical and objective conclusion that one can make regarding the three measures of retention?

    a. Many students find short-answer tests easier than multiple-choice tests.
    b. Many students find the process of encoding easier than storage.
    c. Many students find multiple-choice tests easier than short-answer tests.
    d. Many students find the process of retrieval easier than encoding.

4. Dr. Quarqortog is conducting a replication of a study on the role of neurotransmitters in memory. Which of the following neurotransmitters would this researcher most likely use to demonstrate support for past research that showed how particular neurotransmitters improve memory?

    a. GABA
    b. Endorphins
    c. Serotonin
    d. Norepinephrine

**Use the following text to answer questions 5 and 6:**

Dr. Wallobee wants to conduct a study demonstrating that damage to the hippocampus causes people to have difficulty forming explicit memories.

5. Which of the following reasons best explains why it would be unethical to use human research participants for this work?

   a. It would be unethical to ask participants to disclose their traumatic brain injuries for the sake of memory research.
   b. It would be unethical to use human research participants because it is less invasive to conduct brain imaging studies with nonhuman research participants.
   c. It would be unethical to subject some human research participants to hippocampal damage in the study.
   d. It would be unethical to observe human research participants in their natural environments after they have encountered traumatic brain injury.

6. Which of the following would be the most appropriate operational definition for Dr. Wallobee's dependent variable in this study?

   a. Remembering the steps for baking a cake
   b. Remembering how to ride a bicycle
   c. Remembering a recent vacation
   d. Remembering that thunder and lightning go together

# Module 2.4 Encoding Memories

## LEARNING TARGETS

**2.4-1** Explain the differences between explicit and implicit memories.

**2.4-2** Explain what type of information we process automatically.

**2.4-3** Explain how sensory memory works.

**2.4-4** Explain the capacity of short-term memory.

**2.4-5** Explain the effortful processing strategies that help us remember new information.

**2.4-6** Explain how distributed practice, deep processing, and making new material personally meaningful aid memory.

It's one of the great lessons of psychological science: Our one brain houses two minds—two information processing systems. As with vision and thinking, so with our memory. We have a two-track mind, with most of our thinking, feeling, acting, and remembering taking place effortlessly, outside our conscious awareness (*implicitly*). Yet we also effortfully process *explicit* memories, such as the content of this module, and there are effective strategies for improving those efforts.

## Dual-Track Memory: Effortful Versus Automatic Processing

### 2.4-1 How do explicit and implicit memories differ?

**Explicit** (*declarative*) **memories** are the facts and experiences we can consciously know and "declare." We encode many explicit memories through conscious **effortful processing**. But behind the scenes, other information skips the conscious encoding track and barges directly into storage. This **automatic processing**, which happens without our awareness, produces our **implicit** (*nondeclarative*) **memories**.

Our two-track mind, then, helps us encode, retain, and retrieve information through both effortful and automatic tracks. Let's see how automatic processing assists the formation of implicit memories.

## Automatic Processing and Implicit Memories

### 2.4-2 What information do we process automatically?

Our implicit memories include *procedural* memory for automatic skills (such as how to ride a bike) and classically conditioned *associations* among stimuli. (More on *classical conditioning*—a type of learning in which an organism comes to associate stimuli and anticipate events—in Module 3.7.) If attacked by a dog, years later you might, without recalling the conditioned association, automatically tense up as a dog approaches.

**explicit memory** retention of facts and experiences that we can consciously know and "declare." (Also called *declarative memory*.)

**effortful processing** encoding that requires attention and conscious effort.

**automatic processing** unconscious encoding of incidental information, such as space, time, and frequency, and of familiar or well-learned information, such as sounds, smells, and word meanings.

**implicit memory** retention of learned skills or classically conditioned associations independent of conscious recollection. (Also called *nondeclarative memory*.)

Without conscious effort, you also automatically process information about

- *space.* While studying, you often encode the place on a page or in your notebook where certain material appears; later, you may visualize its location when you want to retrieve the information.

- *time.* While going about your day, you unintentionally note the sequence of its events. Later, realizing you've left your backpack somewhere, the event sequence your brain automatically encoded will enable you to retrace your steps.

- *frequency.* You effortlessly keep track of how many times things happen, as when you realize, "This is the third time I've run into her today!"

Our two-track mind engages in impressively efficient information processing. As one track automatically tucks away routine details, the other track is free to focus on conscious, effortful processing. Mental feats such as vision, thinking, and memory may seem to be single abilities, but they are not. Rather, we split information into different components for separate and simultaneous processing.

## Effortful Processing and Explicit Memories

Automatic processing happens effortlessly. When you see familiar words on the side of a delivery truck, you can't help but read them and register their meaning. *Learning* to read wasn't automatic. You may recall working hard to pick out letters and connect them to certain sounds. But with experience and practice, your reading became automatic. Imagine now learning to read sentences in reverse:

.citamotua emoceb nac gnissecorp luftroffE

At first, this requires effort, but after enough practice, you would also perform this task much more automatically. We develop many skills in this way: driving, texting, and speaking a new language.

### Sensory Memory

> **2.4-3** How does sensory memory work?

Sensory memory (recall Figure 2.3-3) feeds our active working memory, recording momentary images, sounds, and strong scents. But sensory memory, like a lightning flash, is fleeting. How fleeting? In one study, people viewed three rows of three letters each, for only one-twentieth of a second (**Figure 2.4-1**). After the nine letters disappeared, they could recall only about half of them.

Was it because they had insufficient time to glimpse them? *No.* People actually *could* see and recall all the letters, but only momentarily. We know this because rather than ask them to recall all nine letters at once, researcher George Sperling sounded a high, medium, or low tone immediately *after* flashing the letters. The pitch of the tone directed participants to report *only* the top, middle, or bottom row letters, respectively. Now they rarely missed a letter, showing that all nine letters were momentarily available for recall.

Sperling's experiment demonstrated **iconic memory**, a fleeting sensory memory of visual stimuli. For a few tenths of a second, our eyes register a picture-image memory of a scene, and we can recall any part of it in amazing detail. But delaying the tone signal by more than half a second caused the image to fade and memory to suffer. We also have an impeccable, though fleeting, memory for auditory stimuli, called **echoic memory** (Cowan, 1988; Lu et al., 1992). Picture yourself in class being distracted by thoughts of the weekend. If your mildly irked teacher tests you by asking, "What did I just say?" you can recover the last few words from your mind's echo chamber. Auditory echoes linger for 3 or 4 seconds.

**iconic memory** a momentary sensory memory of visual stimuli; a photographic or picture-image memory lasting no more than a few tenths of a second.

**echoic memory** a momentary sensory memory of auditory stimuli; if attention is elsewhere, sounds and words can still be recalled within 3 or 4 seconds.

| K | Z | R |
|---|---|---|
| Q | B | T |
| S | G | N |

**Figure 2.4-1**
**Total recall — briefly**

# Short-Term Memory Capacity

**2.4-4** What is our short-term memory capacity?

Recall that short-term memory—and working memory, its processing manager—refers to what we can briefly retain. What are the limits of what we can hold in this middle, short-term stage?

George Miller (1956) proposed that we can store about seven pieces of information (give or take two) in short-term memory. Miller's magical number seven is psychology's contribution to the list of magical sevens—the seven wonders of the world, the seven seas, the seven deadly sins, the seven colors of the rainbow, the seven-note musical scale, the seven days of the week—seven magical sevens. (After Miller's 2012 death, his daughter recalled his best moment of golf: "He made the one and only hole-in-one of his life at the age of 77, on the seventh green . . . with a seven iron. He loved that" [quoted by Vitello, 2012].)

**SPOTLIGHT ON:**
George Miller

Other research confirms that we can, if nothing distracts us, recall about seven bits of information. But the number varies by task; we tend to remember about six letters and only about five words (Baddeley et al., 1975; Cowan, 2015). And how quickly do our short-term memories disappear? To find out, Lloyd Peterson and Margaret Peterson (1959) asked people to remember three-consonant groups, such as *CHJ*. To prevent rehearsal, the researchers distracted participants (asking them, for example, to start at 100 and begin counting aloud backward by threes). After 3 seconds, people recalled the letters only about half the time; after 12 seconds, they seldom recalled them at all (**Figure 2.4-2**). Without the active processing that we now understand to be a part of our working memory, short-term memories have limited lives.

Working-memory capacity varies, depending on age and other factors. Young adults tend to have greater working-memory capacity—the ability to juggle multiple items while processing information—than do children and older adults (Bopp & Verhaeghen, 2020; Jaroslawska & Rhodes, 2019). This helps young adults to better retain information and to solve problems creatively (De Dreu et al., 2012; Fenn & Hambrick, 2012; Wiley & Jarosz, 2012). But because task switching reduces working memory, everyone does better and more efficient work when focused, without distractions, on one task at a time (Steyvers et al., 2019). *The bottom line*: It's probably a bad idea to simultaneously watch a live stream, text your friends, and write a psychology paper, with your attention switching among them (Willingham, 2010)!

**AP® Science Practice**

### Research

In this study depicted in Figure 2.4-2, the researchers operationally defined memory performance as the percentage of participants who recalled the consonants. You can tell this by how they labeled their graph.

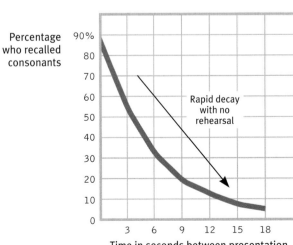

**Figure 2.4-2**
**Short-term memory decay**

(Data from Peterson & Peterson, 1959; see also Brown, 1958.)

# Check Your Understanding

**Examine the Concept**

▶ Explain the difference between *automatic* and *effortful* processing, and offer some examples of each.

▶ At which of Atkinson-Shiffrin's three memory stages would *iconic* and *echoic* memory occur?

*Answers to the Examine the Concept questions can be found in Appendix C at the end of the book.*

**Apply the Concept**

▶ Does it surprise you to learn how much of your memory processing is automatic? What might life be like if *all* memory processing were effortful?

## Effortful Processing Strategies

> **2.4-5** What are some effortful processing strategies that can help us remember new information?

Several effortful processing strategies can boost our ability to form new memories. Later, when we try to retrieve a memory, these strategies can make the difference between success and failure.

### Chunking

Glance for a few seconds at the first set of letters (row 1) in **Figure 2.4-3**, then look away and try to reproduce what you saw. Impossible, yes? But you can easily reproduce set 2, which is no less complex. Similarly, you will probably remember sets 4 and 6 more easily than the same elements in sets 3 and 5. As this demonstrates, **chunking** information into familiar segments enables us to recall it more easily (Thalmann et al., 2019). Try remembering 43 individual numbers and letters. It would be impossible, unless they were chunked into, say, seven meaningful chunks, such as "Try remembering 43 individual numbers and letters." ☺

**chunking** organizing items into familiar, manageable units; often occurs automatically.

**Figure 2.4-3**

**Chunking effects**

Organizing information into meaningful units, such as letters, words, and phrases, helps us recall it more easily (Hintzman, 1978).

1.  Ⅿ Ꮹ Ꭺ Ꙅ Ꭱ Ꮃ Ꚍ

2.  W G V S R M T

3.  VRESLI UEGBN GSORNW CDOUL LWLE NTOD WTO

4.  SILVER BEGUN WRONGS CLOUD WELL DONT TWO

5.  SILVER BEGUN WRONGS CLOUD DONT TWO
    HALF MAKE WELL HAS A
    EVERY IS RIGHT A DONE LINING

6.  WELL BEGUN IS HALF DONE
    EVERY CLOUD HAS A SILVER LINING
    TWO WRONGS DONT MAKE A RIGHT

Chunking usually occurs so naturally that we take it for granted. Native English speakers can reproduce perfectly the 150 or so line segments that make up the words in the three phrases of set 6 in Figure 2.4-3. Similarly amazing is a Mandarin Chinese reader's ability to glance at **Figure 2.4-4** and then reproduce all the strokes, or a varsity basketball player's recall of all the players' positions after a 4-second peek at a basketball play (Allard & Burnett, 1985). We all remember information best when we can organize it into personally meaningful arrangements.

## Mnemonics

To help encode lengthy passages and speeches, ancient Greek scholars and orators developed **mnemonics**. Many of these memory aids use vivid imagery, because we are particularly good at remembering mental pictures. We more easily remember concrete, visualizable words than we do abstract words (Akpinar & Berger, 2015). (When we quiz you later, which three of these words—*bicycle, void, cigarette, inherent, fire, process*—will you most likely recall?) If you still recall the rock-throwing rioter sentence from Module 2.3, it is probably not only because of the meaning you encoded but also because the sentence painted a mental image.

The *peg-word system* harnesses our superior visual-imagery skill. This mnemonic requires you to memorize a jingle: "*One is a bun; two is a shoe; three is a tree; four is a door; five is a hive; six is sticks; seven is heaven; eight is a gate; nine is swine; ten is a hen.*" Without much effort, you will soon be able to count by peg-words instead of numbers: *bun, shoe, tree* . . . and then to visually associate the peg-words with to-be-remembered items. Now you are ready to challenge anyone to give you a grocery list to remember. Carrots? Stick them into the imaginary bun. Milk? Fill the shoe with it. Paper towels? Drape them over the tree branch. Think *bun, shoe, tree* and you see their associated images: carrots, milk, paper towels. Alternatively, you could visualize and recall items at specific spots along a familiar route. Either way, you later would be able to recall the items with great accuracy (Bugelski et al., 1968; Twomey & Kroneisen, 2021).

Memory whizzes understand the power of such systems. Star performers in the World Memory Championships do not usually have exceptional intelligence, but rather are superior at using mnemonic strategies (Maguire et al., 2003b). Frustrated by his ordinary memory, science writer Joshua Foer wanted to see how much he could improve it. After a year of intense practice, he won the U.S. Memory Championship, memorizing a pack of 52 playing cards in under two minutes. How did Foer do it? He used the *method of loci*, in which he added vivid new details to memories of a familiar place—his childhood home. Each card, presented in any order, could then match up with the clear picture in his head. Foer's wild memory experiment showed him the power of painting pretty pictures in his mind (Foer, 2011).

春夏秋冬

▲ **Figure 2.4-4**

**An example of chunking — for those who read Mandarin Chinese**

After looking at these characters, can you reproduce them exactly? If so, you likely are fluent in Chinese.

IT'S EASY TO GET CONFUSED, SO I USE A SIMPLE MNEMONIC: THE FRIDGE ON THE **L**EFT IS FOR **L**UNCH, AND THE FRIDGE ON THE **R**IGHT IS FOR **R**EALLY, **R**EALLY POISONOUS SUBSTANCES.

Tom Gauld/Heart Agency

**mnemonics** [nih-MON-iks] memory aids, especially those techniques that use vivid imagery and organizational devices.

When combined, chunking and mnemonic techniques can be great memory aids for unfamiliar material. Want to remember the planets in order of distance from the Sun? Think of the mnemonic My Very Educated Mother Just Served Us Noodles (*M*ercury, *V*enus, *E*arth, *M*ars, *J*upiter, *S*aturn, *U*ranus, *N*eptune). Need to recall the names of North America's five Great Lakes? Just remember HOMES (*H*uron, *O*ntario, *M*ichigan, *E*rie, and *S*uperior). In many cases, we chunk information into a more familiar form by creating a word (called an *acronym*) from the first letters of the to-be-remembered items.

## Hierarchies

When people develop expertise in an area, they often process information in *hierarchies* composed of a few broad categories divided and subdivided into narrower concepts and facts. (Figure 2.5-3 in Module 2.5 provides a hierarchy of our automatic and effortful memory processing systems.) Organizing knowledge in hierarchies helps us retrieve information efficiently, as Gordon Bower and his colleagues (1969) demonstrated by presenting words either randomly or grouped into categories. When the words were grouped, recall was two to three times better. Such results show the benefits of organizing what you study. In this text, for example, pay special attention to the module headings, Learning Targets, and Check Your Understanding features. Taking class and text notes in outline format—a type of hierarchical organization—may also prove helpful (**Figure 2.4-5**).

**Figure 2.4-5**

**Hierarchies aid retrieval**

When we organize words or concepts into hierarchical groups, as illustrated here with some of the concepts from this section, we remember them better than when we see them presented randomly.

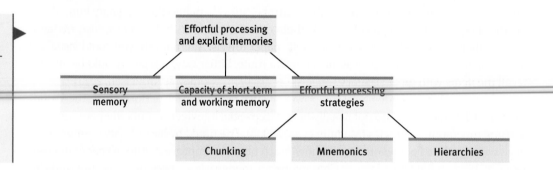

## Distributed Practice

**2.4-6** How do distributed practice, deep processing, and making new material personally meaningful aid memory?

We retain information better when our encoding is distributed over time. Experiments have consistently revealed the benefits of this **spacing effect** (Cepeda et al., 2006; Soderstrom et al., 2016). *Massed practice* (cramming) can produce speedy short-term learning and an inflated feeling of confidence. But to paraphrase memory researcher Hermann Ebbinghaus (1885), those who learn quickly also forget quickly. *Distributed practice* produces better long-term recall. After you've studied long enough to master the material, further study at that time becomes inefficient. Better to spend that extra review time later—a day later if you need to remember something 10 days hence, or a month later if you need to remember something 6 months hence (Cepeda et al., 2008). Reviewing your psychology notes for 10 minutes every night will lead to better retention, and without panic-cramming the day before the test. The spacing effect is one of psychology's most reliable findings, and it extends to motor skills and online game performance, too (Stafford & Dewar, 2014). Memory researcher Henry Roediger (2013) sums it up: "Hundreds of studies have shown that distributed practice leads to more durable learning." The Roman philosopher Seneca had the idea two millennia ago: "The mind is slow in unlearning what it has been long in learning."

**spacing effect** the tendency for distributed study or practice to yield better long-term retention than is achieved through massed study or practice.

220    **Unit 2**  Cognition

One effective way to distribute practice is *repeated* self-testing, a phenomenon that Roediger and Jeffrey Karpicke (2006, 2018) have called the **testing effect**. Testing does more than simply assess learning and memory: It improves them (Su et al., 2020). In this book, the testing questions interspersed throughout and at the end of each module and unit offer opportunities to improve learning and memory. Better to practice retrieval (as any exam will demand) than to merely reread material (which may lull you into a false sense of mastery). Roediger (2013) explains, "Two techniques that students frequently report using for studying—highlighting (or underlining) text and rereading text—[have been found] ineffective." Happily, "retrieval practice (or testing) is a powerful and general strategy for learning." As another memory expert explained, "What we recall becomes more recallable" (Bjork, 2011). No wonder daily quizzing improves introductory psychology students' course performance (Batsell et al., 2017; Pennebaker et al., 2013). So, too, can self-testing with flash cards, responses to teacher questions, and teaching the material to someone else (Fazio & Marsh, 2019).

*The point to remember*: Spaced study and self-assessment beat cramming and rereading. Practice may not make perfect, but smart practice—occasional rehearsal with self-testing—makes for lasting memories.

---

 **Exploring Research Methods & Design**

Suppose you are a researcher interested in examining the effect of distributed practice on academic performance. In preparation for a final exam, you randomly assign 50 students from your high school to engage in self-testing spaced out over several days, while another group of 50 students crams the night before the final exam. You then compare their final exam scores and find that those in the distributed practice group scored significantly higher.

- Identify the research method used in this study.

- What conclusions can or can't you draw based on the method used?

- Who was the sample in this study? Who is the population?

- Identify the independent and dependent variables.

- What ethical problems, if any, are there in this study?

*Remember, you can always revisit Unit 0 to review information related to psychological research.*

---

**AP® Exam Tip**

It's not the studying you do in May that will determine your success on the AP® exam; it's the studying you do now. It's a good idea to take a little time each week to quickly review material from earlier in the course. When was the last time you looked at information from the previous module?

---

**Making things memorable** For suggestions on how to apply the *testing effect* to your own learning, watch my [DM's] 5-minute animation: tinyurl.com/HowToRemember.

**testing effect** enhanced memory after retrieving, rather than simply rereading, information. Also referred to as a *retrieval practice effect* or *test-enhanced learning.*

| Sample Questions to Elicit Different Levels of Processing | Word Flashed | Yes | No |
|---|---|---|---|
| *Shallowest:* Is the word in capital letters? | CHAIR | _____ | _____ |
| *Shallow:* Does the word rhyme with train? | brain | _____ | _____ |
| *Deep:* Would the word fit in this sentence? The girl put the _____ on the table. | puzzle | _____ | _____ |

**TABLE 2.4-1**

## Levels of Processing

Memory researchers have discovered that we process verbal information at different levels, and that depth of processing affects our long-term retention. **Shallow processing** encodes on an elementary level, such as a word's letters (*structural encoding*) or, at a more intermediate level, a word's sound (*phonemic encoding*). Thus, we may type *there* when we mean *their*, *write* when we mean *right*, and *two* when we mean *too*. **Deep processing** encodes *semantically*, based on the meaning of the words. The deeper (more meaningful) the processing is, the better our retention will be.

In one classic study, researchers Fergus Craik and Endel Tulving (1975) flashed words at viewers. Then they asked them questions that would elicit different levels of processing. To experience the task yourself, rapidly answer the questions in **Table 2.4-1**.

Which type of processing would best prepare you to recognize the words at a later time? In this experiment, the deeper, semantic processing triggered by the third question yielded a much better memory than did the shallower processing elicited by the second question or the very shallow processing elicited by the first question (which was especially ineffective).

## Making Material Personally Meaningful

If new information is neither meaningful nor related to our experience, we have trouble processing it. Imagine being asked to remember the following recorded passage:

> The procedure is actually quite simple. First you arrange things into different groups. Of course, one pile may be sufficient depending on how much there is to do. . . . After the procedure is completed, one arranges the materials into different groups again. Then they can be put into their appropriate places. Eventually they will be used once more and the whole cycle will then have to be repeated. However, that is part of life.

When some students heard the paragraph you have just read, without a meaningful context, they remembered little of it (Bransford & Johnson, 1972). When others were told the paragraph described washing clothes (something meaningful), they remembered much more of it—as you probably could now after rereading it.

In the discussion of mnemonics, we gave you six words and told we would quiz you about them later. How many of these words can you now recall? Of these, how many are high-imagery words? How many are low-imagery?[5]

Can you repeat the sentence about the angry rioter that we gave you in Module 2.3?

Perhaps, like the participants in an experiment by William Brewer (1977), you recalled the sentence by the meaning you encoded when you read it (for example, "The angry rioter

**shallow processing**
encoding on a basic level, based on the structure or appearance of words.

**deep processing** encoding semantically, based on the meaning of the words; tends to yield the best retention.

[5] The words were *bicycle, void, cigarette, inherent, fire,* and *process.*

threw the rock *through* the window") and not as it was written ("The angry rioter threw the rock *at* the window"). Asked later what we heard or read, we recall not the literal text but what we encoded. Thus, when studying for a test, you may remember your class notes rather than the class itself.

We can avoid significant mismatches by rephrasing what we see and hear into meaningful terms. From his experiments on himself, Ebbinghaus estimated that, compared with learning nonsense syllables, learning meaningful material required one-tenth the effort. As memory researcher Wayne Wickelgren (1977, p. 346) noted, "The time you spend thinking about material you are reading and relating it to previously stored material is about the most useful thing you can do in learning any new subject matter."

Psychologist-actor team Helga Noice and Tony Noice (2006) have described how actors inject meaning into the daunting task of learning "all those lines." They do it by first coming to understand the flow of meaning: "One actor divided a half-page of dialogue into three [intentions]: 'to flatter,' 'to draw him out,' and 'to allay his fears.'" With this meaningful sequence in mind, the actor more easily remembered the lines.

Most people excel at remembering personally relevant information. Asked how well certain adjectives describe a stranger, we often forget them; asked how well the adjectives describe us, we often remember them. For passwords, people (you, too?) often use self-relevant information (Taylor & Garry, 2019). The tendency to remember self-relevant information, called the *self-reference effect*, is especially strong in individualist Western cultures (Jiang et al., 2019; Symons & Johnson, 1997). In contrast, people from collectivist Eastern cultures tend to remember self-relevant and family-relevant information equally well (Sparks et al., 2016).

*The point to remember:* You can profit from taking time to find personal meaning in what you are studying.

**AP® Exam Tip**

Are you often pressed for time? The most effective way to cut down on the amount of time you need to spend studying is to increase the personal meaningfulness of the material you're trying to remember. If you can relate the material to your own life — and that's pretty easy when you're studying psychology — it takes less time to master it.

**TRY THIS**

Here is another sentence we will ask you about later (in Module 2.7): "The fish attacked the swimmer."

---

**AP® Science Practice**

# Check Your Understanding

**Examine the Concept**

▶ Explain the difference between shallow and deep processing.

▶ Explain the self-reference effect.

**Apply the Concept**

▶ If you try to make the material you are learning personally meaningful, are you processing at a shallow level or a deep level? Describe which level leads to greater retention.

▶ How have you used hierarchies to organize material that you are trying to remember? How would you do so for a section of this module?

▶ Can you think of three ways to employ the principles in this module to improve your own learning and retention of important ideas?

*Answers to the Examine the Concept questions can be found in Appendix C at the end of the book.*

---

# Module 2.4 REVIEW

**2.4-1 How do explicit and implicit memories differ?**

- The human brain processes information on dual tracks, consciously and unconsciously.

- Many *explicit* (declarative) *memories* — our conscious memories of facts and experiences — form through *effortful processing*, which requires conscious effort and attention.

- *Implicit* (nondeclarative) *memories* — of learned skills and classically conditioned associations — happen without our awareness, through *automatic processing*.

### 2.4-2 What information do we process automatically?

- In addition to skills and classically conditioned associations, we automatically process incidental information about space, time, and frequency, and familiar or well-learned information, such as sounds, smells, and word meanings.

### 2.4-3 How does sensory memory work?

- Sensory memory feeds some information into working memory for active processing there.
- An *iconic memory* is a very brief (a few tenths of a second) sensory memory of visual stimuli; an *echoic memory* is a 3- or 4-second sensory memory of auditory stimuli.

### 2.4-4 What is our short-term memory capacity?

- Short-term memory capacity is about seven bits of information, plus or minus two, but this information disappears from memory quickly without rehearsal.
- Our working memory capacity varies, depending on age and other factors, but everyone does better and more efficient work by avoiding task switching.

### 2.4-5 What are some effortful processing strategies that can help us remember new information?

- Effective effortful processing strategies include *chunking*, *mnemonics*, categories, and hierarchies. Each boosts our ability to form new memories.

### 2.4-6 How do distributed practice, deep processing, and making new material personally meaningful aid memory?

- Distributed practice sessions (the *spacing effect*) produce better long-term recall.
- The *testing effect* is the finding that consciously retrieving, rather than simply rereading, information enhances memory.
- Depth of processing also affects long-term retention. In *shallow processing*, we encode words based on their letters or sound. Retention is best when we use *deep processing*, encoding words based on their meaning.
- We also more easily remember material when we learn and rephrase it into personally meaningful terms—the self-reference effect.

## AP® Practice Multiple Choice Questions

1. Meloni's boss gave her the phone number, including the area code, of a client she needed to call. As Meloni goes to enter the number into the contacts list on her phone, she finds that she cannot remember all the numbers in the right order. Which of the following is the best explanation for this failure?

   a. Being 10 digits long, the number is beyond Miller's working memory capacity.
   b. Meloni lacks echoic memory.
   c. Because the number was so short, Meloni did not pay enough attention to it.
   d. Meloni's iconic memory disrupted her encoding of the number.

2. Which of the following is most likely to be encoded automatically?

   a. The side-angle-side geometry theorem
   b. The names of the last 10 presidents of the United States
   c. What you ate for breakfast this morning
   d. The license plate of your new car

3. Which of the following is most likely to lead to semantic encoding of a list of words?

   a. Thinking about how the words relate to your own life
   b. Practicing the words for a single extended period
   c. Breaking up the practice into several relatively short sessions
   d. Focusing on the number of vowels and consonants in the words

Use the following graph to answer questions 4 & 5:

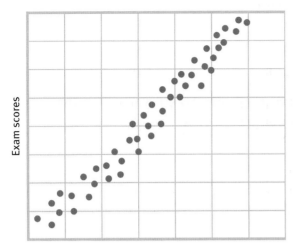

Number of practice quizzes completed

*(y-axis: Exam scores)*

4. Based on the information provided in the graph, what were the researchers most interested in testing?

   a. The impact of chunking on learning
   b. The impact of the testing effect on learning
   c. The impact of the method of loci on learning
   d. The impact of hierarchies on learning

5. Which of the following statements is most accurate?

   a. The researchers used experimental procedures in this study.
   b. The researchers effectively applied random selection in this study.
   c. The researchers minimized sampling bias in this study.
   d. The researchers used quantitative methods in this study.

6. Dr. Tamir conducted a study on echoic memory with a sample of college students, finding that the mean length of echoic memory was 3.47 seconds. Which of the following statements accurately interprets this value?

   a. The most frequent length of time for which the college students remembered visual information was 3.47 seconds.
   b. The most frequent length of time for which the college students remembered auditory information was 3.47 seconds.
   c. The average length of time for which the college students remembered visual information was 3.47 seconds.
   d. The average length of time for which the college students remembered auditory information was 3.47 seconds.

# Module 2.5 Storing Memories

## LEARNING TARGETS

**2.5-1** Explain long-term memory with regard to capacity and location.

**2.5-2** Explain the roles of the frontal lobes and hippocampus in memory processing.

**2.5-3** Explain the roles of the cerebellum and basal ganglia in memory processing.

**2.5-4** Explain how emotions affect our memory processing.

## Retaining Information in the Brain

**2.5-1** What is the capacity of long-term memory? Are our long-term memories processed and stored in specific locations?

As we noted in Modules 2.3 and 2.4, our fleeting *sensory memory* of images, sounds, and scents feeds our *working memory*—our mental "scratch pad" where information is processed, then linked to previously stored information. In this module, we turn to our long-term memory. In Arthur Conan Doyle's *A Study in Scarlet*, Sherlock Holmes offers a popular theory of long-term memory capacity:

> [A] brain originally is like a little empty attic, and you have to stock it with such furniture as you choose. . . . It is a mistake to think that that little room has elastic walls and can distend to any extent. Depend upon it, there comes a time when for every addition of knowledge you forget something that you knew before.

Contrary to Holmes' "memory model," our brain is *not* like an attic, which once filled can store more items only if we discard old ones. Whereas our short-term memory capacity is about seven bits of information, and our working memory capacity varies depending on age and other factors, our capacity for storing long-term memories is essentially limitless. After studying the brain's neural connections, researchers estimated its storage capacity as "in the same ballpark as the World Wide Web" (Sejnowski, 2016).

I [DM] marveled at my aging mother-in-law, a retired pianist and organist. At age 88, her blind eyes could no longer read music. But let her sit at a keyboard and she would flawlessly play any of hundreds of hymns, including ones she had not thought of for 20 years. Where did her brain store those thousands of sequenced notes?

For a time, some surgeons and memory researchers marveled at patients' apparently vivid memories triggered by brain stimulation during surgery. Did this prove that our whole past, not just well-practiced music, is "in there," in complete detail, just waiting to be relived? On closer analysis, the seeming flashbacks appeared to have been invented, not a vivid reliving of long-forgotten experiences (Loftus & Loftus, 1980). In a further demonstration that memories do not reside in single, specific spots, psychologist Karl Lashley (1950) trained rats to find their way out of a maze, then surgically removed pieces of their brain's cortex and retested their memory. No matter which small brain section he removed, the rats retained at least a partial memory of how to navigate the maze. Memories *are* brain-based, but the brain distributes the components of a memory across a network of locations.

These specific locations include some of the neural circuitry involved in the original experience: Some brain cells that fire when we experience something, fire again when we recall it (Miller, 2012; Miller et al., 2013).

*The point to remember*: Despite the brain's vast storage capacity, we do not store information in the way that libraries store their books, in single, precise locations. Instead, brain networks encode, store, and retrieve the information that forms our complex memories.

## Explicit Memory System: The Frontal Lobes and Hippocampus

**2.5-2** What roles do the frontal lobes and hippocampus play in memory processing?

Explicit, conscious memories are either **semantic** (facts and general knowledge) or **episodic** (experienced events). Semantic networks connect concepts, helping us group objects (humans, whales) based on characteristics they share (breathing air, females nurse young) and do not share (walk on two legs, live in the ocean). Our *schemas*—the frameworks we've learned to use in understanding our world—also affect our memory processing. We more readily store new explicit memories if they fit within our existing schemas than if they don't match those understandings.

The brain regions that process and store new explicit memories for facts and episodes include your frontal lobes and hippocampus. When you summon up a mental encore of a past experience, many brain regions send input to your *prefrontal cortex* (the front part of your frontal lobes) for working memory processing (de Chastelaine et al., 2016; Michalka et al., 2015). The left and right frontal lobes process different types of memories. Recalling a password and holding it in working memory, for example, would activate the left frontal lobe. Calling up a visual party scene would more likely activate the right frontal lobe.

Cognitive neuroscientists have found that the **hippocampus**, a temporal lobe neural structure located in the limbic system, can be likened to a "save" button for explicit memories (**Figure 2.5-1**). As children mature, their hippocampus grows, enabling them to construct detailed memories (Keresztes et al., 2017). Brain scans reveal activity in the hippocampus and nearby brain networks as people form explicit memories of names, images, and events (Norman et al., 2019; Terada et al., 2017).

Damage to this structure therefore disrupts the formation and recall of explicit memories. If their hippocampus is severed, chickadees and other birds will continue to cache food in hundreds of places, but later cannot find those places (Kamil & Cheng, 2001; Sherry & Vaccarino, 1989). With left-hippocampus damage, people have trouble remembering verbal information, but they have no trouble recalling visual designs and locations. With right-hippocampus damage, the problem is reversed (Schacter, 1996).

So, the hippocampus is complex, with subregions that serve different functions. One part is active as people and mice learn social information (Okuyama et al., 2016; Zeineh et al., 2003). The rear area processes spatial memory, and it grows bigger as London cabbies learn to navigate the city's complicated maze of streets (Woollett & Maguire, 2011).

Memories are not permanently stored in the hippocampus. Instead, the hippocampus acts as a loading dock where the brain registers and temporarily holds the elements of a to-be-remembered episode—its smell, feel, sound, and location. Then, like older files shifted to be archived, memories migrate to the cortex for storage. This storage process is called **memory consolidation**.

Sleep supports memory consolidation. In one experiment, students who learned material in a study/sleep/restudy condition remembered material better, both a week and 6 months later, than did students who studied in both the morning and the evening without intervening sleep (Mazza et al., 2016). During deep sleep, the hippocampus processes memories for later retrieval. After a training experience, the greater one's hippocampus activity during sleep, the better the next day's memory will be (Peigneux et al., 2004; Whitehurst et al., 2016).

**semantic memory** explicit memory of facts and general knowledge; one of our two conscious memory systems (the other is *episodic memory*).

**episodic memory** explicit memory of personally experienced events; one of our two conscious memory systems (the other is *semantic memory*).

**hippocampus** a neural center located in the limbic system; helps process explicit (conscious) memories—of facts and events—for storage.

**memory consolidation** the neural storage of a long-term memory.

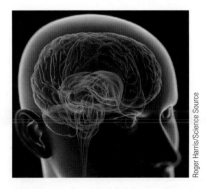

Roger Harris/Science Source

### Figure 2.5-1
### The hippocampus

Explicit memories for facts and episodes are processed in the hippocampus (purple structures) and fed to other brain regions for storage.

**AP® Science Practice**

### Research

Can you identify the independent variable and the dependent variable in the Mazza et al. study? The researchers manipulated whether the participants slept between study sessions (the IV) to see if that had an effect on memory (the DV). It did.

**Hippocampus hero** One contender for champion memorist is a mere birdbrain—the Clark's Nutcracker—which can locate up to 6000 caches of pine seed it had previously buried (Gould et al., 2013; Shettleworth, 1993).

Researchers have watched the hippocampus and brain cortex display simultaneous activity rhythms during sleep, as if they were having a dialogue (Euston et al., 2007; Khodagholy et al., 2017). The brain seems to replay the day's experiences as it transfers them to the cortex for long-term storage (Squire & Zola-Morgan, 1991). When our learning is distributed over days rather than crammed into a single day, we experience more sleep-induced memory consolidation—and that helps explain the spacing effect. The practical take-home lesson: One safe, proven memory enhancer that's available for high schoolers everywhere is effective study followed by adequate *sleep!*

## Implicit Memory System: The Cerebellum and Basal Ganglia

**2.5-3** What roles do the cerebellum and basal ganglia play in memory processing?

Your hippocampus and frontal lobes are processing sites for your *explicit* memories. But you could lose those newer areas of the brain and still, thanks to automatic processing, lay down *implicit* memories for skills and newly conditioned associations. Joseph LeDoux (1996) recounted the story of a patient with brain damage whose amnesia left her unable to recognize her physician as, each day, he shook her hand and introduced himself. One day, she yanked her hand back, for the physician had pricked her with a tack in his palm. The next time he returned to introduce himself she refused to shake his hand but couldn't explain why. Having been classically conditioned—that is, having learned unconsciously to associate the handshake with the pain—she just wouldn't do it. (For more on classical conditioning, see Module 3.7.) Implicitly, she felt what she could not explain.

The *cerebellum* plays a key role in forming and storing the implicit memories created by classical conditioning. With a damaged cerebellum, people cannot develop certain conditioned reflexes, such as associating a tone with an impending puff of air—and thus do not blink in anticipation of the puff (Daum & Schugens, 1996; Green & Woodruff-Pak, 2000). Implicit memory formation needs the cerebellum.

The *basal ganglia*, deep brain structures involved in motor movement, facilitate formation of our procedural memories for skills (Mishkin, 1982; Mishkin et al., 1997). The basal ganglia receive input from the cortex, but do not return the favor by sending information back to the cortex for conscious awareness of procedural learning. If you have learned how to ride a bike, thank your basal ganglia and its communication with your cerebellum.

Our implicit memory system, enabled by these brain areas, helps explain why the reactions and skills we learned during infancy reach far into our future. Yet as adults, our *conscious* memory of our first 4 years is largely blank, due to *infantile amnesia*. As an adult, my [ND's] son, Ellis, will not consciously remember his happy visit to Disney World at age 2. Two influences contribute to infantile amnesia: First, we index much of our explicit memory with a command of language that young children do not possess. Second, the hippocampus is one of the last brain structures to mature, and as it does, more information gets retained (Akers et al., 2014).

## The Amygdala, Emotions, and Memory

**2.5-4** How do emotions affect our memory processing?

Our emotions trigger stress hormones that influence memory formation. When we are excited or stressed, these hormones make more glucose energy available to fuel brain activity, signaling the brain that something important is happening. Moreover, stress hormones focus memory. Stress provokes the *amygdala* (two limbic system emotion-processing clusters) to initiate a *memory trace*—a lasting physical change as the memory forms—that boosts activity in the brain's memory-forming areas (Buchanan, 2007; Kensinger, 2007) **(Figure 2.5-2)**. It's as if the amygdala says, "Brain, encode this moment for future reference!" The result? Emotional arousal can sear certain events into the brain (Brewin et al., 2007; McGaugh, 2015).

Significantly stressful events can form unforgettable memories. After a traumatic experience—a school shooting, a house fire, a sexual assault—vivid recollections of the horrific event may intrude again and again. "Stronger emotional experiences make for stronger, more reliable memories," noted James McGaugh (1994, 2003). Such experiences even strengthen recall for relevant, immediately preceding events (Dunsmoor et al., 2015; Jobson & Cheraghi, 2016). This makes adaptive sense: By waving warning flags, memory protects us from future dangers (Leding, 2019).

Frontal lobes
Hippocampus
Basal ganglia
Amygdala
Cerebellum


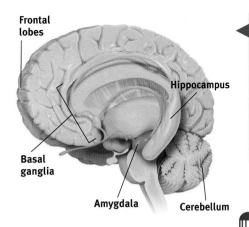

**Figure 2.5-2**
**Review key memory structures in the brain**
*Frontal lobes* and *hippocampus:* explicit memory formation
*Cerebellum* and *basal ganglia:* implicit memory formation
*Amygdala:* emotion-related memory formation

But emotional events produce tunnel-vision memory: They focus our attention and recall on high-priority information, and reduce our recall of irrelevant details (Mather & Sutherland, 2012). Whatever captures our attention is well recalled, at the expense of the surrounding context.

**Flashbulb memories** form when we create mental snapshots of exciting or shocking events, such as our first kiss or our whereabouts when learning of a loved one's death (Brown & Kulik, 1977; Muzzulini et al., 2020). In a 2006 Pew survey, 95 percent of American adults said they could recall exactly where they were or what they were doing when they first heard the news of the 9/11 terrorist attacks.

Our flashbulb memories are noteworthy for their vividness and our confidence in them. But as we relive, rehearse, and discuss them, even our flashbulb memories may become inconsistent, especially among older people (Kopp et al., 2020). With time, some errors crept into people's 9/11 recollections (compared with their reports taken right afterward). Mostly, however, people's memories of 9/11 remained consistent over the next 10 years (Hirst et al., 2015).

Dramatic experiences remain clear in our memory in part because we rehearse them (Hirst & Phelps, 2016). We think about them and describe them to others. Memories of personally important experiences also endure (Storm & Jobe, 2012; Talarico & Moore, 2012).

Figure 2.5-3 summarizes—drawing on our discussions from this module and Module 2.4—the brain's two-track memory processing and storage system for implicit (automatic) and explicit (effortful) memories. *The bottom line*: Learn something and you can change your brain a little.

**AP® Science Practice**

**Research**

A survey, such as the Pew survey, obtains the self-reported attitudes or behaviors of a particular population, usually by questioning a representative, random sample of the group. Survey researchers must ensure that their questions are clearly worded and unbiased. Even small changes in the order or wording of questions can make a big difference in the responses.

**AP® Exam Tip**

Figure 2.5-3 is an excellent summary. Why don't you review it for a few minutes and then see how much of it you can reproduce on a piece of paper? You might even choose to include personal examples of each type of memory to help make the connections. That will give you a good assessment of which parts of the memory process you know and which parts you still need to work on.

**flashbulb memory** a clear memory of an emotionally significant moment or event.

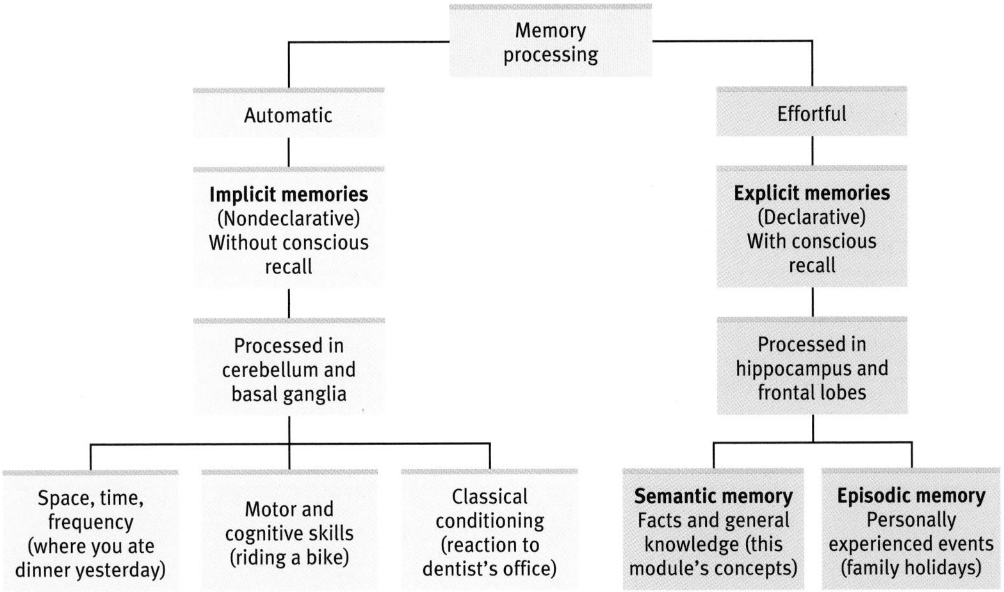

Memory processing
Automatic
Effortful
Implicit memories (Nondeclarative) Without conscious recall
Explicit memories (Declarative) With conscious recall
Processed in cerebellum and basal ganglia
Processed in hippocampus and frontal lobes
Space, time, frequency (where you ate dinner yesterday)
Motor and cognitive skills (riding a bike)
Classical conditioning (reaction to dentist's office)
Semantic memory Facts and general knowledge (this module's concepts)
Episodic memory Personally experienced events (family holidays)


**Figure 2.5-3**
**Our two memory systems**

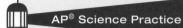

## Check Your Understanding

### Examine the Concept

▶ Which parts of the brain are most important for *implicit* memory processing, and which parts play a key role in *explicit* memory processing?

▶ Which brain area responds to stress hormones by helping to create stronger memories?

### Apply the Concept

▶ Leslie, who has experienced brain damage in an accident, can remember how to tie her shoes but has a hard time remembering anything you say during a conversation. How can implicit versus explicit information processing explain what's going on here?

▶ Can you name an instance in which stress has helped you remember something, and another instance in which stress has interfered with remembering something?

*Answers to the Examine the Concept questions can be found in Appendix C at the end of the book.*

# Module 2.5 REVIEW

**2.5-1 What is the capacity of long-term memory? Are our long-term memories processed and stored in specific locations?**

- Our long-term memory capacity is essentially unlimited.
- Memories are not stored intact in the brain in single spots. Instead, many parts of the brain interact as we encode, store, and retrieve memories.

**2.5-2 What roles do the frontal lobes and hippocampus play in memory processing?**

- The frontal lobes and the *hippocampus* are parts of the brain network dedicated to explicit memory formation.
  - Many brain regions send information to the frontal lobes for processing.
  - The hippocampus, with the help of nearby brain networks, registers and temporarily holds elements of explicit memories (which are either *semantic* or *episodic*) before moving them to other brain regions for long-term storage. The neural storage of long-term memories, which is supported by sleep, is called *memory consolidation*.

**2.5-3 What roles do the cerebellum and basal ganglia play in memory processing?**

- The cerebellum and the basal ganglia are parts of the brain network dedicated to implicit memory formation.
  - The cerebellum is important for forming and storing classically conditioned memories.
  - The basal ganglia are involved in motor movement and help form procedural memories for skills.
- Many reactions and skills learned during our first 4 years continue into our adult lives, but we cannot consciously remember learning these associations and skills (infantile amnesia).

**2.5-4 How do emotions affect our memory processing?**

- Emotional arousal causes an outpouring of stress hormones, which leads the amygdala to boost activity in the brain's memory-forming areas.
- Significantly stressful events can trigger very clear *flashbulb memories*. Through rehearsal, memory of personally important experiences largely endures.

## AP® Practice Multiple Choice Questions

1. Dr. Gusdaw conducted a memory experiment that examined the brain regions associated with forming implicit memories. Which of the following would be the best choice for his independent variable?

   a. Activation in the frontal lobes
   b. Activation in the hippocampus
   c. Activation in the cerebellum
   d. Activation in the occipital lobes

2. Which of the following is an example of a flashbulb memory?

   a. Barry remembers an especially bright sunrise, because he was by the ocean and the sunlight reflected off the water.
   b. Roberto remembers that correlation does not prove a cause-effect relationship because his teacher emphasized this fact over and over again.

c. Anna remembers when her father returned from an overseas military deployment, because the day was very emotional for her.

d. Kristof more clearly remembers second grade than third grade because his second-grade teacher has the same name as his neighbor.

3. While reading about the results of a study on memory, imagine that you read this statement: "After observing hundreds of participants across their lives, researchers found that this type of memory is nearly limitless and lasts, at times, for a lifetime." Which variable is most likely being discussed in this description?

a. Sensory memory
b. Long-term memory
c. Short-term memory
d. Working memory

4. Dr. Pygmal investigates how people group similar concepts together based on their interrelations. What does Dr. Pygmal study?

a. Infantile amnesia
b. Semantic networks
c. Semantic memory
d. Episodic memory

5. Researchers conducted a study in which they first taught 30 new vocabulary words to a group of participants. That evening, the researchers tracked the number of hours the participants slept and the number of new vocabulary words the participants remembered the next day, finding that there was a statistically significant and positive relationship between hours slept and words remembered. Which of the following provides the most accurate interpretation of these results?

a. There is a low likelihood that sleep's effect on memory consolidation was due to chance or error.
b. There is a high likelihood that sleep's effect on semantic network formation was due to chance or error.
c. There is a low likelihood that sleep's effect on episodic memory was due to chance or error.
d. There is a high likelihood that sleep's effect on implicit memory was due to chance or error.

# Module 2.6 Retrieving Memories

After the magic of our brain's encoding and storage, we still have the daunting task of retrieving the information. Accessing stored memories involves either *recall*—our ability to *produce* previously learned information—or *recognition*—our ability to *identify* previously learned items. (See Module 2.3 for more on recall and recognition.)

For stored information to be retrieved and processed, it must migrate from long-term memory storage into working memory—like taking out a box stored in a closet. Once it's in our working memory, the box can be opened, and its contents can enter our consciousness. So, what triggers retrieval, and what strategies can we use to improve our retrieval?

## Retrieval Cues

**2.6-1 How do external cues, internal emotions, and order of appearance influence memory retrieval?**

Imagine a spider suspended in the middle of her web, held up by the many strands extending outward from her in all directions to different points. If you were to trace a pathway to the spider, you would first need to locate an anchor point and then follow the strand into the web.

The process of retrieving a memory follows a similar principle. Within our semantic networks, memories are held in storage by a web of associations, each piece of information interconnected with others. When you encode into memory a target piece of information, such as the name of the person sitting next to you in class, you associate with it other bits of information about your surroundings, mood, seating position, and so on. These bits can serve as *retrieval cues*—like passwords that open memories. The more retrieval cues you have, the better your chances of finding a route to the suspended memory. The best retrieval cues come from associations we form when we encode a memory—smells, tastes, and sights that can evoke our memory of the associated person or event (Tamminen & Mebude, 2019). "Memory is not like a container that gradually fills up; it is more like a tree growing hooks onto which memories are hung" (Russell, 1979).

We need to retrieve memories for both our past (called *retrospective memory*) and our intended future actions (called *prospective memory*). To remember to do something (say, to text someone before you go out), one effective strategy is to mentally associate the act with a cue (perhaps putting your phone by the door) (Rogers & Milkman, 2016). It pays to plan ahead, which helps explain why most people spend more time thinking about their future than about their past (Anderson & McDaniel, 2019).

**Does the unprepared astronaut illustrate a failure of retrospective or prospective memory?**[6]

*"Oh, is that today?"*

[6]It was this astronaut's prospective memory that failed.

## Priming

Often our associations are activated without our awareness. Philosopher-psychologist William James referred to this process, which we call **priming**, as the "wakening of associations." After seeing or hearing the word *rabbit*, we are later more likely to spell the spoken word *hair/hare* as h-a-r-e, even if we don't recall seeing or hearing *rabbit* (Bower, 1986) **(Figure 2.6-1)**.

Priming is often "memoryless memory"—an implicit, invisible memory, without your conscious awareness. If you see a poster of a missing child, you may then unconsciously be primed to interpret an ambiguous adult-child interaction as a possible kidnapping (James, 1986). Although you no longer have the poster in mind, it predisposes your decision-making. Priming can also influence behaviors (Weingarten et al., 2016). Adults and children primed with money-related words and materials change their behavior in various ways, such as by becoming less helpful (Gasiorowska et al., 2016; Lodder et al., 2019). Money may prime our materialism and self-interest.

## Context-Dependent Memory

Have you noticed that putting yourself back in the context where you experienced something earlier can prime your memory retrieval? Remembering, in many ways, depends on our environment (Palmer, 1989). When you visit your childhood home or neighborhood, old memories surface. When scuba divers listened to a word list in one of two different settings (either 10 feet underwater or sitting on the beach), they recalled more words when later tested in the same place where they first heard the list (Godden & Baddeley, 1975).

By contrast, experiencing something outside the usual setting can be confusing. Have you ever run into a former teacher in an unusual place, such as at a store or in a park? Perhaps you felt a glimmer of recognition, but struggled to realize who it was and how you were acquainted. The **encoding specificity principle** helps us understand how *specific* cues will most effectively trigger that memory. In new settings, you may be missing the memory cues needed for speedy face recognition. Our memories are *context-dependent*, and are affected by the cues we have associated with that context.

In several studies, Carolyn Rovee-Collier (1993) found that a familiar context activated memories even in 3-month-olds. After infants learned that kicking would make a crib mobile move (via a connecting ribbon from their ankle), the infants kicked more when tested again in the same crib than when in a different context.

## State-Dependent Memory

Closely related to context-dependent memory is *state-dependent memory*. What we learn in one state may be more easily recalled when we are again in that state. What adults learn when drunk they don't recall well in *any* state (alcohol disrupts memory storage). But they recall it slightly better when again drunk. Adults who hide money when drunk may forget the location until drunk again.

Moods also provide an example of memory's state dependence. Emotions that accompany good or bad events become retrieval cues (Gaddy & Ingram, 2014). Thus, our memories are somewhat **mood congruent**. If you've had a bad day—you argued with a friend, lost your phone, and got a poor grade on your midterm—your gloomy mood may facilitate recalling other bad times. Depression sours memories by priming negative associations, which we then use to

Seeing or hearing the word *rabbit*

Activates concept

Primes spelling the spoken word *hair/hare* as *h-a-r-e*

**Figure 2.6-1**
**Priming associations unconsciously activates related associations**

**TRY THIS**

Ask a friend three rapid-fire questions:

1. What color is the snow?
2. What color are clouds?
3. What do cows drink?

If your friend answers "milk" to the third question, you have demonstrated priming.

**priming** the activation, often unconsciously, of particular associations in memory.

**encoding specificity principle** the idea that cues and contexts specific to a particular memory will be most effective in helping us recall it.

**mood-congruent memory** the tendency to recall experiences that are consistent with one's current good or bad mood.

*"I can't remember what we're arguing about, either. Let's keep yelling, and maybe it will come back to us."*

explain our current mood (Mihailova & Jobson, 2020). In many studies, people put in a happy mood—whether under hypnosis or just by the day's events (a World Cup soccer victory for German participants in one study)—recall the world through rose-colored glasses (DeSteno et al., 2000; Forgas et al., 1984; Schwarz et al., 1987). They recall their behaviors as competent and effective, other people as benevolent, and happy events as more frequent.

Have you ever noticed that your current mood influences your perceptions of others? In one study, adolescents' ratings of parental warmth in one week gave little clue to how they would rate their parents 6 weeks later (Bornstein et al., 1991). When teens were down, their parents seemed cruel; as their mood brightened, their parents morphed from devils into angels. And at age 26, people's recall of their parents' caregiving during their childhood was linked less with the actual caregiving (which had been assessed years earlier) than with their *current* moods and parental relationship (Nivison et al., 2021). Moods modify memories.

We may nod our heads knowingly. Yet, while in a good or bad mood, we persist in attributing to reality our own changing judgments, memories, and interpretations. While in a bad mood, we may read someone's look as a glare and feel even worse. While in a good mood, we may encode the same look as interest and feel even better. Moods magnify.

Mood effects on retrieval help explain why our moods persist. When happy, we recall pleasant events and see the world as a wonderful place, which helps prolong our good mood. When depressed, we recall sad events, which darkens our interpretations of current events. For those of us predisposed to depression, this process can help maintain a vicious, dark cycle.

## Serial Position Effect

**serial position effect** our tendency to recall best the last items in a list initially (a *recency effect*), and the first items in a list after a delay (a *primacy effect*).

Another memory-retrieval quirk, the **serial position effect**, explains why we may have large holes in our memory of a list of recent events. Imagine it's your first day in a new job, and your manager is introducing you to your co-workers. As you meet each person, you silently repeat everyone's name, starting from the beginning. As the last person smiles and turns away, you feel confident you'll be able to greet your new co-workers by name the next day.

Don't count on it. Because you have spent more time rehearsing the earlier names than the later ones, those are the names you'll probably recall more easily the next day. In studies, when people viewed a list of items (words, names, dates) and then immediately tried to recall them in any order, they fell prey to the serial position effect (Daniel & Katz, 2018; Dimsdale-Zucker et al., 2019). They briefly recalled the last items especially quickly and well (a *recency effect*), perhaps because those items were still in working memory. But after a delay, when their attention was elsewhere, their recall was best for the first items (a *primacy effect;* see **Figure 2.6-2**).

### Figure 2.6-2
**The serial position effect**

Immediately after Mahershala Ali made his way down the red carpet at the 2019 Academy Awards, he would probably have best recalled the names of the last few people he greeted (*recency effect*). But later, he may have been able to recall the first few people best (*primacy effect*).

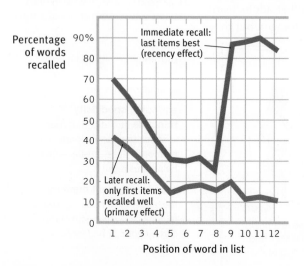

Kevork Djansezian/Getty Images

# Retrieval Practice Strategies

**2.6-2** How do retrieval practice strategies, such as the testing effect, interleaving, and metacognition, support memory retrieval?

So, how can we improve our memory retrieval? Psychology's research has uncovered several effective strategies, including:

*Metacognition.* As we saw in Module 2.2, it pays to think about our thinking! Students who use metacognition—who monitor and evaluate their learning—perform better academically (de Boer et al., 2018). To improve your grades, it helps to figure out what you *don't* know. Self-testing can help.

*Testing effect.* Many students assume that the way to cement new learning is to reread the material. What helps more—and what this book therefore encourages—is *repeated self-testing and rehearsal* of previously studied material. As we noted in Module 2.4, memory researchers call this the *testing effect* (Roediger & Karpicke, 2006). In one study, English-speaking students who had been tested repeatedly recalled the meaning of 20 previously learned Lithuanian words better than did students who had spent the same time restudying the 20 words (Ariel & Karpicke, 2018). Repetitive testing's rewards also make it reinforcing: Students who used repetitive testing once found that it helped, and were more likely to use it later when learning new material. More than 200 studies confirm that *frequent quizzing and self-testing boost students' retention* (Yang et al., 2021).

*Interleaving.* Mixing your study of psychology with your study of other subjects boosts long-term retention and protects against overconfidence (Kornell & Bjork, 2008; Taylor & Rohrer, 2010). **Interleaving** boosts learning by allowing us extra retrieval practice—as we switch between topics of study.

**interleaving** a retrieval practice strategy that involves mixing the study of different topics.

---

**AP® Science Practice**

## Check Your Understanding

### Examine the Concept

▶ Explain *priming*.

▶ When we are tested immediately after viewing a list of words, we tend to recall the first and last items best, which is known as the _____ _____ effect.

▶ Explain the benefits of interleaving.

*Answers to the Examine the Concept questions can be found in Appendix C at the end of the book.*

### Apply the Concept

▶ What sort of mood have you been in lately? Explain how your mood has colored your memories, perceptions, and expectations.

▶ Explain why practicing retrieval improves memory.

---

# Module 2.6 REVIEW

**2.6-1** How do external cues, internal emotions, and order of appearance influence memory retrieval?

- External cues activate associations that help us retrieve memories; this process may occur without our awareness, as it does in *priming*.

- The *encoding specificity principle* is the idea that cues and contexts specific to a particular memory will be most effective in helping us recall it.

- Returning to the same physical context or emotional state *(mood congruency)* in which we formed a memory can help us retrieve it.

- The *serial position effect* is our tendency to recall best the last items (which may still be in working memory) and the first items (which we've spent more time rehearsing) in a list.

> **2.6-2** How do retrieval practice strategies, such as the testing effect, interleaving, and metacognition, support memory retrieval?

- Through metacognition—tracking our understanding—we can figure out what we don't know and use that information to improve our learning and, later, our memory retrieval.

- The testing effect shows that repeated self-testing and retrieval practice work to improve our retention.

- We will learn and remember better if we *interleave* our study of psychology with our studies of other topics.

## AP® Practice Multiple Choice Questions

**1.** John has noticed that he does better on his chemistry exams when he takes them in the same seat in which he sits during class than when he sits in a different seat for exams. Assuming that John is properly prepared for exams, what psychological concept best explains the difference in his scores?

a. Recall
b. Context-dependent memory
c. Explicit memory
d. The serial position effect

**2.** Which of the following is an example of the serial position effect?

a. Remembering the most important assignment you have to complete for school tomorrow
b. Remembering the skills you learned early in life, such as walking
c. Remembering the beginning and end of your grocery list but not the items in the middle
d. Remembering the names of co-workers whom you met over lunch at your new job

**Use the following graph to answer questions 3 and 4.**

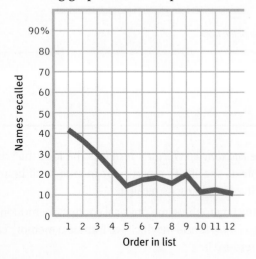

**3.** What psychological concept is depicted in the graph?

a. Recency effect
b. Mood-congruent memory
c. Encoding specificity principle
d. Primacy effect

**4.** Which of the following statements accurately describes the data depicted in the graph?

a. The data in the graph represent qualitative data.
b. The data in the graph represent standard deviations.
c. The data in the graph represent quantitative data.
d. The data in the graph represent ranges.

**5.** Antonia is testing herself in preparation for her upcoming psychology test. She is aware of the value of the testing effect. Which other retrieval practice strategy is she employing by way of her self-testing?

a. Metacognition
b. Interleaving
c. Mood-congruent
d. Priming

**6.** Gabe has tests next week in his biology and psychology classes, and he knows that mixing his study of the two topics—shifting from biology to psychology and back—is an effective way to improve retention. What's the name of the technique described here?

a. Metacognition
b. Interleaving
c. Mood-congruent
d. Priming

7. Dani is at a meeting where everyone goes around the table and introduces themselves. By the end, Dani can only remember the names of the last two people who introduced themselves. This is an example of which concept?

   a. Framing
   b. Mental set
   c. Recency effect
   d. Primacy effect

8. Which of the following involves accessing memory through recognition?

   a. An oral presentation
   b. An essay question
   c. A fill-in-the-blank question
   d. A multiple choice question

# Module 2.7 Forgetting and Other Memory Challenges

**LEARNING TARGETS**

**2.7-1**  Explain why we forget.

**2.7-2**  Explain how misinformation, imagination, and source amnesia influence our memory construction, and describe how we decide whether a memory is real or false.

**2.7-3**  Explain the reliability of young children's eyewitness descriptions.

**2.7-4**  Explain how you can use memory research findings to do better in this and other classes.

## Forgetting

### 2.7-1 Why do we forget?

Amid all the applause for memory—all the efforts to understand it, all the books on how to improve it—have any voices been heard in praise of forgetting? William James (1890, p. 680) was such a voice: "If we remembered everything, we should on most occasions be as ill off as if we remembered nothing." Forgetting unimportant information helps us remember what matters most (Murphy & Castel, 2021). Indeed, the ability to forget out-of-date information—last year's locker combination, our old phone number, restaurant orders already delivered—is a blessing (Nørby, 2015). And letting go of bad memories is good for our mental well-being (Stramaccia et al., 2020). Yet some people seem unable to forget. In the 1920s, Russian journalist and memory whiz Solomon Shereshevsky had merely to listen while other reporters scribbled notes. Performing in front of a crowd, he could memorize streams of nonsensical or random information, such as long sections from Dante's *Inferno* in Italian—despite the fact that he did not speak Italian (Johnson, 2017). But his junk heap of memories dominated his conscious mind (Luria, 1968). He had difficulty thinking abstractly—generalizing, organizing, evaluating. After reading a story, he could recite it but would struggle to summarize its gist.

Jill Price's incredibly accurate memory of her life's events since age 14 has been closely studied by a University of California at Irvine research team. She reports that her super-memory, called *highly superior autobiographical memory*, interferes with her life, with one memory cuing another (McGaugh & LePort, 2014; Parker et al., 2006): "It's like a running movie that never stops. . . . It is nonstop, uncontrollable, and totally exhausting." Although their memories are not perfect, people like Price are prone to having their minds fill up with information that most people ignore—shoes worn on a first date, the day of the week that you first ate at a favorite childhood restaurant—and that, once in memory storage, never leaves (Frithsen et al., 2019; Patihis, 2016). In such rare individuals—60 of whom have been identified worldwide—researchers have found enlarged brain areas and increased brain activity in memory centers (Dutton, 2018; Santangelo et al., 2020). A good memory is helpful, but so is the ability to forget. If a memory-enhancing pill ever becomes available, it had better not be *too* effective.

More often, however, our unpredictable memory dismays and frustrates us. Memories are quirky. My [DM's] memory can easily call up such episodes as that wonderful first kiss with the woman I love, or trivial facts like the driving time from Los Angeles to Detroit. Then it abandons me when I fail to encode, store, or retrieve a student's name, or where I left my keys.

As we process information, we filter, alter, or lose most of it (Figure 2.7-1).

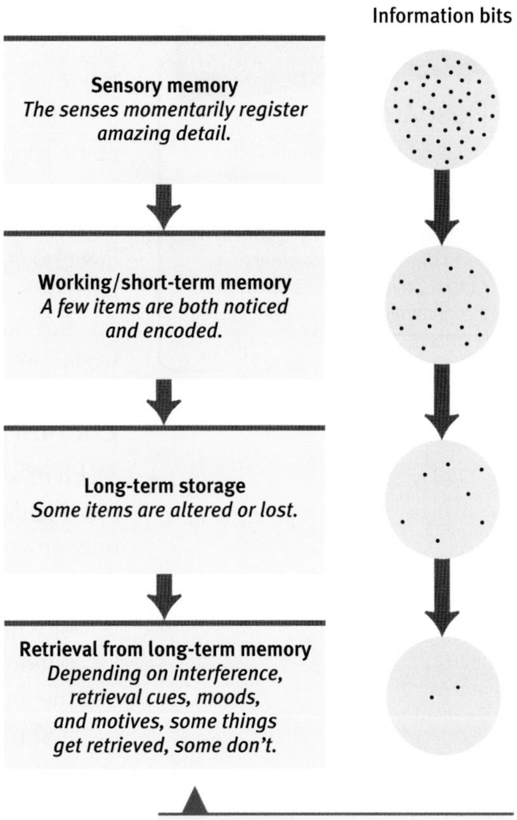

## Forgetting and the Two-Track Mind

For some, memory loss is severe and permanent. Consider Henry Molaison (or H. M., as he was known until his 2008 death). Surgeons removed much of his hippocampus in order to stop his persistent seizures. This resulted "in severe disconnection of the remaining hippocampus" from the rest of the brain (Annese et al., 2014). For his remaining 55 years, he was unable to form new conscious memories. Molaison suffered from **anterograde amnesia**—he could remember his past, but he could not form new memories. (People who *cannot* remember their past—the old information stored in long-term memory—suffer from **retrograde amnesia**.) Just as before his surgery, Molaison was intelligent and did daily crossword puzzles. Yet, reported neuroscientist Suzanne Corkin (2005, 2013), "I've known H. M. since 1962, and he still doesn't know who I am." For about half a minute he could keep something in mind, enough to carry on a conversation. When distracted, he would forget what was just said or what had just occurred. Without the neural tissue for turning new information into long-term memories, he never could name the current U.S. president (Ogden, 2012).

Other patients with amnesia have undergone a post-surgery personality change, yet still have a stable sense of self—perceiving themselves as their former selves (Garland et al., 2021). Patient "R," for example, became extraverted. Yet when responding to a personality test, he perceived himself as still the introvert he formerly was.

Neurologist Oliver Sacks (1985, pp. 26–27) described another patient, Jimmie, who had anterograde amnesia resulting from brain damage. Jimmie had no memories—and, therefore, no sense of elapsed time—beyond his injury in 1945.

When Jimmie gave his age as 19, Sacks set a mirror before him: "Look in the mirror and tell me what you see. Is that a 19-year-old looking out from the mirror?"

Jimmie turned ashen, gripped the chair, cursed, then became frantic: "What's going on? What's happened to me? Is this a nightmare? Am I crazy? Is this a joke?" When his attention was diverted to some children playing baseball, his panic ended, the dreadful mirror forgotten.

Sacks showed Jimmie a photo from *National Geographic*. "What is this?" he asked.

"It's the Moon," Jimmie replied.

"No, it's not," Sacks answered. "It's a picture of the Earth taken from the Moon."

"Doc, you're kidding! Someone would've had to get a camera up there!"

"Naturally."

"Hell! You're joking—how the hell would you do that?" Jimmie's wonder was that of a bright young man from the 1940s, amazed by his travel back to the future.

Careful testing of these unique people reveals something even stranger: Although incapable of recalling new facts or anything they have done recently, Molaison, Jimmie, and others with similar conditions can learn nonverbal tasks. Shown hard-to-find figures in pictures (in the *Where's Waldo?* series, for example), they can quickly spot them again later. They can find their way to the bathroom, though without being able to tell you where it is. They can learn to read mirror-image writing or do a jigsaw puzzle, and they have even learned complicated *procedural* job skills (Schacter, 1992, 1996; Xu & Corkin, 2001). They can be classically conditioned. However, *they do all these things with no awareness of having*

**Information bits**

**Sensory memory**
*The senses momentarily register amazing detail.*

**Working/short-term memory**
*A few items are both noticed and encoded.*

**Long-term storage**
*Some items are altered or lost.*

**Retrieval from long-term memory**
*Depending on interference, retrieval cues, moods, and motives, some things get retrieved, some don't.*

**Figure 2.7-1**
**When do we forget?**
Forgetting can occur at any memory stage.

**anterograde amnesia** an inability to form new memories.

**retrograde amnesia** an inability to remember information from one's past.

*learned them.* "Well, this is strange," Molaison said, after demonstrating his nondeclarative memory of skillful mirror tracing. "I thought that would be difficult. But it seems as though I've done it quite well" (Shapin, 2013).

Molaison and Jimmie lost their ability to form new explicit memories, but their automatic processing ability remained intact. Like individuals with Alzheimer's disease, whose *explicit* memories for new people and events are lost, they could form new *implicit* memories (Lustig & Buckner, 2004). These individuals can learn *how* to do something, but they will have no conscious recall of learning their new skill. Such sad case studies confirm that we have two distinct memory systems, controlled by different parts of the brain.

For most of us, forgetting is a less drastic process. Let's consider some of the reasons we forget.

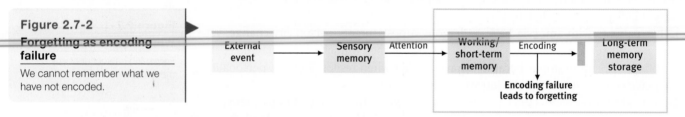
## Encoding Failure

Much of what we sense we never notice, and what we fail to encode, we will never remember (**Figure 2.7-2**). English novelist and critic C. S. Lewis (1967, p. 107) described the enormity of what we never encode:

> [We are] bombarded every second by sensations, emotions, thoughts . . . nine-tenths of which [we] must simply ignore. The past [is] a roaring cataract of billions upon billions of such moments: Any one of them too complex to grasp in its entirety, and the aggregate beyond all imagination. . . . At every tick of the clock, in every inhabited part of the world, an unimaginable richness and variety of "history" falls off the world into total oblivion.

**Figure 2.7-2**

**Forgetting as encoding failure**

We cannot remember what we have not encoded.

External event → Sensory memory → Attention → Working/short-term memory → Encoding → Long-term memory storage

**Encoding failure leads to forgetting**

As we learned in Module 2.3, our short-term memory has limited capacity—just a few items at a time. Information that is not encoded for long-term storage will be lost as new information enters short-term memory—a process called *displacement*. When dialing a list of phone numbers, each new number you dial will displace the previous number in your short-term memory.

Age can affect encoding efficiency. The brain areas that jump into action when young adults encode new information are less responsive in older adults. This slower encoding helps explain age-related memory decline (Grady et al., 1995). (For more on aging's effect on memory, see Module 3.2b.)

But no matter how young we are, we selectively attend to few of the myriad sights and sounds continually bombarding us. Consider: You have surely seen the Apple computer logo thousands of times. Can you draw it? In one study, only 1 of 85 UCLA students (including 52 Apple users) could do so accurately (Blake et al., 2015). Without encoding effort, many potential memories never form.

Lightspring/Shutterstock

**MEMORIES START TO FADE**

## Storage Decay

"You are already beginning to forget the material you just read." So said famed memory researcher Gordon Bower (1973). Indeed, even after encoding something well, we sometimes later forget it. To study the durability of stored memories, Hermann Ebbinghaus (1885)

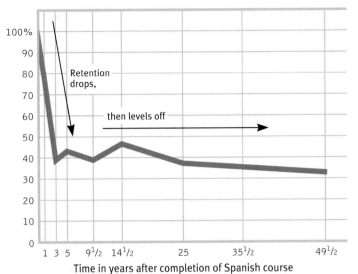

**Figure 2.7-3**

**The forgetting curve for Spanish learned in school**

learned lists of nonsense syllables, such as *YOX* and *JIH*, and measured how much he retained when relearning each list, from 20 minutes to 30 days later. The result was his famous forgetting curve: *The course of forgetting is initially rapid, then levels off with time* (Wixted & Ebbesen, 1991). Another study found a similar forgetting curve for Spanish vocabulary learned in school (Bahrick, 1984). Compared with students just completing a high school or college Spanish course, people 3 years out of school had forgotten much of what they had learned (**Figure 2.7-3**). However, what people remembered then, they still mostly remembered 25 or more years later. Their forgetting had leveled off.

One explanation for these forgetting curves is a gradual fading of the physical *memory trace*. Cognitive neuroscientists are getting closer to solving the mystery of memory's physical storage and are increasing our understanding of how memory storage could decay. Like books you can't find in your high school library, memories may be inaccessible for many reasons. Some were never acquired (not encoded). Others were discarded (stored memories decay). And others are out of reach because we can't retrieve them.

## Retrieval Failure

Often, forgetting is not memories faded, but memories unretrieved. We store in long-term memory what's important to us or what we've rehearsed. But sometimes important events defy our attempts to access them (**Figure 2.7-4**). How frustrating when a name lies poised on the tip of our tongue, just beyond reach. Given retrieval cues (*It begins with an M*), we may easily retrieve the elusive memory. Retrieval problems contribute to the occasional memory failures of older adults, who more frequently are frustrated by tip-of-the-tongue forgetting (Abrams, 2008; Salthouse & Mandell, 2013). (People who are deaf and fluent in sign language experience a parallel "tip of the fingers" phenomenon [Thompson et al., 2005].)

**AP® Science Practice**

### Data

To understand research results, it helps to know how to interpret graphs. In Figure 2.7-3, the variables are retention (operationally defined as percentage of the original vocabulary retained) and time (operationally defined as the time in years after completion of a Spanish course). The researchers clearly were interested in the association between time and retention. Now look at Figure 2.7-5 on the next page. Can you identify the variables? In your own words, can you explain what the researchers found just by looking at the graph?

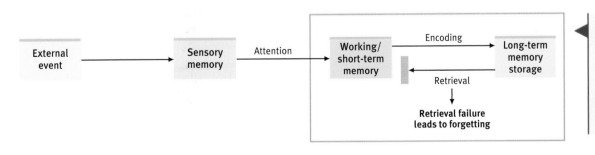

**Figure 2.7-4**

**Retrieval failure**

Sometimes even stored information cannot be accessed, which leads to forgetting.

Do you recall the gist of the sentence about the attacked swimmer that we asked you to remember in Module 2.4's discussion of making material personally meaningful? If not, does the word *shark* serve as a retrieval cue? Studies show that *shark* (likely what you visualized) more readily retrieves the image you stored than does the sentence's actual word, *fish* (Anderson et al., 1976). (The sentence was *The fish attacked the swimmer.*)

Retrieval problems occasionally stem from interference and even from motivated forgetting.

## Interference

As you collect more and more information, your mental attic never fills, but it does get cluttered. Your brain tries to keep things tidy: Using a new password weakens your memory of competing old passwords (Wimber et al., 2015). But sometimes the clutter wins, and new and old learning collide. **Proactive** *(forward-acting)* **interference** occurs when prior learning disrupts your recall of new information. If you buy a new combination lock, your well-rehearsed old combination may interfere with your retrieval of the new one.

**Retroactive** *(backward-acting)* **interference** occurs when new learning disrupts your recall of old information. If someone sings new lyrics to an old song's tune, you may have trouble remembering the original words. Imagine a second stone tossed in a pond, disrupting the waves rippling out from the first.

Information presented in the hour before sleep suffers less retroactive interference because the opportunity for interfering events is minimized (Mercer, 2015). In a classic experiment, two people each learned some nonsense syllables (Jenkins & Dallenbach, 1924). Then they tried to recall them after a night's sleep or after remaining awake. As **Figure 2.7-5** shows, forgetting occurred more rapidly after being awake and involved with other activities. The investigators surmised that "forgetting is not so much a matter of the decay of old impressions and associations as it is a matter of interference, inhibition, or obliteration of the old by the new" (p. 612).

The hour before sleep is a good time to commit information to memory (Scullin & McDaniel, 2010), though information presented in the *seconds* just before sleep is seldom remembered (Wyatt & Bootzin, 1994). If you're considering learning *while* sleeping, forget it. We have little memory for information played aloud in the room during sleep, although the ears do register it (Wood et al., 1992).

Old and new learning do not always compete with each other. Previously learned information (Latin) often facilitates our learning of new information (French). This phenomenon is called *positive transfer.*

**proactive interference** the forward-acting disruptive effect of older learning on the recall of *new* information.

**retroactive interference** the backward-acting disruptive effect of newer learning on the recall of *old* information.

### Figure 2.7-5
**Retroactive interference**

More forgetting occurred when a person stayed awake and experienced other new material. (Data from Jenkins & Dallenbach, 1924.)

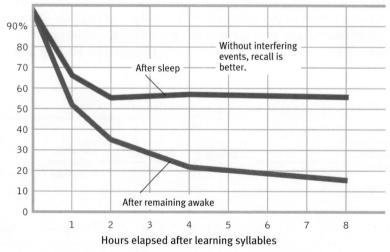

## Motivated Forgetting

To remember our past is often to revise it. Years ago, the huge cookie jar in my [DM's] kitchen was jammed with freshly baked chocolate chip cookies. Still more were cooling across racks on the counter. Twenty-four hours later, not a crumb was left. Who had taken them? During that time, my wife, three children, and I were the only people in the house. So, while memories were still fresh, I conducted a little memory test. Andy admitted wolfing down as many as 20. Peter thought he had eaten 15. Laura guessed she had stuffed her then-6-year-old body with 15 cookies. My wife, Carol, recalled eating 6, and I remembered consuming 15 and taking 18 more to the office. We sheepishly accepted responsibility for 89 cookies. Still, we had not come close; there had been 160.

Why do our memories fail us? This happens in part because memory is an "unreliable, self-serving historian" (Tavris & Aronson, 2007, p. 6). Consider one study, in which researchers told some participants about the benefits of frequent toothbrushing. Those individuals then recalled (more than others did) having frequently brushed their teeth in the preceding 2 weeks (Ross et al., 1981).

So, why were my family and I so far off in our cookie-consumption estimates? Was it an *encoding* problem? (Did we just not notice what we had eaten?) Was it a storage problem? (Might our memories of cookies, like Ebbinghaus' memory of nonsense syllables, have melted away almost as fast as the cookies themselves?) Or was the information still intact but not *retrievable?*[7]

Sigmund Freud might have argued that our memory systems self-censored this information. He proposed that we **repress** painful or unacceptable memories to protect our self-concept (what he called the *ego*) and to minimize anxiety. But the repressed memory lingers, he believed, and can be retrieved by some later cue or during therapy. Repression was central to Freud's psychoanalytic theory and later psychodynamic theory. It remains a popular idea, with many Americans and many clinicians continuing to believe that people repress their traumatic memories (Otgaar et al., 2019; Wake et al., 2020). However, most memory researchers think repression rarely, if ever, occurs. Trauma releases stress hormones, which causes trauma survivors to attend to and remember the threat (Quaedflieg & Schwabe, 2017). Thus, people often have intrusive, persistent memories of the very same traumatic experiences they would most like to forget (Marks et al., 2018).

**AP® Science Practice**

### Research

Nearly all the studies described in this textbook, like the toothbrushing study mentioned here, have been peer reviewed — that is, prior to publication they were evaluated by other scientist experts.

Peter Johansky/Photolibrary/Getty Images

**repression** in psychoanalytic theory, the basic defense mechanism that banishes from consciousness anxiety-arousing thoughts, feelings, and memories.

European Pressphoto Agency/Lages/PORTUGAL/Newscom

**Do people vividly remember — or repress — traumatic experiences?** Imagine yourself several hours into Flight AT236 from Toronto to Lisbon. A fractured fuel line begins leaking. Soon the engines go silent and primary electrical power is lost. In the eerie silence, the pilots instruct you and other terrified passengers to don life jackets and prepare for ocean impact. Before long, the pilot declares above the passengers' screams and prayers, "About to go into the water." Death awaits.

But no! "We have a runway! Brace! Brace! Brace!" The plane makes a hard landing at an Azores airbase, averting death for all 305 on board.

Among the passengers thinking, "I'm going to die," was psychologist Margaret McKinnon. Seizing the opportunity, four years later she tracked down 15 of her fellow passengers to test their trauma memories. Did they repress the experience? No. All exhibited vivid, detailed memories. With trauma comes not repression, but, far more often, "robust" memory (McKinnon et al., 2015).

[7]One of my cookie-scarfing sons, on reading this in his father's textbook years later, confessed he had fibbed "a little."

## Check Your Understanding

**AP® Science Practice**

**Examine the Concept**

▶ Explain what is meant by encoding failure.

▶ Explain the difference between proactive and retroactive interference, providing an example of each.

▶ Freud believed that we _____ unacceptable memories to minimize anxiety.

**Apply the Concept**

▶ Most people, especially as they grow older, wish for a better memory. Is that true of you? Or do you more often wish you could discard old memories?

▶ Compare and contrast anterograde and retrograde amnesia.

*Answers to the Examine the Concept questions can be found in Appendix C at the end of the book.*

# Memory Construction Errors

> **2.7-2** How do misinformation, imagination, and source amnesia influence our memory construction? How do we decide whether a memory is real or false?

Nearly two-thirds of Americans agree: "Human memory works like a video camera, accurately recording the events we see and hear so that we can review and inspect them later" (Simons & Chabris, 2011). Actually, we rarely recall events with such precision. Like scientists who infer a dinosaur's appearance from its remains, we use *constructive memory* to infer our past from stored information, plus what we later imagined, expected, saw, and heard. Memories are constructed: We don't just retrieve them, we reweave them.

Our memories are like Wikipedia pages, capable of constant revision. When we "replay" a memory, we often replace the original with a slightly modified version, rather like what happens in the telephone game, as a whispered message gets progressively altered when passed from person to person (Hardt et al., 2010). Memory researchers call this **reconsolidation** (Elsey et al., 2018). So, in a sense, said Joseph LeDoux (2009), "your memory is only as good as your last memory. The fewer times you use it, the more pristine it is." This means that, to some degree, "all memory is false" (Bernstein & Loftus, 2009b).

Despite knowing all this, I [DM] rewrote my own past at an international conference, where memory researcher Elizabeth Loftus (2012) spoke. Loftus showed attendees a handful of individual faces that we were later to identify, as if in a police lineup. She then showed us some pairs of faces—one face we had seen earlier and one we had not—and asked us to identify the one we had seen. But one pair she had slipped in included *two* new faces, one of which was rather *like* a face we had seen earlier. Most of us understandably but wrongly identified this face as one we had previously seen. To climax the demonstration, she showed us the originally seen face and the previously chosen wrong face, and asked us to choose the original face we had seen. Again, most of us picked the wrong face! As a result of our memory reconsolidation, we—an audience of psychologists who should have known better—had replaced the original memory with a false memory.

Neuroscientists are identifying relevant brain regions and neurochemicals that help or hinder memory reconsolidation (Bang et al., 2018). Meanwhile, clinical researchers have been experimenting. They ask people to recall a traumatic or negative experience and then disrupt the reconsolidation of that memory with a drug (such as propranolol), a brief, painless electroconvulsive shock, or novel distracting images (Phelps & Hofmann, 2019; Scully et al., 2017; Treanor et al., 2017). Someday it might become possible to use memory reconsolidation to erase specific traumatic memories. Would you wish to do this, if you could? If brutally assaulted, would you welcome having your memory of the attack and its associated fears deleted?

**SPOTLIGHT ON:**
Elizabeth Loftus

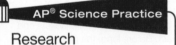

**AP® Science Practice**

**Research**

Human cognition and behavior are often unpredictable and may contradict commonsense expectations. This is why psychological scientists apply the scientific approach detailed in Module 0.5!

**reconsolidation** a process in which previously stored memories, when retrieved, are potentially altered before being stored again.

# Misinformation and Imagination Effects

In more than 200 studies involving more than 20,000 people, Loftus has shown how eyewitnesses reconstruct their memories after a crime or an accident. In one classic experiment, two groups of people watched a traffic accident film clip and then answered questions about what they had seen (Loftus & Palmer, 1974). Those asked, "About how fast were the cars going when they *smashed* into each other?" gave higher speed estimates than those asked, "About how fast were the cars going when they *hit* each other?" A week later, when asked whether they recalled seeing any broken glass, people who had heard *smashed* were more than twice as likely to report seeing glass fragments (**Figure 2.7-6**). In fact, the film showed no broken glass.

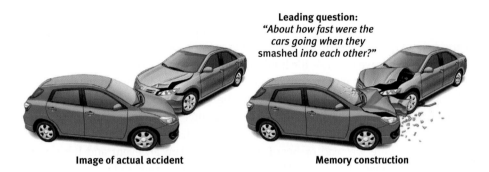

**Leading question:** *"About how fast were the cars going when they smashed into each other?"*

Image of actual accident   Memory construction

**Figure 2.7-6**
**Memory construction**

In many follow-up experiments worldwide, others have witnessed an event, received or not received misleading information about it, and then taken a memory test. The repeated result is a **misinformation effect**: After exposure to subtly misleading information, we may confidently misremember what we've seen or heard (Anglada-Tort et al., 2019; Loftus et al., 1992). Across studies, about half of people show some vulnerability to the misinformation effect (Brewin & Andrews, 2017; Scoboria et al., 2017). A yield sign becomes a stop sign, hammers become screwdrivers, Coke cans become peanut cans, breakfast cereal becomes eggs, and a clean-shaven man morphs into a man with a mustache. These false memories wither away once the trickster researchers *debrief* research participants, letting them know that the study's purpose was to demonstrate the human mind's built-in photo-editing software (Murphy et al., 2020).

So powerful is the misinformation effect that it can influence later attitudes and behaviors (Bernstein & Loftus, 2009a). One experiment falsely suggested to some Dutch university students that, as children, they became ill after eating spoiled egg salad (Geraerts et al., 2008). After absorbing that suggestion, they were less likely to eat egg salad sandwiches, both immediately and 4 months later.

**misinformation effect** occurs when a memory has been corrupted by misleading information.

**Was Alexander Hamilton a U.S. president?** Sometimes our mind tricks us into misremembering dates, places, and names. This often happens because we misuse familiar information. In one study, many Americans mistakenly recalled Alexander Hamilton — whose face appears on the U.S. $10 bill, and who is the subject of Lin-Manuel Miranda's popular Broadway musical — as a U.S. president (Roediger & DeSoto, 2016).

## Research

Can you identify the independent variable in the balloon experiment just described? The IV is the factor that the researchers manipulated; the variable whose effect is being studied. In this case it's the content of the photos. Now, can you identify the dependent variable?

In experiments, researchers have altered photos from a family album to show some family members taking a hot-air balloon ride. After viewing these photos (rather than photos showing just the balloon), children reported more false memories of the balloon ride, and indicated high confidence in those memories. *Imagination inflation* was evident several days later, when they reported even richer details of their false memories (Strange et al., 2008; Wade et al., 2002). Many people—39 percent in one survey—recall improbable first memories from age 2 and before (Akhtar et al., 2018). And in British and Canadian university surveys, nearly one-fourth of students have reported personal memories that they later realized were not accurate (Foley, 2015; Mazzoni et al., 2010). *The bottom line:* Don't believe everything you remember.

## Source Amnesia

What is the frailest part of a memory? Its source. An example: On a recent anniversary of the 9/11 terror attack, I [DM] mentioned to my wife my vivid memory of our Manhattan daughter's call as she witnessed—while we talked—the horror of the second tower's collapse. But no, replied my wife, whose memory is usually far more reliable than mine: "She made that call to *me*."

Clearly, one of us had reported the call to the other, who was now misattributing the source. ("I was definitely speaking to Dad," our daughter later informed us, putting a smug smile on my often error-prone face.) We may cite a statistic when arguing a point, but be unable to recall where we read or heard it. We may dream an event and later be unsure whether it really happened. We may tell a friend some gossip, only to learn we got the news from the friend. Famed child psychologist Jean Piaget was startled as an adult to learn that a vivid, detailed memory from his childhood—a nursemaid's thwarting his kidnapping—was utterly false. He apparently constructed the memory from repeatedly hearing the story (which his nursemaid, after undergoing a religious conversion, later confessed had never happened). In attributing his "memory" to his own experiences, rather than to his nursemaid's stories, Piaget exhibited **source amnesia** (which often occurs as *source misattribution*). Misattribution is at the heart of many false memories. Authors, songwriters, and comedians sometimes suffer from it. They think an idea came from their own creative imagination, when in fact they are unintentionally plagiarizing something they earlier read or heard.

> *Do you ever get that strange feeling of vujà dé? Not déjà vu; vujà dé. It's the distinct sense that, somehow, something just happened that has never happened before. Nothing seems familiar. And then suddenly the feeling is gone. Vujà dé.*
>
> Comedian George Carlin, *Funny Times*, December 2001

Source amnesia also helps explain **déjà vu** (French for "already seen"). Two-thirds of us have experienced this fleeting, eerie sense that "I've been in this exact situation before." The key to déjà vu seems to be familiarity with a stimulus combined with uncertainty about where we encountered it before (Cleary & Claxton, 2018; Urquhart et al., 2018). Normally, we experience a feeling of *familiarity* (thanks to temporal lobe processing) before we consciously remember details (thanks to hippocampus and frontal lobe processing). When these functions (and brain regions) are out of sync, we may experience a feeling of familiarity without conscious recall. Our amazing brains try to make sense of such an improbable situation, and we get an eerie feeling that we're reliving some earlier part of our life. Our source amnesia forces us to do our best to make sense of an odd moment.

**source amnesia** faulty memory for how, when, or where information was learned or imagined (as when *misattributing information to a wrong source*). Source amnesia, along with the misinformation effect, is at the heart of many false memories.

**déjà vu** that eerie sense that "I've experienced this before." Cues from the current situation may unconsciously trigger retrieval of an earlier experience.

## Discerning True and False Memories

Since memory is reconstruction as well as reproduction, we can't be sure whether a memory is real by how real it feels. Much as perceptual illusions may seem like real perceptions, unreal memories *feel* like real memories. Because the misinformation effect and source amnesia happen outside our awareness, it is hard to separate false memories from real ones (Schooler et al., 1986). You can likely recall describing a childhood experience to a friend, constructing your memory to fill in forgotten details with reasonable guesses and assumptions. We all do it, and after more retellings, those guessed details—now absorbed into your memory—may feel as real as if you had actually experienced them (Roediger et al., 1993). False memories, like fake diamonds, seem so real.

False memories can be persistent. Imagine that we were to read aloud a list of words such as *candy, sugar, honey*, and *taste*. Later, we ask you to recognize the presented words from a larger list. If you are at all like the people tested by Henry Roediger and Kathleen McDermott (1995), you would err three out of four times—by falsely remembering a non-presented similar word, such as *sweet*. We more easily remember the gist than the words themselves.

False memories are socially contagious. When we hear others falsely remember events, we tend to make the same memory mistakes (Roediger et al., 2001). We get confused about where we originally learned of the false event—*Did I already know that or am I learning it from others?*—and adopt others' false memories (Hirst & Echterhoff, 2012). It's easy to see how false stories can spread and become false memories.

Memory construction errors also help explain why some people have been sent to prison for crimes they never committed. Of 375 people who were later proven not guilty by DNA testing, 69 percent had been convicted because of faulty eyewitness identification (Innocence Project, 2020; Wells, 2020). Eyewitness accuracy is also influenced by our tendency to recall faces of our own race more accurately than faces of other races. (See Module 4.1's discussion of the *other-race effect*.) Among criminal suspects exonerated with DNA evidence after eyewitness misidentification, more than 40 percent were falsely accused after a cross-racial misidentification (Innocence Project, 2020).

Memory construction errors explain why "hypnotically refreshed" memories of crimes so easily incorporate inaccuracies, some of which may originate with the hypnotist's leading questions *(Did you hear loud noises?)*. And these errors also seem to be at work in many "recovered" memories of childhood abuse. (See Developing Arguments: Can Memories of Childhood Sexual Abuse Be Repressed and Then Recovered? on page 248.)

Memory construction errors explain why dating partners now in love *over* estimate their first impressions of each other *(It was love at first sight)*, while those who have broken up *under* estimate their earlier liking *(We never really clicked)* (McFarland & Ross, 1987). When we love someone, our memory extinguishes the negative and shines a light on the positive (Cortes et al., 2018). And it explains why people who were asked how they felt 10 years ago about marijuana or gender issues recalled attitudes closer to their current views than to the views they had actually reported a decade earlier (Markus, 1986). In one experiment, students who agreed to write an essay supporting a higher tuition policy constructed a false memory of previously supporting the policy, despite initially opposing it (Rodriguez & Strange, 2015). As George Vaillant (1977, p. 197) noted after following adult lives through time, "It is all too common for caterpillars to become butterflies and then to maintain that in their youth they had been little butterflies. Maturation makes liars of us all."

## Children's Eyewitness Recall

**2.7-3** How reliable are young children's eyewitness descriptions?

If memories can be sincere, yet sincerely wrong, how can jurors decide cases in which children's memories of sexual abuse are the only evidence? "It would be truly awful to ever lose sight of the enormity of child abuse," observed Stephen Ceci (1993). Yet Ceci and Maggie Bruck's (1993, 1995) studies of children's memories made them aware of how easily children's memories can be molded. For example, they asked 3-year-olds to show on anatomically correct dolls where a pediatrician had touched them. Of the children who had not received genital examinations, 55 percent pointed to either genital or anal areas.

The researchers also studied the effect of suggestive interviewing techniques (Bruck & Ceci, 1999, 2004). In one study, children chose a card from a deck containing events that,

**AP® Science Practice**

### Research

Recall from Module 0.5 that the APA ethics code outlines standards for safeguarding human participants' well-being, including obtaining their *informed consent*. Parents would have consented for their children to participate in this study of false memories. Would you give consent for your child to participate? Why or why not?

# Developing Arguments

## Can Memories of Childhood Sexual Abuse Be Repressed and Then Recovered?

### Two Possible Tragedies:

**1. People doubt childhood sexual abuse survivors who tell their secret.**

**2. Innocent people are falsely accused,** as therapists prompt "recovered" memories of childhood sexual abuse:

Well-intentioned therapist

"Victims of sexual abuse often have your symptoms. So maybe you were abused and *repressed* the memory. Let's see if I can help you recover the memory, by digging back and visualizing your trauma."

**Misinformation effect** and **source amnesia:** Adult client may form image of threatening person.

With *rehearsal* (repeated therapy sessions), the image grows more vivid.

Client is stunned, angry, and ready to confront or sue the remembered abuser.

Accused person is equally stunned and vigorously denies the accusation of long-ago abuse.

---

**Professional organizations (including the American Medical, American Psychological, and American Psychiatric Associations) are working to find sensible common ground to resolve psychology's "memory war":**[1]

• **Childhood sexual abuse happens** and can leave its victims at risk for problems ranging from sexual dysfunction to depression.[2] But there is no "survivor syndrome" — no group of symptoms that lets us spot victims of sexual abuse.[3]
• **Injustice happens.** Innocent people have been falsely convicted. And guilty people have avoided punishment by casting doubt on their truth-telling accusers.
• **Forgetting happens.** Children abused when very young may not have understood the meaning of their experience or remember it. Forgetting long-ago good and bad events is an ordinary part of everyday life.
• **Recovered memories are common.** Cued by a remark or an experience, we may recover pleasant or unpleasant memories of long-forgotten events. But does the unconscious mind forcibly repress painful experiences,

and can these experiences be recovered by therapist-aided techniques?[4] Memories that surface naturally are more likely to be true.[5]
• **Memories of events before age 4 are unreliable.** Infantile amnesia results from not yet developed brain pathways. Most psychologists therefore doubt "recovered" memories of abuse during infancy.[6] The older a child was when suffering sexual abuse, and the more severe the abuse, the more likely it is to be remembered.[7]
• **Memories "recovered" under hypnosis are especially unreliable.**
• **Memories, whether real or false, can be emotionally upsetting.** What was born of mere suggestion can become, like an actual event, a stinging memory that drives bodily stress.[8]

---

**Psychologists question whether *repression* ever occurs.**
(See Module 4.5 for more on this concept, which is central to Freud's theory.)

---

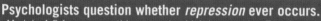

**Traumatic experiences** (witnessing a loved one's murder, being terrorized by a hijacker or rapist, losing everything in a natural disaster) → **TYPICALLY LEAD TO** → vivid, persistent, haunting memories[9]

---

**The Royal College of Psychiatrists Working Group on Reported Recovered Memories of Child Sexual Abuse** advised that "when memories are 'recovered' after long periods of amnesia, particularly when extraordinary means were used to secure the recovery of memory, there is a high probability that the memories are false."[10]

---

## Developing Arguments Questions

**1.** Explain what is meant by *recovered memory*.

**2.** Explain how the misinformation effect and source amnesia play a role in recovered memories. How does this support or refute recovered memories?

**3.** Use the evidence presented here to explain the circumstances when memories are most unreliable.

1. Patihis et al., 2014a. 2. Freyd et al., 2007. 3. Kendall-Tackett et al., 1993. 4. McNally & Geraerts, 2009. 5. Geraerts et al., 2007. 6. Gore-Felton et al., 2000; Knapp & VandeCreek, 2000. 7. Goodman et al., 2003. 8. McNally, 2003, 2007. 9. Porter & Peace, 2007; Goldfarb et al., 2019. 10. Brandon et al., 1998.

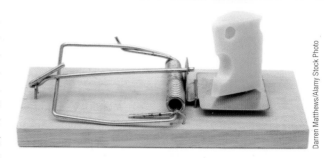

according to their parents, had and had not happened. An adult then asked them a question about the event on the card—for example, "Think real hard, and tell me if this ever happened to you. Can you remember going to the hospital with a mousetrap on your finger?" In subsequent interviews, the same adult repeatedly asked the children to think about the same events, both real and fictitious. After 10 weeks of this, a new adult asked the original question: "Can you remember going to the hospital with a mousetrap on your finger?" The stunning result: 58 percent of preschoolers produced false (often vivid) stories regarding one or more events they had never experienced (Ceci et al., 1994). Here's one:

> My brother Colin was trying to get Blowtorch [an action figure] from me, and I wouldn't let him take it from me, so he pushed me into the wood pile where the mousetrap was. And then my finger got caught in it. And then we went to the hospital, and my mommy, daddy, and Colin drove me there, to the hospital in our van, because it was far away. And the doctor put a bandage on this finger.

Given such detailed stories, professional psychologists who specialize in interviewing children could not reliably separate the real memories from the false ones. Nor could the children themselves. The above child, reminded that his parents had told him several times that the mousetrap incident never happened—that he had imagined it—protested, "But it really did happen. I remember it!" This misinformation effect is common. In one analysis of eyewitness data from over 20,000 participants, children regularly identified innocent suspects as guilty (Fitzgerald & Price, 2015). "[The] research," said Ceci (1993), "leads me to worry about the possibility of false allegations. It is not a tribute to one's scientific integrity to walk down the middle of the road if the data are more to one side."

With carefully trained interviewers, however, both adults and children can be accurate eyewitnesses (Wixted et al., 2018). When questioned about their experiences in neutral words they understand, children often accurately recall what happened and who did it (Brewin & Andrews, 2017; Goodman, 2006). When interviewers have used less suggestive, more effective techniques, even 4- to 5-year-old children have produced more accurate recall (Holliday & Albon, 2004; Pipe et al., 2004). Children are especially accurate when they haven't talked with involved adults prior to the interview, and when their disclosure was made in a first interview with a neutral person who asked nonleading questions.

---

## AP® Science Practice

## Check Your Understanding

### Examine the Concept

▶ Explain the *misinformation effect*.

▶ Explain how source amnesia relates to false memories.

### Apply the Concept

▶ Think of a memory you frequently recall. How might you have changed it without conscious awareness?

▶ What — given the commonness of source amnesia — might life be like if we remembered all our waking experiences and all our dreams?

▶ Imagine being a jury member in a trial for a parent accused of abuse based on a recovered memory. What insights from memory research should you share with the rest of the jury?

*Answers to the Examine the Concept questions can be found in Appendix C at the end of the book.*

# Improving Memory

**2.7-4** How can you use memory research findings to do better in this and other classes?

Biology's findings benefit medicine. Botany's findings benefit agriculture. So, too, can memory researchers' findings benefit education. In particular, they can boost your performance in class and on tests. Here is a summary of some research-based suggestions that can help you remember information when you need it.

*Rehearse repeatedly.* To master material, remember the *spacing effect*—use *distributed (spaced) practice.* To learn a concept, engage in many separate study sessions. Take advantage of life's little intervals—riding a bus, walking to lunch, waiting for class to start. New memories are weak; if you exercise them, they will strengthen. Experts recommend retrieving a to-be-remembered item three times before you stop studying it (Miyatsu et al., 2018). Reading complex material with minimal rehearsal yields little retention. As the *testing effect* has shown, it pays to study actively. Mentally saying, writing, or typing information beats silently reading it (MacLeod & Bodner, 2017). This *production effect* explains why we so often learn something best when teaching it, when explaining it to ourselves, or when rehearsing information out loud (Bisra et al., 2018; Forrin & Macleod, 2018; Koh et al., 2018).

*Make the material meaningful.* Space it. Rehearse it. Personalize it. You can build a network of retrieval cues by forming as many associations as possible. Apply the concepts to your own life. Understand and organize information. Relate the material to what you already know or have experienced. As William James (1890) suggested, "Knit each new thing on to some acquisition already there." You can even try drawing the concept (Fernandes et al., 2018). Mindlessly repeating someone else's words without taking the time to really understand what they mean won't supply many retrieval cues. On an exam, you may find yourself stuck when a question uses phrasing different from the words you memorized.

*Activate retrieval cues.* Remember the importance of *context-dependent* and *state-dependent memory*. Mentally re-create the situation and the mood in which your original learning occurred. Jog your memory by allowing one thought to cue the next.

*Use mnemonic devices.* Make up a story that incorporates *vivid images* of the concepts. *Chunk* information. Create a memorable *mnemonic*. (Did you learn Never Eat Soggy Waffles for the four directions clockwise—*n*orth, *e*ast, *s*outh, and *w*est?)

*Minimize proactive and retroactive interference.* Study before sleep. Do not schedule back-to-back study times for topics that are likely to interfere with each other, such as Spanish and French.

*Sleep more.* During sleep, the brain reorganizes and *consolidates* information for long-term memory. Sleeping more will help you remember what you've learned and what you're planning to do tomorrow (Cousins et al., 2020; Leong et al., 2020).

*Test your own knowledge, both to rehearse it and to find out what you don't yet know.* The testing effect is real, and it is powerful. Don't be lulled into overconfidence by your ability to *recognize* information. Test your *recall* using the Examine the Concept questions found throughout each module and the numbered Learning Targets at each module's end. Outline sections using a blank page. Define the terms and concepts discussed in each module and listed at the end of each unit before turning back to their definitions.

Marc Romanelli/Tetra images/Getty Images

**Thinking and memory** Think actively as you read, by rehearsing and relating ideas, and by making the material personally meaningful. This will yield the best retention.

Use the Exploring Research Methods & Design, Data Interpretation, and Developing Arguments features to rehearse these foundational skills throughout the textbook. Answer the Multiple Choice questions at the end of each module, and complete the AP® Exam Practice Questions at the end of each unit.

---

 **AP® Science Practice**

## Exploring Research Methods & Design

As you learned in this module, explaining and rehearsing new information is a powerful learning tool. To best remember information, we must *do* something with it; we need to actively process it somehow. To demonstrate this, Louis Deslauriers and colleagues (2019) randomly assigned students in a college physics course to either experience passive lectures or engage in active learning. The content covered was identical. As expected, the students learned more in the active classroom as evidenced by higher test scores.

- What was the study's hypothesis?

- Explain why the study is an experiment (rather than a correlational study).

- Can these results be generalized from the sample (college physics students) to the population (all students)? Explain.

---

 **AP® Science Practice**

## Check Your Understanding

### Examine the Concept

▶ Explain how memory researchers' findings can benefit education.

### Apply the Concept

▶ Which memory strategies can help you study smarter and retain more information?

▶ Which three of these study and memory strategies do you feel will be most helpful for *you* to start using to improve your own learning and retention?

*Answers to the Examine the Concept questions can be found in Appendix C at the end of the book.*

---

## Module 2.7 REVIEW

### 2.7-1 Why do we forget?

- Some people experience *anterograde amnesia*, an inability to form new memories, or *retrograde amnesia*, an inability to retrieve old memories.

- Normal forgetting can happen because we have never encoded information (encoding failure), because the physical memory trace has faded (storage decay), or because we cannot retrieve what we have encoded and stored (retrieval failure).

- Retrieval problems may result from *proactive* (forward-acting) *interference,* when prior learning interferes with recall of new information, or from *retroactive* (backward-acting) *interference,* when new learning disrupts recall of old information.

- Motivated forgetting occurs, but researchers have found little evidence of *repression*.

### 2.7-2 How do misinformation, imagination, and source amnesia influence our memory construction? How do we decide whether a memory is real or false?

- Memories can be continually revised when retrieved, a process that memory researchers call *reconsolidation*.

- The *misinformation effect* (exposure to misleading information) and imagination inflation may corrupt our stored memories of what actually happened.

- When we reassemble a memory during retrieval, we may attribute it to the wrong source *(source amnesia).* Source amnesia helps explain *déjà vu.*

- Since memory involves reconstruction as well as reproduction, and the misinformation effect and source amnesia occur outside our awareness, it is difficult to separate false memories from real ones.

**2.7-3** How reliable are young children's eyewitness descriptions?

- Children's eyewitness descriptions are subject to the same memory influences that distort adult reports, and suggestive interviewing techniques can lead to false memories. But if questioned by a carefully trained interviewer who asks nonleading questions—and especially if they have not spoken to involved adults prior to the interview—children can accurately recall events and people involved in them.

**2.7-4** How can you use memory research findings to do better in this and other classes?

- Memory research findings suggest the following strategies for improving memory: Rehearse repeatedly; make the material meaningful; activate retrieval cues; use mnemonic devices; minimize proactive and retroactive interference; sleep more; and test yourself to be sure you can retrieve, as well as recognize, material.

---

# AP® Practice Multiple Choice Questions

1. Which of the following is an example of anterograde amnesia?

   a. Halle can remember her new locker combination but not her old one.
   b. William has lost his memory of the 2 weeks before he had surgery to remove a benign brain tumor.
   c. Louis can remember his past but nothing since experiencing a brain infection 4 years ago.
   d. Maddie can't remember the details of when she was mugged 6 months ago.

2. The cafeteria at Muhammad's school is a large room with nine free-standing pillars that support the roof. Muhammad has been in his school cafeteria hundreds of times. One day, Muhammad's teacher asks him how many pillars there are in the cafeteria. Muhammad has difficulty answering the question, but he finally replies that he thinks there are six pillars. What memory concept does this example illustrate?

   a. Storage decay
   b. Proactive interference
   c. Retroactive interference
   d. Encoding failure

3. Suzanne gets a new phone number. Each time she tries to give someone the new number, she gives her old one instead. The fact that her old number is causing difficulty in her remembering of the new one is an example of

   a. retroactive interference.
   b. retrograde amnesia.
   c. proactive interference.
   d. anterograde amnesia.

4. Regarding therapist-guided "recovered" memories of sexual abuse in infancy, which statement best represents an appropriate conclusion about this issue?

   a. Therapists who use hypnosis are likely to help their patients retrieve repressed memories.
   b. Statistics indicate that childhood sexual abuse rarely occurs; therefore, recovered memories of such abuse are likely false.
   c. Memories are only rarely recovered. Once you are unable to retrieve a memory, you will probably never be able to retrieve it.
   d. Since the brain is not sufficiently mature to store accurate memories of events before the age of 4, memories from the first 4 years of life are not reliable.

**Use the following information to answer questions 5 and 6:**

Kevin composes what he thinks is a unique piece of music. When he plays it for his friend Heidi, she informs him that they heard that song together on the radio last summer.

**5.** Which of the following best describes Kevin's memory error?

a. Source amnesia
b. Retroactive interference
c. Proactive interference
d. Anterograde amnesia

**6.** A few months later when Heidi hears the same song, she tells her mom, "That's my friend Kevin's song!" Which of the following best describes Heidi's memory error?

a. Source misattribution
b. Encoding failure
c. Storage decay
d. Displacement

# Module 2.8a Intelligence and Achievement: Theories of Intelligence

**intelligence** the ability to learn from experience, solve problems, and use knowledge to adapt to new situations.

**2.8-1** How do psychologists define *intelligence*?

### CULTURAL AWARENESS

A person's culture (the behaviors, ideas, attitudes, values, and traditions shared by a group of people and transmitted across generations) influences their definition of intelligence. Can you think of a way that your culture influences your ideas about intelligence?

### CULTURAL AWARENESS

Because culture so heavily influences our understanding of intelligence, we should resist the temptation to impose our values on others. It is easy, for example, to think that Western, urban culture is "more intelligent" than Indigenous or tribal cultures when we use a Western, urban definition as the standard of comparison. Unfortunately, this can fuel prejudice and discrimination (as discussed in Module 4.1).

Few topics have sparked more debate than intelligence: Does each of us have an inborn general mental capacity (intelligence)? Can we quantify this capacity as a meaningful number? How much does intelligence vary within and between groups, and why? Do beliefs about intelligence—whether it is unchangeable or can grow through experience—influence academic achievement?

In many studies, *intelligence* has been defined as whatever *intelligence tests* measure, which has tended to be school smarts. But intelligence is not a quality like height or weight, which has the same meaning to everyone worldwide. People assign this term to the qualities that enable success in their own time and culture (Sternberg & Kaufman, 1998). In Cameroon's equatorial forest, intelligence may reflect understanding the medicinal qualities of local plants. In a North American high school, it may reflect mastering difficult concepts in calculus or chemistry. In both places, **intelligence** is the ability to learn from experience, solve problems, and use knowledge to adapt to new situations. As multibillionaire stock investor Warren Buffett noted, "I happen to have a talent for allocating capital. But my ability to use that talent is completely dependent on the society I was born into. If I'd been born into a tribe of hunters . . . I'd probably end up as some wild animal's dinner."

You probably know some people with talents in science, others who excel in the humanities, and still others gifted in athletics, art, music, or dance. You may also know a talented artist who is stumped by the simplest math problem, or a brilliant math student who struggles when discussing literature. Are all these people intelligent? Could you rate their intelligence on a single scale? Or would you need several different scales?

**Hands-on healing** The socially constructed concept of intelligence varies from culture to culture. This natural healer in Cameroon displays intelligence in his knowledge about medicinal plants and his understanding of the needs of the people he is helping.

imageBROKER/Alamy Stock Photo

# Is Intelligence One General Ability?

**2.8-2** What are the arguments for *general intelligence (g)*?

Charles Spearman (1863–1945) believed we have one **general intelligence** (often shortened to *g*) that lies at the heart of all of our intelligent behavior, from sailing the sea to sailing through school. He granted that people often have special, outstanding abilities. But he noted that those who score high in one area, such as verbal intelligence, typically score higher than average in other areas, such as spatial or reasoning ability. As behavior geneticist Robert Plomin (1999) observed, "*g* is one of the most reliable and valid measures in the behavioral domain . . . and it predicts important social outcomes such as educational and occupational levels far better than any other trait."

Spearman's (1904) belief stemmed in part from his work with **factor analysis**, a statistical procedure that identifies clusters of related variables. His idea of a general mental capacity expressed by a single intelligence score was controversial in Spearman's day, and so it remains. One of Spearman's early critics was L. L. Thurstone (1887–1955). Thurstone gave 56 different tests to people and mathematically identified seven clusters of *primary mental abilities* (word fluency, verbal comprehension, spatial ability, perceptual speed, numerical ability, inductive reasoning, and memory). Thurstone did not rank people on a single scale of general aptitude. But when other investigators studied these profiles, they detected a persistent tendency: Those who excelled in one of the seven clusters generally scored well on the others. So, the investigators concluded, there was still some evidence of a *g* factor.

We might, then, liken mental abilities to physical abilities: Athleticism is not one thing, but many. The ability to run fast is distinct from the eye-hand coordination required to throw a ball on target. Yet there remains some tendency for good things to come packaged together—for running speed and throwing accuracy to correlate. So, too, with intelligence—for humans worldwide (Warne & Burningham, 2019). Several distinct abilities tend to cluster together and to correlate enough to define a general intelligence factor. Distinct brain networks enable distinct abilities, with *g* explained by their coordinated activity (Cole et al., 2015; Kocevar et al., 2019).

## The Cattell-Horn-Carroll Intelligence Theory

**2.8-3** How have the concepts of *Gf* and *Gc*, and the *CHC theory*, affected our understanding of intelligence?

Raymond Cattell (1905–1998) and his student John Horn (1928–2006) formulated a theory of general ability based on two factors: **fluid intelligence** *(Gf)*—our ability to reason speedily and abstractly, as when solving logic problems—and **crystallized intelligence** *(Gc)*—our accumulated knowledge, as reflected in vocabulary and applied skills (Cattell, 1963). An experienced software developer may use her *Gf* to develop creative new theories of computer programming. Her *Gc* may be evident in the way she expertly discusses her work at a conference. Our *Gf* and *Gc* often work together, as when we solve problems by drawing on our accumulated knowledge.

The idea of a single intelligence factor has received support from hundreds of intelligence studies not only for *g*, but also for more specific abilities, with *Gf* and *Gc* bridging the gap between them (Carroll, 1993). Thus, the **Cattell-Horn-Carroll (CHC) theory** was born. This theory affirmed a general intellectual ability factor, along with the existence of *Gf* and *Gc*. And it identified more specific abilities, such as reading and writing ability, memory capacity, and processing speed (Schneider & McGrew, 2012). The CHC theory remains influential because it recognizes that intelligence comprises many abilities, but that these specific abilities exist under a broader umbrella of general intelligence. Thinking about intelligence has inspired other psychologists, particularly since the mid-1980s, to extend the definition of *intelligence* beyond the idea of academic smarts.

**SPOTLIGHT ON:**
Charles Spearman

## Data

The material on intelligence incorporates information about statistics. You can review other statistical concepts in Module 0.6.

**general intelligence (g)** according to Spearman and others, underlies all mental abilities and is therefore measured by every task on an intelligence test.

**factor analysis** a statistical procedure that identifies clusters of related items (called factors) on a test; used to identify different dimensions of performance that underlie a person's total score.

**fluid intelligence** *(Gf)* our ability to reason speedily and abstractly; tends to decrease with age, especially during late adulthood.

**crystallized intelligence** *(Gc)* our accumulated knowledge and verbal skills; tends to increase with age.

**Cattell-Horn-Carroll (CHC) theory** the theory that our intelligence is based on *g* as well as specific abilities, bridged by *Gf* and *Gc*.

# Theories of Multiple Intelligences

**2.8-4** How do Gardner's and Sternberg's theories of multiple intelligences differ, and what criticisms have they faced?

Other psychologists, particularly since the mid-1980s, have extended the definition of intelligence beyond the idea of academic smarts.

## Gardner's Multiple Intelligences

Howard Gardner has identified eight *relatively independent intelligences*, including the verbal and mathematical aptitudes assessed by standardized tests (**Figure 2.8-1**). Thus, the app developer, the poet, the street-smart adolescent, and the basketball team's play-making point guard exhibit different kinds of intelligence (Gardner, 1998). Gardner (1999) has also proposed a ninth possible intelligence—*existential intelligence*—defined as the ability "to ponder large questions about life, death, existence." Gardner's notion of multiple intelligences continues to influence many educators' belief that children have different "learning styles," such as visual and auditory (Newton & Miah, 2017). In one study, 93 percent of British teachers agreed that "individuals learn better when they receive information in their preferred Learning Style" (Dekker et al., 2012). Increasingly, however, research casts doubt on the idea of boosting comprehension in this way (Nancekivell et al., 2019; Papadatou-Pastou et al., 2018). Studies indicate that identifying and teaching to a student's supposed learning style does not produce better student outcomes.

**Figure 2.8-1**

**Gardner's eight intelligences**

Gardner has also proposed *existential intelligence* (the ability to ponder deep questions about life) as a ninth possible intelligence.

Gardner (1983, 2006, 2011; Davis et al., 2011) views these intelligence domains as multiple abilities that come in different packages. Brain damage, for example, may destroy one ability but leave others intact. One man, Dr. P., had visual brain area damage. He spoke fluently and could walk a straight line. But his facial recognition ability suffered, causing him to mistake his wife for, of all things, a hat (Sacks, 1985). And consider people with **savant syndrome**, who have an island of brilliance but often score low on intelligence tests and may have limited or no language ability (Treffert, 2010). Some can compute complicated calculations almost instantly, or identify the day of the week of any given historical date, or render incredible works of art or music (Miller, 1999).

The late memory whiz Kim Peek inspired the movie *Rain Man*. In 8 to 10 seconds, he could read and remember a page. During his lifetime, he memorized 9000 books, including Shakespeare's works and the Bible. He could provide GPS-like travel directions within any major U.S. city. Yet he could not button his clothes, and he had little capacity for abstract

▶ **SPOTLIGHT ON:**
Howard Gardner

**Islands of genius: savant syndrome** After a brief helicopter ride over Singapore followed by 5 days of drawing, British savant artist Stephen Wiltshire accurately reproduced an aerial view of the city from memory.

**savant syndrome** a condition in which a person otherwise limited in mental ability has an exceptional specific skill, such as in computation or drawing.

concepts. Asked by his father at a restaurant to lower his voice, he slid down in his chair to lower his voice box. Asked for Lincoln's Gettysburg Address, he responded, "227 North West Front Street. But he only stayed there one night—he gave the speech the next day" (Treffert & Christensen, 2005).

## Sternberg's Three Intelligences

Robert Sternberg (1985, 2011, 2017) agrees with Gardner that there is more to success than academic intelligence and that we have multiple intelligences. But Sternberg's *triarchic theory* proposes three—not eight or nine—reliably measured intelligences:

- *Analytical (academic problem-solving) intelligence* is assessed by intelligence tests, which present well-defined problems having a single right answer. Such tests predict school grades reasonably well and vocational success more modestly.

- *Creative intelligence* is demonstrated in innovative smarts: the ability to adapt to new situations and generate novel ideas.

- *Practical intelligence* is required for everyday tasks that may be poorly defined and may have multiple solutions.

Gardner and Sternberg agree on two important points: Multiple abilities can contribute to life success, and differing varieties of giftedness bring both spice to life and challenges for education. Trained to appreciate such variety, many teachers have applied multiple intelligence theories in their classrooms.

## General Intelligence, Grit, and Deliberate Practice

Wouldn't it be nice if the world were so fair that a weakness in one area would be compensated by genius in another? Alas, say critics, the world is not fair (Brown et al., 2021; Ferguson, 2009). There *is* a general intelligence factor; *g* matters (Johnson et al., 2008). It predicts performance on various complex tasks and in various jobs (Gottfredson, 2002a,b, 2003a,b). Studies of nearly 70,000 people from 19 countries have revealed that *g* predicts higher incomes (Ganzach et al., 2018; see also **Figure 2.8-2**). Likewise, extremely high cognitive-ability scores predict exceptional achievements, such as doctoral degrees and publications (Kuncel & Hezlett, 2010).

**Street smarts** This child selling candy on the streets of Bogota, Colombia, is developing practical intelligence at a very young age.

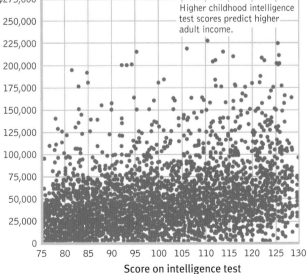

**Figure 2.8-2**
**Smart and rich?**

Jay Zagorsky (2007) tracked 7403 participants in the U.S. National Longitudinal Survey of Youth across 25 years. As shown in this illustrative scatterplot, their intelligence scores correlated +.30 (a moderate positive correlation) with their later income.

## AP® Science Practice

### Data Interpretation

The ability to evaluate graphical representations of data is important in psychology. Figure 2.8-2 illustrates a scatterplot — a graphed cluster of dots, each of which represents the values of two variables. The slope of the points suggests the direction of the relationship between the two variables. Study this figure and then . . .

- Identify the variables represented in this graph.

- Describe the trends in the data depicted in this graph.

- The data presented in this graph reflect a correlation coefficient (abbreviated *r*) of +.30 (a moderate positive correlation). Explain how you could determine this simply by looking at the graph.

*Remember, you can always refer to Module 0.4 for help.*

---

Even so, "success" is not a one-ingredient recipe. Although high academic intelligence will help you get into a profession (via schools and training programs), it alone won't make you successful once there. Success is a combination of talent and **grit**: Highly successful people also tend to be conscientious and persistently energetic.

Skills that breed success seldom sprout spontaneously. It takes time to cultivate a seedling of talent. K. Anders Ericsson and others proposed a *10-year rule*: A common ingredient of expert performance in chess, dance, sports, computer programming, music, and medicine is "about 10 years of intense, daily practice" (Ericsson & Pool, 2016). Becoming a professional musician, chess player, or elite athlete requires, first, native ability (Macnamara et al., 2014, 2016; Vaci et al., 2019). But it also requires years of *deliberate practice*—about 11,000 hours on average (Campitelli & Gobet, 2011). The recipe for success is a gift of nature plus a whole lot of nurture.

**TRY THIS**

For more on how self-disciplined grit feeds achievement, see Module 4.7.

**Talent + opportunity + practice** After winning the New York State chess championship for kindergarten through third grade, Tanitoluwa ("Tani") Adewumi lugged his trophy to his home at the time — a homeless shelter. In the prior year, after his family fled terrorists in northern Nigeria, Tani learned chess at his elementary school, then began hours of daily practice. "He does 10 times more chess puzzles than the average kid," said his chess teacher, after Tani bested privately tutored children from elite schools (Kristof, 2019).

Christopher Lee/The New York Times/Redux Pictures

## Emotional Intelligence

**2.8-5** What are the four components of emotional intelligence?

*Social intelligence* is the know-how involved in understanding social situations and managing yourself successfully (Cantor & Kihlstrom, 1987). Psychologist Edward Thorndike first proposed the concept in 1920, noting that "the best mechanic in a factory may fail as a [supervisor] for lack of social intelligence" (Goleman, 2006, p. 83).

A critical part of social intelligence, **emotional intelligence**, consists of four abilities (Mayer et al., 2002, 2012, 2016):

- *Perceiving emotions* (recognizing them in faces, music, and stories, and identifying our own emotions).

**grit** in psychology, passion and perseverance in the pursuit of long-term goals.

**emotional intelligence** the ability to perceive, understand, manage, and use emotions.

- **Understanding emotions** (predicting them and how they may change and blend).
- **Managing emotions** (knowing how to express them in varied situations, and how to handle others' emotions).
- **Using emotions** to facilitate adaptive or creative thinking.

Emotionally intelligent people are both socially aware and self-aware. They avoid being hijacked by overwhelming depression, anxiety, or anger. They can read others' emotional cues and know what to say to soothe a grieving friend, encourage a workmate, and manage a conflict. They can delay gratification in pursuit of long-range rewards. Thus, emotionally intelligent people tend to succeed in their relationships, careers, and parenting situations where academically smarter but less emotionally intelligent people may fail (Cherniss, 2010a,b; Czarna et al., 2016; Miao et al., 2016). They also tend to be happy and healthy (Sánchez-Álvarez et al., 2016; Sarrionandia & Mikolajczak, 2019). And they do somewhat better academically as well (MacCann et al., 2020). Aware of these benefits, school-based programs have sought to increase teachers' and students' emotional intelligence (Mahoney et al., 2020).

\* \* \*

For a summary of these theories of intelligence, see **Table 2.8-1**.

*"You're wise, but you lack tree smarts."*

**AP® Exam Tip**

Familiarize yourself with Table 2.8-1. Be able to compare and contrast the contributions of the intelligence theorists (Spearman; Cattell, Horn, and Carroll; Gardner; Sternberg).

**TABLE 2.8-1  Comparing Theories of Intelligence**

| Theory | Summary | Strengths | Other Considerations |
|---|---|---|---|
| *Spearman's general intelligence (g)* | A basic intelligence predicts our abilities in varied academic areas. | Different abilities, such as verbal and spatial, do have some tendency to correlate. | Human abilities are too diverse to be encapsulated by a single general intelligence factor. |
| *Cattell-Horn-Carroll (CHC) theory* | Our intelligence is based on a general ability factor as well as other specific abilities, bridged by crystallized and fluid intelligence. | Intelligence is composed of broad and narrow abilities, such as reading ability, memory capacity, and processing speed. | The specific abilities outlined by the CHC theory may be too narrowly cognitive. |
| *Gardner's multiple intelligences* | Our abilities are best classified into eight or nine independent intelligences, which include a broad range of skills beyond traditional school smarts. | Intelligence is more than just verbal and mathematical skills. Other abilities are equally important to our human adaptability. | Should all our abilities be considered *intelligences*? Shouldn't some be called less vital *talents*? |
| *Sternberg's triarchic theory* | Our intelligence is best classified into three areas that predict real-world success: analytical, creative, and practical. | These three domains can be reliably measured. | These three domains may be less independent than the theory suggests, and may actually share an underlying *g* factor. |
| *Emotional intelligence* | Social intelligence is an important indicator of life success. Emotional intelligence is a key aspect of it, consisting of perceiving, understanding, managing, and using emotions. | These four components predict social success and emotional well-being. | Does this stretch the concept of intelligence too far? |

## AP® Science Practice

## Check Your Understanding

### Examine the Concept

▶ Explain how the existence of savant syndrome supports Gardner's theory of multiple intelligences. What supports the concept of *g*?

▶ Explain how the Cattell-Horn-Carroll theory describes intelligence.

▶ Describe the four components of emotional intelligence.

### Apply the Concept

▶ The concept of multiple intelligences assumes that the analytical school smarts measured by traditional intelligence tests are important, but that other abilities are important as well. Different people have different gifts. What are yours?

▶ Compare and contrast Gardner's and Sternberg's theories of intelligence.

▶ Identify how each of the theories in Table 2.8-1 might be influenced by a person's culture.

*Answers to the Examine the Concept questions can be found in Appendix C at the end of the book.*

# Module 2.8a REVIEW

### 2.8-1 How do psychologists define *intelligence*?

- *Intelligence* is the ability to learn from experience, solve problems, and use knowledge to adapt to new situations.

### 2.8-2 What are the arguments for *general intelligence (g)*?

- Charles Spearman proposed that we have one *general intelligence (g)* underlying all mental abilities. Through his work with *factor analysis*, a statistical procedure that identifies clusters of related variables, he noted that those persons who score high in one area typically score higher than average in other areas.

- L. L. Thurstone disagreed and identified seven different clusters of mental abilities. Even so, high scorers in one cluster still tended to score high in other clusters, providing further evidence of a *g* factor.

### 2.8-3 How have the concepts of *Gf* and *Gc*, and the *CHC theory*, affected our understanding of intelligence?

- Raymond Cattell and John Horn formulated a theory of general ability based on two factors: *fluid intelligence (Gf)* and *crystallized intelligence (Gc)*.

- The *Cattell-Horn-Carroll (CHC) theory* affirms a general intellectual ability factor, but also identifies more specific abilities (such as reading and writing ability, memory capacity, and processing speed).

### 2.8-4 How do Gardner's and Sternberg's theories of multiple intelligences differ, and what criticisms have they faced?

- Howard Gardner proposed eight independent intelligences (linguistic, logical-mathematical, musical, spatial, bodily-kinesthetic, intrapersonal, interpersonal, and naturalist), as well as a possible ninth (existential intelligence). The different intelligences of people with *savant syndrome* and certain kinds of brain damage seem to support his view.

- Robert Sternberg's triarchic theory proposes three intelligence areas that contribute to life success: analytical (academic problem solving), creative (innovative smarts), and practical (required for everyday tasks).

- Critics note that research has confirmed the existence of a general intelligence factor, which widely predicts performance. Highly successful people also tend to be conscientious and doggedly energetic; their achievements arise from both ability *and* deliberate practice.

### 2.8-5 What are the four components of emotional intelligence?

- *Emotional intelligence*, which is an aspect of social intelligence, includes the abilities to perceive, understand, manage, and use emotions.

- Emotionally intelligent people tend to be happy, healthy, and more successful personally and professionally.

# AP® Practice Multiple Choice Questions

**1.** Gabrielle has a high capacity to learn, to think, and to adapt, allowing her to function effectively in her environment. What concept is illustrated here?

a. Grit
b. Savant syndrome
c. Intelligence
d. Emotional intelligence

**2.** Dr. Tsai created an intelligence test based on Sternberg's theory that asks a person to come up with solutions for arranging bowls and dishes in a small cabinet. Which type of intelligence is Dr. Tsai most likely testing?

a. Crystallized
b. Analytical
c. Creative
d. Practical

**3.** Brayden believes there are two forms of intelligence— (1) the ability to reason accurately and (2) one's learned knowledge. Which theory best aligns with Brayden's view?

a. Spearman's theory
b. Gardner's theory of multiple intelligences
c. Sternberg's triarchic theory
d. Cattell-Horn-Carroll theory

**4.** Which of the following statements accurately contrasts Spearman's theory of intelligence with the Cattell-Horn-Carroll theory of intelligence?

a. Spearman's theory proposes eight different types of intelligence, while Cattell-Horn-Carroll theory proposes two types of intelligence.
b. Spearman's theory proposes that a single general intelligence exists, while Cattell-Horn-Carroll theory proposes two additional broad forms of intelligence.
c. Spearman's theory proposes eight distinct types of intelligence, while Cattell-Horn-Carroll theory proposes two broad forms of intelligence.
d. Spearman's theory proposes that a single general intelligence exists, while Cattell-Horn-Carroll theory proposes that emotional intelligence exists.

**5.** Marcus solves reasoning problems quickly. What form of intelligence is he most strongly demonstrating?

a. Fluid intelligence
b. Emotional intelligence
c. Crystallized intelligence
d. Creative intelligence

# Module 2.8b Intelligence and Achievement: Assessing Intelligence

## LEARNING TARGETS

**2.8-6** Explain the characteristics of an *intelligence test,* and compare and contrast *achievement tests* and *aptitude tests.*

**2.8-7** Explain when and why intelligence tests were created, and how today's tests differ from early intelligence tests.

**2.8-8** Explain the elements of the *normal curve,* and explain *standardization, reliability,* and *validity.*

---

**intelligence test** a method for assessing an individual's mental aptitudes and comparing them with those of others, using numerical scores.

**achievement test** a test designed to assess what a person has learned.

**aptitude test** a test designed to predict a person's future performance; *aptitude* is the capacity to learn.

---

**2.8-6** What is an *intelligence test,* and how do *achievement tests* and *aptitude tests* differ?

An **intelligence test** assesses people's mental aptitudes and compares them with those of others, using numerical scores. How do psychologists design such tests, and what makes them credible?

By this point in your life, you've taken dozens of mental ability tests: school tests of basic reading and math skills, class quizzes and tests, intelligence tests, maybe a driver's license exam. These tests fall under two general categories:

- **Achievement tests,** which are intended to *reflect* what you have learned. The AP® exam will measure what you learned in this class.

- **Aptitude tests,** which are intended to *predict* what you will be able to learn. A college entrance exam, which is designed to predict your ability to do college or university work, is an aptitude test.

An aptitude test is a "thinly disguised intelligence test," says Howard Gardner (1999b). Indeed, according to Meredith Frey and Douglas Detterman (2004), total scores on the U.S. SAT had a +.82 correlation with general intelligence test scores in a national sample of 14- to 21-year-olds (**Figure 2.8-3**). Aptitude also supports achievement: People who learn quickly are also better at retaining information (Zerr et al., 2018).

Let's consider why psychologists have created and used such tests of mental abilities.

**Figure 2.8-3**

**Close cousins: aptitude and intelligence test scores**

A scatterplot shows the close correlation that has existed between intelligence test scores and verbal and quantitative SAT scores. (Data from Frey & Detterman, 2004.)

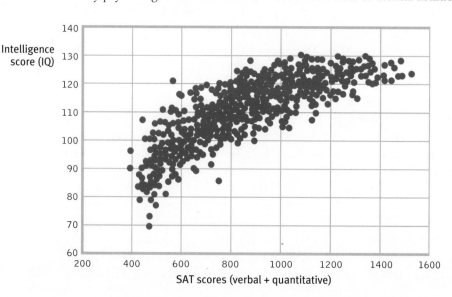

# Early and Modern Tests of Mental Abilities

**2.8-7** When and why were intelligence tests created, and how do today's tests differ from early intelligence tests?

Some cultures emphasize the collective welfare of the family, community, and society (*collectivism*). Other cultures focus on promoting individual opportunity (*individualism*). Plato, a pioneer of the individualist tradition, wrote more than 2000 years ago in *The Republic* that "no two persons are born exactly alike; but each differs from the other in natural endowments, one being suited for one occupation and the other for another." As heirs to Plato's individualism, people in Western societies have pondered how and why individuals differ in mental ability.

## Francis Galton: Presuming Hereditary Genius

Western attempts to assess such differences began in earnest with English scientist Francis Galton (1822–1911), who was fascinated with measuring human traits. When his cousin Charles Darwin proposed that nature selects successful traits through the survival of the fittest, Galton wondered if it might be possible to measure "natural ability." Galton founded *eugenics*—the discriminatory nineteenth- and twentieth-century movement that proposed measuring human traits and encouraging only those deemed "fit" to reproduce. At the 1884 London Health Exhibition, 10,000 visitors received his assessment of their "intellectual strengths" based on such things as reaction time, sensory acuity, muscular power, and body proportions. On these measures, well-regarded adults and students did not outscore others, nor did the measures correlate with each other. Yet Galton's beliefs about the inheritance of intelligence persisted, and were reflected in his book, *Hereditary Genius* (1869).

Galton's contributions include some statistical techniques that we still use, as well as the phrase *nature and nurture*. Yet his story illustrates an important lesson from both the history of intelligence research and the history of science: Although science itself strives for objectivity, individual scientists are affected by their own assumptions and attitudes.

## Alfred Binet: Predicting School Achievement

Modern intelligence testing traces its birth to early twentieth-century France, where a new law required all children to attend school. French officials knew that some children, including many newcomers to Paris, would need special classes. But how could the schools make fair judgments about children's learning potential? Teachers might assess children who had little prior education as slow learners. Or they might sort children into classes by their social backgrounds. To minimize such bias, France's minister of public education gave psychologist Alfred Binet the task of designing fair tests.

Binet and his student, Théodore Simon, began by assuming that all children follow the same course of intellectual development but that some develop more rapidly (Nicolas & Levine, 2012). A child with developmental disabilities should score much like a typical younger child, and an intellectually gifted child should score like a typical older child. Thus, their goal became measuring each child's **mental age**, the level of performance typically associated with a certain chronological age. The average 8-year-old, for example, has a mental age of 8. An 8-year-old with a below-average mental age (perhaps performing at the level of a typical 6-year-old) would struggle with age-appropriate schoolwork.

Binet and Simon tested a variety of reasoning and problem-solving questions on Binet's two daughters, and then on Parisian schoolchildren. Items answered correctly could then predict how well other French children would handle their schoolwork.

**mental age** a measure of intelligence test performance devised by Binet; the level of performance typically associated with children of a certain chronological age. Thus, a child who does as well as an average 8-year-old is said to have a mental age of 8.

**SPOTLIGHT ON:**
Francis Galton

**SPOTLIGHT ON:**
Alfred Binet

Macmillan Learning

**Alfred Binet (1857–1911)** "Some recent philosophers have given their moral approval to the deplorable verdict that an individual's intelligence is a fixed quantity, one which cannot be augmented. We must protest and act against this brutal pessimism" (Binet, 1909, p. 141).

Binet and Simon made no assumptions concerning why a particular child was slow, average, or precocious. Unlike Galton, Binet personally leaned toward an environmental explanation. To raise the capacities of low-scoring children, he recommended "mental orthopedics" that would help develop their attention span and self-discipline. He believed his intelligence test did not measure inborn intelligence as a scale measures weight. Rather, it had a single practical purpose: to identify French schoolchildren needing special attention. Binet hoped his test would be used to improve children's education, but he also feared it would be used to label children and limit their opportunities (Gould, 1981).

## Lewis Terman: Measuring Innate Intelligence

After Binet's death in 1911, others adapted his tests for use as a numerical measure of intelligence. Stanford University professor Lewis Terman (1877–1956) tried the Paris-developed questions and age norms with California kids. Adapting some of Binet's original items, adding others, and establishing new age norms, Terman extended the upper end of the test's range from age 12 to "superior adults." He also gave his revision the name today's version retains—the **Stanford-Binet**.

From such tests, German psychologist William Stern derived the famous **intelligence quotient (IQ)**. The IQ was simply a person's mental age divided by chronological age, multiplied by 100. Thus, the average 8-year-old child, whose mental age and chronological age match, has an IQ of 100. But an 8-year-old who answers questions at the level of a typical 10-year-old has an IQ of 125:

$$IQ = \frac{\text{mental age of } 10}{\text{chronological age of } 8} \times 100 = 125$$

**Stanford-Binet** the widely used American revision (by Terman at Stanford University) of Binet's original intelligence test.

**intelligence quotient (IQ)** defined originally as the ratio of mental age (*ma*) to chronological age (*ca*) multiplied by 100 (thus, IQ = *ma/ca* × 100). On contemporary intelligence tests, the average performance for a given age is assigned a score of 100.

THAT'S MY BOY, MARK... HE'S 39, BUT HE'S ALREADY READING AT A 42-YEAR-OLD LEVEL...

*Mrs. Randolph takes mother's pride too far.*

### CULTURAL AWARENESS

Eugenics is an example of how societies can apply science concepts in inappropriate and discriminatory ways. Even researchers can let their biases get the better of them if they are not careful.

This original IQ formula worked fairly well for children but not for adults. (Should a 40-year-old who does as well on the test as an average 20-year-old be assigned an IQ of only 50?) Most current intelligence tests, including the Stanford-Binet, no longer compute an IQ in this manner (though the term *IQ* still lingers in everyday vocabulary as shorthand for "intelligence test score"). Instead, they represent the test-taker's performance *relative to the average performance* (arbitrarily set at 100) of others the same age. Most people—about 68 percent of those taking an intelligence test—have scores that fall between 85 and 115.

Terman assumed that intelligence tests revealed a mental capacity present from birth. He supported Galton's eugenics—assuming that some ethnic groups were naturally more intelligent than others. With Terman's help, the U.S. government developed new tests to evaluate both newly arriving immigrants and World War I army recruits—the world's first mass administration of an intelligence test. To some psychologists, the results indicated the inferiority of people not sharing their Anglo-Saxon heritage. Such findings led to laws and practices that severely restricted immigration, as well as employment and educational opportunities, for those who were not of Northern or Western European descent.

Binet probably would have been horrified that his test had been adapted and used to draw such conclusions. Indeed, such sweeping judgments became an embarrassment to most of those who championed testing. Even Terman came to appreciate that test scores reflected not only people's innate mental abilities but also their education, native language, and familiarity with the culture assumed by the test. Abuses of the early intelligence tests serve to remind us that science can be value laden. Behind a screen of scientific objectivity, ideology may lurk.

## David Wechsler: Testing Separate Strengths

Psychologist David Wechsler created what is now the most widely used individual intelligence test, the **Wechsler Adult Intelligence Scale (WAIS)**. There is a version for school-age children (the *Wechsler Intelligence Scale for Children [WISC]*), and another for preschool children (Evers et al., 2012). The 2008 edition of the WAIS consists of 15 subtests, including:

- *Similarities*—reasoning the commonality of two objects or concepts ("In what way are wool and cotton alike?")

- *Vocabulary*—naming pictured objects, or defining words ("What is a guitar?")

- *Block design*—visual abstract processing ("Using the four blocks, make one just like this.")

- *Letter-number sequencing*—on hearing a series of numbers and letters ("R-2-C-1-M-3"), repeating the numbers in ascending order, and then the letters in alphabetical order.

The WAIS yields both an overall intelligence score and separate scores for verbal comprehension, perceptual reasoning, working memory, and processing speed. In such ways, this test helps realize Binet's aim: to identify those who could benefit from special educational opportunities for improvement.

**Matching patterns** Block-design puzzles test visual abstract processing ability. Wechsler's individually administered intelligence test comes in forms suited for adults and children.

---

**AP® Science Practice**

## Check Your Understanding

### Examine the Concept

▶ Explain what Binet hoped to achieve by establishing a child's mental age.

▶ What is the IQ score of a 4-year-old with a mental age of 5?

### Apply the Concept

▶ An employer with a pool of applicants for a single available position is interested in testing each applicant's potential. To determine that, she should use an _____ (achievement/aptitude) test. That same employer, wishing to test the effectiveness of a new on-the-job training program would be wise to use an _____ (achievement/aptitude) test.

▶ What achievement or aptitude tests have you taken? In your opinion, how well did these tests assess what you had learned or predict what you were capable of learning?

*Answers to the Examine the Concept questions can be found in Appendix C at the end of the book.*

---

# Three Tests of a "Good" Test

**2.8-8** What is a *normal curve*, and what does it mean to say that a test has been *standardized* and is *reliable* and *valid*?

To be widely accepted, a psychological test must have the **psychometric** properties of being *standardized, reliable,* and *valid*. The Stanford-Binet and Wechsler tests meet these requirements.

## Was the Test Standardized?

To know how well you performed on an intelligence test, you would need some basis for comparison. That's why test-makers give new tests to a representative sample of people. The scores from this pretested group become the basis for future comparisons. If you then take the test following the same procedures, your score, when compared with others, will be meaningful. This process is called **standardization**.

**Wechsler Adult Intelligence Scale (WAIS)** the WAIS and its companion versions for children are the most widely used intelligence tests; they contain verbal and performance (nonverbal) subtests.

**psychometrics** the scientific study of the measurement of human abilities, attitudes, and traits.

**standardization** defining uniform testing procedures and meaningful scores by comparison with the performance of a pretested group.

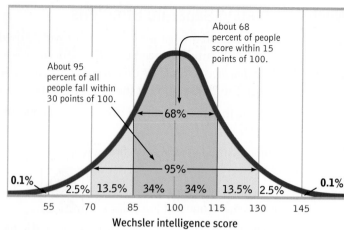

**Figure 2.8-4**

**The normal curve**

Scores on aptitude tests tend to form a normal, or bell-shaped, curve around an average score. For the Wechsler scale, for example, the average score is 100.

 **AP® Science Practice**

**Data**

In the graph in Figure 2.8-4 (which is also included in Module 0.6), intelligence tests are being used to illustrate that 68 percent of a population will be within one standard deviation (a computed measure of how much scores vary around the mean score) of the mean for normally distributed data. Ninety-five percent will be within two standard deviations. This would be a great time to review standard deviation in Module 0.6.

 **AP® Science Practice**

**Data**

In statistical terms, the arithmetic "average" (the total sum of all the scores divided by the number of scores) is referred to as the mean. The mean, along with the mode and the median, are measures of central tendency.

**normal curve** the bell-shaped curve that describes the distribution of many physical and psychological attributes. Most scores fall near the average, and fewer and fewer scores lie near the extremes.

**Flynn effect** the rise in intelligence test performance over time and across cultures.

If we construct a graph of test-takers' scores, the scores typically form a bell-shaped pattern called the *bell curve* or **normal curve**. For many human attributes—height, weight, mental aptitude—the curve's highest point is the average score. On an intelligence test, we give this average score a value of 100 (**Figure 2.8-4**). Moving out from the average, toward either extreme, we find fewer and fewer people. For both the Stanford-Binet and Wechsler tests, a person's score indicates whether that person's performance fell above or below the average. A score of 130 would indicate that only 2.5 percent of test-takers performed better. About 95 percent of all people score within 30 points of 100.

To keep the average score near 100, the Stanford-Binet and Wechsler scales are periodically restandardized. If you recently took the WAIS, Fourth Edition, your performance was compared with that of the standardization sample who took the test in 2007, not with David Wechsler's initial 1930s sample. If you compared the performance of the most recent standardization sample with that of the 1930s sample, do you suppose you would find rising or declining test performance? Amazingly—given that college entrance aptitude scores have sometimes dropped, such as during the 1960s and 1970s—intelligence test performance has improved. This worldwide phenomenon is called the **Flynn effect**, in honor of New Zealand researcher James Flynn (1987, 2012, 2018), who first calculated its magnitude. Flynn observed that the average person's intelligence test score rose three points per decade. Thus, an average person in 1920 would—by today's standard—score only a 76! Such rising performance has been observed in 49 countries, from Sweden to Sudan (Dutton et al., 2018; Wongupparaj et al., 2015). Countries that have shown the greatest growth in IQ score over time have also experienced more economic growth (Rindermann & Becker, 2018). Although some regional reversals have occurred—often related to poverty, discrimination, and educational inequities—the historic increase is now widely accepted as an important phenomenon (Lynn, 2009; Teasdale & Owen, 2008).

The Flynn effect's cause has been a psychological mystery. Did it result from greater test sophistication? *No.* Gains appeared before testing was widespread. Perhaps better nutrition? Thanks to improved nutrition, people have gotten taller as well as smarter. But in postwar Britain, notes Flynn (2009), the lower-class children gained the most from improved nutrition, yet the intelligence performance gains were greater among upper-class children. Might the explanation be greater educational opportunities, smaller families, and rising living standards, such as better health care (Pietschnig & Voracek, 2015; Rindermann et al., 2016)? For example, children around the world now have access to educational programs such as *Sesame Street* that increase their intellectual performance and reduce their prejudice toward children from different ethnic backgrounds (Kwauk et al., 2016). Flynn (2012) attributes the IQ score increases to our need to develop new mental skills to cope with modern environments. Regardless of which combination of factors explains the rise in intelligence test scores, this phenomenon counters a concern of some who see intelligence as inherited—namely, that the higher twentieth-century birthrates among those with lower scores would shift human intelligence scores downward (Lynn & Harvey, 2008).

## Is the Test Reliable?

Knowing where you stand in comparison to a standardization group still won't say much about your intelligence unless the test has **reliability**. A reliable test, when retaken, gives consistent scores. To check a test's reliability, researchers test people many times. They may split the test in half (*split-half*: agreement of odd-numbered question scores and even-numbered question scores), test with alternative forms of the test, or retest with the same test (*test-retest*). The higher the *correlation* between the two scores, the higher the test's reliability is. The tests we have considered—the Stanford-Binet, the WAIS, and the WISC—are very reliable after early childhood (with *correlation coefficients* of about +.9). In retests, sometimes performed decades later, people's scores are generally similar to their first score (Deary et al., 2009b; Lyons et al., 2017).

## Is the Test Valid?

High reliability does not ensure a test's **validity**—the extent to which the test actually measures or predicts what it promises. Imagine using a tape measure with faulty markings. If you use it to measure people's heights, your results will be very reliable. No matter how many times you measure, people's heights will be the same. But your faulty height results will not be valid.

Tests that tap into the pertinent behavior, or *criterion*, have **content validity**. The road test for a driver's license has content validity because it samples the tasks a driver routinely faces. Tests that measure a certain concept have **construct validity**. The test for self-esteem has construct validity because people answer questions about their self-feelings. But we expect intelligence tests to have **predictive validity**: They should predict future performance, and to some extent they do. SAT aptitude scores correlate about +.8 with those for the Graduate Record Examination (GRE; an aptitude test similar to the SAT but intended for those applying to graduate school) (Wai et al., 2018).

Are general aptitude tests as predictive as they are reliable? *No.* Aptitude test scores do predict school grades (Roth et al., 2015). But as critics are fond of noting, the predictive power of aptitude tests peaks in the early school years and weakens later. Academic aptitude test scores are reasonably good predictors of school achievement for children ages 6 to 12, for whom the correlation between intelligence score and school performance is about +.6 (Jensen, 1980). Intelligence scores correlate even more closely with scores on later achievement tests: +.81 in one comparison of 70,000 English children's intelligence scores at age 11 with their academic achievement in national exams at age 16 (Deary et al., 2007, 2009b). The SAT, used in the United States as a college entrance exam, has been less successful in predicting first-year college grades (although the correlation, less than +.5, has been a bit higher when adjusting for high scorers electing tougher courses [Berry & Sackett, 2009; Willingham et al., 1990]). By the time we get to the GRE, the correlation with graduate school performance is an even more modest but still significant +.4 (Kuncel & Hezlett, 2007).

Why does the predictive power of aptitude scores diminish as students move up the educational ladder? Consider a parallel situation: Among all American and Canadian football linemen, body weight correlates with success. A 300-pound player tends to overwhelm a 200-pound opponent. But within the narrow 280- to 320-pound range typically found at the professional level, the correlation between weight and

**AP® Science Practice**

## Data

There are several correlation coefficients presented here. Can you interpret them? Does .+81 indicate a strong or weak relationship between the variables? What direction is the relationship between the variables? You can review this important information in Module 0.4.

**reliability** the extent to which a test yields consistent results, as assessed by the consistency of scores on two halves of the test, on alternative forms of the test, or on retesting.

**validity** the extent to which a test measures or predicts what it is supposed to. (See also *predictive validity*.)

**content validity** the extent to which a test samples the behavior that is of interest.

**construct validity** how much a test measures a concept or trait.

**predictive validity** the success with which a test predicts the behavior it is designed to predict; it is assessed by computing the correlation between test scores and the criterion behavior. (Also called *criterion-related validity*.)

success becomes negligible (**Figure 2.8-5**). The narrower the *range* of weights, the lower the predictive power of body weight becomes. If an elite university takes only those students who have very high aptitude scores, and then gives them a restricted range of high grades, those scores cannot possibly predict much. This will be true even if the test has excellent predictive validity with a more diverse sample of students. Likewise, modern grade inflation has produced less diverse high school grades. With their diminished range, high school grades now predict college grades no better than the SAT scores have (Sackett et al., 2012). So, when we validate a measure using a wide range of scores but then use it with a restricted range of scores, it loses much of its predictive validity.

**Figure 2.8-5**
**Diminishing predictive power**

Let's imagine a correlation between football linemen's body weight and their success on the field. Note how insignificant the relationship becomes when we narrow the range of weight to 280 to 320 pounds. As the range of data under consideration narrows, its predictive power diminishes.

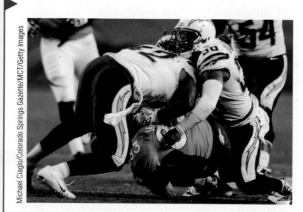

Michael Ciaglo/Colorado Springs Gazette/MCT/Getty Images

---

AP® Science Practice

## Check Your Understanding

### Examine the Concept

▶ Explain the three criteria that a psychological test must meet to be widely accepted.

▶ Compare and contrast content validity and predictive validity.

### Apply the Concept

▶ Are you working to the potential reflected in your standardized test scores? Which factors, other than your aptitude, are affecting your school performance?

*Answers to the Examine the Concept questions can be found in Appendix C at the end of the book.*

---

# Module 2.8b REVIEW

**2.8-6** What is an *intelligence test*, and how do *achievement tests* and *aptitude tests* differ?

● An *intelligence test* assesses an individual's mental aptitudes and compares them with those of other people, using numerical scores.

● *Aptitude tests* measure the ability to learn, while *achievement tests* measure what has already been learned.

**2.8-7** When and why were intelligence tests created, and how do today's tests differ from early intelligence tests?

● Francis Galton, who was fascinated with measuring what he believed to be hereditary genius (so that those

individuals with exceptional abilities might be encouraged to reproduce), attempted but failed to construct a simple intelligence test in the late 1800s.

● Alfred Binet, who tended toward an environmental explanation of intelligence differences, started the modern intelligence-testing movement in France in the early 1900s by developing questions to help predict children's future progress in the Paris school system. Binet hoped his test, which measured children's *mental age*, would improve their education, but he feared it might also be used to label children.

● During the early twentieth century, Lewis Terman of Stanford University revised Binet's work for use in the United States. Terman thought his *Stanford-Binet* could help guide people toward appropriate opportunities, but his belief that intelligence was fixed at birth and differed among ethnic groups realized Binet's fear that intelligence tests would be used to limit children's opportunities.

- William Stern contributed the concept of the intelligence quotient (IQ).

- The most widely used intelligence tests today are the *Wechsler Adult Intelligence Scale (WAIS)* and Wechsler's tests for children. These tests differ from their predecessors by offering an overall intelligence score as well as scores for verbal comprehension, perceptual reasoning, working memory, and processing speed.

> **2.8-8** What is a *normal curve*, and what does it mean to say that a test has been *standardized* and is *reliable* and *valid?*

- The distribution of test scores often forms a *normal* (bell-shaped) *curve* around the central average score, with fewer and fewer scores at the extremes.

- *Standardization* establishes a basis for meaningful score comparisons by giving a test to a representative sample of future test-takers.

- *Reliability* is the extent to which a test yields consistent results (on two halves of the test, on alternative forms of the test, or on retesting).

- *Validity* is the extent to which a test measures or predicts what it is supposed to.
  - A test has *content validity* if it samples the pertinent behavior (for example, a driving test measures driving ability).
  - A test has *construct validity* if it measures a concept or trait (for example, self-esteem).
  - It has *predictive validity* if it predicts the behavior it was designed to predict. (Aptitude tests have predictive ability if they can predict future achievements.)

# AP® Practice Multiple Choice Questions

1. Test developers often define uniform testing procedures and meaningful scores by comparing individuals' scores with the performance of a pretested group. Which of the following best describes this process?

   a. Reliability testing
   b. Validation
   c. Content validation
   d. Standardization

2. Which of the following is the best example of an aptitude test?

   a. Atul answers questions about safe driving.
   b. Mr. Anderson's AP® psychology test covers the material from the current unit.
   c. Sherjeel takes the ACT to gain college admission.
   d. Jeffrey is required to translate 50 Mandarin sentences for his final exam.

3. Dr. Asimov's new intelligence test yields consistent results upon retesting, so it has a high degree of

   a. reliability.
   b. standardization.
   c. construct validity.
   d. predictive validity.

4. Mr. Gaiman shows his class the visual and statistical representation of the distribution of scores around the mean on an intelligence test. What did Mr. Gaiman show his class?

   a. The test's reliability
   b. The test's predictive validity
   c. A test-retest procedure
   d. The normal curve

5. Ms. Skipworth gave her algebra class a quiz on some of the material they learned last week. What type of test did Ms. Skipworth give?

   a. Intelligence test
   b. Aptitude test
   c. Achievement test
   d. Psychometric test

6. The SAT has a +.82 correlation with general intelligence test scores. Based on this information, which statement is most accurate?

   a. As SAT scores increase, so do general intelligence test scores.
   b. As SAT scores decrease, general intelligence scores increase.
   c. The relationship between SAT scores and general intelligence is positive but small.
   d. There is no discernible relationship between SAT scores and general intelligence.

**7.** To assess the reliability of his Spanish test, Mr. Russell gives his classes the test, then gives them the same test a week later. Which technique is Mr. Russell using?

   a. Split-half
   b. Flynn effect
   c. Test-retest
   d. Standardization

**8.** To accurately define the Flynn effect, which of the following should Declan say in his presentation?

   a. A bell-shaped curve depicts the distribution of intelligence.
   b. There is a rise in intelligence test performance over time and across cultures.
   c. Uniform testing procedures should be used for all intelligence tests.
   d. Tests are intended to predict what one will be able to achieve over time.

# Module 2.8c Intelligence and Achievement: Stability of, and Influences on, Intelligence

**LEARNING TARGETS**

**2.8-9** Explain the stability of intelligence test scores over the lifespan.

**2.8-10** Explain how aging affects crystallized intelligence (*Gc*) and fluid intelligence (*Gf*).

**2.8-11** Explain what twin and adoption studies tell us about the nature and nurture of intelligence.

**2.8-12** Explain how environmental influences affect cognitive development.

Researchers are exploring some age-old questions about human intelligence. How stable is a person's intelligence over time? How—and how much—is intelligence influenced by our genetic nature and by our environmental nurture?

## Intelligence Across the Lifespan

What happens to our intellectual muscles as we age? Do they gradually decline, as does our body strength? Or do they remain constant? To see how psychologists have studied intelligence across the lifespan—and for an illustration of psychology's self-correcting process—see Developing Arguments: Cross-Sectional and Longitudinal Studies.

**AP® Science Practice**

# Developing Arguments

## Cross-Sectional and Longitudinal Studies

Researchers using the **cross-sectional** method study different age groups at one time. They have found that *mental ability declines with age.*[1]

Comparing 70-year-olds and 30-year-olds means not only comparing two different people but also two different eras. These researchers were comparing:

 • generally less-educated people (born in the early 1900s) with better-educated people (born after 1950).

 • people raised in large families with people raised in smaller families.

 • people from less-affluent families with people from more-affluent families.

Researchers using the **longitudinal** method study and restudy the same group at different times in their lifespan. They have found that *intelligence remains stable, and on some tests it even increases.*[2]

1950

1985

present

But these studies have their own issue. Participants who survive to the end of these studies may be the healthiest and brightest people. When researchers statistically adjust for the loss of less intelligent participants, intelligence does appear to decline somewhat in later life, especially after age 85.[3]

## Developing Arguments Questions

**1.** Compare and contrast the cross-sectional and longitudinal designs used here.

**2.** The results differed when the researchers used a cross-sectional versus a longitudinal design. Explain why the results were different with each design.

**3.** Suppose a doctor tells an aging patient, "Don't worry, your intelligence will likely remain stable as you get older." Explain how this claim is supported, or not, using the evidence presented here.

1. Wechsler, 1972. 2. Salthouse, 2010, 2014; Schaie & Geiwitz, 1982. 3. Brayne et al., 1999.

## Stability or Change?

### 2.8-9 How stable are intelligence test scores over the lifespan?

What can we predict from a child's early-life intelligence scores? Will a precocious 2-year-old mature into a talented college student and a brilliant senior citizen? Maybe—or maybe not. For most children, intelligence assessments before age 3 only modestly predict future aptitudes (Humphreys & Davey, 1988; Tasbihsazan et al., 2003; Yu et al., 2018a). Some precocious preschoolers become brilliant adults, but even Albert Einstein was once thought "slow"—as he was in learning to talk (Quasha, 1980).

**cross-sectional study** research that compares people of different ages at the same point in time.

**longitudinal study** research that follows and retests the same people over time.

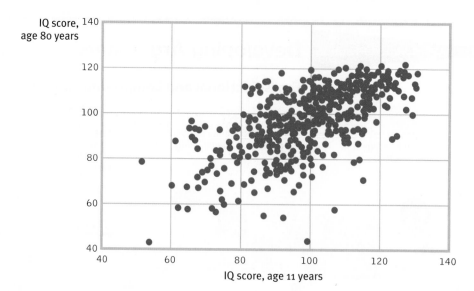

IQ score, age 80 years

IQ score, age 11 years

**AP® Science Practice**

## Research

Testing the same cohort over time is the hallmark of a longitudinal study.

**AP® Science Practice**

## Research

Are the data in Figure 2.8-6 from a correlational or experimental study? If you said correlational, you are correct! The researchers examined the relationship between two variables — IQ scores at age 11, and IQ scores for the same cohort at age 80. Use the graphs throughout this book to practice your data interpretation skills.

By age 4, however, children's performance on intelligence tests begins to predict their adolescent and adult scores. The consistency of scores over time increases with the age of the child (Tucker-Drob & Briley, 2014). By age 11, the stability becomes impressive, as Ian Deary and his colleagues (2004, 2009b, 2013) discovered when they retested the same **cohort**—the same group of people—over many years. Their amazing longitudinal studies have been enabled by their country, Scotland, doing something no nation has done before or since. On June 1, 1932, essentially every child in the country born in 1921—87,498 children around age 11—took an intelligence test. The aim was to identify working-class children who would benefit from further education. Sixty-five years later to the day, Patricia Whalley, the wife of Deary's co-worker, Lawrence Whalley, discovered the test results on dusty storeroom shelves at the Scottish Council for Research in Education, not far from Deary's Edinburgh University office. "This will change our lives," Deary replied when Whalley told him the news.

Since then, Deary has completed dozens of studies of the stability and the predictive capacity of those early test results. One of Deary's studies, for example, retested 542 survivors from the 1932 test group at age 80. The correlation between the two sets of scores—after nearly 70 years of varied life experiences—was striking (**Figure 2.8-6**). Ditto when 106 survivors were retested at age 90 (Deary et al., 2013). Another study that followed Scots born in 1936 from ages 11 to 70 confirmed the remarkable stability of intelligence, independent of life circumstance (Johnson et al., 2010).

Children and adults who are more intelligent tend to live healthier and longer lives (Cadar et al., 2020; Geary, 2019). As Deary (2005) has found, "Whether you live to collect your old-age pension depends in part on your IQ at age 11." High-scoring adolescents, 50 years

**The stability of intelligence** At age 4, James Holzhauer was featured in a *Chicago Tribune* article about his math ability. By age 7, he was in the fifth grade (Jacobs, 2019). At age 34, he won 32 consecutive appearances on the quiz show *Jeopardy!*

later, even *feel* younger than their age (Stephan et al., 2018). Why might this intelligence-health link exist? Deary (2008) has proposed four possible explanations:

1. Intelligence facilitates more education, better jobs, and a healthier environment.

2. Intelligence encourages healthy living: less smoking, better diet, more exercise.

3. Prenatal events or early childhood illnesses can influence both intelligence and health.

4. A "well-wired body," as evidenced by fast reaction speeds, perhaps fosters both intelligence and longevity.

**cohort** a group of people sharing a common characteristic, such as being from a given time period.

# Aging and Intelligence

**2.8-10** How does aging affect crystallized intelligence (*Gc*) and fluid intelligence (*Gf*)?

It matters which questions psychological scientists ask, but sometimes it matters even more *how* they ask them—the research methods they use. Cross-sectional studies had shown that older adults gave fewer correct answers on intelligence tests than did younger adults. These findings caused WAIS-creator David Wechsler (1972) to conclude that "the decline of mental ability with age is part of the general [aging] process of the organism as a whole." For a long time, this rather dismal view went unchallenged. Many corporations established mandatory retirement policies, assuming the companies would benefit from replacing aging workers with younger, more capable employees. As "everyone knows," you can't teach an old dog new tricks.

But thanks to colleges in the 1920s giving intelligence tests to entering students, psychologists years later were able to use longitudinal studies to retest the same cohorts over a period of years. They discovered that intelligence remained stable. On some tests, scores even increased, due partly to experience with the tests (Salthouse, 2014) **(Figure 2.8-7)**. Methods matter.

The more optimistic results from longitudinal studies challenged the presumption that intelligence sharply declines with age. Famed painter Anna Mary Robertson Moses ("Grandma Moses") took up painting in her seventies, and at age 88 a popular magazine named her "Young Woman of the Year." At age 89, architect Frank Lloyd Wright designed New York City's Guggenheim Museum. At age 101, neuropsychologist Brenda Milner was still conducting research and supervising students. As everyone knows, given good health, you're never too old to learn.

So the answers to our age-and-intelligence questions depend on what we assess and how we assess it. For most people, aging leads to both losses and wins. We simultaneously lose recall memory and processing speed, but gain vocabulary and knowledge (Ackerman, 2014; Tucker-Drob et al., 2019) **(Figure 2.8-8)**. *Crystallized intelligence (Gc)*—our accumulated knowledge as

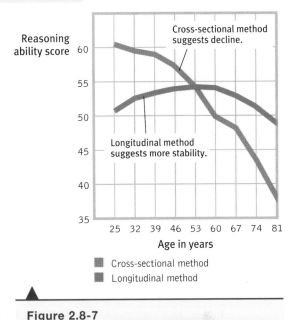

**Figure 2.8-7**

**Cross-sectional versus longitudinal testing of intelligence at various ages**

In this test of one type of verbal intelligence (reasoning ability), the cross-sectional method showed declining scores with age. The longitudinal method (in which the same people were retested over a period of years) showed a slight rise in scores well into adulthood. (Data from Schaie, 1994.)

Joe Raedle/Getty Images

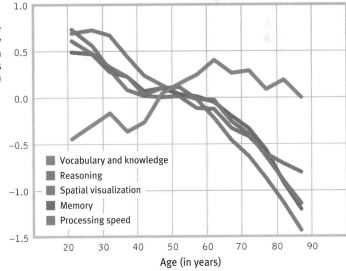

**Figure 2.8-8**

**With age, we lose and we win**

When Joe Biden assumed the U.S. presidency at age 78, many wondered: Would he have the mental agility to be entrusted with the cognitive demands of national and world leadership? With age comes diminishing physical capabilities and a lessening ability to think speedily (fluid intelligence). But later life also offers an accumulation of applicable knowledge (crystallized intelligence) along with an enhanced wisdom that enables older adults to navigate conflicts, to respond with emotional composure, and to appreciate the limits of their knowledge. "In youth we learn, in age we understand," observed the nineteenth-century novelist Marie Von Ebner-Eschenbach.

AP® Science Practice

## Data

The graph in Figure 2.8-8 includes three variables: age (on the *x*-axis), cognitive performance (on the *y*-axis), and type of cognitive ability (as indicated by the color of the lines). Being able to understand graphs is an important skill that grows with practice.

*"We're looking for someone with the wisdom of a 50-year-old, the experience of a 40-year-old, the drive of a 30-year-old, and the payscale of a 20-year-old."*

reflected in vocabulary and analogies tests—can increase up to old age. *Fluid intelligence (Gf)*—our ability to reason speedily and abstractly, as when solving novel logic problems—may decline, but older adults' social reasoning skills increase, as shown by their ability to take multiple perspectives, to appreciate knowledge limits, and to offer helpful wisdom in times of social conflict (Grossman et al., 2010). Decisions also become less distorted by negative emotions such as anxiety, depression, and anger (Blanchard-Fields, 2007; Carstensen & Mikels, 2005).

These lifespan differences in mental abilities help explain why older adults are less likely to embrace new technologies and have more difficulty detecting lies (Brashier & Schacter, 2020; Charness & Boot, 2009; Pew, 2017). The cognitive differences also help explain why mathematicians and scientists produce much of their most creative work, and chess players their best performance, during the late twenties or early thirties, when *Gf* is at its peak (Jones et al., 2014; Strittmatter et al., 2020). In contrast, authors, historians, and philosophers tend to produce their best work in their forties, fifties, and beyond—after building their *Gc*, or accumulated knowledge (Simonton, 1988, 1990).

---

AP® Science Practice

## Check Your Understanding

**Examine the Concept**

▶ Explain the changes in crystallized and fluid intelligence over the lifespan.

**Apply the Concept**

▶ Researcher A wants to study how intelligence changes over the lifespan. Researcher B wants to study the intelligence of people who are now at various life stages. Which researcher should use the cross-sectional method, and which should use the longitudinal method?

*Answers to the Examine the Concept questions can be found in Appendix C at the end of the book.*

---

# Genetic and Environmental Influences on Intelligence

Intelligence runs in families. But why? Are our intellectual abilities mostly inherited? Or are they molded by our environment?

## Heredity and Intelligence

**2.8-11** What do twin and adoption studies tell us about the nature and nurture of intelligence?

*Heritability* is the portion of variation among individuals in a group that we can attribute to genes. Estimates of the heritability of intelligence—the extent to which intelligence test score variation within a group can be attributed to genetic variation—range from 50 percent to 80 percent (Madison et al., 2016; Plomin et al., 2016; Plomin & von Stumm, 2018). Does this mean that we can assume that 50 to 80 percent of *your* intelligence is due to your genes, and the rest to your environment? *No*, it means that genetic influence explains between 50 and 80 percent of the observed *variation among people*. We can never say what percentage of an *individual's* intelligence (or personality) is inherited. It makes no sense to say that your intelligence is due *x* percent to your heredity and *y* percent to your environment. This point is so often misunderstood that we repeat: Heritability refers to *why people in a group differ from one another*—to how much their differences are attributable to their differing genes.

The heritability of traits such as intelligence varies from study to study. Consider humorist Mark Twain's (1835–1910) fictional idea of raising boys in barrels to age 12, feeding them through a hole. If we were to follow his suggestion, the boys would all emerge with lower-than-normal intelligence scores at age 12. Yet given their equal environments, their test score differences could be explained only by their heredity. With the same environment, heritability—differences due to genes—would be near 100 percent.

As environments become more similar, heredity becomes the primary source of differences. If all schools were of uniform quality, all families equally loving, and all neighborhoods equally healthy, then heritability would *increase* (because differences due to environment would *decrease*). But consider the other extreme: If all people had similar heredities but were raised in drastically different environments (some in barrels, some in luxury homes), heritability would be much lower. So, heritability is not a single fixed score. Heritability varies with changing environments.

Identical twins share the same genes, so do they also share mental abilities? As you can see from **Figure 2.8-9**, which summarizes many studies, the answer is clearly *Yes*. Even when adopted by two different families, their intelligence test scores are very similar. When raised together, their scores are nearly as similar as those of the same person taking the same test twice (Haworth et al., 2009; Lykken, 2006; Plomin et al., 2016). Identical twins also exhibit substantial similarity (and heritability) in specific talents, such as music, math, and sports.

Although genes matter, there is no known "genius" gene. When 100 researchers pooled their data on 269,867 people, all of the gene variations analyzed accounted for only about 5 percent of the differences in educational achievement (Savage et al., 2018). Another analysis of genes from 1.1 million people accounted for about 12 percent of their educational attainment differences (Lee et al., 2018). The search continues. Like height, which is predicted by nearly 10,000 known DNA sequences, intelligence is *polygenetic*, involving many genes (Johnson, 2010; Kaiser, 2020). More than 50 specific gene variations together account for 5 percent of our individual height differences, leaving the rest yet to be discovered. What matters for intelligence (as for height, personality, sexual orientation, schizophrenia, or just about any human trait) is the combination of many genes (Sniekers et al., 2017).

**AP® Science Practice**

### Data

Figure 2.8-9 is a histogram, a bar graph depicting a frequency distribution. Can you explain what it shows? Identical twins raised together are much more similar in intelligence scores than unrelated individuals raised together.

**Figure 2.8-9**

**Intelligence: nature and nurture**

The most genetically similar people have the most similar intelligence scores. Remember: 1.00 indicates a perfect correlation; zero indicates no correlation at all. (Data from McGue et al., 1993.)

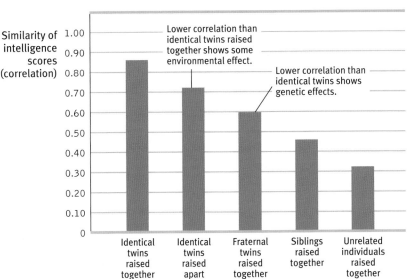

## Environment and Intelligence

Fraternal twins are genetically no more alike than other siblings, but they usually share an environment and are often treated similarly. Their intelligence test scores are also more alike than are the scores of nontwin siblings (see Figure 2.8-9). So, environment does have some effect. Adoption studies help us assess the influence of environment. Seeking to untangle genes and environment, researchers have compared the intelligence test scores of adopted children with those of (a) their *biological parents*, who provided their genes; (b) *adoptive parents*, who provided their home environment; and (c) *adoptive siblings*, who shared that home environment.

Several studies suggest that a shared environment exerts a modest influence on intelligence test scores:

- Adoption from poverty into financially secure homes enhances children's intelligence test scores (Nisbett et al., 2012). One large Swedish study looked at this effect among children adopted into wealthier families with more educated parents. The adopted children's IQ scores were higher, by an average of 4.4 points, than those of their not-adopted biological siblings (Kendler et al., 2015a).

- Adoption of mistreated or neglected children enhances their intelligence scores (Almas et al., 2017).

- The intelligence scores of "virtual twins"—same-age, unrelated children adopted as infants and raised together as siblings—correlate positively: +.28 (Segal et al., 2012).

During childhood, adoptive siblings' test scores correlate modestly. What do you think happens as the years go by and adopted children settle in with their adoptive families? Would you expect the shared-environment effect to grow stronger and the genetic-legacy effect to shrink?

If you said *Yes*, behavior geneticists have a stunning surprise for you. Adopted children's intelligence test scores resemble those of their biological parents much more than those of their adoptive families (Loehlin, 2016). And over time, adopted children's verbal ability scores become *even more* like those of their biological parents (**Figure 2.8-10**). Mental ability similarities between adopted children and their adoptive families wane with age (McGue et al., 1993). Who would have guessed?

Genetic influences become more apparent as we accumulate life experience. Identical twins' similarities, for example, continue or increase into their eighties. In one massive study of 11,000 twin pairs in four countries, the heritability of general intelligence (*g*) increased from 41 percent in middle childhood to 55 percent in adolescence to 66 percent in young adulthood (Haworth et al., 2010). Thus, report Ian Deary and his colleagues (2009a, 2012),

*"Selective breeding has given me an aptitude for the law, but I still love fetching a dead duck out of freezing water."*

Leo Cullum/The New Yorker Collection/The Cartoon Bank

**Figure 2.8-10**

**In terms of their verbal ability, whom do adopted children resemble?**

As the years went by in their adoptive families, children's verbal ability scores became more like their *biological* parents' scores. (Data from Plomin & DeFries, 1998.)

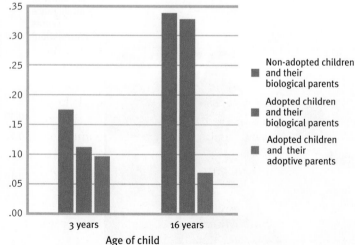

Child–parent correlation in verbal ability scores

- Non-adopted children and their biological parents
- Adopted children and their biological parents
- Adopted children and their adoptive parents

Age of child

the heritability of general intelligence increases from "about 30 percent" in early childhood to "well over 50 percent in adulthood."

## Gene–Environment Interactions

**2.8-12** How can environmental influences affect cognitive development?

Genes and experience together weave the fabric of intelligence. *Epigenetics* studies part of the dynamic biology of this nature–nurture meeting place. With all our abilities—whether mental or physical—*our genes shape the experiences that shape us*. If you have a natural aptitude for dance, you will probably perform more often than others (getting more practice, instruction, and experience). Or, if you have a natural aptitude for academics, you will more likely stay in school, read books, and ask questions—all of which will increase your brain power. The same would be true for your identical twin—who might, not just for genetic reasons, also become a star performer. In these gene–environment interactions, small genetic advantages can trigger social experiences that multiply our original skills (Cheesman et al., 2020; Sauce & Matzel, 2018).

Sometimes, however, environmental conditions work in reverse, depressing physical or cognitive development. Severe deprivation leaves footprints on the brain, as J. McVicker Hunt (1982) observed in a destitute Iranian orphanage. The typical child whom Hunt observed there could not sit up unassisted at age 2 or walk at age 4. The minimal care that infants received was not in response to their crying, cooing, or other behaviors, so the children developed little sense of personal control over their environment. Extreme deprivation had crushed their native intelligence—a finding confirmed by other studies of children raised in poorly run orphanages in Romania and elsewhere (Nelson et al., 2009, 2013; van IJzendoorn et al., 2008).

Aware of both the dramatic effects of early experiences and the impact of early intervention, Hunt began a training program for Iranian caregivers, teaching them to play language-fostering games with 11 infants. They imitated the babies' babbling. They engaged them in vocal follow-the-leader. And, finally, they taught the infants sounds from the Persian language. The results were dramatic. By 22 months of age, the infants could name more than 50 objects and body parts. They so charmed visitors that most were adopted—an unprecedented success for the orphanage.

Hunt's findings are an extreme case of a more general finding: The poor environmental conditions that accompany poverty can depress cognitive development and produce stresses that impede cognitive performance (Heberle & Carter, 2015; Tuerk, 2005). The environment's influence was strikingly apparent after psychologist Harold Skeels in 1934 did an IQ assessment of two toddler girls at an Iowa orphanage, where they were "scarcely touched, never held, rarely spoken to" (Brookwood, 2021). When an overcrowded facility for the "feebleminded" could not accept them, he placed the two toddlers in an institution that housed adult women with mental ages of only 5 to 9 years. The women lavished their new foster children with affection. When Skeels returned nine months later, he was amazed to find the girls "alert, attractive, [and] playful—and after more than two years with their new caregivers, with IQs of 95 and 93. By their late 20s, both were married and with children in loving households." Nurture matters.

If extreme conditions—sensory deprivation, social isolation, poverty—can slow normal brain development, could the reverse also be true? Could an "enriched" environment amplify normal development and give very young children a superior intellect? Most experts doubt it (DeLoache et al., 2010; Reichert et al., 2010; Vance, 2018). There is no environmental recipe for fast-forwarding a normal infant into a genius. All babies should have normal exposure to sights, sounds, and speech. Beyond that, Sandra Scarr's (1984) verdict still is widely shared: "Parents who are very concerned about providing special educational lessons for their babies are wasting their time."

**AP® Science Practice**

**Research**

Hunt's study is another example of a case study. In this instance, a group (children in the Iranian orphanage), rather than an individual, was analyzed in depth.

**Devastating neglect** Some Romanian orphans, such as this child in the Leaganul Pentru Copii orphanage in 1990, had minimal interaction with caregivers, and suffered delayed development.

Josef Polleross/The Image Works

More encouraging results have come from intensive, post-babyhood preschool programs (Dodge et al., 2017; Sasser et al., 2017; Tucker-Drob, 2012). This is particularly true of preschool programs for children living in poverty (Gormley et al., 2013; Heckman & Karapakula, 2019; Magnuson et al., 2007). Intelligence scores also rise with nutritional supplements to pregnant mothers and newborns (3.5 points), with quality preschool experiences (4 points), and with interactive reading programs (6 points) (Protzko et al., 2013).

## Growth Mindset

Schooling and intelligence interact, and both enhance later income (Ceci & Williams, 1997, 2009). But what we accomplish with our intelligence also depends on our own beliefs and motivation. One analysis of 72,431 undergraduates found that study motivation and study skills rivaled aptitude and previous grades as predictors of academic achievement (Credé & Kuncel, 2008). Even intelligence test performance can be affected by motivation. Four dozen studies show that, when promised money for doing well, adolescents score higher on such tests (Duckworth et al., 2011).

These observations would not surprise psychologist Carol Dweck (2018; Dweck & Yeager, 2019). She reports that believing intelligence is changeable fosters a **growth mindset**, a focus on learning and growing. Conversely, believing that intelligence is innately fixed fosters a **fixed mindset**, which involves less optimism about people's capacity for change and growth (Tao et al., 2021). Teachers who adopt a growth mindset tend to view their schools as more likely to improve (Rechsteiner et al., 2021).

Researcher Gregory Walton (2020) teaches growth mindset to his young children, when they tire while riding their bikes home: "It's when you're tired and you keep going that your muscles get stronger." Dweck likewise teaches young teens that the brain is like a muscle, growing stronger with use. Receiving praise for *effort* and for tackling challenges, rather than for being smart or accomplished, helps teens understand the link between hard work and success (Gunderson et al., 2013).

A growth mindset doesn't alter inborn intelligence, so its benefits should not be overstated or lead children to blame themselves for their struggles. But it can make children and youth more resilient when confronted with difficult learning material or frustrating people (Peng & Tullis, 2020; Walton & Wilson, 2018). One national study of 6320 lower-achieving U.S. high school students showed that viewing two 25-minute videos fostering a growth mindset modestly improved their grades (Yeager et al., 2019). Mindset isn't everything, but it does matter.

Courtesy Dr. Carol Dweck

**SPOTLIGHT ON:**
Carol Dweck

**It pays to view intelligence as expandable** Psychologist Carol Dweck has shown several benefits of adopting a growth mindset — believing that intelligence grows through motivated effort. Companies with mission statements that endorse a growth mindset, for example, have more trusting and committed employees (Canning et al., 2020).

❝ *When you [fail], embrace it; learn from it. Don't think . . . that's going to hinder you from becoming whoever you want to become. . . . I wake up every day telling the world: Come on baby, let's ride. What you got for me?* ❞

*Recording artist Pitbull, 2019*

**growth mindset** a focus on learning and growing rather than viewing abilities as fixed.

**fixed mindset** the view that intelligence, abilities, and talents are unchangeable, even with effort.

Dave Nagel/Getty Images

A hungry mind

More than 300 studies confirm that ability + opportunity + motivation = success in fields from sports to science to music (Ericsson et al., 2007). High school students' math proficiency and college students' grades reflect their aptitude but also their self-discipline, their belief in the power of effort, and a curious "hungry mind" (Murayama et al., 2013; Richardson et al., 2012; von Stumm et al., 2011). Consider Zaila Avant-garde, who in 2021 became the first African American to win the U.S. national spelling bee contest after studying thousands of words with her father. Not only was she America's best child speller, but she had also set three world records for basketball dribbling, including for dribbling six balls simultaneously (Cramer & Yuhas, 2021). Zaila Avant-garde shows us how to realize our potential: *Believe* in your ability to learn, and *apply* yourself with sustained effort.

Applying growth mindset findings in large-scale interventions with at-risk students can also have a downside: the social cost of blaming struggling individuals for their circumstances (Ikizer & Blanton, 2016). And researchers and educators sometimes overstate the modest benefit derived from a growth mindset (Burgoyne et al., 2020). Overemphasizing growth mindset power can, as with the motivational concept of *grit*, leave some students feeling that their disappointments reflect a moral flaw. Sometimes people need more than the power of positive thinking to overcome their harsh conditions.

U.S. national spelling bee champion Zaila Avant-garde

Scott McIntyre/The New York Times/Redux Pictures

---

**AP® Science Practice**

## Check Your Understanding

### Examine the Concept

▶ If environments become more equal, the heritability of intelligence will
a. increase.
b. decrease.
c. be unchanged.

▶ The heritability of intelligence scores will be greater in a society of equal opportunity than in a society of extreme economic inequality. Explain why.

*Answers to the Examine the Concept questions can be found in Appendix C at the end of the book.*

### Apply the Concept

▶ How do you feel genetic and environmental influences have shaped your intelligence?

▶ Do you have a growth mindset? How might fostering a growth mindset benefit you?

---

## Module 2.8c REVIEW

**2.8-9** How stable are intelligence test scores over the lifespan?

- The stability of intelligence test scores increases with age.
  - At age 4, scores begin to predict adolescent and adult scores.
  - By age 11, scores are very stable and predictive.

**2.8-10** How does aging affect crystallized intelligence (*Gc*) and fluid intelligence (*Gf*)?

- The answers to age-and-intelligence questions depend on what we assess and how we assess it.
- *Fluid intelligence (Gf)* declines in older adults, who lose recall memory and processing speed.
- Accumulated knowledge, reflected in *crystallized intelligence (Gc)*, tends to increase with age.

**2.8-11** What do twin and adoption studies tell us about the nature and nurture of intelligence?

- Heritability is the proportion of variation among individuals in a group that can be attributed to genes.

- Studies of twins, family members, and adoptive parents and siblings indicate a significant hereditary contribution to intelligence scores.
- Intelligence is polygenetic.

**2.8-12** How can environmental influences affect cognitive development?

- Studies of children raised in impoverished environments with minimal social interaction indicate that life experiences significantly influence cognitive development.
- No evidence supports the idea that normal, healthy children can be molded into geniuses by growing up in an exceptionally enriched environment.
- Environments that foster a *growth mindset* do not alter intelligence, but can positively impact achievement. A *fixed mindset*, which assumes that intelligence, abilities, and talents are unchangeable even with effort, is characterized by less optimism about people's capacity for change and growth.

# AP® Practice Multiple Choice Questions

1. Which of the following best represents the relationship between crystallized intelligence and age?

   a. Jake can solve brain teasers quickly, although his parents can solve them even more quickly.

   b. Grandpa Milt is better than his grandson Artie at crossword puzzles and trivia games.

   c. Aliyah has a knack for training dogs, which she learned from her mother.

   d. Heng writes more creative computer programs than their grandmother does.

2. Hal scored an 89 on an intelligence test when he was 16. Now, at age 56, he is interested in knowing what his score would be as an adult. The score he is most likely to earn on the new test would be

   a. 49.

   b. 70.

   c. 92.

   d. 129.

3. Choose which concept is described in the following statement: "Fifty percent to 80 percent of the variation in intelligence test scores in a group can be explained by genetic variation."

   a. Fixed mindset

   b. Fluid intelligence

   c. Heritability

   d. Polygenetic effects

4. There is a greater correlation between the IQ scores of identical twins raised together than for fraternal twins raised together. What conclusion can be drawn from this finding?

   a. There is no significant hereditary contribution to intelligence.

   b. There is no significant environmental contribution to intelligence.

   c. There is a genetic effect on intelligence.

   d. There is an environmental effect on intelligence.

5. Which of the following is true of the mental similarities between adoptive children and their adoptive parents over time?

   a. Adoptive children become much more similar to their adoptive parents over time.

   b. Adoptive children become slightly more similar to their adoptive parents over time.

   c. There is hardly any similarity when the adoptive children are young or when they are older.

   d. Adoptive children become less similar to their adoptive parents over time.

# Module 2.8d Intelligence and Achievement: Group Differences and the Question of Bias

### LEARNING TARGETS

**2.8-13** Explain male-female similarities and differences in mental ability scores.

**2.8-14** Explain racial and ethnic group similarities and differences in mental ability scores.

**2.8-15** Explain whether intelligence tests are biased or unfair, and explain the influence of *stereotype threat* on test-takers' performance.

## Group Differences in Intelligence Test Scores

If there were no group differences in intelligence test scores, psychologists would have less debate over hereditary and environmental influences. But there are group differences. What are they? And what shall we make of them?

### Gender-Related Similarities and Differences

**2.8-13** How and why are males and females similar and different in their mental ability scores?

In science, as in everyday life, it is differences—not similarities—that excite interest. Men's self-estimated intelligence is often higher than women's self-estimated intelligence, which may fuel a false perception that men are smarter than women (Furnham, 2016). In truth, men's and women's intelligence differences are minor. For example, in that 1932 testing of all Scottish 11-year-olds (Module 2.8c), boys' intelligence scores averaged 100.5 and girls' 100.6 (Deary et al., 2003). As far as *g* is concerned, boys and girls, men and women, are the same.

Yet most people find differences more newsworthy. In cultures where both boys and girls are educated, girls tend to outpace boys in spelling, verbal fluency, reading, and locating objects (Reilly et al., 2019; Voyer & Voyer, 2014). They are better emotion detectors and are more sensitive to touch, taste, and color (Halpern et al., 2007).

In math computation and overall math performance, girls and boys hardly differ (Else-Quest et al., 2010; Hyde & Mertz, 2009; Lindberg et al., 2010). On complex math problems, males outperform females. But the most reliable male edge appears in spatial ability tests like the one shown in **Figure 2.8-11** (Lauer et al., 2019).

[8]The correct answer is *c*.

### Figure 2.8-11

**The mental rotation test**

These kinds of items are often found on a spatial abilities test. See answer below.[8]

**Which one of the options below matches the Original?**

**Original**

(a)

(b)          (c)

**Shrinking the STEM gap** In 2014, Iranian math professor Maryam Mirzakhani (1977–2017) became the first woman to win math's most prestigious award, the Fields Medal (a). In 2018, physicist Donna Strickland (b) and chemist Frances C. Arnold (c) were each awarded a Nobel Prize in scientific fields where women have rarely won. In her acceptance speech, Strickland said, "Not everyone thinks physics is fun, but I do."

(a)  (b)  (c)

*"That's an excellent suggestion, Miss Triggs. Perhaps one of the men would like to suggest it."*

(To solve the problem, you must quickly rotate three-dimensional objects in your mind.) Males' mental ability scores (and brains) also vary more than females' (Wierenga et al., 2020). Worldwide, males outnumber females at both the low and high extremes (Ball et al., 2017; Baye & Monseur, 2016). Males, for example, are more likely than females to need remedial math classes. But they are also more likely to earn the highest math scores.

Psychologist Steven Pinker (2005) has argued for the evolutionary perspective—that biology affects gender-related differences in life priorities (women's somewhat greater interest in people versus men's emphasis on money and things), in risk taking (with men being more reckless), and in math reasoning and spatial abilities. Such differences are, he noted, observed across cultures, stable over time, influenced by prenatal hormones, and observed in genetic boys raised as girls.

But social expectations and opportunities also construct gender by shaping interests and abilities (Jiang et al., 2020). (A reminder: "sex" refers to the biological traits that distinguish male, female, and intersex; "gender" refers to the behavioral traits that people associate with girl/boy/woman/man.) In Asia and Russia, teen girls have outperformed boys in an international science exam; in North America and Britain, boys have scored higher (Fairfield, 2012).

More gender-equal cultures, such as Sweden and Iceland, exhibit little of the gender math gap found in gender-unequal cultures, such as Turkey and Korea (Guiso et al., 2008; Kane & Mertz, 2012). Since the 1970s, as gender equity has increased in the United States, the boy-to-girl ratio among 12- to 14-year-olds with very high SAT math scores (above 700) has declined from 13 to 1 to 3 to 1 (Makel et al., 2016; Nisbett et al., 2012). As we have seen in so many areas of life, cultural expectations and opportunities matter.

## Racial and Ethnic Similarities and Differences

**2.8-14** How and why are racial and ethnic groups similar and different in their mental ability scores?

**Fueling the group-differences debate are two other disturbing but scientifically agreed-upon facts:**

- Racial and ethnic groups mostly overlap, but also differ in their average intelligence test scores.

- High-scoring people (and groups) are more likely to attain high levels of education and income.

There are many group differences in average intelligence test scores. New Zealanders of European descent outscore native Maori New Zealanders. Israeli Jews outscore Israeli

Arabs. Most Japanese outscore most Burakumin, a stigmatized Japanese minority. And White Americans have outscored Black Americans, although this difference has diminished, especially among children (Dickens & Flynn, 2006; Nisbett et al., 2012). Such *group* differences provide little basis for judging individuals. Worldwide, women outlive men by 5 years, but knowing only an individual's sex won't tell us how long that person will live. Similarly, an individual's IQ score may vary significantly from others within their identified group.

We have seen that heredity contributes to *individual* differences in intelligence. But group differences in a heritable trait may be entirely environmental. Consider one of nature's experiments: Allow some children to grow up hearing their culture's dominant language, while others, born deaf, do not. Then give both groups an intelligence test rooted in the dominant language. The result? No surprise: Those with expertise in the dominant language will score higher than those who were born deaf (Braden, 1994; Steele, 1990; Zeidner, 1990).

Might the racial and ethnic gaps be similarly environmental? Consider:

*Genetics research reveals that under the skin, we humans are remarkably alike.* Despite some racial variation, such as in health risks, the average genetic difference between two Icelandic villagers or between two Kenyans greatly exceeds the average group difference between Icelanders and Kenyans (Cavalli-Sforza et al., 1994; Rosenberg et al., 2002). Moreover, looks can deceive. Light-skinned Europeans and dark-skinned Africans are genetically closer than are dark-skinned Africans and dark-skinned Aboriginal Australians.

*Race is not a neatly defined biological category.* Race is primarily a social category without well-defined physical boundaries; each race blends seamlessly into the race of its geographic neighbors (Helms et al., 2005; Smedley & Smedley, 2005). In one genetic analysis of more than 160,000 people living in the United States, most with less than 28 percent African ancestry said they were White; those with more than 28 percent mostly said they were African American (Byrc et al., 2015). Moreover, with increasingly mixed ancestries, more and more people defy neat racial categorization and self-identify as multiracial (Pauker et al., 2009).

*Within the same populations, there are generation-to-generation differences in test scores.* Test scores of today's better-fed, better-educated, and more test-prepared populations exceed those of 1930s populations—by a greater margin than the score difference between today's average Black Americans and White Americans (Flynn, 2012; Pietschnig & Voracek, 2015; Trahan et al., 2014). No one credits genetics for such generation-to-generation differences.

*Schools and culture matter.* Countries whose economies create a large wealth gap between rich and poor tend also to have a large rich-versus-poor intelligence test score gap (Nisbett, 2009). In the United States, rising income inequality has meant less equal access to a college education (Jackson & Holzman, 2020). And fewer educational opportunities can result in lower intelligence test scores. One analysis of 600,000 students showed that each additional year of school predicted 1 to 5 additional IQ points (Ritchie & Tucker-Drob, 2018).

Math achievement, aptitude test differences, and especially grades may reflect conscientiousness more than competence (Poropat, 2014). Women in college and university outperform equally able men, thanks partly to their greater conscientiousness (Keiser et al., 2016). Students in Asia, who have largely outperformed North American students

### CULTURAL AWARENESS

Recall from earlier in this unit that culture even impacts how we define intelligence, and what we value as intelligent behavior.

Larry Williams/Getty Images

on such tests, have also spent more time in school and much more time studying in and out of school (CMEC, 2018; Larson & Verma, 1999; NCEE, 2018). These differences persist within the United States, where Asian American students devote the most time to studying and earn the highest grades (Hsin & Xie, 2014).

*In different eras, different ethnic groups have experienced golden ages — periods of remarkable achievement.* Twenty-five hundred years ago, it was the Greeks and the Egyptians, then the Romans. In the eighth and ninth centuries, genius seemed to reside in the Arab world, which led one Muslim scholar of the era to say of the English and Dutch, "They lack keenness of understanding and clarity of intelligence and are overcome by ignorance and apathy, lack of discernment, and stupidity" (Henrich, 2020). Five hundred years ago, the Aztec Indians and the peoples of Northern Europe were the superachievers. While the gene pool remained relatively stable, cultures rose and fell.

**Intelligence allowed to flourish** The renowned all-women Afghan robotics team stood as a symbol of progress for women in Afghanistan. With the Taliban's return to power in 2021 and the team's welfare and educational opportunities endangered, humanitarian groups helped them escape the country.

## The Question of Bias

**2.8-15** Are intelligence tests biased or unfair? What is *stereotype threat,* and how does it affect test-takers' performance?

Knowing there are group differences in intelligence test scores leads to the question of whether those differences are built into the tests. Are intelligence tests biased? The answer depends on how we define bias.

The *scientific* meaning of *bias* hinges solely on whether a test predicts future behavior for all groups of test-takers, not just for some. For example, if the SAT accurately predicted the college achievement of women but not that of men, then the test would be biased. In this scientific meaning of the term, the near-consensus among psychologists has been that the major U.S. aptitude tests are *not* biased (Berry & Zhao, 2015; Neisser et al., 1996; Wigdor & Garner, 1982). The tests' predictive validity is roughly the same, regardless of gender, race, ethnicity, or socioeconomic level. If an intelligence test score of 95 predicts slightly below-average grades, that rough prediction usually applies equally to all.

But in everyday language, we may consider a test "biased" if it is unfair—if test scores will be influenced by the test-takers' developed abilities, which reflect, in part, their education and cultural experiences. You may have read examples of intelligence test items that make assumptions (for example, that a cup goes with a saucer). Such items bias the test (against those who do not use saucers). Could such questions explain cultural differences in test performance? In such cases, tests can be a vehicle for discrimination, consigning potentially capable children (some of whom may have a different native language) to unchallenging classes and dead-end jobs. Many intelligence researchers therefore recommend creating culture-neutral questions—such as those that assess people's ability to learn novel words, sayings, and analogies—to enable *culture-fair* aptitude tests (Fagan & Holland, 2007, 2009). Today's standardized tests are rigorously reviewed to minimize cultural bias.

Testing proponents also caution us against blaming tests for exposing unequal experiences and opportunities. If, because of malnutrition, people were to suffer stunted growth, should we blame the measuring stick that reveals it? If unequal past experiences predict unequal future achievements, a valid aptitude test will detect such inequalities.

# Test-Takers' Expectations

Throughout this text, you have seen that expectations and attitudes influence perceptions and behaviors. For test-makers, expectations can introduce bias. For test-takers, they can become self-fulfilling prophecies. In one study, equally capable men and women took a difficult math test. The women did not do as well as the men—except when they had been led to expect that women usually do as well as men on the test (Spencer et al., 1997). Otherwise, something affected their performance. There was a "threat in the air" (Spencer et al., 2016). This self-fulfilling **stereotype threat** appeared again when Black students performed worse when reminded of their race just before taking verbal aptitude tests (Steele et al., 2002). Negative stereotypes may undermine people's academic potential (Grand, 2016; Nguyen & Ryan, 2008; Walton & Spencer, 2009). If you worry that your group or "type" often doesn't do well on a certain kind of test or task, your self-doubts and self-monitoring may hijack your working memory and impair attention, performance, and learning (Hutchison et al., 2013; Inzlicht & Kang, 2010; Rydell et al., 2010). If you are confident that your group or "type" does well on a task, being exposed to situations that create stereotype threat in outgroup members may actually improve your performance—an effect called *stereotype lift* (Walton & Cohen, 2003).

Stereotype threat, like growth mindset and grit, is a modest phenomenon that often gets overstated (Flore et al., 2019). Yet it helps explain why Black Americans have scored higher when tested by Black people than when tested by White people (Danso & Esses, 2001). It gives us insight into why women have scored higher on math tests with no men test-takers present.

From such studies, some researchers have concluded that making students believe they probably won't succeed can function as a stereotype and weaken performance. Remedial programs may sometimes have this unintended effect (Steele, 1995, 2010).

Other research teams have demonstrated the benefits of self-affirmation exercises that engage students in writing about their most important values (Borman et al., 2019; Ferrer & Cohen, 2018; Logel et al., 2019). When challenged to believe in their potential, think positively about their diverse life experiences, or increase their sense of belonging, disadvantaged university students have earned higher grades and have had lower dropout rates (Broda et al., 2018; Sarrasin et al., 2018; Townsend et al., 2019).

\* \* \*

What, then, can we realistically conclude about aptitude tests and bias? The tests are not biased in the scientific sense of failing to make valid statistical predictions for different groups. But they may, indeed, be biased in one sense—sensitivity to performance differences caused by cultural experience. Are the tests discriminatory? Again, the answer can be *Yes* or *No*. In one sense, *Yes*, their purpose is to discriminate—to distinguish among individuals. In another sense, *No*, their purpose is to reduce discrimination by decreasing reliance on subjective criteria for school and job placement—who you know, how you dress, or whether you are the "right kind of person." Civil service aptitude tests, for example, were devised to discriminate (distinguish) more fairly and objectively by reducing the political, racial, ethnic, and gender discrimination that preceded their use. Banning aptitude tests would lead those who decide on jobs and admissions to rely more on other considerations, such as personal opinion.

Perhaps, then, our goals for tests of mental abilities should be threefold. First, we should realize the benefits that intelligence-testing pioneer Alfred Binet foresaw—to enable schools to recognize who might profit most from early intervention. Second, we must remain alert to Binet's wish that intelligence test scores not be misinterpreted as literal measures of a person's worth and potential. Third, we must remember that the competence that general intelligence tests measure is important; it helps enable success in some life paths. But these tests reflect only one important aspect of personal competence (Stanovich et al., 2016). Our practical intelligence and emotional intelligence matter, too, as do creativity, talent, and character.

*The point to remember:* There are many ways of being successful; our differences are variations of human adaptability. Life's great achievements result not only from "can do" abilities (and fair opportunity) but also from "will do" motivation. Competence + Diligence → Accomplishment.

**stereotype threat** a self-confirming concern that one will be evaluated based on a negative stereotype.

# Check Your Understanding

**Examine the Concept**

▶ Explain the difference between a test that is culturally biased and a test that is scientifically biased.

▶ Describe the psychological principle that may help explain why women tend to score higher on math tests when none of their fellow test-takers are men.

**Apply the Concept**

▶ How have your expectations influenced your own test performance? What steps could you take to control this influence?

▶ Do you think there is any such thing as a culture-neutral question? Or does the fact that questions use language make them inherently biased?

*Answers to the Examine the Concept questions can be found in Appendix C at the end of the book.*

# Module 2.8d REVIEW

**2.8-13 How and why are males and females similar and different in their mental ability scores?**

- Girls and boys have the same average intelligence test scores, but they tend to differ in some specific abilities.

- Girls, on average, are better spellers, more verbally fluent, better at reading and at locating objects, better at detecting emotions, and more sensitive to touch, taste, and color.

- Boys outperform girls at spatial ability and complex mathematics, though boys and girls hardly differ in math computation and overall math performance. Boys also outnumber girls at both the low and high extremes of mental abilities.

- Evolutionary and cultural explanations have been proposed for these gender-related differences.

**2.8-14 How and why are racial and ethnic groups similar and different in their mental ability scores?**

- Racial and ethnic groups mostly overlap, but also differ in their average intelligence test scores.

- Evidence suggests that environmental differences are responsible for these group differences.

**2.8-15 Are intelligence tests biased or unfair? What is *stereotype threat*, and how does it affect test-takers' performance?**

- The scientific meaning of bias hinges on a test's ability to predict future behavior for all test-takers, not just for some. In this sense, most experts consider the major U.S. aptitude tests unbiased. However, if we consider bias to mean that a test may be influenced by the test-taker's education and cultural experiences, then intelligence tests, by that definition, may be considered unfair.

- *Stereotype threat*, a self-confirming concern that one will be evaluated based on a negative stereotype, affects performance on all kinds of tests. Some research findings suggest effective strategies for reducing stereotype threat.

# AP® Practice Multiple Choice Questions

1. Which of the following statements provides the most logical and objective conclusion regarding gender and mental abilities?

   a. On average, boys have high intelligence test scores but low mathematics achievement test scores.
   b. Boys are better at detecting emotions than are girls.
   c. On average, boys are more verbally fluent than are girls, but they tend to express more interest in mathematics careers.

   d. Boys are more likely to be represented among those scoring extremely low and those scoring extremely high on tests of mental abilities.

2. Which of the following best supports the conclusion that race is more of a social construct than a biological category?

   a. People of varying ancestry may categorize themselves as having the same race.
   b. Scores on tests of mental abilities vary by race.

c. Stereotype threat negatively impacts attention when someone worries about their racial group's performance on a task.

d. Cultural experiences affect mental ability test results regardless of one's racial group membership.

**3.** Dr. Xiao wants his personality test to predict future behaviors similarly for all test takers. What should Dr. Xiao examine?

a. Stereotype threat
b. Stereotype lift
c. Test bias
d. Test fairness

**Use the following text to answer questions 4–6:**

Dr. Yolay wants to conduct a study on how the demographic characteristics of a test administrator impact the performance on an intelligence test among a group of 8-year-old girls. After the girls draw either the number 1 or the number 2 from a hat, she assigns the girls to either (1) take the test with a man as the test administrator or (2) take the test with a woman as the test administrator.

**4.** In this scenario, what is the dependent variable?

a. A group of 8-year-old girls
b. Demographic characteristics of the test administrator
c. Intelligence test performance
d. Test administration

**5.** Based on past research discussed in this unit, what logical and objective result might you expect from this research?

a. The girls in group 1 perform better, on average, compared to the girls in group 2.
b. The girls in group 2 perform better, on average, compared to the girls in group 1.
c. The girls in group 1 perform better on the first half of the test, while the girls in group 2 perform better on the second half of the test.
d. The girls in group 2 perform better on the first half of the test, while the girls in group 1 perform better on the second half of the test.

**6.** Dr. Yolay determined that the gender of the test administrator caused the performance of the girls to differ. What technique did Dr. Yolay employ to be able to make this assertion?

a. Random assignment
b. Random selection
c. Experimental control
d. Operational definitions

# UNIT 2 Review

## KEY TERMS AND CONTRIBUTORS TO REMEMBER

selective attention, p. 166

inattentional blindness, p. 167

change blindness, p. 168

perceptual set, p. 169

gestalt, p. 174

figure-ground, p. 175

grouping, p. 175

depth perception, p. 176

visual cliff, p. 176

binocular cue, p. 177

convergence, p. 177

retinal disparity, p. 177

monocular cue, p. 179

stroboscopic movement, p. 179

phi phenomenon, p. 179

autokinetic effect, p. 179

perceptual constancy, p. 180

color constancy, p. 180

perceptual adaptation, p. 183

cognition, p. 187

metacognition, p. 187

concept, p. 187

prototype, p. 187

Jean Piaget, p. 188

schema p. 188,

assimilation, p. 189

accommodation, p. 189

creativity, p. 189

convergent thinking, p. 189

divergent thinking, p. 189

Robert Sternberg, p. 190

executive functions, p. 193

algorithm, p. 193

heuristic, p. 193

insight, p. 194

Wolfgang Köhler, p. 194

confirmation bias, p. 194

fixation, p. 195

mental set, p. 195

intuition, p. 195

Amos Tversky, p. 195

Daniel Kahneman, p. 195

representativeness heuristic, p. 196

availability heuristic, p. 196

overconfidence, p. 198

belief perseverance, p. 199

framing, p. 200

nudge, p. 200

memory, p. 206

recall, p. 207

recognition, p. 208

relearning, p. 208

Hermann Ebbinghaus, p. 208

encoding, p. 209

storage, p. 209

retrieval, p. 209

parallel processing, p. 209

Richard Atkinson, p. 209

Richard Shiffrin, p. 209

sensory memory, p. 209

short-term memory, p. 209

long-term memory, p. 209

working memory, p. 210

central executive, p. 210

phonological loop, p. 210

visuospatial sketchpad, p. 210

neurogenesis, p. 211

Eric Kandel, p. 211

long-term potentiation (LTP), p. 211

explicit memory, p. 215

effortful processing, p. 215

automatic processing, p. 215

implicit memory, p. 215

iconic memory, p. 216

echoic memory, p. 216

George A. Miller, p. 217

chunking, p. 218

mnemonics [nih-MON-iks], p. 219

spacing effect, p. 220

testing effect, p. 221

shallow processing, p. 222

deep processing, p. 222

semantic memory, p. 227

episodic memory, p. 227

hippocampus, p. 227

memory consolidation, p. 227

flashbulb memory, p. 229

priming, p. 233

encoding specificity principle, p. 233

mood-congruent memory, p. 233

serial position effect, p. 234

interleaving, p. 235

anterograde amnesia, p. 239

retrograde amnesia, p. 239

proactive interference, p. 242

retroactive interference, p. 242

repression, p. 243

reconsolidation, p. 244

Elizabeth Loftus, p. 244

# Unit 2 AP® Practice Multiple Choice Questions

1. Which of the following phrases accurately describes top-down processing?

   a. The entry-level data captured by our various sensory systems
   b. The effect that our experiences and expectations have on perception
   c. Our tendency to scan a visual field from top to bottom
   d. Our ability to detect letters of a word before we know what the word is

2. Which of the following describes a perception process that the Gestalt psychologists would have been interested in?

   a. Depth perception and how it allows us to survive in the world
   b. How an organized whole is formed out of its component pieces
   c. What the smallest units of perception are
   d. The similarities between shape constancy and size constancy

3. As you look down the road, the lines of the road seem to come together in the distance, even though you know they do not. Which depth cue explains this phenomenon?

   a. Texture gradient
   b. Interposition
   c. Light and shadow
   d. Linear perspective

4. Due to an eye infection, Gladys has to wear a patch over her left eye. As a result, she finds that her depth perception is impaired. What best explains this impairment?

   a. Gladys has lost her binocular depth cues.
   b. Gladys no longer experiences perceptual constancy.
   c. Gladys no longer experiences perceptual adaptation.
   d. Gladys has lost her monocular depth cues.

5. The experience of a smooth picture at a movie theater, even though the actual film is made up thousands of separate pictures, is due to

   a. the phi phenomenon.
   b. stroboscopic movement.
   c. relative motion.
   d. the illusory effect.

6. Which of the following represents perceptual constancy?

   a. We recognize the taste of McDonald's food each time we eat it.
   b. In photos of people, the people almost always are perceived as the figure and everything else as the ground.
   c. We know that the color of a printed page has not changed as it moves from sunlight into shadow.
   d. The cold water in a lake doesn't seem so cold after you have been swimming in it for a few minutes.

**7.** When asked to think of a "desk," many students think of the desks in their classroom rather than a large desk used by an executive. This scenario best illustrates

   a. a prototype.
   b. metacognition.
   c. convergent thinking.
   d. functional fixedness.

**8.** Dr. Hansel studies the cognitive frameworks that help us organize and interpret new information in memory. These frameworks are referred to as

   a. prototypes.      c. schemas.
   b. heuristics.      d. intuition.

**9.** Which of the following illustrates a heuristic?

   a. Calculating the area of a rectangle by multiplying the length times the width
   b. Using three dramatic news reports of corporate fraud to estimate how often business fraud occurs
   c. Following a new recipe to bake a cake for your friend
   d. Trying every key on your mom's key ring until you find the one that unlocks the seldom-used storeroom in the basement

**10.** Alice significantly underestimated how long it would take to write her term paper, because she was sure it would be very easy for her. Alice was exhibiting

   a. belief perseverance.      c. the availability heuristic.
   b. intuition.      d. overconfidence.

**11.** People are more concerned about a medical procedure when told it has a 10 percent death rate than they are when told it has a 90 percent survival rate. Which psychological concept explains this difference in concern?

   a. Belief perseverance      c. Framing
   b. Priming      d. Confirmation bias

**12.** Which of the following cognitive strategies is most useful for creativity?

   a. Convergent thinking      c. Heuristics
   b. Divergent thinking      d. Algorithms

**13.** Which of the following best describes long-term potentiation (LTP)?

   a. Constructed memories have the potential to be either accurate or inaccurate.
   b. These synaptic changes allow for more efficient transfer of information.
   c. Implicit memories are processed by the cerebellum instead of by the hippocampus.
   d. Information is transferred from working memory to long-term memory.

**14.** Which of the following is an example of an implicit memory?

   a. Knowing how to tie your shoe
   b. The details of an assignment that is due tomorrow
   c. Vividly recalling significant events, such as the death of a famous person
   d. The names of all U.S. state capitals

**15.** Ms. Pina accurately told her class that the "magical number seven, plus or minus two" refers to

   a. the ideal number of times to rehearse information in the first encoding session.
   b. the number of seconds information stays in short-term memory without rehearsal.
   c. the capacity of short-term memory.
   d. the number of seconds information stays in echoic storage.

**16.** When we provide our phone number to another person, we usually pause after the area code and again after the next three numbers. This pattern underscores the importance of which memory principle?

   a. Chunking
   b. The serial position effect
   c. Semantic encoding
   d. Auditory encoding

**17.** Lewis really wants to do well on his psychology exam. Which strategy should he use to maximize his chances of successfully retrieving the information he will need for the exam?

   a. Iconic memory      c. Automatic processing
   b. Distributed practice      d. Massed practice

**18.** Dr. Jarvis conducted a memory study. Which of his findings replicates the findings from past research?

   a. The amygdala helps process memories of happy experiences.
   b. The amygdala produces long-term potentiation in the brain.
   c. The amygdala enhances memory of events that trigger strong emotional responses.
   d. The amygdala is active when the retrieval of a long-term memory is primed.

**19.** You are more likely to remember happy memories when you are presently happy than when you are sad due to

   a. mood congruence.
   b. iconic memory.
   c. proactive interference.
   d. retroactive interference.

**20.** Which of the following illustrates the serial position effect?

   a. Kimia has trouble remembering information from the book's first unit when she reviews for semester finals.

   b. It's easy for Brittney to remember that carbon's atomic number is 6 because her birthday is on December 6.

   c. Kyle was not able to remember the names of all of his new co-workers after one week on the job, but he could remember them after two weeks.

   d. Alp is unable to remember the middle of a list of vocabulary words as well as he remembers the first or last words on the list.

**21.** Which of the following conclusions can be drawn from the graph?

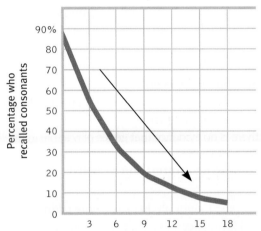

Time in seconds between presentation
of consonants and recall request
(no rehearsal allowed)

   a. Most forgetting occurs early on and then levels off.

   b. Forgetting becomes more rapid as time passes.

   c. Forgetting is relatively constant over time.

   d. Forgetting is unrelated to time.

**22.** Mave got a new car with the license plate "MAVNUM1." She is asked by the school parking clerk what her number is but can only remember her old one, "VANMOM1." Her inability to remember her new plate is most likely due to

   a. retroactive interference.

   b. proactive interference.

   c. anterograde amnesia.

   d. retrograde amnesia.

**23.** Which of the following is an example of source amnesia?

   a. Iva can't remember the details of a horrifying event because she has repressed them.

   b. Mary has entirely forgotten about an incident in grade school until her friend reminds her of the event.

   c. Michael can't remember this year's locker combination because he confuses it with last year's combination.

   d. Stephen misremembers a dream as something that really happened.

**24.** Stephanie received a score on an intelligence test that was much lower than average, though she is exceptional at performing complex calculations. Stephanie might be characterized as having

   a. practical intelligence.

   b. savant syndrome.

   c. advanced mental age.

   d. intelligence heritability.

**25.** If Lanie is able to tell when her husband is upset by noticing subtle changes in his facial expressions, she might be said to have a high degree of

   a. emotional intelligence.

   b. naturalistic intelligence.

   c. practical intelligence.

   d. spatial intelligence.

**26.** How should Dr. Corvus accurately explain the difference between achievement and aptitude tests?

   a. Achievement tests measure verbal performance, while aptitude tests measure spatial performance.

   b. Achievement tests are designed to measure elementary school skills, while aptitude tests are designed to measure secondary school skills.

   c. Achievement tests are intended to reflect what you have learned, while aptitude tests are intended to predict what you will be able to learn.

   d. Achievement tests measure general intelligence, while aptitude tests measure multiple intelligences.

**27.** After creating his intelligence test, Alfred Binet might say, "I wanted to…"

   a. predict how children would do in school.

   b. identify differences among ethnic and racial groups.

   c. help French graduates find the occupation in which they were most likely to succeed.

   d. establish the scientific definition of intelligence.

**28.** Historically, intelligence tests were sometimes used inappropriately to discriminate against specific groups. This is best illustrated by

   a. the Flynn effect.

   b. the eugenics movement.

   c. the Wechsler Adult Intelligence Scale.

   d. test standardization.

**29.** If Aleister wanted to calculate a child's intelligence quotient using the original formula, he should compare a child's

   a. mental age to their chronological age.
   b. intelligence to their siblings' intelligence.
   c. intelligence to their parents' intelligence.
   d. math intelligence to their verbal intelligence.

**30.** If Zowie writes a biography of the creator of the most widely used modern intelligence test, who should she write about?

   a. Alfred Binet
   b. Robert Sternberg
   c. David Wechsler
   d. Howard Gardner

**31.** How might Dr. Duffy explain to his psychology class the purpose of standardizing an intelligence test?

   a. To counter rising intelligence test scores
   b. To measure the extent to which the test actually predicts what it promises
   c. To provide a basis for comparing scores against a pretested group
   d. To determine if the test yields dependably consistent results

**32.** Dr. Pag accurately describes the Flynn effect as the

   a. extreme scores (very high and very low) that are more common for males than for females on math tests.
   b. stereotype threat that might cause some students to underperform on standardized tests.
   c. predictive ability of intelligence tests.
   d. gradual increase in average intelligence score of the general population over the last several decades.

**33.** What would be true of a thermometer that always reads three degrees lower than the actual temperature?

   a. It is valid but not reliable.
   b. It is both reliable and valid.
   c. It is neither reliable nor valid.
   d. It is reliable but not valid.

**34.** Students who do well on college entrance exams generally do well in their first year of college. This helps establish that these exams have

   a. predictive validity.
   b. construct validity.
   c. content validity.
   d. test-retest reliability.

**35.** Yenni studies intelligence. What is he most likely to find regarding crystallized intelligence?

   a. It increases as we age.
   b. It decreases as we age.
   c. It is higher in girls than in boys.
   d. It is higher in boys than in girls.

**36.** If a researcher is interested in exploring the heritability of intelligence, she is most likely going to study

   a. the extent to which a person's intelligence is caused by genetics.
   b. the effect of adoption on the intelligence of adopted children.
   c. the amount of group variation in intelligence that can be attributed to genetics.
   d. the extent to which the quality of schools and other environmental factors determine intelligence.

**37.** To summarize the studies investigating the impact of genes on intelligence, Greg should say that

   a. intelligence is affected by many genes working together.
   b. there is a gene that is involved in the intelligence of men but not women.
   c. there is a gene that is involved in the intelligence of women but not men.
   d. there is no evidence that genes play a role in intelligence.

**Use the following information to answer questions 38 and 39:**

Destini is asked to indicate her sex before taking a complex math test. Having been told that girls aren't as good at math as boys, she enters the test with self-doubts that ultimately impair her performance.

**38.** Destini is experiencing

   a. bottom-up processing.
   b. the Flynn effect.
   c. stereotype threat.
   d. confirmation bias.

**39.** Which of the following conclusions would be most appropriate?

   a. There is not enough information presented to determine if the test itself is biased in any way.
   b. The test Destini is taking is culturally fair.
   c. The test Destini is taking lacks predictive validity.
   d. The test Destini is taking has predictive validity.

**40.** Tori is at a party having a private conversation with a friend. She is able to ignore the music and other conversations due to

a. interleaving.
b. proactive interference.
c. bottom-up processing.
d. selective attention.

**41.** Des is studying for his French test. He encodes his vocabulary words at an elementary level, focusing on the word's letters instead of the meaning. He is engaging in which type of processing?

a. Deep
b. Shallow
c. Bottom-up
d. Top-down

**42.** Seungyeon conducts a study where she compares people of different ages at the same point in time. What method is she using?

a. Cross-sectional
b. Longitudinal
c. Standardization
d. Factor analysis

**43.** Dodge made a new test that assessed depression, making sure to ask questions about each symptom of depression. This allows him to establish

a. predictive validity.
b. test-retest reliability.
c. content validity.
d. split-half reliability.

---

Go to Appendix D to complete the **AP® Practice** Evidence-Based Question and Article Analysis Question for this unit.

UNIT 3

# Development and Learning

Life is a journey, from womb to tomb. So it is for me [DM], and so it will be for you. Across the lifespan, we *develop*, and we *learn*. As infants, we engaged our care providers from the moment we took our first breath—seeking comfort and nourishment. As children, we engaged in social play in preparation for life's work. As teenagers, you and your classmates all smile and cry, love and loathe, and perhaps look forward to greater independence in your adult life ahead. And throughout each day, throughout our lives, we learn—through interactions with the world around us—about how people and things work, what leads to success, and creative ways to overcome challenges.

UNIT **3**
Overview Video

Jose Luis Pelaez Inc/DigitalVision/Getty Images

# Module 3.1 Themes and Methods in Developmental Psychology

**LEARNING TARGETS**

**3.1-1** Explain three themes that have engaged developmental psychologists and two methods they typically use to study human development over time.

My [DM's] story, and yours, began when a man and a woman together contributed 20,000+ genes to an egg that became a unique person. Those genes coded the protein building blocks that, with astonishing precision, form our body and predispose our traits. My grandmother handed down to my mother a rare hearing-loss pattern, which she, in turn, gave to me (the least of her gifts). My father was an amiable extravert, and sometimes I forget to stop talking (although as a child, my talking was impeded by embarrassing stuttering, for which Seattle Public Schools provided speech therapy).

Along with my parents' nature, I also received their nurture. Like you, I was born into a particular family and culture, with its own way of viewing the world. My values have been shaped by a family culture filled with talking and laughter, by a religious culture that speaks of love and justice, and by an academic culture that encourages critical thinking (asking, *What do you mean? How do you know?*).

We are formed by our genes and by our contexts, so our stories all differ. But in many ways we are each like nearly everyone else on Earth. Being human, you and I have a need to belong. My mental video library, which began after age 4, is filled with scenes of social attachment. Over time, my attachments to parents loosened as peer friendships grew. After lacking confidence to date in high school, I fell in love with a college classmate and married at age 20. Natural selection predisposes us to survive and perpetuate our genes. Sure enough, two years later a child entered our lives, and I experienced a new form of love that surprised me with its intensity.

But life is marked by change. That child and his brother now live 2000 miles away, and their sister has found her calling in South Africa. The tight rubber bands linking parent and child have loosened, as yours likely have as well.

Change also marks most vocational lives, which for me transitioned from a teen working in the family insurance agency, to a premed chemistry major and hospital aide, to (after discarding my half-completed medical school applications) a psychology professor and author. I predict that in 10 years you, too, will be doing things you do not currently anticipate.

Stability also marks our development: Our life situations change, but we experience a continuous self. When I look in the mirror, I do not see the person I once was, but I feel like the person I have always been. I am the same person who, as a late teen, played basketball and discovered love. Sixty years later, I still enjoy basketball and still love (with less passion but more security) the life partner with whom I have shared life's griefs and joys.

We experience a continuous self, but that self morphs through stages—for me, growing up, raising children, enjoying a career, and, eventually, life's final stage, which will demand my presence. As I wend my way through this cycle of life and death, I am mindful that life's journey is a continuing process of development, seeded by nature and shaped by nurture, animated by love and focused by work, begun with wide-eyed curiosity and completed, for those blessed to live to a good old age, with peace and never-ending hope.

Across the lifespan, we grow from newborn to toddler, from toddler to teenager, and from teenager to mature adult. At each stage of life there are physical, cognitive, and social-emotional milestones.

## Developmental Psychology's Major Themes

**3.1-1** What three themes have engaged developmental psychologists, and what are two methods they typically use to study human development over time?

Researchers find human development interesting for the same reasons most of us do—they want to understand more about how we've become our current selves, and how we may change in the years ahead. **Developmental psychology** examines our physical, cognitive, and social-emotional development across the lifespan. Developmental psychologists study both the chronological order of this development and its key themes. They often do **cross-sectional studies** (comparing people of different ages) and **longitudinal studies** (following people across time) to explore three major themes:

1. *Nature and nurture:* How does our genetic inheritance (our *nature*) interact with our experiences (our *nurture*) to influence our development? How have your nature and your nurture influenced *your* life story?

2. *Continuity and stages:* Which parts of development are gradual and continuous, like riding an escalator? Which parts change abruptly in separate stages, like climbing rungs on a ladder?

3. *Stability and change:* Which of our traits persist through life? How do we change as we age?

### Nature and Nurture

The unique gene combination created when our mother's egg engulfed our father's sperm helped form us as individuals. Genes predispose both our shared humanity and our individual differences.

But our experiences also shape us, in the womb and in the world. Our families and peer relationships teach us how to think and act. Even differences initiated by our nature may be amplified by our nurture. We are not formed by either nature or nurture, but by the interaction between them. Biological, psychological, and social-cultural forces interact.

Mindful of how others differ from us, however, we often fail to notice the similarities stemming from our shared biology. Regardless of our culture, we humans share the same life cycle. We speak to our infants in similar ways and respond similarly to their coos and cries (Bornstein et al., 1992a,b). Although ethnic groups have differed in some ways, including average school achievement, these differences are "no more than skin deep." To the extent that family structure, peer influences, and parental education predict behavior in one of these ethnic groups, they do so for the others. Compared with the person-to-person differences within groups, between-group differences are small.

### Continuity and Stages

Do adults differ from infants as a giant redwood differs from its seedling—a difference created by gradual, cumulative growth? Or do they differ as a butterfly differs from a caterpillar—a difference of distinct stages?

**AP® Science Practice**

**Research**

Developmental psychology often features longitudinal and cross-sectional studies—because these research design methods help us learn about development across the lifespan (changes over time).

**AP® Exam Tip**

All three of these themes are important for development. Nature and nurture, of course, weave their way through almost every module. Look for the nature/nurture idea throughout this text (and on the AP® exam).

**developmental psychology**
a branch of psychology that studies physical, cognitive, and social-emotional development throughout the lifespan.

**cross-sectional study**
research that compares people of different ages at the same point in time.

**longitudinal study** research that follows and retests the same people over time.

Stages of the life cycle

Researchers who emphasize experience and learning typically see development as a slow, continuous shaping process. Those who emphasize biological maturation tend to see development as a sequence of genetically predisposed stages or steps: Although progress through the various stages may be quick or slow, everyone passes through the stages in the same order.

Are there clear-cut stages of psychological development, as there are physical stages such as walking before running? The *stage theories* we will consider—Jean Piaget's theory of cognitive development, and Erik Erikson's theory of psychosocial development—propose developmental stages (summarized in **Figure 3.1-1**). But as we will also see, some research casts doubt on the idea that life proceeds through neatly defined age-linked stages.

Although many modern developmental psychologists do not identify as stage theorists, the stage concept remains useful. The human brain does experience growth spurts during childhood and puberty that correspond roughly to Piaget's stages (Thatcher et al., 1987). And stage theories contribute a developmental perspective on the whole lifespan by suggesting how people of one age think and act differently when they arrive at a later age.

## Stability and Change

As we follow lives through time, do we find more evidence for stability or change? If reunited with a long-lost childhood friend, do we instantly realize that "it's the same old Jordan"? Or do long-ago friends now seem like strangers? (At least one acquaintance of mine [DM's] would choose the second option. At his 40-year college reunion, he failed to recognize a former classmate. The understandably appalled classmate was his first wife!)

We experience both stability and change. Some of our characteristics, such as *temperament,* are very stable. Following thousands of New Zealanders and Americans over several decades, researchers have been struck by the consistency of temperament and emotionality across time (Kassing et al., 2019; Moffitt et al., 2013; Slutske et al., 2012). Inhibited

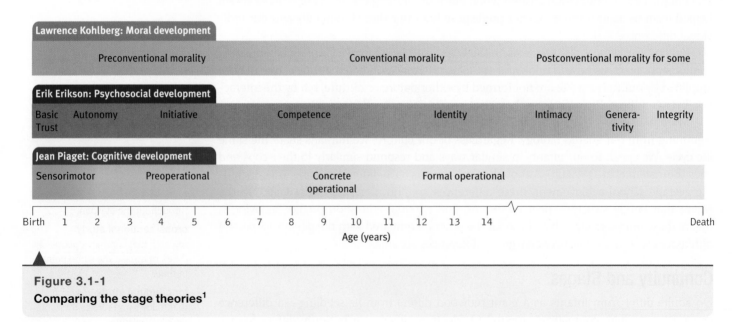

**Figure 3.1-1**
**Comparing the stage theories**[1]

[1]With thanks to Dr. Sandra Gibbs, Muskegon Community College, for inspiring this illustration.

14-month-olds mostly grow up to be reserved, introverted adults (Tang et al., 2020). Out-of-control young children are later the most likely to engage in teen smoking, adult criminal behavior, or out-of-control gambling. Inattentive Canadian kindergarteners are less likely to earn high salaries in their adult careers (Vergunst et al., 2019). Moreover, children observed being repeatedly cruel to animals often become violent adults (Hensley et al., 2018). But on a happier note, the widest smilers in childhood and college photos are the ones most likely to enjoy enduring marriages (Hertenstein et al., 2009).

We cannot, however, predict all aspects of our future selves based on our early life. Our social attitudes, for example, are much less stable than our temperament, especially during the impressionable late adolescent years (Krosnick & Alwin, 1989; Rekker et al., 2015). Older children and adolescents learn new ways of coping. Although delinquent children have elevated rates of later problems, many confused and troubled children blossom into mature, successful adults (Moffitt et al., 2002; Roberts et al., 2013; Thomas & Chess, 1986). Life is a process of becoming. Today's struggles may lay the foundation for tomorrow's happiness.

In some ways, we *all* change with age. Most shy, fearful toddlers begin opening up by age 4, and after adolescence most people gradually become more conscientious, stable, agreeable, and self-confident (Furnham & Cheng, 2019; Lucas & Donnellan, 2009; Van den Akker et al., 2014). Risk-prone adolescents tend, as adults, to become more cautious (Mata et al., 2016). Indeed, many irresponsible 16-year-olds have matured into 40-year-old business or cultural leaders. (If you are the former, you aren't done yet!) But when asked how they have changed in the last decade and will change in the next decade, people—both young and old—exhibit an *end of history illusion*. They recognize that they have changed but presume they will change little in the future (Quoidbach et al., 2013).

Life requires *both* stability and change. Stability provides our identity. Change gives us our hope for a brighter future, allowing us to adapt and grow from experience.

**(a)** **(b)**

**Smiles predict marital stability** In one longitudinal study of 306 U.S. college graduates, 1 in 4 with yearbook expressions like the one in photo (a) later divorced, as did only 1 in 20 with smiles like the one in photo (b) (Hertenstein et al., 2009).

---

### Research

Do inhibited 14-month-olds mostly grow up to be reserved, introverted adults? To answer this question, researchers would use the longitudinal method. They would assess 14-month-olds' inhibition and then retest them again later in life. By following lives through time, longitudinal studies enable researchers to examine whether certain traits remain stable or change over time.

---

### Developing Arguments

Psychological scientists use scientifically derived evidence to support their claims. Which research findings support the idea of stability in personality across the lifespan?

BEFORE AFTER

MUELLER

**As adults grow older, there is continuity of self**

---

## Check Your Understanding

**Examine the Concept**

▶ Explain the difference between longitudinal and cross-sectional studies.

▶ Developmental researchers who emphasize learning and experience are supporting _____; those who emphasize biological maturation are supporting _____.

*Answers to the Examine the Concept questions can be found in Appendix C at the end of the book.*

**Apply the Concept**

▶ Are you the same person you were as a preschooler? As an 8-year-old? As a 12-year-old? How are you different? How are you the same?

## Exploring Research Methods & Design

As you learned in this module, developmental psychologists explore both stability and change. For example, one Spanish research team tested the emotion-detecting ability of 12,198 people ages 17 to 76 (Cabello et al., 2016). When comparing the age groups, they found an inverted-U pattern: Middle-aged adults displayed the best emotion-detecting ability.

- Is this study cross-sectional or longitudinal? Explain your choice.

- Did the researchers use the experimental method in this study? Explain your answer.

- Describe the sample in this study. Who do you think is the intended population?

- Draw a scatterplot depicting these findings. Be sure to label each axis.

---

**AP® Exam Tip**

The AP® Exam focuses on application, not just the ability to define key terms. As you work your way through Modules 3.1–3.6, think of how the material relates to you, your relatives, and your friends. The more often you do this, the easier it will be to apply the material.

---

## Module 3.1 REVIEW

**3.1-1 What three themes have engaged developmental psychologists, and what are two methods they typically use to study human development over time?**

- *Developmental psychologists* study physical, cognitive, and social-emotional changes throughout the lifespan. They explore three issues: nature and nurture (the interaction between our genetic inheritance and our experiences); continuity and stages (which aspects of development are gradual and continuous, and which change relatively abruptly); and stability and change (whether our traits endure or change as we age).

- Developmental psychologists often use *cross-sectional studies* (comparing people of different ages at one point in time) and *longitudinal studies* (retesting the same people over a period of years).

---

## AP® Practice Multiple Choice Questions

**1.** Dr. Lynelle conducts research on how people's bodies, minds, and relationships change over time. In which major area of psychology does Dr. Lynelle conduct research?

a. Biological
b. Developmental
c. Social
d. Cognitive

**2.** Janis gave a presentation on how genes and environment interact. Which of the following was Janis most likely discussing?

a. Stability and change
b. Continuity and stability
c. Continuity and stages
d. Nature and nurture

**Use the following text to answer questions 3–5:**

Dr. Hargen believes that development progresses slowly and steadily. Dr. Hargen followed a group of individuals from birth to age 18 to test her hypothesis.

**3.** Which of the following perspectives best aligns with Dr. Hargen's belief?

   a. Development occurs in stages.
   b. Development occurs longitudinally.
   c. Development occurs continuously.
   d. Development occurs cross-sectionally.

**4.** What type of research method did Dr. Hargen use in her study?

   a. Longitudinal
   b. Cross-sectional
   c. Experimental
   d. Survey

**5.** Which of the following statements best supports Dr. Hargen's hypothesis?

   a. Development occurs like the transformation of a tadpole into a frog, with each stage being distinct from the last.
   b. Development occurs like a caterpillar changing into a butterfly, with clearly different forms emerging at different time points.
   c. Development occurs like a tree grows, with the branches continually growing over time.
   d. Development occurs like the hatching of a chicken from an egg, with the sudden appearance of new abilities.

# Module 3.2a Physical Development Across the Lifespan: Prenatal Development, Infancy, and Childhood

**LEARNING TARGETS**

**3.2-1** Describe the course of prenatal development, and explain how teratogens affect that development.

**3.2-2** Explain some abilities of the newborn, and explain how researchers are able to explore infants' mental abilities.

**3.2-3** Explain key developmental changes in the brain and in motor skills during infancy and childhood.

**3.2-4** Explain how an infant's brain begins processing memories.

Developmental psychologists study physical development, including the developing brain (and blossoming mind), from inside the womb to out in the room, and throughout childhood.

## Prenatal Development and the Newborn

**3.2-1** What is the course of prenatal development, and how do teratogens affect that development?

Your life story began when two lives—and their ancestral genetic histories—merged, and your wonder-filled development began.

### Conception

Nothing is more natural than a species reproducing itself. And nothing is more wondrous. For you, the process started inside your *grandmother*—as an egg formed inside a developing female inside of her. (Your biological mother was born with all the immature eggs she would ever have.) Your biological father, in contrast, began producing sperm cells nonstop at puberty—in the beginning at a rate of more than 1000 sperm during the second it takes to read this phrase.

Some time after puberty, your mother's ovary released a mature egg—a cell roughly the size of the period that ends this sentence. Like space voyagers approaching a huge planet, some 250 million deposited sperm began their frantic race upstream, approaching a cell 85,000 times their own size. The small number reaching the egg released digestive enzymes that ate away the egg's protective coating (**Figure 3.2-1a**). As soon as the one winning sperm penetrated that coating and was welcomed in (Figure 3.2-1b), the egg's surface blocked out the others. Before half a day elapsed, the egg nucleus and the sperm nucleus fused: The two became one.

Consider it your most fortunate of moments. Among some 250 million sperm, the one needed to make you, in combination with that one particular egg, won the race.

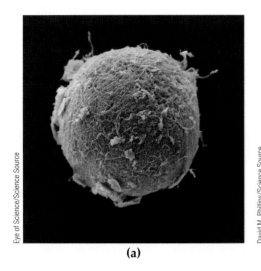 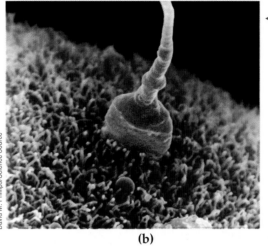

(a)  (b)

**Figure 3.2-1**

**Life is sexually transmitted**

(a) Sperm cells surround an egg. (b) One sperm penetrates the egg's jellylike outer coating, triggering a series of chemical events that will cause sperm and egg to fuse into a single cell. If all goes well, that cell will subdivide again and again to emerge 9 months later as a 37-trillion-cell human being (Bianconi et al., 2013).

(As individual humans, we do not reproduce; we recombine.) And so it was for innumerable generations before us. If any one of our ancestors had been conceived with a different sperm or egg, or died before conceiving, or not chanced to meet their partner, or . . . . The mind boggles at the improbable, unbroken chain of events that produced us.

## Prenatal Development

How many fertilized eggs, called *zygotes*, survive beyond the first 2 weeks? Fewer than half (Grobstein, 1979; Hall, 2004). But for us, good fortune prevailed. One cell became 2, then 4—each just like the first—until this cell division had produced some 100 identical cells within the first week. Then the cells began to differentiate—to specialize in structure and function ("I'll become a brain, you become intestines!").

About 10 days after conception, the *germinal stage* completes as the zygote attaches to the mother's uterine wall, beginning approximately 37 weeks of the closest human relationship. Near the beginning of this maternal bodybuilding feat, the tiny clump of cells forms two parts. The inner cells become the *embryo* (**Figure 3.2-2a**). Many of the outer cells become the *placenta*, the life-link that transfers nutrients and oxygen from mother to embryo. Over the next 6 weeks, the embryo's organs begin to form and function. The heart begins to beat.

By 9 weeks after conception, an embryo looks unmistakably human (Figure 3.2-2b). It is now a *fetus* (Latin for "offspring" or "young one"). During the sixth month, organs such as the stomach develop enough to give the fetus a good chance of surviving and thriving if born prematurely.

**Figure 3.2-2**

**Prenatal development**

(a) The embryo grows and develops rapidly. At 40 days, the spine is visible and the arms and legs are beginning to grow. (b) By the start of the ninth week, when the fetal period begins, facial features, hands, and feet have formed. (c) As the fetus enters the sixteenth week, its 3 ounces could fit in the palm of your hand.

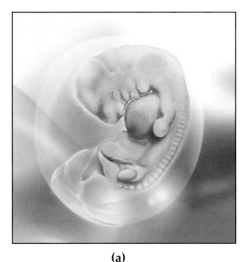 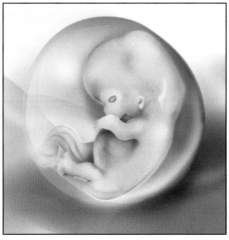 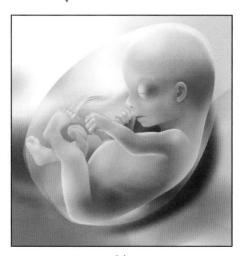

(a)  (b)  (c)

At each prenatal stage, genetic and environmental factors affect our development. By the sixth month, the fetus is responsive to sound. Microphone readings taken inside the uterus reveal that the fetus is exposed to the sound of its mother's muffled voice (Ecklund-Flores, 1992; Hepper, 2005). Immediately after emerging from their underwater world, newborns prefer their mother's voice to another woman's, or to their father's (DeCasper et al., 1986, 1994; Lee & Kisilevsky, 2014).

They also prefer hearing their mother's language. In one study, day-old American and Swedish newborns paused more in their pacifier sucking when listening to familiar vowels from their mother's language (Moon et al., 2013). After repeatedly hearing a fake word (*tatata*) in the womb, Finnish newborns' brain waves displayed recognition when hearing the same word after birth (Partanen et al., 2013). If their mother spoke two languages during pregnancy, newborns displayed interest in both (Byers-Heinlein et al., 2010). And just after birth, the melodic ups and downs of newborns' cries bear the tuneful signature of their mother's native tongue (Mampe et al., 2009). Babies born to French-speaking mothers tended to produce cries with the rising intonation of French; babies born to German-speaking mothers produced cries with the falling tones of German (Mampe et al., 2009). Would you have guessed? The learning of language begins in the womb.

In the 2 months before birth, fetuses demonstrate learning in other ways, as when they adapt to a vibrating, honking device placed on their mother's abdomen (Dirix et al., 2009). Like people who adapt to the sound of trains in their neighborhood, fetuses get used to the honking. Moreover, 4 weeks later, they recall the sound (as evidenced by their mild response, compared with the reactions of those fetuses not previously exposed to such honking).

Sounds are not the only environmental factors that impact fetal development. In addition to transferring nutrients and oxygen from mother to fetus, the placenta screens out many harmful substances. Even so, some slip by. **Teratogens**, agents such as viruses and drugs, can damage an embryo or fetus. This is one reason pregnant women are advised not to drink alcoholic beverages or use nicotine or marijuana (Kuehn, 2019; Saint Louis, 2017). A pregnant woman never smokes, vapes, or drinks alone. When alcohol enters her bloodstream and that of her fetus, it reduces activity in both their central nervous systems. Alcohol use during pregnancy may prime the woman's offspring to like alcohol and put them at risk for heavy drinking and alcohol use disorder during their teen years. In experiments, when pregnant rats drank alcohol, their young offspring later displayed a liking for alcohol's taste and odor (Youngentob & Glendinning, 2009; Youngentob et al., 2007).

Worldwide, 1 in 10 women report consuming alcohol while pregnant (Popova et al., 2019). Even light drinking, occasional binge drinking, or marijuana smoking can affect the fetal brain (CDC, 2018c; Ghazi Sherbaf et al., 2019; Marjonen et al., 2015). Persistent heavy drinking puts the fetus at risk for *congenital* (present at birth) disabilities, future behavior problems, and lower intelligence. For 1 in about 130 children worldwide and 1 in 30 in the United States, the effects are visible as *fetal alcohol spectrum disorder* (Lange et al., 2017; May et al., 2018). Its most serious form is **fetal alcohol syndrome (FAS)**, which is marked by lifelong physical and mental abnormalities. The fetal damage may occur because alcohol has an *epigenetic effect*: It leaves chemical marks on DNA that switch genes abnormally on or off (Liu et al., 2009). Smoking cigarettes or marijuana during pregnancy also leaves epigenetic scars that may increase vulnerability to stress or addiction (Stroud et al., 2014; Szutorisz & Hurd, 2016).

If a pregnant woman experiences extreme stress, the stress hormones flooding her body may indicate a survival threat to the fetus and produce an earlier delivery (Glynn & Sandman, 2011). And malnourishment, maternal illness, and genetic mutations can put a child at risk for health problems and psychiatric disorders (Glynn & Sandman, 2011; Hardie & Landale, 2013; Santavirta et al., 2018).

**teratogens** agents, such as chemicals and viruses, that can reach the embryo or fetus during prenatal development and cause harm.

**fetal alcohol syndrome (FAS)** physical and cognitive function deficits in children caused by their birth mother's heavy drinking during pregnancy. In severe cases, symptoms include a small, out-of-proportion head and distinct facial features.

# The Competent Newborn

**3.2-2** What are some newborn abilities, and how do researchers explore infants' mental abilities?

Babies come with apps preloaded. Having survived prenatal hazards, we as newborns came equipped with automatic reflex responses ideally suited for our survival. We withdraw our limbs to escape pain. If a cloth over our face interferes with our breathing, we turn our head from side to side and swipe at it.

New parents are often in awe of the coordinated sequence of reflexes by which their baby gets food. When something touches their cheek, babies turn toward that touch, open their mouth, and vigorously *root* for a nipple. Finding one, they automatically close on it and begin *sucking*. (Failing to find satisfaction, the hungry baby may cry—a behavior parents find highly unpleasant, and very rewarding to relieve.) Other adaptive reflexes include the *startle* reflex (when arms and legs spring out, quickly followed by fist clenching and loud crying) and the surprisingly strong *grasping* reflex, both of which may have helped infants stay close to their caregivers.

The pioneering American psychologist William James presumed that newborns experience a "blooming, buzzing confusion," an assumption few people challenged until the 1960s. Then scientists discovered that babies can tell you a lot—if you know how to ask. To ask, you must capitalize on what babies can do—gaze, suck, and turn their heads. So, equipped with eye-tracking machines and pacifiers wired to electronic gear, researchers set out to answer parents' age-old questions: What can my baby see, hear, smell, and think?

Consider how researchers exploit **habituation**—decreased responding with repeated stimulation. We saw this earlier when fetuses adapted to a vibrating, honking device placed on their mother's abdomen. The novel stimulus gets attention when first presented. With repetition, the response weakens. This seeming boredom with familiar stimuli gives us a way to ask infants what they see and remember.

As newborns, we prefer sights and sounds that facilitate social responsiveness. We turn our head in the direction of human voices. We gaze longer at a drawing of a face-like image (**Figure 3.2-3**). Even late-stage fetuses look more at face-like patterns in red lights shined into the womb (Reid et al., 2017). As young infants, we also prefer to look at objects 8 to 12 inches away, which—wonder of wonders—just happens to be about the distance between a nursing infant's eyes and its mother's (Maurer & Maurer, 1988). Our brain's default settings help us connect socially.

Within days after birth, our brain's neural networks were stamped with the smell of our mother's body. Week-old nursing babies, placed between a gauze pad from their mother's bra and one from another nursing mother, usually turn toward the smell of their own mother's pad (MacFarlane, 1978). What's more, that smell preference lasts. One study capitalized on the fact that some nursing mothers in a French maternity ward used a chamomile-scented

**habituation** decreasing responsiveness with repeated stimulation. As infants gain familiarity with repeated exposure to a stimulus, their interest wanes and they look away sooner.

**Figure 3.2-3**
**Newborns' preference for faces**

When shown these two images with the same three elements, Italian newborns spent nearly twice as many seconds looking at the face-like image (Valenza et al., 1996). Newborns—average age 53 minutes in one Canadian study—have an apparently inborn preference for looking toward faces (Mondloch et al., 1999).

**Prepared to feed and eat** Like birds and other animals, we are predisposed to respond to our offspring's cries for food—even if we are in the middle of a 314-mile ultramarathon, as I [ND] was when my 18-month-old, Bevy, decided that only Daddy could feed her.

**AP® Science Practice**

## Research

Research on infants can be challenging, because researchers can't ask them directly about their taste or smell preferences. Instead, researchers assess infants' preferences by their gazing time or head turning. Gazing time or head turning is the *operational definition* of infant preferences.

balm to prevent nipple soreness (Delaunay-El Allam et al., 2010). Twenty-one months later, their toddlers preferred playing with chamomile-scented toys! Their peers who had not sniffed the scent while breast-feeding showed no such preference. (This makes us wonder: Will these children grow up to become devoted chamomile tea drinkers?) Such studies reveal the remarkable abilities with which we enter our world.

**AP® Science Practice** **Check Your Understanding**

**Examine the Concept**

► Explain what is meant by "a pregnant woman never smokes, vapes, or drinks alone."

► Explain the effect of teratogens on prenatal development.

**Apply the Concept**

► Are you surprised by the news of infants' competencies? Explain.

► Provide an example of a teratogen.

*Answers to the Examine the Concept questions can be found in Appendix C at the end of the book.*

# Physical Development in Infancy and Childhood

**3.2-3** During infancy and childhood, how do the brain and motor skills develop?

**AP® Exam Tip**

Note that maturation, to developmental psychologists, is a biological sequence. This is much more precise than the general notion that maturation means to become more adult-like.

As a flower unfolds in accordance with its genetic instructions, so do we humans. **Maturation**—the orderly sequence of biological growth—decrees many of our commonalities. Babies first stand, then walk. Toddlers use nouns, then verbs. *Adverse childhood experiences (ACEs),* such as severe deprivation or abuse, can slow development, but genetic growth patterns come "factory-installed"—they are inborn. Maturation (nature) sets the basic course of development; experience (nurture) adjusts it. Genes and scenes interact.

## Brain Development

**maturation** biological growth processes that enable orderly changes in behavior, relatively uninfluenced by experience.

In your mother's womb, your developing brain formed nerve cells at the explosive rate of nearly a quarter million per minute. The developing brain cortex actually overproduces neurons, with the number peaking at 28 weeks (Rabinowicz et al., 1996, 1999).

From infancy on, brain and mind—neural hardware and cognitive software—develop together. On the day you were born, you had most of the brain cells you would ever have. However, your nervous system was immature: After birth, the branching neural networks that eventually enabled all your abilities underwent a wild growth spurt **(Figure 3.2-4)**. This rapid development helps explain why infant brain size increases rapidly in the early days after birth (Holland et al., 2014).

From ages 3 to 6, the most rapid brain growth was in your frontal lobes, which enable rational planning. During those years, your brain required vast amounts of energy (Kuzawa et al., 2014). This energy-intensive process caused rapid progress in your ability to control your attention and behavior (Garon et al., 2008; Thompson-Schill et al., 2009).

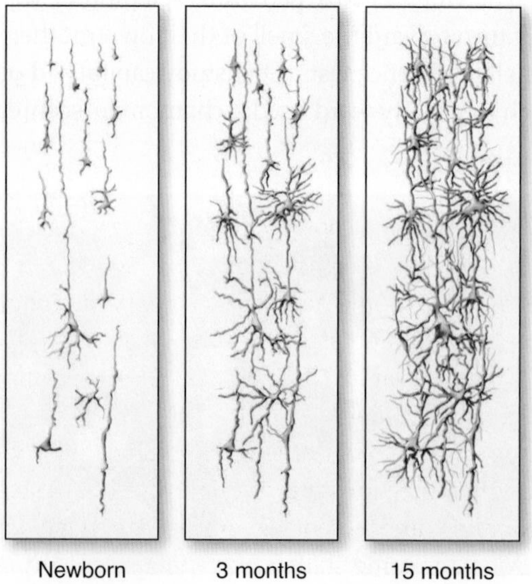

**Figure 3.2-4**
**Infant brain development**

In humans, the brain is immature at birth. As the child matures, the neural networks grow increasingly complex.

Newborn   3 months   15 months

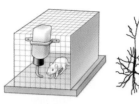

| Impoverished environment | Impoverished rat brain cell | Enriched environment | Enriched rat brain cell |

**Figure 3.2-5**

**Experience affects brain development**

Researchers raised rats either alone in an environment without playthings, or with other rats in an environment enriched with playthings changed daily (Rosenzweig et al., 1962). In 14 of 16 repetitions of this basic experiment, rats in the enriched environment developed significantly more cerebral cortex (relative to the rest of the brain's tissue) than did those in the impoverished environment.

The brain's association areas—those linked with thinking, memory, and language—were the last cortical areas to develop. As they did, your mental abilities surged (Chugani & Phelps, 1986; Thatcher et al., 1987). Fiber pathways supporting agility, language, and self-control proliferated into puberty. Under the influence of adrenal hormones, tens of billions of synapses formed and organized, while a use-it-or-lose-it *synaptic pruning* process shut down unused links (Paus et al., 1999; Thompson et al., 2000).

Your genes dictate your overall brain architecture, rather like the lines of a coloring book, but experience fills in the details (Kenrick et al., 2009). So how do early experiences leave their "fingerprints" in the brain? Mark Rosenzweig, David Krech, and their colleagues (1962) opened a window on that process when they raised some young rats in solitary confinement, and others in a communal playground that simulated a natural environment. When they later analyzed the rats' brains, those who died with the most toys had won: The rats living in the enriched environment had usually developed a heavier and thicker brain cortex (**Figure 3.2-5**).

Rosenzweig was so surprised that he repeated the experiment several times before publishing his findings (Renner & Rosenzweig, 1987; Rosenzweig, 1984). So great were the effects that, if shown brief video clips of the rats, you could tell from their activity and curiosity whether their environment had been impoverished or enriched (Renner & Renner, 1993). After 60 days in the enriched environment, the rats' brain weights increased 7 to 10 percent and the number of brain *synapse* connections mushroomed by about 20 percent (Kolb & Whishaw, 1998). In humans, too, lack of stimulation can slow brain and cognitive development (Farah, 2017).

Such results have motivated improvements in environments for laboratory, farm, and zoo animals—and for children in institutions. Stimulation by touch or massage also benefits both infant rats and premature babies (Field et al., 2007; Sarro et al., 2014). "Handled" infants of these species develop faster neurologically and gain weight more rapidly. Preemies who have had skin-to-skin contact with their parents sleep better, experience less stress, and show better cognitive development 10 years later (Britto et al., 2017; Feldman et al., 2014).

Nature and nurture interact to sculpt our synapses. Brain maturation provides us with an abundance of neural connections. Experiences—sights and smells, touches and tastes, music and movement—activate and strengthen some neural pathways while others weaken from disuse. Like forest pathways, popular neural tracks broaden and less-traveled ones gradually disappear (Dahl et al., 2018; Gopnik et al., 2015). By puberty, this pruning process results in a massive loss of unemployed connections.

Here at the juncture of nurture and nature is the biological reality of early childhood learning. During early childhood—while excess connections are still on call—youngsters can most easily master such skills as the grammar and accent of another language. We seem to have a **critical period**, or *sensitive period*, for some skills. Lacking any exposure to

**AP® Science Practice**

**Research**

As explained in Module 0.4, the *independent variable* is the factor the experimenter manipulates to study its effect on the *dependent variable* (the outcome that is measured). Can you identify the independent variable in the experiment described in Figure 3.2-5?

If you said "type of environment," you are correct!

**Baby brains** This electrode cap allows researchers to detect changes in brain activity triggered by different stimuli.

**critical period** an optimal period early in the life of an organism when exposure to certain stimuli or experiences produces normal development.

**Stringing the circuits starts young** String musicians who started playing before age 12 have larger and more complex neural circuits controlling the note-making left-hand fingers than do string musicians whose training started later (Elbert et al., 1995).

spoken, written, or signed language before adolescence, a person will never master any language (see Module 3.5). Likewise, lacking visual experience during the early years, a person whose vision is later restored by cataract removal will never achieve normal perceptions (see Module 2.1) (Gregory, 1978; Wiesel, 1982). Without that early visual stimulation, the brain cells normally assigned to vision will die or be diverted to other uses. The maturing brain's rule: Use it or lose it.

Although normal stimulation during the early years is critical, brain development does not end with childhood. As we saw in Module 1.4, thanks to the brain's amazing *neuroplasticity*, our neural tissue is ever changing and reorganizing in response to new experiences. New neurons also are born. If a monkey pushes a lever with the same finger many times a day, brain tissue controlling that finger changes to reflect the experience (Karni et al., 1998). Human brains work similarly. Whether learning to keyboard, skateboard, or navigate London's streets, we perform with increasing skill as our brain incorporates the learning (Ambrose, 2010; Maguire et al., 2000).

## Motor Development

The developing brain enables *fine motor* (involving the small muscles of the body) and *gross motor* (involving large muscles and whole-body movement) coordination. Skills emerge as infants exercise their maturing muscles and nervous system. With occasional exceptions, the fine and gross motor development sequence is universal. Babies grasp before they build towers of small blocks, and they roll over before they sit unsupported. These behaviors reflect not imitation but a maturing nervous system.

Genes guide motor development. In the United States, 25 percent of all babies walk by age 11 months, 50 percent within a week after their first birthday, and 90 percent by age 15 months (Frankenburg et al., 1992). Identical twins typically begin walking on nearly the same day (Wilson, 1979). Maturation—including the rapid development of the cerebellum at the back of the brain—creates our readiness to learn walking at about age 1. The same is true for other physical skills, including bowel and bladder control. Before necessary muscular and neural maturation, neither pleading nor punishment will produce successful toilet training. You can't rush a child's first flush.

Still, nurture may amend what nature intends. In some regions of Africa, the Caribbean, and India, caregivers often massage and exercise babies, which can accelerate the process of learning to walk (Karasik et al., 2010). The recommended infant *back to*

**Physical development** Sit, crawl, walk, run — the sequence of these motor development milestones is the same around the world, though babies reach them at varying ages.

(a)

(b)

*sleep position* (putting babies to sleep on their backs to reduce crib-death risk) has been associated with somewhat later crawling but not with later walking (Davis et al., 1998; Lipsitt, 2003).

## Brain Maturation and Infant Memory

**3.2-4** How does an infant's developing brain begin processing memories?

Can you recall your third birthday? Most of us *consciously* recall little from before age 4. Mice and monkeys also forget their early life, as rapid neuron growth disrupts the circuits that stored old memories (Akers et al., 2014). But as children mature, this *infantile amnesia* wanes, and they become increasingly capable of remembering experiences, even for a year or more (Bauer & Larkina, 2014; Morris et al., 2010). The brain areas underlying memory, such as the hippocampus and frontal lobes, continue to mature during and after adolescence (Luby et al., 2016; Murty et al., 2016).

"*Someday we'll look back at this time in our lives and be unable to remember it.*"

Despite consciously recalling little from our early years, our brain was processing and storing information. While finishing her doctoral work in psychology, Carolyn Rovee-Collier observed nonverbal infant memory in action. Her 2-month-old, Benjamin, could be calmed by moving a crib mobile. Weary of hitting the mobile, she strung a cloth ribbon connecting the mobile to Benjamin's foot. Soon, he was kicking his foot to move the mobile. Thinking about her unintended home study, Rovee-Collier realized that, contrary to popular opinion in the 1960s, babies can learn and remember. To know for sure that her son wasn't just a whiz kid, she repeated the study with other infants (Rovee-Collier, 1989, 1999). Sure enough, they, too, soon kicked more when hitched to a mobile, both on the day of the study and the day after. If, however, she hitched them to a different mobile the next day, the infants showed no learning, indicating that they remembered the original mobile and recognized the difference. Moreover, when tethered to the familiar mobile a month later, they remembered the association and again began kicking.

Traces of forgotten childhood languages may also persist. One study tested English-speaking British adults who had no conscious memory of the Hindi or Zulu they had spoken as children. Yet up to age 40, they could relearn subtle sound contrasts in these languages that other English speakers could *not* learn (Bowers et al., 2009). Chinese adoptees living in Canada since age 1 process Chinese sounds as do fluent Chinese speakers, even if they have no conscious recollection of Chinese words (Pierce et al., 2014). We see our two-track mind at work here: What the conscious mind does not know and cannot express in words, the nervous system and unconscious mind somehow remember.

## Check Your Understanding

**AP® Science Practice**

### Examine the Concept

▶ Explain *maturation*.

▶ Explain what is meant by *critical* or *sensitive period*.

### Apply the Concept

▶ What do you regard as your earliest memory? Now that you know about infantile amnesia, has your opinion changed about the accuracy of that memory?

*Answers to the Examine the Concept questions can be found in Appendix C at the end of the book.*

# Module 3.2a REVIEW

**3.2-1** What is the course of prenatal development, and how do teratogens affect that development?

- The life cycle begins at conception, when one sperm cell unites with an egg.
- In the next 6 weeks, body organs begin to form and function.
- *Teratogens* are potentially harmful agents that can pass through the placenta and harm the developing embryo or fetus, as happens with *fetal alcohol syndrome (FAS)*.
- Malnourishment, maternal illness, and genetic mutations can put a child at risk for health problems and psychiatric disorders.

**3.2-2** What are some newborn abilities, and how do researchers explore infants' mental abilities?

- Babies are born with sensory equipment and reflexes that facilitate their survival and their social interactions with adults. For example, they quickly learn to discriminate their mother's smell, and they prefer the sound of human voices.
- Researchers use techniques that test *habituation* to explore infants' abilities.

**3.2-3** During infancy and childhood, how do the brain and motor skills develop?

- The brain's nerve cells are sculpted by heredity and experience.
- As a child's brain develops, neural connections grow more numerous and complex.
- Experiences then trigger a pruning process, in which unused connections weaken and heavily used ones strengthen.
- Complex motor skills—sitting, standing, walking— develop in a predictable sequence, though the timing of that sequence is a function of individual *maturation* and culture. For some skills, we seem to have a *critical* (or *sensitive*) period.

**3.2-4** How does an infant's developing brain begin processing memories?

- We have few or no conscious memories of events occurring before about age 4. This infantile amnesia occurs in part because major brain areas have not yet matured.
- Despite the lack of conscious recall, our brains were still processing and storing information. This is evident in individuals who spoke different languages as young children and are able to relearn their sounds more easily as adults.

## AP® Practice Multiple Choice Questions

1. If a pregnant person contracts the rubella virus, their child may experience lifelong physical and cognitive function deficiencies. The rubella virus is considered to be a(n)

   a. reflex.
   c. teratogen.
   b. embryo.
   d. zygote.

2. FunToys Company is developing a new line of infant toys. Evelyn, a toy designer at FunToys, suggests using face-like images in all their new toys. Which of the following statements provides the best support for Evelyn's idea?

   a. Babies need to practice looking at faces to form effective interpersonal relationships.
   b. Babies prefer sights and sounds that facilitate social responsiveness.
   c. Babies prefer looking at faces rather than abstract images.
   d. Babies will learn to laugh faster by looking at human faces.

3. As infants gain familiarity with repeated exposure to a visual stimulus, their interest wanes and they look away sooner. The decrease in an infant's responsiveness is called

   a. teratogens.
   b. habituation.
   c. stability.
   d. conception.

4. As the infant's brain develops, some neural pathways will decay if not used. This use-it-or-lose-it process is known as

   a. motor development.
   b. synaptic pruning.
   c. infantile amnesia.
   d. maturation.

**5.** Thuy-Linh's example of maturation accurately indicated that

a. we stand before we walk.

b. we like familiar people.

c. we learn the language accents of our peers.

d. we prefer face-like images.

**6.** Dr. Lim wants to conduct a study exploring the effects of color on visual preferences of newborns. Which of the following would be an appropriate operational definition of the dependent variable in her study?

a. Visual preferences

b. Color contrast

c. Habituation to color

d. Being a newborn

**7.** Which of the following is a reflex that helps infants stay close to their caregivers?

a. Maturation

b. Blinking

c. Habituation

d. Grasping

**8.** Researchers found that week-old nursing babies, placed between a gauze pad from their mother's bra and one from another nursing mother, usually turn toward the smell of their own mother's pad. Which of the following statements is true of this study?

a. The researchers can draw causal conclusions because they used an experimental design.

b. The researchers cannot draw causal conclusions because they used an experimental design.

c. The researchers can draw causal conclusions because they used a non-experimental design.

d. The researchers cannot draw causal conclusions because they used a non-experimental design.

# Module 3.2b Physical Development Across the Lifespan: Adolescence and Adulthood

## LEARNING TARGETS

**3.2-5** Define *adolescence*, and explain how the physical changes during this period affect developing teens.

**3.2-6** Explain the physical changes that occur during middle and late adulthood.

Many psychologists once believed that childhood sets our traits. Today's developmental psychologists see development as lifelong. As this *lifespan perspective* emerged, psychologists began to look at how maturation and experience shape us not only in infancy and childhood, but also—after we are no longer handed the children's menu—in adolescence and adulthood.

# Physical Development in Adolescence

**3.2-5** How is *adolescence* defined, and how do physical changes affect developing teens?

**Adolescence**—the years spent morphing from child to adult—starts with the physical beginnings of sexual maturity and ends with the social achievement of independent adult status. Thus, in cultures where postpubertal teens are self-supporting, such as among Aboriginal Australians, adolescence hardly exists (Senior et al., 2021). And in Western cultures, where sexual maturation occurs earlier and independence later, adolescence is lengthening (Sawyer et al., 2018; Worthman & Trang, 2018).

In industrialized countries, what are the teen years like? In Leo Tolstoy's *Anna Karenina*, the teen years were "that blissful time when childhood is just coming to an end, and out of that vast circle, happy and gay, a path takes shape." But another teenager, Anne Frank, writing in her diary while hiding from the Nazis, described tumultuous teen emotions:

> My treatment varies so much. One day Anne is so sensible and is allowed to know everything; and the next day I hear that Anne is just a silly little goat who doesn't know anything at all and imagines that she's learned a wonderful lot from books. . . . Oh, so many things bubble up inside me as I lie in bed, having to put up with people I'm fed up with, who always misinterpret my intentions.

G. Stanley Hall (1904), one of the first psychologists to describe adolescence, believed that the tension between biological maturity and social dependence creates a period of "storm and stress." It's a time of diminishing parental control (Lionetti et al., 2019). It's also a time when teens crave social acceptance, but often feel socially disconnected. Three in four U.S. friendships started in seventh grade dissolve by the end of eighth grade (Hartl et al., 2015). Such social disconnection hits adolescents hard—increasing their risk for substance abuse and depressive symptoms (Hussong et al., 2019). Indeed, after age 30, many who grow up in independence-fostering Western cultures look back on their teenage years as a time they would not want to relive—a time when their peers' social approval was imperative, their sense of direction in life was in flux, and their feeling of alienation from their parents was deepest (Arnett, 1999; Macfarlane, 1964). But for others, adolescence is a time of vitality without the cares of adulthood—a time of rewarding friendships, heightened idealism, and a growing sense of life's exciting possibilities.

Adolescence begins with **puberty**, the time when we mature sexually. Puberty follows a surge of hormones, which may intensify moods and which trigger a series of bodily changes discussed in Module 3.3.

## The Timing of Puberty

Just as in the earlier life stages, the *sequence* of physical changes in puberty (for example, breast buds and visible pubic hair before *menarche*—the first menstrual period) is far more predictable than their *timing*. Some girls start their growth spurt at age 9, some boys as late as age 16.

Early maturation can be a challenge. Early maturing adolescents are at increased risk for mental health problems (Hamlat et al., 2019; Lee et al., 2020; Ullsperger & Nikolas, 2017). This vulnerability is greatest for teen girls and boys with emotionally reactive temperaments. Also, if a girl's physical development outpaces her emotional maturity and her friends' development, she may associate with older adolescents, suffer teasing or sexual harassment, and ruminate more (Alloy et al., 2016; Weingarden & Renshaw, 2012).

**CULTURAL AWARENESS**

Notice the mentions of industrialized countries and Western culture, as well as Aboriginal Australian culture in the discussion of adolescence. Culture plays an important role in how we experience this stage of life. Can you think of a way culture influences the experience of teens? Viewing the experience of others purely through our own cultural lens can lead to misunderstanding.

**adolescence** the transition period from childhood to adulthood, extending from puberty to independence.

**puberty** the period of sexual maturation, during which a person usually becomes capable of reproducing.

# The Teenage Brain

The adolescent brain is a work in progress. Until puberty, brain cells increase their connections, like trees growing more roots and branches. Then, during adolescence, comes a selective *pruning* of unused neurons and connections (Blakemore, 2008). What we don't use, we lose.

As teens mature, their *prefrontal cortex* (in the forward part of the frontal lobes) also continues to develop. The continuing growth of *myelin*, the fatty tissue that forms around axons and speeds neurotransmission, enables better communication with other brain regions (Whitaker et al., 2016). These developments bring improved judgment, impulse control, and long-term planning. A landmark study following 11,000 youth from late childhood to early adulthood is examining influences on teens' brain development, such as drugs, screen time, and sleep (NIMH, 2019; Wadman, 2018).

Maturation of the prefrontal cortex nevertheless lags behind that of the emotional limbic system. Puberty's hormonal surge and limbic system development help explain teens' occasional impulsiveness, risky behaviors, and emotional storms — slamming doors and turning up the music (Smith, 2018; Steinberg & Icenogle, 2019). No wonder younger teens (whose unfinished prefrontal cortex isn't yet fully equipped for making long-term plans and curbing impulses) may succumb to the lure of risky behaviors. Teens actually don't underestimate the risks of vaping, fast driving, and unprotected sex. Their brains are just biased toward immediate rewards, which helps explain why teens worldwide struggle with self-control (Hansen et al., 2019; Steinberg et al., 2018). The teenage brain is like a car with a forceful accelerator and underdeveloped brakes (**Figure 3.2-6**).

So, when Junior drives recklessly and struggles academically, should his parents reassure themselves that "he can't help it; his prefrontal cortex isn't yet fully developed"? They can take hope: Brain changes underlie teens' new self-consciousness about what others are thinking as well as their valuing of risky rewards (Barkley-Levenson & Galván, 2014; Somerville et al., 2013). And the brain with which Junior begins his teens differs from the brain with which he will end his teens. Unless he slows his brain development with heavy drinking — leaving him prone to impulsivity and addiction — his prefrontal cortex will continue maturing until about age 25 (Crews et al., 2007; Giedd, 2015). It will also become better connected with the limbic system, enabling better emotion regulation (Cohen et al., 2016; Steinberg, 2012).

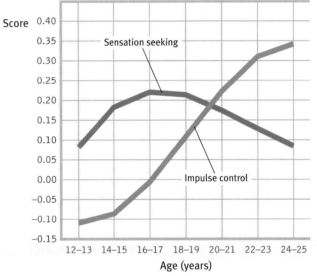

**Figure 3.2-6**

**Impulse control lags reward seeking**

Surveys of more than 7000 American 12- to 24-year-olds reveal that sensation-seeking peaks in the mid-teens, with impulse control developing more slowly as their prefrontal cortex matures. (National Longitudinal Study of Youth and Children and Young Adults survey data presented by Steinberg, 2013.)

---

 **AP® Science Practice**     **Data Interpretation**

Consider Figure 3.2-6.

- Identify the variables represented in the graph.

- Are the data presented in this graph qualitative or quantitative? Explain your choice.

- Which age group shows the most impulse control? Which age group shows the most sensation-seeking?

*"Young man, go to your room and stay there until your cerebral cortex matures."*

In 2004, the American Psychological Association (APA) joined seven other medical and mental health associations in filing U.S. Supreme Court briefs arguing against the death penalty for 16- and 17-year-olds. The briefs documented the teen brain's immaturity "in areas that bear upon adolescent decision making." Brain scans of young teens reveal that prefrontal cortex immaturity is most evident among juvenile offenders and drug users (Shannon et al., 2011; Whelan et al., 2012). Thus, teens are "less guilty by reason of adolescence," suggested psychologist Laurence Steinberg and law professor Elizabeth Scott (2003; Steinberg et al., 2009). In 2005, by a 5-to-4 margin, the Court concurred, declaring juvenile death penalties unconstitutional. In 2012, the APA offered similar arguments against mandatory sentencing of juveniles to life without parole (Banville, 2012; Steinberg, 2013). Once again, the Court, by a narrow 5-to-4 vote, concurred.

**menopause** the time of natural cessation of menstruation; also refers to the biological changes a woman experiences as her ability to reproduce declines.

# Physical Development in Adulthood

> **3.2-6** What physical changes occur during middle and late adulthood?

The unfolding of our lives continues across the lifespan. It is, however, more difficult to generalize about adulthood stages than about life's early years. If you know that James is a 1-year-old and Jamal is a 10-year-old, you could say a great deal about each child. Not so with adults who differ by a similar number of years. The boss may be 30 or 60; the marathon runner may be 20 or 50; the 19-year-old may be a parent who supports a child or a child who receives an allowance. Yet our life courses are in some ways similar. Physically, cognitively, and especially socially, we differ at age 50 from our 25-year-old selves. In the discussion that follows, we recognize these differences and use these terms: *emerging adulthood* (in prosperous communities, from age 18 to mid-twenties), *early adulthood* (roughly twenties and thirties), *middle adulthood* (to age 65), and *late adulthood* (the years after 65). Within each of these stages, people vary widely in their physical, psychological, and social development.

Like the declining daylight after the summer solstice, our physical abilities—muscular strength, reaction time, mobility, flexibility, and cardiac output—all begin an almost imperceptible decline in our mid-twenties. Athletes are often the first to notice. Baseball players peak at about age 27—with 60 percent of Most Valuable Player awardees since 1985 being within 2 years of that age (Silver, 2012). But most of us—especially those of us whose daily lives do not require top physical performance—hardly perceive the early signs of decline.

## Physical Changes in Middle Adulthood

Athletes over 40 know all too well that physical decline gradually accelerates. During early and middle adulthood, physical vigor has less to do with age than with a person's health and exercise habits. Many physically fit 50-year-olds run 4 miles with ease, while sedentary 25-year-olds find themselves huffing and puffing up two flights of stairs.

Aging also brings a gradual decline in fertility, especially for women. For a 35- to 39-year-old woman, the chance of getting pregnant after a single act of intercourse is half that of a woman 19 to 26 years old (Dunson et al., 2002). Women experience **menopause** as their menstrual cycles end, usually within a few years of age 50. Worldwide, early menopause increases women's risk for depression (Georgakis et al., 2016; Zeng et al., 2019). Men experience a gradual decline in sperm count, testosterone

**Adult abilities vary widely** George Blair was, at age 92, the world's oldest barefoot water skier. He is shown here in 2002 when he first set the record, at age 87. (He died at age 98.)

level, and speed of erection and ejaculation. With declining strength and changing appearance, people may experience distress. Seeing their first gray hairs, they may just want to dye.

Sexual activity remains satisfying, though less frequent, after middle age. This was true of 70 percent of Canadians surveyed (ages 40 to 64) and 75 percent of Finns (ages 65 to 74) (Kontula & Haavio-Mannila, 2009; Wright, 2006). And in a sexuality survey, it was not until age 75 or older that most women and nearly half of men reported little sexual desire (DeLamater, 2012; DeLamater & Sill, 2005). As Alex Comfort (2002, p. 226) jested, "The things that stop you having sex with age are exactly the same as those that stop you riding a bicycle (bad health, thinking it looks silly, no bicycle)."

*"Happy fortieth. I'll take the muscle tone in your upper arms, the girlish timbre of your voice, your amazing tolerance for caffeine, and your ability to digest french fries. The rest of you can stay."*

## Physical Changes in Late Adulthood

Is old age "more to be feared than death" (Juvenal, *The Satires*)? Or is life "most delightful when it is on the downward slope" (Seneca, *Epistulae ad Lucilium*)? What is it like to grow old?

### Life Expectancy

From 1950 to 2015, worldwide life expectancy at birth increased from 50 to 73 years (Dicker et al., 2018) (**Figure 3.2-7**). What a gift—two decades more of life! In China, the United States, the United Kingdom, Canada, and Australia (to name some countries where students read this book), life expectancy has risen to 77, 79, 81, 82, and 83 years, respectively (World Bank, 2022). This increasing life expectancy (humanity's greatest achievement, say some) combines with decreasing birthrates: Older adults are a growing population segment, creating an increasing demand for hearing aids, retirement villages, and nursing homes. Today, 13 percent of people worldwide are 60 or older. The United Nations (2017) projects that proportion will more than double by 2100.

Throughout the lifespan, males are more prone to dying. Although 126 male *embryos* begin life for every 100 females, the sex ratio is already down to 105 males for every 100 females at birth (Ritchie & Roser, 2019). During the first year, male infants' death rates exceed females' by one-fourth. And worldwide, women outlive men by 4.7 years (WHO, 2016b). (By age 100, women outnumber men 5 to 1.)

**AP® Science Practice**

**Research**

Notice that the findings cited here came from Canadian, Finnish, and U.S. samples. Researchers conduct similar surveys in various cultures to see if the findings generalize to other older adult populations.

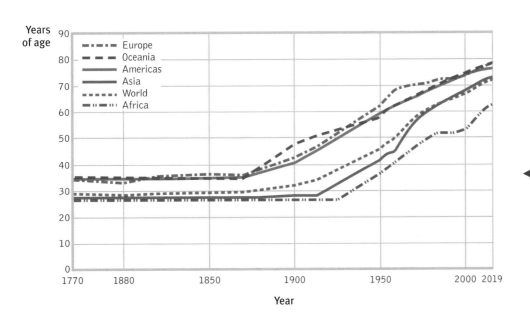

**Figure 3.2-7**

**Life expectancy since 1770, by world regions**

With improved sanitation, modern medicine, and the introduction of antibiotics, infant mortality declined during the twentieth century and life expectancy increased (Roser, 2019).

**World record for longevity?**
French woman Jeanne Calment, the oldest human in history with authenticated age, died in 1998 at age 122 (Robine & Allard, 1999). At age 100, she was still riding a bike.

But few of us live to 100. Disease strikes. The body ages. Its cells stop reproducing. It becomes frail and vulnerable to tiny insults—hot weather, a fall, a mild infection—that at age 20 would have been trivial.

Chronic anger and depression increase our risk of premature death. In contrast, low stress and good health habits enable longevity, as does a positive spirit. Researchers have even observed an intriguing *death-deferral* phenomenon (Shimizu & Pelham, 2008). Across one 15-year period, 2000 to 3000 more Americans died on the 2 days after Christmas than on Christmas and the 2 days before. The death rate also increases when people reach their birthdays, and when they survive until after other milestones, as was true after the first day of the new millennium.

## Sensory Abilities, Strength, and Stamina

Although physical decline begins in early adulthood, we are not usually acutely aware of it until later in life, when the stairs get steeper, other people seem to mumble more, and the print gets smaller. As humorist Dave Barry (1998) mused regarding his own aging, "For some reason, possibly to save ink, [restaurants have] started printing their menus in letters the height of bacteria." Muscle strength, reaction time, and stamina likewise diminish in late adulthood. But even diminished vigor is sufficient for normal activities.

With age, visual sharpness diminishes, as does distance perception and adaptation to light-level changes. The eye's pupil shrinks and its lens becomes less transparent, reducing the amount of light reaching the retina. A 65-year-old retina receives only about one-third as much light as its 20-year-old counterpart (Kline & Schieber, 1985). Thus, to see as well as a 20-year-old when reading or driving, a 65-year-old needs three times as much light—a reason for buying cars with untinted windshields. This also explains why older people sometimes ask younger people, "Don't you need better light for reading?" The senses of smell, hearing, and touch also diminish. In Wales, teens' loitering around a convenience store has been discouraged by a device that emits an aversive high-pitched sound almost no one over 30 can hear (Lyall, 2005).

## Health

As people age, they care less about what their bodies look like and more about how their bodies function. For those growing older, there is both bad and good news about health. The bad news: The body's disease-fighting immune system weakens, making older adults more susceptible to life-threatening ailments such as cancer, pneumonia, and Covid. The good news: Thanks partly to a lifetime's accumulation of antibodies, people over 65 suffer fewer short-term ailments, such as common flu and cold viruses. One study found they were half as likely as 20-year-olds and one-fifth as likely as preschoolers to suffer upper respiratory infections each year (National Center for Health Statistics, 1990).

## The Aging Brain

Up to the teen years, we process information with greater and greater speed (Fry & Hale, 1996; Kail, 1991). But compared with you, older people take a bit more time to react, to solve perceptual puzzles, and even to remember names (Bashore et al., 1997; Verhaeghen & Salthouse, 1997). At video games, most 70-year-olds are no match for a 20-year-old. This

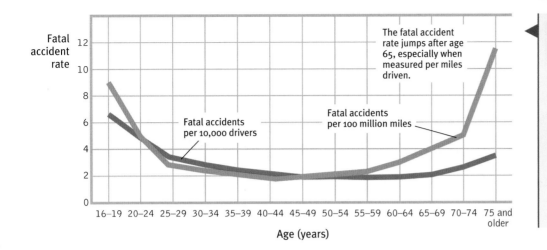

**Figure 3.2-8**

**Age and driver fatalities**

Slowing reactions contribute to increased accident risk among individuals aged 75 and older, and older adults' greater fragility increases their risk of death when accidents happen (NHTSA, 2000). Would you favor driver exams based on performance, not age, to screen out those persons whose slow reactions or sensory impairments indicate a higher accident risk?

processing lag can also have deadly consequences (Aichele et al., 2016). As **Figure 3.2-8** indicates, fatal accident rates per mile driven increase sharply after age 75. By age 85, they exceed the 16-year-old level. Older drivers appear to focus well on the road ahead, but attend less to vehicles approaching from the side (Pollatsek et al., 2012).

Brain regions important to memory begin to atrophy during aging (Fraser et al., 2015; Ritchie et al., 2015). The blood-brain barrier also breaks down beginning in the hippo-campus, which furthers cognitive decline (Montagne et al., 2015). No wonder older adults feel even older after taking a memory test: It's like "aging 5 years in 5 minutes," joked one research team (Hughes et al., 2013). In early adulthood, a small, gradual net loss of brain cells begins, contributing by age 80 to a brain-weight reduction of 5 percent or so. Earlier, we noted that the late-maturing prefrontal cortex, which helps us override our undesirable urges, helps account for teen impulsivity. Late in life, some of that impulsive-ness often returns as that same prefrontal cortex begins to atrophy, seemingly explaining older people's occasional blunt questions ("Have you put on weight?") or inappropriate comments (von Hippel, 2007, 2015). But good news: The aging brain maintains some *neuroplasticity*, which partly compensates for what it loses by recruiting and reorganizing neural networks (Park & McDonough, 2013). During memory tasks, for example, the left frontal lobes are especially active in young adult brains, while older adult brains use both the left and right frontal lobes.

## Exercise and Aging

And more good news: Exercise slows aging, as shown in studies of identical twin pairs in which only one twin exercised (Iso-Markku et al., 2016; Rottensteiner et al., 2015). Midlife and older adults who do more exercising and less sitting around tend to be mentally quick older adults (Kramer & Colcombe, 2018; Won et al., 2019). Physical exercise can even slow the progression of Alzheimer's dis-ease (Kivipelto & Håkansson, 2017; Loprinzi et al., 2015; Smith et al., 2014).

Exercise also appears to stimulate *neurogenesis*—the development of new brain cells—and neural connections, thanks perhaps to increased oxy-gen and nutrient flow (Erickson et al., 2010; Pereira et al., 2007). Seden-tary older adults randomly assigned to aerobic exercise programs exhibited enhanced memory, sharpened judgment, and reduced risk of severe cogni-tive decline (Northey et al., 2018; Raji et al., 2016; Smith, 2016). In the aging brain, exercise reduces brain shrinkage (Gow et al., 2012). And it increases the cellular mitochondria, which help power both muscles and brain cells (Steiner et al., 2011). We are more likely to rust from disuse than to wear out from overuse. Fit bodies support fit minds.

*"I've been working out for six months, but all my gains have been in cognitive function."*

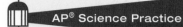
## Check Your Understanding

**Examine the Concept**

▶ Explain what is meant by *adolescence*.

▶ Explain the physical changes in the brain during adolescence.

**Apply the Concept**

▶ Imagining the future, how do you think you might change? How might you stay the same? In what ways do you most want to grow as a person?

▶ Based on what you learned in this module, what logical conclusions can you draw about aging and exercise?

*Answers to the Examine the Concept questions can be found in Appendix C at the end of the book.*

# Module 3.2b REVIEW

**3.2-5** How is *adolescence* defined, and how do physical changes affect developing teens?

- *Adolescence* is the transition period from childhood to adulthood, extending from *puberty* to social independence.

- Early maturation can be a challenge for developing adolescents.

- The brain's prefrontal cortex matures and myelin growth increases during adolescence, enabling improved judgment, impulse control, and long-term planning.

**3.2-6** What physical changes occur during middle and late adulthood?

- Muscular strength, reaction time, mobility, flexibility, sensory abilities, and cardiac output begin to decline almost imperceptibly in the mid-twenties; this downward trajectory accelerates through middle and late adulthood, varying considerably with personal health and exercise habits.

- Women's period of fertility ends with *menopause* around age 50; men experience a more gradual decline.

- In late adulthood, the immune system weakens, increasing susceptibility to life-threatening illnesses.

- Exercise can slow aging; it enhances physical health as well as boosts memory, improves judgment, and reduces the risk of severe cognitive decline.

## AP® Practice Multiple Choice Questions

**1.** When Kaev reached sexual maturity, becoming capable of reproducing, he entered

a. puberty.
b. menopause.
c. fertility.
d. early adulthood.

**2.** Dr. Kamara conducted a study on the transition from childhood to adulthood Dr. Kamara is interested in what variable?

a. Social behavior
b. Puberty
c. Menopause
d. Adolescence

**3.** Compared to when he was 17 years old, Kwame, who is now 25 years old, has noticed that he is better able to resist the urge to play video games all evening. What development in adolescence has allowed for his greater impulse control?

a. Hormonal surges
b. Hindbrain changes
c. Prefrontal cortex maturation
d. Limbic system development

4. Dr. Longoria wants to conduct a study to examine the development of puberty across 30 different countries. Based on past research on brain development in puberty, which of the following would be the best hypothesis Dr. Longoria could make?

   a. In Western countries, limbic system development precedes prefrontal cortex development, while the opposite is true in Eastern countries.
   b. In Eastern countries, puberty's sequence begins with decreased fertility, which should be followed by menopause, while the opposite is true in Western countries.
   c. In all countries, puberty follows the same sequence regardless of the country's geographic location.
   d. In all countries, puberty begins with increased fertility and ends in menopause.

5. Ankit has reached menopause. What is true for her?

   a. She, like men, likely experienced menopause around the age of 50.
   b. She likely experienced menopause around 50 years of age, but men experience menopause around 65 years of age.
   c. She likely experienced menopause around the age of 50, but men don't experience menopause.
   d. Men experience menopause around the age of 65, but she likely experienced menopause in her twenties.

6. Dr. Soq studies the tendency for people to die after major milestones, such as a birthday or a holiday. What does Dr. Soq study?

   a. Menopause and adolescence
   b. Death-deferral phenomenon
   c. Fertility and menopause
   d. Life expectancy

7. Dr. Raley conducted a study on a group of 1000 people who were between 65 and 85 years old and were experiencing difficulties remembering newly presented information. Which of the following is the population of interest in this study?

   a. The 1000 individuals in the study who were in middle adulthood
   b. All individuals in late adulthood
   c. The 1000 individuals in the study who were in late adulthood
   d. All individuals in middle adulthood

# Module 3.3a Gender and Sexual Orientation: Gender Development

**LEARNING TARGETS**

**3.3-1** Explain how the meaning of *gender* differs from the meaning of *sex*.

**3.3-2** Explain some ways in which males and females tend to be alike and tend to differ.

**3.3-3** Explain how sex hormones influence prenatal and adolescent sexual development.

**3.3-4** Explain some cultural influences on gender roles.

**3.3-5** Explain how we form our gender identity.

**3.3-1** How does the meaning of *gender* differ from the meaning of *sex*?

Cultures change, and ideas about gender change, too. After enrolling at Harvard Law School as one of nine women among 500+ men, Ruth Bader Ginsburg was asked by the dean, "Why are you at Harvard Law School, taking the place of a man?" After law school, a Supreme Court justice rejected her clerkship application because he wasn't ready to hire a woman (Lewis, 1993). When Ginsburg was recommended for a law firm job, the managing partner responded flatly, "We don't hire women."

Ginsburg devoted much of her career to changing laws that discriminated against women. In 1993, at age 60, she became the second woman to serve on the U.S. Supreme Court, becoming a champion of gender equality and an icon to younger generations. "Women will have achieved true equality," Ginsburg said, "when men share with them the responsibility of bringing up the next generation" (Sullivan, 2001).

Clearly, social and cultural factors influence our gender expectations. But how do nature and nurture interact to define gender and form our unique gender identities? How are males and females alike, and how and why do they differ? While exploring these issues, we'll also gain insight into the psychology and biology of sexual attraction and intimacy. And as part of the journey, we'll see how evolutionary psychologists explain our sexuality.

Let's start by asking: How does gender develop?

As we saw in Module 2.2a, we humans share an irresistible urge to organize our worlds into simple categories. Among the ways we classify people—as tall or short, dull or smart, cheerful or churlish—one stands out. It's what everyone first wanted to know about you: "Boy or girl?" Your parents may have tried to offer clues with pink or blue clothing; their answer described your birth-assigned **sex**. For most people, biological traits help define their assigned **gender**, their culture's expectations about what it means to be a man or a woman.

Simply said, your body defines your sex; your mind defines your gender. But your mind's understanding of gender arises from the interplay between your biology and your

**sex** in psychology, the biologically influenced characteristics by which people define *male*, *female*, and *intersex*.

**gender** in psychology, the attitudes, feelings, and behaviors that a given culture associates with a person's biological sex. (*See also gender identity.*)

experiences (Eagly & Wood, 2013). Before we consider that interplay, let's look at three ways that males and females differ and how they are alike.

## Similarities and Differences

**3.3-2** What are some of the ways males and females tend to be alike and to differ?

Whether male, female, or **intersex**, most of us receive 23 chromosomes from our mother and 23 from our father. Of those 46 chromosomes, 45 are *unisex*—the same for everyone. Our similar biology helped our evolutionary ancestors face similar adaptive challenges. For example, survival for men and women involved traveling long distances (migration and outrunning threats), which today is reflected biologically in men's and women's similar finishing times for ultralong-distance races. Everyone needed to survive, reproduce, and avoid predators, so we are in most ways alike. Your gender gives no clue to your vocabulary, happiness, or ability to see, learn, and remember, reports gender researcher Janet Shibley Hyde and her colleagues (2019). Whatever our gender, we are, on average, comparably creative and intelligent and feel similar emotions and longings (Hyde, 2014; Lauer et al., 2019; Reilly et al., 2019).

But in some areas, female and male traits do differ, and differences command attention. Some oft-noted differences (such as the gender difference in self-esteem) are actually quite modest (Zell et al., 2015). Others are more striking. The average female enters puberty about 2 years earlier than the average male, and her life expectancy is 4 years longer. She expresses most emotions more freely, smiling and crying more, and, in social media updates, more often expresses "love" and being "sooo excited!!!" (Fischer & LaFrance, 2015; Schwartz et al., 2013). She is better at spelling and reading (Reilly et al., 2019). Ms. Average can detect fainter odors. She also has twice the risk of developing depression and anxiety, and 10 times the risk of developing an eating disorder. By comparison, the average male is 4 times more likely to die by suicide, to abuse tobacco products, and to develop alcohol use disorder. Mr. Average also has greater size and strength, but is more likely to be diagnosed with autism spectrum disorder, color-deficient vision, and attention-deficit/hyperactivity disorder (ADHD). And as an adult, he is more at risk for antisocial personality disorder. Female and male each have their own heightened strengths and risks.

Gender similarities and differences appear throughout this book, but here let's take a closer look at three gender differences. Although individuals vary widely, the *average* male and female differ in aggression, social power, and social connectedness.

## Aggression

To a psychologist, **aggression** is any physical or verbal behavior intended to hurt someone physically or emotionally (Bushman & Huesmann, 2010). Pause to picture in your mind an aggressive person.

Is the person a man? Likely yes. Men generally admit to more aggression, especially extreme physical violence (Yount et al., 2017). Nearly half of 14- to 19-year-old U.S. boys feel pressure to be "willing to punch someone if provoked" (PLAN USA, 2018). In romantic relationships between women and men, minor acts of physical aggression, such as slaps, are roughly equal, but the most violent acts are mostly committed by men (Archer, 2000; Tremblay et al., 2018).

In laboratory experiments, men have been more willing to blast people with what they believed was intense and prolonged noise (Bushman et al., 2007). And outside the laboratory, men worldwide commit more violent crime, including 90 percent of murders (UNODC, 2019). Men also take the lead in hunting, fighting, warring, and supporting war (Liddle et al., 2012; Wood & Eagly, 2002, 2007).

**AP® Science Practice**

### Research

Janet Shibley Hyde based her claims about gender similarities on meta-analyses that she and her team conducted. A meta-analysis, a non-experimental method, is a statistical procedure for summarizing the results of multiple studies to reach an overall conclusion. For example, a researcher might combine the results of 46 studies with hundreds of participants each, thus making her conclusions more generalizable to broader populations.

**SPOTLIGHT ON:**
Janet Shibley Hyde

**AP® Science Practice**

### Data

The statement "Although individuals vary widely, the *average* male and female differ in aggression, social power, and social connectedness" illustrates an important point about psychological science. Researchers do not draw general conclusions from individuals. Instead, they compare group averages. If the difference between the groups is large enough to suggest an actual difference between the populations, the results are said to be statistically significant. (You can revisit Module 0.6 to review these important statistical concepts.)

**intersex** possessing male and female biological sexual characteristics at birth.

**aggression** any physical or verbal behavior intended to harm someone physically or emotionally.

Making history In 2019, West Point's 34 Black female cadets, many shown here, were part of its most diverse graduating class in history.

**relational aggression** an act of aggression (physical or verbal) intended to harm a person's relationship or social standing.

Here's another question: Picture in your mind someone harming others by passing along hurtful gossip, by disclosing private information, by shutting someone out, or by online bullying.

Was the person a woman? Perhaps. Those behaviors are acts of **relational aggression**, which women have been slightly more likely than men to commit (Archer, 2004, 2007, 2009).

## Social Power

Imagine you've walked into a job interview and are taking your first look at the two interviewers. The unsmiling person on the left oozes self-confidence and independence, maintaining steady eye contact. The person on the right gives you a warm, welcoming smile, but makes less eye contact and seems to expect the other interviewer to take the lead.

Which interviewer is male?

If you said the person on the left, you're not alone. Around the world, from Nigeria to New Zealand, people have perceived gender differences in power (Williams & Best, 1990). Even in 2020, a United Nations global survey found almost half of humanity believe men to be superior political leaders, and more than 40 percent believe them to be better business executives (UNDP, 2020). (For more on this, see Developing Arguments: Gender Bias in the Workplace.)

Now picture a heterosexual couple negotiating a car purchase. "If you won't lower your price, we're leaving," says one of them to the salesperson.

Which member of the couple—male or female—made the demand? If you said the male, you're again in good company. People tend to associate negotiation with males, and men often have an advantage in negotiation outcomes (Mazei et al., 2015).

When asked a difficult question—"Do you have any idea why the sky is blue?"—men are more likely than women to hazard answers than to admit they don't know, a phenomenon researchers have called the *male answer syndrome*. Men are also more prone to "mansplaining"—explaining something to women in a condescending and sometimes inaccurate manner (Giuliano et al., 1998; Tramontana, 2020).

## Social Connectedness

Whatever our gender, we all have a need to belong, though we may satisfy this need in different ways (Baumeister, 2010). In the 1980s, many developmental psychologists believed that all children struggle to create a separate, independent identity. Research by Carol Gilligan and her colleagues (1982, 1990), however, suggested that this struggle describes Western individualistic males more than relationship-oriented females. Gilligan believed females tend to differ from males both in being less concerned with viewing themselves as separate individuals and in being more concerned with "making connections." Indeed, males tend to be *independent*. Even as children, males typically form large play groups that brim with activity and competition, with little intimate discussion (Rose & Rudolph, 2006). As adults, men usually enjoy side-by-side activities, and their conversations often focus on problem solving (Baumeister, 2010; Tannen, 1990).

Brain scans show no striking structural sex differences (Ritchie et al., 2018; Wierenga et al., 2019). "Human brains cannot be categorized into two distinct classes—male brain/female brain," reported neuroscientist

*"Oh, you've read it? I'll just describe it to you as if you hadn't."*

 **AP® Science Practice** # Developing Arguments

## Gender Bias in the Workplace

### Differences in **PERCEPTION**

She's so aggressive!

He's so take-charge!

Among politicians who seem power-hungry, women are less successful than men.[1]

Most political leaders are men:

men

**Political leaders**

women

Men held 76% of seats in the world's governing parliaments in 2019.[2]

People around the world tend to see men as more powerful.[3]

When groups form, whether as juries or companies, leadership tends to go to males.[4]

### Differences in **COMPENSATION**

Women in traditionally male occupations have received less than their male colleagues.[5]

**Medicine**
U.S. salary disparity between male and female physicians:[6]

$171,880 **women**

$243,072 **men**

**Academia** Female research grant applicants have received lower quality of researcher ratings and have been less likely to be funded.[7] (But as we will see, gender attitudes and roles are changing.)

### Differences in **FAMILY-CARE RESPONSIBILITY**

**U.S. mothers** still do nearly **twice** as much child care as **fathers**.[8] In the workplace, women are less often driven by money and status, compromise more, and more often opt for reduced work hours.[9]

### What else contributes to **WORKPLACE GENDER BIAS?**

#### Social norms

In most societies, men place more importance on power and achievement, and are socially dominant.[10]

#### Leadership styles

**Men** are more *directive*, telling people what to do and how to do it.

**Women** are more *democratic*, welcoming others' input in decision making.[11]

#### Interaction styles

**Women** are more likely to express support.[12]

**Men** are more likely to offer opinions.[12]

#### Everyday behavior

**Women** smile and apologize more than men.[13]

**Men** are more likely to talk assertively, interrupt, initiate touches, and stare.[13]

### Yet GENDER ROLES VARY WIDELY across place and time.

Women are increasingly represented in leadership (now 50% of Canada's cabinet ministers) and in the workforce. In 1963, the Harvard Business School admitted its first women students. Among its Class of 2020, 41% were women.[14] In 1960, women were 6% of U.S. medical students. Today they are slightly more than half.[15]

## Developing Arguments Questions

**1.** Explain the reasoning that differences in perception lead to gender bias.

**2.** Using scientifically derived evidence, explain how family-care responsibilities contribute to workplace gender bias.

1. Okimoto & Brescoll, 2010. 2. IPU, 2021. 3. Eagly et al., 2020. 4. Colarelli et al., 2006. 5. LMIC, 2020. 6. Willett et al., 2015. 7. Witteman et al., 2019. 8. CEA, 2014; Parker & Wang, 2013; Pew, 2015. 9. Nikolova & Lamberton, 2016; Pinker, 2008. 10. Gino et al., 2015; Schwartz & Rubel-Lifschitz, 2009. 11. Eagly & Carli, 2007; van Engen & Willemsen, 2004. 12. Aries, 1987; Wood, 1987. 13. Leaper & Ayres, 2007; Major et al., 1990; Schumann & Ross, 2010. 14. Harvard Business School, 2019. 15. AAMC, 2018.

(a)

(b)

**Free-for-all, or tend and befriend?** Gender differences in the way we interact with others begin to appear at a very young age.

Daphna Joel and her colleagues (2015). Brain scans do, however, suggest that a female's brain, more than a male's, is usually wired in a way that enables social relationships (Kiesow et al., 2020).

This helps explain why females tend to be more *interdependent*. Across nearly a thousand studies, women have been found to be "more communal than men" (Hsu et al., 2021). In childhood, girls usually play in small groups, often with one friend. They compete less and imitate social relationships more (Maccoby, 1990; Roberts, 1991). Teen girls spend more time with friends and less time alone (Wong & Csikszentmihalyi, 1991). In late adolescence, they spend more time on social media, and average more daily text messages than boys (Pew, 2015a; Yang et al., 2018). Girls' and women's friendships are more intimate, featuring more conversation that explores relationships (Maccoby, 2002). In one analysis of 10 million posts to Facebook (which more women use), women's status updates were as assertive as men's, but used warmer words; men more often swore or expressed anger (Gramlich, 2018; Park et al., 2016). An analysis of more than 700 million Facebook words found women also used more family-related words, whereas men used more work-related words (Schwartz et al., 2013).

When searching for understanding from someone who will share their worries and hurts, people usually turn to women. Women and men have reported that their friendships with women are more intimate, enjoyable, and nurturing (Kuttler et al., 1999; Rubin, 1985; Sapadin, 1988). When stressed, women are also more likely than men to turn to others for support. They are said to *tend and befriend* (Tamres et al., 2002; Taylor, 2002).

Gender differences in both social connectedness and power are greatest in adolescence and early adulthood—the prime years for dating and mating (Hoff et al., 2018; Hsu et al., 2021). By their teen years, girls appear less assertive and more insecure, and boys seem more dominant and less expressive (Chaplin, 2015). In adulthood, attitude and behavior differences often peak with parenthood. Mothers especially may express more traditionally female attitudes and behaviors (Ferriman et al., 2009; Katz-Wise et al., 2010). By age 50, most gender differences subside, especially among parents. Men become less domineering and more empathic, and women—especially those with paid employment—become more assertive and self-confident (Kasen et al., 2006; Maccoby, 1998). Worldwide, fewer women than men work for pay. But, like men, women tend to be more satisfied with their lives when gainfully employed (Ryan, 2016). So, although women and men are more alike than different, there are some behavior differences between the average woman and man, some of which also occur in nonhuman primates (Lonsdorf, 2017). Are such differences dictated by their biology? Shaped by their cultures and other experiences? Read on.

## Check Your Understanding

**Examine the Concept**

▶ Explain what is meant by *gender*.

▶ Explain physical and relational aggression in terms of gender differences.

**Apply the Concept**

▶ Think of two people you've known for a long time: one male and one female. Have you observed differences in their behavior that might, based on what you've learned here, be attributable to their gender? Have these differences changed with age?

*Answers to the Examine the Concept questions can be found in Appendix C at the end of the book.*

# The Nature of Gender

**3.3-3** How do sex hormones influence prenatal and adolescent sexual development?

In most physical ways—regulating heat with sweat, preferring energy-rich foods, growing calluses where the skin meets friction—we are all alike. Although biology does not *dictate* gender, it can influence our sexual development in two ways:

- *Genetically*—We have differing *sex chromosomes*.

- *Physiologically*—We have differing concentrations of *sex hormones*, which trigger other anatomical differences.

These two influences began to form you long before you were born.

## Prenatal Sexual Development

Six weeks after you were conceived, you looked much the same as any other tiny embryo. Then, as your genes kicked in, your biological sexual characteristics—determined by your twenty-third pair of chromosomes (the two sex chromosomes)—became more apparent. Your mother's contribution to that chromosome pair was an **X chromosome**. From your father, you received the 1 chromosome out of the usual 46 that is not unisex—either another X chromosome, making you female, or a **Y chromosome**, making you male. (Occasionally, there are other sexual development variations, as we will see shortly.)

About 7 weeks after conception, a single gene on the Y chromosome throws a master switch, which triggers the testes to develop and to produce **testosterone**, the main *androgen* (male hormone) that promotes male sex organ development. Females also have testosterone, but less of it; the main female sex hormones are the **estrogens**, such as *estradiol*.

Later, during the fourth and fifth prenatal months, sex hormones bathe the fetal brain and influence its wiring. Different patterns for males and females develop under the influence of the male's greater testosterone and the female's estrogens (Hines, 2004; Udry, 2000). If, however, females are prenatally exposed to unusually high levels of male hormones, they tend to grow up with more male-typical interests (Endendijk et al., 2016).

## Adolescent Sexual Development

A flood of hormones triggers another period of dramatic physical change during adolescence, when we enter *puberty*. In this 2-year period of rapid sexual maturation, pronounced female-male differences emerge. A variety of changes begin at about age 10 in girls and at about age 12 in boys, though the subtle beginnings of puberty, such as budding breasts or enlarging testes, appear earlier (Biro et al., 2012; Herman-Giddens et al., 2012). A year or two before visible physical changes, we often feel the first stirrings of sexual attraction (McClintock & Herdt, 1996).

**X chromosome** the sex chromosome found in females and males. Females typically have two X chromosomes; males typically have one. An X chromosome from each parent produces a female child.

**Y chromosome** the sex chromosome typically found only in males. When paired with an X chromosome from the mother, it produces a male child.

**testosterone** the most important male sex hormone. Males and females have it, but the additional testosterone in males stimulates the growth of the male sex organs during the fetal period, and the development of male sex characteristics during puberty.

**estrogens** sex hormones, such as estradiol, that contribute to female sex characteristics and are secreted in greater amounts by females than by males.

**Figure 3.3-1a, b**
**Height differences**
(Data from Tanner, 1978.)

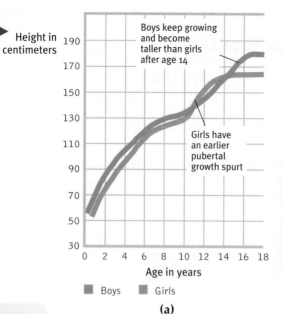

Height in centimeters

Boys keep growing and become taller than girls after age 14

Girls have an earlier pubertal growth spurt

Age in years

■ Boys  ■ Girls

**(a)**

George Doyle/Getty Images

**(b)**

**primary sex characteristics**
the body structures (ovaries, testes, and external genitalia) that make sexual reproduction possible.

**secondary sex characteristics**
nonreproductive sexual traits, such as female breasts and hips, male voice quality, and body hair.

**spermarche** [sper-MAR-key]
the first ejaculation.

**menarche** [meh-NAR-key] the first menstrual period.

Girls' slightly earlier entry into puberty can at first propel them to greater height than boys of the same age (**Figure 3.3-1**). But boys catch up when they begin puberty, and by age 14, they are usually taller than girls. During these growth spurts, the **primary sex characteristics**—the reproductive organs and external genitalia—develop dramatically. So do the nonreproductive **secondary sex characteristics**. Pubic and underarm hair emerges. Girls develop breasts and larger hips. Boys' facial hair begins growing and their voices deepen (**Figure 3.3-2**). (Pubertal boys may not at first like their sparse beard—but then it grows on them.)

For boys, puberty's landmark is the first ejaculation, which often occurs first during sleep (as a "wet dream"). This event, called **spermarche**, usually happens by about age 14.

In girls, the landmark is the first menstrual period, **menarche**, usually within a year of age 12½ (Anderson et al., 2003). Scientists have identified nearly 250 genes that predict age at menarche (Day et al., 2017). But environment matters, too. Early menarche is more likely following stresses related to poverty, father absence, sexual abuse, insecure attachments, or a history of the mother smoking during pregnancy (Richardson et al., 2018;

**Figure 3.3-2**
**Body changes at puberty**

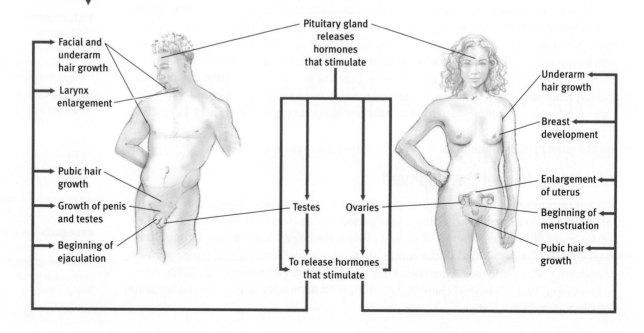

Facial and underarm hair growth

Larynx enlargement

Pubic hair growth

Growth of penis and testes

Beginning of ejaculation

Pituitary gland releases hormones that stimulate

Testes        Ovaries

To release hormones that stimulate

Underarm hair growth

Breast development

Enlargement of uterus

Beginning of menstruation

Pubic hair growth

Shrestha et al., 2011; Sun et al., 2017). Girls in various countries are reaching puberty earlier today than in the past. Suspected triggers include increased body fat, increased hormone-mimicking chemicals in the diet, and increased stress related to family disruption (Biro et al., 2010, 2012; Ellis et al., 2012; Herman-Giddens, 2013). But the good news for children with a secure child-mother attachment is that this bond can provide a buffer against childhood stresses, including those related to early puberty (Sung et al., 2016). Remember: *Nature and nurture interact.*

---

**AP® Science Practice**

## Check Your Understanding

### Examine the Concept

▶ Describe the two major sex hormones.

▶ Explain what is meant by *puberty*.

*Answers to the Examine the Concept questions can be found in Appendix C at the end of the book.*

### Apply the Concept

▶ Compare and contrast primary and secondary sex characteristics.

---

## Sexual Development Variations

Nature sometimes blurs the biological line between males and females. People who are intersex may be born with unusual combinations of male and female chromosomes, hormones, and anatomy. For example, a genetic male may be born with two or more X chromosomes as well as a Y chromosome (*Klinefelter syndrome*), which often results in sterility and small testes. Genetic females born with only one normal X chromosome (*Turner syndrome*) may not have menstrual periods, develop breasts, or be able to have children without reproductive assistance.

In the past, medical professionals often recommended what used to be called "sex-reassignment surgery" to create an unambiguous sex identity for these children. One study reviewed 14 cases of genetic boys who had undergone early surgery and been raised as girls. Of those cases, 6 later identified as male, 5 were living as females, and 3 reported an unclear male or female identity (Reiner & Gearhart, 2004).

In one famous case, a little boy lost his penis during a botched circumcision. His parents followed a psychiatrist's advice to raise him as a girl rather than as a boy. So, with male chromosomes and hormones and a female upbringing, did nature or nurture form this child's gender identity? "Brenda" Reimer was not like most other girls. "She" tore her dresses with rough-and-tumble play, and at puberty wanted no part of kissing boys. Finally, Brenda's parents explained what had happened, which led Brenda immediately to reject the assigned female identity. He underwent surgery to remove the breasts he'd developed from hormone therapy. He cut his hair and chose a male name, David. He eventually married a woman and became a stepfather. Sadly, he later died by suicide — as had his depressed identical twin brother (Colapinto, 2000). Today, most experts recommend postponing *gender-affirming surgery* until a child's naturally developing physical appearance and gender identity become clear.

## The Nurture of Gender

For many people, birth-assigned sex and gender co-exist in harmony. Biology draws the outline, and culture paints the details. The physical traits that define a newborn as male, female, or intersex are the same worldwide. But the gender traits that define how men (or boys) and women (or girls) *should* act, interact, or feel about themselves differ across time and place (Zentner & Eagly, 2015).

MARWAN NAAMANI/AFP/Getty Images

**Driving change** Thanks to the advocacy of Manal al-Sharif and others, driving a car became a universal right for women in 2018, when Saudi Arabia lifted its ban on this practice. She said, "The fight for women's rights anywhere contributes to the fight for women's rights everywhere" (2019).

## CULTURAL AWARENESS

Culture shapes the attitudes, feelings, and behaviors associated with gender. So we're wise to be aware of its influences. Some attitudes (such as "girls are bad at math") can negatively impact people's career goals.

**role** a set of expectations (norms) about a social position, defining how those in the position ought to behave.

**gender role** a set of expected behaviors, attitudes, and traits for men and for women.

dpa picture alliance/Alamy Stock Photo

**Medical miracles to come** Women are gaining ground in STEM fields, as illustrated by awarding of the 2020 Nobel Prize in chemistry to Emmanuelle Charpentier and Jennifer Doudna for creating the DNA-editing technique, CRISPR.

## Gender Roles

**3.3-4 What are some cultural influences on gender roles?**

Cultures shape our behaviors by defining how we ought to behave in a particular social position, or **role**. We can see this shaping power in **gender roles**—the social expectations that guide people's behavior as men or women.

In just a thin slice of history, gender roles worldwide have undergone an extreme makeover. At the beginning of the twentieth century, only one country in the world—New Zealand—granted women the right to vote (Briscoe, 1997). By 2015, that right existed in all countries. A century ago, American women could not vote in national elections, serve in the military, or divorce a husband without cause. If a woman worked for pay, she would more likely have been a cook than a college professor. When asked to draw a scientist in the 1960s and 1970s, fewer than 1 percent of U.S. children drew a woman. In more recent studies, 28 percent did so ( Miller et al., 2018).

Globally, women are often underrepresented in the STEM (science, technology, engineering, and mathematics) fields (UNESCO, 2017). As of 2020, the Nobel Prize in physics had been awarded to three women, and to nine men named *John* (plus 204 other men). Men around the world tend to hold most faculty positions, receive greater financial research support, and have more articles accepted in the most prestigious journals (Odic & Wojcik, 2020; Oliveira et al., 2019; Shen et al., 2018). In many countries, women still experience sexism, subtle or otherwise, that discourages their pursuing a STEM-related career (Kuchynka et al., 2018; Leaper & Starr, 2019).

But signs point to increases in the supply of and demand for women in STEM fields. In high school, U.S. women outperform men on reading and writing (Reilly et al., 2019). At the college level, U.S. women, compared with men, earn more college degrees and higher college grades, and show equal competence in science and math (Stoet & Geary, 2018; Terrell et al., 2017). When researchers invited U.S. professors to recommend candidates for STEM positions, most said they preferred hiring the highly qualified women over the equally qualified men (Williams & Ceci, 2015). This is good news for future female scientists and engineers, who benefit from having capable and motivated female mentors and role models (Dennehy & Dasgupta, 2017; Moss-Racusin et al., 2018).

Gender roles also vary from one place to another. Nomadic societies of food-gathering people have had little division of labor by sex. Boys and girls receive much the same upbringing. In agricultural societies, where women typically work in the nearby fields and men roam while herding livestock, cultures have shaped children to assume more distinct gender roles (Segall et al., 1990; Van Leeuwen, 1978).

Take a minute to check your own gender expectations. Would you agree that "When jobs are scarce, men should have more right to a job?" In Sweden and Spain, barely more than 10 percent of adults agreed in

2016. In Egypt and Jordan, about 90 percent agreed (UNFPA, 2016). We're all human, but my, how our views differ.

Expectations about gender roles also factor into cultural attitudes about **sexual aggression**. In the aftermath of credible accusations of sexual aggression by famous and powerful men, many countries are making efforts to reduce sexual harassment and assault. Still, the problem persists, with a survey of nearly 10,000 people in the Hollywood entertainment industry revealing the power of harassers: "You can fire somebody, you can influence their ability to get another job, or you can just destroy their reputation" (Noveck, 2020).

## Gender Identity

> **3.3-5** How do we form our gender identity?

A *gender role* describes how others expect us to think, feel, and act. Our **gender identity**, when *binary* (involving only two options), is our personal sense of being male or female—regardless of whether this identity matches our birth-assigned sex. Those with a *nonbinary* gender identity may not feel male or female, or they may identify as some combination of male *and* female. How do we develop our gender identity?

**Social learning theory** assumes that we acquire our identity in childhood, by observing and imitating others' gender-linked behaviors and by being rewarded or punished for acting in specific ways ("Tatiana, you're such a good mommy to your dolls"; "Big boys don't cry, Armand"). **Gender typing**—taking on a traditional female or male role—varies from child to child (Tobin et al., 2010). Cultures also differ in their conceptualizations of gender: Some cultures acknowledge nonbinary gender identities or recognize three distinct genders.

Parents help to transmit their culture's views on gender. In one analysis of 43 studies, parents with traditional gender views were more likely to have gender-typed children who shared their expectations about how males and females should act (Tenenbaum & Leaper, 2002). When fathers share equally in housework, their daughters develop higher aspirations for work outside the home (Croft et al., 2014).

But no matter how much parents encourage or discourage traditional gender behavior, children may drift toward what feels right to them. Some organize themselves into "boy worlds" and "girl worlds," each guided by their understanding of the rules. Others conform to these rules more flexibly. Still others prefer **androgyny:** A blend of male and female roles feels right to them. Androgyny has benefits. As adults, androgynous people are more adaptable. They are more flexible in their actions and in their career choices (Bem, 1993). From childhood onward, they tend to be more resilient and self-accepting, and they experience less depression (Lam & McBride-Chang, 2007; Mosher & Danoff-Burg, 2008; Pauletti et al., 2017). Androgyny researchers remind us of the various ways of being male and of being female. One can be fully a boy or a man without being aggressive or loving sports or, for some, being attracted to women. And one can be fully a girl or a woman, accepting one's body, while also being forceful, competitive, or, for some, attracted to other women. A transgender identity is not the only alternative when feeling that one isn't traditionally masculine or feminine.

Our feelings about gender matter, but so does how we think. Early in life, we all form *schemas*, or concepts that help us make sense of our world. Our *gender schemas* organize our experiences of male-female characteristics and help us think about our gender identity—who we are as unique individuals (Bem, 1987, 1993; Martin et al., 2002).

As young children, we were "gender detectives" (Martin & Ruble, 2004). Before our first birthday, we knew the difference between a typically male and female voice or face

**The gendered pandemic**
During the early months of the Covid pandemic, U.S. women were more likely than men to report that their careers had been disrupted "a lot" and to have reduced their work hours (Collins et al., 2020; Hamel & Salganicoff, 2020).

**sexual aggression** any physical or verbal behavior of a sexual nature that is unwanted or intended to harm someone physically or emotionally. Can be expressed as either *sexual harassment* or *sexual assault*.

**gender identity** our personal sense of being male, female, neither, or some combination of male and female, regardless of whether this identity matches our sex assigned at birth, and the social affiliation that may result from this identity.

**social learning theory** the theory that we learn social behavior by observing and imitating and by being rewarded or punished.

**gender typing** the acquisition of a traditional masculine or feminine role.

**androgyny** blending traditionally masculine and traditionally feminine psychological characteristics.

(Martin et al., 2002). After we turned 2 and started talking, language forced us to label the world in terms of gender. The English language has classified people as *he* and *she*, though *they* is increasingly used as a gender-neutral pronoun. Other languages classify objects as masculine ("*le* train") or feminine ("*la* table").

**Learning gender** Environmental cues teach children what to expect from boys and girls.

For young children, gender looms large. It shines through 247 popular children's storybooks (Lewis et al., 2022). For example, *Curious George* and *Amelia Bedelia* model masculine and feminine traits, respectively. Children tend to learn that two sorts of people exist, and that they are supposed to be one of these two sorts, and they begin to search for clues about gender. In every culture, people communicate their gender in many ways. Their *gender expression* drops hints not only in their language but also in their clothing, interests, and possessions. Having picked up such clues, 3-year-olds may divide the human world in half. "Girls," they may decide, are the ones who love *Frozen* and have longer hair. "Boys" think *Captain Underpants* is hilarious and don't wear dresses. Armed with their newly collected "proof," they then adjust their behaviors to fit their concept of gender. These stereotypes are most rigid at about age 5 or 6. If the new neighbor is a girl, a 6-year-old boy may assume he cannot share her interests.

For people who identify as *transgender*, gender identity differs from what is typical for that person's birth-assigned sex (APA, 2010; Bockting, 2014). Brain scans show that individuals who have sought gender-affirming surgery (about 75 percent of whom are men) have had some neural tracts that differ from those whose gender identity matches their birth-assigned sex (Kranz et al., 2014; Van Kesteren et al., 1997). And brain scans have also revealed differences between those who are and are not transgender, suggesting a biological influence on gender identity (Williams, 2018).

In most countries, it's not easy being transgender. In one survey of 27,175 transgender Americans, 46 percent reported being verbally harassed in the last year (James et al., 2016). Transgender people in Europe and Asia also experience frequent insults, prejudice, and discrimination (Amnesty International, 2018). Some transgender people experience profound distress, increasing their risk of gender dysphoria (Mezzalira et al., 2022). To receive a gender dysphoria diagnosis, you must experience clinical levels of distress associated with your gender identity.

American transgender veterans have twice the risk of dying by suicide compared to other military veterans (Tucker, 2019). And in one survey of 27,000 U.S. transgender adults, those who received "conversion therapy"—which aims to change people's gender identity or sexual orientation—had a doubled lifetime risk of attempting suicide (Turban et al., 2020). *Gender identity* is distinct from *sexual orientation* (the direction of one's sexual attraction). Transgender people may be sexually attracted to people of any gender or to no one at all.

Roughly 30 percent of those not identifying with their birth-assigned sex have a nonbinary gender identity—feeling a combination of male and female or feeling neither male nor female (Barr et al., 2016; James et al., 2016; Mikalson et al., 2012). In North America and Europe, the number who identify as transgender is rising, especially among adolescents who were assigned female at birth. Is this increase partly a social phenomenon, or are today's teens simply feeling freer to own their private identities (Shrier, 2020)?

**Constructing identity** Gender expression is one way that people build their personal identity.

Luzo Reis/E+/Getty Images

---

---

# Module 3.3a REVIEW

### 3.3-1 How does the meaning of *gender* differ from the meaning of *sex*?

- In psychology, *gender* refers to the attitudes, feelings, and behaviors that a culture associates with a person's biological sex.

- *Sex* refers to the biologically influenced characteristics by which people define *male*, *female*, and *intersex*.

- Our understanding of gender arises from the interplay between our biology and our experiences.

### 3.3-2 What are some of the ways males and females tend to be alike and to differ?

- Humans are in most ways alike, thanks to our similar genetic makeup—we see, learn, and remember similarly,

with comparable creativity, intelligence, and emotions. Male-female differences include age of onset of puberty, life expectancy, emotional expressiveness, and vulnerability to certain disorders.

- Men display more *aggression* than women do, and they are more likely to be physically (rather than *relationally*) aggressive.

- In most societies, men have more social power. Males tend to be more independent, while females tend to be interdependent.

- Women focus more on social connectedness than do men, and they tend and befriend.

### 3.3-3 How do sex hormones influence prenatal and adolescent sexual development?

- About 7 weeks after conception, males begin producing *testosterone*. This promotes male sex organ development. *Estrogens* contribute to female sex characteristics and are secreted in greater amounts by females than by males.

- During the fourth and fifth prenatal months, sex hormones bathe the fetal brain, with different patterns developing due to the male's greater testosterone levels and the female's estrogen levels. Prenatal exposure of females to unusually high levels of male hormones can later dispose them to more male-typical interests.

- Another flood of hormones occurs in *puberty*, triggering a growth spurt, the development of *primary* and *secondary sex characteristics*, and the landmark events of *spermarche* and *menarche*.

### 3.3-4 What are some cultural influences on gender roles?

- *Gender roles*—a set of expected behaviors, attitudes, and traits for men and women—vary across place and time.

- Gender roles in many parts of the world have changed dramatically in the last century.

- Expectations about gender roles also influence cultural attitudes toward *sexual aggression*.

### 3.3-5 How do we form our gender identity?

- *Social learning theory* proposes that we learn our *gender identity* in the same way that we learn other things: through reward, punishment, observation, and imitation. But *gender typing* varies from child to child, indicating that imitation and reward, by themselves, do not explain gender identity.

- Some children organize themselves into "boy worlds" and "girl worlds"; others prefer *androgyny*.

- Gender identity is distinct from sexual orientation.

# AP® Practice Multiple Choice Questions

1. Uldis was born with male and female biological sexual characteristics. What term or phrase describes this phenomenon?

   a. Transgender
   b. Birth-assigned sex
   c. Intersex
   d. Gender identity

2. Imagine that you are answering a questionnaire. In the demographics section, you come across the following question: "Please provide your sex (how you self-identify)." Which of the following statements best illustrates the problematic language in this survey question?

   a. Instead of using the term *sex*, the researchers should have used the term *sexual orientation*.
   b. Instead of using the term *sex*, the researchers should have used the term *gender*.
   c. Instead of using the term *sex*, the researchers should have used the term *gender role*.
   d. Instead of using the term *sex*, the researchers should have used the term *gender identity*.

3. Dr. Hernandez is conducting a study on the attitudes that people in Honduras hold about biological characteristics of a person at birth, specifically focusing on attitudes about females. Which variable is Dr. Hernandez examining?

   a. Gender roles
   b. Sex
   c. Primary sex characteristics
   d. Gender

4. Males are often perceived to be superior leaders compared to women. Which of the following best supports this finding?

   a. Males often have more social power.
   b. Males exhibit more relational aggression.
   c. Males show more social connectedness.
   d. Males display more androgyny.

**5.** Sharleen, who is a woman, seeks psychological evaluation. Without knowing anything more than her gender and based on past research regarding gender differences in psychological disorders, which diagnosis is her psychologist most likely to make?

a. Antisocial personality disorder
b. Attention-deficit/hyperactivity disorder
c. Anxiety disorder
d. Alcohol use disorder

**6.** Stagger's new development of underarm hair is an example of

a. secondary sex characteristics.
b. primary sex characteristics.
c. menarche.
d. estrogens.

**7.** Sarah learned how to play with dolls by watching how her older sister plays with her dolls. Which of the following is best illustrated in this scenario?

a. Androgyny
b. Gender identity
c. Social learning theory
d. Puberty

---

# Module 3.3b Gender and Sexual Orientation: The Biology and Psychology of Sex

## LEARNING TARGETS

**3.3-6** Explain how hormones influence sexual motivation.

**3.3-7** Explain how external stimuli contribute to sexual arousal.

**3.3-8** Explain the factors that influence teenagers' sexual behavior and use of contraceptives.

**3.3-9** Explain how nature, nurture, and our own choices influence gender roles and sexuality.

**SPOTLIGHT ON:**
Alfred Kinsey

**sexuality** our thoughts, feelings, and actions related to our physical attraction to another.

**asexual** having no sexual attraction toward others.

As you've probably noticed, we can hardly talk about gender without talking about our **sexuality**. For all but the 1 percent of us considered **asexual** (Bogaert, 2004, 2015), dating and mating often become a high priority from puberty on. Biologist Alfred Kinsey (1894–1956) pioneered the study of human sexuality (Kinsey et al., 1948, 1953).

Kinsey and his colleagues' findings ignited debate and controversy, but they also paved the way for future research on the sexual behavior of men and women. Our sexual feelings and behaviors reflect both physiological and psychological influences.

# The Physiology of Sex

Unlike hunger, sex is not an actual *need*. Yet sex is a part of life. Had this not been so for all of your biological ancestors, you would not be alive and reading these words. Sexual motivation is nature's clever way of making people procreate, thus enabling our species' survival. Life is sexually transmitted.

## Hormones and Sexual Behavior

**3.3-6** How do hormones influence sexual motivation?

Among the forces driving sexual behavior are the *sex hormones*. As we saw earlier, the main male sex hormone is *testosterone*, and the main female sex hormones are the *estrogens*, such as *estradiol*. Sex hormones influence us at several points in the lifespan:

- During the prenatal period, they direct our sexual development.

- During puberty, a sex hormone surge ushers us into adolescence. In adolescent males, higher testosterone levels predict more male-typical traits and disorders (Vosberg et al., 2021).

- After puberty and well into the late adult years, sex hormones facilitate sexual behavior.

Women have much less testosterone than men do. Yet women are responsive to their testosterone level (Davison & Davis, 2011; van Anders, 2012). As studies with surgically or naturally menopausal women have demonstrated, testosterone-replacement therapy sometimes helps restore diminished arousal, desire, and sexual activity (Braunstein et al., 2005; Buster et al., 2005; Petersen & Hyde, 2011).

In men, normal fluctuations in testosterone levels have little effect on sexual drive (Byrne, 1982). Indeed, men's hormone levels sometimes vary in *response* to sexual stimulation (Escasa et al., 2011). In one study, Australian skateboarders' testosterone level surged in the presence of an attractive woman, contributing to riskier moves and more crash landings (Ronay & von Hippel, 2010). Thus, sexual arousal can be a *cause* as well as a consequence of increased testosterone levels.

Large hormonal surges or declines affect sexual desire at two predictable points in the lifespan, and sometimes at an unpredictable third point:

1. *The pubertal surge in sex hormones triggers the development of sex characteristics and sexual interest.* If puberty's hormonal surge is precluded—as it was during the 1600s and 1700s for prepubertal boys who were castrated to preserve their soprano voices for Italian opera—sex characteristics and sexual desire do not develop normally (Peschel & Peschel, 1987).

2. *In later life, sex hormone levels fall.* Women experience menopause as their estrogen levels decrease; men experience a more gradual change (see Module 3.2b). Sex remains a part of life, but as hormone levels decline, sexual activity declines as well (Leitenberg & Henning, 1995).

3. ***For some people, surgery or drugs may cause hormonal shifts.*** Male sex offenders who took Depo-Provera, a drug that reduces their testosterone level to that of a prepubertal boy, lost much of their sexual urge (Bilefsky, 2009; Money et al., 1983). If a woman's natural testosterone level drops, as happens with removal of the ovaries, her sexual interest may wane.

To summarize: We might compare sex hormones, especially testosterone, to the fuel in a car. Without fuel, a car will not run. But if the fuel level is minimally adequate, adding more fuel to the gas tank won't change how the car runs. This analogy is imperfect, because hormones and sexual motivation interact. However, it correctly suggests that biology is a necessary but incomplete explanation of human sexual behavior. The hormonal fuel is essential, but so are the psychological stimuli that turn on the engine, keep it running, and shift it into high gear.

# The Psychology of Sex

**3.3-7** How do external stimuli contribute to sexual arousal?

Biological factors powerfully influence sexual motivation and behavior. Yet the wide variations documented over time, across place, and among individuals indicate the great influence of psychological factors as well (**Figure 3.3-3**).

## External Stimuli

Both men and women become aroused when they see, hear, or read erotic material (Heiman, 1975; Stockton & Murnen, 1992). People may find sexual arousal either pleasing or disturbing. With repeated exposure to any stimulus, including an erotic stimulus, the emotional response lessens, or *habituates*. During the 1920s, when Western women's hemlines rose to the knee, an exposed leg made hearts flutter. Today, many people would barely notice it.

Can exposure to sexually explicit material have other effects? Research indicates that it can, in four ways.

- ***Accelerating sexual activity*** When followed over time, teens with high pornography exposure engage in sexual activity earlier and more often (Pirrone et al., 2022). Billie Eilish (2021) has expressed regret over her early pornography exposure, partly because "I was not saying no to things that were not good. It was because I thought that's what I was supposed to be attracted to."

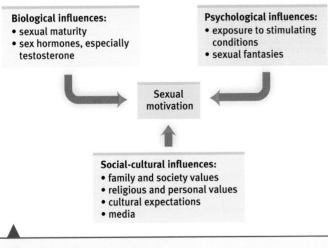

**Figure 3.3-3**

**Biopsychosocial influences on human sexuality**

Human sexuality is less influenced by biological factors than by psychological and social-cultural factors.

- *Believing rape is acceptable* Modern pornography mostly presents women as subservient sexual objects, and often involves physical aggression (Fritz et al., 2020; Fritz & Paul, 2018; Jones, 2018). Depictions of women being sexually coerced—and appearing to enjoy it—have increased viewers' belief in the false idea that women want to be overpowered, and have increased male viewers' expressed willingness to hurt women and to commit rape after viewing such scenes (Allen et al., 1995, 2000; Foubert et al., 2011; Zillmann, 1989).

- *Reducing satisfaction with a partner's appearance or with a relationship* After viewing erotic media of sexually attractive women and men, people have judged their own relationship as less satisfying (Perry, 2020). Perhaps reading or watching erotica's unlikely scenarios creates expectations that few people can fulfill.

- *Desensitization* Extensive online pornography viewing can warp expectations and desensitize young adults to normal sexuality. Repeated exposure to this distorted sexual world may contribute to lowered sexual desire and satisfaction, diminished brain activation in response to sexual images, and, for men, erectile problems (Wright et al., 2018).

## Sexual Risk Taking and Teen Pregnancy

> **3.3-8** Which factors influence teenagers' sexual behavior and use of contraceptives?

Sexual attitudes and behaviors vary dramatically across cultures and eras. "Sex between unmarried adults" is "morally unacceptable," agreed 97 percent of Indonesians and 6 percent of Germans (Pew, 2014). Thanks mostly to decreased sexual activity—from 54 percent of high school students in 1991 reporting ever having intercourse to 38 percent in 2019—U.S. teen pregnancy rates have declined (CDC, 2020h; Livingston & Thomas, 2019). Which social factors contribute to teens' sexual risk taking?

### Communication

Many teenagers are uncomfortable discussing sex and contraception with parents, partners, and peers. But teens who talk freely and openly with their parents and with their partner in an exclusive relationship are more likely to use contraceptives (Aspy et al., 2007; Milan & Kilmann, 1987).

### Impulsivity

If passion overwhelms intentions to use contraceptives or to delay having sex, unplanned sexual activity may result in unsafe sex and pregnancy (Ariely & Loewenstein, 2006; MacDonald & Hynie, 2008).

### Alcohol Use

Among older teens and young adults, most sexual encounters outside of a relationship occur after alcohol use, often without *affirmative consent* (Fielder et al., 2013; Garcia et al., 2013; Johnson & Chen, 2015). Those persons who use alcohol prior to sexual activity are also less likely to use condoms (Kotchick et al., 2001). By depressing the brain centers that control judgment, inhibition, and self-awareness, alcohol disarms normal restraints—a phenomenon well known to sexually coercive people.

**social script** a culturally modeled guide for how to act in various situations.

### Mass Media

Popular media influence teens by providing **social scripts** for sexual behavior. Media also affect peer perceptions: The more sexual content adolescents and young adults view or read (even when controlling for other predictors of early sexual activity), the more likely they are to perceive their peers as sexually active, to develop sexually permissive attitudes, to experience early intercourse, and to use condoms inconsistently (Escobar-Chaves et al., 2005; O'Hara et al., 2012; Parkes et al., 2013; Ward et al., 2018). Perceived peer norms influence teens' sexual behavior (Lyons et al., 2015; van de Bongardt et al., 2015).

## Sexual Restraint

What are the characteristics of teens who delay having sex?

**Distorted social scripts** An analysis of the 60 top-selling video games found 489 characters, 86 percent of whom were males (like most game players). The female characters were much more likely than the male characters to be hypersexualized — partially nude or revealingly clothed, with large breasts and tiny waists (Downs & Smith, 2010). Such depictions can lead to unrealistic expectations about sexuality and body ideals and contribute to the early sexualization of girls (Karsay et al., 2018).

- *High intelligence* Teens with high — rather than average — intelligence test scores have more often delayed sex, partly because they consider possible negative consequences and are more focused on future achievement than on impulsive pleasures (Harden & Mendle, 2011).

- *Religious engagement* Actively religious teens have more often reserved sexual activity for adulthood or long-term relationships (Hull et al., 2011; Schmitt & Fuller, 2015; Štulhofer et al., 2011).

- *Father presence* In studies that followed hundreds of New Zealand and U.S. girls from age 5 to 18, having their father in the household reduced the risk of teen pregnancy and of sexual activity before age 16 (Ellis et al., 2003). These associations held even after adjusting for other influences, such as poverty. Close family attachments — as in families who eat together and where parents know their teens' activities and friends — have also predicted later sexual initiation (Coley et al., 2008).

- *Service learning participation* U.S. teens volunteering as tutors or teachers' aides, or participating in community projects, have had lower pregnancy rates than do comparable teens randomly assigned to control conditions (Kirby, 2002; O'Donnell et al., 2002). Researchers are unsure why. Does service learning promote a sense of personal competence, control, and responsibility? Does it encourage more future-oriented thinking? Or does it simply reduce opportunities for unprotected sex? (After-school activities and later school start times have also reduced unplanned pregnancies [Bryan et al., 2016; Steinberg, 2015].)

Father presence

---

**AP® Science Practice**

**Research**

Intelligence, religious engagement, father presence, and volunteering are *associated* with increased sexual restraint. Because researchers can't easily manipulate these variables, they rely on correlational methods (which are non-experimental) to detect naturally occurring relationships and assess how well one variable predicts another.

**AP® Science Practice** **Check Your Understanding**

**Examine the Concept**

▶ Explain the factors that influence sexual motivation.

▶ Describe four factors that contribute to sexual restraint among teens.

*Answers to the Examine the Concept questions can be found in Appendix C at the end of the book.*

**Apply the Concept**

▶ What strategies could your community use to reduce teen pregnancy?

# Reflections on the Nature and Nurture of Sex, Gender, and Sexuality

> **3.3-9** How do nature, nurture, and our own choices influence gender roles and sexuality?

Evolutionary psychologists point out that our ancestral history helped form us as a species. Nature selects behaviors that increase reproductive success. They suggest that men pair widely, and women pair wisely.

Why do women tend to be choosier than men when selecting sexual partners? Women have more at stake. To send her genes into the future, a woman conceives and protects a fetus growing inside her body for up to 9 months, and may nurse for months following birth. No surprise, then, that straight women prefer partners who will offer their joint offspring support and protection (Meeussen et al., 2019).

Men tend to prefer traits, such as smooth skin and a youthful shape, that convey health and fertility (Buss & Von Hippel, 2018). Mating with such women might increase men's chances of sending their genes into the future.

As mobile gene machines, say evolutionary psychologists, we are designed to prefer whatever worked for our ancestors in their environments. Had they not been genetically predisposed to act in ways that would produce children, we wouldn't be here. As carriers of their genetic legacy, we are similarly predisposed.

But our culture and experiences also shape us. If their genes and hormones predispose males to be more physically aggressive than females, culture can amplify this gender difference through norms that reward dominant men and gentle women. If men are encouraged to assume roles that demand physical power, and women to embrace more nurturing roles, each may act accordingly. Roles remake their players. Lawyers in time become more lawyerly, professors become more professorial. Gender roles similarly shape us.

Although gender roles vary across cultures, gender differences persist. Researchers who analyzed nearly 500,000 global adolescent self-reports concluded, "In every country more girls than boys aspired to a people-oriented occupation, and more boys than girls aspired to a things-oriented or STEM occupation" (Geary & Stoet, 2022).

Nevertheless, in many modern cultures, gender roles are merging. Brute strength has become less important for power and status (recall how teen climate activist Greta Thunberg galvanized millions of people worldwide to environmental protest and action). From 1965 to 2019, the proportion of U.S. medical students who were women soared from 9 percent to 51 percent (AAMC, 2014, 2019). A survey of 30 countries showed a shrinking gender gap in housework and other unpaid work, such as child care (OECD, 2018). Such swift changes signal that biology does not dictate gender roles.

Do cultural expectations also influence gender differences in sexual behavior? Alice Eagly and Wendy Wood (1999, 2013) have found smaller behavioral differences between women and men in cultures with greater gender equality. Eagly and others believe that *social learning theory* offers a helpful explanation of gender differences. We all learn *social scripts*—our culture's guide to how people should act in certain situations. By watching and imitating others in their culture, women, for example, may learn that sexual encounters with strange men can be dangerous, that casual sex may not offer much sexual pleasure, and that women (more than men) who engage in casual sexual activity face reputational harm (Conley, 2011; Muggleton et al., 2019).

If nature and nurture jointly form us, are we "nothing but" the product of nature and nurture? Are we rigidly determined? We *are* the product of nature and nurture, but we are also an open system. Genes are all-pervasive but not all-powerful. People may reject their evolutionary role as transmitters of genes and choose not to reproduce. Culture, too,

**SPOTLIGHT ON:**
Alice Eagly

Ellis Rosen/Cartoon Stock

is all-pervasive but not all-powerful. People may defy peer pressures and resist social expectations.

Moreover, we cannot excuse our failings by blaming them solely on bad genes or bad influences. In reality, we are both creatures and creators of our worlds. So many things about us are the products of our genes and environments. Yet the stream that runs into the future flows through our present choices. Our decisions today design our environments tomorrow. We are the architects. Our hopes, goals, and expectations influence our destiny. And that is what enables cultures to vary and to change.

---

 **AP® Science Practice**

## Check Your Understanding

**Examine the Concept**

▶ Explain some ways in which gender roles are changing.

▶ What is meant by the statement, "We are both creatures and creators of our worlds?"

**Apply the Concept**

▶ Based on what you've learned, how would you say that nature and nurture work together to influence one's sexual development?

*Answers to the Examine the Concept questions can be found in Appendix C at the end of the book.*

---

# Module 3.3b REVIEW

**3.3-6 How do hormones influence sexual motivation?**

- For all but those few individuals considered *asexual*, dating and mating often become a high priority from puberty on.

- The primary female sex hormones (the *estrogens*, such as estradiol) and male sex hormone (*testosterone*) influence human sexual behavior. Women's sexuality is responsive to their testosterone level. Testosterone level also varies in men, partly in response to stimulation.

**3.3-7 How do external stimuli contribute to sexual arousal?**

- External stimuli can trigger sexual arousal.

- Sexually explicit material may diminish relationship satisfaction, and extensive online pornography exposure may warp expectations and desensitize young adults to normal sexuality. Viewing sexually coercive material can lead to increased acceptance of violence toward women.

**3.3-8 Which factors influence teenagers' sexual behavior and use of contraceptives?**

- Teen sexuality varies from culture to culture and from era to era.

- Factors contributing to these variations include communication about sex and contraception, impulsivity, alcohol use, and mass media.

- High intelligence, religious engagement, father presence, and service learning participation predict teen sexual restraint.

**3.3-9 How do nature, nurture, and our own choices influence gender roles and sexuality?**

- Our genes form us, and our culture and experiences shape us, interacting with our biological predispositions. Our biological predispositions may feed gender norms, which can in turn influence our gender roles.

- While we are the product of nature and nurture, our individual choices affect the way these multiple influences interact. We are both products and producers of our worlds.

# AP® Practice Multiple Choice Questions

1. Vadim felt physically attracted to Laima. Which term refers to the thoughts, feelings, and actions he is experiencing?

   a. Sex hormones
   b. Sexuality
   c. Sexual responsiveness
   d. Sexual restraint

2. Dr. Liss studies female sex hormones. What does he study?

   a. Androgens
   b. Menopause
   c. Estrogens
   d. Testosterone

3. Which of the following statements is true concerning the effect of sex hormones?

   a. Hormone injections can be used to easily manipulate sexual behavior in men but not in women.
   b. Sex hormones affect the sexual behavior of men and women.
   c. The levels of sex hormones are more constant in women than in men.
   d. Women's estrogen levels do not vary.

4. Dr. Foxx's findings replicated past research, indicating that high intelligence, religious engagement, father presence, and service-learning participation predicted

   a. sexual maturation.
   b. sexual restraint.
   c. asexuality.
   d. sexual arousal.

# Module 3.3c Gender and Sexual Orientation: Sexual Orientation

## LEARNING TARGETS

**3.3-10** Explain what research has taught us about sexual orientation.

**3.3-11** Explain the biological research that helps us understand sexual orientation.

## Introduction to Sexual Orientation

**3.3-10** What do we know about sexual orientation?

We express the *direction* of our sexual interest in our **sexual orientation**. Our sexual and emotional attractions may be female-male *(heterosexual orientation)*, to our own sex *(same-sex orientation)*, to males and females *(bisexual orientation)*, or to no one at all *(asexual orientation)*.

Cultures vary in their attitudes toward same-sex attractions. Should society accept these feelings and behaviors? *Yes*, say 94 percent of Swedes and 7 percent of Nigerians—with acceptance increasing nearly everywhere worldwide, and with women and younger, more educated adults being more accepting (Poushter & Kent, 2020). Yet whether a culture condemns or accepts same-sex unions, heterosexuality is most common and same-sex attraction and other variations exist. In the African countries in which same-sex relationships are illegal, the ratio of gay and bisexual people "is no different from other countries in the rest of the world," reports the Academy of Science of South Africa (2015). And in cultures in which same-sex behavior has been expected of all boys before marriage, most men have nevertheless grown up straight (Hammack, 2005; Money, 1987). So, same-sex activity spans human history, and sexual behaviors need not indicate *orientation*.

How many people have exclusively same-sex attractions? According to more than a dozen national surveys in Europe and the United States, about 3 or 4 percent of men and 2 percent of women (Chandra et al., 2011; Copen et al., 2016; Savin-Williams et al., 2012). But the percentages vary somewhat over time, with the percentage who feel comfortable self-reporting as gay or bisexual gradually increasing with increased social acceptance (Newport, 2018). Percentages are also slightly higher when reporting is anonymous (Copen et al., 2016). A larger number of Americans—17 percent of women and 6 percent of men—say they have had some same-sex sexual contact during their lives (Copen et al., 2016). In less tolerant places, people are more likely to hide their sexual orientation. About 3 percent of California men express a same-sex preference on Facebook, for example, as do only about 1 percent in Mississippi.

What would it feel like to be straight in a majority same-sex culture? If you are straight, imagine that you have found "the one"—your perfect heterosexual partner. How would you feel if you weren't sure who you could trust with knowing you had these

**AP® Science Practice**

### Research

The data presented illustrate how the wording of surveys can influence their results. The percentages differed if researchers asked about "sexual orientation" rather than "same-sex contact." Recall from Module 0.3 that wording effects matter.

**sexual orientation** according to the APA (2015), "a person's sexual and emotional attraction to another person and the behavior and/or social affiliation that may result from this attraction."

"abnormal" feelings? How would you react if you overheard people telling crude jokes about straight people, or if most movies, TV shows, and advertisements showed only same-sex relationships? And how would you feel if children's organizations thought you might not be safe or trustworthy because you are attracted to people of another sex?

Facing such reactions, some people with same-sex attractions may at first try to ignore or deny their desires, hoping they will go away. But they don't. And these people may—particularly if they live in a region or a country that condemns same-sex attractions—conceal their orientation, which can harm their mental health (Pachankis et al., 2020). Especially during adolescence or when feeling rejected by their parents or peers, people may struggle against same-sex attractions. In surveys of U.S. high schoolers, gay and lesbian youth have been doubly likely as straight youth to report being bullied, feeling unsafe, and experiencing violence. They have also been 3.6 times more likely to report persistent feelings of sadness or hopelessness in the past 12 months, and 4.5 times more likely to have "seriously considered attempting suicide" (CDC, 2020g). Some may try to change their orientation through psychotherapy, willpower, or prayer. But the feelings are typically as enduring as those of straight people—who are similarly unable to change their orientation (Haldeman, 1994, 2002; Myers & Scanzoni, 2005).

Today's psychologists view sexual orientation as neither willfully chosen nor willfully changed. "There is no sound scientific evidence that sexual orientation can be changed," stated the U.K. Royal College of Psychiatrists (2014). Moreover, "[e]fforts to change sexual orientation are unlikely to be successful and involve some risk of harm," declared a 2009 American Psychological Association report. A consensus of British mental health organizations agreed that such attempts are "unethical and potentially harmful" (Gale et al., 2017). Recognizing this, in 2016, Malta became the first European country to outlaw the controversial practice of "conversion therapy" (programs purporting to change people's gender identity or sexual orientation). An increasing number of U.S. states and cities have likewise banned conversion therapy with minors.

Sexual orientation in some ways is like handedness: Most people are one way, some the other. A smaller group experiences some form of ambidexterity. Regardless, the way we are endures, especially in men (Dickson et al., 2013; Norris et al., 2015). Women's sexual orientation tends to be less strongly felt and, for some women, is more fluid and changing. Across time, cultures, situations, and differing levels of education, religious observance, and peer influence, men's sexual drive and interests have been less flexible and varying than have women's. Women, for example, more often prefer to alternate periods of high sexual activity with periods of almost none (Mosher et al., 2005). Social psychologist Roy Baumeister calls this flexibility *erotic plasticity*.

As we continue our exploration of sexual orientation research, note that the scientific question is not "What causes same-sex, heterosexual, or other orientations?" but "What causes differing sexual orientations?" In pursuit of answers, psychological science compares the backgrounds and physiology of people whose sexual orientations *differ*.

## Origins of Sexual Orientation

**3.3-11** What biological research helps us understand sexual orientation?

So, if we do not choose our sexual orientation and (especially for males) cannot change it, where do these feelings come from? In an early search for possible environmental influences on sexual orientation, Kinsey Institute investigators in the 1980s interviewed nearly 1000 lesbian/gay and 500 heterosexual people. They assessed nearly every imaginable psychological "cause" of same-sex attraction—parental relationships, childhood sexual experiences, peer relationships, and dating experiences (Bell et al., 1981; Hammersmith, 1982). Their findings: Gay and lesbian people were no more likely than straight people to have been smothered by maternal love or neglected by their father. And consider this: If "distant fathers" were more likely to produce gay sons, then shouldn't boys growing up in father-absent homes more often be gay? (They are not.) And shouldn't the increasing number of such homes have led to a noticeable increase in the gay population? (It has not.) Most children raised by gay or lesbian parents display gender-typical behavior and are heterosexual (Farr et al., 2018; Gartrell & Bos, 2010). Moreover, they grow up with health and emotional well-being similar to children with straight parents (Bos et al., 2016; Farr, 2017).

*Environment likely contributes to sexual orientation—nature and nurture work together—but the inability to pin down specific environmental influences has led researchers to explore several lines of biological evidence.* These include same-sex attraction in other species, brain differences, and genetic and prenatal influences.

## Same-Sex Attraction in Other Species

In Boston's Public Garden, caretakers solved the mystery of why a much-loved swan couple's eggs never hatched: Both swans were female. In New York City's Central Park Zoo, penguins Silo and Roy spent several years as devoted same-sex partners. Same-sex sexual behaviors have been observed in several hundred other species, including grizzlies, gorillas, giraffes, monkeys, flamingos, and owls (Bagemihl, 1999). Among rams, for example, some 7 to 10 percent display same-sex attraction by shunning ewes and seeking to mount other males (Perkins & Fitzgerald, 1997). Same-sex sexual behavior seems a natural part of the animal world.

SEA LIFE Sydney Aquarium

**Dad and Dad** At Sydney's SEA LIFE Aquarium, Sphen and Magic, a bonded same-sex penguin pair, successfully raised a foster chick (appropriately named "Sphengic").

## Brain Differences

Might the structure and function of gay and straight brains differ? Neuroscientist Simon LeVay (1991) studied sections of the hypothalamus taken from deceased gay and straight people. He found a cell cluster that was indeed reliably larger in straight men than in straight women and gay men.

It should not surprise us that brains differ with sexual orientation. Remember: *Everything psychological is simultaneously biological.* But when did the brain difference begin? At conception? During childhood or adolescence? Did experience produce the difference? Or was it genes or prenatal hormones (or genes activating prenatal hormones)?

### AP® Science Practice

### Research

Throughout this discussion, notice how the conclusions about sexual orientation use evidence from other species, and from human brain differences, genetics, and parental influences. Using multiple research methods to establish valid and reliable results nicely illustrates the scientific process.

LeVay does not view the hypothalamus cell network as a sexual orientation center. Rather, he believes it is an important part of a brain pathway engaged in sexual behavior. He acknowledges that sexual behavior patterns could influence the brain's anatomy. In fish, birds, rats, and humans, brain structures vary with experience—including sexual experience (Breedlove, 1997). But LeVay believes it more likely that brain anatomy influences sexual orientation. His hunch seems confirmed by the discovery of a similar hypothalamic difference between male sheep that do and don't display same-sex attraction (Larkin et al., 2002; Roselli et al., 2002, 2004). Moreover, such differences seem to develop soon after birth, and perhaps even before birth (Rahman & Wilson, 2003).

Since LeVay's brain *structure* discovery, other researchers have reported additional differences in the way that gay and straight brains *function*. One is an area of the hypothalamus that governs sexual arousal (Savic et al., 2005). When straight women were given a whiff of a scent derived from men's sweat, this area became active. Gay men's brains responded similarly to the men's scent. Straight men's brains showed the arousal response only to a female hormone sample. In a similar study, gay women's responses differed from those of straight women (Kranz & Ishai, 2006; Martins et al., 2005). Researcher Qazi Rahman (2015) sums it up: Compared with straight men and women, "gay men appear, on average, more 'female typical' in brain pattern responses and [gay] women are somewhat more 'male typical.'"

On several traits, the average gay man and gay woman fall midway between the average straight man and straight woman. Consider the gay-straight difference in spatial abilities. On mental rotation tasks such as the one in **Figure 3.3-4**, straight men tend to outscore straight women, and the scores of gay men and gay women fall between them (Boone & Hegarty, 2017). But straight women and gay men have both outperformed straight men at remembering objects' spatial locations in memory game tasks (Hassan & Rahman, 2007).

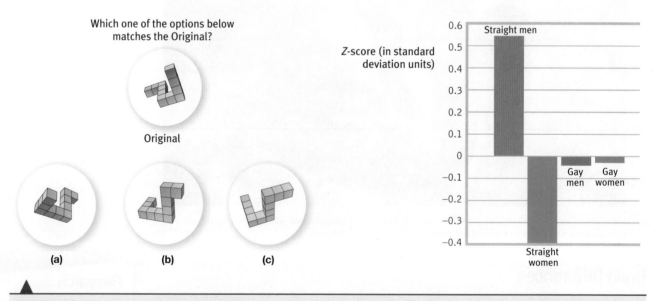

**Figure 3.3-4**

**Spatial abilities and sexual orientation**

Which of the three figures can be rotated to match the original figure?[2] Straight men tend to find this type of mental rotation task easier than do straight women, with gay men and women falling in between them (see graph) (Rahman et al., 2004).

[2]Answer: Figure (c).

# Genetic Influences

Studies indicate that "about a third of variation in sexual orientation is attributable to genetic influences" (Bailey et al., 2016). A same-sex orientation does tend to run in families. And identical twins are somewhat more likely than fraternal twins to share a same-sex orientation (Alanko et al., 2010; Långström et al., 2010). But because sexual orientations differ in many identical twin pairs, especially female twins, we know that other factors besides genes are also at work—including, it appears, *epigenetic marks* that help distinguish gay and straight twins (Balter, 2015; Gavrilets et al., 2018).

By altering a single gene in fruit flies, researchers have changed the flies' sexual orientation and behavior (Dickson, 2005). In search of genes that influence human sexual orientation, researchers have analyzed the genomes of 409 pairs of gay brothers, and of 1231 straight men and 1077 gay men. They found links between sexual orientation and two genes on chromosomes 13 and 14. The first of those chromosome regions influences a brain area that varies in size with sexual orientation. The second influences thyroid function, which has also been associated with sexual orientation (Sanders et al., 2015, 2017). But we should also recall a familiar lesson: Human traits are influenced by *many genes having small effects*. Indeed, a giant study of nearly 500,000 peoples' genes confirmed that "Same-sex behavior is influenced by not one or a few genes but many" (Ganna et al., 2019).

Researchers have speculated about possible reasons why these "gay genes" might exist in the human gene pool, given that same-sex couples cannot naturally reproduce. One possible answer is *kin selection*. Recall from Module 1.1A the evolutionary psychology reminder that many of our genes also reside in our biological relatives. Perhaps, then, gay people's genes live on through their supporting the survival and reproductive success of their relatives.

A *fertile females theory* suggests that maternal genetics may also be at work (Bocklandt et al., 2006). Around the world, gay men tend to have more gay relatives on their mother's side than on their father's side (Camperio-Ciani et al., 2004, 2009, 2012; VanderLaan et al., 2012; VanderLaan & Vasey, 2011). And gay men's heterosexual maternal relatives tend to produce more offspring than do the maternal relatives of straight men. Perhaps the genes that dispose some women to conceive more children with men also dispose some men to be attracted to men (LeVay, 2011). Thus, the decreased reproduction by gay men appears to be offset by the increased reproduction by their maternal extended family.

# Prenatal Influences

Recall that in the womb, sex hormones direct our male and female development. Two sets of findings indicate that, for sexual orientation, the prenatal environment matters. First, in humans, a critical period for fetal brain development seems to be the second trimester (Ellis & Ames, 1987; Garcia-Falgueras & Swaab, 2010; Meyer-Bahlburg, 1995). Exposure to the hormone levels typically experienced by female fetuses during this period may predispose females later to become attracted to males. In contrast, female fetuses most exposed to testosterone appear most likely later to exhibit gender-atypical traits and to experience same-sex desires. When pregnant sheep were injected with testosterone during a similar critical period, their female offspring later showed same-sex sexual behavior (Money, 1987).

Second, the mother's immune system may play a role in the development of sexual orientation. In an amazingly reliable finding of 35 of 36 samples studied, men with older brothers have been somewhat more likely to be gay, reports Ray Blanchard (2004, 2018, 2019)—about one-third more likely for each additional older brother (see also Bogaert, 2003). The odds of same-sex attraction are roughly 2 percent among first sons, but rise to about 2.6 percent among second sons, 3.5 percent for third sons, and so on for each additional older brother (Bailey et al., 2016). This is called the *older-brother* or *fraternal birth-order effect* (see **Figure 3.3-5**).

## Figure 3.3-5
### The older-brother effect

These approximate curves depict a man's likelihood of same-sex attraction as a function of the number of biological (not adopted) older brothers he has (Blanchard, 2008a; Bogaert, 2006a). This correlation has been found in several studies, but only among right-handed men (as about 9 in 10 men, and most research participants, are).

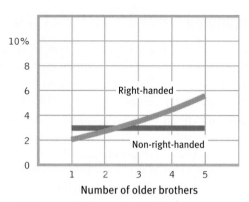

*"Thanks, but I'm in the midst of a lesbian phase that started the day I was born."*

The reason for this older-brother effect is unclear. But the explanation does seem biological, given that this effect does not occur among adopted brothers (Bogaert, 2006a). Blanchard and his colleagues (2020) suspect that male fetuses may stimulate the mother's immune system to produce antibodies. After each pregnancy with a male fetus, the maternal antibodies may become stronger and may prevent a subsequent male fetus' brain from developing in a male-typical pattern (Bogaert et al., 2018).

## Trait Differences and Sexual Orientation

Comparing the traits of gay and straight people is akin to comparing the heights of men and women. The average man is taller than most women, but many women are taller than most men. And just as knowing someone's height doesn't specify their gender, neither does knowing someone's traits tell you their sexual orientation. Yet on several traits, the average gay female or male is intermediate between straight females and males (**Table 3.3-1**; see also LeVay, 2011; Rahman & Koerting, 2008; Rieger et al., 2016).

---

### TABLE 3.3-1 Biological Correlates of Sexual Orientation

**Gay-straight trait differences**

Sexual orientation is part of a package of traits. Studies — some in need of replication — indicate that gay people and straight people tend to differ in the following biological and behavioral traits:

| | | |
|---|---|---|
| • Spatial abilities | • Occupational preferences | • Face structure and birth size/weight |
| • Fingerprint ridge counts | • Relative finger lengths | • Sleep length |
| • Auditory system development | • Gender nonconformity | • Physical aggression |
| • Handedness | • Age of onset of puberty in males | • Walking style |

On average (the evidence is strongest for males), results for gay men and gay women fall between those of straight men and straight women.

Three biological influences — brain, genetic, and prenatal — may contribute to these differences:

**Brain differences**

• One hypothalamic cell cluster is smaller in women and gay men than in straight men.

• Gay men's hypothalamus reacts as does straight women's to the smell of men's sex-related hormones.

**Genetic influences**

• Shared sexual orientation is higher among identical twins than among fraternal twins.

• Sexual attraction in fruit flies can be genetically manipulated.

• Male same-sex attraction often appears to be transmitted from the mother's side of the family.

**Prenatal influences**

• Altered prenatal hormone exposure may lead to same-sex attraction in humans and other animals.

• Men with several older biological brothers are more likely to be gay, possibly due to a maternal immune-system reaction.

*The point to remember*: Taken together, the brain, genetic, and prenatal research findings offer strong support for a biological explanation of sexual orientation, especially for men (LeVay, 2011; Rahman & Koerting, 2008). Women's greater sexual fluidity suggests biopsychosocial influences as well (Diamond et al., 2017).

* * *

Still, some people wonder: Should the cause of sexual orientation matter? Perhaps it shouldn't, but people's assumptions matter. Those who believe sexual orientation is a lifestyle choice often oppose equal rights for people who are sexual minorities. For example, when signing a 2014 bill that made some same-sex sexual acts punishable by life in prison, Uganda's president denied that same-sex attraction is inborn, declaring it rather a matter of "choice" (Balter, 2014; Landau et al., 2014). Those who instead understand the inborn nature of sexual orientation—as shaped by biological and prenatal influences—more often favor equal rights for gay, lesbian, and bisexual people (Bailey et al., 2016).

Do these new concepts such as "nonbinary gender identity" indicate that people have changed? Actually, today's scientists believe that gender identity and sexual orientation have always varied. In all places and times, some people have not fit neatly into binary male/female or gay/straight categories.

---

**AP® Science Practice**

## Check Your Understanding

**Examine the Concept**

▶ Explain what is meant by *sexual orientation*.

▶ Explain two ways that prenatal hormone exposure influences sexual orientation.

**Apply the Concept**

▶ Has learning more about what contributes to sexual orientation influenced how you might interact with people whose sexual orientation differs from yours? Explain.

*Answers to the Examine the Concept questions can be found in Appendix C at the end of the book.*

---

# Module 3.3c REVIEW

### 3.3-10 What do we know about sexual orientation?

- *Sexual orientation* is the direction of our sexual and emotional attractions, and the behavior and social affiliation that may result from these attractions. We may have sexual attraction that is female-male (heterosexual orientation), to our own sex (same-sex orientation), to males and females (bisexual orientation), or to no one at all (asexual orientation).

- About 3 or 4 percent of men and 2 percent of women in Europe and the United States have exclusively same-sex attractions. Scientists have been unable to find specific environmental influences that contribute to sexual orientation, but have found evidence for several biological influences.

### 3.3-11 What biological research helps us understand sexual orientation?

- To understand sexual orientation, researchers have explored same-sex attraction in other species, as well as gay-straight brain differences, genetic influences, and prenatal influences in humans.

# AP® Practice Multiple Choice Questions

1. Dr. Kahinu is interested in studying the role of brain anatomy on college students' sexual and emotional attraction to other people. Which of the following best represents the dependent variable in Dr. Kahinu's study?

   a. Gender
   b. Sex
   c. Gender identity
   d. Sexual orientation

2. Ramone feels no sexual attraction to other people. Ramone has a(n)

   a. bisexual orientation.
   b. asexual orientation.
   c. heterosexual orientation.
   d. same-sex orientation.

3. Keeler, a 14-year-old who identifies as male, has five older brothers. Based on the provided information and past research, which of the following statements is most accurate?

   a. Keeler is more likely than average to have a heterosexual orientation.
   b. Keeler is more likely than average to have an asexual orientation.
   c. Keeler's sexual orientation is not affected by his birth order.
   d. Keeler is more likely than average to have a same-sex orientation.

4. Which of the following is a logical and objective conclusion that can be drawn regarding women's tendency to display higher levels of erotic plasticity compared to men?

   a. Women who primarily identify as heterosexual are more likely to experience same-sex attraction than are men who primarily identify as heterosexual.
   b. Men who primarily identify as heterosexual are more likely to experience same-sex attraction than are women who primarily identify as heterosexual.
   c. Men are more likely to identify as bisexual than are women.
   d. Women are more likely to identify as having a same-sex orientation than are men.

# Module 3.4 Cognitive Development Across the Lifespan

## Cognitive Development in Infancy and Childhood

**3.4-1** How did Piaget broaden our understanding of the way a child's mind develops, and how have today's researchers built on his work?

Somewhere on your journey "from egghood to personhood" (Broks, 2007), you became conscious. When was that? And once conscious, how did your mind grow? Developmental psychologist Jean Piaget [pee-ah-ZHAY] spent his life searching for the answers. He studied children's developing **cognition**—all the mental activities associated with thinking, knowing, remembering, and communicating. His interest in children's cognitive development began in 1920, when he was in Paris developing questions for children's intelligence tests. While administering the tests, Piaget became intrigued by children's wrong answers, which were often strikingly similar among same-age children. Where others saw childish mistakes, Piaget saw developing intelligence at work. Such accidental discoveries are among the fruits of psychological science.

A half-century spent with children convinced Piaget that a child's mind is not a miniature model of an adult's. Thanks partly to his careful observations, we now understand that children reason differently than adults, in "wildly illogical ways" (Brainerd, 1996).

Piaget's studies led him to believe that a child's mind develops through a series of stages, in an upward march from the newborn's simple reflexes to the adult's abstract reasoning power. Thus, an 8-year-old can comprehend things a toddler cannot, such as the analogy that "getting an idea is like having a light turn on in your head." As we saw in Module 2.2A, Piaget proposed that children build **schemas**—concepts that enable us to organize our experiences—and that they actively construct and modify their understanding of the world through the processes of **assimilation** and **accommodation**. Seeing an airplane for the first time, a small child trying to assimilate the new information may point and say "Bird!" When his mother says "That's an airplane," the child is forced to accommodate, adapting his *bird* schema and developing a new schema for *airplane*.

### Piaget's Theory and Current Thinking

Piaget viewed children's cognitive development as a process guided by biological *maturation* (see Module 3.2) and environmental interaction. He believed that children construct their understanding of the world while experiencing it. In Piaget's view, cognitive development

Bill Anderson/Science Source

**Jean Piaget (1896–1980)** "If we examine the intellectual development of the individual or of the whole of humanity, we shall find that the human spirit goes through a certain number of stages, each different from the other" (1930).

 **SPOTLIGHT ON:**
Jean Piaget

**cognition** all the mental activities associated with thinking, knowing, remembering, and communicating.

**schema** a concept or framework that organizes and interprets information.

**assimilation** interpreting our new experiences in terms of our existing schemas.

**accommodation** adapting our current schemas (understandings) to incorporate new information.

© Doug Goodman/Science Source

**Figure 3.4-1**
**Object permanence**

Infants younger than 6 months seldom understand that things continue to exist when they are out of sight. But for this older infant, out of sight is definitely not out of mind.

**sensorimotor stage** in Piaget's theory, the stage (from birth to nearly 2 years of age) at which infants know the world mostly in terms of their sensory impressions and motor activities.

**object permanence** the awareness that things continue to exist even when not perceived.

consists of four major stages—*sensorimotor, preoperational, concrete operational,* and *formal operational*—each with distinctive characteristics that permit specific kinds of thinking.

## Sensorimotor Stage

In the **sensorimotor stage**, from birth to nearly age 2, babies take in the world through their senses and actions—through looking, hearing, touching, mouthing, and grasping. As their hands and limbs begin to move, they learn to make things happen.

Very young babies seem to live in the present: Out of sight is out of mind. In one test, Piaget showed an infant an appealing toy and then flopped his beret over it. Before the age of 6 months, the infant acted as if the toy ceased to exist. Young infants lack **object permanence**—the awareness that objects continue to exist when not perceived. By 8 months, infants begin exhibiting memory for things no longer seen. If you hide a toy, the infant will momentarily look for it (**Figure 3.4-1**). Within another month or two, the infant will look for it even after being restrained for several seconds.

So, does object permanence blossom suddenly at 8 months, much as tulips blossom in spring? Today's researchers believe object permanence unfolds gradually, and they see development as more continuous than Piaget did.

Researchers also believe Piaget and his followers underestimated young children's competence. Young children think like little scientists. They test ideas, make causal inferences, and learn from statistical patterns (Gopnik et al., 2015). Consider these simple experiments:

- ***Baby physics:*** Like adults staring in disbelief at a magic trick (the *"Whoa!"* look), infants look longer at and explore impossible scenes—a car seeming to pass through a solid object, a ball stopping in midair, or an object violating object permanence by magically disappearing (Shuwairi & Johnson, 2013; Stahl & Feigenson, 2015). Why do infants show this visual bias? Because impossible events violate infants' expectations (Baillargeon et al., 2016).

- ***Baby math:*** Karen Wynn (1992, 2000, 2008) showed 5-month-olds one or two objects (**Figure 3.4-2a**). Then she hid the objects behind a screen, and visibly removed

**Figure 3.4-2**
**Baby math**

Shown a numerically impossible outcome, 5-month-old infants stare longer (Wynn, 1992). Clearly, infants are smarter than Piaget appreciated. Even as babies, we have a lot on our minds.

**Then either: possible outcome**
(e) Screen drops revealing 1 object

**or: impossible outcome**
(f) Screen drops revealing 2 objects

(a) Objects placed in case

(b) Screen comes up

(c) Empty hand enters

(d) One object removed
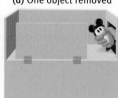

Bianca Moscatelli/Macmillan Learning

## Figure 3.4-3
### Piaget's test of conservation

This visually focused preoperational child does not yet understand the principle of conservation. When the milk is poured into a tall, narrow glass, it suddenly seems like "more" than when it was in the shorter, wider glass. In another year or so, she will understand that the amount stays the same.

or added one (Figure 3.4-2d). When she lifted the screen, the infants sometimes did a double take, staring longer when shown a wrong number of objects (Figure 3.4-2f). But were they just responding to a greater or smaller *mass* of objects, rather than a change in *number* (Feigenson et al., 2002)? Later experiments showed that babies' number sense extends to larger numbers, to ratios, and to such things as drumbeats and motions (Libertus & Brannon, 2009; McCrink & Wynn, 2004; Spelke et al., 2013). If accustomed to a Daffy Duck puppet jumping three times on stage, they showed surprise if it jumped only twice.

## Preoperational Stage

Piaget believed that until about age 6 or 7, children are in a **preoperational stage**—able to represent things with words and images but too young to perform *mental operations* (such as imagining an action and mentally reversing it). For a 5-year-old, the milk that seems "too much" in a tall, narrow glass may become just right if poured into a short, wide glass. Focusing only on the height dimension, this child cannot perform the operation of mentally pouring the milk back. Before about age 6, said Piaget, children lack the concept of **conservation**—the principle that quantity remains the same despite changes in shape (**Figure 3.4-3**).

**Pretend and Parallel Play** Symbolic thinking and the *pretend play* it enables appear at an earlier age than Piaget supposed. Judy DeLoache (1987) showed children a model of a room and hid a miniature stuffed dog behind its miniature couch. The 2½-year-olds easily remembered where to find the miniature toy, but they could not use the model to locate an actual stuffed dog behind a couch in a real room. Three-year-olds—only 6 months older—usually went right to the actual stuffed animal in the real room, showing they *could* think of the model as a symbol for the room. Similarly, 2½-year-olds tend to engage in *parallel play*, in which they play next to other children but do not try to influence others. At a playground, they may play beside a friend, focused on their play and oblivious to their friend's behaviors.

**Egocentrism** Piaget taught us that preschool children are **egocentric:** They have difficulty perceiving things from another's perspective.

**AP® Science Practice**

### Research

The DeLoache study described here is a nice example of a cross-sectional study, one that compares people of different ages at the same point in time to look for developmental differences.

**preoperational stage** in Piaget's theory, the stage (from about 2 to 6 or 7 years of age) at which a child learns to use language but does not yet comprehend the mental operations of concrete logic.

**conservation** the principle (which Piaget believed to be a part of concrete operational reasoning) that properties such as mass, volume, and number remain the same despite changes in the forms of objects.

**egocentrism** in Piaget's theory, the preoperational child's difficulty taking another's point of view.

Dave Myers

Egocentrism in action "Look, Granddaddy, a match!" So said my [DM's] granddaughter, Allie, at age 4, when showing me two memory game cards with matching pictures — that faced her.

*"It's too late, Roger — they've seen us."*

**Roger has not outgrown his early childhood egocentrism**

**AP® Exam Tip**

Careful! *Egocentric* in a preoperational context is not the same as *egotistical*. Egocentric means you can't take someone else's point of view. Egotistical means you're self-centered and conceited.

**AP® Exam Tip**

One good way to master the developmental milestones in Piaget's theory is to see them in action. If you know children of various ages, you can test them using some of the ideas presented in this module. Hide a toy from an infant to see object permanence in action. Pour water between two differently shaped glasses to see if a preschooler understands conservation.

**concrete operational stage** in Piaget's theory, the stage of cognitive development (from about 7 to 11 years of age) at which children can perform the mental operations that enable them to think logically about concrete (actual, physical) events.

**formal operational stage** in Piaget's theory, the stage of cognitive development (normally beginning about age 12) at which people begin to think logically about abstract concepts.

They are like the person who, when asked by someone across a river, "How do I get to the other side?," answered, "You're *on* the other side." Asked to "show Mommy your picture," 2-year-old Gabriella holds the picture up facing her own eyes. Asked what he would do if he saw a bear, 3-year-old Grant replies, "We cover our eyes so the bears can't see us."

Children's conversations also reveal their egocentrism, as one young boy demonstrated (Phillips, 1969, p. 61):

> *"Do you have a brother?"*
> *"Yes."*
> *"What's his name?"*
> *"Jim."*
> *"Does Jim have a brother?"*
> *"No."*

Like Gabriella, TV-watching preschoolers who block your view of the TV assume that you see what they see. They simply have not yet developed the ability to take another's viewpoint. Even adolescents egocentrically overestimate how much others are noticing them (Lin, 2016). And adults may overestimate the extent to which others share their opinions, knowledge, and perspectives. We assume that something will be clear to others if it is clear to us, or that email recipients will "hear" our "just kidding" intent (Epley et al., 2004; Kruger et al., 2005). During the preoperational stage, children may also display *animism*—a belief that inanimate objects are alive or have lifelike feelings and motivations. Animism helps explain why preschoolers become emotionally attached to their stuffed animals and other toys.

## Concrete Operational Stage

By about age 7, said Piaget, children enter the **concrete operational stage**. Given concrete (physical) materials, they begin to grasp more complex operations such as spatial and mathematical relationships. Understanding that change in form does not mean change in quantity, they can mentally pour milk back and forth between glasses of different shapes. They also enjoy jokes that use this new understanding:

> Mr. Jones went into a restaurant and ordered a whole pizza for his dinner. When the waiter asked if he wanted it cut into 6 or 8 pieces, Mr. Jones said, "Oh, you'd better make it 6, I could never eat 8 pieces!" (McGhee, 1976)

Piaget believed that during the concrete operational stage, children become able to comprehend mathematical transformations and conservation. When my [DM's] daughter, Laura, was 6, I was surprised at her inability to reverse simple arithmetic. Asked, "What is 8 plus 4?" she required 5 seconds to compute "12," and another 5 seconds to then compute 12 minus 4. By age 8, she could answer a reversed question instantly.

## Formal Operational Stage

By about age 12, our reasoning expands from the purely concrete (involving actual experience) to encompass abstract thinking (involving symbols or imagined realities, such as beauty). Although young children may struggle to think systematically, as adolescents they can ponder hypothetical propositions and deduce consequences: *If* this, *then* that. Systematic reasoning, what Piaget called **formal operational** thinking, is now likely within their grasp.

Although full-blown logic and reasoning await adolescence, the rudiments of formal operational thinking begin earlier than Piaget realized. Consider this simple problem:

> If John is in school, then Mary is in school. John is in school. What can you say about Mary?

Formal operational thinkers have no trouble answering correctly. But neither do most 7-year-olds (Suppes, 1982). **Table 3.4-1** summarizes the four stages in Piaget's theory.

| TABLE 3.4-1 Piaget's Stages of Cognitive Development | | |
| --- | --- | --- |
| **Typical Age Range** | **Stage and Description** | **Key Milestones** |
| Birth to nearly 2 years | *Sensorimotor* Experiencing the world through senses and actions (looking, hearing, touching, mouthing, and grasping) | • Object permanence<br>• Stranger anxiety |
| About 2 to 6–7 years | *Preoperational* Representing things with words and images; using intuitive rather than logical reasoning | • Pretend play<br>• Egocentrism |
| About 7–11 years | *Concrete operational* Thinking logically about concrete events; grasping concrete analogies and performing arithmetical operations | • Conservation<br>• Mathematical transformations |
| About 12 through adulthood | *Formal operational* Reasoning abstractly | • Abstract logic<br>• Potential for mature moral reasoning |

Liz Banfield/Getty Images

Pretend play

---

**AP® Science Practice**

# Check Your Understanding

**Examine the Concept**

▶ Explain mental operations.

▶ Explain what is meant by *egocentrism*.

**Apply the Concept**

▶ Label each of the following developmental phenomena (i–vi) with the correct cognitive developmental stage: (a) sensorimotor, (b) preoperational, (c) concrete operational, or (d) formal operational.

   i.  Thinking about abstract concepts, such as "freedom"

   ii.  Enjoying imaginary play (such as dress-up)

   iii.  Understanding that physical properties stay the same even when objects change form

   iv.  Having the ability to reverse math operations

   v.  Understanding that something is not gone for good when it disappears from sight

   vi.  Having difficulty taking another's point of view (as when blocking someone's view of the TV)

▶ Can you think of an example from your own childhood, or perhaps that of a sibling, that illustrates one of the theories of cognitive development discussed in this module?

*Answers to the Examine the Concept questions can be found in Appendix C at the end of the book.*

---

## Reflecting on Piaget's Theory

What remains of Piaget's ideas about the child's mind? Plenty—enough to merit his being singled out by *Time* magazine as one of the twentieth century's 20 most influential scientists and thinkers, and his being rated in a survey of British psychologists as the last

## Developing Arguments

Can you identify the reasoning behind the claim that cognitive development is more continuous than Piaget thought?

If you said each stage begins earlier than Piaget thought, that Piaget missed some cognitive abilities, and that formal logic is only a small part of cognition, you would be right! On the AP® exam, you may be asked to develop or critique evidence-based claims.

century's greatest psychologist (*Psychologist*, 2003). Piaget identified significant cognitive milestones and stimulated worldwide interest in how the mind develops. His emphasis was less on the ages at which children typically reach specific milestones than on their sequence. Worldwide studies, from Australia to Algeria to North America, have confirmed that human cognition unfolds basically in the sequence Piaget described (Lourenco & Machado, 1996; Segall et al., 1990).

However, today's researchers see development as more *continuous* (gradual and ongoing) than did Piaget, who mostly focused on the *discontinuous* (occurring in distinct stages) nature of development. Children's minds experience spurts of change, followed by greater stability as they progress from one cognitive plateau to the next. By detecting the beginnings of each type of thinking at earlier ages, modern researchers have revealed conceptual abilities Piaget missed. Moreover, they see formal logic as a smaller part of cognition than he did. Today, as part of our own cognitive development, we are adapting Piaget's ideas to accommodate new findings.

### Implications for Parents and Teachers

Future parents and teachers, remember: Young children are incapable of adult logic. Preschoolers who block your view of the TV simply have not learned to take another person's viewpoint. What seems simple and obvious to us—getting off a seesaw will cause a friend on the other end to crash—may be incomprehensible to a 3-year-old. And it's also important for all of us to remember that children are not passive receptacles waiting to be filled with knowledge. Better to build on what they already know, engaging them in concrete demonstrations and stimulating them to think for themselves. Finally, accept children's cognitive immaturity as adaptive. It is nature's strategy for keeping children close to protective adults and providing time for learning and socialization (Bjorklund & Green, 1992).

## An Alternative Viewpoint: Lev Vygotsky and the Social Child

**3.4-2** How did Vygotsky view children's cognitive development?

**SPOTLIGHT ON:**
Lev Vygotsky

As Piaget was forming his theory of cognitive development, Russian psychologist Lev Vygotsky was also studying how children think and learn. Whereas Piaget emphasized how the child's mind grows through interaction with the physical environment, Vygotsky emphasized how the child's mind grows through interaction with the *social-cultural* environment. If Piaget's child was a young scientist, Vygotsky's was a young apprentice. By giving children new words and mentoring them, parents, teachers, and other children provide what we now call a temporary **scaffold** from which children can step to higher levels of thinking (Renninger & Granott, 2005; Wood et al., 1976).

Effective mentoring occurs when children are developmentally ready to learn a new skill. For Vygotsky, a child's *zone of proximal development* is the zone between what a child can and can't do—it's what a child can do with help. When learning to ride a bike, it's the developmental zone in which a child can ride with training wheels or a steadying parental hand. Children learn best when their social environment presents them with something in the sweet spot between too easy and too difficult.

Language, as an important ingredient of social-cultural mentoring, provides the building blocks for thinking, noted Vygotsky (who was born in the same year as Piaget, but died prematurely of tuberculosis). By age 7, children increasingly think in words and use words to solve problems. They do this, Vygotsky said, by internalizing their culture's language and relying on inner speech (Fernyhough, 2008). Parents who say "No, no, Ellis!" when pulling their child's hand away from a cup of hot coffee are giving him a self-control tool. When

**scaffold** in Vygotsky's theory, a framework that offers children temporary support as they develop higher levels of thinking.

Ellis later needs to resist temptation, he may likewise think, *"No, no, Ellis!"* Second graders who muttered to themselves while doing math problems grasped third-grade math better the following year (Berk, 1994). Whether out loud or inaudibly, talking to themselves helps children control their behavior and emotions and master new skills. (It helps adults, too. Adults who motivate themselves using affirming self-talk—"You can do it!"—experience better performance [Kross et al., 2014].)

**theory of mind** people's ideas about their own and others' mental states—about their feelings, perceptions, and thoughts, and the behaviors these might predict.

## Theory of Mind

> **3.4-3** What does it mean to develop a *theory of mind*?

When Little Red Riding Hood realized her "grandmother" was really a wolf, she swiftly revised her ideas about the creature's intentions and raced away. Preschoolers, although still egocentric, develop this ability to infer others' mental states when they begin forming a **theory of mind** (Premack & Woodruff, 1978).

As the ability to take another's perspective gradually develops, preschoolers come to understand what made a playmate angry, when a sibling will share, and what might make a parent buy a toy. They begin to tease, empathize, and persuade. And when making decisions, they use their understanding of how their actions will make others feel (Repacholi et al., 2016). Preschoolers and young children who have an advanced ability to understand others' minds tend to be well-liked (McElwain et al., 2019; Slaughter et al., 2015).

Between about ages 3 and 4½, children worldwide come to realize that others may hold false beliefs (Callaghan et al., 2005; Rubio-Fernández & Geurts, 2013; Sabbagh et al., 2006). Jennifer Jenkins and Janet Astington (1996) showed Canadian children a Band-Aid box and asked them what was inside. Expecting Band-Aids, the children were surprised to discover that the box actually contained pencils. Asked what a child who had never seen the box would think was inside, 3-year-olds typically answered "pencils." By age 4 to 5, the children's theory of mind had leapt forward, and they anticipated their friends' false belief that the box would hold Band-Aids.

In a follow-up study, children viewed a doll named Sally leaving her ball in a red cupboard (**Figure 3.4-4**). Another doll, Anne, then moved the ball to a blue cupboard. Researchers then posed a question: When Sally returns, where will she look for the ball? Children with *autism spectrum disorder* (Module 5.4) had difficulty understanding that Sally's state of mind differed from their own—that Sally, not knowing the ball had been moved, would return to the red cupboard. Such children also have difficulty reflecting on their own mental states. They are, for example, less likely to use the personal pronouns *I* and *me*. Deaf children with hearing parents and minimal communication opportunities have shown similar difficulty inferring others' states of mind (Peterson & Siegal, 1999).

**Figure 3.4-4**

**Testing children's theory of mind**

This simple problem illustrates how researchers explore children's presumptions about others' mental states. (Inspired by Baron-Cohen et al., 1985.)

*This is Sally.*     *This is Anne.*

*Sally puts her ball in the red cupboard.*

*Sally goes away.*

*Anne moves the ball to the blue cupboard.*

*Where will Sally look for her ball?*

# Cognitive Development in Adolescence

> **3.4-4** How did Piaget and later researchers describe adolescent cognitive and moral development?

During the early teen years, *egocentrism* endures, and reasoning is often self-focused. Capable of thinking about their own and others' thinking, teens also begin imagining what others are thinking about *them* and develop an intense awareness of this *imaginary audience*. (They might worry less if they understood their peers' similar self-focus. Few people will remember our awkward moments, because they're too busy remembering their own.) Teens also have a tendency to develop a *personal fable*—believing that they are unique and special and what happens to "most people" would never happen to them. "My vaping is just for fun; I would never end up an addicted smoker like my uncle."

## Developing Reasoning Power

When adolescents achieve the intellectual summit that Jean Piaget called *formal operations*, they apply their new abstract reasoning tools to the world around them. They may think about what is ideally possible and compare that with the imperfect reality of their society, their parents, and themselves. They may debate human nature, good and evil, truth and justice. Their sense of what's fair changes from simple equality to equity—to what is proportional to merit (Almås et al., 2010). Having left behind the concrete images of early childhood, they may search for spirituality and the deeper meaning of life (Boyatzis, 2012; Elkind, 1970). Reasoning hypothetically and deducing consequences also enable adolescents to detect inconsistencies and spot hypocrisy in others' reasoning, sometimes leading to heated family debates and silent vows never to lose sight of their own ideals (Peterson et al., 1986).

**Fed up with funding cuts** These Oklahoma City high school students are protesting state budget cuts that will reduce their school's funding. According to Piaget, these teens are in the final cognitive stage, formal operations.

## Developing Morality

Two crucial tasks of childhood and adolescence are discerning right from wrong and developing character—the psychological muscles for controlling impulses. Children learn to empathize with others, an ability that continues to develop in adolescence. To be a moral person is to *think* morally and *act* accordingly. Jean Piaget proposed that moral reasoning guides moral actions. A newer view builds on psychology's game-changing recognition that much of our functioning occurs not on the "high road" of deliberate, conscious thinking, but rather on the "low road" of unconscious, automatic thinking.

### Moral Intuition

Psychologist Jonathan Haidt [pronounced HITE] (2002, 2012) believes that much of our morality is rooted in *moral intuitions*—"quick gut feelings." According to this intuitionist view, the mind makes moral judgments quickly and automatically. Feelings of disgust or of elation trigger moral reasoning, says Haidt.

One woman recalled traveling through her snowy neighborhood with three young men as they passed "an elderly woman with a shovel in her driveway. . . . [O]ne of the guys . . . asked the driver to let him off there. . . . [M]y mouth dropped in shock as I realized that he was offering to shovel her walk for her." Witnessing this unexpected goodness triggered elevation: "I felt like jumping out of the car and hugging this guy. I felt like singing and running, or skipping and laughing. I felt like saying nice things about people" (Haidt, 2000).

"Could human morality really be run by the moral emotions," Haidt wonders, "while moral reasoning struts about pretending to be in control?" Consider the desire to punish. Laboratory games reveal that the desire to punish wrongdoing is mostly driven not by reason (such as an objective calculation that punishment deters crime), but rather by emotional reactions, such as moral outrage and the pleasure of revenge (Chester & DeWall, 2016; Darley, 2009). After the emotional fact, moral reasoning—our mind's press secretary—aims to convince us and others of the logic of what we have intuitively felt.

This intuitionist perspective on morality finds support in a study of moral paradoxes. Imagine seeing a runaway trolley headed for five people. All will certainly be killed unless you throw a switch that diverts the trolley onto another track, where it will kill one person. Should you throw the switch? Most say *Yes*. Kill one, save five.

Now imagine the same dilemma, with one change. This time, you must save the five by pushing a stranger onto the tracks, where he will die as his body stops the trolley. In both versions of this famous "trolley problem," the logic is the same—kill one, save five. But worldwide, half say *No* in this second dilemma (Awad et al., 2020). One brain-imaging study showed that only the body-pushing type of moral dilemma activated emotion-area neural responses (Greene et al., 2001). Thus, our moral judgments provide another example of the two-track mind—of dual processing (Feinberg et al., 2012). Moral reasoning, centered in one brain area, says *throw the switch*. Our intuitive moral emotions, rooted in other brain areas, override reason when saying *don't push the man*. We may liken our moral cognition to our phone's camera settings. Usually, we rely on the default settings. Yet sometimes we use reason to manually override those settings or to adjust the resulting image (Greene, 2010; May, 2019).

**Moral reasoning** Bahamians faced a moral dilemma in 2019 when Hurricane Dorian devastated their northern islands. As many took in family and friends who now had no home, their reasons for helping likely reflected different levels of moral thinking, even if they behaved similarly.

THE LITTLE ENGINE THAT FACED A TOUGH MORAL DILEMMA

## Moral Action

Our moral thinking and feeling surely affect our moral talk. But sometimes talk is cheap and emotions are fleeting. Morality involves *doing* the right thing, and what we do also depends on social influences. As political theorist Hannah Arendt (1963) observed, many Nazi concentration camp guards during World War II were ordinary "moral" people corrupted by a powerfully evil situation.

**AP® Science Practice**

### Developing Arguments

Researchers use scientifically derived evidence (such as the trolley problem study) to back up their claims (such as moral judgments are an example of the two-track mind). On the AP® exam, you may be asked to use such evidence to support or dispute claims.

Today's character education programs focus on the whole moral package—thinking, feeling, and *doing* the right thing. In service learning programs, teens have tutored, cleaned up their neighborhoods, and assisted older adults. The result? The participating teens' sense of competence and desire to serve have increased, their school absenteeism and dropout rates have fallen, and their violent behavior has diminished (Andersen, 1998; Heller, 2014; Piliavin, 2003). *Moral action* feeds moral attitudes.

These programs also teach the self-discipline needed to restrain one's own impulses. Those who have learned to *delay gratification*—to live with one eye on the future—have become more socially responsible, academically successful, and productive (Daly et al., 2015; Sawyer et al., 2015). A preference for large-later rather than small-now rewards also minimizes one's risk of problem gambling and delinquency (Callan et al., 2011; Lee et al., 2017).

In one of psychology's best-known experiments, Walter Mischel (2014) gave 4-year-olds a choice between one marshmallow now, or two marshmallows when he returned a few minutes later. The children who delayed gratification went on to have higher college completion rates and incomes, and less often developed addiction problems. A replication of this famous study found a more modest effect (Watts et al., 2018; Watts & Duncan, 2020). But the big idea remains: Maturity and life success grow from the ability to spurn small pleasures now in favor of greater pleasures later (Moreira & Barbosa, 2019). Delaying gratification fosters flourishing.

## AP® Science Practice

# Check Your Understanding

### Examine the Concept

▶ Use Piaget's first three stages of cognitive development to explain why children are not just miniature adults in the way they think.

▶ Explain the theory of mind.

### Apply the Concept

▶ Can you recall making an impulsive decision when you were younger that you later regretted? What did you do? How would you do things differently now?

*Answers to the Examine the Concept questions can be found in Appendix C at the end of the book.*

# Cognitive Development in Adulthood

Along our life's journey from adolescence through adulthood, we continue to develop and change. Very gradually, our thinking, reaction speed, and sensory abilities begin to diminish, even while our impulse control and wisdom grow. Older adults also become prone to *dementia*, a cognitive disorder that impairs memory, cognition, and decision-making.

## Aging and Memory

### AP® Science Practice

#### Research

This module illustrates the complexity of researching seemingly simple questions. It seems as if a question like "Does memory decline with age?" should have a simple answer. But the answer depends on what sort of memory is being considered.

**3.4-5** How does memory change with age?

Among the most intriguing developmental psychology questions is whether adult cognitive abilities, such as memory, intelligence, and creativity, parallel the gradually accelerating decline of physical abilities.

As we age, we remember some things well. Looking back in later life, adults asked to recall the one or two most important events over the last half-century tend to name events from their teens or twenties (Conway et al., 2005; Rubin et al., 1998). They also display

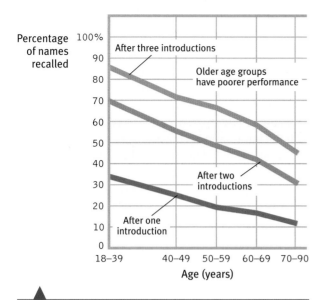

**Figure 3.4-5**
**Tests of recall**

Recalling new names introduced once, twice, or three times is easier for younger adults than for older ones. (Data from Crook & West, 1990.)

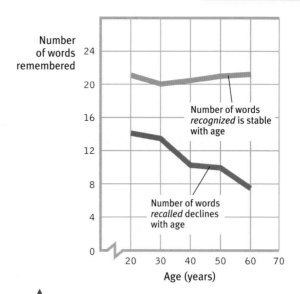

**Figure 3.4-6**
**Recall and recognition in adulthood**

In this experiment, the ability to *recall* new information declined during early and middle adulthood, but the ability to *recognize* new information did not. (Data from Schonfield & Robertson, 1966.)

this "reminiscence bump" when asked to name their all-time favorite music, movies, and athletes (Janssen et al., 2012). Whatever people experience around this time of life—the Vietnam war, the Covid pandemic, the Ukraine war—becomes pivotal (Pillemer, 1998; Schuman & Scott, 1989). Our teens and twenties hold so many memorable "firsts"—first kiss, first job, first day at college or university, first apartment.

Early adulthood is indeed a peak time for some types of learning and remembering. In one test of recall, people watched video clips as 14 strangers said their names, using a common format: "Hi, I'm Larry" (Crook & West, 1990). As **Figure 3.4-5** shows, even after a second and third replay of the introductions with more personal information, younger adults consistently remembered more names than older adults. How well older people remember depends in part on the task. In another study, when asked to *recognize* 24 words they had earlier tried to memorize, older adults showed no memory decline. When they were asked to *recall* that information without clues, however, the decline was greater (**Figure 3.4-6**).

Teens and young adults surpass both young children and 70-year-olds at *prospective memory*, our memory for doing future behaviors ("Remember to . . .") (Zimmermann & Meier, 2006). But older people's prospective memory remains strong when events help trigger a memory (as when walking by a convenience store triggers "Pick up milk!"). By comparison, time-based tasks ("Client meeting at 3:00 P.M.") and especially habitual tasks ("Take medications at 9:00 A.M., 2:00 P.M., and 6:00 P.M.") can be challenging (Einstein & McDaniel, 1990; Einstein et al., 1995, 1998). To minimize such problems, older adults rely more on time management and reminder cues, such as notes to themselves (Henry et al., 2004). This might have helped John Basinger, who, at age 76, memorized all 12 volumes of John Milton's epic poem *Paradise Lost* and became the subject of a psychology journal article (Seamon et al., 2010; Weir, 2010). A local paper scheduled an interview with Basinger, which he forgot to attend. Calling the reporter to apologize, he noted the irony of forgetting his interview about memory!

**AP® Science Practice**

**Data**

Figure 3.4-5 provides an opportunity to practice your data interpretation skills. Can you identify the three variables in the graph? Can you describe the trends you see in the data? (Answers: Age, number of introductions, and recall; Older groups had poorer recall, though all ages did better after three introductions).

"I'm concerned about his memory. He keeps asking, 'Who's a good boy? Who's a good boy?'"

Paul Karasik/Cartoon Stock

In our capacity to learn and remember, as in other areas of development, we show individual differences. Younger adults vary in their abilities to learn and remember, but 70-year-olds vary much more. "Differences between the most and least able 70-year-olds become much greater than between the most and least able 50-year-olds," reported Oxford University researcher Patrick Rabbitt (2006). Some 70-year-olds perform below nearly all 20-year-olds; other 70-year-olds match or outdo the average 20-year-old.

No matter how quick or slow we are, remembering seems also to depend on the type of information we are trying to retrieve. If the information is meaningless—nonsense syllables or unimportant events or experiences—then the older we are, the more errors we are likely to make. If the information is *meaningful*, as was *Paradise Lost* for John Basinger, older people's rich web of existing knowledge will help them to hold it. But they may take longer than younger adults to *produce* the words and things they know. Older adults also more often experience tip-of-the-tongue forgetting (Ossher et al., 2012). Quick-thinking game show winners are usually young or middle-aged adults (Burke & Shafto, 2004).

## Maintaining Mental Abilities

More education earlier in life predicts better cognitive ability late in life (Lövdén et al., 2020). Psychologists who study the aging mind therefore debate whether computer-based "brain fitness" training programs can simulate education, by building mental muscles that stave off cognitive decline. Our brain remains plastic throughout life (Gutchess, 2014). So, can exercising our brain on a "cognitive treadmill"—with memory, visual tracking, and problem-solving exercises—help us avoid losing our mind? One analysis of cognitive training programs showed that they consistently improved scores on tests related to their training (Simons et al., 2016). Video game playing may also enhance people's attention (Bediou et al., 2018).

Based on such findings, some computer game makers have been marketing daily brain-exercise programs for older adults. But other researchers, after reviewing all the available studies, advise skepticism (Redick et al., 2017; Sala et al., 2018). Across more than 200 studies, brain-exercise programs improved performance on closely related tasks but not on unrelated tasks (Basak et al., 2020). As researcher Zach Hambrick (2014) explains, "Play a video game and you'll get better at that video game, and maybe at very similar video games"—but not at driving a car or filling out your tax return. One experiment found that, compared with mere online video game playing, a prominent brain-training program by Lumosity did not improve mental performance more (Kable et al., 2017).

Module 2.8 explored another dimension of cognitive development: intelligence. As we saw, *cross-sectional studies* (comparing people of different ages) and *longitudinal studies* (restudying the same people over time) have identified mental abilities that do and do not change as people age. Age is less a predictor of memory and intelligence than is proximity to a natural death, which does give a clue to someone's mental ability. In the last three or four years of life, and especially as death approaches, cognitive decline typically accelerates (Vogel et al., 2013; Wilson et al., 2007). Researchers call this near-death drop *terminal decline* (Backman & MacDonald, 2006). Our goals also shift: We're driven less to learn and more to connect socially (Carstensen, 2011).

**AP® Science Practice**

## Check Your Understanding

**Examine the Concept**

▶ Explain the evidence on brain-exercise programs for older adults.

**Apply the Concept**

▶ Suppose a friend asks you, does memory decline with age? Now that you have read this module, how would you respond?

▶ What experiences from your high school years do you think you may never forget? (These years, and the next few, will be among the times of your life you may remember most easily when you are 50.)

*Answers to the Examine the Concept questions can be found in Appendix C at the end of the book.*

# Module 3.4 REVIEW

### 3.4-1 How did Piaget broaden our understanding of the way a child's mind develops, and how have today's researchers built on his work?

- When studying children's *cognitive* development, Jean Piaget proposed that children actively construct and modify their understanding of the world through the processes of *assimilation* and *accommodation*. They form *schemas* that help them organize their experiences.

- Progressing from the simplicity of the *sensorimotor stage* of the first two years, in which they develop *object permanence*, children move to more complex ways of thinking. In the *preoperational stage* (about age 2 to about 6 or 7), children are *egocentric* and unable to perform simple logical operations. By about age 7, they enter the *concrete operational stage* and are able to comprehend the principle of conservation. By age 12, children enter the formal operational stage and can reason systematically.

- Research supports the sequence Piaget proposed, but it also shows that young children are more capable, and their development more continuous, than he believed.

### 3.4-2 How did Vygotsky view children's cognitive development?

- Lev Vygotsky's studies of child development focused on the ways a child's mind grows by interacting with the social environment. In his view, parents, teachers, and other children provide temporary *scaffolds* enabling children to step to higher levels of thinking.

### 3.4-3 What does it mean to develop a *theory of mind*?

- Our *theory of mind*—our ideas about our own and others' mental states—develops during early childhood.

- Children with *autism spectrum disorder (ASD)* have difficulty understanding that others' state of mind may differ from their own.

### 3.4-4 How did Piaget and later researchers describe adolescent cognitive and moral development?

- Piaget theorized that adolescents develop a capacity for formal operations and that this development is the foundation for moral judgment.

- Other researchers believe that morality lies in moral intuition and moral action as well as thinking.

- Life success can grow from the ability to delay gratification.

### 3.4-5 How does memory change with age?

- Recall begins to decline, especially for meaningless information, but recognition memory remains strong.

- Developmental researchers study age-related changes such as in memory with *cross-sectional studies* and *longitudinal studies*.

- "Terminal decline" describes the cognitive decline in the final few years of life.

---

## AP® Practice Multiple Choice Questions

**1.** If you showed a 2-year-old a model of her bedroom where you had hidden a toy behind the bed, she would

   a. neither be able to find the toy in the model bedroom nor find the toy in her own room.

   b. be able to find the toy in the model but not in her actual room due to lack of symbolic thinking.

   c. understand that the model represented her room and be able to find the toy in her own room.

   d. misunderstand the instructions due to her lack of theory of mind.

**2.** What psychological concept is being depicted in this graph?

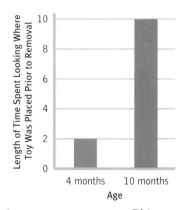

   a. Egocentrism
   b. Theory of mind
   c. Object permanence
   d. Scaffolding

3. Dr. Tchoupitoulas wants to conduct a study on the formal operational stage of development. Which of the following is an appropriate operational definition of the formal operational stage?

   a. Reversing arithmetic operations
   b. Using hypothetical situations as the basis of moral reasoning
   c. Using symbolic thinking for pretend play
   d. Understanding basic physics to recognize impossible situations

4. Cesaire, a 4-year-old child, comes into the room and tells his parent, "I broke it" without feeling the need to tell his parent what is broken because 4-year-olds often

   a. lack an understanding of conservation.
   b. cannot remember what was broken.
   c. struggle with reversing operations.
   d. are egocentric.

5. Which of the following examples indicates that a child understands conservation?

   a. She would continue to seek a toy hidden under a blanket.
   b. She would "hide" in a game of hide-and-seek by covering her eyes with her hands.
   c. She would believe that a clay snake would have the same amount of clay as the clay ball that was used to make it.
   d. She would recognize that 7 + 3 involves the same mathematical relationship as 10 − 7.

6. Which of the following is a current belief of researchers that differs from Piaget's original theories?

   a. The formal operational stage is narrower than Piaget believed.
   b. Object permanence develops earlier than Piaget believed.
   c. Infants learn more by verbal explanations than Piaget believed.
   d. Schemas do not form until later than Piaget believed.

7. Ms. Quintron accurately taught her class about Vygotsky's theory. What might she say to her class?

   a. Theory of mind refers to one's thoughts about oneself and others.
   b. Conservation refers to the idea that properties remain the same despite changes in form.
   c. The sensorimotor stage refers to a period when babies and toddlers engage the world via their senses and motor movements.
   d. The zone of proximal development refers to the space between what a child is capable of doing and what the child cannot yet do.

# Module 3.5 Communication and Language Development

## LEARNING TARGETS

**3.5-1** Explain how we acquire language, and explain the concept of *universal grammar*.

**3.5-2** Explain the milestones in language development, and identify the critical period for acquiring language.

**3.5-3** Identify the brain areas involved in language processing and speech.

**3.5-4** Explain the relationship between thinking and language, and discuss the value of thinking in images.

Imagine an alien species that could pass thoughts from one head to another merely by pulsating air molecules in the space between them. Perhaps these weird creatures could inhabit a future science fiction movie? Actually, we are those creatures! When we speak, our brain and voice apparatus transmit air pressure waves that we send banging against another person's eardrum—enabling us to transfer thoughts from our brain into theirs. As cognitive psychologist Steven Pinker (1998) noted, we sometimes sit for hours "listening to other people make noise as they exhale, because those hisses and squeaks contain *information*." Depending on how you vibrate the air, you may get a scowl or a kiss.

**Language** is more than vibrating air—it is our spoken, written, or signed words, and the ways we combine them to communicate meaning. When I [DM] created this paragraph, my fingers on the keyboard generated electronic binary numbers that morphed into the squiggles in front of you. When transmitted by light rays into your retina (or by sound waves into your ear), these squiggles trigger formless nerve impulses that travel to several areas of your brain, which integrate the information, compare it to stored information, and decode meaning. Thanks to language, information is moving from my mind to yours. Many animals know little more than what they sense. Thanks to language, we comprehend much that we've never seen and that our distant ancestors never knew. And thanks to technology, we can use language to communicate across vast distances—through spoken, written, and even pictorial "emoticon" words (including the 2015 *Oxford English Dictionary* "word of the year," the emoji: 😂).

> **language** our agreed-upon systems of spoken, written, or signed words, and the ways we combine them to communicate meaning.

M. Spencer Green/AP Photo

**Language transmits knowledge**
Whether spoken, written, or signed, language — the original wireless communication — enables mind-to-mind information transfer, and with it the transmission of civilization's accumulated knowledge across generations.

## Language Acquisition and Development

We humans have an astonishing knack for language. With little effort, we draw from tens of thousands of words in our memory; assemble them, on the fly, using the rules of our language; and spew them out, three words a second (Vigliocco & Hartsuiker, 2002). Given how many ways we can mess up, our language capacity is truly amazing.

**SPOTLIGHT ON:**

Noam Chomsky

**Creating a language** Brought together as if on a desert island (actually a school), Nicaragua's young deaf children over time drew upon sign gestures from home to create their own Nicaraguan Sign Language, complete with words and intricate grammar. Activated by a social context, nature and nurture work creatively together (Osborne, 1999; Sandler et al., 2005; Senghas & Coppola, 2001).

**phoneme** in a language, the smallest distinctive sound unit.

**morpheme** in a language, the smallest unit that carries meaning; may be a word or a part of a word (such as a prefix).

**grammar** in a language, a system of rules that enables us to communicate with and understand others. Semantics is the language's set of rules for deriving meaning from sounds, and syntax is its set of rules for combining words into grammatically sensible sentences.

**universal grammar (UG)** humans' innate predisposition to understand the principles and rules that govern grammar in all languages.

## Language Acquisition: How Do We Learn Language?

> **3.5-1** How do we acquire language, and what did Chomsky mean by *universal grammar*?

Linguist Noam Chomsky has argued that language is an unlearned human trait, separate from other parts of human cognition. He initially proposed that we are born with a *language acquisition device*, which allows us to learn any human language. Spoken languages require three building blocks. **Phonemes** are the smallest distinctive sound units in a language. (To say *that*, English speakers utter the phonemes *th, a,* and *t*.) **Morphemes** are the smallest language units that carry meaning. (The word *readers* contains three morphemes: *read; er*, signaling that we mean "one who reads"; and *s*, signaling that we mean not one, but multiple readers.) Every word in a language contains one or more morphemes. **Grammar** is a language's set of rules that enable people to communicate. Grammatical rules guide us in deriving meaning from sounds (*semantics*) and in ordering words into sentences (*syntax*).

Chomsky later expanded his thinking and suggested that we are born with a built-in predisposition to learn grammar. This ability, which he called **universal grammar (UG)**, helps explain why preschoolers pick up language so readily and use grammar so well. It happens so naturally—as naturally as birds learn to fly—that training hardly helps. Whether we're born in Indiana or Indonesia, we intuitively follow similar grammatical rules that transform arbitrary symbols to generate an infinity of ideas (Aryawibawa & Ambridge, 2019). Whatever language we experience as children, whether spoken or signed, we will readily learn its specific grammar and vocabulary (Bavelier et al., 2003). And we always start speaking mostly in nouns (*kitty, da-da*) rather than in verbs and adjectives (Bornstein et al., 2004). Biology and experience work together.

## Language Development: When Do We Learn Language?

> **3.5-2** What are the milestones in language development, and when is the critical period for acquiring language?

Make a quick guess: How many words of your native language will you have learned between your first birthday and your high school graduation? Although you use only 150 words for about half of what you say, you probably will have learned about 60,000 words (Bloom, 2000; McMurray, 2007). That averages (after age 2) to nearly 3500 words each year, or about 10 each day! How you do this—how those 3500 words could so far outnumber the roughly 200 words your schoolteachers consciously taught you each year—is one of the great human wonders.

Could you even now state the structural rules—for example, the correct way to string words together to form sentences—for the language(s) you speak fluently? Most of us cannot. Yet before you were able to add 2 + 2, you were creating your own original sentences and applying these rules. As a preschooler, you comprehended and spoke with a facility that far outpaced even the brightest adult's ability to learn a new language.

### Receptive Language

Children's language development moves from simplicity to complexity. Babies come prepared to learn any language, with a slight bent toward the language they heard in the womb. By 4 months of age, babies can recognize differences in speech sounds (Stager & Werker, 1997). They can also read lips: We know this because in studies by Patricia Kuhl and Andrew Meltzoff (1982), babies have preferred looking at a face that matches a sound—an "*ah*" coming from wide open lips and an "*ee*" from a mouth with corners pulled back. Recognizing such differences marks the beginning of the development of babies' *receptive language*, their ability to understand what is said to and about them. At 7 months and beyond, they grow in their power to do what adults find difficult when listening to an unfamiliar language: to segment spoken sounds into individual words.

## Productive Language

Long after the beginnings of receptive language, babies' *productive language*—their ability to produce words—matures. Before nurture molds babies' speech, nature enables a wide range of possible sounds, such as cooing and babbling. In the **babbling stage**, beginning around 4 months, babies seem to sample all the sounds they can make, such as *ah-goo*. Babbling does not imitate the adult speech babies hear—it includes sounds from various languages. From this early babbling, a listener could not identify an infant as being, say, French, Korean, or Ethiopian.

By about 10 months, infants' babbling has changed so that a trained ear can identify the household language (de Boysson-Bardies et al., 1989). Deaf infants who observe their deaf parents using sign language begin to babble more with their hands (Petitto & Marentette, 1991). Without exposure to other languages, babies lose their ability to do what adults cannot—to discriminate and produce sounds and tones outside their native language (Kuhl et al., 2014; Meltzoff et al., 2009). Thus, by adulthood, those who speak only English cannot discriminate certain sounds in Japanese speech. Nor can Japanese adults with no training in English hear the difference between the English *r* and *l*. For a Japanese-speaking adult, "*la-la-ra-ra*" may sound like the same syllable repeated.

Around their first birthday, most children enter the **one-word stage**. They know that sounds carry meanings, and they begin to use sounds—usually only one barely recognizable syllable, such as *ma* or *da*—to communicate meaning. But gradually the infant's language conforms more to the family's language. Across the world, baby's first words are often nouns that label objects or people (Tardif et al., 2008). At this one-word stage, "*Doggy!*" may mean "*Look at the dog out there!*"

At about 18 months, children's word learning explodes from about a word per week to a word per day. By their second birthday, most have entered the **two-word stage** (**Table 3.5-1**). They start uttering two-word sentences in **telegraphic speech**. Like yesterday's telegrams that charged by the word ("TERMS ACCEPTED. SEND MONEY"), a 2-year-old's speech contains mostly nouns and verbs (*"Want juice"*). They may also overgeneralize grammar rules, such as saying "tooths" rather than "teeth." Also like telegrams, their speech arranges words in a sensible order. English-speaking children typically place adjectives before nouns—*white house* rather than *house white*. Spanish reverses this order, as in *casa blanca*.

Moving out of the two-word stage, children quickly begin uttering longer phrases (Fromkin & Rodman, 1983). By early elementary school, they understand complex sentences and begin to enjoy the humor conveyed by double meanings: "You never starve in the desert because of all the *sand-which-is* there."

All the while, babies also communicate without words—with *gestures* (Zubler et al., 2022). They learn to lift arms to be picked up, to wave goodbye, to clap hands when excited, and to point when asking for something or answering a question. To help them communicate, many care providers now teach babies basic signs, such as for "more" and "all done."

**A natural talent** Human infants come with a remarkable capacity to soak up language. But the particular language they learn reflects their unique interactions with others.

Purestock/AGE Fotostock

**babbling stage** the stage in speech development, beginning around 4 months, during which an infant spontaneously utters various sounds that are not all related to the household language.

**one-word stage** the stage in speech development, from about age 1 to 2, during which a child speaks mostly in single words.

**two-word stage** the stage in speech development, beginning about age 2, during which a child speaks mostly in two-word sentences.

**telegraphic speech** the early speech stage in which a child speaks like a telegram—"go car"—using mostly nouns and verbs.

| TABLE 3.5-1 Summary of Language Development | |
|---|---|
| **Month (approximate)** | **Stage** |
| 4 | Babbles many speech sounds ("ah-goo") |
| 10 | Babbling resembles household language ("ma-ma") |
| 12 | One-word speech ("Kitty!") |
| 24 | Two-word speech ("Get ball.") |
| 24+ | Rapid development into complete sentences |

*"Got idea. Talk better. Combine words. Make sentences."*

Human language evolved from gestured communications (Corballis, 2002, 2003; Pollick & de Waal, 2007). Even today, our gestures naturally accompany our spontaneous speech, even for those persons who are blind (Özçaliskan et al., 2016). Both gesture and speech communicate, and when they convey the same information, we humans understand faster and more accurately (Dargue et al., 2019; Hostetter, 2011; Kelly et al., 2010).

## Critical Periods

Some children—such as those who receive a cochlear implant to enable hearing, or those who are adopted by a family who use another language—get a late start on learning a language. For these late bloomers, language development follows the same sequence, although usually at a faster pace (Ertmer et al., 2007; Snedeker et al., 2007). But there is a limit on how long language learning can be delayed. Childhood seems to represent a *critical* (or *sensitive*) *period* for mastering certain aspects of language before the language-learning window gradually closes (Hernandez & Li, 2007; Lenneberg, 1967). If not exposed to either a spoken or a signed language until age 7 or beyond, children lose their ability to master *any* language.

Cultural and other environmental variations affect children's language exposure. Children exposed to low-quality language—such as American 4-year-olds in classrooms with 3-year-olds, or some children from impoverished homes—often display less language skill (Ansari et al., 2015; Hirsh-Pasek et al., 2015). Reading to children increases language exposure. Jessica Logan and her colleagues (2019) found that frequent exposure to children's books boosts children's school readiness: "Kids who hear more vocabulary words are going to be better prepared to see those words in print when they enter school."

Language-learning ability is universal, but learning any language is easiest when we're children. If we learn a new language as adults, we will usually speak it with the accent of our native language, and with imperfect grammar (Hartshorne et al., 2018). In one study, U.S. immigrants from South Korea and China considered 276 English sentences ("*Yesterday the hunter shoots a deer*") and decided whether each was grammatically correct or incorrect (Johnson & Newport, 1991). All had been in the United States for approximately 10 years; some had arrived in early childhood, others as adults. As **Figure 3.5-1** reveals, those who learned their second language early learned it best.

The older we are when we move to a new country, the harder it is to learn its language and to absorb its culture (Cheung et al., 2011; Hakuta et al., 2003). When I [ND] first went to Japan, I was told not even to bother trying to bow, that there were something like a dozen different bows and I was always going to "bow with an accent."

### Figure 3.5-1

### Our ability to learn a new language diminishes with age

Ten years after coming to the United States, Asian immigrants took an English grammar test. Those who arrived before age 8 understood American English grammar as well as native speakers. Those who arrived later did not. (Data from Johnson & Newport, 1991.)

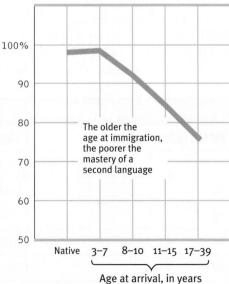

Percentage correct on grammar test

The older the age at immigration, the poorer the mastery of a second language

Age at arrival, in years

# Deafness and Language Development

The impact of early experiences is evident in language learning in deaf children of hearing-nonsigning parents. These children typically do not experience language during their early years. And natively deaf children who learn sign language after age 9 never learn it as well as those who learned it early in life. Those who learn to sign as teens or adults never become as fluent as native signers in producing and comprehending subtle grammatical differences (Newport, 1990). As a flower's growth requires nourishment, so, too, children's language acquisition requires early life language exposure.

Worldwide, 466 million people live with hearing loss (WHO, 2019). Some are profoundly deaf; most (more men than women) have hearing loss (Agrawal et al., 2008). Some were deaf from birth; others have known the hearing world. Some sign and identify with the language-based Deaf culture. Others, especially those who lost their hearing after speaking a language, are "oral" and converse with the hearing world by reading lips or written notes. Still others move between the two cultures.

The challenges of life without hearing may be greatest for children. Unable to communicate in customary ways, signing playmates may struggle to coordinate their play with speaking playmates. School achievement may also suffer; academic subjects are usually rooted in *spoken* languages. Adolescents may feel socially excluded, with a resulting low self-confidence. Deaf children who grow up around other deaf people more often identify with Deaf culture and feel positive self-esteem. If raised in a signing household, whether by deaf or hearing parents, they also express higher self-esteem and feel more accepted (Bat-Chava, 1993, 1994).

Adults who lose hearing ability also face challenges. Expending effort to hear words drains their capacity to perceive, comprehend, and remember them (Wingfield et al., 2005). In several studies, people with hearing loss, especially those not wearing hearing aids, have reported more sadness, less social engagement, and worrying that they irritate others (Kashubeck-West & Meyer, 2008; National Council on Aging, 1999).

I [DM] understand. My mother, with whom we communicated by writing notes on an erasable "magic pad," spent her last dozen years in an utterly silent world, largely withdrawn from the stress and strain of trying to interact with people outside a small circle of family and old friends. My own hearing is declining on a trajectory toward hers (with my hearing aids out at night, I cannot understand my wife speaking from her adjacent pillow). I do benefit from cool technology (see HearingLoop.org) that, at the press of a button, can transform my hearing aids into in-the-ear loudspeakers for the broadcast of phone, TV, and public address system sound. Yet I still experience frustration when I can't hear the joke everyone else is guffawing over; when, after repeated tries, I just can't catch that exasperated person's question and can't fake my way around it; when family members give up and say, "Oh, never mind," after trying three times to tell me something unimportant. Yet for me, communication is worth the effort. To reach out, to connect, to communicate with others is to affirm our humanity as social creatures.

## CULTURAL AWARENESS

Notice the use of the word *culture* here. Culture goes beyond simply one's country of origin. It encompasses the shared ideas and values of any group, including deaf people. Even your school has its own unique culture. Critical thinkers are aware that our culture can create biases, but with conscious effort, we can transcend those biases.

### AP® Science Practice

#### Research

The studies mentioned here were correlational. The researchers measured sadness, social engagement, and worry to see if they were associated with hearing loss. Therefore, they can't conclude that being a person with hearing loss *causes* the reported relationships. That would require an experiment with random assignment.

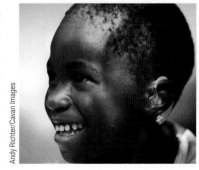

**Hearing improved** A boy in Malawi experiences new hearing aids.

---

### AP® Science Practice

## Check Your Understanding

### Examine the Concept

▶ Explain Noam Chomsky's view of language development.

▶ Explain the difference between *receptive* language and *productive* language. Give an example to illustrate each.

▶ Identify three pieces of evidence to support the claim that it is difficult to learn a new language in adulthood.

*Answers to the Examine the Concept questions can be found in Appendix C at the end of the book.*

### Apply the Concept

▶ Have you tried to start learning a new language *after* learning your first language? If so, how did learning this other language differ from learning your first language? Does speaking it feel different?

# The Brain and Language

**3.5-3** Which brain areas are involved in language processing and speech?

We think of speaking and reading, or writing and reading, or singing and speaking as merely different examples of the same general ability—language. But consider this curious finding: Damage to any of several cortical areas can produce **aphasia**, impairment of language. Even more curious, some people with aphasia can speak fluently but cannot read (despite good vision). Others can comprehend what they read but cannot speak. Still others can write but not read, read but not write, read numbers but not letters, or sing but not speak. These cases suggest that language is complex, and that different brain areas must serve different language functions.

Indeed, in 1865, French physician Paul Broca confirmed a fellow physician's observation that after damage to an area of the left frontal lobe (later called **Broca's area**) a person would struggle to *speak* words, yet could still sing familiar songs and comprehend speech. A decade later, German investigator Carl Wernicke discovered that after damage to a specific area of the left temporal lobe (**Wernicke's area**), people could not *understand* others' sentences and could speak only meaningless sentences.

Brain scans have confirmed brain activity in Broca's and Wernicke's areas during language processing (**Figure 3.5-2**). For people with aphasia, electrical stimulation of Broca's area can help restore speaking abilities (Marangolo et al., 2016). But we also now know that the brain's processing of language is complex. Broca's area coordinates the brain's processing of language in other areas as well (Flinker et al., 2015; Tremblay & Dick, 2016). Although you experience language as a single, unified stream, functional magnetic resonance imaging (fMRI) scans would show that your brain is busily multitasking and networking. Different neural networks are activated by nouns and verbs (or objects and actions); by different vowels; by stories of visual versus motor experiences; by who spoke and what was said; and by many other stimuli (Perrachione et al., 2011; Shapiro et al., 2006; Speer et al., 2009).

If you're lucky enough to be natively fluent in two languages, your brain processes them in similar areas (Kim et al., 2017). But your brain doesn't use the same areas if you learned a second language *after* the first or if you sign rather than speak your second language (Berken et al., 2015; Kovelman et al., 2014).

*The point to remember*: In processing language, as in other forms of information processing, the brain operates by dividing its mental functions—speaking, perceiving, thinking, remembering—into subfunctions. Your conscious experience of learning about the brain and language *seems* indivisible, but thanks to your parallel processing, many different neural networks are pooling their work to give meaning to the words, sentences, and paragraphs (Fedorenko et al., 2016; Snell & Grainger, 2019). *E pluribus unum*: Out of many, one.

**aphasia** impairment of language, usually caused by left hemisphere damage either to Broca's area (impairing speaking) or to Wernicke's area (impairing understanding).

**Broca's area** a frontal lobe brain area, usually in the left hemisphere, that helps control language expression by directing the muscle movements involved in speech.

**Wernicke's area** a brain area, usually in the left temporal lobe, involved in language comprehension and expression.

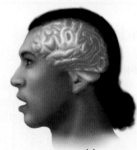
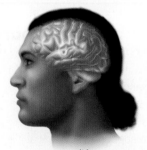

**(a)**
**Speaking words**
**(Broca's area and the motor cortex)**

**(b)**
**Hearing words**
**(Wernicke's area and the auditory cortex)**

**Figure 3.5-2**
**Brain activity when speaking and hearing words**

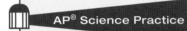

## Check Your Understanding

**Examine the Concept**

▶ _____ is one part of the brain that, if damaged, might impair your ability to speak words. Damage to _____ might impair your ability to understand language.

**Apply the Concept**

▶ There has been controversy at some universities about allowing fluency in sign language to fulfill a second-language requirement for an undergraduate degree. Given what you've learned about sign language, what position would you take on the issue, and what evidence would you use to argue your point?

*Answers to the Examine the Concept questions can be found in Appendix C at the end of the book.*

## Thinking and Language

**3.5-4** What is the relationship between thinking and language, and what is the value of thinking in images?

Thinking and language—which comes first? This is one of psychology's great chicken-and-egg questions. Do our ideas come first and then the words to name them? Or are our thoughts conceived in words and therefore unthinkable without them?

The theory of **linguistic determinism** was developed by linguist Benjamin Lee Whorf (1956), who believed that those peoples who use languages with no past tense, such as the Hopi, could not readily *think* about the past. But Whorf's theory was too extreme. We all think about things for which we have no words. (Can you think of a shade of blue you cannot name?) And we routinely have wordless, imageless thoughts, as when someone, watching two men carry a load of bricks, wondered whether the men would drop them (Heavey & Hurlburt, 2008; Hurlburt et al., 2013).

A less extreme idea, **linguistic relativism**, recognizes that our words *influence* our thinking (Gentner, 2016). To those who speak two dissimilar languages, such as English and Japanese, this point seems obvious (Brown, 1986). Unlike English, which has a rich vocabulary for self-focused emotions such as anger, Japanese has more words for interpersonal emotions such as sympathy (Markus & Kitayama, 1991). Many bilingual individuals report having different senses of self—that they feel like different people—depending on which language they are using (Matsumoto, 1994; Pavlenko, 2014).

Depending on which emotion they want to express, bilingual people often switch languages. "When my mom gets angry at me, she'll speak in Mandarin," explained one Chinese American student. "If she's really mad, she'll switch to Cantonese" (Chen et al., 2012). Bilingual individuals may even reveal different personality profiles when taking the same test in two languages, with their differing cultural associations (Chen & Bond, 2010; Dinges & Hull, 1992). When China-born, bilingual University of Waterloo students described themselves in English, their responses fit typical Canadian profiles, expressing mostly positive self-statements and moods. When responding in Chinese, the same students gave typically Chinese self-descriptions, reporting more agreement with Chinese values and roughly equal positive and negative self-statements and moods (Ross et al., 2002). Similar attitude and personality changes have been shown when switching between Spanish and English or between Arabic and English (Ogunnaike et al., 2010; Ramírez-Esparza et al., 2006). "Learn a new language and get a new soul," says a Czech proverb.

**TRY THIS**

Before reading on, use a pen or pencil to sketch this idea: "The girl pushes the boy." Now see the footnoted comment.[3]

**linguistic determinism** Whorf's hypothesis that language determines the way we think.

**linguistic relativism** the idea that language influences the way we think.

[3]How did you illustrate "the girl pushes the boy"? Anne Maass and Aurore Russo (2003) report that people whose language reads from left to right mostly position the pushing girl on the left. Those who read and write Arabic, a right-to-left language, mostly place her on the right. This spatial bias appears only in those old enough to have learned their culture's writing system (Dobel et al., 2007).

**Culture and color** In Papua New Guinea, Berinmo children have words for different shades of yellow, which might enable them to spot and recall yellow variations more quickly. Here and everywhere, "the languages we speak profoundly shape the way we think, the way we see the world, the way we live our lives," noted psychologist Lera Boroditsky (2009).

### AP® Science Practice

## Research

Recall from Module 0.4 that a control group in an experiment is the group *not* exposed to the treatment (for example, the French-immersion schooling mentioned below). It serves as a source of comparison for the experimental group when evaluating the effect of the treatment.

**Figure 3.5-3**

**Language and perception**

When people view blocks of equally different colors, they perceive those with different names as more different. Thus, the "green" and "blue" in contrast A may appear to differ more than the two equally different blues in contrast B (Özgen, 2004).

So, our words do *influence* our thinking (Boroditsky, 2011). Words define our mental categories, influencing even our thinking about colors. Whether we live in New Mexico, New South Wales, or New Guinea, we *see* the same colors, but we use our native language to *classify* and *remember* them (Davidoff, 2004; Roberson et al., 2004, 2005). Imagine viewing three colors and calling two of them "yellow" and one of them "blue." Later you would likely see and recall the yellows as being more similar. But if you speak the language of Papua New Guinea's Berinmo people, which has words for two different shades of yellow, you would more readily perceive and better recall the variations between the two yellows. And if your native language is Russian or Greek, which have distinct names for various shades of blue, you would perceive and recall the yellows as more similar and remember the shades of blue better (Maier & Abdel Rahman, 2018). Words matter.

On the color spectrum, blue blends into green—until we draw a dividing line between the portions we call "blue" and "green." Although equally different on the color spectrum, two different items that share the same color name (as the two "blues" do in **Figure 3.5-3**, contrast B) are harder to distinguish than two items with different names ("blue" and "green," as in Figure 3.5-3, contrast A) (Özgen, 2004). Likewise, $4.99 perceptually differs more from $5.01 than from $4.97. And to doctors, a patient who is 80 seems, relative to a 79-year-old, older than does a 79-year-old compared to one who is 78 (Olenski et al., 2020).

Given their subtle influence on thinking, we do well to choose our words carefully. When hearing the generic *he* (as in "the artist and his work"), people are more likely to picture a male (Henley, 1989; Ng, 1990). If *he* and *his* were truly gender free, we shouldn't skip a beat when hearing that "man, like other mammals, nurses his young." Transgender and gender-nonconforming youth, too, report feeling respected and included when their preferred pronouns are used—*he/she, him/her, they/their* (Olson & Gülgöz, 2018; Rae et al., 2019). And consider this: Gender prejudice also occurs more in gendered languages, such as French, in which, for example, *la table* is feminine and *le téléphone* is masculine (DeFranza et al., 2020; Lewis & Lupyan, 2020).

To expand language is to expand the ability to think. Young children's thinking develops hand in hand with their language (Gopnik & Meltzoff, 1986). Indeed, it is very difficult to think about or conceptualize certain abstract ideas (*commitment, freedom,* or *rhyming*) without language. And what is true for preschoolers is true for everyone: *It pays to increase your word power.* That's why most textbooks, including this one, introduce new words—to teach new ideas and new ways of thinking.

Increased word power helps explain some benefits of bilingualism. McGill University researcher Wallace Lambert (1992; Lambert et al., 1993) reports that bilingual people are skilled at inhibiting their use of one language while speaking another—for example, blocking out the thought of "crayón amarillo" while saying "yellow crayon" to English speakers, then doing the reverse for Spanish speakers (Tsui et al., 2019). Bilingual children also exhibit enhanced social skills, as they are better able to understand another's perspective (Fan et al., 2015; Gampe et al., 2019). Bilingual preschool children have also displayed less racial bias (Singh et al., 2020).

Working with bilingual education advocates Olga Melikoff, Valerie Neale, and Murielle Parkes, Lambert helped implement a Canadian program that has given millions of English-speaking children a natural French fluency via French-immersion schooling (Statistics Canada, 2019a). Compared with similarly capable children in control groups, these children exhibit no loss of English fluency. They also display increased creativity and appreciation for French-Canadian culture (Genesee & Gándara, 1999; Lazaruk, 2007).

One lingering dispute concerns whether there exists, as some have claimed, a "bilingual advantage" in cognitive tasks such as planning, focusing attention, and then, when needed, switching attention (Antoniou, 2019; Bialystok, 2017). After reviewing all the available research, critics argue that any bilingual advantage on overall cognitive

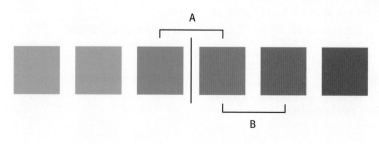

performance is unreliable and small (Gunnerud et al., 2020; Lowe et al., 2021; Nichols et al., 2020). Stay tuned: This research story is still being written.

Whether we are in the linguistic minority or majority, language links us to one another. Language also connects us to the past and the future. "To destroy a people," goes a saying, "destroy their language."

## Thinking in Images

To turn on the cold water in your bathroom, in which direction do you turn the handle? To answer, you probably thought not in words but with *implicit* (nondeclarative, procedural) memory—a mental picture of how you do it.

Indeed, we often think in images; mental practice relies on it. Pianist Liu Chi Kung harnessed this power. One year after placing second in the 1958 Tchaikovsky piano competition, Liu was imprisoned during China's cultural revolution. Soon after his release, after 7 years without touching a piano, he was back on tour. Critics judged Liu's musicianship as better than ever. How did he continue to develop without practice? "I did practice," said Liu, "every day. I rehearsed every piece I had ever played, note by note, in my mind" (Garfield, 1986).

For someone who has learned a skill, such as ballet dancing, even *watching* the activity will activate the brain's internal simulation of it (Calvo-Merino et al., 2004). So, too, will *imagining* a physical experience, which activates some of the same neural networks that are active during the actual experience (Grèzes & Decety, 2001). Small wonder, then, that mental practice has become a standard part of training for Olympic athletes (Blumenstein & Orbach, 2012; Ungerleider, 2005).

One study of mental practice and basketball free-throw shooting tracked the University of Tennessee women's team over 35 games (Savoy & Beitel, 1996). During that time, the team's free-throw accuracy increased from approximately 52 percent in games following standard physical practice, to some 65 percent after mental practice. Players had repeatedly imagined making free throws under various conditions, including being "trash-talked" by their opposition. In a dramatic conclusion to this study, Tennessee won the national championship game in overtime, thanks in part to their free-throw shooting.

Researchers also demonstrated the academic benefits of mental rehearsal with two groups of introductory psychology students facing a midterm exam 1 week later (Taylor et al., 1998). (Students not engaged in any mental rehearsal formed a third control group.) The first group spent 5 minutes each day visualizing themselves scanning the posted grade list, seeing their A, beaming with joy, and feeling proud. This daily *outcome simulation* added only 2 points to their average exam score. The second group spent 5 minutes each day visualizing themselves reading their text, going over notes, eliminating distractions, and declining an invitation out. This daily *process simulation* paid off: The second group began studying sooner, spent more time at it, and beat the others' average score by 8 points. *The point to remember*: It's better to imagine *how* to reach your goal than merely to fantasize your desired destination.

**AP® Science Practice**

### Research

Review independent and dependent variables in Module 0.4. Can you identify the independent and dependent variables in the study of the academic benefits of mental rehearsal described below?

Blend Images/Getty Images

---

**AP® Science Practice**

## Check Your Understanding

### Examine the Concept

▶ Explain the theory of linguistic determinism.

▶ Explain what is meant by *linguistic relativism*.

### Apply the Concept

▶ How could you use mental practice to improve your performance in some area of your life — for example, in your schoolwork, personal relationships, or hobbies?

*Answers to the Examine the Concept questions can be found in Appendix C at the end of the book.*

# Module 3.5 REVIEW

### 3.5-1 How do we acquire language, and what did Chomsky mean by *universal grammar?*

- Spoken languages require three building blocks: *phonemes* (the smallest distinctive sound units in a language), *morphemes* (the smallest language units that carry meaning), and *grammar* (a language's set of rules that enable communication). Grammatical rules guide us in deriving meaning from sounds (semantics) and in ordering words into sentences (syntax).

- As our biology and experience interact, we readily learn the specific grammar and vocabulary of the language we experience as children. Linguist Noam Chomsky has proposed that humans are born with a built-in predisposition to learn grammar rules, which he called *universal grammar.*

- Human languages do share some commonalities, but other researchers note that children learn grammar as they discern language patterns.

### 3.5-2 What are the milestones in language development, and when is the critical period for acquiring language?

- The timing of language development varies, but all children follow the same sequence. Receptive language (the ability to understand what is said to or about you) develops before productive language (the ability to produce words).

- At about 4 months of age, infants coo and *babble*, making sounds found in languages from all over the world; by about 10 months, their babbling has narrowed to include only the sounds found in their household language. Around 12 months of age, children begin to speak in single words. This *one-word* stage evolves into *two-word* (*telegraphic*) utterances before their second birthday, after which they begin speaking in full sentences.

- Childhood is a critical period for learning language. Children who get a late start on language learning follow the usual developmental sequence, though at a faster pace. But children not exposed to either a spoken or a signed language before age 7 will never master any language. The importance of early language experiences is often evident in deaf children born to hearing-nonsigning parents.

### 3.5-3 Which brain areas are involved in language processing and speech?

- *Aphasia* is an impairment of language, usually caused by left-hemisphere damage. Two important language- and speech-processing areas are *Broca's area*, a region of the left frontal lobe that controls language expression, and *Wernicke's area*, a region in the left temporal lobe that controls language reception.

- Language processing is spread across other brain areas as well, with different neural networks handling specific linguistic subtasks.

### 3.5-4 What is the relationship between thinking and language, and what is the value of thinking in images?

- Although Benjamin Lee Whorf's *linguistic determinism* hypothesis suggested that language determines thought, it is more accurate to say that language influences thought (*linguistic relativism*).

- Different languages embody different ways of thinking, and bilingualism can enhance thinking.

- We often think in images when we use implicit (nondeclarative, procedural) memory.

- Thinking in images can increase our skills when we mentally practice an activity. Process simulation (focusing on the steps needed to reach a goal) is effective, but outcome simulation (fantasizing about having achieved the goal) does little.

# AP® Practice Multiple Choice Questions

1. Eighteen-month-old Becca is in the telegraphic speech phase. Which of the following best represents something she might say?
   a. "Mama"
   b. "Katie fall"
   c. "The dog is fuzzy."
   d. "I love you, Mommy."

2. The word *cat* has how many phonemes?
   a. None
   b. One
   c. Two
   d. Three

3. Marta believes that language develops because of an inborn tendency to learn grammar rules. Which theory best aligns with Marta's views?
   a. Critical period
   b. Broca's aphasia
   c. Universal grammar
   d. Productive language

**Use the following graph to answer questions 4–5:**

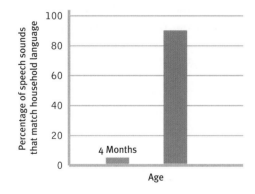

4. Which of the following is the label for the red bar in the graph?
   a. 10 months
   b. 2 months
   c. 6 months
   d. 3 months

5. In which stage of language development are the babies represented by the red bar?
   a. One-word stage
   b. Two-word stage
   c. Telegraphic speech stage
   d. Babbling stage

6. Yolay wrote a story about a young girl named Neko who was raised by cats, not having any contact with humans until she was 12 years old. In the story, Neko became a great orator who detailed her life experiences living with cats to large audiences. Which of the following explains why Yolay's story is implausible based on past psychological research?
   a. Because Neko was not exposed to human language during the critical period for language, she would likely not become a great speaker and would likely not master human language.
   b. Because Neko experienced early-life aphasia, she would likely not become a great speaker and would likely not master human language.
   c. Because Neko was not exposed to universal grammar during her early life, she would likely not become a great speaker and would likely not master human language.
   d. Because Neko was only exposed to productive language and not to receptive language, she would likely not become a great speaker and would likely not master human language.

# Module 3.6a Social-Emotional Development Across the Lifespan: Infancy & Childhood

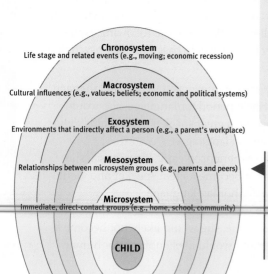

## LEARNING TARGETS

**3.6-1** Explain how caregiver-infant attachment bonds form.

**3.6-2** Explain how psychologists have studied attachment differences, and synthesize what they have learned.

**3.6-3** Explain how experiencing adversity affects children's social development.

**3.6-4** Explain the onset and development of children's self-concepts.

**3.6-5** Explain the differences among the four main parenting styles.

**Figure 3.6-1**

**The ecological systems theory**

Directly and indirectly, our social environments influence our development.

A s Aristotle recognized long ago, we are, from infancy onward, social animals. Thanks to our ancient ancestors surviving in groups that together hunted, gathered, and shared, nature has given us a need to belong. Whether babies, teens, or retirees, we flourish when supported by close relationships. Psychologist Urie Bronfenbrenner's (1977) **ecological systems theory** argued that different environments we encounter affect our cognitive, social, and biological development (see **Figure 3.6-1**). As Pope Francis has said, "Everyone's existence is deeply tied to that of others."

## Social-Emotional Development in Infancy and Childhood

**3.6-1** How do caregiver-infant attachment bonds form?

**ecological systems theory**
a theory of the social environment's influence on human development, using five nested systems (microsystem; mesosystem; exosystem; macrosystem; chronosystem) ranging from direct to indirect influences.

**stranger anxiety** the fear of strangers that infants commonly display, beginning by about 8 months of age.

From birth, most babies are social creatures, developing an intense attachment to their caregivers. Infants come to prefer familiar faces and voices, then to coo and gurgle when given a caregiver's attention. By 4.5 months, infants can distinguish between familiar and unfamiliar languages (Fecher & Johnson, 2019). After about 8 months, soon after object permanence emerges and children become mobile, a curious thing happens: They develop *separation anxiety* when away from caregivers, and **stranger anxiety** in the presence of strangers. They may greet strangers by crying and reaching for familiar caregivers, as if to say "No! Don't leave me!" Children this age have schemas for familiar faces—and may resist being handed to someone unfamiliar (Quinn et al., 2019). Once again, we see an important principle: *The brain, mind, and social-emotional behavior develop together.*

## Origins of Attachment

One-year-olds typically cling tightly to a caregiver when they are frightened or expect separation. Reunited after being apart, they often shower the caregiver with smiles and hugs. This striking caregiver-infant **attachment** bond is a powerful survival impulse that keeps infants close to their caregivers. Infants usually become attached to those—typically their parents—who are comfortable and familiar. For many years, psychologists reasoned that infants became attached to those who satisfied their need for nourishment. But an accidental finding overturned this explanation.

### Body Contact

During the 1950s, psychologists Harry Harlow and Margaret Harlow bred monkeys for their learning studies. To equalize experiences and to isolate any disease, they separated the infant monkeys from their mothers shortly after birth and raised them in individual cages, each of which included a cheesecloth baby blanket (Harlow et al., 1971). Then came a surprise: When their soft blankets were taken to be washed, the monkeys became distressed.

The Harlows recognized that this intense attachment to the blanket contradicted the idea that attachment derives from an association with nourishment. But how could they show this more convincingly? To pit the drawing power of a food source against the contact comfort of the blanket, they created two artificial mothers. One was a bare wire cylinder with a wooden head and an attached feeding bottle; the other was a cylinder with no bottle, but covered with foam rubber and wrapped with terry cloth.

When raised with both artificial mothers, the monkeys overwhelmingly preferred the comfy cloth mother (**Figure 3.6-2**). Like other infants clinging to their live mothers, anxious monkey babies would cling to their cloth mothers, soothed by this *contact comfort*. When exploring their environment, they used her as a *secure base*, as if attached to her by an invisible elastic band that stretched only so far before pulling them back. Researchers soon learned that other qualities—rocking, warmth, and feeding—made the cloth mother even more appealing.

Human infants, too, become attached to parents who are soft and warm and who rock, feed, and pat. Much parent-infant emotional communication occurs via touch, which can be either soothing (snuggles) or arousing (tickles) (Hertenstein et al., 2006). People across the globe agree that the ideal mother "shows affection by touching" (Mesman et al., 2015). Such parental affection not only feels good, but also boosts brain development and later cognitive ability (Davis et al., 2017).

Another aspect of human attachment is one person providing another with a secure base from which to explore and a safe haven when distressed. As we mature, our secure base shifts—from parents to peers and partners (Cassidy & Shaver, 1999; Schmidt et al., 2019). But at all ages we are social creatures. We gain strength when someone offers, by words and actions, a safe haven: "I will be here. I am interested in you. Come what may, I will support you" (Crowell & Waters, 1994).

### Familiarity

Contact is one key to attachment. Another is familiarity. In many animals, attachments based on familiarity form during a *critical period*—an optimal period when certain events must take place to facilitate proper development (Bornstein, 1989). As we saw in Module 3.5, humans seem to have a critical period for language. Goslings, ducklings, and chicks have a critical period for attachment, called **imprinting**, which falls in the hours shortly after hatching, when the first moving object they see is normally their mother. From then on, the young fowl follow her, and her alone.

Children—unlike ducklings—do not imprint. However, they do become attached, during a less precisely defined *sensitive period*, to

PR INC/Science Source

**Figure 3.6-2**

**The Harlows' monkey mothers**

The Harlows' discovery surprised many psychologists: The infants much preferred contact with the comfortable cloth mother, even while feeding from the nourishing wire mother.

**SPOTLIGHT ON:**

Harry Harlow and Margaret Harlow

**attachment** an emotional tie with others; shown in young children by their seeking closeness to caregivers and showing distress on separation.

**imprinting** the process by which certain animals form strong attachments during early life.

Nina Leen/Getty Images

**Daddy duck?** While researching imprinting, Konrad Lorenz (1937) wondered: What would ducklings do if he was the first moving creature they observed? What they did was follow him around: Everywhere that Konrad went, the ducks were sure to go.

**strange situation** a procedure for studying child-caregiver attachment; a child is placed in an unfamiliar environment while their caregiver leaves and then returns, and the child's reactions are observed.

**secure attachment** demonstrated by infants who comfortably explore environments in the presence of their caregiver, show only temporary distress when the caregiver leaves, and find comfort in the caregiver's return.

**insecure attachment** demonstrated by infants who display a clinging, *anxious attachment*; an *avoidant attachment* that resists closeness; or a *disorganized attachment* with no consistent behavior when separated from or reunited with caregivers.

**temperament** a person's characteristic emotional reactivity and intensity.

**SPOTLIGHT ON:**
Mary Ainsworth

**Figure 3.6-3**
**Social deprivation and fear**

In the Harlows' experiments, monkeys raised with artificial mothers were overwhelmed when placed in strange situations without those mothers.

Science Source

**AP® Science Practice**

**Research**

The Harlows' monkey studies would likely not be permitted today because the American Psychological Association now has guidelines that protect animal welfare. You can revisit Module 0.5 to review these guidelines.

what they've known. *Mere exposure* to people and things fosters fondness. Children like to reread the same books, rewatch the same movies, and reenact family traditions. They prefer to eat familiar foods, live in the same familiar neighborhood, and attend school with the same old friends. Familiarity is a safety signal. Familiarity breeds content.

## Attachment Differences: Temperament and Parenting

> **3.6-2** How have psychologists studied attachment differences, and what have they learned?

What accounts for children's attachment differences? To answer this question, Mary Ainsworth (1979) designed the **strange situation**. She observed mother-infant pairs at home during their first 6 months. Later she observed the 1-year-old infants in a strange situation (usually a laboratory playroom) with and without their mothers. Such research has shown that about 60 percent of infants and young children display **secure attachment** (Moulin et al., 2014). In their mother's presence they play comfortably, happily exploring their new environment. When she leaves, they become distressed; when she returns, they seek contact with her.

Other infants show **insecure attachment**, marked by *anxiety* or by *avoidance* of trusting relationships. These infants are less likely to explore their surroundings; they may even cling to their mother. When she leaves, they either cry loudly and remain upset or seem indifferent to her departure and return (Ainsworth, 1973, 1989; Kagan, 1995; van IJzendoorn & Kroonenberg, 1988). Infants who display *disorganized attachment* show no consistent behavior during these separations and reunions.

Ainsworth and others found that sensitive, responsive mothers—those who noticed what their babies were doing and responded appropriately—had infants who exhibited secure attachment (De Wolff & van IJzendoorn, 1997). Insensitive, unresponsive mothers—mothers who attended to their babies when they felt like doing so but ignored them at other times—often had infants who were insecurely attached. The Harlows' monkey studies, with unresponsive artificial mothers, produced even more striking effects. When put in strange situations without their artificial mothers, the deprived infants were terrified (**Figure 3.6-3**).

Many remember Harry Harlow as the researcher who tortured helpless monkeys, and today's climate of greater respect for animal welfare would likely prevent such primate studies. But Harlow defended his methods: "Remember, for every mistreated monkey there exist a million mistreated children," he said, expressing the hope that his research would sensitize people to child abuse and neglect. "No one who knows Harry's work could ever argue that babies do fine without companionship, that a caring mother doesn't matter," noted Harlow biographer Deborah Blum (2011, pp. 292, 307). "And since we . . . didn't fully believe that before Harry Harlow came along, then perhaps we needed—just once—to be smacked really hard with that truth so that we could never again doubt."

So, caring parents (and other caregivers) matter. But is attachment style the *result* of parenting? Or are other factors also at work?

## Temperament and Attachment

How does **temperament**—a person's characteristic emotional reactivity and intensity—affect attachment style? Studies reveal that heredity affects temperament, and that temperament affects attachment style (Picardi et al., 2011; Raby et al., 2012).

As most parents with multiple children will report, babies differ right out of the womb (Willoughby et al., 2019). Some babies are noticeably *difficult*—irritable, intense, and unpredictable. Others are *easy*—cheerful, relaxed, and on predictable feeding and sleeping schedules (Chess & Thomas, 1987). Identical twins, more than fraternal twins, often have similar temperaments (Fraley & Tancredy, 2012; Kandler et al., 2013). And differences in temperament appear in physiological differences. Anxious, inhibited infants have high and variable heart rates and a reactive nervous system. When facing new or strange situations, they become more physiologically aroused (Kagan & Snidman, 2004; Roque et al., 2012).

Temperament differences typically persist. The most emotionally reactive newborns tend also to be the most reactive 9-month-olds (Wilson & Matheny, 1986; Worobey & Blajda, 1989). Emotionally intense preschoolers tend to become relatively intense young adults (Larsen & Diener, 1987). One study of 1037 New Zealanders found that a 45-minute assessment of 3-year-olds' frustration tolerance, impulsivity, and intelligence could predict "with considerable accuracy" which of them would, by age 38, consume the most welfare benefits, parent and then abandon the most children, and commit the most crimes (Caspi et al., 2016).

Parenting studies that neglect such inborn differences, noted Judith Harris (1998), do the equivalent of "comparing foxhounds reared in kennels with poodles reared in apartments." To separate the effects of nature and nurture on attachment, we would need to vary parenting while controlling temperament. (Pause and think: If you were the researcher, how might you do this?)

Dutch researcher Dymphna van den Boom's (1994) solution was to randomly assign 100 temperamentally difficult 6- to 9-month-olds to either an experimental group, in which mothers received personal training in sensitive responding, or a control group, in which they did not. At 12 months of age, 68 percent of the infants in the experimental group were securely attached, compared to only 28 percent of the control group infants. Other studies confirm that intervention programs can increase parental sensitivity and, to a lesser extent, infant attachment security (Bakermans-Kranenburg et al., 2003; Van Zeijl et al., 2006). Such "positive parenting" interventions seem to be especially beneficial for children with difficult temperaments (Slagt et al., 2016).

As many of these examples indicate, researchers have more often studied mother care than father care, but fathers are more than just mobile sperm banks. Despite the widespread attitude that "fathering a child" means impregnating, and "mothering" means nurturing, nearly 100 studies worldwide have shown that a father's love and acceptance are comparable with a mother's love in predicting an offspring's health and well-being (Rohner & Veneziano, 2001; see also **Table 3.6-1**). Fathers matter.

**TABLE 3.6-1  Dual Parenting Positives**

- *Active dads are caregiving more.* Today's co-parenting fathers are more engaged, with a doubling in the weekly hours spent with their children, compared with fathers in 1965 (Livingston & Parker, 2011).

- *Couples who share housework and child care are happier in their relationships and less divorce-prone* (Wilcox & Marquardt, 2011).

- *Dual parenting supports children.* After controlling for other factors, children average better life outcomes "if raised by both parents" (Taylor, 2014).

- *Parents' gender and sexual orientation do not affect children's well-being.* The American Academy of Pediatrics (2013) reports that what matters is competent, secure, nurturing parents. The American Sociological Association (2013) concurs: Parental stability and resources matter, but "whether a child is raised by same-sex or opposite-sex parents has no bearing on a child's well-being." One analysis of 21,000 American children aged 4 to 17 found that, compared to those with straight parents, children with gay or lesbian parents experienced similar levels of well-being (Calzo et al., 2019).

Lorie Hailey

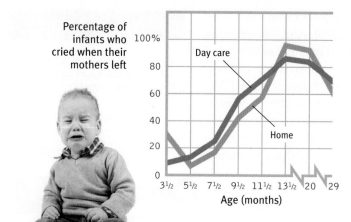

Percentage of infants who cried when their mothers left

Jouke van Keulen/Shutterstock

**Figure 3.6-4**

**Infants' distress over separation**

In this study, infants were left by their mothers in an unfamiliar room. Regardless of whether the infant had experienced day care, the percentage who cried when the mother left peaked at about 13 months of age (Kagan, 1976).

A large British study following 7259 children from birth to adulthood showed that those whose fathers were most involved in parenting (through outings, reading to them, and taking an interest in their education) tended to achieve more in school, even after controlling for other factors such as parental education and family wealth (Flouri & Buchanan, 2004). Fathers can also help children cope with stress. Among children exposed to Northern Ireland's "the Troubles" conflict (from the late 1960s to 1998), those with engaged fathers experienced fewer mental health problems (Luningham et al., 2020). Girls with supportive fathers expect that other men will treat them with care and respect, and they are less prone to engage in risky sexual behaviors (DelPriore et al., 2017, 2019).

Increasing nonmarital births and the greater instability of cohabiting versus married partnerships has, however, meant more father-absent families (Hymowitz et al., 2013). In Europe and the United States, for example, children born to married parents are (compared to cohabiting parents) about half as likely to experience their parents' separation, which often entails diminished father care (Brown et al., 2016; Wilcox & DeRose, 2017). Even after controlling for parents' income, education, and race, children whose parents are married experience a lower rate of school problems (Zill, 2020).

Children's anxiety over separation from parents peaks at around 13 months, then gradually declines (**Figure 3.6-4**). This happens whether they live with one parent or two, are cared for at home or in day care, and live in North America, Guatemala, or the Kalahari Desert. Does this mean our need for and love of others also fades away? Hardly. Our capacity for love grows, and our pleasure in touching and holding those we love never ceases.

## Attachment Styles and Later Relationships

Developmental psychologist Erik Erikson (1902–1994), working with his wife, Joan Erikson (1902–1997), believed that securely attached children approach life with a sense of **basic trust**—a sense that the world is predictable and reliable. He attributed basic trust not to environment or inborn temperament, but to early parenting. He theorized that infants blessed with sensitive, loving caregivers form a lifelong attitude of trust rather than fear.

Many researchers now believe that our early attachments form the foundation for our adult relationships (Birnbaum et al., 2006; Fraley et al., 2020). People who report secure relationships with their parents tend to enjoy secure friendships (Gorrese & Ruggieri, 2012). Students leaving home to attend college or university—another kind of "strange situation"— tend to adjust well if they're securely attached to parents (Mattanah et al., 2011). Children with sensitive, responsive mothers tend to flourish socially and academically (Raby et al., 2014).

Feeling insecurely attached to others may take either of two main forms (Fraley, 2019). One is *anxious attachment*, in which people constantly crave acceptance but remain alert to signs of possible rejection. The other is *avoidant attachment*, in which people experience discomfort when getting close to others and use avoidant strategies to maintain distance from others. In romantic relationships, an anxious attachment style creates constant concern over rejection, leading people to cling to their partners. An avoidant style decreases commitment and increases conflict (DeWall et al., 2011; Overall et al., 2015).

Adult attachment styles can also affect relationships with one's own children. But say this for those (nearly half of all people) who exhibit wary, insecure attachments: Across the ages, anxious or avoidant tendencies have helped humans detect or escape dangers (Ein-Dor et al., 2010).

**basic trust** according to Erik Erikson, a sense that the world is predictable and trustworthy; said to be formed during infancy by appropriate experiences with responsive caregivers.

## AP® Science Practice

# Check Your Understanding

**Examine the Concept**

▶ Explain the difference between imprinting and attachment.

**Apply the Concept**

▶ How has your upbringing affected your attachment style?

*Answers to the Examine the Concept questions can be found in Appendix C at the end of the book.*

## Facing Adversity

**3.6-3** How does experiencing adversity affect children's social development?

### Deprivation of Attachment

If secure attachment fosters social competence, what happens when circumstances prevent a child from forming any attachments? In all of psychology, there is no sadder research than adverse childhood experiences (ACEs) related to deprivation of attachment. Babies locked away at home under conditions of abuse or extreme neglect are often withdrawn, frightened, and even speechless. The same is true of those raised in institutions without the stimulation and attention of a regular caregiver, as was tragically illustrated during the 1970s and 1980s in Romania. Having decided that economic growth for his impoverished country required more human capital, Nicolae Ceauşescu, Romania's Communist dictator, outlawed contraception, forbade abortion, and taxed families with fewer than five children. The birthrate skyrocketed. But unable to afford the children they had been coerced into having, many families had to leave them at government-run orphanages with untrained and overworked staff. Child-to-caregiver ratios often were 15 to 1, so the children were deprived of healthy attachments with at least one adult.

When the deprived children were tested years later, and compared with children assigned to quality foster care, they had lower intelligence scores, abnormal stress responses, and quadruple the rate of attention-deficit/hyperactivity disorder (ADHD) (van IJzendoorn et al., 2020). Hundreds of other studies across 19 countries have shown that orphaned children generally fare better on later intelligence tests when raised in family homes from an early age (van IJzendoorn et al., 2020).

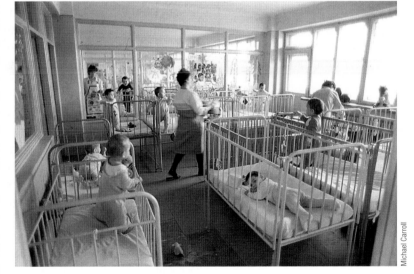

**The deprivation of attachment** In this 1980s Romanian orphanage, children between ages 1 and 5 outnumbered caregivers by 15 to 1.

Michael Carroll

### Trauma, Abuse, and Poverty

Most children who grow up under adversity (including child survivors of the Holocaust) are *resilient*; they withstand the trauma and become well-adjusted adults (Helmreich, 1992; Masten, 2001). So do most victims of childhood sexual abuse (Clancy, 2010). Hardship short of trauma often boosts mental toughness (Seery, 2011). Children who have coped with some adversity become hardier when facing future stresses (Ellis et al., 2017).

But many others who experience enduring abuse don't bounce back so readily. The Harlows' monkeys raised in total isolation, without even an artificial mother, bore lifelong scars. As adults, when placed with other monkeys their age, they either cowered in fright or lashed out in aggression. When they reached sexual maturity, most were incapable of mating. If artificially

"We've created a safe, nonjudgmental environment that will leave your child ill-prepared for real life."

## AP® Science Practice

### Research

The research on childhood abuse and adult characteristics is correlational, a non-experimental method used to assess how well one variable (in this case, childhood abuse) *predicts* another (for example, suicide attempts).

impregnated, females often were neglectful, abusive, and even murderous toward their first-born. Another primate study confirmed the abuse-breeds-abuse phenomenon: 9 of 16 female monkeys that had been abused by their mothers became abusive parents, compared to *none* of the females raised by a nonabusive mother (Maestripieri, 2005).

In humans, too, the abused may become the abusers. Most abusive parents—and many condemned murderers—have reported being neglected or battered as children (Kempe & Kempe, 1978; Lewis et al., 1988). Some 30 percent of people who have been abused later abuse their children—four times the U.S. national rate of child abuse (Dumont et al., 2007; Kaufman & Zigler, 1987). And abusive parents tend to abuse their own children in the ways they were abused as children, such as through neglect, emotional abuse, physical abuse, or sexual abuse (Madigan et al., 2019).

Although most abused children do *not* later become violent criminals or abusive parents, extreme early trauma may nevertheless leave footprints on the brain (McLaughlin et al., 2019). Like battle-stressed soldiers, abused children's brains respond to angry faces with heightened activity in threat-detecting areas (McCrory et al., 2011). In conflict-plagued homes, even sleeping infants' brains show heightened reactivity to hearing angry speech (Graham et al., 2013). As adults, abused children are more uncomfortable when touched (Maier et al., 2020). They tend to struggle in adulthood to regulate their negative emotions. They exhibit stronger startle responses, and are twice as likely to attempt suicide (Angelakis et al., 2019; Jovanovic et al., 2009; Lavi et al., 2019).

If repeatedly threatened and attacked while young, normally placid golden hamsters grow up to be cowards when caged with same-sized hamsters, or bullies when caged with weaker ones (Ferris, 1996). Such animals show changes in their levels of the brain chemical serotonin, which calms aggressive impulses. A similarly sluggish serotonin response has been found in abused children who become aggressive teens and adults. Children raised in poverty face unique hardships. They complete less schooling, and as adolescents and adults commit more crimes and have more problems with anxiety, depression, substance abuse, and getting a job (Akee et al., 2010; National Academy of Sciences, 2019). The Covid pandemic increased unemployment and closed schools, which led to more child poverty and child hunger (Sinha et al., 2020). By sensitizing the stress response system, such early stress can permanently heighten reactions to later stress and increase stress-related disease (Fagundes & Way, 2014; van Zuiden et al., 2012; Wei et al., 2012). Child abuse can also leave epigenetic marks—chemical tags—that alter normal gene expression (Lutz et al., 2017; McKinney, 2017).

Such findings help explain why young children who have survived severe or prolonged physical abuse, sexual abuse, bullying, or wartime atrocities are at increased risk for health problems, psychological disorders, substance abuse, criminality, and, for women, earlier death (Chen et al., 2016; Jakubowski et al., 2018; Schaefer et al., 2018). A study of 135,000 adolescents in 48 countries found that those who were bullied had triple the normal rate of attempted suicide (Koyanagi et al., 2019). In one national study of 43,093 U.S. adults, 8 percent reported experiencing physical abuse at least fairly often before age 18 (Sugaya et al., 2012). Among these individuals, 84 percent had experienced at least one psychiatric disorder. Moreover, the greater the abuse, the greater the odds of anxiety, depression, substance use disorder, and attempted suicide are.

Abuse victims are at especially heightened risk for depression if they carry a gene variation that spurs stress-hormone production (Bradley et al., 2008). As we will see again and again, behavior and emotion arise from a particular environment interacting with particular genes. Nature *and* nurture matter.

Adults also suffer when their attachment bonds are severed. Whether it occurs through death or separation, such a break produces a predictable sequence. Agitated preoccupation with the lost partner is followed by deep sadness and, eventually, the beginnings of emotional detachment and a return to normal living (Hazan & Shaver, 1994). Newly separated couples who have long ago ceased feeling affection are sometimes surprised at their desire to be near the former partner. Detaching is a process, not an event.

# Developing a Self-Concept

**3.6-4** How do children's self-concepts develop?

*Infancy's* major social achievement is attachment. *Childhood's* major social achievement is a positive sense of self. By the end of childhood, at about age 12, most children have developed a **self-concept**—an understanding and assessment of who they are. (Their *self-esteem* is how they *feel* about who they are.) Parents often wonder when and how this sense of self develops. "Is my baby aware of herself—does she know she is a person distinct from everyone else?"

Of course, we cannot ask the baby directly, but we can again capitalize on what she can do—letting her *behavior* provide clues to the beginnings of her self-awareness. In 1877, biologist Charles Darwin offered one idea: Self-awareness begins when we recognize ourselves in a mirror. To see whether a child recognizes that the girl in the mirror is indeed herself, researchers sneakily dabbed color on her nose. At about 6 months, children reach out to touch their mirror image as if it were another child (Courage & Howe, 2002; Damon & Hart, 1982, 1988, 1992). By 15 to 18 months, they begin to touch their own noses when they see the colored spot in the mirror (Butterworth, 1992; Gallup & Suarez, 1986). Apparently, 18-month-olds have a schema of how their face should look, and they wonder, "What is that spot doing on *my* face?"

By the time they reach school age, children's self-concept blossoms. It now includes their gender identity, group memberships, psychological traits, and similarities and differences compared with other children (Newman & Ruble, 1988; Stipek, 1992). They come to see themselves as good and skillful in some ways but not others. They form a concept of which traits, ideally, they would like to have. By age 8 or 10, their self-image is quite stable.

Children's views of themselves affect their actions. Children who form a positive self-concept are more confident, independent, optimistic, assertive, and sociable (Maccoby, 1980). So how can parents encourage a positive, yet realistic self-concept?

**Self-awareness** Mirror images fascinate infants from the age of about 6 months. Only at about 18 months, however, does the child recognize that the image in the mirror is "me."

---

## AP® Science Practice

### Research

Measuring self-awareness by determining if an infant touches the color on the nose in the mirror or on her own nose is another example of a clever operational definition.

---

# Parenting Styles

**3.6-5** What are the four main parenting styles?

Some parents spank; others reason. Some are strict; others are lax. Some show little affection; others liberally hug and kiss. How do such parenting-style differences affect children?

The most heavily researched aspect of parenting has been how, and to what extent, parents seek to control their children. Parenting styles can be described as a combination of two traits: how *responsive* and how *demanding* parents are (Kakinami et al., 2015). Investigators have identified four parenting styles (Baumrind, 1966, 1989, 1991; Maccoby & Martin, 1983; Steinberg et al., 1994):

1. *Authoritarian* parents are *coercive*. They impose rules and expect obedience: "Don't interrupt." "Keep your room clean." "Don't stay out late or you'll be grounded." "Why? Because I said so."

2. *Permissive* parents are *unrestraining*. They make few demands, set few limits, and use little punishment.

3. *Neglectful* parents are *uninvolved*. They are neither demanding nor responsive. They are careless and inattentive, and do not seek a close relationship with their children.

4. *Authoritative* parents are *confrontive*. They are both demanding and responsive. They exert control by setting rules, but, especially with older children, they encourage open discussion and allow exceptions.

Too hard, too soft, too uncaring, and just right, these styles have been called, especially by pioneering researcher Diana Baumrind and her followers. For more on parenting styles and their associated outcomes, see Developing Arguments: Parenting Styles.

**self-concept** all our thoughts and feelings about ourselves, in answer to the question, "Who am I?"

# Developing Arguments

### Parenting Styles

**Researchers have identified four parenting styles,[1] which have been associated with varying outcomes.**

## 1 Authoritarian parents

*Children with less social skill and self-esteem, and a brain that overreacts when they make mistakes[2]*

## 2 Permissive parents

*Children who are more aggressive and immature[3]*

## HOWEVER, Correlation ≠ Causation!

What other factors might explain this parenting-competence link?
• Children's traits may influence parenting. Parental warmth and control vary somewhat from child to child, even in the same family.[6] Maybe socially mature, agreeable, easygoing children get greater trust and warmth from their parents? Twin studies have supported this possibility.[7]
• Some underlying third factor may be at work. Perhaps, for example, competent parents and their competent children share genes that make social competence more likely. Twin studies have also supported this possibility.[8]

## 3 Neglectful parents

*Children with poor academic and social outcomes[4]*

## 4 Authoritative parents

*Children with the highest self-esteem, self-reliance, self-regulation, and helpfulness[5]*

## Developing Arguments Questions

**1.** Based on the evidence presented here, which parenting style would you recommend to new parents? Explain your choice.

**2.** Identify other factors that might explain the link between parenting style and children's competence.

1. Kakinami et al., 2015. 2. Meyer et al., 2019. 3. Luyckx et al., 2011. 4. Pinquart, 2016; Steinberg et al., 1994. 5. Baumrind, 1996, 2013; Buri et al., 1988; Coopersmith, 1967; Wong et al., 2021. 6. Holden & Miller, 1999; Klahr & Burt, 2014. 7. Kendler, 1996. 8. South et al., 2008.

Parents who struggle with conflicting advice should also remember that *all advice reflects the advice-giver's values.* For parents who prize unquestioning obedience, or whose children live in dangerous environments, an authoritarian style may have the desired effect. For those who value children's sociability and self-reliance, there is wisdom in authoritative, firm-but-open parenting.

## Culture and Child Raising

In a study of 414 mothers, most, regardless of cultural background, believed it was important to establish rules, encourage child safety, encourage socializing, and teach right from wrong (Cho et al., 2021). Yet cultural traditions differ in ways that can affect parental preferences and children's attachment styles. Do you prefer children who are independent, or children who comply with what others think? Compared with families in Asian cultures, families in Western cultures more often prefer independence: "You are responsible for yourself. Follow your conscience. Be true to yourself. Discover your gifts." Such child raising practices may help explain why Western children are more likely than others to report an avoidant attachment style (Strand et al., 2019). Today, many parents with Western cultural values no longer prioritize obedience, respect, and sensitivity to others (Alwin, 1990; Remley, 1988). In the 1950s, however, Western parents were more likely to teach their children, "Be true to your traditions. Be loyal to your heritage and country. Show respect toward your parents and other superiors." Cultures vary. And cultures change.

Children across time and place have thrived under various child-raising systems. Upper-class British parents traditionally handed off routine caregiving to nannies, then sent their 10-year-olds away to boarding school.

Those from Asian and African cultures more often value physical and emotional closeness. Children often sleep with their parents and spend their days close to a family member (Shweder et al., 1995; Xiong et al., 2020). Such expectations of physical and emotional closeness (and anxiety of it being taken away) helps explain why children from collectivist cultures are prone to attachment anxiety. Many of these cultures encourage a strong sense of *family self*—meaning that what shames the child shames the family, and what honors the family honors the self.

In western Kenya's traditional Gusii society, babies nurse freely but spend most of the day on their mother's or siblings' back—with lots of body contact but little face-to-face and language interaction. What might appear as a lack of interaction to many Westerners might, to these Gusii parents, seem far preferable to the lesser body contact experienced by babies pushed in strollers, carried in car seats, and left in playpens (Small, 1997). In some rural villages in Senegal, cultural traditions discourage caregivers' talking with young children. Programs encouraging verbal interaction improved the children's language development one year later (Weber et al., 2017). But were the programs worth the cultural disruption? Diversity in child raising cautions us against presuming that any one culture's way is the only way to raise children successfully.

* * *

One thing is certain: Whatever our culture, the investment in raising a child buys many years of joy and love, but also a lot of worry and irritation. Yet for most people who become parents, a child is part of one's legacy—one's personal investment in the human future. To paraphrase psychiatrist Carl Jung, we reach backward into our parents and forward into our children, and through their children into a future we will never see, but about which we must therefore care.

**AP® Exam Tip**

It's understandable if you are struggling to remember the differences between authoritarian and authoritative. Maybe it will help to realize that authoritative parents will engage in a little more give and take, while authoritarian parents do not negotiate. The words *give* and *authoritative* both end in the letters *ive*.

**Cultures vary** Parents everywhere care about their children, but raise and protect them differently depending on the surrounding culture. What some may judge as an adverse childhood experience (ACE) in one culture may seem typical in another. For example, in big cities, parents keep their children close. In smaller, close-knit communities, such as Scotland's Orkney Islands' town of Stromness, social trust has enabled parents to park their toddlers outside shops.

Stephen H. Reehl

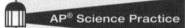 

## Check Your Understanding

**Examine the Concept**

▶ Explain what is meant by *self-concept*.

▶ Explain the differences among the four parenting styles.

**Apply the Concept**

▶ How would you describe the style of your parents or primary caregivers? How has this impacted your attachment style or your other traits and behaviors?

▶ What mistakes do you think parents of the past most often made? What mistakes do you think today's parents might be making, and that as a parent you would want to avoid?

*Answers to the Examine the Concept questions can be found in Appendix C at the end of the book.*

# Module 3.6a REVIEW

**3.6-1 How do caregiver-infant attachment bonds form?**

- The *ecological systems theory* outlines the social environment's influence on human development.

- At about 8 months, soon after object permanence develops, children separated from their caregivers display separation and *stranger anxiety*. Infants form *attachments* with caregivers who gratify their biological needs but, more importantly, who are comfortable, familiar, and responsive.

- Many birds and other animals have a more rigid attachment process, called *imprinting*, that occurs during a critical period.

**3.6-2 How have psychologists studied attachment differences, and what have they learned?**

- Attachment has been studied in strange situation experiments, which show that some children are securely attached and others are insecurely attached (exhibiting anxious, avoidant, or disorganized attachments). Infants' differing attachment styles reflect both their individual *temperament* and the responsiveness of their caregivers.

- Adult relationships seem to reflect the attachment styles of early childhood, lending support to Erik Erikson's idea that basic trust is formed in infancy by our experiences with responsive caregivers.

**3.6-3 How does experiencing adversity affect children's social development?**

- Most children growing up under adversity are resilient, and they may be hardier when facing future stresses. But extreme trauma in childhood can alter the brain, affecting stress responses or leaving epigenetic marks.

- Children who experience severe or prolonged abuse, neglect, bullying, poverty, or wartime atrocities are at increased risk for health problems, psychological disorders, substance abuse, and criminality.

**3.6-4 How do children's self-concepts develop?**

- *Self-concept*, an understanding and evaluation of who we are, emerges gradually. By 15 to 18 months, children can recognize themselves in a mirror. By school age, they can describe many of their own traits; and by age 8 or 10, their self-image is stable.

**3.6-5 What are the four main parenting styles?**

- The main parenting styles are authoritarian (coercive), permissive (unrestraining), neglectful (uninvolved), and authoritative (confrontive).

# AP® Practice Multiple Choice Questions

**1.** Erma, an 18-month-old, typically recognizes herself in a mirror. Based on this information, Erma has developed

 a. an attachment bond.
 b. her self-concept.
 c. strong self-esteem.
 d. basic trust.

**Use the following scenario to answer questions 2–3:**

After Daisy forgot to water the plants in the front yard, she was grounded for a week—even before her parents heard what might have caused Daisy to forget about her chore.

**2.** Which parenting style do Daisy's parents exhibit?

 a. Authoritative
 b. Authoritarian
 c. Permissive
 d. Neglectful

**3.** Which of the following conclusions can we draw about Daisy's behavior in adulthood based on the information provided in the scenario?

 a. Daisy is more likely to behave immaturely.
 b. Daisy is more likely to have poor academic performance.
 c. Daisy is more likely to have high self-esteem.
 d. Daisy is more likely to have poor social skills.

**4.** Which of the following would be considered a sign of secure attachment in a 1-year-old?

 a. Davis shows no sign of stranger anxiety whether his parents are present or not.
 b. Antoine pays no attention to his parents who return after a brief separation.
 c. Nola becomes distressed when her parents leave but seeks contact on return.
 d. Delmond does not react to his parents leaving or returning after a brief separation.

**5.** Osman and Eun-Ji have secure attachment styles. Based on research on attachment, they are also likely to

 a. be parented by authoritarian parents.
 b. develop a sense of basic trust.
 c. be raised in a neglectful environment.
 d. be able to think in an abstract manner.

**6.** Dr. Hannon is studying a group of 3-year-olds, who tend to cling to their parent's leg at separation and remain distressed throughout the day. Dr. Hannon plans to measure the length of time the children cry upon separation from their parents at preschool. Which variable is Dr. Hannon most likely interested in studying?

 a. Insecure attachment
 b. Self-concept
 c. Stranger anxiety
 d. Contact comfort

# Module 3.6b Social-Emotional Development Across the Lifespan: Adolescence, Emerging Adulthood, and Adulthood

## LEARNING TARGETS

**3.6-6** Explain the social tasks and challenges of adolescence.

**3.6-7** Explain the differences between parental and peer influences during adolescence.

**3.6-8** Explain the characteristics of *emerging adulthood*.

**3.6-9** Describe the themes and influences that mark our social journey from early adulthood to death.

**3.6-10** Explain changes in well-being across the lifespan.

**3.6-11** Describe the range of reactions to the death of a loved one.

## Social-Emotional Development in Adolescence

**3.6-6** What are the social tasks and challenges of adolescence?

**AP® Exam Tip**

Become familiar with Table 3.6-2, Erikson's Stages of Psychosocial Development, and be able to identify an individual who may be dealing with the issue in each stage. For example, a teenager may be dealing with the identity and role confusion issue.

Psychologist Erik Erikson (1963) contended that each stage of life has its own *psychosocial task*, a crisis that needs resolution. Young children wrestle with issues of *trust*, then *autonomy* (independence), then *initiative*. School-age children strive for *competence* (also called *industry*), feeling able and productive. But for people your age, the task is to synthesize past, present, and future possibilities into a clearer sense of self (**Table 3.6-2**). Adolescents wonder, "Who am I as an individual? What do I want to do with my life? What values should I live by? What do I believe in?" Erikson called this quest the adolescent's *search for identity*.

### Forming an Identity

To refine their sense of identity, adolescents in individualist cultures usually try out different "selves" in different situations. They may act out one self at home, another with friends, another online, and still another at school. If two situations overlap—as when a teenager brings new friends home—the discomfort can be considerable (Klimstra et al., 2015). The teen often wonders, "Which self should I be? Which is the real me?" The eventual resolution is a self-definition that unifies the various selves into a consistent and comfortable sense of who one is—an **identity**.

For both adolescents and adults, group identities are often formed based on how we differ from those around us—in gender and sexual orientation, in age and relative wealth, in

**identity** our sense of self; according to Erikson, the adolescent's task is to solidify a sense of self by testing and integrating various roles.

## TABLE 3.6-2 Erikson's Stages of Psychosocial Development

| Stage (approximate age) | Issue | Description of Task |
|---|---|---|
| *Infancy* (to 1 year) | Trust and mistrust | If needs are dependably met, infants develop a sense of basic trust. |
| *Toddlerhood* (1–3 years) | Autonomy and shame and doubt | Toddlers learn to exercise their will and do things for themselves, or they doubt their abilities. |
| *Preschool* (3–6 years) | Initiative and guilt | Preschoolers learn to initiate tasks and carry out plans, or they feel guilty about their efforts to be independent. |
| *Elementary school* (6 years to puberty) | Competence (industry) and inferiority | Children learn the pleasure of applying themselves to tasks, or they feel inferior. |
| *Adolescence* (teen years into 20s) | Identity and role confusion | Teenagers work at refining a sense of self by testing roles and then integrating them to form a single identity, or they become confused about who they are. |
| *Young adulthood* (20s to early 40s) | Intimacy and isolation | Young adults learn to form close relationships and gain the capacity for intimate love, or they feel socially isolated. |
| *Middle adulthood* (40s to 60s) | Generativity and stagnation | Middle-aged people discover a sense of contributing to the world, usually through family and work, or they may feel a lack of purpose. |
| *Late adulthood* (late 60s and older) | Integrity and despair | Reflecting on their lives, older adults may feel a sense of satisfaction or failure. |

abilities and beliefs. When living in Britain, I [DM] become conscious of my Americanness. When spending time in Hong Kong, I [ND] become conscious of my White race. For international students, for those of a minority ethnic or religious group, for gay and transgender people, or for people with a disability, a **social identity** often forms around their distinctiveness. (Stay tuned for more on social identity and prejudice in Module 4.1.)

Erikson noticed that some adolescents forge their identity early, simply by adopting their parents' values and expectations (a familial identity). Other adolescents may develop a racial or ethnic identity, gender identity, religious identity, or occupational identity. Traditional, collectivist cultures teach adolescents who they are, rather than encouraging them to decide on their own. Multicultural adolescents form complex identities as they integrate group memberships and their feelings about them (Marks et al., 2011). Teens' consideration of *possible selves*—the versions of themselves they imagine becoming in the future—may facilitate their identity formation (see Module 4.6).

Researchers have contended that identity formation proceeds through a series of stages, as adolescents explore and gradually commit to who they will become. They begin in the *diffusion* stage, without a clear commitment to a particular identity and perhaps with little sense of who they are. This is followed by *foreclosure:* a premature commitment to an identity with little exploration ("I'm a jock"). In the *moratorium* stage, teens more actively seek a meaningful identity. Finally, they reach identity *achievement*—a committed sense of self, and a desire to accomplish something personally meaningful that contributes to the world beyond oneself (Fuligni, 2019; Marcia, 1966, 1980).

Most young people develop a sense of contentment with their lives. Which statement best describes you: "I would choose my life the way it is right now" or "I wish I were somebody else"? When U.S. teens answered, 81 percent picked the first option, and 19 percent chose the second (Lyons, 2004). Reflecting on their existence, 76 percent of U.S. college and university students say they "discuss religion/spirituality" with friends (Stolzenberg et al., 2019).

### AP® Science Practice

**Research**

Findings such as 81 percent of U.S. teens selecting "I would choose my life the way it is right now" come from survey methods. Recall from Module 0.3 that surveys are vulnerable to the wording effect. Would you answer differently if the option was "There is nothing I would change about my life" instead?

**social identity** the "we" aspect of our self-concept; the part of our answer to "Who am I?" that comes from our group memberships.

**Who shall I be today?** By varying the way they look, adolescents try out different "selves." Although we eventually form a consistent and stable sense of identity, the self we present may change with the situation.

## CULTURAL AWARENESS

When talking about attending college or working, the authors qualify their statement by specifying industrialized countries. This is because adolescents' expectations and experiences are culture-bound. Although there are some universal experiences (for example, teens and parents have conflicts), notice how often the findings described in this module are culture-specific.

**intimacy** in Erikson's theory, the ability to form close, loving relationships; a primary developmental task in young adulthood.

"She says she's someone from your past who gave birth to you, and raised you, and sacrificed everything so you could have whatever you wanted."

Interventions that aim to boost adolescents' health and well-being work best when appealing to their desires for self-esteem, status, and respect (Yeager et al., 2018). (Which of these arguments do you find more convincing: "Eating well is important for your health" or "Buying junk food gives money to rich adults who disrespect you by thinking you don't know better"?)

During the early to mid-teen years, self-esteem typically falls and, for girls, depression scores often increase (Kwong et al., 2019; Salk et al., 2017). Teen depression and suicide rates have increased since the spread of social media and the peer comparisons they enable. (More on this in Module 4.7.) If your life feels dull compared with all of the fun experiences your online friends are posting, be consoled: Most of your friends feel the same way (Deri et al., 2017). But self-image rebounds during the late teens and twenties, and self-esteem gender differences shrink (Zuckerman et al., 2016). Agreeableness and emotional stability scores also increase in late adolescence (Klimstra et al., 2009).

The late teens and twenties are the years when many people in industrialized countries begin exploring new opportunities by attending college or working full time. Many college and university seniors have achieved a clearer identity and a more positive self-concept than they had as first-year students (Waterman, 1988). Those who have achieved a clear sense of identity are less prone to alcohol misuse (Bishop et al., 2005).

Erikson contended that adolescent identity formation (which continues into adulthood) is followed in young adulthood by a developing capacity for **intimacy**, the ability to form emotionally close relationships. When Mihaly Csikszentmihalyi [chick-SENT-me-hi] and Jeremy Hunter (2003) used a beeper to sample the daily experiences of U.S. teens, they found them to be unhappiest when alone and happiest when with friends. Romantic relationships, which tend to be emotionally intense during the teenage years, are reported by some two in three North American 17-year-olds, but by fewer in collectivist countries such as China (Collins et al., 2009; Li et al., 2010). Those individuals who enjoy high-quality (intimate, supportive) relationships with family and friends also tend to enjoy similarly high-quality romantic relationships in adolescence, which set the stage for healthy adult relationships. Such relationships are, for most of us, a source of great pleasure.

## Parent and Peer Relationships

**3.6-7** How do parents and peers influence adolescents?

This next research finding will not surprise you: As adolescents in Western cultures seek to form their own identities, they begin to pull away from their parents. Adolescence is typically a time of diminishing parental influence and growing peer influence (Blakemore, 2018; Giletta et al., 2021). The preschooler who can't be close enough to her mother, who loves to touch and cling to her, gradually becomes the 14-year-old who wouldn't be caught dead holding hands with Mom. As children, we recognize adult faces more readily than other children's faces; by adolescence, we display superior recognition for our peers' faces (Picci & Scherf, 2016). Puberty alters attachments and primes perceptions.

As Aristotle long ago recognized, we humans are "the social animal." At all ages, but especially during childhood and adolescence, we seek to fit in with our groups (Blakemore, 2018; Harris, 1998, 2000). Preschoolers who disdain a certain food often will eat that food if put at a table with a group of children who like it. Children who hear English spoken with one accent at home and another in the neighborhood and at school will invariably adopt the accent of their peers, not their parents. Accents (and slang) reflect culture, "and children get their culture from their peers," as Judith Rich Harris (2007) noted. And teens who start vaping or smoking typically have friends who model smoking, suggest its pleasures, and share supplies (Liu et al., 2017). Part of this peer similarity may result from a *selection effect,* as adolescents seek out peers with similar attitudes, interests, and traits (Domingue et al., 2018). Those who smoke (or don't) may select as friends those who also smoke (or don't).

By adolescence, parent-child arguments occur more often, usually over mundane things—household chores, bedtime, homework (Tesser et al., 1989). Conflict during the transition to adolescence tends to be greater with first-born than with second-born children, and greater with mothers than with fathers (Burk et al., 2009; Shanahan et al., 2007).

For a minority of parents and their adolescents, differences lead to real splits and great stress (Steinberg & Morris, 2001). But most disagreements are at the level of harmless bickering. With sons, the issues often are behavior problems, such as acting out or hygiene; for daughters, the issues commonly involve relationships, such as dating and friendships (Schlomer et al., 2011). In a survey of nearly 6000 adolescents in 10 countries—from Australia to Bangladesh to Turkey—most said they like

**Peer power** As we develop, we play and partner with peers. No wonder children and youths are so sensitive and responsive to peer influences.

their parents (Offer et al., 1988). "We usually get along but . . . ," adolescents often reported (Galambos, 1992; Steinberg, 1987). Positive parent-teen relations and positive peer relations often go hand in hand. High school girls who have the most affectionate relationships with their mothers also tend to enjoy the most intimate friendships with girlfriends (Gold & Yanof, 1985). And teens who feel close to their parents tend to be healthy and happy and to do well in school (Resnick et al., 1997). Of course, we can state this correlation the other way: Misbehaving teens are more likely to have tense relationships with parents and other adults.

Although heredity does much of the heavy lifting in forming individual temperament and personality differences, parents and peers influence teens' behaviors and attitudes. When with peers, teens discount the future and focus more on immediate rewards (O'Brien et al., 2011). Most teens are herd animals, talking, dressing, and acting more like their peers than their parents. What their friends are, they often become, and what "everybody's doing," they usually do. Teens' social media use illustrates the power of peer influence. Compared to photos with few likes, teens prefer photos with many likes. Moreover, when viewing many-liked photos, teens' brains become more active in areas associated with reward processing and imitation (Sherman et al., 2016). Liking and doing what everybody else likes and does feels good.

When excluded or bullied, whether online or face-to-face, children and teens feel acute pain. Most excluded "students suffer in silence. . . . A small number act out in violent ways against their classmates" (Aronson, 2001). The pain of exclusion also persists. In one large study, those who were bullied as children showed poorer physical health and greater psychological distress 40 years later (Takizawa et al., 2014).

The power to select a child's neighborhood and schools gives some parents the ability to influence the culture that shapes the child's peer group. And because neighborhood influences matter, parents may want to become involved in intervention programs aimed at a whole school or neighborhood. If the vapors of a toxic climate are seeping into a child's life, that climate—not just the child—needs reforming. Even so, peers are but one medium of cultural influence. As an African proverb declares, "It takes a village to raise a child."

### AP® Science Practice

**Research**

Do you recognize the design of the large study that spanned 40 years? If not, go back and review Module 3.1. It is a design commonly used by developmental psychologists.

## How Much Credit or Blame Do Parents Deserve?

Biological parents shuffle their gene decks and deal a life-forming hand to their child-to-be, who is then subjected to countless influences beyond their control. But all parents—whether biological or adoptive—feel enormous satisfaction in their children's successes or guilt and

*"First, I did things for my parents' approval, then I did things for my parents' disapproval, and now I don't know why I do things."*

shame over their failures. They beam over the child who wins trophies and titles. They wonder where they went wrong with the child who is repeatedly in trouble. Freudian psychiatry and psychology encouraged such ideas, blaming problems from asthma to schizophrenia on "bad mothering."

Do parents really produce wounded future adults by being (take your pick from the toxic-parenting lists) overbearing—or uninvolved? Pushy—or indecisive? Overprotective—or distant? Should we then blame our parents for our failings, and ourselves for our children's failings? Or does talk of wounding fragile children through normal parental mistakes trivialize the brutality of real abuse? To paraphrase developmental psychologist Alison Gopnik (2016), parents may be less like potters who mold clay, and more like gardeners who provide the soil for their children's natural growth.

Parents do matter. But parenting wields its largest effects at the extremes: the abused children who sometimes become abusive, the deeply loved but firmly handled children who become self-confident and socially competent adults. Evidence of the power of the family environment also can be seen in the remarkable academic and vocational successes of many children of people who leave their home countries, such as those of refugees who fled war-torn Vietnam and Cambodia—successes attributed to close-knit, supportive, even demanding families (Caplan et al., 1992). Asian Americans, Hispanic Americans, and European Americans often differ in their parenting expectations. An Asian American mother may push her children to do well, but usually not in a way that strains their relationship (Fu & Markus, 2014). Having a "Tiger Mother"—one who pushes her children and works alongside them—tends to motivate children (whose culture prepares them to expect such pushing) to work harder. Latina mothers may expect their children to obey authority and not interrupt adults, and they may view a child's public behavior as reflecting on the entire family. These views can enhance harmonious mother-child relationships when children expect such cultural parenting practices (Calzada et al., 2015; Tamis-LeMonda et al., 2019). European Americans, however, might see such support as going overboard, reducing perceived freedom, and undermining children's motivation.

Nevertheless, personality measures reveal that shared environmental influences from the womb onward typically account for less than 10 percent of children's differences. Referring to our traits rather than our values, behavior geneticist Robert Plomin (2018b) noted, "We would essentially be the same person if we had been adopted at birth and raised in a different family." So, knowing that children's personalities are not easily sculpted by parental nurture, perhaps parents can relax and love their children for who they are.

---

## Check Your Understanding

### Examine the Concept

▶ Match the psychosocial development stage (i–viii) with the issue that Erikson believed we wrestle with at that stage (a–h).

| | |
|---|---|
| i. Infancy | a. Generativity and stagnation |
| ii. Toddlerhood | b. Integrity and despair |
| iii. Preschool | c. Initiative and guilt |
| iv. Elementary school | d. Intimacy and isolation |
| v. Adolescence | e. Identity and role confusion |
| vi. Young adulthood | f. Competence and inferiority |
| vii. Middle adulthood | g. Trust and mistrust |
| viii. Late adulthood | h. Autonomy and shame and doubt |

*Answers to the Examine the Concept questions can be found in Appendix C at the end of the book.*

### Apply the Concept

▶ What is the *selection effect*, and how might it affect a teen's decision to join sports teams at school?

▶ What have been your best and worst experiences during adolescence? Who do you credit or blame more — your parents or your peers?

# Emerging Adulthood

**3.6-8** What is *emerging adulthood*?

In the Western world, adolescence now roughly corresponds to the teen years. At earlier times, and in other parts of the world today, this slice of life has been much smaller (Baumeister & Tice, 1986). Shortly after sexual maturity, young people would assume adult responsibilities and status. The event might be celebrated with an elaborate initiation—a public rite of passage. The new adult would then work, marry, and have children.

When schooling became compulsory in many Western countries, independence was put on hold until after graduation. Adolescents are now taking more time to establish themselves as adults. Today's adolescents are less likely to work for pay, drive, or have romantic attachments (Twenge & Park, 2019). In the United States, the average age at first marriage has increased more than 5 years since 1960 (to 29 for men and 27 for women). In 1960, three in four women and two in three men had, by age 30, finished school, left home, become financially independent, married, and had a child. In the early twenty-first century, this was true for fewer than half of 30-year-old women and one-third of 30-year-old men (Henig, 2010). In 2016, 15 percent of 25- to 35-year-old Americans—double the 1981 proportion—were living in their parents' home (Fry, 2017).

Together, later independence and earlier sexual maturity have widened the once-brief interlude between biological maturity and social independence (**Figure 3.6-5**). In prosperous communities, the time from age 18 to the mid-twenties is an increasingly not-yet-settled phase of life, now often called **emerging adulthood** (Arnett, 2006, 2007; Reitzle, 2006). No longer adolescents, these emerging adults—having not yet assumed full adult responsibilities and independence—feel somewhere "in between." Those furthering their education or working may be managing their own time and priorities. Yet they may be doing so from their parents' home, unable to afford their own place and perhaps still emotionally dependent as well (Fry, 2017). Recognizing today's more gradually emerging adulthood, the U.S. government now allows dependent children up to age 26 to remain on their parents' health insurance plans (HHS, 2020b).

> **emerging adulthood** a period from about age 18 to the mid-twenties, when many persons in prosperous Western cultures are no longer adolescents but have not yet achieved full independence as adults.

*"I just don't know what to do with myself in that long stretch after college but before social security."*

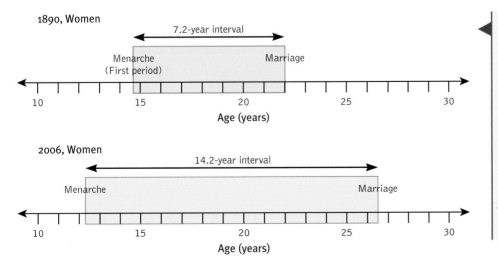

**Figure 3.6-5**

**The transition to adulthood is being stretched from both ends**

In the 1890s, the average interval between a woman's first menstrual period and marriage, which typically marked a transition to adulthood, was about 7 years. By 2006 in industrialized countries, that gap had widened in well-off communities to about 14 years (Finer & Philbin, 2014; Guttmacher Institute, 1994). Although many adults are unmarried, later marriage combines with prolonged education and earlier menarche to help stretch out the transition to adulthood.

# Social-Emotional Development in Adulthood

> **3.6-9** What themes and influences mark our social journey from early adulthood to death?

Try completing this statement five times: "I am _____."

In response, teens mostly describe their individual traits. Young adults more often define themselves in terms of their social roles, such as their occupation or being a parent (Hards et al., 2019). Many differences between teens, younger adults, and older adults are created by significant life events. A new job means new relationships, new expectations, and new demands. Marriage brings the joy of intimacy and the stress of merging two lives. The 3 years surrounding the birth of a child bring increased life satisfaction for most couples (Dyrdal & Lucas, 2011). The death of a loved one creates an irreplaceable loss. How do these life events shape the course of our adulthood?

## Adulthood's Ages and Stages

As people enter their forties, they undergo a transition to middle adulthood, a time when they realize that life will soon be mostly behind instead of ahead of them. Some psychologists have argued that for many people the *midlife transition* is a crisis, a time of great struggle, regret, or even feeling struck down by life. The popular image of the midlife crisis—an early-forties man who forsakes his family for a younger romantic partner and a hot sports car—is more a myth than reality. In surveys in many countries, unhappiness does *not* surge during the early forties (Galambos et al., 2020). One study of emotional instability in nearly 10,000 men and women found "not the slightest evidence" that distress peaks anywhere in the midlife age range (McCrae & Costa, 1990).

For the 1 in 4 adults who report experiencing a life crisis, the trigger is not age, but rather a major event, such as illness, divorce, or job loss (Lachman, 2004). Some middle-aged adults describe themselves as a "sandwich generation," simultaneously supporting their aging parents and their emerging adult children or grandchildren (Riley & Bowen, 2005). With others depending on their support, middle-aged adults become especially sensitive to their social status rising or falling (Weiss & Kunzmann, 2020). Later in life, status changes matter less for people's happiness.

Life events trigger transitions to new life stages at varying ages. The **social clock**—the definition of "the right time" to leave home, get a job, marry, have children, or retire—varies from era to era and culture to culture. This once-rigid sequence has loosened; the social clock still ticks, but people feel freer to keep their own time.

Even *chance events* can have lasting significance, by deflecting us down one road rather than another. Albert Bandura (1982, 2005) recalled the ironic true story of a book editor who came to one of Bandura's lectures on the "Psychology of Chance Encounters and Life Paths"—and ended up marrying the woman who happened to sit next to him. Chance events can change our lives.

## Adulthood's Commitments

Two basic aspects of our lives dominate adulthood. Erik Erikson called them *intimacy* (forming close relationships) and *generativity* (being productive and supporting future generations). Sigmund Freud (1935) put this idea more simply: The healthy adult, he said, is one who can *love* and *work*.

### Love

Although more and more people are living single lives, most eventually pair up romantically. People typically flirt, fall in love, and commit—one person at a time. "Pair-bonding is

**social clock** the culturally preferred timing of social events such as marriage, parenthood, and retirement.

a trademark of the human animal," observed anthropologist Helen Fisher (1993). From an evolutionary perspective, relatively monogamous pairing makes sense: Parents who cooperated to nurture their children to maturity were more likely to have their genes passed along to posterity than were parents who didn't.

Adult bonds of love are most satisfying and enduring when marked by a similarity of interests and values, a sharing of emotional and material support, and intimate self-disclosure. And for better or for worse, our standards have risen over the years: We now hope not only for an enduring bond, but also for a mate who is a wage earner, caregiver, intimate friend, and warm and responsive lover (Finkel, 2017). There also appears to be "vow power." Straight and gay relationships sealed with commitment more often endure (Rosenfeld, 2014; Wilcox et al., 2019). Such bonds are especially likely to last when couples marry after age 20 and are well educated. Compared with their counterparts of 70 years ago, people in Western countries *are* better educated and marrying much later—7 to 8 years later for first marriages in the United States (Census, 2021). These trends may help explain why the U.S. divorce rate, which surged from 1960 to 1980, has since declined.

Might test-driving life together minimize divorce risk? In Europe, Canada, and the United States, those couples who live together before marriage (and especially before engagement) have had *higher* rates of divorce and marital troubles than those who have not lived together (Rosenfeld & Roesler, 2019, 2021). Across developed countries, cohabiting partners were more likely than married spouses to agree that they have had recent serious doubts their relationship will last (Wang & Wilcox, 2019). Three factors contribute. First, those who live together tend to be initially less committed to the idea of enduring marriage. Second, they may become even less marriage-supporting while living together. Third, it's more awkward to break up with a cohabiting partner than with a dating partner, leading some cohabiters to marry someone "they otherwise would have left behind" (Stanley & Rhoades, 2016a, 2016b).

Although there is more variety in relationships today, the institution of marriage endures. More than 9 in 10 U.S. adults either have married during their lifetime or want to marry (Newport & Wilke, 2013). In Western countries, what counts as a "very important" reason to marry? In the United States, 31 percent say financial stability, and 93 percent say love (Cohn, 2013). Moreover, marriage is a predictor of happiness, sexual satisfaction, income, and physical and mental health (Scott et al., 2010; Wilcox & Wolfinger, 2017). Between 1972 and 2018, U.S. surveys of more than 60,000 people revealed that 40 percent of married adults were "very happy," compared with 23 percent of those who had never married (NORC, 2019). Gay and lesbian adults similarly report greater happiness if married. Finally, neighborhoods with high marriage rates typically have low rates of social pathologies such as crime, delinquency, and emotional disorders among children (Myers & Scanzoni, 2005; Wilcox et al., 2018).

Of course, relationships that last are not always devoid of conflict. Some couples fight but also shower each other with affection. Other couples never raise their voices yet also seldom praise each other or nuzzle. Both styles can last. After observing the interactions of 2000 couples, John Gottman and Julie Gottman (2018) reported one indicator of marital success: at least *a five-to-one ratio of positive to negative interactions*. Stable marriages provided five times more instances of smiling, touching, complimenting, and laughing than of sarcasm, criticism, and insults. So, if you want to predict which couples will stay together, don't pay attention to how passionately they are in love—the pairs who make it are more often those who refrain from putting down their partners. To prevent a cancerous negativity, successful couples learn to fight fair (to state feelings without insulting) and to steer conflict away from chaos with comments like "I know it's not your fault" or "I'll just be quiet for a moment and listen."

Often, love bears children. For most people, this most enduring of life changes is a happy event—one that adds occasional stress but also meaning and joy (Nelson-Coffey et al., 2019; Witters, 2014). "I feel an overwhelming love for my children unlike anything

Andersen Ross/Blend Images/Alamy Stock Photo

**Love** Intimacy, attachment, commitment — love by whatever name — is central to healthy and happy adulthood.

**AP® Science Practice**

### Research

Does marriage correlate with happiness because marital support and intimacy breed happiness, because happy people more often marry and stay married, or both? Or is there a third variable, such as social skills, that accounts for this relationship? We can't say for sure because this research is correlational. It would be unethical (indeed, impossible) to randomly assign individuals to marry or not, and only random assignment provides the control necessary to draw cause-and-effect conclusions.

I feel for anyone else," said 93 percent of U.S. mothers in a national survey (Erickson & Aird, 2005). Many fathers feel the same. A few weeks after the birth of my first child, I [DM] was suddenly struck by a realization: "So *this* is how my parents felt about me!" As a Chinese proverb says, "To understand your parents' love, bear your own children."

When children begin to absorb time, money, and emotional energy, parents' satisfaction with their own relationship may decline (Doss et al., 2009). This is especially likely among employed women, who—more than they expected—may also carry the burden of doing more chores at home. Putting effort into creating an equitable relationship can thus pay double dividends: greater satisfaction, which breeds better parent-child relations (Erel & Burman, 1995).

Eventually, most children leave home. This departure is a significant and sometimes difficult event. But for most parents, an empty nest is a happy place (Adelmann et al., 1989; Gorchoff et al., 2008). Many parents experience a "postlaunch honeymoon," especially if they maintain close relationships with their children (White & Edwards, 1990). As Daniel Gilbert (2006) said, "The only known symptom of 'empty nest syndrome' is increased smiling."

### Work

For many adults, the answer to "Who are you?" depends a great deal on the answer to "What do you do?" Choosing a career path is difficult, especially during uncertain economic times. Even in the best of times, few students in their first 2 years of college or university can predict their later careers. Moreover, career plans change. Physicist Albert Einstein started out as a patent clerk. Before becoming a Nobel laureate novelist, William Faulkner was a postal clerk. Actor Whoopi Goldberg was a bricklayer and mortuary beautician.

In the end, happiness is about having work that fits your interests and provides you with a sense of competence and accomplishment. It is about having a close, supportive companion, or family and friends, who notice and cheer your accomplishments (Campos et al., 2015). And for some, it includes having children who love you and whom you love and feel proud of.

**Job satisfaction and life satisfaction** Work can provide us with a sense of identity and competence, and opportunities for accomplishment. Perhaps this is why challenging and interesting occupations enhance people's happiness. For more on work, including discovering your own strengths, see Module EM.2: Psychology at Work.

### Well-Being Across the Lifespan

**3.6-10** How does our well-being change across the lifespan?

To live is to grow older. This moment marks the oldest you have ever been and the youngest you will henceforth be. That means we all can look back with satisfaction or regret, and forward with hope or dread. When asked what they would have done differently if they could relive their lives, people's most common answer has been "taken my education more seriously and worked harder at it" (Kinnier & Metha, 1989; Roese & Summerville, 2005).

Other regrets—"I should have told my father I loved him," "I regret that I never went to Europe"—have also focused less on mistakes made than on the things one *failed* to do (Gilovich & Medvec, 1995).

But until the very end, the over-65 years are not notably unhappy. Self-esteem and psychological well-being remain stable (Jebb et al., 2020; Wagner et al., 2016). Gallup asked 658,038 people worldwide to rate their lives on a ladder from 0 ("the worst possible life") to 10 ("the best possible life"). Age—from 15 to over 90 years—gave no clue to life satisfaction (Morrison et al., 2014). Positive feelings, supported by enhanced emotional control, tend to grow after midlife, and negative feelings subside (Stone et al., 2010; Urry & Gross, 2010). Compared with younger Chinese and American adults, for example, older adults are *more* attentive to positive news (Isaacowitz, 2012; Wang et al., 2015a).

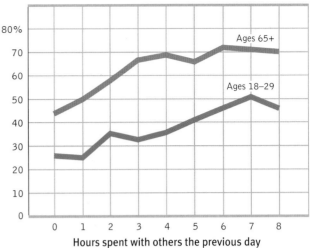

Percentage of Americans reporting a lot of stress-free enjoyment and happiness the previous day

Ages 65+

Ages 18–29

Hours spent with others the previous day

**Figure 3.6-6**

**We are social creatures**

Both younger and older adults report greater happiness when spending time with others. (Note that this correlation could also reflect happier people being more social.) (Gallup survey data reported by Crabtree, 2011.)

Like people of all ages, older adults are happiest when not alone (**Figure 3.6-6**). Compared with teens and young adults, older adults do tend to have a smaller social network, with fewer friendships and greater loneliness (Luhmann & Hawkley, 2016; Wagner et al., 2016). However, older adults experience fewer problems in their relationships—less attachment anxiety, stress, and anger (Chopik et al., 2013; Fingerman & Charles, 2010). With age, we become more stable and trusting (Bailey & Leon, 2019; Shallcross et al., 2013).

Cultures differ in their expectations for old age. Older adults from a Western cultural tradition tend to live independently and to seek opportunities for personal growth, such as ticking off items on their "bucket list" (Kitayama et al., 2020; Tsai et al., 2018). My [ND] own grandmother fit this mold, as she lived independently until age 97. In East Asian cultures, older adults more often move in with family and help care for grandkids.

The aging brain may help nurture positive feelings. Brain scans of older adults show that the amygdala, a neural processing center for emotions, responds less actively to negative events, but still responds to positive events (Mather et al., 2004). Brain-wave reactions to negative images also diminish with age (Kisley et al., 2007). As we reach the later chapters of our lives, our brain enables a contented culmination (Mather, 2016). As former U.S. First Lady Eleanor Roosevelt reflected, "At age 70, I would say the advantage is that you take life more calmly. You know that 'this, too, shall pass'!"

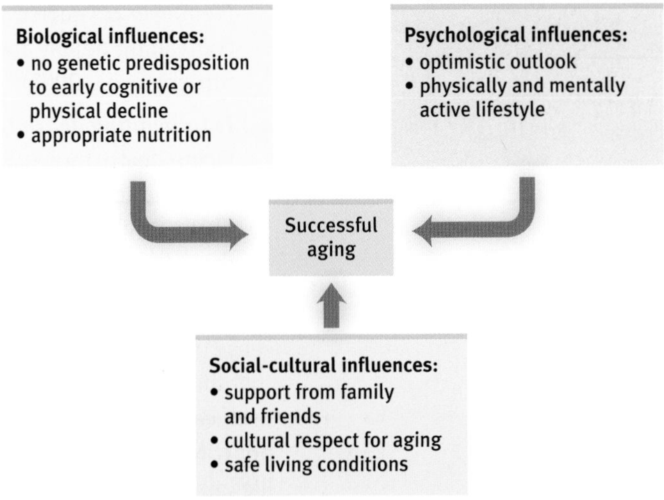

Moreover, unlike younger people, older adults remember the good more than the bad events of their lives (Addis et al., 2010). This happy phenomenon leaves most older people with the comforting feeling that life, on balance, has been mostly good. Thanks to biological, psychological, and social-cultural influences, more and more people flourish into later life (**Figure 3.6-7**).

The resilience of well-being across the lifespan obscures some interesting age-related emotional differences. When researchers mapped people's emotional terrain by periodically signaling them with electronic beepers to report their current activities and feelings, they found that teenagers typically come down from elation or up from gloom in less than an hour, but that adult moods are less extreme and more enduring (Csikszentmihalyi & Larson, 1984). As the years go by, feelings mellow (Brose et al., 2015). Highs become less high, lows less low.

**Figure 3.6-7**

**Biopsychosocial influences on successful aging**

**Biological influences:**
• no genetic predisposition to early cognitive or physical decline
• appropriate nutrition

**Psychological influences:**
• optimistic outlook
• physically and mentally active lifestyle

**Successful aging**

**Social-cultural influences:**
• support from family and friends
• cultural respect for aging
• safe living conditions

Compliments provoke less elation and criticisms less despair, as both become merely additional feedback atop a mountain of accumulated praise and blame. As we age, life becomes less of an emotional roller coaster.

## Death and Dying

> **3.6-11** What range of reactions does a loved one's death trigger?

"Time is a great teacher," noted the nineteenth-century composer Hector Berlioz, "but unfortunately it kills all its pupils."

Most of us will cope with the deaths of relatives and friends. Typically, the most difficult separation a person experiences is the death of a partner—a loss suffered by four times more women than men. That's because women tend to be younger than their mates, and also because, worldwide, women outlive men by 4.4 years (Ritchie, 2019; WHO, 2019a).

Maintaining everyday engagements and relationships increases resilience in the face of such a loss (Infurna & Luthar, 2016). But for some, grief is severe, especially when a loved one's death comes suddenly and before its expected time on the social clock. I [ND] experienced this when a tragic accident claimed the life of my mother at age 60. Such tragedies may trigger a year or more of memory-laden mourning (Lehman et al., 1987).

For some, the loss is unbearable. One Danish long-term study of more than 1 million people found that about 17,000 of them had suffered the death of a child under 18. In the 5 years following that death, 3 percent of them had a first psychiatric hospitalization—a 67 percent higher rate than among other parents (Li et al., 2005).

Reactions to a loved one's death range more widely than most suppose. Some cultures encourage public weeping and wailing; others hide grief. Within any culture, individuals differ. Given similar losses, some people grieve hard and long, others less so (Ott et al., 2007). Some popular misconceptions persist, however:

- *Are there stages of grieving?* Terminally ill and bereaved people do not go through identical predictable stages, such as denial before anger (Friedman & James, 2008; Nolen-Hoeksema & Larson, 1999).

- *Should we purge our grief?* Those who express the strongest grief immediately do not purge their grief more quickly (Bonanno & Kaltman, 1999; Wortman & Silver, 1989). But grieving parents who try to protect their partner by "staying strong" and not discussing their child's death may actually prolong the grieving (Stroebe et al., 2013).

- *Is therapy needed?* Bereavement therapy and self-help groups offer support, but there is similar healing power in the passing of time, the support of friends, and the act of giving support and help to others (Baddeley & Singer, 2009; Brown et al., 2008; Neimeyer & Carrier, 2009). Grieving spouses who talk often with others or receive grief counseling adjust about as well as those who grieve more privately (Bonanno, 2004; Stroebe et al., 2005).

- *Is impending death terrifying?* Compared to what people *imagine* they would feel when facing death, those actually facing imminent death due to terminal illness are more positive and less sad and despairing. After studying terminally ill patients' blog posts and death row inmates' last words, Amelia Goranson and her colleagues (2017) concluded that "Meeting the grim reaper may not be as grim as it seems."

Facing death with dignity and openness helps people complete the life cycle with a sense of life's meaningfulness and unity—the sense that their existence has been good and that life and death are parts of an ongoing cycle. Although death may be unwelcome, life itself can be affirmed even at death. This is especially so for people who review their lives not with despair but with what Erik Erikson called a sense of *integrity*—a feeling that one's life has been meaningful and worthwhile.

## Check Your Understanding

**Examine the Concept**

▶ Explain what is meant by *emerging adulthood*. How does culture/geographic region impact this?

▶ Explain the relationship between cohabitation and divorce.

*Answers to the Examine the Concept questions can be found in Appendix C at the end of the book.*

**Apply the Concept**

▶ In what ways are you looking forward to adulthood? What concerns do you have about your own transition into adulthood, and how do you think you might address them?

# Module 3.6b REVIEW

**3.6-6** What are the social tasks and challenges of adolescence?

- Erik Erikson proposed eight stages of psychosocial development across the lifespan. He believed we need to achieve trust, autonomy, initiative, competency (industry), *identity* (in adolescence), *intimacy* (in young adulthood), generativity, and integrity. Each life stage has its own psychosocial task.

- Solidifying one's sense of self in adolescence means trying out a number of different roles. *Social identity* is the part of the self-concept that comes from a person's group memberships.

**3.6-7** How do parents and peers influence adolescents?

- During adolescence, parental influence diminishes and peer influence increases. Adolescents tend to seek out peers with similar attitudes, interests, and traits—due in part to the selection effect—and to adopt their peers' ways of dressing, acting, and communicating. Positive parent-teen relationships correlate with positive peer relationships, however.

- Personalities and temperaments are shaped by both nature and nurture, including parental and peer influences.

**3.6-8** What is *emerging adulthood*?

- Due to earlier sexual maturity and later independence, the transition from adolescence to adulthood is taking longer than it once did. *Emerging adulthood* is the period from age 18 to the mid-twenties, when many young people are not yet fully independent. This stage is found mostly in today's Western cultures.

**3.6-9** What themes and influences mark our social journey from early adulthood to death?

- Adults do not progress through an orderly sequence of age-related social stages. Chance events can determine life choices.

- The *social clock* is a culture's preferred timing for events such as marriage, parenthood, and retirement, but people today feel freer than they once did about keeping their own time.

- Adulthood's dominant themes are love and work (Erikson's intimacy and generativity, respectively).

**3.6-10** How does our well-being change across the lifespan?

- Surveys show that until the very end of life, life satisfaction is unrelated to age. Self-esteem and psychological well-being remain stable. Positive emotions increase after midlife and negative ones decrease, and older adults experience fewer extremes in their emotions and mood.

- While older adults do have smaller social networks, with fewer friendships and greater loneliness, they also experience fewer relationship problems.

**3.6-11** What range of reactions does a loved one's death trigger?

- People do not grieve in predictable stages, as was once supposed, and bereavement therapy is not significantly more effective than grieving without such aid. Life can be affirmed even at death, especially for those who experience what Erikson called a sense of integrity—a feeling that one's life has been meaningful.

# AP® Practice Multiple Choice Questions

1. In some prosperous Western societies, it is common for adolescents to graduate from high school, go to college, and still live at home with their parents. They have not yet assumed full adult responsibilities and independence. Psychologists have identified this period of time as
   a. middle adulthood.
   b. early adulthood.
   c. emerging adulthood.
   d. late adolescence.

2. Kayden just turned 14. Which of the following changes will Kayden most likely exhibit?
   a. Kayden will distance herself from her parents, and her relationships with her friends will become more important.
   b. Kayden's relationship with her mother will deteriorate, while her relationships with her youngest siblings will improve.
   c. Kayden's relationship with her parents will become the most important influence in her life in high school, and she will not be affected by peers.
   d. Kayden will connect with her school teachers, but her familial relationships and friendships will decrease in importance.

3. EK is an adolescent. According to Erikson, her primary developmental task is to develop a sense of
   a. trust.
   b. intimacy.
   c. competence.
   d. identity.

4. Interpreting the graph below, which shows data about females from Western cultures, which of the following statements is most accurate?
   a. Compared with the late nineteenth century, the average number of years between puberty and marriage is smaller in current Western cultures.
   b. Compared with the late nineteenth century, puberty is starting later and marriage is happening earlier, on average, in current Western cultures.
   c. Compared with the late nineteenth century, puberty is starting earlier and marriage is happening earlier, on average, in current Western cultures.
   d. Compared with the late nineteenth century, puberty is starting earlier and marriage is happening later, on average, in current Western cultures.

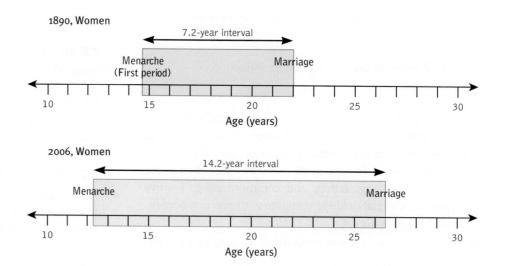

**5.** Megan, a third grader, is having trouble with math. She is starting to do poorly in other subjects, because she feels she cannot master math. Based on Erikson's stages of psychosocial development, which stage is Megan in?

   a. Autonomy and shame and doubt
   b. Initiative and guilt
   c. Competence and inferiority
   d. Identity and role confusion

**6.** Okoye is 15 years old. Her teacher gave her an assignment to describe herself with the prompt, "I am _____." Which of the following is Okoye most likely to write in the blank space?

   a. a student
   b. a sister
   c. kind
   d. a babysitter

**7.** Olivia and Jackson plan to get married next year. This significant life event will allow them to achieve Erikson's stage of

   a. competence (industry).
   b. generativity.
   c. intimacy.
   d. identity.

# Module 3.7a  Classical Conditioning: Basic Concepts

## LEARNING TARGETS

**3.7-1**  Define *learning*, and explain some basic forms of learning.

**3.7-2**  Explain behaviorism's view of learning.

**3.7-3**  Identify Pavlov, and explain the basic components of classical conditioning.

**3.7-4**  Explain the processes of *acquisition*, *extinction*, *spontaneous recovery*, *generalization*, and *discrimination in classical conditioning*.

**3.7-5**  Explain why Pavlov's work remains so important.

We humans, across our lifespan, learn from experience. Indeed, nature's most important gift may be our *adaptability*—our capacity to learn new behaviors that can help us cope with our changing world. We can learn how to build grass huts or snow shelters, submarines or space stations, thereby adapting to almost any environment.

Learning breeds hope. What is learnable, we may be able to teach—a fact that encourages parents, educators, and coaches. What has been learned, we may be able to change by new learning—an assumption underlying stress management and counseling programs. No matter how unhappy or unsuccessful or unloving we are, that need not be the end of our story.

No topic is closer to the heart of psychology than *learning*. In this unit, we have considered infants' and children's learning; language learning; the learning of culture, social behavior, and gender roles; and how the capacity to learn and remember changes as we develop across the lifespan. In earlier modules, we discussed the learning of visual perceptions and of a drug's expected effect. And in later modules, we will see how learning shapes our motivations and emotions, personalities, and attitudes. In Modules 3.7, 3.8, and 3.9, we will examine the heart of learning: classical conditioning, operant conditioning, the effects of biology and cognition on learning, and learning by observation.

## How Do We Learn?

**3.7-1** How do we define *learning*, and what are some basic forms of learning?

By **learning**, we adapt to our environments. We learn to expect and prepare for significant events such as the arrival of food or pain (*classical conditioning*). We learn to repeat acts that bring rewards and to avoid acts that bring unwanted results (*operant conditioning*; see Module 3.8). We learn new behaviors by observing events and people, and through language, we learn things we have neither experienced nor observed (*cognitive learning*; see Module 3.9). But *how* do we learn?

One way we learn is by *association*. Our mind naturally connects events that occur in sequence. Suppose you see and smell freshly baked bread, eat some, and find it satisfying. The next time you see and smell fresh bread, you will expect that eating it will again be satisfying. So, too, with sounds. If you associate a sound with a frightening consequence, hearing the sound alone may trigger your fear. As one 4-year-old exclaimed after watching a TV character get mugged, "If I had heard that music, I wouldn't have gone around the corner!" (Wells, 1981).

**learning** the process of acquiring through experience new and relatively enduring information or behaviors.

Learned associations feed our habitual behaviors (Urcelay & Jonkman, 2019; Wood, 2017). Habits can form when we repeat behaviors in a given context—sleeping in the same comfy bed position, biting our nails when taking an exam, or switching off the lights when leaving a room. As behavior becomes linked with the context, our next experience of that context will evoke our habitual response. Especially when we are mentally fatigued, we tend to fall back on our habits (Neal et al., 2013). That's true of both good habits (eating fruit) and bad (overindulging in potato chips) (Graybiel & Smith, 2014). To increase your self-control, and to achieve your academic goals, the key is to form helpful habits (Fiorella, 2020).

How long does it take to form a helpful habit? To find out, one British research team asked 96 university students to choose a healthy behavior (such as running before dinner or eating fruit with lunch), to do it daily for 84 days, and to record whether the behavior felt automatic (something they did without thinking and would find it hard not to do). On average, behaviors became habitual after about 66 days (Lally et al., 2010). Is there something you'd like to make a routine or essential part of your life? Just do it every day for two months, or a bit longer for exercise, and you likely will find yourself with a new habit.

Other animals also learn by association. Disturbed by a squirt of water, the sea slug *Aplysia* protectively withdraws its gills. If the squirts continue, as happens naturally in choppy water, the withdrawal response diminishes. (We say the slug **habituates**: Recall from Module 3.2 that *habituation* is what happens when repeated stimulation produces waning responsiveness.) But if the sea slug repeatedly receives an electric shock just after being squirted, its protective response to the squirt instead grows stronger. The animal has associated the squirt with the impending shock.

Complex animals can learn to associate their own behavior with its outcomes. An aquarium seal will repeat behaviors, such as slapping and barking, that prompt people to toss it a herring. After five speech-imitating African grey parrots were adopted and housed together at England's Lincolnshire Wildlife park, they started swearing, which put the park staff in hysterics. Their "fowl" language prompted their removal from public display. "The more they swear, the more you usually laugh, which then triggers them to swear again," explained the park manager (Franklin & Merrifield, 2020).

By linking two events that occur close together, both sea slugs and seals are exhibiting **associative learning**. The sea slug associates the squirt with an impending shock; the seal associates slapping and barking with a herring treat. Each animal has learned something important to its survival: anticipating the immediate future.

This process of learning associations is *conditioning*. It takes two main forms:

- In *classical conditioning* (**Figure 3.7-1**), we learn to associate two stimuli and thus to anticipate events. (A **stimulus** is any event or situation that evokes a response.) We learn

**habituation** decreasing responsiveness with repeated stimulation.

**associative learning** learning that certain events occur together. The events may be two stimuli (as in classical conditioning) or a response and its consequence (as in operant conditioning).

**stimulus** any event or situation that evokes a response.

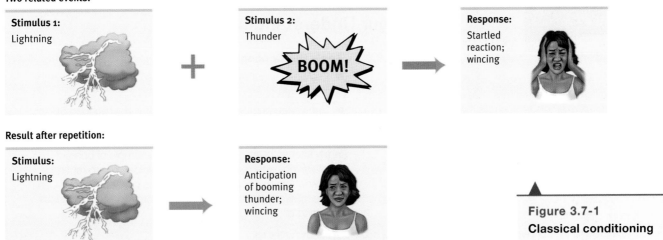

Two related events:

Stimulus 1: Lightning + Stimulus 2: Thunder BOOM! → Response: Startled reaction; wincing

Result after repetition:

Stimulus: Lightning → Response: Anticipation of booming thunder; wincing

**Figure 3.7-1**
**Classical conditioning**

**Figure 3.7-2**
**Operant conditioning**

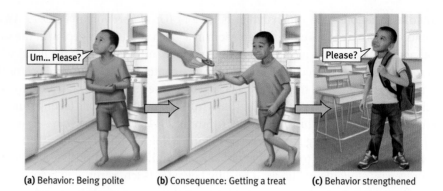

**(a)** Behavior: Being polite    **(b)** Consequence: Getting a treat    **(c)** Behavior strengthened

**TRY THIS**

Most of us could not list in order the songs on our favorite album or playlist. Yet hearing the end of one piece cues (by association) our anticipation of the next. Likewise, when singing your national anthem, you associate the end of each line with the beginning of the next. (Pick a line out of the middle and notice how much harder it is to recall the *previous* line.)

that a flash of lightning signals an impending crack of thunder; when lightning flashes nearby, we start to brace ourselves. We associate stimuli that we do not control, and we respond automatically (exhibiting **respondent behavior**).

● In *operant conditioning*, we learn to associate a response (our behavior) and its consequence. Thus, we (and other animals) learn to repeat acts that are followed by good results (**Figure 3.7-2**) and avoid acts that are followed by bad results. These associations produce **operant behaviors** (which operate on the environment to produce consequences).

To simplify, we will explore these two types of associative learning separately in this module and the next. But they often occur together, as on one Japanese cattle ranch, where the clever rancher outfitted his herd with electronic pagers that he could call. After a week of training, the animals learned to associate two stimuli—their pager's beep and the arrival of food (classical conditioning). But they also learned to associate their hustling to the food trough with the pleasure of eating (operant conditioning), which simplified the rancher's work. Classical conditioning + operant conditioning did the trick.

Conditioning is not the only form of learning. Through **cognitive learning**, we acquire mental information that guides our behavior. *Observational learning*, a form of cognitive learning, lets us learn from others' experiences. Chimpanzees, for example, sometimes learn behaviors merely by watching other chimpanzees perform them. If one animal sees another solve a puzzle and gain a food reward, the observer may perform the trick more quickly. So, too, in humans: We look and we learn. (We will discuss this more in Module 3.9.)

**respondent behavior** behavior that occurs as an automatic response to some stimulus.

**operant behavior** behavior that operates on the environment, producing a consequence.

**cognitive learning** the acquisition of mental information, whether by observing events, by watching others, or through language.

---

**Check Your Understanding**

**Examine the Concept**

▶ What is learning?

▶ Explain the difference between associative and cognitive learning. Provide an example to illustrate the differences.

**Apply the Concept**

▶ Explain why habits, such as having something sweet with a cup of coffee or tea, are so hard to break.

▶ Can you remember an example from your childhood of learning through classical conditioning — perhaps salivating at the sound or smell of some delicious food cooking in your family kitchen? Can you remember an example of operant conditioning, when you repeated (or decided not to repeat) a behavior because you liked (or hated) its consequences? Can you recall watching someone else perform some act and later repeating or avoiding that act?

*Answers to the Examine the Concept questions can be found in Appendix C at the end of the book.*

# Classical Conditioning

**3.7-2** What is behaviorism's view of learning?

For many people, the name Ivan Pavlov (1849–1936) rings a bell. The Russian physiologist's early twentieth-century experiments—now psychology's most famous research—are classics, and the phenomenon he explored we justly call **classical conditioning**.

Pavlov's work laid the foundation for many of psychologist John B. Watson's ideas. In searching for laws underlying learning, Watson (1913) urged his colleagues to avoid referring to inner thoughts, feelings, and motives. The science of psychology should instead study how organisms respond to stimuli in their environments, said Watson: "Its theoretical goal is the prediction and control of behavior. Introspection forms no essential part of its methods." Simply put, psychology should be an objective science—based on observable behavior.

This view, which Watson called **behaviorism**, influenced North American psychology, especially during the first half of the twentieth century. Pavlov and Watson came to share both a disdain for "mentalistic" concepts (such as consciousness) and a belief that the basic laws of learning were the same for all animals—whether dogs or humans. Few researchers today agree that psychology should ignore mental processes, but most agree that classical conditioning is a basic form of learning by which all organisms adapt to their environment.

**SPOTLIGHT ON:**
John B. Watson

Ivan Pavlov "Experimental investigation . . . should lay a solid foundation for a future true science of psychology" (1927).

**John B. Watson** Watson (1924) admitted to "going beyond my facts" when offering his famous boast: "Give me a dozen healthy infants, well-formed, and my own specified world to bring them up in and I'll guarantee to take any one at random and train him to become any type of specialist I might select—doctor, lawyer, artist, merchant-chief, and, yes, even beggar-man and thief, regardless of his talents, penchants, tendencies, abilities, vocations, and race of his ancestors."

## Pavlov's Experiments

**3.7-3** Who was Pavlov, and what are the basic components of classical conditioning?

**SPOTLIGHT ON:**
Ivan Pavlov

Pavlov was driven by a lifelong passion for research. After setting aside his initial plan to follow his father into the Russian Orthodox priesthood, Pavlov earned a medical degree at age 33 and spent the next two decades studying dogs' digestive system. This work earned him, in 1904, Russia's first Nobel Prize. But Pavlov's novel experiments on learning, which consumed the last three decades of his life, earned this feisty, intense scientist his place in history (Todes, 2014).

Pavlov's new direction came when his creative mind seized on an incidental observation: Without fail, putting food in a dog's mouth caused the animal to salivate. Moreover, the dog began salivating not only when it tasted the food, but also in response to the mere sight of the food, or the food dish, or the person delivering the food, or even the sound of that person's approaching footsteps. At first, Pavlov considered these "psychic secretions" an annoyance—until he realized they pointed to a simple but fundamental form of learning.

Pavlov and his team of researchers—more than half of whom were women (Hill, 2019)—tried to imagine what the dog was thinking and feeling as it drooled in anticipation of the food. This line of thought only led them into fruitless debates. So, to explore the phenomenon more objectively, they experimented. To eliminate other possible influences,

**classical conditioning** a type of learning in which we link two or more stimuli; as a result, to illustrate with Pavlov's classic experiment, the first stimulus (a tone) comes to elicit behavior (drooling) in anticipation of the second stimulus (food).

**behaviorism** the view that psychology (1) should be an objective science that (2) studies behavior without reference to mental processes. Most research psychologists today agree with (1) but not with (2).

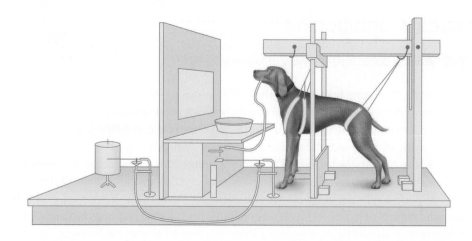

**Figure 3.7-4**
**Pavlov's classic experiment**

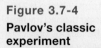

Pavlov presented a neutral stimulus (a tone) just before an unconditioned stimulus (food in mouth). The neutral stimulus then became a conditioned stimulus, producing a conditioned response.

they isolated the dog in a small room, secured it in a harness, and attached a device to divert its saliva to a measuring instrument (**Figure 3.7-3**). From the next room, they presented food—first by sliding in a food bowl, later by blowing meat powder into the dog's mouth at a precise moment. They then paired various **neutral stimuli (NS)**—events the dog could see or hear but didn't associate with food—with food in the dog's mouth. If a sight or sound regularly signaled the arrival of food, would the dog learn the link? If so, would it begin salivating in anticipation of the food?

The answers proved to be *Yes* and *Yes*. Just before placing food in the dog's mouth to produce salivation, Pavlov sounded a tone. After several pairings of tone and food, the dog, now anticipating the meat powder, began salivating upon just hearing the tone. In later experiments, a buzzer,[4] a light, a touch on the leg, and even the sight of a circle set off the drooling. (This procedure works with people, too. When hungry young Londoners viewed abstract figures before smelling peanut butter or vanilla, their brain soon responded in anticipation to the abstract images alone [Gottfried et al., 2003].)

A dog does not learn to salivate in response to food in its mouth. Rather, food in the mouth automatically, *unconditionally*, triggers a dog's salivary reflex (**Figure 3.7-4**). Thus,

**BEFORE CONDITIONING**

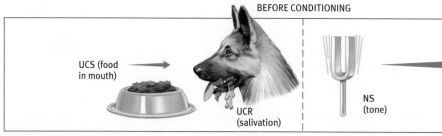

An unconditioned stimulus (UCS) produces an unconditioned response (UCR).

A neutral stimulus (NS) produces no salivation response.

**DURING CONDITIONING**

**AFTER CONDITIONING**

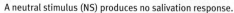

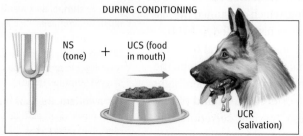

The UCS is repeatedly presented just after the NS. The UCS continues to produce a UCR.

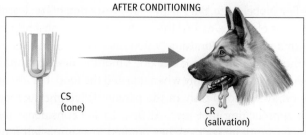

The previously neutral stimulus alone now produces a conditioned response (CR), thereby becoming a conditioned stimulus (CS).

[4]The "buzzer" (English translation) was perhaps the bell people commonly associate with Pavlov (Tully, 2003). Pavlov used various stimuli, but some have questioned whether he used a bell.

THE EARS HEAR THE CAN OPENER..

RIGHT AWAY THE STOMACH KNOWS THAT SUPPER IS COMING..

HOW DO THE EARS TELL THE STOMACH?

I'VE NEVER BEEN ABLE TO FIGURE THAT OUT..

Peanuts reprinted with permission of United Features Syndicate

Peanuts

Pavlov called this drooling an unlearned or **unconditioned response (UCR)**. And he called the food an **unconditioned stimulus (UCS)**.

Salivation in response to a tone, however, is learned. It is *conditional* upon the dog's associating the tone with the food. Thus, we call this response the **conditioned response (CR)**. The stimulus that used to be neutral (in this case, a previously meaningless tone that now triggers salivation) is the **conditioned stimulus (CS)**. Distinguishing these two kinds of stimuli and responses is easy: Conditioned = learned; *un*conditioned = *un*learned.

If Pavlov's demonstration of associative learning was so simple, what did he do for the next three decades? What discoveries did his research factory publish in his 532 papers on salivary conditioning (Windholz, 1997)? Pavlov and his associates explored five major conditioning processes: *acquisition, extinction, spontaneous recovery, generalization,* and *discrimination*.

## Acquisition

**3.7-4** In classical conditioning, what are the processes of *acquisition*, *extinction*, *spontaneous recovery*, *generalization*, and *discrimination*?

**Acquisition** is the initial learning of an association. Pavlov and his associates wondered: How much time should elapse between presenting the NS (the tone, the light, the touch) and the UCS (the food)? In most cases, not much—half a second usually works well.

What do you suppose would happen if the food (UCS) appeared before the tone (NS) rather than after it? Would conditioning occur? Not likely. Conditioning usually won't occur when the NS follows the UCS. Remember: *Classical conditioning is biologically adaptive because it helps humans and other animals prepare for good or bad events*. To Pavlov's dogs, the originally neutral tone became a CS after signaling an important biological event—the arrival of food (UCS). To deer in the forest, a snapping twig (CS) may signal a predator's approach (UCS).

Research on male Japanese quail shows how a CS can signal another important biological event (Domjan, 1992, 1994, 2005). Just before presenting an approachable female quail, the researchers turned on a red light. Over time, as the red light continued to herald the female's arrival, the light alone caused the male quail to become excited. They developed a preference for their cage's red-light district, and when a female appeared, they mated with her more quickly and released more semen and sperm (Matthews et al., 2007). This capacity for classical conditioning supports reproduction.

In humans, too, objects, smells, sounds, and sights associated with sexual pleasure—even a geometric figure in one experiment—can become conditioned stimuli for sexual arousal (Byrne, 1982; Hoffmann, 2012, 2017). Onion breath, for example, is an NS—it does not typically produce sexual arousal. But when repeatedly paired with a passionate kiss, it can become a CS and do just that (**Figure 3.7-5**).

*The larger lesson: Conditioning helps an animal survive and reproduce—by responding to cues that help it gain food, avoid dangers, locate mates, and produce offspring* (Hollis, 1997).

**neutral stimulus (NS)** in classical conditioning, a stimulus that elicits no response before conditioning.

**unconditioned response (UCR)** in classical conditioning, an unlearned, naturally occurring response (such as salivation) to an unconditioned stimulus (UCS) (such as food in the mouth).

**unconditioned stimulus (UCS)** in classical conditioning, a stimulus that unconditionally—naturally and automatically—triggers an unconditioned response (UCR).

**conditioned response (CR)** in classical conditioning, a learned response to a previously neutral (but now conditioned) stimulus (CS).

**conditioned stimulus (CS)** in classical conditioning, an originally neutral stimulus that, after association with an unconditioned stimulus (UCS), comes to trigger a conditioned response (CR).

**acquisition** in classical conditioning, the initial stage—when one links a neutral stimulus and an unconditioned stimulus so that the neutral stimulus begins triggering the conditioned response. (In operant conditioning, the strengthening of a reinforced response.)

Figure 3.7-5

**An unexpected CS**

Psychologist Michael Tirrell (1990) recalled: "My first girlfriend loved onions, so I came to associate onion breath with kissing. Before long, onion breath sent tingles up and down my spine. Oh what a feeling!"

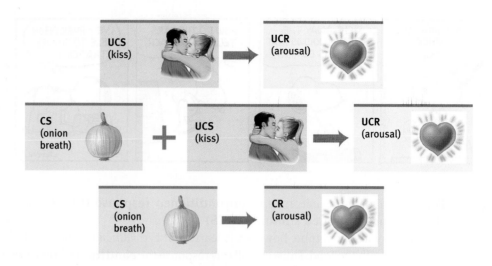

### AP® Exam Tip

You may find it helpful to note that spontaneous recovery is, in fact, spontaneous (Figure 3.7-6). In other words, the extinguished conditioned response returns without any additional pairing with the unconditioned stimulus. It is not a form of acquisition.

### AP® Science Practice

## Data

If you saw the graph in Figure 3.7-6 without the labels "acquisition," "extinction," or "spontaneous recovery," could you identify these concepts? Re-create the graph without the labels and test yourself. On the AP® exam, you will likely be asked to identify psychological concepts depicted in graphs.

**higher-order conditioning**
a procedure in which the conditioned stimulus in one conditioning experience is paired with a new neutral stimulus, creating a second (often weaker) conditioned stimulus. For example, an animal that has learned that a tone predicts food might then learn that a light predicts the tone and begin responding to the light alone. (Also called *second-order conditioning*.)

**extinction** in classical conditioning, the diminishing of a conditioned response when an unconditioned stimulus does not follow a conditioned stimulus. (In operant conditioning, when a response is no longer reinforced.)

**spontaneous recovery** the reappearance, after a pause, of a weakened conditioned response.

**Higher-order conditioning** occurs when a neutral stimulus becomes associated with a previously conditioned stimulus. If a tone regularly signals food and produces salivation, then a light that becomes associated with the tone (light → tone → food) may also begin to trigger salivation. In this way, a conditioned stimulus can be used as an unconditioned stimulus in higher-order conditioning. Although this higher-order conditioning (also called *second-order conditioning*) tends to be weaker than first-order conditioning, it influences our everyday lives. If a dog bites you, just the sound of a barking dog may later make you feel afraid.

## Extinction and Spontaneous Recovery

What would happen, Pavlov wondered, if, after conditioning, the CS occurred repeatedly without the UCS? If the tone sounded again and again, but no food appeared, would the tone still trigger salivation? The answer was mixed. The dogs salivated less and less, a reaction known as **extinction**. Extinction is diminished responding that occurs when the CS (tone) no longer signals an impending UCS (food). But, if after several hours' delay, Pavlov sounded the tone again, the dogs drooled in response (**Figure 3.7-6**). This **spontaneous recovery**—the reappearance of a (weakened) CR after a pause—suggested to Pavlov that extinction was suppressing the CR, rather than truly eliminating it.

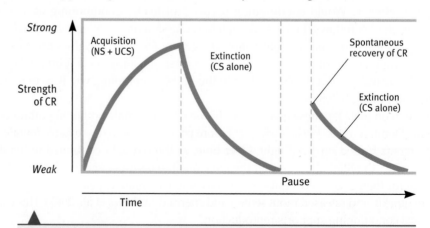

**Figure 3.7-6**

**Idealized curve of acquisition, extinction, and spontaneous recovery**

The rising curve shows the CR rapidly growing stronger as the NS becomes a CS due to repeated pairing with the UCS (*acquisition*). The CR then weakens rapidly as the CS is presented alone (*extinction*). After a pause, the (weakened) CR reappears (*spontaneous recovery*).

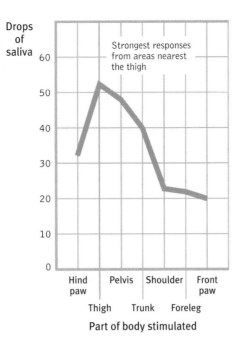

**Figure 3.7-7**
**Generalization**

Pavlov demonstrated generalization by attaching miniature vibrating devices to various parts of a dog's body. After conditioning salivation to stimulation of the thigh, he stimulated other areas. The closer a stimulated spot was to the dog's thigh, the stronger the conditioned response was. (Data from Pavlov, 1927.)

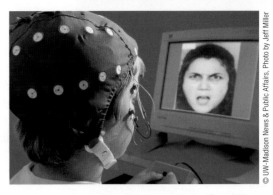

**Figure 3.7-8**
**Child abuse leaves tracks in the brain**

Abused children's sensitized brains react more strongly to angry faces (Pollak et al., 1998). This generalized anxiety response may help explain their greater risk of psychological disorder.

## Generalization

Pavlov and his students noticed that a dog conditioned to the sound of one tone also responded somewhat to the sound of a new and different tone. Likewise, a dog conditioned to salivate when rubbed would also drool a bit when scratched (Windholz, 1989) or when touched on a different body part (**Figure 3.7-7**). This tendency to respond to stimuli similar to the CS is called **generalization** (or *stimulus generalization*).

Generalization can be adaptive, as when toddlers who learn to fear moving cars also become afraid of moving trucks and motorcycles. And generalized fears can linger, sticking in our memory (Simon-Kutscher et al., 2019; Stout et al., 2018). For two months after being in a car collision, sensitized young drivers are less vulnerable to repeat collisions (O'Brien et al., 2017). Years after being tortured in an Argentinian prison, one journalist reported still flinching with fear at the sight of black shoes—his first glimpse of his torturers as they approached his cell (Timerman, 1980). Generalized anxiety reactions have also been demonstrated in laboratory studies comparing abused with nonabused children (**Figure 3.7-8**).

Stimuli related to naturally disgusting or morally objectionable objects will, by association, also evoke some physical or moral disgust. Would most people eat otherwise desirable fudge shaped to resemble dog feces? Or hold a dictionary apparently owned and used by Adolf Hitler? Or wrap themselves in a blanket thought to have been previously owned by members of the al-Qaeda terrorist group? *No, No,* and *No.* These situations cause people to feel repulsed (Fedotova & Rozin, 2018; Rozin et al., 1986, 2015). Such examples show how people's emotional reactions to one stimulus can generalize to other, related stimuli.

*"I don't care if she's a tape dispenser. I love her."*

Which conditioning principle is influencing the snail's affections?

## Discrimination

Pavlov's dogs also learned to respond to the sound of a particular tone and *not* to other tones. One stimulus tone predicted the UCS, and the others

**generalization** (also called *stimulus generalization*) in classical conditioning, the tendency, once a response has been conditioned, for stimuli similar to the conditioned stimulus to elicit similar responses. (In operant conditioning, when responses learned in one situation occur in other, similar situations.)

did not. This learned ability to *distinguish* between a conditioned stimulus (which predicts the UCS) and other, irrelevant stimuli is called **discrimination**. Being able to recognize differences is adaptive: Slightly different stimuli can cause vastly different consequences. After eating a poisonous butterfly, birds will generalize—they will avoid preying on similar butterflies. But they will also discriminate such butterflies from other butterfly species that are edible (Sims, 2018). Kenyan elephants flee the scent of Maasai hunters, whom they have learned to fear, but not the scent of the nonthreatening Kamba people (Rhodes, 2017). Facing a guard dog, your heart may race; facing a guide dog, it probably will not.

---

## Check Your Understanding

**Examine the Concept**

▶ The first step of classical conditioning, when an NS becomes a CS, is called _____. When the UCS no longer follows the CS, and the CR becomes weakened, this is called _____.

▶ Explain the difference between discrimination and generalization.

**Apply the Concept**

▶ An experimenter sounds a tone just before delivering an air puff that causes your eye to blink. After several repetitions, you blink to the tone alone. What is the NS? The UCS? The UCR? The CS? The CR?

▶ A psychologist recalled coming to associate his girlfriend's onion breath with arousal. Can you remember ever experiencing something that would normally be neutral (or even unpleasant), but came to mean something special to you?

▶ Do Pavlov's experiments, showing that dogs learned to anticipate meat powder, surprise you? Why or why not?

*Answers to the Examine the Concept questions can be found in Appendix C at the end of the book.*

---

## Pavlov's Legacy

### 3.7-5 Why does Pavlov's work remain so important?

What remains today of Pavlov's ideas? A great deal. Most psychologists now agree that classical conditioning is a basic form of learning. Modern neuroscience has also supported Pavlov's ideas—by identifying neural circuits that link a conditioned stimulus (warning signal) with an impending unconditioned stimulus (threat) (Harnett et al., 2016; Yau & McNally, 2018). Other researchers have applied Pavlov's ideas to shopping. Conditioning that associates neutral brand logos with positive or negative images can cause people to like or loathe those brands (Alves et al., 2020). With today's knowledge of the interplay of our biology, psychology, and social-cultural environment, some of Pavlov's ideas seem incomplete. But if we see further than Pavlov did, it is because we stand on his shoulders.

Why does Pavlov's work remain so important? If he had merely taught us that old dogs can learn new tricks, his experiments would long ago have been forgotten. Why should we care that dogs can be conditioned to salivate to the sound of a tone? The importance lies first in this finding: *Many other responses to many other stimuli can be classically conditioned in many other organisms*—in fact, in every species tested, from microscopic creatures to earthworms to fish to dogs to monkeys to people (Schwartz, 1984; Zhou et al., 2019). Thus, classical conditioning is one way that virtually all organisms learn to adapt to their environment.

Second, *Pavlov showed us how a process such as learning can be studied objectively*. He was proud that his methods involved virtually no subjective judgments or guesses about what went on in a dog's mind. The salivary response is a behavior measurable in cubic centimeters of saliva. Pavlov's success suggested a scientific model for how the young discipline of psychology might proceed—by isolating the basic building blocks of complex behaviors and studying them with objective laboratory procedures.

**discrimination** in classical conditioning, the learned ability to distinguish between a conditioned stimulus and other stimuli that have not been associated with a conditioned stimulus. (In operant conditioning, the ability to distinguish responses that are reinforced from similar responses that are not reinforced.)

408    **Unit 3**   Development and Learning

## Check Your Understanding

**Examine the Concept**

▶ Explain two important contributions of Pavlov's research.

**Apply the Concept**

▶ Companies often pay to make their products visible in popular movies — such as when admired actors drink certain beverages. Based on classical conditioning principles, what might be an effect of this pairing?

▶ How have your emotions or behaviors been classically conditioned?

*Answers to the Examine the Concept questions can be found in Appendix C at the end of the book.*

# Module 3.7a REVIEW

### 3.7-1 How do we define *learning*, and what are some basic forms of learning?

- *Learning* is the process of acquiring through experience new and relatively enduring information or behaviors.

- In *associative learning*, we learn that certain events occur together.

- In classical conditioning, we learn to associate two *stimuli* and thus to anticipate events. Automatically responding to stimuli we do not control is called *respondent behavior*.

- In operant conditioning, we learn to associate a response and its consequence. These associations produce operant behaviors.

- Through *cognitive learning*, we acquire mental information that guides our behavior. For example, in observational learning, we learn new behaviors by observing events and watching others.

### 3.7-2 What is behaviorism's view of learning?

- Ivan Pavlov's work on classical conditioning laid the foundation for *behaviorism*, the view that psychology should be an objective science that studies behavior without reference to mental processes. The behaviorists believed that the basic laws of learning are the same for all animals, including humans.

### 3.7-3 Who was Pavlov, and what are the basic components of classical conditioning?

- Ivan Pavlov, a Russian physiologist, performed novel experiments on learning. His early twentieth-century research over the last three decades of his life demonstrated that *classical conditioning* is a basic form of learning.

- Classical conditioning is a type of learning in which an organism comes to associate stimuli and anticipate events.
  - A *UCR* (unconditioned response) is an event that occurs naturally (such as salivation), in response to some stimulus.
  - A *UCS* (unconditioned stimulus) is something that naturally and automatically (without learning) triggers the unlearned response (for example, food in the mouth triggers salivation).
  - A *CS* (conditioned stimulus) is originally an *NS* (neutral stimulus, such as a tone) that, after association with a UCS (such as food) comes to trigger a CR.
  - A *CR* (conditioned response) is the learned response (salivating) to the originally neutral (but now conditioned) stimulus.

### 3.7-4 In classical conditioning, what are the processes of *acquisition, extinction, spontaneous recovery, generalization*, and *discrimination*?

- In classical conditioning, the first stage is *acquisition*, associating an NS with the UCS so that the NS begins triggering the CR. Acquisition occurs most readily when the NS is presented just before (ideally, about a half-second before) a UCS, preparing the organism for the upcoming event. This finding supports the view that classical conditioning is biologically adaptive.

- *Extinction* is diminished responding, which occurs if the CS appears repeatedly by itself without the UCS.

- *Spontaneous recovery* is the reappearance of a weakened conditioned response following a rest period.
- *Generalization* is the tendency to respond to stimuli that are similar to a CS.
- *Discrimination* is the learned ability to distinguish between a CS and other irrelevant stimuli.

**3.7-5** Why does Pavlov's work remain so important?

- Pavlov taught us that significant psychological phenomena can be studied objectively, and that classical conditioning is a basic form of learning that applies to all species.

---

# AP® Practice Multiple Choice Questions

**1.** Which of the following is the best example of learning?

   a. A dog salivates when food is placed in its mouth.

   b. A honeybee stings when the hive is threatened.

   c. A child cries when his brother hits him.

   d. A child flinches when he sees a balloon, because he is afraid of it popping.

**2.** In classical conditioning, a person learns to anticipate events by

   a. associating a response with its consequence.

   b. avoiding spontaneous recovery.

   c. using operant behaviors.

   d. associating two stimuli.

**3.** A family uses the microwave to prepare their cat's food. The cat comes running into the room when the microwave timer sounds but not when it hears the oven timer. The cat is demonstrating the concept of

   a. generalization.

   b. discrimination.

   c. spontaneous recovery.

   d. extinction.

**4.** Courtney is the supervisor of all the cashiers at a local grocery store. When cashiers have questions, they flip on a light to signal Courtney to come assist them. Initially, Courtney walked quickly immediately upon seeing lights flash at the grocery store. Now, after seeing hundreds of lights flash over the course of a week, Courtney finds that she does not walk as quickly over to the cashiers when she sees a light. This example best illustrates the concept of

   a. habituation.

   b. spontaneous recovery.

   c. extinction.

   d. discrimination.

**Use the following scenario to answer questions 5–6:**

Every day for a week, Juliette, a 2-year-old, hears a loud honk and sees a red truck pass by her house, which leads her to cry. The next week, Juliette begins crying when she sees the red truck, even though it did not honk. The red truck never honks again, but every so often, Juliette will cry when she sees this red truck and other red vehicles, although she never cries when seeing vehicles of other colors.

**5.** What is the red truck in this example?

   a. Conditioned response

   b. Unconditioned stimulus

   c. Conditioned stimulus

   d. Unconditioned response

**6.** Which of the following statements best explains why Juliette cries every so often even when the truck no longer honks?

   a. Juliette has become habituated to the truck.

   b. Juliette is experiencing spontaneous recovery.

   c. Extinction of Juliette's conditioned response has occurred.

   d. Juliette has yet to acquire an association between the truck and the honking.

**7.** Which of the following is a reason Pavlov's work remains so important today?

a. He demonstrated that learning can be studied objectively.

b. He showed that learning is a subjective process.

c. He discovered that only mammals can be classically conditioned.

d. He identified the neural circuits used in classical conditioning.

**8.** Dr. Bernstein classically conditioned babies to smile every time they saw a bottle full of milk. He then repeatedly showed the babies a picture of a tree before they were presented with a bottle of milk. He noticed that 98 percent of the time, babies smiled at the tree picture when it was presented alone, which was a rate that was beyond what could be expected by chance or error. Which of the following statements most accurately describes Dr. Bernstein's results?

a. The bottle of milk caused the babies to smile because Dr. Bernstein conducted an experiment.

b. There was a statistically significant effect of higher-order conditioning in this study.

c. Babies smiled at the tree picture, because the tree served as an unconditioned stimulus.

d. The bottle of milk allowed the babies to spontaneously recover a response to the tree image.

# Module 3.7b Classical Conditioning: Applications and Biological Limits

## LEARNING TARGETS

**3.7-6** Explain some applications of Pavlov's work to human health and well-being, and explain how Watson applied Pavlov's principles to learned fears.

**3.7-7** Explain how biological constraints affect classical conditioning.

## Applications of Classical Conditioning

**3.7-6** What have been some applications of Pavlov's work to human health and well-being? How did Watson apply Pavlov's principles to learned fears?

Other modules in this text—on consciousness, motivation, emotion, health, psychological disorders, and therapy—show how Pavlov's principles can influence human health and well-being. Three examples:

- *Drug cravings*. Classical conditioning may inform treatments for substance use disorder. People who formerly abused drugs often feel a craving when they are again in the drug-using context, because their brain has become conditioned to associate that context with a drug's reward (Wilar et al., 2019). Breaking this association can reduce cravings (Ananth et al., 2019; Martínez-Rivera et al., 2019). Many drug counselors advise clients to steer clear of the people and settings associated with previous highs (NIDA, 2017; Siegel, 2005).

- *Food cravings*. Classical conditioning makes avoiding sweets difficult. Sugary substances evoke sweet sensations. Researchers have conditioned healthy volunteers to experience cravings after only one instance of eating a sweet food (Blechert et al., 2016). So, the next time you think, "I can definitely eat just one cookie," you might be wise to think twice.

- *Immune responses*. Classical conditioning even works on the body's disease-fighting immune system. When a particular taste accompanies a drug that influences immune responses, the taste by itself may come to produce an immune response (Ader & Cohen, 1985).

Pavlov's work also provided a basis for Watson's (1913) idea that human emotions and behaviors, though biologically influenced, are mainly a bundle of conditioned responses. Watson and his graduate student Rosalie Rayner (1920; Harris, 1979) studied an 11-month-old infant to show how specific fears might be conditioned. Like most infants, "Little Albert" feared loud noises but not white rats. Watson and Rayner presented a white rat and, as Little Albert reached to touch it, struck a hammer against a steel bar just behind his head. After seven repeats of seeing the rat and hearing the frightening noise, Albert burst into tears at the mere sight of the rat. Five days later, he reportedly generalized this startled fear reaction to the sight of a rabbit, a dog, and even a furry coat. A modern reanalysis questioned Watson's evidence for Albert's conditioning, but the case remains legendary (Powell & Schmaltz, 2020).

For years, people wondered what became of Little Albert. Sleuthing by Russell Powell and his colleagues (2014) found a well-matched child of one of the hospital's wet nurses. The child, William Albert Barger, went by Albert B.—precisely the name used by Watson and Rayner. This Albert was an easygoing person, though, perhaps coincidentally, he had an aversion to dogs. He died in 2007 without ever knowing of his role in psychology's history.

People also wondered what became of Watson. After losing his Johns Hopkins professorship over an affair with Rayner (whom he later married), he joined an advertising agency as the company's resident psychologist. There, he used his knowledge of associative learning to conceive many successful advertising campaigns, including one for Maxwell House that helped make the "coffee break" an American custom (Hunt, 1993).

**Little Albert** In Watson and Rayner's experiments, "Little Albert" learned to fear a white rat after repeatedly experiencing a loud noise as the rat was presented. In these experiments, what was the UCS? The UCR? The NS? The CS? The CR?[5]

*Archives of the History of American Psychology, The Center for the History of Psychology, The University of Akron*

[5]*Answer:* The UCS was the loud noise; the UCR was the fear response to the noise; the NS was the rat before it was paired with the noise; the CS was the rat after pairing; and the CR was fear of the rat.

Some psychologists had difficulty repeating Watson and Rayner's findings with other children. (These studies would also be unethical by today's standards, making replication attempts difficult.) Nevertheless, Little Albert's learned fears led many psychologists to wonder whether each of us might be a walking warehouse of conditioned emotions. If so, might extinction procedures or new conditioning help us change our unwanted responses to emotion-arousing stimuli? Psychologist Mary Cover Jones (1924) was the first to extend Watson and Rayner's results by showing how conditioning can also reduce children's fear.

Therapists began using conditioning to reduce their clients' fears. One person used his therapist's conditioning strategy to treat a longtime fear of entering an elevator alone. For 10 days, the client entered 20 elevators a day. By the end of the treatment, the client's fear of elevators had nearly vanished (Ellis & Becker, 1982). Comedian-writer Mark Malkoff extinguished his fear of flying by taking 135 flights in 30 days, spending 14 hours a day in the air (NPR, 2009). After a week and a half, his fears had faded, and he began playing games with fellow passengers. His favorite was the "toilet paper experiment": Put one end of a roll in the toilet, unroll the rest down the aisle, and flush, sucking down the whole roll in three seconds! In Module 5.5, we will see more examples of how psychologists use behavioral techniques such as *counterconditioning* to treat psychological disorders and promote personal growth.

# Biological Constraints on Classical Conditioning

**3.7-7** How do biological constraints affect classical conditioning?

Ever since Charles Darwin, scientists have assumed that all animals share a common evolutionary history and, therefore, share commonalities in their makeup and functioning. Pavlov, Watson, and later B. F. Skinner (see Module 3.8) believed the basic laws of learning were essentially similar in all animals. So it should make little difference whether one studied pigeons or people. Moreover, it seemed that any natural response could be conditioned to any neutral stimulus.

In 1956, learning researcher Gregory Kimble proclaimed, "Just about any activity of which the organism is capable can be conditioned and . . . these responses can be conditioned to any stimulus that the organism can perceive" (p. 195). Twenty-five years later, he humbly acknowledged that "half a thousand" scientific reports had proven him wrong (Kimble, 1981). More than the early behaviorists realized, an animal's capacity for conditioning is limited by biological constraints. For example, each species' predispositions *prepare* it to learn the associations that enhance its survival—a phenomenon called **preparedness**. Environments are not the whole story. Biology matters.

John Garcia (1917–2012) was among those who challenged the prevailing idea that all associations can be learned equally well. While researching the effects of radiation on laboratory animals, Garcia and Robert Koelling (1966) noticed that rats began to avoid drinking water from the plastic bottles in radiation chambers. Could classical conditioning be the culprit? Might the rats have linked the plastic-tasting

**preparedness** a biological predisposition to learn associations, such as between taste and nausea, that have survival value.

John Garcia  As the laboring son of California farmworkers, Garcia attended school only in the off-season during his early childhood years. After entering junior college in his late twenties, and earning his Ph.D. in his late forties, he received the American Psychological Association's Distinguished Scientific Contribution Award "for his highly original, pioneering research in conditioning and learning." He was also elected to the National Academy of Sciences.

**One-trial conditioning: taste aversion** Our biology prepares us to readily learn taste aversions to toxic foods.

water (a CS) to the sickness (UCR) triggered by the radiation (UCS)?

To test their hunch, Garcia and Koelling exposed the rats to a particular taste, sight, or sound (CS) and later also to radiation or drugs (UCS) that led to nausea (UCR). Two startling findings emerged: First, even if sickened as late as several hours after tasting a particular novel flavor, the rats thereafter avoided that flavor. This appeared to violate the notion that for conditioning to occur, the UCS must immediately follow the CS.

Second, the sickened rats developed aversions to tastes but not to sights or sounds. This contradicted the behaviorists' idea that any perceivable stimulus could serve as a CS. But it made adaptive sense. For rats, the easiest way to identify tainted food is to taste it; if sickened after sampling new food, they later avoid it. This *taste aversion response*, which can occur with just one bad experience, makes it difficult to eradicate a population of "bait-shy" rats by poisoning.

Humans, too, seem biologically prepared to learn certain associations. If you become violently ill four hours after eating contaminated oysters, you will probably develop an aversion to the taste of oysters more readily than to the sight of the restaurant or the music you listened to while eating. You may also experience *one-trial conditioning:* The single pairing of stimulus (oysters) and response (illness) will be enough to create an association, and your new aversion won't be strengthened by further pairings.

Garcia and Koelling's taste-aversion research is but one instance in which psychological studies that began with the discomfort of some laboratory animals ended by enhancing many others' welfare. In one conditioned taste-aversion study, coyotes and wolves were tempted into eating sheep carcasses laced with a sickening poison. Thereafter, they developed an aversion to sheep meat; two wolves later penned with a live sheep seemed actually to fear it (Gustavson et al., 1974, 1976). These studies not only saved the sheep from their predators, but also saved the sheep-shunning coyotes and wolves from angry ranchers and farmers who had wanted to destroy them. Similar applications have prevented baboons from raiding African gardens, raccoons from attacking chickens, and ravens and crows from feeding on crane eggs. In all these cases, research helped preserve both the prey and their predators, all of which occupy important ecological niches (Dingfelder, 2010; Garcia & Gustavson, 1997).

Such research supports Darwin's principle that natural selection favors traits that aid survival. Our ancestors learned to avoid foods and situations that made them sick, which helped them survive and leave descendants (Bernal-Gamboa et al., 2018). Nausea, like anxiety, pain, and other bad feelings, serves a good purpose. Like a car's low-fuel warning light, each alerts the body to a threat (Davidson & Riley, 2015; Neese, 1991).

Our preparedness to associate a CS with a UCS that follows predictably and immediately is adaptive. "Once bitten, twice shy," says a proverb.

Causes often do immediately precede effects. But as we saw in the taste-aversion findings, our predisposition to associate an effect with a preceding event can trick us. When chemotherapy triggers nausea and vomiting more than an hour following treatment, cancer patients may, over time, develop classically conditioned nausea (and sometimes anxiety) to

**AP® Science Practice**

## Research

As illustrated by Garcia's work, replication is an important part of the scientific process. It is through replication that researchers can build consensus about the validity and reliability of their conclusions.

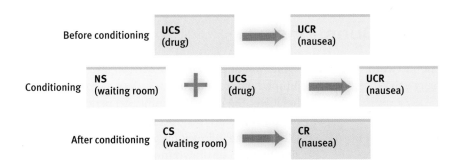

Figure 3.7-9
**Nausea conditioning in cancer patients**

the sights, sounds, and smells associated with the clinic (Hall, 1997) (**Figure 3.7-9**). Merely returning to the clinic's waiting room or seeing the nurses can provoke these conditioned feelings (Burish & Carey, 1986; Davey, 1992). Under normal circumstances, such revulsion to sickening stimuli would be adaptive.

* * *

It's one thing to classically condition a dog to salivate to the sound of a tone, or a child to fear moving cars. But to teach an elephant to walk on its hind legs or a child to say *please*, we turn to operant conditioning—the topic of the next module.

---

**AP® Science Practice**

## Check Your Understanding

### Examine the Concept

▶ Explain how therapists might use conditioning to reduce their clients' fears.

▶ Explain what is meant by *biological preparedness*. Give an example to illustrate the concept.

*Answers to the Examine the Concept questions can be found in Appendix C at the end of the book.*

### Apply the Concept

▶ Which foods or beverages have you eventually grown to like — or dislike — since you were a child? Has falling ill after enjoying a food ever changed a one-time like to a definite dislike?

---

# Module 3.7b REVIEW

**3.7-6** What have been some applications of Pavlov's work to human health and well-being? How did Watson apply Pavlov's principles to learned fears?

- Classical conditioning techniques are used to improve human health and well-being in many areas, including behavioral therapy for some types of psychological disorders.

- The body's immune system may also respond to classical conditioning.

- Pavlov's work provided a basis for Watson's idea that human emotions and behaviors, though biologically influenced, are mainly a bundle of conditioned responses. Watson applied classical conditioning principles in his studies of "Little Albert" to demonstrate how specific fears might be conditioned.

**3.7-7** How do biological constraints affect classical conditioning?

- An animal's capacity for conditioning is limited by biological constraints, so some associations are easier to learn.

- Each species has a biological predisposition to learn associations that aid its survival—a phenomenon called *preparedness*. Those who readily learned taste aversions were unlikely to eat the same toxic food again and were more likely to survive and leave descendants.

# AP® Practice Multiple Choice Questions

1. Dr. Cao studies the biological predisposition to learn associations that will increase a species' survival. What does Dr. Cao study?

   a. Taste aversion
   b. Preparedness
   c. Conditioning
   d. Counterconditioning

2. Which of the following is an example of taste aversion?

   a. Mick does not like avocados because he dislikes their texture.
   b. Tran avoids eating dessert after 9:00 P.M. to avoid staying up too late.
   c. Esther vomited after eating hamburgers and thereafter avoided eating them.
   d. Blythe has never liked chocolate since she was a young child.

3. While walking home from school, Yaya's best friend, Ari, jumped out from behind a wall of a grocery store, scaring her. Over the next six months, Ari periodically jumped out from behind the grocery store wall to scare Yaya. Which of the following is a logical and objective conclusion that can be drawn from this example?

   a. Yaya will begin to crave the food at the grocery store.
   b. Yaya will develop a taste aversion to the food at the grocery store.
   c. Yaya will begin to fear the grocery store.
   d. Yaya will develop preparedness toward the grocery store.

4. Due to a traumatic brain injury, Leslie cannot taste or smell the food she eats. She becomes sick after eating string cheese and later notices that she feels nauseous when seeing pictures of string cheese. Which of the following best explains Leslie's experience?

   a. Leslie has developed a conditioned emotional reaction to the presence of string cheese due to her negative experiences.
   b. Leslie has developed an aversion to the sight of string cheese, since she cannot rely on the way food tastes to develop an aversion to tainted food.
   c. Leslie has developed taste aversion to string cheese because it is the easiest way to determine which foods might make her sick.
   d. Leslie has learned to associate fear with string cheese based on getting sick after eating it.

# Module 3.8a Operant Conditioning: Basic Concepts

## LEARNING TARGETS

**3.8-1** Explain *operant conditioning*.

**3.8-2** Identify Skinner, and explain how operant behavior is reinforced and shaped.

**3.8-3** Explain the difference between positive reinforcement and negative reinforcement, and explain the basic types of reinforcers.

**3.8-4** Explain how different reinforcement schedules affect behavior.

**3.8-5** Explain the difference between punishment and negative reinforcement, and explain how punishment affects behavior.

**3.8-6** Explain why Skinner's ideas provoked controversy.

---

**3.8-1** What is *operant conditioning*?

Classical conditioning and operant conditioning are both forms of associative learning. But their differences are straightforward:

- *Classical conditioning* (see Module 3.7) forms associations between stimuli (a CS and the UCS it signals). It also involves *respondent behavior*—automatic responses to a stimulus (such as salivating in response to meat powder, and later in response to a tone).

- In **operant conditioning**, organisms associate their own actions with consequences. Actions followed by reinforcers increase; those followed by punishers often decrease. Behavior that *operates* on the environment to *produce* rewarding or punishing stimuli is called *operant behavior*.

## Skinner's Experiments

**SPOTLIGHT ON:**
B. F. Skinner

**3.8-2** Who was Skinner, and how is operant behavior reinforced and shaped?

B. F. Skinner (1904–1990), initially a college English major and aspiring writer, went on to become modern behaviorism's most influential and controversial figure. Skinner's work elaborated on what psychologist Edward L. Thorndike (1874–1949) called the **law of effect**: Rewarded behavior tends to recur (**Figure 3.8-1**). Using Thorndike's law of effect as a starting point, Skinner developed a behavioral technology that revealed principles of *behavior control*. Working from a rooftop office in a Minneapolis flour mill in 1943, Skinner and his students looked at the flocks of pigeons sitting on the windowsills and jokingly wondered, "Could we teach a pigeon how to bowl?" (Goddard, 2018; Skinner, 1960). By shaping pigeons' natural walking and pecking behaviors, they did just that (Peterson, 2004). Skinner later used his new learning principles to teach pigeons other unpigeon-like behaviors, including how to walk in a figure 8, play table tennis, and keep a missile on course by pecking at a screen target.

**operant conditioning** a type of learning in which a behavior becomes more likely to recur if followed by a reinforcer or less likely to recur if followed by a punisher.

**law of effect** Thorndike's principle that behaviors followed by favorable (or *reinforcing*) consequences become more likely, and that behaviors followed by unfavorable (or *punishing*) consequences become less likely.

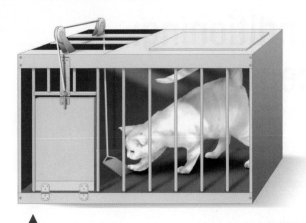

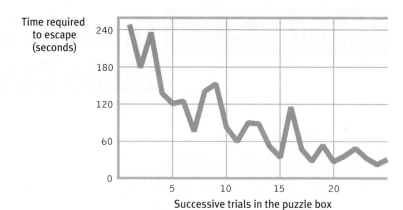

Time required to escape (seconds)

Successive trials in the puzzle box

**Figure 3.8-1**

**Cat in a puzzle box**

Thorndike used a fish reward to entice cats to find their way out of a puzzle box through a series of maneuvers. The cats' performance tended to improve with successive trials, illustrating Thorndike's *law of effect.* (Data from Thorndike, 1898.)

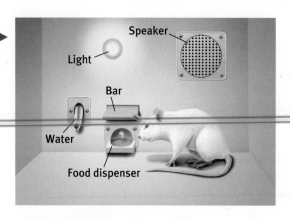

**Figure 3.8-2**

**A Skinner box**

Inside the box, the rat presses a bar for a food reward. Outside, measuring devices (not shown here) record the animal's accumulated responses.

Speaker

Light

Bar

Water

Food dispenser

For his pioneering studies, Skinner designed an **operant chamber**, popularly known as a *Skinner box* (**Figure 3.8-2**). The box has a bar (a lever) that an animal presses—or a key (a disk) the animal pecks—to release a reward of food or water. It also has a device that records these responses. This creates a stage on which rats and other animals act out Skinner's concept of **reinforcement**, defined as any event that strengthens (increases the frequency of) a preceding response. What is reinforcing depends on the animal and the conditions. For people, it may be praise, attention, or a paycheck. For hungry and thirsty rats, food and water work well. Skinner's experiments have done far more than teach us how to pull habits out of a rat—they have explored the precise conditions that foster efficient and enduring learning.

## Shaping Behavior

Imagine that you wanted to condition a hungry rat to press a bar. Like Skinner, you could tease out this action with **shaping**, gradually guiding the rat's actions toward the desired behavior. First, you would observe the animal's natural behavior so that you could build on its existing behaviors. You might give the rat a bit of food each time it approaches the bar. Once the rat is approaching regularly, you would give the food only when it moves close to the bar, then closer still. Finally, you would require it to touch the bar to get food. By rewarding *successive approximations*, you reinforce responses that are ever closer to the final desired behavior. By making rewards contingent on desired behaviors, researchers and animal trainers gradually shape complex behaviors. In one study, 11 cows were potty trained with a treat that reinforced their entering and urinating in a stall that collected their urine (Dirksen et al., 2021). If widely implemented, "MooLoo training" could cut ammonia emissions and capture nitrogen and phosphorus for fertilizer.

We can also shape our own behavior. Suppose you want to train for your first 5K race. You set up a daily plan with a mixture of walking and running. At each stage, you give yourself a

**operant chamber** in operant conditioning research, a chamber (also known as a *Skinner box*) containing a bar or key that an animal can manipulate to obtain a food or water reinforcer; attached devices record the animal's rate of bar pressing or key pecking.

**reinforcement** in operant conditioning, any event that *strengthens* the behavior it follows.

**shaping** an operant conditioning procedure in which reinforcers guide behavior toward closer and closer approximations of the desired behavior.

nice reward—perhaps first for a 15-minute walk, then for walking and running that distance, then for running it, then for running a bit more each week—rewarding successive approximations of your target behavior.

Shaping can also help us understand what nonverbal organisms can perceive. Can a dog distinguish between red and green? Can a baby hear the difference between lower- and higher-pitched tones? If we can shape them to respond to one stimulus and not to another, then we know they can perceive the difference. Such experiments have even shown that some nonhuman animals can form concepts. When experimenters reinforced pigeons for pecking after seeing a human face, but not after seeing other images, the pigeons' behavior showed that they could recognize human faces (Herrnstein & Loveland, 1964). In this experiment, the human face was a **discriminative stimulus**. Like a green traffic light, discriminative stimuli signal that a response will be reinforced. After being trained to discriminate among classes of events or objects—flowers, people, cars, chairs—pigeons can usually identify the category in which a new pictured object belongs (Bhatt et al., 1988; Wasserman, 1993). They have even been trained to discriminate between the music of Bach and Stravinsky (Porter & Neuringer, 1984).

Will Burgess/Reuters/Newscom

**Reinforcers vary with circumstances** What is reinforcing (a heat lamp) to one animal (a cold meerkat) may not be to another (an overheated bear). What is reinforcing in one situation (a cold snap at the Taronga Zoo in Sydney) may not be in another (a sweltering summer day). Reinforcers also vary among humans. A chocolate treat that is reinforcing to Clarice might not be to Clarence, who prefers vanilla.

Levenson RM, Krupinski EA, Navarro VM, Wasserman EA (2015) Pigeons (Columba livia) as Trainable Observers of Pathology and Radiology Breast Cancer Images. PLoS ONE 10(11): e0141357.

**Bird brains spot tumors** After being rewarded with food when correctly spotting breast tumors, pigeons became as skilled as humans at discriminating cancerous from healthy tissue (Levenson et al., 2015). Other animals have been shaped to sniff out explosives and drugs, or to locate people amid rubble (La Londe et al., 2015).

Skinner noted that we continually reinforce and shape others' everyday behaviors, though we may not mean to do so. Erlinda's nagging annoys her mother, for example, but consider how Mom typically responds:

ERLINDA: *Could you take me to the store?*

MOM: *(Continues checking her phone.)*

ERLINDA: *Mom, I need to go to the store.*

MOM: *Uh, yeah, in a few minutes.*

ERLINDA: *MOM! The store!*

MOM: *Show some manners! Okay, where are my keys . . .*

Erlinda's nagging is reinforced, because she gets something desirable—a drive to the store. Her mother's response is also reinforced, because it gets rid of something aversive—Erlinda's nagging.

Or consider a teacher who sticks gold stars on a wall chart beside the names of children scoring 100 percent on spelling tests. As everyone can then see, some children consistently do perfect work. The others, who may have worked harder than the academic all-stars, get no rewards. The teacher would be better advised to apply the principles of operant conditioning—to reinforce all spellers for gradual improvements (successive approximations toward perfect spelling of words they find challenging).

**discriminative stimulus** in operant conditioning, a stimulus that elicits a response after association with reinforcement (in contrast to related stimuli not associated with reinforcement).

**Examine the Concept**

▶ With classical conditioning, we learn associations between events we _____ (do/do not) control. With operant conditioning, we learn associations between our behavior and _____ (resulting/random) events.

▶ Explain the process of shaping.

*Answers to the Examine the Concept questions can be found in Appendix C at the end of the book.*

**Apply the Concept**

▶ Can you recall a time when a teacher, coach, family member, or employer helped you learn something by shaping your behavior in little steps until you achieved your goal?

## Types of Reinforcers

**3.8-3** How do positive and negative reinforcement differ, and what are the basic types of reinforcers?

Until now, we've mainly been discussing **positive reinforcement**, which strengthens responding by *presenting* a typically *pleasurable* stimulus immediately after a response. But, as the nagging Erlinda story illustrates, there are two basic kinds of reinforcement (Table 3.8-1). **Negative reinforcement** strengthens a response by *reducing or removing* something *negative*. Erlinda's nagging was *positively* reinforced, because Erlinda got something desirable—a ride to the store. Her mother's response (doing what Erlinda wanted) was *negatively* reinforced, because it ended an aversive event—Erlinda's nagging. Similarly, taking aspirin may relieve your headache, giving your dog a treat may silence its barking, and hitting the snooze button will silence your irritating alarm. These welcome results provide negative reinforcement and increase the odds that you will repeat these behaviors. For people with a drug addiction, the negative reinforcement of ending withdrawal pangs can be a compelling reason to resume using the drug (Baker et al., 2004). Note that *negative reinforcement is not punishment.* (Some friendly advice: Repeat the italicized words in your mind.) Rather, negative reinforcement—psychology's most misunderstood concept—*removes* a punishing (aversive) event. Think of negative reinforcement as something that provides relief—from that bad headache, yapping dog, or annoying alarm clock.

Sometimes negative and positive reinforcement coincide. Imagine a worried student who, after goofing off and getting a bad test grade, studies harder for the next test. This increased effort may be *negatively* reinforced by reduced anxiety, and *positively* reinforced by a better grade. We reap the rewards of escaping the aversive stimulus, which increases the chances that we will repeat our behavior. *The point to remember*: Whether it works by reducing something aversive or by providing something desirable, *reinforcement is any consequence that strengthens behavior.*

### AP® Exam Tip

Prepare to identify specific examples of positive and negative reinforcements. Pay particular attention to Table 3.8-1 for guidance.

**positive reinforcement** increasing behaviors by presenting a pleasurable stimulus. A positive reinforcer is any stimulus that, when *presented* after a response, strengthens the response.

**negative reinforcement** increasing behaviors by stopping or reducing an aversive stimulus. A negative reinforcer is any stimulus that, when *removed* after a response, strengthens the response. (*Note:* Negative reinforcement is not punishment.)

**TABLE 3.8-1 Ways to Increase Behavior**

| Operant Conditioning Term | Description | Examples |
|---|---|---|
| *Positive reinforcement* | Add a desirable stimulus | Pet a dog that comes when you call it; pay someone for work done. |
| *Negative reinforcement* | Remove an aversive stimulus | Take painkillers to end pain; fasten seatbelt to end loud beeping. |

How is operant conditioning at work in this cartoon?[6]

## Primary and Conditioned Reinforcers

Getting food when you're hungry or having a painful headache go away is innately satisfying. These **primary reinforcers** are unlearned. **Conditioned reinforcers**, also called *secondary reinforcers*, get their power through learned association with primary reinforcers. If a rat in a Skinner box learns that a light reliably signals a food delivery, the rat will work to turn on the light (see Figure 3.8-2). The light has become a conditioned reinforcer. Our lives are filled with conditioned reinforcers—money, good grades, approving words, social media "likes" (Rosenthal-von der Pütten et al., 2019).

## Immediate and Delayed Reinforcers

Let's return to the imaginary shaping experiment in which you were conditioning a rat to press a bar. In addition to performing this "wanted" behavior, the hungry rat will engage in other "unwanted" behaviors—scratching, sniffing, and moving around. If you present food immediately after any one of these behaviors, the rat will likely repeat that rewarded behavior. But what if the rat presses the bar while you are distracted, and you delay giving the reinforcer? If the delay lasts longer than about 30 seconds, the rat will not learn to press the bar (Austen & Sanderson, 2019; Cunningham & Shahan, 2019). Delays also decrease human learning. Students learn class material better when they complete frequent quizzes that provide them with immediate feedback (Healy et al., 2017). Immediate feedback produces immediate learning.

But unlike rats, humans *can* respond to delayed reinforcers: the paycheck for completed work, the good grade at the term's end, the trophy at the sport season's end. Indeed, to function effectively, we must learn how to master the difficult task of delaying gratification. In one of psychology's most famous studies, some 4-year-olds showed this ability. When choosing a piece of candy or a marshmallow, these impulse-controlled children preferred having a big one tomorrow to munching on a small one right away. The children who delayed gratification tended to become socially competent and high-achieving adults (Mischel, 2014). Later studies showed a similar (though weaker) relationship between delay of gratification and later achievement (Watts et al., 2018). Learning to control our impulses to earn more valued future rewards reduces our later likelihood of committing impulsive crimes (Åkerlund et al., 2016; Logue, 1998a, 1998b). *The bottom line*: It pays to delay.

To our detriment, small but immediate pleasures (late-night binge-watching) are sometimes more alluring than big but delayed rewards (feeling rested for a big test tomorrow). For many teens, the immediate gratification of risky, unprotected sex in passionate moments prevails over the delayed gratifications of safe or saved sex. And for many people, the immediate rewards of today's gas-guzzling vehicles and air conditioning prevail over the bigger future consequences of the global climate crisis, including rising seas and more extreme weather.

### Research

The marshmallow study is a good example of the correlational method. Researchers only collected data on the variables, such as impulse control and social competence. The researchers did not manipulate the variables.

**primary reinforcer** an innately reinforcing stimulus, such as one that satisfies a biological need.

**conditioned reinforcer** a stimulus that gains its reinforcing power through its association with a primary reinforcer. (Also known as a *secondary reinforcer*.)

[6]*Answer:* The baby negatively reinforces her parents' behavior when she stops crying once they grant her wish. Her parents positively reinforce her cries by letting her sleep with them.

# Reinforcement Schedules

In most of our examples, the desired response has been reinforced every time it occurs. But **reinforcement schedules** can vary. With a **continuous reinforcement schedule**, learning occurs rapidly, which makes it the best choice for mastering a behavior. But extinction also occurs rapidly. When the reinforcement stops—when we stop delivering food after the rat presses the bar—the behavior soon stops (is *extinguished*). If a normally dependable vending machine fails to deliver a chocolate bar twice in a row, we stop putting money into it (although a week later we may exhibit *spontaneous recovery* by trying again).

The New Yorker Collection, 1993, Tom Cheney/
The Cartoon Bank.

*"Oh, not bad. The light comes on, I press the bar, they write me a check. How about you?"*

Real life rarely provides continuous reinforcement. Salespeople do not make a sale with every pitch. But they persist because their efforts are occasionally rewarded. This persistence is typical with **partial (intermittent) reinforcement schedules**, in which responses are sometimes reinforced, sometimes not. Learning is slower to appear, but *resistance to extinction* is greater than with continuous reinforcement. Imagine a pigeon that has learned to peck a key to obtain food. If you gradually phase out the food delivery until it occurs only rarely, in no predictable pattern, the pigeon may peck 150,000 times without a reward (Skinner, 1953). Slot machines reward gamblers in much the same way—occasionally and unpredictably. And like pigeons, slot players keep trying, time and time again. With intermittent reinforcement, hope springs eternal.

Sometimes, the accidental timing of rewards can produce *superstitious behaviors*. If a Skinner box food dispenser gives a pellet of food unpredictably, whatever the animal happened to be doing just before the food arrives (perhaps scratching itself) is more likely to be repeated and reinforced, which occasionally can produce a persistent superstitious behavior. A gambler may wear the same "lucky" bracelet again after a big win. And a baseball or softball player who gets a hit after tapping the plate with the bat may be more likely to do so again. Over time, we may experience partial reinforcement for what becomes a superstitious behavior.

*Lesson for parents and babysitters*: Whether intended or not, partial reinforcement also affects children. *Occasionally* giving in to children's tantrums for the sake of peace and quiet intermittently reinforces the tantrums. This is the very best procedure for making a behavior persist!

Skinner (1961) and his collaborators compared four schedules of partial reinforcement and their effects on behavior: fixed ratio, variable ratio, fixed interval, and variable interval.

**Fixed-ratio schedules** reinforce behavior after a set number of responses. Coffee shops may reward us with a free coffee after every 10 purchased. Once conditioned, rats may be reinforced on a fixed ratio of, say, one food pellet for every 30 responses. Once conditioned, animals will pause only briefly after a reinforcer before returning to a high rate of responding.

**Variable-ratio schedules** provide reinforcers after a seemingly unpredictable number of responses. This unpredictable reinforcement is what slot-machine players and anglers experience, and it's what makes gambling and fishing so hard to extinguish even when they don't produce the desired results. Because reinforcers increase as the number of responses increases, variable-ratio schedules produce high rates of responding.

**reinforcement schedule** a pattern that defines how often a desired response will be reinforced.

**continuous reinforcement schedule** reinforcing the desired response every time it occurs.

**partial (intermittent) reinforcement schedule** reinforcing a response only part of the time; results in slower acquisition of a response but much greater resistance to extinction than does continuous reinforcement.

**fixed-ratio schedule** in operant conditioning, a reinforcement schedule that reinforces a response only after a specified number of responses.

**variable-ratio schedule** in operant conditioning, a reinforcement schedule that reinforces a response after an unpredictable number of responses.

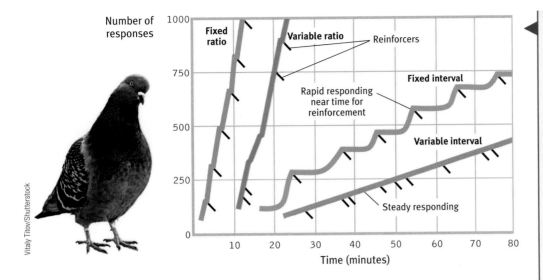

**Figure 3.8-3**
**Intermittent reinforcement schedules**

Skinner's (1961) laboratory pigeons produced these response patterns to each of four reinforcement schedules. (Reinforcers are indicated by diagonal marks.) For people, as for pigeons, reinforcement linked to number of responses (a *ratio schedule*) produces a higher response rate than reinforcement linked to amount of time elapsed (an *interval schedule*). But the predictability of the reward also matters. An unpredictable (*variable*) schedule produces more consistent responding than does a predictable (*fixed*) schedule. (Data from Skinner, 1961.)

**Fixed-interval schedules** reinforce a response after a fixed time period. Animals on this type of schedule tend to respond more frequently as the anticipated time for reward draws near. People check more frequently for the mail as delivery time approaches. Pigeons peck keys more rapidly as the time for reinforcement draws closer. This produces a scalloped pattern rather than a steady rate of response (**Figure 3.8-3**).

**Variable-interval schedules** reinforce the first response after *varying* time intervals. At unpredictable times, a food pellet rewarded Skinner's pigeons for persistence in pecking a key. Like the longed-for message that finally rewards persistence in checking our phone, variable-interval schedules tend to produce slow, steady responding. This makes sense, because there is no way to know when the waiting will be over (**Table 3.8-2**). Pigeons keep pecking—and we keep checking—hoping that *this time* we'll get the reward.

In general, response rates are higher when reinforcement is linked to the number of responses (a ratio schedule) rather than to time (an interval schedule). But responding is more consistent when reinforcement is unpredictable (a variable schedule) than when it is predictable (a fixed schedule). (See Figure 3.8-3.) Animal behaviors differ, yet Skinner (1956) contended that the reinforcement principles of operant conditioning are universal. It matters little, he said, which response, which reinforcer, or which species is considered. The effect of a given reinforcement schedule is pretty much the same: "Pigeon, rat, monkey, which is which? It doesn't matter. . . . Behavior shows astonishingly similar properties."

**AP® Exam Tip**

Sometimes the schedules of reinforcement can be confusing. The word *interval* in schedules of reinforcement means that an interval of time must pass before reinforcement. There is nothing the learner can do to shorten the interval. The word *ratio* refers to the ratio of responses to reinforcements. If the learner responds with greater frequency, there will be more reinforcements.

| TABLE 3.8-2 | Schedules of Partial Reinforcement | |
|---|---|---|
| | **Fixed** | **Variable** |
| Ratio | *Every so many*: reinforcement after every *n*th behavior, such as a "buy 10 coffees, get 1 free" offer, or paying workers per product unit produced | *After an unpredictable number*: reinforcement after a random number of behaviors, as when playing slot machines or fishing |
| Interval | *Every so often*: reinforcement for behavior after a fixed time, such as Tuesday discount prices | *Unpredictably often*: reinforcement for behavior after a random amount of time, as when checking our phone for a message |

**fixed-interval schedule**
in operant conditioning, a reinforcement schedule that reinforces a response only after a specified time has elapsed.

**variable-interval schedule**
in operant conditioning, a reinforcement schedule that reinforces a response at unpredictable time intervals.

# Check Your Understanding

**Examine the Concept**

▶ Explain the difference between primary and conditioned reinforcers.

**Apply the Concept**

▶ Compare and contrast positive and negative reinforcement.

▶ People who send spam email are reinforced by which type of schedule? Home bakers checking the oven to see if the cookies are done are reinforced by which type of schedule? Sandwich shops that offer a free sandwich after every 10 purchased are using which reinforcement schedule?

▶ In your everyday life, which type of reinforcement schedule do you respond to most strongly? Explain why.

*Answers to the Examine the Concept questions can be found in Appendix C at the end of the book.*

## Punishment

> **3.8-5** How does punishment differ from negative reinforcement, and how does punishment affect behavior?

Reinforcement increases a behavior; **punishment** does the opposite. A *punisher* is any consequence that *decreases* the frequency of a preceding behavior (see **Table 3.8-3** for examples of *positive* and *negative punishment*). Swift and sure punishers can powerfully restrain unwanted behavior. The rat that is shocked after touching a forbidden object (positive punishment) and the child who has their favorite doll taken away after they hit the dog with it (negative punishment) will learn not to repeat those behaviors.

Criminal behavior, much of it impulsive, is also influenced more by swift and sure punishment than by the threat of severe sentences (Darley & Alter, 2013). Thus, when Arizona introduced an exceptionally harsh sentence for first-time drunk drivers, the drunk-driving rate changed very little. But when Kansas City police started patrolling a high crime area to increase the swiftness and sureness of punishment, that city's crime rate dropped dramatically.

What do punishment studies imply for parenting? One analysis of more than 160,000 children found that physical punishment rarely corrects unwanted behavior (Gershoff & Grogan-Kaylor, 2016). With support from an American Psychological Association resolution on the ineffectiveness and potential harm of physical punishment, psychologists have noted its five major drawbacks (APA, 2019a; Finkenauer et al., 2015; Gershoff et al., 2018, 2019; Marshall, 2002):

1. ***Punished behavior is suppressed, not forgotten. This temporary state may (negatively) reinforce parents' punishing behavior.*** The child swears, the parent swats, the child stops swearing when the parent is nearby, so the parent believes the punishment successfully stopped the behavior. No wonder that spanking is a hit with so many parents—with more than 2 in 3 children in less developed countries being spanked or otherwise physically punished (UNICEF, 2020).

**AP® Exam Tip**

You should be able to explain the difference between reinforcement and punishment. Remember that *any kind of reinforcement* (positive, negative, primary, conditioned, immediate, delayed, continuous, or partial) encourages the behavior. *Any kind of punishment* discourages the behavior. Positive and negative do not refer to values — it's not that positive reinforcement (or punishment) is the good kind and negative is the bad. Think of positive and negative mathematically; a stimulus is added with positive reinforcement (or punishment) and a stimulus is subtracted with negative reinforcement (or punishment).

**punishment** an event that tends to *decrease* the behavior that it follows.

**TABLE 3.8-3 Ways to Decrease Behavior**

| Type of Punisher | Description | Examples |
|---|---|---|
| *Positive punishment* | Administer an aversive stimulus. | Spray water on a barking dog; give a traffic ticket for speeding. |
| *Negative punishment* | Withdraw a rewarding stimulus. | Take away a misbehaving teen's driving privileges; block a rude commenter on social media. |

2. ***Physical punishment does not replace the unwanted behavior.*** Physical punishment may reduce or even eliminate unwanted behavior, but it does not provide direction for appropriate behavior. A child who is slapped for screaming in the car may stop yelling but continue to throw her food or take her brother's toys.

3. ***Punishment teaches discrimination among situations.*** In operant conditioning, discrimination occurs when an organism learns that certain responses, but not others, will be reinforced. Did the punishment effectively end the child's swearing? Or did the child simply learn not to swear in front of their parents?

4. ***Punishment can teach fear.*** In operant conditioning, generalization occurs when responses learned in one situation occur in other, similar situations. A punished child may associate fear not only with the undesirable behavior, but also with the person who delivered the punishment or with the place it occurred. Thus, children may learn to fear a punishing teacher and try to avoid school, or may become anxious (Gershoff et al., 2010). For such reasons, most European countries and 31 U.S. states now ban hitting children in public schools (EndCorporalPunishment.org). As of 2022, 63 countries had outlawed all corporal punishment of children, including in the home. A large survey in Finland, the second country to pass such a law, revealed that children born after the law passed were, indeed, less often slapped and beaten (Österman et al., 2014).

5. ***Physical punishment may increase aggression by modeling violence as a way to cope with problems.*** Studies find that spanked children are at increased risk for aggression (MacKenzie et al., 2013). We know, for example, that many aggressive adults come from abusive families (Fitton et al., 2020).

Some researchers question this logic. Physically punished children may be more aggressive, they say, for the same reason that people who have undergone psychotherapy are more likely to suffer depression—because they had preexisting problems that triggered the treatments (Ferguson, 2013; Larzelere, 2000; Larzelere et al., 2019). So, does spanking cause misbehavior, or does misbehavior trigger spanking? Or do physically aggressive parents give their children aggression-disposing genes? Correlations don't hand us an answer.

How *should* parents and caregivers discipline children? Many psychologists encourage *time-out from positive reinforcement*: removing a misbehaving child from access to desired stimuli such as siblings' and parents' attention (Dadds & Tully, 2019). Effective time-outs come with clear expectations for replacing problem behavior (hitting siblings) with alternative positive behaviors (telling siblings they have hurt your feelings) (O'Leary et al., 1967; Patterson et al., 1968). Children learn that time-out helps the family enjoy positive and caring interactions.

Parents of delinquent youths are often unaware of how to achieve desirable behaviors without screaming, hitting, or threatening their children with punishment (Patterson et al., 1982). Training programs can help transform dire threats ("You clean up your room this minute or no dinner!") into positive incentives ("You're welcome at the dinner table after you get your room cleaned up"). Stop and think about it. Aren't many threats of punishment just as forceful, and perhaps more effective, when rephrased positively? Thus, "If you don't get your homework done, there'll be no allowance" could be phrased more positively as . . . .

In classrooms, too, teachers can give feedback by saying, "No, but try this . . ." and "Yes, that's it!" Such responses reduce unwanted behavior while reinforcing more desirable alternatives. Other studies show that people learn and grow more from feedback that tells them where they've succeeded rather than where they have failed (Eskreis-Winkler & Fishbach, 2019). A pat on the back outdoes a kick in the pants. *Remember*: Punishment tells you what not to do; reinforcement tells you what to do. Thus, punishment trains a particular sort of morality—one focused on prohibition (what *not* to do) rather than on positive obligations (Sheikh & Janoff-Bulman, 2013).

What punishment often teaches, said Skinner, is how to avoid it. Most psychologists now favor an emphasis on reinforcement: Focus on what people do right and praise them for it.

**AP® Science Practice**

## Research

Why don't correlations "hand us an answer"? Because correlation (a non-experimental method) does not equal causation. You can revisit Module 0.4 if you need to review this fundamental point.

# Check Your Understanding

# Skinner's Legacy

**3.8-6** Why did Skinner's ideas provoke controversy?

B. F. Skinner "I am sometimes asked, 'Do you think of yourself as you think of the organisms you study?' The answer is *Yes*. So far as I know, my behavior at any given moment has been nothing more than the product of my genetic endowment, my personal history, and the current setting" (1983).

Macmillan Learning

B. F. Skinner stirred a hornet's nest with his outspoken beliefs. He repeatedly insisted that external influences, not internal thoughts and feelings, shape behavior. He argued that brain science isn't needed for psychological science, saying that "a science of behavior is independent of neurology" (Skinner, 1938/1966, pp. 423–424). And he urged people to use operant conditioning principles to influence others' behavior at school, work, and home. Knowing that behavior is shaped by its results, he argued that we should use rewards to evoke more desirable behavior.

Skinner's critics objected, saying that he dehumanized people by neglecting their personal freedom and by seeking to control their actions. Skinner's reply: External consequences already haphazardly control people's behavior. Why not administer those consequences toward human betterment? Wouldn't reinforcers be more humane than the punishments used in homes, schools, and prisons? And if it is humbling to think that our history has shaped us, doesn't this very idea give us hope that we can apply operant conditioning to shape our future?

# Data Interpretation

Dr. Gonzales studies conditioning in rats using a Skinner box. Consider her data set, shown here.

| Number of Responses per Hour |
| --- |
| 20 |
| 20 |
| 50 |
| 100 |
| 150 |

- What is the mean for this data set? The median? The mode?

- Collectively, the mean, median, and mode are referred to as measures of _____ _____.

*Remember, you can always revisit Module 0.6 to review information related to data interpretation in psychological research.*

# Module 3.8a REVIEW

**3.8-1** What is *operant conditioning?*

- *Operant conditioning* is a type of learning in which a behavior becomes more likely to recur if followed by a reinforcer or less likely to recur if followed by a punisher.

**3.8-2** Who was Skinner, and how is operant behavior reinforced and shaped?

- B. F. Skinner was a college English major and aspiring writer who later entered graduate school for psychology. He became modern behaviorism's most influential and controversial figure.

- Expanding on Edward Thorndike's *law of effect*, Skinner and others found that the behavior of rats or pigeons placed in an *operant chamber* (Skinner box) can be *shaped* by using reinforcers to guide successive approximations of the desired behavior.

**3.8-3** How do positive and negative reinforcement differ, and what are the basic types of reinforcers?

- *Reinforcement* is any event that strengthens the behavior it follows. *Positive reinforcement* adds a desirable stimulus to increase the frequency of a behavior. *Negative reinforcement* reduces or removes an aversive stimulus to increase the frequency of a behavior.

- *Primary reinforcers* (such as receiving food when hungry or having nausea end during an illness) are innately satisfying—no learning is required. *Conditioned* (or secondary) *reinforcers* (such as money) are satisfying because we have learned to associate them with more basic rewards (such as the desirable things we buy).

- Immediate reinforcers (such as a food reward given immediately after a desired behavior) offer immediate payback; delayed reinforcers (such as a paycheck) require the ability to delay gratification.

**3.8-4** How do different reinforcement schedules affect behavior?

- A *reinforcement schedule* defines how often a response will be reinforced.

- In *continuous reinforcement* (reinforcing desired responses every time they occur), learning is rapid, but so is extinction if rewards cease. In *partial (intermittent) reinforcement* (reinforcing responses only sometimes), initial learning is slower, but the behavior is much more resistant to extinction.

- *Fixed-ratio schedules* reinforce behaviors after a set number of responses; *variable-ratio schedules*, after an unpredictable number.

- *Fixed-interval schedules* reinforce behaviors after set time periods; *variable-interval schedules*, after unpredictable time periods.

**3.8-5** How does punishment differ from negative reinforcement, and how does punishment affect behavior?

- *Punishment* administers an undesirable consequence (such as a time-out) or withdraws something desirable (such as taking away a favorite toy) to decrease the frequency of a behavior (a child's disobedience).

- Negative reinforcement (taking an aspirin) removes an aversive stimulus (a headache). This desired consequence (freedom from pain) increases the likelihood that the behavior (taking aspirin to end pain) will be repeated.

- Physical punishment rarely corrects unwanted behavior and has five major drawbacks: suppressing rather than changing unwanted behaviors; failing to provide a direction for appropriate behavior; encouraging discrimination (so that the undesirable behavior appears when the punisher is not present); creating fear; and teaching aggression.

**3.8-6** Why did Skinner's ideas provoke controversy?

- Critics of Skinner's principles believed the approach dehumanized people by neglecting their personal freedom and seeking to control their actions.

- Skinner replied that people's actions are already controlled by external consequences, and that reinforcement is more humane than punishment as a means for controlling behavior.

# AP® Practice Multiple Choice Questions

1. Colleen uses reinforcement with her kids to cause a behavior to
   a. stop.
   b. weaken.
   c. continue.
   d. occur for only a limited amount of time.

2. Which of the following scenarios best demonstrates negative reinforcement?
   a. Joachim stops fouling other players in basketball because his coach benches him when he does.
   b. Beatriz studies hard because it earns him "A" grades in math.
   c. Charles often does yoga, because he feels less anxious after doing yoga.
   d. Osel stopped walking by his neighbor's house because a dog growls at him each time he walks by.

3. Dr. Bumpers studies how behaviors followed by a favorable consequence become more likely to be repeated. Dr. Bumpers studies Thorndike's principle called
   a. the law of effect.
   b. operant conditioning.
   c. shaping.
   d. respondent behavior.

4. Which of the following is a conditioned reinforcer?
   a. Rats are rewarded with food in a Skinner box.
   b. Becca drinks cold water on a hot day.
   c. Xavier earns a high score on an exam after studying.
   d. Marco receives a big hug from his mother.

5. Rey's chore in her home is to feed the dog. Her mother wanted Rey to remember to feed the dog each day, so she tested some methods to try to ensure that Rey fed the dog every day. For 2 weeks, she gave Rey $1 each time Rey fed the dog (Method A). For another 2 weeks, she gave Rey $5 if she remembered to feed the dog at least once in the past week (Method B). Her mother tracked how each method affected Rey's dog-feeding behavior. Which schedule of reinforcement corresponds to Method B?
   a. Fixed-ratio schedule of reinforcement
   b. Fixed-interval schedule of reinforcement
   c. Variable-ratio schedule of reinforcement
   d. Variable-interval schedule of reinforcement

6. Looking at the graph shown here, which label should be applied to the bar that is black?

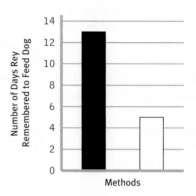

   a. Method A
   b. Method B
   c. Methods A and B
   d. No label is needed here.

7. Every time he prepares to putt a golf ball into the hole, Loxley looks up at the sky, because he has made winning putts after he first checked for rain clouds in the sky. Which of the following best explains Loxley's superstitious behavior?
   a. Loxley experienced a conditioned response (CR) before a conditioned stimulus (CS).
   b. Loxley gradually reduced the reward associated with putting.
   c. Loxley was accidentally reinforced for a response that is unrelated to golfing.
   d. Loxley failed to monitor how often he engaged in his desired behaviors.

**8.** Dad is frustrated because three-year-old Maya has started to throw her toys often. He takes away one of her toys every time she throws one, and eventually Maya stops throwing her toys. This is an example of

a. positive reinforcement.

b. negative reinforcement.

c. punishment.

d. shaping.

**9.** Lennox agrees with the law of effect. Which statement would she most likely say?

a. Punished behaviors tend to reoccur.

b. Rewarded behaviors tend to reoccur.

c. Positive reinforcement is more effective than negative reinforcement.

d. A fixed ratio schedule of reinforcement is more effective than a fixed interval schedule.

## Module 3.8b Operant Conditioning: Applications, Biological Limits, and Contrasts with Classical Conditioning

### LEARNING TARGETS

**3.8-7** Explain ways to apply operant conditioning principles in everyday life.

**3.8-8** Explain how biological constraints affect operant conditioning.

**3.8-9** Explain the characteristics that distinguish operant conditioning from classical conditioning.

## Applications of Operant Conditioning

**3.8-7** How might operant conditioning principles be applied in everyday life?

Would you like to apply operant conditioning principles to your own life—to be a healthier person, a more successful student, or a high-achieving athlete? Reinforcement techniques have been widely used in schools, sports, computer programs, workplaces, and homes, and these principles can support our self-improvement as well (Flora, 2004).

**At School** In 1953, while visiting his daughter's fourth-grade math class, Skinner observed that some students finished their work quickly and then squirmed awaiting the next task, while others squirmed as they struggled to comprehend (Watters, 2021). In response, Skinner envisioned a day when "machines and textbooks" would individualize learning and shape it in small steps, by immediately reinforcing correct responses. Such machines and texts, he thought, would revolutionize education and free teachers to focus on each student's unique needs. "Good instruction demands two things," said Skinner (1989). "Students must be told immediately whether what they do is right or wrong and, when right, they must be directed to the step to be taken next."

Skinner might be pleased to know that many of his ideals for education are now being implemented. Teachers used to find it difficult to pace material to each student's learning rate and provide prompt feedback. The personalized testing available with this text does both. Students move through quizzes at their own pace, according to their own level of understanding. And they get immediate feedback on their efforts, including personalized study plans.

**In Sports** The key to shaping behavior in athletic performance, as elsewhere, is first reinforcing small successes and then gradually increasing the challenge. Golf students can learn putting by starting with very short putts, and then, as they build mastery, stepping back farther and farther. Novice batters can begin with half swings at an oversized ball pitched from 10 feet away, giving them the immediate pleasure of smacking the ball. As the hitters' confidence builds with their success and they achieve mastery at each level, the pitcher gradually moves back and eventually introduces a standard baseball. Compared with children taught by conventional methods, those trained by this behavioral method have shown faster skill improvement (Simek & O'Brien, 1981, 1988).

**In Computer Programs** Using reinforcement principles, developers have created computer programs that mimic human learning. Such *artificial intelligence (AI)* programs perform actions—playing chess, poker, or the multiplayer videogame *Quake III*—faster than humans do, enabling the programs to quickly learn to repeat reinforced actions (what leads to winning) and avoid punished responses (what leads to losing) (Botvinick et al., 2019; Jaderberg et al., 2019). AI programs are teaching humans about the limits of human learning.

**At Work** How might managers successfully motivate their employees? People do respond to delayed positive and negative reinforcement, but it's better to make the reinforcement *immediate*. It's also better to reward *specific, achievable behaviors* rather than vaguely defined "merit." General Motors CEO Mary Barra understood this point. In 2015, she observed workers' high performance and awarded record bonuses (Vlasic, 2015). But rewards don't have to be monetary. An effective manager may simply walk the floor and sincerely praise people for good work.

**In Parenting** As we have seen, parents can learn from operant conditioning practices. Parent-training researchers remind us that by saying, "Get ready for bed" and then caving in to protests or defiance, parents reinforce such whining and arguing (Wierson & Forehand, 1994). Exasperated, they may then yell or gesture menacingly. When the child, now frightened, obeys, that response reinforces the parent's angry behavior. Over time, a destructive parent-child relationship develops.

To disrupt this cycle, parents should remember the basic rule of shaping: *Notice people doing something right and affirm them for it.* Give children attention and other reinforcers when they are behaving *well*. Parents who want teens to drive safely can reward them for safe driving (Hinnant et al., 2019). Target a specific behavior, reward it, and watch it increase. When children misbehave, don't yell at them or hit them. Simply explain the misbehavior and take away their screen time, remove a misused toy, or give a brief time-out.

Chuck Burton/AP Photo

**Immediate reinforcement** Muffet McGraw, the coach of Notre Dame's 2018 national championship women's basketball team, spent her career focusing on catching her players doing something right and applauding them for it on the spot.

**To Change Your Own Behavior**   Finally, we can use operant conditioning in our own lives. To reinforce your own desired behaviors (perhaps to improve your study habits) and extinguish the undesired ones (to stop texting while studying, for example), psychologists suggest taking these steps:

1. *State a realistic goal in measurable terms and announce it.* You might, for example, aim to boost your study time by an hour a day. To increase your commitment and odds of success, share that goal with friends.

2. *Decide how, when, and where you will work toward your goal.* Take time to plan. From North American undergraduates to Swedish entrepreneurs, those who specify how they will implement goals become more focused on those goals and more often fulfill them (Gollwitzer & Oettingen, 2012; van Gelderen et al., 2018).

3. *Monitor how often you engage in your desired behavior.* You might log your current study time, noting under which conditions you do and don't study. (When we began writing textbooks, we each logged our time and were amazed to discover how much time we were wasting.)

4. *Reinforce the desired behavior.* People's persistence toward long-term goals is powered mostly by immediate rewards (Woolley & Fishbach, 2017). So, to increase your study time, reward yourself (a snack or some activity you enjoy) only after you finish your extra hour of study. Agree to join your friends for weekend activities only if you have met your realistic weekly study goal. Apps can help you track and reinforce your progress toward desired goals, whether those goals are to exercise, get more sleep, or eat a healthy diet.

5. *Reduce the rewards gradually.* As your new behaviors become more habitual, give yourself a mental pat on the back instead of a cookie.

## Biological Constraints on Operant Conditioning

**3.8-8** How do biological constraints affect operant conditioning?

As is the case with classical conditioning (see Module 3.7), nature constrains each species' capacity for operant conditioning. Science fiction writer Robert Heinlein said it well: "Never try to teach a pig to sing; it wastes your time and annoys the pig."

We most easily learn and retain behaviors that reflect our biological and psychological predispositions (Iliescu et al., 2018). Thus, using food as a reinforcer, you could easily condition a hamster to dig or to rear up, because these are among the animal's natural food-searching behaviors. But you won't be so successful if you use food as a reinforcer to shape face washing and other hamster behaviors that aren't normally associated with food or hunger (Shettleworth, 1973). Similarly, you could easily teach pigeons to flap their wings to avoid being shocked, and to peck to obtain food: Fleeing with their wings and eating with their beaks are natural pigeon behaviors. However, pigeons would have a hard time learning to peck to avoid a shock, or to flap their wings to obtain food (Foree & LoLordo, 1973). The principle: *Biological constraints predispose organisms to learn associations that are naturally adaptive.*

In the early years of their work, animal trainers Marian Breland and Keller Breland presumed that operant principles would work on almost any response an animal could make. But they, too, learned about biological constraints. In one act, pigs trained to pick up large wooden "dollars" and deposit them in a piggy bank began to drift back to their natural ways. They dropped the coin, pushed it with their snout as pigs are prone to do, picked it up again, and then repeated the sequence—delaying their food reinforcer. This **instinctive drift** occurred as the animals reverted to their biologically predisposed patterns.

**AP® Science Practice**

**Research**

What would you need to do to make the claim that specifying how an individual will implement a goal *causes* that person to be more focused on that goal? That's right, you would need to perform an experiment! Design an experiment to test this claim. What are your independent and dependent variables? Recall from Module 0.4 that random assignment of conditions is required in experiments.

*"I wrote another five hundred words. Can I have another cookie?"*

Mick Stevens/Cartoon Stock

**Natural athletes** Animals can most easily learn and retain behaviors that draw on their biological predispositions, such as this horse's inborn ability to move around obstacles with speed and agility.

Jeffery Jones/The Gallup Independent/AP Photo

**instinctive drift** the tendency of learned behavior to gradually revert to biologically predisposed patterns.

# Contrasting Classical and Operant Conditioning

**AP® Exam Tip**

You will need to understand the difference between classical conditioning and operant conditioning for the AP® exam. Classical conditioning is involuntary (respondent) behavior, while operant conditioning is voluntary (operant) behavior.

**3.8-9** How does operant conditioning differ from classical conditioning?

Both classical and operant conditioning are forms of *associative learning*. Both involve *acquisition, extinction, spontaneous recovery, generalization,* and *discrimination*. But these two forms of learning also differ. Through classical (Pavlovian) conditioning, we associate different stimuli we do not control, and we respond automatically *(respondent behaviors)* (**Table 3.8-4**). Through operant conditioning, we associate our own behaviors—which act on our environment to produce rewarding or punishing stimuli *(operant behaviors)*—with their consequences.

| TABLE 3.8-4 **Comparison of Classical and Operant Conditioning** | | |
| --- | --- | --- |
| | **Classical Conditioning** | **Operant Conditioning** |
| *Basic idea* | Learning associations between events we do not control. | Learning associations between our behavior and its consequences. |
| *Response* | Involuntary, automatic. | Voluntary, operates on the environment. |
| *Acquisition* | Associating events; NS is paired with UCS and becomes CS. | Associating a response with a consequence (reinforcer or punisher). |
| *Extinction* | CR decreases when CS is repeatedly presented alone. | Responding decreases when reinforcement stops. |
| *Spontaneous recovery* | The reappearance, after a rest period, of a weakened CR. | The reappearance, after a rest period, of a weakened response. |
| *Generalization* | The tendency to respond to stimuli similar to the CS. | Responses learned in one situation occurring in other, similar situations. |
| *Discrimination* | Learning to distinguish between a CS and other stimuli that do not signal a UCS. | Learning that some responses, but not others, will be reinforced. |

---

**AP® Science Practice**

## Check Your Understanding

**Examine the Concept**

▶ Explain how artificial intelligence uses reinforcement principles to mimic human learning.

▶ Salivating in response to a tone paired with food is a(n) _____ (involuntary/voluntary) behavior; pressing a bar to obtain food is a(n) _____ (involuntary/voluntary) behavior.

**Apply the Concept**

▶ Joslyn constantly misbehaves at preschool even though her teacher scolds her repeatedly. Why does Joslyn's misbehavior continue, and what can her teacher do to stop it?

▶ Think of a personal bad habit you'd like to break. How could you use operant conditioning to break it?

*Answers to the Examine the Concept questions can be found in Appendix C at the end of the book.*

\* \* \*

In this module and Module 3.7, we've discussed classical and operant conditioning principles, and we've seen the limits that biology places on conditioning. In Module 3.9, we will explore other factors—social, cognitive, and neurological—that also influence our learning.

# Module 3.8b REVIEW

### 3.8-7 How might operant conditioning principles be applied in everyday life?

- Teachers can use shaping techniques to guide students' behaviors, and they can use interactive media to provide immediate feedback.
- Coaches can build players' skills and self-confidence by rewarding small improvements.
- Artificial intelligence (AI) programs developed using reinforcement principles are teaching us about the limits of human learning.
- Managers can boost productivity and morale by rewarding specific, achievable behaviors.
- Parents can reward desired behaviors but not undesirable ones.
- We can shape our own behaviors by stating realistic goals, planning how to work toward those goals, monitoring the frequency of desired behaviors, reinforcing desired behaviors, and gradually reducing rewards as behaviors become habitual.

### 3.8-8 How do biological constraints affect operant conditioning?

- We most easily learn and retain behaviors that reflect our biological and psychological predispositions.
- During operant training, animals may display *instinctive drift* by reverting to biologically predisposed patterns.

### 3.8-9 How does operant conditioning differ from classical conditioning?

- In operant conditioning, an organism learns associations between its own behavior and resulting events; this form of conditioning involves operant behavior (behavior that operates on the environment, producing rewarding or punishing consequences).
- In classical conditioning, the organism forms associations between stimuli—events it does not control; this form of conditioning involves respondent behavior (automatic responses to some stimulus).

## AP® Practice Multiple Choice Questions

1.  Kelbi has refused to eat dinner this entire week. Based on operant conditioning principles, which of the following is the best advice to give Kelbi's parents?

    a.  Do not allow Kelbi to watch television for a week for each day Kelbi does not eat dinner.
    b.  Allow Kelbi to watch her parents eat dinner each night.
    c.  Give Kelbi a small reward each day that she eats her dinner.
    d.  Allow Kelbi to have dessert, even if she does not eat her dinner, in the hopes that she will eat dinner the next day.

2.  Glynnis wrote a report on how biological patterns of behavior emerge and replace learned behaviors in animals. What did Glynnis write about?

    a.  Shaping
    b.  Instinctive drift
    c.  Punishment
    d.  Immediate feedback

3. Which of the following statements provides a logical and objective conclusion about the difficulty of teaching a dog to climb trees based on biological constraints?

   a. Because dogs require realistic goals set in measurable terms, it would be difficult to train a dog to climb trees without first operationalizing what it means to climb trees.

   b. If dogs' behavior is appropriately shaped, they can easily learn to climb trees.

   c. Since dogs do not have retractable claws and do not typically climb trees, it may be difficult to teach a dog to climb trees.

   d. When dogs are provided with immediate punishment for remaining on the ground, they can learn to climb trees with ease.

4. Daneel is the manager for car sales at a local car dealership. Greg started working at the car dealership this month but has not yet sold a car. Which of the following plans should Daneel implement to increase the likelihood that Greg will sell a car?

   a. Daneel should tell Greg that he needs to sell 10 cars by the end of the month, and if he fails to meet this goal, Daneel will fire Greg.

   b. Daneel should tell Greg that he needs to sell at least 5 cars this week, and if he fails to meet this goal, he will have to sell 3 times the number of cars next week.

   c. Daneel should tell Greg that he needs to sell a car by the end of the week, and if he meets this goal, the dealership will throw a party for Greg.

   d. Daneel should tell Greg that he needs to stop worrying about selling a car, and that instinctive drift will help Greg sell a car soon.

5. Tiffany claims that computers are "just smarter than humans." Which of the following modifies Tiffany's statement to more accurately reflect computers' advantage over humans regarding learned behavior?

   a. Computers are superior to humans in setting realistic goals.

   b. Computers are superior to humans due to instinctive drift.

   c. Computers are superior to humans in removing rewards gradually.

   d. Computers are superior to humans in learning to repeat reinforced behaviors.

# Module 3.9 Social, Cognitive, and Neurological Factors in Learning

From drooling dogs, running rats, and pecking pigeons, we have learned much about the basic processes of learning. But conditioning principles don't tell us the whole story. Today's learning theorists recognize that learning is the product of the interaction of biological, psychological, and social-cultural influences (**Figure 3.9-1**).

## Cognition's Influence on Conditioning

**3.9-1** How do cognitive processes affect classical and operant conditioning?

Conditioning, we've noted, is learning by association. In classical conditioning, we associate a neutral stimulus with an unconditioned stimulus. In operant conditioning, we learn to associate our behavior with its consequences. Yet, there is more to the story than simple associations. Our interpretations and expectations also influence conditioned behaviors. Mind matters.

## Cognition and Classical Conditioning

In their dismissal of "mentalistic" concepts such as consciousness, Pavlov and Watson underestimated the importance of not only biological constraints such as *preparedness* (see Module 3.7) and *instinctive drift* (see Module 3.8), but also the effects of cognitive processes (thoughts, perceptions, and expectations). The early behaviorists believed that rats' and dogs' learned behaviors could be reduced to mindless mechanisms, so there was no need to consider cognition. But Robert Rescorla and Allan Wagner (1972) argued that an animal can learn an event's *predictability*. If a shock always is preceded by a tone, and then may also be preceded by a light that accompanies the tone, a rat will react with fear to the tone but not to the light. Although the light is always followed by the shock, it adds no new information; the tone is a better predictor. The more predictable the association, the stronger the conditioned response will be. It's as if the animal learns an *expectancy*, an awareness of how likely it is that the UCS will occur.

**Figure 3.9-1**

**Biopsychosocial influences on learning**

Our learning results not only from environmental experiences, but also from cognitive and biological influences.

**Biological influences:**
- genetic predispositions
- unconditioned responses
- adaptive responses
- neural mirroring

**Psychological influences:**
- previous experiences
- predictability of associations
- generalization
- discrimination
- expectations

**Learning**

**Social-cultural influences:**
- culturally learned preferences
- motivation, affected by presence of others
- modeling

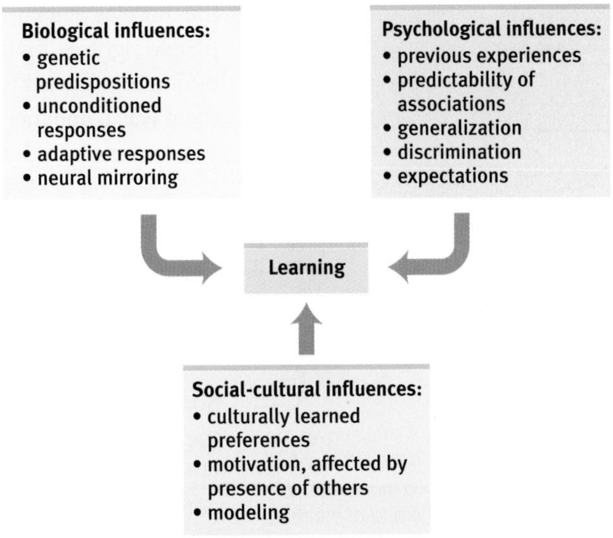

### AP® Science Practice

## Research

In rat studies that use mazes, the time to complete the maze is the operational definition of learning. The quicker the time, the stronger the learning.

**Latent learning** Animals, like people, can learn from experience, with or without reinforcement. In a classic experiment, rats in one group repeatedly explored a maze, always with a food reward at the end. Rats in another group explored the maze with no food reward. But once given a food reward at the end, rats in the second group thereafter ran the maze as quickly as (and even faster than) the always-rewarded rats (Tolman & Honzik, 1930).

*"Bathroom? Sure, it's just down the hall to the left, jog right, left, another left, straight past two more lefts, then right, and it's at the end of the third corridor on your right."*

Classical conditioning treatments that ignore cognition often have limited success. For example, people receiving therapy for alcohol use disorder may be given alcohol spiked with a nauseating drug. Will they then associate alcohol with sickness? If classical conditioning were merely a matter of "stamping in" stimulus associations, we might hope so, and to some extent this does occur (as we will see in Module 5.5). However, a person's awareness that the drug, not the alcohol, induces nausea often weakens the association between drinking alcohol and feeling sick, reducing the treatment's effectiveness. So, even in classical conditioning, it is—especially with humans—not simply the CS-UCS association but also the thought that counts.

## Cognition and Operant Conditioning

B. F. Skinner acknowledged the biological underpinnings of behavior and the existence of private thought processes. Nevertheless, many psychologists criticized him for discounting cognition's importance.

A mere 8 days before dying of leukemia at age 86, Skinner stood before the American Psychological Association convention. In this final address, he still resisted the growing belief that cognition has a necessary place in the science of psychology and even in our understanding of conditioning. He viewed "cognitive science" as a throwback to early twentieth-century introspectionism. For Skinner, thoughts and emotions were behaviors that follow the same laws as other behaviors.

Nevertheless, the evidence of cognitive processes cannot be ignored.

### Latent Learning

Evidence of cognitive processes has come from studying rats in mazes, including classic studies done in Skinner's youth by Edward Chase Tolman (1886–1959) and Charles Honzik. Rats exploring a maze, given no obvious rewards, seem to develop a **cognitive map**—a mental representation of the maze, much like your mental map of your school. When an experimenter then places food in the maze's goal box, these rats run the maze as quickly as other rats that were previously reinforced with food for this result. Like people sightseeing in a new town, the exploring rats seemingly experienced **latent learning** during their earlier tours (Tolman & Honzik, 1930). That learning became apparent only when there was some incentive to demonstrate it. Children, too, may learn from watching a parent but demonstrate the learning only much later, as needed.

*The point to remember*: There is more to learning than simply associating a response with a consequence; there is also cognition. In Unit 2, we explored other striking evidence of cognitive abilities in solving problems. In Unit 4, we will see how, due to cognition, excessive rewards can make us *less* motivated to perform a desired behavior.

### Insight Learning

Some learning occurs after little or no systematic interaction with our environment—when there is no learned association, consequence, or model. Psychologist Wolfgang Köhler (1925) noted that **insight learning** occurs when we puzzle over a problem and suddenly perceive the solution. In one classic study, a chimpanzee named Sultan was given a stick that he used to gather fruit. The fruit was then removed out of Sultan's reach, leading him to search for solutions. Suddenly, Sultan had a flash of insight: He could use his short stick to reach a longer stick, which made it possible to grasp the out-of-reach fruit. Insight also helped 10-year-old Johnny Appleton solve a problem that had stumped construction workers: how to rescue a young robin from a narrow 30-inch-deep hole in a cement-block wall. Johnny's solution: Slowly pour in sand, giving the bird enough time to keep its feet on top of the constantly rising pile (Ruchlis, 1990).

Table 3.9-1 compares the biological and cognitive influences on classical and operant conditioning.

| TABLE 3.9-1 Biological and Cognitive Influences on Conditioning | Classical Conditioning | Operant Conditioning |
| --- | --- | --- |
| Biological influences | Natural predispositions constrain which stimuli and responses can easily be associated. | Organisms most easily learn behaviors similar to their natural behaviors; unnatural behaviors instinctively drift back toward natural ones. |
| Cognitive influences | Organisms develop an expectation that a CS signals the arrival of a US. | Organisms develop an expectation that a response will be reinforced or punished; they also exhibit latent learning, without reinforcement. |

### AP® Science Practice
## Check Your Understanding

**Examine the Concept**

▶ Explain latent learning. Provide an example.

▶ Explain insight learning.

**Apply the Concept**

▶ Can you think of a cognitive map that you have? Perhaps you have one for your school or neighborhood. Explain how your map is evidence of cognitive processes.

▶ Compare and contrast the cognitive influences on classical and operant conditioning.

*Answers to the Examine the Concept questions can be found in Appendix C at the end of the book.*

# Learning by Observation

**3.9-2** What is *observational learning*?

Cognition supports **observational learning**, also called *social learning*. As we saw in Module 3.3, *social learning theory* proposes that we learn social behavior by observing and imitating others. Observational learning does not require that we experience a consequence ourselves. A child who sees his sister burn her fingers on a hot stove learns not to touch it. Likewise, nonhuman animals learn by observing others responding to threats, such as predators (Olsson et al., 2020). Observational learning does have its limits: Merely observing someone who is proficient at, say, dart-throwing, can lead people to overestimate their talent at doing the same (Kardas & O'Brien, 2018). Imitative *practice* matters, too. We learn our native languages and various other specific behaviors by observing and by imitating others, a process called **modeling**.

Picture this scene from an experiment by Albert Bandura (1925–2021), the pioneering researcher of observational learning (Bandura et al., 1961): A preschool child is working on a drawing, while an adult in another part of the room builds with Tinkertoys. As the child

**observational learning**
learning by observing others. (Also called *social learning*.)

**modeling** the process of observing and imitating a specific behavior.

**Albert Bandura (1925–2021)**
An analysis of citations, awards, and textbook coverage identified Bandura — shown here receiving a 2016 U.S. National Medal of Science from U.S. President Barack Obama — as the world's most eminent psychologist (Diener et al., 2014). In 2005, Bandura wrote, "The Bobo doll follows me wherever I go. The photographs are published in every introductory psychology text and virtually every undergraduate takes introductory psychology. I recently checked into a Washington hotel. The clerk at the desk asked, 'Aren't you the psychologist who did the Bobo doll experiment?' I answered, 'I am afraid that will be my legacy.' He replied, 'That deserves an upgrade. I will put you in a suite in the quiet part of the hotel.'"

▶ **SPOTLIGHT ON:**
Albert Bandura

watches, the adult gets up and for nearly 10 minutes pounds, kicks, and throws around the room a large inflated toy clown called a Bobo doll, yelling, "Sock him in the nose. . . . Hit him down. . . . Kick him."

The child is then taken to another room filled with appealing toys. Soon the experimenter returns and tells the child she has decided to save these good toys "for the other children." She takes the now-frustrated child to a third room containing a few toys, including a Bobo doll. Left alone, what does the child do?

Unlike children not exposed to the adult model, those who viewed the model's actions often lashed out at the doll (Bandura, 2017). Observing the aggressive outburst apparently lowered their inhibitions. But *something more* was also at work, because the children imitated the very acts they had observed and used the very words they had heard (**Figure 3.9-2**). Additionally, reported Bandura (2017), the children displayed "non-modeled" aggressive behaviors, such as "assaults with dart guns and fights among toy animals."

**Figure 3.9-2**
**The famous Bobo doll experiment**

Notice how the children's actions directly imitate the adult's.

AP® Science Practice

# Exploring Research Methods & Design

Let's take a deeper look at the Bobo doll experiment. Bandura randomly assigned children to either view the aggressive adult model (his experimental group) or not (his control group). Then he measured all children's level of aggression toward the doll. He found that children who viewed the aggressive model often imitated the aggression, while those who did not view the aggressive model showed no aggression toward the doll. Address the following research methods and design questions about this study. If you need to refresh yourself on any of the research terminology, revisit Module 0.4.

• Explain why this study is an experiment.

• What is the independent variable? The dependent variable?

• Based on this experiment, can Bandura conclude that viewing aggressive models *causes* children to behave more aggressively? (*Hint*: Think about how experimental controls and random assignment allow for causal conclusions.)

• Bandura's results were statistically significant. Explain what that means and why it is relevant to his conclusion.

That "something more," Bandura suggested, was this: By watching models, we experience *vicarious conditioning*—*vicarious reinforcement* or *vicarious punishment*. We also learn to anticipate a behavior's consequences in situations like those we are observing. We are especially likely to learn from people whom we perceive as powerful, successful, or similar to ourselves. fMRI scans show that when people observe someone winning a reward (and especially when it's someone likable and similar to themselves), their own brain reward systems become activated, much as if they themselves had won the reward (Mobbs et al., 2009). When we identify with someone, we experience their outcomes vicariously. Even our learned fears may be extinguished as we observe someone else safely navigating the feared situation (Golkar et al., 2013). Lord Chesterfield (1694–1773) had the idea: "We are, in truth, more than half what we are by imitation."

Bandura's work provides an example of how basic research "pursued for its own sake" can have a broader purpose. Insights derived from his research have been used not only to place limits on televised violence, but also to offer positive social models. In this way, African, Asian, and Latin American television and radio programs have helped reduce unplanned childbearing, protect against AIDS, and promote environmental conservation.

So, we learn by observation—but how does our brain do so?

## Mirrors and Imitation in the Brain

**3.9-3** How may observational learning be enabled by neural mirroring?

In 1991, on a hot summer day in Parma, Italy, a lab monkey awaited its researchers' return from lunch. The researchers had implanted electrodes next to its motor cortex, in a frontal lobe brain region that enabled the monkey to plan and enact movements. The monitoring device would alert the researchers to activity in that region of the monkey's brain. When the monkey moved a peanut into its mouth, for example, the device would buzz. That day, as one of the researchers reentered the lab, ice cream cone in hand, the monkey stared at him. As the researcher raised the cone to lick it, the monkey's monitor buzzed—as if the motionless monkey had itself moved (Blakeslee, 2006; Iacoboni, 2008, 2009).

The same buzzing had been heard earlier, when the monkey watched humans or other monkeys move peanuts to their mouths. The flabbergasted researchers had, they believed, stumbled onto a previously unknown type of neuron (Rizzolatti et al., 2002, 2006). These presumed **mirror neurons**, they argued, provide a neural basis for everyday imitation and observational learning. When one monkey sees, its neurons mirror what another monkey does. (For a debate regarding the importance of mirror neurons, which have been overblown in the popular press, see Gallese et al., 2011; Hickok, 2014.)

Imitation is widespread in other species. As Module EM.3 describes, primates observe and imitate all sorts of behaviors, such as how to crack nuts using stone hammers (Fragaszy et al., 2017). These types of behaviors are then transmitted from generation to generation within their local culture (Hopper et al., 2008; Whiten et al., 2007). In one study, Erica van de Waal and her co-researchers (2013) trained groups of vervet monkeys to prefer either blue or pink corn by soaking one color in a disgusting-tasting solution. Four to six months later, after a new generation of monkeys was born, the adults stuck with whatever color they had learned to prefer—and, on observing them, so did all but one of 27 infant monkeys. Moreover, when blue- (or pink-) preferring males migrated to the other group, they switched preferences and began eating as the other group did. Monkey see, monkey do.

In humans, imitation is pervasive. Our catchphrases, fashions, ceremonies, foods, traditions, morals, and fads all spread by one person copying another. Children, and even infants, are natural imitators (Davis et al., 2021). From ages 8 to 16 months, infants come to imitate various novel gestures

**mirror neurons** neurons that some scientists believe fire when we perform certain actions or observe another doing so. The brain's mirroring of another's action may enable imitation and empathy.

"Your back is killing me!"

Mirror neurons at work?

David Sipress/Cartoon Stock

**(a)**　　　　　　　　　　　　　　　　　　　**(b)**

*Masa Ushioda/AGE Fotostock*

*Erica van de Waal*

**Animal social learning**

Humpback whales' whacking the water, which drives prey fish into a clump and thus boosts feeding, has spread through social learning (Allen et al., 2013). Likewise, monkeys learn to prefer whatever color corn they observe other monkeys eating.

(Jones, 2007, 2017). By age 12 months (**Figure 3.9-3**), they look where an adult is looking (Meltzoff et al., 2009). And by age 14 months, children imitate acts modeled on TV (Meltzoff, 1988; Meltzoff & Moore, 1989, 1997). Even as 2½-year-olds, when many of their mental abilities are near those of adult chimpanzees, young humans surpass chimps at social tasks such as imitating another person's solution to a problem (Herrmann et al., 2007). Children see, children do.

So strong is the human predisposition to learn from watching adults that 2- to 5-year-old children *overimitate*. Whether living in urban Australia or rural Africa, they copy even irrelevant adult actions. Before reaching for a toy in a plastic jar, they will first stroke the jar with a feather if that's what they have observed (Lyons et al., 2007). Or, imitating an adult, they will wave a stick over a box and then use the stick to push on a knob that opens the box—when all they needed to do to open the box was to push on the knob (Nielsen & Tomaselli, 2010).

Humans, like monkeys, have brains that support empathy and imitation. Researchers cannot insert experimental electrodes in human brains, but they can use fMRI scans to see brain activity associated with performing and with observing actions. So, is the human capacity to simulate another's action and share in another's experience due to specialized mirror neurons? Or is it due to distributed brain networks? That issue remains the subject of debate (Bekkali et al., 2020; Jeon & Lee, 2018). Regardless, children's brains do enable their empathy and their ability to infer another's mental state, an ability known as *theory of mind*.

Our brain's response to observing others makes emotions contagious. Our brain simulates and vicariously experiences what we observe. So real are these mental instant replays that we may misremember an action we have observed as one we have performed (Lindner et al., 2010). When research participants watched someone experience

*Meltzoff, A. N., Kuhl, P. K., Movellan, J. & Sejnowski, T. J. (2009). Foundations for a new science of learning. Science, 325, 284–288.*

**Figure 3.9-3**

**Imitation**

This 12-month-old infant sees an adult look left, and immediately follows her gaze (Meltzoff et al., 2009).

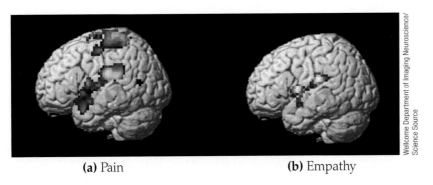

**(a)** Pain        **(b)** Empathy

Wellcome Department of Imaging Neuroscience/Science Source

**Figure 3.9-4**

**Experienced and imagined pain in the brain**

In these fMRI scans, brain activity related to actual pain (a) is mirrored in the brain of an observing loved one (b) (Singer et al., 2004). Empathy in the brain shows up in areas that process emotions, but not in the somatosensory cortex, which receives the physical pain input.

electric shocks, they became more fearful in their own choices—as if they had experienced the shocks themselves (Lindström et al., 2019). Through these reenactments, we grasp others' states of mind. Observing others' postures, faces, voices, and writing styles, we unconsciously synchronize our own to theirs—which helps us feel what they are feeling (Bernieri et al., 1994; Ireland & Pennebaker, 2010). Imitation helps us gain friends, leading us to mimic those whom we like, who then like us more in return (Chartrand & Lakin, 2013; Salazar Kämpf et al., 2018). We find ourselves yawning when they yawn, smiling when they smile, laughing when they laugh.

Seeing a loved one's pain, our faces mirror their emotion. But as **Figure 3.9-4** shows, so do our brains. Observing others' pain also releases our body's natural painkillers, thus calming our distress and enabling our helping (Haaker et al., 2017). Even fiction reading may trigger such activity, as we mentally simulate (and vicariously experience) the feelings and actions described in the story (Mar & Oatley, 2008; Speer et al., 2009). In a series of experiments, reading about kid wizard Harry Potter and his acceptance of people such as the "Mudbloods" reduced readers' prejudice against immigrants, refugees, and gay people (Vezzali et al., 2015).

## Applications of Observational Learning

**3.9-4** What is the impact of prosocial modeling and of antisocial modeling?

The big news from Bandura's studies and the mirror-neuron research is that we look, we mentally imitate, and we learn. Models—in our family, our neighborhood, or the media we consume—have effects, both good and bad.

**prosocial behavior** positive, constructive, helpful behavior. The opposite of antisocial behavior.

### Prosocial Effects

The good news is that people's modeling of **prosocial** (positive, helpful) **behaviors** can have prosocial effects. Many business organizations effectively use *behavior modeling* to help new employees learn communication, sales, and customer service skills (Taylor et al., 2005). Trainees gain these skills faster when they can observe the skills being modeled effectively by experienced workers (or actors simulating them).

People who exemplify nonviolent, helpful behavior can also prompt similar behavior in others (Jung et al., 2020). After observing someone helping (assisting a woman with dropped books), people became more helpful, such as by assisting someone who dropped a dollar (Burger et al., 2015). India's Mahatma Gandhi and America's Martin Luther King, Jr., both drew on the power of modeling, making nonviolent action a powerful, enduring force for social change in both countries (Matsumoto et al., 2015). Likewise, the media can offer models of prosocial behaviors. Across many countries and dozens of studies, viewing prosocial TV, movies, and video games boosted later helping behavior (Coyne et al., 2018).

**A model caregiver** As a sixteenth-century proverb states, "Example is better than precept." Nineteenth-century French essayist Joseph Joubert agreed: "Children need models more than they need critics."

Thinkstock Images/Stockbyte/Getty Images

Children see, children do?

"Screen time . . . screen time . . ."

**antisocial behavior** negative, destructive, harmful behavior. The opposite of prosocial behavior.

Parents are also powerful models. European Christians who risked their lives to rescue Jews from the Nazis usually had a close relationship with at least one parent who modeled a strong moral or humanitarian concern; this was also true for U.S. civil rights activists in the 1960s (London, 1970; Oliner & Oliner, 1988). The observational learning of morality begins early. Socially responsive toddlers, who readily imitate their parents, tend to become preschoolers with a strong internalized conscience (Forman et al., 2004). To encourage children's honesty, let them overhear adults praising honesty (Sai et al., 2020).

Models are most effective when their actions and words are consistent. To increase the odds that your children will practice your religion, worship and attend religious activities with them (Lowicki & Zajenkowski, 2020). To teach your children persistence, let them see *you* practice persistence (Butler, 2017). Sometimes, however, models say one thing and do another. Many parents seem to operate according to the principle "Do as I *say*, not as I *do*." Experiments suggest that children learn to do both (Rice & Grusec, 1975; Rushton, 1975). Exposed to a hypocrite, they tend to imitate the hypocrisy—by doing what the model did and saying what the model said.

### Antisocial Effects

The bad news is that observational learning can also increase **antisocial behavior**. This helps us understand why abusive parents might have aggressive children, why children who are lied to become more likely to cheat and lie, and why many men who abuse their wives had wife-abusing fathers (Hays & Carver, 2014; Jung et al., 2019; Stith et al., 2000). Aggressiveness could have a genetic link. But with monkeys, we know it can be environmental. In study after study, young monkeys separated from their mothers and subjected to high levels of aggression grew up to be aggressive themselves (Chamove, 1980). The lessons we learn as children are not easily replaced as adults, and they are sometimes visited on future generations.

Observational learning influences adults, too. People who are repeatedly exposed to hate speech become desensitized to hateful words and more prejudiced toward its targets (Soral et al., 2018). As social psychologists Chris Crandall and Mark White (2016) remind us, political leaders have the power to influence *norms*, and norms matter: "People express the prejudices that are socially acceptable and they hide the ones that are not."

TV shows, movies, and videos are sources of observational learning. While watching, children may learn that bullying is an effective way to control others, that free and easy sex brings pleasure without consequence, or that men should be tough and women gentle. Do films that glorify high-speed and risky driving teach viewers that such driving is acceptable? An analysis of nearly 200,000 speeding tickets showed increased average speed among drivers who received them on the weekends following the release of the *Fast & Furious* films (Jena et al., 2018). And most U.S. children have ample time to learn such lessons.

Viewers are learning about life from a peculiar storyteller, one that reflects the culture's mythology rather than its reality. Between 1998 and 2006, prime-time violence on TV reportedly increased 75 percent (PTC, 2007). An analysis of more than 3000 network and cable programs aired during one closely studied year revealed that nearly 6 in 10 featured violence, that 74 percent of the violence went unpunished, that 58 percent did not show the victims' pain, that nearly half the incidents involved "justified" violence, and that nearly half involved an attractive perpetrator. These conditions define the recipe for the *violence-viewing effect* described in many studies around the world and recognized by most media researchers (Bushman & Anderson, 2021; Martins & Weaver, 2019; Teng et al., 2019). (See Developing Arguments: on The Effects of Viewing Media Violence.)

**AP® Science Practice** Developing Arguments

## The Effects of Viewing Media Violence

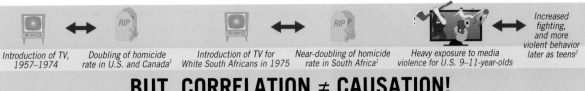

*Introduction of TV, 1957–1974* · *Doubling of homicide rate in U.S. and Canada[1]* · *Introduction of TV for White South Africans in 1975* · *Near-doubling of homicide rate in South Africa[1]* · *Heavy exposure to media violence for U.S. 9–11-year-olds* · *Increased fighting, and more violent behavior later as teens[2]*

# BUT, CORRELATION ≠ CAUSATION!

***Experimental* studies have also found that media violence viewing can cause aggression:**
Viewing violence (compared to entertaining nonviolence) ➡ participants react more cruelly when provoked. (Effect is strongest if the violent person is attractive, the violence seems justified and realistic, the act goes unpunished, and the viewer does not see pain or harm caused.)

## What prompts the *violence-viewing effect*?

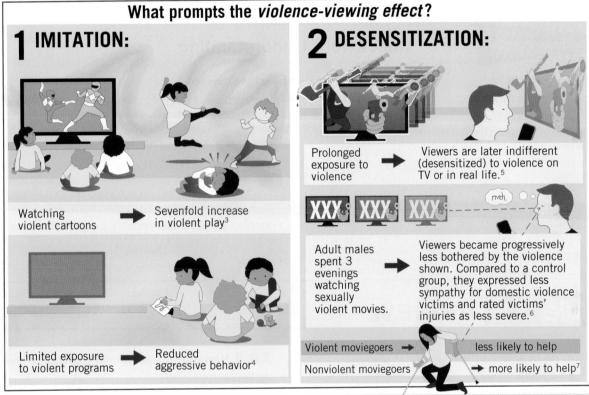

### 1 IMITATION:

Watching violent cartoons ➡ Sevenfold increase in violent play[3]

Limited exposure to violent programs ➡ Reduced aggressive behavior[4]

### 2 DESENSITIZATION:

Prolonged exposure to violence ➡ Viewers are later indifferent (desensitized) to violence on TV or in real life.[5]

Adult males spent 3 evenings watching sexually violent movies. ➡ Viewers became progressively less bothered by the violence shown. Compared to a control group, they expressed less sympathy for domestic violence victims and rated victims' injuries as less severe.[6]

Violent moviegoers ➡ less likely to help
Nonviolent moviegoers ➡ more likely to help[7]

- **APA Task Force on Violent Media (2015)** found that the "research demonstrates a consistent relation between violent video game use and increases in aggressive behavior, aggressive cognitions, and aggressive affect, and decreases in prosocial behavior, empathy, and sensitivity to aggression."

- **American Academy of Pediatrics (2009)** has advised pediatricians that "media violence can contribute to aggressive behavior, desensitization to violence, nightmares, and fear of being harmed."

**Critics** suggest that these statements may ignore some weakness in media violence research, such as reliability and the size of the effect. They also note that some places, such as Japan, have similarly violent media but much less violent behavior.[8]

## Developing Arguments Questions

**1.** Identify the reasoning that supports the claim that media violence viewing can cause aggression.

**2.** A friend is thinking about getting her young niece a violent video game as a gift. Use scientifically derived evidence to explain to her why this might be a bad idea.

**3.** Explain how prolonged exposure to violence might lead to increased violent behaviors.

1. Centerwall, 1989. 2. Boxer et al., 2009; Gentile et al., 2011; Gentile & Bushman, 2012. 3. Boyatzis et al., 1995. 4. Christakis et al., 2013. 5. Fanti et al., 2009; Jin et al., 2018; Rule & Ferguson, 1986. 6. Mullin & Linz, 1995. 7. Bushman & Anderson, 2009. 8. Elson et al., 2019.

Netflix/Photofest

**Viewing violence** Many popular streamed programs, such as *Squid Game*, prominently feature violence.

* * *

Bandura's work—like that of Ivan Pavlov, John Watson, B. F. Skinner, and thousands of others who advanced our knowledge of learning principles—illustrates the impact that can result from single-minded devotion to a few well-defined problems and ideas. These researchers defined the issues and impressed on us the importance of learning. As their legacy demonstrates, intellectual history is often made by people who risk going to extremes in pushing ideas to their limits (Simonton, 2000).

---

**AP® Science Practice**

## Check Your Understanding

**Examine the Concept**

▶ Explain how both observation and imitation are important in modeling.

▶ What are mirror neurons? Explain how they relate to imitation and empathy.

**Apply the Concept**

▶ Hannah's parents and older friends all drive faster than the speed limit, but they advise her not to. Breonna's parents and friends drive within the speed limit, but they say nothing to deter her from speeding. Will Hannah or Breonna be more likely to speed? Explain your answer.

▶ Most of us spend plenty of time with various types of screens. What prosocial and antisocial role models do you see on your screens? Which ones have you chosen to imitate?

▶ For whom are you a role model? How might you become a better role model for others?

*Answers to the Examine the Concept questions can be found in Appendix C at the end of the book.*

---

# Module 3.9 REVIEW

**3.9-1 How do cognitive processes affect classical and operant conditioning?**

● In classical conditioning, animals may learn when to expect a UCS and may be aware of the link between stimuli and responses.

● In operant conditioning, *cognitive mapping* and *latent learning* research demonstrates the importance of cognitive processes in learning.

● Other research shows that some learning can occur after little or no systematic interaction with our environment (*insight learning*).

**3.9-2 What is *observational learning*?**

● *Observational learning* (also called social learning) involves learning by watching and imitating, rather than through direct experience.

**3.9-3 How may observational learning be enabled by neural mirroring?**

● Our brain's frontal lobes have a demonstrated ability to mirror the activity of another's brain, which may enable imitation and observational learning.

● Some scientists argue that *mirror neurons* are responsible for this ability, while others attribute it to distributed brain networks.

**3.9-4 What is the impact of prosocial modeling and of antisocial modeling?**

● Children tend to imitate what a model does and says, whether the behavior being *modeled* is *prosocial* (positive, constructive, and helpful) or *antisocial*.

● If a model's actions and words are inconsistent, children may imitate the hypocrisy they observe.

# AP® Practice Multiple Choice Questions

1. Eliza easily remembers how to walk from her classroom to the bathroom and how to walk to the library from the bathroom in her school. Which of the following concepts most applies to this scenario?
   a. Latent learning
   b. Insight
   c. Cognitive map
   d. Mirror neurons

2. Khalefah had been pondering a brain teaser for days and was about to give up when, suddenly, the solution came to her. Which of the following best explains her experience?
   a. Cognitive mapping
   b. Insight learning
   c. Latent learning
   d. Social learning

3. Which of the following studies would best replicate the findings of Bandura's famous Bobo doll experiment?
   a. Dr. Franz conducted a study on how children only show their knowledge about how to draw a tree when they know they will be given a reward after drawing.
   b. Dr. Smalarz conducted a study to examine how quickly children learn the association between lightning and thunder.
   c. Dr. Pika conducted a study to examine whether children can learn how to navigate from one house in their neighborhood to another house.
   d. Dr. Singh conducted a study on whether children will learn to pretend they are superheroes after watching older children play superheroes.

4. Which of the following most logically contributes to our learning of languages?
   a. Classical conditioning
   b. Latent learning
   c. Modeling
   d. Insight learning

5. Which of the following best demonstrates when modeling is most effective?
   a. Kiara watched a toddler she was babysitting build a sandcastle in the sandbox while Kiara was building sandcastles.
   b. Sansa watched an employee of a coffee shop get fired while Sansa ordered coffee.
   c. Alcide watched his boss successfully sell a couch while Alcide was learning how to do his new job.
   d. Tawnya watched her friend's grandmother make tamales while Tawnya was visiting her friend's home.

6. After observing his older sibling walk across a balance beam, Joe's brain reacts in a way that will help him to copy the action later. Which neurological structure is implicated in this example?
   a. Hippocampus
   b. Somatosensory cortex
   c. Mirror neurons
   d. Amygdala

# UNIT 3 Review

## KEY TERMS AND CONTRIBUTORS TO REMEMBER

developmental psychology, p. 297

cross-sectional study, p. 297

longitudinal study, p. 297

teratogens, p. 304

fetal alcohol syndrome (FAS), p. 304

habituation, p. 305, 401

maturation, p. 306

critical period, p. 307

adolescence, p. 312

puberty, p. 312

menopause, p. 314

sex, p. 320

gender, p. 320

intersex, p. 321

aggression, p. 321

relational aggression, p. 322

Carol Gilligan, p. 322

X chromosome, p. 325

Y chromosome, p. 325

testosterone, p. 325

estrogens, p. 325

primary sex characteristics, p. 326

secondary sex characteristics, p. 326

spermarche [sper-MAR-key], p. 326

menarche [meh-NAR-key], p. 326

role, p. 328

gender role, p. 328

sexual aggression, p. 329

gender identity, p. 329

social learning theory, p. 329

gender typing, p. 329

androgyny, p. 329

sexuality, p. 333

asexual, p. 333

Alfred Kinsey, p. 333

social script, p. 336

Alice Eagly, p. 338

sexual orientation, p. 341

Jean Piaget, p. 349

cognition, p. 349

schema, p. 349

assimilation, p. 349

accommodation, p. 349

sensorimotor stage, p. 350

object permanence, p. 350

preoperational stage, p. 351

conservation, p. 351

egocentrism, p. 351

concrete operational stage, p. 352

formal operational stage, p. 352

Lev Vygotsky, p. 354

scaffold, p. 354

theory of mind, p. 355

language, p. 363

Noam Chomsky, p. 364

phoneme, p. 364

morpheme, p. 364

grammar, p. 364

universal grammar (UG), p. 364

babbling stage, p. 365

one-word stage, p. 365

two-word stage, p. 365

telegraphic speech, p. 365

aphasia, p. 368

Paul Broca, p. 368

Broca's area, p. 368

Carl Wernicke, p. 368

Wernicke's area, p. 368

linguistic determinism, p. 369

Benjamin Lee Whorf, p. 369

linguistic relativism, p. 369

ecological systems theory, p. 374

stranger anxiety, p. 374

attachment, p. 374

Harry Harlow, p. 375

Margaret Harlow, p. 375

imprinting, p. 375

Konrad Lorenz, p. 375

Mary Ainsworth, p. 376

strange situation, p. 376

secure attachment, p. 376

insecure attachment, p. 376

temperament, p. 376

Erik Erikson, p. 378

basic trust, p. 378

self-concept, p. 381

Diana Baumrind, p. 381

identity, p. 386

social identity, p. 387

intimacy, p. 388

emerging adulthood, p. 391

social clock, p. 392

learning, p. 400

associative learning, p. 401

stimulus, p. 401

respondent behavior, p. 402

operant behavior, p. 402

cognitive learning, p. 402

Ivan Pavlov, p. 403

# Unit 3 AP® Practice Multiple Choice Questions

1. Which of these is an example of a cross-sectional study?

   a. The depth perception of infants is measured once a month for 6 months in a row, starting at age 6 months.
   b. Researchers compare the reaction time of 20 sixth graders.
   c. The memory of one group of 50-year-olds is measured and compared to a different group of 70-year-olds.
   d. Researchers compare curiosity ratings for a group of toddlers with that same group's SAT scores 15 years later.

2. As teens mature, they start to show improved judgment, impulse control, and long-term planning. These improvements are due to development of which brain area?

   a. Prefrontal cortex
   b. Thalamus
   c. Occipital lobe
   d. Hippocampus

3. If a pregnant person drinks alcohol, their child may experience lifelong physical and mental abnormalities. In this case, alcohol is considered to be a

   a. syndrome.
   b. congenital defect.
   c. teratogen.
   d. sensitive period.

4. Dr. Holliday informed new parents about the period when certain events must take place to facilitate proper development. Dr. Holliday taught them about the

   a. conservation stage.
   b. preoperational stage.
   c. attachment period.
   d. critical period.

5. What should Ching say to be accurate in her speech about gender differences?

   a. Men show more relational aggression than women do.
   b. Women show more physical aggression than men do.
   c. Women show more relational aggression than men do.
   d. There are no gender differences in physical or relational aggression.

6. To replicate past research, Dr. Shadow should expect to find differences between gay men and straight men in the brain region known as the

   a. hippocampus.
   b. amygdala.
   c. medulla.
   d. hypothalamus.

7. Vy is 11 years old and knows $10 - 7 = 3$ and $3 + 7 = 10$ but finds it difficult to solve a math problem, such as $3x - 5$, because she cannot understand why there is a letter in the problem. Piaget would most likely place her in the

   a. concrete operational stage.
   b. formal operational stage.
   c. preoperational stage.
   d. sensorimotor stage.

8. By providing increasingly difficult words for his second grader to spell, Logan is making use of

   a. scaffolding.
   b. assimilation.
   c. accommodation.
   d. imprinting.

9. Most adolescents can ponder and debate human nature, good and evil, and truth and justice. According to Piaget, this thinking ability is due to the emergence of which stage?

   a. Concrete operational
   b. Sensorimotor
   c. Preoperational
   d. Formal operational

10. Brianna wants to encourage her teenage niece to delay having sex until she is older. What might Briana do to encourage sexual restraint?

   a. Avoid talking to her niece about sex
   b. Increase her niece's exposure to sexual content in the media
   c. Get her niece involved in volunteer community service
   d. Make her niece feel ashamed of her sexual feelings

11. After a brain injury, Aivars was unable to understand other people's speech. Which of the following best describes Aivars' experience?

   a. Aphasia
   b. Universal grammar
   c. Linguistic relativism
   d. Telegraphic speech

12. Which of the following words has three morphemes?

   a. Cat
   b. Greeters
   c. Choose
   d. Nonstop

13. Based on past research, Bristle is likely securely attached to his parents because he was exposed to

   a. a caregiver with the right temperament.
   b. consistent, responsive caregivers.
   c. an imprinting experience shortly after birth.
   d. enriched motor development experiences.

14. Dr. Adjika wants to study temperament. Which aspect of an infant's development should she examine?

   a. Susceptibility to infection and disease
   b. Fine motor skills
   c. Emotional reactivity
   d. General intelligence

15. Ellie and Ella's parents set clear rules, but also have discussions with their daughters about the types of rules and what the consequences should be for breaking the rules. Their parents are evidently following the

   a. authoritarian parenting style.
   b. neglectful parenting style.
   c. authoritative parenting style.
   d. permissive parenting style.

16. When she was 45, Sophie decided to go to nursing school because she felt that her corporate job was not fulfilling. Erikson would argue that her career change was an attempt to find a sense of

   a. integrity.
   b. intimacy.
   c. generativity.
   d. identity.

17. Jayden, age 15, is struggling with how his political views fit with those of his peers and his parents as he moves toward developing what Erikson would call his sense of

   a. initiative.
   b. worth.
   c. autonomy.
   d. identity.

18. In her speech about self-esteem, Klarity accurately explained that self-esteem decreases from the early to mid-teen years, after which

a. self-image rebounds in the late teens and twenties.
b. self-image does not rebound until age 30.
c. self-image rebounds in males by age 20 but not until age 30 for females.
d. females continue to have low self-image scores until age 40.

19. Mason retired at age 50 and was called "lucky" by his peers. This is because age 65 is the normal retirement age according to the

a. theory of mind.
b. critical period.
c. lifespan.
d. social clock.

20. The first time Tresh tried hot sauce, he thought it was extremely spicy. However, he experienced a decrease in response intensity after frequently eating hot sauce due to

a. stagnation.
b. attachment.
c. imprinting.
d. habituation.

**Use the following graph to answer questions 21 and 22:**

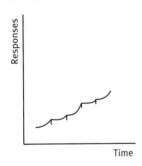

21. The graph above depicts the typical rate of response produced by which schedule of reinforcement?

a. Fixed interval
b. Fixed ratio
c. Variable interval
d. Variable ratio

22. The data depicted in the graph above were most likely collected by a psychological scientist studying

a. classical conditioning.
b. operant conditioning.
c. social learning.
d. theory of mind.

23. Which of the following processes would produce the acquisition of a conditioned response?

a. Repeatedly present an unconditioned response.
b. Administer the conditioned stimulus without the unconditioned stimulus.
c. Make sure that the conditioned stimulus comes at least 1 minute before the unconditioned stimulus.
d. Pair a neutral stimulus with an unconditioned stimulus several times.

24. After being conditioned to salivate to the sound of a tone that had been paired with food, a dog stops salivating when the tone is repeatedly presented without the food. After a few weeks, the dog hears the tone and starts salivating again. Which of the following best explains the dog's renewed salivation?

a. Spontaneous recovery
b. Extinction
c. Generalization
d. Discrimination

25. Which of the following illustrates generalization?

a. A rabbit that has been conditioned to blink to a tone also blinks when a different tone is sounded.
b. A dog salivates to a tone but not to a buzzer.
c. A light is turned on repeatedly until a rat stops flexing its paw when it's turned on.
d. A pigeon whose disk-pecking response has been extinguished is placed in a Skinner box.

26. Nola learns how to apply her makeup by watching her older sister apply her makeup. In this case, Nola's older sister is serving as a

a. conditioned stimulus.
b. source of positive reinforcement.
c. model.
d. secure base.

27. Taste-aversion studies led researchers to which of the following conclusions?

a. Taste is the most fundamental of the senses.
b. Animals must watch another animal have a taste reaction before they exhibit the aversion.
c. Animals must evaluate a situation cognitively before taste aversion develops.
d. Taste aversion is a universal survival mechanism.

**Use the following scenario to answer questions 28 and 29:**

Jazz is determined to quit drinking and enters a therapy program. The program places a nausea-inducing drug into each drink she takes. After a few weeks, the sight or thought of a drink makes Jazz sick.

**28.** Her sickness as a result of the drug is a(n)

   a. UCR.
   c. CS.
   b. NS.
   d. CR.

**29.** The drug that makes Jazz sick is a(n)

   a. UCS.
   c. CS.
   b. UCR.
   d. CR.

**30.** Which of the following best demonstrates the law of effect?

   a. Tommy keeps asking Josie to the prom even though she has said no several times.
   b. Gloria refuses to make her bed and is grounded.
   c. A dog whines at the door and is let out, so later she whines again.
   d. A baseball player drops a ball and is cut from the team.

**31.** Which of the following is an application of shaping?

   a. A mother who wants her daughter to hit a baseball first praises her for holding a bat, then for swinging it, and then for hitting the ball.
   b. A pigeon pecks a disk 25 times for an opportunity to receive a food reinforcement.
   c. A rat gradually stops pressing a bar when it no longer receives a food reinforcement.
   d. A gambler continues to play a slot machine, even though he has won nothing on his last 20 plays, and he has lost a significant amount of money.

**32.** A student studies diligently to avoid the bad feelings associated with a previously low grade on a test. In this case, the studying behavior is being strengthened by which of the following concepts?

   a. Positive reinforcement
   b. Negative reinforcement
   c. Positive punishment
   d. Negative punishment

**33.** Tunde checks her phone every 30 minutes for incoming text messages, but she finds messages only some of the time. Her behavior is being maintained by which kind of reinforcement schedule?

   a. Fixed interval
   c. Variable ratio
   b. Variable interval
   d. Fixed ratio

**34.** When asked why he punishes his employees, Mr. Massey accurately stated that

   a. punishment is a good way to increase a behavior.
   b. punishment may create problems in the short term but rarely produces long-term side effects.
   c. punishment can be effective at stopping specific behaviors quickly.
   d. punishment is an ineffective means of controlling behavior.

**35.** To summarize research on operant conditioning, what should Kenya say?

   a. Positive punishment continues a behavior; negative punishment discontinues a behavior.
   b. Positive punishment discontinues a behavior; negative punishment continues a behavior.
   c. Positive punishment continues a behavior; positive reinforcement continues a behavior.
   d. Positive reinforcement continues a behavior; negative reinforcement continues a behavior.

**36.** Latent learning is evidence for which of these conclusions?

   a. Positive reinforcement is an effective means of controlling behavior.
   b. Cognition plays an important role in operant conditioning.
   c. Conditioned reinforcers are more effective than primary reinforcers.
   d. Shaping is usually not necessary for operant conditioning.

**37.** What did Albert Bandura's Bobo doll experiments demonstrate?

   a. Children are likely to imitate the behavior of adults.
   b. There may be a negative correlation between televised violence and aggressive behavior.
   c. Children are more likely to copy what adults say than what adults do.
   d. Observational learning can explain the development of fears in children.

**38.** Dr. Munoz's research on mirror neurons most likely demonstrates that their function is

   a. to allow an organism to replace an unconditioned response with a conditioned response.
   b. to be the mechanism by which the brain accomplishes observational learning.
   c. to allow an organism to react differently to various schedules of reinforcement.
   d. to explain why modeling prosocial behavior is more effective than modeling antisocial behavior.

**39.** Torian regularly helps his grandmother with her shopping, and he volunteers after school. What is he displaying with these positive, constructive, helpful behaviors?

a. Modeling
b. Prosocial behavior
c. Associative learning
d. Moral development

**40.** Little Lulu is afraid of dogs. She observes her older sister playing with the neighbor's dog and enjoying it. As a result, Lulu's fear diminishes. This is an example of

a. scaffolding.
b. negative reinforcement.
c. shaping.
d. vicarious conditioning.

Go to Appendix D to complete the **AP® Practice** Evidence-Based Question and Article Analysis Question for this unit.

# UNIT 4

# Social Psychology and Personality

irk Willems faced a moment of decision in 1569. Threatened with torture and death as a member of a persecuted religious minority, he escaped from his Asperen, Holland, prison and fled across an ice-covered pond. His stronger and heavier jailer pursued him but fell through the ice. Unable to climb out, the jailer pleaded for help.

With his freedom in front of him, Willems acted with ultimate selflessness. He turned back and rescued his pursuer, who, under orders, took him back to captivity. A few weeks later, Willems was condemned to be "executed with fire, until death ensues." For his martyrdom, present-day Asperen has a street named in honor of its folk hero (Toews, 2004).

What drives groups to feel contempt for minority-group members, such as Dirk Willems, and to act so spitefully? What motivates people, such as his jailer, to carry out unfair orders? And what inspired the selflessness of Willems' response, and of so many who have died trying to save others? Indeed, what motivates any of us who volunteer kindness and generosity?

**Personality psychologists** focus on the person. They study the personal traits and dynamics that explain why, in a given situation, *different people* may act differently. (Would you have helped your jailer out of the icy water?) **Social psychologists** focus on the situation. They study the social influences that explain why *the same person* acts differently in *different situations*. (Might Willems' jailer have released him under other circumstances?)

In this unit, we begin with social psychology: how we think about and influence one another, and how we *relate* to one another. We will look at the interactions of people and situations: What causes people sometimes to hate and harm, and at other times to love and help? We will then explore *personality*—that enduring sense of "who I am," which colors our interactions with our world. Finally, we will examine the motivations that direct and drive us, and the emotions that influence our thoughts, actions, and interactions.

**personality psychology** the scientific study of personality and its development, structure, traits, processes, variations, and disordered forms (personality disorders).

**social psychology** the scientific study of how we think about, influence, and relate to one another.

## MODULES

UNIT **4**

**Overview Video**

453

**person perception** how we form impressions of ourselves and others, including attributions of behavior.

**attribution theory** the theory that we explain someone's behavior by crediting either the situation (a *situational attribution*) or the person's stable, enduring traits (a *dispositional attribution*).

**fundamental attribution error** the tendency for observers, when analyzing others' behavior, to underestimate the impact of the situation and to overestimate the impact of personal disposition.

Thinking about ourselves and others, we form judgments. Our **person perception** refers to how we form impressions of people. We try to explain why others act as they do, and why we act as we do. We compare ourselves to others. We categorize (and sometimes stereotype) people. We define ourselves by our *social identity*, our sense of who *we* are.

This module examines person perception, including *attribution theory* (how we explain our own and others' behaviors) and *social comparison*. And it explores how our social identity and social categorizations sometimes lead to prejudice.

## The Fundamental Attribution Error

**4.1-1** What is *person perception*, and how do we tend to explain others' behavior and our own?

An etching of Dirk Willems by Dutch artist Jan Luyken (From *The Martyrs Mirror*, 1685)

Dirk Willemſz. 1569.

Mennonite Library and Archives/Bethel College

Psychologists study our *attributions*, or how we explain the causes of events. (If you do well in this class, to what will you attribute your success?) People may demonstrate a predictable pattern of attributions called *explanatory style* (Module 5.1), interpreting good and bad events in ways that are pessimistic ("It's all my fault!") or optimistic ("I did the best I could, and I'll do better next time").

We also make assumptions about why people behave the way they do. After studying this, Fritz Heider (1958) proposed an **attribution theory**.

For example, in class, we notice that Jill seldom talks. Over coffee, Jack talks nonstop. That must be the sort of people they are, we decide: shy or outgoing. Such attributions—to their dispositions—can be valid. But sometimes we fall prey to the **fundamental attribution error** (Ross, 1977, 2018). In class, Jack may be as quiet as Jill. Catch Jill as the lead in the high school musical and you may hardly recognize her.

In one experiment, college students talked, one at a time, with a woman who acted either cold and critical or warm and friendly (Napolitan & Goethals, 1979). Before the conversations, the researchers told half the students that the woman's behavior would be spontaneous. They told the other half the truth—that they had instructed her to *act* friendly or unfriendly.

Did hearing the truth affect students' impressions of the woman? Not at all! If the woman acted friendly, both groups decided she was a warm person. If she acted unfriendly, both decided she was a cold person. They attributed her behavior to her personal disposition *even when told that her behavior was situational*—that she was merely acting that way for the experiment.

We all commit the fundamental attribution error. Consider: Is your AP® Psychology teacher shy or outgoing?

If you answer "outgoing," remember that you know your teacher from only one situation—the classroom, where teaching demands talking. Your teacher might disagree: "Me, outgoing? It all depends on the situation. In class or with good friends, yes, I'm outgoing. But at professional meetings I'm really rather shy." Outside their assigned roles, teachers seem less teacherly, presidents less presidential, managers less managerial.

## Which Factors Affect Our Attributions?

One influence on our attributions is culture. Westerners more often attribute behavior to people's personal traits. People in China and Japan are more sensitive to the power of the situation (Feinberg et al., 2019; Miyamoto & Kitayama, 2018). In experiments that asked people to view scenes, such as a big fish swimming among smaller fish and plants, U.S. viewers focused more on the attributes of the big fish. Japanese viewers focused more on the setting and context—the situation (Chua et al., 2005; Nisbett, 2003).

*Whose* behavior also matters: We exhibit an **actor-observer bias**. When we explain *our own* behavior, we are sensitive to how behavior changes with the situation (Idson & Mischel, 2001). After behaving badly, for example, we recognize how the situation affected our actions. People with high self-esteem and self-confidence typically credit their good deeds and accomplishments to their own traits, and blame their mistakes and failures on the situation: "I aced my history test because I studied hard, but I did poorly on my chem test because it was unfair." (More on this perceptual error—the *self-serving bias*—in Module 4.6.) We also are sensitive to the power of the situation when we have prior experience to draw on—for example, when we have observed someone's behavior in many different contexts. We more often commit the fundamental attribution error when a stranger misbehaves. Having only seen that enraged fan screaming at the referee in the heat of competition, we may assume they have a negative, disagreeable temperament. But outside the stadium, this person may be a good neighbor and a loving parent.

Would taking an observer's viewpoint make us judge our behavior differently? Researchers tested this idea by using separate cameras to film two people interacting. When they showed each person a replay of the interaction—filmed from the other person's perspective—participants credited their own behavior more to their *disposition* (personal character), much as an observer typically would (Lassiter & Irvine, 1986; Storms, 1973). Similarly, when people assess a police officer's actions from the officer's body camera perspective (rather than a dashcam that also shows the officer), they become more attuned to the situation—and more sympathetic to the officer (Turner et al., 2019).

Two important exceptions to our usual view of our own actions: We often attribute our deliberate and *admirable* actions to our own good reasons, not to the situation (Malle, 2006; Malle et al., 2007). And as we age, we tend to attribute our younger selves' behavior mostly to our traits (Pronin & Ross, 2006). In 5 or 10 years, your current self may seem like another person.

## How Do Our Attributions Matter?

The way we explain others' actions, attributing them to the person or the situation, can have important real-life effects (Fincham & Bradbury, 1993; Fletcher et al., 1990). Does a warm greeting reflect romantic interest or social courtesy? Does a manager's tart-tongued

**Personal versus situational attributions** Should the 2018 slaughter of 11 Jewish worshippers at Pittsburgh's Tree of Life synagogue be attributed to the shooter's hateful disposition? To social media, where the shooter and like-minded others promoted anti-Semitism and White nationalism? To America's gun culture? (The shooter used four guns.) Or to all of these? And to what should we attribute the compassion of the emergency room nurse — a Jew and the son of a rabbi — who treated the hate-spewing shooter (Flynn, 2018)?

remark reflect a job threat or just a bad day? Was a shooting malicious or an act of self-defense? In one study, 181 U.S. state judges gave lighter sentences to a violent offender who a scientist testified had a gene that altered brain areas related to aggressiveness (Aspinwall et al., 2012). Attributions matter.

Do you attribute poverty or unemployment to social circumstances, or to personal traits and bad choices? In Britain, India, Australia, and the United States, political conservatives have tended to attribute responsibility to the personal dispositions of the poor and unemployed (Dunn, 2018; Furnham, 1982; Pandey et al., 1982; Wagstaff, 1982; Zucker & Weiner, 1993). "People make their own choices. Those who take initiative can still get ahead." In experiments, participants who reflect on the power of choice — either by recalling their own choices or by taking note of another's choices — become more likely to think that people get what they deserve (Savani & Rattan, 2012). Political liberals, and those not primed to consider the power of choice, are more likely to blame past and present situations: "If you or I had to live with the same poor education, lack of opportunity, and discrimination, would we be any better off?"

*The point to remember:* Our attributions — to a person's disposition or to the situation — have real consequences.

---

**AP® Science Practice**

## Check Your Understanding

**Examine the Concept**

▶ Explain the *fundamental attribution error*.

**Apply the Concept**

▶ Driving to school one snowy day, Marco narrowly misses a car that slides through a red light. "Slow down! What a terrible driver," he thinks. Moments later, Marco himself slips through an intersection and yelps, "Wow! These roads are awful. The city plows need to get out here." What social psychology principle has Marco just demonstrated? Explain.

*Answers to the Examine the Concept questions can be found in Appendix C at the end of the book.*

---

## Social Comparison

**4.1-2** How does social comparison influence our perceptions of ourselves and others?

When we evaluate others and ourselves, we often engage in *social comparison*. By comparing ourselves to others, we judge whether we're succeeding or failing. When we succeed, our self-esteem rises. When we come up short, our self-esteem plummets.

Today's online world offers many opportunities for social comparison — for better or for worse. Scrolling through our social media feeds, we may feel inspired and elevated by others' stories and successes. But comparing our lives to a highlight reel of others' best moments can also harm our self-concept. We wonder: "Am I as attractive? Funny? Smart? Talented? Popular?" An Instagram research report acknowledged that its platform "make[s] body image issues worse for one in three teen girls" (Wells et al., 2021).

## Check Your Understanding

**Examine the Concept**

▶ How can social comparison both help and harm us?

**Apply the Concept**

▶ Think of a time when you engaged in social comparison. How did this experience influence your self-concept?

*Answers to the Examine the Concept questions can be found in Appendix C at the end of the book.*

# Prejudice

**4.1-3** What is *prejudice?* How do explicit and implicit prejudice differ?

Our evaluations of ourselves and others sometimes lead us down a dark path. **Prejudice,** which means "prejudgment," is an unjustifiable and usually negative *attitude* toward a group and its members—who often are people of a particular racial or ethnic group, gender, or sexual orientation. Attitudes are feelings, influenced by beliefs, that predispose us to act in certain ways. The ingredients in prejudice's three-part mixture are

- *negative emotions,* such as hostility or fear.

- **stereotypes,** which are generalized beliefs about a group of people. Our stereotypes sometimes reflect reality. As Texas Senator Ted Cruz (2018) explained, "It's a stereotype that Texans like barbecue. It also happens that pretty much all Texans like barbecue." Stereotypes can reduce the effort, or *cognitive load,* it takes to make decisions or judgments. But stereotypes often overgeneralize or exaggerate. In the United States, for example, strongly partisan Republicans and Democrats exhibit a "perception gap"—they overestimate the extremism of the other side (Yudkin et al., 2019a).

- a predisposition to **discriminate**—to *act* in negative and unjustifiable ways toward members of the group. Sometimes prejudice is blatant. People with anti-Black attitudes, for example, are less likely to judge as guilty a White police officer who killed a Black man (Cooley et al., 2019). At other times it is more subtle, taking the form of *microaggressions,* such as race-related traffic stops or a reluctance to choose a train seat next to someone of a different race (Pierson et al., 2020; Wang et al., 2011). In experiments, Americans seeking Airbnb reservations and Uber and Lyft pickups have received better treatment when calling themselves John rather than Jamal, or Emily rather than Lakisha (Edelman et al., 2017; Ge et al., 2016).

> **AP® Exam Tip**
>
> Be sure you understand the distinctions among *discrimination, prejudice,* and *stereotype.* They are related, but different.

> **CULTURAL AWARENESS**
>
> In the Airbnb studies described here, having a culturally specific name (such as Jamal) can lead to bias from others (such as the Airbnb owners). As we will learn, this bias might even be implicit, but it can still influence someone's perceptions and behaviors.

## Explicit and Implicit Prejudice

Again and again, we have seen that our brain processes thoughts, memories, and attitudes on two different tracks. Sometimes that processing is *explicit*—on the radar screen of our awareness. More often, it is *implicit*—an unthinking knee-jerk response operating below the radar, leaving us unaware of how our attitudes are influencing our behavior. In 2015, the U.S. Supreme Court, in upholding the Fair Housing Act, recognized implicit bias research, noting that "unconscious prejudices" can cause discrimination even when people do not consciously intend to discriminate.

Psychologists study implicit prejudice by

- ***testing for unconscious group associations.*** Tests in which people quickly pair a person's image with a trait demonstrate that even people who deny any racial prejudice may exhibit negative associations (Greenwald & Banaji, 2017). Millions of people have taken the Implicit Association Test (as you can, too, at Implicit.Harvard.edu).

**prejudice** an unjustifiable and usually negative attitude toward a group and its members. Prejudice generally involves negative emotions, stereotyped beliefs, and a predisposition to discriminatory action.

**stereotype** a generalized (sometimes accurate but often overgeneralized) belief about a group of people.

**discrimination** unjustifiable negative behavior toward a group or its members.

Beata Zawrzel/NurPhoto/Getty Images

KEREM YUCEL/AFP/Getty Images

**Implicit bias? Explicit prejudice?**
In May 2020, a White police officer killed George Floyd by kneeling on his neck for more than 9 minutes while Floyd cried, "I can't breathe!" and subordinate officers stood by without intervening. Only two months earlier, police shot unarmed medical worker Breonna Taylor six times in a botched raid on her home. Commentators and Black Lives Matter protesters asked: Had Floyd and Taylor been White, would they have been perceived and treated the same way? In the wake of the tragedy, more police departments are training officers to intervene when they witness racially motivated misconduct.

- *considering unconscious patronization*. In one experiment, White university women assessed flawed student essays they believed had been written by either a White or a Black student. The women gave low evaluations, often with harsh comments, to the essays supposedly written by a White student. When the same essay was attributed to a Black student, their assessment was more positive (Harber, 1998). In real-world evaluations, such low expectations and the resulting "inflated praise and insufficient criticism" could hinder minority student achievement, the researcher noted. Thus, many teachers read essays while "blind" to their authors' race.

- *monitoring reflexive bodily responses*. Even people who consciously express little prejudice may give off telltale signals as their body responds selectively to an image of a person from another ethnic group. Neuroscientists can detect signals of implicit prejudice in the viewer's facial-muscle responses and in the activation of the emotion-processing amygdala (Cunningham et al., 2004; Eberhardt, 2005; Stanley et al., 2008).

## Targets of Prejudice

**4.1-4** What group distinctions tend to elicit prejudice?

### Racial and Ethnic Prejudice

Americans' expressed racial attitudes have changed dramatically in the last half-century. Support for interracial marriage between Black people and White people, for example, increased from a mere 4 percent approval in 1959 to 87 percent in 2013 (Saad, 2019a). Three in four Americans (including nearly 9 in 10 college graduates) now agree that their nation's having "many different races and ethnicities" is good for the country (Horowitz, 2019). The diversity benefit appeared in one analysis of 9 million scientific papers and 6 million scientists: Ethnically diverse scientific teams produced the most influential research (AlShebli et al., 2018).

Yet, even as overt interracial prejudice has waned, prejudice lingers, including *subtle* prejudices:

- **Colorism**. Among Black and Hispanic people, and also among people in India and some East Asian cultures, those with darker skin tones experience greater prejudice and discrimination (Bettache, 2020; Gonzales-Barrera, 2019; Landor & Smith, 2019; Yasir & Gettleman, 2020).

- **Criminal stereotypes**. Black men are judged more harshly than White men when they commit "stereotypically Black" crimes (drive-by shooting, gang violence, street gambling) rather than "stereotypically White" crimes (embezzlement, computer hacking, and insider trading) (Petsko & Bodenhausen, 2019).

❝ Data [show] plunges in extreme poverty, illiteracy, war, violent crime, racism, sexism, homophobia, domestic violence, disease lethal accidents and just about every other scourge. ❞

— Psychologist Steven Pinker, "Scared by the News? Take the Long View," 2018

- **Medical care**. Health professionals spend more money to treat White patients than to treat equally unhealthy Black patients (Obermeyer et al., 2019). Such unequal medical treatment helps explain why Black Americans were nearly three times more likely than White Americans to die from Covid (COVID Tracking Project, 2020).

Many wonder how such prejudice persists. One reason is that few people muster the courage to challenge prejudicial or hate speech. Although many *say* they would feel upset with someone making racist (or homophobic) comments, they often respond indifferently when hearing prejudice-laden language (Kawakami et al., 2009). *The bottom line:* If you disapprove of prejudice, ask yourself, "What message am I sending when I remain silent while others make racist, homophobic, transphobic, or sexist remarks?"

As noted, prejudice is not just subtle, but often unconscious (implicit). The Implicit Association Test (IAT), its critics and defenders agree, should not be used to judge individuals. But it does offer some intriguing findings (Greenwald & Lai, 2020). One IAT study found 9 in 10 White respondents taking longer to identify pleasant words (such as *peace* and *paradise*) as "good" when presented with Black-sounding names (such as *Latisha* and *Darnell*) than when shown White-sounding names (such as *Katie* and *Ian*). Moreover, people who more quickly associate good things with White names or faces also are the quickest to perceive anger and apparent threat in Black faces (Hugenberg & Bodenhausen, 2003). In the 2008 U.S. presidential election, those demonstrating explicit *or* implicit prejudice were less likely to vote for candidate Barack Obama. His election, however, reduced implicit prejudice (Bernstein et al., 2010; Payne et al., 2010; Stephens-Davidowitz, 2014).

Our perceptions can also reflect implicit bias. In 1999, Amadou Diallo, who was Black, was accosted as he approached his doorway by police officers looking for a rapist. When he pulled out his wallet, the officers, perceiving a gun, riddled his body with 19 bullets from 41 shots. In one analysis of 59 unarmed suspect shootings in Philadelphia over seven years, 49 involved the misidentification of an object (such as a phone) or movement (such as pants tugging). Black suspects were more than twice as likely to be misperceived as threatening, even by Black officers (Blow, 2015). Across the United States, about 1 in 1000 Black men have been killed by a police officer—more than double the rate for White men (Edwards et al., 2019). One research team analyzed implicit bias scores from more than 2 million Americans, while accounting for several other factors. Their finding: A region's implicit bias toward African Americans predicted its number of African Americans killed by police (Hehman et al., 2018).

To better understand implicit prejudice, researchers have also simulated situations (Correll et al., 2007, 2015; Plant & Peruche, 2005; Sadler et al., 2012). They asked viewers to press buttons quickly to "shoot" or not shoot men who suddenly appeared on screen. Some of the on-screen men held a gun. Others held a harmless object, such as a flashlight or bottle. People (whether Black or White, including police officers) more often shot Black men holding a harmless object. Priming people with a flashed Black face rather than a White face also made them more likely to misperceive a flashed tool as a gun (**Figure 4.1-1**). Fatigue, which diminishes one's conscious control and increases automatic reactions, amplifies racial bias in decisions to shoot (Ma et al., 2013).

**Figure 4.1-1**

**Race primes perceptions**

In experiments by Keith Payne (2006), people viewed (a) a White or Black face, instantly followed by (b) a flashed gun or hand tool, which was then followed by (c) a masking screen. Participants were more likely to misperceive a tool as a gun when it was preceded by a Black face rather than a White face.

(a)

(b)

(c)

## Gender Prejudice

Overt gender prejudice has declined sharply. The one-third of Americans who in 1937 told Gallup pollsters that they would vote for a qualified woman whom their party nominated for president soared to 95 percent in 2012 (Jones, 2012; Newport, 1999). Although women worldwide still represent nearly two-thirds of illiterate adults, and 30 percent have experienced intimate-partner violence, 94 percent of people surveyed across 34 countries agree that it's important "that women have the same rights as men" (Horowitz & Fetterolf, 2020).

Nevertheless, both implicit and explicit gender prejudice and discrimination persist. Consider:

- **Work and pay**. In Western countries, we pay more to those (usually men) who care for our streets than to those (usually women) who care for our children. Despite expressed support for women having the "same rights," 40 percent of the global survey respondents agreed that men have more right to a job when work is scarce. (Agreement varied greatly by country, ranging from 7 percent in Sweden to about 80 percent in India and Tunisia.)

- **Leadership**. From 2007 through 2016, male directors of 1000 popular films (the top 100 for each year) outnumbered female directors by 24 to 1 (Smith et al., 2017). Implicit gender bias also contributes to females' not being promoted in other fields (Régner et al., 2019).

- **Perceived intelligence**. Gender bias even applies to beliefs about intelligence: Despite equality between males and females in intelligence test scores, people tend to perceive their fathers as more intelligent than their mothers and their sons as brighter than their daughters (Furnham, 2016).

- **Masculine norms**. Organizations often value and reward masculine ideas, values, and interaction styles (Cheryan & Markus, 2020). For example, people are encouraged to work independently, nominate themselves for awards and promotions, and use an assertive interaction style to influence others. These "masculine defaults" can reduce women's opportunities for inclusion and success.

Unwanted female infants are no longer left out on a hillside to die of exposure, as was the practice in ancient Greece. Yet the normal male-to-female newborn ratio (105-to-100) doesn't explain what some have estimated as the world's millions of "missing women." In many places, parents value sons more than daughters. In India, there are 3.5 times more Google searches asking how to conceive a boy than how to conceive a girl (Stephens-Davidowitz, 2014). With scientific testing that enables sex-selective abortions, some countries are experiencing a shortfall in female births. India's newborn sex ratio was recently 112 boys for every 100 girls. China's has been 111 to 100, despite China's declaring sex-selective abortions a criminal offense (CIA, 2014). In China and India, which together have 50 million more males than females younger than age 20, many heterosexual bachelors will be without mates (Denyer & Gowen, 2018; Gupta, 2017). A shortage of women also contributes to increased crime, violence, prostitution, and trafficking of women (Brooks, 2012).

## LGBTQ Prejudice

In most of the world, LGBTQ people experience prejudice. Although 29 countries allowed same-sex marriage by 2021, dozens more had laws criminalizing same-sex relationships. Cultural variation is enormous—ranging from the 98 percent in Ghana to the 6 percent in Spain for whom "homosexuality is morally unacceptable" (Pew, 2014). Worldwide, anti-gay attitudes are most common among men, older adults, and those who are unhappy, unemployed, and less educated (Haney, 2016; Jäckle & Wenzelburger, 2015).

Explicit anti-LGBTQ prejudice persists, even in countries with legal protections in place. When U.S. and U.K. experimenters sent thousands of responses to employment ads, those whose resumes included "Treasurer, Progressive and Socialist Alliance" received more replies than did those whose resumes specified "Treasurer, Gay and Lesbian Alliance"

(Agerström et al., 2012; Bertrand & Mullainathan, 2004; Drydakis, 2009, 2015). Other evidence has appeared in national surveys of LGBTQ Americans:

- 39 percent reported having been "rejected by a friend or family member" because of their sexual orientation or gender identity (Pew, 2013b).
- 58 percent reported being "subject to slurs or jokes" (Pew, 2013b).
- 54 percent reported having been harassed at school and at work (Grant et al., 2011; James et al., 2016).

Do attitudes and practices that label, disparage, and discriminate against gay, lesbian, and transgender people increase their risk of psychological disorder and ill health? *Yes.* In U.S. states without protections against LGBTQ hate crimes and discrimination, gay and lesbian people experience substantially higher rates of depression and related disorders, even after controlling for income and education differences. In communities where anti-gay prejudice is high, so are gay and lesbian suicides and cardiovascular deaths. In 16 states that banned same-sex marriage between 2001 and 2005, gay and lesbian people (but not straight people) experienced a 37 percent increase in depressive disorder rates, a 42 percent increase in alcohol use disorder, and a 248 percent increase in generalized anxiety disorder. Meanwhile, gay and lesbian people in other states did not experience increased psychiatric disorders (Hatzenbuehler, 2014).

So, do laws that promote acceptance of gay, lesbian, and transgender people *reduce* bias? Again, *Yes.* As happened after the passage of desegregation and civil rights laws, attitudes have followed the newly legislated behavior. In the various U.S. states, people became more gay-supportive when and where same-sex marriages became legal (Ofosu et al., 2019).

## Exploring Research Methods & Design

As you learned, explicit anti-LGBTQ prejudice persists. Consider a study that explored the effect of perceived sexual identity on employment. Experimenters randomly selected employment ads and sent in fake resumes to apply for the jobs. All resumes were identical, except for one point. By random assignment, half of the resumes included "Treasurer, Progressive and Socialist Alliance" while the other half included "Treasurer, Gay and Lesbian Alliance." The latter resume received fewer replies than did the former.

- Explain which research design is being employed — correlational or experimental?
- Identify the operational definition of the independent variable.
- Explain the difference between random assignment and random selection in this study.

## Roots of Prejudice

**4.1-5** What are some social, emotional, and cognitive roots of prejudice?

Prejudice springs from a culture's divisions, the heart's passions, and the mind's natural workings.

### Social Inequalities and Divisions

When some people have money, power, and prestige and others do not, the "haves" usually develop attitudes that justify things as they are. The **just-world phenomenon** reflects an idea we commonly teach our children—that good is rewarded and evil is punished. From this, it is but a short and sometimes automatic leap to assume that those who succeed must be good and those who suffer must be bad. Such reasoning enables the rich to see both their

**just-world phenomenon** the tendency for people to believe the world is just and that people therefore get what they deserve and deserve what they get.

**social identity** the "we" aspect of our self-concept; the part of our answer to "Who am I?" that comes from our group memberships.

**ingroup** "us"—people with whom we share a common identity.

**outgroup** "them"—those perceived as different or apart from our ingroup.

**ingroup bias** the tendency to favor our own group.

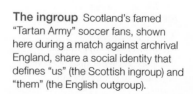

wealth and the poor's misfortune as justly deserved. When slavery existed in the United States, slaveholders perceived enslaved people as innately lazy, ignorant, and irresponsible—as having the very traits that supposedly justified enslaving them. Stereotypes rationalize inequalities.

Victims of discrimination may react in ways that feed prejudice through the classic *blame-the-victim* dynamic (Allport, 1954). Do the circumstances of poverty breed a higher crime rate? If so, that higher crime rate can be used to justify discrimination against those who live in poverty.

Dividing the world into "us" and "them" can result in conflict, racism, and war, but it also provides the benefits of communal solidarity. Thus, we cheer for our groups, kill for them, die for them. Indeed, we define who we are—our **social identity**—partly in terms of our groups (Thomas et al., 2020; Whitehouse, 2018). When Oliver identifies himself as a man, a Brit, a Liverpool native, and a Brexit supporter, he knows who he is, and so do we. Mentally drawing a circle defines "us," the **ingroup**. But the social definition of who we are also states who we are not. People outside that circle are "them," the **outgroup**. An **ingroup bias** soon follows. In experiments, people, beginning in early childhood, have favored their own group when dividing rewards—even a group that is created by a mere coin toss (Tajfel, 1982; Wynn et al., 2018). Across 17 countries, ingroup bias appears more as ingroup favoritism than as harm to the outgroup (Romano et al., 2017). Discrimination is triggered less by outgroup hostility than by ingroup networking and mutual support—such as hiring a friend's child at the expense of other candidates (Greenwald & Pettigrew, 2014).

We have inherited our Stone Age ancestors' need to belong, to live and love in groups. There was safety in solidarity: Whether hunting, defending, or attacking, 10 hands were better than 2. Evolution prepared us, when encountering strangers, to make instant judgments: friend or foe? This urge to distinguish enemies from friends, and to dehumanize or "otherize" those not like us, predisposes prejudice against strangers (Kteily & Bruneau, 2017; Whitley, 1999). To Greeks of the classical era, all non-Greeks were "barbarians." In our own era, most children believe their school is better than all other schools in town. (Can you recall being conscious of your school identity when competing with an archrival school?) Many high school students form cliques—jocks, preps, nerds—and disparage those outside their own group. Even chimpanzees have been seen to wipe clean the spot where they were touched by a chimpanzee from another group (Goodall, 1986). They also display ingroup empathy by yawning more after seeing ingroup (rather than outgroup) members yawn (Campbell & de Waal, 2011). Although an ideal world might prioritize justice and love for all, in our real world, ingroup love often outranks universal justice.

**The ingroup** Scotland's famed "Tartan Army" soccer fans, shown here during a match against archrival England, share a social identity that defines "us" (the Scottish ingroup) and "them" (the English outgroup).

## Negative Emotions

Negative emotions nourish prejudice. When facing death, fearing threats, or experiencing frustration, people cling more tightly to their ingroup. When frustrated by extreme inequality, people worldwide wish for a strong leader to restore order (Sprong et al., 2019). Fearing terrorism increases patriotism, along with loathing and aggression toward those perceived as threats (Pyszczynski et al., 2002, 2008).

**Scapegoat theory** proposes that when things go wrong, finding someone to blame can provide a target for our negative emotions. During the Covid pandemic, some government officials in White-majority countries referred to the virus as the "Chinese virus" or "China virus." Associating the virus with a country fueled prejudice and discrimination, contributing to 650 reported U.S. incidents of discrimination against Asian Americans in just 1 week (Hong, 2020; Van Bavel et al., 2020). One man was stabbed; others were spit on or told, "You people brought the virus. Go back to China" (Loffman, 2020). New York Congresswoman Grace Meng (2022) noted that "No person deserves to live in fear of physical attacks, but sadly . . . Asian Americans continue to be victims of senseless violence, as we are scapegoated for the spread of Covid-19."

Researchers report that "frequent and repetitive exposure to hate speech leads to desensitization" to such speech and to "increasing outgroup prejudice" (Soral et al., 2018). Political leaders have the power to influence norms, and norms matter: "People express the prejudices that are socially acceptable and they hide the ones that are not" (Crandall & White, 2016; Ruisch & Ferguson, 2022). In England and Wales, following the 2016 anti-immigrant Brexit referendum, reported hate crimes soared from 52,000 in 2015–2016 to 103,000 in 2018–2019 (Home Office, 2019). There, and in Germany and the United States, anti-Semitic crimes have also been on the increase (ADL, 2019; Statista, 2019).

Evidence for the scapegoat theory comes in two forms: (1) *social trends*—economically frustrated people often express heightened prejudice, and during economic downturns racial prejudice intensifies (Bianchi et al., 2018); and (2) *experiments*—temporarily frustrating people intensifies their prejudice. Students who experience failure or are made to feel insecure often restore their self-esteem by disparaging a rival school or another person (Cialdini & Richardson, 1980; Crocker et al., 1987). Denigrating others may boost our own sense of status, which explains why a rival's misfortune sometimes provides a twinge of pleasure. (The German language has a word—*Schadenfreude*—for this secret joy that we sometimes take in another's failure.) By contrast, those made to feel loved and supported become more open to and accepting of others who differ (Mikulincer & Shaver, 2001).

## Cognitive Shortcuts

Stereotyped beliefs are in part a by-product of how we cognitively simplify the world. To help understand the world around us, we frequently form categories. Chemists categorize molecules as organic and inorganic. A basketball coach categorizes offensive players as guards and post players. Therapists categorize psychological disorders. We all categorize people by gender, ethnicity, race, age, and many other characteristics—including their warmth and their competence (Fiske, 2018). But when we categorize people into groups, we often stereotype. We may exhibit *ethnocentrism*—the tendency to view our own ethnic or racial group as superior. We recognize how greatly *we* differ from other individuals in *our* groups. But we overestimate the extent to which members of other groups are alike (Bothwell et al., 1989). We perceive *outgroup homogeneity*—uniformity of attitudes, personality, and appearance. Our greater recognition for individual own-race faces—called the **other-race effect** (or *cross-race effect* or *own-race bias*)—emerges during infancy, between 3 and 9 months of age (Anzures et al., 2013; Telzer et al., 2013). (We also have an *own-age bias*—better memory for faces of our own age group [Rhodes & Anastasi, 2012].)

*Schadenfreude is a German word meaning "taking pleasure in another's misery."*

**scapegoat theory** the theory that prejudice offers an outlet for anger by providing someone to blame.

**other-race effect** the tendency to recall faces of one's own race more accurately than faces of other races. Also called the *cross-race effect* and the *own-race bias*.

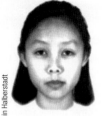     

| 100% Chinese | 80% Chinese 20% White | 60% Chinese 40% White | 40% Chinese 60% White | 20% Chinese 80% White | 100% White |

Dr. Jamin Halberstadt

### Figure 4.1-2

**Categorizing mixed-race people**

When New Zealanders quickly classified 104 photos by race, those of European descent more often than those of Chinese descent classified the ambiguous middle two as Chinese (Halberstadt et al., 2011).

Sometimes, however, people don't fit easily into our racial categories. When that happens, we often assign them to their minority identity. Researchers believe this happens because, after learning the features of a familiar racial group, the observer's *selective attention* is drawn to the distinctive features of the less-familiar minority. Jamin Halberstadt and his colleagues (2011) illustrated this learned-association effect by showing New Zealanders blended Chinese-White faces. Compared with participants of Chinese descent, European-descent New Zealanders more readily classified ambiguous faces as Chinese (**Figure 4.1-2**). With effort and with experience, people get better at recognizing individual faces from another group (Hugenberg et al., 2010; Young et al., 2012).

## Remembering Vivid Cases

As we saw in Module 2.2, we also simplify our world by employing *heuristics*—mental shortcuts that enable snap judgments. The *availability heuristic* is the tendency to estimate the frequency of an event by how readily it comes to mind. Vivid cases come to mind easily, so it's no surprise that they feed our stereotypes. In a classic experiment, researchers showed two groups of students lists containing information about 50 men (Rothbart et al., 1978). The first group's list included 10 men arrested for *nonviolent* crimes, such as forgery. The second group's list included 10 men arrested for *violent* crimes, such as assault. Later, both groups were asked how many men on their list had committed *any* sort of crime. The second group overestimated the number. Violent crimes form vivid memories.

© Dave Coverly/speedbump.com

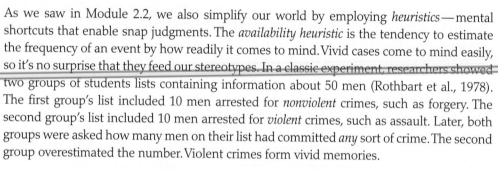

AP® Science Practice

## Exploring Research Methods & Design

Consider the Rothbart et al. (1978) experiment described above, and address each of the following:

- Explain why this is an experiment (as opposed to a non-experimental method).

- Identify the independent and dependent variables.

- Explain why the researchers can draw causal conclusions about the relationship between vividness and judgments.

## Victim Blaming

As we noted earlier, people often justify their prejudices by blaming victims. If the world is just, they assume, people must get what they deserve. As one German civilian is said to have remarked when visiting the Bergen-Belsen concentration camp shortly after World War II, "What terrible criminals these prisoners must have been to receive such treatment."

*Hindsight bias* amplifies victim blaming (Carli & Leonard, 1989). Have you ever heard people say that rape victims, abused spouses, or people with AIDS got what they deserved? In some countries, such as Pakistan, rape victims have been sentenced to severe punishment for violating adultery prohibitions (Mydans, 2002). In one experiment, two groups were given a detailed account of a date (Janoff-Bulman et al., 1985). The first group's account ended with the woman being raped. Members of that group perceived the woman's behavior as at least partly to blame, and in hindsight, they thought, "She should have known better." The second group, given the same account with the rape ending deleted, did not perceive the woman's behavior as inviting rape. In the first group, hindsight bias promoted a blame-the-victim mentality. Blaming the victim also serves to reassure people that it couldn't happen to them.

People also have a basic tendency to justify their culture's social systems (Jost, 2019). We're inclined to see the way things are as the way they ought to be and deserve to be: If people are rich, they must be smart (Hussak & Cimpian, 2015). Once social policies based on these assumptions are in place, our "system justification" tends to preserve them.

\*\*\*

If your own gut-check reveals you sometimes have feelings you would rather not have about other people, remember this: It is what we *do* with our feelings that matters. By monitoring our feelings and actions, by replacing old habits with new ones, and by seeking out new friendships, we can work to free ourselves from prejudice.

---

 **AP® Science Practice**    **Check Your Understanding**

**Examine the Concept**

▶ Explain the differences among stereotyping, prejudice, and discrimination.

▶ Explain scapegoat theory.

*Answers to the Examine the Concept questions can be found in Appendix C at the end of the book.*

**Apply the Concept**

▶ What are some examples of ingroup bias in your own life, and in your community? How can you help break down barriers that you or others may face?

---

## Module 4.1 REVIEW

**4.1-1 What is *person perception*, and how do we tend to explain others' behavior and our own?**

- Person perception describes how we form impressions of ourselves and others, including attributions of behavior.

- When explaining others' behavior, we may—especially if we come from an individualist Western culture—exhibit an *actor-observer bias*. This contributes to the *fundamental attribution error*, when we underestimate the influence of the situation and overestimate the effects of stable, enduring traits. When explaining our own behavior, we more readily attribute it to the influence of the situation.

**4.1-2 How does social comparison influence our perceptions of ourselves and others?**

- When we evaluate others and ourselves, we often engage in *social comparison*. By comparing ourselves to others, we judge whether we're succeeding or failing.

- When we feel as though we're coming up short, social comparisons can negatively impact our self-concept and self-esteem.

**4.1-3 What is *prejudice*? How do explicit and implicit prejudice differ?**

- *Prejudice* is an unjustifiable, usually negative attitude toward a group and its members. Prejudice's three components are negative emotions, beliefs (often *stereotypes*), and a predisposition to action (*discrimination*).

- Prejudice may be explicit (overt), or it may be implicit—an unthinking knee-jerk response operating below conscious awareness. Implicit prejudice can cause discrimination even when people do not consciously intend to discriminate.

## 4.1-4 What group distinctions tend to elicit prejudice?

- Prejudice involves explicit and implicit negative attitudes toward people of a particular racial or ethnic group, gender, or sexual orientation.

- In the United States, frequently targeted groups include Black Americans, women, and LGBTQ people.

## 4.1-5 What are some social, emotional, and cognitive roots of prejudice?

- The social roots of prejudice include social inequalities and divisions. Higher-status groups often justify their privileged position with the *just-world* phenomenon. We tend to favor our own group (*ingroup bias*) as we divide ourselves into "us" (the *ingroup*) and "them" (the *outgroup*).

- Prejudice can also be a tool for protecting our emotional well-being, as when we focus our anger by blaming events on a *scapegoat*.

- The cognitive roots of prejudice grow from our natural ways of processing information: forming categories, remembering vivid cases, and believing that the world is just (and that our own and our group's ways of doing things are the right ways).

---

# AP® Practice Multiple Choice Questions

**1.** Claire has had several car accidents that she blames on other drivers, believing that they are just bad at driving. Which of the following psychological concepts applies to this scenario?

  a. Social comparison
  b. Implicit prejudice
  c. Fundamental attribution error
  d. Ingroup bias

**Use the following text to answer questions 2–4:**

Sandro attends State University, and he loves being a student there. He believes that everyone at nearby Tech College is rude and a bully. When the air conditioning stopped working on his campus, he blamed the students of Tech College, believing that they sabotaged State University's air-conditioning system.

**2.** Which of these cognitive shortcuts best explains Sandro's biased beliefs about the students of Tech College?

  a. Availability heuristic
  b. Hindsight bias
  c. Other-race effect
  d. Outgroup homogeneity

**3.** Which of the following best explains Sandro's willingness to blame the students of Tech College for the air-conditioning malfunction?

  a. Scapegoat theory
  b. Social comparison
  c. Just-world phenomenon
  d. Social identity

**4.** Which of the following best describes Sandro's perception of himself as a student of State University?

  a. Stereotype
  b. Social identity
  c. Social comparison
  d. Other-race effect

**5.** Dr. Chavez is conducting a study on attitudes toward women athletes. In the study, he monitors the facial responses of sportscasters who are discussing women in sports. What variable is Dr. Chavez interested in investigating?

  a. Attribution theory
  b. Implicit prejudice
  c. Just-world phenomenon
  d. Ingroup bias

**6.** On a game show, Zeke is asked to describe the just-world phenomenon. How should he answer?

  a. It is the reduction in prejudice that has resulted from improvements in our laws and judicial system.
  b. It is the belief that most people get what they deserve and deserve what they get.
  c. It is the tendency of people to deny that prejudice is still a problem.
  d. It is a reflection of our desire to categorize daily events as "unfair."

**7.** Which of the following is an example of ingroup bias?

    a.  Hinata is a member of the drama club, but she also plays tuba in the marching band.

    b.  Sabrina has been a New York Yankees fan since she was in fourth grade.

    c.  Kimia believes she is the best student in her AP® Psychology class, but her grades are not as high as those of several other students.

    d.  Derek believes his T-ball team is the best in the league and that the other teams have no talented players.

**8.** Clarence, who is White, has just begun a new job. In the morning, he meets three coworkers: Tony and Nat, who are Black, and Cole, who is White. Later, when he walks into the break room for lunch and finds a big group of employees talking and eating, Clarence recognizes Cole more easily than Tony or Nat. Which of the following explains why Clarence remembered Cole's face best?

    a.  Scapegoat theory

    b.  Actor-observer bias

    c.  The other-race effect

    d.  Ingroup bias

# Module 4.2 Attitude Formation and Attitude Change

**AP® Science Practice**

## Research

In the tanning experiment described below, experimental group participants (the group exposed to the "treatment") received vivid information about skin cancer; those in the control group (the group *not* exposed to the treatment) received no such information.

### LEARNING TARGETS

**4.2-1** Describe how our attitudes and actions interact.

**4.2-2** Describe how *peripheral route persuasion* and *central route persuasion* differ.

## Attitudes and Actions

**4.2-1** How do our attitudes and actions interact?

**attitudes** feelings, often influenced by our beliefs, that predispose us to respond in a particular way to objects, people, and events.

As we learned in Module 4.1, **attitudes** predispose our reactions to objects, people, and events. If we *believe* someone is threatening us, we may *feel* fear and anger toward the person and *act* defensively. The traffic between our attitudes and our actions is two-way. Our attitudes affect our actions. Hateful attitudes feed violent behavior. And, as we will see, our actions affect our attitudes.

### Attitudes Affect Actions

Attitudes affect our behavior. But situational factors, such as intense social pressures, can override the attitude-behavior connection (Wallace et al., 2005). Politicians may vote as their supporters demand, despite privately disagreeing (Nagourney, 2002). Or they may publicly espouse behaviors they don't privately practice.

Attitudes are especially likely to affect behavior when external influences are minimal, and when the attitude is stable, specific to the behavior, and easily recalled (Glasman & Albarracín, 2006). One experiment used vivid, easily remembered information to convince White sun-tanning college students that repeated tanning put them at risk for future skin cancer. One month later, 72 percent of the participants, and only 16 percent of those in a control group, had lighter skin (McClendon & Prentice-Dunn, 2001). Changed attitudes (about skin cancer risk) changed behavior (less tanning).

**Figure 4.2-1**

**Attitudes follow behavior**

Cooperative actions, such as those performed by people on sports teams (including Germany's national soccer team, shown here celebrating a World Cup victory), feed mutual liking. Such attitudes, in turn, promote positive behavior.

Actions

Matthias Hangst/Getty Images

Attitudes

### Actions Affect Attitudes

Now consider a more surprising principle: Not only will we stand up for what we believe, but we also will more strongly believe in what we have stood up for. Many streams of evidence confirm the *attitudes-follow-behavior* principle (Figure 4.2-1).

### The Foot-in-the-Door Phenomenon

How would you react if someone induced you to act against your beliefs? In many cases, people adjust their attitudes. During the Korean war, many U.S. prisoners were held in Chinese communist war camps. The captors secured prisoners' collaboration in various activities, ranging from simple tasks (running errands to gain privileges) to more serious actions (false confessions, informing on other prisoners, and divulging U.S. military information).

After doing so, the prisoners sometimes adjusted their beliefs to be more consistent with their public acts (Lifton, 1961). When the war ended, 21 prisoners chose to stay with the communists. Some others returned home convinced that communism was good for Asia (though not literally "brainwashed," as has often been said).

The captors succeeded in part thanks to the **foot-in-the-door phenomenon**: People who agree to a small request find it easier to comply later with a larger one. The captors began with harmless requests, such as copying a trivial statement, but gradually escalated their demands (Schein, 1956). The next statement to be copied might list flaws of capitalism. Then, to gain privileges, the prisoners would move up to participating in group discussions, writing self-criticisms, and, finally, uttering public confessions. The point is simple: To get people to agree to something big, start small and build (Cialdini, 1993). A trivial act makes the next act easier. A small lie paves the way to a bigger lie. Fibbers may become frauds. Succumb to a temptation and the next temptation becomes harder to resist. (Experiments also reveal a *door-in-the-face* effect. Approach someone with an unreasonable request: "Could you volunteer daily for two weeks?" After you get turned down—the door in the face—a follow-up moderate request becomes more acceptable: "Could you volunteer for the next 30 minutes?")

In dozens of studies, researchers have coaxed people into acting against their attitudes or violating their moral standards, with the same result: Doing becomes believing. After giving in to an order to harm an innocent victim—by making nasty comments or delivering presumed electric shocks—people begin to look down on their victim. After speaking or writing on behalf of a position they have qualms about, they begin to believe their own words.

Fortunately, the attitudes-follow-behavior principle works with good deeds as well. In one experiment, researchers sought permission to place a large "Drive Carefully" sign in people's yards (Freedman & Fraser, 1966). The 17 percent agreement rate soared to 76 percent among those who first did a small favor—displaying a 3-inch-high "Be a Safe Driver" window sign.

The foot-in-the-door tactic has helped boost charitable contributions, blood donations, and U.S. school desegregation. With the passage of the Civil Rights Act of 1964, school desegregation became law. In the years that followed, White Americans expressed diminishing racial prejudice. And as Americans in different regions came to *act* more alike—thanks to more uniform national standards against discrimination—they began to *think* more alike. Research confirms the point: *Moral actions strengthen moral convictions.*

## Role-Playing Affects Attitudes

When you adopt a new **role**—when you become a college student or begin a new job—you strive to follow the social norms. At first, your behaviors may feel phony, because you are *acting* a role. Soldiers, who at first feel they are playing war games, come to embrace military attitudes. When you first move out on your own, you may feel like a child playing at "adulting" rather than an actual adult. Before long, however, what began as play-acting in the theater of life becomes *you*. To choose a vocation is also to choose who you will become (Woods et al., 2020).

In the real world, step-by-step role-playing has even been used to train torturers (Staub, 1989). In the early 1970s, the Greek military government eased men into these roles. First, a trainee played the role of guard outside an interrogation cell. After this foot-in-the-door

**foot-in-the-door phenomenon** the tendency for people who have first agreed to a small request to comply later with a larger request.

**role** a set of expectations (*norms*) about a social position, defining how those in the position ought to behave.

**New nurse** Pulling on scrubs for the first time can feel like playing dress-up. But over time, that role defines the players, as they jump into the day-to-day work and follow the social cues in their new environment.

step, he stood guard inside. Only then was he ready to become actively involved in the questioning-and-torture role. In one study of German men, military training toughened their personalities, leaving them less agreeable even five years later, after leaving the military (Jackson et al., 2012). Every time we act like the people around us, we slightly change ourselves to be more like them and less like who we used to be.

Yet people differ. In real-life atrocity-producing situations, some people have succumbed to the situation and others have not (Haslam & Reicher, 2007, 2012; Mastroianni & Reed, 2006; Zimbardo, 2007). Person and situation interact.

## Cognitive Dissonance: Relief From Tension

We have seen that actions can affect attitudes, sometimes turning prisoners into collaborators and role-players into believers. But why? One explanation is that when we become aware that our attitudes and actions don't coincide, we experience tension, or *cognitive dissonance*. To relieve this tension, according to Leon Festinger's (1957) **cognitive dissonance theory**, we may adjust our actions to match our attitudes. But we might also adjust our attitudes, bringing them into line with our past actions.

Dozens of experiments have tested cognitive dissonance theory (Levy et al., 2018). Many have made people feel responsible for behavior that clashed with their attitudes and had foreseeable consequences. As a participant in one of the experimental groups, you might agree, for little money, to write an essay supporting something you don't believe in (perhaps a tuition increase). Participants in the control group might agree to do the same for a large sum of money. Feeling responsible for your written statements (which are inconsistent with your attitudes), you would probably feel dissonance, especially if you thought your essay might influence an administrator. To reduce the uncomfortable tension, you might start believing your phony words. It's as if we rationalize, "If I chose to do it (or say it) for just a small amount of money, I must believe in it." The less coerced and more responsible we feel for a troubling act, the more dissonance we feel. The more dissonance we feel, the more motivated we are to find and project consistency, such as changing our attitudes to justify the act.

The *attitudes-follow-behavior* principle has a heartening implication: We cannot directly control all our feelings, but we can influence them by altering our behavior. If we are depressed, we can change our attributions and explain events in more positive terms, with more self-acceptance and fewer self-put-downs (Rubenstein et al., 2016). If we are unloving, we can become more loving by behaving *as if* we were—by doing thoughtful things, expressing affection, giving affirmation. "Each time you ask yourself, 'How should I act?'" observes Robert Levine (2016), "you are also asking, 'Who is the person I want to become?'" That helps explain why teens' participation in volunteer work promotes a compassionate identity. Act as if you like someone, and you soon may. Pretense can become reality. Conduct sculpts character. What we do we become.

*The point to remember:* Not only can we think ourselves into action, but we can also act ourselves into a way of thinking.

**cognitive dissonance theory** the theory that we act to reduce the discomfort (dissonance) we feel when two of our thoughts (cognitions) are inconsistent. For example, when we become aware that our attitudes and our actions clash, we can reduce the resulting dissonance by changing our attitudes.

---

**AP® Science Practice**

## Check Your Understanding

### Examine the Concept

▶ Explain the *foot-in-the-door phenomenon*.

▶ Explain how cognitive dissonance can lead to attitude change.

### Apply the Concept

▶ Do you have an attitude or a tendency you would like to change? Using the attitudes-follow-behavior principle, how might you go about changing that attitude?

*Answers to the Examine the Concept questions can be found in Appendix C at the end of the book.*

# Persuasion

**4.2-2** How do *peripheral route persuasion* and *central route persuasion* differ?

**Persuasion** is powerful—whether others are trying to convince us of something ("My candidate is the one who has your best interests at heart!"), or we're trying to convince ourselves ("It's better that I didn't get a callback; I don't really like singing anyway."). Often, people may try to influence our actions by using persuasion to change our attitudes. For example, during the recent pandemic public health officials aimed to persuade Covid skeptics, and to encourage mask-wearing and vaccinations. The *elaboration likelihood model* suggests that when we actively process a message—when we mentally elaborate on it—we more often retain it. According to this model, persuasion usually takes one of two forms:

- **Peripheral route persuasion** uses attention-getting cues to trigger speedy, emotion-based judgments. One experiment gave some people information that debunked the vaccines-cause-autism myth; others viewed photos of unvaccinated children suffering mumps, measles, or rubella, along with a parent's description of measles. Only those given the vivid photos and description became more supportive of vaccines (Horne et al., 2015). Celebrity endorsements can also influence us, as we may believe beautiful or famous people are especially smart or trustworthy (the *halo effect*). When environmental activist and actor Cate Blanchett urges action to counter climate change disaster, or when Pope Francis (2015) states that "Climate change is a global problem with grave implications," they hope to harness their appeal for peripheral route persuasion. The same is true of advertisements that use heart-tugging imagery to sell products.

- **Central route persuasion** offers evidence and arguments that aim to trigger careful thinking. To persuade consumers to purchase a new gadget, an ad might itemize all the latest features. To marshal support for climate change intervention, convincing arguments have focused on the accumulating greenhouse gases, melting arctic ice, rising world temperatures and seas, and increasing extreme weather (van der Linden et al., 2015). Central route persuasion works well for people who are naturally analytical or involved in an issue. And because it is more thoughtful and less superficial, it is more durable.

With time and persuasion, attitudes can change dramatically. What yesterday's people mostly accepted—slavery, climate destruction, anti-gay policies, orca captures—today's people mostly mourn. So, how can we be more successful at getting others to see our point of view? And how can we more effectively counter misinformation, such as from antivaccine activists or conspiracy theorists? For more on effective persuasion strategies, see Developing Arguments: How to Be Persuasive.

**persuasion** changing people's attitudes, potentially influencing their actions.

**peripheral route persuasion** occurs when people are influenced by incidental cues, such as a speaker's attractiveness.

**central route persuasion** occurs when interested people's thinking is influenced by considering evidence and arguments.

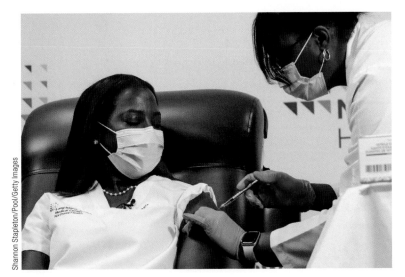

Shannon Stapleton/Pool/Getty Images

**Symbol of health and hope** New York nurse Sandra Lindsay made history when she became the first American vaccinated for the coronavirus. Mindful of historically unequal and racist medical treatment of people of color, Lindsay said she wanted to "inspire people who look like me, who are skeptical in general about taking vaccines" (Otterman, 2020).

# Developing Arguments

## How to Be Persuasive

# Do not:

### Loudly argue your position before listening. Yelling backfires.

### Humiliate people, or imply that they are ignorant. Insults breed defensiveness.

^%*&#!!

idiot

Stupid

*#*&#!!

### Bore people with complex and forgettable information.

Therefore, with that said, direct your attention to this very dull and wonky and boring statistic that you will never remember. Now, however, on the other hand, here are yet more data points that are even more dry and overly complicated than the last... Let us continue...

# Do:

### Identify your shared values or goals,

such as, "We all want to graduate, yes? Find a good job eventually? Let's study for the test before we take time off to hang out."

### Appeal to others' admirable motives.

Relate your aims to their yearnings.[1] For example:

"I would like us to *recover the good old days*, when people owned hunting rifles and pistols, but not assault rifles."

"I would prefer to *make a change*, so that in the future people may own hunting rifles and pistols, but no one will have assault rifles."

**Political conservatives** tend to respond to nostalgia. Those promoting gun safety legislation to this group should frame their message as an affirmation of yesteryear.

**Political liberals** respond better to future-focused messages.

### Make your message vivid. People remember dramatic visual examples well. Pictures of unvaccinated children suffering from preventable diseases, or hungry children starving speak to the heart as well as the head.

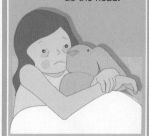

### Repeat your message.
People often come to believe repeated falsehoods, but they also tend to believe oft-repeated truths.

### Engage your audience in restating your message or, better yet, acting on it. Engage them in actively owning it—not just passively listening.

## Developing Arguments Questions

**1.** When trying to persuade someone, which strategies should you avoid?

**2.** Using scientifically derived evidence, explain how you can appeal to other's admirable motives.

**3.** Explain the reasoning behind the assertion that repeating a message is persuasive.

1. Lammers & Baldwin, 2018.

**AP® Science Practice**

## Check Your Understanding

### Examine the Concept

▶ Under what circumstances would peripheral route persuasion be most effective? What about central route persuasion?

### Apply the Concept

▶ Can you think of some commercials or advertisements that utilize peripheral route persuasion? What about central route persuasion?

*Answers to the Examine the Concept questions can be found in Appendix C at the end of the book.*

## Module 4.2 REVIEW

### 4.2-1 How do our attitudes and actions interact?

- Our *attitudes* and our actions influence one another. When other influences are minimal, attitudes that are stable, specific, and easily recalled can affect our actions.

- Actions can modify attitudes, as in the *foot-in-the-door phenomenon* and *role-playing*.

- When our attitudes don't fit with our actions, *cognitive dissonance theory* suggests that we will reduce tension by changing either our actions or our attitudes.

### 4.2-2 How do *peripheral route persuasion* and *central route persuasion* differ?

- *Peripheral route persuasion* uses attention-getting cues (such as celebrity endorsement) to trigger fast but relatively thoughtless judgments.

- *Central route persuasion* offers evidence and arguments to trigger thoughtful responses.

## AP® Practice Multiple Choice Questions

1. Lawrence dislikes Freddy and avoids him because he believes Freddy is a liar. This scenario portrays

   a. central route persuasion.
   b. a role.
   c. the foot-in-the-door phenomenon.
   d. an attitude.

2. Eddie considers himself to be an honest person, so he feels tension when he is dishonest with his friend. Eddie is experiencing

   a. cognitive dissonance.
   b. persuasion.
   c. the foot-in-the-door phenomenon.
   d. role-playing.

3. What psychological concept is depicted in the graph?

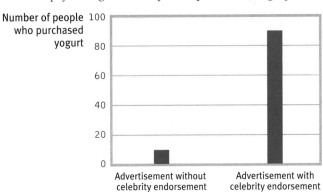

   a. Peripheral route persuasion
   b. Cognitive dissonance
   c. Foot-in-the-door phenomenon
   d. Central route persuasion

4. Dr. Demouy conducted a study in which she divided participants into two groups. With the first group, she pretended she needed to borrow a quarter from each participant; later, she asked to borrow $5 to buy a snack. With the second group, she immediately asked to borrow $5 to buy a snack. She found that when participants first lent her a quarter, they were more likely to give her $5 than if she'd immediately asked for $5. What variable is represented in this description?

   a. Peripheral route persuasion
   b. Central route persuasion
   c. Foot-in-the-door phenomenon
   d. Cognitive dissonance

5. Which of the following is the most accurate statement about cognitive dissonance?

   a. There is a positive correlation between the amount of dissonance felt and the motivation to change attitudes to create consistency between attitudes and thoughts: Higher levels of dissonance are linked with higher levels of motivation to change attitudes.
   b. There is a negative correlation between the amount of dissonance felt and the motivation to change attitudes to create consistency between attitudes and thoughts: Higher levels of dissonance are linked with higher levels of motivation to change attitudes.
   c. There is a positive correlation between the amount of dissonance felt and the motivation to change attitudes to create consistency between attitudes and thoughts: Higher levels of dissonance are linked with lower levels of motivation to change attitudes.
   d. There is a negative correlation between the amount of dissonance felt and the motivation to change attitudes to create consistency between attitudes and thoughts: Higher levels of dissonance are linked with lower levels of motivation to change attitudes.

6. In which of the following examples are attitudes most likely to affect behavior?

   a. Cat, whose favorite color is green, is asked what her favorite color is when she is in a group of people who all love purple.
   b. Kareem, who believes he is a kind person, is walking to class when he sees someone drop their books on the floor.
   c. Sophia, who is usually hard-working and dedicated to her studies, is asked by her soccer team to watch movies all night.
   d. Nancy, who sees herself as a careful driver, notices that everyone else is speeding down the highway.

# Module 4.3a Psychology of Social Situations: Conformity and Obedience

## LEARNING TARGETS

**4.3-1** Explain how social contagion is a form of conformity, and explain how conformity experiments reveal the power of social influence.

**4.3-2** Explain what Milgram's obedience experiments teach us about the power of social influence.

**4.3-3** Explain what social influence studies teach us about ourselves and the power we have as individuals.

Social psychology's great lesson is the enormous power of social influence. This influence stems in part from social **norms**. At high school, jeans are the norm; on New York's Wall Street or London's Bond Street, business attire is expected. When we know how to act, how to groom, how to talk, life functions smoothly.

But sometimes social pressure moves people in dreadful directions. Isolated with others who share their grievances, dissenters may gradually become rebels, and rebels may become terrorists. Shootings, suicides, bomb threats, and airplane hijackings all have a curious tendency to come in clusters. After a mass killing (of four or more people), the probability of another such attack increases for the ensuing 13 days (Towers et al., 2015).

In this module, we will examine the pull of our social strings: How strong are they? How do they operate? When do we break them?

**norms** a society's understood rules for accepted and expected behavior. Norms prescribe "proper" behavior in individual and social situations.

## Conformity: Complying with Social Pressures

**4.3-1** How is social contagion a form of conformity, and how do conformity experiments reveal the power of social influence?

Fish swim in schools. Birds fly in flocks. And humans, too, tend to go with their group, to do what it does and think what it thinks.

### Social Contagion

Our actions are influenced by *social contagion*—the spontaneous spread of behaviors. A lion that sees another member of its pride yawn becomes 100+ times more likely to yawn in the next 3 minutes (Casetta et al., 2021). If one of us humans yawns, laughs, coughs, scratches, stares at the sky, or checks our phone, others in our group will often do the same (Holle et al., 2012). Even just reading about yawning increases people's yawning (Provine, 2012)—as perhaps you've just noticed?

Tanya Chartrand and John Bargh (1999) call this social contagion the *chameleon effect*, likening it to chameleon lizards' ability to mimic the color of their surroundings. In one experiment, students worked in a room alongside another person (actually the experimenter's accomplice). Sometimes the accomplices rubbed their own face.

*I CAN'T STOP YAWNING, EITHER...*

CLAMS

Sometimes they shook their foot. Sure enough, students tended to rub their face along with the face-rubbing person and shake their foot along with the foot-shaking person.

Social contagion also affects emotions. We human chameleons take on the emotional tones of those around us—their expressions, postures, and voice tones—and even their grammar (Ireland & Pennebaker, 2010). Just hearing someone reading a neutral text in either a happy- or sad-sounding voice creates *mood contagion* in listeners (Neumann & Strack, 2000).

This natural mimicry enables us to *empathize*—to feel what others are feeling. This helps explain why we feel happier around happy people than around depressed people. It also helps explain why studies of groups of British workers have revealed *mood linkage*—the sharing of moods (Totterdell et al., 1998). Empathic mimicking—as when a conversation partner nods their head as you do—fosters fondness (Chartrand & van Baaren, 2009; Lakin et al., 2008). We tend to mimic those whom we like, and to like those who mimic us (Kämpf et al., 2018). Just going for a walk with someone—perhaps someone with whom you disagreed—not only synchronizes your movements but increases rapport and empathy (Webb et al., 2017).

Social networks serve as contagious pathways for moods, drug use, and even the behaviors that contribute to obesity and sleep loss (Christakis & Fowler, 2009). On websites, positive product ratings generate more positive ratings—a phenomenon called *positive herding,* as when great reviews of a movie or product generate more positive reviews (Muchnik et al., 2013).

Suggestibility and mimicry can also lead to tragedy. Following highly publicized mass shootings, people are more likely to purchase guns and threaten violence (Cooper, 1999; Porfiri et al., 2019). Spikes in suicide rates sometimes also follow a highly publicized suicide (Phillips et al., 1985, 1989).

What causes behavior clusters? Do people act similarly because they influence one another? Or because they are simultaneously exposed to the same events and conditions? Seeking answers to such questions, social psychologists have conducted experiments on conformity.

## Conformity and Social Norms

Suggestibility and mimicry are subtle types of **conformity**. To study conformity, Solomon Asch (1955) devised a simple test. Imagine yourself a participant in a supposed study of visual perception. You arrive in time to take a seat at a table with five other people. The experimenter asks the group members to state, one by one, which of three comparison lines is identical to a standard line. You see clearly that the answer is Line 2, and you wait your turn to say so. Your boredom begins to show when the next set of lines proves equally easy.

**SPOTLIGHT ON:**
Solomon Asch

**conformity** adjusting our behavior or thinking to coincide with a group standard.

NON SEQUITUR                                                     by WILEY

BANKING on the YOUTH MARKET...

TATTOO & PIERCING

BE LIKE ALL YOUR FRIENDS AND EXPRESS YOUR INDIVIDUALITY

OPEN

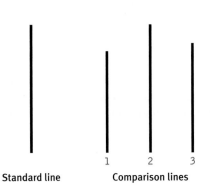

Standard line  Comparison lines

1 2 3

### Figure 4.3-1
### Asch's conformity experiments

Which of the three comparison lines is equal to the standard line? What do you suppose most people would say after hearing five others say, "Line 3"? In this photo from one of Asch's experiments, the student in the center shows the severe discomfort that comes from disagreeing with the responses of other group members (in this case, accomplices of the experimenter).

Now comes the third trial, and the correct answer seems just as clear-cut (**Figure 4.3-1**). But the first person gives what strikes you as a wrong answer: "Line 3." When the second person and then the third and fourth give the same wrong answer, you sit up straight and squint. When the fifth person agrees with the first four, you feel your heart begin to pound. The experimenter then looks to you for your answer. Torn between the unanimity voiced by the five others and the evidence of your own eyes, you feel tense and suddenly unsure. You hesitate before answering, wondering whether you should suffer the discomfort of being the oddball. What answer do you give?

In Asch's experiments, college students, answering questions alone, erred less than 1 percent of the time. But what happened when several others—accomplices of the experimenter—answered incorrectly? Although most people told the truth even when others did not, Asch was disturbed by his result: More than one-third of the time, these "intelligent and well-meaning" college students were "willing to call white black" by going along with the group.

Later investigations have not always found as much conformity as Asch found, but they have revealed that we are more likely to conform when we

- are made to feel incompetent or insecure.
- are in a group with at least three other people.
- are in a group in which everyone else agrees. (If just one other person disagrees, the odds of our disagreeing greatly increase.)
- admire the group's status and attractiveness.
- have not made a prior commitment to any response.
- know that others in the group will observe our behavior.
- are from a culture that strongly encourages respect for social standards.

Why do we so often do as others do and think as they think? Why, when asked controversial questions, are students' answers more similar when they raise their hands and more diverse when they use anonymous electronic clickers (Stowell et al., 2010)? Why do we clap when others clap, eat as others eat, believe what others believe, say what others say, even see what others see? *Social influence* principles provide some answers.

### AP® Science Practice

#### Research

After Asch's original studies, other researchers extended his work, yielding the findings in the bulleted list. Replicating, refining, and expanding knowledge is how psychological science works.

**Tattoos: Yesterday's nonconformity, today's conformity?** Steven Pinker (2019) recalls the unnoticed irony of the college administrator who bragged: "Our students are nonconformists. They all have tattoos and piercings."

**normative social influence**
influence resulting from a person's desire to gain approval or avoid disapproval.

**informational social influence**
influence resulting from a person's willingness to accept others' opinions about reality.

Frequently, we conform to avoid rejection or to gain social approval. In such cases, we are responding to **normative social influence**. We need to belong. People are most conforming to social norms in collectivist cultures, which prize group harmony (Stamkou et al., 2019). People also are responsive to "dynamic norms"—to how norms are *changing*, such as toward eating less meat, consuming fewer sugary drinks, or supporting gay rights (Sparkman & Walton, 2017, 2019).

At other times, we conform because we want to be accurate. Groups provide information, and only an uncommonly stubborn person will never listen to others. When we accept others' opinions about reality, as when reading online movie and product reviews, we are responding to **informational social influence**. Sometimes it pays to assume others are right and to follow their lead. One Welsh driver set a record for the longest distance driven on the wrong side of a British divided highway—30 miles, with only one minor sideswipe, before the motorway ran out and police were able to puncture her tires. The driver, who was intoxicated, later explained that she thought the hundreds of other drivers coming at her were all on the wrong side of the road (Woolcock, 2004).

Is conformity bad or good? Conformity can be bad—leading people to agree with falsehoods or go along with bullying. Or it can be good—leading people to give more generously after observing others' generosity (Nook et al., 2016). The answer also depends partly on our culturally influenced values. Studies across 17 countries have found lower conformity rates in individualist cultures (Bond & Smith, 1996).

*"I love the little ways you're identical to everyone else."*
Mike Twohy The New Yorker Collection/ The Cartoon Bank

AP® Science Practice

## Check Your Understanding

**Examine the Concept**

▶ Which of the following strengthens conformity to a group?
a. Finding the group attractive
b. Feeling secure
c. Coming from an individualist culture
d. Having made a prior commitment

**Apply the Concept**

▶ Despite her mother's pleas to use a more comfortable backpack, Antonia insists on carrying her books to school in an oversized purse, the way her fashionable friends do. Antonia is affected by what type of social influence?

▶ How have you found yourself conforming, or perhaps "conforming to nonconformity"? In what ways have you seen others identifying themselves with those of the same culture?

*Answers to the Examine the Concept questions can be found in Appendix C at the end of the book.*

# Obedience: Following Orders

**4.3-2** What did Milgram's obedience experiments teach us about the power of social influence?

▶ SPOTLIGHT ON:
Stanley Milgram

**obedience** complying with an order or a command.

Complying with an order or a command is to exhibit **obedience**. Social psychologist Stanley Milgram (1963, 1974), a student of Solomon Asch, knew that people often give in to social pressures. But what about outright commands? Would they respond as did those who carried out Holocaust atrocities? (Some of Milgram's family members had survived Nazi concentration camps.) To find out, the 26-year-old Yale professor undertook what have become social psychology's most famous and controversial experiments (Benjamin & Simpson, 2009).

Imagine yourself as one of the nearly 1000 people, mostly White men aged 20 to 50, who took part in Milgram's 23 experiments. You respond to an ad for participants in a Yale

University psychology study of the effect of punishment on learning. Professor Milgram's assistant asks you and another person to draw slips from a hat to see who will be the "teacher" and who will be the "learner." You draw a "teacher" slip (unknown to you, both slips say "teacher"). The supposed learner, a mild and submissive-seeming man, is led to an adjoining room and strapped into a chair. From the chair, wires run through the wall to a shock machine. You sit down in front of the machine and are given your task: Teach and then test the learner on a list of word pairs. If the learner gives a wrong answer, you are to flip a switch to deliver a brief electric shock. For the first wrong answer, you will flip the switch labeled "15 Volts—Slight Shock." With each succeeding error, you will move to the next higher voltage. With each flip of a switch, lights flash and electronic switches buzz.

The experiment begins, and you deliver the shocks after the first and second wrong answers. If you continue, you hear the learner grunt when you flick the third, fourth, and fifth switches. After you activate the eighth switch ("120 Volts—Moderate Shock"), the learner cries out that the shocks are painful. After the tenth switch ("150 Volts—Strong Shock"), he begins shouting: "Get me out of here! I won't be in the experiment anymore! I refuse to go on!" You draw back, but the stern experimenter prods you: "Please continue—the experiment requires that you continue." You resist, but the experimenter pressures you, making statements such as "It is absolutely essential that you continue" or "You have no other choice, you *must* go on."

If you obey, you hear the learner shriek in apparent agony as you continue to raise the shock level after each new error. After the 330-volt level, the learner refuses to answer and falls silent. Still, the experimenter pushes you toward the final, 450-volt switch. "Ask the question," he says, "and if no correct answer is given, administer the next shock level."

Would you follow the experimenter's commands to shock someone? At what level would you refuse to obey? Previously, Milgram had asked nonparticipants what they would do. Most were sure they would stop soon after the learner first indicated pain, certainly before he shrieked in agony. Forty psychiatrists agreed with that prediction. Were the predictions accurate? Not even close. When Milgram actually conducted the experiment, he was astonished. More than 60 percent complied fully—right up to the last switch. When he ran a new study, with 40 new "teachers" and a learner who complained of a "slight heart condition," the results were similar. A full 65 percent of the new teachers obeyed the experimenter, right up to 450 volts (**Figure 4.3-2**). In 10 later studies, women obeyed at rates similar to men's (Blass, 1999).

**Stanley Milgram (1933–1984)**
This social psychologist's obedience experiments "belong to the self-understanding of literate people in our age" (Sabini, 1986).

**Figure 4.3-2**
**Milgram's follow-up obedience experiment**

(b)

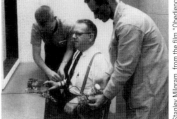

(c)

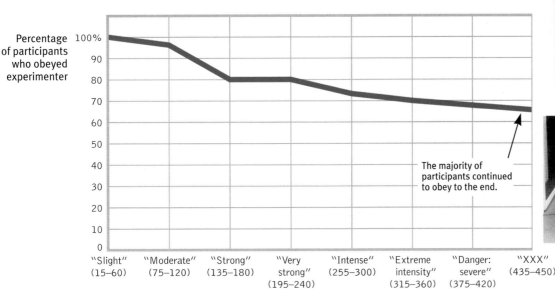

The majority of participants continued to obey to the end.

Shock levels in volts
(a)

AP® Science Practice

## Data Interpretation

Use the graph in Figure 4.3-2 on the preceding page to review your data interpretation skills.

- What do the data show?

- Are these data qualitative or quantitative? Explain.

Remember, you can revisit Module 0.6 to review this material.

Were Milgram's results a product of the 1960s U.S. mindset? *No.* In a more recent replication, 70 percent of the California participants obeyed up to the 150-volt point (only a modest reduction from Milgram's 83 percent at that level) (Burger, 2009). A Polish research team found 90 percent obedience to the same level (Doliński et al., 2017). And in a French reality TV show replication, 81 percent of participants, egged on by a cheering audience, obeyed and tortured a screaming "victim" (Beauvois et al., 2012).

Did Milgram's teachers figure out the hoax—that no real shock was being delivered and the learner was actually an accomplice pretending to feel pain? Did they realize the experiment was really testing their willingness to obey commands to inflict punishment? Some did, and then became willing to play along, report Milgram's critics (Griggs et al., 2020). But Milgram reported that the teachers were often genuinely distressed: Many sweated, trembled, laughed nervously, and bit their lips.

Milgram's use of deception and stress triggered a debate over his research ethics. In his own defense, Milgram pointed out that after the participants learned of the deception and actual research purposes, virtually none regretted taking part (though perhaps by then the participants had reduced their *cognitive dissonance*—the discomfort they felt when their actions conflicted with their attitudes). When a psychiatrist later interviewed 40 of the teachers who had agonized most, none appeared to be suffering emotional aftereffects. All in all, said Milgram, the experiments provoked less enduring stress than university students experience when facing and failing big exams (Blass, 1996). Other scholars, after delving into Milgram's archives, report that his debriefing was less extensive and his participants' distress greater than he had suggested (Nicholson, 2011; Perry, 2013). Critics have also speculated that participants may have been identifying with the researcher and his scientific goals rather than merely being blindly obedient (Haslam et al., 2014, 2016).

In later experiments, Milgram discovered some conditions that influence people's behavior. When he varied the situation, full obedience ranged from 0 to 93 percent. Obedience was highest when

- **the person giving the orders was close at hand and was perceived to be a legitimate authority figure.** This was the case in 2005 when Temple University's basketball coach sent a 250-pound bench player, Nehemiah Ingram, into a game with instructions

**The power of disobedience** The U.S. civil rights movement was ignited when one Black woman, Rosa Parks, was arrested after spontaneously refusing to relinquish her Montgomery, Alabama, bus seat to a White man.

Bettmann/Getty Images

to commit "hard fouls." Following orders, Ingram fouled out in 4 minutes after breaking an opposing player's right arm.

- *a powerful or prestigious institution supported the authority figure*. Compliance was somewhat lower when Milgram dissociated his experiments from Yale University. People have wondered: Why, during the 1994 Rwandan genocide, did so many Hutu citizens slaughter their Tutsi neighbors? It was partly because they were part of "a culture in which orders from above, even if evil," were understood as having the force of law (Kamatali, 2014).

- *the victim was depersonalized or at a distance, even in another room*. Similarly, many soldiers in combat either have not fired their rifles at an enemy they could see, or have not aimed them properly. Such refusals to kill are rarer among soldiers operating long-distance artillery or aircraft weapons (Padgett, 1989). Those who kill from a distance—by operating remotely piloted drones—also suffer stress, though much less posttraumatic stress than do veterans of on-the-ground conflict in Afghanistan and Iraq (G. Miller, 2012a).

- *there were no role models for defiance*. "Teachers" did not see any other participant disobey the experimenter.

---

**AP® Science Practice**

### Exploring Research Methods & Design

Critics question the ethics of Milgram's studies. Explain how he incorporated (or didn't) each of the four guidelines for human research described in Module 0.5:

1. Informed consent

2. Protection from harm and discomfort

3. Confidentiality

4. Debriefing after deception

If you were a member of an Institutional Review Board, based on your assessment of the guidelines, would you approve this study?

---

The power of legitimate, close-at-hand authorities was apparent among those who followed orders to carry out the Nazis' Holocaust atrocities. Obedience alone does not explain the Holocaust—anti-Semitic ideology produced eager killers as well (Fenigstein, 2015; Mastroianni, 2015). But obedience was a factor. In the summer of 1942, nearly 500 middle-aged German reserve police officers were dispatched to German-occupied Jozefow, Poland. On July 13, the group's visibly upset commander informed his recruits, mostly family men, of their orders. They were to round up the village's Jews, who were said to be aiding the enemy. Able-bodied men would be sent to work camps, and the rest would be shot on the spot.

The commander gave the recruits a chance to refuse to participate in the executions. Only about a dozen immediately refused. Within 17 hours, the remaining 485 officers killed 1500 helpless citizens, including women, children, and the elderly, shooting them in the back of the head as they lay face down. Hearing the victims' pleas, and seeing the gruesome results, some 20 percent of the officers did dissent eventually, managing either to miss their victims or to slip away and hide until the slaughter was over (Browning, 1992). In real life, as in Milgram's experiments, those who resisted were the minority.

A different story played out in the French village of Le Chambon. There, villagers openly defied orders to cooperate with the "New Order": They sheltered French Jews destined for

> *The Holocaust . . . did not start from gas chambers. This hatred gradually developed from words, stereotypes & prejudice through legal exclusion, dehumanisation & escalating violence.*
> — Auschwitz Museum tweet, 2018

deportation to Germany, and they sometimes helped them escape across the Swiss border. The villagers' Protestant ancestors had themselves been persecuted, and their pastors taught them to "resist whenever our adversaries will demand of us obedience contrary to the orders of the Gospel" (Rochat, 1993). Ordered by police to give a list of sheltered Jews, the head pastor modeled defiance: "I don't know of Jews, I only know of human beings." At great personal risk, the people of Le Chambon made an initial commitment to resist. Throughout the long, terrible war, they suffered poverty and were punished for their disobedience. Still, supported by their beliefs, their role models, their interactions with one another, and their own initial acts, they remained defiant to the war's end.

Lest we presume that obedience is always evil and resistance is always good, consider the heroic obedience of British soldiers who, in 1852, were traveling with civilians aboard the steamship *Birkenhead*. As they neared their South African port, the *Birkenhead* became impaled on a rock. The soldiers calmed passengers and helped them onto three available lifeboats—not nearly enough for everyone. "Steady, men!" ordered their officer as the lifeboats filled. Heroically, no one frantically rushed to claim a lifeboat seat. As the boat sank, all left onboard were plunged into the sea, most to be drowned or devoured by sharks. For almost a century, noted James Michener (1978), "the Birkenhead drill remained the measure by which heroic behavior at sea was measured."

## Lessons From the Conformity and Obedience Studies

**4.3-3** What do the social influence studies teach us about ourselves? How much power do we have as individuals?

How do the laboratory experiments on social influence relate to real life? How does judging the length of a line or flicking a shock switch relate to everyday social behavior? Psychological experiments aim not to re-create the actual, complex behaviors of everyday life, but rather to capture and explore the underlying processes that shape those behaviors. Solomon Asch and Stanley Milgram devised experiments that forced a familiar choice: Do I adhere to my own standards, even when they conflict with the expectations of others?

In Milgram's experiments and their modern replications, participants were torn. Should they respond to the pleas of the victim or the orders of the experimenter? Their moral sense warned them not to harm another, yet it also prompted them to obey the experimenter and to be a good research participant. With kindness and obedience on a collision course, obedience usually won.

These experiments demonstrated that strong social influences induce many people to conform to falsehoods or capitulate to cruelty. Milgram saw this as the fundamental lesson of his work: "Ordinary people, simply doing their jobs, and without any particular hostility on their part, can become agents in a terrible destructive process" (1974, p. 6).

Focusing on the end point—450 volts, or someone's real-life violence—we can hardly comprehend the inhumanity. But Milgram did not entrap his teachers by asking them first to zap learners with enough electricity to make their hair stand on end. Using the *foot-in-the-door technique*, he instead began with a little tickle of electricity and escalated step by step. To those throwing the switches, the small action became justified, making the next act tolerable. So it happens when people succumb, gradually, to evil.

In any society, great evils often grow out of people's compliance with lesser evils. The Nazi leaders suspected that most German civil servants would resist shooting or gassing Jews directly, but they found them willing to handle the paperwork of the Holocaust (Silver & Geller, 1978).

Milgram found a similar reaction in his experiments. When he asked 40 men to administer the learning test while someone else did the shocking, 93 percent complied. Cruelty

(a)

(b)

does not require devilish villains. All it takes is ordinary people corrupted by an evil situation. Ordinary students may follow orders to haze initiates into their group. Ordinary employees may follow orders to produce and market harmful products. Among people abducted into a violent group, those forced to perpetrate violence are most likely then to identify with the group (Littman, 2018). Attitudes follow behavior.

In Jozefow and Le Chambon, as in Milgram's experiments, those who resisted usually did so early. After the first acts of compliance or resistance, attitudes began to follow and justify behavior.

What have social psychologists learned about the power of the individual? *Social control* (the power of the situation) and *personal control* (the power of the individual) interact. Much as water dissolves salt but not sand, so rotten situations turn some people into bad apples while others resist (Johnson, 2007).

When feeling pressured, some people react by doing the opposite of what is expected (Rosenberg & Siegel, 2018). The power of one or two individuals to sway majorities is *minority influence* (Moscovici, 1985). One research finding repeatedly stands out. When you are the minority, you are far more likely to sway the majority if you hold firmly to your position and don't waffle. This tactic won't make you popular, but it may make you influential, especially if your self-confidence stimulates others to consider why you react as you do. Even when a minority's influence is not yet visible, people may privately develop sympathy for the minority position and rethink their views (Wood et al., 1994).

The powers of social influence are enormous, but so are the powers of the committed individual. Were this not so, communism would have remained an obscure theory, Christianity would be a small Middle Eastern sect, and Rosa Parks' refusal to sit at the back of the bus would not have ignited the U.S. civil rights movement. Social forces matter. But individuals matter, too.

**A minority of one** To be August Landmesser (a), standing defiantly with arms folded as everyone else salutes their allegiance to the Nazi Party and Adolf Hitler, requires extraordinary courage. Such is also true of Marina Ovsyannikova (b), an editor who crashed Russia's most-watched news program to protest her country's invasion of Ukraine. But sometimes such individuals have inspired others, demonstrating the power of minority influence.

**The power of one** In August 2018, 15-year-old Greta Thunberg sat alone outside the Swedish Parliament. Her action was the first school strike protesting climate change. Thirteen months after her act ignited a movement, some 4 million people worldwide joined her for the September 2019 climate strike, and *Time* magazine honored her as its 2019 Person of the Year.

**Examine the Concept**

▶ Explain the difference between conformity and obedience.

▶ Which situations have researchers found to be most likely to encourage obedience in participants?

*Answers to the Examine the Concept questions can be found in Appendix C at the end of the book.*

**Apply the Concept**

▶ Can you think of a time when you or others followed orders and it was beneficial? What about a time when it would have been better to disobey?

# Module 4.3a REVIEW

**4.3-1** How is social contagion a form of conformity, and how do conformity experiments reveal the power of social influence?

- Social contagion (the chameleon effect)—our tendency to unconsciously imitate others' behavior, expressions, postures, inflections, and moods—is a form of *conformity*.

- Solomon Asch and others found that we are most likely to conform when we feel incompetent or insecure, our group has at least three people, everyone else agrees, we admire the group's status and attractiveness, we have not already committed to another response, we know we are being observed, and our culture encourages respect for social standards.

- We may conform to gain approval (*normative social influence*) or because we are willing to accept others' opinions as new information (*informational social influence*).

**4.3-2** What did Milgram's obedience experiments teach us about the power of social influence?

- Stanley Milgram's experiments—in which people obeyed orders even when they thought they were harming

another person—demonstrated that strong social influences can make ordinary people conform to falsehoods or capitulate to cruelty.

- Obedience was highest when the person giving orders was nearby and was perceived as a legitimate authority figure, the research was supported by a prestigious institution, the victim was depersonalized or at a distance, and there were no role models for defiance.

**4.3-3** What do the social influence studies teach us about ourselves? How much power do we have as individuals?

- These experiments have demonstrated that strong social influences can influence behavior. The power of the individual (personal control) and the power of the situation (social control) interact.

- Minority influence can also be powerful: A small minority that consistently expresses its views may sway the majority, as may even a single committed individual.

## AP® Practice Multiple Choice Questions

**1.** Which of the following refers to the tendency of people to mimic others' behaviors?

  a. Obedience

  b. Minority influence

  c. Social contagion

  d. Informational social influence

2. Which of the following is an example of conformity?

   a. Malik is the manager of a grocery store, and he expects his employees to be on time for work every day.
   b. Renee buys the same brand of sweatshirt that most of the kids in her school are wearing.
   c. Jonah makes sure to arrive home before his curfew because he knows he will be grounded if he doesn't.
   d. Terry exerts more effort during volleyball practice because the team captain scolded her for not showing enough effort.

3. Jon does what his friends are doing and throws eggs at houses on Halloween, even though he knows that he should not. Jon's egg throwing is most likely due to

   a. obedience.
   b. normative social influence.
   c. minority influence.
   d. informational social influence.

4. Lyudmila hires a consultant to learn how to increase conformity and obedience in her organization. What advice will the consultant likely give?

   a. People are more likely to obey and to conform in large groups.
   b. People are more likely to obey and to conform when others have high perceived status.
   c. People are more likely to obey and to conform when the victim is depersonalized.
   d. People are more likely to obey and to conform when they come from individualist cultures.

5. Which of the following illustrates a reason why Milgram's study would not pass the ethical guidelines of an institutional review board today? (See Module 0.5 if you need a reminder.)

   a. Milgram did not obtain the informed consent of the participants, and he deceived them in his study.
   b. Milgram put participants under intense psychological distress by making them think they greatly harmed another human.
   c. Milgram did not employ either random sampling or random assignment.
   d. Milgram drew conclusions from the study that would not generalize to broader populations.

# Module 4.3b Psychology of Social Situations: Group Behavior

**4.3-4** How does the presence of others influence our actions, via social facilitation, social loafing, and deindividuation?

Imagine standing in a room holding a fishing pole. Your task is to wind the reel as fast as you can. On some occasions you wind in the presence of another participant, who is also winding as fast as possible. Will the other's presence affect your own performance?

In one of social psychology's first experiments, Norman Triplett (1898) reported that adolescents would wind a fishing reel faster in the presence of someone doing the same thing than they would alone. Although a modern reanalysis revealed that the difference was modest (Stroebe, 2012), Triplett inspired later social psychologists to study how others' presence affects our behavior. Group influences operate both in simple groups—one person in the company of another—and in more complex groups.

**Social facilitation** Skilled athletes often find they are "on" before an audience. What they do well, they do even better when people are watching.

## Social Facilitation

Triplett's claim—of strengthened performance in others' presence—is called **social facilitation**. But studies revealed that the truth is more complicated. The presence of others strengthens our most *likely* response—the correct one on an easy task, an incorrect one on a difficult task (Guerin, 1986; Zajonc, 1965). Why? Because when others observe us, we become aroused, and this arousal amplifies our reactions. Perhaps you, like most people, tend to eat more when eating with others (Ruddock et al., 2019)? Or consider the expert pool players who made 71 percent of their shots when alone, and 80 percent when four people came to watch them (Michaels et al., 1982). Poor shooters, who made 36 percent of their shots when alone, made only 25 percent when watched.

The energizing effect of an enthusiastic audience probably contributes to the home advantage. Studies of more than a quarter-million college and professional athletic events in various countries have shown a home team advantage of 54 percent in Major League Baseball games, 60 percent in National Basketball Association games, and 63 percent in English Premier League soccer games (Allen & Jones, 2014; Jamieson, 2010; Moskowitz & Wertheim, 2011). But in pandemic-era empty stadiums, the home advantage dissipated or disappeared in German and British professional soccer matches (Hamilton, 2021; Tilp & Thaller, 2020).

**social facilitation** in the presence of others, improved performance on simple or well-learned tasks, and worsened performance on difficult tasks.

*The point to remember:* What you do well, you are likely to do even better in front of an audience, especially a friendly audience. What you usually find difficult may seem all but impossible when you are being watched.

Social facilitation also helps explain a funny effect of crowding. Comedians know that a "good house" is a full one. What they may not know is that crowding triggers arousal. Comedy routines that are mildly amusing in an uncrowded room seem funnier in a densely packed room (Aiello et al., 1983; Freedman & Perlick, 1979). When seated close to one another, people like a friendly person even more and an unfriendly person even less (Schiffenbauer & Schiavo, 1976; Storms & Thomas, 1977). So, to energize your next event, choose a room or set up seating that will just barely accommodate everyone.

## Social Loafing

Social facilitation experiments test the effect of others' presence on the performance of an individual task, such as shooting pool. But what happens when people perform as a group—say, in a team tug-of-war? Would you exert more, less, or the same effort as you would exert in a one-on-one match?

To find out, a University of Massachusetts research team asked blindfolded students "to pull as hard as [they] can" on a rope. When they fooled the students into believing three others were also pulling behind them, students exerted only 82 percent as much effort as when they knew they were pulling alone (Ingham et al., 1974). And consider what happened when blindfolded people seated in a group clapped or shouted as loudly as they could while hearing (through headphones) other people clapping or shouting loudly (Latané, 1981). When they thought they were part of a group effort, the participants produced about one-third less noise than when clapping or shouting "alone."

This diminished effort is called **social loafing** (Jackson & Williams, 1988; Latané, 1981). Experiments in the United States, India, Thailand, Japan, China, and Taiwan have found social loafing on various tasks, though it was especially common among men in individualist cultures (Karau & Williams, 1993). What causes social loafing? When people act as part of a group, they may

- *feel less accountable* and therefore worry less about what others think.
- *view individual contributions as dispensable* (Harkins & Szymanski, 1989; Kerr & Bruun, 1983).
- *overestimate their own contributions*, downplaying others' efforts (Schroeder et al., 2016).
- *free ride on others' efforts*. Unless highly motivated and strongly identified with the group, people may slack off (as you perhaps have observed on group assignments)—especially when they share equally in the benefits, regardless of how much they contribute.

FatCamera/E+/Getty Images

**Working hard, or hardly working?** In group projects, social loafing often occurs, as individuals free ride on the efforts of others.

## Deindividuation

We've seen that the presence of others can arouse people (social facilitation), or it can diminish their feelings of responsibility (social loafing). But sometimes the presence of others does both. The uninhibited behavior that results can range from a food fight to vandalism or rioting. Perhaps you can recall following the crowd in yelling at a referee or an opposing team? This process of losing self-awareness and self-restraint, called **deindividuation**, often occurs when group participation makes people both *aroused* and *anonymous*. Compared with identifiable women in a control group, New York University women dressed in depersonalizing Ku Klux Klan–style hoods delivered twice as much presumed electric shock to a victim (Zimbardo, 1970).

**social loafing** the tendency for people in a group to exert less effort when pooling their efforts toward attaining a common goal than when individually accountable.

**deindividuation** the loss of self-awareness and self-restraint occurring in group situations that foster arousal and anonymity.

Jessica Kourkounis/Reuters/Newscom

**Deindividuation** In the excitement that followed the Philadelphia Eagles winning their first National Football League Super Bowl in 2018, some fans, disinhibited by social arousal and the anonymity provided by their "underdog" masks, became destructive.

Deindividuation thrives in many settings. Internet anonymity enables people to feed and freely express their anger, sometimes with bullying and hate speech (Chetty & Alathur, 2018; Kowalski et al., 2018). Online trolls report enjoying their unleashed abuse of others (Buckels et al., 2014; Sest & March, 2017). They might never say "You're disgusting!" to someone's face, but they can hide behind their anonymity online. Tribal warriors wearing face paint or masks are more likely than those with exposed faces to kill, torture, or mutilate captured enemies (Watson, 1973). When we shed self-awareness and self-restraint—whether in a mob, at a concert, at a ball game, or at worship—we become more responsive to the group experience, bad or good. For a comparison of social facilitation, social loafing, and deindividuation, see **Table 4.3-1**.

**TABLE 4.3-1 Behavior in the Presence of Others: Three Phenomena**

| Phenomenon | Social Context | Psychological Effect of Others' Presence | Behavioral Effect |
|---|---|---|---|
| *Social facilitation* | Individual being observed | Increased arousal | Amplified dominant behavior, such as doing better what one does well, or doing worse what is difficult |
| *Social loafing* | Group projects | Diminished feelings of responsibility when not individually accountable | Decreased effort |
| *Deindividuation* | Group setting that fosters arousal and anonymity | Reduced self-awareness | Lowered self-restraint |

\* \* \*

We have examined the conditions under which the *presence* of others can motivate people to exert themselves or tempt them to free ride on the efforts of others, make easy tasks easier or difficult tasks harder, and enhance humor or fuel mob violence. Research also shows that *interacting* with others can similarly have both bad and good effects.

**AP® Science Practice**

## Check Your Understanding

**Examine the Concept**

▶ What is *social facilitation*, and why does it improve performance with a well-learned task?

▶ Explain social loafing, and identify one way it has been operationally defined.

**Apply the Concept**

▶ You are organizing a meeting of fiercely competitive political candidates and their supporters. To add to the fun, friends have suggested handing out masks of the candidates' faces for supporters to wear. What phenomenon might these masks engage?

▶ What steps could you take to reduce social loafing in your next group project assignment?

*Answers to the Examine the Concept questions can be found in Appendix C at the end of the book.*

## Group Polarization

**4.3-5** How can group interaction enable group polarization?

We live in an increasingly polarized world. The Middle East is torn by warring factions. The European Union is struggling with nationalist divisions. In 1990, a 1-minute speech in the U.S. Congress would enable you to guess the speaker's party just 55 percent of the time;

by 2009, partisanship was evident 83 percent of the time (Gentzkow et al., 2016). In 2016, for the first time in survey history, most U.S. Republicans and Democrats reported having "*very* unfavorable" views of the other party (Doherty & Kiley, 2016). People in both parties believe that "my side" is objective, and the other side is biased (Schwalbe et al., 2020).

A powerful principle helps us understand this increasing polarization: The beliefs and attitudes we bring to a group grow stronger as we discuss them with like-minded others. This process, called **group polarization**, can have beneficial results, as when low-prejudice students become even more accepting while discussing racial issues. As George Bishop and I [DM] discovered, it can also be socially toxic, as when high-prejudice students who discuss racial issues together become *more* prejudiced (Myers & Bishop, 1970) (**Figure 4.3-3**). Our repeated finding: Like minds polarize.

Analyses of terrorist organizations around the world reveal that the terrorist mentality emerges slowly among those who share a grievance (McCauley, 2002; McCauley & Segal, 1987; Merari, 2002). As susceptible individuals interact in isolation (sometimes with other "brothers" and "sisters" in camps or prisons), their views grow more and more extreme. Increasingly, they categorize the world as "us" against "them" (Chulov, 2014; Moghaddam, 2005). Knowing that group polarization occurs when like-minded people segregate, a 2006 U.S. National Intelligence estimate speculated "that the operational threat from self-radicalized cells will grow."

The internet offers us a connected global world, but also provides an easily accessible medium for group polarization. When I [DM] got my start in social psychology with experiments on group polarization, I never imagined the potential power of polarization in *virtual* groups. In the online world, progressives friend progressives and share links to sites that affirm their shared views. Conservatives connect with conservatives and likewise share conservative perspectives. With news feeds and retweets, we fuel one another with information—and misinformation—and click on content with which we agree (Hills, 2019). Social media connects us with like-minded people in self-reinforcing echo chambers that amplify extremist messages—the very messages we're most likely to see and to share (Bail, 2021). As comedian Steve Martin tweeted, "Dear Satan, thank you for having my Internet news feeds tailored especially for ME!"

The result is an outrage machine: Our biases may lead us to welcome and share misinformation that supports our beliefs, which strengthens our biases, and leads to even more polarization.

Mindful of the viral false-news phenomenon, tech companies are working on ways to promote media literacy. For more on the internet's role in group polarization—toward ends that are good as well as bad—see Developing Arguments: The Internet as Social Amplifier.

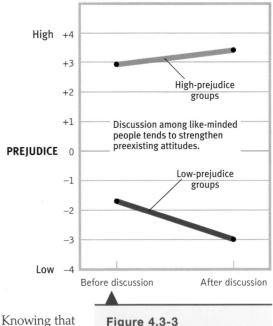

**Figure 4.3-3**
**Group polarization**

**Toxic group polarization**
As illustrated in this 2017 Charlottesville, Virginia, White nationalist rally, the interaction of like minds — both online and face-to-face — can strengthen preexisting attitudes. The 2019 U.S. Department of Homeland Security's *Strategic Framework for Countering Terrorism and Targeted Violence* declared, "Similar to how ISIS inspired and connected with potential . . . terrorists, white supremacist violent extremists connect with like-minded individuals online."

**AP® Science Practice**

**Data**

The graph in Figure 4.3-3 includes three variables. Can you identify them? (They are time in the discussion, prejudice levels of the groups, and individual prejudice levels.)

**group polarization** the enhancement of a group's prevailing inclinations through discussion within the group.

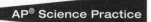

# Developing Arguments
## The Internet as Social Amplifier

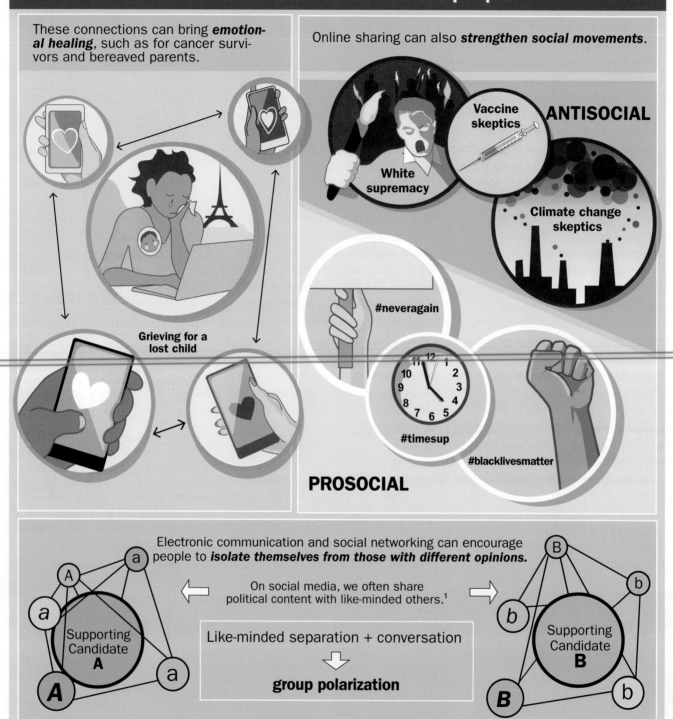

## The internet connects like-minded people.

These connections can bring **emotional healing**, such as for cancer survivors and bereaved parents.

Grieving for a
lost child

Online sharing can also **strengthen social movements**.

White
supremacy

Vaccine
skeptics

**ANTISOCIAL**

Climate change
skeptics

#neveragain

#timesup

#blacklivesmatter

**PROSOCIAL**

Electronic communication and social networking can encourage people to *isolate themselves from those with different opinions.*

On social media, we often share political content with like-minded others.[1]

Like-minded separation + conversation

**group polarization**

A

Supporting
Candidate
**A**

B

Supporting
Candidate
**B**

## Developing Arguments Questions

**1.** Provide reasoning that supports the claim that connecting with like-minded people online can lead to both prosocial and antisocial outcomes.

**2.** Using scientifically derived evidence, explain how connecting with like-minded people online can lead to group polarization.

1. Bakshy et al., 2015; Barberá et al., 2015.

# Groupthink

**4.3-6** How can group interaction enable groupthink?

Does group influence ever distort important national decisions? Consider the Bay of Pigs fiasco. In 1961, U.S. President John F. Kennedy and his advisers decided to invade Cuba with 1400 CIA-trained Cuban exiles. When the invaders were easily captured and quickly linked to the U.S. government, Kennedy wondered aloud, "How could I have been so stupid?"

Social psychologist Irving Janis (1982) studied the decision-making process leading to the ill-fated invasion. He discovered that the soaring morale of the recently elected president and his advisers fostered undue confidence. To preserve the good feeling, group members suppressed or self-censored their dissenting views, especially after President Kennedy voiced his enthusiasm for the scheme. Since no one spoke strongly against the idea, everyone assumed the support was unanimous. To describe this harmonious but unrealistic group thinking, Janis coined the term **groupthink**.

Later studies showed that groupthink—fed by overconfidence, conformity, self-justification, and group polarization—contributed to other fiascos as well. Among them were the failure to anticipate the 1941 Japanese attack on Pearl Harbor; the escalation of the Vietnam war; the U.S. Watergate cover-up; the Chernobyl nuclear reactor accident (Reason, 1987); the U.S. space shuttle *Challenger* explosion (Esser & Lindoerfer, 1989); and the Iraq war, launched on the false idea that Iraq had weapons of mass destruction (U.S. Senate Intelligence Committee, 2004).

Despite the dangers of groupthink, two heads are often better than one. Great minds often *don't* think alike. Knowing this, Janis also studied instances in which U.S. presidents and their advisers collectively made good decisions, such as when the Truman administration formulated the Marshall Plan, which offered assistance to Europe after World War II, and when the Kennedy administration successfully prevented the Soviets from installing missiles in Cuba. His conclusion? Groupthink is prevented when a leader—whether in government or in business—welcomes various opinions, invites experts' critiques of developing plans, and assigns people to be devil's advocates—to identify possible problems. Just as the suppression of dissent bends a group toward bad decisions, open debate often shapes good ones. This is especially the case with small but diverse groups, whose varied backgrounds and perspectives often enable creative or superior outcomes (Shi et al., 2019; Wang et al., 2019; Wu et al., 2019). None of us is as smart as all of us.

# Cultural Influences

**4.3-7** How does culture affect our behavior?

So far, we have seen how the presence of others—and our interactions with them—can affect our actions, for better or for worse. On a grand scale, we see these influences in our *culture*, which shapes how we live our lives and impacts generations to come.

Compared with the narrow path taken by flies, fish, and foxes, the road along which the environment drives humans is wider. Our species' success is born of our ability to imitate and invent. We absorb the collected wisdom of those who came before us, and we sometimes improve upon it. We come equipped with a powerful cerebral mobile device, ready to download specific cultural apps.

How do you cook rice? Dry your wet clothes? Care for yourself when you're sick? Rather than use trial and error, we imitate people close to us. **Culture** consists of the behaviors, ideas, and values shared by a group of people and passed down from generation to generation (Brislin, 1988; Cohen, 2009). Humans are social animals, but more. Wolves are also social animals; they live and hunt in packs. Ants are incessantly social, never alone.

**groupthink** the mode of thinking that occurs when the desire for harmony in a decision-making group overrides a realistic appraisal of alternatives.

**culture** the enduring behaviors, ideas, attitudes, values, and traditions shared by a group of people and transmitted from one generation to the next.

**Humans are cultural animals**
More than any other species, humans imitate and invent. They absorb the wisdom of previous generations, build upon it, and pass it along through teaching.

But "culture is a better way of being social," observed social psychologist Roy Baumeister (2005). Wolves function pretty much as they did 10,000 years ago. We enjoy electricity, indoor plumbing, antibiotics, and the internet—things unknown to most of our ancestors. Culture works.

Social living, imitation, and language have ensured the *preservation of innovation*. Culture also enables *division of labor*. Although three lucky people get their names on this book (which transmits accumulated cultural wisdom), it actually results from the coordination and commitment of a team of gifted people, no one of whom could produce it alone.

Across cultures, we differ in our language, money, sports, religion, and customs. But beneath these differences lies our great similarity—our capacity for culture. Culture works. It transmits the customs and beliefs that enable us to communicate, to exchange money for things, to play, to eat, and to drive with agreed upon rules and without crashing into one another.

## Variation Across Cultures

We see our adaptability in cultural variations among our beliefs and our values, in how we nurture our children and bury our dead, and in what we wear (or whether we wear anything at all). We are ever mindful that the worldwide readers of this book are culturally diverse. You and your ancestors reach from Australia to Algeria and from Singapore to Sweden. Cultures influence how we sleep, eat, dress, learn, and worship.

**tight culture** a place with clearly defined and reliably imposed norms.

**loose culture** a place with flexible and informal norms.

Everyday practices in many Asian, African, and Latin American countries, for example, place a higher value on *collectivism*. Situations focus on "we," on meeting group standards and accommodating others. Western European and English-speaking countries tend to prioritize *individualism*. They more often focus on "me" as an independent, separate self (Triandis, 1994). Very diverse countries may also have a high degree of *multiculturalism*, which places value on cultural and ethnic groups' maintenance of their unique identities, beliefs, and practices.

Cultures also differ in how strictly people follow norms. In **tight cultures**, people more often obey social norms: A pedestrian might wait for the light to say "WALK," even on a deserted corner at midnight. In such cultures, people arrive on time, rarely drop a piece of trash, and might not kiss their sweetheart in public. **Loose cultures** have norms, too (as drivers appreciate), but people expect variability (Gelfand, 2018). In loose cultures, people tolerate some jaywalking, late arrivals, littering, and public affection. Each cultural pattern has benefits.

**Pandemic response: individual "freedom" or group protection?**
(a) Individualist nations, such as Germany, saw more defiance in response to community safeguarding measures during the Covid pandemic. (b) Residents in collectivist nations, such as Japan, demonstrated greater compliance with protective restrictions.

(a)

(b)

Riding along with a unified culture is like biking with the wind. As it carries us along, we hardly notice it. When we try traveling against the wind, though, we feel its force. Face-to-face with a different culture, we become aware of the cultural winds. Visiting Europe, Americans may notice the small cars and tiny coffee cups. Visiting North America, Japanese may wonder why people wear their dirty street shoes in the house and can't seem to line up properly.

When cultures collide, their differing norms often befuddle. Should we greet people by shaking hands, bowing, or kissing each cheek? Knowing what sorts of gestures and compliments are culturally appropriate, we can relax and enjoy one another without fear of embarrassment or insult.

When we don't understand what's expected or accepted, we may experience *culture shock*. People from Mediterranean cultures have perceived northern Europeans as efficient but cold, and preoccupied with punctuality (Triandis, 1981). People from time-conscious Japan—where pedestrians walk briskly and postal clerks fill requests speedily—have found themselves growing impatient when visiting Indonesia, where the pace of life is more leisurely (Levine & Norenzayan, 1999).

## Variation Over Time

Like biological creatures, cultural groups vary, compete for resources, and, over time, evolve (Mesoudi, 2009). Cultures change when many people copy the innovations of a few. Not long ago, humans roamed Earth in groups of 150; today, we mostly live in stable, cooperative societies of millions (Johnson & Earle, 2000). What changed? The cultural inventions of agriculture and animal domestication provided dependable sources of calories (Diamond, 1997). And when religion encouraged people to control their selfish impulses and cooperate, the settlements that developed typically grew and became more successful (Heinrich, 2020; Norenzayan et al., 2016).

Cultures can change rapidly. At the beginning of the last century, people lived in a world without cars, radio broadcasting, or electric lighting. If you could sit down to chat with your great-great-grandparents, you'd likely have trouble understanding one another's accents, words, and expressions. And in the thin slice of history since 1960, most Western cultures have changed with astonishing speed. People enjoy expanded human rights. Middle-class people enjoy the convenience of air-conditioned housing, online shopping, anywhere/anytime electronic communication, and doubled per-person real income.

But some changes seem not so wonderfully positive. Had you fallen asleep in the United States in 1960 and awakened today, you would open your eyes to a culture with more depression and more economic inequality. You would also find North Americans—like their counterparts in Britain, Australia, and New Zealand—spending more hours working, fewer hours with friends and family, and fewer hours asleep (BLS, 2011; Twenge, 2017).

Whether we love or loathe these changes, we cannot fail to be impressed by their breathtaking speed. And we cannot explain them by changes in the human gene pool, which evolves far too slowly to account for high-speed cultural transformations. Cultures vary. Cultures change. Cultures shape our lives.

---

 **AP® Science Practice**

## Check Your Understanding

**Examine the Concept**

▶ Explain groupthink.

▶ What is *culture*, and why do humans need it more than other social animals do?

*Answers to the Examine the Concept questions can be found in Appendix C at the end of the book.*

**Apply the Concept**

▶ How have you been influenced by group polarization online?

▶ How does your culture influence your thoughts, feelings, and actions?

**4.3-4 How does the presence of others influence our actions, via social facilitation, social loafing, and deindividuation?**

- In *social facilitation*, the mere presence of others arouses us, improving our performance on easy or well-learned tasks but decreasing it on difficult ones.

- In *social loafing*, participating in a group project makes us feel less responsible, and we may free ride on others' efforts.

- When the presence of others both arouses us and makes us feel anonymous, we may experience *deindividuation*—loss of self-awareness and self-restraint.

**4.3-5 How can group interaction enable group polarization?**

- In *group polarization*, group discussions with like-minded others strengthen members' prevailing beliefs and attitudes.

**4.3-6 How can group interaction enable groupthink?**

- *Groupthink* is driven by a desire for harmony within a decision-making group, overriding realistic appraisal of alternatives.

- Group leaders can harness the benefits of group interaction by assigning people to identify possible problems, and by welcoming various opinions and expert critique.

- Small but diverse groups, with varied backgrounds and perspectives, can enable superior outcomes.

**4.3-7 How does culture affect our behavior?**

- A *culture* is an enduring set of behaviors, ideas, attitudes, values, and traditions shared by a group and transmitted from one generation to the next.

- Culture enables innovation and division of labor.

- Cultural *norms*, which differ across time and place, are understood rules that inform members of a culture about accepted and expected behaviors.

- Cultures differ in how strictly people follow norms: People more often obey norms in *tight cultures*, but those in *loose cultures* expect greater variability.

# AP® Practice Multiple Choice Questions

**Use the following text to answer questions 1 & 2:**

Kat, who is an excellent hockey player, is playing in the final game of her high school career. In the packed arena, to the sound of roaring fans, Kat easily scores three goals—until she is knocked over and injures her leg. Kedi, one of the team's weaker players, replaces her. Kedi appears unusually confused and nervous, and has more difficulty than ever handling the puck during the game.

**1.** The most likely explanation for Kat's stellar performance is

   a. social loafing.
   b. group polarization.
   c. social facilitation.
   d. deindividuation.

**2.** The most likely explanation for Kedi's poor performance is

   a. social loafing.
   b. group polarization.
   c. social facilitation.
   d. deindividuation.

**3.** Which psychological concept is depicted in the graph?

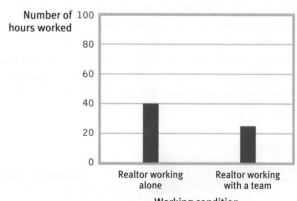

   a. Social facilitation
   b. Groupthink
   c. Group polarization
   d. Social loafing

**Use the following text to answer questions 4 & 5:**

While trying to figure out a topic for their group project, Marie's group chooses the first option proposed without discussing other ideas. Everyone in the group, including Marie, says that the idea is "fine" and "okay," even though the topic does not excite any member of the group.

**4.** Which psychological concept best applies to this scenario?

   a. Social loafing
   b. Group polarization
   c. Loose culture
   d. Groupthink

**5.** What logical and objective advice might you give to Marie to avoid the issues discussed in the example?

   a. "Make sure that there are no free riders in your group."
   b. "Make sure to ask your group members for divergent opinions."
   c. "Make sure to hold each group member accountable."
   d. "Make sure to work on your project in a crowded area."

**6.** Dr. Oslo studies the enduring behaviors, ideas, attitudes, values, and traditions shared by a group of people that are transmitted across generations. What does Dr. Oslo study?

   a. Deindividuation
   b. Groupthink
   c. Social facilitation
   d. Culture

**7.** After students wearing face paint tore down the goal-posts following a stunning win, the school's principal banned students from football games. Which of the following explains the problem with this policy and proposes a better alternative?

   a. The principal's policy is not effective because group polarization tends to happen when groups of like-minded people discuss shared beliefs. The principal should instead instruct students to sit with their families rather than in a separate student section.
   b. The principal's policy is not effective because deindividuation tends to happen when anonymous people lose self-restraint. The principal should ban the use of face paint for all students rather than banning students from games.
   c. The principal's policy is not effective because groupthink tends to happen when people want to keep the peace and don't consider alternative solutions. The principal should ensure that everyone discusses a behavioral plan before the game with a behavioral expert.
   d. The principal's policy is not effective because social facilitation tends to happen when people perform simple tasks better in front of other people. The principal should ask everyone to watch the games online rather than attending the games in person.

# Module 4.3c Psychology of Social Situations: Aggression

**LEARNING TARGETS**

**4.3-8** Explain how psychology's definition of *aggression* differs from everyday usage, and explain the biological factors that make us more prone to hurt one another.

**4.3-9** Explain the psychological and social-cultural triggers of aggression.

**4.3-8** How does psychology's definition of *aggression* differ from everyday usage? What biological factors make us more prone to hurt one another?

In psychology, **aggression** is any physical or verbal behavior intended to harm someone, whether done out of hostility or as a calculated means to an end. The assertive, persistent salesperson is not aggressive. Nor is the dentist who makes you wince with pain. But the high school gossip who invents a vicious rumor about you, the bully who torments you in person or online, and the attacker who robs you are aggressive. Like discrimination, which we explored in Module 4.1, aggression is an *antisocial* behavior—behavior that defies social norms or violates others' rights. (As we will see, social psychologists also study *prosocial* behavior—behavior that helps or benefits someone.)

Aggressive behavior emerges from the interaction of biology and experience. Let's look first at some biological factors that influence our thresholds for aggressive behavior, then at the psychological factors that trigger aggression.

**Do guns in the home save or take more lives?** "Personal safety/protection" is the number one reason Americans have given for gun ownership (Swift, 2013). However, firearms ownership can backfire: Guns in the home are much more often used to kill loved ones or oneself than in self-defense (Kivisto et al., 2019; Stroebe et al., 2017). In 2020, 45,222 Americans died from firearms injuries; 54 percent were suicides (Gramlich, 2022). Compared with people of the same sex, race, age, and neighborhood, those who keep a gun in the home are twice as likely to be murdered and three times as likely to die by suicide (Anglemyer et al., 2014; Stroebe, 2013). States and countries with high gun ownership rates also tend to have high gun death rates (VPC, 2016). It takes Japan nearly a decade to accumulate as many violent gun deaths as occur in an average U.S. day. More guns → more deaths.

## The Biology of Aggression

Aggression varies too widely from culture to culture, era to era, and person to person to be considered an unlearned instinct. But biology does *influence* aggression. We can look for biological influences at three levels—genetic, neural, and biochemical.

### Genetic Influences

Genes influence aggression. Animals have been bred for aggressiveness—sometimes for sport, sometimes for research. The effect of genes also appears in human *twin studies* (Miles & Carey, 1997; Rowe et al., 1999). If one identical twin admits to "having a violent temper," the other twin will often independently admit the same. Fraternal twins are much less likely to respond similarly.

Researchers continue to search for genetic markers in those who commit violent acts. One is already well known and is carried by half the human race: the Y chromosome.

**aggression** any physical or verbal behavior intended to harm someone physically or emotionally.

Another such marker is the *monoamine oxidase A (MAOA) gene*, which is involved in breaking down neurotransmitters such as dopamine and serotonin. People who have low *MAOA* gene expression tend to behave aggressively when provoked. In one experiment, low (compared with high) *MAOA* gene carriers gave more unpleasant hot sauce to someone who provoked them (McDermott et al., 2009; Tiihonen et al., 2015).

## Neural Influences

There is no one spot in the brain that controls aggression. Aggression is a complex behavior, and it occurs in particular contexts. But animal and human brains have neural systems that, given provocation, will either inhibit or facilitate aggression (Falkner et al., 2016; Fields, 2019). Consider:

- Researchers implanted a radio-controlled electrode in the brain of the domineering leader of a caged monkey colony. The electrode was in an area that, when stimulated, inhibits aggression. When researchers placed the control button for the electrode in the colony's cage, one small monkey learned to push it every time the boss became threatening.

- A neurosurgeon, seeking to diagnose a disorder, implanted an electrode in the amygdala of a mild-mannered woman. Because the brain has no sensory receptors, she was unable to feel the stimulation. But at the flick of a switch she snarled, "Take my blood pressure. Take it now," then stood up and began to strike the doctor.

- If the impulse-controlling frontal lobes are damaged, inactive, disconnected, or not yet fully mature, aggression may be more likely (Amen et al., 1996; Davidson et al., 2000; Raine, 2013). One study of 203 convicted murderers revealed reduced tissue in the frontal lobes (Sajous-Turner et al., 2020).

## Biochemical Influences

Our genes engineer our individual nervous systems, which operate electrochemically. The hormone testosterone, for example, circulates in the bloodstream and influences the neural systems that control aggression. A raging bull becomes a gentle giant when castration reduces its testosterone level. Conversely, when injected with testosterone, gentle, castrated mice once again become aggressive.

Humans are less sensitive to hormonal changes. But drugs that sharply reduce testosterone levels also subdue men's aggressive tendencies. And as men's testosterone levels diminish with age, hormonally charged, aggressive 17-year-olds mature into quieter and gentler 50-year-olds. As psychologist David Lykken (1995) wryly observed, "We could avoid two-thirds of all crime simply by putting all able-bodied young men in cryogenic sleep from the age of 12 through 28."

*"It's a guy thing."*

**A lean, mean fighting machine — the testosterone-laden female hyena** The hyena's unusual embryology pumps testosterone into female fetuses. The result is revved-up young female hyenas that seem born to fight.

**AP® Science Practice**

### Research

Different areas within psychology tend to rely on particular research methods to draw conclusions. For example, the biological perspective uses animal studies and case studies to examine the brain's role in aggression.

Another drug that sometimes circulates in the bloodstream—alcohol—*unleashes* aggressive responses to frustration. Across police data, prison surveys, and experiments, aggression-prone adults are more likely to drink, and to become violent when intoxicated (White et al., 1993). Alcohol is a disinhibitor—it slows the brain activity that controls judgment and inhibitions. Under its influence, people may interpret ambiguous acts (such as being bumped in a crowd) as provocations and react aggressively (Bègue et al., 2010; Giancola & Gorman, 2007). Alcohol has been a factor in 73 percent of homicides in Russia and 57 percent in the United States (Landberg & Norström, 2011). When alcohol sales have been restricted—as when Sydney, Australia, outlawed late-night pub sales, or when South Africa temporarily banned alcohol during the Covid pandemic—assaults have dropped (Anna, 2020; BBC, 2020; Kypri & Livingston, 2020).

Even people who just *think* they've imbibed alcohol can become more aggressive (Bègue et al., 2009). But so, too, will those who unknowingly ingest alcohol slipped into a drink. Thus, alcohol affects aggression both biologically and psychologically (Bushman, 1993; Ito et al., 1996).

# Psychological and Social-Cultural Factors in Aggression

> **4.3-9** What psychological and social-cultural factors may trigger aggressive behavior?

Biological factors influence how easily aggression is triggered. But what psychological and social-cultural factors pull the trigger?

## Aversive Events

Suffering sometimes builds character. In laboratory experiments, however, those made miserable have often made others miserable (Berkowitz, 1983, 1989). Aversive stimuli—hot temperatures, physical pain, personal insults, foul odors, cigarette smoke, crowding, and a host of others—can evoke hostility. Even hunger can feed anger—making people "hangry" (Bushman et al., 2014). A prime example of this phenomenon is the **frustration-aggression principle**: Frustration creates anger, which can spark aggression.

The frustration-aggression link was illustrated in an analysis of 27,667 hit-by-pitch Major League Baseball incidents between 1960 and 2004 (Timmerman, 2007). Pitchers were most likely to hit batters when the previous batter had hit a home run, the current batter had hit a home run the last time at bat, or a pitch had hit the pitcher's teammate in the previous half-inning. A separate study found a similar link between rising temperatures and the number of hit batters (Reifman et al., 1991; see **Figure 4.3-4**). Overheated temperatures → overheated tempers.

In the wider world, higher rates of violent crime and spousal abuse have been recorded during hotter years, seasons, months, and days (Anderson et al., 1997; Heilmann & Kahn, 2019). Studies from other social science fields converge in finding that throughout history, higher temperatures have predicted increased individual violence, wars, and revolutions (Hsiang et al., 2013). One projection from available data estimates that global warming of 4 degrees Fahrenheit (about 2 degrees Celsius) could induce tens of thousands of additional assaults and murders (Anderson & Delisi, 2011; Miles-Novelo & Anderson, 2019). And that's before the added violence inducements from climate change–related drought, poverty, food insecurity, and migration.

## Reinforcement and Modeling

Aggression may naturally follow aversive events, but learning can alter natural reactions. As Unit 3 explained, we learn when our behavior is reinforced, and we learn by watching others.

In situations where experience has taught us that aggression pays, we are likely to act aggressively again. Children whose aggression has successfully intimidated other children

**frustration-aggression principle** the principle that frustration—the blocking of an attempt to achieve some goal—creates anger, which can generate aggression.

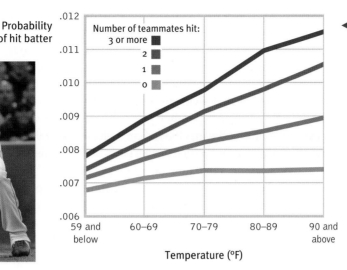

**Figure 4.3-4**
**Temperature and retaliation**
Researchers looked for occurrences of batters hit by pitches during 4,566,468 pitcher-batter matchups across 57,293 Major League Baseball games since 1952 (Larrick et al., 2011). The probability of a hit batter increased if one or more of the pitcher's teammates had been hit, and also with higher temperatures.

may become bullies. Animals that have successfully fought to get food or mates become increasingly ferocious. To foster a kinder, gentler world, we had best model and reward sensitivity and cooperation from an early age, perhaps by training parents to discipline without modeling violence. Parent-training programs often advise parents to avoid screaming and hitting; instead, they can reinforce desirable behaviors and frame statements positively ("When you clean your room, you can go play," rather than "If you don't clean your room, you'll be in big trouble").

Different cultures model, reinforce, and evoke different tendencies toward violence. For example, crime rates have been higher and average happiness lower in times and places marked by a great disparity between rich and poor (Messias et al., 2011; Oishi et al., 2011; Wilkinson & Pickett, 2009). And fathers matter (Triandis, 1994). Even after controlling for parental education, race, income, and teen motherhood, U.S. male youths from father-absent homes are incarcerated at twice the rate of their peers (Harper & McLanahan, 2004). A study of 1.3 million Danish individuals also showed that, even after controlling for parents' income, father absence increased youths' risk for later violent crime (Mok et al., 2018).

Violence can vary by culture within a country. The U.S. South, for example, has long had a "culture of honor." In one study, researchers analyzed violence among White Americans in southern towns settled by Scots-Irish herders whose tradition encouraged violent response to insult, the use of arms to protect one's flock, and slavery (Nisbett & Cohen, 1996). Compared with their White counterparts in New England towns settled by the more traditionally peaceful Puritan, Quaker, and Dutch farmer-artisans, the cultural descendants of those herders had triple the homicide rates and were more supportive of physically punishing children, of wars, and of uncontrolled gun ownership. In more recent years, southern culture-of-honor states have had higher rates of students bringing weapons to school and of school shootings (Brown et al., 2009).

## Media Models for Violence

Parents are hardly the only models for their children's aggression. Television, films, video games, and the internet offer supersized portions of violence. An adolescent boy faced with a real-life challenge may "act like a man"—at least an action-film man—by intimidating or eliminating the threat. Media violence teaches us **social scripts**—culturally provided mental files for how to act in certain situations. As more than 100 studies confirm, we sometimes imitate what we've viewed. Watching media depictions of risk-glorifying behaviors (dangerous driving, extreme sports, unprotected sex) increases real-life risk taking (Fischer et al., 2011). Watching violent behaviors (murder, robbery) can increase real-life aggressiveness (Anderson et al., 2017).

**AP® Exam Tip**

This is a good opportunity to review Unit 3. If you don't recognize the basic components of operant conditioning and observational learning in this material, refer to Unit 3 for a quick review.

**CULTURAL AWARENESS**

Culture influences our behavior because, as you will learn later in this module, it determines our social scripts. Mindful that cultures often have different scripts, critical thinkers guard against having biased thoughts, feelings, or actions toward members of other cultures.

**social script** a culturally modeled guide for how to act in various situations.

## Research

In the German study described here, participants who heard woman-hating lyrics made up the experimental group, whereas those who heard neutral lyrics were in the control group. These groups enabled researchers to isolate the effects of the independent variable. Can you identify the experimental and control groups in the pornography study detailed here?

Music lyrics also write social scripts. In one study, German university men who listened to woman-hating lyrics poured the most hot chili sauce for a woman to consume. Listening to man-hating lyrics had a similar effect on women (Fischer & Greitemeyer, 2006).

How does repeatedly watching pornographic films affect viewers? Just as repeated viewing of on-screen violence helps immunize us to aggression, repeated viewing of pornography—even nonviolent pornography—makes sexual aggression seem less serious (Harris, 1994). In one experiment, undergraduates viewed six brief films each week for six weeks (Zillmann & Bryant, 1984). Some viewed sexually explicit films; others viewed films with no sexual content. Three weeks later, both groups, after reading a report about a man convicted of raping a female hitchhiker, suggested an appropriate prison term. Compared with the sentences recommended by the control group, the sex film viewers recommended terms that were half as long. In other studies exploring pornography's effects on aggression toward relationship partners, pornography consumption predicted both self-reported aggression and participants' willingness to administer laboratory noise blasts to their partner (Lambert et al., 2011; Peter & Valkenburg, 2016). Pornography acts mostly by adding fuel to a fire: It heightens the risk of sexual aggression primarily among aggression-prone men (Malamuth, 2018).

Pornography with violent sexual content can also increase men's readiness to behave aggressively toward women. As a statement by 21 social scientists noted, "Pornography that portrays sexual aggression as pleasurable for the victim increases the acceptance of the use of coercion in sexual relations" (Surgeon General, 1986). Contrary to much popular opinion, viewing such scenes does not provide an outlet for bottled-up impulses. Rather, said the statement, "in laboratory studies measuring short-term effects, exposure to violent pornography increases punitive behavior toward women."

## Do Violent Video Games Teach Social Scripts for Violence?

AFP/Getty Images

**Coincidence or cause?** In 2011, Norwegian Anders Behring Breivik bombed government buildings in Oslo, and then went to a youth camp where he shot and killed 69 people, mostly teens. As a player of first-person shooter games, Breivik stirred debate when he commented, "I see MW2 [*Modern Warfare 2*] more as a part of my training-simulation than anything else." Did his violent game playing — and that of the 2012 mass murderer of Newtown, Connecticut's first-grade children — contribute to the violence, or was it a merely coincidental association? Psychologists explore such questions with experimental research.

Experiments worldwide indicate that playing positive games produces positive effects (Greitemeyer & Mügge, 2014; Prot et al., 2014). For example, playing the classic video game *Lemmings*, where a goal was to help others, increased real-life helping. So, might a parallel effect occur after playing games that enact violence? Violent video games became an issue for public debate after teenagers in more than a dozen places seemed to mimic the carnage in the shooter games they had so often played (Anderson, 2004, 2013).

Such incidents of violent mimicry make us wonder: What are the effects of actively role-playing aggression? Does it cause people to become less sensitive to violence and more open to violent acts? Amid conflicting findings, nearly 400 studies of 130,000 people offer some answers (Calvert et al., 2017). Violent video game playing tends to make us less sensitive to cruelty (Arriaga et al., 2015). Video games can prime aggressive thoughts, decrease empathy, and induce us to respond aggressively when provoked. Two dozen longitudinal studies, which followed children and youth for up to 4 years, found that violent video game playing predicts "greater levels of overt physical violence over time" (Prescott et al., 2018).

In experiments, people who were randomly assigned to play a game involving bloody murders with groaning victims (rather than to play nonviolent games) became more hostile. Studies of young adolescents reveal that those who play a lot of violent video games become more aggressive and see the world as more hostile (Bushman, 2016; Exelmans et al., 2015; Gentile, 2009). Compared with nongaming kids, they get into more arguments and fights and earn poorer grades. In another experiment, children who played a video game with gun violence (rather than sword violence or no violence) later became more likely to touch, pick up, and pull the trigger on a real (but disabled) gun (Chang & Bushman, 2019).

Ah, but is this merely because naturally hostile kids are drawn to such games (Greitemeyer et al., 2019)? Apparently not. Comparisons of gamers and nongamers who scored low on hostility measures revealed a difference in the number of fights they reported. Almost 4 in 10 violent-game players had been in fights, compared with only 4 in 100 of the nongaming kids (Anderson, 2004). Some researchers believe that, due partly to the more active participation and rewarded violence of game play, violent video games have even greater effects on aggressive behavior and cognition than do violent TV shows and movies (Anderson & Warburton, 2012).

Other researchers are unimpressed by such findings (Ferguson et al., 2020; Markey & Ferguson, 2018). They note that from 1996 to 2006, video game sales increased, yet youth violence declined. They argue that the best studies find minimal effects and that other factors — depression, family violence, peer influence, and a gun-toting culture — better predict aggression. Although some commentators have tried to blame modern mass shootings on violent video games, most researchers agree that they are, at worst, but one modest contributor to social violence (APA, 2019b; Mathur & VanderWeele, 2019).

\* \* \*

To sum up, research reveals biological, psychological, and social-cultural influences on aggressive behavior. Complex behaviors, including violence, have many causes, making any single explanation an oversimplification. Asking what causes violence is therefore like asking what causes cancer. Those who study the effects of asbestos exposure on cancer rates may remind us that asbestos is indeed a cancer cause, but it is only one among many. Like so much else, aggression is a biopsychosocial phenomenon (**Figure 4.3-5**).

A happy concluding note: Historical trends suggest that the world is becoming less violent over time (Pinker, 2011, 2018). The fact that people vary across time and place reminds us that environments differ. Yesterday's plundering Vikings have become today's peace-promoting Scandinavians. Like all behavior, aggression arises from the interaction of persons and situations.

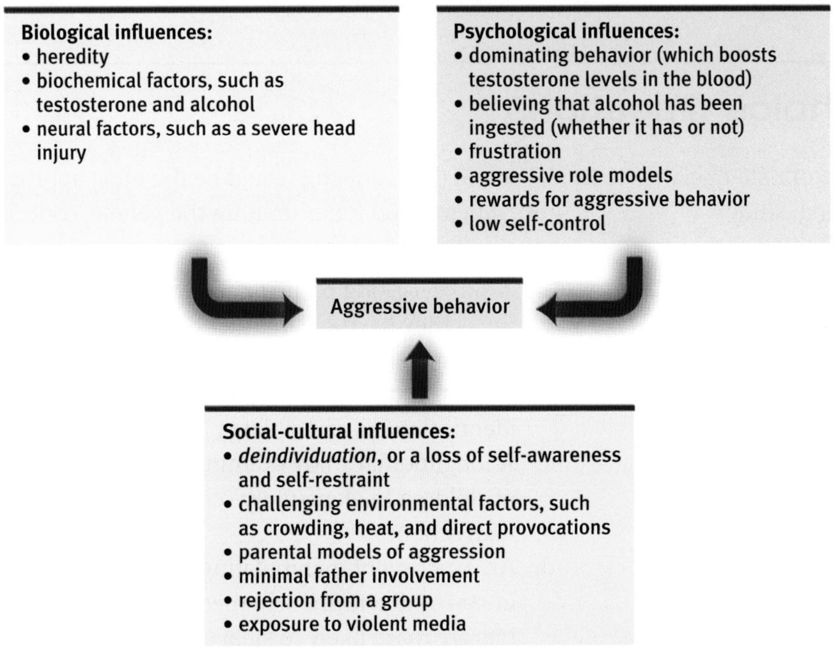

**AP® Science Practice**

**Research**

In the experiments described here, the participants in the studies make up the *sample*, whereas the researchers are hoping to generalize the results to the *population* — all young people who play violent video games.

**Biological influences:**
• heredity
• biochemical factors, such as testosterone and alcohol
• neural factors, such as a severe head injury

**Psychological influences:**
• dominating behavior (which boosts testosterone levels in the blood)
• believing that alcohol has been ingested (whether it has or not)
• frustration
• aggressive role models
• rewards for aggressive behavior
• low self-control

**Aggressive behavior**

**Social-cultural influences:**
• *deindividuation*, or a loss of self-awareness and self-restraint
• challenging environmental factors, such as crowding, heat, and direct provocations
• parental models of aggression
• minimal father involvement
• rejection from a group
• exposure to violent media

**Figure 4.3-5**

**Biopsychosocial understanding of aggression**

Because many factors contribute to aggressive behavior, there are many ways to change such behavior, including learning anger management and communication skills, and avoiding violent media and video games.

## Check Your Understanding

**Examine the Concept**

▶ Explain the frustration-aggression principle.

▶ What biological, psychological, and social-cultural influences interact to produce aggressive behaviors?

**Apply the Concept**

▶ In what ways have you been affected by social scripts for aggression? Have your viewing and gaming habits influenced these social scripts?

▶ Do you think there should be laws to prevent children's exposure to violent media? Why or why not?

*Answers to the Examine the Concept questions can be found in Appendix C at the end of the book.*

---

# Module 4.3c REVIEW

**4.3-8** How does psychology's definition of *aggression* differ from everyday usage? What biological factors make us more prone to hurt one another?

- In psychology's more specific meaning, *aggression* is any physical or verbal behavior intended to harm someone physically or emotionally.

- Biology influences our threshold for aggressive behaviors at three levels: genetic (inherited traits), neural (activity in key brain areas), and biochemical (such as alcohol or excess testosterone in the bloodstream).

- Aggression is a complex behavior resulting from the interaction of biology and experience.

**4.3-9** What psychological and social-cultural factors may trigger aggressive behavior?

- Frustration (the *frustration-aggression principle*), previous reinforcement for aggressive behavior, observing an aggressive role model, and poor self-control can all contribute to aggression.

- Media violence provides *social scripts* that children learn to follow.

- Viewing sexual violence contributes to greater aggression toward women.

- Playing violent video games increases aggressive thoughts, emotions, and behaviors.

---

# AP® Practice Multiple Choice Questions

1. Which of the following would be an appropriate operational definition of aggression in a research study?

   a. The number of car accidents that occur between midnight and 2:00 A.M.

   b. The number of rumors spread at lunchtime in a middle school

   c. The number of times a crowd yells loudly during a basketball game

   d. The number of times cell phones sound alerts during a movie

2. Which of the following would be the most appropriate research method for examining the genetic contributions to aggression?

   a. A survey asking participants to rate the number of times they have called other people names after playing violent video games

   b. A twin study comparing the *MAOA* levels between identical twins and siblings

   c. A longitudinal study examining the neural activity of children in elementary school, middle school, and high school

   d. An experiment manipulating the levels of testosterone in rats to determine whether the high-testosterone rats are more likely to steal other rats' cheese

**3.** From a learning perspective, which of the following is a possible implication of parents screaming or hitting to try to decrease aggressive actions in their children?

   a. Children may feel frustrated, which may increase aggression.

   b. Children may imitate their parents' aggressive actions.

   c. Children may become disinhibited and act more aggressively.

   d. Children may experience decreased activation in the frontal lobes, leading to more aggression.

**4.** Brandt's baseball team just lost the state championship game after a questionable call made by the umpire. As a result, Brandt gets angry and starts shouting insults at the umpire. Which of the following best applies to this scenario?

   a. Stimulation of the amygdala

   b. Biochemical influences

   c. Frustration-aggression principle

   d. Social scripts

**5.** Dwayne is acting violently toward his friends and family. A positron emission tomography (PET) scan of his brain may show

   a. increased temporal lobe activity.

   b. diminished activity in the hypothalamus.

   c. decreased frontal lobe activity.

   d. a decrease in the size of the hippocampus.

**6.** Which of the following is an example of a social-cultural influence on aggressive behavior?

   a. Demarsha reads an anxiety-provoking novel.

   b. Martina feels frustrated when she sees her spelling test grade.

   c. Kendall has higher-than-average levels of testosterone.

   d. Hatch plays violent video games every day after school.

**7.** Dr. Jordison conducted a study in which he measured testosterone levels in 10-year-old boys, then counted the number of times they called other children unkind names over the next week. Which of the following statements is a plausible conclusion Dr. Jordison might draw from his study?

   a. Higher levels of testosterone cause young boys to behave more aggressively.

   b. Aggressive actions cause testosterone levels to increase significantly.

   c. Higher levels of testosterone appear to be related to aggression.

   d. Boys who are frustrated feel more anger, which leads to higher levels of aggression.

# Module 4.3d Psychology of Social Situations: Attraction

As social animals—as people who need people—we often approach others not with closed fists, but with open arms. Social psychologists focus not only on the dark side of social relationships, but also on the bright side, by studying *prosocial* behavior—behavior that intends to help or benefit someone. Our positive behaviors toward others are evident from explorations of this module's focus, attraction, and those of the next module, altruism and peacemaking.

Pause a moment and think about your relationships with two people—a close friend and someone who has stirred your romantic feelings. What psychological chemistry binds us together in friendship or love? Social psychology suggests some answers.

## The Psychology of Attraction

**4.3-10** Why do we befriend or fall in love with some people but not others?

We endlessly wonder how we can win others' affection and what makes our own affections flourish or fade. Does familiarity breed contempt, or does it amplify affection? Do birds of a feather flock together, or do opposites attract? Is it what's inside that counts, or does physical attractiveness matter, too? To explore these questions, let's consider three ingredients of our liking for one another: proximity, attractiveness, and similarity.

### Proximity

Before friendships become close, they must begin. *Proximity*—geographic nearness—is friendship's most powerful predictor. Proximity can provide opportunities for aggression. But much more often it breeds liking (and sometimes even marriage) among those who live in the same neighborhood, sit nearby in class, work in the same office, share the same parking lot, or eat in the same cafeteria. Look around. Matching starts with meeting.

The power of proximity was illustrated at a "Seeds of Peace" Israeli summer camp (White et al., 2021). The camp sought to reduce intergroup conflict among outgroup pairs (Jewish and Palestinian teens) with one of three strategies: share a sleeping bunk, eat at the same table, or attend the same 110-minute dialogue group. Proximity mattered most. Outgroup pairs who shared a sleeping bunk, versus those who did not, were 11 times more likely to become friends.

Proximity breeds liking partly because of the **mere exposure effect**. Repeated exposure to novel visual stimuli increases our liking for them. By age 3 months, infants prefer photos of the race they most often see—usually their own race (Kelly et al., 2007). Familiarity with a face also makes it look happier (Carr et al., 2017). For our ancestors, this mere exposure effect likely had survival value. What was familiar was generally safe and approachable. What was unfamiliar was more often dangerous and threatening. Evolution may therefore have hard-wired into us the tendency to bond with those who look familiar and to be wary of those who look unfamiliar (Sofer et al., 2015; Zajonc, 1998).

Brendan Beirne/REX/Shutterstock

**Familiarity breeds acceptance** When this rare white penguin was born in the Sydney, Australia, zoo, his tuxedoed peers ostracized him. Zookeepers thought they would need to dye him black to gain acceptance. But after three weeks of contact, the other penguins came to accept him.

**mere exposure effect** the tendency for repeated exposure to novel stimuli to increase our liking of them.

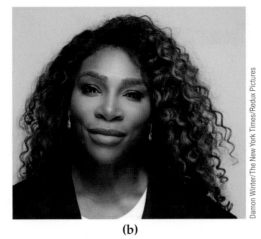

(a)     (b)

**Which is the real Serena Williams?** The mere exposure effect applies even to ourselves. Because the human face is not perfectly symmetrical, the face we see in the mirror is not the same face our friends see. Most of us prefer the familiar mirror image, while our friends like the reverse (Mita et al., 1977). The person tennis star Serena Williams sees in the mirror each morning is (b), and that's the photo she would probably prefer.

Mere exposure increases our liking not only for faces, but also for musical selections, geometric figures, Chinese characters, and the letters of our own name (Moreland & Zajonc, 1982; Nuttin, 1987; Zajonc, 2001). So, up to a point (after which the effect wears off), familiarity feeds fondness (Bornstein, 1989, 1999; Montoya et al., 2017). This would come as no surprise to the young Taiwanese man who wrote more than 700 letters to his girlfriend, urging her to marry him. She did marry—the mail carrier (Steinberg, 1993).

No face is more familiar than your own. And that helps explain an interesting finding by Lisa DeBruine (2002, 2004): We like other people when their faces incorporate some morphed features of our own. When university students played an electronic game with a supposed other player, they were more trusting and cooperative when the other person's image had some of their own facial features morphed into it. In me I trust.

### AP® Science Practice

#### Research

The data from U.S. women's experiences on online dating sites were gathered using a survey — a technique for obtaining the self-reported attitudes of a particular group. But crafting questions is tricky, because their wording can influence respondents' answers. This is called the wording effect.

## Modern Matchmaking

Those who have not found a romantic partner in their immediate proximity may cast a wider net. Millions search for love on one of 8000 dating sites (Hatfield, 2016). In 2015, 27 percent of 18- to 24-year-old Americans tried an online dating service or mobile dating app (Smith, 2016). Despite some risks—which, for about half of young U.S. women using online dating sites and apps, include receiving unwanted sexual messages (Anderson et al., 2020)—some 10 million Americans are using online matchmaking (Statista, 2018).

Online matchmaking definitely expands the pool of potential mates, especially for same-sex couples (Finkel et al., 2012a,b; Rosenfeld et al., 2019). Among couples surveyed in 2017 who had met during the internet age, 39 percent of straight couples and 65 percent of same-sex couples met online (Rosenfeld et al., 2019; see **Figure 4.3-6**). Compared to couples meeting offline, those who meet online also more often differ in race or ethnicity (Brown, 2019).

*". . .and if anyone here suspects that the algorithm that put these two together might be flawed, speak now . . ."*

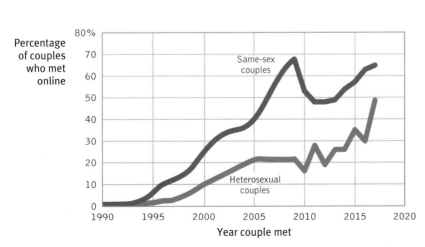

**Figure 4.3-6**

**The changing way we meet our partners**

The internet's increasing role is clear in U.S. surveys of straight and same-sex couples. (Data from Rosenfeld, 2011; Rosenfeld et al., 2018, 2019.)

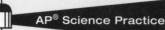

How effective is the matchmaking? Compared with those formed in person, internet-formed friendships and romantic relationships are, on average, slightly more likely to last and be satisfying (Bargh & McKenna, 2004; Bargh et al., 2002; Cacioppo et al., 2013). In one study, people disclosed more, with less posturing, to those whom they met online (McKenna et al., 2002). When conversing online with someone for 20 minutes, they felt more liking for that person than they did for someone they had met and talked with face-to-face. This was true even when (unknown to them) it was the same person!

*Speed dating* pushes the search for romance into high gear. In a process pioneered by a matchmaking rabbi, people meet a succession of prospective partners, either in person or via webcam (Bower, 2009). After a 3- to 8-minute conversation, people move on to the next prospect. (In an in-person meeting of straight daters, one group—usually the women—remains seated while the other group circulates.) Those who want to meet again can arrange for future contact. For many participants, 4 minutes is enough time to form a feeling about a conversational partner and to register whether the partner likes them (Eastwick & Finkel, 2008a,b).

For researchers, speed dating offers a unique opportunity for studying influences on our first impressions of potential romantic partners. Some recent findings:

- *People who fear rejection often elicit rejection*. After a 3-minute speed date, those who most feared rejection were least often selected for a follow-up date (McClure & Lydon, 2014).

- *Given more options, people make more superficial choices*. When people meet lots of potential partners, they focus on more easily assessed characteristics, such as height and weight (Lenton & Francesconi, 2010).

- *Men wish for future contact with more of their speed dates; women tend to be choosier*. But this difference disappears if the conventional roles are reversed, so that men stay seated while women circulate (Finkel & Eastwick, 2009).

- *Compatibility is difficult to predict*. In two speed-dating studies, participants answered more than 100 self-report measures beforehand. Alas, nothing predicted successful matches (Joel et al., 2017).

## Physical Attractiveness

Once proximity affords us contact, what most affects our first impressions? The person's sincerity? Intelligence? Personality? Hundreds of experiments reveal that it is something more superficial: physical appearance. This finding is unnerving for those of us taught that "beauty is only skin deep" and "appearances can be deceiving."

In one early study, researchers randomly matched new university students for heterosexual blind dates in a Welcome Week dance (Walster et al., 1966). Before the dance, the researchers gave each student a battery of personality and aptitude tests, and they rated each student's physical attractiveness. The couples danced and talked for more than 2 hours and then took a brief intermission to rate their dates. What predicted whether they liked each other? Only one thing: appearance. Both the men and the women liked good-looking dates best. Women are more likely than men to say that another person's looks don't affect them (Lippa, 2007). But studies show that a man's looks do affect women's behavior (Eastwick et al., 2014a,b). In speed-dating experiments, attractiveness influences first impressions (Belot & Francesconi, 2006; Finkel & Eastwick, 2008).

Physical attractiveness also predicts how often people date and how popular they feel. And it affects initial impressions of people's personalities. We perceive attractive people as healthier, happier, more sensitive, more successful, and more socially skilled (Eagly et al., 1991; Hatfield & Sprecher, 1986).

For those who find the importance of looks unfair and unenlightened, three other findings may be reassuring.

- People's attractiveness is surprisingly unrelated to their self-esteem and happiness (Diener et al., 1995; Major et al., 1984). Unless we have just compared ourselves with superattractive people, few of us (thanks, perhaps, to the mere exposure effect) view ourselves as unattractive (Thornton & Moore, 1993).

- Strikingly attractive people are sometimes suspicious that praise for their work may simply be a reaction to their looks. Less attractive people are more likely to accept praise as sincere (Berscheid, 1981).

- For couples who were friends before lovers—who became romantically involved long after first meeting—looks matter less (Hunt et al., 2015). With slow-cooked love, shared values and interests matter more.

Beauty is also in the eye of the culture. Hoping to look attractive, people across the globe have pierced and tattooed their bodies, lengthened their necks, bound their feet, artificially lightened or darkened their skin and hair, and bulked up their muscles. They have gorged themselves to achieve a full figure or liposuctioned fat to achieve a slim one, applied chemicals to rid themselves of unwanted hair or to regrow wanted hair, and used undergarments to change the proportions of waists, hips, and breasts. Cultural ideals also change over time and with the context. For women in North America, for example, the ultrathin ideal of the Roaring Twenties gave way to the soft, voluptuous Marilyn Monroe ideal of the 1950s. And during the Covid pandemic, the cosmetics and clothing industries took a hit as many people, isolating at home, embraced a more natural look.

Some aspects of heterosexual attractiveness, however, do cross place and time (Cunningham et al., 2005; Langlois et al., 2000). By providing reproductive clues, bodies influence sexual attraction. As evolutionary psychologists explain (and as you may recall from Module 3.3), heterosexual men in cultures worldwide judge women as more attractive if they have a youthful, fertile appearance (Walter et al., 2020). Heterosexual women also feel attracted to men who are healthy- and fertile-looking, as well as to men who seem mature, dominant, and affluent.

"Cosmetic dentistry changed my life."

Peter Steiner/Cartoon Stock

**CULTURAL AWARENESS**

By understanding how cultural traditions influence beauty ideals, we can appreciate and respect the beauty in humanity within and across cultures. Differences are not deficits.

Sean Caffrey/Getty Images

Blend Images/Alamy Stock Photo

svetikd/Getty Images

**What is "attractive"?** The answer varies by culture and over time. Yet some adult physical features, such as a healthy appearance and a relatively symmetrical face, seem attractive everywhere.

David Perrett/University of St. Andrews

**Figure 4.3-7**

**Average is attractive**

Which of these faces offered by University of St. Andrews psychologist David Perrett (2002, 2010) is most attractive? Most people say it's the face on the right — of a nonexistent person that is the average composite of these 3 plus 57 other actual faces.

Faces matter, too. When people rate faces and bodies separately, the face tends to be the better predictor of overall physical attractiveness (Currie & Little, 2009; Peters et al., 2007). So what makes a face attractive? Attractive faces have average features—neither unusually large nor unusually small. Symmetrical faces are also perceived as more attractive (Rhodes, 2006). This helps explain why an averaged (and therefore symmetrical) face is attractive (**Figure 4.3-7**). In one clever demonstration, researchers digitized the faces of up to 32 college students and used a computer to average them (Langlois & Roggman, 1990). The result? Viewers judged the averaged, composite faces as more attractive than 96 percent of the individual faces. (If only we could merge either half of our face with its mirror image: Our symmetrical new face would be a notch more attractive.)

Our feelings also influence our attractiveness judgments. Imagine two people: One is honest, humorous, and polite. The other is rude, unfair, and abusive. Which one is more attractive? Most people perceive the person with the appealing traits as more physically attractive (Lewandowski et al., 2007). Or imagine being paired with a stranger of the gender you find attractive, who listens intently to your self-disclosures. Might you feel a twinge of sexual attraction toward that empathic person? Student volunteers did, in several experiments (Birnbaum & Reis, 2012). Our feelings influence our perceptions. Those we like we find attractive.

In a Rodgers and Hammerstein production of *Cinderella*, Prince Charming asks, "Do I love you because you're beautiful, or are you beautiful because I love you?" Chances are it's both. As we see our loved ones again and again, their physical imperfections grow less noticeable and their attractiveness grows more apparent (Beaman & Klentz, 1983; Gross & Crofton, 1977). Shakespeare said it in *A Midsummer Night's Dream:* "Love looks not with the eyes, but with the mind." Come to love someone and watch beauty grow. Love sees loveliness.

## Similarity

So, proximity has brought you into contact with someone, and your appearance has made an acceptable first impression. What influences whether you will become friends? As you get to know each other, will the chemistry be better if you are opposites or if you are alike?

It makes a good story—extremely different types liking or loving each other. Consider unlikely friends Frog and Toad in Arnold Lobel's books, or unlikely couple Hermione and Ron in the Harry Potter series. These stories delight us by expressing what we seldom experience. In real life, opposites tend to retract (Montoya & Horton, 2013; Rosenbaum, 1986). Tall people typically find true love with other tall people; short people show a soft spot for other short people (Yengo et al., 2018). Compared with randomly paired people, friends and couples are far more likely to share—and to like those with whom they share—attitudes, beliefs, and interests (and, for that matter, age, religion, race, education, intelligence, smoking behavior, and economic status). As C. S. Lewis (1960) observed, "What draws people to be friends is that they see the same truth."

Moreover, people feel attracted to people when they share a rare attitude, such as an unusual hobby or a favorite musician (Alves, 2018). One journalist was right to suppose that love lasts "when the lovers love many things together, and not merely each other" (Lippmann, 1929). Similarity breeds content.

Proximity, attractiveness, and similarity are not the only determinants of attraction. We also like those who like us. This is especially true when our self-image is low. When we believe someone likes us, we feel good and respond to them warmly, which leads them to like us even more (Curtis & Miller, 1986). To be liked is powerfully rewarding. And good news, when we're fretting over our words or looks after meeting someone: Most people immediately like us more than we realize (Boothby et al., 2018).

Indeed, all the findings we have considered so far can be explained by a simple *reward theory of attraction:* We will like those whose behavior is rewarding to us, including those who are both able and willing to help us achieve our goals (Montoya & Horton, 2014). When people live or work in close proximity to us, it requires less time and effort to develop the friendship and enjoy its benefits. When people are attractive, they are aesthetically pleasing, and associating with them can be socially rewarding. When people share our views, they reward us by validating our beliefs.

*Similarity attracts; perceived dissimilarity does not.*

---

### AP® Science Practice

## Check Your Understanding

**Examine the Concept**

▶ Explain how proximity relates to attraction.

▶ How does being physically attractive influence others' perceptions?

**Apply the Concept**

▶ To what extent have your closest relationships been affected by proximity, physical attractiveness, and similarity?

*Answers to the Examine the Concept questions can be found in Appendix C at the end of the book.*

---

# Romantic Love

**4.3-11** How does romantic love typically change as time passes?

Sometimes people move from initial impressions to friendship to the more intense, complex, and mysterious state of romantic love. If love endures, temporary *passionate love* will mellow into a lingering *companionate love* (Hatfield, 1988).

## Passionate Love

**Passionate love** mixes something new with something positive (Aron et al., 2000; Coulter & Malouff, 2013). We intensely desire to be with our partner, and seeing our partner stimulates blood flow to a brain region linked to craving and obsession (Acevedo et al., 2012; Hatfield et al., 2015).

The *two-factor theory of emotion,* which we will learn more about in Module 4.8, explains the intense positive absorption of passionate love (Hatfield, 1988). That theory assumes that

- emotions have two ingredients—*physical arousal* plus *cognitive appraisal.*

- arousal from any source can enhance one emotion or another, depending on how we interpret and label the arousal.

In one classic study, researchers studied men crossing two bridges above British Columbia's rocky Capilano River (Dutton & Aron, 1974, 1989). One, a swaying footbridge, was 230 feet (70 meters) above the rocks; the other was low and solid. As the men came off each bridge, an attractive young woman (working for the researchers) intercepted them

**passionate love** an aroused state of intense positive absorption in another, usually present at the beginning of a romantic relationship.

and asked them to fill out a short questionnaire. She then offered her phone number in case they wanted to hear more about her project. Far more of the men who had just crossed the high bridge—which left their hearts pounding—accepted the number and later called the woman.

So, if you're looking for romance, perhaps you should go work out at a climbing gym. To be revved up and to associate some of that arousal with a desirable person is to feel the pull of passion. Adrenaline makes the heart grow fonder. Sexual desire + a growing attachment = passionate love (Berscheid, 2010).

## Companionate Love

Although the desire and attachment of romantic love often endure, the intense absorption in the other, the thrill of the romance, the giddy "floating on a cloud" feelings typically fade. Does this mean the French are correct in saying that "love makes the time pass and time makes love pass"? Or can friendship and commitment keep a relationship going after the passion cools?

As love matures, it typically becomes a steadier **companionate love**—a deep, affectionate attachment (Hatfield, 1988). Like a passing storm, the flood of passion-facilitating hormones (testosterone, dopamine, adrenaline) subsides. But another hormone, *oxytocin*, remains, supporting feelings of trust, calmness, and bonding with the mate. This shift from passion to attachment may have adaptive value (Reis & Aron, 2008). Passionate love often produces children; companionate love aids children's survival as the parents lose their obsession with each other.

In the most satisfying of marriages, attraction and sexual desire endure, minus the obsession of early romance (Acevedo & Aron, 2009). Recognizing the short duration of obsessive passionate love, some societies deem such feelings an irrational reason for marrying. Better, they say, to seek (or have someone seek for you) a partner with a compatible background and interests. Cultures where people rate love as less important for marriage do have lower divorce rates (Levine et al., 1995).

One key to a gratifying and enduring relationship is **equity**. When equity exists—when both partners receive in proportion to what they give—the chances for sustained and satisfying companionate love have been good (Gray-Little & Burks, 1983; Van Yperen & Buunk,

**companionate love** the deep affectionate attachment we feel for those with whom our lives are intertwined.

**equity** a condition in which people receive from a relationship in proportion to what they give to it.

**Love is an ancient thing** This 5000- to 6000-year-old "Romeo and Juliet" young couple was unearthed locked in embrace, near Rome.

1990). In one national survey, on a list of nine things people associated with successful marriages, "sharing household chores" ranked third—after "having shared interests" and a "satisfying sexual relationship" (Geiger, 2016). As the Pew Research Center (2007) summarized, "I like hugs. I like kisses. But what I really love is help with the dishes."

Equity's importance extends beyond marriage. Mutually sharing one's self and possessions, making decisions together, giving and getting emotional support, promoting and caring about each other's welfare—all of these acts are at the core of every type of loving relationship (Sternberg & Grajek, 1984). It's true for lovers, for parents and children, and for close friends.

Sharing includes **self-disclosure**, revealing intimate details about ourselves—our likes and dislikes, our dreams and worries, our proud and shameful moments. "When I am with my friend," noted the Roman statesman Seneca, "methinks I am alone, and as much at liberty to speak anything as to think it." Self-disclosure breeds liking, and liking breeds self-disclosure (Collins & Miller, 1994). As one person reveals a little, the other reciprocates, the first then reveals more, and on and on, as lovers (and friends) move to deeper intimacy (Baumeister & Bratslavsky, 1999).

One experiment marched some student pairs through 45 minutes of increasingly self-disclosing conversation—from "What is the greatest accomplishment of your life?" to "When did you last cry in front of another person? By yourself?" Other pairs spent the time with small-talk questions, such as "What was your high school like?" (Aron et al., 1997). By the experiment's end, those experiencing the escalating intimacy felt much closer to their conversation partner than did the small-talkers. Likewise, after dating couples spent 45 minutes answering such questions, they felt increased love (Welker et al., 2014).

In addition to equity and self-disclosure, a third key to enduring love is *positive support*. Our acute sensitivity to criticism impacts our relationships (Tierney & Baumeister, 2019). It takes multiple compliments to equal the attention-getting and emotion-affecting power of one criticism. Relationship conflicts are inevitable, but hurtful communications are not. Do we more often express sarcasm or support, scorn or sympathy, sneers or smiles? For unhappy couples, disagreements, criticisms, and put-downs are routine. For happy couples in enduring relationships, positive interactions (compliments, touches, laughing) outnumber negative interactions (sarcasm, disapproval, insults) by at least 5 to 1 (Gottman, 2007; see also Sullivan et al., 2010).

In the mathematics of love, self-disclosing intimacy + mutually supportive equity = enduring companionate love.

> **self-disclosure** the act of revealing intimate aspects of ourselves to others.

THEY HATED ME.

Carolita Johnson/Conde Nast/The Cartoon Bank

### AP® Science Practice

#### Research

In the self-disclosure study described here, what is the independent variable? What is the dependent variable? (Answer: Type of conversation and feelings of closeness, respectively.)

---

### AP® Science Practice

## Check Your Understanding

**Examine the Concept**

▶ Explain the difference between passionate and companionate love.

▶ Describe self-disclosure.

*Answers to the Examine the Concept questions can be found in Appendix C at the end of the book.*

**Apply the Concept**

▶ When you think of some of the older couples you know, which ones seem to experience companionate love? How do you think they've achieved it?

**4.3-10** Why do we befriend or fall in love with some people but not others?

- Proximity (geographic nearness) increases liking, in part because of the *mere exposure effect*—exposure to novel stimuli increases liking of those stimuli.

- Physical attractiveness increases social opportunities and improves the way we are perceived.

- Similarity of attitudes and interests greatly increases liking, especially as relationships develop. We also like those who like us.

**4.3-11** How does romantic love typically change as time passes?

- Intimate love relationships start with *passionate love*—an intensely aroused state.

- Over time, the strong affection of *companionate love* may develop, especially if enhanced by an *equitable* relationship, by intimate *self-disclosure*, and by positive support.

## AP® Practice Multiple Choice Questions

1. "I am friends with Kaci because she lives close to me," said Adam. This example illustrates
   a. the mere exposure effect.
   b. proximity.
   c. similarity.
   d. symmetry.

2. Which of the following is an example of the mere exposure effect?
   a. Adrianna has started arriving tardy to her second period class to avoid a group of kids in the hall who constantly tease her.
   b. Daiyu has seen the same toothpaste ad on television a hundred times, and she hates it more each time she views it.
   c. Abdul has always loved dogs, and after he asked his parents repeatedly, they allowed him to adopt one from the local shelter.
   d. Although Guiren didn't like sushi the first time he tried it, his friend encouraged him to keep eating it, and now it's his favorite food.

3. Dr. Pina conducted a study in which she examined the extent to which physical attractiveness predicted whether someone was asked on a date. Which of the following would be an appropriate independent variable in Dr. Pina's study?
   a. Facial symmetry
   b. Whether someone was asked on a date
   c. Number of miles between participants' homes
   d. Shared hobbies

4. Chandler and Alex just met and are beginning to get to know each other. They are sharing information such as their past accomplishments and life goals. They are engaging in which of the following?
   a. Mere exposure
   b. Proximity
   c. Equity
   d. Self-disclosure

**5.** Dr. Velez is conducting a study in which she asks participants to examine three photos and select the person who seems most likeable. The participant shown in this image chooses face B—which, unbeknownst to her, blends some features from an actual face with features of her own face.

**Participant**

**Choice A**

**Choice B**

**Choice C**

This demonstrates the influence of

a. physical attractiveness.
b. the mere exposure effect.
c. equity.
d. the reward theory of attraction.

**6.** Which of the following provides a logical and objective explanation of why online dating appears to lead to slightly longer and more satisfying relationships?

a. Individuals are better able to choose mates who fit their criteria for physical attractiveness via online dating.
b. Individuals are able to screen out mates who do not have shared interests via online dating.
c. Individuals are more likely to self-disclose in a genuine manner via online dating.
d. Individuals are better able to reap social rewards via online dating.

**7.** Dr. Auerbach believes that people are attracted to others who reward them and help them achieve their goals. Dr. Auerbach's beliefs align with

a. passionate love.
b. the reward theory of attraction.
c. equity.
d. the mere exposure effect.

# Module 4.3e Psychology of Social Situations: Altruism, Conflict, and Peacemaking

> ## LEARNING TARGETS
>
> **4.3-12** Define *altruism*, and explain when people are most — and least — likely to help.
>
> **4.3-13** Explain how social exchange theory and social norms explain helping behavior.
>
> **4.3-14** Explain how social traps and mirror-image perceptions fuel social conflict.
>
> **4.3-15** Describe what we can do to promote peace.

## Altruism

> **4.3-12** What is *altruism?* When are people most — and least — likely to help?

"We are made for goodness," observed South African Archbishop Desmond Tutu (1931–2021). "Why else do we get so outraged by wrong?"

So it seemed during the first two weeks of March 2022. Outraged by Russia's violence against Ukraine, people from 165 countries booked more than 430,000 nights at Ukrainian Airbnbs, most belonging to people they did not know (Friedman, 2022). The purchasers had no intention of using the reservation; they simply wanted to donate money to people in need. In the invasion's first two weeks, other people worldwide donated nearly $400 million to support Ukrainians (Roohi, 2022).

Among those fleeing Ukraine were cousins Lesia Orshoko and Alona Chugai. On their arrival in Israel, they were welcomed by Sharon Bass, who owed her own existence to the long-ago altruism of the cousins' Ukrainian grandmother, Maria Blyshchik. Blyshchik, who was not Jewish, hid Bass' Jewish grandmother Fania Rosenfeld—then a teen—for two years during the Holocaust, which killed Rosenfeld's parents and five siblings.

After later relocating to Israel, Fania Rosenfeld Bass would tell "the story over and over to her children and grandchildren, letting them know about the good people who held on to their humanity and quietly rebelled against the horrors of the war" (Greenbaum, 2022). Eight decades later, as war ravaged Ukraine, Sharon Bass reciprocated that heroic goodness by enabling the cousins' escape to Israel and welcoming them into her home. For as long as they wish, she said, her house is their house. We humans are capable of great evil, but also, as we shall see, of great goodness.

Like Dirk Willems (who we met at the beginning of Unit 4) rescuing his trapped jailer, Maria Blyshchik and Sharon Bass exemplified **altruism**.

Altruism became a major concern of social psychologists after a vile act on March 13, 1964. A stalker repeatedly stabbed Kitty Genovese, then raped her as she lay dying outside her Queens, New York, apartment at 3:30 A.M. "Oh, my God, he stabbed me!" Genovese

Chagit Bass Nussbaum

**An altruistic act** At great personal risk, Maria Blyshchik (right) sheltered a teenage Fania Rosenfeld Bass during the Holocaust. The pair reunited in 1999, more than 50 years later.

**altruism** unselfish regard for the welfare of others.

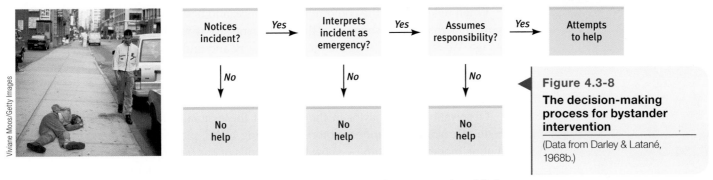

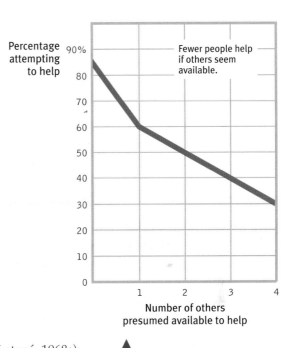

**Figure 4.3-8**

**The decision-making process for bystander intervention**

(Data from Darley & Latané, 1968b.)

screamed into the early morning stillness. "Please help me!" Windows opened and lights went on as some neighbors heard her screams. Her attacker fled and then returned to stab and rape her again. Until it was too late, no one called police or came to her aid.

## Bystander Intervention

Although initial accounts of the murder misreported the number and inaction of witnesses—one of whom cradled Genovese's body as she lay bleeding—the reports triggered outrage over the bystanders' apparent "apathy" and "indifference." Rather than blaming the onlookers, social psychologists John Darley and Bibb Latané (1968b) attributed their inaction to an important situational factor—the presence of others. Given certain circumstances, they suspected, most of us might behave similarly. To paraphrase the French writer Voltaire, we all are guilty of the good we did not do.

After staging emergencies under various conditions, Darley and Latané assembled their findings into a decision scheme: We will help only if the situation enables us first to *notice* the incident, then to *interpret* it as an emergency, and finally to *assume responsibility* for helping (**Figure 4.3-8**). At each step, the presence of others can turn us away from the path that leads to helping.

One of Darley and Latané's experiments staged a fake emergency as students in separate laboratory rooms took turns talking over an intercom. Only the person whose microphone was switched on could be heard. When his turn came, one student (actually an accomplice) pretended to have an epileptic seizure, and he called for help (Darley & Latané, 1968a).

How did the others react? As **Figure 4.3-9** shows, those who believed only they could hear the victim—and therefore thought they alone were responsible for helping him—usually went to his aid. Students who thought others could also hear the victim's cries were more likely to do nothing. When more people shared responsibility for helping—when there was a *diffusion of responsibility*—any single listener was less likely to help. Indeed, inattention and diffused responsibility contribute to the "global bystander nonintervention" as millions of far-away people die of hunger, disease, and genocide (Pittinsky & Diamante, 2015).

Hundreds of additional experiments have confirmed this **bystander effect**. For example, researchers and their assistants took 1497 elevator rides in three cities and "accidentally" dropped coins or pencils in front of 4813 fellow passengers (Latané & Dabbs, 1975). When alone with the person in need, 40 percent helped; in the presence of 5 other bystanders, only 20 percent helped. Ironically, Kitty Genovese's killer, Winston Moseley, was captured thanks to the intervention of a single bystander who confronted him as he later burgled a home. Disbelieving Moseley's explanation that he was helping the owners move, the bystander called another neighbor—who called police—and then pulled wires to disable Moseley's car (Kassin, 2017).

**Figure 4.3-9**

**Responses to a simulated emergency**

When people thought they alone heard the calls for help from a person they believed to be having an epileptic seizure, they usually helped. But when they thought four others were also hearing the calls, fewer than one-third responded. (Data from Darley & Latané, 1968a.)

**bystander effect** the tendency for any given bystander to be less likely to give aid if other bystanders are present.

When reflecting on the conformity, obedience, and bystander experiments, it's tempting to think that, unlike so many of the participants, we would have responded with moral courage. We tend to overestimate our own bravery and underestimate the power of social constraints (Swim & Hyers, 1999). To say and do something that is deeply unpopular in our world, and that may cause us to be scorned and ridiculed, such as objecting to sexist remarks or a racial slur, requires substantial moral courage.

Observations of behavior in thousands of these situations—relaying an emergency phone call, aiding a stranded motorist, donating blood, picking up dropped books, contributing money, giving time—show that the odds of our helping someone depend on the characteristics of that person, the situation, and our own internal state. The odds of helping are highest when

## Data

Ask yourself: Are the data presented in Figure 4.3-9 on the preceding page qualitative or quantitative? How do you know? (The answer is quantitative, because they are numerical data that represent degrees of a variable — the percentage of participants attempting to help.)

- the person appears to need and deserve help.
- the person is in some way similar to us.
- the person is a woman.
- we have just observed someone else being helpful.
- we are not in a hurry.
- we are in a small town or rural area.
- we are feeling guilty.
- we are focused on others and not preoccupied.
- we are in a good mood.

The "good mood" result—that happy people are helpful people—is one of psychology's most consistent findings. As poet Robert Browning (1868) observed, "Oh, make us happy and you make us good!" It doesn't matter how we are cheered. Whether by being made to feel successful and intelligent, by thinking happy thoughts, by finding money, or even by receiving a posthypnotic suggestion, we become more generous and more eager to help (Aknin et al., 2019).

## Research

To establish a causal relationship between helping and happiness, researchers use random assignment to control for confounding variables. In the money and helping experiment, participants were randomly assigned to either an experimental group (spend money on others) or a control group (spend money on yourself).

So, happiness breeds helpfulness. But it's also true that helpfulness breeds happiness. Helping those in need activates brain areas associated with reward (Harbaugh et al., 2007; Kawamichi et al., 2015). That helps explain a curious finding: People who give money away are happier than those who spend it almost entirely on themselves. In one experiment, researchers gave people money and instructed one group to spend it on themselves and another to spend it on others (Aknin et al., 2020). Which group was happiest? It was, indeed, those randomly assigned to the spend-it-on-others condition. And in a survey of more than 200,000 people worldwide, people in both rich and developing countries were happier with their lives if they had donated to a charity in the last month (Dunn et al., 2008).

# Check Your Understanding

## Examine the Concept

▶ Explain the social psychology principle the Kitty Genovese incident illustrates.

## Apply the Concept

▶ Imagine being a newcomer needing directions at a busy bus terminal. What could you do to increase the odds that someone will assist you, and what sort of person would be most likely to help?

*Answers to the Examine the Concept questions can be found in Appendix C at the end of the book.*

# Norms for Helping

**4.3-13** How do social exchange theory and social norms explain helping behavior?

*Why* do we help? One widely held view is that self-interest underlies all human interactions, that our constant goal is to maximize rewards and minimize costs. Accountants call it *cost-benefit analysis*. Philosophers call it *utilitarianism*. Social psychologists call it **social exchange theory**. If you are considering donating blood, you may weigh the costs of doing so (time, discomfort, anxiety) against the benefits (reduced guilt, social approval, good feelings). If the rewards exceed the costs, you will help.

Others believe we help because we have been socialized to do so, through norms that prescribe how we *ought* to behave (Everett et al., 2015). Two such norms are the *reciprocity norm* and the *social-responsibility norm*.

The **reciprocity norm** is the expectation that we should return help, not harm, to those who have helped us. Those for whom we do favors will often return favors. (Be kind to others and you may elicit future kindness from them.) With similar others, the reciprocity norm motivates us to give (in favors, gifts, or social invitations) about as much as we receive. Sometimes this means "paying it forward," as happened in one experiment, when people who were treated generously became more likely to be generous to a stranger (Tsvetkova & Macy, 2014). Returning favors feels good, so we tend to find the reciprocity norm a pleasant way to help others (Hein et al., 2016).

The reciprocity norm kicked in after Dave Tally, a man experiencing homelessness, found $3300 in a backpack that an Arizona State University student had misplaced on his way to buy a used car (Lacey, 2010). Instead of using the cash for much-needed bike repairs, food, and shelter, Tally turned the backpack in to the social services agency where he volunteered. To reciprocate Tally's help, the backpack's owner thanked him with a cash reward. Hearing about Tally's self-giving deeds, dozens of others also sent him money and job offers.

The **social-responsibility norm** is the expectation that we should help those who need our help—young children and others who cannot give as much as they receive—even if the costs outweigh the benefits. Europeans are most welcoming of the most vulnerable asylum seekers—those, for example, who have been tortured or have no surviving family (Bansak et al., 2016). During the Covid pandemic, many people—despite the risk of infection—cared for the sick, shopped for older neighbors, and distributed food to those in need. And many people responded affirmatively to persuasion that defined mask-wearing as an act of kindness and concern.

Construction worker Wesley Autrey exemplified the social-responsibility norm on January 2, 2007. He and his 6- and 4-year-old daughters were awaiting a New York City subway train when, before them, a man collapsed in a seizure, got up, then stumbled to the platform's edge and fell onto the tracks. With train headlights approaching, "I had to make a split-second decision," Autrey later recalled (Buckley, 2007). His decision, as his girls looked on in horror, was to leap from the platform, push the man off the tracks and into a foot-deep space between them, and lay atop him. As the train screeched to a halt, five cars traveled just above his head, leaving grease on his knit cap. When Autrey cried out, "I've got two daughters up there. Let them know their father is okay," onlookers erupted into applause.

Many world religions encourage their followers to practice the social-responsibility norm, and sometimes this leads to prosocial behavior (Heinrich, 2020). Between 2006 and 2008, Gallup polls sampled more than 300,000 people across 140 countries, comparing the "highly religious" (who said religion was important to them and who had attended a religious service in the prior week) to the less religious. The highly religious, despite being poorer, were about 50 percent more likely to report having "donated money to a charity in the last month" and to have volunteered time to an organization (Pelham & Crabtree, 2008). New surveys of 32,000 New Zealanders replicate this association of religious engagement with volunteerism (Van Tongeren et al., 2021).

**CULTURAL AWARENESS**

Culture refers to a group's shared and enduring behaviors, ideas, attitudes, values, and traditions. Culture may help explain group differences in how people think, feel, and act. However, some traditions are universal across cultures, such as religious social-responsibility norms.

Denis Poroy/AP Photo

**Heroic helping** In 2019, when a gunman entered a California synagogue, 60-year-old Lori Gilbert-Kaye was murdered when she selflessly used her body to shield her rabbi. Social psychologists study what prompts people to help.

**social exchange theory** the theory that our social behavior is an exchange process, the aim of which is to maximize benefits and minimize costs.

**reciprocity norm** an expectation that people will help, not hurt, those who have helped them.

**social-responsibility norm** an expectation that people will help those needing their help.

# From Conflict to Peace

Positive social norms encourage generosity and enable group living. But conflicts often divide us. One response to recent global conflict- and scarcity-driven mass migrations has been increasing nationalism and nativism (favoring native-born citizens over newcomers). Moreover, *every day* the world continues to spend almost $5 billion for arms and armies—money that could be used for needed housing, nutrition, education, and health care. Knowing that wars begin in human minds, psychologists have wondered: What in the human mind causes destructive conflict? How might a spirit of cooperation replace the perceived threats of social diversity?

## Elements of Conflict

**4.3-14** How do social traps and mirror-image perceptions fuel social conflict?

To a social psychologist, **conflict** is a perceived incompatibility of actions, goals, or ideas. The elements of conflict are much the same, whether it involves partners sparring, political groups feuding, or nations at war. In each situation, conflict may seed positive change, or it may be a destructive process that can produce unwanted results. Among the destructive processes are *social traps* and *distorted perceptions*.

### Social Traps

In some situations, pursuing our personal interests also supports our collective well-being. As capitalist Adam Smith wrote in *The Wealth of Nations* (1776), "It is not from the benevolence of the butcher, the brewer, or the baker that we expect our dinner, but from their regard to their own interest." In other situations, we *harm* our collective well-being by pursuing our personal interests. Such situations are **social traps**.

Researchers have created mini social traps in laboratory games that require two participants to choose between pursuing their immediate self-interest, at others' expense, versus cooperating for mutual benefits. Many real-life situations similarly pit our individual interests against our communal well-being. In 2020, anticipating Covid-related shutdowns, people bought and hoarded toilet paper, leaving shelves empty for others. Individual car owners reason, "Electric cars are a bit more expensive to buy. Besides, the fuel that I burn in my one car doesn't noticeably add to the greenhouse gases." When enough people reason similarly, the collective result threatens disaster—climate change, rising seas, and more extreme weather.

Social traps challenge us to reconcile our right to pursue our personal well-being with our responsibility for the well-being of all. Psychologists have therefore explored ways to convince people to cooperate for their mutual betterment—through agreed-upon *regulations*, through better *communication*, and through promoting *awareness* of our responsibilities toward community, nation, and the whole of humanity (Dawes, 1980; Linder, 1982; Sato, 1987). Given effective regulations, communication, and awareness, people more often cooperate, whether playing a laboratory game or the real game of life.

Social traps challenge us to balance our self-interest and our responsibility for the well-being of all. Imagine two friends, Roger and Chris, commit a crime together. The police catch them and question them separately. Should Roger and Chris betray each other, hoping to avoid a serious criminal conviction? Or should they remain silent?

Here is the deal:

*Option A:* If Roger and Chris betray each other, each of them serves five years in prison.

*Option B:* If Roger betrays Chris but Chris remains silent, Roger is free and Chris serves three years in prison. The same is true for the reverse scenario, in which Chris betrays Roger (and gets no prison sentence) and Roger remains silent (and gets three years in prison).

*Option C:* If both Roger and Chris remain silent, both of them serve only one year in prison.

Jeff J Mitchell/Getty Images

**Not in my ocean!** Many people support alternative energy sources, including wind turbines. But proposals to construct wind farms in real-world places elicit less support. Wind turbines in the Highlands and off the coast of Scotland have produced heated debate over the benefits of clean energy versus the costs of altering treasured scenic views.

**conflict** a perceived incompatibility of actions, goals, or ideas.

**social trap** a situation in which two parties, by each pursuing their self-interest rather than the good of the group, become caught in mutually destructive behavior.

This scenario illustrates what psychologists call the *prisoner's dilemma* (Axelrod, 1984). Roger and Chris would do best if they both remain silent. But chances are they will both instead betray each other. Most people focus on their self-interest, even when trusting and cooperating with each other would help them more personally.

## Enemy Perceptions

Psychologists have noted that those in conflict have a curious tendency to form diabolical images of each other. These distorted images are, ironically, so similar that we call them **mirror-image perceptions**: As we see "them"—as untrustworthy, with evil intentions—so "they" see us. Each demonizes the other. "My political party, unlike the other party, has the nation's best interests at heart" (Waytz et al., 2014).

Mirror-image perceptions can often feed a vicious cycle of hostility. If Juan believes Maria is annoyed with him, he may snub her, causing her to act in ways that justify his perception. As with individuals, so with countries. Perceptions can become **self-fulfilling prophecies**—beliefs that confirm themselves by influencing the other country to react in ways that seem to justify those beliefs.

Individuals and nations alike tend to see their own actions as responses to provocation, not as the causes of what happens next. Perceiving themselves as returning tit for tat, they often hit back harder, as University College London volunteers did in one study (Shergill et al., 2003). After feeling pressure on their own finger, they were to use a mechanical device to press on another volunteer's finger. Although told to reciprocate with the same amount of pressure, they typically responded with about 40 percent more force than they had just experienced. Despite seeking only to respond in kind, their touches soon escalated to hard presses, much as when each child after a fight claims that "I just touched him, but he hit me!" Mirror-image perceptions feed similar cycles of hostility on the world stage. To most people, torture seems more justified when done by "us" rather than by "them" (Tarrant et al., 2012).

The point is not that truth must lie midway between two such views (one may be more accurate). The point is that enemy perceptions often form mirror images. Moreover, as enemies change, so do perceptions. In U.S. minds and media, the "bloodthirsty, cruel, treacherous" Japanese of World War II later became our "intelligent, hardworking, self-disciplined, resourceful allies" (Gallup, 1972).

## Promoting Peace

**4.3-15** What can we do to promote peace?

How can we make peace? Can contact, cooperation, communication, and conciliation transform the antagonisms fed by prejudice and conflict into attitudes that promote peace? Research indicates that, in some cases, they can.

## Contact

Does it help to put two conflicting parties into close contact? It depends. Negative contact increases *dis*liking (Kotzur & Wagner, 2021). But positive contact—especially noncompetitive contact between parties of equal status, such as fellow store clerks—typically helps. Initially prejudiced co-workers of different races have, in such circumstances, usually come to accept one another. This finding is confirmed by studies of face-to-face contact between majority people and outgroups, such as ethnic minorities, older people, LGBTQ people, and people with disabilities. Among the quarter-million people studied across 38 nations, contact has correlated with (and in experiments has led to) more positive and empathic attitudes (Paluck et al., 2018; Pettigrew & Tropp, 2011; Tropp & Barlow, 2018). Some examples:

- Countries and U.S. states with the most immigrants tend to be the most supportive of immigrants; outgroup prejudice is strongest in places with few immigrants (Myers, 2018a; Shrira, 2020; Wagner et al., 2020).

**mirror-image perceptions** mutual views often held by conflicting parties, as when each side sees itself as ethical and peaceful and views the other side as evil and aggressive.

**self-fulfilling prophecy** a belief that leads to its own fulfillment.

- People's attitudes toward gay and transgender people are influenced not only by *what* they know but also by *whom* they know (Brown, 2017; DellaPosta, 2018). In surveys, the reason people most often give for becoming more supportive of same-sex marriage is "having friends, family, or acquaintances who are gay or lesbian" (Pew Research Center, 2013a). And in the United States, where 87 percent of people now say they know someone who is gay, attitudes toward same-sex marriage have become much more accepting (McCarthy, 2019; Pew Research Center, 2016).
- Friendly contact—say, between Black and White students as roommates—improves explicit and implicit attitudes toward others of the different race, and even toward other racial groups (Gaither & Sommers, 2013; Onyeador et al., 2020).

However, contact is not always enough. Despite laws that forbid school segregation, ethnic groups often resegregate themselves in lunchrooms, in classrooms, and elsewhere on school grounds (Alexander & Tredoux, 2010; Clack et al., 2005; Schofield, 1986). People in each group often think that they would welcome more contact with the other group, but they assume the other group does not reciprocate the wish (Richeson & Shelton, 2007). "I don't reach out to them, because I don't want to be rebuffed; they don't reach out to me, because they're just not interested." When such mirror-image misperceptions are corrected, friendships may form and prejudices melt.

## Cooperation

To see if enemies could overcome their differences, researcher Muzafer Sherif (1966) set a conflict in motion at a boys' summer camp. He separated 22 Oklahoma City boys into two separate camp areas. Then he had the two groups compete for prizes in a series of activities. Before long, each group became intensely proud of itself and hostile to the other group's "sneaky," "smart-alecky stinkers." Food wars broke out. Cabins were ransacked. Fistfights had to be broken up by camp counselors. Brought together, the two groups avoided each other, except to taunt and threaten. Little did they know that within a few days, they would be friends.

Sherif accomplished this by giving them **superordinate goals**—shared goals that could be achieved only through cooperation. When he arranged for the camp water supply to "fail," all 22 boys had to work together to restore the water. To rent a movie in those pre-Netflix days, they all had to pool their resources. To move a stalled truck, everyone needed to combine their strength, pulling and pushing together. Having used isolation and competition to make strangers into enemies, Sherif used shared predicaments and goals to turn enemies into friends. What reduced conflict was not mere contact, but *cooperative* contact.

Critics suggest that Sherif's research team encouraged the conflict, hoping the study would illustrate their expectations about socially toxic competition and socially beneficial cooperation (Perry, 2018). Yet shared predicaments have powerfully unifying effects. Minority-group members facing rejection or discrimination have developed strong ingroup identification (Bauer et al., 2014; Ramos et al., 2012). Children and youth exposed to war or conflict also develop strong social identities. Israeli children growing up in conflict areas often develop conflict-supportive perceptions, beliefs, and emotions regarding their shared adversary (Nasie et al., 2016). Such interpretations build ingroup solidarity but also insensitivity to the pain experienced by those in the outgroup (Levy et al., 2016).

In the aftermath of a divisive U.S. primary election, party members will usually eventually reunify when facing their shared threat—the opposing party's candidate. At such times, cooperation can lead people to define a new, inclusive group that dissolves their former subgroups

**Strangers coming together** When a family got stuck in a Florida rip current, no fewer than 80 of their fellow beachgoers formed a human chain, rescuing them. Wrote one of the witnesses, Rosalind Beckton: "All races & ages join[ed] together to save lives" (AP, 2017).

Rosalind Beckton

**superordinate goals** shared goals that override differences among people and require their cooperation.

(Dovidio & Gaertner, 1999). If this were a social psychology experiment, you might seat members of two groups not on opposite sides, but alternately around a table. Give them a new, shared name. Have them work together. Then watch "us" and "them" become "we."

Could cooperative learning in classrooms create interracial friendships, while also enhancing student achievement? Experiments with adolescents from 11 countries confirm that it can (Roseth et al., 2008). Members of multiethnic groups who work together on projects typically come to feel friendly toward one another. Knowing this, thousands of teachers have made multiethnic cooperative learning part of their classroom experience. And *industrial-organizational psychologists*, who apply psychology's principles in the workplace, might use such techniques to improve relationships among people working together or for a common company or program. (I/O psychologists also study work performance, work management, and avoiding burnout; see EM.2, Psychology at Work, for more on this topic.)

The power of cooperative activity to make friends of former enemies has led psychologists to urge increased international exchange and cooperation. Some experiments have found that just imagining the shared threat of global climate change reduces international hostilities (Pyszczynski et al., 2012). From adjacent Brazilian tribes to European countries, formerly conflicting groups have managed to build interconnections, interdependence, and a shared social identity as they seek to achieve common goals (Fry, 2012). As we engage in mutually beneficial trade, as we work to protect our common destiny on this fragile planet, and as we become more aware that our hopes and fears are shared, we can transform misperceptions that feed conflict into feelings of solidarity based on common interests.

## Communication

When real-life conflicts become intense, a third-party mediator—a marriage counselor, labor mediator, diplomat, community volunteer—may facilitate communication (Rubin et al., 1994). Mediators help each party voice its view and understand the other's needs and goals. If successful, mediators can replace a competitive *win-lose* orientation with a cooperative *win-win* orientation that leads to a mutually beneficial resolution. A classic example: Two friends, after quarreling over an orange, agreed to split it. One squeezed his half for juice. The other used the peel from her half to flavor a cake. If only the two had communicated, they could have hit on the win-win solution of one having all the juice, the other all the peel.

## Conciliation

Understanding and cooperative resolution are most needed, and yet least likely to occur, in times of anger or crisis (Bodenhausen et al., 1994; Tetlock, 1988). When conflicts intensify, images become more stereotyped, judgments more rigid, and communication more difficult, or even impossible. Each party is likely to threaten, coerce, or retaliate.

Under such conditions, is there an alternative to war or surrender? Social psychologist Charles Osgood (1962, 1980) advocated a strategy of *Graduated and Reciprocated Initiatives in Tension-Reduction*, nicknamed **GRIT**. In applying GRIT, one side first announces its recognition of mutual interests and its intent to reduce tensions. It then initiates one or more small, conciliatory acts. Without weakening one's retaliatory capability, this modest beginning opens the door for reciprocity by the other party. Should the enemy respond with hostility, one reciprocates in kind. But so, too, with any conciliatory response.

In laboratory experiments, small conciliatory gestures—a smile, a touch, a word of apology—have allowed both parties to begin edging down the tension ladder to a safer rung where communication and mutual understanding can begin (Lindskold, 1978;

Justin Tafoya/Getty Images

**Superordinate goals override differences** Cooperative efforts to achieve shared goals are an effective way to break down social barriers, as these jubilant Baylor University 2019 U.S. Women's National Champion basketball players make clear. Likewise, when Iraqi Christians were assigned to play with Muslims (versus with other Christians) on the same soccer team, they were later more likely to train with Muslims and register to play on a Christian-Muslim mixed soccer team (Mousa, 2020).

**Finding common ground** In local communities across the United States, mediators are helping "red" (conservative) and "blue" (liberal) citizens discover their common ground and form friendships (see BraverAngels.org). My Country Talks is an international platform with similar goals. It sets up "one-on-one discussions between people with completely different views" to encourage civil political dialogue (MyCountryTalks.org, 2021).

Byron Buck

**GRIT** Graduated and Reciprocated Initiatives in Tension-Reduction; a strategy designed to decrease international tensions.

Lindskold & Han, 1988). In a real-world international conflict, U.S. President John F. Kennedy's gesture of stopping atmospheric nuclear tests began a series of U.S./Russia reciprocated conciliatory acts that culminated in the 1963 atmospheric test-ban treaty.

As working toward shared goals reminds us, we are more alike than different. Civilization advances not by conflict and cultural isolation, but by tapping the knowledge, the skills, and the arts that are each culture's legacy to the whole human race. Open societies are enriched by cultural sharing (Sowell, 1991). We have China to thank for paper and printing and for the magnetic compass that enabled the great explorations. We have Egypt to thank for trigonometry. We have the Islamic world and India's Hindus to thank for our Arabic numerals. While celebrating and claiming these diverse cultural legacies, we can also welcome the continuing enrichment of today's cultural diversity. We can view ourselves as instruments in a human orchestra. And we can therefore affirm our own culture's heritage while building bridges of communication, understanding, and cooperation across our cultural traditions.

---

**AP® Science Practice**

## Check Your Understanding

**Examine the Concept**

▶ Explain the *self-fulfilling prophecy*.

▶ Describe four ways to reconcile conflicts and promote peace.

**Apply the Concept**

▶ How does group identity enable sports fans to feel a sense of satisfaction when their archrival team loses? Do such feelings, in other settings, make conflict resolution more challenging?

▶ Do you regret arguing with a friend or not getting along with a family member? How might you use these peace-promoting principles to resolve such conflicts, now or in the future?

*Answers to the Examine the Concept questions can be found in Appendix C at the end of the book.*

---

# Module 4.3e REVIEW

**4.3-12** What is *altruism?* When are people most — and least — likely to help?

- *Altruism* is unselfish regard for the well-being of others.

- We are most likely to help when we notice an incident, interpret it as an emergency, and assume responsibility for helping. Other factors, including our mood and our similarity to the victim, also affect our willingness to help.

- We are least likely to help if other bystanders are present (the *bystander effect*).

**4.3-13** How do social exchange theory and social norms explain helping behavior?

- *Social exchange theory* is the view that we help others because it is in our own self-interest; in this view, the goal of social behavior is maximizing personal benefits and minimizing costs.

- Others believe that helping results from socialization, in which we are taught guidelines for expected behaviors in social situations, such as the *reciprocity norm* and the *social-responsibility norm*.

**4.3-14** How do social traps and mirror-image perceptions fuel social conflict?

- *Social traps* are situations in which people in *conflict* pursue their own individual self-interest, harming the collective well-being.

- Individuals and cultures in conflict also tend to form *mirror-image perceptions:* Each party views the opponent as untrustworthy and evil-intentioned, and itself as an ethical, peaceful victim. Perceptions can become *self-fulfilling prophecies.*

### 4.3-15 What can we do to promote peace?

- Peace can result when individuals or groups work together to achieve *superordinate* (shared) *goals*.

- Research indicates that contact, cooperation, communication, and conciliation—such as the Graduated and Reciprocated Initiatives in Tension-Reduction (GRIT) strategy—help promote peace.

---

## AP® Practice Multiple Choice Questions

**1.** Balash helped Rovshan, even though he did not get anything in return. Balash displayed

    a. social exchange theory.
    b. the bystander effect.
    c. altruism.
    d. the reciprocity norm.

**2.** Ms. Skipworth challenged the students in her class to complete an extra-credit assignment, promising to add three points to everyone's final grade if every single student turned it in. Believing that other students wouldn't complete the assignment and not wanting to spend his free time doing work for no reason, Chase did not complete the assignment. What psychological concept does this scenario illustrate?

    a. Social trap
    b. Bystander effect
    c. GRIT
    d. Social-responsibility norm

**3.** Which of the following studies would best replicate the "good mood" result associated with helpfulness?

    a. Dr. Vogel designed an experiment in which participants were randomly assigned to read a blurb about a person who either shared their gender identity and college major or who shared no characteristics with them, later measuring how willing the participants would be to help the person in the blurb.
    b. Dr. Scott designed an experiment in which participants were randomly assigned to either interact with a woman or to interact with a man, later measuring how willing the participants would be to help the person with whom they interacted.
    c. Dr. Wade designed an experiment in which participants were randomly assigned either to pick a prize or to receive no prize, later measuring how willing the participants were to help another person.
    d. Dr. Krizan designed an experiment in which participants were randomly assigned to visit either a big city or a small town, later measuring how willing the participants were to help another person.

**4.** Gulnaz studies social exchange theory. Which hypothesis would she most likely make?

    a. People will be more likely to help others when there are fewer people present.
    b. People will be more likely to help others when the pros outweigh the cons of helping.
    c. People will be more likely to help others who have helped them.
    d. People will be more likely to help others when they share a common goal.

**5.** In an experiment, Dr. Westwood randomly assigned participants to one of two ethnically diverse groups. Group 1 was given a task of working together to solve brain teasers, which would enable them to "escape" from a room in which they were locked. Group 2 was given a task of mingling with one another. All other conditions, including the room in which the groups interacted, were the same. After the tasks, Dr. Westwood measured how connected the members of the group felt to one another. She found that the Group 1 members tended to feel more connected with one another than the Group 2 members. Which of the following best describes the outcome of Dr. Westwood's use of experimental control?

    a. Dr. Westwood is able to infer that superordinate goals caused greater connection among members of Group 1.
    b. Dr. Westwood is able to apply the results regarding the reciprocity norm to the broader population of people.
    c. Dr. Westwood is able to replicate the results regarding the bystander effect with better precision.
    d. Dr. Westwood is able to calculate confidence intervals and effect size regarding the social responsibility norm.

6. Based on this image, what logical and objective conclusion about helpfulness can be drawn?

Tetra Images/Alamy Stock Photo

a. The people in this town are prone to help one another.
b. The people in this town are prone to the prisoner's dilemma.
c. The people in this town are prone to being influenced by social exchange theory.
d. The people in this town are prone to being impacted by mirror image perceptions.

7. Anke is running for class president on a platform of decreasing the cost of school snacks to improve food accessibility. Dario is running for class president on a platform of increasing the cost of school snacks to make needed repairs to the school's lockers. Anke and Dario each see the other as unethical and aggressive. Which of the following psychological concepts is illustrated in this scenario?

a. Diffusion of responsibility
b. GRIT
c. Mirror-image perceptions
d. Superordinate goals

# Module 4.4 Introduction to Personality

## LEARNING TARGETS

**4.4-1** Explain what psychologists mean by *personality*, and identify the theories that inform our understanding of personality.

Lady Gaga dazzles millions with her unique musical arrangements, tantalizing outfits, and provocative performances. Her most predictable feature is her unpredictability. At the MTV Video Music Awards, she stirred up debate by wearing a meat dress. In 2021, she inspired viewers with her rendition of the National Anthem at U.S. President Joseph Biden's inauguration.

Yet even unpredictable Lady Gaga exhibits distinctive and enduring ways of thinking, feeling, and behaving. Her fans and critics alike can depend on her openness to new experiences and the energy she gets from the spotlight. And they can also rely on her painstaking dedication to her performances. She describes her high school self as "very dedicated, very studious, and very disciplined." Now, in adulthood, she shows similar self-discipline: "I'm very detailed—every minute of the show has got to be perfect." The next three modules focus on our *personality*—our unique and persistent patterns of thinking, feeling, and behaving.

Much of this book deals with personality. Other modules and units consider biological influences on personality; personality development across the lifespan; how personality relates to learning, motivation, emotion, and health; social influences on personality; and disorders of personality. Modules 4.4, 4.5, and 4.6 focus on personality itself—what it is and how researchers study it.

(a)

(b)

**Predictably unpredictable** The young Stefani Joanne Angelina Germanotta, who would one day be known as Lady Gaga, shared many of her older self's distinctive and enduring ways of thinking, feeling, and behaving — her *personality*.

**personality** an individual's characteristic pattern of thinking, feeling, and acting.

We begin with two important theories of personality that have become part of Western culture: *psychodynamic theories* and *humanistic theories*. These sweeping perspectives on human nature laid the foundation for later personality theories and for what this unit presents next: newer scientific explorations of personality.

Today's personality researchers study the basic dimensions of personality, and the interaction of persons and environments—our inherited traits, our experiences, and our cultural beliefs and values. They also study self-esteem, self-serving bias, and cultural influences on our concept of self—that sense of "who I am." And they study the unconscious mind—with findings that probably would have surprised even Sigmund Freud.

## Classic Perspectives on Personality

**4.4-1** What is *personality*, and what theories inform our understanding of personality?

Psychologists have varied ways to view, assess, and study **personality**. Sigmund Freud's *psychoanalytic theory* proposed that childhood sexuality and unconscious motivations influence personality. The *humanistic theories* focused on our inner capacities for growth and self-fulfillment. Later theorists built upon these two broad perspectives. *Trait theories* examine characteristic patterns of behavior (*traits*). *Social-cognitive theories* explore the interaction between people's traits (including their thinking) and their social context. In the next module, we'll begin with Freud's work, and its modern-day descendant, *psychodynamic theories*.

---

**AP® Science Practice**

## Check Your Understanding

### Examine the Concept

▶ Explain what is meant by *personality*.

▶ Differentiate among the five theoretical perspectives of personality.

*Answers to the Examine the Concept questions can be found in Appendix C at the end of the book.*

### Apply the Concept

▶ Do you think of yourself as predictable or unpredictable? What characteristics of your personality have remained relatively constant?

---

## Module 4.4 REVIEW

**4.4-1** Explain what psychologists mean by *personality*, and identify the theories that inform our understanding of personality.

- Personality is an individual's characteristic pattern of thinking, feeling, and acting.

- Psychoanalytic (and later psychodynamic) theory and humanistic theory have become part of Western culture. They also laid the foundation for later theories, such as trait and social-cognitive theories of personality.

# AP® Practice Multiple Choice Questions

1. Ilham thinks each person has a different characteristic pattern of thinking, feeling, and acting. Ilham believes that people differ in terms of
   a. social-cognitive theory.
   b. personality.
   c. cultural beliefs.
   d. humanistic theory.

2. Dzhabar wants to study the offshoot of Freud's psychoanalytic theory. What theories should he study?
   a. Humanistic theories
   b. Trait theories
   c. Social-cognitive theories
   d. Psychodynamic theories

3. Dr. Richmond believes that people are capable of growing throughout their lives. Which personality theory does Dr. Richmond most likely support?
   a. Humanistic
   b. Psychoanalytic
   c. Trait
   d. Social-cognitive

4. Elman uses self-report questionnaires to measure personality characteristics. Elman most likely adheres to which theory?
   a. Psychoanalytic
   b. Social-cognitive
   c. Trait
   d. Psychodynamic

# Module 4.5a Psychodynamic and Humanistic Theories of Personality: Psychoanalytic and Psychodynamic Theories

## LEARNING TARGETS

**4.5-1** Explain how Freud's treatment of psychological disorders led to his view of the unconscious mind, and describe his view of personality.

**4.5-2** Explain how Freud thought people defended themselves against anxiety.

**4.5-3** Explain which of Freud's ideas his followers accepted or rejected.

**4.5-4** Explain how contemporary psychologists view Freud's psychoanalysis, and describe how modern research has developed our understanding of the unconscious.

**4.5-5** Explain *projective tests* and how they are used, and describe some criticisms of them.

**Sigmund Freud (1856–1939)**
"I was the only worker in a new field."

▶ **SPOTLIGHT ON:**
Sigmund Freud

**psychodynamic theories** of personality view human behavior as a dynamic interaction between the conscious mind and the unconscious mind, including associated motives and conflicts. These theories descended from Freud's **psychoanalysis**—his theory of personality and the associated treatment techniques. Freud's work is so famous that you may assume it's psychology's most important theory. It's not—other theories have more scientific support. However, Freud's focus on our unconscious mind has been followed by today's scientific studies of unconscious information processing.

## Freud's Psychoanalytic Perspective: Exploring the Unconscious

**4.5-1** How did Freud's treatment of psychological disorders lead to his view of the unconscious mind, and what was his view of personality?

Ask 100 people on the street to name a notable deceased psychologist, suggested Keith Stanovich (1996, p. 1), and "Freud would be the winner hands down." In the popular mind, he is to psychology what Elvis Presley is to rock music. Freud's influence lingers not only in psychiatry and clinical psychology, but also in literary and film interpretation. Almost 9 in 10 U.S. college courses that reference psychoanalysis have been offered outside of psychology departments (Cohen, 2007). Freud's early twentieth-century concepts penetrate our twenty-first-century language. Without realizing their source, we may speak of *ego, repression, projection, sibling rivalry, Freudian slips,* and *fixation.* So, who was Freud, and what did he teach?

---

**psychodynamic theories**
theories that view personality with a focus on the unconscious mind and the importance of childhood experiences.

**psychoanalysis** Freud's theory of personality that attributes thoughts and actions to unconscious motives and conflicts; the techniques used in treating psychological disorders by seeking to expose and interpret unconscious tensions.

Like all of us, Sigmund Freud was a product of his times. The late 1800s, the tail end of the Victorian era, was a time of tremendous discovery and scientific advancement, but also of sexual suppression and men's dominance. Gender roles were clearly defined and men's superiority assumed. Men's sexuality was generally acknowledged (discreetly), while women's sexuality was dismissed or ignored. These assumptions influenced Freud's thinking about personality. He believed that psychological troubles resulted from men's and women's unresolved conflicts with their expected roles.

Long before he entered the University of Vienna in 1873, young Freud showed signs of independence and brilliance. He so loved reading plays, poetry, and philosophy that he once ran up a bookstore debt beyond his means. As a teen he often took his evening meal in his tiny bedroom to focus on his studies. After medical school he set up a private practice specializing in nervous disorders. Before long, however, he faced patients whose disorders made no neurological sense. A patient might have lost all feeling in a hand—yet there is no sensory nerve that, if damaged, would numb the entire hand and nothing else. Freud's search for a cause for such disorders set his mind running in a direction destined to change human self-understanding.

Do some neurological disorders have psychological causes? Observing patients led Freud to his "discovery" of the **unconscious**. He speculated that lost feeling in one's hand might be caused by a fear of touching one's genitals; that unexplained blindness or deafness might be caused by not wanting to see or hear something that aroused intense anxiety. How might such disorders be treated? After some early unsuccessful trials with hypnosis, Freud turned to **free association**, in which he told the patient to relax and say whatever came to mind, no matter how embarrassing or trivial. He assumed that a line of mental dominoes had fallen from his patients' distant past to their troubled present, and that the chain of thought revealed by free association would allow him to retrace that line into his patients' unconscious. There, painful memories, often from childhood, could then be retrieved, reviewed, and released.

Basic to Freud's theory was this belief that the mind is mostly hidden (**Figure 4.5-1**). Our *conscious* awareness is like the part of an iceberg that floats above the surface. Beneath this awareness is the larger *unconscious* mind, with its thoughts, wishes, feelings, and memories. We store some of these thoughts temporarily in a *preconscious* area, from which we can retrieve them into conscious awareness. Of greater interest to Freud was the mass of unacceptable passions and thoughts that he believed we *repress*, or forcibly block from our consciousness because they would be too unsettling to acknowledge. Freud believed that without our awareness, these troublesome feelings and ideas powerfully influence us. Such feelings, he said, sometimes surface in disguised forms—the work we choose, the beliefs we hold, our daily habits, our upsetting symptoms.

## Personality Structure

Freud believed that human personality, including its emotions and strivings, arises from a conflict between impulse and restraint—between our aggressive, pleasure-seeking biological urges and our internalized social controls over these urges. Freud believed personality springs from our efforts to resolve this basic conflict—to express these impulses in ways that bring satisfaction without also bringing guilt or punishment. To understand the mind's dynamics during this conflict, Freud proposed three interacting systems: the *id, ego,* and *superego* (Figure 4.5-1).

**unconscious** according to Freud, a reservoir of mostly unacceptable thoughts, wishes, feelings, and memories. According to contemporary psychologists, information processing of which we are unaware.

**free association** in psychoanalysis, a method of exploring the unconscious in which the person relaxes and says whatever comes to mind, no matter how trivial or embarrassing.

### AP® Science Practice

#### Research

By basing his theory on observations of his patients, Freud implemented a case study approach (a non-experimental method). As a result, his findings might not generalize to others. Recall from Module 0.3 that findings must be replicated to build consensus for their validity and generalizability.

### Figure 4.5-1

#### Freud's idea of the mind's structure

Psychologists have used an iceberg image to illustrate Freud's idea that the mind is mostly hidden beneath the conscious surface.

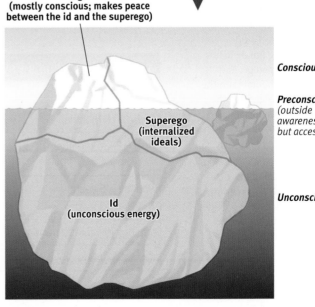

Ego (mostly conscious; makes peace between the id and the superego)

Superego (internalized ideals)

Id (unconscious energy)

*Conscious mind*

*Preconscious (outside awareness but accessible)*

*Unconscious mind*

The unconscious psychic energy of the **id** constantly strives to satisfy basic drives to survive, reproduce, and aggress. The id operates on the *pleasure principle:* It seeks immediate gratification. Freud believed that the *libido* is a life energy force that fuels our pleasure-seeking. To understand the id's power, think of a newborn infant crying out for satisfaction, caring nothing for the outside world's conditions and demands. Or think of people who focus on the present more than the future—those who abuse tobacco, alcohol, and other drugs, and would sooner party now than sacrifice today's temporary pleasure for future success and happiness (Fernie et al., 2013; Friedel et al., 2014; Keough et al., 1999).

As the **ego** develops, a young child responds to the real world. The ego, operating on the *reality principle*, seeks to gratify the id's impulses in realistic ways to bring long-term pleasure. It is the "executive" that weighs a decision's risks and rewards. (Imagine what would happen if, lacking an ego, we acted on our unrestrained sexual or aggressive impulses.) The ego tries to satisfy the id's impulses in realistic ways that bring long-term benefits rather than pain or destruction.

Around age 4 or 5, Freud theorized, a child's ego recognizes the demands of the newly emerging **superego**, the partly conscious voice of our moral compass (conscience) that forces the ego to consider not only the real but also the *ideal*. The superego focuses on how we *ought* to behave. It strives for perfection, judging actions and producing positive feelings of pride or negative feelings of guilt. Someone with an exceptionally strong superego may be virtuous yet guilt-ridden; another with a weak superego may be outrageously self-indulgent and remorseless.

Because the superego's demands often oppose the id's, the ego struggles to reconcile the two. As the executive, the ego mediates among the impulsive demands of the id, the restraining demands of the superego, and the real-life demands of the external world. If virtuous Conner feels sexually attracted to Tatiana, his ego may satisfy both his id and superego by joining an organization where Tatiana volunteers regularly.

## Personality Development

Analysis of his patients' histories convinced Freud that personality forms during life's first few years. He concluded that children pass through a series of *psychosexual stages*, during which the id's pleasure-seeking energies focus on distinct pleasure-sensitive areas of the body called *erogenous zones* (**Table 4.5-1**). Each stage offers its own challenges, which Freud saw as conflicting tendencies.

**id** a reservoir of unconscious psychic energy that, according to Freud, strives to satisfy basic sexual and aggressive drives. The id operates on the *pleasure principle*, demanding immediate gratification.

**ego** the partly conscious, "executive" part of personality that, according to Freud, mediates among the demands of the id, the superego, and reality. The ego operates on the *reality principle*, satisfying the id's desires in ways that will realistically bring pleasure rather than pain.

**superego** the partly conscious part of personality that, according to Freud, represents internalized ideals and provides standards for judgment (the conscience) and for future aspirations.

| TABLE 4.5-1 Freud's Psychosexual Stages | |
|---|---|
| **Stage** | **Focus** |
| *Oral* (0–18 months) | Pleasure centers on the mouth — sucking, biting, chewing |
| *Anal* (18–36 months) | Pleasure focuses on bowel and bladder elimination; coping with demands for control |
| *Phallic* (3–6 years) | Pleasure zone is the genitals; coping with incestuous sexual feelings |
| *Latency* (6 years to puberty) | A phase of dormant sexual feelings |
| *Genital* (puberty on) | Maturation of sexual interests |

Freud believed that during the *phallic stage*, for example, boys develop both unconscious sexual desires for their mother and jealousy and hatred for their father, whom they consider a rival. He believed these feelings cause boys to feel guilty and to fear punishment, perhaps by castration, from their father. Such was Freud's (1897) own experience: "I have found, in my own case too, [the phenomenon of] being in love with my mother and jealous of my father, and I now consider it a universal event in early childhood." He called this collection of feelings the *Oedipus complex* after the Greek legend of Oedipus, whose failure to understand his unconscious desires led him to unknowingly kill his

"I heard that as soon as we become aware of our sexual impulses, whatever they are, we'll have to hide them."

father and marry his mother. In Freud's era, some psychoanalysts believed that girls experience a parallel *Electra complex* (named after a mythological daughter who helped kill her mother to avenge her father's murder).

Children eventually cope with the threatening feelings, said Freud, by repressing them and by trying to become like the rival parent. It's as though something inside the child decides, "If you can't beat 'em [the same-sex parent], join 'em." Through this *identification* process, children's superegos gain strength as they incorporate many of their parents' values. Freud believed that identification with the same-sex parent provides what psychologists now understand more broadly as our *gender identity*—our sense of being male, female, neither, or some combination of male and female (see Module 3.3). Freud presumed that our early childhood relations—especially with our parents and other caregivers—influence our developing identity, personality, and frailties.

In Freud's view, conflicts that go unresolved during earlier psychosexual stages could surface as maladaptive behavior in the adult years. At any point in the oral, anal, or phallic stages, strong conflict could lock, or *fixate*, the person's pleasure-seeking energies in that stage. A person who had been either orally overindulged or deprived (perhaps by abrupt, early weaning) might fixate at the oral stage. This orally fixated adult could exhibit either passive dependence (like that of a nursing infant) or an exaggerated denial of this dependence (by acting tough or uttering biting sarcasm). Or the person might continue to seek oral gratification by smoking or excessive eating. In such ways, Freud suggested, the twig of personality is bent at an early age.

## Defense Mechanisms

**4.5-2** How did Freud think people defended themselves against anxiety?

Anxiety, said Freud, is the price we pay for civilization. As members of social groups, we must control our sexual and aggressive impulses, not act them out. But sometimes the ego fears losing control of this inner id-superego war. The presumed result is a dark cloud of unfocused anxiety that leaves us feeling unsettled but unsure why.

The differences between these
defense mechanisms can be
subtle. To identify different defense
mechanisms, focus on each
example's key feature. If the key
feature is seeing your own impulse
in someone else, it's projection.
If the key feature is shifting your
aggression from one target to
another, it's displacement.

Freud proposed that the ego protects itself with **defense mechanisms**—tactics that reduce or redirect anxiety by distorting reality (Table 4.5-2). For Freud, *all defense mechanisms functioned indirectly and unconsciously.* Just as the body unconsciously defends itself against disease, the ego also unconsciously defends itself against anxiety. For example, **repression** banishes anxiety-arousing wishes and feelings from consciousness. According to Freud, *repression underlies all the other defense mechanisms.* However, because repression is often incomplete, repressed urges may appear as symbols in dreams or as slips of the tongue in casual conversation.

Freud believed he could glimpse the unconscious seeping through when a financially stressed patient, not wanting any large pills, said, "Please do not give me any bills, because I cannot swallow them." (Today we call these "Freudian slips.")

Regression

**defense mechanisms** in psychoanalytic theory, the ego's protective methods of reducing anxiety by unconsciously distorting reality.

**repression** in psychoanalytic theory, the basic defense mechanism that banishes from consciousness anxiety-arousing thoughts, feelings, and memories.

### TABLE 4.5-2 Seven Defense Mechanisms

Freud believed that *repression*, the basic mechanism that banishes anxiety-arousing impulses, enables other defense mechanisms. Seven of those defense mechanisms are listed here, with examples of how they might play out in a high school student who was just cut from the soccer team.

| Defense Mechanism | Unconscious Process Employed to Avoid Anxiety-Arousing Thoughts or Feelings | Example (How an Imaginary Student Might Employ These Mechanisms After Being Cut From the Soccer Team) |
|---|---|---|
| *Regression* | Retreating to an earlier psychosexual stage, where some psychic energy remains fixated | Curls up with an old stuffed animal and watches cartoons for comfort |
| *Reaction formation* | Switching unacceptable impulses into their opposites | Feeling the urge to cry with disappointment, instead declares loudly that "Getting cut from the soccer team was the best thing that ever happened to me" |
| *Projection* | Disguising one's own threatening impulses by attributing them to others | Tells everyone how mad his parents are at the coach |
| *Rationalization* | Offering self-justifying explanations in place of the real, more threatening unconscious reasons for one's actions | Explains that he wasn't working very hard in tryouts and could have made the team if he'd really wanted to |
| *Displacement* | Shifting sexual or aggressive impulses toward a more acceptable or less threatening object or person | Yells at his little brother for no reason |
| *Sublimation* | Transferring of unacceptable impulses into socially valued motives | Feels an urge to go to a practice and yell at the coach; instead, offers to teach his little brother to play soccer that day |
| *Denial* | Refusing to believe or even perceive painful realities | Insists there was an error on the team list and he's going to set things right with the coach |

Freud also viewed jokes as expressions of repressed sexual and aggressive tendencies, and dreams as the "royal road to the unconscious." The remembered content of dreams (their *manifest content*) he believed to be a censored expression of the dreamer's unconscious wishes (the dream's *latent content*). In his dream analyses, Freud searched for patients' inner conflicts.

"Good morning, beheaded—uh, I mean beloved."

**66** *I remember your name perfectly but I just can't think of your face.* **99**
— Oxford professor W. A. Spooner (1844–1930) , famous for his linguistic flip-flops (spoonerisms). Spooner rebuked one student for "fighting a liar in the quadrangle" and another who "hissed my mystery lecture," adding, "You have tasted two worms."

---

**AP® Science Practice**

# Check Your Understanding

**Examine the Concept**

▶ How does Freud define the unconscious?

▶ Explain the purpose of defense mechanisms.

**Apply the Concept**

▶ Which Freudian terms have you found yourself using, or heard others using, in everyday conversation (e.g., Freudian slip, projection, repression, ego)? Do they reflect Freud's ideas accurately?

*Answers to the Examine the Concept questions can be found in Appendix C at the end of the book.*

---

# The Neo-Freudian and Later Psychodynamic Theorists

**4.5-3** Which of Freud's ideas did his followers accept or reject?

Freud's writings sparked intense debate. Remember that Freud lived at a time when people seldom talked about sex, and certainly not about unconscious sexual desires for one's parent. So it's no surprise that Freud was harshly criticized. In a letter to a trusted friend, Freud wrote, "In the Middle Ages, they would have burned me. Now they are content with burning my books" (Jones, 1957).

Despite the controversy, Freud attracted followers. Several young, ambitious physicians formed an inner circle around their strong-minded leader. These pioneering psychoanalysts, whom we often call *neo-Freudians*, adopted Freud's interviewing techniques and accepted his basic ideas: the personality structures of id, ego, and superego; the importance of the unconscious; the childhood roots of personality; and the dynamics of anxiety and the defense mechanisms. But they broke away from Freud in two important ways. First, they emphasized the conscious mind's role in interpreting experience and in coping with the environment. Second, they doubted that sex and aggression were all-consuming motivations. Instead, they tended to emphasize loftier motives and social interactions.

Alfred Adler and Karen Horney [HORN-eye], for example, agreed with Freud that childhood is important. But they believed that childhood *social*—not sexual—tensions are crucial for personality formation (Ferguson, 2003, 2015). Adler (who gave us the still popular *inferiority complex* idea) had struggled to overcome childhood illnesses and accidents. He believed that much of our behavior is driven by efforts to conquer childhood inferiority feelings that trigger our strivings for superiority and power. Horney said childhood anxiety triggers our desire for love and security. She also opposed Freud's assumptions that women have weak superegos and suffer "penis envy," and she attempted to balance his masculine bias.

**Alfred Adler (1870–1937)** "The individual feels at home in life and feels his existence to be worthwhile just so far as he is useful to others and is overcoming feelings of inferiority" (*Problems of Neurosis*, 1964).

**Karen Horney (1885–1952)** "The view that women are infantile and emotional creatures, and as such, incapable of responsibility and independence is the work of the masculine tendency to lower women's self-respect" (*Feminine Psychology*, 1932).

**Carl Jung (1875–1961)** "From the living fountain of instinct flows everything that is creative; hence the unconscious is the very source of the creative impulse" (*The Structure and Dynamics of the Psyche*, 1960).

**collective unconscious** Carl Jung's concept of a shared, inherited reservoir of memory traces from our species' history.

Carl Jung [Yoong], Freud's disciple-turned-dissenter, placed less emphasis on social factors and agreed with Freud that the unconscious exerts a powerful influence. But to Jung, the unconscious contains more than our repressed thoughts and feelings. He believed we also have a **collective unconscious**, a common reservoir of images, or *archetypes*. Jung said that the collective unconscious explains why, for many people, spiritual concerns are deeply rooted and why people in different cultures share certain myths and images. Today's psychologists assume that our shared evolutionary history has indeed shaped some universal dispositions, and that experience can leave *epigenetic* marks affecting gene expression (see Module 1.1).

Freud died in 1939. Since then, some of his ideas have been incorporated into the diverse perspectives that make up modern psychodynamic theory. "Most contemporary [psychodynamic] theorists and therapists are not wedded to the idea that sex is the basis of personality," noted Drew Westen (1996). They "do not talk about ids and egos, and do not go around classifying their patients as oral, anal, or phallic characters." They assume, as did Freud and with much support from today's psychological science, that much of our mental life is unconscious. Like Freud, they also assume that we often struggle with inner conflicts among our wishes, fears, and values, and that childhood shapes our personality and ways of becoming attached to others.

## Evaluating Freud's Psychoanalytic Perspective and Modern Views of the Unconscious

**4.5-4** How do contemporary psychologists view Freud's psychoanalysis, and how has modern research developed our understanding of the unconscious?

"Many aspects of Freudian theory are indeed out of date," observed psychologist Drew Westen (1998). "And they should be: Freud died in 1939, and he has been slow to undertake further revisions." So how should we critique Freud from a twenty-first-century perspective?

### Modern Research Contradicts Many of Freud's Ideas

Freud did not have access to neurotransmitter or DNA studies, or to all that we have since learned about human development, thinking, and emotion. To criticize his theory by comparing it with today's thinking is like criticizing the Ford Model T by comparing it with a new Tesla S. How tempting it always is to judge the past from the perspective of our present.

Nevertheless, both Freud's devotees and his detractors agree that recent research contradicts many of his specific ideas. Today's developmental psychologists see our development as lifelong, not fixed in childhood. They doubt that infants' neural networks are mature enough to sustain as much emotional trauma as Freud assumed. Some think Freud overestimated parental influence and underestimated peer influence. These critics also doubt that conscience and gender identity form as the child resolves the Oedipus (or Electra) complex at age 5 or 6. We gain our gender identity earlier, and those who become strongly masculine or feminine do so even without a same-sex parent present. And they note that Freud's ideas about childhood sexuality arose from stories of childhood sexual abuse told by his female patients—stories that some scholars believe Freud doubted, and attributed to his patients' own childhood sexual wishes and conflicts (Esterson, 2001; Powell & Boer, 1994). Today, we know that *childhood sexual abuse happens*, and we also understand how Freud's questioning might have created false memories of abuse.

As we saw in Module 1.5, modern dream research disputes Freud's belief that dreams disguise and fulfill wishes. And slips of the tongue can be explained as competition between similar verbal choices in our memory network. Someone who says, "I don't want to do that—it's a lot of brothel," may simply be blending *bother* and *trouble* (Foss & Hakes, 1978). History also has failed to support Freud's idea that suppressed sexuality causes psychological disorders. From Freud's time to ours, sexual inhibition has diminished; psychological disorders have not.

Psychologists further criticize Freud's theory for its scientific shortcomings. As we discuss in Unit 0, good scientific theories explain observations and offer testable hypotheses. Freud's theory rests on few objective observations, and parts of it offer few testable hypotheses. For Freud, his own recollections and interpretations of patients' free associations, dreams, and slips—sometimes selected to support his theory—were evidence enough.

What is the most serious problem with Freud's theory? It offers after-the-fact explanations of any characteristic (of one person's smoking, another's fear of horses, another's sexual orientation), yet fails to *predict* such behaviors and traits. If you feel angry at your mother's death, you illustrate Freud's theory because "your unresolved childhood dependency needs are threatened." If you do not feel angry, you again illustrate his theory because "you are repressing your anger." That "is like betting on a horse after the race has been run" (Hall & Lindzey, 1978, p. 68). A good theory makes testable predictions.

So, should psychology post an "Allow Natural Death" order on this old theory? Freud's supporters object. To criticize Freudian theory for not making testable predictions is, they say, like criticizing baseball for not being an aerobic exercise—something it was never intended to be. Freud never claimed that psychoanalysis was predictive science. He merely claimed that, looking back, psychoanalysts could find meaning in our state of mind (Rieff, 1979).

Freud's supporters also note that some of his ideas *are* enduring. It was Freud who drew our attention to the unconscious and the irrational, at a time when such ideas were not popular. Many researchers have since studied our irrationality (Ariely, 2010; Thaler, 2015). Psychologist Daniel Kahneman (in 2002) and behavioral economist Richard Thaler (in 2017) each won Nobel Prizes for their studies of our faulty decision making. Freud also drew our attention to the importance of human sexuality, and to the tension between our biological impulses and our social well-being. It was Freud who challenged our self-righteousness, exposed our self-protective defenses, and reminded us of our potential for evil.

**AP® Science Practice**

### Research

Technology that allows us to study neurotransmitters and DNA has moved the science of psychology forward. As a result, our conclusions and theories have evolved. This is how science works!

## Modern Research Challenges the Idea of Repression

Psychoanalytic theory hinges on the assumption that our mind often *represses* offending wishes, banishing them into the unconscious until they resurface, like long-lost books in a dusty attic. Recover and resolve childhood's conflicted wishes, and emotional healing should follow. Repression became a widely accepted concept, used to explain hypnotic phenomena and psychological disorders. Some psychodynamic followers extended repression to explain apparently lost and recovered memories of childhood traumas (Boag, 2006; Cheit, 1998; Erdelyi, 2006). These psychodynamic beliefs have seeped into popular culture. In one survey, 88 percent of university students believed that painful experiences commonly get pushed out of awareness and into the unconscious (Garry et al., 1994).

Today's researchers agree that we sometimes preserve our self-esteem by neglecting threatening information (Green et al., 2008). Yet they also find that repression is rare, even in response to terrible trauma. Even those who have witnessed a parent's murder or survived Nazi death camps have retained their unrepressed memories of the horror (Helmreich, 1992, 1994; Malmquist, 1986; Pennebaker, 1990).

Some researchers do believe that extreme, prolonged stress, such as the stress some severely abused children experience, might disrupt memory by damaging the hippocampus, which is important for processing conscious memories (Schacter, 1996). But the far more common reality is that high stress and associated stress hormones *enhance* memory. Indeed, rape, torture, and other traumatic events haunt survivors, who experience unwanted flashbacks. They are seared onto the soul. "You see the babies," said Holocaust survivor Sally H. (1979). "You see the screaming mothers. You see hanging people. You sit and you see that face there. It's something you don't forget."

## The Modern Unconscious Mind

**AP® Exam Tip**

It's important to understand the differences between Freud's view of the unconscious and modern psychology's view of the unconscious. Read this section carefully.

Freud was right about a big idea that underlies today's psychodynamic thinking: We have limited access to all that goes on in our mind (Erdelyi, 1985, 1988; Norman, 2010). Our two-track mind has a vast unseen realm. Some researchers even argue that "most of a person's everyday life is determined by unconscious thought processes" (Bargh & Chartrand, 1999). (Perhaps, for example, you can recall being sad or mad without consciously knowing why.)

Many research psychologists now think of the unconscious not as a mass of seething passions and repressive censoring but as a form of information processing that occurs without our awareness. To these researchers, the unconscious also involves

- the *schemas* that automatically control our perceptions and interpretations (Module 2.2).
- the *priming* by stimuli to which we have not consciously attended (Module 2.6).
- the right-hemisphere activity that enables the *split-brain* patient's left hand to carry out an instruction the patient cannot verbalize (Module 1.4).
- the *implicit memories* of learned skills that operate without conscious recall, even in people with amnesia (Module 2.4).
- the *emotions* that are activated instantly, before conscious analysis occurs (Module 4.8).
- the *stereotypes* and *implicit prejudice* that automatically and unconsciously influence how we process information about others (Module 4.1).

More than we realize, we fly on autopilot. Our lives are guided by off-screen, out-of-sight, unconscious information processing. The unconscious mind is vast. However, our current understanding of unconscious information processing is more like the pre-Freudian view, of an underground, unattended stream of thought from which spontaneous behavior and creative ideas surface (Bargh & Morsella, 2008).

Research also supports two of Freud's defense mechanisms. One study demonstrated *reaction formation* (trading unacceptable impulses for their opposite) in men who reported strong anti-gay attitudes. Compared with those who did not report such attitudes, these anti-gay men experienced greater physiological arousal when watching videos of gay men having sex, even though they said the films did not make them sexually aroused (Adams et al., 1996). Likewise, some evidence suggests that people who have an unconscious same-sex sexual orientation—but who consciously identify as straight—report more negative attitudes toward gay men and lesbians (Weinstein et al., 2012).

Freud's *projection* (attributing our own threatening impulses to others) has also been confirmed. People do tend to see their traits, attitudes, and goals in others (Baumeister et al., 1998b; Maner et al., 2005). Aggressive people, for example, tend to see ambiguous faces as angry (Brennan & Baskin-Sommers, 2020). Today's researchers call this the *false consensus effect*—the tendency to overestimate the extent to which others share our beliefs and behaviors. People who cheat on their assignments or shoplift petty items "for thrills" tend to think many others do the same. Shortly before the 2020 U.S. presidential election, 83 percent of Democrats and 84 percent of Republicans predicted that voters would elect *their* party's presidential candidate (ISR, 2020). As we are, so we see others.

Jack Ziegler/Cartoon Stock

---

**AP® Science Practice**  ▷  **Data Interpretation**

This is a good time to practice your data interpretation skills. As cheating becomes more frequent, more students perceive that others cheat.

- Create a scatterplot depicting this finding.

- Does this finding represent a positive or negative correlation? Explain.

---

Finally, research has supported Freud's idea that we unconsciously defend ourselves against anxiety. Researchers have proposed that one source of anxiety is "the terror resulting from our awareness of vulnerability and death" (Greenberg et al., 1997). Hundreds of experiments testing **terror-management theory** show that thinking about one's mortality—for example, by writing a short essay on dying and its associated emotions—provokes various terror-management defenses (Burke et al., 2010). For example, death anxiety increases aggression toward rivals and heightens esteem for oneself (Cohen & Solomon, 2011; Koole et al., 2006).

**terror-management theory** a theory of death-related anxiety; explores people's emotional and behavioral responses to reminders of their impending death.

Carolita Johnson The New Yorker Collection/ The Cartoon Bank

Faced with a threatening world, people not only act to enhance their self-esteem, but also adhere more strongly to worldviews that answer questions about life's meaning. The prospect of death promotes religious sentiments (Norenzayan & Hansen, 2006). Moreover, when contemplating death, people prioritize their close relationships (Cox & Arndt, 2012; Mikulincer et al., 2003). The actual death of loved ones can provoke protective responses as well. For years, I [ND] have studied the way people respond to thoughts about death—but it took the shock of my own mother's unexpected death to motivate me to live a healthier lifestyle. Facing death can inspire us to affirm life.

*"It says, 'Someday you will die.'"*

## Check Your Understanding

### Examine the Concept

▶ What do critics see as the most serious problem with Freud's theory?

▶ Describe how modern-day research psychologists think of the unconscious.

*Answers to the Examine the Concept questions can be found in Appendix C at the end of the book.*

### Apply the Concept

▶ What understandings and impressions of Freud did you bring to this course? Are you surprised to find that some of his ideas have value, or that others have been called into question?

## Assessing Unconscious Processes

**Thematic Apperception Test (TAT)** a projective test in which people express their inner feelings and interests through the stories they make up about ambiguous scenes.

**projective test** a personality test, such as the TAT or Rorschach, that provides ambiguous images designed to trigger projection of one's inner dynamics and explore the preconscious and unconscious mind.

**Rorschach inkblot test** a projective test designed by Hermann Rorschach; seeks to identify people's inner feelings by analyzing how they interpret 10 inkblots.

**4.5-5** What are *projective tests*, how are they used, and what are some criticisms of them?

Personality tests reflect the basic ideas of particular personality theories. So, what might be the assessment tool of choice for someone working in the Freudian tradition? It would need to provide some sort of road into the unconscious—to unearth the residue of early childhood experiences, move beneath surface thoughts, and reveal hidden conflicts and impulses. Objective assessment tools, such as agree-disagree or true-false questionnaires, would be inadequate because they would merely tap the conscious surface.

Henry Murray (1933) demonstrated a possible basis for such a test at a party hosted by his 11-year-old daughter. Murray engaged the children in a frightening game called "Murder." When shown some photographs after the game, the children perceived the photos as more malicious than they had before the game. These children, it seemed to Murray, had *projected* their inner feelings into the pictures.

### Figure 4.5-2
### The TAT

This clinician presumes that the hopes, fears, and interests expressed in this boy's descriptions of a series of ambiguous pictures in the Thematic Apperception Test (TAT) are projections of his inner feelings.

Lewis J. Merrim/Science Source

A few years later, Murray introduced the **Thematic Apperception Test (TAT)**—a **projective test** in which people view ambiguous pictures and then make up stories about them (**Figure 4.5-2**). Shown a daydreaming boy, those who imagine he is fantasizing about an achievement are presumed to be projecting their own goals. "As a rule," said Murray, "the subject leaves the test happily unaware that he has presented the psychologist with what amounts to an X-ray of his inner self" (quoted by Talbot, 1999).

Numerous studies suggest that Murray was right: The TAT provides a valid and reliable map of people's implicit motives (Jenkins, 2017). For example, such storytelling has been used to assess *achievement* and *affiliation motivation*, which we will discuss in Module 4.7 (Drescher & Schultheiss, 2016; Schultheiss et al., 2014). TAT responses also show consistency over time (Lundy, 1985; Schultheiss & Pang, 2007). Show people a picture today, and they'll imagine a story similar to one they will tell when, a month later, they see the same picture.

Swiss psychiatrist Hermann Rorschach [ROAR-shock; 1884–1922] created the most widely used projective test. He based his famous **Rorschach inkblot test** (Figure 4.5-3) on a childhood game. Unlike the TAT's natural life images, Rorschach and his friends would drip ink on a paper, fold it, and then say what they saw in the resulting inkblot (Sdorow, 2005). Do you see predatory animals or weapons? If so, perhaps you have aggressive tendencies. But is this a reasonable assumption, considering that inkblots don't have any real-life meaning? The answer varies.

Some clinicians cherish the Rorschach test, convinced that it projects a client's inner motives to the outside world. Others view the test as a source of suggestive leads, an ice-breaker, or a revealing interview technique.

But critics insist the Rorschach is no emotional MRI. They argue that only a few of the many Rorschach-derived scores, such as those for cognitive impairment and thought disorder, have demonstrated reliability and validity (Mihura et al., 2013, 2015; Wood et al., 2015). And inkblot assessments have inaccurately diagnosed many healthy adults as pathological (Wood, 2003; Wood et al., 2006).

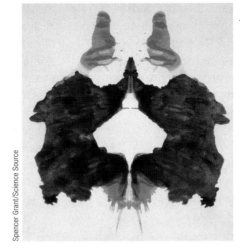
Spencer Grant/Science Source

**Figure 4.5-3**
**The Rorschach inkblot test**
In this projective test, people describe what they see in a series of symmetrical inkblots. Some psychologists believe that the interpretation of ambiguous images reveals unconscious aspects of the test-taker's personality.

 **AP® Science Practice**

**Research**

The "Assessing Unconscious Processes" section describes various *operational definitions* of unconsciousness. Each assessment offers a unique and specific way to assess the same variable.

 **AP® Science Practice**

**Research**

Researchers strive for both validity (making sure a test or experiment measures what it is supposed to measure) *and* reliability (the extent to which findings can be replicated) as described in Module 0.3.

## Module 4.5a REVIEW

**4.5-1** How did Freud's treatment of psychological disorders lead to his view of the unconscious mind, and what was his view of personality?

- *Psychodynamic theories* of personality view behavior as a dynamic interaction between the conscious and unconscious mind. These theories trace their origin to Sigmund Freud's theory of *psychoanalysis*.

- In treating patients whose disorders had no clear physical explanation, Freud concluded that these problems reflected unacceptable thoughts and feelings, hidden away in the *unconscious* mind. To explore this hidden part of a patient's mind, Freud used *free association*.

- Freud believed that personality results from conflict arising from the interaction among the mind's three systems: the *id* (pleasure-seeking impulses), *ego* (reality-oriented executive), and *superego* (internalized set of ideals, or conscience).

**4.5-2** How did Freud think people defended themselves against anxiety?

- For Freud, anxiety was the product of tensions between the demands of the id and superego. The ego copes by using unconscious *defense mechanisms*, such as *repression*, which he viewed as the basic mechanism underlying and enabling all the others.

**4.5-3** Which of Freud's ideas did his followers accept or reject?

- Freud's early followers, the neo-Freudians, accepted many of his ideas. They differed in placing more emphasis on the conscious mind and in stressing social motives more than sex or aggression.

- Most contemporary psychodynamic theorists and therapists reject Freud's emphasis on sexual motivation. They stress, with support from modern research findings, the view that much of our mental life is unconscious, and they believe that our childhood experiences influence our adult personality and attachment patterns. Many also believe that our species' shared evolutionary history shaped some universal predispositions.

**4.5-4** How do contemporary psychologists view Freud's psychoanalysis, and how has modern research developed our understanding of the unconscious?

- Freud is credited with drawing attention to the unconscious and the irrational, the importance of human sexuality, and the conflict between biological impulses and social restraints, and for formulating some science-backed defense mechanisms. But his concept of repression, and his view of the unconscious as a collection of repressed and unacceptable thoughts, wishes, feelings, and memories, cannot survive scientific scrutiny. Freud offered after-the-fact explanations, which are hard to test scientifically.

- Research does not support many of Freud's specific ideas, such as the view that development (which we now know is lifelong) is fixed in childhood. Research confirms that we do not have full access to all that goes on in our mind, though today's science views the unconscious as a separate and parallel track of information processing that occurs outside our awareness. This processing includes schemas that control our perceptions, priming, implicit memories of learned skills, instantly activated emotions, and the implicit prejudice and stereotypes that filter our information processing of others' traits and characteristics. Research also supports reaction formation and projection (the false consensus effect).

**4.5-5** What are *projective tests*, how are they used, and what are some criticisms of them?

- *Projective tests* show people stimuli that are open to many possible interpretations, treating their answers as revelations of inner dynamics. The *Thematic Apperception Test (TAT)* and the *Rorschach inkblot test* are two such tests.
- The TAT provides a valid and reliable map of people's implicit motives that is consistent over time. The Rorschach inkblot test has low reliability and validity, but some clinicians value it as a source of suggestive leads, an icebreaker, or a revealing interview technique.

# AP® Practice Multiple Choice Questions

1. Carly's therapist asks her to simply say what is on her mind rather than responding to specific questions or topics. Her therapist is making use of a psychoanalytic technique known as

   a. rationalization.  
   b. sublimation.  
   c. free association  
   d. identification.

2. Ella was an aggressive child in middle school. In high school, she is a successful three-sport athlete because she channels her aggression into sports. Which of the following defense mechanisms best applies to this scenario?

   a. Sublimation  
   b. Reaction formation  
   c. Displacement  
   d. Projection

3. Which of the following statements would Freud make to best describe this image?

   Nacivet/Getty Images

   a. The child is using reaction formation while in the latency stage.  
   b. The child is using regression to reduce anxiety.  
   c. The child is using displacement to replace anxiety.  
   d. The child is using denial to resolve the phallic stage.

**4.** Amberlyn studies the shared, inherited reservoir of memory traces from our species' history to better understand Carl Jung's ideas. She studies the

a. collective unconscious.
b. inferiority complex.
c. terror management.
d. superego.

**5.** Ralph was tasked to differentiate between Freud's perspective of the unconscious and current views of the unconscious. What should he say?

a. Freud's perspective of the unconscious focuses on the activation of instantaneous emotions, while current perspectives emphasize the role of childhood experiences on the unconscious mind.
b. Freud's perspective of the unconscious focuses on implicit memories of learned skills, while current perspectives emphasize the role of hidden wishes and desires.
c. Freud's perspective of the unconscious focuses on schemas that affect interpretations of situations, while current perspectives emphasize the role of stereotypes and implicit prejudice.
d. Freud's perspective on the unconscious focuses on the role of hidden wishes and desires, while current perspectives focus on the role of information processing that occurs outside of awareness.

**6.** Every morning, Marlie finds that one of her neighbors has left trash in her front yard. Although Marlie wants to pound on her neighbor's door and scream at him, she instead brings him some muffins she's just baked. Which of the following defense mechanisms best explains Marlie's behavior?

a. Repression
b. Displacement
c. Projection
d. Reaction formation

# Module 4.5b Psychodynamic and Humanistic Theories of Personality: Humanistic Theories

**humanistic theories** theories that view personality with a focus on the potential for healthy personal growth.

**hierarchy of needs** Maslow's levels of human needs, beginning at the base with physiological needs. Often visualized as a pyramid, with needs nearer the base taking priority until they are satisfied.

**self-actualization** according to Maslow, one of the ultimate psychological needs that arises after basic physical and psychological needs are met and self-esteem is achieved; the motivation to fulfill one's potential.

**self-transcendence** according to Maslow, the striving for identity, meaning, and purpose beyond the self.

## LEARNING TARGETS

**4.5-6** Explain how humanistic psychologists viewed personality, and explain their goal in studying personality.

**4.5-7** Explain how humanistic psychologists assessed a person's sense of self.

**4.5-8** Explain how humanistic theories have influenced psychology, and explain the criticisms they have faced.

---

**4.5-6** How did humanistic psychologists view personality, and what was their goal in studying personality?

By the 1960s, some personality psychologists had become discontented with the sometimes bleak focus on drives and conflicts in psychodynamic theory, and the mechanistic psychology of B. F. Skinner's *behaviorism* (see Modules 3.7 and 3.8). Two pioneering theorists—Abraham Maslow and Carl Rogers—offered a *third-force perspective* that emphasized our potential for healthy personal growth. In contrast to Freud's emphasis on disorders born out of dark conflicts, these **humanistic theorists** emphasized the ways people strive for self-determination and self-actualization. In contrast to behaviorism's scientific objectivity, they studied people through self-reported experiences and feelings.

## Abraham Maslow's Self-Actualizing Person

Maslow proposed that we are motivated by a **hierarchy of needs**, which others later portrayed as a pyramid (Bridgman et al., 2019; **Figure 4.5-4**). Our physiological needs, such as for food and water, form the pyramid's base. As these needs become met, our focus shifts to our need for safety, and then to satisfying our needs to give and receive love and to enjoy self-esteem. Having achieved self-esteem, we ultimately seek **self-actualization** (the process of fulfilling our potential) and **self-transcendence** (meaning, purpose, and identity beyond the self).

Maslow (1970) developed his ideas by studying healthy, creative people rather than clinical cases of troubled people. His description of self-actualization grew out of his study of people, such as Abraham Lincoln, who seemed notable for their meaningful and productive lives. Maslow reported that such people shared certain characteristics: They were self-aware and self-accepting, open and spontaneous, loving and caring, and not paralyzed by others' opinions (Kaufman, 2018). Secure in their sense of who they were, their interests were task-centered rather than self-centered. Curious about the world,

Macmillan Learning

**Abraham Maslow (1908–1970)**
"Any theory of motivation that is worthy of attention must deal with the highest capacities of the healthy and strong person as well as with the defensive maneuvers of crippled spirits" (*Motivation and Personality*, 1970, p. 33).

**SPOTLIGHT ON:**
Abraham Maslow

they embraced uncertainties and stretched themselves to seek out new experiences (Compton, 2018; Kashdan, 2009). Once they focused their energies on a particular task, they often regarded it as their life mission, or "calling" (Hall & Chandler, 2005). Most enjoyed a few deep relationships rather than many superficial ones. Many had been moved by spiritual or personal *peak experiences* that surpassed ordinary consciousness.

Maslow (1970) considered these to be adult qualities. These healthy people had outgrown their mixed feelings toward their parents and had found their calling. They had "acquired enough courage to be unpopular, to be unashamed about being openly virtuous." (Test your own level of self-actualization in Figure 4.5-5.)

**Self-transcendence needs**
Need to find meaning and identity beyond the self

**Self-actualization needs**
Need to live up to our fullest and unique potential

**Esteem needs**
Need for self-esteem, achievement, competence, and independence; need for recognition and respect from others

**Belongingness and love needs**
Need to love and be loved, to belong and be accepted; need to avoid loneliness and separation

**Safety needs**
Need to feel that the world is organized and predictable; need to feel safe, secure, and stable

**Physiological needs**
Need to satisfy hunger and thirst

Jalal Morchidi/Anadolu Agency/Getty Images

**Figure 4.5-4**

**Maslow's hierarchy of needs**

During the month of Ramadan, many Muslims refrain from eating and drinking from dawn to sunset. They end their daily fast by satisfying their lower-level needs for food and drink and engaging their middle-level needs for belongingness and love, often having a large communal meal (called *iftar*, meaning "break fast").

---

### Characteristics of Self-Actualization Scale (CSAS)

Here are a number of characteristics that may or may not describe you. Please select the answer that best indicates the extent to which you agree or disagree with each statement. Be as honest as possible, but rely on your initial feeling and do not think too much.

| 1 | 2 | 3 | 4 | 5 |
|---|---|---|---|---|
| Strongly disagree | Disagree | Neutral | Agree | Strongly agree |

1. ____I often feel gratitude for the good in my life no matter how many times I encounter it.

2. ____I accept all sides of myself, including my shortcomings.

3. ____I take responsibility for my actions.

4. ____I am often undisturbed and unruffled by things that seem to bother most people.

5. ____I have a purpose in life that will help the good of humankind.

6. ____I often have a clear perception of reality.

7. ____I have a genuine desire to help the human race.

8. ____I often have experiences in which I feel one with all people and things on this planet.

9. ____I have a strong sense of right and wrong in my daily life.

10. ____I bring a generally creative attitude to all of my work.

**Scoring Guide:**
Add up your scores and divide by 10 for your total score. The items above represent the 10 characteristics of self-actualization studied by Scott Barry Kaufman (2018):
(1) Continued freshness of appreciation, (2) Acceptance, (3) Authenticity, (4) Equanimity (mental calmness), (5) Purpose, (6) Truth seeking, (7) Humanitarianism (concern with human welfare), (8) Peak experiences, 9) Good moral intuition, and (10) Creative spirit.

Kaufman found that those with higher scores experienced "greater life satisfaction, self-acceptance, positive relations, personal growth, purpose in life, and self-transcendent experiences" as well as "creativity across multiple domains of achievement."

**Figure 4.5-5**

**Characteristics of Self-Actualization Scale (CSAS)**

This shortened version of the CSAS represents the 10 self-actualization characteristics studied by Scott Barry Kaufman (2018).

## AP® Science Practice

## Data Interpretation

The humanistic theories of personality focused on our inner capacities for growth and self-actualization. Self-actualization can be measured using the Characteristics of Self-Actualization Scale (CSAS; Kaufman, 2018). This 10-item questionnaire uses a scale from 1 (strongly disagree) to 5 (strongly agree). A sample item is "I have a genuine desire to help the human race." Higher scores indicate higher self-actualization. Research shows there is a statistically significant, positive correlation between self-actualization and being curious about the world.

- Are the data gathered from the CSAS quantitative or qualitative? Explain your choice.

- Explain the relationship between self-actualization and being curious about the world.

- Explain what is meant by statistically significant, in this case.

Remember, you can always refer to Module 0.6 for help.

**Carl Rogers (1902–1987)** "The curious paradox is that when I accept myself just as I am, then I can change" (*On Becoming a Person*, 1961).

P. BYRNES.

**A father *not* offering unconditional positive regard**
*"Just remember, son, it doesn't matter whether you win or lose — unless you want Daddy's love."*

**unconditional positive regard**
a caring, accepting, nonjudgmental attitude, which Carl Rogers believed would help people develop self-awareness and self-acceptance. (Also known as *unconditional regard*.)

## Carl Rogers' Person-Centered Perspective

Fellow humanistic psychologist Carl Rogers agreed with much of Maslow's thinking. Rogers' *person-centered perspective* held that people are basically good and are, as Maslow said, endowed with self-actualizing tendencies. Unless thwarted by a growth-inhibiting environment, each of us is like an acorn, primed for growth and fulfillment. Rogers (1980) believed that a growth-promoting social climate provides

- *acceptance*. When people are *accepting*, they offer **unconditional positive regard** (also known as *unconditional regard*), an attitude of grace that values us even knowing our failings. It is a profound relief to drop our pretenses, confess our worst feelings, and discover that we are still accepted. In a good marriage, a close family, or an intimate friendship, we are free to be spontaneous without fearing the loss of others' esteem.

- *genuineness*. When people are *genuine*, they are open with their own feelings, drop their facades, and are transparent and self-disclosing.

- *empathy*. When people are *empathic*, they share and mirror others' feelings and reflect their meanings. "Rarely do we listen with real understanding, true empathy," said Rogers. "Yet listening, of this very special kind, is one of the most potent forces for change that I know." (When others talk do you generally listen closely, or just wait for your turn to talk?)

Acceptance, genuineness, and empathy are, Rogers believed, the water, Sun, and nutrients that enable people to grow from acorns into vigorous oak trees. For "as persons are accepted and prized, they tend to develop a more caring attitude toward themselves" (Rogers, 1980, p. 116). When heard and accepted, said Rogers, people can listen to and accept their thoughts and feelings.

The educator Alice Stewart Trillin discovered parental acceptance and genuineness at a camp for children with severe disorders. L., a "magical child," had genetic diseases that meant she had to be tube-fed and could walk only with difficulty. Alice wondered "what this child's parents could have done . . . to make her the most optimistic, most enthusiastic, most hopeful human being I had ever encountered" (quoted in Trillin, 2006). One day Alice spotted a note that L. received from her mom, which read, "If God had given us all of the children in the world to choose from, L., we would only have chosen you." Inspired, Alice approached a co-worker. "Quick. Read this," she whispered. "It's the secret of life."

Maslow and Rogers would have smiled knowingly. For them, a central feature of personality is one's **self-concept**—all the thoughts and feelings we have in response to the question, "Who am I?" If our self-concept is positive, we tend to act and perceive the world positively. If it is negative—if we fall far short of our *ideal self*—said Rogers, we feel dissatisfied and unhappy. A worthwhile goal for therapists, parents, teachers, and friends, he said, is therefore to help others know, accept, and be true to themselves.

## Assessing the Self

**4.5-7** How did humanistic psychologists assess a person's sense of self?

Humanistic psychologists sometimes assessed personality by asking people to fill out questionnaires that would evaluate their self-concept. One questionnaire, inspired by Carl Rogers, asked people to describe themselves both as they would *ideally* like to be and as they *actually* are. When the ideal and the actual self are nearly alike, said Rogers, the self-concept is positive. Assessing his clients' personal growth during therapy, he looked for successively closer ratings of actual and ideal selves.

Some humanistic psychologists believed that any standardized assessment of personality, even a questionnaire, is depersonalizing. Rather than forcing the person to respond to narrow categories, these humanistic psychologists presumed that interviews and intimate conversation would provide a better understanding of each person's unique experiences. Some researchers today believe our identity may be revealed using the *life story approach*—collecting a rich narrative detailing each person's unique life history (Adler et al., 2016; McAdams & Guo, 2015). A lifetime of stories can show more of a person's complete identity than can the responses to a few questions (Waters et al., 2019).

## Evaluating Humanistic Theories

**4.5-8** How have humanistic theories influenced psychology? What criticisms have they faced?

One thing said of Freud can also be said of the humanistic psychologists: Their impact has been pervasive. Maslow's and Rogers' ideas have influenced counseling, education, child raising, and management. And they laid the groundwork for today's scientific *positive psychology* subfield (Module 5.2).

These theorists have also influenced—sometimes in unintended ways—much of today's popular psychology. Is a positive self-concept the key to happiness and success? Do acceptance and empathy nurture positive feelings about ourselves? Are people basically good and capable of self-improvement? Many people answer *Yes*, *Yes*, and *Yes*. In 2006, U.S. high school students reported notably higher self-esteem and greater expectations of future career success than did students living in 1975, before humanistic psychology's feelgood philosophy infused U.S. culture (Twenge & Campbell, 2008). Given a choice, North American college students have said they would rather get a self-esteem boost, such as a compliment or good grade on a paper, than enjoy a favorite food (Bushman et al., 2011). When you hear talk about the importance of "loving yourself," you can give some credit to the humanistic theorists.

But the prominence of the humanistic perspective set off a backlash of criticism. First, said the critics, its concepts are vague and subjective. Consider Maslow's description of self-actualizing people as open, spontaneous, loving, self-accepting, and productive. Is this

**The picture of empathy** Being open and sharing confidences is easier when the listener shows real understanding. Within such relationships, we can relax and fully express our true selves.

**self-concept** all our thoughts and feelings about ourselves, in answer to the question, "Who am I?"

Even scientists have cultural and
cognitive biases. As illustrated here,
one's cultural values and ideals can
influence the theory one proposes.

a scientific description? Or is it merely a description of the theorist's own values and ideals? Maslow, noted M. Brewster Smith (1978), offered impressions of his own personal heroes, such as Abraham Lincoln and Albert Einstein. Imagine another theorist who began with a different set of heroes—perhaps Russian President Vladimir Putin or U.S. media personality Kim Kardashian. This theorist might describe self-actualizing people as "undeterred by others' opinions" and "comfortable with attention."

Critics also objected to the idea that, as Rogers (1985) put it, "The only question which matters is, 'Am I living in a way which is deeply satisfying to me, and which truly expresses me?'" This emphasis on *individualism*—trusting and acting on one's feelings, being true to oneself, fulfilling oneself—could lead to self-indulgence, selfishness, and an erosion of moral restraint (Campbell & Specht, 1985; Wallach & Wallach, 1983). Imagine working on a group project with people who refuse to complete any task that is not deeply satisfying or does not truly express their identity.

Humanistic psychologists have replied that a secure, nondefensive self-acceptance is actually the first step toward loving others. Indeed, people who feel intrinsically liked and accepted—for who they are, not just for their achievements—exhibit less defensive attitudes (Schimel et al., 2001). Those feeling liked and accepted by a romantic partner report being happier in their relationships and acting more kindly toward their partner (Gordon & Chen, 2010).

A final critique has been that humanistic psychology is naive—that it fails to appreciate the reality of our human capacity for evil (May, 1982). Psychological science reminds us of this unfortunate capacity. As we saw earlier in this unit, situations can prompt us to follow falsehoods or capitulate to cruelty. *Deindividuation*, *groupthink*, and *group polarization* may accentuate our worst tendencies. And mere disliking can become prejudiced despising. But as the humanistic psychologists remind us, there is another mountain of research that testifies to our potential for goodness—for growth and gratitude, for humility and hope, for empathy and compassion.

**Are we humans born to be bad or good?** The lessons of psychological science mirror our cultural experience of human evil: senseless killings, White supremacism, barefaced lies spreading virally. But they also reveal the potential for human good: courageous first responders, volunteers staffing food banks, pandemic health care workers risking their own health to care for those who are alone and suffering.

Faced with a looming climate crisis, economic woes, and systemic racism, we may become apathetic from either of two rationalizations. One is a starry-eyed optimism that denies the threat ("Everything will work out for the best"). The other is a dark despair ("It's hopeless; why try?"). Action requires enough realism to fuel concern and enough optimism to provide hope.

---

### AP® Science Practice

## Check Your Understanding

### Examine the Concept

▶ Explain how the humanistic theories provided a fresh perspective.

▶ Explain the difference between self-actualization and self-transcendence.

### Apply the Concept

▶ Think back to a conversation you had when you knew someone was just waiting for their turn to speak instead of listening to you. Now consider the last time someone heard you with empathy. How did those two experiences differ?

▶ Have you had someone in your life who accepted you unconditionally? How did this person help you to know yourself better and to develop a better image of yourself?

*Answers to the Examine the Concept questions can be found in Appendix C at the end of the book.*

# Module 4.5b REVIEW

**4.5-6 How did humanistic psychologists view personality, and what was their goal in studying personality?**

- The *humanistic* psychologists' view of personality focused on the potential for healthy personal growth and people's striving for self-determination and self-realization.

- Abraham Maslow proposed that human motivations form a *hierarchy of needs;* if basic needs are fulfilled, people will strive toward *self-actualization* and *self-transcendence*.

- Carl Rogers believed that the ingredients of a growth-promoting environment are acceptance (including *unconditional positive regard*), genuineness, and empathy.

- *Self-concept* was a central feature of personality for both Maslow and Rogers.

**4.5-7 How did humanistic psychologists assess a person's sense of self?**

- Some rejected any standardized assessments and relied on interviews and conversations.

- Others, like Rogers, sometimes used questionnaires in which people described their ideal and actual selves; these were later used to judge progress during therapy.

- Some now use the life story approach, which creates a rich narrative detailing each person's unique life history.

**4.5-8 How have humanistic theories influenced psychology? What criticisms have they faced?**

- Humanistic psychology has had a pervasive cultural impact; it also laid the groundwork for today's scientific subfield of positive psychology.

- Critics have said that humanistic psychology's concepts are vague and subjective, its values self-centered, and its assumptions naively optimistic.

## AP® Practice Multiple Choice Questions

1. What psychological concept is depicted in this pie chart?

I am...

20% Studious
30% Kind
25% Friendly
25% Creative

   a. Self-transcendence
   b. Self-actualization
   c. Self-awareness
   d. Self-concept

2. What do we call the process of fulfilling our potential?

   a. Belongingness
   b. Unconditional positive regard
   c. Self-actualization
   d. Self-concept

3. Emiko feels grateful that he has food to eat, a home, and good friends, but he cannot stop feeling as if he is doing a bad job at work. With which level of Maslow's hierarchy of needs is Emiko struggling?

   a. Physiological
   b. Safety
   c. Self-transcendence
   d. Esteem

4. Humanistic psychologists may assess personality by

   a. asking people to complete surveys about their ideal selves versus their actual selves.
   b. doing case studies on what a person sees in ambiguous inkblots.
   c. having a person describe their dreams over multiple years.
   d. conducting experiments on the impact of stressful situations on people's behavior under pressure.

**5.** Which of the following is an example of unconditional positive regard?

   a. The Prohaskas credit the success of their marriage to accepting the faults of the other without criticism.

   b. Mr. Lopez, a second-grade teacher, gives smiley-face stickers to students who sit quietly at their desks during math.

   c. Jacqueline got a promotion and a raise at work after filling in for a manager one day, because she did a better job than the manager typically does.

   d. Chen's parents praise him when he does well and ignore him when he engages in minor misbehavior.

**6.** Dr. Kumar conducted a study in which he randomly assigned participants either to complete a questionnaire about the dreams they had during the last week or to tell their life stories. Then, he asked them to indicate the extent to which they felt more secure in their sense of self. Dr. Coneja conducted a study in which she asked college students in her classes to write stories about their lives over the semester. At the end of the semester, she asked her students to indicate the extent to which they felt more secure in their sense of self. Which of the following best differentiates the conclusions that Dr. Kumar and Dr. Coneja can draw from their studies?

   a. Dr. Kumar can claim that the life story approach caused the participants' self-concepts to solidify, while Dr. Coneja cannot make this claim because she did not use random assignment.

   b. Dr. Kumar can claim that the life story approach caused the participants' self-concepts to solidify, while Dr. Coneja cannot make this claim because she did not use random sampling.

   c. Dr. Kumar can claim that there is a statistically significant difference between dream analysis and the life story approach, while Dr. Coneja cannot make this claim because she used a qualitative method.

   d. Dr. Kumar can claim that there is a statistically significant difference between dream analysis and the life story approach, while Dr. Coneja cannot make this claim because she used an experimental design.

# Module 4.6a Social-Cognitive and Trait Theories of Personality: Trait Theories

## LEARNING TARGETS

**4.6-1** Explain how psychologists use traits to describe personality.

**4.6-2** Describe *personality inventories*, and explain their strengths and weaknesses as trait-assessment tools.

**4.6-3** Identify the traits that seem to provide the most useful information about personality variation.

**4.6-4** Explain whether research supports the consistency of personality traits over time and across situations.

---

### 4.6-1 How do psychologists use traits to describe personality?

Rather than focusing on unconscious forces and thwarted growth opportunities, some researchers attempt to define personality in terms of stable and enduring behavior patterns, such as Lady Gaga's self-discipline and openness to new experiences. This perspective can be traced in part to a remarkable meeting in 1919, when Gordon Allport, a curious 22-year-old psychology student, interviewed Sigmund Freud in Vienna. During the interview, Allport quickly discovered just how preoccupied the founder of psychoanalysis was with finding hidden motives, even in Allport's own behavior. That experience ultimately led Allport to do what Freud did not do: to describe personality in terms of fundamental **traits,** or people's characteristic behaviors and conscious motives (such as the curiosity that actually motivated Allport to see Freud). Meeting Freud, said Allport, "taught me that [psychoanalysis], for all its merits, may plunge too deep, and that psychologists would do well to give full recognition to manifest motives before probing the unconscious." Allport came to define personality in terms of identifiable behavior patterns. He was concerned less with *explaining* individual traits than with *describing* them.

Like Allport, Isabel Briggs Myers (1987) and her mother, Katharine Briggs, wanted to describe important personality differences. They attempted to sort people according to Carl Jung's *personality types*, based on their responses to 126 questions. The *Myers-Briggs Type Indicator (MBTI)*, available in 20+ languages, has been taken by millions of people, mostly for counseling, leadership training, and work-team development (CPP, 2017). It offers choices, such as "Do you usually value sentiment more than logic, or value logic more than sentiment?" Then it counts the test-taker's preferences; labels them as indicating, say, a "feeling type" or "thinking type"; and feeds them back to the person in complimentary terms. Feeling types, for example, are told they are "sympathetic, appreciative, and tactful"; thinking types are told they are "good at analyzing." (Every type has its strengths, so everyone is affirmed.)

Most people agree with their announced MBTI profile, which mirrors their declared preferences. They may also accept their label as a basis for being matched with work or dating partners, and with tasks that supposedly suit their temperaments. But a National Research Council report noted that despite the test's popularity in business and career counseling, its use has outrun research on its validity as a job performance predictor: "The popularity

**trait** a characteristic pattern of behavior or a disposition to feel and act in certain ways, as assessed by self-report inventories and peer reports.

"Hello. This is Dial-a-Grump. What the hell do you want?"

**Figure 4.6-1**

**Two personality dimensions**

Mapmakers can tell us a lot by using two axes (north–south and east–west). Two primary personality factors (extraversion–introversion and stability–instability) are similarly useful as axes for describing personality variation. Varying combinations define other, more specific traits (Eysenck & Eysenck, 1963). Although many actors are extraverted, some, such as Issa Rae, are introverts — particularly capable of solitary study to become each character they portray. Professional comedians, such as Jimmy Fallon, are often natural extraverts (Irwing et al., 2020).

of this instrument in the absence of proven scientific worth is troublesome" (Druckman & Bjork, 1991, p. 101; see also Al-Shawaf, 2021). Although research on the MBTI has been accumulating since those cautionary words were expressed, the test remains mostly a counseling and coaching tool, not a research instrument. Fortunately, newer research offers reliable and valid tools to explore traits.

## Exploring Traits

We are each a unique complex of multiple traits. As Dr. Seuss put it, "There is no one alive who is Youer than You." So how can we describe our personalities in a way that captures our individuality? We might describe an apple by placing it along several trait dimensions—relatively large or small, red or green, sweet or tart. By placing people on several trait dimensions simultaneously, psychologists can describe countless individual personality variations.

What trait dimensions describe personality? If you were looking at profiles on an online dating service, what personality traits would give you the best sense for each person? Allport and his associate H. S. Odbert (1936) counted all the words in an unabridged dictionary that could be used to describe people. There were almost 18,000! How, then, could psychologists condense the list to a manageable number of basic traits?

## Factor Analysis

One technique is *factor analysis*, a statistical procedure that identifies clusters (factors) of test items that tap basic components of a trait (McCabe & Fleeson, 2016). Imagine that people who describe themselves as outgoing also tend to say that they like excitement and practical jokes and dislike quiet reading. Such a statistically correlated cluster of behaviors reflects a basic factor, or trait—in this case, *extraversion*.

British psychologists Hans Eysenck [EYE-zink] and Sybil Eysenck believed that we can reduce many of our normal individual variations to two dimensions: *extraversion–introversion* and *emotional stability–instability* (**Figure 4.6-1**).[1] People in 35 countries worldwide, from China to Uganda to Russia, took the *Eysenck Personality Questionnaire*. When their answers were analyzed, the extraversion and emotionality (later called neuroticism) factors inevitably emerged as basic personality dimensions (Eysenck, 1990, 1992). The Eysencks believed, and research confirms, that these factors are genetically influenced.

(a)

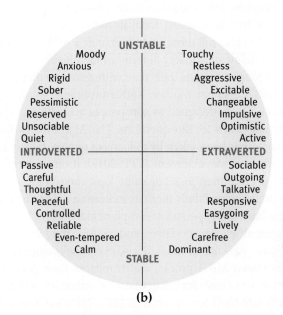

UNSTABLE

Moody    Touchy
Anxious    Restless
Rigid    Aggressive
Sober    Excitable
Pessimistic    Changeable
Reserved    Impulsive
Unsociable    Optimistic
Quiet    Active

INTROVERTED ——— EXTRAVERTED

Passive    Sociable
Careful    Outgoing
Thoughtful    Talkative
Peaceful    Responsive
Controlled    Easygoing
Reliable    Lively
Even-tempered    Carefree
Calm    Dominant

STABLE

(b)

(c)

[1]Some of the late Hans Eysenck's views have been deemed racist and some of his other research has been judged untrustworthy, but his personality concepts remain accepted (O'Grady, 2020).

## Biology and Personality

Brain-activity scans of extraverts add to the growing list of traits and mental states now being explored. Such studies indicate that extraverts seek stimulation because their normal *brain arousal* is relatively low. For example, PET scans have shown that a frontal lobe area involved in behavior inhibition is less active in extraverts than in introverts (Johnson et al., 1999). Dopamine and dopamine-related neural activity tend to be higher in extraverts (Kim et al., 2008; Wacker et al., 2006).

Our biology influences our personality. Recall from the twin and adoption studies in Module 1.1 that, compared with fraternal twins, identical twin personalities are more similar (Loehlin & Martin, 2018; Mõttus et al., 2019). What's true of so much of human nature is also true of personality and life outcomes, which are influenced by many genes having small effects (Smith-Woolley et al., 2019; van den Berg et al., 2016). Our genes also influence the *temperament* and behavioral style that shape our personality. Jerome Kagan (2010), for example, has explained differences in children's shyness and inhibition as a function of their autonomic nervous system reactivity. Those with a reactive autonomic nervous system respond to stress with greater anxiety and inhibition. The fearless, curious child may become the extreme skier or mountain biker with a GoPro. (See Developing Arguments: The Stigma of Introversion.)

---

**AP® Science Practice** ## Developing Arguments

### The Stigma of Introversion

#### Western cultures are hard on introverts:

Extraverts are often celebrated in comics and film. Black Panther unites five tribes of people with his engaging strength of character. Take-charge Elastigirl saves the day in *The Incredibles*.

**87% of Westerners want to be more extraverted.**[1]

**Being introverted seems to imply that we don't have the "right stuff."**[2]

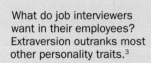

What do job interviewers want in their employees? Extraversion outranks most other personality traits.[3]

Attractive, successful people are presumed to be extraverts.[4]

#### What is introversion?

Introverts tend to gain energy from time alone, and may find social interactions exhausting. Extraverts, by contrast, tend to draw energy from time spent with others.

Introverts are not "shy." (Shy people remain quiet because they fear others will evaluate them negatively.)

 Introverted people seek low levels of stimulation from their environment because they have more sensitive nervous systems. For example, when given lemon juice, introverted people salivated more than extraverted people.[5]

#### Introversion has many benefits:

· Introverted leaders outperform extraverted leaders in some contexts, such as when their employees voice new ideas and challenge existing norms.[6]

· Introverts handle conflict well. In response, they seek solitude rather than revenge.[7]

· Many introverts have flourished, including Sir Isaac Newton, Mother Teresa, and Oprah Winfrey. "A true extravert," Winfrey explains, "gets energy,...feeds off people,...and I get sucked dry."[8]

### Developing Arguments Questions

**1.** Explain what scientifically derived evidence has revealed about the nature of introversion.

**2.** Use the scientifically derived evidence presented here to support the claim that there is a bias toward extraversion.

**3.** Explain the scientifically derived evidence that refutes the introversion stigma.

1. Hudson & Roberts, 2014. 2. Cain, 2012. 3. Kluemper et al., 2015; Salgado & Moscoso, 2002. 4. McCord & Joseph, 2020. 5. Corcoran, 1964. 6. A. Grant et al., 2011. 7. Ren et al., 2016. 8. OWN, 2018.

---

**Octopus personality** The real-life Otto the octopus seems to love getting attention from visitors. But when his German aquarium closes during the winter, Otto acts like a bored prankster. He has juggled hermit crabs, squirted water at staff members, and broken his light by spraying it with water.

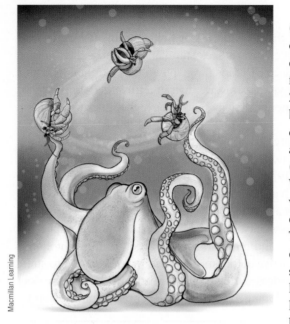

Macmillan Learning

❝ *People have had fun spoofing the MMPI with their own mock items: "Weeping brings tears to my eyes," "Frantic screams make me nervous," and "I stay in the bathtub until I look like a raisin" (Frankel et al., 1983).* ❞

**personality inventory** a questionnaire (often with *true-false* or *agree-disagree* items) on which people respond to items designed to gauge a wide range of feelings and behaviors; used to assess selected personality traits.

**Minnesota Multiphasic Personality Inventory (MMPI)** the most widely researched and clinically used of all personality tests. Originally developed to identify emotional disorders (still considered its most appropriate use), this test is now used for many other screening purposes.

**empirically derived test** a test (such as the MMPI) created by selecting from a pool of items those that discriminate between groups.

**Big Five factors** five traits— *openness, conscientiousness, extraversion, agreeableness,* and *neuroticism*—that describe personality. (Also called the *five-factor model*.)

Personality differences among dogs (in energy, affection, reactivity, and curious intelligence) are as evident, and as consistently judged, as personality differences among humans (Gosling et al., 2003; Jones & Gosling, 2005). Monkeys, bonobos, chimpanzees, orangutans, orcas, sea lions, and even birds and fish also have distinct and stable personalities (Altschul et al., 2018; Úbeda et al., 2018; Weiss et al., 2017). Even conscientiousness varies among individual animals, from chimps to bees (Delgado & Sulloway, 2017). Through selective breeding, researchers can produce bold or shy birds. Both personality types have their place in natural history: In lean years, bold birds are more likely to find food; in abundant years, shy birds feed with less risk.

## Assessing Traits

**4.6-2** What are *personality inventories*, and what are their strengths and weaknesses as trait-assessment tools?

If stable and enduring traits guide our actions, can we devise valid and reliable tests of them? Several trait-assessment techniques exist—some more valid than others. Some provide quick assessments of a single trait, such as extraversion, anxiety, or self-esteem. **Personality inventories**—longer questionnaires covering a wide range of feelings and behaviors—assess several traits at once.

The classic personality inventory is the **Minnesota Multiphasic Personality Inventory (MMPI)**. Although the MMPI was originally developed to identify emotional disorders, it also assesses people's personality traits. One of its creators, Starke Hathaway (1960), compared his effort with that of Alfred Binet (who, as you saw in Module 2.8, developed the first intelligence test by selecting items that identified children who would likely struggle to progress in French schools). Like Binet's items, the MMPI items were **empirically derived**: From a large pool of items, Hathaway and his colleagues selected those on which particular diagnostic groups differed. "My hands and feet are usually warm enough" may seem superficial, but it just so happened that anxious people were more likely to answer *False.* The researchers grouped the questions into 10 clinical scales, including scales that assess depressive tendencies, masculinity–femininity, and introversion–extraversion. Today's MMPI-2 has additional scales that assess work attitudes, family problems, and anger.

Whereas most projective tests (such as the Rorschach inkblot test) are scored subjectively, personality inventories are scored objectively. Objectivity does not, however, guarantee validity. Individuals taking the MMPI for employment purposes can give socially desirable answers to create a good impression. But in so doing they may also score high on a *lie scale* that assesses faking (as when people respond *False* to a universally true statement, such as "I get angry sometimes"). In other cases, the MMPI can be used to identify people pretending to have a disorder in an effort to avoid their responsibilities (Chmielewski et al., 2017). The MMPI's objectivity has contributed to its popularity and its translation into more than 100 languages.

## Data Interpretation

Dr. Pramar is interested in personality. She randomly selects five students from two classes and administers a 50-item extraversion scale. The items are true or false, and scores can range from 0 to 50. Higher scores indicate higher extraversion. Consider the following data set.

| Extraversion Scores | |
|---|---|
| Dr. Pramar's 9:00 A.M. Class | Dr. Pramar's 3:00 P.M. Class |
| 48 | 34 |
| 25 | 20 |
| 32 | 14 |
| 25 | 28 |
| 40 | 14 |

- Calculate the mean, median, and mode for each class.

- If the difference in extraversion between the two classes is statistically significant, what does this mean?

- Explain what conclusions Dr. Pramar can draw from these data.

The ability to calculate and interpret measures of central tendency is an important skill in psychology that will be assessed on the AP® exam. Remember, you can always refer to Module 0.6 for help.

# The Big Five Factors

**4.6-3** Which traits seem to provide the most useful information about personality variation?

Today's trait researchers believe that simple trait factors, such as the Eysencks' introversion–extraversion and stability–instability dimensions, are important, but they do not tell the whole story. A slightly expanded set of factors developed by Robert McCrae and Paul Costa — dubbed the **Big Five factors** (also called the *five-factor model*) — does a better job (Costa & McCrae, 2011; Soto & John, 2017). If a test specifies where you are on the five dimensions (*openness, conscientiousness, extraversion, agreeableness,* and *neuroticism* [OCEAN]; see **Table 4.6-1**), it has said much of what there is to say about

**TABLE 4.6-1** **The Big Five Personality Factors**

Researchers use a self-report inventory to assess and score the Big Five personality factors.

(*Memory tip*: Picturing an **OCEAN** will help you recall these.)

| | | |
|---|---|---|
| Practical, prefers routine, conforming | **O**penness | Imaginative, prefers variety, independent |
| Disorganized, careless, impulsive | **C**onscientiousness | Organized, careful, disciplined |
| Retiring, sober, reserved | **E**xtraversion | Sociable, fun-loving, affectionate |
| Ruthless, suspicious, uncooperative | **A**greeableness | Soft-hearted, trusting, helpful |
| Calm, secure, self-satisfied | **N**euroticism (emotional stability vs. instability) | Anxious, insecure, self-pitying |

Information from McCrae & Costa (1986, 2008).

your personality. The Big Five factors can also be used to understand both psychological flourishing and dysfunction (Bleidorn et al., 2020; Oltmanns et al., 2018; Wimmelmann et al., 2020).

Around the world—across 56 nations and 29 languages in one study (Schmitt et al., 2007)—people describe others in terms roughly consistent with this list. The Big Five—today's "common currency for personality psychology" (Funder, 2001)—has been the most active personality research topic since the early 1990s and is currently our best approximation of the basic trait dimensions.

Big Five research has explored various questions:

**AP® Science Practice**

## Research

Do you recall the research method that would allow researchers to determine the stability of a person's personality over their lifespan? It is the longitudinal method.

- ***How stable are these traits?*** Research teams have analyzed the traits of Americans, Australians, Icelanders, and Germans up to age 50 (Damian et al., 2019; Hoff et al., 2020; Wagner et al., 2019). People's personalities remained generally stable, but most exhibited a *maturity principle:* From adolescence onward, they became more conscientious and agreeable, and less neurotic (emotionally unstable) (Allemand et al., 2019; Klimstra et al., 2018; Rohrer et al., 2018). People in Japan, who more often adapt their personality to their social environment, show somewhat more Big Five trait variation (Haas & vanDellen, 2020).

- ***Do self-ratings on these traits match others' ratings?*** The ratings of family and friends of our Big Five trait levels do resemble the ratings we give ourselves (Finnigan & Vazire, 2018; Luan et al., 2019).

- ***Do these traits reflect differing brain structure?*** The size and thickness of brain tissue correlates with several Big Five traits (DeYoung & Allen, 2019; Li et al., 2017; Riccelli et al., 2017). For example, those who score high on conscientiousness tend to have a larger frontal lobe area that aids in planning and controlling behavior. Brain connections also influence the Big Five traits (Toschi et al., 2018). People high in neuroticism have brains that are wired to experience stress intensely (Shackman et al., 2016; Xu & Potenza, 2012).

*"I do think it would speed things up
if you followed my social media."*

- *Do these traits reflect birth order?* After controlling for other variables such as family size, are first-born children, for example, more conscientious and agreeable? Contrary to popular opinion, several massive studies failed to find any association between birth order and personality, even after controlling for family size and other variables (Damian & Roberts, 2015; Harris, 2009; Rohrer et al., 2015).

- *How well do these traits apply to various cultures?* The Big Five dimensions describe personality in various cultures reasonably well (Fetvadjiev et al., 2017; Kim et al., 2018; Schmitt et al., 2007). From herders in Kenya and Tanzania to gardeners in Mali, these traits help us understand basic features of personality (Thalmayer et al., 2020). After studying people from 50 cultures, Robert McCrae and 79 co-researchers (2005) concluded that "features of personality traits are common to all human groups."

- *Do the Big Five traits predict our everyday behaviors?* *Yes*, the Big Five traits reliably predict important life outcomes (Soto, 2019). Conscientiousness predicts better school performance and workplace success (McCredie & Kurtz, 2020; Nickel et al., 2019). Agreeable people are caring and law-abiding, as when following mobility restrictions to minimize Covid spread (Chan et al., 2020; Zajenkowski et al., 2020). Extraverts post more on social media and more often become leaders (Bowden-Green, 2020; Scott & Medeiros, 2020).

By exploring such questions, Big Five research has sustained trait psychology and has renewed appreciation for the importance of personality. (To describe your personality, try the brief self-assessment in **Figure 4.6-2**.) Traits matter.

**How do you vote? Let me count the likes** Researchers can use Facebook likes to predict Big Five traits, opinions, and political attitudes (Youyou et al., 2015). Companies sell these "big data" to advertisers, which then personalize the ads you see, and to political campaigns, which then target you with persuasive messages (Matz et al., 2017).

---

**Figure 4.6-2**
**The Big Five Self-assessment**

**How Do You Describe Yourself?**

Describe yourself as you generally are now, not as you wish to be in the future. Describe yourself as you honestly see yourself, in relation to other people you know of the same sex and roughly the same age. Use the scale below to enter a number for each statement. Then, use the scoring guide at the bottom to see where you fall on the spectrum for each of the Big Five traits.

| 1 | 2 | 3 | 4 | 5 |
|---|---|---|---|---|
| Very Inaccurate | Moderately Inaccurate | Neither Accurate Nor Inaccurate | Moderately Accurate | Very Accurate |

1. ___Am the life of the party
2. ___Sympathize with others' feelings
3. ___Get stressed out easily
4. ___Am always prepared
5. ___Am full of ideas
6. ___Start conversations
7. ___Take time out for others
8. ___Follow a schedule
9. ___Worry about things
10. ___Have a vivid imagination

**SCORING GUIDE SORTED BY BIG FIVE PERSONALITY TRAITS**

**Openness:** statements 5, 10

**Conscientiousness:** statements 4, 8

**Extraversion:** statements 1, 6

**Agreeableness:** statements 2, 7

**Neuroticism:** statements 3, 9

**How to score:**
Separate your responses by each Big Five personality trait, as noted at left, and divide by two to obtain your score for each trait. So, for example, for the "Agreeableness" trait let's say you scored 3 for statement 2 ("Sympathize with others' feelings") and 4 for statement 7 ("Take time out for others"). That means on a scale from 1 to 5, your overall score for the "Agreeableness" trait is 3 + 4 = 7 ÷ 2 = **3.5.**

Scale data from: International Personality Item Pool: A Scientific Collaboratory for the Development of Advanced Measures of Personality Traits and Other Individual Differences (ipip.ori.org)

# Check Your Understanding

**Examine the Concept**

▶ Explain what is meant by *trait*.

▶ Describe the Big Five personality factors. Why are they scientifically useful?

**Apply the Concept**

▶ Before you tried the self-assessment in Figure 4.6-2, where would you have placed yourself on the Big Five personality dimensions? Where might your family and friends place you? Did the actual results surprise you, and do you think these results would surprise them?

*Answers to the Examine the Concept questions can be found in Appendix C at the end of the book.*

## Evaluating Trait Theories

> **4.6-4** Does research support the consistency of personality traits over time and across situations?

Are our personality traits stable and enduring? Or does our behavior depend on where and with whom we find ourselves? Cheerful, friendly children do tend to become cheerful, friendly adults. At a college reunion, I [DM] was amazed to find that my jovial former classmates were still jovial, the shy ones still shy, the happy-seeming people still smiling and laughing *50 years later*. But it's also true that a fun-loving jokester can suddenly turn serious and respectful at a job interview. New situations and major life events can shift the personality traits we express. Transitioning from high school to university or the workforce, we often become more agreeable, conscientious, and open-minded, and less neurotic (Bleidorn et al., 2018). Losing our job may make us less agreeable and open-minded (Boyce et al., 2015). But when we retire—losing our job *by choice*—we often become more agreeable and open-minded (Schwaba & Bleidorn, 2019).

## The Person-Situation Controversy

Roughly speaking, the external influences on behavior are the focus of *social psychology*, and the inner influences are the focus of *personality psychology*. But all behavior is influenced by the interaction of our environment with our inner disposition. Still, the question lingers: Which is more important? When we explore this *person-situation controversy*, we look for genuine personality traits that persist over time *and* across situations. Are some people dependably conscientious and others unreliable? Some cheerful and others dour? Some outgoing and others quiet? If we are to consider friendliness a trait, friendly people must act in a friendly manner at different times and in different places. Do they?

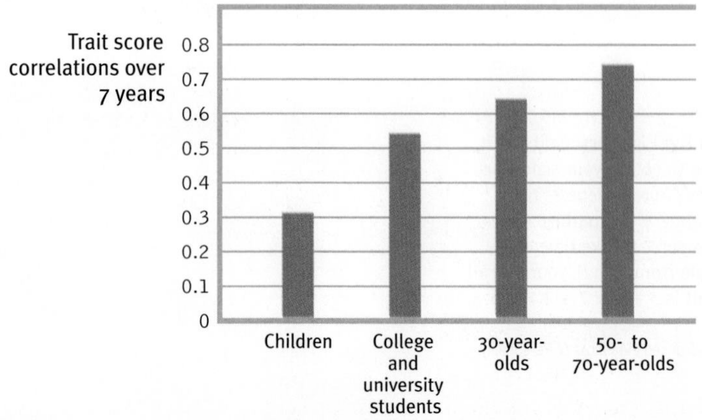

In earlier modules and units, we considered research that has followed lives through time. We noted that some scholars (especially those who study infants) are impressed with personality change; others are struck by personality stability during adulthood. As **Figure 4.6-3** illustrates, data from 152 long-term (*longitudinal*) studies reveal that personality trait scores are positively correlated with scores obtained 7 years later, and that as people grow older, their personality stabilizes. Interests may change—the avid tropical-fish collector may become an avid gardener. Careers may change—the determined salesperson may become a determined social worker. Relationships may change—the hostile son may become a hostile husband. But most people come to recognize and accept just who they are. As Robert McCrae and

**Figure 4.6-3**

**Personality stability**

With age, personality traits become more stable, as reflected in the stronger correlation of trait scores with follow-up scores 7 years later. (Data from Roberts & DelVecchio, 2000.)

Trait score correlations over 7 years

0.8
0.7
0.6
0.5
0.4
0.3
0.2
0.1
0

Children | College and university students | 30-year-olds | 50- to 70-year-olds

Paul Costa (1994) observed, recognizing the inevitability of our personality is "the culminating wisdom of a lifetime."

So most people—including most psychologists—would probably presume the stability of personality traits. Moreover, our traits are socially significant. They influence our health, our thinking, and our job choices and performance (Hogan, 1998; Jackson et al., 2012; Mueller et al., 2018). Studies that follow thousands of people through time show that personality traits rival socioeconomic status and cognitive ability as predictors of mortality, divorce, and occupational attainment (Graham et al., 2017; Roberts et al., 2007).

Although our personality *traits* may be both stable and potent, the consistency of our specific *behaviors* from one situation to the next is another matter. What relationship would you expect to find between being conscientious in one situation (say, showing up for class on time) and being conscientious in another (say, avoiding unhealthy foods)? If you've noticed how outgoing you are in some situations and how reserved you are in others, perhaps you said, "Very little." That's what researchers have found—only a small correlation (Mischel, 1968; Sherman et al., 2015). This inconsistency in behaviors also makes personality test scores weak predictors of behaviors. People's scores on an extraversion test, for example, do not neatly predict how sociable they actually will be on any given occasion.

If we remember such results, we will be more cautious about labeling and pigeonholing individuals (Mischel, 1968). Years in advance, science can tell us the phase of the Moon for any given date. A day in advance, meteorologists can often predict the weather. But we are much further from being able to predict how *you* will feel and act tomorrow.

However, people's *average* outgoingness, happiness, or carelessness over many situations is predictable (Epstein, 1983a,b). This tendency toward trait-consistent actions occurs worldwide, from the United States to Venezuela to Japan (Locke et al., 2017). By tracking their daily phone activity, researchers confirmed that extraverts really do talk and text more (Harari et al., 2020). (All three of this book's authors are extraverts. I [DM] repeatedly vowed to cut back on my jabbering and joking during my noontime pickup basketball games with friends. Alas, moments later, the irrepressible chatterbox would inevitably reoccupy my body. Likewise, when buying groceries, I [ND] always end up chatting with the cashier! And I [EYH] regularly strike up cheery conversations with strangers.) As our best friends can verify, we do have persistent, genetically influenced personality traits. And our personality traits get expressed in our

- *music preferences*. Your playlist reveals something of your personality. Folk, reggae, and nontraditional ambient music lovers tend to be open to experience and verbally intelligent. Agreeable people tend to like jazz and avoid punk music. Blues, old country, and soul music lovers tend to be emotionally stable. Extraverts like country, R&B, and funk music—and enjoy listening to their friends' playlists (Anderson et al., 2021). On first meeting, students often disclose their music preferences to one another; in doing so, they are swapping information about their personalities.

- *written communications*. If you have ever felt you could detect someone's personality from their writing voice, you are right!! What a cool finding!!! ☺ People's writings—even their brief tweets and Facebook posts—often express their extraversion and agreeableness (Bowden-Green et al., 2020; Park et al., 2015). "Off to meet a friend. Woohoo!!!" posted one Facebook user who had scored high on extraversion (Kern et al., 2014). Extraverts also use more adjectives.

- *online and personal spaces*. Are online profiles, websites, and avatars also a canvas for self-expression? Or are they an opportunity for people to present themselves in false or misleading ways? It's more the former (Akhtar et al., 2018a; Hinds & Joinson, 2019).

## my hair over time

childhood

teens and twenties - experimentation

thirties and up

*mitra farmand*

© Mitra Farmand, www.tuffermutter.com

**It's not just personality that stabilizes with age.**

### AP® Science Practice

#### Research

The research presented here represents the correlational method, which is a non-experimental approach. It assesses the degree to which two variables (personality and musical preference) are related. Remember, you can't draw causal conclusions from correlational research.

"You tend to overuse the exclamation point."

Studies show that people who seem most likable on Facebook or Twitter also seem most likable in person (Qiu et al., 2012; Weisbuch et al., 2009). Even mere photos, with their associated clothes, expressions, and postures, can give clues to personality and how people act in person (Gunyadin et al., 2017; Naumann et al., 2009). Our living and working spaces also help us express our identity. They all offer clues to our extraversion, agreeableness, conscientiousness, and openness (Back et al., 2010; Fong & Mar, 2015; Gosling, 2008).

In unfamiliar, formal situations—perhaps when we're a guest in the home of a person from another culture—our traits remain hidden as we carefully attend to social cues. In familiar, informal situations—just hanging out with friends—we feel less constrained, allowing our traits to emerge (Buss, 1989). In these informal situations, our expressive styles—our animation, manner of speaking, and gestures—are impressively consistent. Viewing "thin slices" of someone's behavior—such as seeing a photo for a mere fraction of a second, or seeing several 2-second clips of a teacher in action—can tell us a lot about the person's basic personality traits (Ambady, 2010; Tackett et al., 2016).

**Room with a cue** Even at "zero acquaintance," people can catch a glimpse of others' personality from looking at their online and personal spaces. So, what's your read on the occupants of these two rooms?

Some people are naturally expressive (and therefore talented at pantomime and charades); others are less expressive (and therefore better poker players). To evaluate people's voluntary control over their expressiveness, Bella DePaulo and her colleagues (1992) asked people to act as expressive or inhibited as possible while stating opinions. Their remarkable findings: Inexpressive people, even when feigning expressiveness, were less expressive than expressive people acting naturally. Similarly, expressive people, even when trying to seem inhibited, were less inhibited than inexpressive people acting naturally. It's hard to be someone you're not, or not to be who you are.

To sum up, we can say that at any moment the immediate situation powerfully influences a person's behavior. Social psychologists have learned that this is especially so when a "strong situation" makes clear demands (Cooper & Withey, 2009). We can better predict drivers' behavior at traffic lights from knowing the color of the lights than from knowing the drivers' personalities. Thus, teachers may perceive certain students as subdued (based on their classroom behavior), but friends may perceive them as pretty wild (based on their behavior outside of school). Averaging our behavior across many occasions does, however, reveal distinct personality traits. Traits exist. We differ. And our differences matter.

---

**AP® Science Practice**

## Check Your Understanding

**Examine the Concept**

▶ Explain some ways that personality test scores predict our behavior.

**Apply the Concept**

▶ How do you think your own personality traits shine through in your music preferences, communication style, and online and personal spaces?

*Answers to the Examine the Concept questions can be found in Appendix C at the end of the book.*

# Module 4.6a REVIEW

**4.6-1** How do psychologists use traits to describe personality?

- *Trait* theorists see personality as a stable and enduring pattern of behavior. They have been more interested in trying to describe our differences than in explaining them.

- Using factor analysis, they identify clusters of behavior tendencies that occur together. Genetic predispositions influence many traits.

**4.6-2** What are *personality inventories*, and what are their strengths and weaknesses as trait-assessment tools?

- *Personality inventories* (such as the *MMPI*) are questionnaires on which people respond to items designed to gauge a wide range of feelings and behaviors.

- Test items are *empirically derived*, and the tests are objectively scored. Objectivity does not guarantee validity; people can fake their answers to create a good impression (but may then score high on a lie scale that assesses faking).

**4.6-3** Which traits seem to provide the most useful information about personality variation?

- The *Big Five* personality factors—openness, conscientiousness, extraversion, agreeableness, and neuroticism (OCEAN)—currently offer our best approximation of the basic trait dimensions.

- These factors are generally stable and describe personality in various cultures reasonably well.

**4.6-4** Does research support the consistency of personality traits over time and across situations?

- A person's average traits persist over time and are predictable over many different situations. But traits cannot predict behavior in any one particular situation.

## AP® Practice Multiple Choice Questions

1. Nearly all the time, Estrella is kind, thinks fondly of her friends, and feels warmly about others. What concept is illustrated in this example?

   a. A Myers-Briggs indicator
   b. A factor analysis
   c. A self-report inventory
   d. A trait

2. Even though her friends have tried to show her a copy of the exam she is about to take, Jayne refuses to cheat. Jayne would rank high on the Big Five trait of

   a. conscientiousness.
   b. neuroticism.
   c. openness to experience.
   d. extraversion.

3. Which of the following best describes the person depicted in this image?

   a. Agreeableness
   b. Openness to experience
   c. Extraversion
   d. Neuroticism

**Use the text below to answer questions 4 & 5:**

Dr. Barbieri conducted a study on extraversion in which she asked participants to rate the extent to which they agreed with a variety of statements about their behaviors. For example, she asked participants to rate their agreement with the following statement: "I easily trust other people I meet, and I enjoy being around other people."

4. What kind of assessment technique did Dr. Barbieri use to assess extraversion in her study?

   a. Free association
   b. Personality inventory
   c. Factor analysis
   d. Dream analysis

**5.** Which of the following best captures why the wording of her statement may be confusing to participants?

   a. In addition to asking participants about a behavior related to extraversion, it asked about a behavior related to conscientiousness.

   b. In addition to asking participants about a behavior related to extraversion, it asked about a behavior related to neuroticism.

   c. In addition to asking participants about a behavior related to extraversion, it asked about a behavior related to agreeableness.

   d. In addition to asking participants about a behavior related to extraversion, it asked about a behavior related to openness to experience.

**6.** Geri just had her 75th birthday. Which of the following is a logical and objective conclusion about Geri's personality?

   a. Geri's personality is more stable than when she was 40 years old.

   b. Geri's level of neuroticism has likely increased.

   c. Geri's birth order plays a bigger role in the expression of her personality.

   d. Geri likely rates her personality very differently than her friends rate her personality.

# Module 4.6b Social-Cognitive and Trait Theories of Personality: Social-Cognitive Theories

## LEARNING TARGETS

**4.6-5** Explain how social-cognitive theorists view personality development and how they explore behavior.

**4.6-6** Explain the criticisms social-cognitive theories have faced.

**4.6-5** How do social-cognitive theorists view personality development, and how do they explore behavior?

The **social-cognitive perspective** on personality, proposed by Albert Bandura (1986, 2006, 2008), emphasizes the interaction of our traits with our situations. Much as nature and nurture always work together, so do individuals and their situations.

Those who take the **behavioral approach** to personality development emphasize the effects of learning. We are conditioned to repeat certain behaviors, and we learn by observing and imitating others. For example, a child with a very controlling parent may learn to follow orders rather than think independently, and may exhibit a more timid personality.

Social-cognitive theorists do consider the behavioral perspective, believing that we learn many of our behaviors through conditioning or by observation and imitation. (That's the "social" part.) They also emphasize the importance of mental processes: What we *think* about a situation affects our behavior in that situation. (That's the "cognitive" part.) Instead of focusing solely on how our environment *controls* us (behaviorism), social-cognitive theorists focus on how we and our environment *interact:* How do we interpret and respond to external events? How do our schemas, our memories, and our expectations influence our behavior patterns?

**social-cognitive perspective** a view of behavior as influenced by the interaction between people's traits (including their thinking) and their social context.

**behavioral approach** focuses on the effects of learning on our personality development.

**reciprocal determinism** the interacting influences of behavior, internal cognition, and environment.

## Reciprocal Influences

Bandura (1986, 2006) views the person-environment interaction as **reciprocal determinism**. "Behavior, internal personal factors, and environmental influences," he said, "all operate as interlocking determinants of each other" (**Figure 4.6-4**). We can see this interaction in

(a)

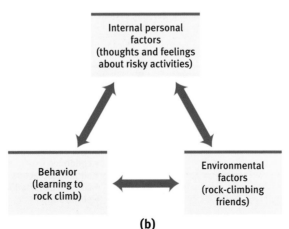

Internal personal factors (thoughts and feelings about risky activities)

Behavior (learning to rock climb)

Environmental factors (rock-climbing friends)

(b)

◄ **Figure 4.6-4 Reciprocal determinism**

people's daily lives. For example, Rosa's high self-esteem and self-efficacy contribute to her positive self-concept (internal factors). Thus, when facing a challenge (environmental factor), she confidently tackles it (behavior). These influences also work in reverse: When praised (environmental factor), Rosa's self-esteem rises (internal factor) and so does her determined effort (behavior).

Consider three specific ways in which individuals and environments interact:

- *Different people choose different environments.* What do you read? What social media do you use? What extracurricular activities do you pursue? What music do you listen to? With whom do you enjoy spending time? All these choices are part of the environment you choose, based partly on your personality (Denissen et al., 2018; Funder, 2009). And the environments we choose then shape us. People with inflated self-esteem may post frequent selfies, which may lead to public attention and praise, and even greater self-love (Halpern et al., 2016).

- *Our personalities shape how we interpret and react to events.* If we perceive the world as threatening, we will watch for threats and be prepared to defend ourselves. Anxious people often attend to and react strongly to relationship threats (Campbell & Marshall, 2011).

- *Our personalities help create situations to which we react.* How we view and treat people influences how they then treat us. If we expect that others will not like us, our efforts to win their approval (such as bragging) might actually cause them to reject us (Scopelliti et al., 2015).

In addition to the interaction of internal personal factors, the environment, and our behaviors, we experience *gene-environment interaction* (Module 1.1). Our genetically influenced traits evoke certain responses from others, which may nudge us in one direction or another. In one well-replicated finding, people with the interacting factors of (1) having a specific gene associated with aggression and (2) being raised in a difficult environment were most likely to demonstrate adult antisocial behavior (Byrd & Manuck, 2014; Caspi et al., 2002).

In such ways, we are both the products and the architects of our environments: *Behavior emerges from the interplay of external and internal influences.* Boiling water turns an egg hard and a potato soft. A threatening environment turns one person into a hero, another into a scoundrel. *At every moment,* our behavior is influenced by our biology, our social and cultural experiences, and our cognition and dispositions (**Figure 4.6-5**).

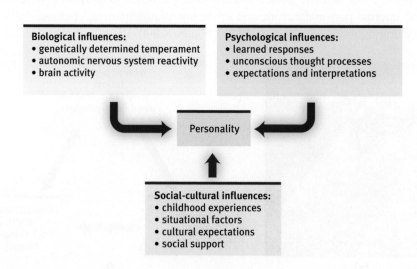

**Figure 4.6-5**

**The biopsychosocial approach to the study of personality**

As with other psychological phenomena, personality is fruitfully studied at multiple levels.

**Biological influences:**
- genetically determined temperament
- autonomic nervous system reactivity
- brain activity

**Psychological influences:**
- learned responses
- unconscious thought processes
- expectations and interpretations

**Personality**

**Social-cultural influences:**
- childhood experiences
- situational factors
- cultural expectations
- social support

## Check Your Understanding

**Examine the Concept**

▶ Explain the social-cognitive perspective, including reciprocal determinism.

*Answers to the Examine the Concept questions can be found in Appendix C at the end of the book.*

**Apply the Concept**

▶ How have your experiences shaped your personality? How has your personality helped shape your environment?

## Assessing Behavior in Situations

To predict behavior, social-cognitive psychologists often observe behavior in realistic situations. One ambitious example was the U.S. Army's World War II strategy for assessing candidates for spy missions. Rather than using paper-and-pencil tests, Army psychologists subjected the candidates to simulated undercover conditions. They tested their ability to handle stress, solve problems, maintain leadership, and withstand intense interrogation without blowing their cover. Although time-consuming and expensive, this assessment of behavior in a realistic situation helped predict later success on actual spy missions (OSS Assessment Staff, 1948).

Military and educational organizations and many *Fortune* 500 companies have adopted similar strategies, known as the *assessment center* approach (Bray & Byham, 1991, 1997; Eurich et al., 2009). The U.S. telecommunications giant AT&T has observed prospective managers doing simulated managerial work. Student teachers are observed and evaluated several times during the term they spend in your school. Some European universities give student applicants material to study, and then test their learning—thus mimicking the educational program (Niessen & Meijer, 2017). Many colleges assess nursing students' potential by observing their clinical work. And they assess potential faculty members' teaching abilities by observing them teach.

The assessment center approach applies the principle that the best means of predicting future behavior is neither a personality test nor an interviewer's intuition; rather, it is *the person's past behavior patterns in similar situations* (Lyons et al., 2011; Mischel, 1981; Schmidt & Hunter, 1998). As long as the situation and the person remain much the same, the best predictor of future job performance is past job performance; the best predictor of future

**Singing success** On the television show *The Voice*, contestants compete against one another in stressful situations. The winner receives a cash prize and a music recording contract. The show presumes a valid point: People's behavior in job-relevant situations helps predict their job performance. This was true for English singer and songwriter Becky Hill, whose career took off following her success on the show.

grades is past grades; the best predictor of future aggressiveness is past aggressiveness. If you can't check the person's past behavior, the next best thing is to create an assessment situation that simulates the task so you can see how the person handles it (Lievens et al., 2009; Meriac et al., 2008).

# Evaluating Social-Cognitive Theories

**4.6-6** What criticisms have social-cognitive theories faced?

Social-cognitive theories of personality sensitize researchers to how situations affect, and are affected by, individuals. More than other personality theories (see **Table 4.6-2**), they build from psychological research on learning and cognition.

**TABLE 4.6-2** Comparing the Major Personality Theories

| Personality Theory | Key Proponents | Assumptions | View of Personality | Personality Assessment Methods |
|---|---|---|---|---|
| *Psychoanalytic* | Freud | Emotional disorders spring from unconscious dynamics, such as unresolved sexual and other childhood conflicts, and fixation at various developmental stages. Defense mechanisms fend off anxiety. | Personality consists of pleasure-seeking impulses (the id), a reality-oriented executive (the ego), and an internalized set of ideals (the superego). | Free association, projective tests, dream analysis |
| *Psychodynamic* | Adler, Horney, Jung | The unconscious and conscious minds interact. Childhood experiences and defense mechanisms are important. | The dynamic interplay of conscious and unconscious motives and conflicts shapes our personality. | Projective tests, therapy sessions |
| *Humanistic* | Maslow, Rogers | Rather than focusing on disorders born of dark conflicts, it's better to emphasize how healthy people may strive for self-realization. | If our basic human needs are met, we will strive toward self-actualization. In a climate of unconditional positive regard, we can develop self-awareness and a more realistic and positive self-concept. | Questionnaires, therapy sessions, life story approach |
| *Trait* | Allport, Costa, H. Eysenck, S. Eysenck, McCrae | We have certain stable and enduring characteristics, which are influenced by genetic predispositions. | Scientific study of traits has isolated important dimensions of personality, such as the Big Five traits (openness, conscientiousness, extraversion, agreeableness, and neuroticism). | Personality inventories |
| *Social-cognitive* | Bandura | Our traits interact with the social context to produce our behaviors. | Conditioning and observational learning interact with cognition to create behavior patterns. Our behavior in one situation is best predicted by considering our past behavior in similar situations. | Observing behavior in realistic situations |

Critics charge that social-cognitive theories focus so much on the situation that they fail to appreciate the person's inner traits. Where is the person in this view of personality, ask the dissenters, and where are human emotions? True, the situation does guide our behavior. But, say the critics, in many instances our unconscious motives, our emotions, and our pervasive traits shine through. Personality traits predict behavior at work, in love, and at play. Our biologically influenced traits really do matter. Consider Percy Ray Pridgen and Charles Gill. Each faced the same situation: They had jointly won a $90 million lottery jackpot (Harriston, 1993). When Pridgen learned of the winning numbers, he began trembling uncontrollably, huddled with a friend behind a bathroom door while confirming the win, and then sobbed. When Gill heard the news, he told his wife and then went to sleep.

**AP® Science Practice**

**Research**

Notice the varying methods of assessing personality in Tables 4.6-2 and 4.6-3. Different theoretical perspectives use different research methods and measures to draw conclusions.

\* \* \*

As we have seen, researchers investigate personality using various methods that serve differing purposes. For a synopsis and comparison of these methods, see **Table 4.6-3**.

**TABLE 4.6-3** **Comparing Research Methods and Assessments to Investigate Personality**

| Method/Assessment | Description | Perspectives Incorporating This Method/Assessment | Benefits | Weaknesses |
|---|---|---|---|---|
| *Case study* | In-depth study of one individual. | Psychoanalytic, humanistic | Less expensive than other methods. | May not generalize to the larger population. |
| *Survey* | Systematic questioning of a random sample of the population. | Trait, social-cognitive | Results tend to be reliable and can be generalized to the larger population. | May be expensive; correlational findings. |
| *Projective tests* (e.g., TAT and Rorschach inkblot test) | Ambiguous stimuli designed to trigger projection of inner dynamics. | Psychodynamic | Designed to get beneath the conscious surface of a person's self-understanding; may be a good ice-breaker. | Results have weak validity and reliability. |
| *Personality inventories*, such as the MMPI (to determine scores on Big Five personality factors) | Objectively scored groups of questions designed to identify personality dispositions. | Trait | Generally reliable and empirically validated. | Explore a limited number of traits. |
| *Observation* | Studying how individuals react in different situations. | Social-cognitive | Allows researchers to study the effects of environmental factors on the way an individual's personality is expressed. | Results may not apply to the larger population. |
| *Experimentation* | Manipulate variables, with random assignment to conditions. | Social-cognitive | Discerns cause and effect. | Some variables cannot feasibly or ethically be manipulated. |

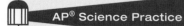
## Check Your Understanding

**Examine the Concept**

▶ Explain three specific ways in which individuals and environments interact.

**Apply the Concept**

▶ Can you think of a recent situation in which your personality led you to react differently than did someone else — maybe a family member, friend, or classmate — who experienced the same event?

*Answers to the Examine the Concept questions can be found in Appendix C at the end of the book.*

# Module 4.6b REVIEW

**4.6-5** How do social-cognitive theorists view personality development, and how do they explore behavior?

- Albert Bandura's *social-cognitive perspective* emphasizes the interaction of our traits with our situations.

- The *behavioral approach* contributes an understanding that our personality development is affected by learned responses.

- Social-cognitive researchers apply principles of learning, cognition, and social behavior to personality.

- *Reciprocal determinism* describes the interaction and mutual influence of behavior, internal cognition, and environment.

- Assessment situations involving simulated conditions applies the principle that the best predictor of future behavior is a person's actions in similar situations.

**4.6-6** What criticisms have social-cognitive theories faced?

- Social-cognitive theories of personality build on well-established concepts of learning and cognition, sensitizing researchers to the ways situations affect, and are affected by, individuals.

- They have been faulted for underemphasizing the importance of unconscious motives, emotions, and biologically influenced traits.

## AP® Practice Multiple Choice Questions

**1.** Kylan supports social-cognitive theory. Which statement would he most likely make?

a. Unconscious sexual and childhood conflicts create personality.

b. Humans strive for self-actualization.

c. Personality can be described by stable and enduring characteristics.

d. Behavior is affected by traits and by the environment.

**2.** Which of the following assessment techniques is most likely to be used by a social-cognitive psychologist?

a. A new teacher is formally observed and evaluated while teaching in a training classroom.

b. A person applying for a managerial position takes a personality questionnaire.

c. In a pre-marriage counseling session, a young couple responds to ambiguous inkblots.

d. A young man experiencing depression is asked by his therapist to relax on a couch and talk about whatever comes to mind.

**Use the following text to answer questions 3–5:**

Dr. Orca, a psychoanalytic theorist and researcher, wanted to carry out a case study on the impact of childhood experiences on anxiety. Dr. Orca randomly assigned 100 participants to either a condition in which they were asked to write about their most difficult childhood memories or a condition in which they were asked to write about their favorite type of fish. Dr. Orca later measured the participants' anxiety levels, finding that the group who recalled their childhoods reported higher anxiety levels than the group who wrote about fish.

**3.** Which of the following best describes a way that this research scenario does not follow appropriate methodology?

a. Although Dr. Orca wanted to carry out a case study, he actually conducted an experiment.
b. Although Dr. Orca wanted to carry out a case study, he actually conducted a survey.
c. Although Dr. Orca wanted to carry out a case study, he actually conducted a naturalistic observation study.
d. There were no problems with Dr. Orca's study.

**4.** Based on the study that Dr. Orca actually conducted, what conclusion can he draw from his research?

a. Dr. Orca can conclude that recalling childhood memories is related to anxiety levels.
b. Dr. Orca can conclude that writing about fish causes people to discontinue the study.
c. Dr. Orca can conclude that recalling childhood memories causes anxiety levels to increase.
d. Dr. Orca can conclude that writing about fish is related to relaxation.

**5.** Which personality theory do the conclusions from Dr. Orca's research study best support?

a. Humanistic
b. Psychoanalytic
c. Trait
d. Reciprocal determinism

**6.** Fyonah is a skilled singer, and she thinks that singing for other people is the most fun she can have. As such, she often seeks out opportunities to sing for large crowds, who, seeing her enjoyment and enthusiasm, tend to cheer loudly for her. Which of the following psychological concepts is captured in this scenario?

a. Personality traits
b. Gene-environment interaction
c. Reciprocal determinism
d. Modeling

# Module 4.6c Social-Cognitive and Trait Theories of Personality: Exploring the Self

**4.6-7** Why has psychology generated so much research on the self? How important is self-esteem to our well-being?

Our personality feeds our sense of self. Asked to consider "who I am," people draw on their distinctive and enduring ways of thinking, feeling, and acting. Psychology's concern with our sense of self dates back at least to William James, who devoted more than 100 pages of his 1890 *Principles of Psychology* to the topic. But by 1943, Gordon Allport lamented that the self had become "lost to view." Although humanistic psychology's later emphasis on the self did not instigate much scientific research, it did help renew the concept of self and keep it alive. Now, more than a century after James, the self is one of Western psychology's most vigorously researched topics. Every year, new studies galore appear on self-esteem, self-disclosure, self-awareness, self-schemas, self-monitoring, and more. Even neuroscientists have searched for the self, by identifying a central frontal lobe region that activates when people respond to self-reflective questions about their traits and dispositions (Damasio, 2010; Mitchell, 2009; Pauly et al., 2013). The **self**, as organizer of our thoughts, feelings, and actions, occupies the center of personality.

Consider the concept of *possible selves* (Markus & Nurius, 1986; Rathbone et al., 2016). Your possible selves include your visions of the self you dream of becoming (the rich self, the successful self, the loved and admired self), and also the self you fear becoming (the unemployed self, the academically failed self, the lonely and unpopular self). Possible selves motivate us to lay out specific goals that direct our energy effectively and efficiently (Landau et al., 2014). Eighth- and ninth-grade students whose families struggle financially are more likely to earn high grades if they have a clear vision of themselves succeeding in school (Duckworth et al., 2013). Dreams do often give birth to achievements.

Carried too far, our self-focus can lead us to fret that others are noticing and evaluating us, a phenomenon called the **spotlight effect**. In one experiment, university students who were asked to put on an embarrassing T-shirt before meeting other students guessed that nearly half their peers would notice the shirt. But only 23 percent did (Gilovich, 1996). To turn down the spotlight's brightness, we can use two strategies. The first is simply to know and remember the spotlight effect. Public speakers perform better if they understand that their natural nervousness is hardly noticeable (Savitsky & Gilovich, 2003). The second is to

**AP® Science Practice**

## Research

In the embarrassing T-shirt experiment described below, participants were randomly assigned to wear either an embarrassing T-shirt (the experimental group) or a neutral shirt (the control group). By randomly assigning participants to experimental and control groups, the researchers minimized preexisting differences between the different groups.

**self** in modern psychology, assumed to be the center of personality, the organizer of our thoughts, feelings, and actions.

**spotlight effect** overestimating others' noticing and evaluating our appearance, performance, and blunders (as if we presume a spotlight shines on us).

take the audience's perspective. When we imagine audience members empathizing with our situation, we usually expect to be judged less harshly (Epley et al., 2002). *The point to remember:* We stand out less than we imagine, even with dorky clothes and bad hair, and even after a blunder like setting off a library alarm (Gilovich & Savitsky, 1999; Savitsky et al., 2001).

## The Benefits of Self-Esteem

**Self-esteem**—our feelings of high or low self-worth—matters. So does **self-efficacy**, our sense of competence on a task (Bandura, 1977, 2018). (A student might feel high self-efficacy in a math class yet low overall self-esteem.) People who feel good about themselves (who strongly agree with self-affirming questionnaire statements, such as "I am fun to be with") have fewer sleepless nights. They tend to be outgoing, responsible, and open to new experiences (Fetvadjiev & He, 2019). Online and in person, they communicate positively, causing others to like and include them more (Cameron & Granger, 2019; Mahadevan et al., 2019). They feel less shy, anxious, and lonely, and are just plain happier (Greenberg, 2008; Orth & Robins, 2014; Swann et al., 2007). Our self-esteem grows from venturesome experiences and achievement, so it changes as we age (Hutteman et al., 2015). Self-esteem often increases dramatically from adolescence to middle adulthood, then continues to climb until peaking between ages 50 and 60 (Bleidorn et al., 2016; Orth et al., 2018; van Soest et al., 2018).

LOW SELF-ESTEEM

But most psychologists doubt that high self-esteem is "the armor that protects kids" from life's problems (Baumeister & Vohs, 2018; McKay, 2000; Seligman, 2002). Children's academic self-efficacy—their confidence that they can do well in a subject—predicts school achievement. But general self-image does not (Marsh & Craven, 2006; Swann et al., 2007; Trautwein et al., 2006). Maybe self-esteem simply reflects reality. Maybe self-esteem is a side effect of meeting challenges and surmounting difficulties, or a gauge that reports the state of our relationships with others (Bleidorn et al., 2021; Reitz et al., 2016). If so, isn't pushing the gauge artificially higher with empty compliments much like forcing a car's low fuel gauge to display "full"?

If feeling good *follows* doing well, then giving praise in the absence of good performance may actually harm people. After receiving weekly self-esteem-boosting messages, struggling students earned *lower*-than-expected grades (Forsyth et al., 2007). Other research showed that giving people random rewards hurt their effort. Martin Seligman (2012) reported that "when good things occurred that weren't earned, like nickels coming out of slot machines, it did not increase people's well-being. It produced helplessness. People gave up and became passive."

There are, however, important *effects* when self-esteem is threatened. When researchers temporarily deflated participants' self-image (by telling them they did poorly on an aptitude test or by disparaging their personality), those participants became more likely to disparage others or to express heightened racial prejudice (vanDellen et al., 2011; van Dijk et al., 2011; Ybarra, 1999). Self-image threat even increases *unconscious* racial bias (Allen & Sherman, 2011). Those who are negative about themselves have also tended to be oversensitive and judgmental (Baumgardner et al., 1989; Pelham, 1993).

Such findings are consistent with humanistic psychology's ideas about the benefits of a healthy self-image. Accept yourself and you'll find it easier to accept others. Disparage yourself and you will be prone to the floccinaucinihilipilification[2] of others. People who are down on themselves tend to be down on others.

**AP® Exam Tip**

Note the difference between *self-esteem* and *self-efficacy*. Although your feeling of self-worth might be related to your beliefs about how competent you are, they are not the same thing.

**AP® Science Practice**

**Research**

To study the *effects* of threatened self-esteem, researchers use the experimental method. They control for confounding variables by using random assignment of participants to groups. This allows the researchers to determine the effect of the independent variable on the dependent variable.

**self-esteem** our feelings of high or low self-worth.

**self-efficacy** our sense of competence and effectiveness.

[2]We couldn't resist throwing that in. But don't worry, you won't be tested on *floccinaucinihilipilification*, which is the act of estimating something as worthless (and was the longest nontechnical word in the first edition of the *Oxford English Dictionary*).

# The Costs of Self-Esteem

**4.6-8** How do blindness to one's own incompetence and self-serving bias reveal the costs of self-esteem, and how do defensive and secure self-esteem differ?

Healthy self-esteem can support our well-being. But inflated self-esteem may come at a cost—as when we overestimate our abilities, overlook our misdeeds, and respond defensively to criticisms rather than with self-reflection.

## Blindness to One's Own Incompetence

People often are most overconfident when most incompetent. They are often "unskilled and unaware of it," observed Justin Kruger and David Dunning (1999), after finding that most students scoring at the low end on grammar and logic *believed* they had scored in the top half. Likewise, one-third of Americans, when asked their opinions about vaccines, claimed to be as knowledgeable as doctors and scientists about the causes of autism (Motta et al., 2018). This "ignorance of one's own incompetence" is now famously called the *Dunning-Kruger effect*. As comedian Trevor Noah (2020) quipped, "This is the problem when the dumbest person in the room thinks they're the smartest."

Because it takes competence to recognize competence, "Our ignorance is invisible to us," summarizes Dunning (2019). "The first rule of the Dunning-Kruger club," he says, "is you don't know you're a member of the Dunning-Kruger club." Thus, to judge our competence and predict our future performance, it pays to invite others' assessments (Dunning, 2006; Grossmann & Kross, 2014).

Based on studies in which both individuals and their acquaintances predict their future, we can hazard some advice: Ask your peers for their candid prediction. If you're in love and want to predict whether it will last, don't listen to your heart—ask your friends.

## Self-Serving Bias

Imagine dashing to class, hoping not to miss the first few minutes. But you arrive 5 minutes late, huffing and puffing. As you sink into your seat, what sorts of thoughts go through your mind? Do you go through a negative door, thinking "I'm such a loser"? Or do you go through a positive door, telling yourself, "I did my very best to arrive on time"?

*"That's strange. I remember it differently, in a way that aligns with my world view and casts me in a positive light."*

Personality psychologists have found that most people choose the second door because it leads to positive self-thoughts. We have a good reputation with ourselves. We show a **self-serving bias**—a readiness to perceive ourselves favorably (Myers, 2010). Consider:

***People accept more responsibility for good deeds than for bad, and for successes than for failures***. When athletes succeed, they often credit their own talent. When they fail, they might blame poor weather, bad luck, lousy officials, or the other team's exceptional performance (Allen et al., 2020). Most students who receive poor exam grades criticize the exam or the teacher, not themselves. On insurance claims, drivers have explained accidents in such words as "A pedestrian hit me and went under my car." The question "What have I done to deserve this?" is one we usually ask of our troubles, not our successes. Although a self-serving bias can lead us to avoid uncomfortable truths, it can also motivate us to approach difficult tasks with confidence instead of despair (Tomaka et al., 1992; von Hippel & Trivers, 2011). Indeed, across many studies, self-enhancement predicts emotional well-being (Dufner et al., 2019).

***Most people see themselves as better than average***. Compared with most other people, how moral are you? How easy to get along with? On each question, where would you rank yourself, from the 1st to the 99th percentile? Most people put themselves well above the 50th percentile. This better-than-average effect appears for nearly any subjectively assessed and

**self-serving bias** a readiness to perceive ourselves favorably.

socially desirable trait or behavior. Most people rate themselves as having better-than-average intelligence, kindness, humor, and ethics (Zell et al., 2020). Nine in ten drivers rate themselves as more skilled than the average driver (Koppel et al., 2021). Self-serving bias is weaker in Asia, where social practices emphasize modesty (Church et al., 2014; Falk et al., 2009). Yet in every one of 53 countries surveyed, people expressed self-esteem above the midpoint of the most widely used scale (Schmitt & Allik, 2005). The average person thinks they're better than average.

Self-serving bias often underlies conflicts, such as blaming a partner for relationship problems or a colleague for work problems. We all tend to see our own *groups*—our school, organization, region, or country—as superior. Although there are 50 U.S. states, Americans on average estimate that their home state made 18 percent of the contributions to U.S. history (Putnam et al., 2018). Likewise, people from 35 countries rate their own country as making outsized contributions to world history (Zaromb et al., 2018). Such *group-serving bias*—"My group is better"—fueled Nazi horrors and Rwandan genocide. No wonder literature and religion so often warn against the perils of self-love and pride. Ingroup love often feeds outgroup hate (Golec de Zavala & Lantos, 2020).

**PEANUTS**

Finding their self-esteem threatened, people with inflated egos may react violently. Researchers Brad Bushman and Roy Baumeister (1998; Bushman et al., 2009) had undergraduate volunteers write a brief essay, in response to which another supposed student gave them either praise ("Great essay!") or stinging criticism ("One of the worst essays I have read!"). The essay writers were then allowed to lash out at their evaluators by blasting them with unpleasant noise. Can you anticipate the result?

After criticism, those with inflated self-esteem were "exceptionally aggressive." They delivered three times the auditory torture than did those with normal self-esteem. More than 80 studies have replicated the dangerous effect of **narcissism** (excessive self-love and self-focus) on aggression (Rasmussen, 2016). Researchers have concluded that "conceited, self-important individuals turn nasty toward those who puncture their bubbles of self-love" (Baumeister, 2001).

---

**AP® Science Practice**

## Exploring Research Methods & Design

Let's focus on the Bushman and Baumeister experiment described above. Read the description in the text again, and answer the following questions.

- What makes this study experimental, as opposed to correlational?
- Identify the independent and dependent variables.
- State the operational definition of the dependent variable.
- Create a bar graph (or histogram) of their findings.
- What conclusion can Bushman and Baumeister draw at the end of their experiment?

Revisit Module 0.4 if you need help.

**narcissism** excessive self-love and self-absorption.

After tracking self-importance across several decades, psychologist Jean Twenge (2006; Twenge & Foster, 2010) reported that what she called *Generation Me*—born in the 1980s and early 1990s—expressed more narcissism (by agreeing more often with statements such as "If I ruled the world, it would be a better place" or "I think I am a special person"). Why does a rise in narcissism matter? Narcissists tend to be materialistic, desire fame, have inflated expectations, hook up more often without commitment, and gamble and cheat more—all of which have been increasing as narcissism has increased. Humility, by contrast, is the attitude that, no matter your accomplishments, you are not entitled to special treatment (Banker & Leary, 2020).

Narcissistic people (more often men) tend to be unforgiving, take a game-playing approach to romantic relationships, and engage in sexually forceful behavior (Johnson, 2020; Lamarche & Seery, 2019). They're often charismatic and ambitious, making them popular until others tire of their cold-hearted arrogance (Leckelt et al., 2020; Poorthuis et al., 2019). From moment to moment, they crave status and adulation and often become defensive or enraged when criticized (Grapsas et al., 2020; Sedikides, 2021). Many had parents who told them they were superior to others (Brummelman et al., 2015). Reality TV stars are often especially narcissistic (Rubinstein, 2016; Young & Pinsky, 2006).

Some critics of the concept of self-serving bias claim that it overlooks those who feel worthless and unlovable: If self-serving bias prevails, why do so many people disparage themselves? For five reasons:

1. Self-directed put-downs can be *subtly strategic*—they elicit reassuring strokes. Saying "No one likes me" may at least elicit "But not everyone has met you!"

2. Before an important event, such as a game or a test, self-disparaging comments *prepare us for possible failure*. The coach who extols the superior strength of the upcoming opponent makes a loss understandable, a victory noteworthy.

3. A self-disparaging "How could I have been so stupid!" can help us *learn from our mistakes*.

4. Sometimes false humility is actually a *humblebrag*: "I barely studied, so I'm amazed I got an A" (Sezer et al., 2018).

5. Self-disparagement frequently *pertains to one's old self*. Asked to remember their really bad behaviors, people recall things from long ago; good behaviors more easily come to mind from their recent past (Escobedo & Adolphs, 2010). Even when they have not changed, people are much more critical of their distant past selves than of their current selves (Wilson & Ross, 2001). Chumps yesterday, champs today: "At 18, I was a jerk; today I'm more sensitive."

Even so, all of us some of the time (and some of us much of the time) do feel inferior. This is especially true when we compare ourselves with those who are a step or two higher on the ladder of status, looks, income, or ability. The more frequently we feel comparatively inferior, the more unhappy or even depressed we become. But for most people, thinking has a naturally positive bias.

Some researchers identify two types of self-esteem—defensive and secure (Kernis, 2003; Lambird & Mann, 2006; Ryan & Deci, 2004). *Defensive self-esteem* is fragile. It focuses on sustaining itself, which makes failure and criticism feel threatening. Defensive people may respond to such perceived threats with anger or aggression (Crocker & Park, 2004; Donnellan et al., 2005).

*Secure self-esteem* is less fragile, because it is less contingent on external evaluations. Feeling accepted for who we are, and not for our looks, wealth, or acclaim, relieves pressures to succeed and enables us to focus beyond ourselves. Those who accept their own flaws also more compassionately accept others' flaws (Zhang et al., 2020).

By losing ourselves in relationships and purposes larger than ourselves, we may achieve a more secure self-esteem, satisfying relationships, and greater quality of life (Crocker & Park, 2004). Authentic pride, rooted in actual achievement, supports self-confidence and leadership (Tracy et al., 2009; Weidman et al., 2016; Williams & DeSteno, 2009).

---

**AP® Science Practice**

## Check Your Understanding

### Examine the Concept

▶ Explain two negative effects of high self-esteem.

▶ Explain what is meant by *self-serving bias*.

### Apply the Concept

▶ What possible selves do you dream of — or fear — becoming? To what extent do these imagined selves motivate you now?

*Answers to the Examine the Concept questions can be found in Appendix C at the end of the book.*

---

## Culture and the Self

**4.6-9** How do individualist and collectivist cultures shape values and goals?

Our personality—our characteristic ways of thinking, feeling, and acting—is culturally influenced. Consider, for example, how you are shaped by your culture's individualism (or collectivism). School, work, and family settings that are **individualist** encourage people to express an independent sense of "me," to celebrate their unique personal convictions and values. In such contexts, classroom posters cheer, "Just be yourself!" Military recruiters promise young candidates the opportunity to "Be all that you can be." Graduation speakers advise, "Follow your passion." Individualism prioritizes personal goals. People define their identity mostly in terms of personal traits and they seek personal control and individual achievement.

The human need to belong is universal. So, even in individualist cultures, people seek out and join groups. But individualists focus less on group harmony or their social duty (Brewer & Chen, 2007). Being more self-contained, individualists move in and out of social groups more easily. They feel relatively free to switch places of worship, change jobs, or leave their extended families and migrate to a new place. Marriage is often for as long as they both shall love.

When individualists feel coerced, they often rebel—sometimes with devastating consequences. Western individualist cultures suffered the worst Covid death rates, due mainly to many citizens rejecting social distancing and masking (Garland et al., 2020; Leonhardt, 2020) (Figure 4.6-6). Within the United States, people living in the most individualist regions

**AP® Science Practice**

### Data

Can you recall the type of graph depicted in Figure 4.6-6? It's called a scatterplot. Be sure you can interpret and understand the data in this graph. You will likely be asked to demonstrate this skill on the AP® exam.

**individualism** a cultural pattern that emphasizes people's own goals over group goals and defines identity mainly in terms of unique personal attributes.

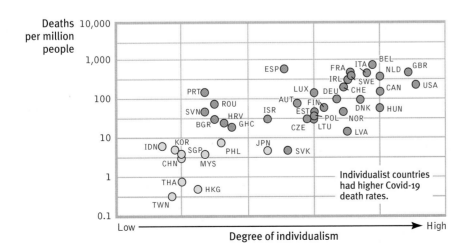

**Figure 4.6-6**

**Deadly individualism**

Worldwide, countries' levels of individualism correlated positively with Covid death rates ($r = .75$). (Data from Garland et al., 2020.)

collectivism a cultural pattern that prioritizes the goals of important groups (often one's extended family or work group).

were the least likely to socially distance or mask, and the most likely to contract the virus (Bazzi et al., 2020; CovidCast, 2020). Promoting **collectivism**, suggested one group of psychological researchers, "may be a way to increase engagement with efforts to reduce the spread of COVID-19" (Biddlestone et al., 2020, p. 663).

In collectivist settings, people are considered mature when they accommodate important groups. Identity is shaped by family, groups, and friends. People's *group identifications* provide a sense of belonging, a set of values, and an assurance of security. Collectivists have deep attachments to their groups—their family, clan, company, or country. Adults in collectivist countries often feel duty-bound to support their aging parents, such as by paying part of their retirement living expenses (Sethi, 2021; Yang, 2015).

Sportscasters in collectivist contexts credit coaches and teammates as much as individual athletes for success (Markus et al., 2006). Collectivists find satisfaction in advancing their groups' interests while keeping their personal needs in the background. They may preserve group spirit by avoiding direct confrontation, blunt honesty, and uncomfortable topics. Norms favor humility, not self-importance (Bond et al., 2012). Collectivists view forgiveness as a way to strengthen group harmony (Joo et al., 2019). Given the priority on "we," not "me," that satisfying, super-customized North American latte might seem selfishly demanding in Seoul (Kim & Markus, 1999).

Culture teaches us which behaviors are "good" and which are "bad." What do you think of people who willingly change their behavior to suit different people and situations? People in largely individualist countries, such as the United States and Brazil, tend to believe that opposites cannot coexist, such as someone being both extraverted and introverted (Choi & Choi, 2002). This thinking leads people in individualist countries to label people who frequently switch their behavior as "dishonest," "untrustworthy," and "insincere" (Levine, 2016). Traditionally collectivist countries (China and Japan, for example) emphasize adopting more flexible perceptions (Peng & Nisbett, 1999). Thus, people in collectivist countries more often describe behavior-switching as indicative of being "mature," "honest," "trustworthy," and "sincere."

A country's cultural values are powerful, but not absolutely so. Even though Christmas permeates U.S. spaces every December, many Americans do not celebrate it. Similarly, even when a country's dominant messages are collectivist (or individualist), its people vary. All countries host distinct subcultures related to religion, economic status, and region (Cohen, 2009).

Patterns within cultures reflect economic practices, too. Southern Chinese farmers typically grow rice, a crop that requires intense labor and rewards farmers' coordination. Northern Chinese farmers often grow wheat, a crop that can be farmed independently

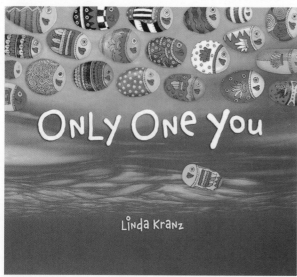

The tolerance of a Starbucks barista is severely tested.

" I'D LiKE a DeCAFFACiNNO FRAPPA CHAPPA DAPPA DiNGO ICE BLENDED LAST of THe MOCCA-HiCANS VANiLLA ICE ICE BETTER LATTe' THAN NeveR SMOOTHie WiTH a SHOT of SELF-EXPRESSO. "

Cartoon by Buddy Hickerson

**Me or we?** U.S. school systems are likely to favor books, such as *Only One You*, that encourage individuality and taking pride in one's personal identity. In contrast, Japanese stories, such as *A Big Turnip*, describe how groups are stronger together (Imada, 2012).

(Dong et al., 2019; Obschonka et al., 2018; Talhelm et al., 2014). In one clever study, researchers used chairs to block aisles in Starbucks coffeehouses across China. They observed who acted like a typical individualist, controlling the environment by moving one of the chairs out of the way, and who acted like a typical collectivist, adapting to the environment by squeezing through the chairs (Talhelm et al., 2018). Compared with the more collectivist Southern Chinese, the Northern Chinese were more likely to simply move the chair.

In collectivist Japan, a spirit of individualism marks the "northern frontier" island of Hokkaido (Kitayama et al., 2006). And even in the most individualist countries, people hold some collectivist values. But in general (and especially for men), competitive, individualist cultures encourage more personal freedom and independence from family, enable more privacy, and induce folks to take pride in personal achievements (**Table 4.6-4**).

People even value unusual names in individualist contexts, as psychologist Jean Twenge noticed while seeking a name for her first child. When she and her colleagues (2010a, 2016)

| TABLE 4.6-4 **Value Contrasts Between Individualism and Collectivism** | | |
|---|---|---|
| **Concept** | **Individualism** | **Collectivism** |
| *Self* | Independent (identity from internal, individual traits) | Interdependent (identity from group roles) |
| *Life task* | Discover and express one's uniqueness | Maintain connections, fit in, perform role |
| *What matters* | Me — personal achievement and fulfillment; rights and liberties; self-esteem | Us — group goals and solidarity; responsibilities and relationships; family duty |
| *Coping method* | Change reality | Accommodate to reality |
| *Morality* | Defined by the individual (choice-based) | Defined by social networks (duty-based) |
| *Relationships* | Easier to enter and leave relationships | Fewer but closer and more stable relationships |
| *Attributing behavior* | Behavior reflects the individual's personality and attitudes | Behavior also reflects social norms and roles |
| Information from Thomas Schoeneman (1994) and Harry Triandis (1994). | | |

Sam Harrel/ZUMA Press/Newscom

**Culture** Although the United States emphasizes individualism, many cultural subgroups remain collectivist. This is true for Alaska Natives, who demonstrate respect for tribal elders, and whose identity springs largely from their group affiliations.

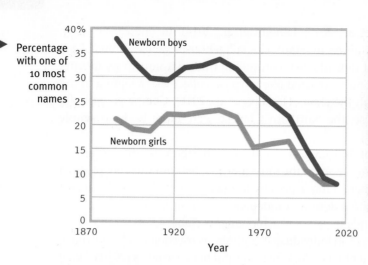

**Figure 4.6-7**

**A child like no other**

Americans' individualistic tendencies are reflected in their choice of names for their babies. In recent years, the percentage of U.S. babies receiving one of that year's 10 most common names has plunged. (Data from Twenge et al., 2010a, 2016.)

Percentage with one of 10 most common names (vertical axis, 0 to 40%)

Newborn boys

Newborn girls

Year (horizontal axis: 1870, 1920, 1970, 2020)

"Remember—we want her to stand out and fit in."

William Haefeli/The New Yorker Collection/The Cartoon Bank

analyzed the first names of 358 million U.S. babies born between 1880 and 2015, they discovered that the most common baby names had become less common. As **Figure 4.6-7** illustrates, the percentage of boys and girls given one of the 10 most common names for their birth year has plunged. Collectivist Japan provides a contrast: Half of Japanese baby names are among the country's 10 most common names, though unique names are also increasing in that culture (Ogihara et al., 2015).

Individualists frequently demand romance and personal fulfillment in marriage (Dion & Dion, 1993). In contrast, collectivist love songs have often expressed enduring commitment and friendship, as in this one from China: "We will be together from now on . . . . I will never change from now to forever" (Rothbaum & Tsang, 1998). Marriages unite two families, not just two individuals.

What predicts cultural change over time, or differences between cultures? Social history matters. Individualism and independence have been fostered by voluntary emigration, a capitalist economy, and a sparsely populated, challenging environment (Kitayama et al., 2009, 2010; Varnum et al., 2010). In Western cultures over the last century and now in all but the poorest countries, individualism has increased, following closely on the heels of increasing affluence (Grossmann & Varnum, 2015; Hamamura, 2012; Santos et al., 2017).

---

**AP® Science Practice**

## Check Your Understanding

**Examine the Concept**

▶ Explain the difference between individualist and collectivist cultures.

**Apply the Concept**

▶ Is the culture you live in more collectivist or individualist? How have your culture's values influenced your behavior, emotions, and thoughts?

*Answers to the Examine the Concept questions can be found in Appendix C at the end of the book.*

---

## Module 4.6c REVIEW

**4.6-7 Why has psychology generated so much research on the self? How important is self-esteem to our well-being?**

● The *self* is vigorously researched as the center of personality, organizing our thoughts, feelings, and actions.

● Considering possible selves helps motivate us toward positive development, but focusing too intensely on ourselves can lead to the *spotlight effect*.

● High *self-esteem* and *self-efficacy* correlate with benefits such as greater high school achievement and the ability to meet challenges. But the direction of the correlation is unclear.

- Rather than unrealistically promoting self-worth, it's better to reward achievements, thus promoting feelings of competence.

---

**4.6-8 How do blindness to one's own incompetence and self-serving bias reveal the costs of self-esteem, and how do defensive and secure self-esteem differ?**

- People are often most overconfident when they are most incompetent (the Dunning-Kruger effect). Inviting others' candid assessments can help combat this effect.

- *Self-serving bias* is our tendency to perceive ourselves favorably, as when viewing ourselves as better than average or when accepting credit for our successes but not blame for our failures.

- Self-serving bias often underlies conflicts, both individual and group (group-serving bias), and narcissistic people may react violently if their self-esteem is threatened.

- Defensive self-esteem is fragile, focuses on sustaining itself, and views failure or criticism as a threat. Secure self-esteem enables us to feel accepted for who we are.

---

**4.6-9 How do individualist and collectivist cultures shape values and goals?**

- Our personality is culturally influenced. Although individuals vary, different cultures tend to emphasize either individualism or collectivism.

- Cultures based on self-reliant *individualism* tend to value personal independence and individual achievement. They define identity in terms of self-esteem, personal goals and attributes, and personal rights and liberties.

- Cultures based on socially connected *collectivism* tend to value group goals, social identity, and commitments. They define identity in terms of interdependence, tradition, and harmony.

---

## AP® Practice Multiple Choice Questions

1. Madison knows that there is an internal organizer of her thoughts, feelings, and behavior. Madison has a sense of
   a. self-esteem.
   b. self.
   c. self-efficacy.
   d. self-serving bias.

2. Which of the following is an example of self-efficacy?
   a. Manuela believes she is better than others.
   b. Abraham believes he is a good person.
   c. Rasheed believes that he is a competent skater.
   d. Igor maintains his optimism despite doing poorly in his math class.

3. Nigel, who believes that he is a good person, has high self-worth; Jinella, who believes she is not good enough, has poor self-worth. Which of the following statements draws logical and objective conclusions about Nigel and Jinella?
   a. Because he has higher self-efficacy than Jinella, Nigel likely is more outgoing than Jinella.
   b. Because he has higher self-esteem than Jinella, Nigel likely is happier than Jinella.
   c. Because he has higher narcissism than Jinella, Nigel likely responds aggressively to threats to his competence.
   d. Because he has higher collectivism than Jinella, Nigel likely seeks other people's support more often than Jinella.

4. Jean thinks she is a special person and hopes to become famous. Her friends describe her as self-absorbed and materialistic. Jean is exhibiting
   a. a self-serving bias.
   b. secure self-esteem.
   c. narcissism.
   d. the spotlight effect.

5. Timothy is from an individualist culture. Which of the following is most likely to be true about Timothy?
   a. He would choose a career based on his personal interests and goals.
   b. He would view his life task as fitting in and maintaining connections.
   c. He would strive to develop a few close and enduring relationships.
   d. He would focus on his duty to his family.

6. Karl was late to his interview because he left the house late and got lost. If Karl exhibits the self-serving bias, which of the following statements will he use to explain his lateness?

   a. "I thought I knew where I was going, but I got lost."
   b. "I spent too much time trying to find a tie that matched this shirt."
   c. "There were too many cars on the road today, which made me late."
   d. "Sometimes I procrastinate and do not leave enough time to get places."

Motivation: Motivational Concepts

## LEARNING TARGETS

**4.7-1** Explain *motivation* as psychologists use the term, and identify four key motivation theories.

**4.7-2** Explain how the idea that some needs are more compelling than others is a useful framework for thinking about motivation.

---

**4.7-1** How do psychologists define *motivation*? What are four key motivation theories?

How well I [DM] remember asking my first discussion question in a new introductory psychology class. Several hands rose, along with one left foot. The foot belonged to Chris Klein, who was the unlikeliest person to have made it to that class. At birth, Chris suffered oxygen deprivation that required 40 minutes of CPR. "One doctor wanted to let him go," recalled his mother.

The result was severe cerebral palsy. With damage to the brain area that controls muscle movement, Chris can't contain his constantly moving hands. He can't feed, dress, or care for himself. And he can't speak. But what Chris can control are his keen mind and left foot. With that blessed foot, he operates the joystick on his motorized wheelchair. Using his left big toe, he can type sentences, which his communication system can store, send, or speak. And Chris is motivated—very motivated.

When Chris was a high school student in suburban Chicago, three teachers doubted he would be able to leave home for college. Yet he persisted, and, with much support, attended my college called Hope. Five years later, as his left foot drove him across the stage to receive his diploma, Chris's admiring classmates honored his achievement with a spontaneous standing ovation.

Today, Chris is an inspirational speaker for schools, churches, and community events, giving "a voice to those that have none, and a helping hand to those with disabilities." He is writing a book, *Lessons from the Big Toe*. And he has found love and married.

Few of us face Chris Klein's challenges. But we all seek to direct our energy in ways that will produce satisfaction and success. Our feelings move us, and we inspire feelings in others. We are pushed by social motives, such as affiliation and achievement, and biological ones, such as hunger. We feel hope and happiness, sadness and pain, tenderness and triumph. Chris' fierce will to live, learn, and love highlights the close ties between our *motivations*—the topic of this module—and our *emotions*, which we will explore in Module 4.8. Together, motivations and emotions energize, direct, and enrich our lives.

Our **motivations** arise from the interplay between nature (the bodily "push") and nurture (the "pulls" from our personal experiences, thoughts, and culture). That is usually, but not always, for the better. When our bodies tell us we're hungry, we respond by eating foods we have learned to trust and enjoy. But when our motivations get hijacked, our lives go awry.

**motivation** a need or desire that energizes and directs behavior.

**A motivated man: Chris Klein** To see and hear Chris presenting his story, visit tinyurl.com/ChrisPsychStudent.

Katie Green/MLive.com

Those with *substance use disorder*, for example, may find their cravings for an addictive substance override their longings for sustenance, safety, and social support.

Psychologists have viewed motivated behavior from four perspectives:

- *Instinct theory* (now replaced by the *evolutionary perspective*) focuses on genetically predisposed behaviors.
- *Drive-reduction theory* focuses on how we respond to inner pushes and external pulls.
- *Arousal theory* focuses on finding the right level of stimulation.
- *Abraham Maslow's hierarchy of needs* focuses on the priority of some needs over others.

Psychologists have also examined Kurt Lewin's *motivational conflicts theory*, which we will discuss in Module 5.1.

## Instincts and Evolutionary Theory

To qualify as an **instinct**, a complex behavior must have a fixed pattern throughout a species and be unlearned (Tinbergen, 1951). Such unlearned behaviors include *imprinting* in birds (which you learned about in Module 3.6) and the return of salmon to their birthplace. A few human behaviors, such as infants' innate reflexes to root for a nipple and suck (Module 3.2), exhibit unlearned fixed patterns. But many more are directed by both physiological needs and psychological wants.

**Same motive, different wiring**
The more complex the nervous system, the more adaptable the organism. Both humans and weaverbirds satisfy their need for shelter in ways that reflect their inherited capacities. Human behavior is flexible; we can learn whatever skills we need to build a house. The bird's behavior pattern is fixed; it can build only this kind of nest.

Although instincts cannot explain most human motives, the underlying assumption endures in *evolutionary psychology:* Genes do predispose some species-typical behavior. Module 3.7 discussed the limits that biological predispositions place on conditioning. In Module 4.3, we saw how evolution might influence our helping behaviors and our romantic attractions. And later in this module, we'll see how our taste preferences aid our survival.

## Drives and Incentives

In addition to our predispositions, we have *drives.* **Physiological needs** (such as for food or water) create an aroused, motivated state—a drive (such as hunger or thirst)—that pushes us to reduce the need. **Drive-reduction theory** explains that, with few exceptions, when a physiological need increases, so does our psychological drive to reduce it.

Drive reduction is one way our bodies strive for **homeostasis** (literally "staying the same")—the maintenance of a steady internal state. For example, our body regulates its temperature in a way similar to a room's thermostat. Both systems operate through feedback loops: Sensors feed room temperature to a control device. If the room's temperature cools, the control device switches on the furnace. Likewise, if our body's temperature cools,

**instinct** a complex behavior that is rigidly patterned throughout a species and is unlearned.

**physiological need** a basic bodily requirement.

**drive-reduction theory** the idea that a physiological need creates an aroused state (a drive) that motivates an organism to satisfy the need.

**homeostasis** a tendency to maintain a balanced or constant internal state; the regulation of any aspect of body chemistry, such as blood glucose, around a particular level.

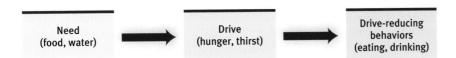

Need
(food, water)
→
Drive
(hunger, thirst)
→
Drive-reducing
behaviors
(eating, drinking)

**Figure 4.7-1**
**Drive-reduction theory**
Drive-reduction motivation arises
from *homeostasis*—our body's
natural tendency to maintain a
steady internal state. Thus, if we
are water-deprived, our thirst
drives us to drink to restore the
body's normal state.

our blood vessels constrict (to conserve warmth) and we feel driven to put on more clothes or seek a warmer environment (**Figure 4.7-1**).

According to *incentive theory*, not only are we *pushed* by our need to reduce drives, but we are also *pulled* by **incentives**—positive or negative environmental stimuli that lure or repel us. Such stimuli (when positive) increase our dopamine levels, causing our underlying drives (such as for food or love) to become active impulses (Hamid et al., 2016). And the more these impulses are satisfied and reinforced, the stronger the drive may become: As Roy Baumeister (2015) noted, "Getting begets wanting." If you are hungry, the aroma of good food will motivate you. Whether that aroma comes from roasted peanuts or toasted tarantula will depend on your culture and experience. Incentives can also be negative: If teasing others on social media causes others to unfollow or unfriend us, we may feel motivated to treat others better.

When there is both a need and an incentive, we feel strongly driven. The food-deprived person who smells pizza baking may feel an intense hunger drive, and the baking pizza may become a compelling incentive. For each motive, we can ask, "How is it pushed by our inborn physiological needs and pulled by learned incentives in the environment?"

## Arousal Theory

We are much more than calm homeostatic systems, however. Some motivated behaviors *increase* rather than decrease arousal. Well-fed animals will leave their shelter to explore and gain information, seemingly in the absence of any need-based drive. Curiosity drives monkeys to monkey around trying to figure out how to unlock a latch that opens nothing or opens a window that allows them to see outside their room (Butler, 1954). It drives newly mobile infants to investigate every accessible corner of the house. It drives the scientists whose work this text discusses. And it drives the explorers and adventurers who enjoy high arousal and novel sensations. According to *sensation seeking theory*, these "sensation seekers" may display traits such as *experience seeking* (a desire for novel sensory or mental experiences), *thrill or adventure seeking* (an attraction to risky or fear-inspiring activities, like skydiving), *disinhibition* (a loss of self-control), and *boredom susceptibility* (the inability to tolerate monotony or repetition) (Zuckerman, 1979, 2009).

So, human motivation aims not to eliminate arousal but to seek optimal levels of arousal. Having all our biological needs satisfied, we feel driven to experience stimulation. Lacking stimulation, we feel bored and look for a way to increase arousal. Most people, worldwide,

**incentive** a positive or negative
environmental stimulus that
motivates behavior.

**Driven by curiosity** Young
monkeys and children are fascinated
by the unfamiliar. Their drive to
explore maintains an optimal level of
arousal. It is one of several motives
that do not fill any immediate
physiological need.

prefer to *do* something—even (when given no other option while waiting in a lab) to self-administer mild electric shocks (Buttrick et al., 2019; Wilson et al., 2014). Why might people seek to increase their arousal? Moderate arousal and even anxiety can be motivating—leading to higher levels of math achievement, for example (Z. Wang et al., 2015). Yet *too much* stimulation or stress motivates us to decrease arousal. In experiments, people have felt less stress when they limited email-checking and phone notifications to three times a day rather than being continually accessible (Fitz et al., 2019; Kushlev & Dunn, 2015).

**Yerkes-Dodson law** the principle that performance increases with arousal only up to a point, beyond which performance decreases.

Two early twentieth-century psychologists studied the relationship of arousal to performance and identified the **Yerkes-Dodson law**: *Moderate arousal leads to optimal performance* (Yerkes & Dodson, 1908). When taking an exam, it pays to be moderately aroused—alert but not trembling with nervousness. (If you're already nervous, it's better to avoid becoming further aroused with caffeine.) Between bored low arousal and anxious hyperarousal lies a flourishing life. But optimal arousal levels depend on the task, with more difficult tasks requiring lower arousal for best performance (Hembree, 1988).

---

**AP® Science Practice**

## Check Your Understanding

**Examine the Concept**

▶ Explain what is meant by *motivation*.

▶ Explain the Yerkes-Dodson law.

**Apply the Concept**

▶ Performance peaks at lower levels of arousal for difficult tasks, and at higher levels for easy or well-learned tasks. (a) How might this affect marathon runners? (b) How might this affect anxious test-takers facing a difficult test?

▶ Does boredom ever motivate you to do things just to figure out something new? When was the last time that happened, and what did you find?

*Answers to the Examine the Concept questions can be found in Appendix C at the end of the book.*

---

## A Hierarchy of Needs

**4.7-2** Why is the idea that some needs are more compelling than others a useful framework for thinking about motivation?

Some needs take priority over others. At this moment, with your needs for air and water hopefully satisfied, other motives—such as your desire to learn and achieve (discussed later in this module)—are energizing and directing your behavior. Let your need for water go unsatisfied, however, and your thirst will preoccupy you. Deprived of air, your thirst will disappear.

As we learned in Module 4.5, Abraham Maslow (1970) described these priorities as a *hierarchy of needs* (see Figure 4.5-4). If our physiological needs are met, we become concerned with personal safety. If we feel safe, we then seek to love and to be loved. With our love needs satisfied, we seek self-esteem. Beyond this, said Maslow (1971), lies the need to actualize one's full potential.

Near the end of his life, Maslow proposed that some of us also reach a level of *self-transcendence*. At the self-actualization level, we seek to realize our own potential. At the self-transcendence level, we strive for meaning, purpose, and communion in a way that is transpersonal—beyond the self (Kaufman, 2020). Maslow's contemporary, psychiatrist Viktor Frankl (1962), a Nazi concentration camp survivor, concurred that the search for meaning is an important human motive: "Life is never made unbearable by circumstances, but only by lack of meaning and purpose."

"Do you feel your life has an important purpose or meaning?" When Gallup asked this question of people in 132 countries, 91 percent answered *Yes* (Oishi & Diener, 2014). People sense meaning when they experience their life as having *purpose* (goals), *significance* (value), and *coherence* (sense)—sentiments that may be nourished by strong social connections, a religious faith, an orderly world, and social status (King et al., 2016; Martela & Steger, 2016). People's sense of life's meaning predicts their psychological and physical well-being, and their capacity to delay gratification (Heine et al., 2006; Van Tongeren et al., 2018). Meaning matters.

The order of Maslow's hierarchy is not universally fixed: U.S. suffragist Alice Paul starved herself to make a political statement (enduring force-feeding by her jailers). Culture also influences our priorities: Self-esteem matters more in modern individualist nations, where people prioritize personal achievements over family and community identity (Oishi et al., 1999). And, while agreeing with Maslow's basic levels of need, today's psychologists add that gaining and retaining mates, parenting offspring, and desiring social status are also universal human motives (Anderson et al., 2015; Kenrick et al., 2010).

Nevertheless, the simple idea that some motives are more compelling than others provides a framework for thinking about motivation. Worldwide life-satisfaction surveys support this basic idea (Oishi et al., 1999; Tay & Diener, 2011). In poorer nations that lack easy access to money and the food and shelter it buys, financial satisfaction more strongly predicts feelings of well-being. In wealthy countries, where most people can meet their basic needs, social connections better predict well-being.

With these classic motivation theories in mind (**Table 4.7-1**), let's now take a closer look at several key human motives. Some higher-level motives, such as our needs for belongingness and achievement, are driven by psychological factors, such as the social rewards that come from affiliation and success. Other motives, such as hunger, have identifiable physiological mechanisms that drive them (though learned tastes and cultural expectations matter, too). What unifies *all* motives is their common effect: the energizing and directing of behavior. Let's begin with two specific, higher-level motives: the *need to belong* and the *need to achieve*. After that, we will explore that powerful physiological motive, hunger. As you read about these motives, watch for ways that incentives (the psychological "pull") interact with physiological needs (the biological "push").

**CULTURAL AWARENESS**

Throughout this text, you will notice culture's influence on our attitudes, beliefs, and behaviors. Understanding and appreciating cultural differences can help you avoid cultural biases. *Different* doesn't mean *deviant*.

| TABLE 4.7-1 | Classic Motivation Theories |
|---|---|
| **Theory** | **Its Big Idea** |
| *Instincts and evolutionary theory* | There is a genetic basis for unlearned, species-typical behavior (such as birds building nests or infants rooting for a nipple). |
| *Drive-reduction theory* | Physiological needs (such as hunger and thirst) create an aroused state that drives us to reduce the need (for example, by eating or drinking). |
| *Arousal theory* | Our need to maintain an optimal level of arousal motivates behaviors that meet no physiological need (such as our yearning for stimulation and our hunger for information). |
| *Maslow's hierarchy of needs* | We prioritize survival-based needs and then social needs more than the needs for esteem and meaning. |

# Check Your Understanding

**Examine the Concept**

▶ Explain the differences among the big ideas of the classic motivation theories.

**Apply the Concept**

▶ Your aunt tells you a story of a family vacation she took as a child. After hours of driving through an isolated stretch, she and her parents finally spotted a diner. Although it looked deserted and creepy, they stopped because they were *really* hungry and thirsty. How would Maslow's hierarchy of needs explain their behavior?

▶ Consider your own experiences in terms of Maslow's hierarchy of needs. Do you remember experiencing hunger or thirst that displaced your concern for other, higher-level needs?

*Answers to the Examine the Concept questions can be found in Appendix C at the end of the book.*

---

# Data Interpretation

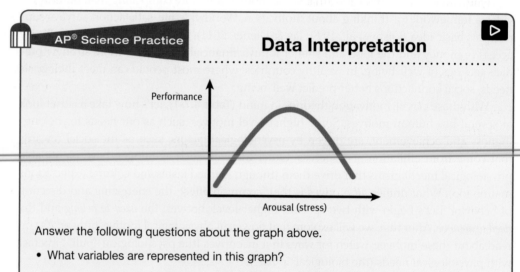

Answer the following questions about the graph above.

• What variables are represented in this graph?

• What psychological concept is depicted in this graph?

Being able to recognize and evaluate graphical representations of psychological concepts demonstrates that you have strong data interpretation skills.

---

# Module 4.7a REVIEW

**4.7-1 How do psychologists define *motivation*? What are four key motivation theories?**

• *Motivation* is a need or desire that energizes and directs behavior.

• The *instinct*/evolutionary perspective explores genetic influences on complex behaviors.

• *Drive-reduction theory* explores how *physiological needs* create aroused, motivated states (drives) that direct us to satisfy those needs. Environmental *incentives* can intensify

drives. Drive reduction's goal is *homeostasis*, maintaining a steady internal state.

• Arousal theory proposes that some behaviors (such as those driven by sensation-seeking or curiosity) do not reduce physiological needs, but rather are prompted by a search for certain kinds of novel experiences or an optimal level of arousal. The *Yerkes-Dodson law* describes the relationship between arousal and performance.

• Abraham Maslow's *hierarchy of needs* proposes a pyramid of human needs, from basic needs up to higher-level needs.

**4.7-2** Why is the idea that some needs are more compelling than others a useful framework for thinking about motivation?

- Theories such as Maslow's hierarchy of needs address the fact that some needs take priority. Although the order of this hierarchy is not universally fixed (as seen when people refuse to eat to make a political statement), worldwide surveys support this basic idea.

# AP® Practice Multiple Choice Questions

1. Ansley experiences an energizing desire that drives her to work hard at school. What is Ansley experiencing?
   a. Homeostasis
   b. Arousal
   c. Motivation
   d. Instinct

**Use the following text to answer questions 2–4:**

Karl arrives home hungry. He smells a delicious fragrance coming from the kitchen. When he walks in, he finds a loaf of freshly baked bread.

2. Which of the following psychological concepts describes Karl's hunger?
   a. Incentive
   b. Homeostasis
   c. Arousal
   d. Physiological need

3. Which of the following psychological concepts describes the freshly baked bread?
   a. Incentive
   b. Physiological need
   c. Drive-reduction
   d. Arousal

4. Based on drive-reduction theory, which of the following best describes Karl's likely behavior?
   a. Karl will feel an instinct to eat the bread.
   b. Feeling a physiological need and met with an incentive, Karl will eat the bread.
   c. If Karl feels an optimal level of hunger and interest in eating the bread, he will eat the bread.
   d. Karl will immediately eat the bread to satisfy a physiological need, after which he can pursue safety and security needs.

5. Dr. Kepler was interested in the impact of arousal on performance. She studied high school students' abilities to quickly and accurately complete calculus problems in front of three calculus experts. She later had the same students complete the calculus problems alone in the classroom, finding much better performance under these conditions. What psychological concept is represented in this description?
   a. Instinct
   b. Yerkes-Dodson law
   c. Self-transcendence
   d. Drive-reduction theory

6. Renaldo, a biological psychologist, studies genetics. Which theory does he most likely support?
   a. Drive-reduction theory
   b. Arousal theory
   c. Maslow's hierarchy of needs
   d. Instinct theory

7. To feel less thirsty and return to a steady state, Prunella drinks water. Which theory best explains her behavior?
   a. Drive-reduction theory
   b. Maslow's hierarchy of needs
   c. Evolutionary theory
   d. Arousal theory

**8.** Nolan is motivated to study because his teacher praises him for it. For Nolan, his teacher's praise serves as a(n)

a. incentive.
b. instinct.
c. need.
d. drive.

**9.** Which of the following is true according to the Yerkes-Dodson law?

a. When taking an exam, you should be extremely relaxed.
b. When taking an exam, you should make sure your physiological needs have been met.
c. When taking an exam, you should strive for self-transcendence.
d. When taking an exam, you should be moderately aroused, but not trembling with nervousness.

# Module 4.7b Motivation: Affiliation and Achievement

> ### LEARNING TARGETS
>
> **4.7-3** Identify the evidence that points to our human affiliation need — our need to belong.
>
> **4.7-4** Explain how social networking influences us.
>
> **4.7-5** Describe *achievement motivation*, and identify some ways to encourage achievement.

## The Need to Belong

> **4.7-3** What evidence points to our human affiliation need — our need to belong?

We are what the ancient Greek philosopher Aristotle called *the social animal*. Cut off from friends or family—at a new school, alone in prison or a foreign land, or isolating during a pandemic—most people feel keenly their lost connections with important others. This deep *need to belong*—our **affiliation need**—is a key human motivation (Baumeister & Leary, 1995). It is normal and healthy to seek some privacy and solitude (Ren et al., 2021). But most of us also seek to affiliate—to become strongly attached to certain others in enduring, close relationships. Across 27 countries, people's strongest motives were to maintain their romantic relationship and care for family members (Ko et al., 2020).

**affiliation need** the need to build and maintain relationships and to feel part of a group.

## The Benefits of Belonging

Social bonds boosted our early ancestors' chances of survival. Adults who formed attachments were more likely to survive and reproduce, and to co-nurture their offspring to maturity. Attachment bonds motivated caregivers to keep children close, calming them and protecting them from threats (Esposito et al., 2013).

Cooperating with friends and acquaintances also enhanced survival. As hunters, our ancestors learned that six hands were better than two. As food gatherers, they gained protection from two-footed and four-footed enemies by traveling in groups. Those who felt a need to belong survived and reproduced most successfully, and their genes now predominate. Our innate need to belong drives us to befriend people who cooperate and to avoid those who exploit (Feinberg et al., 2014; Kashima et al., 2019). People in every society on Earth belong to groups and prefer and favor "us" over "them." Having a *social identity*—feeling part of a group—boosts people's health and well-being (Allen et al., 2015; Haslam et al., 2019).

Do you have close friends—people with whom you freely disclose your ups and downs? Having someone who rejoices with us over good news helps us feel better about both the news and the friendship (Reis, 2018). Such companionship creates connection and cooperation (Canavello & Crocker, 2017). The need to belong runs deeper, it seems, than any need to be rich. Very happy university students are distinguished not by their money, but rather by their "strong social relationships" (Diener et al., 2018).

The need to belong colors our thoughts and emotions. We spend a great deal of time thinking about actual and hoped-for relationships. Falling in mutual love, people have been known to feel their cheeks ache from their irrepressible grins. Asked, "What is necessary for your happiness?" or "What is it that makes your life meaningful?" most people have mentioned—before anything else—close, satisfying relationships with family, friends, or romantic partners (Berscheid, 1985). Happiness hits close to home.

According to **self-determination theory**, we strive to satisfy three needs: *competence*, *autonomy* (a sense of personal control), and *relatedness* (Deci & Ryan, 2012; Ryan & Deci, 2000). Fulfilling these motives reduces stress and boosts health and self-esteem (Guertin et al., 2017; Uysal et al., 2020). One analysis of 200,000 people from nearly 500 studies concluded that "self-determination is key to explaining human motivation" (Howard et al., 2017, p. 1346). Self-determined behaviors tend to be **intrinsically motivated**—we perform them because they are inherently meaningful or satisfying, and they *enhance* our feelings of competence, autonomy, and relatedness. Behaviors that are **extrinsically motivated** tend to *undermine* these feelings.

Self-determination theory can help leaders motivate people. Employees who feel empowered perform better. They also feel more autonomous, competent, and socially included (Slemp et al., 2018; Van den Broeck et al., 2016). Ditto for teachers motivating their students and military leaders motivating their soldiers (Bakadorova & Raufelder, 2018; Chambel et al., 2015; Hagger & Chatzisarantis, 2016).

To gain acceptance, we generally conform to group standards. We monitor our behavior, hoping to make a good impression. We spend billions on clothes, cosmetics, and diet and fitness aids—all motivated, in part, by our search for love and acceptance.

Thrown together in groups at school, at camp, or in team sports, we form bonds. Upon parting, we feel distressed. We promise to stay in touch and return for reunions. By drawing a sharp circle around "us," the need to belong feeds both deep attachments to those inside the circle (loving families, faithful friendships, team loyalty) and hostilities toward those outside (rival gangs, ethnic conflicts, fanatic nationalism). Feelings of love activate brain reward and safety systems. In one experiment, deeply in love university students exposed to heat felt less pain when looking at their beloved's picture (Younger et al., 2010). Pictures of our loved ones activate a brain region—the prefrontal cortex—that dampens feelings of physical pain (Eisenberger et al., 2011). Love is a natural painkiller.

Even when bad relationships end, people suffer. In one 16-nation survey, and in repeated U.S. surveys, separated and divorced people have been half as likely as married people to

Photodisc/Getty Images

**AP® Science Practice**

### Research

In the experiment described here, university students exposed to heat when looking at their beloved's picture felt less pain than they did when viewing pictures of an equally attractive and familiar acquaintance. The students in the study are the sample, but the findings are generalizable to the population: people in love.

**self-determination theory** the theory that we feel motivated to satisfy our needs for competence, autonomy, and relatedness.

**intrinsic motivation** the desire to perform a behavior effectively for its own sake.

**extrinsic motivation** the desire to perform a behavior to receive promised rewards or avoid threatened punishment.

say they are "very happy" (Inglehart, 1990; NORC, 2016a). Is that simply because happy people more often marry and stay married? A national study following British lives through time revealed that, even after controlling for premarital life satisfaction, "the married are still more satisfied, suggesting a causal effect" of marriage (Grover & Helliwell, 2014). Divorce also predicts earlier mortality. Data from more than 600 million(!) people in 24 countries reveal that, compared with married people, separated and divorced people are at greater risk for early death (Shor et al., 2012). This massive study's finding was no fluke: An independent study of 7.8 million people replicated the association between being separated or divorced and risk of early death (Wang et al., 2020). As one data scientist noted, "[A happy marriage] is perhaps as important as not smoking, which is to say: huge" (Ungar, 2014).

Children who endure a series of foster homes or repeated family relocations experience repeated disruptions of budding relationships. They may then have difficulty forming deep connections with others (Oishi & Schimmack, 2010). The evidence is clearest at the extremes. Children who grow up in institutions without a sense of belonging to anyone, or who are locked away at home and severely neglected, often become withdrawn, frightened, even speechless. Feeling insecurely attached to others during childhood can persist into adulthood in two main forms (Fraley et al., 2011). One is *anxiety:* constantly craving acceptance but remaining vigilant to signs of possible rejection. The other is *avoidance:* feeling such discomfort over getting close to others that avoidant strategies are used to maintain distance.

No matter how secure our early years were, we all experience anxiety, loneliness, jealousy, or guilt when something threatens or dissolves our social ties. Much as life's best moments occur when close relationships begin—making a new friend, falling in love, having a baby—life's worst moments happen when close relationships end (Beam et al., 2016). Bereaved, we may feel life is empty or pointless, and we may overeat to fill that emptiness (Yang et al., 2016). Even the first months of living away from home on a college campus can be distressing (English et al., 2017).

Gregory Walton and Timothy Wilson (2018) note that a lonely new college student may wonder, "Can people like me belong here?" Entering African American students who experienced a 1-hour session explaining the normality of that worry, with reassuring stories from older peers, achieved higher grades over the next 3 years—and greater life and career satisfaction after college. Boosting belonging had big benefits.

Social isolation can put our mental health at risk. In separate U.S. surveys during the early months of the Covid pandemic:

- 48 percent of 18- to 29-year-olds reported repeatedly feeling lonely or isolated (Cox & Bowman, 2020).

- 70 percent of all adults reported experiencing "moderate or severe distress"—triple the 22 percent in a prior survey (Twenge & Joiner, 2020a).

- 36 percent of all adults showed signs of clinical depression or anxiety—again, triple the level of a year earlier (NCHS, 2020).

British researchers also reported surging rates of mental distress during the pandemic restrictions (Pierce et al, 2020). The benefits of belonging make it worth the effort to nurture our relationships with family or friends in whatever ways we can.

## The Pain of Being Shut Out

Can you recall feeling excluded, ignored, or shunned? Perhaps your texts went unanswered, or you were unfriended or ghosted online. Perhaps others gave you the silent treatment, avoided you, looked away, mocked you, or shut you out in some other way. Or perhaps you have felt excluded when among people speaking an unfamiliar language (Dotan-Eliaz et al., 2009).

**Creative graduation "ceremonies"** As social animals with a need to belong, we thrive on our connections with others. Social distancing slowed the Covid pandemic, but it also disrupted our relationships and challenged us to create new ways to celebrate.

Keith Birmingham/MediaNews Group/Pasadena Star-News/Getty Images

We feel the sting even from small-scale exclusions like being *phubbed*—an Australian-coined term meaning *phone-snubbed*—when our conversation partner seems more interested in their phone than in us (Roberts & David, 2016). Frequent phubbing, with partners placing their phone where they can check it during conversational lulls, distracts attention and predicts a less satisfying relationship (Kushlev et al., 2019; Sbarra et al., 2019).

All these experiences are instances of **ostracism**—of social exclusion (Williams, 2007, 2009). Worldwide, humans use many forms of ostracism—shunning, exile, imprisonment, solitary confinement—to punish, and therefore control, social behavior. For children, even a brief time-out in isolation can be punishing. Asked to describe personal episodes that made them feel especially *bad* about themselves, people will—about four times in five—describe a broken or painful social relationship (Pillemer et al., 2007). Ostracism—even just being excluded from ball tosses during a virtual game—also increases suicidal thinking (Chen et al., 2021).

Being ostracized threatens one's need to belong (Vanhalst et al., 2015). "It's the meanest thing you can do to someone, especially if you know they can't fight back. I never should have been born," said Lea, a lifelong victim of silent treatment from her mother and grandmother (Wirth et al., 2010). Like Lea, people often respond to ostracism with initial efforts to restore their acceptance, followed by depressed mood, and finally withdrawal. To many, social exclusion is a sentence worse than death. Prisoner William Blake (2013) has spent more than a quarter-century in solitary confinement. "I cannot fathom how dying any death could be harder and more terrible than living through all that I have been forced to endure," he observed.

To experience ostracism is to experience real pain, as social psychologists Kipling Williams and his colleagues were surprised to discover in their studies of exclusion on social media (Gonsalkorale & Williams, 2006). Such ostracism elicits increased activity in brain areas, such as the *anterior cingulate cortex*, that also respond to physical pain (Lieberman & Eisenberger, 2015; Rotge et al., 2015).

When people view pictures of romantic partners who broke their heart, their brain and body begin to ache (Kross et al., 2011). That helps explain some other surprising findings: The pain reliever acetaminophen (marketed as Tylenol) lessens *social* as well as physical pain (DeWall et al., 2010). Ditto for marijuana (Deckman et al., 2014). Across cultures, people use the same words (for example, *hurt*, *crushed*) to describe social pain and physical pain (MacDonald & Leary, 2005). Psychologically, we seem to experience social pain with the same unpleasantness that marks physical pain. Compared with collectivist cultures, rejection tends to hurt more in individualist cultures—where people have weaker social support networks (Heu et al., 2019; Uskul & Over, 2017).

"A bunch of friends are coming over to stare at their phones."

**Enduring the pain of ostracism**
White cadets at the U.S. Military Academy at West Point ostracized Henry Flipper for years, hoping he would drop out. He persevered in spite of their cruelty, and in 1877 he became the first African American West Point graduate.

**ostracism** deliberate social exclusion of individuals or groups.

**Social acceptance and rejection**
Successful participants on the reality TV show *Survivor* form alliances and gain acceptance among their peers. The rest receive the ultimate social punishment by being "voted off the island."

Ostracism can also make people disagreeable, uncooperative, and hostile, which leads to further ostracism (Rudert et al., 2019; Walasek et al., 2019). In one series of experiments, researchers told some students that people they had met earlier didn't want them in a group that was forming (Gaertner et al., 2008; Twenge et al., 2001).[3] Others heard good news: "Everyone chose you as someone they'd like to work with." Those who were excluded became much more likely to engage in self-defeating behaviors and to act in disparaging or aggressive ways against those who had excluded them (blasting them with noise, for example).

**AP® Science Practice**

## Check Your Understanding

**Examine the Concept**

▶ Describe our affiliation need.

▶ Describe the three needs we are motivated to satisfy, according to self-determination theory.

**Apply the Concept**

▶ Have there been times when you felt lonely or ostracized? What are some strategies that might help you to cope the next time you feel this way?

*Answers to the Examine the Concept questions can be found in Appendix C at the end of the book.*

## Connecting and Social Networking

**4.7-4** How does social networking influence us?

As social creatures, we live for connection. Researcher George Vaillant (2013) was asked what he had learned from studying 238 Harvard University men from the 1930s to the end of their lives. He replied, "Happiness is love." A South African Zulu saying captures the idea: *Umuntu ngumuntu ngabantu*—"a person is a person through other persons."

### Mobile Networks and Social Media

Look around and see humans connecting: talking, tweeting, posting, gaming, emailing. Today, have you observed more students engaging with each other face-to-face or by silently checking their phones, as one research team's phone app counted students doing 56 times per day (Elias et al., 2016)? The changes in how we connect have been fast and vast:

- *Mobile phones:* By 2020's end, 96 percent of the world's 7.8 billion people lived in an area covered by a mobile-cellular network, and most humans—5.8 billion—had broadband mobile subscriptions (ITU, 2020).

- *Texting and instant messaging:* The average American sends and receives 94 texts/messages per day (Burke, 2018). Half of 18- to 29-year-olds check their phone multiple times per hour, and "can't imagine . . . life without [it]" (Newport, 2015; Saad, 2015).

- *Social networking:* More than half of entering U.S. college students report using social networking sites at least 6+ hours per week (Stolzenberg et al., 2020). With our friends online, it's hard to avoid social networks: Check in or miss out.

Increased online time displaces other activities. Compared to teens before 2010, today's teens spend fewer hours dating, driving, working, talking face-to-face, and reading books (Livingston et al., 2019; Twenge, 2019). Time spent networking is time spent not-working. Technology has radically changed the teen experience.

**AP® Science Practice**

**Research**

The research supporting the claim that technology has radically changed the teen experience was conducted in the United States. These findings might not generalize to other cultures. It would require replication and cross-cultural research to determine if the results generalize to other populations.

---

[3]The researchers later *debriefed* and reassured the participants.

## The Net Result: Social Effects of Social Networking

By connecting like-minded people, the internet serves as a social amplifier. In times of social crisis or personal stress, it provides information and supportive connections. The internet can also function as a matchmaker (as I [ND] can attest: I met my wife online). While dating websites aren't adept at matchmaking, they do expand the pool of potential romantic matches (Joel et al., 2017).

But social media also leads people to compare their lives with others. When others seem happier, more popular, or more successful, this *social comparison* can trigger envy and depressed feelings (Verduyn et al., 2017; Whillans et al., 2017; see Module 5.2 for more on *relative deprivation*). In study after study, most people perceive that others' social lives are more active than their own (Deri et al., 2017). Do you feel that others party more, dine out more, and have more friends and fun? Take comfort: Most of your friends feel the same.

Smartphones have become pervasive: Their number tripled between 2011 and 2018 in the United States, and similarly elsewhere. Simultaneously—and merely coincidentally?—Canadian, British, and U.S. teen depression, anxiety, self-harm, and suicide rates mushroomed. From 2010 to 2018, for example, major depression episodes increased from 8 to 14 percent among both 12- to 17-year-old and 18- to 25-year-old Americans (SAMHSA, 2019). Rates of depression, anxiety, self-injury, and suicidal thinking similarly increased for college students (Duffy et al., 2019).

So, is there a causal connection between these concurrent increases in screen time and mental health problems? Under the leadership of Jonathan Haidt and Jean Twenge (2021), researchers are accumulating and debating findings. They have reached tentative conclusions from three types of explorations:

- **Correlational studies ask:** *Is social media use associated with teen mental health?* Studies vary, but overall there is a small positive correlation between adolescents' social media time and their risk of depression, anxiety, and self-harm. The screen time–disorder association is stronger for social media use than for TV and gaming time. The link is also stronger for teen girls. And it increases only with daily screen time of 3 hours or more.

- **Longitudinal studies ask:** *Does teens' social media use predict their future mental health?* The answer is *Maybe*. Of 27 studies, 14 confirmed that excessive teen social media use (defined as more than 3 hours per day) predicted worse future mental health.

- **Experiments ask:** *Do volunteers randomly assigned to restricted social media use fare better than those not assigned on outcomes such as loneliness and depression?* On balance, *Yes*, but the few such studies have produced mixed results. One recent study, which randomly assigned nearly 3000 paid volunteers to either deactivate their Facebook account or not, found that "four weeks without Facebook improves subjective well-being" (Allcott et al., 2020).

Is screen time the primary culprit because it displaces other healthy activities—face-to-face connection, sleep, exercise, reading, watching movies together, and spending time outdoors? Or is the problem with social media specifically, because it drives envy when comparing one's own mundane life with the lives of cooler-seeming others? What other social forces might be at work? And what can be done to protect and improve youth and young adult well-being? Stay tuned: This important story is still being written.

Online networking is a double-edged sword. Nature has designed us for face-to-face relationships, and those who spend hours online daily are *less* likely to know and draw help from their real-world neighbors. But social media does help us connect with friends, stay in touch with family, and find support when we're facing challenges (Clark et al., 2018). When used in moderation, social networking supports our face-to-face relationships and therefore predicts longer life (Hobbs et al., 2016; Waytz & Gray, 2018).

*"Well, if it's any consolation, your social media makes it look like you're absolutely thriving."*

Maddie Dai/Cartoon Stock

### AP® Exam Tip

The comparison of three types of research methods described here is very informative. Be sure you understand the differences between them and the different conclusions you can draw from each. These research methods and design practices will be on the AP® exam.

## Data

The narcissism measure mentioned below is quantitative because it provides numerical data to represent degrees of the variable (narcissism).

*"The women on these dating sites don't seem to believe I'm a prince."*

### Does Electronic Communication Stimulate Healthy Self-Disclosure?

*Self-disclosure* is sharing ourselves—our joys, worries, and weaknesses—with others. Confiding can be a healthy way of coping with day-to-day challenges. When communicating electronically rather than face-to-face, we often are less focused on others' reactions. We are less self-conscious, and thus less inhibited. Sometimes, these disinhibitions become toxic: Political extremists post inflammatory messages, online bullies hound victims, hate groups promote bigotry, and people send selfies they later regret (Frimer et al., 2019). But more often, the increased self-disclosure strengthens friendships (Valkenburg & Peter, 2009).

### Does Social Networking Promote Narcissism?

As we saw in Module 4.6, *narcissism* is self-esteem gone wild. Narcissistic people are self-important, self-focused, and self-promoting. To measure your narcissistic tendencies, you might rate your agreement with personality test items such as "I like to be the center of attention." People who agree with such statements tend to have high narcissism scores—and they are especially active on social networking sites (Casale & Banchi, 2020). They collect more superficial "friends." They offer more staged, glamorous photos. They retaliate more against negative comments. And, not surprisingly, they *seem* more narcissistic to strangers (Buffardi & Campbell, 2008; Weiser, 2015).

For narcissists, social networking sites are more than a gathering place; they are a feeding trough. In one study, college students were *randomly assigned* either to edit and explain their online profiles for 15 minutes, or to use that time to study and explain a Google Maps routing (Freeman & Twenge, 2010). After completing their tasks, all were tested. Who then scored higher on a narcissism measure? Those who had spent the time focused on themselves.

## Exploring Research Methods & Design

Consider the Freeman and Twenge (2010) study described here.

- Why do you think random assignment is emphasized here?

- What conclusions can you draw from this study?

- If the researchers had not used random assignment, how would your conclusions differ?

Review Module 0.4 if you have trouble addressing these questions.

**Self-esteem or narcissism?**
Social networking can help people share self-relevant information and stay connected with family and friends. But it can also feed narcissistic tendencies and enable self-glamorization.

## Maintaining Balance and Focus

It will come as no surprise that excessive online socializing and gaming have been correlated with lower grades and with increased anxiety and depression (Brooks, 2015; Lepp et al., 2014; Walsh et al., 2013). In one U.S. survey, 47 percent of the heaviest users of the internet and other media were receiving mostly C grades or lower, as were just 23 percent of the lightest users (Kaiser Family Foundation, 2010). In another national survey, young adults who used seven or more social media platforms were three times more likely to be depressed or anxious than those who used two or fewer (Primack et al., 2016).

In today's world, it can be challenging to maintain a healthy balance between our real-world and online time. Experts offer some practical suggestions:

- *Monitor your time*. Use a time-tracking app to measure your time online. Then ask yourself, "Does my time use reflect my priorities? Am I spending more time online than I intended? Does it interfere with my school or work performance or my relationships?"

- *Monitor your feelings*. Ask yourself, "Am I emotionally distracted by my online interests? When I disconnect and move to another activity, how do I feel?"

- *When needed, hide from your online friends who post more frequently*. And in your own postings, practice the golden rule: Ask yourself, "Is this something I'd care about if someone else posted it?"

- *Break the phone-checking habit*. Selective attention—the flashlight of your mind—can be in only one place at a time. When we try to do two things at once, we don't do either one of them very well (Willingham, 2010). If you want to study or work productively—or just give a friend your full attention—resist the temptation to be always available. Disable sound alerts, vibration, and pop-ups. (To reduce distraction, I [ND] am writing while using an app that blocks distracting websites.)

- *Refocus by taking a nature walk*. People learn better after connecting with nature, which—unlike a walk on a busy street—refreshes our capacity for focused attention (Berman et al., 2008). Connecting with nature boosts our spirits and sharpens our mind (Pritchard et al., 2019; Zelenski & Nisbet, 2014).

As psychologist Steven Pinker (2010) said, "The solution is not to bemoan technology but to develop strategies of self-control, as we do with every other temptation in life."

*"It keeps me from looking at my phone every two seconds."*

Liam Walsh/Cartoon Stock

---

## Check Your Understanding

**Examine the Concept**

▶ Explain how social media use is associated with teen mental health.

**Apply the Concept**

▶ Do your connections on social media increase your sense of belonging? Do they sometimes make you feel lonely? Which of the strategies discussed will you find most useful to maintain balance and focus?

*Answers to the Examine the Concept questions can be found in Appendix C at the end of the book.*

# Achievement Motivation

**4.7-5** What is *achievement motivation*, and what are some ways to encourage achievement?

Some motives seem to have little obvious survival value. Billionaires may be motivated to make ever more money, internet celebrities to attract ever more social media followers, politicians to achieve ever more power. And motives vary across cultures. In an individualist culture, employees may work to receive an "employee of the month" award; in a collectivist culture, they may strive to join a company's hardest-working team. The more we achieve, the more we may need to achieve. Psychologist Henry Murray (1938) called this **achievement motivation**.

Achievement motivation matters. One famous study followed the lives of 1528 California children whose intelligence test scores were in the top 1 percent. Forty years later, researchers compared those who were most and least successful professionally. What did the researchers discover? A motivational difference. The most successful were more ambitious, energetic, and persistent. As children, they had more active hobbies. As adults, they participated in more groups and sports (Goleman, 1980). Gifted children are able learners. Accomplished adults are tenacious doers. Most of us are energetic doers when starting and when finishing a project. It's easiest—have you noticed?—to get stuck in the middle. That's when high achievers keep going (Bonezzi et al., 2011). Once they get in a groove, their motivation keeps them in an orbit of goal striving (Foulk et al., 2019). It's no wonder that people with high achievement motivation tend to have greater financial success, healthy social relationships, and good physical and mental health (Steptoe & Wardle, 2017).

In some studies of both secondary school and university students, self-discipline has surpassed intelligence test scores in predicting school performance, attendance, and graduation honors. For school performance, "discipline outdoes talent," concluded researchers Angela Duckworth and Martin Seligman (2005, 2006).

Discipline focuses and refines talent. By their early twenties, top violinists have fiddled away thousands of lifetime practice hours—in fact, double the practice time of other violin students aiming to be teachers (Ericsson 2001, 2006, 2007). A study of outstanding scholars, athletes, and artists found that all were highly motivated and self-disciplined, willing to dedicate hours every day to the pursuit of their goals (Bloom, 1985). But as young Mozart composing at age 8 illustrates, native talent matters, too (Hambrick & Meinz, 2011; Ruthsatz & Urbach, 2012). In sports, music, and chess, people's practice-time differences, while significant, account for a third or less of their performance differences (Hambrick et al., 2014a,b; Macnamara et al., 2014, 2016; Ullén et al., 2016). High achievers benefit from passion and perseverance, but the superstars among them are also distinguished by their extraordinary natural talent.

Duckworth (2016) has a name for passionate dedication to an ambitious, long-term goal: **grit**. Other researchers see grit as similar to conscientiousness or self-control (Credé, 2018; Schmidt et al., 2018; Vazsonyi et al., 2019). Researchers have begun to sleuth the neural and genetic markers of grit (Nemmi et al., 2016; Rimfeld et al., 2016; Wang et al., 2018). Passion and perseverance fuel gritty goal-striving, which can produce great achievements (Jachimowicz et al., 2018; Muenks et al., 2018). Consider Elinor Ostrom: When seeking to enter a PhD economics program, she faced rejection. So she obtained a PhD in political science—and then, four decades later (in 2009), became the first woman to receive the Nobel Prize in economics.

Gritty students are most likely to avoid school burnout and persist in school (Saunders-Scott et al., 2018; Tang et al., 2021). When they experience setbacks, gritty students keep working until they achieve their goal. As basketball star Damian Lillard (2015)

**achievement motivation**
a desire for significant accomplishment, for mastery of skills or ideas, for control, and for attaining a high standard.

**grit** in psychology, passion and perseverance in the pursuit of long-term goals.

**Calum's road: what grit can accomplish** Having spent his life on the Scottish island of Raasay, farming a small patch of land, tending its lighthouse, and fishing, Malcolm ("Calum") MacLeod (1911–1988) felt anguished. His local government repeatedly refused to build a road that would enable vehicles to reach his north end of the island. With the once-flourishing population there having dwindled to two — MacLeod and his wife — he responded with heroic determination. One spring morning in 1964, MacLeod, then in his fifties, gathered an ax, a chopper, a shovel, and a wheelbarrow. By hand, he began to transform the existing footpath into a 1.75-mile road (Miers, 2009).

"With a road," a former neighbor explained, "he hoped new generations of people would return to the north end of Raasay," restoring its culture (Hutchinson, 2006). Day after day he worked through rough hillsides, along hazardous cliff faces, and over peat bogs. Finally, 10 years later, he completed his supreme achievement. The road, which the government has since surfaced, remains a visible example of what vision plus determined grit can accomplish. It bids us each to ponder: What "roads" — what achievements — might we, with sustained effort, build in the years to come?

has said, "If you want to look good in front of thousands, you have to outwork thousands in front of nobody."

Although intelligence is distributed like a bell curve, achievements are not. This tells us that achievement involves much more than raw ability. That's why it pays to know how best to engage people's motivations to achieve. Promising people a reward for an enjoyable task can backfire. Excessive rewards can destroy *intrinsic motivation*. In experiments, children have been promised a payoff for playing with an interesting puzzle or toy. Later, they played with the toy *less* than did unpaid children (Deci et al., 1999; Tang & Hall, 1995). Likewise, rewarding children with toys or candy (or money or screen time) for reading diminishes the time they spend reading (Marinak & Gambrell, 2008). It is as if they think, "If I have to be bribed into doing this, it must not be worth doing!"

To sense the difference between intrinsic motivation and *extrinsic motivation*, think about your experience in this course. Like most students, you probably want to earn a high grade. But what motivates your actions to achieve your goal? Do you feel pressured to finish this reading before a deadline? Are you worried about your grade? Eager for college credit by doing well on the AP® exam? If *Yes*, then you are extrinsically motivated (as, to some extent, all students must be). Do you also find the material interesting? Does learning it make you feel more competent? If there were no grade at stake, might you be curious enough to want to learn the material for its own sake? If *Yes*, intrinsic motivation also fuels your efforts.

People who focus on their work's meaning and significance not only do better work but ultimately earn more extrinsic rewards (Wrzesniewski et al., 2014). Elementary school students with greater-than-average academic intrinsic motivation — who love learning for its own sake — go on to perform better in school, take more challenging classes, and earn more advanced degrees (Fan & Williams, 2018; Gottfried et al., 2006). Wanting to do something, rather than having to do something, seems to pay off (Converse et al., 2019).

Extrinsic rewards work well when people perform tasks that don't naturally inspire complex, creative thinking (Hewett & Conway, 2015). They're also effective when used to signal a job well done (rather than to bribe or control someone) (Boggiano et al., 1985). When administered wisely, rewards can improve performance and spark creativity (Eisenberger & Aselage, 2009; Henderlong & Lepper, 2002). "Most improved player" awards, for example, can boost feelings of competence and increase enjoyment of a sport.

And the rewards that often follow academic achievement, such as scholarships and job opportunities, can have long-lasting benefits.

*Organizational psychologists* seek ways to engage and motivate ordinary people doing ordinary jobs (see Module EM.2).

## Goal Setting

Each of us can adopt some research-based strategies for achieving our goals:

1. *Do make that resolution*. Challenging goals motivate achievement (Harkin et al., 2016). SMART goals are specific, *m*easurable, *a*chievable, realistic, and *t*imely. Such goals—"finish that psychology assignment by Tuesday"—direct attention and motivate persistence.

2. *Announce the goal to friends or family*. We're more likely to follow through after making a public commitment.

3. *Develop an action plan*. Be specific about when, where, and how you'll progress toward your goal. Identify potential challenges and decide how you'll revisit and adjust your plan. People who flesh out goals with detailed plans become more focused and more likely to succeed (Gollwitzer & Oettingen, 2012). Better to concentrate on small steps—spending 5 to 10 minutes learning Arabic vocabulary words each week—than to fantasize about conversing in Arabic.

4. *Create short-term rewards that support long-term goals*. Although delayed rewards motivate us to set goals, immediate rewards best predict our persistence toward those goals (Woolley & Fishbach, 2018).

5. *Monitor and record progress*. If you're striving to perform more exercise, use a wearable fitness tracker or enter your activity in a free fitness app. It's even more motivating when progress is shared rather than hidden (Harkin et al., 2016).

6. *Create a supportive environment*. When trying to eat healthily, keep junk food out of the cupboards. When focusing on a project, hole up in the library. When sleeping, stash the phone. Have your gym bag ready the night before. Such "situational self-control strategies" prevent tempting impulses (Duckworth et al., 2016; Schiffer & Roberts, 2018).

7. *Transform the hard-to-do behavior into a must-do habit*. Habits form when we repeat behaviors in a given context (Module 3.7). Do something every day for about two months and see it become an ingrained habit.

To achieve important life goals, we often know what to do. We *know* that a full night's sleep boosts our alertness, energy, and mood. We *know* that exercise lessens depression and anxiety, builds muscle, and strengthens our heart and mind. We *know* that what we put into our body—junk food or balanced nutrition, addictive substances or clean air—affects our health and longevity. Alas, as T. S. Eliot foresaw, "Between the idea / And the reality . . . / Falls the Shadow." Nevertheless, by taking these seven steps—resolving, announcing, planning, rewarding, monitoring, controlling, and persistently acting—we can create a bridge between the idea and the reality.

AP® Science Practice

## Check Your Understanding

**Examine the Concept**

▶ Explain what is meant by *achievement motivation*.

**Apply the Concept**

▶ What goal would you like to achieve? How might you use the seven strategies offered in this section to meet that goal?

*Answers to the Examine the Concept questions can be found in Appendix C at the end of the book.*

# Module 4.7b REVIEW

### 4.7-3 What evidence points to our human affiliation need — our need to belong?

- Our *affiliation need*—to feel connected and identified with others—had survival value for our ancestors, which may explain why humans in every society live in groups.

- According to *self-determination theory*, we strive to satisfy our needs for competence, autonomy, and relatedness. Self-determined behaviors tend to be *intrinsically motivated* and satisfy these needs. Behaviors that are *extrinsically motivated* tend to undermine these needs.

- Social bonds help us to be healthier and happier, and feeling loved activates brain regions associated with reward and safety systems.

- *Ostracism* is the deliberate exclusion of individuals or groups.

- Social isolation can put us at risk mentally and physically.

### 4.7-4 How does social networking influence us?

- We connect with others through social networking, strengthening our relationships, meeting new friends or romantic partners, and finding support at difficult times.

- But increased online time displaces other activities, and social media use leads people to compare their lives with others. Researchers are investigating possible connections between increasing screen time and a rise in teen mental health problems.

- When networking, people tend toward increased self-disclosure. People with high levels of *narcissism* are especially active on social networking sites.

- Working out strategies for self-control and disciplined usage can help people maintain a healthy balance between their real-world and online time.

### 4.7-5 What is *achievement motivation*, and what are some ways to encourage achievement?

- *Achievement motivation* is a desire for significant accomplishment, for mastery of skills or ideas, for control, and for attaining a high standard.

- High achievement motivation leads to greater success, especially when combined with determined, persistent *grit*.

- Research shows that excessive rewards (driving extrinsic motivation) can undermine intrinsic motivation.

- To achieve our own goals, we can make a resolution; announce the goal; develop an implementation plan; create short-term rewards; monitor and record progress; create a supportive environment; and transform the behavior into a habit.

## AP® Practice Multiple Choice Questions

1. Yancy is a motivational speaker. Based on self-determination theory, what is he most likely to encourage people to pursue in order to find meaning in life?

   a. Money
   b. Close relationships
   c. An average level of intelligence
   d. Traveling

2. Dr. Vulvokov wants to conduct a study on the extent to which affiliation need impacts happiness levels. Which of the following would be an appropriate operational definition of affiliation need in this study?

   a. The amount of money earned
   b. The amount of free time someone uses to pursue their hobbies
   c. The number of degrees someone has earned
   d. The number of close friends someone has

3. Alan plays video games every day after school until 11:00 P.M. Which of the following would be a logical and objective conclusion that one might draw about Alan?

   a. Alan's grades are similar to his peers' grades, although he has lower levels of anxiety than his peers.
   b. Alan's grades are higher than his peers' grades, but he has higher levels of anxiety than his peers.
   c. Alan's grades are lower than his peers' grades, and he has higher levels of anxiety than his peers.
   d. Alan's grades are lower than his peers' grades, but he has lower levels of anxiety than his peers.

**4.** Which of the following graphs roughly depicts the relationship between achievement motivation and mental health?

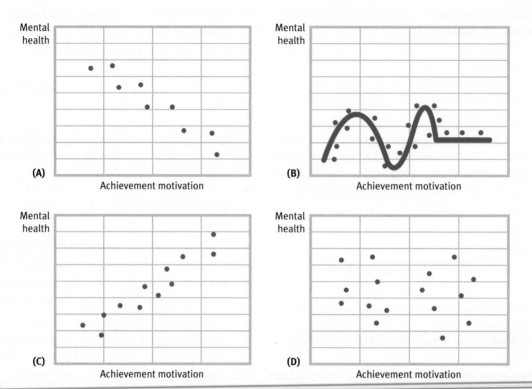

a. Graph A
b. Graph B
c. Graph C
d. Graph D

**5.** Fergie wants to earn the highest possible score on her final chemistry exam. What advice would you give her to help her achieve her goal?

a. "Avoid giving yourself immediate rewards, which diminish motivation."
b. "Visualize how satisfied you'll be when you get your test back and see that A."
c. "Tell your friends and family about your goal rather than keeping it to yourself."
d. "Avoid over-monitoring yourself, which leads to performance anxiety."

**6.** Fifth-graders Josslyn and JaCorie each got an A on their science project. Josslyn worked hard because her parents give her money whenever she earns a grade above a B on an assignment. JaCorie worked hard because he enjoys learning. Which of the following are logical and objective future outcomes for Josslyn and JaCorie?

a. Josslyn is likely to earn more extrinsic rewards than JaCorie.
b. Josslyn is likely to perform better in school than JaCorie.
c. JaCorie is likely to earn more advanced degrees than Josslyn.
d. JaCorie is likely to take fewer challenging classes than Josslyn.

7. Paola believes that humans are "social animals." Which of the following best aligns with Paola's views?
   a. Affiliation need
   b. Achievement motivation
   c. Self-determination theory
   d. Social comparison

8. Sandra's friends excluded her from a party, and she is feeling shunned and left out. Sandra is experiencing
   a. belonging.
   b. ostracism.
   c. self-determination.
   d. affiliation.

# Module 4.7c Motivation: Hunger Motivation

## LEARNING TARGETS

**4.7-6** Explain the physiological factors that produce hunger.

**4.7-7** Explain the cultural and situational factors that influence hunger.

Physiological needs are powerful. In a vivid demonstration, Ancel Keys and his research team (1950) studied semistarvation among volunteers, who participated as an alternative to military service. After feeding 200 men normally for 3 months, researchers halved the food intake for 36 of them. These semistarved men became listless and apathetic as their bodies conserved energy. Eventually, their body weights stabilized about 25 percent below their starting weights.

Consistent with Abraham Maslow's idea of a needs hierarchy, the men became food-obsessed. They talked food. They daydreamed food. They collected recipes, read cookbooks, and feasted their eyes on delectable forbidden food. Preoccupied with their unmet basic need, they lost interest in sex and social activities. As one man reported, "If we see a show, the most interesting part of it is

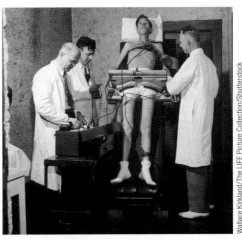

Wallace Kirkland/The LIFE Picture Collection/Shutterstock

**Studying starvation in conscientious objectors**
Researchers carefully recorded and analyzed the physiological and psychological effects of 6 months of starvation, and various methods for rehabilitation. They hoped to support the recovery of World War II famine victims.

**AP® Science Practice**

### Research

The starvation study likely could not be conducted today. Modern psychological scientists must follow ethical guidelines that, among other things, protect participants from greater-than-usual harm and discomfort. You can review these guidelines in Module 0.5.

*"Never hunt when you're hungry."*

contained in scenes where people are eating. I couldn't laugh at the funniest picture in the world, and love scenes are completely dull." The semistarved men's preoccupations illustrate how powerful motives can hijack our consciousness.

## The Physiology of Hunger

**4.7-6** What physiological factors produce hunger?

Deprived of a normal food supply, Keys' semistarved volunteers were clearly hungry. But what precisely triggers hunger? Is it the pangs of an empty stomach? So it seemed to A. L. Washburn. Working with Walter Cannon, Washburn agreed to swallow a balloon attached to a recording device (Cannon & Washburn, 1912) (**Figure 4.7-2**). When inflated to fill his stomach, the balloon transmitted his stomach contractions. Washburn supplied information about his *feelings* of hunger by pressing a key each time he felt a hunger pang. The discovery: Whenever Washburn felt hungry, he was indeed having stomach contractions.

### Figure 4.7-2
### Monitoring stomach contractions

(Information from Cannon, 1929.) Can hunger exist without stomach pangs? To answer that question, researchers removed some rats' stomachs, creating a direct path to their small intestines (Tsang, 1938). Did the rats continue to eat? Indeed they did. Some hunger similarly persists in humans whose stomachs have been removed due to ulcers or cancer. So the pangs of an empty stomach are not the *only* source of hunger. What else might trigger hunger?

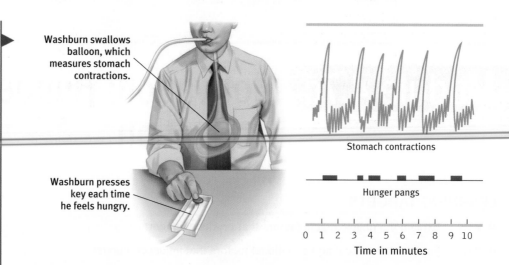

Washburn swallows balloon, which measures stomach contractions.

Washburn presses key each time he feels hungry.

Stomach contractions

Hunger pangs

Time in minutes

## Body Chemistry and the Brain

Somehow, somewhere, your body is keeping tabs on the energy it takes in and the energy it uses. If this weren't true, you would be unable to maintain a stable body weight. A major source of energy in your body is the blood sugar **glucose**. If your blood glucose level drops, you won't consciously feel the lower blood sugar, but your stomach, intestines, and liver will signal your brain to motivate eating. Your brain, which is automatically monitoring your blood chemistry and your body's internal state, will then trigger hunger.

How does the brain integrate these messages and sound the alarm? Several neural areas—some housed in the *hippocampus* and the *hypothalamus*—do the work (Stevenson & Francis, 2017; **Figure 4.7-3**). Hormones, regulated by the hypothalamus via the pituitary gland, influence feelings of hunger and satiety. One neural network in the hypothalamus has a center that secretes appetite-stimulating hormones. When it is stimulated electrically, well-fed animals begin to eat. If it is destroyed, even starving animals have no interest in food. Another neural center secretes appetite-suppressing hormones. When it is stimulated electrically, animals will stop eating. Destroy this area and animals can't stop eating (see Figure 4.7-3b) (Duggan & Booth, 1986; Hoebel & Teitelbaum, 1966).

Blood vessels connect the hypothalamus to the rest of the body, so it can respond to our current blood chemistry and other incoming information. One of its tasks is monitoring

**glucose** the form of sugar that circulates in the blood and provides the major source of energy for body tissues. When its level is low, we feel hunger.

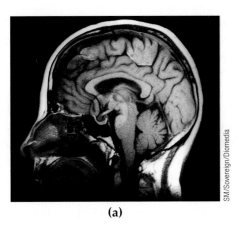 

(a) (b)

SM/Sovereign/Diomedia

Voisin/Phanie/Science Source

**Figure 4.7-3**
**The hypothalamus**

(a) The hypothalamus (colored orange) performs various body maintenance functions, including control of hunger. Blood vessels supply the hypothalamus, enabling it to respond to our current blood chemistry as well as to incoming neural information about the body's state. (b) The overweight mouse on the left has nonfunctioning receptors in the appetite-suppressing part of the hypothalamus.

levels of appetite hormones, such as *ghrelin*, a hunger-arousing hormone secreted by an empty stomach. During bypass surgery for severe *obesity*, surgeons seal off or remove part of the stomach. The remaining stomach then produces much less ghrelin, reducing the person's appetite and making food less enticing (Ammori, 2013; Lemonick, 2002; Scholtz et al., 2013). Other appetite hormones include *orexin*, *leptin*, and *PYY;* **Figure 4.7-4** describes how they influence our feelings of hunger.

If you lose some extra weight and later find it creeping back, you can also blame your brain for your weight regain (Cornier, 2011). The interaction of appetite hormones and brain activity suggests that the body has some sort of "weight thermostat." When semistarved rats fall below their normal weight, this system signals the body to restore the lost weight. It's as though fat cells cry out "Feed me!" and grab glucose from the bloodstream (Ludwig & Friedman, 2014). Hunger increases and energy output decreases. In this way, rats (and humans) tend to hover around a stable weight, or **set point**, influenced in part by heredity (Keesey & Corbett, 1984).

 **AP® Science Practice**

## Research

The American Psychological Association has ethical guidelines for the care and treatment of animals in research, just as it does for human participants.

**set point** the point at which the "weight thermostat" may be set. When the body falls below this weight, increased hunger and a lowered metabolic rate may combine to restore lost weight.

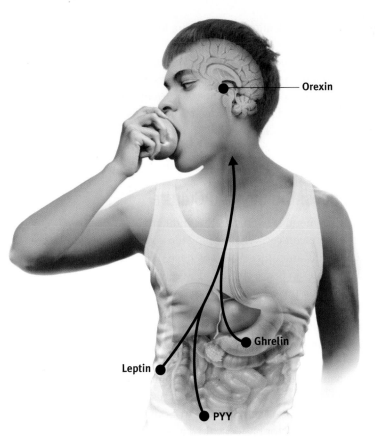

— Orexin

Ghrelin

Leptin

PYY

**Figure 4.7-4**
**The appetite hormones**
**Increases appetite**
- *Ghrelin*: Hormone secreted by empty stomach; sends "I'm hungry" signals to the brain.
- *Orexin*: Hunger-triggering hormone secreted by hypothalamus.

**Decreases appetite**
- *Leptin*: Protein hormone secreted by fat cells; when abundant, causes the brain to increase metabolism and decrease hunger.
- *PYY*: Digestive tract hormone; sends "I'm *not* hungry" signals to the brain.

**basal metabolic rate** the body's resting rate of energy output.

We humans (and other species, too) vary in our **basal metabolic rate**, the resting rate of energy expenditure for maintaining basic body functions. But we share a common response to decreased food intake: Our basal metabolic rate drops, as it did for participants in Keys' experiment. After 24 weeks of semistarvation, they stabilized at three-fourths of their normal weight, even though they were taking in only *half* their previous calories. How did they achieve this dieter's nightmare? They reduced their energy expenditure, partly because they were less active, but partly because their basal metabolic rate dropped by 29 percent.

Some researchers, however, doubt that our bodies have a preset tendency to maintain optimal weight (Assanand et al., 1998). They point out that slow, sustained changes in body weight can alter a person's set point, and that psychological factors also sometimes drive our feelings of hunger. Given unlimited access to a wide variety of tasty foods, people and other animals tend to overeat and gain weight (Raynor & Epstein, 2001). Thus, many researchers prefer the term *settling point* to indicate the level at which a person's weight settles in response to caloric intake and expenditure (which are influenced by environment as well as biology).

AP® Science Practice

## Check Your Understanding

### Examine the Concept

▶ Explain the body's set point and how it relates to hunger.

▶ Explain how ghrelin levels relate to hunger.

### Apply the Concept

▶ Have you ever been extremely hungry and experienced the kind of food-distracted thoughts Ancel Keys' volunteers experienced? How did that affect your behavior?

*Answers to the Examine the Concept questions can be found in Appendix C at the end of the book.*

## The Psychology of Hunger

**4.7-7** What cultural and situational factors influence hunger?

Our internal hunger is pushed by our physiology—our body chemistry and brain activity. Yet there is more to hunger than meets the stomach. This was strikingly apparent when researchers tested two patients who had no memory for events occurring more than a minute ago (Rozin et al., 1998). If offered a second lunch 20 minutes after eating a normal lunch, both patients readily consumed it . . . and usually a third meal offered 20 minutes after they finished the second. This suggests that one part of our decision to eat is our memory of our last meal. As time passes, we think about eating again, and those thoughts trigger feelings of hunger.

## Taste Preferences: Biology and Culture

Body cues and environmental factors together influence not only the *when* of hunger, but also the *what*—our taste preferences. When feeling tense or depressed, do you tend to take solace in high-calorie foods, as ardent football fans have done after a big loss (Cornil & Chandon, 2013)? The carbohydrates in pizza, chips, and sweets help boost levels of the neurotransmitter serotonin, which has calming effects. When dieting and stressed, both rats and many humans find it extra rewarding to gobble up Oreos (Boggiano et al., 2005; Sproesser et al., 2014). And people living stressed lives tend to put on more weight (Mehlig et al., 2020).

Our preferences for sweet and salty tastes are genetic and universal, but conditioning can intensify or alter those preferences. People given highly salted foods may develop a liking for excess salt (Beauchamp, 1987). People sickened by a food may develop an aversion to it. (The frequency of children's illnesses provides many chances for them to learn to avoid certain foods.)

Culture affects taste, too. Many people in Southeast Asian countries enjoy *durian*, a fruit that one Western detractor has described as smelling like "turpentine and onions, garnished with a gym sock" (Sterling, 2003). East Asians may be similarly repulsed by what

(a)            (b)

**An acquired taste** People everywhere learn to enjoy the fatty, bitter, or spicy foods common in their culture. (a) For these Alaska Natives, but not for most other North Americans, whale blubber is a tasty treat. (b) For Peruvians, roasted guinea pig is similarly delicious.

many Westerners love—"the rotted bodily fluid of an ungulate" (a.k.a. cheese, some varieties of which have the same bacteria and odor as stinky feet) (Herz, 2012).

But there is biological wisdom to many of our taste preferences. For example, in regions with hot climates where foods spoil more quickly, recipes often include spices that inhibit bacterial growth (**Figure 4.7-5**). Pregnancy-related food dislikes—and the nausea associated with them—peak about the tenth week, when the developing embryo is most vulnerable to toxins. Thus, many pregnant women naturally avoid potentially harmful foods and other substances, such as alcoholic and caffeinated beverages (Forbes et al., 2018; Gaskins et al., 2018).

Rats tend to avoid unfamiliar foods (Sclafani, 1995). So do we humans, especially those that are animal-based. This dislike of unfamiliar things surely was adaptive for our ancestors by protecting them from potentially toxic substances. In experiments, people who repeatedly try small samples of an unfamiliar food or drink begin to dislike it less (Pliner, 1982; Pliner et al., 1993).

## Situational Influences on Eating

Situations also influence our eating—a phenomenon psychologists have called the *ecology of eating*. Time of day, for example, can affect both our feelings of hunger and the kinds of foods we crave. Here are some other situational influences you may have noticed:

- *Friends and food:* Do you eat more when eating with friends? Most of us do (Cummings & Tomiyama, 2019). But when we're trying to impress an attractive date, we often eat less (Baker et al., 2019).

- *Serving size:* Researchers studied the effects of portion size by offering people varieties of free snacks: full or half pretzels, big or little Tootsie Rolls, or a small or large serving scoop with a bowl of M&M'S (Geier et al., 2006). Offered a supersized portion, people put away more calories. Larger portions induce bigger bites, which may increase intake by decreasing oral exposure time (Herman et al., 2015). Portion size matters.

- *Stimulating selections:* Food variety also stimulates eating. Offered a dessert buffet, people eat more than they do when choosing a portion from one favorite dessert. For our early ancestors, variety was healthy. When foods were abundant and varied, eating more provided a wide range of vitamins and minerals and produced protective fat for winter cold or famine. When a bounty of varied foods was unavailable, eating less extended the food supply until winter or famine ended (Polivy et al., 2008; Remick et al., 2009).

- *Nudging nutrition:* When carrots appeared early (rather than late) in a lunch line, schoolchildren took four times more carrots (Redden et al., 2015). In other ways, too—nutrition labeling, healthy food defaults, taxing what's unhealthy—we can structure an environment that promotes healthier eating (Roberto, 2020). Such "nudges" show how psychological science can improve our everyday life.

### Data

Consider the scatterplot in Figure 4.7-5. Do these data represent a positive or negative correlation? Unsure? Review correlation coefficients in Module 0.4.

**Figure 4.7-5**
**Hot climates and hot spices**

Countries with hot climates, in which food historically spoiled more quickly, feature recipes with more bacteria-inhibiting spices (Sherman & Flaxman, 2001). India averages nearly 10 spices per meat recipe; Finland, 2 spices.

# Check Your Understanding

## Examine the Concept

▶ Explain some ways in which culture influences taste preferences.

## Apply the Concept

▶ After an 8-hour hike without food, your long-awaited favorite dish is placed in front of you, and your mouth waters in anticipation. Why?

▶ Do you usually eat only when your body sends hunger signals? How much does the sight or smell of delicious food tempt you even when you're full?

*Answers to the Examine the Concept questions can be found in Appendix C at the end of the book.*

---

**obesity** defined as a body mass index (BMI) measurement of 30 or higher, which is calculated from our weight-to-height ratio. (Individuals who are *overweight* have a BMI of 25 or higher.)

\* \* \*

To consider how hunger and other factors affect our risks for **obesity**, see Developing Arguments: The Challenges of Obesity and Weight Control. And for tips on improving eating habits, see **Table 4.7-2**.

---

### TABLE 4.7-2 Tips for Healthy Eating

For those seeking healthier eating habits that can boost energy and longevity, here are some evidence-based guidelines (Sole-Smith, 2020):

- *Healthy eating requires a healthy attitude.* Those who believe their weight is malleable most often succeed in healthful monitoring (Ehrlinger et al., 2017).

- *Exercise and get enough sleep.* Especially when supported by 7 to 8 hours of sleep a night, exercise empties fat cells, builds muscle, speeds up metabolism, helps lower your settling point, and reduces stress and stress-induced craving for carbohydrate-rich comfort foods (Bennett, 1995; Ruotsalainen et al., 2015; Thompson et al., 1982). Among TV's *Biggest Loser* competitors, exercise predicted less weight regain (Kerns et al., 2017).

- *Minimize exposure to tempting food cues.* Food-shop on a full stomach. Keep unhealthy foods out of your home, and tuck away special-occasion foods. You can't eat it if you can't reach it.

- *Limit variety and eat healthy foods.* Given more variety, people consume more. So, eat simple meals with protein, vegetables, fruits, and whole grains. Healthy fats, such as those found in olive oil and fish, help regulate appetite (Taubes, 2001, 2002). Water- and vitamin-rich veggies can fill the stomach with few calories. Better crispy greens than Krispy Kremes.

- *Reduce portion sizes and relabel your portions.* When offered less, people consume less. People also eat less when they think of a portion as a number of items (10 chips) rather than as a general quantity (1 serving of chips) (Lewis & Earl, 2018).

- *Time your intake.* We tend to have a healthier weight (and better sleep) when we eat our last meal in the early evening and then hold off eating or drinking more until the next morning's breakfast (Wilkinson et al., 2020). Eating our heavier meals earlier in the day boosts metabolism, and eating a balanced breakfast helps us to feel more alert and less fatigued by late morning (Spring et al., 1992).

- *Beware of the binge*. The urge to eat can be unleashed in adults who drink alcohol or start feeling anxious or depressed (Herman & Polivy, 1980; Mehlig et al., 2020). And take note: Eating slowly can lead to eating less (Hurst & Fukuda, 2018; Martin et al., 2007).

- *Before eating with others, decide what and how much you want to eat.* Eating with friends can distract us from monitoring our own eating (Ward & Mann, 2000).

- *Allow for an occasional treat.* A lapse need not become a collapse in a move toward healthier eating.

- *Chart your progress online.* Those who record and publicly disclose their progress toward a goal more often achieve it (Harkin et al., 2016).

- *Connect to a support group.* Join with others, either face-to-face or online, to share goals and progress updates (Freedman, 2011).

AP® Science Practice

# Developing Arguments

## The Challenges of Obesity and Weight Control

## Obesity and Its Health Effects

Obesity is associated with:
- **physical health risks**, including diabetes, high blood pressure, heart disease, gallstones, arthritis, and certain types of cancer.[1]
  - **increased depression,** especially among women.[2]
  - **bullying,** outranking race and sexual orientation as the biggest reason for youth bullying in Western cultures.[3]

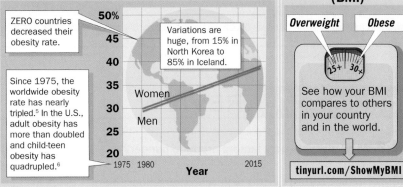

**Percentage Overweight in 195 Countries Studied[4]**

ZERO countries decreased their obesity rate.

Variations are huge, from 15% in North Korea to 85% in Iceland.

Since 1975, the worldwide obesity rate has nearly tripled.[5] In the U.S., adult obesity has more than doubled and child-teen obesity has quadrupled.[6]

Women
Men

Year
1975 1980 2015

**Body Mass Index (BMI)**

Overweight   Obese

25+   30+

See how your BMI compares to others in your country and in the world.

tinyurl.com/ShowMyBMI

## How Did We Get Here?

Does obesity reflect a simple lack of willpower, as some people presume?[7]
**No.** Many factors contribute to obesity.

### PHYSIOLOGY FACTORS

#### Storing fat was adaptive.

- This ideal form of stored energy carried our ancestors through periods of famine. People in some impoverished places still find heavier bodies attractive, as plumpness signals affluence and status.[8]
- In food-rich countries, the drive for fat has become dysfunctional.[9]

fat cell

#### Set point and metabolism matter.

- Fat (lower metabolic rate than muscle) requires less food intake to maintain than it did to gain.
- If weight drops below *set point/settling point*, the brain triggers more hunger and a slowed metabolism.
  - Body perceives STARVATION; adapts by burning fewer calories. Most dieters in the long run regain what they lose on weight-loss programs.[10]
  - After 30 weeks of competition on TV's *The Biggest Loser*, 6 years later only 1 of 14 contestants had kept the weight off. On average, they regained 70% of what they lost, and their metabolism remained slow.[11]

#### Genes influence us.

- Lean people seem naturally disposed to move about, burning more calories than energy-conserving overweight people, who tend to sit still longer.[12]
- Adoptive siblings' body weights are uncorrelated with one another or with their adoptive parents, instead resembling their biological parents' weight.[13]
- Identical twins have closely similar weights, even if raised apart.[14] Much lower *fraternal* twin weight correlation suggests genes explain 2/3 of our varying body mass.[15]
- More than 100 genes have been identified as each affecting weight in some small way.[16]

### ENVIRONMENTAL FACTORS

- **Sleep loss** makes us more vulnerable to obesity.[17]

*Increasing*

*Decreasing*

**Sleep deprivation**

**Ghrelin**—appetite-stimulating stomach hormone

**Leptin**—reports body fat to the brain

**NOTE:** With weight, as with intelligence and other characteristics, there can be high levels of *heritability* (genetic influence on *individual* differences) without heredity explaining *group* differences. Genes mostly determine why one person is heavier than another. Environment mostly determines why people today are heavier than people were 50 years ago.

- **Social influences:** Our own odds of becoming obese triple if a close friend becomes obese.[18]
- **Food and activity levels:** Worldwide, we eat more energy-dense foods and we move less, with 31% of adults (including 43% of Americans and 25% of Europeans) now sedentary—averaging <20 minutes per day of moderate activity such as walking.[19]

## Developing Arguments Questions

**1.** Identify scientifically derived evidence that obesity impacts health.

**2.** Use scientifically derived evidence to support the claim that factors other than willpower contribute to obesity.

1. Kitahara et al., 2014. 2. Haynes et al., 2019; Jung et al., 2017; Rivera et al., 2017. 3. Puhl et al., 2015. 4. GBD, 2017. 5. NCD, 2016. 6. Flegal et al., 2010, 2012, 2016. 7. NORC, 2016b.
8. Furnham & Baguma, 1994; Nettle et al., 2017; Swami, 2015. 9. Hall, 2016. 10. Mann et al., 2015. 11. Fothergill et al., 2016. 12. Levine et al., 2005. 13. Grilo & Pogue-Geile, 1991.
14. Hjelmborg et al., 2008; Plomin et al., 1997. 15. Maes et al., 1997. 16. Akiyama et al., 2017. 17. Keith et al., 2006; Nedeltcheva et al., 2010; Taheri, 2004; Taheri et al., 2004.
18. Christakis & Fowler, 2007. 19. Hallal et al., 2012.

## Check Your Understanding

**Examine the Concept**

▶ Why can two people of the same height, age, and activity level maintain the same weight, even if one of them eats much less than the other does?

**Apply the Concept**

▶ How would you rate your eating habits? What would you like to improve, and which healthy-eating strategies would help you the most?

*Answers to the Examine the Concept questions can be found in Appendix C at the end of the book.*

# Module 4.7c REVIEW

**4.7-6 What physiological factors produce hunger?**

● Hunger pangs correspond to stomach contractions, but hunger also has other causes.

● Brain areas, some within the hippocampus and the hypothalamus, monitor blood chemistry (including *glucose* level) and incoming information about the body's state.

● Appetite hormones include ghrelin (secreted by an empty stomach), leptin (secreted by fat cells), orexin (secreted by the hypothalamus), and PYY (secreted by the digestive tract).

● *Basal metabolic rate* is the body's resting rate of energy expenditure.

● The body may have a *set point* (a biologically fixed tendency to maintain an optimal weight) or a looser settling point (also influenced by the environment).

**4.7-7 What cultural and situational factors influence hunger?**

● Hunger reflects our memory of when we last ate and our expectation of when we should eat again.

● Humans as a species prefer certain tastes (such as sweet and salty), but our individual preferences are also influenced by conditioning, culture, and situation.

● Some taste preferences have survival value.

● Situational influences include time of day, the presence of others, serving size, and the variety of foods offered.

# AP® Practice Multiple Choice Questions

**1.** Dr. Gavin studies the sugar found in the bloodstream that provides energy for the human body. Gavin studies

  a. orexin.
  b. leptin.
  c. PYY.
  d. glucose.

**2.** Which of the following would be an appropriate operational definition for a researcher who wants to study hunger-arousing factors?

  a. Leptin levels
  b. PYY levels
  c. Orexin levels
  d. Set point levels

**3.** Which of the following best explains, in terms of ethical principles, why Ancel Keys' semistarvation study would be unlikely to be conducted today?

  a. The participants experienced greater-than-usual harm in the study because the participants likely experienced permanently decreased glucose levels.
  b. The participants experienced greater-than-usual harm in the study because the participants' basal metabolic rates were possibly impacted past the duration of the study.
  c. The participants experienced greater-than-usual harm in the study because the participants experienced a disruption in the ecology of eating.
  d. The participants experienced greater-than-usual harm in the study because the participants' arcuate nuclei were destroyed.

**Use the following text to answer questions 4 & 5:**

Harvey's weight has remained approximately the same over the last 10 years. However, when he turned 38, he decided that he wanted to eat smaller portions at each meal. He lost weight quickly after this decrease in caloric intake, but he noticed that his weight loss slowed over time.

4. Which of the following best explains why Harvey's weight remained the same for a decade?

   a. Arcuate nucleus
   b. Set point
   c. Ecology of eating
   d. PYY

5. Which of the following best explains Harvey's slowed weight loss over time after he reduced the amount of food he ate at each meal?

   a. His PYY level increased.
   b. His orexin level increased.
   c. His basal metabolic rate decreased.
   d. His ghrelin level decreased.

6. Which of the following research methods has been used to support the genetic influence on weight?

   a. Case studies
   b. Twin studies
   c. Experiments
   d. Surveys

# Module 4.8a Emotion: Theories and Physiology of Emotion

## LEARNING TARGETS

**4.8-1** Explain how arousal, expressive behavior, and cognition interact in emotion.

**4.8-2** Explain whether we can experience emotions without consciously interpreting and labeling them.

**4.8-3** Identify some of the basic emotions.

**4.8-4** Explain the link between emotional arousal and the autonomic nervous system.

**4.8-5** Explain how emotions activate different physiological and brain-pattern responses.

Motivated behavior is often connected to powerful emotions. You can surely recall a time when emotion overwhelmed you. I [DM] retain a flashbulb memory of the day I went to a huge store and brought along Peter, my toddler first-born child. As I set Peter down on his feet for a moment so I could do some paperwork, a passerby warned, "You'd better be careful or you'll lose that boy!" Not more than a few breaths later, I turned and found no Peter beside me.

With mild anxiety, I looked around one end of the store aisle. No Peter in sight. With slightly more anxiety, I peered around the other side. No Peter there, either. Now, with my heart accelerating, I circled the neighboring counters. Still no Peter anywhere. As anxiety turned to panic, I began racing up and down the store aisles. He was nowhere to be found. The alerted store manager used the intercom to ask customers to assist in looking for a missing child. Soon after, I passed the customer who had warned me. "I told you that you were going to lose him!" he now scolded. With visions of kidnapping (strangers routinely adored that beautiful child), I braced for the unthinkable possibility that my negligence had caused me to lose what I loved above all else, and—dread of all dreads—that I might have to return home and face my wife after losing our only child.

But then, as I passed the customer service counter yet again, there he was, having been found and returned by some obliging customer. In an instant, the arousal of terror spilled into ecstasy. Clutching my son, with tears suddenly flowing, I found myself unable to speak my thanks and stumbled out of the store awash in grateful joy.

Emotions are subjective. But they are real. As researcher Lisa Feldman Barrett (2012, 2013) notes, "My experience of anger is not an illusion. When I'm angry, I feel angry. That's real." Where do our emotions come from? Why do we have them? What are they made of?

Emotions are our body's adaptive response. They "are our body's way of ensuring we do what is best for us," observes Frans de Waal (2019). Anger can elicit a concession. Gratitude strengthens relationships. Pride motivates hard work (Weidman & Kross, 2021). "I look at fear not as cowardice," wrote poet Amanda Gorman (2022), "but as a call forward, a summons to fight for what we hold dear."

When we face challenges, emotions focus our attention and energize our actions (Cyders & Smith, 2008). Our heart races. Our pace quickens. All our senses go on high alert.

Courtesy of David Myers

By integrating data from our environment, our body, and our experiences, we feel emotional stress (Francis, 2018).

Emotions can also be positive. Receiving unexpected good news, we may find our eyes tearing up. We raise our hands triumphantly. We feel exuberance and a newfound confidence. Yet negative and prolonged emotions can harm our health.

# Emotion: Arousal, Behavior, and Cognition

**4.8-1** How do arousal, expressive behavior, and cognition interact in emotion?

**Emotion**, or *affect*, is a complex process distinct from knowledge and reasoning. As my panicked search for Peter illustrates, emotions are a mix of:

- **bodily arousal** (heart pounding).
- **expressive behaviors** (quickened pace).
- **conscious experience** (*Is this a kidnapping?*) and **feelings** (panic, fear, joy).

Not only emotion, but most psychological phenomena (vision, sleep, memory, sex, and so forth) can be approached these three ways—physiologically, behaviorally, and cognitively. The puzzle for psychologists is fitting these three pieces together. To do that, the first researchers of emotion considered two big questions:

1. A chicken-and-egg debate: Does your bodily arousal come *before* or *after* your emotional feelings? (Did I first notice my racing heart and faster step, and then feel terror about losing Peter? Or did my sense of fear come first, stirring my heart and legs to respond?)

2. How do *thinking* (cognition) and *feeling* interact? Does cognition always come before emotion? (Did I think about a kidnapping threat before I reacted emotionally?)

The psychological study of emotion began with the first question: How do bodily responses relate to emotions? Two of the earliest emotion theories offered different answers.

## Arousal Comes Before Emotion

Common sense tells most of us that we cry because we are sad, lash out because we are angry, tremble because we are afraid. But to pioneering psychologist William James, this commonsense view of emotion had things backward. Rather, "We feel sorry because we cry, angry because we strike, afraid because we tremble" (James, 1890, p. 1066). To James, emotions result from attention to our bodily activity. James' idea was also proposed by Danish physiologist Carl Lange, and so is called the *James-Lange theory*. James and Lange would have guessed that I noticed my racing heart and then, shaking with fright, felt the whoosh of emotion—that my feeling of fear *followed* my body's response.

## Arousal and Emotion Occur Simultaneously

Physiologist Walter Cannon (1871–1945) disagreed with the James-Lange theory. Does a racing heart signal fear or anger or love? The body's responses—heart rate, perspiration, and body temperature—are too similar, and they change too slowly, to *cause* the different emotions, said Cannon. He, and later another physiologist, Philip Bard, concluded that our bodily responses and experienced emotions occur separately but simultaneously. So, according to the *Cannon-Bard theory*, my heart began pounding *as* I experienced fear. The emotion-triggering stimulus traveled to my sympathetic nervous system, causing my body's arousal. *At the same time*, it traveled to my brain's cortex, causing my awareness of my emotion. My pounding heart did not cause my feeling of fear, nor did my feeling of fear cause my pounding heart.

MATT SULLIVAN/REUTERS/Newscom

**Joy expressed** According to the James-Lange theory, we don't just smile because we share our teammates' joy. We also share the joy because we are smiling with them.

**emotion** a response of the whole organism, involving (1) physiological arousal, (2) expressive behaviors, and, most importantly, (3) conscious experience resulting from one's interpretations.

### Research

Obviously, researchers could never intentionally sever someone's spinal cord — so, they rely on case studies, which are a non-experimental method. Case studies show us what can happen and offer ideas for further study.

But are they really independent of each other? Countering the Cannon-Bard theory are studies of people with severed spinal cords, including a survey of 25 World War II soldiers (Hohmann, 1966). Those with *lower-spine injuries*, who had lost sensation only in their legs, reported little change in their emotions' intensity. Those with *high spinal cord injury*, who could feel nothing below the neck, did report changes. Some reactions were much less intense than before the injuries. Anger, one man with this injury type revealed, "just doesn't have the heat to it that it used to. It's a mental kind of anger." Other emotions, those expressed mostly in body areas above the neck, were felt *more* intensely. These men reported increases in weeping, lumps in the throat, and getting choked up when saying good-bye, worshiping, or watching a touching movie. Such evidence has led some researchers to view feelings as "mostly shadows" of our bodily responses and behaviors (Damasio, 2003).

But our emotions also involve cognition (Averill, 1993; Barrett, 2006, 2017). Here we arrive at psychology's second big emotion question: How do thinking and feeling interact? Whether we fear the man behind us on a dark street depends entirely on whether we interpret him as threatening.

## Arousal + Label = Emotion

**4.8-2** To experience emotions, must we consciously interpret and label them?

Stanley Schachter and Jerome Singer (1962) demonstrated that how we *appraise* (interpret) our experiences also matters. Our physical reactions *and our thoughts* (perceptions, memories, and interpretations) together create emotion. In their *two-factor theory*, emotions have two ingredients: physical arousal and cognitive appraisal. An emotional experience, they argued, requires a conscious interpretation of arousal.

Consider how arousal spills over from one event to the next. Imagine returning home after an invigorating run and finding that you'd received a longed-for college acceptance letter. With arousal lingering from the run, would you feel more elated than if you heard this news after staying awake all night studying?

To explore this *spillover effect*, Schachter and Singer injected college men with the hormone *epinephrine*, which triggers feelings of arousal. One group of men was told to expect feelings of arousal from the injection. Others were told by the trickster researchers that it would help test their eyesight. Picture yourself as a participant: After receiving the injection, you go to a waiting room, where you find yourself with another person (actually an accomplice of the experimenters) who is acting either euphoric or irritated. As you observe this person, you begin to feel your heart race, your skin flush, and your breathing become

**The spillover effect** Arousal from a soccer match can fuel anger, which can descend into rioting or other violent confrontations.

more rapid. If you had been in the group told to expect these effects from the injection, what would you feel? In the experiment, these volunteers felt little emotion—because they correctly attributed their arousal to the drug. But if you had been told the injection would help assess your eyesight, what would you feel? Perhaps you would react as this group of participants did. They "caught" the apparent emotion of the other person in the waiting room. They became happy if the accomplice was acting euphoric, and testy if the accomplice was acting irritated.

This discovery—that a stirred-up state can be experienced as one emotion or another, depending on how we interpret and label it—has been replicated in dozens of experiments and continues to influence modern emotion research (MacCormack & Lindquist, 2016; Reisenzein, 1983; Sinclair et al., 1994). *The point to remember:* Arousal fuels emotion; cognition channels it.

# Does Cognition Always Precede Emotion?

But is the heart always subject to the mind? Must we *always* interpret our arousal before we can experience an emotion? Robert Zajonc [ZI-unts] (1923–2008) didn't think so. He contended that we actually have many emotional reactions apart from, or even before, our conscious interpretation of a situation (Zajonc, 1980, 1984). Perhaps you can recall liking (or disliking) something or someone immediately, without knowing why.

Even when people repeatedly view stimuli flashed too briefly for them to interpret, they come to prefer those stimuli (Kunst-Wilson & Zajonc, 1980). Unaware of having previously seen them, they nevertheless like them. We also have an acutely sensitive automatic radar for emotionally significant information; even a subliminally flashed stimulus can prime us to feel better or worse about a follow-up stimulus (Murphy et al., 1995; Zeelenberg et al., 2006).

Neuroscientists are charting the neural pathways of emotions (Ochsner et al., 2009). Our emotional responses can follow two different brain pathways. Some emotions (especially more complex feelings such as hatred and love) travel a "high road." A stimulus following this path would travel (by way of the thalamus) to the brain's cortex (**Figure 4.8-1**). There, it would be analyzed and labeled before the response command is sent out, via the amygdala (an emotion-control center).

But sometimes our emotions (especially simple likes, dislikes, and fears) take what Joseph LeDoux (2002, 2015) has called the more direct "low road," a neural shortcut that bypasses the cortex. Following the low road, a fear-provoking stimulus would travel from the eye or ear (again via the thalamus) directly to the amygdala (Figure 4.8-1b). This shortcut enables our greased-lightning emotional response before our intellect intervenes. Like speedy reflexes (which also operate separately from the brain's thinking cortex), the amygdala's reactions are so fast that we may be unaware of what's transpired (Dimberg et al., 2000). A conscious fear experience then occurs as we become aware that our brain has detected danger (LeDoux & Brown, 2017).

The amygdala sends more neural projections up to the cortex than it receives back, which makes it easier for our feelings to hijack our thinking than for our thinking to rule our feelings (LeDoux & Armony, 1999). Thus, in the forest, we can jump at the sound of rustling bushes nearby, leaving it to our cortex to decide later whether the sound was made by a snake or by the wind. Such experiences support Zajonc's and LeDoux's belief that *some* of our emotional reactions involve no deliberate thinking.

Emotion researcher Richard Lazarus (1991, 1998) agreed that our brain processes vast amounts of information without our conscious awareness, and that some emotional responses do not require *conscious* thinking. Much of our emotional life operates via the automatic, speedy low road. But he further wondered: How would we *know* what we are reacting to if we did not in some way appraise the situation? The appraisal may be effortless and we may not be conscious of it, but it is still a mental function. To know whether a stimulus is good or bad, the brain must have some

### Figure 4.8-1
**The brain's pathways for emotions**

In the two-track brain, sensory input may be routed (a) to the cortex (via the thalamus) for analysis and then transmission to the amygdala; or (b) directly to the amygdala (via the thalamus) for an instant emotional reaction.

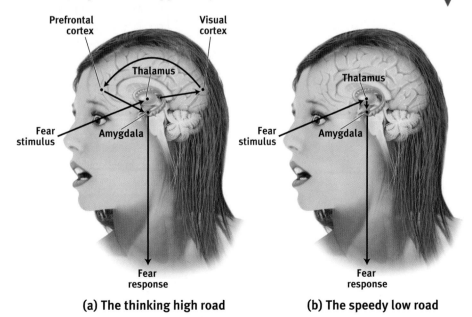

(a) The thinking high road

(b) The speedy low road

idea of what it is (Storbeck et al., 2006). Thus, said Lazarus, emotions arise when we *appraise* an event as harmless or dangerous. We appraise the sound of the rustling bushes as the presence of a threat. Then we realize that it was "just the wind."

So, let's sum up (see also **Table 4.8-1**). As Zajonc and LeDoux have demonstrated, some simple emotional responses involve no conscious thinking. When I [ND] see a big spider trapped behind glass, I experience fear, even though I *know* the spider can't hurt me. Such responses are difficult to alter by changing our thinking. Within a fraction of a second, we may automatically perceive one person as more likable or trustworthy than another (Willis & Todorov, 2006). This instant appeal can even influence our political decisions if we vote (as many people do) for the candidate we *like* over the candidate who expresses positions closer to our own (Westen, 2007).

But other emotions—including depressive moods and complex feelings—are greatly affected by our conscious and unconscious information processing: our memories, expectations, and interpretations. For these emotions, we have more conscious control. When we feel emotionally overwhelmed, we can change our interpretations (Gross, 2013). Such *reappraisal* often reduces distress and the corresponding amygdala response (Ford & Troy, 2019; Liu et al., 2019). Reappraisal not only reduces stress, but also helps students achieve better school performance (Borman et al., 2019). Don't stress about your stress. Embrace it, and approach your next test with this mindset: "Stress evolved to help maintain my focus and solve problems." Although the emotional low road functions automatically, the thinking high road allows us to retake some control over our emotional life. *The bottom line:* Together, automatic emotion and conscious thinking weave the fabric of our emotional lives.

| TABLE 4.8-1 | Summary of Emotion Theories | |
| --- | --- | --- |
| **Theorist** | **Explanation of Emotions** | **Example** |
| *James; Lange* | Emotions arise from our awareness of our specific bodily responses to emotion-arousing stimuli. | We observe our heart racing after a threat and then feel afraid. |
| *Cannon; Bard* | Emotion-arousing stimuli trigger our bodily responses and simultaneous subjective experience. | Our heart races at the same time that we feel afraid. |
| *Schachter; Singer* | A two-factor theory: Our experience of emotion depends on a) general arousal and b) a conscious cognitive label. | We may interpret our arousal as fear or excitement, depending on the context. |
| *Zajonc; LeDoux* | Some embodied responses happen instantly, without conscious appraisal. | We automatically feel startled by a sound in the forest before labeling it as a threat. |
| *Lazarus* | Cognitive appraisal ("Is it dangerous or not?") — sometimes without our awareness — defines emotion. | The sound is "just the wind." |

## Check Your Understanding

**Examine the Concept**

▶ Emotion researchers have disagreed about whether emotional responses occur in the absence of cognitive processing. How would you characterize the approach of each of the following researchers: Zajonc, LeDoux, and Lazarus?

*Answers to the Examine the Concept questions can be found in Appendix C at the end of the book.*

**Apply the Concept**

▶ Can you remember a time when you began to feel upset or uneasy and only later labeled those feelings?

# Embodied Emotion

Whether you are falling in love or grieving a death, you need little convincing that emotions involve the body. Feeling without a body is like breathing without lungs. Some physical responses are easy to notice. Other emotional responses we experience without awareness. Before examining our physical responses to specific emotions, consider another big question: How many distinct emotions are there?

## The Basic Emotions

**4.8-3** What are some of the basic emotions?

When surveyed, most emotion scientists agreed that anger, fear, disgust, sadness, and happiness are basic human emotions (Ekman, 2016). Carroll Izard (1977) isolated 10 basic emotions (joy, interest-excitement, surprise, sadness, anger, disgust, contempt, fear, shame, and guilt), most of which are present in infancy (**Figure 4.8-2**). Others believe that as many as 28 emotions exist, including awe, love, and pride (Cowen & Keltner, 2020).

(a) Joy (mouth forming smile, cheeks lifted, twinkle in eye)

(b) Anger (brows drawn together and downward, eyes fixed, mouth squarish)

(c) Interest (brows raised or knitted, mouth softly rounded, lips may be pursed)

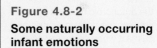

**Figure 4.8-2**

**Some naturally occurring infant emotions**

To identify the emotions generally present in infancy, Carroll Izard analyzed the facial expressions of infants.

(d) Disgust (nose wrinkled, upper lip raised, tongue pushed outward)

(e) Surprise (brows raised, eyes widened, mouth rounded in oval shape)

(f) Sadness (brows' inner corners raised, mouth corners drawn down)

(g) Fear (brows level, drawn in and up, eyelids lifted, mouth corners retracted)

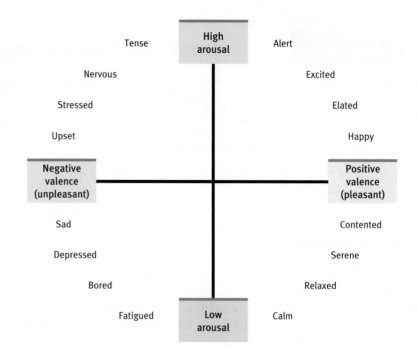

**Figure 4.8-3**

**A tale of two emotional dimensions**

You can feel good with little arousal (the calmness that often accompanies meditation) or lots of arousal (excitement at a friend's birthday party). Likewise, negative feelings can involve low arousal (fatigue at the end of a taxing day) or high arousal (nervousness before a class presentation).

Emotions are categorized along two dimensions: *valence* (positive versus negative) and *arousal* (low versus high) (Feldman Barrett & Russell, 1998; Russell, 2003) (**Figure 4.8-3**). But are emotions biologically distinct? Does our body, for example, know the difference between fear and anger?

## Emotions and the Autonomic Nervous System

**4.8-4** What is the link between emotional arousal and the autonomic nervous system?

As we saw in Module 1.2, in a crisis, the *sympathetic division* of your *autonomic nervous system (ANS)* mobilizes your body for action (**Figure 4.8-4**). It triggers the release of the stress hormones epinephrine (adrenaline) and norepinephrine (noradrenaline). To provide

**Figure 4.8-4**

**Emotional arousal**

Like a crisis management center, the autonomic nervous system arouses the body in a crisis and calms it when danger passes.

**Autonomic Nervous System Controls Physiological Arousal**

| Sympathetic division (arousing) | | Parasympathetic division (calming) |
|---|---|---|
| Pupils dilate | EYES | Pupils contract |
| Decreases | SALIVATION | Increases |
| Perspires | SKIN | Dries |
| Increases | RESPIRATION | Decreases |
| Accelerates | HEART | Slows |
| Inhibits | DIGESTION | Activates |
| Secrete stress hormones | ADRENAL GLANDS | Decrease secretion of stress hormones |
| Reduced | IMMUNE SYSTEM FUNCTIONING | Enhanced |

energy, your liver pours extra sugar (glucose) into your bloodstream. To help burn the sugar, your respiration increases to supply needed oxygen. Your heart rate and blood pressure increase. Your digestion slows, diverting blood from your internal organs to your muscles. With blood sugar driven into the large muscles, action becomes easier. Your pupils dilate, letting in more light. To cool your stirred-up body, you perspire. If wounded, your blood would clot more quickly.

When the crisis passes, the *parasympathetic division* of your ANS gradually calms your body, as stress hormones slowly leave your bloodstream. After your next crisis, think of this: Without any conscious effort, your body's response to danger is wonderfully coordinated and adaptive—preparing you to *fight* or *flee*. So, do the different emotions have distinct arousal fingerprints?

## The Physiology of Emotions

**4.8-5** How do emotions activate different physiological and brain-pattern responses?

Imagine conducting an experiment measuring the physiological responses of different emotions. In each of four rooms, you have someone watch a movie. In the first room, the person views a horror film; in the second, an anger-provoking film; in the third, a sexually arousing film; in the fourth, a boring film. From the control center, you monitor each person's perspiration, pupil size, breathing, and heart rate. Could you tell who is frightened? Who is angry? Who is sexually aroused? Who is bored?

With training, you could probably pick out the bored viewer. But discerning physiological differences among fear, anger, and sexual arousal is much more difficult (Siegel et al., 2018). Different emotions can share common biological signatures. As C. S. Lewis (1963) recalled after his wife's death, "No one ever told me that grief felt so much like fear. I am not afraid, but the sensation is like being afraid. The same fluttering in the stomach, the same restlessness, the yawning."

A single brain region can also serve as the seat of seemingly different emotions. Consider the broad emotional portfolio of the *insula*, a neural center deep inside the brain. The insula is activated when we experience various negative social emotions, such as lusting after another's partner, pridefulness, and disgust. In brain scans, it becomes active when people bite into some disgusting food, smell disgusting food, think about biting into a disgusting cockroach, or feel moral disgust over a sleazy business-person exploiting a saintly widow (Sapolsky, 2010). Similar multitasking regions are found in other brain areas.

Yet our varying emotions *feel* different to us, and they often *look* different to others. We may appear "paralyzed with fear" or "ready to explode." Fear and joy prompt a similar increased heart rate, but they stimulate different facial muscles. When fearful, your brow muscles tense. When joyful, muscles in your cheeks and under your eyes pull into a smile (Witvliet & Vrana, 1995).

Some of our emotions also have distinct brain circuits (Dixon et al., 2017; Panksepp, 2007). Observers watching fearful faces show more amygdala activity than do other observers who view angry faces (Whalen et al., 2001). Emotions also activate different areas of the brain's cortex.

**Scary thrills** Elated excitement and panicky fear involve similar physiological arousal. This allows us to flip rapidly between the two emotions.

Jacob Lund/Shutterstock

When you experience a negative emotion, such as disgust, your right prefrontal cortex tends to be more active than the left. Depression-prone people, and those with generally negative perspectives, have also shown more right frontal lobe activity (Harmon-Jones et al., 2002).

Positive moods tend to trigger more left frontal lobe activity. People with positive personalities—from exuberant infants to alert, energized, and persistently goal-directed adults—have also shown more activity in the left frontal lobe than in the right (Davidson, 2000; Urry et al., 2004).

To sum up, we can't easily see differences in emotions from tracking heart rate, breathing, and perspiration. But facial expressions and brain activity can vary with the emotion. So, do we, like Pinocchio, give off telltale signs when we lie? (For more on that question, see Developing Arguments: Lie Detection.)

**polygraph** a machine used in attempts to detect lies; measures emotion-linked changes in perspiration, heart rate, and breathing.

---

### AP® Science Practice

# Developing Arguments

## Lie Detection

**Polygraphs** are not actually lie detectors, but rather arousal detectors. They measure emotion-linked changes in breathing, heart rate, and perspiration. Can we use these results to detect lies?

In the last 20 years, have you ever taken something that didn't belong to you?

No!

Did you ever steal anything from your previous employer?

Uh, no.

EEG — Many people tell a little white lie in response to this *control question*, prompting elevated arousal readings that give the examiner a baseline for comparing responses to other questions.

EEG — This person shows greater arousal in response to the *critical question* than she did to the control question, so the examiner may infer she is lying.

**But is it true that _only a thief becomes nervous when denying a theft?_**

1. We have similar bodily arousal in response to anxiety, irritation, and guilt. So, is she really guilty, or just anxious?

2. Many innocent people do get tense and nervous when accused of a bad act. (Many of those sexually assaulted, for example, have "failed" these tests because they had strong emotional reactions while telling the truth about the event.[1])

About one-third of the time, polygraph test results are *just wrong*.[2]

**Innocent people**

**Guilty people**

○ Judged innocent by polygraph   ● Judged guilty by polygraph

If these polygraph experts had been the judges, more than one-third of the innocent would have been declared guilty, and nearly one-fourth of the guilty would have gone free.

The CIA and other U.S. agencies have spent millions of dollars testing tens of thousands of employees. Yet the U.S. National Academy of Sciences (2002) has reported that "no spy has ever been caught [by] using the polygraph."

**The Concealed Information Test is more effective.** Innocent people are seldom wrongly judged to be lying.

Questions focus on specific crime-scene details known only to the police and the guilty person.[3] (If a camera and computer had been stolen, for example, only a guilty person should react strongly to the brand names of the stolen items. A slow response time may also indicate a lie. It typically takes less time to tell the truth than to make up a lie.[4])

## Developing Arguments Questions

1. Identify the reasoning supporting the claim that lie detectors are actually arousal detectors.

2. Should courts use results from lie detectors in determining guilt or innocence? Use scientifically derived evidence to support your response.

1. Lykken, 1991. 2. Kleinmuntz & Szucko, 1984. 3. Ben-Shakhar & Elaad, 2003; Verschuere & Meijer, 2014; Vrij & Fisher, 2016. 4. Suchotzki et al., 2017.

**AP® Science Practice**

## Check Your Understanding

**Examine the Concept**

▶ What roles do the two divisions of the autonomic nervous system play in our emotional responses?

**Apply the Concept**

▶ Can you think of a time when you noticed your body's reactions to an emotionally charged situation, such as a tense social setting, or perhaps before an important test or game? How would you describe your sympathetic nervous system's responses?

*Answers to the Examine the Concept questions can be found in Appendix C at the end of the book.*

# Module 4.8a REVIEW

**4.8-1 How do arousal, expressive behavior, and cognition interact in emotion?**

- *Emotion*, or affect, is a complex process distinct from knowledge and reasoning. Emotions are responses of the whole organism, involving bodily arousal, expressive behaviors, and conscious experience resulting from one's interpretations.

- Theories of emotion generally address two major questions: (1) Does physiological arousal come before or after emotional feelings? and (2) How do feeling and cognition interact?

- James and Lange maintain that emotion occurs when we become aware of our body's response to emotion-inducing stimuli (we observe our heart pounding and feel fear).

- Cannon and Bard propose that our physiological response to an emotion-inducing stimulus occurs at the same time as our subjective experience of the emotion (one does not cause the other).

**4.8-2 To experience emotions, must we consciously interpret and label them?**

- Two-factor theory holds that our emotions have two ingredients: physical arousal and a cognitive label. The cognitive labels we put on our states of arousal are an essential ingredient of emotion.

- Zajonc and LeDoux have contended that some simple emotional responses occur instantly, not only outside our conscious awareness, but before any cognitive processing occurs. This interplay between emotion and cognition illustrates our two-track mind.

- Lazarus agreed that some emotional responses do not require conscious thinking, but asserted that appraisals can occur outside of conscious awareness and give rise to emotions.

**4.8-3 What are some of the basic emotions?**

- Most emotion scientists agree that anger, fear, disgust, sadness, and happiness are basic human emotions.

- Carroll Izard's 10 basic emotions are joy, interest-excitement, surprise, sadness, anger, disgust, contempt, fear, shame, and guilt.

**4.8-4 What is the link between emotional arousal and the autonomic nervous system?**

- The arousal component of emotion is regulated by the autonomic nervous system's sympathetic (arousing) and parasympathetic (calming) divisions.

- In a crisis, the fight-or-flight response automatically mobilizes your body for action.

**4.8-5 How do emotions activate different physiological and brain-pattern responses?**

- The large-scale body changes that accompany fear, anger, and sexual arousal are very similar (increased perspiration, breathing, and heart rate), though they feel different. Emotions may be similarly arousing, but some subtle physiological responses (such as facial muscle movements) distinguish them.

- More meaningful differences have been found in activity in some brain pathways and cortical areas.

# AP® Practice Multiple Choice Questions

1. Johari noticed he was having an emotional reaction. Which responses did he likely experience?

    a. Bodily arousal and expressive behaviors only
    b. Expressive behaviors and conscious experience only
    c. Bodily arousal, expressive behaviors, and conscious experience
    d. Bodily arousal and conscious experience only

2. Kellen started his paper on emotion theories with a common question that these theories address, writing

    a. Does cognition always come before emotion?
    b. Is nature or nurture more important in emotional response?
    c. Which division of the nervous system is activated first in an emotional response?
    d. What is the evolutionary purpose of emotions?

3. Amanda felt fear, which traveled on the "low road" neural pathway. Which is true of her experience?

    a. Information travels directly from the thalamus to the amygdala.
    b. The emotional response happens more slowly than it would via the "high road."
    c. This pathway is more likely to be utilized for complex feelings.
    d. This pathway passes through the brain's cortex.

4. Nellie believes that when she gives a speech in front of her class, she gets sweaty and feels nervous at exactly the same moment. What research finding shows that Nellie's belief is not accurate?

    a. Research indicates that bodily arousal precedes the subjective experience of emotions.
    b. Research indicates that bodily arousal and the subjective experience of emotions are not entirely independent of each other.
    c. Research indicates that bodily arousal must be interpreted prior to the subjective experience of emotions.
    d. Research indicates that bodily arousal occurs without conscious awareness, and the subjective experience of emotions occurs after interpretation.

5. While vigorously dancing at a concert, Wanda heard the band play a new song. The crowd cheered wildly, and Wanda noticed herself feeling ecstatic due to

    a. bodily arousal.
    b. the spillover effect.
    c. valence.
    d. lie detection.

6. Kennedy is walking in the park and jumps at the sound of rustling bushes nearby. A few seconds later he realizes the sound was made by the wind, and he calms down. This scenario supports which of the following statements?

   a. Our physiological responses are dependent on our interpretation of a situation.
   b. Our arousal can spill over from one situation into the next.
   c. We experience most emotions without conscious awareness.
   d. We can have emotional reactions apart from our conscious interpretation of a situation.

7. Who is displaying one of the 10 basic human emotions?

   a. David, who is showing interest by raising his eyebrows
   b. Zach, who is showing jealousy by pursing his lips
   c. Kristin, who is showing boredom by rolling her eyes
   d. Maggie, who is showing empathy by making eye contact

8. When given a pop quiz, Valero's sympathetic nervous system activated. Which effect did he likely experience?

   a. Contracted pupils
   b. Enhanced immune functioning
   c. Inhibited digestion
   d. Decreased respiration

# Module 4.8b Emotion: Expressing and Experiencing Emotion

## LEARNING TARGETS

**4.8-6** Explain our ability to communicate nonverbally.

**4.8-7** Explain how men and women differ in nonverbal communication.

**4.8-8** Explain how gestures and facial expressions are understood within and across cultures.

**4.8-9** Explain how our facial expressions influence our feelings.

Expressive behavior implies emotion. Dolphins, with smiles seemingly plastered on their faces, appear happy. Basset hounds, with their long faces and droopy eyes, seem sad. To decipher people's emotions we read their bodies, listen to their vocal tones, and study their faces. Does nonverbal language vary with culture—or is it universal? And do our expressions influence our experienced emotions?

## Detecting Emotion in Others

**4.8-6** How do we communicate nonverbally?

**4.8-6** How do we communicate nonverbally?

To Westerners, a firm handshake conveys an outgoing, expressive personality (Chaplin et al., 2000). A gaze can communicate intimacy, while darting eyes may signal anxiety (Kleinke, 1986; Perkins et al., 2012). When two people are passionately in love, they typically spend time—lots of time—gazing into each other's eyes (Bolmont et al., 2014; Rubin, 1970). Would such gazes stir loving feelings between strangers? To find out, researchers asked unacquainted, heterosexual pairs to gaze intently for 2 minutes either at each other's hands or into each other's eyes. After separating, the eye gazers reported feeling a tingle of attraction and affection (Kellerman et al., 1989).

Our brain is an amazing detector of subtle expressions, helping most of us read nonverbal cues well. We are adept at detecting a hint of a smile (Maher et al., 2014). Shown 10 seconds of video from the end of a speed-dating interaction, people can often tell whether one person is attracted to the other (Place et al., 2009). Signs of status are also easy to spot. When shown someone with arms raised, chest expanded, and a slight smile, people—from Canadian undergraduates to Fijian villagers—perceive that person as experiencing pride and having high status (Tracy et al., 2013). Even glimpsing a face for one-tenth of a second has enabled viewers to judge people's attractiveness or trustworthiness, or to rate politicians' competence and predict their voter support (Willis & Todorov, 2006). "First impressions . . . occur with astonishing speed," note Christopher Olivola and Alexander Todorov (2010).

We also excel at detecting nonverbal threats. We readily sense subliminally presented negative words, such as *snake* or *bomb* (Gomes et al., 2018). An angry face will "pop out" of

**A silent language of emotion**
Hindu classic dance uses the face and body to effectively convey 10 different emotions (Hejmadi et al., 2000).

Zohaib Hussain/Getty Images

a crowd (Öhman et al., 2001; Stjepanovic & Labar, 2018). Even 2-year-olds attend to angry faces, suggesting we come hard-wired to detect threats (Burris et al., 2019). Experience can sensitize us to particular emotions, as shown by studies using a series of faces (like those in **Figure 4.8-5**) that morph from anger to fear (or sadness). Shown a face that is 50 percent fear and 50 percent anger, physically abused children are more likely than other children to perceive anger. Their perceptions become sensitively attuned to more quickly spot glimmers of danger.

Hard-to-control facial muscles can reveal signs of emotions you may be trying to conceal. Lifting just the inner part of your eyebrows, which few people do consciously, reveals distress or worry. Eyebrows raised and pulled together signal fear. Raised cheeks and activated muscles under the eyes suggest a natural smile. A feigned smile, such as the one we make for a photographer, is often frozen in place for several seconds, then suddenly switched off; genuine happy smiles tend to be briefer but to fade less abruptly (Bugental, 1986) (**Figure 4.8-6**). Women—who, as psychologist Marianne LaFrance noted, "get completely socialized that smiling should be the default expression on their face"—may have found some relief from this pressure to feign smiles during the Covid pandemic, while wearing face masks (Bennett, 2020). True smiles cause others to perceive us as trustworthy, authentic, and attractive (Gunnery & Ruben, 2016).

Despite our brain's emotion-detecting skill, we find it difficult to discern deceit. The behavioral differences between liars and truth tellers are too minute for most people to detect (Hartwig & Bond, 2011). One digest of 206 studies found that people were just 54 percent accurate in discerning truth from lies—barely better than a coin toss (Bond & DePaulo, 2006). Virtually no one—except perhaps police professionals in high-stakes situations—beats chance by much, not even when detecting children's lies (Gongola et al., 2017; O'Sullivan et al., 2009; ten Brinke et al., 2016).

Some of us, more than others, are sensitive to the physical cues of various emotions. In one study, people were asked to name the emotion displayed in brief film clips. The clips showed portions of a person's emotionally expressive face or body, sometimes accompanied by a garbled voice (Rosenthal et al., 1979). For example, after a 2-second scene—a brief sample of behavior known as a *thin slice*— revealing only the face of an upset woman, viewers were asked if the woman was criticizing someone for being late or was talking about her divorce. Introverts tend to excel at reading others' emotions, while extraverts are generally easier to read (Ambady et al., 1995).

Gestures, facial expressions, and vocal tones, which are absent in written communication, convey important information. The difference was clear when study participants in one group heard 30-second recordings of people describing their marital separations. Participants in the other group read a script of the recording. Those who *heard* the recording were better able to predict the people's current and future adjustment (Mason et al., 2010). Just hearing a stranger say "hello" is enough to give listeners some clue to the speaker's personality.

Online communications lack vocal and facial nuances. Without the normal expressive cues, we run the risk of what developmental psychologist Jean Piaget called *egocentrism;* we may fail to perceive how others interpret our "just kidding" message (Kruger et al., 2005). So, to help people understand whether our online comment is serious, kidding, or sarcastic, we may insert emojis. 😊

**Figure 4.8-5**

**Experience influences how we perceive emotions**

Viewing the morphed middle face, which evenly mixes anger with fear, physically abused children were more likely than nonabused children to perceive the face as angry (Pollak & Kistler, 2002; Pollak & Tolley-Schell, 2003).

**Figure 4.8-6**

**Which of researcher Paul Ekman's smiles is feigned, which natural?**

The smile on the right engages the facial muscles of a natural smile.

**AP® Science Practice**

**Research**

The digest of 206 studies that examined how accurately people could discern truth from lies is a meta-analysis. A meta-analysis combines the results of multiple studies to reach an overall conclusion.

# Gender, Emotion, and Nonverbal Behavior

**4.8-7** How do men and women differ in nonverbal communication?

Do women have greater sensitivity than men to nonverbal cues? An analysis led by Judith Hall (2016) of 176 *thin slice* studies indicated that women do outperform men at emotion detection. This advantage emerges early in infancy (McClure, 2000). Women's nonverbal sensitivity helps explain their greater emotional literacy. When invited to describe how they would feel in certain situations, men tend to describe simpler emotional reactions (Barrett et al., 2000). You might like to try this yourself: Ask some people how they might feel when saying good-bye to friends after graduating from high school. Research suggests young men are more likely to say, simply, "I'll feel bad," and young women to express more complex emotions: "It will be bittersweet; I'll feel both happy and sad."

Women's skill at decoding others' emotions may also contribute to their greater emotional responsiveness and expressiveness, especially for positive emotions (Fischer & LaFrance, 2015; McDuff et al., 2017). In studies of 23,000 people from 26 cultures, women more than men reported themselves open to feelings (Costa et al., 2001). Girls also express stronger emotions than boys do, hence the extremely strong perception that emotionality is "more true of women"—a perception expressed by nearly 100 percent of 18- to 29-year-old Americans (Chaplin & Aldao, 2013; Newport, 2001).

One exception: Quickly—imagine an angry face. What gender is the person? If you are like three in four Arizona State University students, you imagined a man (Becker et al., 2007). And when a gender-neutral face was made to look angry, most people perceived it as a man; if the face was smiling, they were more likely to perceive it as a woman (Becker et al., 2007; **Figure 4.8-7**). Anger strikes most people as a more masculine emotion.

Vaughn Becker/© APA

**Figure 4.8-7**
**Gendered perceptions?**

The perception of women's emotionality also feeds—and is fed by—people's habit of attributing women's emotionality to their disposition and men's emotionality to their circumstances: "She's emotional" versus "He's having a bad day" (Barrett & Bliss-Moreau, 2009). Many factors influence our attributions, including cultural norms (Mason & Morris, 2010). Nevertheless, researchers have identified some gender differences in descriptions of emotional experiences. When surveyed, women are far more likely than men to describe themselves as empathic (Benenson et al., 2021). If you have *empathy*, you identify with others and imagine being in their skin. You appraise a situation as they do, rejoicing with those who rejoice and weeping with those who weep (Wondra & Ellsworth, 2015). Fiction readers, who immerse themselves in others' lives, report higher empathy levels (Mar et al., 2009).

Women are also more likely to *express* empathy—to display more emotion when observing others' emotions. As **Figure 4.8-8** shows, this gender difference was clear when students watched film clips that were sad (children with a dying parent), happy (slapstick comedy), or frightening (a man nearly falling off the ledge of a tall building) (Kring & Gordon, 1998). Women also tend to experience upsetting emotional events, such as viewing pictures of mutilation, more deeply and with more brain activation in areas sensitive to emotion. And they remember the scenes better 3 weeks later (Canli et al., 2002).

You may wonder: Are gender differences in empathy the result of nature or nurture? As we have seen repeatedly, nature and nurture often interact. Evolutionary biologists and neuroscientists note that similar female-male empathy differences occur in nonhuman animals, too (Christov-Moore et al., 2014). To these researchers, biology powerfully predicts empathy. But cultural learning also matters. People who occupy positions of high power and privilege are less motivated to empathize (Dietze & Knowles, 2021; Kraus et al., 2012). Those lower in power, as women historically have been, often feel the urge to understand others' emotions (Dietze & Knowles, 2016).

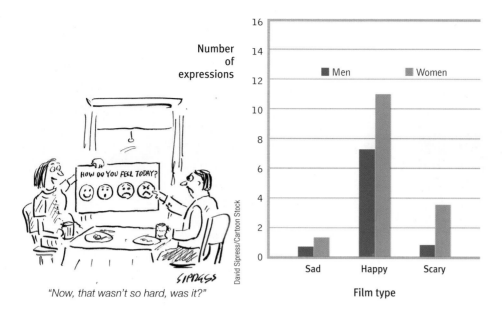

"Now, that wasn't so hard, was it?"

David Sipress/Cartoon Stock

**Figure 4.8-8**
**Gender and expressiveness**
Male and female film viewers did not differ dramatically in self-reported emotions or physiological responses, but women's faces *showed* much more emotion than men's. (Data from Kring & Gordon, 1998.)

## Culture and Emotion

**4.8-8** How are gestures and facial expressions understood within and across cultures?

The meaning of *gestures* varies from culture to culture. In 1968, North Korea publicized photos of supposedly happy officers from a captured U.S. Navy spy ship. In the photo, three men had raised their middle finger, telling their captors it was a "Hawaiian good luck sign" (Fleming & Scott, 1991). I [ND] have taught my children the thumbs-up gesture so they can let me know that something is good. But I will also teach them not to make that gesture if we travel to certain West African and Middle Eastern countries, where it can mean "Up yours!" (Koerner, 2003).

Do *facial expressions* also have different meanings in different cultures? To find out, researchers have traveled the world, showing people photos of different posed faces (Ekman, 2016; Ekman & Friesen, 1975; Izard, 1994; Nelson et al., 2013). You can try one such task yourself by labeling the emotions in **Figure 4.8-9**.

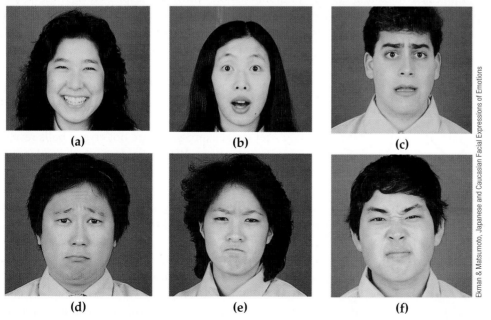

(a)　(b)　(c)

(d)　(e)　(f)

Ekman & Matsumoto, Japanese and Caucasian Facial Expressions of Emotions

**Figure 4.8-9**
**Culture-specific or culturally universal expressions?**
Which pose expresses disgust? Anger? Fear? Happiness? Sadness? Surprise?[4] (From Matsumoto & Ekman, 1989.)

[4]The original researchers suggested: (a) happiness, (b) surprise, (c) fear, (d) sadness, (e) anger, (f) disgust.

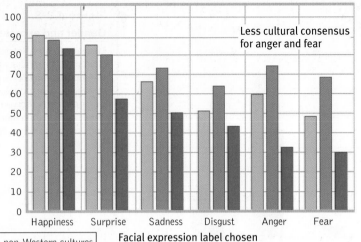

**Figure 4.8-10**

**Cultural consensus in question**

In global studies, most people agree that a smiling face represents happiness. Other expressions, such as in the face shown here, have offered less cross-cultural consensus (Nelson et al., 2013). What emotion do you see in this face?

Graph legend:
- Literate, non-Western cultures
- Literate, Western cultures
- Illiterate, isolated cultures

Percentage cultural agreement (y-axis: 0–100)

Facial expression label chosen (x-axis: Happiness, Surprise, Sadness, Disgust, Anger, Fear)

Less cultural consensus for anger and fear

**AP® Science Practice**

**Data**

Can you identify the three variables depicted in the graph in Figure 4.8-10? The answer is (1) type of culture, (2) facial expression label chosen, and (3) percentage of cultural agreement.

**Figure 4.8-11**

**Anger expressed**

Cover up faces (c) and (d) and ask a friend if they would select image (a) or image (b) as the angry one. Even without the obvious facial cues, most people easily choose (b) (Franklin et al., 2019).

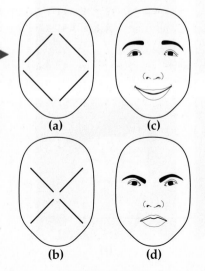

(a)  (c)
(b)  (d)

You probably labeled the smiling face as "happiness"—and so would people around the world. But people differ on the other expressions, especially anger and fear, even when matching exaggerated poses to a limited set of emotion words (Crivelli et al., 2016a) (Figure 4.8-10). We're also better at judging faces from our own culture, as if we learn a local emotional dialect (Crivelli et al., 2016b; Elfenbein & Ambady, 2002; Laukka et al., 2016).

Some emotion categories are clear universals: A smile's a smile the world around. The same with laughter: People everywhere can discriminate real from fake laughs (Bryant et al., 2018). Even people blind from birth spontaneously exhibit the common facial expressions associated with such emotions as joy, sadness, fear, anger, and pride (Galati et al., 1997; Tracy & Matsumoto, 2008).

Do these shared emotional categories reflect shared *cultural* experiences, such as movies and TV shows seen everywhere? Apparently not. Paul Ekman and Wallace Friesen (1971) asked isolated people in New Guinea to respond to such statements as, "Pretend your child has died." When North American undergraduates viewed the recorded responses, they easily read the New Guineans' facial reactions.

Such results would not have surprised evolutionary theorist Charles Darwin (1809–1882), who argued that before our prehistoric ancestors communicated in words, they communicated threats, greetings, and submission with facial expressions. These shared expressions helped them survive (Hess & Thibault, 2009). In confrontations, for example, a human sneer retains elements of an animal baring its teeth in a snarl (Figure 4.8-11).

Emotional expressions may enhance our survival in other ways, too. Surprise raises the eyebrows and widens the eyes, enabling us to take in more information. Disgust wrinkles the nose, reducing intake of foul odors.

Yet facial expressions are not crystal balls revealing our emotions. We routinely control our faces to fit in with, influence, or deceive others. Euphoric Olympic gold-medal winners typically don't smile when they are waiting alone for their award ceremony. But they wear broad grins when interacting with officials and when facing the crowd and cameras (Fernández-Dols & Ruiz-Belda, 1995). The same expression may also convey different messages (Barrett et al., 2019). When worn by a villain, a smile may be terrifying. A fearful face set in a painful

**(a)**

**(b)**

Masashi Hara/Getty Images

Elsa/Getty Images

**Display rules differ** Soccer players from more collectivist cultures, such as Japanese Yu Kobayashi, tend to celebrate a goal with fellow players in a way that deflects attention from themselves (a). Those from more individualist cultures, such as American Megan Rapinoe — shown here after scoring at the 2019 Women's World Cup — are more comfortable making themselves distinct from others (b).

situation looks pained (Carroll & Russell, 1996). Film directors harness this phenomenon by creating scenes and soundtracks that amplify our perceptions of particular emotions.

Emotional expressions are also cultural events, with different triggers (*elicitors*), and *display rules* on how *much* emotion to express. Westerners are biased toward enthusiastic positivity. On one U.S. campus, 40 percent of students were seen smiling as they walked around, as were only 20 percent of college students in Beijing (Talhelm et al., 2019). Compared with job applicants in Hong Kong, where calmness is emphasized, European American applicants use excited smiles and words more frequently. Likewise, European American leaders express broad smiles six times more frequently in their official photos (Bencharit et al., 2019).

In cultures that encourage individuality and personal influence, as in Western Europe, Australia, New Zealand, and North America, people prefer high-intensity emotions (Tsai, 2007). Those cultures that encourage people to adjust to others, as in Japan, China, India, and Korea, often value less intense emotional displays (Cordaro et al., 2018; Matsumoto et al., 2009). Moreover, in Japan, the mouth—often so expressive in North Americans—conveys less emotion than do the telltale eyes (Masuda et al., 2008; Yuki et al., 2007). If we're happy and we know it, our culture will teach us how to show it.

Cultural differences also exist *within* nations. The Irish and their Irish American descendants have tended to be more expressive than the Scandinavians and their Scandinavian American descendants (Tsai & Chentsova-Dutton, 2003). Even within cultures, what elicits emotion, and how people display emotion, can differ by gender, age, and status. Like most psychological events, facial expressions are best understood not only as biological and cognitive phenomena, but also as social-cultural phenomena.

## The Effects of Facial Expressions

**4.8-9** How do our facial expressions influence our feelings?

As William James (1890) struggled with feelings of depression and grief, he came to believe that we can control emotions by going "through the outward movements" of any emotion we want to experience. "To feel cheerful," he advised, "sit up cheerfully, look around cheerfully, and act as if cheerfulness were already there." In *The Expression of the Emotions in Man and Animals*, Charles Darwin (1872) contended that "the free expression by outward signs of an emotion intensifies it. . . . He who gives way to violent gestures will increase his rage."

Were they right? You can test this hypothesis: Fake a big grin. Now scowl. Can you feel the "smile therapy" difference? Participants in dozens of experiments have felt a difference. Researchers subtly induced students to make a frowning expression by asking them to contract certain muscles and pull their brows together (supposedly to help the researchers attach facial electrodes) (Laird, 1974, 1984; Laird & Lacasse, 2014). The results? The students reported feeling a little angry, as do people naturally frowning (by squinting) when

Figure 4.8-12

**How to make people smile without telling them to smile**

Do as Kazuo Mori and Hideko Mori (2009) did with students in Japan: Attach rubber bands to the sides of the face with adhesive bandages, and then run them either over the head or under the chin. Based on the *facial feedback effect*, how might students report feeling when the rubber bands raise their cheeks as though in a smile? How might they report feeling when the rubber bands pull their cheeks downward?

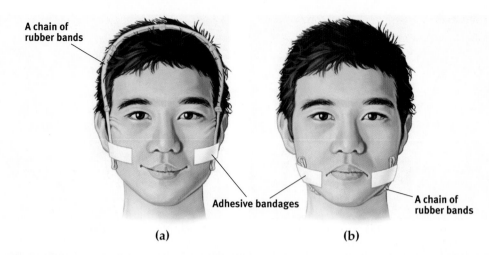

A chain of rubber bands

Adhesive bandages

A chain of rubber bands

(a)    (b)

facing the Sun (Marzoli et al., 2013). So, too, for other basic emotions. For example, people reported feeling more fear than anger, disgust, or sadness when made to construct a fearful expression: "Raise your eyebrows. And open your eyes wide. Move your whole head back, so that your chin is tucked in a little bit, and let your mouth relax and hang open a little" (Duclos et al., 1989).

James and Darwin were right: Expressions not only communicate emotion, but also amplify and regulate it. This **facial feedback effect** has been found many times, in many places, for many basic emotions (Coles et al., 2019; see **Figure 4.8-12**). We're just a little happier when smiling, angrier when scowling, and sadder when frowning. Merely activating one of the smiling muscles by holding a pen in the teeth (rather than gently between the lips, which produces a neutral expression) makes stressful situations less upsetting (Kraft & Pressman, 2012). A hearty smile — with raised cheeks that crinkle the eyes — enhances positive feelings even more when you are reacting to something pleasant or funny (Soussignan, 2001). While research has produced mixed results, replicating the original pen-in-teeth study—without distracting participants by videotaping them—reliably demonstrates the effect (Marsh et al., 2019; Noah et al., 2018; Strack, 2016). So there's practical wisdom in advice to "put on a happy face." As Buddhist spiritual monk Thich Nhât Hanh reportedly observed, "Sometimes your joy is the source of your smile, but sometimes your smile can be the source of your joy."

So, your face is more than a billboard that displays your feelings; it also feeds your feelings. Scowl and the whole world scowls back. No wonder some depressed patients reportedly felt better after Botox injections paralyzed their frowning muscles (Parsaik et al., 2016). Botox paralysis of the frowning muscles slows people's reading of sadness- or anger-related sentences, and it slows activity in emotion-related brain circuits (Havas et al., 2010; Hennenlotter et al., 2008). The opposite happens when Botox paralyzes laughter muscles: People feel more depressed (Lewis, 2018).

Researchers have also observed a broader **behavior feedback effect** (Carney et al., 2015; Flack, 2006). You can duplicate the participants' experience: Walk for a few minutes with short, shuffling steps, keeping your eyes downcast. Now walk around taking long strides, with your arms swinging and your eyes looking straight ahead. Can you feel your mood shift? Or when angry, lean back in a reclined sitting position and feel the anger lessen (Krahé et al., 2018). Going through the motions awakens the emotions. The next time you're angry or stressed, lean back and take a few deep breaths.

You can use your understanding of feedback effects to become more empathic: Let your own face mimic another person's expression. Acting as another acts helps us feel what another feels (Vaughn & Lanzetta, 1981). Losing this ability to mimic others can leave us struggling to make emotional connections, as social worker Kathleen Bogart, who has Moebius syndrome (a rare facial paralysis disorder), discovered while working with Hurricane Katrina evacuees: When people made a sad expression, "I wasn't able to return it.

**facial feedback effect** the tendency of facial muscle states to trigger corresponding feelings such as fear, anger, or happiness.

**behavior feedback effect** the tendency of behavior to influence our own and others' thoughts, feelings, and actions.

I tried to do so with words and tone of voice, but it was no use. Stripped of the facial expression, the emotion just dies there, unshared" (Carey, 2010).

Our natural mimicry of others' emotions helps explain why emotions are contagious (Dimberg et al., 2000; Neumann & Strack, 2000; Peters & Kashima, 2015). Positive, upbeat social media posts create a ripple effect, leading friends to also express more positive emotions (Kramer, 2012).

**AP® Science Practice**

## Check Your Understanding

### Examine the Concept

▶ Describe some gender differences in nonverbal behavior.

▶ Explain the difference between the facial feedback effect and the behavioral feedback effect.

*Answers to the Examine the Concept questions can be found in Appendix C at the end of the book.*

### Apply the Concept

▶ Imagine a situation in which you would like to change the way you feel. How could you do so by altering your facial expressions or the way you carry yourself? In what other settings could you apply your knowledge of these feedback effects?

\* \* \*

We have seen how our motivated behaviors, triggered by the forces of nature and nurture, frequently go hand in hand with significant emotional responses. Our often-adaptive psychological emotions likewise come equipped with physical reactions. Nervous about an important encounter, we feel stomach butterflies. Anxious over public speaking, we frequent the bathroom. Smoldering over a family conflict, we get a splitting headache. As this text's discussion of stress and health next shows, negative emotions and the prolonged high arousal that may accompany them can tax the body and harm our health.

## Module 4.8b REVIEW

### 4.8-6 How do we communicate nonverbally?

● Much of our communication is through body movements, facial expressions, and vocal tones. Even seconds-long filmed slices of behavior can reveal feelings.

### 4.8-7 How do men and women differ in nonverbal communication?

● Women tend to read emotional cues more easily and to be more empathic. They also show greater emotional responsiveness and expressiveness, especially for positive emotions.

### 4.8-8 How are gestures and facial expressions understood within and across cultures?

● The meaning of gestures varies with culture, but some facial expressions, such as those of happiness and sadness, are universal.

● Context and culture can influence the interpretation of facial expressions. Cultural display rules also influence the amount of emotion expressed, and elicitors of emotion may differ between or within cultures.

### 4.8-9 How do our facial expressions influence our feelings?

● Research on the *facial feedback effect* shows that our facial expressions can trigger emotional feelings and signal our body to respond accordingly. We also mimic others' expressions, which helps us empathize.

● A similar *behavior feedback effect* is the tendency of behavior to influence our own and others' thoughts, feelings, and actions.

# AP® Practice Multiple Choice Questions

1. Carla, an introvert, lives with Cindy, an extravert. Cindy ate Carla's last granola bar, but she told Carla that she did not know where the granola bar went. Which of the following is the most logical and objective conclusion that can be drawn about Carla's ability to figure out the truth?

   a. Carla, being an introvert, is skilled at reading other people's emotions; so, she will likely figure out that Cindy is lying.
   b. Cindy, being an extravert, is emotionally expressive; so, Carla will likely figure out that Cindy is lying.
   c. Because nearly everyone has difficulty detecting deceit, Carla will not likely figure out that Cindy is lying.
   d. As a woman, Carla will be able to use her strong emotion detection skills to figure out that Cindy is lying.

2. Dr. Bumpers asserted that, when shown photos of a variety of facial expressions, participants in his cross-cultural study were statistically significantly more accurate in detecting happiness than in detecting other emotions. Which of the following statements provides the most accurate interpretation of her results?

   a. Similar to the findings of past research, people in the study were so much better at detecting happiness compared to other emotions that the result was unlikely to have occurred by chance or by error.
   b. Counter to findings of past research, people in the study were so much better at detecting happiness compared to other emotions that the result was unlikely to have occurred by chance or by error.
   c. Similar to the findings of past research, people in the study were not any better at detecting happiness compared to other emotions, such that any difference could be attributed to merely chance or error alone.
   d. Counter to the findings of past research, people in the study were not any better at detecting happiness compared to other emotions, such that any difference could be attributed to merely chance or error alone.

**Use the following graph to answer questions 3 & 4:**

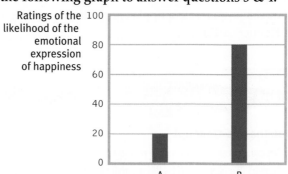

3. Based on the graph and what you know about people's perceptions of emotional expressiveness, what are the likely labels for A and for B?

   a. The likely label for A is younger adults, and the likely label for B is older adults.
   b. The likely label for A is men, and the likely label for B is women.
   c. The likely label for A is older adults, and the likely label for B is younger adults.
   d. The likely label for A is women, and the likely label for B is men.

4. If the graph's $y$-axis was changed to read "Ratings of the likelihood of the emotional expression of anger," what changes, if any, should be made to the A and B labels on the $x$-axis?

   a. The labels should remain the same.
   b. The labels should be switched.
   c. The labels should be removed.
   d. The labels should be consolidated into a single label.

5. Trixie, a 20-year-old woman, is watching the news with her roommate, Miguel, a 19-year-old man. They both become tearful when hearing a story about an abandoned dog who found his forever home. When their third roommate, Calliope, enters the room, which of the following best captures how she is likely to explain Trixie's and Miguel's tearfulness?

   a. Calliope will believe that both Trixie and Miguel became tearful because they are emotional people.
   b. Calliope will believe that Miguel became tearful because he is an emotional person, and that Trixie became tearful because she had a difficult day.
   c. Calliope will believe that both Trixie and Miguel became tearful because they had a difficult day.
   d. Calliope will believe that Trixie became tearful because she is an emotional person, and that Miguel became tearful because he had a difficult day.

6. Paul Ekman found that facial expressions tend to be the same around the world. Which of the following statements best uses empirical evidence to explain the nuances of this finding?

a. Although people around the world often display similar facial expressions, they tend to differ in their expression of happiness.

b. Although people around the world often display similar facial expressions, they tend to differ in the amount of emotion expressed.

c. Although people around the world often display similar facial expressions, they tend to differ in their ability to distinguish fake laughter from real laughter.

d. Although people around the world often display similar facial expressions, they tend to differ in their susceptibility to the facial feedback effect.

7. Kimi grew up in Japan. When she moved to the United States, she was surprised by the intensity with which people expressed their emotions: Smiles seemed more exuberant, and scowls seemed angrier. Which of the following best explains Kimi's experience?

a. The facial feedback effect
b. Display rules
c. The behavior feedback effect
d. Empathy

# UNIT 4 Review

## KEY TERMS AND CONTRIBUTORS TO REMEMBER

personality psychology, p. 453

social psychology, p. 453

person perception, p. 454

attribution theory, p. 454

fundamental attribution error, p. 454

actor-observer bias, p. 455

prejudice, p. 457

stereotype, p. 457

discrimination, p. 457

just-world phenomenon, p. 461

social identity, 462

ingroup, p. 462

outgroup, p. 462

ingroup bias, p. 462

scapegoat theory, p. 463

other-race effect, p. 463

attitudes, p. 468

foot-in-the-door phenomenon, p. 469

role, p. 469

Leon Festinger, p. 470

cognitive dissonance theory, p. 470

persuasion, p. 471

peripheral route persuasion, p. 471

central route persuasion, p. 471

norms, p. 475

Solomon Asch, p. 476

conformity, p. 476

normative social influence, p. 478

informational social influence, p. 478

obedience, p. 478

Stanley Milgram, p. 478

social facilitation, p. 486

social loafing, p. 487

deindividuation, p. 487

group polarization, p. 489

groupthink, p. 491

culture, p. 491

tight culture, p. 492

loose culture, p. 492

aggression, p. 496

frustration-aggression principle, p. 498

social script, p. 499

mere exposure effect, p. 504

passionate love, p. 509

companionate love, p. 510

equity, p. 510

self-disclosure, p. 511

altruism, p. 514

John Darley, p. 515

Bibb Latané, p. 515

bystander effect, p. 515

social exchange theory, p. 517

reciprocity norm, p. 517

social-responsibility norm, p. 517

conflict, p. 518

social trap, p. 518

mirror-image perceptions, p. 519

self-fulfilling prophecy, p. 519

superordinate goals, p. 520

GRIT, p. 521

personality, p. 526

psychodynamic theories, p. 528

psychoanalysis, p. 528

Sigmund Freud, p. 529

unconscious, p. 529

free association, p. 529

id, p. 530

ego, p. 530

superego, p. 530

defense mechanisms, p. 532

repression, p. 532

Alfred Adler, p. 533

Karen Horney, p. 533

Carl Jung, p. 534

collective unconscious, p. 534

terror-management theory, p. 537

Thematic Apperception Test (TAT), p. 538

projective test, p. 538

Rorschach inkblot test, p. 539

Abraham Maslow, p. 542

humanistic theories, p. 542

hierarchy of needs, p. 542

self-actualization, p. 542

self-transcendence, p. 542

Carl Rogers, p. 544

unconditional positive regard, p. 544

self-concept, p. 545

trait, p. 549

personality inventory, p. 552

Minnesota Multiphasic Personality Inventory (MMPI), p. 552

empirically derived test, p. 552

Robert McCrae, p. 553

Paul Costa, p. 553

Big Five factors, p. 553

social-cognitive perspective, p. 561

Albert Bandura, p. 561

behavioral approach, p. 561

reciprocal determinism, p. 561

## Unit 4 AP® Practice Multiple Choice Questions

**1.** When Pick stepped on Querc's foot, Querc believed Pick was a mean person, which illustrates

   a. the foot-in-the-door phenomenon.
   b. the fundamental attribution error.
   c. social loafing.
   d. social thinking.

**2.** Which of the following is an example of prejudice?

   a. Ann has a negative attitude toward children.
   b. Antoine chooses professors who are women over professors who are men.
   c. Anquelle believes all people should be treated equitably.
   d. Annette hits her younger brother when he angers her.

**3.** Tim pulls into traffic behind a woman and immediately gets irritated, muttering "Women are terrible drivers." Tim's belief is

   a. a norm.
   b. a stereotype.
   c. the frustration-aggression principle.
   d. discrimination.

**4.** Students at Interlake High School believe they are superior to students at West Lake High School in every way possible. This is a demonstration of

   a. ingroup bias.
   b. conformity.
   c. discrimination.
   d. groupthink.

**5.** Samir does not feel any obligation to help the people experiencing homelessness he sees each morning in the subway. He assumes the situation is their fault and that they must have done something to deserve it. Samir's assumptions represent

   a. an ingroup bias.
   b. altruism.
   c. aggression.
   d. the just-world phenomenon.

**6.** Jacob feels tension after he flirts with other people even though he is in a committed relationship, which illustrates

   a. the fundamental attribution error.
   b. social pressure.
   c. social influence.
   d. cognitive dissonance.

**7.** Which of the following is the clearest example of conformity?

   a. Sharing a mood with your friends
   b. Unconsciously mimicking the behaviors and reactions of strangers
   c. Adjusting your behavior to be more like your friends
   d. Changing your thinking about a situation to please your parents

8. Lily is more likely to challenge her teacher when
   a. she is alone with the teacher.
   b. the teacher is male.
   c. she is in a group with more than three people.
   d. she has seen someone else disobey.

9. Ayshia is less self-conscious and less restrained when she is in a large group. Ayshia is demonstrating which of the following concepts?
   a. Social loafing
   b. Deindividuation
   c. Social facilitation
   d. Cognitive dissonance

10. Xavier's mother is in a very bad mood. Xavier attributes this bad mood to the fact that his mother has a headache. Xavier is exhibiting which of the following social psychological concepts?
    a. The fundamental attribution error
    b. The just-world phenomenon
    c. An external attribution
    d. A stereotype

11. Caroline hates to do group projects with Jake because she ends up doing much more of the work than he does. Jake is engaging in
    a. social facilitation.
    b. a social trap.
    c. social loafing.
    d. altruism.

12. Marcus and Todd tried to buy tickets to see their favorite band, but they were unable to do so because the show sold out by the time they filled in the online form. Marcus swipes his laptop onto the floor in anger. The best explanation for why he does this is
    a. the proximity effect.
    b. the frustration-aggression principle.
    c. social scripting.
    d. deindividuation.

13. Jaxson downloaded an album, even though she liked only one of the songs. Over time she found that she likes the other songs on the album as well. This is best explained by
    a. the mere exposure effect.
    b. hindsight bias.
    c. the just-world phenomenon.
    d. GRIT.

14. Cora, a 4-month-old infant, looked longer at people of her race than people of different races, which demonstrates
    a. similarity.
    b. the mere exposure effect.
    c. the mirror image perception.
    d. cognitive dissonance.

15. Carol believes that Paul is mad at her so she chooses to ignore him, which serves to actually make him mad at her. This is an example of
    a. superordinate goals.
    b. a social trap.
    c. a mirror-image perception.
    d. a self-fulfilling prophecy.

16. Elaine's friends know that she should never be trusted with a secret, as she will tell everyone almost immediately. Elaine, however, complains that her friends can't be trusted. Elaine is making use of the defense mechanism of
    a. projection.
    b. rationalization.
    c. regression.
    d. sublimation.

17. A psychoanalytic psychologist might use the TAT and the Rorschach inkblot test to
    a. get a glimpse of a person's ideal self.
    b. determine if a person is an introvert.
    c. gain insight into a person's unconscious mind.
    d. gain insight into where a person falls in Maslow's hierarchy of needs.

18. What theory should Abe study if he wants to help people find healthy personal growth?
    a. Neo-Freudian
    b. Psychodynamic
    c. Humanistic
    d. Behavioral

19. Shelley supports Carl Rogers' idea that we are our best selves when we feel accepted for who we are. What does Shelley believe in?
    a. A peak experience
    b. Unconditional positive regard
    c. Self-transcendence
    d. Humanistic psychology

20. When Marty reflected on who she is, all the thoughts and feelings she had in response to this question represent her
    a. self-concept.
    b. ideal self.
    c. self-esteem.
    d. self-efficacy.

21. When analyzing his data, Dr. Lannin used factor analysis to
    a. develop ambiguous pictures.
    b. identify clusters of behaviors that occur together.
    c. analyze the most common defense mechanisms.
    d. determine how people feel about themselves in the present moment.

22. Children's TV-viewing habits (past behavior) influence their viewing preferences (internal personal factor), which influence how television (environmental factor) affects their current behavior. What is this an example of?
    a. Spotlight effect
    b. Reciprocal determinism
    c. The Big Five traits
    d. Implicit learning

23. Paola and Juliana went to a baseball game and were shown on the centerfield screen. Juliana was embarrassed, because she had mustard on her face from her hot dog. In reality, no one in the crowd noticed the mustard. Juliana was overestimating how much attention people were paying to her due to the
    a. self-efficacy effect.
    b. self-serving bias.
    c. self-transcendent effect.
    d. spotlight effect.

24. Athletes who often privately credit their victories to their own abilities, and their losses to bad breaks, lousy officiating, or the other team's exceptional performance, are exhibiting which psychological concept?
    a. The self-serving bias
    b. Pessimism
    c. The spotlight effect
    d. Conscientiousness

25. Augie is from a collectivist culture. He is more likely to
    a. develop a strong sense of self.
    b. give priority to group goals.
    c. achieve personal goals.
    d. focus on how he is different from the group.

26. Marcelo has a good job, a nice house, and plenty of food. On weekends, he skydives for fun. His weekend behavior is best explained by which of the following theories?
    a. Incentive
    b. Drive-reduction
    c. Arousal
    d. Instinct

27. A hungry person eats so as to maintain an internal balance known as
    a. hierarchy of needs.
    b. basal metabolic rate.
    c. homeostasis.
    d. instinct.

28. Cylee is thirsty and takes a drink. Her motivation to reduce the need for water is best explained by (the)
    a. instinct theory.
    b. drive-reduction theory.
    c. arousal theory.
    d. hierarchy of needs.

29. When individuals were placed on a semistarvation diet, researchers found that these individuals
    a. became obsessed with physical exercise.
    b. were more interpersonally outgoing.
    c. were in a state of homeostasis.
    d. lost interest in social activities.

30. Dr. Stevenson told her patients about the best biological explanation for why the human body stores fat, saying
    a. fat is a fuel reserve during periods when food is scarce.
    b. fat is a display of abundant food sources.
    c. fat keeps the body warm in winter climates.
    d. fat contributes to the global epidemic of diabetes.

31. A person who eats excessively and never seems to feel full may have which of the following conditions?
    a. Tumor in the hypothalamus
    b. Too much insulin
    c. Tumor in the hippocampus
    d. Too much of the hormone PYY

32. Amari noticed a change to his thoughts, his behaviors, and his physiological arousal. What did Amari most likely experience?
    a. Facial feedback
    b. Homeostasis
    c. Reciprocal determinism
    d. Emotion

33. What is Dr. Van Brunt most likely to find in her research on facial expressions and gestures?

    a. Facial expressions and gestures both tend to be culture-specific.
    b. Facial expressions and gestures both tend to be universally understood.
    c. Facial expressions tend to be culture-specific, and gestures tend to be universally understood.
    d. Facial expressions tend to be universally understood, and gestures tend to be culture-specific.

34. Dr. Copeland replicated research on emotion detection in facial expressions, finding that people can most readily detect

    a. sadness.
    b. happiness.
    c. anger.
    d. fear.

35. What psychological concept did Dr. Tumminia examine when he predicted that smiling warmly on the outside would cause someone to feel better on the inside?

    a. Drive-reduction theory
    b. Homeostasis
    c. Ideal self
    d. Facial feedback effect

36. Which psychological concept is represented in the following graph?

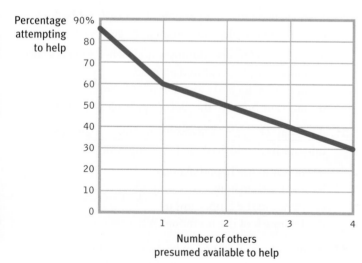

Percentage attempting to help (y-axis, 0 to 90%) vs. Number of others presumed available to help (x-axis, 1 to 4)

    a. The spotlight effect
    b. Social exchange theory
    c. Empathy
    d. The bystander effect

**Use the following text to answer questions 37 & 38:**

Abi has been singing since she was a child. Recently, she moved from her small rural hometown to a large city to pursue her singing career. She was soon hired for an important and popular choral performance. She was nervous but excited about this new opportunity.

37. How might social facilitation affect Abi's performance?

    a. Because she is well practiced at singing, Abi's performance should improve in front of larger crowds.
    b. Because she is well practiced at singing, Abi's performance should be worse in front of larger crowds.
    c. If Abi receives positive feedback from the audience, she will be motivated to give extra effort in her performances.
    d. Because Abi is performing in a group, her individual effort will decrease.

38. Imagine that Abi's singing career does not progress, and she is forced to look for other jobs. As a result, she changes her attitude and decides she never wanted a singing career in the first place. This is best explained by which of the following psychological concepts?

    a. Self-fulfilling prophecy
    b. Frustration-aggression model
    c. Cognitive dissonance
    d. Reciprocity norm

39. McKenna wanted $20 to buy a new T-shirt. She asked her mother for $5 to buy some snacks, and her mother said yes. McKenna then asked for $20, which her mother gave her. McKenna was utilizing which persuasion technique?

    a. Foot-in-the-door
    b. Cognitive dissonance
    c. Central route
    d. Reciprocity norm

40. Korbin is organized, careful, and disciplined. He would score high on which of the Big Five factors?

    a. Agreeableness
    b. Conscientiousness
    c. Openness
    d. Extraversion

**41.** Roman has the tendency to view his own ethnic group as superior to others. This tendency is known as

a. self-transcendence.

b. ethnocentrism.

c. social identity.

d. deindividuation.

**42.** Jackal used peripheral route persuasion to get her friend to give her money. Which method did she use?

a. The door-in-the-face technique

b. The halo effect

c. Unconditional positive regard

d. Repression

Go to Appendix D to complete the **AP® Practice** Evidence-Based Question and Article Analysis Question for this unit.

UNIT 5

# Mental and Physical Health

"It's killing me inside. I'm kind of broken. I'm broken. And my colleagues are broken. And people say, 'It's not that big a deal.' And I want to take them by the collar and say you don't know what you're talking about. Come see my world." So explained Montana nurse Joey Traywick (2021), choking back tears while his hospital's intensive care unit was overwhelmed with Covid-19 patients.

Patients' loved ones, restricted from visiting, also experienced deep distress. That emotional pain was witnessed by Nebraska nurse Antonia Brune (2020) as she accompanied a patient to life's finish line: "I could feel how my patient's three daughters were tormented by not being able to be there physically with their mom." Brune used an iPad to enable the daughters to spend "the whole night talking to their mother—sharing stories, laughter, tears, memories, and music." When their mother's breathing ceased, Brune recalled, "[the daughters] asked me, 'Could you touch her face?' I softly stroked her forehead. 'Could you touch her cheek?' I caressed her cheek. 'Could you hold her hand?' I took her hand. Her daughters gained peace from the sense that they were touching their mom, through me. We were all united in a beautiful, ephemeral moment—patient, family, and caregiver—as they said their final goodbyes."*

The Covid pandemic caused stress: loss of loved ones, illness, fear of becoming ill, social isolation, job loss, and the upheaval of normal routines. This stress affected people's mental health worldwide: In the pandemic's first year, anxiety and depression soared 25 percent (WHO, 2022). As we will see, our mental and our physical health are intimately linked. People with preexisting physical conditions were more likely, during the pandemic, to develop symptoms of psychological disorders. And people with preexisting psychological disorders, if infected with Covid, have been more likely to experience hospitalization, severe illness, and death. Many countries therefore included mental health support in their Covid response plans.

Covid's impact illustrates what this unit explores: our mental and physical health, and the interplay between them. We will discuss what causes stress, how different stressors affect our mental and physical health, and how we manage stress and setbacks. We'll examine evidence-based ways to manage our stress and live a happy, flourishing life. Finally, we will discuss psychological disorders—how they are diagnosed, how they are classified, and the various therapies used to treat them.

**UNIT 5**
**Overview Video** ▶

*Excerpt from Nebraska Nurses Association

Santiago Íñiguez/EyeEm/Getty Images

# Module 5.1a Introduction to Health Psychology: Stress and Illness

To study how stress—and healthy and unhealthy behaviors—influence health and illness, psychologists and physicians created the interdisciplinary field of *behavioral medicine*, integrating behavioral and medical knowledge. **Health psychology**, which provides psychology's contribution to behavioral medicine, explores the impact of psychological, behavioral, and cultural factors on health and wellness. A branch of health psychology called **psychoneuroimmunology** focuses on mind-body interactions (Kiecolt-Glaser, 2009; Kipnis, 2018). This awkward name makes sense: Your thoughts and feelings (*psycho*) influence your brain (*neuro*), which influences the endocrine hormones that affect your disease-fighting *immune* system. And this subfield is the study (*ology*) of those interactions.

Health psychologists use psychological science to enhance health and health care. As we will see throughout this unit, research has identified behaviors that influence health and well-being, such as regular exercise, nutritious eating, sufficient sleep, and not smoking. Health psychologists may work with individuals, hospitals, corporations, or government agencies to promote lifestyle changes that incorporate health-enhancing behaviors, and they may advocate for public policies that promote wellness. Health psychologists also aim to increase the well-being of people with medical conditions, such as by managing chronic pain—which, as we saw in Module 1.6, is influenced by both bottom-up sensory input and top-down cognition. Body and mind form one human system.

Often, people think about their health only when something goes wrong that requires medical attention. That, say health psychologists, is like ignoring a car's maintenance and going to a mechanic only when the car breaks down. Health maintenance begins with implementing strategies that prevent illness by alleviating stress, managing anger, and enhancing well-being.

Let's begin by taking a closer look at stress—what it is, and how it affects our health and well-being.

**health psychology** a subfield of psychology that explores the impact of psychological, behavioral, and cultural factors on health and wellness.

**psychoneuroimmunology** the study of how psychological, neural, and endocrine processes together affect our immune system and resulting health.

# Stress: Some Basic Concepts

**5.1-1** How does our appraisal of an event affect our stress reaction, and what are the three main types of stressors?

To live is to experience stress. Worldwide, 35 percent of people reported experiencing "a lot of stress" the day before (Gallup, 2019a). We may experience stress as positive and motivating (*eustress*) or negative and debilitating (*distress*).

How often do you experience negative stress in your daily life? For many students, the high school years, with their new relationships and more demanding challenges, prove stressful. Deadlines loom at the end of each term. The time demands of volunteering, sports, music and theater, work, and college applications combine with occasional family tensions and success pressures. Sometimes it's enough to give you a headache or disrupt sleep.

Some stresses we anticipate: the upcoming surgery, the visit to an ailing relative, the first day at a new school. Reading or viewing horrific events may also cause stress. (Although helpfully intended, *trigger warnings* that alert people to, say, graphic video content to come, do little to prevent distress and may even increase anxiety [Bellet et al., 2020; Sanson et al., 2019].)

Other stress strikes without warning. Imagine being 21-year-old Ben Carpenter, who experienced the world's wildest and fastest wheelchair ride. As he crossed a street, the light changed and a semitruck moved into the intersection. When they bumped, Carpenter's wheelchair handles got stuck in the truck's grille. The driver, who hadn't seen Carpenter and couldn't hear his cries for help, took off down the highway, pushing the wheelchair at 50 miles per hour until, after two miles, passing police flagged down the truck. As Carpenter tried to cope with his loss of control, his heart raced, his hands sweated, and his breathing sped up: "It was very scary."

**Extreme stress** From a 911 caller reporting Ben Carpenter's horrifying ride: "You are not going to believe this. There is a semitruck pushing a guy in a wheelchair on Red Arrow highway!"

*Michigan State Police*

---

**AP® Science Practice**

## Exploring Research Methods & Design ▷

As you learned above, a Gallup poll surveyed people worldwide and found that 35 percent reported experiencing "a lot of stress" the day before.

- Explain the difference between the population and the sample used in this research.

- Explain why random sampling is important in this research.

---

**Stress** is a slippery concept. We sometimes use the word informally to describe threats or challenges ("Ben Carpenter was under a lot of stress"), and at other times our responses ("Carpenter experienced acute stress"). To a psychologist, the terrifying truck ride was a *stressor*. Carpenter's physical and emotional responses were a *stress reaction*. And the process by which he related to the threat was *stress*. Stress often arises less from events themselves than from how we appraise them (Lazarus, 1998). One person, alone in a house, ignores its creaking sounds and experiences no stress; someone else suspects an intruder and becomes alarmed. One person regards a new job as a welcome challenge; someone else appraises it as risking

**stress** the process by which we perceive and respond to certain events, called *stressors*, that we appraise as threatening or challenging.

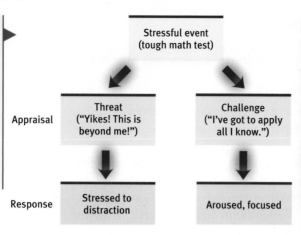

**Figure 5.1-1**
**Stress appraisal**

The events of our lives flow through a psychological filter. How we appraise an event influences how much stress we experience and how effectively we respond.

Stressful event (tough math test)

Appraisal

Threat ("Yikes! This is beyond me!")

Challenge ("I've got to apply all I know.")

Response

Stressed to distraction

Aroused, focused

Fuse/Getty Images

failure (**Figure 5.1-1**). Once we've assessed ("appraised") an event as a stressor (the *primary appraisal*), we then assess our ability to respond to it (the *secondary appraisal*).

When short-lived, or when perceived as challenges, stressors can have positive effects. A momentary stress can mobilize the immune system to fend off infections and heal wounds (Segerstrom, 2007). Stress also arouses and motivates us to conquer problems. Championship athletes, successful entertainers, motivated students, and great teachers and leaders all thrive and excel when aroused by a challenge (Blascovich & Mendes, 2010; Wang et al., 2015). In games and athletic contests, the stress of not knowing who will win makes the competition enjoyable (Abuhamdeh et al., 2015). Having conquered cancer or rebounded from a lost job, some people emerge with stronger self-esteem and a deepened spirituality and sense of purpose. Indeed, experiencing some stress builds *resilience*, the personal strength to cope and recover (Seery, 2011). When we experience hardship, we sometimes discover hidden talents we didn't know we had (Frankenhuis et al., 2020). Adversity can produce growth.

But extreme or prolonged stress can harm us. Stress can trigger risky decisions and unhealthy behaviors (Cohen et al., 2016; Starcke & Brand, 2016). *Adverse childhood experiences (ACEs)*, such as abuse or other traumas, can influence long-term stress responses and negatively impact health and well-being. And stress can affect health directly, increasing infectious-disease–related deaths (Hamer et al., 2019). Pregnant women with overactive stress systems tend to have shorter pregnancies, which pose health risks for their infants (Guardino et al., 2016). What is your perceived stress level (**Figure 5.1-2**)?

There is an interplay between our head and our health. Psychological states are physiological events that influence other parts of our physiological system. Just pausing to *think* about biting into an orange wedge—the sweet, tangy juice from the pulpy fruit flooding across your tongue—can trigger salivation. We'll explore that interplay shortly, but first, let's look more closely at stressors and stress reactions.

**AP® Science Practice**

## Research

On surveys, such as the Perceived Stress Scale, people report their behavior or opinions. But designing questions isn't easy, because people's answers can depend on how questions are framed (or worded). Suppose Question 9 in Figure 5.1-2 said *aggressive* instead of *angered*. Would that change your response?

## Stressors: Things That Push Our Buttons

Stressors fall into three main types: catastrophes, significant life changes, and daily hassles (including social stress). All can be toxic.

### Catastrophes

Catastrophes are large-scale disasters: Think earthquakes, hurricanes, wildfires, pandemics, and wars. After such events, damage to emotional and physical health can be significant. In the four months after Hurricane Katrina in 2005, the suicide rate in New Orleans (my [EYH's] hometown) tripled (Saulny, 2006). And in surveys taken in the 3 weeks after the 9/11 terrorist attacks, 58 percent of Americans said they were experiencing greater-than-average arousal and anxiety (Silver et al., 2002). In the New York City area, people were especially likely to report such symptoms, and sleeping pill prescriptions rose by 28 percent (HMHL, 2002; NSF, 2001). Extensively watching 9/11 television footage predicted worse health

**Figure 5.1-2**
**Perceived stress scale**

## Perceived Stress Scale

The questions in this scale ask about your feelings and thoughts *during the last month*. In each case, indicate how often you felt or thought a certain way.

| 0 | 1 | 2 | 3 | 4 |
|---|---|---|---|---|
| Never | Almost never | Sometimes | Fairly often | Very often |

**In the last month...**

1. ___ ...how often have you been upset because of something that happened unexpectedly?

2. ___ ...how often have you felt that you were unable to control the important things in your life?

3. ___ ...how often have you felt nervous and "stressed"?

4. ___ ...how often have you felt confident about your ability to handle your personal problems?

5. ___ ...how often have you felt that things were going your way?

6. ___ ...how often have you found that you could not cope with all the things you had to do?

7. ___ ...how often have you been able to control irritations in your life?

8. ___ ...how often have you felt that you were on top of things?

9. ___ ...how often have you been angered because of things that were outside of your control?

10. ___ ...how often have you felt difficulties were piling up so high that you could not overcome them?

### SCORING:

- First, reverse your scores for questions 4, 5, 7, and 8.
  On these four questions, change the scores like this: 0 = 4, 1 = 3, 2 = 2, 3 = 1, 4 = 0.
- Next, add up your scores to get a **total score**.
- Scores range from 0 to 40, with higher scores indicating higher perceived stress.
- Scores ranging from 0 to 13 would be considered *low perceived stress.*
- Scores ranging from 14 to 26 would be considered *moderate perceived stress.*
- Scores ranging from 27 to 40 would be considered *high perceived stress.*

Scale data from Cohen, S., Kamarck, T., & Mermelstein, R. (1983). A global measure of perceived stress. *Journal of Health and Social Behavior, 24*, 385–396.

outcomes 2 to 3 years later (Silver et al., 2013). A similar uptick in health issues, from heart problems to suicides, immediately followed the 2011 terrorist attacks in Norway (Strand et al., 2016).

For those who respond to catastrophes by relocating to another country, the stress may be twofold. The trauma of uprooting and family separation may combine with the challenges of adjusting to a different environment and a new culture's language, ethnicity, and social norms (Pipher, 2002; Williams & Berry, 1991). Newcomers often feel marginalized and experience culture shock, leading to stress-related inflammation (Gonzales et al., 2018; Scholaske et al., 2018). This *acculturative stress* declines over time, especially when people engage in meaningful activities and connect socially (Bostean & Gillespie, 2017; Kim et al., 2012).

## Significant Life Changes

Life transitions—having a loved one die, a friend move away, parents get divorced—are often keenly felt. Even happy transitions, such as graduating from high school or leaving home for college, can be stressful. Many such changes happen during adolescence and young adulthood. One massive Canadian survey investigating people's ability to handle unexpected and difficult problems revealed that adolescents struggled the most (Statistics Canada, 2019b). When 650,000 Americans were asked if they had experienced a lot of stress "yesterday," young adults reported the most stress (Newport & Pelham, 2009).

Some psychologists study the health effects of life changes by following people over time. Others compare the life challenges previously experienced by those who have (or have not)

Scott Olson/Getty Images

**A hurricane of destruction and distress** Hurricane Michael raged across Central America and the Florida Panhandle in 2018, killing 74 people and destroying the homes and possessions of thousands more—from the distraught neighbors shown here to my own [ND's] in-laws. "The community at large is suffering from trauma and grief," said officials one year later. "Citizens are fatigued . . . and anxious" (Schneider, 2019).

suffered a health problem, such as a heart attack. In such studies, those recently widowed, fired, or divorced have been more vulnerable to disease (Dohrenwend et al., 1982; Sbarra et al., 2015; Strully, 2009). One Finnish study of 96,000 widowed people found that the survivor's risk of death doubled in the week following a partner's death (Kaprio et al., 1987). A cluster of crises—losing a job, home, and partner—puts a person even more at risk.

## Daily Hassles and Social Stress

Events don't have to remake our lives to cause stress. Stress also comes from *daily hassles*—aggravating siblings, incessant social media interruptions, and overflowing to-do lists (Lazarus, 1990; Pascoe & Richman, 2009; Ruffin, 1993). We might have to give a public speech or do difficult math problems or do our first driving in traffic (Balodis et al., 2010; Dickerson & Kemeny, 2004) (**Figure 5.1-3**). During the Covid pandemic, people from China to Germany to the United States experienced quarantine-related mental distress (Sibley et al., 2020; Xin et al., 2020; Zacher & Rudolph, 2020).

Some people shrug off such hassles; others cannot. This is especially the case for adults who wake up each day facing housing problems, unreliable child care, budgets that won't stretch to the next payday, disability challenges, and poor health. Inequality can likewise take a toll on health and well-being (Piazza et al., 2013; Sapolsky, 2018; Sin et al., 2015). Chronic workplace stress can cause worker "burnout"—feeling ineffective, emotionally depleted, and disconnected (Guthier et al., 2020). Compared with people in 1990, people today report more stress in their day-to-day lives (Almeida et al., 2020). That matters, because persistent (chronic) stress can harm physical health years later—and even shorten life (Chiang et al., 2018; Leger et al., 2018).

Daily pressures may be compounded by prejudice, which—like other stressors—can have both psychological and physical consequences (Benner et al., 2018; Pascoe & Richman, 2009).

### Figure 5.1-3
### Studying stress

Most people experience stress when giving a public speech. To study stress, researchers re-create this type of situation. At the end, they *debrief* and reassure each participant.

1. Participants chew gum so that collecting saliva is easy. The researcher takes a saliva sample from each participant at the beginning of the experiment to measure levels of the stress hormone *cortisol*.

What is 1223 minus 37?

2. Participant gives simulated job interview speech to a critical panel. Next, the participant is asked to complete difficult math problems out loud.

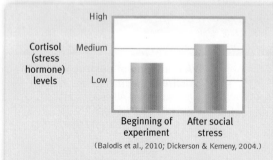

(Balodis et al., 2010; Dickerson & Kemeny, 2004.)

3. Measuring cortisol in participants' saliva before and after tells us that although they enter the lab experiencing some stress, that level goes up 40 percent after they experience social stress.

4. Research team thanks and *debriefs* the participant—explaining the purpose of the experiment and the role she played.

Thinking that some of the people you encounter each day will dislike, distrust, or doubt you is a toxic stress. Many transgender and gender-nonconforming people experience the stress of stigma and discrimination (Valentine & Shipherd, 2018). People with a same-sex sexual orientation who face frequent prejudice in their communities have died, on average, 12 years earlier than have those who live in more accepting communities (Hatzenbueler, 2014). For many Black Americans, the stress of racial discrimination can lead to less healthy behaviors and to unhealthy blood pressure, increased risk for brain disease, and sleep deprivation (Beatty Moody et al., 2019; Brody et al., 2018; Michaels et al., 2022; Pascoe et al., 2022).

Stress also arises from the daily conflicts we face between our different **approach and avoidance motives**, which Kurt Lewin identified in his theory of motivational conflicts (Hovland & Sears, 1938; Lewin, 1935). Least stressful are the *approach-approach* conflicts, in which two attractive but incompatible goals pull us—to choose tacos or pizza, a dance or a music class, the green or the gray hoodie. At other times, we face an *avoidance-avoidance* conflict between two undesirable alternatives. Do you avoid studying a disliked subject, or avoid failure by doing your reading? Do you suffer someone's wrath for admitting the truth, or feelings of guilt for having lied?

In times of *approach-avoidance* conflict, we feel simultaneously attracted and repelled. You may adore some things about your romantic partner but dislike others. From a distance, the goal—a happy relationship—looks appealing. But as you approach that goal, your avoidance tendency may begin to overtake your approach tendency and you feel an urge to escape. Stepping back, the negative aspects fade and you again feel attracted. Stress multiplies when we face several approach-avoidance conflicts simultaneously—whom to date, which courses to take, which college to attend.

**approach and avoidance motives** the drive to move toward (approach) or away from (avoid) a stimulus.

## The Stress Response System

### 5.1-2 How do we respond and adapt to stress?

Medical interest in stress dates back to Hippocrates (460–377 B.C.E.). Centuries later, Walter Cannon (1929) confirmed that the stress response is part of a unified mind-body system. He observed that extreme cold, lack of oxygen, and emotion-arousing events all trigger an outpouring of the adrenal stress hormones epinephrine (adrenaline) and norepinephrine (noradrenaline). When alerted by any of a number of brain pathways, the sympathetic nervous system arouses us, preparing the body for the wonderfully adaptive response Cannon called *fight or flight*. It increases heart rate and respiration, diverts blood from digestion to the skeletal muscles, dulls feelings of pain, and releases sugar and fat from the body's stores. The sympathetic nervous system helps more with immediate threats (a poisonous snake nearby) than with distant or looming threats (a climate apocalypse). By fighting or fleeing, and sometimes by *freezing* (no response), we increase our chances of survival.

Since Cannon's time, physiologists have identified an additional stress response system. On orders from the cerebral cortex, the endocrine system secretes *glucocorticoid* stress hormones such as *cortisol*. The two systems work at different speeds, explained biologist Robert Sapolsky (2003): "In a fight-or-flight scenario, epinephrine is the one handing out guns; glucocorticoids are the ones drawing up blueprints for new aircraft carriers needed for the war effort." Speedy epinephrine took over during an experiment inadvertently conducted on a British Airways San Francisco to London flight. Three hours after takeoff, a mistakenly played message told passengers the plane was about to crash into the sea. Although the flight crew immediately recognized the error and tried to calm the terrified passengers, several required medical assistance (Associated Press, 1999).

Canadian scientist Hans Selye's (1936, 1976) 40 years of research on stress extended Cannon's findings. His studies of animals' reactions to various stressors, such as electric shock and surgery, helped make stress a major concept in both psychology and medicine. Selye proposed that the body's adaptive response to stress is so general

**AP® Science Practice**

**Research**

Notice how Selye's research built upon Cannon's research. Building upon prior findings is how scientific theories evolve.

**AP® Exam Tip**

Be able to differentiate Walter Cannon's fight-or-flight theory from Hans Selye's general adaptation syndrome. These have been on the AP® exam in the past.

**AP® Science Practice**

## Data

Consider the graph in Figure 5.1-4.
- What variables are depicted in the graph?
- What psychological concept is illustrated in the graph?
- What conclusions about stress resistance can you draw from this graph?

that, like a single burglar alarm, it sounds, no matter what intrudes. He named this response the **general adaptation syndrome (GAS)**, which he saw as a three-phase process.

Let's say you suffer a physical or an emotional trauma:

- In **Phase 1**, you have an ***alarm reaction***, as your sympathetic nervous system is suddenly activated. Your heart rate zooms. Blood is diverted to your skeletal muscles. With your resources mobilized, you are now ready to fight back.

- During **Phase 2**, ***resistance***, your temperature, blood pressure, and respiration remain high. Your endocrine system pumps epinephrine and norepinephrine into your bloodstream. You are fully engaged, summoning all your resources to meet the challenge. As time passes, with no relief from stress, your body's reserves dwindle.

- You have reached **Phase 3**, ***exhaustion***. With exhaustion, you become more vulnerable to illness or even, in extreme cases, collapse and death.

Selye's basic point: Although the human body copes well with temporary stress, prolonged stress can damage it. Syria's civil war, for example, has taken a toll on its people's health (Al Ibraheem et al., 2017) (**Figure 5.1-4**). Severe childhood stress gets under the skin, leading to greater adult stress, sleeplessness, and heart disease (Jakubowski et al., 2018; Puterman et al., 2016; Talvitie et al., 2019). In one two-decade longitudinal study, severely stressed Welsh children were three times more likely to develop heart disease as adults (Ashton et al., 2016).

We respond to stress in other ways, too. One response is common after a loved one's death: Withdraw. Isolate. Conserve energy. Faced with an extreme disaster, such as a ship sinking, some people become paralyzed by fear. Another response, found often among women, is to give and receive support—what's called the **tend-and-befriend response** (Lim & DeSteno, 2016; Taylor, 2006; von Dawans et al., 2019).

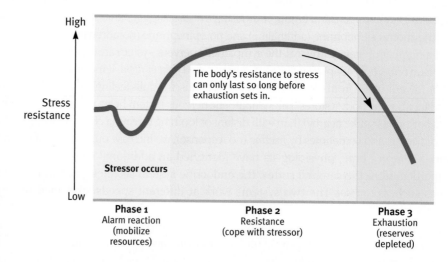

### Figure 5.1-4

**Selye's general adaptation syndrome**

Due to the ongoing conflict, Syria's White Helmets (volunteer rescuers) are perpetually in "alarm reaction" mode, rushing to pull victims from the rubble after each fresh attack. As their resistance depletes, they risk exhaustion.

## AP® Science Practice

## Check Your Understanding

### Examine the Concept

▶ The field of _____ studies mind-body interactions, including the effects of psychological, neural, and endocrine functioning on the immune system and overall health.

▶ Explain the stages in Selye's general adaptation syndrome (GAS).

*Answers to the Examine the Concept questions can be found in Appendix C at the end of the book.*

### Apply the Concept

▶ How often is your stress response system activated? What are some of the things that have triggered a fight, flight, or freeze response for you?

**Friendly foes** Tending and befriending helped U.S. marathon rivals and good friends Kara Goucher and Shalane Flanagan cope with stress and excel. During the 2012 London Olympics marathon, they battled intense rain and physical pain, finishing 1 second apart.

# Stress and Vulnerability to Disease

### 5.1-3 How does stress make us more vulnerable to disease?

It often pays to spend our resources in fighting or fleeing an external threat. But we do so at a cost. When stress is momentary, the cost is small. When stress persists, the cost may be greater, in the form of lowered resistance to infections and other threats to mental and physical well-being.

If you've ever had a stress headache, or felt your blood pressure rise with anger, you know that our psychological states have physiological effects. Stress can even leave you less able to fight off disease because your nervous and endocrine systems influence your immune system (Sternberg, 2009). You can think of your immune system as a complex surveillance system. When it functions properly, it keeps you healthy by isolating and destroying bacteria, viruses, and other invaders. Four types of cells are active in these search-and-destroy missions (**Figure 5.1-5**).

Your age, nutrition, genetics, and stress level all influence your immune system's activity. If it doesn't function properly, your immune system can err in two directions:

1. *Overreacting*, the immune system may attack the body's own tissues, causing an allergic reaction or a self-attacking disease such as lupus, multiple sclerosis, or some forms of arthritis. Women, who are immunologically stronger than men, are more susceptible to such *autoimmune diseases* (Nussinovitch & Schoenfeld, 2012; Schwartzman-Morris & Putterman, 2012).

2. *Underreacting*, the immune system may allow a bacterial infection to flare, a dormant virus to erupt, or cancer cells to multiply.

Immune system suppression has been observed in animals stressed by physical restraints, unavoidable electric shocks, noise, crowding, cold water, social defeat, or separation from their mothers (Maier et al., 1994). One study monitored immune responses in 43 monkeys over 6 months (Cohen et al., 1992). Half were left in stable groups. The rest were stressed by being housed with new roommates—3 or 4 new monkeys each month. By the end of the experiment, the socially disrupted monkeys had weaker immune systems.

Human immune systems react similarly. Three examples:

- *Surgical wounds heal more slowly in stressed people*. In one experiment, dental students received punch wounds (precise small holes punched in the skin). Compared with wounds placed during summer vacation, those placed three days before a major exam healed 40 percent more slowly (Kiecolt-Glaser et al., 1998). In other studies, marital conflict has also slowed punch-wound healing (Kiecolt-Glaser et al., 2005).

 **AP® Science Practice**

## Research

According to American Psychological Association guidelines, animal researchers must provide "humane care and healthful conditions," and testing should "minimize discomfort" (APA, 2012). Using these ethical guidelines, do you think the monkey study described here would be approved by an institutional review board?

**general adaptation syndrome (GAS)** Selye's concept of the body's adaptive response to stress in three phases—alarm, resistance, exhaustion.

**tend-and-befriend response** under stress, people (especially women) may nurture themselves and others (*tend*) and bond with and seek support from others (*befriend*).

Figure 5.1-5

**A simplified view of immune responses**

Romariolen/Shutterstock

Intruders!

Is it a bacterial infection?

Is it a cancer cell, virus, or other "foreign substance"?

Is it some other harmful intruder, or perhaps a worn-out cell needing to be cleaned up?

Are there diseased cells (such as those infected by viruses or cancer) that need to be cleared out?

**Possible Responses:**

Send in: *B lymphocytes,* which fight bacterial infections. (This one is shown in front of a macrophage.)

CNRI/Science Source

Send in: *T lymphocytes,* which attack cancer cells, viruses, and foreign substances.

NIBSC/Science Source

Send in: *macrophage cells* ("big eaters"), which attack harmful invaders and worn-out cells. (This one is engulfing tuberculosis bacteria.)

SPL/Science Source

Send in: *natural killer cells* (NK cells), which attack diseased cells. (These two are attacking a cancer cell.)

Eye of Science/Science Source

- ***Stressed people are more vulnerable to colds***. Major life stress increases the risk of a respiratory infection (Pedersen et al., 2010). When researchers dropped a cold virus into people's noses, 47 percent of those living stress-filled lives developed colds (**Figure 5.1-6**). Among those living relatively free of stress, only 27 percent did. In follow-up research, the happiest and most relaxed people were likewise markedly less vulnerable to an experimentally delivered cold virus (Cohen et al., 2003, 2006; Cohen & Pressman, 2006).

- ***Stress can hasten the course of disease***. As its name tells us, *acquired immune deficiency syndrome (AIDS)* is an immune disorder, caused by the *human immunodeficiency virus (HIV)*. Stress cannot give people AIDS. But an analysis of 33,252 participants from around the world found that stress and negative emotions sped the transition from HIV infection to AIDS. And stress predicted a faster decline in those persons with AIDS (Chida & Vedhara, 2009).

The stress effect on immunity makes physiological sense. It takes energy to track down invaders, produce swelling, and maintain fevers. Thus, when diseased, your body reduces its

Figure 5.1-6

**Stress and colds**

People with the highest life stress scores were also most vulnerable when exposed to an experimentally delivered cold virus (Cohen et al., 1991).

Laurent/Yakou/Science Source

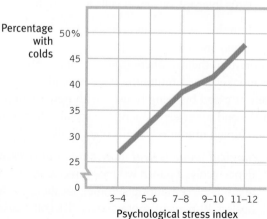

Percentage with colds

50%

45

40

35

30

25

0

3–4   5–6   7–8   9–10   11–12

Psychological stress index

muscular energy output by decreasing activity (and increasing sleep). Stress creates a competing energy need. During an aroused fight-or-flight reaction, your stress responses divert energy from your disease-fighting immune system and send it to your muscles and brain. This increases your vulnerability to illness. Those experiencing the stress of depression tend to age faster and die sooner (McIntosh & Relton, 2018). *The point to remember:* Stress gets under the skin. It does not make us sick, but it does alter our immune functioning, which leaves us less able to resist infection.

## Check Your Understanding

**Examine the Concept**

▶ Explain three effects of stress on our immune system.

**Apply the Concept**

▶ How have changes in stress levels — such as increased stress around finals week — affected your health, and the health of other students in your classes?

*Answers to the Examine the Concept questions can be found in Appendix C at the end of the book.*

## Stress and Cancer

Stress does not create cancer cells. In a healthy, functioning immune system, lymphocytes, macrophages, and natural killer (NK) cells search out and destroy cancer cells and cancer-damaged cells. If stress weakens the immune system, might this weaken a person's ability to fight off cancer? To explore a possible stress-cancer connection, experimenters have implanted tumor cells in rodents or given them *carcinogens* (cancer-producing substances). They then exposed some rodents to uncontrollable stress, such as inescapable shocks, which weakened their immune systems (Sklar & Anisman, 1981). Stressed rodents, compared with their unstressed counterparts, developed cancer more often, experienced tumor growth sooner, and grew larger tumors.

Does this stress-cancer link also hold with humans? The results are generally the same (Lutgendorf & Andersen, 2015). Some studies have found that people are at increased risk for cancer within a year after experiencing significant stress or bereavement (Chida et al., 2008; Steptoe et al., 2010). In one large Swedish study, the risk of colon cancer was 5.5 times greater among people with a history of workplace stress than among those who reported no such problems. This difference was not due to group differences in age, smoking, drinking, or physical characteristics (Courtney et al., 1993). Other studies, however, have found no link between stress and human cancer risk (Butow et al., 2018; Petticrew et al., 1999, 2002). Concentration camp survivors and former prisoners of war, for example, do not have elevated cancer rates.

Overstating the link between emotions and cancer may lead some patients to blame themselves for their illness. A corollary danger is a sense of virtuousness among those who remain cancer-free and assume, incorrectly, that anyone could do the same if they changed their lifestyle.

This point is important enough to repeat: *Stress does not create cancer cells.* At worst, it may affect their growth by weakening the body's natural defenses against multiplying malignant cells (Lutgendorf et al., 2008; Nausheen et al., 2010; Sood et al., 2010). Although a relaxed, hopeful state may enhance these defenses against the powerful biological processes at work in advanced cancer, we should be aware of the thin line that divides science from wishful thinking (Andersen, 2002). For patients with both cancer and depression, treating the depression typically improves quality of life—but it does not increase survival rates (Mulick et al., 2018).

# Stress and Heart Disease

> **5.1-4** Why are some of us more prone than others to coronary heart disease?

Imagine a world where you wake up each day, eat your breakfast, and check the news. In the headlines, you see that four 747 jumbo jets crashed again yesterday, killing another 1642 passengers. You finish your breakfast, grab your bag, and head to class. It's just an average day.

Replace airline crashes with **coronary heart disease**, the United States' leading cause of death, and you have reentered reality. About 655,000 Americans die annually from heart disease (CDC, 2020c). High blood pressure (hypertension) and a family history of the disease increase the risk. So do smoking, obesity, an unhealthy diet, physical inactivity, and a high cholesterol level. Such factors—along with more homicides, opioid deaths, and inequality—help explain why, despite spending much more on health care, the United States has a lower life expectancy than other rich countries, and U.S. longevity has been declining since 2014 (Roser, 2020).

Stress and personality also play a big role in heart disease. The more psychological trauma people experience, the more their bodies generate *inflammation*, which is associated with heart and other health problems, including depression (Haapakoski et al., 2015; O'Donovan et al., 2012).

## The Effects of Personality, Pessimism, and Depression

In a classic study, Meyer Friedman, Ray Rosenman, and their colleagues tested the idea that stress increases vulnerability to heart disease by measuring, at different times of year, the blood cholesterol level and clotting speed of 40 U.S. men who were tax accountants (Friedman & Ulmer, 1984). The test results were initially normal. But as the accountants began scrambling to finish their clients' tax returns before the April 15 filing deadline, their cholesterol and clotting measures rose to dangerous levels. After the deadline, these measures returned to normal. For these men, stress predicted heart attack risk.

The researchers then launched a *longitudinal study* of more than 3000 healthy middle-aged men. They interviewed each man for 15 minutes, noting his work and eating habits, manner of talking, and other behavior patterns, and then identified him as either **Type A** or **Type B** (with a roughly equal number of each type).

Nine years later, 257 men in Friedman and Rosenman's study had suffered heart attacks—69 percent of them Type A. Moreover, not one of the "pure" Type Bs—the most mellow and laid-back of their group—had suffered a heart attack.

As often happens in science, this exciting discovery provoked both enormous public interest and researchers' curiosity. Was the finding reliable? If so, what was the toxic component of the Type A profile? Time-consciousness? Competitiveness? Anger?

Hundreds of other studies have since explored possible psychological correlates or predictors of cardiovascular health (Chida & Hamer, 2008; Chida & Steptoe, 2009). They reveal that Type A's toxic core is negative emotions—especially the anger associated with an aggressively reactive temperament. As Type A individuals' often-active sympathetic nervous system redistributes blood flow to their muscles, it pulls blood away from their internal organs. The liver, which normally removes cholesterol and fat from the blood, can't do its job. Thus, excess cholesterol and fat may continue to circulate in the blood and later get deposited around the heart. Hostility also correlates with other risk factors, such as smoking, drinking, and obesity (Bunde & Suls, 2006). Our mind and heart interact.

In Western cultures, suppressing negative emotions increases depression, relationship problems, and health risks (Cameron & Overall, 2018; Kitayama et al., 2015). Yet hundreds of studies

**coronary heart disease** the clogging of the vessels that nourish the heart muscle; a leading cause of death in many developed countries.

**Type A** Friedman and Rosenman's term for competitive, hard-driving, impatient, verbally aggressive, and anger-prone people.

**Type B** Friedman and Rosenman's term for easygoing, relaxed people.

of young and middle-aged people confirm that those who react with anger over little things are the most prone to coronary heart disease. Rage "seems to lash back and strike us in the heart muscle" (Spielberger & London, 1982).

Pessimism seems to be similarly toxic (Pänkäläinen et al., 2016). One longitudinal study followed 1306 initially healthy men who a decade earlier had been scored as optimists, pessimists, or neither (Kubzansky et al., 2001). Even after adjusting for other risk factors, such as smoking, pessimists were more than twice as likely as optimists to develop heart disease (**Figure 5.1-7**).

Happiness also matters. "A cheerful heart is a good medicine," offered the ancient book of Proverbs. Happy and consistently satisfied people tend to be healthy and to outlive their unhappy peers (Diener et al., 2017; Gana et al., 2016; Martín-María et al., 2017). People with big smiles tend to have extensive social networks, which predict longer life (Hertenstein et al., 2009). Having a happy spouse also predicts better health. Happy you, healthy me (Chopik & O'Brien, 2017).

As we noted earlier, depressed people tend to age faster and die sooner (Han et al., 2018). In one study, nearly 4000 English women and men (ages 52 to 79) provided mood reports from a single day. Compared with those in a good mood, those in a depressed mood were twice as likely to be dead 5 years later (Steptoe & Wardle, 2011). In a U.S. survey of 164,102 adults, those who had experienced a heart attack were twice as likely to report also having been depressed at some point in their lives (Witters & Wood, 2015). And in the years following a heart attack, people with high scores for depression were four times more likely than their low-scoring counterparts to develop further heart problems (Frasure-Smith & Lesperance, 2005). Depressed people tend to smoke more and exercise less (Whooley et al., 2008). Depression is disheartening.

## Stress and Inflammation

Stress is also disheartening: Work stress, job loss, and trauma-related stress symptoms increase heart disease risk (Allesøe et al., 2010; Gallo et al., 2006; Kubzansky et al., 2009; Slopen et al., 2010).

Both heart disease and depression may result when chronic stress triggers blood vessel inflammation, disrupting the body's disease-fighting immune system (Miller & Blackwell, 2006; Mommersteeg et al., 2016). People who experience social threats, including harshly raised children, are more prone to inflammation responses (Dickerson et al., 2009; Miller & Chen, 2010). Persistent inflammation can lead to asthma or clogged arteries, and can worsen depression.

Stress can affect our health in many ways. (See Developing Arguments: Stress and Health.) The stress-illness connection is a price we pay for the benefits of stress. Stress invigorates our lives by arousing and motivating us. An unstressed life would hardly be challenging, productive, or even safe.

**Figure 5.1-7**

**Pessimism and heart disease**

A Harvard School of Public Health team found pessimistic men had a doubled risk of developing heart disease over a 10-year period. (Data from Kubzansky et al., 2001.)

(a)           (b)

**A broken heart?** Fans were shocked by the unexpected death of actor and writer Carrie Fisher in 2016. They were shocked again when — a day later — her mother, the actor and singer Debbie Reynolds, also died (a). In 2022, Uvalde, Texas teacher Irma Garcia was among 21 people massacred at Robb Elementary School. Two days later, her distraught husband, Joe Garcia, died of a heart attack (b). People wondered: Might grief-related depression and stress hormones have contributed to Reynolds' stroke and Garcia's heart failure?

# Developing Arguments

### Stress and Health

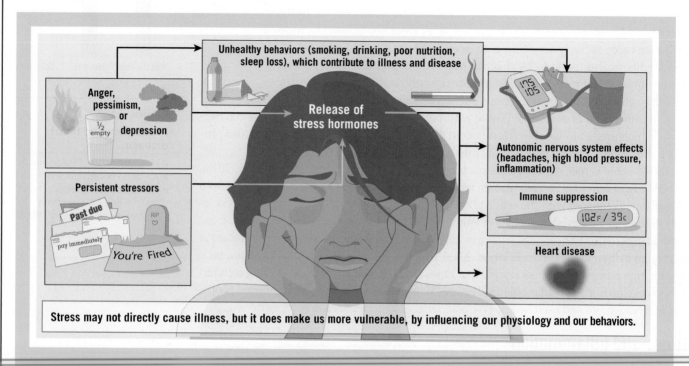

Unhealthy behaviors (smoking, drinking, poor nutrition, sleep loss), which contribute to illness and disease

Anger, pessimism, or depression

½ empty

Release of stress hormones

Persistent stressors

Past due

RIP

pay immediately

You're Fired

Autonomic nervous system effects (headaches, high blood pressure, inflammation)

Immune suppression

102F / 39c

Heart disease

**Stress may not directly cause illness, but it does make us more vulnerable, by influencing our physiology and our behaviors.**

## Developing Arguments Questions

**1.** Using scientifically derived evidence presented here, support the claim that stress makes us more vulnerable to illness.

**2.** What type of research method would you need to use to address the question "Does stress *cause* illness?" Explain your choice.

## Anger Management

> **5.1-5** What are the causes and consequences of anger?

When we face a threat or challenge, fear triggers flight but anger triggers fight—each at times an adaptive behavior. Yet chronic hostility, as in the Type A personality, is linked to heart disease. How, then, can we manage our anger?

Individualist cultures encourage people to vent their rage. Such advice is seldom heard in cultures where people's identity is centered more on the "we" than "me." People who keenly sense their *inter*dependence see anger as a threat to group harmony (Markus & Kitayama, 1991). In Tahiti, for instance, people learn to be considerate and gentle. In Japan, from infancy on, angry expressions are less common than in Western cultures.

The Western vent-your-anger advice presumes that aggression enables emotional release, or **catharsis**. Expressing anger can indeed be *temporarily* calming if it does not leave us feeling guilty or anxious (Geen & Quanty, 1977; Hokanson & Edelman, 1966). But catharsis usually fails to cleanse our rage. More often, expressing anger breeds more anger. It may provoke further retaliation, causing a minor conflict to escalate into a major confrontation. And it can magnify anger: As we learned from the *behavior feedback* research in Module 4.8, *acting* angry can make us *feel* angrier (Flack, 2006; Snodgrass et al., 1986). Anger's backfire potential appeared in a study of people who were asked to wallop a punching bag while

**catharsis** in psychology, the idea that "releasing" aggressive energy (through action or fantasy) relieves aggressive urges.

ruminating about a person who had recently angered them (Bushman, 2002). Later, when given a chance for revenge, those who vented their anger became even more aggressive.

Angry outbursts that temporarily calm us may also become reinforcing and therefore habit forming. If stressed managers find they can temporarily drain off some of their tension by berating an employee, then the next time they feel irritated and tense they may be more likely to explode again.

What are some better ways to manage anger? Experts offer three suggestions:

- **Wait**. Doing so will reduce your physiological arousal. "What goes up must come down," noted Carol Tavris (1982). "Any emotional arousal will simmer down if you just wait long enough."

- **Find a healthy distraction or support instead of ruminating**. Calm yourself by exercising, reading, or talking it through with a friend. Brain scans show that ruminating inwardly about why you are angry increases blood flow to the brain's anger-processing amygdala (Fabiansson et al., 2012).

- **Distance yourself**. Try to move away from the situation mentally, as if you are watching it unfold from a distance or the future. Self-distancing reduces rumination, anger, and aggression (Kross & Ayduk, 2011; Mischkowski et al., 2012; White et al., 2015).

Used wisely, anger communicates strength and competence (Tiedens, 2001). Anger also motivates people to act courageously and achieve goals (Aarts & Custers, 2012; Halmburger et al., 2015). Controlled expressions of anger are more adaptive than either hostile outbursts or pent-up angry feelings. Civility means not only keeping silent about trivial irritations but also communicating about important ones clearly and assertively. A nonaccusatory statement of feeling—perhaps letting a friend know that "I get upset when you cancel plans at the last minute"—can help resolve conflicts. Anger that expresses a grievance in ways that promote reconciliation rather than retaliation can benefit a relationship.

**When anger is all the rage** Fans seem to experience a *temporary* release while cheering at World Cup soccer matches, such as this one in South Africa. My [DM's] daughter, a South Africa resident, noted, "Every time I got angry at Uruguay, blowing that vuvuzela and joining the chorus of dissent released something in me."

---

**AP® Science Practice**

## Check Your Understanding

### Examine the Concept

▶ Which component of the Type A personality has been linked most closely to coronary heart disease?

▶ Which one of the following is an effective strategy for reducing angry feelings?

   a. Retaliate verbally or physically.

   b. Wait or "simmer down."

   c. Express anger in action or fantasy.

   d. Review the grievance silently.

*Answers to the Examine the Concept questions can be found in Appendix C at the end of the book.*

### Apply the Concept

▶ Do you think you are Type A, Type B, or somewhere in between? In what ways has this tendency been helpful to you, and in what ways has it been a challenge?

▶ What changes could you make to avoid the persistent stressors in your life?

---

# Module 5.1a REVIEW

**5.1-1 How does our appraisal of an event affect our stress reaction, and what are the three main types of stressors?**

- *Stress* is the process by which we perceive and respond to stressors that we appraise as challenging or threatening.

If we appraise an event as challenging, we will be aroused and focused in preparation for success. If we appraise an event as a threat, we will experience a stress reaction, and our health may suffer.

- The three main types of stressors are catastrophes, significant life changes, and daily hassles—including social stress. Daily hassles and social stress may include inequality and prejudice, chronic workplace stress (which may lead to worker "burnout"), and the conflicts we face between our different *approach and avoidance motives*.

### 5.1-2 How do we respond and adapt to stress?

- Walter Cannon viewed the stress response as a fight-or-flight system.

- Later researchers identified an additional stress response system in which the endocrine system secretes glucocorticoid stress hormones, such as cortisol.

- Hans Selye proposed a three-phase (alarm, resistance, exhaustion) *general adaptation syndrome (GAS)*.

- Some people may react to stress by withdrawing. Others, especially women, may demonstrate a *tend-and-befriend* response.

### 5.1-3 How does stress make us more vulnerable to disease?

- *Psychoneuroimmunology* is the study of how psychological, neural, and endocrine processes together affect our immune system and resulting health.

- Along with factors such as age, nutrition, and genetics, stress can prompt the immune system to either overreact (causing an allergic reaction or autoimmune disease) or underreact (allowing an infection to flare or cancer cells to multiply).

- Stress diverts energy from the immune system, inhibiting the activities of its B and T lymphocytes, macrophages, and NK cells.

- Stress does not cause illness, but by altering our immune functioning it may make us more vulnerable to diseases and influence their progression.

### 5.1-4 Why are some of us more prone than others to coronary heart disease?

- *Coronary heart disease* has been linked with the reactive, anger-prone *Type A* personality.

- Compared to people with relaxed, easygoing *Type B* personalities, the sympathetic nervous system in Type A people is more active; it may divert blood flow from the liver to the muscles, leaving excess cholesterol and fat circulating in the bloodstream and allowing these substances to eventually become deposited around the heart.

- Chronic stress also contributes to persistent inflammation, which is associated with heart and other health problems, including depression.

### 5.1-5 What are the causes and consequences of anger?

- Facing a threat or a challenge may trigger anger, and chronic hostility is linked to heart disease. Our culture can influence how we express anger.

- Emotional *catharsis* may be temporarily calming, but it does not reduce anger; expressing anger can make us angrier.

- Experts suggest reducing the level of physiological arousal of anger by waiting, finding a healthy distraction or support, and trying to move away from the situation mentally. Controlled assertions of feelings may resolve conflicts, and expressing grievances in ways that promote reconciliation can benefit a relationship.

## AP® Practice Multiple Choice Questions

1. Dr. Fyneburge wants to help people change their behaviors to improve their wellness. What area of psychology should Dr. Fyneburge pursue?

   a. Evolutionary psychology
   b. Cognitive psychology
   c. Health psychology
   d. Social psychology

2. Ana's family was directly exposed to a recent hurricane in Puerto Rico. Which phase of the general adaptation syndrome (GAS) would they have experienced first?

   a. Resistance
   b. Appraisal
   c. Exhaustion
   d. Alarm

**3.** Regan conducted a study about how psychological, neural, and hormonal factors impact people's health. What did Regan study?

    a. Health psychology

    b. Psychoneuroimmunology

    c. General adaptation

    d. Catharsis

**Use the following scenario to answer questions 4 and 5:**

Dr. Roberto is conducting a study on a sample of 30 people who always want to win, become angry easily, and have a hard time waiting their turn. Dr. Roberto is especially interested in this population because they tend to have a higher risk of coronary heart disease.

**4.** Based on this description, what variable is Dr. Roberto most likely examining?

    a. Type A personality

    b. Type B personality

    c. General adaptation syndrome

    d. Overreactive immune systems

**5.** What advice should Dr. Roberto give to his sample of participants to reduce their risk of coronary heart disease?

    a. When you feel angry, release it in the most aggressive way possible to maximize catharsis.

    b. When you feel angry, wait for a period before expressing your anger.

    c. When you feel angry, try to ruminate about the causes of your anger.

    d. When you feel angry, think about all the downsides to being angry.

**6.** Dr. McNulty conducted a study in which high school students were seated in a hot, crowded room, with loud clanging noises sounding nearby. He then sent them to a comfortable room, and randomly divided them into two groups. One group conversed with other members about the negative experience, while the other group was asked simply to sit in the new room. Dr. McNulty found that, at the study's conclusion, the conversation group reported less stress. Which of the following illustrates a conclusion that Dr. McNulty could draw from his study?

    a. The general adaptation syndrome caused the students in the supportive group to have less stress.

    b. There was an association between secondary appraisals and the amount of stress the students experienced.

    c. Experiencing an avoidance-avoidance motive was correlated with lower stress.

    d. A tend-and-befriend response led to lower stress levels.

**7.** Janie needs to decide whether to attend State University or City College, and she finds that she is excited about each one. Which of the following is most likely to be true for Janie?

    a. Janie is experiencing an extreme amount of stress in her approach-avoidance conflict.

    b. Janie is experiencing some stress in her approach-approach conflict.

    c. Janie is experiencing a moderate amount of stress in her avoidance-avoidance conflict.

    d. Janie is experiencing an extreme amount of stress in her avoidance-avoidance conflict.

# Module 5.1b Introduction to Health Psychology: Coping With Stress

> **LEARNING TARGETS**
>
> **5.1-6** Explain two ways in which people try to alleviate stress.
>
> **5.1-7** Explain how a perceived lack of control can affect health.
>
> **5.1-8** Explain why self-control is important and whether it can be depleted.
>
> **5.1-9** Explain how an optimistic outlook affects health and longevity.
>
> **5.1-10** Explain how social support promotes good health.

### 5.1-6 In what two ways do people try to alleviate stress?

Stressors are unavoidable. This fact, coupled with the fact that persistent stress correlates with heart disease, depression, and lowered immunity, gives us a clear message: We need to learn to **cope** with the stress in our lives.

Some stressors we address directly, with **problem-focused coping**. If our impatience leads to a family fight, we may go directly to that family member to work things out. We tend to use problem-focused strategies when we believe stress is a problem to be solved—when we feel a sense of control over a situation and think we can change the circumstances. We turn to **emotion-focused coping** when we believe we cannot change a situation. If, despite our best efforts, we cannot get along with that family member, we may relieve stress by meditating, reaching out to family or friends, or seeking psychiatric care. Some emotion-focused strategies can harm our health, such as when we respond by eating unhealthy comfort foods. When challenged, some of us tend to respond with cool problem-focused coping, others with emotion-focused coping (Connor-Smith & Flachsbart, 2007). Our feelings of personal control, our optimistic outlook, our sense of humor, and our supportive connections all influence our ability to cope successfully.

## Personal Control

### 5.1-7 How does a perceived lack of control affect health?

Picture the scene: Two rats receive simultaneous shocks. Only one of them can turn a wheel to stop the shocks. The helpless rat, but not the wheel turner, becomes more susceptible to ulcers and lowered immunity to disease (Laudenslager & Reite, 1984). In humans, too, uncontrollable threats trigger the strongest stress responses (Dickerson & Kemeny, 2004).

Any of us may feel helpless, hopeless, and depressed after experiencing a series of bad events beyond our **personal control**. Martin Seligman and his colleagues have shown that for some animals and people, a series of uncontrollable events creates a state of

**coping** alleviating stress using emotional, cognitive, or behavioral methods.

**problem-focused coping** attempting to alleviate stress directly—by changing the stressor or the way we interact with that stressor.

**emotion-focused coping** attempting to alleviate stress by avoiding or ignoring a stressor and attending to emotional needs related to our stress reaction.

**personal control** our sense of controlling our environment rather than feeling helpless.

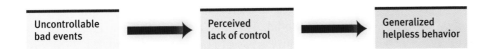

| Uncontrollable bad events | → | Perceived lack of control | → | Generalized helpless behavior |

**Figure 5.1-8**
**Learned helplessness**
When animals and people experience no control over repeated bad events, they often learn helplessness.

**learned helplessness** (Figure 5.1-8). In experiments, dogs were strapped in a harness and given repeated shocks, with no opportunity to avoid them (Seligman & Maier, 1967). Later, when placed in another situation where they *could* escape the punishment by simply leaping a hurdle, the dogs displayed learned helplessness; they cowered as if without hope. Other dogs that had been able to escape the first shocks reacted differently. They had learned they were in control and easily escaped the shocks in the new situation (Seligman & Maier, 1967). People have shown similar patterns of learned helplessness (Abramson et al., 1978, 1989; Seligman, 1975).

Perceiving a loss of control, we become more vulnerable to ill health. This is an especially serious problem for older people, who are highly susceptible to health problems and also perceive the greatest loss of control (Drewelies et al., 2017). In a famous study of elderly nursing home residents, those who perceived the least amount of control over their activities declined faster and died sooner than those given more control (Rodin, 1986). Workers able to adjust office furnishings and control interruptions and distractions in their work environment have experienced less stress (O'Neill, 1993). Such findings help explain why British executives have tended to outlive those in clerical or laboring positions, and why Finnish workers with low job stress have been less than half as likely to die of stroke or heart disease as those with a demanding job and little control. The more control workers have, the longer they live (Bosma et al., 1997, 1998; Kivimaki et al., 2002; Marmot et al., 1997).

Poverty entails less control of one's life, which helps explain the link between economic status and longevity (Jokela et al., 2009). In one study of 843 grave markers in an old cemetery in Glasgow, Scotland, those with the costliest, highest pillars (indicating the most affluence) tended to have lived the longest (Carroll et al., 1994). Likewise, U.S. presidents, who are generally wealthy and well educated, have had above-average lifespans (Olshansky, 2011). Across cultures, high economic status predicts a lower risk of heart and respiratory diseases (Sapolsky, 2005). Wealthy parents also tend to have healthy, advantaged children (Savelieva et al., 2016). With higher economic status comes reduced risk of low birth weight, infant mortality, smoking, and violence. Sometimes, it pays to be rich. Even among other primates, those at the bottom of the social pecking order have been more likely than their higher-status counterparts to become sick when exposed to a cold-like virus (Cohen et al., 1997).

When rats cannot control shock or when humans or other primates feel unable to control their environment, stress hormone levels rise, blood pressure increases, and immune responses drop (Rodin, 1986; Sapolsky, 2005). The greater nurses' workload, the higher their cortisol level and blood pressure—but only among nurses who reported little control over their environment (Fox et al., 1993). The crowding in high-density neighborhoods, prisons, and college and university dorms is another source of diminished feelings of control—and of elevated levels of stress hormones and blood pressure (Fleming et al., 1987; Ostfeld et al., 1987).

Increasing control—allowing prisoners to move chairs and to control room lights and the TV, having workers participate in decision making, allowing people to personalize their work space—has noticeably improved health and morale (Humphrey et al., 2007; Ng et al., 2012; Ruback et al., 1986). In the case of nursing home residents, 93 percent of those who

Adrees Latif/Reuters/Newscom

**Separation stress** In 2018, new U.S. immigration policies led to thousands of immigrating children being separated from their parents at the southern border. Children taken from parents and held in detention camps lose a sense of control over their own fate. Psychological research suggests that such extreme stress will make these children vulnerable to future physical and psychological problems.

**learned helplessness** the hopelessness and passive resignation humans and other animals learn when unable to avoid repeated aversive events.

**Taking control of tragedy**
Brothers Fatu Matagi (left) and Samoana "Sam" Matagi (right) experienced accidents that resulted in the amputation of one hand for Fatu and both hands for Sam. As amputees, they retook control, which has left them happy and socially connected. "Being an amputee is like being born again — you have to relearn how to do everything," said Sam, whose YouTube tutorials teach others who have lost limbs how to brush their teeth or even play basketball. "I remember that feeling of helplessness and hopelessness. Helping somebody else is good for my soul."

were encouraged to exert more control became more alert, active, and happy (Rodin, 1986). As researcher Ellen Langer concluded, "Perceived control is basic to human functioning" (1983, p. 291).

People thrive when they live in conditions of personal freedom and empowerment. At the national level, citizens of stable democracies report higher levels of happiness (Inglehart et al., 2008). Freedom and personal control foster human flourishing. But does ever-increasing choice breed ever-happier lives? Today's Western cultures may offer an "excess of freedom" — too many choices. The result can be decreased life satisfaction, increased depression, or even behavior paralysis (Schwartz, 2000, 2004). In one study, people offered a choice of one of 30 brands of jam or chocolate were less satisfied with their decision than were others who had chosen from only 6 options (Iyengar & Lepper, 2000). This *tyranny of choice* brings information overload and a greater likelihood that we will feel regret over some of the things we left behind. Do you, too, ever waste time agonizing over too many choices?

## Internal Versus External Locus of Control

Consider your own perceptions of control, and how they have been influenced by your upbringing and culture. Do you believe that your life is beyond your control? That getting a good job depends mainly on being in the right place at the right time? Or do you more strongly believe that you control your own fate? That being a success is a matter of hard work?

Hundreds of studies have compared people who differ in their perceptions of control. On one side are those who have what psychologist Julian Rotter called an **external locus of control**. In one study of more than 1200 Israeli individuals exposed to missile attacks, those with an external locus of control experienced the most *posttraumatic stress* symptoms (Hoffman et al., 2016). On the other side are those who perceive an **internal locus of control**. In study after study, the "internals" have achieved more in school and work, acted more independently, enjoyed better health, and felt less depressed than did the "externals" (Lefcourt, 1982; Ng et al., 2006). In longitudinal research on more than 7500 people, those who had expressed a more internal locus of control at age 10 exhibited less obesity, lower blood pressure, and less distress at age 30 (Gale et al., 2008). Compared with nonleaders, military and business leaders have lower-than-average levels of stress hormones and report less anxiety, thanks to their greater sense of control (Sherman et al., 2012).

Another way to say that we believe we are in control of our own life is to say we have *free will*. Studies show that people who believe they have free will behave more helpfully, learn better, and persist and perform better at work (Job et al., 2010; Li et al., 2018; Stillman et al., 2010). Across varied cultures, those who believe in free will also experience greater job satisfaction (Feldman et al., 2018). Belief in free will feeds *self-control* — to which we turn next.

---

**external locus of control** the perception that outside forces beyond our personal control determine our fate.

**internal locus of control** the perception that we control our own fate.

---

## The Importance of Self-Control

**5.1-8** Why is self-control important, and can our self-control be depleted?

When we have a sense of personal control over our lives, we are more likely to develop **self-control**—the ability to control impulses and delay short-term gratification for longer-term rewards. Self-control predicts good health, higher income, and better school performance (Bub et al., 2016; Keller et al., 2016; Moffitt et al., 2011). In studies of American, Asian, and New Zealander children, self-control outdid intelligence test scores in predicting future academic and life success (Duckworth & Seligman, 2005, 2017; Poulton et al., 2015; Wu et al., 2016).

Strengthening self-control is key to coping effectively with stress. Doing so requires attention and energy—similar to strengthening a muscle. It's easy to form bad habits, but it takes hard work to break them. With frequent practice in overcoming unwanted urges, people have improved their self-management of anger, dishonesty, smoking, and impulsive spending (Beames et al., 2017; Wang et al., 2017a).

Like a muscle, self-control tends to weaken after use, recover after rest, and grow stronger with exercise (Baumeister & Vohs, 2016). Does exercising willpower temporarily gobble up the mental energy we need for self-control on other tasks (Garrison et al., 2019)? In one famous experiment, hungry people who had spent some of their willpower resisting tempting chocolate chip cookies then abandoned a tedious task sooner than did others (Baumeister et al., 1998a). Although some researchers debate the reliability of this willpower "depletion effect" (Hagger et al., 2016), the big lesson of self-control research remains: Develop self-discipline to help yourself to a healthier, happier, and more successful life (Baumeister et al., 2018; Tuk et al., 2015). Delaying a little fun now can lead to bigger future rewards. And persevering through today's struggles builds an inner strength that enables us to tackle tomorrow's challenges. Think of it this way: Immediate gratification makes today easy but tomorrow hard; self-discipline—delayed gratification—makes today hard and tomorrow easy.

**Extreme self-control** Our ability to exert self-control increases with practice, and some of us have a lot of practice! This performer has made her living as a very convincing human statue on The Royal Mile in Edinburgh, Scotland.

# Optimism Versus Pessimism

**5.1-9** How does an optimistic outlook affect health and longevity?

Our coping with stress is influenced by our outlook—what we expect from the world. Pessimists expect things to go badly (Aspinwall & Tedeschi, 2010). They attribute their poor performance to a basic lack of ability ("I can't do this") or to situations enduringly beyond their control ("There is nothing I can do about it"). Optimists do the opposite by expecting more control, coping ability, and better health (Aspinwall & Tedeschi, 2010; Boehm & Kubzansky, 2012; Hernandez et al., 2015). During a semester's final month, optimistic students reported the least fatigue and fewer coughs, aches, and pains. And during the stressful first few weeks of law school, optimists enjoyed better moods and stronger immune systems (Segerstrom et al., 1998). Optimists tend to have optimal health.

Optimists have tended to get better grades because they respond to setbacks with a hopeful attitude—that is, by believing they can improve (Noel et al., 1987; Peterson & Barrett, 1987). Optimists and their romantic partners generally manage conflict constructively, resulting in feeling more supported and satisfied with the resolution and with their relationship (Srivastava et al., 2006). Optimism relates to well-being and success in many places, from Europe and North America to China and Japan (Qin & Piao, 2011).

**self-control** the ability to control impulses and delay short-term gratification for greater long-term rewards.

Consider the consistency and startling magnitude of the optimism and positive emotions factor in several other longitudinal studies:

- *Long-lived nurses and veterans.* One research team followed 70,021 nurses over time; those scoring in the top quarter on optimism were nearly 30 percent less likely to have died than those scoring in the bottom quarter (Kim et al., 2017). Even greater optimism-longevity differences have been found in studies of Finnish men and American Vietnam War veterans (Everson et al., 1996; Phillips et al., 2009). In long-term studies of nurses and veterans, the most optimistic were 50 to 70 percent more likely than pessimists to live beyond age 85 (Lee et al., 2019).

- *The famous "Nuns Study."* A classic study followed up on 180 Catholic nuns who had written brief autobiographies at about 22 years of age and had thereafter lived similar lifestyles. Those who had expressed happiness, love, and other positive feelings in their autobiographies lived an average 7 years longer than their more dour counterparts (Danner et al., 2001). By age 80, some 54 percent of those expressing few positive emotions had died, as had only 24 percent of the most positive-spirited.

- *Optimism and the end of life.* Optimists not only live longer lives—they approach the end of life positively. One study followed more than 68,000 American women, ages 50 to 79 years, for nearly 2 decades (Zaslavsky et al., 2015). As death grew nearer, the optimistic women tended to feel more life satisfaction than did the pessimists.

Optimism runs in families, so some people are born with a sunny, hopeful outlook. If one identical twin is optimistic, the other typically will be, too (Bates, 2015; Mosing et al., 2009).

The good news is that all of us, even the most pessimistic, can learn to become more optimistic. Compared with a control group of pessimists who simply kept diaries of their daily activities, pessimists in a skill-building group—who learned ways of seeing the bright side of difficult situations and of viewing their goals as achievable—reported lower levels of depression (Sergeant & Mongrain, 2014). In other experiments, people who were instructed to imagine their best possible future—one where they have worked hard and succeeded in all their life goals—become more optimistic (Malouff & Schutte, 2017). Positive expectations often motivate eventual success: Optimism is the light bulb that can brighten anyone's life.

"We just haven't been flapping them hard enough."

## Social Support

**5.1-10** How does social support promote good health?

Social support—feeling liked and encouraged by intimate friends and family—promotes both happiness and health. When randomly prompted by a researcher's phone app, people report more happiness when with others (Quoidbach et al., 2019). In international studies following thousands of people over several years, close relationships have predicted happiness and health in both individualist and collectivist cultures (Brannan et al., 2013; Chu et al., 2010; Rueger et al., 2016). People supported by close relationships tend to live longer (Smith et al., 2018; Whisman et al., 2018). When researchers combined data from 70 studies of 3.4 million people worldwide, they confirmed a striking social support benefit: Compared with those who had ample social connections, socially isolated or lonely people had a 30 percent greater death rate during the 7-year study period (Holt-Lunstad et al., 2010, 2015, 2017). "Loneliness [predicts] a reduction of life span," former U.S. Surgeon General Vivek H. Murthy (2017) noted, that is "similar to that caused by smoking 15 cigarettes a day."

To combat social isolation, we need to do more than collect acquaintances. We need people who genuinely care about us (Cacioppo et al., 2014; Hawkley et al., 2008). Some fill this need by connecting with friends, family, co-workers, members of a faith community, or support groups. Others connect in positive, supportive marriages. Happy marriages

**Laughter among friends is good medicine** Laughter arouses us, massages muscles, and then leaves us feeling relaxed (Robinson, 1983). Humor (though not hostile sarcasm) may ease pain and strengthen immune activity (Ayan, 2009; Berk et al., 2001; Dunbar et al., 2011). Humor buffers stress (Fritz et al., 2017). People who laugh a lot also tend to have lower rates of heart disease (Clark et al., 2001).

**Funny business** Part of our pleasure in authoring this text — and, we hope, yours in reading it — is finding cartoons that offer comic relief while illustrating and reinforcing psychological concepts. Many have come from *The New Yorker*, whose longtime cartoonist and cartoon editor was Bob Mankoff — a former psychology major who lectures on the psychology of humor and is president of CartoonCollections.com. Mankoff explains: "Humor, like other forms of play, has three main benefits. First, it's physically and psychologically healthy, especially in the way it blocks stress. Second, humor makes us mentally flexible — able to manage change, take risks, and think creatively. And third, humor serves as a social lubricant, making us more effective in dealing with colleagues and clients."

bathe us in social support, leading to less weight gain and a longer life (Chen et al., 2018; VanderWeele, 2017). One 7-decade-long study found that at age 50, healthy aging was better predicted by a good marriage than by a low cholesterol level (Vaillant, 2002). On the flip side, divorce predicts poor health. In one analysis of 600 million people in 24 countries, separated and divorced people were more likely to die early (Shor et al., 2012). But it's less marital status than marital *quality* that predicts health—to about the same extent as a healthy diet and physical activity do (Robles, 2015; Smith & Baucom, 2017).

*Social support calms us*, *improves our sleep*, *and reduces blood pressure* (Baron et al., 2016; Kent de Grey et al., 2018; Uchino et al., 2017). To see if social support might calm people's response to threats, one research team subjected happily married women, while lying in an fMRI machine, to the threat of electric shock to an ankle (Coan et al., 2006). During the experiment, some women held their husband's hand. Others held the hand of an unknown person or no hand at all. While awaiting the occasional shocks, women holding their husband's hand showed less activity in threat-responsive areas. This soothing benefit was greatest for those reporting the highest-quality marriages. Simply holding your romantic partner's hand while resolving a conflict may help you handle stress and improve communication (Jakubiak & Feeney, 2019).

*Social support fosters stronger immune functioning*. Stress hampers immune functioning, but social connections strengthen it (Leschak & Eisenberger, 2019). Volunteers exposed to cold viruses showed this effect while being quarantined for 5 days (Cohen, 2004; Cohen et al., 1997). (In these experiments, the more than 600 participants were well-paid volunteers.) Age, race, sex, and health habits being equal, those with close social ties were least likely to catch a cold. People whose daily life included frequent hugs likewise experienced fewer cold symptoms and less symptom severity (Cohen et al., 2015). The cold fact: The effect of social ties is nothing to sneeze at!

### AP® Science Practice

**Argumentation**

Being able to identify the reasoning that supports a claim is an important skill. Explain how the fMRI study described here supports the claim that "holding your romantic partner's hand while resolving a conflict may help you handle stress."

### AP® Science Practice

**Research**

Ethical guidelines ensure that participants are volunteers and that they provide informed consent. Under what conditions would you volunteer to be in a study that might expose you to a cold virus?

**Pets are friends, too** Having a pet may increase the odds of survival after a heart attack, relieve depression among people with AIDS, and lower blood pressure and other coronary risk factors (Allen, 2003; McConnell et al., 2011; Wells, 2009). Pets are no substitute for effective drugs and exercise. But for people who enjoy animals, and especially for those who live alone, pets are a healthy pleasure (Reis et al., 2017; Siegel, 1990). During the Covid pandemic, many people coping with stress and social isolation became new pet owners.

*Close relationships give us an opportunity for "open heart therapy"—a chance to confide painful feelings* (Frattaroli, 2006). Talking about a stressful event can temporarily arouse us, but in time it calms us (Lieberman et al., 2007; Mendolia & Kleck, 1993; Niles et al., 2015). In one study, 33 Holocaust survivors spent 2 hours recalling their experiences, many in intimate detail never before disclosed (Pennebaker et al., 1989). Those who disclosed the most had the most improved health 14 months later. In another study of surviving spouses of people who had died by suicide or in car accidents, those who bore their grief alone had more health problems than those who shared it with others (Pennebaker & O'Heeron, 1984). As the ancient writer of Ecclesiastes noted, "Woe to one who is alone and falls and does not have another to help." Self-disclosure is good for the body and the soul.

Suppressing emotions can be detrimental to physical health. When psychologist James Pennebaker (1985) surveyed more than 700 undergraduate women, those who had experienced a traumatic sexual experience in childhood reported more headaches and stomach ailments than those who had experienced other traumas—possibly because survivors of sexual abuse are less likely than other trauma survivors to confide in others. Another study, of 437 Australian ambulance drivers, confirmed the ill effects of suppressing one's emotions after witnessing a trauma (Wastell, 2002).

Even writing about personal traumas in a diary can help (Burton & King, 2008; Kállay, 2015; Lyubomirsky et al., 2006). For trauma victims, writing therapy reduces posttraumatic stress (Pavlacic et al., 2019). In one experiment, volunteers who kept trauma diaries (rather than diaries about trivial topics) had fewer health problems during the ensuing 4 to 6 months (Pennebaker, 1990). As one participant explained, "Although I have not talked with anyone about what I wrote, I was finally able to deal with it, work through the pain instead of trying to block it out. Now it doesn't hurt to think about it."

If we are aiming to exercise more, eat healthy, or reach our full academic potential, our social ties can tug us away from, or toward, our goal. If you are trying to achieve some goal, think about whether your social network is helping or hindering you.

---

**AP® Science Practice** ┊ **Check Your Understanding**

**Examine the Concept**

▶ Explain some ways that social support enhances health.

**Apply the Concept**

▶ Can you remember a time when you felt better after discussing a problem with a friend or family member? How did doing so help you to cope?

*Answers to the Examine the Concept questions can be found in Appendix C at the end of the book.*

# Module 5.1b REVIEW

### 5.1-6 In what two ways do people try to alleviate stress?

- We use *problem-focused coping* to change the stressor or the way we interact with it.
- We use *emotion-focused coping* to avoid or ignore stressors and attend to emotional needs related to stress reactions.

### 5.1-7 How does a perceived lack of control affect health?

- A perceived lack of *personal control* provokes a rise in stress hormones and blood pressure and a lowered immune response, which puts people's health at risk. Being unable to avoid repeated aversive events can lead to *learned helplessness*.
- Poverty entails less control, which helps explain the link between economic status and longevity.
- People who perceive an *internal locus of control* achieve more, enjoy better health, and are happier than those who perceive an *external locus of control*. Belief in free will is linked to more helpful behavior, better learning, and superior persistence, performance, and satisfaction at work.

### 5.1-8 Why is self-control important, and can our self-control be depleted?

- *Self-control* requires attention and energy, but it predicts good health, higher income, and better school performance.

It does better than an intelligence test score in predicting future academic and life success.

- Self-control tends to weaken after use, recover after rest, and grow stronger when exercised.
- Researchers disagree about whether self-control can be depleted, but strengthening self-control can lead to a healthier, happier, and more successful life.

### 5.1-9 How does an optimistic outlook affect health and longevity?

- Studies of people with an optimistic outlook show that they are more likely than pessimists to have optimal health, to be successful, and to have a longer life expectancy.

### 5.1-10 How does social support promote good health?

- Social support promotes health by calming us, improving our sleep, and reducing blood pressure, and it fosters stronger immune functioning. We can significantly reduce our stress and increase our health by building and maintaining relationships, and by confiding rather than suppressing painful feelings.

## AP® Practice Multiple Choice Questions

1. Tomas' psychologist recommended that he should alleviate stress using emotional, cognitive, and behavioral strategies. What did his psychologist recommend?
   a. Personal control
   b. Coping
   c. Optimism
   d. Social support

2. JerryLynn was worried about her upcoming math exam. Which of the following illustrates a problem-focused strategy that JerryLynn could use to cope with her stress?
   a. JerryLynn went to get ice cream to treat herself before her exam.
   b. JerryLynn did yoga before her exam.
   c. JerryLynn talked to a friend about her stress before her exam.
   d. JerryLynn met with her teacher to review before her exam.

3. Golden believes that he can earn better grades in his English class if he studies for 10 additional minutes each day. Which psychological concept does this example illustrate?
   a. Emotion-focused coping
   b. Optimism
   c. Internal locus of control
   d. Social support

4. When conducting a study, Dr. Mehari found that one variable caused better health and school performance. Which of the following was most likely to be Dr. Mehari's independent variable?
   a. Self-control
   b. An external locus of control
   c. Learned helplessness
   d. Emotion-focused coping

**Use the following graph to answer questions 5–7:**

Dr. Hennessey is interested in how perceptions of control play a role in the workplace. She conducted a study examining the relationship between the number of decisions employees make at work and their corresponding stress levels. Participants rated their stress levels on a scale from 0 to 10, with 10 indicating the highest level of stress.

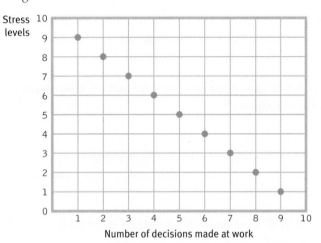

5. What psychological concept is depicted in the graph?

   a. Pessimism
   b. Emotion-focused coping
   c. Learned helplessness
   d. Social support

6. Considering the data in the graph, what outcome is most likely for employees who make the fewest decisions at work?

   a. Their internal locus of control will increase.
   b. They will report poor health.
   c. Their optimism will increase.
   d. They will seek social support.

7. Dr. Bernstein believes that Dr. Hennessey's study does not fully capture the relationship between employees' decisions and their stress levels. Which of the following statements might Dr. Bernstein make to best explain her doubts?

   a. Although having few choices is linked to higher stress levels, optimism is also linked to stress.
   b. Although having few choices is linked to higher stress levels, when people experience an excess of freedom, they experience some distress.
   c. Although having few choices is linked to higher stress levels, using emotion-focused coping strategies buffers against the negative effects of limited choices.
   d. Although having few choices is linked to higher stress levels, social support is the most important factor in assessing people's stress levels.

# Module 5.2a Positive Psychology: Positive Emotions and Positive Traits

## LEARNING TARGETS

**5.2-1** Explain the *feel-good, do-good phenomenon*, and describe the focus of positive psychology research.

**5.2-2** Explain how time, wealth, adaptation, and comparison affect our happiness levels.

**5.2-3** Explain the predictors of happiness.

**5.2-4** Explain the broaden-and-build theory of emotions and its relationship to coping.

**5.2-5** Explain the factors that contribute to positive psychology's 24 character strengths and virtues.

As early as 1902, psychologist William James was writing about the importance of happiness ("the secret motive for all [we] do"). By the 1960s, the *humanistic psychologists* were interested in advancing human fulfillment. In the twenty-first century, under the leadership of American Psychological Association (APA) past-president Martin Seligman, **positive psychology** has used scientific methods to study human flourishing. This young subfield includes studies of **subjective well-being**.

Taken together, satisfaction with the past, happiness with the present, and optimism about the future define the positive psychology movement's first pillar: *positive well-being*.

Positive psychology is about building not just a pleasant life, says Seligman, but also a good life that engages one's skills, and a meaningful life that points beyond oneself. Thus, the second pillar, *positive traits*, focuses on exploring and enhancing creativity, courage, compassion, integrity, self-control, leadership, wisdom, and spirituality. Happiness is a by-product of a pleasant, engaged, and meaningful life.

The third pillar, *positive groups, communities, and cultures*, seeks to foster a positive social ecology. This includes healthy families, friendly neighborhoods, effective schools, socially responsible media, and civil dialogue.

"Positive psychology," Seligman and colleagues have said (2005), "is an umbrella term for the study of positive emotions, positive character traits, and enabling institutions." Its focus differs from psychology's traditional interests in understanding and alleviating negative states—abuse and anxiety, depression and disease, prejudice and poverty. (Psychology articles published since 1887 mentioning "depression" have outnumbered those mentioning "happiness" by 16 to 1.)

In ages past, times of relative peace and prosperity have enabled cultures to turn their attention from repairing weakness and damage to promoting what Seligman (2002) has called "the highest qualities of life." Prosperous fifth-century Athens nurtured philosophy and democracy. Flourishing fifteenth-century Florence nurtured great art. Victorian England, flush with the bounty of the British Empire, nurtured honor, discipline, and duty. In this millennium, Seligman believes, thriving Western cultures have a parallel opportunity to create, as a "humane, scientific monument," a more positive psychology, concerned not only with weakness and damage but also with strength and virtue. Thanks to his leadership, and to more than $200 million in funding, the movement has gained strength, with supporters in 77 countries (IPPA, 2017; Seligman, 2016).

**Martin E. P. Seligman** "The main purpose of a positive psychology is to measure, understand, and then build the human strengths and the civic virtues."

**positive psychology** the scientific study of human flourishing, with the goals of promoting strengths and virtues that foster well-being, resilience, and positive emotions, and that help individuals and communities to thrive.

**subjective well-being** self-perceived happiness or satisfaction with life. Used along with measures of objective well-being (for example, physical and economic indicators) to evaluate people's quality of life.

# Positive Emotions

Positive psychology began with the scientific pursuit of happiness. It asked: What are the roots and the fruits of human happiness?

## Happiness

> **5.2-1** What is the *feel-good, do-good phenomenon*, and what is the focus of positive psychology research?

People aspire to, and wish one another, health and happiness. And for good reason: Our state of happiness or unhappiness colors everything. Happy people perceive the world as safer. Their eyes are drawn toward emotionally positive information (Raila et al., 2015). They are more confident and decisive, and they cooperate more easily. They experience more career success (Walsh et al., 2018). They rate job applicants more favorably, savor their positive past experiences without dwelling on the negative, and are more socially connected. They live healthier and more energized and satisfied lives (Boehm et al., 2015; Kushlev et al., 2020; Willroth et al., 2020). And they are more generous (Boenigk & Mayr, 2016).

The simple conclusion: *Moods matter.* When your mood is gloomy, life seems depressing and meaningless—and you think more skeptically and attend more critically to your surroundings. Let your mood brighten and your positive emotions take over, and then—as we will see—your thinking broadens, becoming more playful and creative (Baas et al., 2008; Forgas, 2008; Fredrickson, 2013).

Young adults' happiness helps predict their future life course. One study showed that the happiest 20-year-olds were later more likely to marry and less likely to divorce (Stutzer & Frey, 2006). When researchers surveyed thousands of U.S. college students in 1976 and restudied them at age 37, happy students had gone on to earn significantly more money than their less-happy-than-average peers (Diener et al., 2002). When we are happy, our relationships, self-image, and hopes for the future also seem more promising.

Moreover—and this is one of psychology's most consistent findings—happiness doesn't just feel good, it *does* good. A mood-boosting experience such as recalling a happy event has made people more likely to give money, pick up someone's dropped papers, volunteer time, and do other good deeds. Psychologists call it the **feel-good, do-good phenomenon** (Salovey, 1990).

The reverse is also true: Doing good promotes good feeling. Spending money on others, rather than on ourselves, increases happiness (Aknin et al., 2020). Young children, too, show more positive emotion when they give (Aknin et al., 2015). In a Spanish corporate workplace, helping co-workers caused employees to experience greater well-being, and those they helped also became happier and more helpful (Chancellor et al., 2018). Even donating a kidney, despite the pain, leaves donors feeling good (Brethel-Haurwitz & Marsh, 2014).

Why does doing good feel so good? One reason is that it strengthens our social relationships (Aknin & Human, 2015; Yamaguchi et al., 2015). Some happiness coaches harness this *do-good, feel-good phenomenon* as they assign people to perform a daily "random act of kindness" and to record the results.

## The Short Life of Emotional Ups and Downs

> **5.2-2** How do time, wealth, adaptation, and comparison affect our happiness levels?

Are some days of the week happier than others? Social psychologist Adam Kramer (at my [DM's] request and in cooperation with Facebook) did a *naturalistic observation* of emotion words in *billions* (!) of Facebook status updates. After eliminating exceptional days, such as

**AP® Science Practice**

### Research

The claim that young adults' happiness *predicts* (as opposed to causes) their future life course implies correlational methods. To draw cause-effect conclusions, researchers have to use the experimental method. And in this case, it would be difficult to randomly assign happiness.

**feel-good, do-good phenomenon** people's tendency to be helpful when in a good mood.

**AP® Science Practice**

### Research

Recall that naturalistic observation is a non-experimental method of observing and recording behavior in naturally occurring situations without trying to manipulate and control the situation.

holidays, he tracked the frequency of positive and negative emotion words by day of the week. The days with the most positive moods? Friday and Saturday (**Figure 5.2-1**). Similar analyses of questionnaire responses and 59 million Twitter messages found Friday to Sunday the week's happiest days (Golder & Macy, 2011; Helliwell & Wang, 2015; Young & Lim, 2014). For you, too?

Over the long run, our emotional ups and downs tend to balance out, even over the course of the day. Positive emotion rises over the early to middle part of most days and then drops off (Kahneman et al., 2004; Watson, 2000). A stressful event—an argument, a team loss, a poor grade—can trigger a bad mood. No surprise there. But by the next day, the gloom nearly always lifts (Affleck et al., 1994; Bolger et al., 1989; Stone & Neale, 1984). Our overall judgments of our lives often show lingering effects of good or bad events, but our daily moods typically rebound (Luhmann et al., 2012). If anything, people tend to bounce back from a bad day to a *better*-than-usual good mood the following day.

**Human resilience** Helen Keller, blind and deaf from early childhood, went on to become a prominent author, activist, and speaker. In her autobiography (1902), she noted, "Everything has its wonders, even darkness and silence, and I learn, whatever state I may be in, therein to be content."

Worse events—the loss of a pet or the end of a friendship—can drag us down for longer periods (Infurna & Luthar, 2016). But eventually, most bad moods end. People involved in romantic relationships expected a breakup would deflate their lives. Actually, after a recovery period, their happiness level was about the same as for those who didn't break up (Gilbert et al., 1998).

Grief over the loss of a loved one or anxiety after a severe trauma (such as child abuse, rape, or the terrors of war) can linger. But usually, even tragedy is not permanently depressing. People who become blind or paralyzed may not completely recover their previous well-being, but those with an agreeable personality usually recover near-normal levels of day-to-day happiness (Boyce & Wood, 2011; Hall et al., 1999). Even if you become paralyzed, explained Daniel Kahneman (2005), "you will gradually start thinking of other things, and the more time you spend thinking of other things the less miserable you are going to be."

The surprising reality: *We overestimate the duration of our emotions and underestimate our resiliency.* (As one who inherited hearing loss with a trajectory toward that of my mother, who spent the last 13 years of her life completely deaf, I [DM] take heart from these findings.)

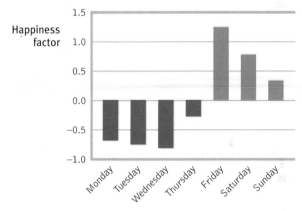

Happiness factor

**Figure 5.2-1**

**Emotion notification**

A pattern emerged in tracked positive and negative emotion words in many "billions" (the exact number is proprietary information) of status updates of U.S. Facebook users over a 3-year period (Kramer, 2010).

## Can Money Buy Happiness?

**Effects of Income and Inequality** Would you be happier if you made more money? How important is "being very well off financially"? "Very important" or "essential," say 82 percent of entering U.S. college students (Eagan et al., 2016). But can money truly buy happiness? Research shows that:

*National wealth matters*. People in countries where most people have a secure livelihood tend to be happier than those in poor countries (Diener & Tay, 2015).

*Personal income (up to a satiation point) predicts happiness*. Having enough money to eat, to feel control over your life, and to occasionally treat yourself to something special predicts greater happiness (Fischer & Boer, 2011; Ruberton et al., 2016). As Australian

## Figure 5.2-2

### Does money buy happiness?

It surely helps us to avoid certain types of pain. But, although average buying power has nearly tripled since the 1950s, Americans' reported happiness has remained almost unchanged. (Happiness data from National Opinion Research Center surveys; income data from *Historical Statistics of the United States* and *Economic Indicators*.)

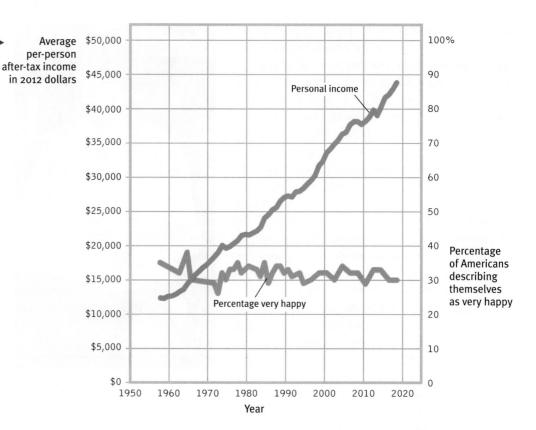

data confirm, the power of more money to increase happiness is strongest at low incomes (Cummins, 2006). A $2000 wage increase does more for someone making $20,000 annually than for someone making $200,000.

Once we have enough money for comfort and security, we reach an "income satiation" point, beyond which piling up more and more matters less and less (Donnelly et al., 2018; Jebb et al., 2018). Experiencing luxury diminishes our savoring of life's simpler pleasures (Cooney et al., 2014; Quoidbach et al., 2010). If you ski the Alps once, your neighborhood sledding hill pales. If you ski the Alps every winter, it becomes an ordinary part of life rather than an experience to treasure (Quoidbach et al., 2015).

***Over time**, a rising economic tide has not produced increased happiness or decreased depression*. Consider: Since the late 1950s, the average U.S. citizen's buying power almost tripled. Did it also buy more happiness? As **Figure 5.2-2** shows, Americans have become no happier. In 1957, some 35 percent said they were "very happy," as did slightly fewer—31 percent—in 2018. Much the same has been true of Europe, Canada, Australia, and Japan, where increasing real incomes have *not* produced increasing happiness (Australian Unity, 2008; Diener & Biswas-Diener, 2008; Di Tella & MacCulloch, 2010; Zuzanek, 2013). Ditto for China, where living standards have risen but happiness and life satisfaction have not (Davey & Rato, 2012; Graham et al., 2018). These findings lob a bombshell at modern materialism: *Economic growth in affluent countries has provided no apparent boost to people's morale or social well-being.*

***Extreme inequality is socially toxic**. Why has economic growth not made us happier? Economic growth has been accompanied by rising inequality, which, across time and place, predicts unhappiness (Cheung & Lucas, 2016; Graafland & Lous, 2019). In countries such as the United States, China, and India, the last half-century's rising tide has lifted the yachts faster than the rowboats (Hasell, 2018). In countries and states with greater inequality, people with lower incomes tend to experience more ill health,

### Research

The data depicted in Figure 5.2-2 are quantitative. This graph uses numerical data (dollar amounts) to represent degrees of a variable (income). In contrast, qualitative research methods rely on non-numerical, narrative data, such as from interviews or focus groups.

social problems, and mental disorders (Payne, 2017; Sommet et al., 2018; Wilkinson & Pickett, 2017a,b). Across the world, we seem to understand this. Regardless of their political party, most people say they would prefer smaller pay gaps between the rich and the poor (Arsenio, 2018; Kiatpongsan & Norton, 2014).

## Happiness Is Relative: Adaptation and Comparison

Two other psychological principles explain why more money does not, except when scarce, buy more happiness. In its own way, each principle suggests that happiness is relative.

*"But on the positive side, money can't buy happiness—so who cares?"*

**Happiness Is Relative to Our Own Experience** Psychologist Harry Helson (1898–1977) explained an **adaptation-level phenomenon**: We adjust our *neutral* levels—the points at which sounds seem neither loud nor soft, temperatures neither hot nor cold, events neither pleasant nor unpleasant—based on our experience. We then notice and react to variations up or down from these levels. Have you noticed how the first chilly fall day feels colder than the same temperature in mid-winter?

So, could we ever create a permanent social paradise? Probably not (Campbell, 1975; Di Tella et al., 2010). People who have experienced a recent windfall—from a lottery, an inheritance, or a surging economy—typically feel elated (Diener & Oishi, 2000; Gardner & Oswald, 2007). So would you, if you woke up tomorrow to your utopia—perhaps a world with no bills, no ills, and perfect test scores. But eventually, your utopia would become your new normal. Before long, you would again sometimes feel gratified (when events exceed your expectations) and sometimes feel deprived (when they fall below). *The point to remember:* Feelings of satisfaction and dissatisfaction, and of success and failure, are judgments we make based partly on expectations formed by our recent experience (Rutledge et al., 2014).

**Happiness Is Relative to Others' Success** We are always comparing ourselves with others. And as psychologist Sonja Lyubomirsky (2001) has noted, whether we feel good or bad depends on who those others are. Believing that others have more friends or are more socially successful makes us feel worse (Whillans et al., 2017; Zell et al., 2018). This sensation is called **relative deprivation**.

When expectations soar above attainments, we feel disappointed. Worldwide, life satisfaction suffers when people with low incomes compare themselves to those with higher incomes (Macchia et al., 2020). One analysis of 2.4 million participants in 357 studies found that happiness depended less on actual financial success than on how participants *compared* themselves financially to their peers (Tan et al., 2020). As we saw in Module 4.7, social media can enable social comparisons, leading us to feel dissatisfied with our seemingly mundane lives. As Theodore Roosevelt reportedly remarked, "Comparison is the thief of joy."

Just as comparing ourselves with those who are better off creates envy, so counting our blessings as we compare ourselves with those worse off boosts our contentment. In one study, university women considered others' deprivation and suffering (Dermer et al., 1979). They viewed vivid depictions of grim city life in 1900. They imagined and then wrote about various personal tragedies, such as being burned and disfigured. Later, the women expressed greater satisfaction with their own lives. Similarly, when mildly depressed people have read about someone who was even more depressed, they felt somewhat better (Gibbons, 1986). "I cried because I had no shoes," states a Persian saying, "until I met a man who had no feet."

**adaptation-level phenomenon** our tendency to form judgments (of sounds, of lights, of income) relative to a neutral level defined by our prior experience.

**relative deprivation** the perception that we are worse off relative to those with whom we compare ourselves.

# What Predicts Our Happiness Levels?

**5.2-3** What predicts happiness?

Happy people share many characteristics (**Table 5.2-1**). But why are some people normally so joyful and others so somber? Here, as in so many other areas, the answer is found in the interplay between nature and nurture.

| TABLE 5.2-1 **Happiness Is . . .** | |
|---|---|
| **Researchers Have Found That Happy People Tend to** | **However, Happiness Seems Not Much Related to Other Factors, Such as** |
| Have high self-esteem (in individualist countries). | Age. |
| Be optimistic, outgoing, and agreeable, and have a humorous outlook. | Gender (women are more often joyful, but also more often depressed). |
| Have close, positive, and lasting relationships. | Physical attractiveness. |
| Have work and leisure that engage their skills. | |
| Have an active religious faith (especially in more religious cultures). | |
| Sleep well and exercise. | |

Information from Batz-Bararich et al., 2018; De Neve & Cooper, 1998; Diener et al., 2003, 2011; Headey et al., 2010; Lucas et al., 2004; Myers, 1993, 2000; Myers & Diener, 1995, 1996; Steel et al., 2008. Veenhoven (2014, 2015) offers a database of 13,000+ correlates of happiness at WorldDatabaseofHappiness.eur.nl.

**CULTURAL AWARENESS**

Our culture influences many of our beliefs and attitudes, including our happiness. When we are aware of this, it is easier to resist the temptation to impose our cultural views on others.

Genes matter. In one analysis of 55,000+ identical and fraternal twins, 36 percent of the differences among people's happiness ratings was heritable—attributable to genes (Bartels, 2015). Even identical twins raised apart are often similarly happy. The quest for specific genes that influence happiness confirms a familiar lesson: Human traits are influenced by many genes having small effects (Røysamb & Nes, 2019).

But our personal history and our culture matter, too. At the personal level, as we have seen, our emotions tend to balance around a level defined by our experience. At the cultural level, groups vary in the traits they value. Self-esteem and achievement matter more in Western cultures, which value individualism. Social acceptance and harmony matter more in communal cultures such as Japan, which stress family and community (Diener et al., 2003; Fulmer et al., 2010; Uchida & Kitayama, 2009).

Depending on our genes, outlook, and recent experiences, our happiness seems to fluctuate around a "happiness set point," which disposes some people to be ever upbeat and others more negative. Even so, after following thousands of lives over two decades, researchers have determined that our satisfaction with life can change (Lucas & Donnellan, 2007). Happiness rises and falls, and can be influenced by factors that are under our control (Layous & Lyubomirsky, 2014; Nes et al., 2010).

If we can enhance our happiness on an *individual* level, could we use happiness research to refocus our *national* priorities more on the pursuit of happiness? Many psychologists believe we could. Happy societies are not only prosperous, but also places where people trust one another, feel free, and enjoy close relationships (Helliwell et al.,

2013; Oishi & Schimmack, 2010). Thus, in debates about the minimum wage, economic inequality, tax rates, divorce laws, health care, and city planning, people's psychological well-being can be a consideration. Many political leaders agree: 43 nations have begun measuring their citizens' well-being, and many have undertaken interventions to boost national well-being (Diener et al., 2015, 2019). Britain's Annual Population Survey, for example, asks its citizens how satisfied they are with their lives, how worthwhile they judge their lives, and how happy and how anxious they felt yesterday (ONS, 2018).

**AP® Science Practice**

## Check Your Understanding

### Examine the Concept

▶ Does personal income predict happiness?

▶ Explain the adaptation-level phenomenon.

### Apply the Concept

▶ Were you surprised by any of the findings about income related to happiness? How might you increase your happiness?

*Answers to the Examine the Concept questions can be found in Appendix C at the end of the book.*

## The Broaden-and-Build Theory of Positive Emotions

**5.2-4** What is the broaden-and-build theory of positive emotions, and how does it help us cope?

Emotions influence our perceptions and actions. The **broaden-and-build theory** argues that everyday positive emotions *broaden* awareness, which over time helps people *build* skills and resilience that boost their well-being (Fredrickson, 2001, 2013).

In one experiment, participants viewed an array of positive, negative, and neutral images, with an instruction to view "whatever interests you — as if watching a television show" (Wadlinger & Isaacowitz, 2006). An eye-tracking device measured participants' attention. By random assignment, some participants received candy treats before viewing the images (positive emotion group), whereas other participants received their candy treats after viewing the images (neutral emotion group). Consistent with the broaden-and-build theory, participants in a positive emotional state spent more time gazing at a variety of images than did participants in a neutral emotional state. Brightened moods beget broadened attention.

Using a healthier strategy to increase positive emotions, psychologist Barbara Fredrickson and her colleagues (2008) randomly assigned some people to complete a 7-week meditation workshop designed to teach them how to reduce stress. Other participants were assigned to a waitlist control group. At the end of each day, all participants reported their emotional experiences of that day. Meditation boosted participants' positive emotions, which built strong coping resources that improved their mental health. For example, compared with participants in the waitlist condition, those in the meditation condition reported greater purpose in life, positive relations with others, ability to savor the future, and lower physical illness symptoms. A follow-up experiment replicated these findings (Kok et al., 2013).

Whether it is the joy of spending time with friends, expressive gratitude when we receive a gift, or contentment when we focus on the good in our lives, positive emotions broaden our mental awareness, which over time helps people build resources that improve well-being.

**broaden-and-build theory**
proposes that positive emotions broaden our awareness, which over time helps us build novel and meaningful skills and resilience that improve well-being.

# Positive Traits

**5.2-5** What factors contribute to positive psychology's 24 character strengths and virtues?

In keeping with positive psychologists' goal of promoting the **character strengths and virtues** that foster well-being, resilience, and positive emotions, Christopher Peterson and Martin Seligman (2004) constructed the Values in Action (VIA) classification. In this system, 24 *character strengths* are organized into six broad *virtue* categories:

- *Wisdom*: creativity, curiosity, judgment, love of learning, and perspective
- *Courage*: bravery, honesty, perseverance, and zest
- *Humanity*: kindness, love, and social intelligence
- *Justice*: fairness, leadership, and teamwork
- *Temperance*: forgiveness, humility, prudence, and self-regulation
- *Transcendence*: appreciation of beauty and excellence, gratitude, hope, humor, and spirituality

**character strengths and virtues** a classification system to identify positive traits; organized into categories of wisdom, courage, humanity, justice, temperance, and transcendence.

Positive psychologists maintain that we all possess these traits, which are not unique to any culture. But we possess them to different degrees, giving each of us a unique character strengths profile. Developing and exercising our character strengths can boost our happiness. (A free survey to assess your own character strengths is available at viacharacter.org; you must be 13 years or older to register for an account.)

---

## AP® Science Practice

## Check Your Understanding

**Examine the Concept**

▶ Explain the broaden-and-build theory.

**Apply the Concept**

▶ Think about your own strengths and virtues. Which categories are you strong in? Which categories would you like to improve on?

▶ Do you think all people possess some degree of the character strength and virtues? Explain how your response relates to the humanistic approach to behavior.

*Answers to the Examine the Concept questions can be found in Appendix C at the end of the book.*

---

# Module 5.2a REVIEW

**5.2-1** What is the *feel-good, do-good phenomenon*, and what is the focus of positive psychology research?

- Happy people tend to be healthy, energized, and satisfied with life, making them more willing to help others (the *feel-good, do-good phenomenon*).
- *Positive psychology*, which includes studies of subjective well-being, uses scientific methods to study human flourishing. It aims to discover and promote strengths and virtues that foster well-being, resilience, and positive emotions and help individuals and communities to thrive.

**5.2-2** How do time, wealth, adaptation, and comparison affect our happiness levels?

- With time, our positive and negative emotions tend to balance out—even over the course of the day. Even significantly bad events are usually not permanently depressing.
- Having enough money to assure comfort, security, and a sense of control predicts happiness; having more than enough does not increase it. Economic growth in many countries has produced rising inequality, which predicts unhappiness; in countries and states with greater

inequality, people with lower incomes experience more ill health, social problems, and mental disorders.

- The moods triggered by good or bad events seldom last beyond that day. Even significant good events, such as sudden wealth, seldom increase happiness for long.

- Happiness is relative to our own experiences (the *adaptation-level phenomenon*) and to others' success (the *relative deprivation* principle).

### 5.2-3 What predicts happiness?

- Some individuals, because of their genetic predispositions and personal histories, are happier than others.

- Cultures, which vary in the traits they value and the behaviors they expect and reward, also influence personal levels of happiness.

### 5.2-4 What is the broaden-and-build theory of emotions, and how does it help us cope?

- The *broaden-and-build theory* argues that positive emotions broaden our awareness and help us to build skills that improve well-being.

- By boosting our positive emotions, we can build the skills and resilience that facilitate our coping.

### 5.2-5 What factors contribute to positive psychology's 24 character strengths and virtues?

- Positive psychology's Values in Action (VIA) classification includes *24 character strengths and virtues* that foster well-being, resilience, and positive emotions.

- The 24 character strengths are organized into six virtue categories; wisdom, courage, humanity, justice, temperance, and transcendence.

- These strengths are universal, but we each possess them to different degrees. Harnessing and developing our character strengths can help us to thrive.

## AP® Practice Multiple Choice Questions

1. Harlan is taking a positive psychology class. What might he learn in the class?

   a. Positive psychology seeks to enable people to be happy all the time.
   b. Positive psychology seeks to treat stress with medication.
   c. Positive psychology seeks to enable people to flourish.
   d. Positive psychology seeks to reduce daily hassles in people's lives.

2. Which of the following is an example of the feel-good, do-good phenomenon?

   a. After Niko is praised by his teacher, he volunteers to help his teacher clean the classroom.
   b. Carson often feels happiest on the weekend because he can spend time painting.
   c. Anagha receives more allowance from her parents when she is kind to her sister.
   d. Rowen is glad to finally be over the flu so he can return to his volunteer work.

3. Which of the following best describes the trends in the data shown in the graph?

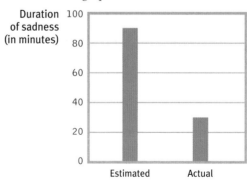

   a. People tend to underestimate the length of time emotions last.
   b. People tend to feel happiest over a long period of time.
   c. People tend to overestimate the length of time emotions last.
   d. Negative events tend to worsen mood for a prolonged period.

**4.** Renaldo was just fired from his job. Without considering any additional information, which of the following is a logical and objective conclusion that can be drawn about Renaldo?

   a. Renaldo will remain sad for the rest of his life, tending to take a pessimistic outlook.

   b. Renaldo will be unaffected by his job loss unless he is high in neuroticism.

   c. Renaldo will remain sad unless he is agreeable.

   d. Renaldo will feel sad for a period, after which he will feel positive emotions again.

**5.** A U.S. presidential candidate promises to improve middle income citizens' subjective well-being by increasing their annual income to $200,000 per citizen. Which of the following explains why $200,000 income would not effectively increase well-being?

   a. Although an increase in income will likely increase citizens' subjective well-being, this level of income may exceed the income satiation point; once citizens have enough to feed themselves, feel in control of their lives, and occasionally have a treat, more money will not make them much happier.

   b. Although an increase in income will likely increase citizens' subjective well-being, this level of income will make only the wealthiest people happier; the power of more income is stronger for individuals with the highest incomes.

   c. Although an increase in income will likely increase citizens' subjective well-being, this effect will be observed only in wealthier states; people tend to compare their past wealth to their new wealth as a result of the adaptation-level phenomenon.

   d. Although an increase in income will likely increase citizens' subjective well-being, this effect will be observed only among individuals in more collectivistic cultures; people from more individualistic cultures will tend to be less affected by monetary gains.

**6.** What main takeaway should Dr. Yula state to her positive psychology students about the broaden-and-build theory of emotions?

   a. When we experience positive emotions, we are motivated to build new skills.

   b. When we experience negative emotions, we are motivated to reduce the negative feelings.

   c. When we experience positive emotions, we are motivated to sleep more often.

   d. When we experience negative emotions, we are motivated to seek out social connections.

**7.** Helga participated in a study about positive psychology's 24 character strengths and virtues. During her debriefing, she received feedback indicating that, according to researchers, she is someone who greatly values creativity, curiosity, and learning. Which virtue category best captures Helga's character strengths?

   a. Wisdom

   b. Transcendence

   c. Humanity

   d. Justice

# Module 5.2b Positive Psychology: Enhancing Well-Being

As we saw in Module 5.1, having a sense of control, developing more optimistic thinking, and building social support can help us minimize stress and maximize health. Positive psychology strategies can also promote **resilience**. Aerobic exercise, relaxation, mindfulness, gratitude, and active spiritual engagement have helped people to become resilient when facing challenges and to experience well-being.

## Aerobic Exercise

**5.2-6** How effective is aerobic exercise as a way to manage stress and improve well-being?

It's hard to find a medicine that works for most people most of the time. But **aerobic exercise**—sustained, oxygen-consuming exertion—is one of those rare near-perfect "medicines." Estimates vary, but some studies suggest that exercise adds to your quantity of life—about *seven hours longer life for every exercise hour* (Lee et al., 2017; Mandsager et al., 2018; Zahrt & Crum, 2017). Think about it: Nature generously gives a 7-to-1 return for time spent exercising. It also boosts your quality of life, with more energy, better mood, and stronger relationships (Buecker et al., 2020; Wiese et al., 2018). As author Bill Bryson (2019) noted, "If someone invented a pill that could do for us all that a moderate amount of exercise achieves, it would instantly become the most successful drug in history."

In the late 1940s, British government doctor Jeremy Morris and his colleagues (1953) sought a low-cost way to test their belief that exercise reduced people's risk of heart attacks. While busing to work one day, it occurred to Morris that every double-decker bus offered a perfect laboratory: Each had a driver who sat while working, and a conductor who was moving constantly and climbing 600 steps in a typical shift. After following 31,000 drivers and conductors for 2 years and adjusting for other factors, he had the first solid evidence of exercise affecting health: Compared with drivers, the conductors suffered fewer than half as many heart attacks.

Exercise helps fight heart disease by strengthening the heart, increasing blood flow, keeping blood vessels open, lowering blood pressure, and reducing the hormone and blood pressure reaction to stress (Ford, 2002; Manson, 2002). Compared with inactive adults, people who exercise suffer about half as many heart attacks (Evenson et al., 2016;

**resilience** the personal strength that helps people cope with stress and recover from adversity and even trauma.

**aerobic exercise** sustained exercise that increases heart and lung fitness; also helps alleviate depression and anxiety.

Visich & Fletcher, 2009). It's a fact: Fitness predicts longevity (Lee et al., 2011; Moholdt et al., 2018). Dietary fat contributes to clogged arteries, but exercise makes our muscles hungry for those fats and cleans them out of our arteries (Barinaga, 1997). A study of 1.44 million Americans and Europeans found that exercise predicted "lower risks of many cancer types" (Moore et al., 2016). Scottish mail carriers, who spend their days walking, have lower heart disease risk than Scottish mail office workers (Tigbe et al., 2017). Regular exercise in later life also predicts better cognitive functioning and reduced risk of neurocognitive disorder and Alzheimer's disease (Kramer & Erickson, 2007).

The genes passed down to us from our distant ancestors enabled the physical activity essential to hunting, foraging, and farming (Raichlen & Polk, 2013; Shave et al., 2019). In muscle cells, those genes, when activated by exercise, respond by producing proteins. We are made for exercise. In the modern inactive person, these genes produce lower quantities of proteins and leave us susceptible to more than 20 chronic diseases, such as type 2 diabetes, coronary heart disease, stroke, and cancer (Booth & Neufer, 2005). Inactivity is thus potentially toxic. Physical activity can weaken the influence of some genetic risk factors. In one analysis of 45 studies, physical activity lowered the obesity rate by 27 percent (Kilpeläinen et al., 2012).

Does exercise also boost the spirit? In a 21-country survey of university students, physical exercise was a strong and consistent predictor of life satisfaction (Grant et al., 2009). Americans, Canadians, and Britons who do aerobic exercise at least three times a week manage stress better, exhibit more self-confidence, have more vigor, and feel less depressed and fatigued than their inactive peers (Rebar et al., 2015; Smits et al., 2011). One analysis of 1.2 million Americans compared exercisers with nonexercisers. After controlling for other physical and social differences among them, the exercisers experienced 43 percent "fewer days of poor mental health in the last month" (Chekroud et al., 2018). "Exercise has a large and significant antidepressant effect," concluded one digest of 49 controlled studies (Schuch et al., 2018). "If the body be feeble," observed Thomas Jefferson (1786), "the mind will not be strong."

But we could state this observation another way: Stressed and depressed people exercise less. Remember, these correlations do not imply causation. To sort out cause and effect, researchers experiment. They *randomly assign* stressed, depressed, or anxious people either to an aerobic exercise group or to a control group. Next, they measure whether aerobic exercise (compared with a control activity not involving exercise) produces a change in stress, depression, anxiety, or some other health-related outcome. One classic experiment randomly assigned mildly depressed female college students to three groups. One-third participated in a program of aerobic exercise, one-third took part in a program of relaxation exercises, and the remaining third (the control group) formed a no-treatment group (McCann & Holmes, 1984). As **Figure 5.2-3** shows, 10 weeks later, the women in the aerobic exercise program reported the greatest decrease in depression. Many had, quite literally, run away from their troubles.

Dozens of other experiments and longitudinal studies confirm that exercise reduces or prevents depression and anxiety (Catalan-Matamoros et al., 2016; Harvey et al., 2018; Stubbs et al., 2017). When experimenters randomly assigned depressed people to an exercise group, an antidepressant group, or a placebo pill group, exercise reduced depression as effectively as antidepressants—and with longer-lasting effects (Hoffman et al., 2011).

Vigorous exercise provides a substantial and immediate mood boost (Watson, 2000). Even a 10-minute walk stimulates 2 hours of increased well-being by raising energy levels and lowering tension (Thayer, 1987, 1993). Exercise works its magic in several ways. It increases arousal, thus counteracting depression's low arousal state. It enables muscle relaxation and sounder sleep. It produces toned muscles, which filter out a depression-causing

Paik Photography/Alamy Stock Photo

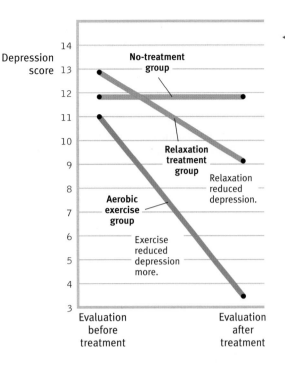

Depression score

14
13 — No-treatment group
12
11
10
9 — Relaxation treatment group
8 — Relaxation reduced depression.
7 — Aerobic exercise group
6 — Exercise reduced depression more.
5
4
3

Evaluation before treatment | Evaluation after treatment

**Figure 5.2-3**
**Aerobic exercise reduces mild depression**
(Data from McCann & Holmes, 1984.)

toxin (Agudelo et al., 2014). Like an antidepressant drug, it orders up mood-boosting chemicals from our body's internal pharmacy—neurotransmitters such as norepinephrine, serotonin, and the endorphins (Jacobs, 1994; Salmon, 2001). Exercise also promotes *neurogenesis*. In mice, exercise causes the brain to produce a molecule that stimulates the production of new, stress-resistant neurons (Hunsberger et al., 2007; Reynolds, 2009; van Praag, 2009).

On a simpler level, the sense of accomplishment and improved physique and body image that often accompany a successful exercise routine may enhance one's self-image, leading to a better emotional state. Frequent exercise is like a drug that prevents and treats disease, increases energy, calms anxiety, and boosts mood—a drug we would all take, if available. Yet few people (only 1 in 4 in the United States) take advantage of it (Mendes, 2010).

Kathryn Brownson

Alice DeWall

Elliott Hammer

**The mood boost** When energy or spirits are sagging, few things reboot the day better than exercising — as I [DM] can confirm from my biking, jogging, and basketball; I [ND] from my running; and I [EYH] from my hiking in nature.

**AP® Science Practice**

## Data Interpretation

Suppose researchers randomly assigned mildly depressed female high school students to two groups. One half did aerobic exercise by running on a treadmill for 30 minutes, three days a week. The other half formed the no-treatment group, behaving as usual. After 10 weeks, the researchers measured all students' depression levels. They found that there was a statistically significant difference between the two groups, with less depression in the exercise group. As a result, they concluded that aerobic exercise causes a reduction in depression.

• What is the control group in this experiment?

• Explain how the use of random assignment strengthens the researchers' ability to make a cause-effect conclusion.

• Determine whether their data are qualitative or quantitative.

• What does it mean for the results to be *statistically significant*?

• Describe one ethical procedure researchers would need to have in place in this study.

# Relaxation, Meditation, and Mindfulness

**5.2-7** In what ways might relaxation, meditation, and mindfulness influence stress and health?

Knowing the damaging effects of stress, could we learn to counteract our stress responses by altering our thinking and lifestyle? In the late 1960s, psychologists began experimenting with *biofeedback*, a system of recording, amplifying, and feeding back information about subtle physiological responses in an effort to help people control them. Today's psychologists have shown the effectiveness of biofeedback in reducing depression and tension-type headaches (Nestoriuc et al., 2008; Pizzoli et al., 2021).

Simple relaxation methods, which require no expensive equipment, produce many of the results biofeedback once promised. Massage helps relax premature infants, and it helps people who are suffering pain by relaxing their muscles and easing their depression (Hou et al., 2010). Figure 5.2-3 pointed out that aerobic exercise reduces depression. But did you notice in that figure that depression also decreased among women in the relaxation treatment group? More than 60 studies have found that relaxation procedures can also help alleviate headaches, hypertension, anxiety, and insomnia (Nestoriuc et al., 2008; Stetter & Kupper, 2002).

Such findings would not surprise Meyer Friedman, Ray Rosenman, and their colleagues. They tested relaxation in a program designed to help hard-driving *Type A* heart attack survivors (who are more prone to heart attacks than their relaxed *Type B* peers) reduce their risk of future attacks. Among hundreds of randomly assigned middle-aged men, half received standard advice from cardiologists about medications, diet, and exercise habits. The other half received similar advice, but also learned to slow down and relax by walking, talking, and eating more slowly; to smile at others and laugh at themselves; and to admit their mistakes, take time to enjoy life, and renew their religious faith. The training paid off (**Figure 5.2-4**). During the next 3 years, the lifestyle modification group had half as many repeat heart attacks as did the first group. This, wrote the exuberant Friedman, was an unprecedented, spectacular reduction in heart attack recurrence. A smaller-scale British study spanning 13 years similarly showed a halved death rate among high-risk individuals trained to alter their thinking and lifestyle (Eysenck & Grossarth-Maticek, 1991). After suffering a heart attack at age 55, Friedman started taking his own behavioral medicine—and lived to age 90 (Wargo, 2007).

Time may heal all wounds, but relaxation can help speed that process. In one study, surgery patients were randomly assigned to two groups. Both groups received standard

**AP® Science Practice**

## Research

Can you identify the independent and dependent variables in the lifestyle modification experiment described here? *Hint:* The independent variable is the factor manipulated by the investigator, and the dependent variable is the outcome that is measured.

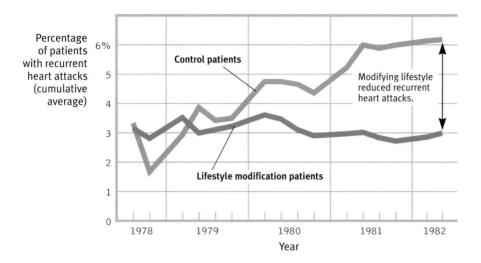

treatment, but the second group also experienced a 45-minute relaxation session and received relaxation recordings to use before and after surgery. A week after surgery, patients in the relaxation group reported lower stress and showed better wound healing (Broadbent et al., 2012).

*Meditation* is a practice with a long history. In many world religions, meditation has been used to reduce suffering and improve awareness, insight, and compassion. Today, meditation apps offer free, guided techniques that can improve health (Adams et al., 2018). Numerous studies have confirmed meditation's benefits (Goyal et al., 2014; Rosenberg et al., 2015; Sedlmeier et al., 2012). One type, **mindfulness meditation**, has found a new home in stress management programs. If you were taught this practice, you would relax and silently attend to your inner state, without judging it (Goldberg et al., 2018, 2019; Kabat-Zinn, 2001). You would sit down, close your eyes, and mentally scan your body from head to toe. Zooming in on certain body parts and responses, you would remain aware and accepting. You would also pay attention to your breathing, attending to each breath as if it were a material object.

Practicing mindfulness boosts happiness and lessens anxiety and depression (de Abreu Costa et al., 2019; Goldberg et al., 2022). In one experiment, Korean participants were asked to think about their own mortality. Compared with nonmeditators, those who meditated were less anxious when reminded of their inevitable death (Park & Pyszczynski, 2019). Mindfulness practices have also been linked with improved sleep, helpfulness, and immune system functioning, and a reduced risk of cancer and heart disease (Conklin et al., 2018; Donald et al., 2018; Rusch et al., 2019; Villalba et al., 2019). Just a few minutes of daily mindfulness meditation is enough to improve concentration and decision making (Hafenbrack et al., 2014; Rahl et al., 2017).

**Furry friends relieve stress** As EYH (pictured here with her dogs, Booker and Darby) can attest, pets reduce stress. In fact, some colleges and universities bring cuddly critters on campus to help students relax and lower disruptive stress levels. In one study, exam-stressed college students who interacted with therapy dogs felt less stressed 10 hours later (Ward-Griffin et al., 2018).

*❝ Meditation is an ancient practice with deep roots in many world religions. Gregory of Sinai (d. 1346) offered this guidance: "Sit down alone and in silence. Lower your head, shut your eyes, breathe out gently, and imagine yourself looking into your own heart. . . . As you breathe out, say 'Lord Jesus Christ, have mercy on me.' . . . Try to put all other thoughts aside. Be calm, be patient, and repeat the process very frequently." ❞*

**Is music a natural antistress medicine?** One analysis of more than 100 studies showed that listening to music (especially slower tempo music) reduced heart rate, blood pressure, and psychological distress (de Witte et al., 2019). The next time you find yourself stressed, remember that music may help you mellow out.

**mindfulness meditation** a reflective practice in which people attend to current experiences in a nonjudgmental and accepting manner.

Nevertheless, some researchers caution that mindfulness is overhyped and sometimes has unpleasant side effects, such as anxiety (Britton et al., 2021; Van Dam et al., 2018). Mere solitude can similarly relax us and reduce stress (Nguyen et al., 2018). But the positive results make us wonder: What's going on in the brain as we practice mindfulness? Correlational and experimental studies offer three explanations.

- *Mindfulness strengthens connections among brain regions*. The affected regions are those associated with focusing our attention, processing what we see and hear, and being reflective and aware (Berkovich-Ohana et al., 2014; Ives-Deliperi et al., 2011; Kilpatrick et al., 2011).

- *Mindfulness activates brain regions associated with more reflective awareness* (Davidson et al., 2003; Way et al., 2010). When labeling emotions, mindful people show less activation in the amygdala, a brain region associated with fear, and more activation in the prefrontal cortex, which aids emotion regulation (Creswell et al., 2007; Gotink et al., 2016).

- *Mindfulness calms brain activation in emotional situations*. This lower activation was clear in one study in which participants watched two movies—one sad, one neutral. Those in the control group, who were not trained in mindfulness, showed strong brain activation differences when watching the two movies. Those who had received mindfulness training showed little change in brain response to the two movies (Farb et al., 2010). Emotionally unpleasant images also trigger weaker electrical brain responses in mindful people than in their less mindful counterparts (Brown et al., 2013). A mindful brain is strong, reflective, and calm.

Barbara Smaller/Cartoon Stock

*"We don't have a time-out chair in our Classroom Community. That's our mindfulness chair."*

## Practicing Gratitude

**5.2-8** How does expressing gratitude enhance our well-being?

**gratitude** an appreciative emotion people often experience when they benefit from other's actions or recognize their own good fortune.

Think of a time when you received another person's kindness, gift, or help. How did you feel? Perhaps you felt **gratitude**. Experiencing and expressing gratitude predicts positive mental well-being. One study of 26,000 children, adolescents, and adults showed that people who experience more gratitude report less depression (Iodice et al., 2021). People who count their blessings, compared with those who do not, report greater happiness (Davis et al., 2016).

As country music star Willie Nelson noted, "When I started counting my blessings, my whole life turned around" (Nelson & Pipkin, 2006).

Gratitude helps people enjoy their present and become optimistic about their future. Gratitude also supports health, thanks to its association with a strong immune system and low blood pressure (Emmons & Stern, 2013). Being grateful benefits relationships, by increasing helpfulness and empathy and lowering aggression (Bartlett & DeSteno, 2006; DeWall et al., 2012; McCullough et al., 2001).

To increase your gratitude, count your blessings in a daily gratitude journal. If you're grateful for someone's help, tell them so or write them an email. By practicing gratitude, we appreciate the good in our lives and live a healthier and happier life.

## Faith Communities and Health

**5.2-9** What is the *faith factor*, and what are some possible explanations for the link between faith and health?

A wealth of studies—more than 2000 in the twenty-first century's first two decades alone—have revealed another curious correlation: the *faith factor* (Balboni, VanderWeele, Doan-Soares, et al., 2022). Religiously active people (especially in more-religious cultures) tend to live longer than those not religiously active (Ebert et al., 2020). One such study compared the death rates for 3900 people living in two Israeli communities. The first contained 11 religiously Orthodox collective settlements; the second was home to 11 matched, nonreligious collective settlements (Kark et al., 1996). Over a 16-year period, "belonging to a religious collective was associated with a strong protective effect" not explained by age or economic differences. In every age group, religious community members were about half as likely to have died as were their nonreligious counterparts. This difference is roughly comparable to the gender difference in mortality. Another study followed 74,534 American nurses over 20 years. After controlling for various health risk factors, those who attended religious services more than weekly were a third less likely to have died than were nonattenders, and were much less likely to have died by suicide (Li et al., 2016; VanderWeele et al., 2016). In U.S. obituaries, mention of a religious affiliation predicted 7.5 years of additional life compared with no religious affiliation (Wallace et al., 2018).

How should we interpret such findings, recalling that researchers cannot randomly assign people to be religiously engaged or not? Correlations are not cause-effect statements, and they leave many factors uncontrolled (Sloan, 2005; Sloan & Bagiella, 2002; Sloan et al., 1999, 2000). Here is another possible interpretation: Women are more religiously active than men, and women outlive men. Might religious involvement merely reflect this gender-longevity link?

Apparently not. One 8-year National Institutes of Health study followed 92,395 women, ages 50 to 79. After controlling for many factors, researchers found that women attending religious services at least weekly experienced an approximately 20 percent reduced risk of death during the study period (Schnall et al., 2010). Moreover, the association between religious involvement and life expectancy is also found among men

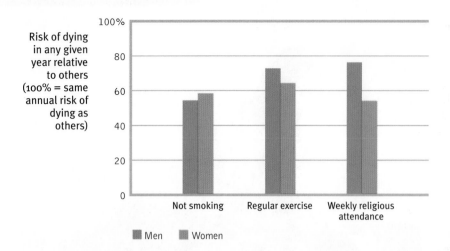

Risk of dying in any given year relative to others (100% = same annual risk of dying as others)

Not smoking    Regular exercise    Weekly religious attendance

■ Men    ■ Women

**Figure 5.2-5**

**Predictors of longer life**

Researchers found that among adult participants, not smoking, regular exercise, and religious attendance all predicted a lower risk of death in any given year (Oman et al., 2002; Strawbridge, 1999; Strawbridge et al., 1997). Women attending weekly religious services, for example, were only 54 percent as likely to die in a typical study year as were nonattenders.

(Benjamins et al., 2010; McCullough et al., 2000; McCullough & Laurenceau, 2005). A 28-year study that followed 5286 Californians found that, after controlling for age, gender, ethnicity, and education, frequent religious attenders were 36 percent less likely to have died in any year (**Figure 5.2-5**). In another 8-year controlled study of more than 20,000 people (Hummer et al., 1999), this effect translated into a life expectancy of 83 years for those frequently attending religious services and 75 years for nonattenders.

Research points to three possible explanations for the religiosity-longevity correlation (**Figure 5.2-6**):

- *Healthy behaviors* Religion promotes self-control (DeWall et al., 2014; McCullough & Willoughby, 2009). This helps explain why religiously active people tend to smoke and drink much less and to have healthier lifestyles (Islam & Johnson, 2003; Koenig & Vaillant, 2009; Masters & Hooker, 2013; Park, 2007). In one large U.S. Gallup survey, 15 percent of the very religious were smokers, as were 28 percent of the nonreligious (Newport et al., 2010). But such lifestyle differences are not great enough to explain the dramatically reduced mortality in the Israeli religious settlements. In U.S. studies, too, about 75 percent of the longevity difference remained when researchers controlled for unhealthy behaviors, such as inactivity and smoking (Musick et al., 1999).

- *Social support* To belong to a faith community is to participate in a support network. Religiously active people are there for one another when misfortune strikes. In the 20-year nurses study, for example, religious people's social support was the best predictor of their good health. Moreover, religion encourages marriage, another predictor (when happy) of health and longevity (Bookwala & Gaugler, 2020).

- *Positive emotions* Even after controlling for social support, unhealthy behaviors, gender, and preexisting health problems, studies have found that religiously engaged people tend to live longer (Chida et al., 2009). Researchers speculate that religiously active people may benefit from a stable, coherent worldview, a sense of hope for the long-term future, feelings of ultimate acceptance, and the relaxed meditation of prayer or other religious observances. The religiously active seem to have healthier immune functioning, fewer hospital admissions, and, for people with AIDS, fewer stress hormones and longer survival (Ironson et al., 2002; Koenig & Larson, 1998; Lutgendorf et al., 2004).

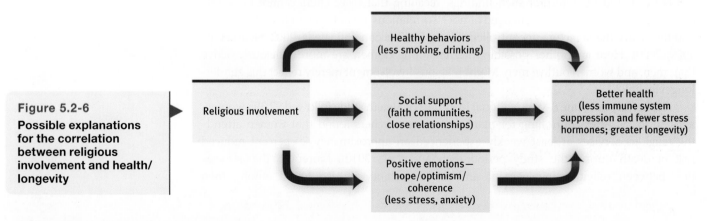

**Figure 5.2-6**

**Possible explanations for the correlation between religious involvement and health/longevity**

Religious involvement

Healthy behaviors (less smoking, drinking)

Social support (faith communities, close relationships)

Positive emotions— hope/optimism/ coherence (less stress, anxiety)

Better health (less immune system suppression and fewer stress hormones; greater longevity)

Table 5.2-2 offers some research-based suggestions for improving your mood and increasing your satisfaction with life.

### TABLE 5.2-2 Evidence-Based Suggestions for Improving Well-Being

- **Take control of your time**. Happy people feel in control of their lives and less time-stressed (Whillans, 2019). Too little time is stressful; too much is boring. So, set goals and divide them into manageable daily aims. We all tend to overestimate how much we will accomplish in any given day, but the good news is that we generally *underestimate* how much we can accomplish in a year, given just a little daily progress.

- **Act happy**. Research shows that people who are manipulated into a smiling expression feel better. So, put on a happy face. Talk *as if* you feel positive self-esteem, are optimistic, and are outgoing. We can often act our way into a happier state of mind.

- **Seek work and leisure that engage your skills**. Happy people often are in a zone called *flow* — absorbed in tasks that challenge but don't overwhelm them. Passive forms of leisure (streaming movies and television shows) often provide less flow experience than exercising, socializing, or expressing artistic interests. Turn off the smartphone and turn on your focus.

- **Buy experiences rather than things**. For those who are not struggling financially, money buys more happiness when spent on experiences — especially socially shared experiences — that you look forward to, enjoy, remember, and talk about (Caprariello & Reis, 2013; Kumar & Gilovich, 2013, 2015; Lee et al., 2018). As pundit Art Buchwald said, "The best things in life aren't things."

- **Join the "movement" movement**. Aerobic exercise not only promotes health and energy, but also helps relieve mild depression (McIntyre et al., 2020; Willis et al., 2018). Sound minds often reside in sound bodies.

- **Give your body the sleep it wants**. Happy people live active lives yet reserve time for renewing, refreshing sleep. Sleep debt results in fatigue, diminished alertness, and gloomy moods. If you sleep now, you'll smile later.

- **Give priority to close relationships**. Compared with unhappy people, happy people engage in more meaningful conversations (Milek et al., 2018). Resolve to nurture your closest relationships by *not* taking your loved ones for granted: Give them the sort of kindness and affirmation you give others. Relationships matter.

- **Focus and find meaning beyond self**. Reach out to those in need. Perform acts of kindness. Happiness increases helpfulness, but doing good also fills us with happiness, meaning, and purpose. And meaning matters mightily: A meaningful life is often a long, active, and healthy life (Alimujiang et al., 2019; Hooker & Masters, 2018).

- **Challenge your negative thinking**. Reframe "I failed" to "I can learn from this!" Remind yourself that stuff happens, and that in a month or a year, a bad experience may not seem like that big a deal.

- **Live mindfully**. When participating in your daily activities — eating, walking, doing chores — attend to your inner states and your surroundings without judging them. When you eat, for example, appreciate the experience of the food: Savor each bite, attend to the internal cues that signal your hunger or fullness, and take the time to be fully present for your meal.

- **Count your blessings and record your gratitude**. Keeping a gratitude journal heightens well-being (Davis et al., 2016). Take time to savor positive experiences and achievements, and to appreciate why they occurred (Sheldon & Lyubomirsky, 2012). Share your gratitude with others and prepare for smiles all around (Dickens, 2017; Kumar & Epley, 2018).

- **Nurture your spiritual self**. Relaxation and meditation help us stay emotionally steady. And for many people, faith provides a support community, a reason to focus beyond self, and a sense of purpose and hope. That helps explain why, worldwide, people active in faith communities report greater-than-average happiness and often cope well with crises (Pew Research Center, 2019).

RubberBall Selects /Alamy Stock Photo

**Examine the Concept**

▶ Explain the relationship between aerobic exercise and psychological health.

**Apply the Concept**

▶ What strategies have you used to cope with struggles in your life? How well have they worked? What other strategies could you try?

*Answers to the Examine the Concept questions can be found in Appendix C at the end of the book.*

# Module 5.2b REVIEW

**5.2-6 How effective is aerobic exercise as a way to manage stress and improve well-being?**

- *Aerobic exercise* helps fight heart disease, predicts longevity, and, in later life, is associated with better cognitive functioning.

- It boosts mood by promoting muscle relaxation and sounder sleep, triggering the production of neurotransmitters, fostering neurogenesis, and enhancing self-image. It increases arousal and can reduce or prevent depression and anxiety.

**5.2-7 In what ways might relaxation, meditation, and mindfulness influence stress and health?**

- Relaxation and meditation have been shown to lower stress, improve immune functioning, and lessen anxiety and depression.

- *Mindfulness meditation* is a reflective practice of attending to current experiences in a nonjudgmental and accepting manner. Massage therapy also promotes relaxation and reduces depression.

**5.2-8 How does expressing gratitude enhance our well-being?**

- People who express gratitude report greater happiness than those who do not. Gratitude helps people enjoy their present and become optimistic about their future.

- Being grateful benefits relationships, increasing helpfulness and empathy and lowering aggression. Gratitude also supports health, boosting the immune system and lowering blood pressure.

**5.2-9 What is the *faith factor*, and what are some possible explanations for the link between faith and health?**

- The faith factor is the finding that religiously active people tend to live longer than those who are not religiously active. Possible explanations may include the effect of intervening variables, such as the healthy behaviors, social support, or positive emotions often found among people who regularly attend religious services.

## AP® Practice Multiple Choice Questions

1. Dr. Salah wanted to conduct a study on how sleep impacts people's sense of their personal strength and ability to overcome adversity. Which of the following is Dr. Salah's dependent variable?

   a. Relaxation
   b. Mindfulness
   c. Faith
   d. Resilience

2. At the end of the day, Rafael enjoys eating his favorite chocolate. He accepts this enjoyment within himself, and he makes sure to savor each part of the process: He listens to the sounds the wrapper makes when he opens the chocolate, feels the chocolate in his hand before eating it, and pays attention to the aroma and flavors as he eats. What psychological concept is depicted in this example?

   a. Aerobic exercise
   b. Meditation
   c. Mindfulness
   d. Gratitude

**Use the following scenario to answer questions 3–4:**

Dr. Batista conducted a study in which he randomly divided participants into two groups. Group A wrote essays about the television shows they had watched in the previous week, while Group B ran on treadmills. At the end of the study, Dr. Batista found that Group B displayed lower stress levels than Group A.

**3.** Which of the following conclusions can Dr. Batista draw from the results of this study?

   a. Aerobic exercise decreased stress levels for Group B.
   b. Meditation increased stress levels for Group A.
   c. Relaxation was associated with increased stress levels.
   d. Gratitude was associated with lower stress levels.

**4.** Which of the following is a logical and objective conclusion that can be drawn about Dr. Batista's study?

   a. During the study, Group A likely had better cognitive functioning than Group B.
   b. During the study, Group A likely had more illnesses than Group B.
   c. During the study, Group A likely had better sleep than Group B.
   d. During the study, Group A likely had more vigor than Group B.

# Module 5.3 Explaining and Classifying Psychological Disorders

**LEARNING TARGETS**

**5.3-1**    Explain how we draw the line between typical behavior and a disorder.

**5.3-2**    Explain how the biopsychosocial approach and the diathesis-stress model frame our understanding of psychological disorders.

**5.3-3**    Describe how and why clinicians classify psychological disorders, and explain why some psychologists criticize diagnostic labels.

**5.3-4**    Identify the factors that increase the risk of suicide, and explain what we know about nonsuicidal self-injury.

**5.3-5**    Explain whether psychological disorders predict violent behavior.

**5.3-6**    Describe how many people have, or have had, a psychological disorder, and identify some of the risk factors.

You lose entire blocks of your day to obsessive thoughts or actions. I spend so much time finishing songs in my car before I can get out or redoing my entire shower routine because I lost count of how many times I scrubbed my left arm.

> —*Kelly, diagnosed with obsessive-compulsive disorder (from Schuster, 2015)*

Whenever I get depressed it's because I've lost a sense of self. I can't find reasons to like myself. I think I'm ugly. I think no one likes me.

> —*Greta, diagnosed with depression (from Thorne, 1993, p. 21)*

Voices, like the roar of a crowd, came. I felt like Jesus; I was being crucified.

> —*Stuart, diagnosed with schizophrenia (from Emmons et al., 1997)*

Now and then, all of us feel, think, or act in ways that resemble a psychological disorder. We feel anxious, depressed, withdrawn, or suspicious. So it's no wonder that we sometimes see ourselves in the mental illnesses we study.

Many of us will know—or love someone who knows—the confusion and pain of unexplained physical symptoms, irrational fears, or a feeling that life is not worth living. Worldwide, 1.1 billion people suffer from mental or substance use disorders (James et al., 2018). In a survey of first-year university students in eight countries, 1 in 3 reported a mental health problem during the prior year (Auerbach et al., 2018).

Most of us would agree that someone who is depressed and stays mostly in bed for 3 months has a psychological disorder. But what about a grieving father who can't resume his usual social activities 3 months after his child has died? Where do we draw the line between understandable grief and clinical depression? Between a fear and a phobia? Between typical distractedness and attention-deficit/hyperactivity disorder? In their search for answers, theorists and clinicians ask:

- How should we *define* psychological disorders?

- How should we *understand* disorders? How do underlying biological factors contribute? How do troubling environments influence our well-being? And how do these effects of nature and nurture interact?

**AP® Science Practice**

## Research

There are many questions about psychological disorders listed here. The research method an investigator uses is driven by the question they ask. Does having a specific disorder predict self-harm (correlational)? Does exposure to extreme stress (versus low stress) cause certain disorders (experimental)? You can review these foundational methods in Unit 0.

- How should we *classify* psychological disorders? And can we do so in a way that allows us to help people without stigmatizing or labeling them?
- Are people with psychological disorders at risk of harming themselves or others?
- What do we know about *rates* of psychological disorders? How many people have them? Who is vulnerable, and when?

This module and the next will examine these disorders, and Module 5.5 considers their treatment.

**psychological disorder** a disturbance in people's thoughts, emotions, or behaviors that causes distress or suffering and impairs their daily lives.

## Defining Psychological Disorders

> **5.3-1** How should we draw the line between typical behavior and a disorder?

A **psychological disorder** is a collection of symptoms marked by a disruption to people's thoughts, emotions, or behaviors that causes distress or suffering. Such thoughts, emotions, or behaviors are *dysfunctional* or *maladaptive*—they interfere with normal day-to-day life. Believing your home must be thoroughly cleaned every weekend is not a disorder. But if daily cleaning rituals interfere with work and leisure, they may be signs of a disorder. Occasional sadness is part of life, but a sadness that persists and becomes disabling likewise signals a psychological disorder. Being energized enables productive work, but being hyped may indicate a psychological disorder when it leads you to sleep too little, drive dangerously, or spend money recklessly.

*Distress* often accompanies such dysfunction. Kelly, Greta, and Stuart were all distressed by their thoughts, emotions, or behaviors.

Social norms, or what is seen as acceptable behavior, change over time. As a result, definitions of what makes for a "significant disturbance" also vary over time. In 1973, the American Psychiatric Association voted that "homosexuality" no longer be classified as a psychological disorder. Its members made this change because they now viewed same-sex attraction as a natural biological predisposition that need not cause people distress or impair their daily lives. What was once considered social deviance—that fueled prejudice and discrimination—became socially acceptable. Such is the power of shifting societal beliefs. In the twenty-first century, controversies continue to swirl over other new or altered diagnoses in the most recent edition of psychiatry's manual for describing disorders (Conway et al., 2019; Widiger et al., 2019).

## Understanding Psychological Disorders

> **5.3-2** How do the biopsychosocial approach and the diathesis-stress model frame our understanding of psychological disorders?

Our view of a problem influences how we try to solve it. In earlier times, people often thought that strange behaviors were evidence of strange forces—the movements of the stars, godlike powers, or evil spirits—at work. Had you lived during the Middle Ages, you might have said, "The devil made me do it." To drive out demons, people suffering from "madness" (as mental illness was then known) have been chained, caged, or given "therapies" such as genital mutilation, beatings, removal of teeth or lengths of intestines, or transfusions of animal blood (Farina, 1982).

Reformers, such as Philippe Pinel (1745–1826) in France, opposed such brutal treatments. Madness is not demonic possession, Pinel insisted, but a sickness of the mind caused by severe stress and inhumane conditions. He argued that curing the illness requires *moral treatment*, including boosting patients' spirits by unchaining them and talking with them. He and others worked to replace brutality with gentleness, isolation with activity, and filth with clean air and sunshine.

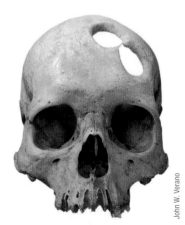

John W. Verano

**Yesterday's "therapy"** Through the ages, psychologically disordered people have received brutal treatments, including the trephination evident in this Stone Age patient's skull. Drilling skull holes like these may have been an attempt to release evil spirits and cure people with mental disorders. Did this patient survive the "cure"?

In some places, cruel treatments for mental illness—including chaining people to beds or confining them in spaces with wild animals—linger even today. The World Health Organization has launched a reform that aims to transform hospitals "into patient-friendly and humane places with minimum restraints" (WHO, 2014b).

## The Medical Model

A medical breakthrough around 1900 prompted further reforms. Researchers discovered that syphilis, a sexually transmitted infection, invades the brain and distorts the mind. This discovery triggered an eager search for physical causes of other mental disorders, and for treatments that would cure them. Hospitals replaced asylums, and the **medical model** of mental disorders was born. Under its influence we still speak of the mental *health* movement. A mental *illness* (also called a psycho*pathology*) needs to be *diagnosed* on the basis of its *symptoms*. It needs to be *treated* through *therapy*, which may include treatment in a psychiatric *hospital*. The medical perspective has been energized by recent discoveries that many genes together influence the brain and biochemistry abnormalities that contribute to all major disorders (Smoller, 2019). A growing number of clinical psychologists now work in medical hospitals, where they collaborate with physicians to determine how the mind and body operate together.

## The Biopsychosocial Approach and the Diathesis-Stress Model

To call psychological disorders "sicknesses" tilts research heavily toward the influence of biology. But as in so many other areas, biological, psychological, and social-cultural influences together weave our lived experiences. As individuals, we differ in how much we experience and how we cope with stressors. Cultures also differ in the sources of stress and in their traditional ways of coping. We are physically embodied and socially embedded.

Two disorders—major depressive disorder and schizophrenia—occur worldwide. Other disorders tend to be *culture-bound*, or associated with specific cultures. In Latin America, some experience *susto*—severe anxiety or panic in response to an emotional trauma or fear of black magic. In Japanese culture, people may experience *taijin kyofusho*—fear that others are judging their bodies as undesirable, offensive, or unpleasing. The eating disorders *anorexia nervosa* and *bulimia nervosa* occur mostly in food-abundant Western cultures. Such disorders may share an underlying dynamic (such as anxiety) while differing in the symptoms (an eating problem or a specific fear) manifested in a particular culture. Even disordered aggression may have varying explanations in different cultures. In Malaysia, *amok* describes a sudden outburst of violent behavior (as in the English phrase "run amok").

*Interaction models* can help us understand the interacting influences on psychological disorders. The biopsychosocial approach emphasizes that mind and body are inseparable (**Figure 5.3-1**). Negative emotions can trigger physical problems, and vice versa. The biopsychosocial approach gave rise to the **diathesis-stress model**[1] (also called the *vulnerability-stress model*), which assumes that individual genetic predispositions combine with environmental stressors to influence psychological disorder (Monroe & Simons, 1991; Zuckerman, 1999). Research on **epigenetics** (see Module 1.1) supports the diathesis-stress model by showing how our DNA and our environment interact. A gene may be *expressed* in one environment, but not in another. For some people, that will be the difference between developing a disorder or not.

Disorders often appear together (Jacobson & Newman, 2017; Plana-Ripoli et al., 2019). People diagnosed with one disorder, such as major depressive disorder, are at higher risk for being diagnosed with another, such as an anxiety disorder. Such *comorbidity* results from overlapping genes that predispose individuals to different disorders (Brainstorm Consortium, 2018; Gandal et al., 2018).

[1]"Diathesis"—meaning predisposed vulnerability—derives from a Greek word for predisposition.

**AP® Science Practice**

**Research**

Because the experience of a disorder may differ by culture, the results from one sample might not generalize to other populations. For example, if participants in a study on anxiety are U.S. adults, the results might not generalize to adults in Latin America.

**medical model** the concept that diseases—in this case, psychological disorders—have physical causes that can be *diagnosed, treated*, and, in most cases, *cured*, often through treatment in a *hospital*.

**diathesis-stress model** the concept that genetic predispositions (diathesis) combine with environmental stressors (stress) to influence psychological disorder.

**epigenetics** "above" or "in addition to" (*epi*) genetics; the study of the molecular mechanisms by which environments can influence genetic expression (without a DNA change).

**Biological influences:**
- evolution
- individual genes
- brain structure and chemistry

**Psychological influences:**
- stress
- trauma
- learned helplessness
- mood-related perceptions and memories

Psychological disorder

**Social-cultural influences:**
- roles
- expectations
- definitions of *disorder*

Wavebreakmedia Ltd/Getty Images

**Figure 5.3-1**

**The biopsychosocial approach to psychological disorders**

Today's psychology studies how biological, psychological, and social-cultural factors interact to produce specific psychological disorders.

# Classifying Disorders — and Labeling People

**5.3-3** How and why do clinicians classify psychological disorders, and why do some psychologists criticize diagnostic labels?

In biology, classification creates order. To classify an animal as a "mammal" says a great deal—that it is likely to be warm-blooded, has hair or fur, and produces milk to feed its young. In psychiatry and psychology, too, classification aims to order and describe symptoms. To classify a person's disorder as "schizophrenia" suggests that the person talks incoherently, has irrational beliefs, shows either little emotion or inappropriate emotion, or is socially withdrawn. "Schizophrenia" is a quick way of describing a complex disorder.

Moreover, diagnostic classification gives more than a thumbnail sketch of a disorder. In psychiatry and psychology, classification also aims to *predict* a disorder's future course, *suggest* appropriate treatment, and *prompt research* into its causes. To study a disorder, we must first name and describe it. Psychology's varied perspectives offer different ways of explaining psychological disorders (**Table 5.3-1**). (We will discuss the treatments informed by these perspectives in Module 5.5.)

In many countries, the most common tool for describing disorders is the American Psychiatric Association's *Diagnostic and Statistical Manual of Mental Disorders*, released in

*"I'm always like this, and my family was wondering if you could prescribe a mild depressant."*

**AP® Exam Tip**

Notice how often you have seen the model in Figure 5.3-1. Human behavior is influenced by biological, psychological, and social-cultural influences. Be sure you can identify these influences on relevant topics.

| TABLE 5.3-1  Perspectives on Psychological Disorders | |
|---|---|
| **Perspective** | **Explanation for Psychological Disorders** |
| *Psychodynamic* | Unresolved childhood conflicts and unconscious thoughts |
| *Humanistic* | Lack of social support and the inability to fulfill one's potential |
| *Behavioral* | Maladaptive learned associations |
| *Cognitive* | Maladaptive thoughts, beliefs, attitudes, or emotions |
| *Biological* | Genetic or physiological predispositions |
| *Evolutionary* | Maladaptive forms of behaviors that enabled human survival |
| *Sociocultural* | Problematic social and cultural contexts |

**TABLE 5.3-2  Insomnia Disorder**

- Feeling unsatisfied with amount or quality of sleep (trouble falling asleep, staying asleep, or returning to sleep)
- Sleep disruption causes distress or diminished everyday functioning
- Happens three or more nights each week
- Occurs during at least three consecutive months
- Happens even with sufficient sleep opportunities
- Independent from other sleep disorders (such as narcolepsy)
- Independent from substance use or abuse
- Independent from other mental disorders or medical conditions

*Information from:* American Psychiatric Association (2013).

2022 as an updated Text Revision of the fifth edition (**DSM-5-TR**). Physicians and trained mental health workers use the detailed DSM-5-TR to guide diagnoses and treatment. For example, someone who meets *all* of the criteria in **Table 5.3-2** may be diagnosed with insomnia disorder. Other disorders, such as *posttraumatic stress disorder* and *major depressive disorder*, require people to meet only a certain number of criteria to be diagnosed. The DSM-5-TR includes diagnostic codes from the World Health Organization's *International Classification of Diseases* (ICD), which makes it easy to track worldwide trends in psychological disorders. (A book of case illustrations accompanying a previous DSM edition provided several examples for this module.)

In real-world tests (*field trials*) assessing the DSM-5-TR categories' reliability, some diagnoses fared well and others fared poorly (Freedman et al., 2013). Clinician agreement on adult *posttraumatic stress disorder* and childhood *autism spectrum disorder*, for example, was near 70 percent. (If one psychiatrist or psychologist diagnosed someone with one of these disorders, there was a 70 percent chance that another mental health worker would independently give the same diagnosis.) But for *antisocial personality disorder* and *generalized anxiety disorder*, agreement was closer to 20 percent.

Critics have long faulted the DSM for casting too wide a net and bringing "almost any kind of behavior within the compass of psychiatry" (Eysenck et al., 1983). Some worried that the current DSM's even wider net would extend the pathologizing of everyday behavior. For example, the DSM-5 classified bereavement grief and distress following loss as a *depressive disorder*. Critics wondered whether such grief could instead simply be considered a common human reaction to tragic life events. The DSM-5-TR (2022) responded to this concern with the newly classified *prolonged grief disorder*, which is diagnosed only when bereavement-related grief lasts more than a year (or 6 months for children and adolescents) and disrupts daily life. Still, critics objected. As one grieving person remarked: "How dare you tell me how long I may grieve . . . six months, one year? . . . Grief is not a problem to be solved, but a process to be lived through" (Perry, 2022).

Other critics of classification register a more basic complaint—that diagnostic labels can be subjective, or even value judgments masquerading as science. Once we label a person, we view that person differently. Labels can change reality by putting us on alert for evidence that confirms our view. If we hear that a new co-worker is mean-spirited, we may treat them suspiciously. They may, in turn, react to us as a mean-spirited person would. Ditto if we're led to believe that someone is smart. Teachers who were told certain students were "gifted" then acted in ways that brought out the behaviors they expected (Snyder, 1984). Labels can be self-fulfilling, and, if negative, they can be stigmatizing.

**DSM-5-TR** the American Psychiatric Association's *Diagnostic and Statistical Manual of Mental Disorders*, Fifth Edition, Text Revision; a widely used system for classifying psychological disorders.

In one study, people watched recorded interviews. If told the interviewees were job applicants, viewers perceived the interviewees as typical people (Langer & Abelson, 1974; Langer & Imber, 1980). Other viewers who were told they were watching psychiatric patients perceived the same interviewees as "different from most people." Therapists who thought they were watching an interview of a psychiatric patient perceived him as "frightened of his own aggressive impulses," a "passive, dependent type," and so forth.

People tend to stigmatize individuals with psychological disorders, but activism, education, and contact between people with psychological disorders and those without reduce this stigma (Corrigan et al., 2012, 2014).

Labels also have power outside the laboratory. Getting a job or finding a place to rent can be a challenge for people recently released from a psychiatric hospital. Label someone as "mentally ill" and people may fear them as potentially violent. That reaction is fading as people come to better understand psychological disorders. Public figures have helped foster this understanding by speaking openly about their own struggles with disorders such as anxiety, depression, and substance abuse—and how beneficial it was to seek help, receive a diagnosis, and get better through treatment.

So, labels matter. Despite their risks, diagnostic labels have benefits. They help mental health professionals communicate about their cases and study the causes and treatments of disorders. Clients are often relieved to learn that their suffering has a name, and that they are not alone in experiencing their symptoms.

**The struggle is real** Actor Dwayne "The Rock" Johnson has been vocal about his struggle with depression. "Struggle and pain is real," he said. "I was devastated and depressed" (Parker, 2018). But he "found that, with depression, one of the most important things you could realize is that you're not alone" (Mosbergen, 2015).

**Struggles and recovery** U.S. Secretary of Labor and former Boston Mayor Martin Walsh has spoken openly about his past struggles with alcohol and involvement in a 12-step program. His honesty helped him reduce stigma and win political races in both 2014 and 2017.

---

**AP® Science Practice**

# Check Your Understanding

### Examine the Concept

▶ Describe ways that psychological disorders are both universal and culture-specific.

▶ Explain the biopsychosocial approach. Why is it important in our understanding of psychological disorders?

▶ Explain the value and the dangers of labeling individuals with disorders.

*Answers to the Examine the Concept questions can be found in Appendix C at the end of the book.*

### Apply the Concept

▶ Have you or someone you know been diagnosed with a psychological disorder? How do you think a diagnostic label has helped or hurt?

# Risk of Harm to Self and Others

People with psychological disorders are more likely to harm themselves than are people without such disorders. Are they also more likely to harm others?

## Understanding Suicide

> **5.3-4** What factors increase the risk of suicide, and what do we know about nonsuicidal self-injury?

> "But life, being weary of these worldly bars,
> Never lacks power to dismiss itself."
>
> —William Shakespeare, *Julius Caesar*, 1599

Each year some 160,000 Americans are among the drug, alcohol, or suicide "deaths of despair" (Case & Deaton, 2020). Among the many who entertain the thought, each year some 800,000 despairing people worldwide will complete the act, electing a permanent solution to what might have been a temporary problem (WHO, 2018c). Someone will likely die by suicide in the 40-odd seconds it takes you to read this paragraph. For those who have been anxious, the risk of suicide is tripled, and for those who have been depressed, the risk is quintupled (Bostwick & Pankratz, 2000; Kanwar et al., 2013). Yet people seldom elect suicide while in the depths of depression, when energy and initiative are lacking. The risk increases when they begin to rebound and become capable of following through (Chu et al., 2016).

Comparing the suicide rates of different groups, researchers have found a number of differences:

- **National differences** Russia has double the suicide rate of the United States, which has double that of Spain (WHO, 2018c). Within Europe, Lithuanians have been seven times more likely to die by suicide than Greeks.

- **Racial differences** Within the United States, White and Native American people die by suicide roughly twice as often as Black, Hispanic, and Asian people (Curtin & Hedegaard, 2019). The rate among Indigenous Canadians is triple that of other Canadians (Kumar & Tjepkema, 2019).

- **Gender differences** Women and girls are much more likely than men to consider or attempt suicide. But worldwide, men are twice as likely to actually die by suicide (ONS, 2019; Ritchie et al., 2019b; WHO, 2018c). The methods men use, such as firing a bullet into the head, are more lethal.

- **Trait differences** Suicidal thoughts increase when perfectionist people feel driven to reach a goal or standard—to become thin or straight or rich—and find it unattainable (Chatard & Selimbegović, 2011; Smith et al., 2018).

- **Age differences and trends** In late adulthood, suicide rates increase worldwide, with the highest rate found among those older than age 70 (Ritchie et al., 2019a).

- **Other group differences** Suicide rates have been much higher among the rich, the non-religious, and the unmarried (Chen et al., 2020; Norko et al., 2017; VanderWeele et al., 2016, 2017). Gay, transgender, and gender-nonconforming youth facing an unsupportive environment, including family or peer rejection, are also at increased risk of attempting suicide (Goldfried, 2001; Haas et al., 2011; Hatzenbuehler, 2011; Testa et al., 2017). One in four transgender adults has attempted suicide, a very high rate that doubles among First Nations people (Adams & Vincent, 2019).

- **Year-by-year differences** In most countries, suicides have been increasing (Ritchie et al., 2020). For example, between 2009 and 2019, U.S. high school students' suicide rate increased by 62 percent (CDC, 2019f; SAMHSA, 2019).

**AP® Science Practice**

## Research

The research described here is correlational. The researchers are attempting to see if variables such as nationality or age *predict* suicide rates. A positive correlation does not mean that everyone in that category will be suicidal or that membership in that category *causes* someone to be suicidal.

Social suggestion may trigger suicidal thinking and behavior. One analysis of 17 million Twitter users' data showed that sharing suicidal thoughts had a ripple effect, spreading suicidal thinking through one's social network (Cero & Witte, 2020). Following highly publicized suicides and TV programs featuring suicide, rates of suicide sometimes increase (Niederkrotenthaler et al., 2019). So do fatal auto and private airplane "accidents." One 6-year study tracked suicide cases among all 1.2 million people who lived in metropolitan Stockholm during the 1990s (Hedström et al., 2008). Men became 3.5 times more likely to take their life if exposed to a co-worker's suicide.

Suicide is not usually an act of hostility or revenge. People—especially older adults—may choose death as an alternative to current or future suffering, a way to switch off unendurable pain and relieve a perceived burden on family members. Suicidal urges typically arise when people feel like they don't belong or are a burden to others, when they feel trapped by a seemingly inescapable situation, or when they feel incapable of experiencing joy (Chu et al., 2018; Ducasse et al., 2018; Taylor et al., 2011). The Covid pandemic brought widespread unemployment and social isolation, and a tripling of suicidal thinking (CDC, 2020d). Wartime stress has been followed by increased soldier suicides.

In most countries, suicides have been increasing (Ritchie et al., 2020). For example, between 2009 and 2019, U.S. high school students' suicide rate increased 62 percent (CDC, 2019; SAMSHA, 2019). What cultural shift helps explain rising teen depression and suicide? One proposed answer is smartphone and social media use, which grew dramatically after 2009, while face-to-face time with friends decreased (Haidt, 2022). Especially among teen girls, social media use exceeding 3 or 4 hours a day predicts increased suicidal thinking and depression (Twenge et al., 2020).

Looking back, families and friends may recall signs they believe should have forewarned them—verbal hints, giving possessions away, a sudden mood change, or withdrawal and preoccupation with death (Bagge et al., 2017). To judge from surveys of 84,850 people across 17 nations, about 9 percent of people at some point in their lives contemplate suicide. About 3 in 10 of those who think about it will actually attempt suicide; of those, fewer than 1 in 20 will die by suicide (Han et al., 2016; Nock et al., 2008; WHO, 2020a). In one study that followed people for up to 25 years after a first suicide attempt, some 5 percent eventually died by suicide (Bostwick et al., 2016).

As one research team summarized, suicide is hard to predict: "The vast majority of people who possess a specific risk factor [for suicide] will never engage in suicidal behavior" (Franklin et al., 2017, p. 217). Might today's genetic testing give us a clue? "The short answer," reports National Institutes of Health expert David Goldman (2020), is "No."

But researchers continue to try to solve the suicide puzzle. Using an app that harvests phone data, investigative teams have gained clues to suicide risk by studying teen volunteers' tone of voice, language, photos, music choice, sleep disturbances, and angry words in text messages (Glenn et al., 2020; Servick, 2019). Some researchers are seeking to identify how our genes predict suicide risk (Goldman, 2020; Kendler et al., 2020). Other research teams are developing suicide-predicting AI (artificial intelligence) algorithms using psychological assessments, health records, or social media posts (Ribeiro et al., 2019; Simon et al., 2018; Walsh et al., 2017).

About 47,000 Americans a year die by suicide—half using guns (CDC, 2019c). (Poison and drug overdoses account for about 80 percent of suicide *attempts*, but only 14 percent of suicide fatalities.) States with high gun ownership are states with high suicide rates, even after controlling for poverty and urbanization (Siegel & Rothman, 2016). After Missouri repealed its tough handgun law, its suicide rate went up 15 percent; when Connecticut enacted such a law, its suicide rate dropped 16 percent (Crifasi et al., 2015). Thus, although U.S. gun owners often keep a gun to feel safer, having a gun in the home actually makes one less safe, because it substantially *increases* the odds of a family member dying by suicide or homicide (Kposowa et al., 2016; VPC, 2015; Vyse, 2016).

How can we be helpful to someone who is talking suicide—who says, for example, "I wish I could just end it all" or "I hate my life; I can't go on"? If people write such things online, you can anonymously contact various social media safety teams (including on Facebook, Twitter, Instagram, YouTube, and Snapchat). If a classmate, friend, or family member talks about suicide, you can

1. *listen*, empathize, and offer hope.

2. *connect* the person with your school psychologist or counselor; with (in the United States) the National Suicide Prevention Lifeline (1-800-273-8255[TALK]) or Crisis Text Line (by texting HOME to 741741); or with their counterparts in other countries (such as CrisisServicesCanada.ca).

3. *protect* someone who appears at immediate risk by seeking help from a trusted adult—a parent, a teacher, a school nurse or school counselor—or calling 911. Better to share a secret than to attend a funeral. Remain connected—online or in-person—until the person gets the help they need.

## Nonsuicidal Self-Injury

Self-harm takes many forms. Some people—mostly adolescents and females—engage in *nonsuicidal self-injury (NSSI)* (Mercado et al., 2017) (**Figure 5.3-2**). They may, for example, cut or burn their skin, hit themselves, or insert objects under their nails or skin.

### Figure 5.3-2

**Rates of U.S. nonsuicidal self-injury emergency room visits**

Self-injury rates peak higher for 15- to 19-year-old females than for same-age males (Mercado et al., 2017). Canada and England have simultaneously experienced the same gender difference and upward trend (Data from Campeau et al., 2022; data from McManus et al., 2019).

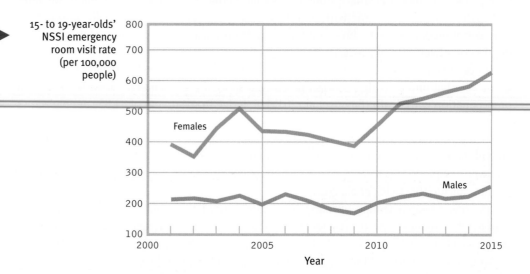

15- to 19-year-olds' NSSI emergency room visit rate (per 100,000 people)

Year

**AP® Science Practice**

## Data Interpretation

Figure 5.3-2 provides a nice opportunity to practice your data interpretation skills, which you will likely be asked to demonstrate on the AP® exam. Consider the graph and address each of the following questions.

- Identify the three variables represented in this graph.

- What do the graph's data tell you about gender differences in NSSI emergency room visits?

- What do the data tell you about NSSI emergency room visits over time?

- Given that these data were collected in the United States, are the trends in the data generalizable to all populations? Explain.

- Are these data quantitative or qualitative? Explain your choice.

Those who engage in NSSI often have experienced bullying, harassment, or stress (Miller et al., 2019; van Geel et al., 2015). They are generally less able to tolerate and regulate emotional distress (Hamza et al., 2015). And they are often both self-critical and impulsive (Beauchaine et al., 2019; Cha et al., 2016).

NSSI is often self-reinforcing (Hooley & Franklin, 2018; Selby et al., 2019). People who engage in NSSI may

- find relief from intense negative thoughts through the distraction of pain.
- attract attention and possibly get help.
- relieve guilt by punishing themselves.
- get others to change their negative behavior (bullying, criticism).
- fit in with a peer group.

Does NSSI lead to suicide? Usually not. Those who engage in NSSI are typically suicide gesturers, not suicide attempters (Evans & Simms, 2019; Nock & Kessler, 2006). Nevertheless, NSSI is a risk factor for suicidal thoughts and future suicide attempts, especially when coexisting with a bipolar disorder (Geulayov et al., 2019). If people do not find help, their nonsuicidal behavior may escalate to suicidal thoughts and, finally, to suicide attempts.

## Does Disorder Equal Danger?

**5.3-5** Do psychological disorders predict violent behavior?

September 16, 2013, started like any other Monday at the Navy Yard in Washington, D.C., with people arriving early to begin work. Then government contractor Aaron Alexis entered the building and began shooting. An hour later, 13 people were dead—including Alexis, who had a history of mental illness and had earlier written that an "ultra low frequency attack is what I've been subject to for the last three months. And to be perfectly honest, that is what has driven me to this."

This mass shooting, like many others, reinforced public perceptions that people with psychological disorders pose a threat (Barry et al., 2013; Jorm et al., 2012). In one survey, 84 percent of Americans agreed that "increased government spending on mental health screening and treatment" would be a "somewhat" or "very" effective "approach to preventing mass shootings at schools" (Newport, 2012). In the aftermath of each devastating new U.S. mass shooting, many politicians have suggested a preventive solution: keeping guns from mentally ill people. U.S. President Donald Trump proposed opening more mental hospitals that could house would-be mass murderers: "When you have some person like this, you can bring them into a mental institution."

Can clinicians indeed predict who is likely to do harm? *No.* Most violent criminals are not mentally ill, and most mentally ill people are not violent (Leshner, 2019; Verdolini et al., 2018). Moreover, clinical prediction of violence is unreliable. The few people with disorders who commit violent acts tend to be either those, like the Navy Yard shooter, who experience threatening delusions and hallucinated voices that command them to act, or those who abuse substances (Douglas et al., 2009; Elbogen et al., 2016; Fazel et al., 2009, 2010).

People with disorders are more likely to be *victims* than perpetrators of violence (Buchanan et al., 2019). According to the U.S. Surgeon General's Office (1999, p. 7), "there is very little risk of violence or harm to a stranger from casual contact with an individual who has a mental disorder." Better predictors of violence are alcohol or drug use, previous violence, gun availability, and—as in the case of the repeatedly head-injured and ultimately homicidal National Football League player Aaron Hernandez—brain damage (Belson, 2017). Mass-killing shooters have one more thing in common: They are mostly young males.

ADREES LATIF/REUTERS/Newscom

**Could mental health screenings prevent mass shootings?**
Following the 2012 Newtown, Connecticut, slaughter of 20 schoolchildren and 6 adults, and again following the 2018 Parkland, Florida, massacre of 14 youths and 3 adults, people wondered: Could the tiny percentage of people with psychological disorders who are violence-prone be identified in advance by mental health workers and prevented from gun ownership? But in 85 percent of U.S. mass killings between 1982 and 2017, the killer had no known prior contact with mental health professionals. Most homicide "is committed by healthy people in the grip of everyday emotions using guns" (Friedman, 2017).

# Rates of Psychological Disorders

**5.3-6** How many people have, or have had, a psychological disorder? What are some of the risk factors?

Who is most vulnerable to psychological disorders? At what times of life? To answer such questions, many countries have conducted lengthy, structured interviews with their citizens. After asking hundreds of questions that probed for symptoms—"Has there ever been a period of two weeks or more when you felt like you wanted to die?"—researchers have estimated the current, prior-year, and lifetime prevalence of various disorders.

*How many people have a psychological disorder?* "Mental and addictive disorders affected more than 1 billion people globally in 2016," reported a major worldwide study (Rehm & Shield, 2019). In the United States, 47 million adults—19 percent—experienced a mental illness within the last year (SAMHSA, 2018) (**Table 5.3-3**).

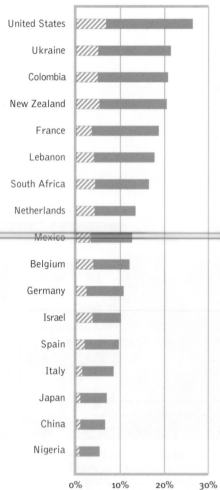

**Figure 5.3-3**

**Prior-year prevalence of disorders in selected areas**

From interviews in 28 countries. (Data from Kessler et al., 2009.)

Legend:
- Percentage with any mental disorder
- Proportion of those disorders considered "serious"

**TABLE 5.3-3 Percentage of Americans Reporting Selected Psychological Disorders "in the Past Year"**

| Psychological Disorder | Percentage |
|---|---|
| Phobia of specific object or situation | 9.1 |
| Major depressive disorder | 7.8 |
| Social anxiety disorder | 7.1 |
| Attention-deficit/hyperactivity disorder (ADHD) | 4.4 |
| Posttraumatic stress disorder (PTSD) | 3.6 |
| Bipolar disorders | 2.8 |
| Generalized anxiety disorder | 2.7 |
| Obsessive-compulsive disorder (OCD) | 1.2 |
| Schizophrenia | <0.5 |
| Data from: National Institute of Mental Health (2018). | |

*Do rates of psychological disorder vary by place?* A World Health Organization study—based on 90-minute interviews with thousands of people who were representative of their country's population—estimated the number of prior-year mental disorders in 28 countries (Kessler et al., 2009). Cultures vary, and as **Figure 5.3-3** illustrates, the lowest rate of reported mental disorders was in Nigeria; the highest rate was in the United States. Moreover, immigrants to the United States from Mexico, Africa, and Asia averaged better mental health than their U.S.-born counterparts with the same ethnic heritage (Breslau et al., 2007; Maldonado-Molina et al., 2011). For example, compared with Mexican Americans born in the United States, Mexican Americans who have recently immigrated are less at risk of mental disorder—a phenomenon known as the *immigrant paradox* (Salas-Wright et al., 2018).

*What increases vulnerability to mental disorders?* As **Table 5.3-4** indicates, there are various risk and protective factors for mental disorders. One predictor—poverty—crosses ethnic and gender lines. The incidence of serious psychological disorders

## TABLE 5.3-4 Risk and Protective Factors for Mental Disorders

| Risk Factors | Protective Factors |
|---|---|
| Academic failure | Aerobic exercise |
| Birth complications | Community offering empowerment, opportunity, and security |
| Caring for those who are chronically ill or who have a neurocognitive disorder | Economic independence |
| Child abuse and neglect | Effective parenting |
| Chronic insomnia | Feelings of mastery and control |
| Chronic pain | Feelings of security |
| Family disorganization or conflict | High self-esteem |
| Low birth weight | Literacy |
| Low socioeconomic status | Positive attachment and early bonding |
| Medical illness | Positive parent-child relationships |
| Neurochemical imbalance | Problem-solving skills |
| Parental mental illness | Resilient coping with stress and adversity |
| Parental substance abuse | Social and work skills |
| Personal loss and bereavement | Social support from family and friends |
| Poor work skills and habits | |
| Reading disabilities | |
| Sensory disabilities | |
| Social incompetence | |
| Stressful life events | |
| Substance abuse | |
| Trauma experiences | |

Data from: World Health Organization (2004a, 2004b).

is 2.5 times higher among those below the poverty line (CDC, 2014). This poverty-disorder *correlation* raises further questions: Does poverty cause disorders? Or do disorders cause poverty? The answer varies with the disorder. Schizophrenia understandably leads to poverty. Yet poverty can beget suffering that increases the risk of certain disorders. A recession-related financial, job, or housing loss may produce lingering depression and anxiety (Forbes & Krueger, 2019).

One natural experiment investigated the poverty-pathology link. Researchers tracked rates of behavior problems in North Carolina children from the Eastern Band of Cherokee Indians over time, as economic development enabled a dramatic reduction in the poverty rate for part of their community. When the study began, children of poverty exhibited more deviant and aggressive behaviors. After 4 years, children whose families had moved above the poverty line exhibited a 40 percent decrease in behavior problems. But children whose families remained in poverty or were never in poverty exhibited no change (Costello et al., 2003).

***At what times of life do disorders strike?*** About half of people with a disorder experience their first symptoms by their mid-teens, and three-quarters do so by their mid-twenties (Kessler et al., 2007; Robins & Regier, 1991). Among the earliest to appear are the symptoms of antisocial personality disorder (median age 8) and of phobias (median age 10). Alcohol use disorder, obsessive-compulsive disorder, bipolar disorders, and schizophrenia symptoms appear at a median age near 20. Major depressive disorder often hits somewhat later, at a median age of 25.

**AP® Science Practice**

### Research

Recall from Module 0.4 that while a correlation can indicate the possibility of a cause-effect relationship, it does not indicate the direction of the influence or whether an underlying third variable may explain the correlation. For example, socioeconomic stress or lack of access to health care may account for the poverty-disorder link.

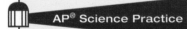
## Check Your Understanding

**Examine the Concept**

▶ Explain the relationship between poverty and psychological disorders.

**Apply the Concept**

▶ Why do you think people often believe the stereotype that individuals with psychological disorders are dangerous?

*Answers to the Examine the Concept questions can be found in Appendix C at the end of the book.*

# Module 5.3 REVIEW

**5.3-1** How should we draw the line between typical behavior and a disorder?

- According to psychologists and psychiatrists, *psychological disorders* are marked by a clinically significant disturbance in an individual's cognition, emotion regulation, or behavior.

- Such dysfunctional or maladaptive thoughts, emotions, or behaviors—which are often accompanied by distress—interfere with daily life, and thus are disordered.

**5.3-2** How do the biopsychosocial approach and the diathesis-stress model frame our understanding of psychological disorders?

- The biopsychosocial perspective assumes that disordered behavior comes from the interaction of biological characteristics, psychological dynamics, and social-cultural circumstances.

- This approach has given rise to the *diathesis-stress model*, in which individual genetic predispositions and environmental stressors combine to increase or decrease the likelihood of developing a psychological disorder—a model supported by *epigenetics* research.

**5.3-3** How and why do clinicians classify psychological disorders, and why do some psychologists criticize diagnostic labels?

- The American Psychiatric Association's *DSM-5-TR* (*Diagnostic and Statistical Manual of Mental Disorders*, Fifth Edition, Text Revision) contains diagnostic labels and descriptions that provide a common language and shared concepts for communication and research.

- Classification helps psychiatrists and psychologists to *predict* a disorder's future course, *suggest* treatment, and *prompt* research into its causes.

- Some critics believe the DSM casts too wide a net and may pathologize typical behaviors.

- Any classification attempt produces diagnostic labels that may create preconceptions, which may then bias perceptions of the labeled person's past and present behavior.

**5.3-4** What factors increase the risk of suicide, and what do we know about nonsuicidal self-injury?

- Suicide rates differ by nation, race, gender, age group, income, religious involvement, marital status, and other factors. In most countries, suicide rates have been increasing.

- People lacking social support, such as many gay, transgender, and gender-nonconforming youth, are at increased risk of suicide, as are people who have been anxious or depressed. Isolation and unemployment can also heighten this risk.

- Forewarnings of suicide may include verbal hints, giving away possessions, social withdrawal, and preoccupation with death.

- People who talk about suicide should be taken seriously: Listen and empathize, connect them to help, and protect those who appear at immediate risk.

- Nonsuicidal self-injury (NSSI) does not usually lead to suicide but may escalate to suicidal thoughts and acts if untreated.

- People who engage in NSSI do not tolerate stress well and tend to be self-critical and impulsive.

**5.3-5** Do psychological disorders predict violent behavior?

- Mental disorders seldom lead to violence, and clinicians cannot predict who is likely to harm others. Most people with disorders are nonviolent and are more likely to be victims than attackers.

- Better predictors of violence are alcohol or drug use, previous violence, gun availability, and brain damage.

**5.3-6** How many people have, or have had, a psychological disorder? What are some of the risk factors?

- Psychological disorder rates vary, depending on the time and place of the survey. In one multinational survey, the lowest rate of reported mental disorders was in Nigeria, and the highest rate in the United States.

- Poverty is a risk factor. But some disorders, such as schizophrenia, can also drive people into poverty. Immigrants to the United States may average better mental health than their U.S.-born counterparts with the same ethnic heritage, a phenomenon known as the immigrant paradox.

## AP® Practice Multiple Choice Questions

1. Traci, a soybeans farmer, has become preoccupied with personal hygiene over the last several months. The moment she becomes dirty from farm work, she feels she must wash or bathe, leading her to spend much of each day washing or bathing. Many of her crops have suffered as a result, decreasing her income for the year. Which of the following factors is present that might contribute to Traci's being diagnosed with a psychological disorder?

   a. Social deviance
   b. Suffering
   c. Atypicality
   d. Dysfunction

2. Dr. Costner, a psychologist, is meeting with a client who is currently experiencing depression and has a family history of depressive disorders. The client shares that she feels sad because she has very few friends and a job she doesn't enjoy in her small town, but she cannot afford to move somewhere with more social and professional opportunities. What approach might Dr. Costner use when assessing this client?

   a. The medical model
   b. Moral treatment
   c. The diathesis-stress model
   d. Epigenetics research

3. Which of the following best illustrates the impact of historical and cultural context on judgments of whether particular behaviors, thoughts, and emotions constitute psychological disorders?

   a. Reformers advocated for moral treatment in the 1700s and 1800s.
   b. The medical model indicates that psychological disorders have physical causes that can be diagnosed and treated.
   c. Same-sex attractions were classified as a psychological disorder until 1973.
   d. Many psychologists use an eclectic approach to treating psychological disorders.

4. Asale is training to become a psychologist, and she plans to work with clients who are experiencing anxiety and depression. Once Asale is a licensed clinician, which of the following tools will enable her to diagnose psychological disorders?

   a. Medical model
   b. Moral treatment
   c. DSM-5-TR
   d. An eclectic approach

5. Dr. Fetter uses a variety of theoretical perspectives when working with her therapy clients. Which of the following does Dr. Fetter use?

   a. An eclectic approach
   b. The medical model
   c. Field trials
   d. Moral treatment

**6.** Which of the following illustrates an appropriate operational definition derived from a study examining the medical model?

a. Dr. Swan conducted a study examining the extent to which brain anatomy, brain activation, and neurochemical markers result in the same psychological disorder diagnosis.

b. Dr. Vrazel conducted a study examining how the average temperature of the town in which a person lives affects the development of psychological disorders.

c. Dr. Fedor conducted a study examining how differences in language processing affect emotion, and whether this might influence the development of psychological disorders.

d. Dr. Zhao conducted a study examining how the number of televisions in a family's home affect the interactions between family members, and whether this might influence the development of psychological disorders.

**7.** Which of the following provides the most accurate interpretation of the following statement: "The median age for developing a phobia is 10 years old"?

a. On average, people develop phobias at 10 years old.

b. The most common age at which people develop a phobia is 10 years old.

c. The average amount of variability around the mean associated with developing a phobia is 10 years.

d. Ten years old is the midpoint of all individuals who develop phobias.

# Module 5.4a Selection of Categories of Psychological Disorders: Anxiety Disorders, Obsessive-Compulsive and Related Disorders, and Trauma- and Stressor-Related Disorders

## LEARNING TARGETS

**5.4-1** Describe generalized anxiety disorder, panic disorder, and specific phobias.

**5.4-2** Describe *obsessive-compulsive disorder (OCD)*.

**5.4-3** Describe *posttraumatic stress disorder (PTSD)*.

**5.4-4** Describe how conditioning, cognition, and biology contribute to the feelings and thoughts that mark anxiety disorders, obsessive-compulsive and related disorders, and trauma- and stressor-related disorders.

Anxiety is part of life. Speaking in front of a class, peering down from a ladder, or waiting to learn the results of a final test can make any of us feel nervous. Anxiety may even cause us to avoid talking or making eye contact—"shyness," we call it. We also feel anxiety when we agonize over terrible things that might happen or flash back to traumatic events. Fortunately for most of us, our uneasiness is not intense and persistent. Some, however, are especially prone to fear the unknown and notice and remember perceived threats (Gorka et al., 2017; Mitte, 2008). When the brain's danger-detection system becomes hyperactive, we are at greater risk for an *anxiety disorder*, and for other disorders that involve anxiety, such as *obsessive-compulsive disorder (OCD)* and *posttraumatic stress disorder (PTSD)*.

## Anxiety Disorders

**5.4-1 How do generalized anxiety disorder, panic disorder, and specific phobias differ?**

The **anxiety disorders** are marked by distressing, persistent anxiety or by dysfunctional anxiety-reducing behaviors. For example, people with **social anxiety disorder** become extremely anxious in social settings where others might judge them, such as parties, class presentations, or even eating in public (a symptom of *agoraphobia*; see below for more discussion). One student experienced palpitations, tremors, blushing, and sweating when

**anxiety disorders** a group of disorders characterized by excessive fear and anxiety and related maladaptive behaviors.

**social anxiety disorder** intense fear and avoidance of social situations.

giving a presentation, taking an exam, or meeting an authority figure, fearing he would embarrass himself. By staying home, he avoided the anxious feelings. But it was maladaptive: Avoiding others prevented him from learning to cope and left him feeling lonely (Leichsenring & Leweke, 2017).

Let's take a closer look at three other anxiety disorders:

- *generalized anxiety disorder*, in which a person, for no obvious reason, worries about many things they cannot control and is continually tense and uneasy;
- *panic disorder*, in which a person experiences *panic attacks*—sudden episodes of intense dread and physical arousal—and fears the next attack; and
- *specific phobias*, in which a person is intensely and excessively afraid of something.

## Generalized Anxiety Disorder

For two years, Tom, a 27-year-old electrician, was bothered by dizziness, sweating palms, and irregular heartbeat. He felt on edge and sometimes found himself shaking. Tom mostly hid his symptoms from his family and co-workers. But he allowed himself few other social contacts, and occasionally his symptoms caused him to leave work. Neither his family doctor nor a neurologist could find any physical problem.

Tom's unfocused, out-of-control, agitated feelings suggest **generalized anxiety disorder**, which is marked by excessive and uncontrollable worry that persists for six months or more. People with this condition (two-thirds are women) worry continually, and they are often jittery, on edge, and sleep-deprived (McLean & Anderson, 2009). Their *autonomic nervous system* arousal may leak out through furrowed brows, twitching eyelids, trembling, perspiration, or fidgeting. Concentration suffers as everyday worries demand continual attention.

Those affected usually cannot identify, relieve, or avoid their anxiety. To use Sigmund Freud's term, the anxiety is *free-floating* (not linked to a specific stressor or threat). Generalized anxiety disorder and depression often go hand in hand. But even without depression, generalized anxiety disorder tends to be disabling. Moreover, it may lead to physical problems, such as high blood pressure.

## Panic Disorder

Some people experience intense anxiety that escalates into a terrifying panic attack—a minutes-long episode of intense fear that something horrible is about to happen. Irregular heartbeat, chest pains, shortness of breath, choking, trembling, or dizziness may accompany the panic. One woman recalled suddenly feeling

> hot and as though I couldn't breathe. My heart was racing and I started to sweat and tremble and I was sure I was going to faint. Then my fingers started to feel numb and tingly and things seemed unreal. It was so bad I wondered if I was dying and asked my husband to take me to the emergency room. By the time we got there (about 10 minutes) the worst of the attack was over and I just felt washed out. (Greist et al., 1986)

For the 3 percent of people with **panic disorder**, panic attacks are recurrent. These anxiety tornados strike suddenly, wreak havoc, and disappear, but are not forgotten. Ironically, worries about anxiety—perhaps fearing another panic attack, or fearing anxiety-related symptoms in public—can amplify anxiety symptoms (Olatunji & Wolitzky-Taylor, 2009). Panic disorder can also manifest as a culture-bound anxiety disorder, such as *ataque de nervios* (experienced mainly by people of Caribbean or Iberian descent). After several panic attacks, people may come to fear the fear itself (**Figure 5.4-1**). This may trigger **agoraphobia**—a specific phobia involving fear or avoidance of public situations from which escape might be difficult. People with agoraphobia may avoid being outside the home, in a crowd, in public spaces (such as theaters or shops), or on public transportation.

**generalized anxiety disorder** an anxiety disorder in which a person is continually tense, apprehensive, and in a state of autonomic nervous system arousal.

**panic disorder** an anxiety disorder marked by unpredictable, minutes-long episodes of intense dread in which a person may experience terror and accompanying chest pain, choking, or other frightening sensations; often followed by worry over a possible next attack.

**agoraphobia** fear or avoidance of situations, such as crowds or wide open places, where one may experience a loss of control and panic.

**specific phobia** an anxiety disorder marked by a persistent, irrational fear and avoidance of a specific object, activity, or situation.

**Panic Attacks (repeated and unexpected)**
*With four or more of the following symptoms:*

Heart racing
Trembling
Difficulty breathing
Choking sensation
Chest pain
Sweating
Hot flashes/chills

Dizziness, light-headedness
Feeling separate from oneself or as if things are not real
Fearing loss of control
Worries about dying
Intestinal distress or nausea
Feelings of numbness or tingling

**+**

One month or more of intense and persistent fear of future panic attacks; may lead to maladaptive avoidance behaviors

**=**

**Panic Disorder**

Smokers have at least a doubled risk of panic disorder and greater symptoms when they do have an attack (Knuts et al., 2010; Zvolensky & Bernstein, 2005). Because nicotine is a stimulant, lighting up doesn't lighten us up.

Charles Darwin began experiencing panic disorder at age 28, after spending 5 years sailing the world. He moved to the country, avoided social gatherings, and traveled only in his wife's company. But the relative seclusion did free him to elaborate his evolutionary theory. "Even ill health," he reflected, "has saved me from the distraction of society and its amusements" (quoted in Ma, 1997).

## Specific Phobias

We all live with some fears. But people with **specific phobias** are consumed by a persistent, irrational fear and avoidance of some object, activity, or situation—for example, heights (acrophobia) or spiders (arachnophobia) (**Figure 5.4-2**). Many people avoid the triggers, such as high places, that arouse their fear. Marilyn, an otherwise healthy and happy 28-year-old, so feared thunderstorms that she felt anxious as soon as a weather forecaster mentioned possible storms later in the week. If her husband was away and a storm was forecast, she often stayed with a close relative. During a storm, she hid from windows and buried her head to avoid seeing the lightning.

**Figure 5.4-1**

**Panic attack and panic disorder**

A person who experiences four or more of the symptoms noted here may be having a *panic attack* (American Psychiatric Association, 2022). They may be diagnosed with a *panic disorder* if a disruptive fear of future panic attacks persists for a month or more.

**Figure 5.4-2**

**Some common specific fears**

Researchers surveyed Dutch people to identify the most common events or objects they feared. An intense fear becomes a specific phobia if it provokes a compelling, irrational desire to avoid the dreaded object or situation. (Data from Depla et al., 2008.)

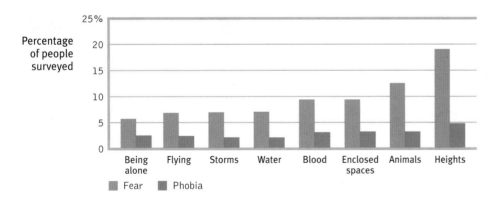

Martin Harvey/Getty Images

---

**AP® Science Practice**

## Check Your Understanding

**Examine the Concept**

▶ Describe the symptoms of generalized anxiety disorder.

▶ Describe the difference between generalized anxiety disorder and a specific phobia.

**Apply the Concept**

▶ Have you ever seen a movie or TV character exhibit anxiety disorder symptoms? Based on what you've read, how realistic was the portrayal of the disorder?

*Answers to the Examine the Concept questions can be found in Appendix C at the end of the book.*

# Obsessive-Compulsive and Related Disorders

> **5.4-2** What is *OCD*?

*Obsessive-compulsive and related disorders* are characterized by obsessions and compulsions. *Obsessive thoughts* are unwanted and seemingly unending. *Compulsive behaviors* are responses to those thoughts. As with the anxiety disorders, we can see aspects of our own behavior in **obsessive-compulsive disorder (OCD)**.

We all are at times obsessed with thoughts, and we may behave compulsively. Have you ever felt a bit anxious about how your living space will appear to others and found yourself compulsively cleaning one last time before your guests arrived? Or, perhaps worried about an upcoming test, have you ever caught yourself lining up your study materials "just so" before studying? Our everyday lives are full of little rehearsals and fussy behaviors. They cross the fine line between normality and disorder only when they *persistently interfere* with everyday living and cause distress. Checking that you locked the door is a typical behavior that can ensure your survival; checking 10 times is not. (**Table 5.4-1** offers more examples.) At some time during their lives, often during their late teens or early adulthood, about 2 percent of people cross that line from normal preoccupations and fussy behaviors to debilitating disorder (Kessler et al., 2012). Although people know their anxiety-fueled obsessive thoughts are irrational, these thoughts can become so haunting, and the compulsive rituals so intensely time-consuming, that effective functioning—including school success—becomes nearly impossible (Pérez-Vigil et al., 2018).

**obsessive-compulsive disorder (OCD)** a disorder characterized by unwanted repetitive thoughts (obsessions), actions (compulsions), or both.

"Wait—did you wash your hands?"

"Not until you've arranged your pillows."

**Writing with OCD** Author John Green's personal experience with obsessive-compulsive disorder informed his bestselling novel, *Turtles All the Way Down* (Flood, 2017). Green described his intrusive thoughts: "It's like there is an invasive weed that just spreads out of control. It starts out with one little thought and then slowly that becomes the only thought that you're able to have, the thought that you're constantly either forced to have or trying desperately to distract yourself from" (Gross, 2018).

**TABLE 5.4-1** Common Obsessions and Compulsions Among Children and Adolescents With Obsessive-Compulsive Disorder

| Thought or Behavior | Percentage Reporting Symptom |
|---|---|
| Obsessions (repetitive *thoughts*) | |
|    Concern with dirt, germs, or toxins | 40 |
|    Something terrible happening (fire, death, illness) | 24 |
|    Symmetry, order, or exactness | 17 |
| Compulsions (repetitive *behaviors*) | |
|    Excessive hand washing, bathing, toothbrushing, or grooming | 85 |
|    Repeating rituals (in/out of a door, up/down from a chair) | 51 |
|    Checking doors, locks, appliances, car brakes, homework | 46 |
| Data from: Rapoport, 1989. | |

OCD is more common among teens and young adults than among older people (Samuels & Nestadt, 1997). A 40-year follow-up study of 144 Swedes diagnosed with the disorder found that, for most, the obsessions and compulsions had gradually lessened, though only 1 in 5 had completely recovered (Skoog & Skoog, 1999).

Some people experience other OCD-related disorders, such as **hoarding disorder** (cluttering their space with acquired possessions they can't part with), *body dysmorphic disorder* (preoccupation with perceived body defects; repeatedly checking their appearance in the mirror), or *trichotillomania* (hair-pulling disorder). Many people have some clutter in their living space or feel sensitive about their appearance. But for these common behaviors and feelings to be considered an OCD-related disorder, they would need to occur frequently and disrupt people's lives—their social life, work, or daily functioning.

**hoarding disorder** a persistent difficulty parting with possessions, regardless of their value.

**posttraumatic stress disorder (PTSD)** a disorder characterized by haunting memories, nightmares, hypervigilance, avoidance of trauma-related stimuli, social withdrawal, jumpy anxiety, numbness of feeling, and/or insomnia that lingers for 4 weeks or more after a traumatic experience.

**trauma- and stressor-related disorders** a group of disorders in which exposure to a traumatic or stressful event is followed by psychological distress.

---

## AP® Science Practice

### Data Interpretation

Consider the data below.

| Thought or Behavior | Percentage Reporting Symptom |
|---|---|
| Obsessions (repetitive *thoughts*) | |
| Concern with dirt, germs, or toxins | 40% |
| Something terrible happening (fire, death, illness) | 24% |
| Symmetry, order, or exactness | 17% |

- What research method is represented in these data — qualitative or quantitative? Explain.

- Create a histogram (or bar graph) depicting these data. Label each axis.

- What conclusion can you draw from your histogram?

---

# Trauma- and Stressor-Related Disorders

### 5.4-3 What is *PTSD*?

While serving overseas, Jesse, a soldier, saw the killing "of children and women. It was just horrible for anyone to experience." Back home, he suffered "real bad flashbacks" (Welch, 2005).

Jesse is not alone. In one study of 104,000 veterans returning from Iraq and Afghanistan, 25 percent were diagnosed with a psychological disorder (Seal et al., 2007). The most frequent diagnosis was **posttraumatic stress disorder (PTSD)**, one of the **trauma- and stressor-related disorders**. Survivors of terror, torture, sexual assault, earthquakes, and refugee displacement have also exhibited PTSD (Charlson et al., 2016; Westermeyer, 2018). The hallmark symptoms are recurring vivid, distressing memories and nightmares. PTSD also often entails laser-focused attention on possible threats, hostility, social withdrawal, jumpy anxiety, and trouble sleeping (Fried et al., 2018; Lazarov et al., 2019; Malaktaris & Lynn, 2019).

**PTSD from Parkland** In the 2018 Parkland, Florida, school shooting, Samantha Fuentes (at right) witnessed friends dying, and shrapnel struck her face and legs. She later reported PTSD symptoms, including a fear of returning to the school and jumping at the sound of a slammed door. Two other student survivors died by apparent suicide in 2019, including one who had been diagnosed with PTSD (Mazzei, 2019).

Chip Somodevilla/Getty Images

Many of us will experience a traumatic event. And many people will display *survivor resiliency*—by recovering with healthy functioning (Galatzer-Levy et al., 2018). During the early months of the Covid pandemic, people's self-reported anxiety and depression rose sharply, and then—illustrating human resilience—subsided (Banks et al., 2021; Fancourt et al., 2021; Helliwell et al., 2021). Although philosopher Friedrich Nietzsche's (1889/1990) idea that "what does not kill me makes me stronger" is not true for all, about half of trauma victims report *posttraumatic growth* (Wu et al., 2019). Sometimes, tears become triumphs.

Why do some 5 to 10 percent of people develop PTSD after a traumatic event while others do not (Bonanno et al., 2011)? One factor is the amount of emotional distress: The higher the level of distress (such as the level of physical torture suffered by prisoners of war), the greater the risk for posttraumatic symptoms (King et al., 2015; Ozer et al., 2003). Among U.S. soldiers in Iraq and Afghanistan, those experiencing both high-combat intensity and self-blaming catastrophic thinking were especially vulnerable to PTSD (Seligman et al., 2019). Among survivors of the 9/11 terrorist attack on New York's World Trade Center, the rates of subsequent PTSD diagnoses for those who had been inside the buildings were double the rates of those who had been outside (Bonanno et al., 2006).

---

 **AP® Science Practice**      **Data Interpretation**

Consider this finding: The more distress people experience during a traumatic event, the greater their risk for posttraumatic symptoms.

- Make up data to create a scatterplot depicting this finding.

- What statistical measure would you use to analyze the data in your scatterplot? Why?

- What does it mean if the results of your analysis are statistically significant?

*Remember, you can always review these data interpretation concepts in Module 0.6.*

---

What else influences PTSD development? Individual differences in memory processing matter. On a novel laboratory memory task, those who experienced PTSD following a Paris terror attack exhibited more difficulty inhibiting unwanted memories than did those who had not experienced PTSD after the trauma (Mary et al., 2020).

Violent victimization also increases the risk of PTSD. One study found that African Americans and Puerto Ricans who experienced repeated violent crime, such as being threatened with a weapon or assaulted, also faced higher than average risk of experiencing PTSD (Pahl et al., 2020). Other studies show that 1 in 4 U.S. college women have experienced sexual assault and, in turn, a dramatically higher than average risk of PTSD (AAU, 2020; Dworkin et al., 2017).

Some psychologists believe that PTSD has been overdiagnosed (Dobbs, 2009; McNally, 2003). "Trauma"—which initially referred to physical injury, and then to severe emotional suffering—has, critics say, been inflated to include stressful life experiences within the range of normal human experience (job loss, serious illness, relationship breakups) (Haslam & McGrath, 2020). Too often, say critics, PTSD gets stretched to include normal stress-related bad memories and dreams. And some well-intentioned procedures—such as "debriefing" people by asking them to revisit the experience and vent their emotions—may worsen normal stress reactions (Bonanno et al., 2010; Wakefield & Spitzer, 2002).

## Check Your Understanding

### Examine the Concept

▶ Describe the symptoms of posttraumatic stress disorder.

### Apply the Concept

▶ Have you ever seen a TV or movie character exhibiting obsessive-compulsive disorder or a related disorder (hoarding, for example)? Based on what you've learned, how accurately were the symptoms portrayed? Explain your response.

*Answers to the Examine the Concept questions can be found in Appendix C at the end of the book.*

# Understanding Anxiety Disorders, Obsessive-Compulsive and Related Disorders, and Trauma- and Stressor-Related Disorders

**5.4-4** How do conditioning, cognition, and biology contribute to the feelings and thoughts that mark anxiety disorders, obsessive-compulsive and related disorders, and trauma- and stressor-related disorders?

How do anxious, obsessive, and trauma- and stress-related feelings and thoughts arise? Most psychologists attribute them to conditioning, cognition, and biology.

## Conditioning

Through *classical conditioning*, our fear responses can become linked with formerly neutral objects and events. To understand the link between learning and anxiety, researchers have given lab rats unpredictable electric shocks (Schwartz, 1984). The rats, like assault victims who report feeling anxious when returning to the scene of the crime, then become uneasy in their lab environment.

Likewise, anxious or traumatized people learn to associate their anxiety with certain cues (Bar-Haim et al., 2007; Duits et al., 2015). In one survey, 58 percent of people with social anxiety disorder said their disorder began after a traumatic event (Öst & Hugdahl, 1981). Anxiety or an anxiety-related disorder is more likely to develop when bad events happen unpredictably and uncontrollably (Field, 2006; Mineka & Oehlberg, 2008). Even a single painful and frightening event may trigger a full-blown phobia, thanks to classical conditioning's *stimulus generalization* and operant conditioning's *reinforcement*.

*Stimulus generalization* occurs when a person experiences a fear-provoking event and later develops a fear of similar events. My [DM's] car was once struck by a driver who missed a stop sign. For months afterward, I felt a twinge of unease when any car approached from a side street. If as a child you suffered a dog bite, you likely then similarly had a fear of most dogs.

*Reinforcement* helps maintain learned fears and anxieties. Anything that enables us to avoid or escape a feared situation can reinforce maladaptive behaviors. Fearing a panic attack, we may decide not to leave the house. Reinforced by feeling calmer, we are likely to repeat that behavior (Antony et al., 1992). So, too, with compulsive behaviors. If washing our hands relieves our feelings of anxiety, we may wash our hands again when those feelings return.

### AP® Exam Tip

Review time: Think about the reinforcement examples provided here. Do they describe *positive* or *negative* reinforcement?[2]

[2]Because the behaviors result in removal or reduction of unpleasant anxiety, they are examples of *negative reinforcement*.

## Cognition

Conditioning influences our feelings of anxiety, but so do our thoughts, memories, interpretations, and expectations. We learn some fears by observing others. Nearly all monkeys raised in the wild fear snakes, but lab-raised monkeys do not. Surely, most wild monkeys do not actually suffer snake bites. Do they learn their fear through observation?

To find out, Susan Mineka (1985, 2002) studied six monkeys raised in the wild (all strongly fearful of snakes) and their lab-raised offspring (virtually none of which feared snakes). The young monkeys repeatedly observed their parents or peers refusing to reach for food in the presence of a snake. Can you predict what happened? The monkeys also developed a strong fear of snakes that persisted when retested 3 months later. We humans similarly learn fears by observing others (Helsen et al., 2011; Olsson et al., 2007).

Although it pays to be alert to dangers, anxiety is often a response to self-produced fake news. One study that followed people with anxiety disorder found that more than 9 in 10 worries proved groundless (LaFreniere & Newman, 2020). Such people tend to be *hypervigilant*. They more often *interpret* stimuli as threatening (Everaert et al., 2018). A pounding heart signals a heart attack; a lone spider indicates an infestation; an everyday disagreement with a friend spells a doomed relationship. And they more readily *remember* threatening events (Van Bockstaele et al., 2014). Anxiety is especially common when people cannot switch off such intrusive thoughts and feel helpless (Franklin & Foa, 2011).

## Biology

Conditioning and cognition can't explain all aspects of anxiety disorders, OCD, and PTSD. Our biology also plays a role.

### Genes

Among monkeys, fearfulness runs in families. A monkey reacts more strongly to stress if its close biological relatives have sensitive, high-strung temperaments (Suomi, 1986). So, too, with people. Although twins in general are not at higher risk for disorders, if one identical twin has an anxiety disorder, the other is also at risk (Polderman et al., 2015). Even when raised separately, identical twins may develop similar specific phobias (Carey, 1990; Eckert et al., 1981). One pair of separated identical twins independently became so afraid of water that each would wade into the ocean backward and only up to her knees. Another pair of twins with OCD rarely left their house, took hours-long showers, used five bottles of disinfecting rubbing alcohol daily, and, tragically, died together in an apparent suicide pact (Schmidt, 2018).

Given the genetic contribution to anxiety disorders, researchers are sleuthing the culprit genes. Among their findings are gene variations associated with typical anxiety disorder symptoms or with specific disorders such as OCD (Purves et al., 2020; Smoller, 2020).

Some genes influence anxiety disorders by regulating brain levels of neurotransmitters. These include *serotonin*, which influences sleep, mood, and attending to threats, and *glutamate*, which heightens activity in the brain's alarm centers (Pergamin-Hight et al., 2012; Welch et al., 2007).

So genes matter. Some of us have genes that make us like orchids—fragile, yet capable of beauty under favorable circumstances. Others of us are like dandelions—hardy, and able to thrive in varied circumstances (Ellis & Boyce, 2008; Pluess & Belsky, 2013).

But experience affects gene expression. A history of wartime trauma or child abuse can leave long-term *epigenetic marks* (see Module 1.1). These molecular tags turn certain genes on or off. Thus, experiences such as abuse can increase the likelihood that a genetic vulnerability to a disorder such as PTSD will be expressed (Mehta et al., 2013; Zannas et al., 2015).

## The Brain

Our experiences change our brain, paving new pathways. Traumatic fear-learning experiences can leave tracks in the brain, creating fear circuits within the amygdala (Etkin & Wager, 2007; Herringa et al., 2013; Kolassa & Elbert, 2007). These fear pathways provide easy inroads for more fear experiences (Armony et al., 1998). Some antidepressant drugs dampen this fear-circuit activity and associated obsessive-compulsive behaviors.

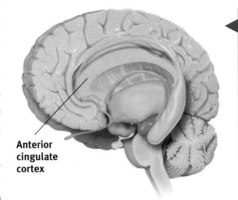

**Anterior cingulate cortex**

**Figure 5.4-3**

**An obsessive-compulsive brain**

When people engaged in a challenging cognitive task, those with OCD showed the most activity in the anterior cingulate cortex in the brain's frontal lobe (Maltby et al., 2005).

Generalized anxiety disorder, panic attacks, specific phobias, OCD, and PTSD express themselves biologically as overarousal of brain areas involved in impulse control and habitual behaviors. These disorders reflect the brain's danger-detection system gone hyperactive—producing anxiety when little danger exists. In OCD, for example, when the brain detects that something is amiss, it seems to generate a mental hiccup of repeating thoughts (obsessions) or actions (compulsions) (Gehring et al., 2000). Brain scans reveal elevated activity in specific brain areas during behaviors such as compulsive hand washing, checking, organizing, and hoarding (Insel, 2010; Mataix-Cols et al., 2004, 2005). The *anterior cingulate cortex*, a brain region that monitors our actions and checks for errors, is often especially hyperactive (Maltby et al., 2005) (**Figure 5.4-3**). Scientists are even identifying specific brain cells that contribute to anxiety in the hope of helping people control it (Jimenez et al., 2018).

## Natural Selection

We seem biologically prepared to fear the threats our ancestors faced. Our specific phobias focus on specific fears such as spiders and snakes, enclosed spaces and heights, storms and darkness. Those who did not fear these threats were less likely to survive and leave descendants. Nine-month-old infants attend more to sounds signaling ancient threats (hisses, thunder) than they do to sounds representing modern threats (a bomb exploding, breaking glass) (Erlich et al., 2013). It is easy to condition and hard to extinguish fears of such "evolutionarily relevant" stimuli (Coelho & Purkis, 2009; Davey, 1995; Öhman, 2009).

Peter Bohler/Redux Pictures

**(a)**

**Fearless** The biological perspective helps us understand why most people fear heights more than Alex Honnold does. In 2017, he became the first person to free solo (climb without safety ropes) Yosemite National Park's massive El Capitan granite wall. (*Free Solo*, a documentary about this feat, won a 2019 Oscar.) When psychologist Jane Joseph showed Honnold fear-inducing images in the lab, an fMRI scan found his fear-processing amygdala was minimally responsive. (The red and yellow indicate normal amygdala activation in the control subject.)

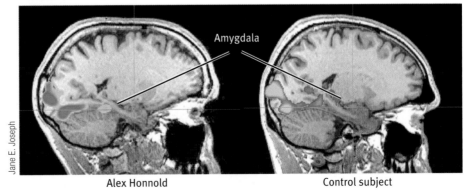

Jane E. Joseph

Amygdala

Alex Honnold          Control subject

**(b)**

Some of our modern fears (such as fear of flying) might also have an evolutionary explanation (a biological predisposition to fear confinement and heights).

Just as our specific phobias focus on the dangers our ancestors faced, our compulsive acts typically exaggerate the behaviors that helped them survive. Grooming had survival value. Gone wild, it becomes compulsive hair pulling. Washing up becomes ritual hand washing. And checking territorial boundaries becomes checking and rechecking already locked doors (Rapoport, 1989).

---

 **AP® Science Practice**

## Check Your Understanding

**Examine the Concept**

▶ Researchers believe that conditioning and cognitive processes are aspects of learning that contribute to anxiety disorders. Explain some *biological* factors that also contribute to these disorders.

*Answers to the Examine the Concept questions can be found in Appendix C at the end of the book.*

**Apply the Concept**

▶ What is a fear that you have learned? How was conditioning or cognition involved?

---

# Module 5.4a REVIEW

**5.4-1 How do generalized anxiety disorder, panic disorder, and specific phobias differ?**

- *Anxiety disorders* are psychological disorders characterized by excessive fear and anxiety and related maladaptive behaviors.

- People with *generalized anxiety disorder* feel persistently and uncontrollably tense and apprehensive, for no apparent reason.

- In the more extreme *panic disorder*, anxiety escalates into periodic episodes of intense dread.

- Those with a *specific phobia* may be irrationally afraid of some object, activity, or situation.

**5.4-2 What is OCD?**

- Unwanted repetitive thoughts (obsessions), actions (compulsions), or both characterize *obsessive-compulsive disorder* (OCD).

- *Hoarding disorder* is characterized by a persistent difficulty parting with possessions, regardless of their value.

**5.4-3 What is PTSD?**

- Symptoms of *posttraumatic stress disorder* (PTSD) include 4 weeks or more of haunting memories, nightmares, hypervigilance, avoidance of trauma-related stimuli, social withdrawal, jumpy anxiety, numbness of feeling, and/or insomnia following some traumatic experience.

**5.4-4 How do conditioning, cognition, and biology contribute to the feelings and thoughts that mark anxiety disorders, obsessive-compulsive and related disorders, and trauma- and stressor-related disorders?**

- The learning perspective views these disorders as products of fear conditioning, stimulus generalization, fearful-behavior reinforcement, and observational learning of others' fears and cognitions.

- The biological perspective considers genetic predispositions for high levels of emotional reactivity and neurotransmitter production; abnormal responses in the brain's fear circuits; and the role that fears of life-threatening dangers played in natural selection and evolution.

# AP® Practice Multiple Choice Questions

1. Reyne often feels fear, which makes it difficult for him to work and to do his tasks around his house. What set of psychological disorders might Reyne be experiencing?
   a. Obsessive-compulsive and related disorders
   b. Anxiety disorders
   c. Specific phobias
   d. Trauma- and stressor-related disorders

2. Dr. Lopez wants to conduct a study on all individuals at a local psychological clinic who have been diagnosed with a disorder characterized by intense fear and avoidance of social situations. Dr. Lopez would like for the study participants to represent all individuals diagnosed with this disorder. Which of the following best captures an appropriate population and an appropriate sample for Dr. Lopez's study?

   a. The population includes all individuals at the psychological clinic, and the sample includes all individuals at the psychological clinic diagnosed with generalized anxiety disorder.
   b. The population includes all individuals diagnosed with agoraphobia, and the sample includes just the participants in the study diagnosed with agoraphobia.
   c. The population includes all individuals at the psychological clinic, and the sample includes all individuals at the psychological clinic diagnosed with panic disorder.
   d. The population includes all individuals diagnosed with social anxiety disorder, and the sample includes just the participants in the study diagnosed with social anxiety disorder.

3. Jerome seeks therapy to help with symptoms of what he believes might be generalized anxiety disorder. Jerome has been feeling quite tense and worried about many things for the last three months. Which of the following might a psychologist tell Jerome to explain why he does not meet the criteria for generalized anxiety disorder?

   a. "Jerome, you do not meet the criteria for generalized anxiety disorder because you do not avoid situations where help or escape might be difficult."
   b. "Jerome, you do not meet the criteria for generalized anxiety disorder because you do not display a persistent fear of a specific thing."

   c. "Jerome, you do not meet the criteria for generalized anxiety disorder because you have not shown these symptoms for at least six months."
   d. "Jerome, you do not meet the criteria for generalized anxiety disorder because you do not experience unwanted, repetitive thoughts."

4. Dr. Andrews wants to conduct a study of people who fear birds to the point that they have difficulty leaving their homes. What psychological disorder does Dr. Andrews intend to study?
   a. Agoraphobia
   b. Specific phobia
   c. Panic disorder
   d. Generalized anxiety disorder

**Use the following scenario to answer questions 5 and 6:**

After a town was impacted by a major tornado, Dr. Gramlich conducted a study to determine the extent to which catastrophic thinking was associated with study participants' developing nightmares, haunting memories, and hypervigilance.

5. Which of the following is most likely to be one of the variables in Dr. Gramlich's study?

   a. The development of agoraphobia
   b. The development of panic disorder
   c. The development of trichotillomania
   d. The development of posttraumatic stress disorder

6. Which brain area might be most involved in the symptoms displayed by the participants in Dr. Gramlich's study?

   a. Amygdala
   b. Hypothalamus
   c. Temporal lobe
   d. Occipital lobe

7. Sarah has been diagnosed with obsessive-compulsive disorder (OCD). Which of the following scenarios best represents a compulsive behavior in OCD?

   a. Sarah arranges her books on the shelf in alphabetical order so she can easily find them.

   b. Sarah experiences intrusive thoughts about harming her loved ones, but she doesn't act on them.

   c. Sarah constantly feels the urge to wash her hands when she is in public, fearing contamination and germs.

   d. Sarah has trouble leaving home because she repeatedly double-checks if she has locked the front door.

8. Which of the following scenarios best represents an obsession in obsessive-compulsive disorder (OCD)?

   a. Lisa frequently rearranges her furniture to create a more aesthetically pleasing living space.

   b. Mark meticulously follows a daily routine, adhering to specific timings for meals, work, and leisure activities.

   c. Christiana experiences unwanted and repetitive thoughts about getting sick from germs when she is in public.

   d. Robert has a strong aversion to certain colors and avoids them in his clothing choices and home decor.

9. Dr. Karns found that some genes influence anxiety disorders by regulating the levels of the neurotransmitter involved in sleep and mood. What neurotransmitter did Dr. Karns most likely measure in her study?

   a. Serotonin
   b. Glutamate
   c. Acetylcholine
   d. Dopamine

10. Drake once got lost in a crowded mall as a child. Now he feels anxious and fearful in crowded places. This scenario best exemplifies

   a. an epigenetic mark.
   b. a compulsion.
   c. posttraumatic growth.
   d. classical conditioning.

# Module 5.4b Selection of Categories of Psychological Disorders: Depressive Disorders and Bipolar Disorders

## LEARNING TARGETS

**5.4-5** Describe depressive disorders and bipolar disorders.

**5.4-6** Explain how the biological and social-cognitive perspectives help us understand depressive disorders and bipolar disorders.

### 5.4-5 How do depressive disorders and bipolar disorders differ?

How do sadness and depression differ? We feel sad when bad things happen—getting a poor test grade, suffering a relationship breakup, or losing someone we love. But when feelings of despair or void last most of the day for days (or even weeks) and we can no longer sleep well, eat, or do things we enjoy, psychologists consider this not just sadness, but depression.

In the past year, have you at some time "felt so depressed that it was difficult to function"? If so, you were not alone. In one national survey, 31 percent of American college students answered *Yes* (ACHA, 2009). In a survey of American high school students, 32 percent "felt so sad or hopeless almost every day for 2 or more weeks in a row that they stopped doing some usual activities" (Kann et al., 2018). You may feel deeply discouraged about the future, dissatisfied with your life, or socially isolated. You may lack the energy to get things done, to see people, or even to force yourself out of bed. You may be unable to concentrate, eat, or sleep normally. You might even wonder if you would be better off dead. Perhaps academic success came easily to you before, but now you find that disappointing grades jeopardize your goals (Levine et al., 2020). Maybe loneliness, discrimination, or a romantic breakup has plunged you into despair. And perhaps low self-esteem increases your brooding, worsening your self-torment or leading you to "doomscroll" through depressing news (NPR, 2020; Orth et al., 2016). Comparing yourself to seemingly happy, successful others on social media, you might mistakenly think it's just you feeling this way (Jordan et al., 2011). Most of us will have some direct or indirect experience with depression. Misery has more company than most suppose.

AaronAmat/iStock/Getty Images

While anxiety is a response to the threat of future loss, depression is often a response to past and current stress. To feel bad in reaction to very sad events is to be in touch with reality. In such times, depression is like a car's low-fuel light—a signal to stop and take appropriate measures. As one book title reminds us, there are "good reasons for bad feelings."

Biologically speaking, life's purpose is survival and reproduction, not happiness. Just as coughing, vomiting, and various sorts of pain protect our body from dangerous toxins, depression protects us. It slows us down, prompting us to conserve energy (Beck & Bredemeier, 2016; Gershon et al., 2016). When we grind temporarily to a halt and reassess our life, as depressed people do, we can redirect our energy in more promising ways (Watkins, 2008). There is sense to suffering. As psychologist Daniel Gilbert (2006) noted, "If someone offered you a pill that would make you permanently happy, you would be well advised to run fast and run far. Emotion is a compass that tells us what to do, and a compass that is perpetually stuck on NORTH is worthless."

Even mild sadness helps people process and recall faces more accurately (Hills et al., 2011). They also tend to pay more attention to details, think more critically (with less gullibility), and make better decisions (Forgas, 2009, 2013, 2017). Bad moods can serve useful purposes. But sometimes depression becomes seriously maladaptive. How do we recognize the fine line between a blue mood and a disorder?

In this section, we consider disorders in which depression impairs daily living. People with **depressive disorders** experience hopelessness and lethargy lasting several weeks or months. Among the depressive disorders are *major depressive disorder* and *persistent depressive disorder*. Those with **bipolar disorders** (formerly called *manic-depressive disorder*) alternate between depression and overexcited hyperactivity.

## Depressive Disorders

Joy, contentment, sadness, and despair are different points on a continuum—points at which any of us may be found at any given moment. The difference between a blue mood

**depressive disorders** a group of disorders characterized by an enduring sad, empty, or irritable mood, along with physical and cognitive changes that affect a person's ability to function.

**bipolar disorders** a group of disorders in which a person alternates between the hopelessness and lethargy of depression and the overexcited state of mania. (Formerly called *manic-depressive disorder.*)

after bad news and **major depressive disorder** is like the difference between breathlessness after climbing stairs and chronic breathing problems (**Table 5.4-2**).

| TABLE 5.4-2 Diagnosing Major Depressive Disorder |
|---|
| The DSM-5-TR classifies major depressive disorder as the presence of at least five of the following symptoms over a two-week period (minimally including depressed mood or reduced interest) (American Psychiatric Association, 2022): |
| • Depressed mood most of the time |
| • Dramatically reduced interest or enjoyment in most activities most of the time |
| • Significant challenges regulating appetite and weight |
| • Significant challenges regulating sleep |
| • Physical agitation or lethargy |
| • Feeling listless or with much less energy |
| • Feeling worthless, or feeling unwarranted guilt |
| • Problems in thinking, concentrating, or making decisions |
| • Thinking repetitively of death and suicide |

Adults diagnosed with **persistent depressive disorder** (formerly called dysthymia) have experienced a depressed mood more often than not for at least two *years* (American Psychiatric Association, 2022). They also display at least two of the following symptoms:

- Difficulty with decision making and concentration
- Feeling hopeless
- Poor self-esteem
- Reduced energy levels
- Problems regulating sleep
- Problems regulating appetite

Depression can look different across people. You can also be depressed in different ways and for different amounts of time. You can be depressed for two weeks or more in the case of major depressive disorder. You can also feel depressed with symptoms that last a much longer period of time (persistent depressive disorder), feel unusually depressed a week before your menses (premenstrual dysphoric disorder), experience aspects of depression and anxiety at the same time (mixed anxiety-depressive disorder), or feel depressed combined with severe irritability that starts at a young age (disruptive mood dysregulation disorder) (American Psychiatric Association, 2022). But the most common form of depression is major depressive disorder.

Depression is the number-one reason people seek mental health services. Indeed, the World Health Organization declared depression "the leading cause of disability worldwide" (WHO, 2017a). In one survey conducted in 21 countries, 4.6 percent of people interviewed were experiencing moderate or severe depression, as have 1 in 10 U.S. adults at some point during the prior year (Hasin et al., 2018; Thornicroft et al., 2017). U.S. depression levels rose dramatically during the Covid pandemic. Younger adults, women, people of color, and those who were unemployed were hardest hit (Czeisler et al., 2020; Fitzpatrick et al., 2020; Twenge & Joiner, 2020b). At least one in five health care professionals — feeling socially isolated, overworked, and stressed from caring for people dying from Covid — reported symptoms of depression (Pappa et al., 2020; Rossi et al., 2020).

**major depressive disorder** a disorder in which a person experiences five or more symptoms lasting two or more weeks, in the absence of drug use or a medical condition, at least one of which must be either (1) depressed mood or (2) loss of interest or pleasure.

**persistent depressive disorder** a disorder in which people experience a depressed mood on more days than not for at least two years. (Formerly called dysthymia.)

Some people believe that depression has a *seasonal pattern*, returning each winter. Canadians aged 12 to 24 in one large study, for example, reported feeling worse about themselves and experiencing more trouble falling or staying asleep during the winter (Lukmanji et al., 2020). Antidepressant prescriptions follow this same seasonal pattern (Lansdall-Welfare et al., 2019). Although the DSM-5-TR recognizes a seasonal pattern in major depressive disorder and bipolar disorders, some researchers challenge the presumption of widespread "seasonal affective disorder." Based on national data sets, they report that people in northerly or cloudier places do *not* experience more wintertime depression (Øverland et al., 2020; Traffanstedt et al., 2016). So, is seasonal affective disorder a myth? Stay tuned.

## Bipolar Disorders

People with *bipolar disorders* have periods of extremely excited mood and increased energy that can last several days or more. Like depressive disorders, bipolar disorders can take different forms depending on how severe the symptoms are and how long they last. People with **bipolar I disorder**, the most severe form, experience a euphoric, talkative, highly energetic, and overly ambitious state called **mania** that lasts a week or longer. Psychiatrist Kay Redfield Jamison, who was diagnosed with bipolar I disorder, described her mania: "When you're high it's tremendous. The ideas and feelings are fast and frequent like shooting stars, and you follow them until you find better and brighter ones" (Jamison, 1995). As Kanye West said on one of his album covers, "I hate being Bi-Polar / Its [sic] awesome."

But before long, many people with bipolar I disorder can plunge back into depression. Sometimes, they go back and forth, experiencing *rapid cycling* between the highs and lows. Those with **bipolar II disorder** move between depression and a milder *hypomania* (**Figure 5.4-4**).

If depression is living in slow motion, mania is fast forward. During the manic phase, people with bipolar disorders typically have less need for sleep. They show fewer sexual inhibitions. Their positive emotions persist abnormally (Gruber et al., 2019; Stanton et al., 2019). Their speech is loud, flighty, and hard to interrupt. They find advice irritating. Yet they need protection from their own poor judgment, which may lead to reckless spending or unsafe sex. Thinking fast feels good, but it also increases risk-taking (Chandler & Pronin, 2012; Pronin, 2013).

Genes that increase bipolar risk also predict creativity (Taylor, 2017). George Frideric Handel (1685–1759), who may have suffered from a mild form of bipolar disorder, composed

**bipolar I disorder** the most severe form, in which people experience a euphoric, talkative, highly energetic, and overly ambitious state that lasts a week or longer.

**mania** a hyperactive, wildly optimistic state in which dangerously poor judgment is common.

**bipolar II disorder** a less severe form of bipolar in which people move between depression and a milder hypomania.

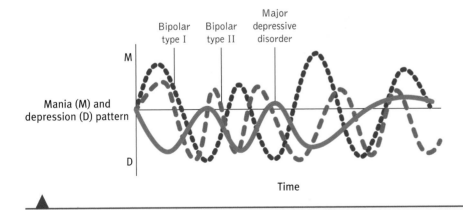

**Figure 5.4-4**

**Mood fluctuation in bipolar disorders, compared with major depressive disorder**

For individuals with major depressive disorder, their moods move up and down but barely make it above the midline. For those with bipolar I, there is deeper depression than for those with major depressive disorder, along with dramatic swings into mania. Those with bipolar II experience similar depression but less severe mania than those with bipolar I.

**Bipolar disorders** Artist Abigail Southworth illustrated her experience of a bipolar disorder.

*Life as a Two-Headed Beast: Bipolar, Abigail Southworth*

his nearly three-hour-long *Messiah* during three weeks of intense, creative energy in 1742 (Keynes, 1980). Bipolar disorders may strike more often among those who rely on emotional expression and vivid imagery, such as poets and artists, and less often among those who rely on precision and logic, such as architects and journalists (Jamison, 1993, 1995; Kaufman & Baer, 2002; Ludwig, 1995). Indeed, one analysis of more than a million individuals showed that the only psychiatric condition linked to working in a creative profession was a bipolar disorder (Kyaga et al., 2013).

Bipolar disorders are much less common than major depressive disorder, but they are often more dysfunctional. Unlike major depressive disorder, for which women are at highest risk, bipolar disorders affect as many men as women. This diagnosis has been increasing among adolescents, whose mood swings may vary from raging to bubbly. Between 1994 and 2003, bipolar diagnoses in Americans under age 20 showed an astonishing 40-fold increase — from an estimated 20,000 to 800,000 (Carey, 2007; Flora & Bobby, 2008; Moreno et al., 2007). The DSM-5 classifications became stricter, however, which reduced the number of child and adolescent bipolar diagnoses.

*Axelle/Bauer-Griffin/Getty Images*

**Creativity and bipolar disorders**

There have been many creative artists, composers, writers, and musical performers with a bipolar disorder. Some struggle secretly, as did Mariah Carey for 17 years.

Recording artist Mariah Carey

## Understanding Depressive Disorders and Bipolar Disorders

> **5.4-6** How can the biological and social-cognitive perspectives help us understand depressive disorders and bipolar disorders?

Today's psychologists continue to investigate why people have depressive disorders and bipolar disorders, and to design more effective ways to treat and prevent these disorders. Here, we focus primarily on depressive disorders. Any theory of depression must explain the following (Lewinsohn et al., 1985, 1998, 2003):

- *Behaviors and thoughts change with depression.* People trapped in a depressed mood become inactive and feel alone, empty, and without a meaningful future. Depression may be triggered by a sad or stressful event, but people with depression may feel a heavy sadness even when nothing bad happens. They also more often recall and expect negative happenings (my team will lose, my grades will fall, my love will fail) (Zetsche et al., 2019).

- ***Depression is widespread, with women at greater risk.*** Worldwide, 350 million people have major depressive disorder and 60 million people have a bipolar disorder (WHO, 2017a). Globally, women's risk for major depressive disorder is roughly double men's (Kuehner, 2017; see also **Figure 5.4-5**). The depression gender gap fits a bigger pattern: Women are generally more vulnerable to disorders involving internal states, such as depression, anxiety, and inhibited sexual desire. Women also experience more situations that increase their risk for depression, such as receiving less pay for equal work, juggling multiple roles, and caring for children and elderly family members (Freeman & Freeman, 2013). Men's disorders tend to be more external—alcohol use disorder, and disorders related to antisocial conduct and lack of impulse control. Women often get sadder than men do; men often get madder than women do.

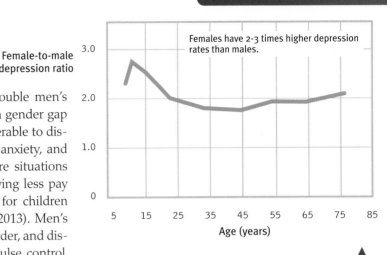

**Female-to-male depression ratio**

Females have 2-3 times higher depression rates than males.

Age (years)

▲

**Figure 5.4-5**

**Female-to-male depression ratio, worldwide**

Researchers Rachel Salk, Janet Hyde, and Lyn Abramson (2017) found that, compared with males, females have twice the risk of depression, and a tripled rate during early adolescence. For many girls, the early teen years are tough.

- ***Most major depressive episodes end on their own.*** Therapy often speeds recovery. But even without professional help, most people recover from depression. Some do so without future depression and with "optimal well-being" (Rottenberg et al., 2019).

- ***Depression sometimes returns.*** For many people, the black cloud of depression comes and, after sustained struggle, it often goes. But for about half of these people, the depression returns (Curry et al., 2011; Klein & Kotov, 2016). For some 20 percent, the condition will be chronic (Klein, 2010). An enduring recovery is more likely if the first episode strikes later in life, there were no previous episodes, the person experiences minimal physical or psychological stress, and there is ample social support (Fuller-Thomson et al., 2016).

- ***Stress and negative events often precede depression.*** About 1 person in 4 diagnosed with depression has been brought down by a significant loss or trauma, such as a loved one's death, a ruptured marriage, a physical assault, or a lost job (LeMoult, 2020). Moving to a new culture also increases risk for depression, especially among younger people who have not yet formed their identities (Zhang et al., 2013). And childhood abuse doubles a person's risk of adult depression (Nelson et al., 2017).

- ***Compared with generations past, depression strikes earlier and more often, with the highest rates among older teens and young adults*** (Cross-National Collaborative Group, 1992; Kessler et al., 2010; Olfson et al., 2015). From 2009 to 2020, depression doubled among U.S. 12- to 17-year-olds (SAMHSA, 2021).

## The Biological Perspective

Depression is a whole-body disorder. It involves genetic predispositions, brain connectivity issues, and biochemical imbalances, as well as negative thoughts and a gloomy mood.

### Genes and Depression

Depressive disorders and bipolar disorders run in families. The risk of being diagnosed with one of these disorders increases if your parent or sibling has the disorder (Sullivan et al., 2000; Weissman et al., 2016). If one identical twin is diagnosed with major depressive disorder, the chances are about 1 in 2 that at some time the other twin will be, too. If one identical twin has a bipolar disorder, the chances of a similar diagnosis for the co-twin are even higher—7 in 10—even for twins raised apart (DiLalla et al., 1996).

Summarizing the major twin studies, two research teams independently estimated the *heritability*—the extent to which individual differences are attributable to genes—of

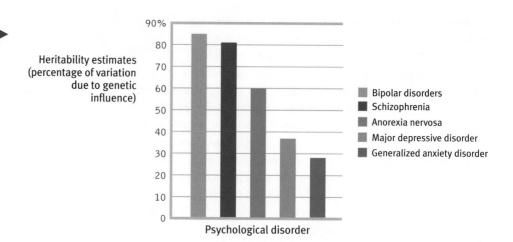

major depressive disorder at 40 percent (Kendler et al., 2018; Polderman et al., 2015; see also **Figure 5.4-6**). But nurture matters, too. A Swedish national study examined children who had a biological parent with depression. Among families in which at least one child was home-raised and another adopted into a different family, those raised in the adoptive homes "had a significantly reduced risk for major depression" (Kendler et al., 2020a).

Emotions are "postcards from our genes" (Plotkin, 1994). To tease out the genes that put people at risk for depression, researchers may use *linkage analysis*. First, geneticists find families in which the disorder appears across several generations. Next, the researchers look for differences in DNA from affected and unaffected family members. Linkage analysis points them to a chromosome neighborhood: "A house-to-house search is then needed to find the culprit gene" (Plomin & McGuffin, 2003). But depression is a complex condition. Many genes work together, producing a mosaic of small effects that interact with other factors to put some people at greater risk. Nevertheless, researchers are identifying culprit gene variations in depressive and bipolar disorders that may open the door to more effective drug therapy (Halldorsdottir et al., 2019; Stahl et al., 2019).

## Brain Structure and Activity

Nearly 100 studies have identified brain abnormalities linked with depression (Gray et al., 2020). Scanning devices offer a window into the brain's activity during depressed and manic states in people with a bipolar disorder. During depression, brain activity slows; during mania, it increases (**Figure 5.4-7**). Depression often lowers activity in the brain's reward centers, whereas bipolar disorders increase reward center activity (Dutra et al., 2015; Nusslock et al., 2012).

At least two neurotransmitter systems are at work during the periods of brain inactivity and hyperactivity that accompany major depressive disorder and bipolar disorders. *Norepinephrine*, which increases arousal and boosts mood, is scarce during depression and overabundant during mania. Drugs that decrease mania reduce norepinephrine levels.

## Figure 5.4-7

### The ups and downs of a bipolar disorder

These top-facing PET scans show that brain energy consumption rises and falls with the patient's emotional changes. Red areas are where the brain rapidly consumes *glucose,* an important energy source.

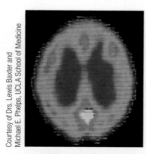

**Depressed state**
(May 17)

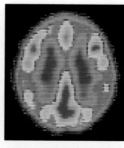

**Manic state**
(May 18)

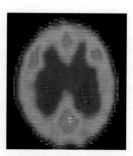

**Depressed state**
(May 27)

Courtesy of Drs. Lewis Baxter and Michael E. Phelps, UCLA School of Medicine

Serotonin is also scarce or inactive during depression, but its level increases when depression fades (Carver et al., 2008; Svensson et al., 2021). Drugs that relieve depression tend to increase serotonin or norepinephrine supplies by blocking either their reuptake (as Prozac, Zoloft, and Paxil do with serotonin) or their chemical breakdown. Repetitive physical exercise, such as jogging, reduces depression in part because it increases serotonin (Airan et al., 2007; Harvey et al., 2018; Ilardi, 2009). To get away from a bad mood, some people use their own two feet.

## AP® Science Practice

## Data Interpretation

Dr. Singleton is researching a new drug for major depressive disorder. She randomly selects 10 individuals diagnosed with major depressive disorder from her clinic. She randomly assigns five of those individuals to take the new drug, and five to receive a placebo. Neither the participants nor Dr. Singleton knows which group they are in. After 6 months, she measures depressive symptoms using a self-report questionnaire. Scores range from 1 to 30, with higher scores indicating more intense symptoms. Consider the following data set:

| New Drug | Placebo |
|---|---|
| 5 | 30 |
| 10 | 25 |
| 5 | 20 |
| 15 | 15 |
| 20 | 15 |

- Calculate the mean, median, and mode for each group.

- Explain why the use of a placebo is important in this study.

- Explain the difference between random sampling and random assignment in this study.

- How did Dr. Singleton operationally define the dependent variable?

- Explain how Dr. Singleton employed the double-blind procedure.

- Describe two ethical guidelines Dr. Singleton would have to follow in her study.

- If the results are statistically significant, what conclusion can Dr. Singleton draw at the end of her study?

*Need help with any of the answers? Revisit Unit 0.*

**Minding the gut** Does food modify mood? Digestive system bacteria produce serotonin and other neurotransmitters that influence emotions. Although some researchers think the happy gut/happy brain relationship is over-hyped, healthy, diverse gut microbes predict less risk of anxiety and depression (Cruz-Pereira et al., 2020; Pennisi, 2020; Simpson et al., 2021).

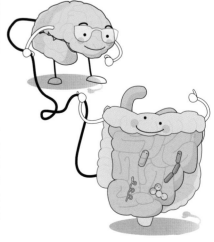

## Nutritional Effects

What's good for the heart is also good for the brain and mind. People who eat a heart-healthy "Mediterranean diet" (heavy on vegetables, fish, whole grains, and olive oil) have a comparatively low risk of developing heart disease, stroke, late-life cognitive decline, and depression—all of which are associated with inflammation in the body (Kaplan et al., 2015; Psaltopoulou et al., 2013; Rechenberg, 2016). Excessive alcohol use also correlates with depression, partly because depression can increase alcohol use but mostly because alcohol misuse *leads to* depression (Fergusson et al., 2009).

**rumination** compulsive fretting; *overthinking* our problems and their causes.

**Rumination runs wild** It's normal to think about our flaws. But dwelling constantly on negative thoughts — particularly negative thoughts about ourselves — makes it difficult to believe in ourselves and solve problems. People sometimes seek therapy to reduce their rumination.

# The Social-Cognitive Perspective

The *social-cognitive perspective* explores how people's assumptions and expectations influence what they perceive. Many depressed people have intensely negative views of themselves, their situation, and their future (Nieto et al., 2020). Norman, a Canadian university professor, recalled his depression this way:

> I [despaired] of ever being human again. I honestly felt subhuman, lower than the lowest vermin. Furthermore, I . . . could not understand why anyone would want to associate with me, let alone love me. . . . I was positive that I was a fraud and a phony and that I didn't deserve my Ph.D. . . . I didn't deserve the research grants I had been awarded; I couldn't understand how I had written books and journal articles. . . . I must have conned a lot of people. (Endler, 1982, pp. 45–49)

Expecting the worst, depressed people magnify bad experiences and minimize good ones (Wenze et al., 2012). Their *self-defeating beliefs* and *negative explanatory style* feed their depression.

## Negative Thoughts, Negative Moods, and Gender

Do you agree or disagree that you "at least occasionally feel overwhelmed by all I have to do"? In a survey, 38 percent of women and 17 percent of men entering U.S. colleges and universities agreed (Pryor et al., 2006). Relationship stresses also affect teen girls more than boys (Hamilton et al., 2015). Why are women nearly twice as vulnerable as men to depression, and twice as likely to take antidepressant drugs (Pratt et al., 2017)?

Susan Nolen-Hoeksema (2003) related women's higher risk of depression to what she described as their tendency to ruminate or *overthink*. Staying focused on a problem — thanks to the continuous activation of an attention-sustaining frontal lobe area — can be adaptive (Altamirano et al., 2010; Andrews & Thomson, 2009a,b). But relentless, self-focused **rumination** can distract us, increase negative emotions, and disrupt daily activities (Johnson et al., 2016; Leary, 2018; Yang et al., 2017). We can even ruminate about our excessive rumination — by thinking too much about how we're thinking about something too much.

Comparisons can also feed misery. Lonely Lori scrolls through her social media feed and sees Maria having a blast at a party, Angelique enjoying a family vacation, and Amira looking super in a swimsuit. In response, Lori broods: "My life is terrible."

But why do life's unavoidable failures lead only some people to become depressed? The answer lies partly in their *explanatory style*, which may be pessimistic or optimistic. Imagine two people who do poorly on a test. The first person, who has a pessimistic explanatory style ("I'm such a failure! I'll never pass this class"), feels hopeless and depressed. The second person, who has an optimistic explanatory style ("I didn't study enough, but I'll work hard and do better next time"), feels more positive and copes more successfully.

Depression-prone people respond to bad events in an especially self-focused, self-blaming way (LeMoult & Gotlib, 2019). As **Figure 5.4-8** illustrates, they explain bad events in terms that are *stable*, *global*, and *internal*.

**Figure 5.4-8**
**Explanatory style and depression**

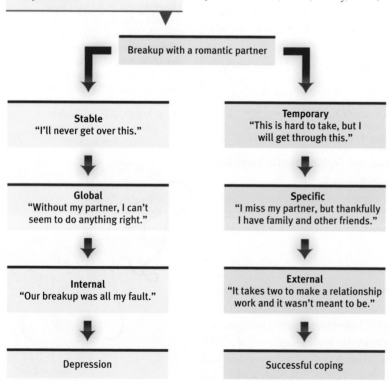

Breakup with a romantic partner

**Stable**
"I'll never get over this."

**Temporary**
"This is hard to take, but I will get through this."

**Global**
"Without my partner, I can't seem to do anything right."

**Specific**
"I miss my partner, but thankfully I have family and other friends."

**Internal**
"Our breakup was all my fault."

**External**
"It takes two to make a relationship work and it wasn't meant to be."

**Depression**

**Successful coping**

Self-defeating beliefs may arise from *learned helplessness*, the hopelessness and passive resignation that humans and other animals learn when they experience uncontrollable painful events (Maier & Seligman, 2016; see Module 5.1). Pessimistic, overgeneralized, self-blaming attributions may create a depressing sense of hopelessness (Abramson et al., 1989; Groß et al., 2017). As researcher Martin Seligman (1991, p. 78) has noted, "A recipe for severe depression is preexisting pessimism encountering failure." What, then, might we expect of new college students who exhibit a pessimistic explanatory style? Lauren Alloy and her colleagues (1999) monitored several hundred students every 6 weeks for 2.5 years. Among those identified as having a pessimistic thinking style, 17 percent had a first episode of major depression, as did only 1 percent of those who began college with an optimistic thinking style.

Critics note a chicken-and-egg problem nesting in the social-cognitive explanation of depression. Which comes first—the pessimistic explanatory style or the depressed mood? The negative explanations *coincide* with a depressed mood, and they are *indicators* of depression. But do negative thoughts *cause* depression, any more than a speedometer's reading causes a car's speed? In experiments, temporarily putting people in a bad or sad mood does make their memories, judgments, and expectations more pessimistic—a phenomenon that memory researchers call *state-dependent memory* (see Module 2.6).

Cultural forces may also nudge people toward or away from depression. Why is depression so common among young Westerners? Seligman (1991, 1995) has pointed to the rise of individualism and the decline of commitment to religion and family. In non-Western cultures, where close-knit relationships and cooperation are the norm, major depressive disorder is less common and less tied to self-blame for failure (DeVaus et al., 2018; Ferrari et al., 2013). In Japan, for example, depressed people instead tend to report feeling shame over letting others down (Draguns, 1990).

"You should never engage in unsupervised introspection."

The New Yorker Collection, 2009, William Haefeli/The Cartoon Bank

## Depression's Vicious Cycle

Depression is both a cause and an effect of stressful experiences that disrupt our sense of who we are and why we matter. Such disruptions can lead to brooding, which is rich soil for growing negative feelings. And that negativity—being withdrawn, self-focused, and complaining—can by itself cause others to reject us (Furr & Funder, 1998; Gotlib & Hammen, 1992). Indeed, people deep in depression are at high risk for divorce, job loss, and other stressful life events. Weary of the person's fatigue, hopeless attitude, and negativity, a spouse may threaten to leave, or a boss may begin to question the person's competence. Rejection and depression feed each other. Misery may love another's company, but company does not love another's misery.

We can now assemble the pieces of the depression puzzle (Figure 5.4-9): (1) Stressful experiences interpreted through (2) a brooding, negative explanatory style create (3) a hopeless, depressed state that (4) hampers the way the person thinks and acts. These thoughts and actions, in turn, fuel (1) further stressful experiences such as rejection. Depression is a snake that bites its own tail.

It is a cycle we can all recognize. When we feel down, we think negatively and remember bad experiences. Britain's Prime Minister Winston Churchill called depression a "black dog" that periodically hounded him. U.S. President Abraham Lincoln was so withdrawn and brooding as a young man that his friends feared he might take his own life (Kline, 1974). As their lives remind us, "depression" can be an anagram for "I pressed on." Many people struggle through depression and regain their capacity to love, to work, and to succeed.

### Figure 5.4-9

**The vicious cycle of depressed thinking**

Therapists recognize this cycle, and they work to help depressed people break out of it by changing their negative thinking, turning their attention outward, and engaging them in more pleasant and competent behaviors.

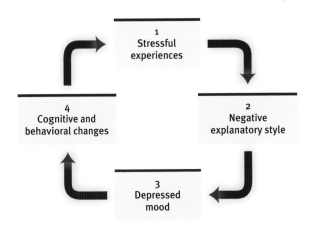

1 Stressful experiences

2 Negative explanatory style

3 Depressed mood

4 Cognitive and behavioral changes

## Check Your Understanding

**Examine the Concept**

▶ Describe the relationship between explanatory style and depression.

▶ Describe the vicious cycle of depressed thinking.

*Answers to the Examine the Concept questions can be found in Appendix C at the end of the book.*

**Apply the Concept**

▶ Compare and contrast the symptoms of major depressive disorder and bipolar disorder.

▶ Have you ever ruminated about something? How did it make you feel? What can you do to reduce rumination?

# Module 5.4b REVIEW

**5.4-5** How do depressive disorders and bipolar disorders differ?

- *Depressive disorders* are characterized by a sad, empty, or irritable mood, along with physical and cognitive changes that affect a person's ability to function.

- A person with *major depressive disorder* experiences at least five symptoms of depression (including either depressed mood or loss of interest or pleasure) for two or more weeks.

- A person with *persistent depressive disorder* experiences a depressed mood more often than not for at least two years, as well as at least two symptoms of depression.

- A person with a *bipolar disorder* experiences not only depression but also *mania*—episodes of hyperactive and wildly optimistic, impulsive behavior.

**5.4-6** How can the biological and social-cognitive perspectives help us understand depressive disorders and bipolar disorders?

- The biological perspective on depressive disorders and bipolar disorders focuses on genetic predispositions, abnormalities in brain structures and function (including those found in neurotransmitter systems), and nutritional (and drug) effects.

- The social-cognitive perspective views depression as an ongoing cycle of stressful experiences—interpreted through negative beliefs, attributions, and memories, often with relentless *rumination*—leading to negative moods, thoughts, and actions, thereby fueling new stressful experiences.

## AP® Practice Multiple Choice Questions

1. Loralynn has been feeling sad and empty most of the time for the past few weeks, which has gotten in the way of her ability to function in important life areas. With what disorder might she be diagnosed?

   a. Bipolar disorders
   b. Persistent depressive disorder
   c. Mania
   d. Major depressive disorder

2. After spending several weeks barely able to get out of bed, Haroun is experiencing a period of intense energy, sleeplessness, and impulsive, reckless behavior. Haroun's symptoms most closely match those of

   a. a bipolar disorder.
   b. persistent depressive disorder.
   c. rumination.
   d. a depressive disorder.

**3.** Dr. Navarro conducted a study with individuals who experienced a depressed mood for most days over a three-year period to determine their occupational outcomes. What variable did Dr. Navarro study?

   a. Bipolar I disorder

   b. Persistent depressive disorder

   c. Major depressive disorder

   d. Bipolar II disorder

**4.** Delfina was first diagnosed with major depressive disorder when she was 53 years old. Which of the following conclusions is most likely to be true for Delfina?

   a. Delfina will experience persistent depressive disorder.

   b. Delfina will recover from this episode of major depressive disorder without recurrence.

   c. Delfina will experience recurrent major depressive episodes for the duration of her life.

   d. Delfina will develop a bipolar disorder.

**5.** Emogene has been experiencing a high degree of wild optimism, hyperactivity, and poor judgment. What is she experiencing?

   a. Bipolar disorder

   b. Rumination

   c. Learned helplessness

   d. Mania

# Module 5.4c Selection of Categories of Psychological Disorders: Schizophrenia Spectrum Disorders

## LEARNING TARGETS

**5.4-7** Describe the patterns of perceiving, thinking, and feeling that characterize schizophrenia.

**5.4-8** Contrast *chronic schizophrenia* and *acute schizophrenia*.

**5.4-9** Describe the brain abnormalities associated with schizophrenia.

**5.4-10** Describe the prenatal events associated with increased risk of developing schizophrenia.

**5.4-11** Explain how genes influence schizophrenia.

**schizophrenia spectrum disorders** a group of disorders characterized by delusions, hallucinations, disorganized thinking or speech, disorganized or unusual motor behavior, and negative symptoms (such as diminished emotional expression); includes *schizophrenia* and *schizotypal personality disorder*.

**psychotic disorders** a group of disorders marked by irrational ideas, distorted perceptions, and a loss of contact with reality.

During their most severe periods, people with a **schizophrenia spectrum disorder** live in a private inner world, preoccupied with strange ideas and images. The word *schizophrenia* means "split" (*schizo*) "mind" (*phrenia*). This "split" does not refer to multiple identities; rather, people with schizophrenia have a mind that is split from reality. They often have disturbed perceptions and beliefs, disorganized speech, and diminished, inappropriate emotions and actions. Schizophrenia is the chief example of a **psychotic disorder**.

People with *schizotypal personality disorder*—another disorder in this group—experience discomfort in close relationships, have distorted thoughts and perceptions, and engage in eccentric behaviors. Both people with schizophrenia and people with schizotypal personality disorder have irrational beliefs and unusual behaviors, but only schizophrenia is characterized by frequent and intense hallucinations and delusions—and an inability to abandon such thoughts and perceptions when it's clear that they are disconnected from reality.

As you can imagine, these characteristics profoundly disrupt relationships and work. Given a supportive environment and medication, more than 40 percent of people with schizophrenia will have periods of a year or more of normal life experience (Jobe & Harrow, 2010). Unfortunately, only 1 in 7 experiences a full and enduring recovery (Jääskeläinen et al., 2013).

## Symptoms of Schizophrenia

**5.4-7** What patterns of perceiving, thinking, and feeling characterize schizophrenia?

### AP® Exam Tip

When psychologists refer to "positive" and "negative" schizophrenia symptoms (as with positive and negative *reinforcement* in Unit 3), the terms *positive* and *negative* don't mean "good" and "bad." Symptoms are positive and negative in a mathematical sense (adding or subtracting behaviors).

Schizophrenia comes in varied forms. People with schizophrenia display symptoms that are *positive* (*inappropriate* behaviors are *present*) or *negative* (*appropriate* behaviors are *absent*). Those with positive symptoms may experience disturbed perceptions, talk in disorganized and deluded ways, or exhibit inappropriate laughter, tears, or rage. Those with negative symptoms may exhibit an absence of emotion in their voices, expressionless faces, or mute and rigid bodies.

## Disturbed Perceptions and Beliefs

People with schizophrenia sometimes *hallucinate*—they see, hear, feel, taste, or smell things that exist only in their minds. Most often, the hallucinations are voices, which sometimes make insulting remarks or give orders. The voices may tell the person that they are bad or that they must set fire to their living space. Imagine your own reaction if a dream broke into your waking consciousness, making it hard to separate your experience from your imagination. When the unreal seems real, the resulting perceptions are at best bizarre, at worst terrifying.

Hallucinations are false *perceptions*. People with schizophrenia also have disorganized, fragmented thinking, often distorted by false *beliefs* called **delusions**. If they have *paranoid* delusions, they may believe they are being threatened or pursued.

One cause of disorganized thinking may be a breakdown in *selective attention*. Recall from Module 2.1 that we normally have a remarkable capacity for giving our undivided attention to one set of sensory stimuli while filtering out others. People with schizophrenia are easily distracted by tiny unrelated stimuli, such as the grooves on a brick or the tones in a voice. This selective-attention difficulty is but one of dozens of cognitive differences associated with schizophrenia (Reichenberg & Harvey, 2007).

## Disorganized Speech

Maxine, a young woman with schizophrenia, believed she was Mary Poppins. Communicating with Maxine was difficult because her thoughts spilled out in no logical order. Her biographer, Susan Sheehan (1982, p. 25), observed her saying aloud to no one in particular, "This morning, when I was at Hillside [Hospital], I was making a movie. I was surrounded by movie stars. . . . I'm Mary Poppins. Is this room painted blue to get me upset? My grandmother died four weeks after my eighteenth birthday."

Jumbled ideas may make no sense even within sentences, forming what is known as *word salad*. One young man begged for "a little more allegro in the treatment," and suggested that "liberationary movement with a view to the widening of the horizon" will "ergo extort some wit in lectures."

## Diminished and Inappropriate Emotions

The expressed emotions of schizophrenia are often utterly inappropriate, split off from reality (Kring & Caponigro, 2010). Maxine laughed after recalling her grandmother's death. On other occasions, she cried when others laughed, or became angry for no apparent reason. Others with schizophrenia lapse into an emotionless *flat affect* state of no apparent feeling.

Most also have an *impaired theory of mind*—they have difficulty reading other peoples' facial expressions and states of mind (Bora & Pantelis, 2016). Unable to understand others' mental states, individuals with schizophrenia struggle to feel sympathy and compassion (Bonfils et al., 2016). These emotional deficiencies occur early in the illness and have a genetic basis (Bora & Pantelis, 2013). *Motor behavior* may also be inappropriate and disruptive. People with schizophrenia may experience *catatonia*, which can present as positive symptoms (the restlessness, agitation, and compulsive movements of *catatonic excitement*) or negative symptoms (the motionlessness of *catatonic stupor*).

# Onset and Development of Schizophrenia

**5.4-8** How do *chronic schizophrenia* and *acute schizophrenia* differ?

An estimated 20 million people worldwide—about 1 in 270—have schizophrenia (WHO, 2019b). This disorder knows no national boundaries and typically strikes as young people are maturing into adulthood. Men tend to be diagnosed more often than women, and to be

© Craig Geiser

**Art by someone diagnosed with schizophrenia** After his schizophrenia diagnosis, Michigan artist Craig Geisler said he "started drawing as a way to relax and escape the real world" (Geiser, 2021). Medication and therapy have helped quiet Geiser's hallucinations and delusions, enabling him to lead a meaningful life (Geiser, 2019).

**delusion** a false belief, often of persecution or grandeur, that may accompany psychotic disorders.

struck earlier and with more severity (Aleman et al., 2003; Eranti et al., 2013; Picchioni & Murray, 2007).

When schizophrenia is a slow-developing process, called **chronic schizophrenia**, recovery is doubtful (Harrison et al., 2001; Jääskeläinen et al., 2013). This was the case with Maxine, whose schizophrenia took a slow course, emerging from a long history of social inadequacy and poor school performance (MacCabe et al., 2008). Although people with both chronic and *acute schizophrenia* can exhibit positive or negative symptoms, social withdrawal—a negative symptom—is often found among those with chronic schizophrenia (Kirkpatrick et al., 2006). Men more often exhibit negative symptoms and chronic schizophrenia (Räsänen et al., 2000).

When previously well-adjusted people develop schizophrenia rapidly following particular life stresses, the condition is called **acute schizophrenia**, and recovery is much more likely. These individuals more often have positive symptoms that respond to drug therapy (Fenton & McGlashan, 1991, 1994; Fowles, 1992).

# Understanding Schizophrenia

Schizophrenia is one of the most intensely researched psychological disorders. Most studies now link it with abnormal brain tissue and genetic predispositions. Schizophrenia is a disease of the brain manifested in symptoms of the mind.

## Brain Abnormalities

**5.4-9** What brain abnormalities are associated with schizophrenia?

Might chemical imbalances in the brain explain schizophrenia? Scientists have long known that strange behavior can have strange chemical causes. Have you ever heard the saying "as mad as a hatter"? That phrase is often thought to refer to the psychological deterioration of British hatmakers whose brains, it was later discovered, were slowly poisoned by the mercury-laden felt material (Smith, 1983). Could schizophrenia symptoms have a similar biochemical key? Scientists are searching for blood proteins that might predict schizophrenia onset (Chan et al., 2015). And they are tracking the mechanisms by which chemicals produce hallucinations and other symptoms.

### Dopamine Overactivity

The *dopamine hypothesis* provides one possible answer. When researchers examined schizophrenia patients' brains after death, they found an excess number of *dopamine* receptors (Seeman et al., 1993; Wong et al., 1986). The resulting hyper-responsive dopamine system may intensify brain signals in schizophrenia, creating positive symptoms such as hallucinations and paranoia (Maia & Frank, 2017). Drugs that block dopamine receptors often lessen these symptoms. Drugs that increase dopamine levels, such as nicotine, amphetamines, and cocaine, sometimes intensify them (Basu & Basu, 2015; Farnia et al., 2014).

### Abnormal Brain Activity and Anatomy

Abnormal brain activity and brain structures accompany schizophrenia. Some people diagnosed with schizophrenia have abnormally low brain activity in the brain's frontal lobes, which help us reason, plan, and solve problems (Morey et al., 2005; Pettegrew et al., 1993; Resnick, 1992). The brain waves that reflect synchronized neural firing in the frontal lobes decline noticeably (Spencer et al., 2004; Symond et al., 2005).

One study took PET scans of brain activity while people with schizophrenia were hallucinating (Silbersweig et al., 1995). When participants heard a voice or saw something, their brain became vigorously active in several core regions. One was the thalamus, the structure

**chronic schizophrenia** (also called *process schizophrenia*) a form of schizophrenia in which symptoms usually appear by late adolescence or early adulthood. As people age, psychotic episodes last longer and recovery periods shorten.

**acute schizophrenia** (also called *reactive schizophrenia*) a form of schizophrenia that can begin at any age, frequently occurs in response to a traumatic event, and from which recovery is much more likely.

that filters incoming sensory signals and transmits them to the brain's cortex. Another PET scan study of people with paranoia found increased activity in the amygdala, a fear-processing center (Epstein et al., 1998).

In schizophrenia, fluid-filled brain cavities called *ventricles* become enlarged; cerebral tissue also shrinks (Goldman et al., 2009; van Haren et al., 2016). People often inherit these brain differences. If one affected identical twin shows brain abnormalities, the odds are at least 1 in 2 that the other twin's brain will have them (van Haren et al., 2012). Some studies have even found these abnormalities in people who *later* developed the disorder (Karlsgodt et al., 2010). The greater the brain shrinkage, the more severe the thought disorder (Collinson et al., 2003; Nelson et al., 1998; Shenton, 1992).

Smaller-than-normal areas may include the cortex, the hippocampus, and the corpus callosum connecting the brain's two hemispheres (Arnone et al., 2008; Bois et al., 2016). Often, the thalamus is also smaller than normal, which may explain why filtering sensory input and focusing attention can be difficult for people with schizophrenia (Andreasen et al., 1994; Ellison-Wright et al., 2008). Schizophrenia also tends to involve a loss of neural connections across the brain network (Bohlken et al., 2016; Kambeitz et al., 2016). *The bottom line:* Schizophrenia involves not just a single isolated brain abnormality but problems with several brain regions and their interconnections (Andreasen, 1997, 2001; Arnedo et al., 2015).

**Storing and studying brains**
Psychiatrist E. Fuller Torrey has collected the brains of hundreds of people who died as young adults and suffered disorders such as schizophrenia and bipolar disorders.

## Prenatal Environment and Risk

**5.4-10** What prenatal events are associated with increased risk of developing schizophrenia?

What causes these brain abnormalities in people with schizophrenia? Some scientists point to prenatal development or delivery (Fatemi & Folsom, 2009; Walker et al., 2010). Risk factors include low birth weight, maternal diabetes, older paternal age, and oxygen deprivation during delivery (King et al., 2010). Famine may also increase the risks. People conceived during the peak of World War II's Dutch famine and during the famine of 1959 to 1961 in eastern China later developed schizophrenia at twice the usual rate (St. Clair et al., 2005; Susser et al., 1996). And extreme maternal stress may be a culprit: A study of 200,000 Israeli mothers showed that exposure to terror attacks during pregnancy doubled their children's risk of schizophrenia (Weinstein et al., 2018).

Let's consider another possible culprit. Might a midpregnancy viral infection impair fetal brain development (Brown & Patterson, 2011)? To test this fetal-virus idea, scientists have asked these questions:

- *Are people at increased risk of schizophrenia if their country experienced a flu epidemic during the middle of their fetal development?* The repeated answer has been *Yes* (Mednick et al., 1994; Murray et al., 1992; Wright et al., 1995).

- *Are people born in densely populated areas, where viral diseases spread more readily, at greater risk for schizophrenia?* The answer, confirmed in a study of 1.75 million Danes, has again been *Yes* (Jablensky, 1999; Mortensen, 1999).

- *Are people born during the winter and spring months—those who were in utero during the fall-winter flu season—also at increased risk?* The answer is again *Yes* (Fox, 2010; Schwartz, 2011; Torrey & Miller, 2002; Torrey et al., 1997).

- *In the Southern Hemisphere, where the seasons are the reverse of the Northern Hemisphere, are the months of above-average pre-schizophrenia births similarly reversed?* Again, the answer has been *Yes*. In Australia, people born between August and October are at greater risk. But people born in the Northern Hemisphere who later moved to Australia still have a greater risk if they were born between January and March (McGrath et al., 1995; McGrath & Welham, 1999).

- *Are mothers who report being sick with influenza during pregnancy more likely to bear children who develop schizophrenia?* In one study of nearly 8000 women, the answer was *Yes*. The schizophrenia risk increased from the customary 1 percent to about 2 percent—but only when infections occurred during the second trimester (Brown et al., 2000). Maternal influenza infection during pregnancy affects brain development in monkeys as well (Short et al., 2010).

- *Does blood drawn from pregnant women whose offspring develop schizophrenia show higher-than-normal levels of antibodies that suggest a viral infection?* In several studies, the answer has again been *Yes* (Brown et al., 2004; Buka et al., 2001; Canetta et al., 2014).

These converging lines of evidence suggest that fetal-virus infections contribute to the development of schizophrenia. They also strengthen the World Health Organization's (2012b) recommendation that pregnant women be given highest priority for the seasonal flu vaccine.

**Research**

Notice how the studies on the fetal-virus link to schizophrenia build upon each other, and how the results support the overarching theory. Replicating and expanding on studies builds consensus for the reliability and validity of conclusions.

## Genetic Influences

### 5.4-11 How do genes influence schizophrenia?

Fetal-virus infections may increase the odds that a child will develop schizophrenia. But many women get the flu during their second trimester of pregnancy, and only 2 percent of them bear children who develop schizophrenia. Why are only some children at risk? Might some people be more genetically vulnerable to schizophrenia? *Yes.* The roughly 1-in-270 lifetime odds of any one person being diagnosed with schizophrenia become about 1 in 10 among those who have a sibling or parent with the disorder. If the affected sibling is an identical twin, the odds increase to nearly 1 in 2 (**Figure 5.4-10**). Those odds are unchanged even when the twins are reared apart (Plomin et al., 1997). (Only about a dozen such cases are on record.)

Remember, though, that identical twins share more than their genes—they share a prenatal environment. About two-thirds also share a placenta and the blood it supplies; the other third have separate placentas. Shared placentas matter. If the co-twin of an identical twin with schizophrenia shared the placenta, the chances of developing the disorder are 6 in 10. If the identical twins had separate placentas, the co-twin's chances of developing schizophrenia drop to 1 in 10 (Davis et al., 1995; Davis & Phelps, 1995; Phelps et al., 1997). Twins who share a placenta are more likely to share the same prenatal viruses. So perhaps shared germs as well as shared genes produce identical twin similarities (**Figure 5.4-11**).

**Data**

Which three variables are depicted in the histogram (or bar graph) in Figure 5.4-10?
(The variables are country of origin, type of twin, and schizophrenia risk.)

**Figure 5.4-10**

**Risk of developing schizophrenia**

The lifetime risk of developing schizophrenia varies with a person's genetic relatedness to someone who has this disorder. Worldwide, barely more than 1 in 10 fraternal twins, but some 5 in 10 identical twins, share a schizophrenia diagnosis. (Data from Gottesman, 2001; Hilker et al., 2018.)

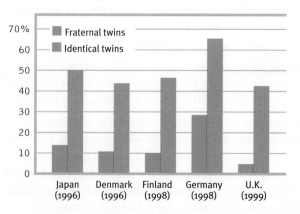

Adoption studies help untangle genetic and environmental influences. Children adopted by someone who develops schizophrenia do not "catch" the disorder. Rather, adopted children have a higher risk if a *biological* parent has schizophrenia (Gottesman, 1991). Genes do, indeed, matter.

The search is on for specific genes that, in some combination, predispose schizophrenia-inducing brain abnormalities. In the largest genetic studies of schizophrenia, scientists analyze worldwide data from the genomes of tens of thousands of people with and without schizophrenia (Lam et al., 2019; Pardiñas et al., 2018). One analysis found 176 genome locations linked with this disorder, including some affecting dopamine and other neurotransmitters. Another study of more than 100,000 people identified 413 schizophrenia-associated genes (Huckins et al., 2019).

Although genes matter, the genetic formula is not as straightforward as the inheritance of eye color. Schizophrenia is influenced by (no surprise by now) many genes, each with small effects (Binder, 2019; Weinberger, 2019). As we have seen in so many different contexts, nature and nurture interact. Recall that *epigenetic* factors influence whether genes will be expressed. Like hot water activating a tea bag, environmental factors such as viral infections, nutritional deprivation, and maternal or severe life stress can "turn on" the genes that put some of us at higher risk for schizophrenia. Identical twins' differing histories in the womb and beyond explain why they may show differing gene expressions (Dempster et al., 2013; Walker et al., 2010). Our heredity and our life experiences work together. Neither hand claps alone.

Thanks to our expanding understanding of genetic and brain influences on maladies such as schizophrenia, the general public increasingly recognizes the potency of biological factors in psychiatric disorders (Pescosolido et al., 2010).

* * *

Few of us can relate to the strange thoughts, perceptions, and behaviors of people with schizophrenia spectrum disorders. Sometimes our thoughts jump around, but we rarely talk nonsensically. Occasionally we feel unjustly suspicious of someone, but we do not believe the world is plotting against us. Often our perceptions err, but rarely do we see or hear things that are not there. We feel regret after laughing at someone's misfortune, but we rarely giggle in response to our own bad news. At times we just want to be alone, but we do not retreat into fantasy worlds. However, millions of people worldwide do talk strangely, suffer delusions, hear nonexistent voices, see things that are not there, laugh or cry at inappropriate times, or withdraw into private imaginary worlds. The quest to solve the cruel puzzle of schizophrenia therefore continues, more vigorously than ever.

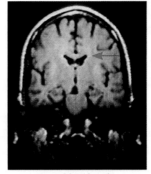
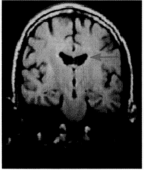

**No schizophrenia**
**(a)**

**Schizophrenia**
**(b)**

Daniel Weinberger, M.D., CBDB, NIMH

**Figure 5.4-11**

**Schizophrenia in only one identical twin**

When identical twins differ, only the brain of the twin with schizophrenia typically has enlarged, fluid-filled cranial cavities (b) (Suddath et al., 1990). The difference between the twins implies some nongenetic factor, such as a virus, is also at work.

---

**AP® Science Practice**

## Check Your Understanding

**Examine the Concept**

▶ Describe the positive and negative symptoms of schizophrenia.

▶ Describe the factors that contribute to the onset and development of schizophrenia.

**Apply the Concept**

▶ Compare and contrast *chronic schizophrenia* and *acute schizophrenia*.

▶ Can you recall a time when you heard something or someone casually (and inaccurately) described as "schizophrenic"? Now that you know more about this disorder, how might you correct such descriptions?

*Answers to the Examine the Concept questions can be found in Appendix C at the end of the book.*

**5.4-7 What patterns of perceiving, thinking, and feeling characterize schizophrenia?**

- Schizophrenia and schizotypal personality disorder are *schizophrenia spectrum disorders*. Disorders in this group are characterized by delusions, hallucinations, disorganized thinking or speech, disorganized or unusual motor behavior, and negative symptoms.

- Both schizophrenia and schizotypal personality disorder involve irrational beliefs and unusual behaviors, but only schizophrenia—the chief example of a *psychotic disorder*—is characterized by frequent, intense hallucinations and delusions, and an inability to abandon such thoughts and perceptions when their disconnection from reality is clear.

- Hallucinations are sensory experiences without sensory stimulation; *delusions* are false beliefs.

- Schizophrenia symptoms may be positive (the presence of inappropriate behaviors) or negative (the absence of appropriate behaviors).

**5.4-8 How do *chronic schizophrenia* and *acute schizophrenia* differ?**

- Schizophrenia typically strikes during late adolescence or early adulthood, affects men more often than women, and occurs in all cultures.

- In *chronic* (or process) *schizophrenia*, the disorder develops gradually and recovery is doubtful.

- In *acute* (or reactive) *schizophrenia*, onset is sudden—often in reaction to a traumatic event—and prospects for recovery are brighter.

**5.4-9 What brain abnormalities are associated with schizophrenia?**

- People with schizophrenia have an excess number of dopamine receptors, which may intensify brain signals, creating positive symptoms such as hallucinations and paranoia.

- Brain scans have revealed abnormal activity in the frontal lobes, thalamus, and amygdala, as well as a loss of neural connections across the brain network.

- Brain abnormalities associated with schizophrenia include enlarged, fluid-filled areas and corresponding shrinkage and thinning of cerebral tissue. Smaller-than-normal areas may include the cortex, the hippocampus, the corpus callosum, and the thalamus.

**5.4-10 What prenatal events are associated with increased risk of developing schizophrenia?**

- Possible contributing factors include maternal diabetes; older paternal age; viral infections, famine conditions, or extreme maternal stress during pregnancy; and low birth weight or oxygen deprivation at birth.

**5.4-11 How do genes influence schizophrenia?**

- Twin and adoption studies indicate that the predisposition to schizophrenia is inherited.

- Multiple genes interact to produce schizophrenia. No environmental causes invariably produce schizophrenia, but environmental events (such as prenatal viruses or maternal stress) may "turn on" genes in those individuals who are predisposed to this disorder.

## AP® Practice Multiple Choice Questions

1. Tenny is doing a report on schizophrenic spectrum disorders. In his report, he should describe them as

   a. a group of disorders marked by irrational ideas, distorted perceptions, and loss of contact with reality.

   b. a group of disorders marked by discomfort in close relationships, distorted thoughts and perceptions, and eccentric behavior.

   c. a group of disorders marked by delusions, hallucinations, disorganized thinking and speech, disorganized or unusual motor behavior, and negative symptoms.

   d. a group of disorders marked by the absence of appropriate behaviors.

2. Over several years, Charles gradually developed schizophrenia. As a result, the prognosis for recovery is poor. His type of schizophrenia would be referred to as

   a. acute.

   b. chronic.

   c. catatonic.

   d. positive.

**3.** Dr. Nemcek conducted a study on a group of individuals who remained motionless for a long period of time and did not display emotionality. Which of the following variables was Dr. Nemcek likely investigating?

a. Genetic influences of schizophrenia
b. Schizotypal personality disorder
c. Acute schizophrenia
d. Negative symptoms of schizophrenia

**Use the following graph, which shows the symptoms of individuals diagnosed with a psychological disorder, to answer questions 4 and 5:**

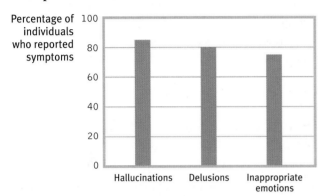

**4.** What psychological concept is depicted along the *x*-axis of the graph?

a. Positive symptoms
b. Theory of mind
c. Negative symptoms
d. Selective attention

**5.** What conclusion can you draw about the likely diagnostic label of the individuals depicted in the graph?

a. Schizotypal personality disorder
b. Chronic schizophrenia
c. Acute schizophrenia
d. Theory of mind

**6.** Dr. Kealoha examined CT scans of the brains of 10 people with schizophrenia, all of which showed some degree of cerebral tissue shrinkage. What conclusion should Dr. Kealoha draw from his comparisons of these scans?

a. The individuals with the greatest shrinkage are more likely to experience severe symptoms associated with schizophrenia.
b. The individuals with the least shrinkage are most likely to have a reduction in dopamine activity.
c. The individuals with the greatest shrinkage are more likely to experience schizotypal personality disorder.
d. The individuals with the least shrinkage are more likely to have enlarged ventricles.

**7.** Poppy falsely believes she is a flower. What is she experiencing?

a. A hallucination
b. Word salad
c. Theory of mind
d. A delusion

# Selection of Categories of Psychological Disorders: Dissociative Disorders, Personality Disorders, Feeding and Eating Disorders, and Neurodevelopmental Disorders

## LEARNING TARGETS

**5.4-12** Describe *dissociative disorders*, and explain why they are controversial.

**5.4-13** Describe the three clusters of personality disorders, and explain what behaviors and brain activity characterize antisocial personality disorder.

**5.4-14** Describe the three main eating disorders, and explain how biological, psychological, and social-cultural influences make people more vulnerable to them.

**5.4-15** Describe *neurodevelopmental disorders*, and explain how they impact thinking and behavior.

## Dissociative Disorders

**5.4-12** What are *dissociative disorders*, and why are they controversial?

**dissociative disorders**
a controversial, rare group of disorders characterized by a disruption of or discontinuity in the normal integration of consciousness, memory, identity, emotion, perception, body representation, motor control, and behavior.

**dissociative identity disorder (DID)** a rare dissociative disorder in which a person exhibits two or more distinct and alternating identities. (Formerly called *multiple personality disorder*.)

Among the most bewildering disorders are the rare **dissociative disorders**, in which a person's conscious awareness *dissociates* (separates) from painful memories, thoughts, and feelings. The result may be a *dissociative fugue state*, a sudden loss of memory or change in identity, often in response to an overwhelmingly stressful situation (Harrison et al., 2017). Such was the case for one Vietnam War veteran who was haunted by his comrades' deaths, and who had left his World Trade Center office shortly before the 9/11 terrorist attack. Later, he disappeared. Six months later, when he was discovered in a Chicago homeless shelter, he reported no memory of his identity or family (Stone, 2006).

### Dissociative Identity Disorder

Dissociation itself is not so rare. Any one of us may have a fleeting sense of being unreal, of being separated from our body, of watching ourselves as if in a movie. A massive dissociation of self from ordinary consciousness occurs in **dissociative identity disorder (DID)**, in which two or more distinct identities—each with its own voice and mannerisms—seem to control a person's behavior. Thus, the person may be prim and proper one moment, loud and flirtatious the next. Typically, the original identity denies any awareness of the other(s).

## Dissociative Amnesia

Forgetting is a part of life. You may forget your homework's due date, your friend's birthday, or where you left your keys. But people with **dissociative amnesia**, which may or may not involve fugue, reportedly experience gaps in memory that go beyond typical forgetting. They are said to forget specific events (a car accident), periods of time (months or even years—such as when a person was kidnapped or held hostage), or aspects of their identity and life history (being a high school student whose hometown is Boston). Dissociative amnesia is reportedly triggered by traumatic or stressful events. Some cases, however, may reflect "ordinary forgetting and malingering [faking a condition to avoid responsibilities]" (Mangiulli et al., 2022).

One case study described Mr. A., a 20-year-old man who experienced a stressful romantic breakup and later showed symptoms of dissociative amnesia (Sharma et al., 2015). Two weeks after the breakup, Mr. A. went to work but could not recognize his friends or remember his typical job activities. His supervisor sent him home, but Mr. A. continued to exhibit impaired memory. He failed to recognize his family members and possessions. Mr. A.'s concerned mother took him to the hospital, where doctors first ruled out brain damage and then diagnosed Mr. A. with dissociative amnesia. Over the next several months, Mr. A. worked with psychotherapists to remember past details. Little by little, his memories returned.

## Understanding Dissociative Disorders

Skeptics question dissociative disorders. They find it suspicious that these disorders have such a short and localized history. Between 1930 and 1960, the number of North American DID diagnoses averaged two per decade. By the 1980s, when the DSM first included a formal code for this disorder, the number had exploded to more than 20,000 (McHugh, 1995). The average number of displayed identities also mushroomed—from 3 to 12 per patient (Goff & Simms, 1993). And although diagnoses have been increasing in countries where DID has been publicized, the disorder is much less prevalent outside North America (Lilienfeld, 2017). As skeptics note, once a disorder becomes widely known, reported cases of it tend to soar.

Are clinicians who discover multiple identities merely triggering role playing by fantasy-prone people in a particular social context (Giesbrecht et al., 2008, 2010; Lynn et al., 2014; Merskey, 1992)? After all, clients do not enter therapy saying, "Allow me to introduce myselves." Rather, charge the critics, some therapists go fishing for multiple identities: *"Have you ever felt like another part of you does things you can't control?" "Does this part of you have a name?" "Can I talk to the angry part of you?"* Once clients permit a therapist to talk, by name, "to the part of you that says those angry things," they begin acting out the fantasy. Like actors who lose themselves in their roles, vulnerable patients may "become" the parts they are acting out. The result may be the experience of another self. Or perhaps dissociative identities are simply a more extreme version of the varied "selves" we normally present—a goofy self around our friends, a subdued self around our employer?

Despite some hoaxes, other researchers and clinicians believe DID and dissociative amnesia are real disorders. They cite findings of distinct body and brain states associated with differing identities (Putnam, 1991). Abnormal brain anatomy and activity can also accompany dissociative disorders. Brain scans show shrinkage in areas that aid memory and detection of threats (Vermetten et al., 2006). Other research has shown lower activity in the hippocampus—the brain's memory center—among people with dissociative amnesia (Kikuchi et al., 2015).

Both the psychodynamic and learning perspectives have interpreted DID symptoms as ways of coping with anxiety. Some psychodynamic theorists see them as defenses against

**Multiple identities in the movies**
Chris Sizemore's story, told in the book and movie *The Three Faces of Eve*, gave early visibility to what is now called dissociative identity disorder. This controversial disorder continues to influence modern media, as in the 2019 movie *Glass*, where James McAvoy's character (pictured here) displays 24 different identities.

**dissociative amnesia** a disorder in which people with intact brains reportedly experience memory gaps; people with dissociative amnesia may report not remembering trauma-related specific events, people, places, or aspects of their identity and life history.

**Widespread dissociation** Shirley Mason was a psychiatric patient diagnosed with dissociative identity disorder. Her life formed the basis of the bestselling book, *Sybil* (Schreiber, 1973), and of two movies. The book and movies' popularity contributed to increased DID diagnoses. Audio recordings later revealed that Mason's psychiatrist manipulated her and that she did not have the disorder (Nathan, 2011).

the anxiety caused by unacceptable impulses. In this view, a second identity enables the discharge of forbidden impulses. Learning theorists see dissociative disorders as behaviors reinforced by anxiety reduction.

Some clinicians include dissociative disorders under the umbrella of posttraumatic stress disorder as a natural, protective response to traumatic experiences during childhood (Brand et al., 2016; Spiegel, 2008). Many people being treated for dissociative disorders recall being physically, sexually, or emotionally abused as children (Chu et al., 1999; Gleaves, 1996; Lilienfeld et al., 1999). Critics wonder, however, whether such recollections are false memories (Kihlstrom, 2005; McNally, 2007). So the scientific debate continues.

## Personality Disorders

> **5.4-13** What are the three clusters of personality disorders? What behaviors and brain activity characterize antisocial personality disorder?

The inflexible and enduring behavior patterns of **personality disorders** interfere with social functioning. These 10 disorders in the DSM-5-TR tend to form three clusters (**Table 5.4-3**):

- In Cluster A, people appear ***eccentric or odd***, as in the suspiciousness of *paranoid personality disorder;* the social detachment of *schizoid personality disorder;* or the magical thinking of *schizotypal personality disorder.*

- In Cluster B, people appear ***dramatic***, ***emotional***, ***or erratic***, as in the unstable, attention-getting *borderline personality disorder;* the self-focused and self-inflating *narcissistic personality disorder;* the excessively emotional *histrionic personality disorder;* and—what we next discuss as an in-depth example—the callous, and often dangerous, *antisocial personality disorder.*

- In Cluster C, people appear ***anxious or fearful***, as in the fearful sensitivity to rejection that predisposes the withdrawn *avoidant personality disorder;* the clinging behavior of *dependent personality disorder;* and the preoccupation with orderliness, perfectionism, and control that characterizes *obsessive-compulsive personality disorder.*

### Antisocial Personality Disorder

People with **antisocial personality disorder**, usually male, can display symptoms by age 8. Their lack of conscience becomes plain before age 15, as they begin to lie, steal, fight, or display unrestrained sexual behavior (Cale & Lilienfeld, 2002). Not all children with these traits become antisocial adults, and for many males, antisocial behavior often subsides after adolescence (Moffitt, 2018). (Note that *antisocial* means socially harmful and remorseless, not merely unsociable.) Those who do develop the disorder—about half—will generally act in violent or otherwise criminal ways, be unable to keep a job, and behave irresponsibly toward family members (Farrington, 1991).

**personality disorders** a group of disorders characterized by enduring inner experiences or behavior patterns that differ from someone's cultural norms and expectations, are pervasive and inflexible, begin in adolescence or early adulthood, are stable over time, and cause distress or impairment.

**antisocial personality disorder** a personality disorder in which a person (usually a man) exhibits a lack of conscience for wrongdoing, even toward friends and family members; may be aggressive and ruthless or a clever con artist.

## TABLE 5.4-3 Personality Disorders (American Psychiatric Association, 2022)

The DSM-5-TR identifies 10 personality disorders. People with these disorders display the following characteristics:

- **Paranoid personality disorder:** suspiciousness; distrust of others

- **Schizoid personality disorder:** social detachment; limited emotional expression

- **Schizotypal personality disorder:** intense social discomfort; distorted cognitions or perceptions; behavioral eccentricity

- **Antisocial personality disorder:** indifference to (and willingness to violate) others' rights; impulsiveness; criminal behavior

- **Borderline personality disorder:** impulsivity; unstable relationships and self-image

- **Histrionic personality disorder:** extreme emotional expression; a need for attention

- **Narcissistic personality disorder:** grandiosity; admiration-seeking behavior; deficient empathy

- **Avoidant personality disorder:** social inhibition; feeling inadequate; sensitivity to criticism

- **Dependent personality disorder:** submissive behavior; emotional neediness

- **Obsessive-compulsive personality disorder:** a fixation on orderliness; the need for perfection and control

But criminality is not an essential component of antisocial behavior (Skeem & Cooke, 2010). And many criminals do not exhibit antisocial personality disorder; rather, they show responsible concern for their friends and family members. In contrast to most criminals, people with antisocial personality disorder (sometimes called *sociopaths* or *psychopaths*) are more socially deficient. They often exhibit less *emotional intelligence*—the ability to understand, manage, and perceive emotions (Ermer et al., 2012b; Gillespie et al., 2019).

Antisocial personalities behave impulsively, and then feel and fear little (Fowles & Dindo, 2009). Their impulsivity can have horrific consequences, including homicide (Camp et al., 2013; Fox & DeLisi, 2019). Consider the case of Tommy Lynn Sells. He said he killed his first victim when he was 15. He felt little regret then or later. During his years of crime, he brutally murdered at least 17 women, men, and children. "I am hatred," Sellers told one interviewer while on death row (ABC, 2014). "When you look at me, you look at hate."

*"Thursday is out. I have jury duty."*

**Many criminals, like this one, display a sense of conscience and responsibility in other areas of their life, and thus do not exhibit antisocial personality disorder.**

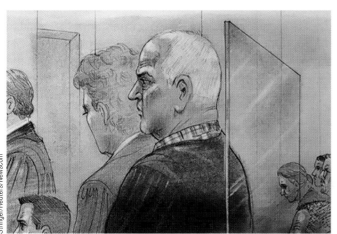

**No remorse** A 66-year-old Toronto landscaper, shown here in a courtroom sketch, was convicted in 2019 of killing eight people over eight years. He often targeted men who were gay, homeless, or immigrants, storing their remains in boxes at his job sites. He exhibited the extreme lack of remorse that marks antisocial personality disorder.

## Understanding Antisocial Personality Disorder

Antisocial personality disorder is woven of both biological and psychological strands. Twin and adoption studies reveal that biological relatives of people with antisocial and unemotional tendencies are at increased risk for antisocial behavior (Frisell et al., 2012; Kendler et al., 2015a). No single gene codes for a complex behavior such as crime. But genes that predispose individuals to lower mental ability and self-control predict a higher crime risk (Wertz et al., 2018).

As with other disorders, geneticists have identified some specific genes that are more common in those with antisocial personality disorder (Gunter et al., 2010; Tielbeek et al., 2017). The genes that put people at risk for antisocial behavior also increase the risk for substance use disorder (Dick, 2007). Disorders often do appear together—for example, depressive disorders and anxiety disorders (Jacobson & Newman, 2017; Plana-Ripoll et al., 2019). People diagnosed with one disorder are at higher risk for being diagnosed with another. Such *comorbidity* results from overlapping genes that predispose people to different disorders (Brainstorm Consortium, 2018; Gandal et al., 2018).

Genetic influences, often in combination with negative environmental factors such as childhood abuse, family instability, or poverty, help wire the brain (Dodge, 2009). This gene–environment combination also occurs in chimpanzees, which, like humans, vary in their antisocial (mean/bold/disinhibited) tendencies (Latzman et al., 2017). In people with antisocial criminal tendencies, the emotion-controlling amygdala is smaller (Pardini et al., 2014).

The genetic vulnerability of people with antisocial tendencies appears as low arousal in response to threats. Awaiting events that most people would find unnerving, such as electric shocks or loud noises, they show little autonomic nervous system arousal (Hare, 1975; Ling et al., 2019). Long-term studies show that their stress hormone levels were lower than average as teens, before they had ever committed a crime (**Figure 5.4-12**). And those who were slow to develop conditioned fears at age 3 were also more likely to commit a crime later in life (Gao et al., 2010). Likewise, preschool boys who later become aggressive or antisocial adolescents tend to be impulsive, uninhibited, unconcerned with social rewards, and low in anxiety (Caspi et al., 1996; Tremblay et al., 1994).

Traits such as fearlessness and dominance can be adaptive. If channeled in more productive directions, fearlessness may lead to athletic stardom, adventurism, or courageous heroism (Costello et al., 2018; Patton et al., 2018). Indeed, 42 U.S. presidents exhibited higher than usual fearlessness and dominance (Lilienfeld et al., 2012, 2016). Patient S. M., a 49-year-old woman with amygdala damage, showed fearlessness and impulsivity but also heroism: She gave a man in need her only coat and scarf, and donated her hair to the Locks of Love charity after befriending a child with cancer (Lilienfeld et al., 2017). Lacking a sense of social responsibility, however, the same disposition may produce a cool con artist or killer (Lykken, 1995).

With antisocial personality disorder—as with all other personality disorders—nature and nurture interact. Once again, the biopsychosocial perspective helps us understand the whole story. To further investigate the neural basis of antisocial personality disorder, neuroscientists are exploring the antisocial brain (Brazil & Buades-Rotger, 2020). Shown emotionally evocative photographs, such as a man holding a knife to a woman's throat, criminals with antisocial personality disorder display blunted heart rate and perspiration responses, and less activity in brain areas that typically respond to emotional stimuli (Harenski et al., 2010; Kiehl & Buckholtz, 2010). They also have a larger and hyperreactive dopamine reward system, which predisposes their impulsive drive to do something rewarding despite the consequences (Buckholtz et al., 2010; Glenn et al., 2010).

**Figure 5.4-12**

**Cold-blooded arousability and risk of crime**

Levels of the stress hormone adrenaline were measured in two groups of 13-year-old Swedish boys. In both stressful and nonstressful situations, those who would later be convicted of a crime as 18- to 26-year-olds showed relatively low arousal. (Data from Magnusson, 1990.)

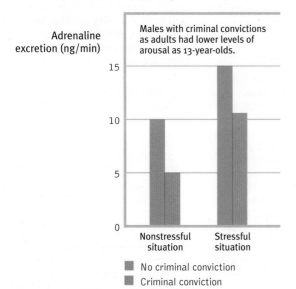

Males with criminal convictions as adults had lower levels of arousal as 13-year-olds.

Adrenaline excretion (ng/min)

- No criminal conviction
- Criminal conviction

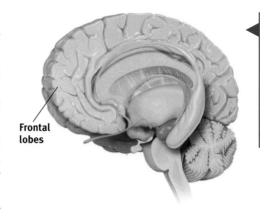

One study compared PET scans of 41 murderers' brains with those from people of similar age and sex. The murderers' frontal lobes—an area that helps control impulses—displayed reduced activity (Raine, 1999, 2005; **Figure 5.4-13**). The reduced activation was especially apparent in those who murdered impulsively. Researchers later found that violent repeat offenders had 11 percent less frontal lobe tissue than normal (Raine et al., 2000). This helps explain another finding: People with antisocial personality disorder fall far below normal in aspects of thinking such as planning, organization, and inhibition, which are all frontal lobe functions (Morgan & Lilienfeld, 2000). Such data remind us: Everything psychological is also biological.

**Frontal lobes**

**Figure 5.4-13**
**Murderous minds**
Researchers have found reduced activation in a murderer's frontal lobes. This brain area (shown in a left-facing brain) helps curb impulsive, aggressive behavior (Raine, 1999).

---

**AP® Science Practice**

## Check Your Understanding

**Examine the Concept**

▶ Describe the differences among the behavioral patterns in Cluster A, Cluster B, and Cluster C personality disorders.

▶ Explain how biological and psychological factors contribute to antisocial personality disorder.

*Answers to the Examine the Concept questions can be found in Appendix C at the end of the book.*

**Apply the Concept**

▶ Given what we have learned in earlier modules and units about the powers and limits of parental influence, how much do you think parents affect the risk of a child's developing antisocial personality disorder?

---

# Feeding and Eating Disorders

**5.4-14** What are the three main eating disorders, and how do biological, psychological, and social-cultural influences make people more vulnerable to them?

Our bodies are naturally disposed to maintain a steady weight, including storing energy for times when food becomes unavailable. But sometimes psychological influences overwhelm biological wisdom. This becomes painfully clear in the **feeding and eating disorders**.

- In **anorexia nervosa**, people—often female adolescents—starve themselves. Anorexia often begins as an attempt to lose weight, but the dieting becomes a habit (Steinglass et al., 2018). Regardless of their actual weight, the self-starved person feels fat, fears being fat, and focuses obsessively on losing weight, sometimes exercising excessively.

- In **bulimia nervosa**, a cycle of repeated episodes of binge eating alternates with behaviors to compensate, such as vomiting, laxative use, fasting, or excessive exercise (Wonderlich et al., 2007). Unlike anorexia, bulimia is marked by weight fluctuations within or above normal ranges, making the disorder easier to hide. Bulimia may also be triggered by a weight-loss diet that is broken by gorging on forbidden foods. People with this disorder—mostly women in their late teens or early twenties (but also some men)—eat in spurts, sometimes influenced by negative emotions or by friends who are bingeing (Crandall, 1988; Haedt-Matt & Keel, 2011). Preoccupied with food (craving sweet and high-fat foods) and fearful of becoming overweight, binge-purge eaters experience bouts of depression, guilt, and anxiety during and following binges (Hinz & Williamson, 1987; Johnson et al., 2002).

- People with *binge-eating disorder*—about 1 in 200 females and 1 in 100 males—engage in significant bouts of bingeing, followed by remorse (Giel et al., 2022). But they do not purge, fast, or exercise excessively.

**feeding and eating disorders**
a group of disorders characterized by altered consumption or absorption of food that impairs health or psychological functioning. (Feeding disorders typically occur in infants and young children, whereas eating disorders affect people who self-feed.)

**anorexia nervosa** an eating disorder in which a person (usually an adolescent female) maintains a starvation diet despite being significantly underweight, and has an inaccurate self-perception; sometimes accompanied by excessive exercise.

**bulimia nervosa** an eating disorder in which a person's binge eating (usually of high-calorie foods) is followed by inappropriate weight-loss-promoting behavior, such as vomiting, laxative use, fasting, or excessive exercise.

A distorted body image underlies anorexia.

At some point during their lifetime, about 2.6 million Americans (0.8 percent) met the DSM-5-TR defined criteria for anorexia, 2.6 million met the criteria for bulimia, and 2.7 million met the criteria for binge-eating disorder (Udo & Grilo, 2019). All three disorders can be deadly. They harm the body and mind, resulting in shorter life expectancy and greater risk of suicide and nonsuicidal self-injury (Cucchi et al., 2016; Fichter & Quadflieg, 2016; Mandelli et al., 2019).

## Understanding Feeding and Eating Disorders

Eating disorders are *not* (as some have speculated) a telltale sign of childhood sexual abuse (Smolak & Murnen, 2002; Stice, 2002). The family environment may influence eating disorders in other ways, however. For example, the families of people with anorexia tend to be competitive, high achieving, and protective (Ahrén et al., 2013; Berg et al., 2014; Yates, 1989, 1990).

Eating disorders share some commonalities with anxiety disorders (Schaumberg et al., 2021). Those with eating disorders often have low body satisfaction, set perfectionist standards, and ruminate about falling short of expectations and how others perceive them (Farstad et al., 2016; Smith et al., 2018; Wang et al., 2019). Some of these factors also predict teen boys' pursuit of unrealistic muscularity (Karazsia et al., 2017; Ricciardelli & McCabe, 2004).

Heredity also matters. Identical twins share these disorders more often than do fraternal twins—to an extent indicating 50 to 60 percent *heritability* for anorexia (Yilmaz et al., 2015). Scientists are searching for culprit genes. The largest study identified gene differences by comparing the genomes of nearly 17,000 patients with anorexia with 56,000 people who did not have the disorder (Watson et al., 2019).

But eating disorders also have cultural and gender components. Ideal shapes vary across culture and time. In countries with high poverty rates, plump may mean prosperity and thin may signal poverty or illness (Knickmeyer, 2001; Swami et al., 2010). Not so in wealthy Western cultures. In one analysis of 222 studies, the rise in eating disorders in the last half of the twentieth century coincided with a dramatic decline in Western women's body image (Feingold & Mazzella, 1998).

*"Up until that point, Bernice had never once had a problem with low self-esteem."*

Today's weight-obsessed culture—a culture that says "fat is bad" in countless ways—motivates millions of women to diet constantly, and invites eating binges by pressuring women to live in a constant state of semistarvation. One former model recalled walking into a meeting with her agent, starving and with her organs failing due to anorexia (Carroll, 2013). Her agent's greeting: "Whatever you are doing, keep doing it." Women who view real and doctored images of unnaturally thin models and celebrities often feel ashamed, depressed, and dissatisfied with their own bodies—the very attitudes that predispose eating disorders (Bould et al., 2018; Tiggeman & Miller, 2010). Even ultrathin models do not reflect the impossible standard of the original Barbie doll, who had, when adjusted to a height of 5 feet 7 inches, a 32–16–29 figure (in centimeters, 82–41–73) (Norton et al., 1996).

Most people diagnosed with an eating disorder do improve. In one 22-year study, 2 in 3 women with anorexia nervosa or bulimia nervosa had recovered (Eddy et al., 2017). Prevention is also possible. Interactive programs that teach teen girls to accept their bodies have reduced the risk of eating disorders (Beintner et al., 2012; Melioli et al., 2016; Vocks et al., 2010). By combating cultural learning, those at risk may instead live long and healthy lives.

---

 **AP® Science Practice**

## Check Your Understanding

### Examine the Concept

▶ Describe anorexia nervosa, bulimia nervosa, and binge-eating disorders.

### Apply the Concept

▶ How does culture influence eating disorders? What depictions have you seen — in movies or TV shows, advertisements, magazines, or social media — that promote an unhealthy body ideal?

*Answers to the Examine the Concept questions can be found in Appendix C at the end of the book.*

---

# Neurodevelopmental Disorders

> **5.4-15** What are *neurodevelopmental disorders*, and how do they impact thinking and behavior?

Our thoughts and behaviors change as we grow older. For people with **neurodevelopmental disorders**, these typical changes are disrupted in childhood because of unusual features of the central nervous system, leading people to exhibit behaviors inappropriate for their age or maturity range. As we will see, environmental, physiological, and genetic factors may increase or decrease the risk for neurodevelopmental disorders. This section focuses on four common neurodevelopmental disorders: *specific learning disorders*, *motor disorders*, *autism spectrum disorder*, and *attention-deficit/hyperactivity disorder*.

## Specific Learning Disorders

Everyone experiences setbacks when learning new information. "The expert at anything," a motivational phrase reminds us, "was once a beginner." But people with *specific learning disorders* experience chronic difficulties perceiving and processing information, making it difficult for them to transition from beginner to expert. People with specific learning disorders are typically of average or above-average intelligence. These disorders usually begin in early childhood, leading children to underperform academically. As adults, people with specific learning disorders may struggle to learn their job tasks.

Children with specific learning disorders may experience difficulties reading, spelling, writing, or understanding numbers and mathematical reasoning. Their learning difficulties are persistent, lasting at least six months, and are not due to other mental or neurological disorders. Children with specific learning disorders may do well academically until they face challenging situations, such as timed tests, completing complex written assignments on a deadline, or juggling a demanding academic workload.

Many people who learn to manage their specific learning disorders go on to achieve success. Comedian Jay Leno, actress Keira Knightley, and entrepreneur and *Shark Tank* investor Daymond John have been open about living with a specific learning disorder with impaired reading (often referred to as *dyslexia*). They have adjusted their lives to coexist with their learning disorder, overcoming obstacles to discover their unique talents. Social support

**neurodevelopmental disorders** central nervous system abnormalities (usually in the brain) that start in childhood and alter thinking and behavior (as in intellectual limitations or a psychological disorder).

often makes a positive difference. "I had wonderful teachers," Leno said. "My English teacher said to me, 'You know, you're always telling jokes in the hall. Why don't you write some of those stories down and maybe you can tell them to the class?'" (Salomon, 2014).

## Motor Disorders

*Motor disorders* impair people's ability to communicate, interact with others, or perform necessary tasks. These disorders—which usually appear before age 18, and sometimes as young as age 5—affect the parts of our brain involved in planning and executing actions, causing people to display movements that are atypical or involuntary. People with *developmental coordination disorder* show extreme clumsiness and slowness when performing tasks that require motor skill, such as writing by hand, riding a bike, or eating with utensils. Those with *stereotypic movement disorder* engage in repetitive and unnecessary motor movements, such as hand waving, body rocking, or self-biting. And people with *tic disorders* produce sudden, rapid, and involuntary movements or vocalizations. Those with *Tourette's disorder* (a type of tic disorder), for example, may repetitively utter "No way!" and turn their head to the side, even if they recognize that such behaviors are inappropriate. In rare cases, people with Tourette's disorder involuntarily curse or make vulgar gestures.

Motor disorders are often distressing. Unable to control their motor or verbal actions, people with motor disorders are prone to anxiety and depression (Draghi et al., 2020; Liu et al., 2020). One study of 7736 people with tic disorders showed that they were four times more likely than others to die by suicide (de la Cruz et al., 2017). A lack of motor coordination may also make people hesitant to exercise, which helps to explain why some motor disorders also predict poor physical fitness (Rivilis et al., 2011).

Symptoms of motor disorders can improve over time. People with developmental coordination disorder can benefit from occupational or physical therapy to help them integrate sensory information and build muscle strength (Harris et al., 2015). Likewise, behavior therapy can improve symptoms among children with stereotypic movement disorder (Specht et al., 2016). Tics can wax and wane, with some people experiencing them less frequently as they age. In people with severe Tourette's disorder, implanting electrodes deep in the brain can reduce motor and verbal tics (Martinez-Ramirez et al., 2018).

## Autism Spectrum Disorder

**autism spectrum disorder (ASD)** a disorder that appears in childhood and is marked by limitations in communication and social interaction, and by rigidly fixated interests and repetitive behaviors.

**Autism spectrum disorder (ASD)** is a cognitive and social-emotional disorder that is marked by social deficiencies and repetitive behaviors. Once believed to affect 1 in 2500 children (and referred to simply as *autism*), ASD is now diagnosed in 1 in 38 children in South Korea, 1 in 54 in the United States, 1 in 62 in Canada, and 1 in 166 in Germany

**Autism spectrum disorder** This speech-language pathologist is helping a boy with ASD learn to form sounds and words. ASD is marked by limited communication ability and difficulty grasping others' states of mind.

(CDC, 2020e; Chiarotti & Venerosi, 2020). The increase in ASD diagnoses has been offset by a decrease in the number of children with a "cognitive disability" or "learning disability," which suggests a relabeling of children's disorders (Gernsbacher et al., 2005; Grinker, 2007; Shattuck, 2006).

The underlying source of ASD's symptoms seems to be poor communication among brain regions that normally work together to let us take another's viewpoint. From age two months on, children typically spend more and more time looking into others' eyes; those who later develop ASD do so less and less (Baron-Cohen, 2017; Wang et al., 2020). Researchers are debating whether people with autism spectrum disorder have an *impaired theory of mind* (Gernsbacher & Yergeau, 2019; Matthews & Goldberg, 2018; Velikonja et al., 2019). The kind of mind reading that most of us find intuitive *(Is that face conveying a smile or a sneer?)* is often difficult for individuals with ASD. They have difficulty inferring how others think differently than they do (Deschrijver & Palmer, 2020). For example, they may not appreciate that playmates and parents view things differently, or understand that their teachers know more than they do (Boucher et al., 2012; Frith & Frith, 2001; Knutsen et al., 2015).

Partly for such reasons, a national survey of parents and school staff reported that 46 percent of adolescents with ASD had suffered the taunts and torments of bullying—about four times the 11 percent rate for other children (Sterzing et al., 2012). Children with ASD do make friends, but their peers often find such relationships emotionally unsatisfying (Mendelson et al., 2016). This helps explain why people with ASD have a quadrupled risk of experiencing depression in their lifetime (Hudson et al., 2019).

ASD has differing levels of severity. Some people (those diagnosed with what used to be called *Asperger syndrome*) generally function at a high level. They have normal intelligence, often accompanied by exceptional skill or talent in a specific area. But those with ASD may lack the motivation and ability to interact and communicate socially, and they tend to become distracted by irrelevant stimuli (Clements et al., 2018; Remington et al., 2009). Those at the spectrum's more severe end struggle to use language.

ASD gets diagnosed in four boys for every girl (CDC, 2020e). Psychologist Simon Baron-Cohen (2010) believes this is because boys, more often than girls, are "systemizers." They tend to understand things according to rules or laws, as in mathematical and mechanical systems. Girls, he contends, are more often predisposed to be "empathizers." They tend to excel at reading facial expressions, predicting what others will feel, and knowing what to do in social situations.

Whether male or female, people with ASD are systemizers who have more difficulty reading facial expressions, intuitively knowing what others feel, and understanding how to have smooth social interactions (Greenberg et al., 2018; Velikonja et al., 2019). People working

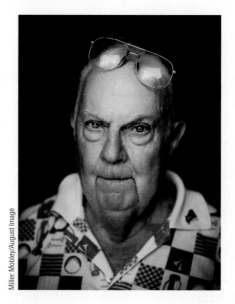

**"Autism" case number 1** In 1943, Donald Gray Triplett, an "odd" child with unusual gifts and social limitations, was the first person to receive the diagnosis of "autism." (After a 2013 change in the DSM, his condition is now called *autism spectrum disorder*.) In 2016, at age 82, Triplett — a retired bank teller who often played golf — was living independently in his family home and Mississippi town (Atlas, 2016).

in STEM (science, technology, engineering, or mathematics) careers are also somewhat more likely than others to exhibit some ASD-like traits (Ruzich et al., 2015). Some people with autism, like Erin McKinney (2015), view these unique ways of thinking, feeling, and perceiving as a gift: "Autism makes my life difficult, but it also makes my life beautiful. When everything is more intense, then the everyday, the mundane, the typical, the normal—those things become outstanding."

Biological factors contribute to ASD (Zhou et al., 2019). Prenatal environment matters, especially when it is altered by maternal infection, psychiatric drug use, or stress hormones (NIH, 2013; Wang, 2014). Genes also matter. One five-nation study of two million individuals found the heritability of ASD was near 80 percent (Bai et al., 2019). If one identical twin is diagnosed with ASD, the chances are nearly 9 in 10 that the co-twin will be as well, though such twins often differ in symptom severity (Castelbaum et al., 2020). No one "autism gene" accounts for the disorder. Rather, many genes—with more than 400 identified so far—appear to contribute (Krishnan et al., 2016; Yuen et al., 2016). Random genetic mutations in sperm cells may also play a role. As men age, these mutations become more frequent, which helps explain why a man older than 40 has a much higher risk of fathering a child with ASD than does a man younger than 30 (Wu et al., 2017).

Researchers are also sleuthing ASD's telltale signs in the brain's structure. Several studies have revealed "underconnectivity"—fewer-than-normal fiber tracts connecting the front of the brain to the back (Picci et al., 2016). With underconnectivity, there is less of the whole-brain synchrony that, for example, integrates visual and emotional information. In children as young as three months, EEG-recorded brain activity can foretell ASD (Bosl et al., 2018).

Biology's role in ASD also appears in the brain's functioning. People without ASD often yawn after seeing others yawn. And as they view and imitate another's smiling or frowning, they feel something of what the other person is feeling. Scientists are exploring whether treatment with oxytocin, the hormone that promotes social bonding, might improve social understanding in individuals with ASD (Gordon et al., 2013; Lange & McDougle, 2013).

What does *not* contribute to ASD? Childhood vaccinations—despite a fraudulent 1998 study claiming otherwise—have *no* relationship to the disorder (Taylor et al., 2014). The autism vaccine myth arose partly because autism symptoms coincidentally appear about the same time children are first inoculated. But science is decisive: There's no causal link. In fact, in one recent study following nearly 700,000 Danish children, those receiving the measles/mumps/rubella vaccine were actually slightly *less* likely to later be among the 6517 children diagnosed with ASD (Hviid et al., 2019).

## Attention-Deficit/Hyperactivity Disorder

For children who experience the challenging symptoms of **attention-deficit/hyperactivity disorder (ADHD)**, diagnosis and treatment can help (Kupfer, 2012; Maciejewski et al., 2016). The DSM has broadened the diagnostic criteria for this disorder, prompting critics to wonder whether the criteria are now too broad (Frances, 2013). Shall we say such a child is hyperactive—or energetic? Impulsive—or spontaneous? Excessively talkative—or excited? One 10-year study in Sweden found children's attentional behaviors unchanging, while national ADHD diagnoses increased fivefold (Rydell et al., 2018). (See Developing Arguments: ADHD—Normal High Energy or Disordered Behavior?)

**attention-deficit/hyperactivity disorder (ADHD)** a psychological disorder marked by extreme inattention and/or hyperactivity and impulsivity.

**AP® Science Practice**

# Developing Arguments

## ADHD — Normal High Energy or Disordered Behavior?

### Diagnosis in the U.S.

9.4%[1] ⬤ 2- to 17-year-olds

2.5%[2] ⬤ adults

Less often in many other countries, such as Norway and Sweden[3]

Twice as often in BOYS as in girls

### Symptoms

- inattention and distractibility[4]
- hyperactivity[5]
- impulsivity

### SKEPTICS note:

**Energetic child** + **boring school** = **ADHD overdiagnosis**

- Children are not meant to sit for hours in chairs inside.
- The youngest children in a class tend to be more fidgety — and more often diagnosed.[6]
- Older students may seek out stimulant ADHD prescription drugs — "good-grade pills."[7]
- We don't know the long-term effects of drug treatment.
- There is no clear explanation for increases in ADHD diagnoses and drugs.[8]

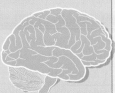

### SUPPORTERS note:

- More diagnoses reflect increased awareness.
- "ADHD is a real neurobiological disorder whose existence should no longer be debated."[9]
- ADHD is associated with abnormal brain structure, abnormal brain activity patterns, and future risky or antisocial behavior.[10]

### Causes?

- May co-exist with a learning disorder or with defiant and temper-prone behavior.
- May be genetic.[11]

### Treatment

- Stimulant drugs (Ritalin and Adderall) calm hyperactivity, and increase ability to sit and focus.[12] So do behavior therapy and aerobic exercise.[13]
- Psychological therapies help with the distress of ADHD.[14]

### The bottom line:

Extreme inattention, hyperactivity, and impulsivity can derail social, academic, and work achievements. These symptoms can be treated with medication and other therapies. But the debate continues over whether normal high energy is too often diagnosed as a psychiatric disorder, and whether there is a cost to the long-term use of stimulant drugs in treating ADHD.

## Developing Arguments Questions

**1.** Identify the reasoning used by those who claim ADHD is overdiagnosed.

**2.** What scientifically derived evidence is used by supporters of the ADHD diagnosis?

**3.** Where do you fall in the high energy-versus-disorder debate? Use evidence presented here to support your position.

1. CDC, 2019a. 2. Simon et al., 2009. 3. MacDonald et al., 2019; Smith, 2017. 4. Martel et al., 2016. 5. Kofler et al., 2016. 6. Chen, M. et al., 2016. 7. Schwarz, 2012. 8. Ellison, 2015. Hales et al., 2018; Sayal et al., 2017. 9. World Federation for Mental Health, 2005. 10. Ball et al, 2019; Hoogman et al., 2019. 11. Nikolas & Burt, 2010; Poelmans et al., 2011; Volkow et al., 2009; Williams et al., 2010. 12. Barbaresi et al., 2007. 13. Cerrillo-Urbina et al., 2015; Pelham et al., 2016. 14. Fabiano et al., 2008.

* * *

The bewilderment, fear, and sorrow caused by psychological disorders are real. But as our next topic—therapy—shows, hope, too, is real.

## Check Your Understanding

**Examine the Concept**

▶ Describe the symptoms of ASD.

**Apply the Concept**

▶ Do you or does anyone you know have ADHD? How does this affect daily experiences at school?

*Answers to the Examine the Concept questions can be found in Appendix C at the end of the book.*

# Module 5.4d REVIEW

**5.4-12 What are *dissociative disorders*, and why are they controversial?**

- *Dissociative disorders* are a controversial, rare group of disorders characterized by a disruption of or discontinuity in the normal integration of consciousness, memory, identity, emotion, perception, body representation, motor control, and behavior.

- Skeptics note that *dissociative identity disorder (DID)* increased dramatically in the late twentieth century, is rarely found outside North America, and may reflect role-playing by people vulnerable to therapists' suggestions. Others view DID as a manifestation of feelings of anxiety, or as a response learned when behaviors are reinforced by anxiety reduction.

**5.4-13 What are the three clusters of personality disorders? What behaviors and brain activity characterize antisocial personality disorder?**

- *Personality disorders* are a group of disorders characterized by enduring inner experiences or behavior patterns that differ from someone's cultural norms and expectations; are pervasive and inflexible; begin in adolescence or early adulthood; are stable over time; and cause distress or impairment.

- The 10 DSM-5-TR personality disorders tend to form three clusters in which people appear eccentric or odd (Cluster A); dramatic, emotional, or erratic (Cluster B); or anxious or fearful (Cluster C).

- *Antisocial personality disorder* (a disorder in Cluster B) is characterized by a lack of conscience and, sometimes, by aggressive and fearless behavior. The amygdala is smaller and the frontal lobes less active in people with this disorder, leading to impaired frontal lobe cognitive functions and decreased responsiveness to others' distress. Genetic predispositions may interact with the environment to produce these characteristics.

**5.4-14 What are the three main eating disorders, and how do biological, psychological, and social-cultural influences make people more vulnerable to them?**

- The *feeding and eating disorders* are characterized by altered consumption or absorption of food that impairs health or psychological functioning. Feeding disorders typically occur in infants or young children, whereas eating disorders affect people who self-feed.

- In people with eating disorders, psychological factors overwhelm the body's tendency to maintain a normal weight.

- Despite being significantly underweight, people with *anorexia nervosa* (usually adolescent females) maintain a starvation diet, sometimes exercise excessively, and have an inaccurate self-perception.

- People with *bulimia nervosa* (usually women in their late teens and early twenties, but also some men) binge and then compensate by purging, fasting, or excessively exercising.

- Cultural pressures, low self-esteem, and negative emotions interact with stressful life experiences and genetics to produce eating disorders.

**5.4-15** What are *neurodevelopmental disorders,* and how do they impact thinking and behavior?

- *Neurodevelopmental disorders* are central nervous system abnormalities, usually in the brain, that begin in childhood and alter thinking and behavior.

- *Attention-deficit hyperactivity disorder* is marked by extreme inattention and/or hyperactivity and impulsivity, which can impact social, academic, and work success.

- *Autism spectrum disorder* is marked by limitations in communication and social interaction, as well as rigidly fixated interests and repetitive behaviors.

## AP® Practice Multiple Choice Questions

1. Joplin has been experiencing a disruption in his integration of consciousness, memory, identity, emotion, perception, body representation, and motor control. Joplin might be diagnosed with what type of disorders?

   a. Feeding disorders
   b. Personality disorders
   c. Dissociative disorders
   d. Neurodevelopmental disorders

2. Dr. Tremblay believes that dissociative amnesia should be removed from the DSM-5-TR, while Dr. Bhatt believes it should remain. Which of the following is an argument Dr. Bhatt might cite for retaining this disorder in the DSM-5-TR?

   a. Research shows that individuals with dissociative amnesia have larger and hyper-reactive dopamine reward systems.
   b. Research shows that individuals with dissociative amnesia have families that are competitive and high achieving.
   c. Research shows that individuals with dissociative amnesia have decreased brain activity associated with mirroring others' actions.
   d. Research shows that individuals with dissociative amnesia have lower activity in the hippocampus.

3. Buford, who has been diagnosed with a Cluster C personality disorder, most likely experiences

   a. anxiety.
   b. eccentricity.
   c. impulsivity.
   d. emotionality.

4. What psychological disorder is most likely portrayed in this graph?

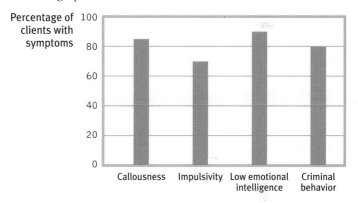

   a. Narcissistic personality disorder
   b. Autism spectrum disorder
   c. Tourette's disorder
   d. Antisocial personality disorder

5. Dr. Cruz conducted a study of 50 clients at a college counseling center with diagnosed psychological disorders. She identified seven who tended to eat large amounts of high-calorie food in one sitting, and who then exercise excessively. Based on this description, what was the likely diagnosis of these participants?

   a. Anorexia nervosa
   b. Bulimia nervosa
   c. Stereotypic movement disorder
   d. Attention-deficit/hyperactivity disorder

**6.** Dr. Privitera wants to conduct a study of individuals diagnosed with autism spectrum disorder. Which of the following would be an appropriate sample for his study?

a. All individuals in the world who exhibit differences in social communication and interaction and also demonstrate repetitive and restricted behaviors

b. Twenty volunteers from a local college who exhibit differences in social communication and interaction and also demonstrate repetitive and restricted behaviors

c. All individuals in the world who exhibit extreme inattention and hyperactivity/impulsivity

d. Twenty volunteers from a local college who exhibit extreme inattention and hyperactivity/impulsivity

**7.** If Olga has a tic disorder, she likely displays

a. extreme clumsiness.

b. repetitive and unnecessary motor movements.

c. hyperactivity.

d. involuntary movements or vocalizations.

# Module 5.5a  Treatment of Psychological Disorders: Introduction to Therapy, and Psychodynamic and Humanistic Therapies

## LEARNING TARGETS

**5.5-1** Contrast *psychotherapy* and the *biomedical therapies*.

**5.5-2** Describe the goals and techniques of psychoanalysis, and explain how they have been adapted in psychodynamic therapy.

**5.5-3** Describe the basic themes of humanistic therapy, and describe the goals and techniques of Rogers' person-centered approach.

Kay Redfield Jamison is both an award-winning clinical psychologist and a world expert on the emotional extremes of bipolar disorders. She knows her subject firsthand, as she recalled in *An Unquiet Mind:*

For as long as I can remember, I was frighteningly, although often wonderfully, beholden to moods. Intensely emotional as a child, mercurial as a young girl, first severely depressed as an adolescent, and then unrelentingly caught up in the cycles of manic-depressive illness [now known as *bipolar I disorder*] by the time I began my professional life, I became, both by necessity and intellectual inclination, a student of moods. (1995, pp. 4–5)

Jamison's life was blessed with times of intense sensitivity and passionate energy. But like her father's, it was also sometimes plagued by reckless spending, racing conversation, and sleeplessness, alternating with swings into "the blackest caves of the mind."

Then, "in the midst of utter confusion," she made a life-changing decision. Risking professional embarrassment, she made an appointment with a therapist, a psychiatrist she would visit weekly for years to come:

He kept me alive a thousand times over. He saw me through madness, despair, wonderful and terrible love affairs, disillusionments and triumphs, recurrences of illness, an almost fatal suicide attempt, the death of a man I greatly loved, and the enormous pleasures and aggravations of my professional life. . . . He was very tough, as well as very kind, and even though he understood more than anyone how much I felt I was losing—in energy, vivacity, and originality—by taking medication, he never [lost] sight of the overall perspective of how costly, damaging, and life threatening my illness was. . . . Although I went to him to be treated for an illness, he taught me . . . the total beholdenness of brain to mind and mind to brain. (pp. 87–88)

**deinstitutionalization** the process, begun in the late twentieth century, of moving people with psychological disorders out of institutional facilities.

**psychotherapy** treatment involving psychological techniques; consists of interactions between a trained therapist and someone seeking to overcome psychological difficulties or achieve personal growth.

**biomedical therapy** prescribed medications or procedures that act directly on the person's physiology.

**SPOTLIGHT ON:**
Dorothea Dix

Macmillan Learning

**Dorothea Dix** "I . . . call your attention to the state of the Insane Persons confined within this Commonwealth, in cages" (*Memorial to the Legislature of Massachusetts*, 1843).

**The history of treatment** Visitors to eighteenth-century psychiatric hospitals paid to gawk at patients, as though they were viewing zoo animals. William Hogarth's (1697–1764) painting captured one of these visits to London's St. Mary of Bethlehem hospital (commonly called Bedlam).

Actor Kerry Washington and singer Katy Perry have also shared openly the benefits they received from psychotherapy. "I've been going to therapy for about five years," Perry says, "and I think it has really helped my mental health incredibly" (Chen, 2017). Catherine, Duchess of Cambridge (a.k.a. Kate Middleton), has worked on reducing the stigma surrounding mental illness and therapy: "We need to help young people and their parents understand that it's not a sign of weakness to ask for help" (Holmes, 2015).

This module explores some of the healing options available to therapists and the people who seek their help. We begin by exploring and evaluating *psychotherapies*, and then focus on *biomedical therapies* and preventing disorders.

## Treating Psychological Disorders

**5.5-1** How do *psychotherapy* and the *biomedical therapies* differ?

The long history of treating psychological disorders has included a bewildering mix of harsh and gentle methods. Would-be healers have cut holes in people's heads and restrained, bled, or "beat the devil" out of them. But they also have given warm baths and massages and placed people in sunny, serene environments. They have given them drugs. And they have talked with them about childhood experiences, current feelings, and maladaptive thoughts and behaviors.

Reformers Philippe Pinel (1745–1826) and Dorothea Dix (1802–1887) pushed for gentler, more humane treatments and for constructing psychiatric hospitals. Their efforts largely paid off. Since the 1950s, the introduction of effective *psychotropic* drug therapies and community-based treatment programs has emptied most of those hospitals. Unfortunately, this **deinstitutionalization** has left many people with mental illness untreated, which has contributed to increased homelessness and incarceration. Today's therapists prefer to treat people with chronic mental illness in *decentralized ways*, combining medication and psychological therapies in outpatient or inpatient community-based facilities.

Modern Western therapies can be classified into two main categories.

- In **psychotherapy**, a trained therapist uses psychological techniques to help someone overcome difficulties and achieve personal growth. The therapist may explore a client's early relationships, encourage the client to adopt new ways of thinking, or coach the client in replacing old behaviors with new ones.

- **Biomedical therapy** offers medication or other biological treatments. For example, a person with severe depression may receive antidepressants, electroconvulsive shock therapy (ECT), or deep brain stimulation.

The Granger Collection

Today, 1 in 5 Americans receives some form of outpatient mental health therapy (Olfson et al., 2019). The care provider's training and expertise, and the disorder itself, influence the choice of treatment. Psychotherapy and medication are often combined. Kay Redfield Jamison received psychotherapy in her meetings with her psychiatrist, and she took medications to control her wild mood swings.

Let's look first at some influential psychotherapy options for those treated with "talk therapies." Each is built on one or more of psychology's major theories: psychodynamic, humanistic, behavioral, and cognitive. Most of these techniques can be used one-on-one or in groups, in person or online. Some therapists combine techniques. Indeed, most psychotherapists describe their approach as **eclectic**, using a blend of therapies.

# Psychoanalysis and Psychodynamic Therapies

> **5.5-2** What are the goals and techniques of psychoanalysis, and how have they been adapted in psychodynamic therapy?

The first major psychological therapy was Sigmund Freud's **psychoanalysis**. Although few clinicians today practice therapy as Freud did, his work deserves discussion. It helped form the foundation for treating psychological disorders, and it continues to influence modern therapists working from the *psychodynamic* perspective.

## The Goals of Psychoanalysis

Freud believed that in therapy, people could achieve healthier, less anxious living by releasing the energy they had previously devoted to id-ego-superego conflicts (Module 4.5). Freud assumed that we do not fully know ourselves. He believed that there are threatening things we *repress*—things we do not want to know, so we disavow or deny them. Psychoanalysis was Freud's method of helping people to bring these repressed feelings into conscious awareness. By helping them reclaim their unconscious thoughts and feelings, and by giving them *insight* into the origins of their disorders, the therapist (*analyst*) could help them reduce growth-impeding inner conflicts.

## The Techniques of Psychoanalysis

Psychoanalytic theory emphasizes the power of childhood experiences to mold the adult. Thus, psychoanalysis is historical reconstruction. It aims to unearth the past in the hope of loosening its bonds on the present. After discarding hypnosis as an unreliable excavator, Freud turned to *free association.*

Imagine yourself as a patient using free association. You begin by relaxing, perhaps by lying on a couch. The psychoanalyst, who sits out of your line of vision, asks you to say aloud whatever comes to mind. At one moment, you're relating a childhood memory. At another, you're describing a dream or recent experience. It sounds easy, but soon you notice how often you edit your thoughts as you speak. You pause for a second before uttering an embarrassing thought. You omit what seems trivial, irrelevant, or shameful. Sometimes your mind goes blank or you clutch up, unable to remember important details. You may joke or change the subject to something less threatening.

Freud thought that these mental blocks indicate **resistance**. They hint that anxiety lurks and you are defending against sensitive material. The analyst will note your resistance and then provide insight into its meaning. If offered at the right moment, this **interpretation**—of, say, your reluctance to call or message your mother—may illuminate the underlying wishes, feelings, and conflicts you are avoiding. The analyst may also offer an explanation of how this resistance fits with other pieces of your psychological puzzle, including those based on analysis of your dream content.

Over many such sessions, your relationship patterns surface in your interaction with your analyst. You may find yourself experiencing strong positive or negative feelings for this confidant. The analyst may suggest you are **transferring** feelings, such as dependency or mingled love and anger, that you experienced in earlier relationships with family members or other important people. By exposing such feelings, you may gain insight into your current relationships.

Relatively few North American therapists now offer traditional psychoanalysis. Much of its underlying theory is not supported by scientific research (Module 4.5). Analysts'

**AP® Exam Tip**

Most of the treatments discussed in this module come from the perspectives you've learned about in other modules (for example, the psychoanalytic, psychodynamic, and humanistic perspectives discussed in Module 4.5). As you reach each major section — like the upcoming one on psychoanalytic and psychodynamic therapy — try to anticipate how someone from that perspective would approach therapy (for example, "What would Rogers do?"). This should help you organize and retain the information as you read.

**AP® Exam Tip**

As you read, think about the various disorders previously studied and consider how a particular form of therapy might be most effective in treating that disorder.

**eclectic approach** an approach to psychotherapy that uses techniques from various forms of therapy.

**psychoanalysis** Sigmund Freud's therapeutic technique. Freud believed the patient's free associations, resistances, dreams, and transferences—and the analyst's interpretations of them—released previously repressed feelings, allowing the patient to gain self-insight.

**resistance** in psychoanalysis, the blocking from consciousness of anxiety-laden material.

**interpretation** in psychoanalysis, the analyst's noting of supposed dream meanings, resistances, and other significant behaviors and events in an effort to promote insight.

**transference** in psychoanalysis, the patient's transfer to the analyst of emotions linked with other relationships (such as love or hatred for a parent).

*"I'm more interested in hearing about the eggs you're hiding from yourself."*

interpretations cannot be supported or refuted. And psychoanalysis takes considerable time and money, often years of several expensive sessions per week. Some of these problems have been addressed in the modern *psychodynamic perspective* that has evolved from psychoanalysis.

## Psychodynamic Therapy

Although influenced by Freud's ideas, **psychodynamic therapists** don't talk much about id-ego-superego conflicts. Instead, they try to help people understand their current symptoms by focusing on important relationships and events, including childhood experiences and the therapist-client relationship. "We can have loving feelings and hateful feelings toward the same person," observed psychodynamic therapist Jonathan Shedler (2009), and "we can desire something and also fear it." Client-therapist meetings occur once or twice a week (rather than several times weekly), and often for only a few weeks or months. Clients may engage in free association or have their dreams interpreted, but they often do so meeting with their therapist face-to-face (in-person or online) rather than while lying on a couch, out of their therapist's line of vision. And in contrast to Freud's prescribing cocaine to his depressed patients (!), today's patients receiving psychodynamic therapy sometimes take antidepressant drugs that have been researched, tested, and deemed safe for use (Driessen et al., 2020).

Therapist David Shapiro (1999, p. 8) illustrated this with the case of a young man who had told women he loved them when he knew that he didn't. The client's explanation: They expected it, so he said it. But later, with his wife, who wished he would say that he loved her, he found himself unable — "I don't know why, but I can't."

**Therapist:** Do you mean, then, that if you could, you would like to?

**Patient:** Well, I don't know. . . . Maybe I can't say it because I'm not sure it's true. Maybe I don't love her.

Further interactions revealed that the client could not express real love because it would feel "mushy" and "soft" and therefore unmanly. He was "in conflict with himself, and . . . cut off from the nature of that conflict." Shapiro noted that with such patients, who are estranged from themselves, therapists using psychodynamic techniques "are in a position to introduce them to themselves. We can restore their awareness of their own wishes and feelings, and their awareness, as well, of their reactions against those wishes and feelings."

## Humanistic Therapies

**5.5-3** What are the basic themes of humanistic therapy? What are the goals and techniques of Rogers' person-centered approach?

The *humanistic* perspective (Module 4.5) emphasizes people's innate potential for self-fulfillment. Not surprisingly, humanistic therapies attempt to reduce the inner conflicts that interfere with natural development and growth. To achieve this goal, humanistic therapists try to help clients discover new insights. Indeed, because they share this goal, the psychodynamic and humanistic therapies are often referred to as **insight therapies**. But humanistic therapies differ from psychodynamic therapies in many ways, including their focus on

- *growth*. Humanistic therapists focus not on illness, but on helping people grow in self-awareness and self-acceptance. Thus, they call those in therapy "persons" or "clients" rather than "patients" (a change many other therapists have adopted).

- *the present*. The path to growth is not uncovering hidden causes, but rather taking immediate responsibility for one's feelings and actions. The present and future are more

**psychodynamic therapy** therapy deriving from the psychoanalytic tradition; views individuals as responding to unconscious forces and childhood experiences, and seeks to enhance self-insight.

**insight therapies** therapies that aim to improve psychological functioning by increasing a person's awareness of underlying motives and defenses.

important than the past. Therapy thus focuses on exploring feelings as they occur, rather than on achieving insight into the childhood origins of those feelings.

- *the conscious mind*. Conscious thoughts are more important than unconscious thoughts.

All of these themes are present in the widely used **person-centered therapy**, a humanistic technique that Carl Rogers (1902–1987) developed. In this *nondirective therapy*, the client leads the discussion. The therapist listens, without judging or interpreting, and refrains from directing the client toward certain insights.

Believing that most people possess the resources for growth, Rogers (1961, 1980) encouraged therapists to foster that growth by exhibiting *acceptance*, *genuineness*, and *empathy*. By being *accepting*, therapists may help clients feel freer and more open to change. By being *genuine*, therapists hope to encourage clients to express their true feelings. By being *empathic*, therapists try to sense, validate, and reflect their clients' feelings, helping them experience a deeper self-understanding and self-acceptance (Hill & Nakayama, 2000). As Rogers (1980) explained:

> Hearing has consequences. When I truly hear a person and the meanings that are important to him at that moment, hearing not simply his words, but him, and when I let him know that I have heard his own private personal meanings, many things happen. There is first of all a grateful look. He feels released. He wants to tell me more about his world. He surges forth in a new sense of freedom. He becomes more open to the process of change.
>
> I have often noticed that the more deeply I hear the meanings of the person, the more there is that happens. Almost always, when a person realizes he has been deeply heard, his eyes moisten. I think in some real sense he is weeping for joy. It is as though he were saying, "Thank God, somebody heard me. Someone knows what it's like to be me." (p. 10)

To Rogers, "hearing" was **active listening**. The therapist echoes, restates, and seeks clarification of what the client expresses (verbally or nonverbally). The therapist also acknowledges those expressed feelings. Active listening is now an accepted part of counseling practices in many schools, colleges, and clinics. Counselors listen attentively. They interrupt only to restate and confirm feelings, to accept what was said, or to check their understanding of something. In the following brief excerpt, note how Rogers tried to provide a psychological mirror that would help the client see himself more clearly (Meador & Rogers, 1984, p. 167):

**Rogers:** Feeling that now, hm? That you're just no good to yourself, no good to anybody. Never will be any good to anybody. Just that you're completely worthless, huh?—Those really are lousy feelings. Just feel that you're no good at all, hm?

**Client:** Yeah. (Muttering in a low, discouraged voice) That's what this guy I went to town with just the other day told me.

**Rogers:** This guy that you went to town with really told you that you were no good? Is that what you're saying? Did I get that right?

**Client:** M-hm.

**Rogers:** I guess the meaning of that if I get it right is that here's somebody that meant something to you and what does he think of you? Why, he's told you that he thinks you're no good at all. And that just really knocks the props out from under you. (Client weeps quietly.) It just brings the tears. (Silence of 20 seconds)

**Client:** (Rather defiantly) I don't care though.

**Rogers:** You tell yourself you don't care at all, but somehow I guess some part of you cares because some part of you weeps over it.

**person-centered therapy** a humanistic therapy, developed by Carl Rogers, in which the therapist uses techniques such as *active listening* within an accepting, genuine, empathic environment to facilitate clients' growth. (Also called *client-centered therapy*.)

**active listening** empathic listening in which the listener echoes, restates, and seeks clarification. A feature of Rogers' person-centered therapy.

**Active listening** Carl Rogers (right) empathized with a client during this group therapy session.

Michael Rougier/Getty Images

Can a therapist be a perfect mirror, without selecting and interpreting what is reflected? Rogers conceded that no one can be *totally* nondirective. Nevertheless, he said, the therapist's most important contribution is to accept and understand the client. Given a nonjudgmental, grace-filled environment that provides **unconditional positive regard**, people may accept even their worst traits and feel valued and whole.

How can we improve communication in our own relationships by listening more actively? Three Rogers-inspired hints may help:

1. *Paraphrase*. Check your understanding by summarizing the person's words out loud, in your own words.

2. *Invite clarification*. "What might be an example of that?" may encourage the person to say more.

3. *Reflect feelings*. "It sounds frustrating" might mirror what you're sensing from the person's body language and intensity.

**unconditional positive regard** a caring, accepting, nonjudgmental attitude, which Carl Rogers believed would help clients develop self-awareness and self-acceptance. (Also known as *unconditional regard*.)

---

### AP® Science Practice

## Check Your Understanding

**Examine the Concept**

▶ Why do relatively few North American therapists now offer traditional psychoanalysis?

▶ Describe the eclectic approach to therapy.

▶ Describe the difference between psychodynamic therapy and person-centered therapy.

*Answers to the Examine the Concept questions can be found in Appendix C at the end of the book.*

**Apply the Concept**

▶ Think of your closest friends. Do they tend to express more empathy than those you feel less close to? How might *you* more deeply and actively listen to your friends?

---

## Module 5.5a REVIEW

**5.5-1 How do *psychotherapy* and the *biomedical therapies* differ?**

- *Psychotherapy* is treatment involving psychological techniques; it consists of interactions between a trained therapist and someone seeking to overcome psychological difficulties or achieve personal growth.

- The major psychotherapies derive from psychology's psychodynamic, humanistic, behavioral, and cognitive perspectives.

- Many therapists take an *eclectic approach* that blends therapies.

- *Biomedical therapy* treats psychological disorders with medications or procedures that act directly on a patient's physiology.

**5.5-2** What are the goals and techniques of psychoanalysis, and how have they been adapted in psychodynamic therapy?

- Through *psychoanalysis*, Sigmund Freud tried to give people self-insight and relief from their disorders by bringing anxiety-laden feelings and thoughts into conscious awareness.
  - Psychoanalytic techniques included free association and *interpretation* of instances of *resistance* and *transference*.
- *Psychodynamic therapy* has been influenced by traditional psychoanalysis but differs from it in many ways, paying little attention to the concepts of id, ego, and superego. This contemporary therapy is briefer, less expensive, and more focused on helping the client find relief from current symptoms.
  - Psychodynamic therapists help clients understand how past relationships create themes that may be acted out in present relationships.

**5.5-3** What are the basic themes of humanistic therapy? What are the goals and techniques of Rogers' person-centered approach?

- Both psychoanalytic and humanistic therapies are *insight therapies*—they attempt to improve functioning by increasing people's awareness of motives and defenses.
- Humanistic therapy's goals include helping people grow in self-awareness and self-acceptance, promoting personal growth rather than curing illness, helping people take responsibility for their feelings and actions, focusing on conscious thoughts rather than unconscious motivations, and seeing the present and future as more important than the past.
- Carl Rogers' *person-centered therapy* proposed that therapists' most important contribution is to function as a psychological mirror through *active listening* and to provide a growth-fostering environment of *unconditional positive regard*.

# AP® Practice Multiple Choice Questions

**1.** In the 1950s, Dr. Tanaka conducted a study to determine how being discharged from a mental hospital impacted participants' subjective well-being. She found that 8 weeks after their discharge, 85 percent of participants reported improved subjective well-being, compared to the 23 percent who reported improved subjective well-being while still hospitalized. Which of the following is a variable in Dr. Tanaka's study?

a. Acceptance
b. Psychodynamic therapy
c. Deinstitutionalization
d. Person-centered therapy

**2.** Blacklawn Outpatient Clinic treats clients who have been diagnosed with a bipolar disorder. What is a logical conclusion about the treatment methods used for these clients?

a. These clients likely receive psychoanalytic therapy.
b. These clients likely receive a combination of psychotherapy and biomedical therapies.
c. These clients likely receive biomedical therapy.
d. These clients likely receive a combination of psychodynamic therapy and psychoanalytic therapy.

**3.** Dr. Carlson works with individuals diagnosed with major depressive disorder. He encourages them to discuss their childhoods, internal conflicts, and present lives, believing that an open and empathic environment will help his clients accept not only past events but also their current selves. His therapeutic style would be best described as

a. biomedical.
b. psychoanalytic.
c. humanistic.
d. eclectic.

**4.** When Harriet could not consciously remember her difficult childhood, her psychoanalytic therapist said she was experiencing

a. resistance.
b. interpretation.
c. transference.
d. free association.

**5.** In her application for funding for her treatment center, Verna needs to advocate for humanistic therapies. What should she say?

a. Humanistic therapies assert that the past is more important than the present and future.

b. Humanistic therapies assert that the best path to growth is found by uncovering hidden determinants.

c. Humanistic therapies assert that unconscious thoughts are more important than conscious thoughts.

d. Humanistic therapies focus on promoting growth, not curing illness.

**6.** Xiaoming uses active listening, acceptance, genuineness, and empathy in her work with therapy clients to promote their growth. Xiaoming uses

a. insight therapy.

b. humanistic therapy.

c. person-centered therapy.

d. psychodynamic therapy.

# Module 5.5b Treatment of Psychological Disorders: Behavioral, Cognitive, and Group Therapies

## Behavior Therapies

**5.5-4** How does the basic assumption of behavior therapy differ from the assumptions of psychodynamic and humanistic therapies? What classical conditioning techniques are used in exposure therapies and aversive conditioning?

The insight therapies assume that self-awareness and psychological well-being go hand in hand. For example, psychodynamic therapists expect people's problems to lessen as they gain insight into their unresolved and unconscious tensions. And humanistic therapists expect problems to diminish as people get in touch with their feelings. **Behavior therapists**, influenced by the *behavioral perspective*, doubt the healing power of self-awareness. Rather than delving deeply below the surface looking for inner causes, behavior therapists assume that problem behaviors *are* the problems. (You can become aware of why you are highly anxious during tests and still be anxious.) Using learning principles, behavior therapists offer clients strategies for reducing unwanted behaviors. Behavior therapists view a specific phobia of heights, for example, as a learned response. So why not replace old, unwanted behaviors with new, constructive behaviors?

**behavior therapy** therapy that uses learning principles to reduce unwanted behaviors.

### Classical Conditioning Techniques

One cluster of behavior therapies derives from principles developed in Ivan Pavlov's early twentieth-century conditioning experiments (Module 3.7). As Pavlov and others showed, we learn various behaviors and emotions through classical conditioning. If a dog attacks us, we may thereafter have a conditioned fear response when other dogs approach.

(If our fear generalizes and all dogs become conditioned stimuli, we may even develop a dog phobia.)

Could maladaptive symptoms be examples of conditioned responses? If so, might reconditioning be a solution? Learning theorist O. H. Mowrer (1907–1982) thought so. He developed a successful conditioning therapy for chronic bed-wetting, using a liquid-sensitive pad connected to an alarm. If the sleeping child wets the bed pad, moisture triggers the alarm, waking the child. After several trials, the child associates bladder relaxation with waking. In three out of four cases, the treatment has been effective and the success has boosted the child's self-esteem (Christophersen & Edwards, 1992; Houts et al., 1994).

Can we unlearn fear responses, such as to public speaking or flying, through new conditioning? Many people have. An example: The fear of riding in an elevator is often a learned aversion to being in a confined space. **Counterconditioning**, such as with *exposure therapy*, pairs the trigger stimulus (in this case, the enclosed space of the elevator) with a new response (relaxation) that is incompatible with fear.

## Exposure Therapies

Picture this scene: Behavioral psychologist Mary Cover Jones is working with 3-year-old Peter, who is petrified of rabbits and other furry objects. To rid Peter of his fear, Jones plans to associate the fear-evoking rabbit with the pleasurable, relaxed response associated with eating. As Peter begins his midafternoon snack, she introduces a caged rabbit on the other side of the huge room. Peter, eagerly munching away on his crackers and drinking his milk, hardly notices. On succeeding days, she gradually moves the rabbit closer and closer. Within two months, Peter is holding the rabbit in his lap, even stroking it while he eats. Moreover, his fear of other furry objects subsides as well, having been *countered*, or replaced, by a relaxed state that cannot coexist with fear (Fisher, 1984; Jones, 1924).

Unfortunately for many people who might have been helped by Jones' counterconditioning procedures, her story of Peter and the rabbit didn't become well known when it was reported in 1924. It was more than 30 years before psychiatrist Joseph Wolpe (1958; Wolpe & Plaud, 1997) refined Jones' counterconditioning technique into the **exposure therapies** used today. These therapies are a good example of *applied behavior analysis*—using what we know about conditioning to address disordered behaviors. Therapists try to change people's reactions by repeatedly exposing them to stimuli that trigger unwanted reactions. We all experience this process in everyday life. A person moving to a new apartment may be annoyed by nearby loud traffic noise, but only for a while. With repeated exposure, the person adapts. So, too, with people who have fear reactions to specific events, such as people with PTSD (Thompson-Hollands et al., 2018). By being exposed repeatedly to the situation that once petrified them, they can learn to react less anxiously (Holder et al., 2020). Exposure therapy is neither pleasant nor easy, so it helps to have supportive family and friends (Meis et al., 2019).

One exposure therapy widely used to treat specific phobias is **systematic desensitization**. You cannot simultaneously be anxious and relaxed. Therefore, if you can repeatedly relax when facing fear-provoking stimuli, you can gradually eliminate your fear. The trick is to proceed gradually. If you fear public speaking, a behavior therapist might first help you construct a *fear hierarchy*—a kind of ladder of speaking situations that trigger increasing levels of fear. Yours might range from mildly anxiety-provoking situations (perhaps speaking up in a small group of friends) to panic-provoking situations (having to address a large audience).

Next, the therapist would train you in *progressive relaxation*. You would learn to release tension in one muscle group after another, until you achieve a comfortable, complete state of relaxation. Then the therapist might ask you to imagine, with your eyes closed, a mildly anxiety-arousing situation: You are having coffee with a group of friends and are trying to decide whether to speak up. If imagining the scene causes you to feel any anxiety, you are told to signal by raising your finger. Seeing the signal, the therapist will instruct you to switch off the mental image and go back to deep relaxation. This imagined scene is repeatedly paired with relaxation until you feel no trace of anxiety.

**counterconditioning** behavior therapy procedures that use classical conditioning to evoke new responses to stimuli that are triggering unwanted behaviors; include *exposure therapies* and *aversive conditioning*.

**exposure therapies** behavioral techniques, such as *systematic desensitization* and *virtual reality exposure therapy*, that treat anxieties by exposing people (in imaginary or actual situations) to the things they fear and avoid.

**systematic desensitization** a type of exposure therapy that associates a pleasant relaxed state with gradually increasing anxiety-triggering stimuli. Commonly used to treat specific phobias.

The therapist will then move to the next item in your anxiety hierarchy, again using relaxation techniques to desensitize you to each imagined situation. After several sessions, you move to actual situations and practice what you had only *imagined* before. You begin with relatively easy tasks (like speaking up with friends) and gradually move to more anxiety-filled ones (like giving a public speech). Conquering your anxiety in an actual situation, not just in your imagination, will increase your self-confidence (Foa & Kozak, 1986; Williams, 1987). Eventually, you may even become a confident public speaker. Often people fear not just a situation, such as public speaking, but also being incapacitated by their own fear response. As their fear subsides, so does their fear of the fear.

If anxiety-arousing situations (such as flying, heights, particular animals, and public speaking) are too expensive, difficult, or embarrassing to re-create, the therapist may recommend **virtual reality exposure therapy**. Imagine donning a head-mounted display unit that projects a lifelike three-dimensional virtual world tailored to your particular fear (**Figure 5.5-1**). If you fear flying, for example, you could peer out of a simulated plane, feel the engine's vibrations, and hear it roar as the plane taxis down the runway and takes off. If you fear social interactions, you could experience simulated stressful situations, such as entering a roomful of people. In controlled studies, people treated with virtual reality exposure therapy have experienced relief from real-life fear and social anxiety (Anderson et al., 2017; Freeman et al., 2018; Minns et al., 2019).

## Aversive Conditioning

Exposure therapy helps you learn what you *should* do; it enables a more relaxed, positive response to an upsetting *harmless* stimulus. **Aversive conditioning** helps you learn what you *should not* do; it creates a negative (aversive) response to a *harmful* stimulus (such as alcohol). The aversive conditioning procedure is simple: It associates the unwanted behavior with unpleasant feelings. To treat compulsive nail biting, the therapist may suggest painting the fingernails with a nasty-tasting nail polish (Baskind, 1997). To treat alcohol use disorder, the therapist may offer the client appealing drinks laced with a drug that produces severe nausea. If that therapy links alcohol with violent nausea, the person's reaction to alcohol may change from positive to negative (**Figure 5.5-2**).

**Figure 5.5-1**
**Scary spider**

Guided by a therapist, virtual reality technology exposes people to vivid simulations of feared stimuli and helps them gradually overcome their fear.

**virtual reality exposure therapy** a counterconditioning technique that treats anxiety through creative electronic simulations in which people can safely face specific fears, such as flying, spiders, or public speaking.

**aversive conditioning** associates an unpleasant state (such as nausea) with an unwanted behavior (such as drinking alcohol).

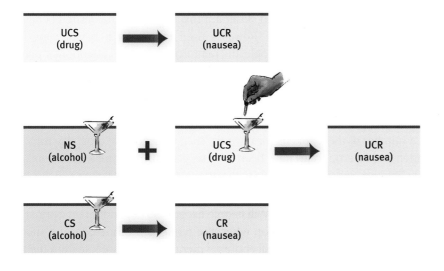

**Figure 5.5-2**
**Aversion therapy for alcohol use disorder**

After repeatedly imbibing an alcoholic drink mixed with a drug that produces severe nausea, some people with a history of alcohol use disorder develop at least a temporary conditioned aversion to alcohol. (Remember: UCS is unconditioned stimulus, UCR is unconditioned response, NS is neutral stimulus, CS is conditioned stimulus, and CR is conditioned response.)

Taste aversion learning has been a successful alternative to killing predators in some animal protection programs (Dingfelder, 2010; Garcia & Gustavson, 1997). After being sickened by eating a tainted sheep, wolves may later avoid sheep. Does aversive conditioning also transform humans' reactions to alcohol? In the short run it may. In one classic study, 685 patients hospitalized with alcohol use disorder completed an aversion therapy program (Wiens & Menustik, 1983). Over the next year, they returned for several booster treatments that paired alcohol with sickness. At the end of that year, 63 percent were not drinking alcohol. But after three years, only 33 percent were alcohol free.

In therapy, as in research, cognition influences conditioning. People know that outside the therapist's office they can drink without fear of nausea. This ability to discriminate between the therapy situation and all others can limit aversive conditioning's effectiveness. Thus, therapists often combine aversive conditioning with other treatments.

## Operant Conditioning Techniques

**5.5-5** What is the main premise of behavior therapy based on operant conditioning principles, and what are the views of its proponents and critics?

If you have learned to swim, you learned how to hold your breath with your head under water, how to pull your body through the water, and perhaps even how to dive safely. Operant conditioning shaped your swimming. You were reinforced for safe, effective behaviors. And you were naturally punished, as when you swallowed water, for improper swimming behaviors.

Pioneering researcher B. F. Skinner helped us understand the basic principle of operant conditioning (Module 3.8): Consequences strongly influence our voluntary behaviors. Knowing this, behavior therapists can apply *behavior modification*. They reinforce desirable behaviors, and they fail to reinforce—or sometimes punish—undesirable behaviors.

John D. Buffington/DigitalVision/Getty Images

Using operant conditioning principles to solve specific behavior problems has raised hopes for some seemingly hopeless cases. *Applied behavior analysis* (ABA), for example, uses principles of learning theory to increase positive behavior and decrease unwanted behavior. For example, therapists have used ABA to help socially withdrawn children with autism spectrum disorder learn to interact (Virués-Ortega, 2010). People with schizophrenia have been helped to behave more rationally. In such cases, therapists use positive reinforcers to *shape* behavior. In a step-by-step manner, they reward closer and closer approximations of the desired behavior.

Rewards used to modify behavior vary. For some people, the reinforcing power of attention or praise is sufficient. Others require concrete rewards, such as food. In institutional settings, therapists may create a **token economy**. When people display a desired behavior, such as getting out of bed, washing, dressing, eating, talking meaningfully, cleaning their rooms, or playing cooperatively, they receive a token or plastic coin. Later, they can exchange a number of these tokens for rewards, such as candy, TV time, day trips, or better living quarters. Token economies have been used successfully in homes, classrooms, and correctional institutions, and among people with various disabilities (Matson & Boisjoli, 2009).

Behavior modification critics express two concerns:

**token economy** an operant conditioning procedure in which people earn a token for exhibiting a desired behavior and can later exchange tokens for privileges or treats.

- *How durable are the behaviors?* Will people become so dependent on extrinsic rewards that the desired behaviors will stop when the reinforcers stop? Behavior modification advocates believe the behaviors will endure if therapists wean people from the tokens by shifting them toward other, real-life rewards, such as social approval. As people become more socially competent, the intrinsic satisfaction of social interaction may sustain the behaviors.

- **Is it right for one human to control another's behavior?** Those who set up token economies deprive people of something they desire and decide which behaviors to reinforce. To critics, this whole process feels too authoritarian. Advocates reply that control already exists: People's destructive behavior patterns are being maintained and perpetuated by natural reinforcers and punishers in their environments. Isn't using positive rewards to reinforce adaptive behavior more humane than institutionalizing or punishing people? Advocates also argue that the right to effective treatment and an improved life justifies temporary deprivation.

---

**AP® Science Practice**

## Check Your Understanding

### Examine the Concept

▶ Describe the difference between behavior therapies and insight therapies.

▶ Exposure therapies and aversive conditioning are applications of _____ conditioning. Token economies are an application of _____ conditioning.

### Apply the Concept

▶ What might a psychodynamic therapist say about Mowrer's therapy for bed-wetting? How might a behavior therapist defend it?

▶ Some maladaptive behaviors are learned. What hope does this fact provide?

▶ Have you had any experience with behavior therapy techniques in your own life, perhaps to eliminate some childhood behavior problem or to shape some good behavior? Were they effective? Why or why not?

*Answers to the Examine the Concept questions can be found in Appendix C at the end of the book.*

---

## Cognitive Therapies

**5.5-6** What are the goals and techniques of the cognitive therapies and of cognitive-behavioral therapy?

People with specific fears and problem behaviors may respond to behavior therapy. But how might behavior therapists modify the wide assortment of behaviors that accompany depressive disorders? Or treat people with generalized anxiety disorder, where unfocused anxiety doesn't lend itself to a neat list of anxiety-triggering situations? The *cognitive perspective* that has profoundly changed other areas of psychology since the 1960s has influenced therapy as well.

The **cognitive therapies** assume that our *thinking* colors our *feelings* (**Figure 5.5-3**). Between an event and our response lies the mind. Anxiety, for example, can arise from

**cognitive therapy** therapy that teaches people new, more adaptive ways of thinking; based on the assumption that thoughts intervene between events and our emotional reactions.

**Figure 5.5-3**

**A cognitive perspective on psychological disorders**

The person's emotional reactions are produced not directly by the event, but rather by the person's thoughts in response to the event.

an "attention bias to threat" (MacLeod & Clarke, 2015). Self-blaming and overgeneralized explanations of bad events feed depression. If depressed, we may interpret a suggestion as criticism, disagreement as dislike, praise as flattery, friendliness as pity. Dwelling on such thoughts sustains or worsens negative thinking. If depression is sometimes nature's way of getting us to slow down and solve a problem, cognitive therapies may speed up that problem solving (Hollon, 2020). Cognitive therapies help people change their mind with new, more constructive ways of perceiving and interpreting events (Schmidt et al., 2019). By engaging in such *cognitive restructuring*, they echo the presumption of second-century emperor-philosopher Marcus Aurelius: "You have power over your mind."

## Rational-Emotive Behavior Therapy

According to Albert Ellis (1962, 1987, 1993), the creator of **rational-emotive behavior therapy (REBT)**, many problems arise from irrational thinking. For example, he described how therapy might challenge one client's illogical, self-defeating assumptions (Ellis, 2011, pp. 198–199):

> [She] does not merely believe it is undesirable if her lover rejects her. She tends to believe, also, that (a) it is awful; (b) she cannot stand it; (c) she should not, must not be rejected; (d) she will never be accepted by any desirable partner; (e) she is a worthless person because one lover has rejected her; and (f) she deserves to be rejected for being so worthless. Such common covert [hidden] hypotheses are illogical, unrealistic, and destructive. . . . They can be easily elicited and demolished by any scientist worth his or her salt; and the rational-emotive therapist is exactly that: an exposing and nonsense-annihilating scientist.

Change people's thinking by revealing the "absurdity" of their self-defeating ideas, the sharp-tongued Ellis believed, and you will change their self-defeating feelings and enable healthier behaviors. As the author and humorist Mark Twain observed, "Life does not consist mainly, or even largely, of facts and happenings. It consists mainly of the storm of thoughts that are forever blowing through one's mind."

## Beck's Cognitive Therapy

In the late 1960s, a woman left a party early. Things had not gone well. She felt disconnected from the other partygoers and assumed no one liked her. A few days later, she visited cognitive therapist Aaron Beck (1921–2021). Rather than go down the traditional path to her childhood, Beck questioned her current thinking. After she then listed a dozen people who *did* like her, Beck realized that challenging people's automatic negative thoughts could be therapeutic. And thus was born his cognitive therapy (Spiegel, 2015).

People with depression view life through dark glasses. They ignore good news and perceive the world as full of loss, rejection, and abandonment. In therapy, they recall and rehearse their failings and worst impulses (Kelly, 2000). Beck and his colleagues (1979) used cognitive therapy to reverse clients' negativity about themselves, their situations, and their futures. With this technique, gentle questioning seeks to reveal irrational thinking, and then to persuade people to reduce the negative bias that colors their thoughts and perceptions (Beck et al., 1979, pp. 145–146):

**Client:** I agree with the descriptions of me but I guess I don't agree that the way I think makes me depressed.

**Beck:** How do you understand it?

**Client:** I get depressed when things go wrong. Like when I fail a test.

**Beck:** How can failing a test make you depressed?

**Client:** Well, if I fail I'll never get into law school.

**Aaron Beck** "Cognitive therapy seeks to alleviate psychological stresses by correcting faulty conceptions and beliefs. By correcting erroneous beliefs we can lower excessive reactions" (Beck, 1978).

Macmillan Learning

**Beck:** So failing the test means a lot to you. But if failing a test could drive people into clinical depression, wouldn't you expect everyone who failed the test to have a depression? . . . Did everyone who failed get depressed enough to require treatment?

**Client:** No, but it depends on how important the test was to the person.

**Beck:** Right, and who decides the importance?

**Client:** I do.

**Beck:** And so, what we have to examine is your way of viewing the test (or the way that you think about the test) and how it affects your chances of getting into law school. Do you agree?

**Client:** Right.

**Beck:** Do you agree that the way you interpret the results of the test will affect you? You might feel depressed, you might have trouble sleeping, not feel like eating, and you might even wonder if you should drop out of the course.

**Client:** I have been thinking that I wasn't going to make it.

**Beck:** Now what did failing mean?

**Client:** (tearful) That I couldn't get into law school.

**Beck:** And what does that mean to you?

**Client:** That I'm just not smart enough.

**Beck:** Anything else?

**Client:** That I can never be happy.

**Beck:** And how do these thoughts make you feel?

**Client:** Very unhappy.

**Beck:** So it is the meaning of failing a test that makes you very unhappy. In fact, believing that you can never be happy is a powerful factor in producing unhappiness. So, you get yourself into a trap—by definition, failure to get into law school equals "I can never be happy."

We often think in words. Therefore, getting people to change what they say to themselves is an effective way to change their thinking. Perhaps you can identify with the anxious students who, before a test, make matters worse with self-defeating thoughts: "This test's going to be impossible. Everyone else seems so relaxed and confident. I didn't study hard enough. I'll probably forget everything." Psychologists call this sort of relentless, overgeneralized, self-blaming behavior *catastrophizing*.

To change such negative self-talk, cognitive therapists have offered *stress inoculation training*, which teaches people to restructure their thinking in stressful situations (Meichenbaum, 1977, 1985). Sometimes it may be enough simply to say more positive things to yourself: "Relax. The test may be hard, but it will be hard for everyone else, too. I studied really hard. Besides, I don't need a perfect score to get a good grade." After learning to "talk back" to negative thoughts, depression-prone children, teens, and college students have shown a greatly reduced rate of future depression (Reivich et al., 2013; Seligman et al.,

2009). Ditto for anxiety (Krueze et al., 2018). To a large extent, it *is* the thought that counts. For a sampling of commonly used cognitive therapy techniques, see **Table 5.5-1**.

### TABLE 5.5-1 Selected Cognitive Therapy Techniques

| Aim of Technique | Technique | Therapists' Directives |
|---|---|---|
| *Reveal beliefs* | Question your interpretations | Explore your beliefs, revealing faulty assumptions such as "I need to be liked by everyone." |
| | Rank thoughts and emotions | Gain perspective by ranking your thoughts and emotions from mildly to extremely upsetting. |
| *Test beliefs* | Examine consequences | Explore difficult situations, assessing possible consequences and challenging faulty reasoning. |
| | Decatastrophize thinking | Work through the actual worst-case consequences of the situation you face (it is often not as bad as imagined). Then determine how to cope with the real situation you face. |
| *Change beliefs* | Take appropriate responsibility | Challenge total self-blame and negative thinking, noting aspects for which you may be truly responsible, as well as aspects that aren't your responsibility. |
| | Resist extremes | Develop new ways of thinking and feeling to replace maladaptive habits. For example, change from thinking "I am a total failure" to "I got a failing grade on that paper, and I can make these changes to succeed next time." |

**cognitive-behavioral therapy (CBT)** a popular integrative therapy that combines cognitive therapy (changing self-defeating thinking) with behavior therapy (changing behavior).

It's not just depressed people who can benefit from positive self-talk. We all talk to ourselves (thinking "I'm glad I stayed calm," for example, can protect us from future overreacting). The findings of nearly three dozen sport psychology studies show that self-talk interventions can even enhance the learning of athletic skills (Hatzigeorgiadis et al., 2011). Novice basketball players may be trained to think "focus" and "follow through," swimmers to think "high elbow," and tennis players to think "look at the ball." People anxious about public speaking have grown in confidence if asked to recall a speaking success, and then asked this: "Explain WHY you were able to achieve such a successful performance" (Zunick et al., 2015).

## Cognitive-Behavioral Therapy

"The trouble with most therapy," said therapist Albert Ellis (1913–2007), "is that it helps you to feel better. But you don't get better. You have to back it up with action, action, action." **Cognitive-behavioral therapy (CBT)** takes a combined approach to treating depressive and other disorders. This widely practiced *integrative* therapy aims to alter not only the way people *think* but also the way they *act*. Like other cognitive therapies, CBT seeks to make people aware of their irrational negative thinking and to replace it with new ways of thinking. And like other behavior therapies, it trains people to *practice* the more positive approach in everyday settings.

Anxiety, depressive, and bipolar disorders share a common problem: unhealthy emotion regulation (Aldao & Nolen-Hoeksema, 2010; Szkodny et al., 2014). An effective CBT program for these emotional disorders trains people both to replace their catastrophizing *thinking* with more realistic appraisals and, as homework, to practice *behaviors* that are incompatible with their problem (Kazantzis et al., 2010; Moses & Barlow, 2006). A person might keep a log of daily situations associated

**CBT for eating disorders aided by journaling** Cognitive-behavioral therapists guide people with eating disorders toward new ways of explaining their good and bad food-related experiences (Linardon et al., 2017). By recording positive events and how she has enabled them, this woman may become more mindful of her self-control and more optimistic.

with negative and positive emotions, and engage more in activities that lead to feeling good. Those who fear social situations might learn to restrain the negative thoughts surrounding their social anxiety and practice approaching people.

## Exploring Research Methods & Design

Research has found that keeping a daily log or journal of positive emotions increases optimism. Imagine you are a researcher who wants to replicate this finding. Design a study to do so, and then address the following questions.

- Is the study you designed to test this research question non-experimental or experimental? Why?

- State your hypothesis.

- Identify your variables. What are your operational definitions of each?

- Identify one ethical guideline your study will have to follow.

- Explain why replication is important in the scientific process.

*Remember, you can always revisit Unit 0 to review information related to psychological research.*

CBT has been used to effectively treat people with obsessive-compulsive and related disorders (Öst et al., 2015; Tolin et al., 2019). In one classic study, people learned to prevent their compulsive behaviors by relabeling their obsessive thoughts (Schwartz et al., 1996). Feeling the urge to wash their hands again, they would tell themselves, "I'm having a compulsive urge." They would explain to themselves that the hand washing urge was a result of their brain's abnormal activity, which they had previously viewed in PET scans. Then, instead of giving in, they would spend 15 minutes in an enjoyable, alternative behavior—practicing an instrument, taking a walk, gardening. This helped "unstick" the brain by shifting attention and engaging other brain areas. For two or three months, the weekly therapy sessions continued, with relabeling and refocusing practice at home. By the study's end, most participants' symptoms had diminished, and their PET scans revealed normalized brain activity. Many other studies confirm CBT's effectiveness for treating other disorders, such as PTSD and alcohol or other substance use disorders (Lewis et al., 2020; Magill et al., 2020).

Newer CBT variations have shown promise in altering clients' thinking and behavior. *Dialectical behavior therapy (DBT)* helps change harmful and even suicidal behavior patterns (Linehan, 2020; McCauley et al., 2018). *Dialectical* means "opposing," and this therapy attempts to make peace between two opposing forces—acceptance and change. Therapists create an accepting and encouraging environment, helping clients feel they have an ally who will offer them constructive feedback and guidance. In individual sessions, clients learn new ways of thinking that help them tolerate distress and regulate their emotions. They may also receive training in social skills and in *mindfulness meditation*, which helps alleviate depression (Wielgosz et al., 2019). Group training sessions offer additional opportunities to practice new skills in a social context, with further practice as homework. Another CBT variation, *acceptance and commitment therapy (ACT)*, helps clients learn to *accept* their feelings and *commit* to actions that are more consistent with their life values (Hayes et al., 2009). ACT effectively treats depression and anxiety, and even chronic pain (Bai et al., 2020; van Agteren et al., 2021).

# Group and Family Therapies

**5.5-7** What are the aims and benefits of group and family therapies?

So far, we have focused mainly on therapies in which one therapist treats one client. Most therapies (though not traditional psychoanalysis) can also occur in small groups.

## Group Therapy

In **group therapy**, people share and interact with others. While group therapy does not provide the same degree of therapist involvement with each client, it offers other benefits:

- *It saves therapists' time and clients' money* and often is no less effective than individual therapy (Burlingame et al., 2016).

- *It offers a social laboratory for exploring social behaviors and developing social skills*. Therapists frequently suggest group therapy for people experiencing frequent conflicts or whose behavior distresses others. The therapist guides people's interactions as they discuss issues and try out new behaviors.

- *It enables people to see that others share their problems*. It can be a relief to discover that others have experienced similar stressors, troublesome feelings, and behaviors (Rahman et al., 2019).

- *It provides feedback as clients try out new ways of behaving*. Hearing that you look or sound poised, even though you feel anxious and self-conscious, can be very reassuring—and the presence of others can promote accountability.

## Family Therapy

*"We are communicating better, but we are still not out of the woods."*

One special type of group interaction, **family therapy**, assumes that no person is an island. Our social and cultural environments (the *social-cultural perspective*) form us. We live and grow in relation to others, especially our family. We struggle to differentiate ourselves from our families, but also need to connect with them emotionally. These two opposing tendencies can create stress for both the individual and the family.

Family therapists view families as systems, in which each person's actions trigger reactions from others. A child's rebellion, for example, affects and is affected by other family tensions. Therapists are often successful in helping family members identify their roles within the family's social system, improve communication, and discover new ways of preventing or resolving conflicts (Hazelrigg et al., 1987; Shadish et al., 1993).

**group therapy** therapy conducted with groups rather than individuals, providing benefits from group interaction.

**family therapy** therapy that treats people in the context of their family system. Views an individual's unwanted behaviors as influenced by, or directed at, other family members.

**Family therapy** As a preventive mental health strategy, family therapy includes *couples therapy*, as shown here at a retreat for U.S. military families. The therapist helps family members understand how their ways of relating to one another create problems. The treatment's emphasis is not only on changing the individuals, but also on changing their relationships and interactions. Couples therapy often increases emotional intimacy, healthy communication, and relationship satisfaction (Roddy et al., 2020).

## Self-Help Groups

More than 100 million Americans have belonged to religious, special-interest, or support groups that meet regularly—with 9 in 10 reporting that group members "support each other emotionally" (Gallup, 1994). Self-help groups often provide support to people who struggle to find it elsewhere (Dingle et al., 2021). One analysis of more than 14,000 self-help groups reported that most focus on stigmatized, hard-to-discuss problems (Davison et al., 2000).

Many self-help groups use a 12-step program modeled on that of Alcoholics Anonymous (AA), the grandparent of support groups and "the largest organization on Earth that nobody wanted to join" (Finlay, 2000). Such a program asks members to admit their powerlessness, to seek help from a higher power and from one another, and (the twelfth step) to take the message to others in need of it (Galanter, 2016). Studies of 12-step programs such as AA have found that they help reduce alcohol use disorder at rates comparable to other treatment interventions (Ferri et al., 2006; Moos & Moos, 2005). An 8-year, $27 million investigation found that AA participants reduced their drinking sharply, as did those assigned to CBT or an alternative therapy (Project Match, 1997). The more meetings AA members attend, the greater their alcohol abstinence is (Moos & Moos, 2006). Those whose personal stories include a "redemptive narrative"—who see something good as having come from their struggles—more often sustain sobriety (Dunlop & Tracy, 2013).

In an individualist age, with more and more people living alone or feeling isolated, the popularity of support groups—for the addicted, the bereaved, the divorced, or simply those seeking fellowship and growth—may reflect a longing for community and connectedness.

\* \* \*

For a synopsis of these modern psychotherapies, see **Table 5.5-2**.

**AP® Science Practice**

### Data

Research shows that the more meetings AA members attend, the greater their alcohol abstinence is. This finding represents a positive correlation: The two variables increase (or decrease) together. Using data that you make up, can you create a scatterplot to depict this relationship?

**AP® Exam Tip**

Review Table 5.5-2. You'll want to be able to compare and contrast the psychotherapies.

| TABLE 5.5-2 **Comparing Modern Psychotherapies** | | | |
| --- | --- | --- | --- |
| **Therapy** | **Presumed Problem** | **Therapy Aim** | **Therapy Technique** |
| *Psychodynamic* | Unconscious conflicts from childhood experiences | Reduce anxiety through self-insight. | Interpret clients' memories, dreams, and feelings. |
| *Person-centered* | Barriers to self-understanding and self-acceptance | Enable growth via unconditional positive regard, acceptance, genuineness, and empathy. | Listen actively and reflect clients' feelings. |
| *Behavior* | Dysfunctional behaviors | Learn adaptive behaviors; extinguish problem ones. | Use classical conditioning (via exposure or aversion therapy) or operant conditioning (as in token economies). |
| *Cognitive* | Negative, self-defeating thinking | Promote healthier thinking and self-talk. | Train people to dispute their negative thoughts and attributions. |
| *Cognitive-behavioral* | Self-harmful thoughts and behaviors | Promote healthier thinking and adaptive behaviors. | Train people to counter self-harmful thoughts and to act out their new ways of thinking. |
| *Group and family* | Stressful relationships | Heal relationships. | Develop an understanding of family and other social systems, explore roles, and improve communication. |

## Check Your Understanding

**Examine the Concept**

▶ Describe how person-centered and cognitive therapies differ.

▶ Describe *cognitive-behavioral therapy*. What sorts of problems does this therapy best address?

▶ Describe some benefits of group therapy.

*Answers to the Examine the Concept questions can be found in Appendix C at the end of the book.*

**Apply the Concept**

▶ Have you ever struggled to reach a goal because of your own self-defeating thoughts? How could you challenge those thoughts?

# Module 5.5b REVIEW

**5.5-4 How does the basic assumption of behavior therapy differ from the assumptions of psychodynamic and humanistic therapies? What classical conditioning techniques are used in exposure therapies and aversive conditioning?**

- *Behavior therapies* are not insight therapies, but instead assume that problem behaviors *are* the problem. Their goal is to apply learning principles to modify these problem behaviors.

- Classical conditioning techniques, including *exposure therapies* (such as *systematic desensitization* and *virtual reality exposure therapy*) and *aversive conditioning*, attempt to change behaviors through *counterconditioning*—evoking new responses to old stimuli that trigger unwanted behaviors.

**5.5-5 What is the main premise of behavior therapy based on operant conditioning principles, and what are the views of its proponents and critics?**

- Operant conditioning assumes that voluntary behaviors are strongly influenced by their consequences. Therapy based on operant conditioning principles therefore uses behavior modification techniques to change unwanted behaviors by positively reinforcing desired behaviors and ignoring or punishing undesirable behaviors.

- Critics maintain that (1) techniques such as those used in *token economies* may produce behavior changes that disappear when rewards end, and (2) deciding which behaviors should change is authoritarian and unethical.

- Proponents argue that treatment with positive rewards is more humane than punishing people or institutionalizing them for undesired behaviors.

**5.5-6 What are the goals and techniques of the cognitive therapies and of cognitive-behavioral therapy?**

- The *cognitive therapies*, such as Aaron Beck's cognitive therapy for depression, assume that our thinking colors our feelings, and that the therapist's role is to change clients' self-defeating thinking by training them to perceive and interpret events in more constructive ways.

- *Rational-emotive behavior therapy (REBT)* is a confrontational cognitive therapy that actively challenges irrational beliefs.

- The widely researched and practiced *cognitive-behavioral therapy (CBT)* combines cognitive therapy and behavior therapy by helping clients regularly try out their new ways of thinking and behaving in their everyday life.

- A newer CBT variation, dialectical behavior therapy (DBT), combines cognitive tactics for tolerating distress and regulating emotions with social skills training and mindfulness meditation.

**5.5-7 What are the aims and benefits of group and family therapies?**

- *Group therapy* sessions can help more people at a lower cost compared to individual therapy. Clients may benefit in person or online from exploring feelings and developing social skills in a group situation, from learning that others have similar problems, and from getting feedback on new ways of behaving.

- *Family therapy* aims to help family members discover the roles they play within the family's interactive social system, improve communication, and learn new ways to prevent or resolve conflicts.

# AP® Practice Multiple Choice Questions

**1.** Dr. Welle helps her clients by teaching them to modify the way they think when they are under stress or when they are experiencing symptoms. What form of therapy does Dr. Welle most likely practice?

a. Behavioral
b. Cognitive
c. Group
d. Family

**Use the following graph to answer questions 2 and 3:**

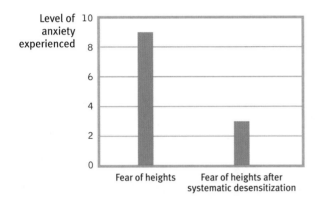

**2.** What form of therapy is depicted in the graph?

a. Cognitive
b. Group
c. Family
d. Behavioral

**3.** Which of the following best describes the trends in the variables as depicted by the data in the graph?

a. The participants' anxiety decreased after they were repeatedly exposed to heights while practicing relaxation techniques.
b. The participants' anxiety increased after they were repeatedly exposed to heights while practicing relaxation techniques.
c. The participants' anxiety decreased after they were repeatedly exposed to heights while undergoing aversive conditioning.
d. The participants' anxiety increased after they were repeatedly exposed to heights while undergoing aversive conditioning.

**4.** Jayne has been diagnosed with major depressive disorder. Her therapist suggested that she interact with her friends more frequently, and she helped Jayne learn how to decrease her worries about whether her friends want to be around her. What form of therapy is Jayne's therapist using?

a. Cognitive-behavioral therapy
b. Group therapy
c. Rational-emotive behavior therapy
d. Behavior modification

**5.** Dr. Laremy meets with adolescents and their parents together to help them develop effective communication strategies. What form of therapy does Dr. Laremy use?

a. Self-help
b. Cognitive-behavioral
c. Dialectical behavioral
d. Family

**6.** Dr. Mehari believes that the best way to treat clients is to use active listening and to help clients gain self-acceptance, while Dr. Rodriguez believes that the best way to treat clients is to help them change their thoughts and behaviors. Which statement is most accurate about Dr. Mehari's and Dr. Rodriguez's preferred therapy?

a. Dr. Mehari prefers psychodynamic therapy, while Dr. Rodriguez prefers cognitive-behavioral therapy.
b. Dr. Mehari prefers person-centered therapy, while Dr. Rodriguez prefers cognitive-behavioral therapy.
c. Dr. Mehari prefers person-centered therapy, while Dr. Rodriguez prefers cognitive therapy.
d. Dr. Mehari prefers psychodynamic therapy, while Dr. Rodriguez prefers behavioral therapy.

**7.** Javi's parents give him a marble each day he completes his homework. He can exchange marbles for privileges, such as a later weekend bedtime or a trip to the ice-cream store. Which of the following is described in this example?

a. Aversive conditioning
b. Token economy
c. Acceptance and commitment therapy
d. Systematic desensitization

**8.** Which of the following scenarios best illustrates the concept of counterconditioning?

   a. Kendall's fear of flying gradually diminishes after he takes several flights without experiencing any turbulence.

   b. Roman's dislike for broccoli increases over time because he always has to eat it as part of his meals.

   c. Jerri's fear of dogs intensifies after a negative encounter with an aggressive dog at a park.

   d. Logan's preference for chocolate decreases when he repeatedly pairs its consumption with a foul taste.

**9.** After repeatedly drinking an alcoholic drink mixed with a drug that produces severe nausea, Xander, who has a history of alcohol use disorder, developed a temporary conditioned aversion to alcohol. In this example of aversive conditioning, the nausea-producing drug is the

   a. UCS, because it naturally elicits the response.

   b. CS, because it naturally elicits the response.

   c. UCS, because the association must be learned in order to elicit the response.

   d. CS, because the association must be learned in order to elicit the response.

# Module 5.5c   Treatment of Psychological Disorders: Evaluating Psychotherapies

## LEARNING TARGETS

**5.5-8**   Describe the effectiveness of psychotherapy and explain how we can make this judgment.

**5.5-9**   Describe which psychotherapies are more effective for specific disorders.

**5.5-10**   Describe the three elements shared by all forms of psychotherapy.

**5.5-11**   Describe the personal factors that influence the therapist-client relationship.

**5.5-12**   Explain when a person should seek therapy, and describe what people should look for when selecting a therapist.

**5.5-13**   Describe the ethical principles that guide psychotherapy.

Many people have great confidence in psychotherapy's effectiveness. "Seek counseling" or "Ask your mate to find a therapist," advice columnists often urge. Before 1950, psychiatrists were the primary providers of mental health care. Today's providers include clinical and counseling psychologists; clinical social workers; pastoral, marital, abuse, and school counselors; and psychiatric nurses. With such an enormous outlay of time as well as money and effort, it is important to ask: Are the millions of people worldwide justified in placing their hopes in psychotherapy?

# Is Psychotherapy Effective?

> **5.5-8** Does psychotherapy work? How can we know?

This question, though simply put, is not simply answered. If an infection quickly clears, we may assume an antibiotic has been effective. But how can we assess psychotherapy's effectiveness? By how we feel about our progress? By how our therapist feels about it? By how our friends and family feel about it? By how our behavior has changed?

## Client Perceptions

If client testimonials were the only measuring stick, we could strongly affirm psychotherapy's effectiveness. Consider one early survey of 2900 people who related their experiences with mental health professionals (*Consumer Reports*, 1995; Kotkin et al., 1996; Seligman, 1995). How many were at least "fairly well satisfied"? Almost 90 percent (as was Kay Redfield Jamison, as we saw at this module's beginning). Among those who recalled feeling *fair* or *very poor* when beginning therapy, 9 in 10 now were feeling *very good*, *good*, or at least *so-so*. Worldwide, most people report benefiting from psychotherapy (Stein et al., 2020). We have clients' word for it—and who should know better?

We should not dismiss these testimonials. But consider some reasons for skepticism:

- **People often enter therapy in crisis**. When, with the normal ebb and flow of events, the crisis passes, people may attribute their improvement to the therapy. Depressed people often get better no matter what they do.

- **Clients believe that treatment will be effective**. The *placebo effect* is the healing power of positive expectations.

- **Clients generally speak kindly of their therapists**. Even if the problems remain, clients "work hard to find something positive to say. The therapist had been very understanding, the client had gained a new perspective, he learned to communicate better, his mind was eased, anything at all so as not to have to say treatment was a failure" (Zilbergeld, 1983, p. 117).

- **Clients want to believe the therapy was worth the effort**. If you invested time and money in something, wouldn't you be motivated to find something positive about it? Psychologists call this *effort justification*.

## Clinician Perceptions

If clinician perceptions were proof of therapy's effectiveness, we would have even more reason to celebrate. Case studies of successful treatment abound. The problem is that clients enter psychotherapy focused on their unhappiness and leave it focused on their well-being. Therapists treasure compliments from those clients saying good-bye or later expressing their gratitude. But they hear little from clients who experience only temporary relief and seek out new therapists for their recurring problems. Thus, therapists are most aware of the failures of *other* therapists. With the same recurring anxieties, depression, or marital difficulty, the same person may be a "success" story in several therapists' files. Moreover, therapists, like the rest of us, are vulnerable to cognitive errors. **Confirmation bias** can lead them to unconsciously seek evidence that confirms their beliefs and to ignore contradictory evidence, and *illusory correlations* can lead them to perceive associations that don't really exist (Lilienfeld et al., 2015b). Thus, clients may seem to verify their therapists' theories.

**confirmation bias** a tendency to search for information that supports our preconceptions and to ignore or distort contradictory evidence.

**meta-analysis** a statistical procedure for analyzing the results of multiple studies to reach an overall conclusion.

## Outcome Research

How, then, can we objectively measure the effectiveness of psychotherapy? What *outcomes* can we expect—what types of people and problems are helped, and by what type of psychotherapy?

In search of answers, psychologists have turned to the well-traveled path of controlled research. Similar research in the 1800s transformed the field of medicine when skeptical physicians began to realize that many patients were dying despite receiving then-mainstream treatments (such as bloodletting), and many others were getting better on their own. Sorting fact from superstition required observing patients and recording outcomes with and without a particular treatment. Patients with typhoid fever, for example, often improved after being bled, convincing most physicians that the treatment worked. Then came the shock. A control group was given mere bed rest, and after five weeks of fever, 70 percent improved, showing that the bloodletting was worthless (Thomas, 1992).

A similar shock—and a spirited debate—followed the summary of 24 studies of psychotherapy outcomes (Eysenck, 1952). Two-thirds of people who received psychotherapy for disorders not involving hallucinations or delusions improved markedly. To this day, no one disputes that optimistic estimate. But there was a catch: Similar improvement occurred among people who were *untreated*, such as those on treatment waiting lists. With or without psychotherapy, roughly two-thirds improved noticeably. Time was a great healer.

Later research revealed shortcomings in the summary's analyses and methods. The sample was small—only 24 outcome studies in 1952, compared with thousands available today. The best of these are *randomized clinical trials*, in which researchers randomly assign people on a waiting list to therapy or to no therapy. Later, they evaluate everyone and compare outcomes, using tests and assessments done by others who don't know whether therapy was given.

A glimpse of psychotherapy's overall effectiveness can then be provided by means of a **meta-analysis**, a statistical procedure that combines the conclusions of a large number of different studies. Simply said, a meta-analysis summarizes lots of studies' results. Therapists welcomed the first meta-analysis of some 475 psychotherapy outcome studies (Smith et al., 1980). It showed that the average client who receives therapy ends up better off than 80 percent of the untreated individuals on waiting lists (**Figure 5.5-4**). Psychologist Mary Lee Smith and her colleagues summed it up: "Psychotherapy benefits people of all ages as reliably as schooling educates them, medicine cures them, or business turns a profit" (p. 183).

### Figure 5.5-4

**Treatment versus no treatment**

These two normal distribution curves based on data from 475 studies show the improvement of untreated people and clients receiving psychotherapy. The outcome for the average client receiving therapy surpassed the outcomes for 80 percent of the untreated people. (Data from Smith et al., 1980.)

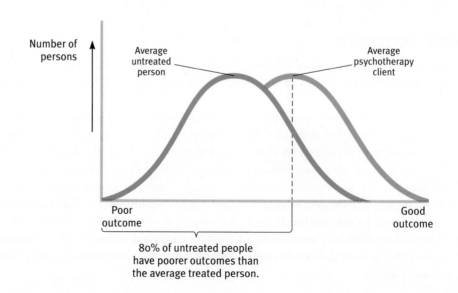

Dozens of subsequent summaries have replicated the older outcome studies: *People not undergoing therapy often improve, but those undergoing therapy are more likely to improve—and to improve more quickly and with less risk of relapse* (Eckshtain et al., 2020; Weisz et al., 2017). (One qualification: Compared with studies that find no therapy benefit, those that do find a positive therapy effect are more likely to get published [Driessen et al., 2015].) After therapy, many people exhibit improved insight and emotional awareness, with a more patient, outgoing personality (Høglend & Hagtvet, 2019; Roberts et al., 2017). Some people with depression or anxiety also experience sudden symptom reductions between their treatment sessions (Aderka et al., 2012). Those *sudden gains* bode well for long-term improvement (Shalom & Aderka, 2020).

Psychotherapy also can be cost-effective. Studies show that when people seek psychological treatment, their search for other medical treatment drops substantially—by 16 percent in one digest of 91 studies (Chiles et al., 1999). Substance abuse and other psychological disorders exert a staggering cost on society, including crime, accidents, and lost work. By one estimate, the opioid epidemic cost the United States more than $1 trillion between 2001 and 2017 (Altarum, 2018). Given such costs, psychotherapy is a good investment, much like investing time and money in healthy foods and exercise (Johnson et al., 2019). Both *reduce* long-term costs. Boosting employees' psychological well-being can lower medical costs, improve work efficiency, and decrease absenteeism. It's no wonder that U.S. health insurers and the National Health Service in Britain have increasingly funded psychotherapy (Hockenberry et al., 2019; NHS, 2020).

But note that the claim—that psychotherapy, *on average*, is somewhat effective—refers to no one therapy in particular. It is like reassuring patients with lung cancer that "on average," medical treatment of health problems is effective. What people want to know is whether a *particular* treatment is effective for their specific problem.

**Trauma** People who experience trauma, such as these women in China mourning the devastating loss of lives and homes in the 2010 Yushu earthquake, may benefit from counseling. But many people recover on their own or with the help of supportive relationships with family and friends. "Life itself still remains a very effective therapist," noted psychodynamic therapist Karen Horney (*Our Inner Conflicts*, 1945).

## Which Psychotherapies Work Best?

**5.5-9** Are some psychotherapies more effective than others for specific disorders?

The early statistical summaries and surveys did not find that any one type of psychotherapy is generally better than others (Smith & Glass, 1977; Smith et al., 1980). Later studies have similarly found that clients can benefit from psychotherapy regardless of their clinicians' experience, training, supervision, and licensing (Cuijpers, 2017; Kivlighan et al., 2015; Wampold et al., 2017). A *Consumer Reports* survey found the same result (Seligman, 1995). Were clients treated by a psychiatrist, psychologist, marriage counselor, or other mental health professional? Were they seen in a group or an individual context? Did the therapist have extensive or relatively limited training and experience? It didn't matter.

So, was *Alice in Wonderland's* dodo bird right: "Everyone has won and all must have prizes"? Not quite. One general finding emerges from the studies: The more specific the problem, the greater the hope that psychotherapy might solve it (Singer, 1981; Westen & Morrison, 2001). Individuals who experience panic or specific phobias, who are unassertive, or who are frustrated by sexual performance problems can hope for improvement. Those with less-focused problems, such as depression and anxiety, usually benefit in the short term but often relapse later.

Nevertheless, some forms of therapy do get prizes for effectively treating *particular* problems. As an English proverb says, "Different sores have different salves."

- *Cognitive and cognitive-behavioral therapies*—primarily anxiety, posttraumatic stress disorder, insomnia, and depression (Qaseem et al., 2016; Scaini et al., 2016; Tolin, 2010).

- *Behavioral conditioning therapies*—behavior problems such as bed-wetting, specific phobias, compulsions, marital difficulties, and sexual dysfunctions (Baker et al., 2008; Hunsley & DiGiulio, 2002; Shadish & Baldwin, 2005).

**AP® Science Practice**

### Data

Studies show that when people seek psychological treatment, their search for other medical treatment drops. This represents a negative correlation. As one variable increases (seeking psychological treatment), the other decreases (seeking medical treatment). Using data you make up, create a scatterplot to depict this relationship.

- *Psychodynamic therapy*—depression and anxiety (Driessen et al., 2010; Leichsenring & Rabung, 2008; Shedler, 2010). Some analyses suggest that psychodynamic therapy and cognitive-behavioral therapy are equally effective in reducing depression (Driessen et al., 2017; Steinert et al., 2017).

- *Nondirective (person-centered) counseling*—mild to moderate depression (Cuijpers et al., 2012).

The tendency of many disordered states of mind to return to better health, combined with the placebo effect (the healing power of mere belief in a treatment), creates fertile soil for pseudotherapies. No prizes—and no scientific support—go to certain alternative therapies (Arkowitz & Lilienfeld, 2006; Lilienfeld et al., 2015a). We would all be wise to avoid therapies that propose to manipulate invisible "energy fields," therapies that reenact the supposed trauma of a client's birth, and therapies that use touch to "facilitate" communication with noncommunicative people.

Like some pseudomedical treatments, some pseudopsychological treatments are not only ineffective but actually harmful. The American Psychiatric Association, the Canadian Psychological Association, and the British Psychological Society have warned against conversion therapies that purport to change people's gender identity or sexual orientation. These therapies aim to "repair . . . something that is not a mental illness and therefore does not require therapy," declared American Psychological Association president Barry Anton (2015). Indeed, conversion therapy entails "a significant risk of harm" (APA, 2018; Turban et al., 2020). Such evidence has led to many conversion therapy bans, especially for minors. Other initiatives—the Scared Straight program designed to tame teenage delinquency, weight-reduction programs, and pedophile rehabilitation efforts—have also proven unsuccessful (Walton & Wilson, 2018).

The evaluation question—which therapies get prizes and which do not?—lies at the heart of what some call psychology's civil war. To what extent should science guide both clinical practice and insurers' willingness to pay for psychotherapy? On one side are research psychologists using scientific methods to extend the list of well-defined and validated therapies for various disorders. They decry clinicians who seem to "give more weight to their personal experience than to science" (Baker et al., 2008). On the other side are some nonscientist therapists who view their practice more as an art, arguing that people are too complex and psychotherapy is too intuitive to describe in a manual or test in an experiment.

Between these two factions stand the science-oriented clinicians calling for **evidence-based practice**, which has been endorsed by the American Psychological Association (APA) and others (APA, 2006; Holmes et al., 2018; Sakaluk et al., 2019; **Figure 5.5-5**). After rigorous evaluation, clinicians apply therapies suited to their own skills and their clients' unique situations. Some are using technology, too. By analyzing many pieces of clients' information, computer programs can help clinicians offer personalized therapeutic solutions (Ewbank et al., 2019; Webb et al., 2020). Increasingly, insurer and government support for mental health services requires evidence-based practice.

**Figure 5.5-5**

**Evidence-based practice**

Ideal clinical decision making can be visualized as a three-legged stool, upheld by research evidence, clinical expertise, and knowledge of the client.

**AP® Science Practice**

**Research**

Psychology's conclusions are based on scientifically derived evidence. Evidence-based practice offers treatments that have research support.

**evidence-based practice**
clinical decision making that integrates the best available research with clinical expertise and client characteristics and preferences.

## How Do Psychotherapies Help People?

**5.5-10** What three elements are shared by all forms of psychotherapy?

Why have studies found little correlation between therapists' training and experience and clients' outcomes? One answer seems to be that all psychotherapies offer three basic benefits (Cuijpers et al., 2019; Frank, 1982; Wampold, 2007):

- *Hope for discouraged people* People seeking therapy typically feel anxious, depressed, self-disapproving, and incapable of turning things around. What any psychotherapy offers is the expectation that, with commitment from the therapy seeker, things can and will get better. This belief, apart from any therapy technique, may improve morale, create feelings of self-efficacy, and diminish symptoms (Corrigan, 2014; Meyerhoff & Rohan, 2016).

- *A new perspective* Every psychotherapy offers people a plausible explanation of their symptoms. Armed with a believable fresh perspective, they may approach life with a new attitude, open to making changes in their behaviors and their views of themselves.

- *An empathic, trusting, caring relationship* No matter what technique they use, effective therapists are empathic. They seek to understand the client's experience. They communicate care and concern, and they earn trust through respectful listening and guidance (Ovenstad et al., 2020). These qualities were clear in recorded therapy sessions from 36 recognized master therapists (Goldfried et al., 1998). Some took a cognitive-behavioral approach. Others used psychodynamic principles. Although the master therapists used different approaches, they showed some striking *similarities*. They helped clients evaluate themselves, link one aspect of their life with another, and gain insight into their interactions with others. The emotional bond between therapist and client—the **therapeutic alliance**—helps explain why empathic, caring therapists are especially effective (Flückiger et al., 2020). Whether experienced in Canada or Cambodia, a strong therapeutic alliance fosters psychological health (Falkenström et al., 2019; Gold, 2019). It may even save lives. In one analysis of a dozen studies, a strong therapeutic alliance predicted less frequent suicidal thoughts, self-harming behaviors, and suicide attempts (Dunster-Page et al., 2017).

**therapeutic alliance** a bond of trust and mutual understanding between a therapist and client, who work together constructively to overcome the client's problem.

These three common elements—hope, a fresh perspective, and an empathic, caring relationship—help us understand why *paraprofessionals* (briefly trained caregivers) can assist many troubled people so effectively (Bryan & Arkowitz, 2015; Christensen & Jacobson, 1994). They are also part of what the growing number of in-person and online self-help and support groups offer their members. And they are part of what traditional healers have offered (Jackson, 1992). Healers everywhere—special people to whom others disclose their suffering, whether psychiatrists or shamans—have listened to understand and to empathize, reassure, advise, console, interpret, or explain (Torrey, 1986). Such qualities may explain why people who feel supported by close relationships—who enjoy the fellowship and friendship of caring people—have been less likely to seek therapy (Frank, 1982; O'Connor & Brown, 1984).

*"The thing is, you have to really want to change."*

* * *

To recap, people who seek help usually improve. So do many of those who do not, which is a tribute to our human resourcefulness and our capacity to care for one another. Nevertheless, though the therapist's orientation and experience appear not to matter much, people who receive some psychotherapy usually improve more than those who do not. People with clear-cut, specific problems tend to improve the most.

**Friendship bench** Some Zimbabwe health clinics have added outdoor "friendship benches," where paraprofessional community health workers offer therapy (Chibanda et al., 2016). Psychiatrist Dixon Chibanda created this free therapy for rural communities after a client, lacking bus fare to get to his office, died by suicide. "We have to take [psychiatry] to the community," Chibanda said (Rosenberg, 2019).

# Check Your Understanding

**Examine the Concept**

▶ Describe how the *placebo effect* can bias clients' and clinicians' appraisals of the effectiveness of psychotherapies.

▶ What is *evidence-based practice*?

▶ Describe the three elements that are shared by all forms of psychotherapy.

*Answers to the Examine the Concept questions can be found in Appendix C at the end of the book.*

**Apply the Concept**

▶ Based on what you've read, would you seek therapy if you were struggling with a problem? Why or why not? If you've experienced therapy, how does what you've learned alter your feelings about the experience?

# Human Diversity and Psychotherapy

> **5.5-11** What personal factors influence the therapist-client relationship?

All psychotherapies offer hope. Nearly all psychotherapists attempt to enhance their clients' sensitivity, openness, personal responsibility, and sense of purpose (Jensen & Bergin, 1988). But in matters of culture, values, and personal identity, psychotherapists differ from one another and may differ from their clients (Delaney et al., 2007; Kelly, 1990).

These differences can create a mismatch—for example, when a therapist from one culture interacts with a client from another. In North America, Europe, and Australia, most psychotherapists reflect their culture's *individualism*, which often gives priority to personal desires and identity. Clients with a *collectivist* perspective, including many from Asian cultures, may be more mindful of social and family responsibilities, harmony, and group goals. These clients may have trouble relating to therapists who ask them to think only of their own well-being (Markus & Kitayama, 1991). In one experiment, Asian American clients matched with counselors who shared their cultural values (rather than mismatched with those who did not) perceived more counselor empathy and felt a stronger alliance with the counselor (Kim et al., 2005).

**Shared values** Psychotherapy works best when clients and therapists have matching cultural values.

Client-therapist mismatches may also stem from other personal differences. For example, highly religious people may prefer and benefit from religiously similar therapists who share their values and beliefs (Masters, 2010; Pearce et al., 2015).

Cultural differences help explain some groups' reluctance to use mental health services. People living in "cultures of honor" prize being strong and tough. They may feel that seeking mental health care is an admission of weakness rather than an opportunity for growth (Brown et al., 2014). Refugees, despite having frequently endured trauma and discrimination, tend to avoid seeking mental health services due to distrust, poverty, and language barriers (Byrow et al., 2020). And some cultural groups tend to be both reluctant to seek therapy and quick to leave it (Chen et al., 2009; Sue et al., 2009).

The bottom line: By building their *cultural competence*—understanding and respecting different cultural groups' values, beliefs, and traditions—therapists can better serve their clients (Soto et al., 2018).

# Seeking Psychotherapy

**5.5-12** When should a person seek therapy, and what should people look for when selecting a therapist?

Life for everyone is marked by a mix of serenity and stress, blessing and bereavement, good moods and bad. So, when should we seek a mental health professional's help? The APA offers this list of common trouble signals:

- Feelings of hopelessness
- Deep and lasting depression
- Self-destructive behavior, such as substance abuse and self-injury
- Disruptive fears
- Sudden mood shifts
- Thoughts of suicide
- Compulsive rituals, such as hand washing
- Hearing voices or seeing things that others don't experience

When looking for a therapist, you may want to have a preliminary consultation with two or three therapists. Meeting with more than one gives you more opportunities to find someone with whom you feel comfortable. High school counseling offices are generally good starting points.

Many people also use the internet to search for therapists, and many receive help online or via one of the more than 10,000 mental health apps (Kocsis, 2018; Levin et al., 2018; Nielssen et al., 2019). Therapist-guided, online and app-based therapy can help reduce depression, social anxiety disorder, and panic disorder (Niles et al., 2021). Being able to meet with an online therapist has helped people who—because of their location, income, or embarrassment—may struggle to attend in-person sessions (Dadds et al., 2019; Markowitz et al., 2021). Such online therapy also offered a useful alternative solution when it was unsafe to attend in-person therapy sessions during the Covid pandemic.

During your in-person or online meetings, you can describe your problem and learn about each therapist's treatment approach. You can ask questions about the therapist's values, credentials (**Table 5.5-3**), and fees. And you can assess your own feelings about each therapist. The emotional bond between therapist and client is perhaps the most important factor in effective therapy.

| TABLE 5.5-3 | Therapists and Their Training |
|---|---|
| **Type** | **Therapy Description** |
| *Clinical psychologists* | Most are psychologists with a Ph.D. (includes research training) or Psy.D. (focuses on therapy) supplemented by a supervised internship and, often, postdoctoral training. About half work in agencies and institutions, half in private practice. |
| *Psychiatrists* | Psychiatrists are physicians who specialize in the treatment of psychological disorders. Not all psychiatrists have had extensive training in psychotherapy, but as M.D.s or D.O.s they can prescribe medications. Thus, they tend to see those individuals with the most serious problems. Many have their own private practice. |
| *Clinical or psychiatric social workers* | A two-year master of social work graduate program plus postgraduate supervision prepares some social workers to offer psychotherapy, mostly to people with everyday personal and family problems. About half in the United States have earned the National Association of Social Workers' designation of clinical social worker. |
| *Counselors* | Family and couples counselors specialize in problems arising from family relations. Clergy provide counseling to countless people. Counselors may work with people with substance use disorders and with spouse and child abusers and victims of abuse. Mental health and other counselors may be required to have a two-year master's degree. |

The APA recognizes the importance of a strong therapeutic alliance, and it welcomes diverse therapists who can relate well to diverse clients. It accredits programs that provide training in cultural sensitivity (for example, differing values, communication styles, and language) and that recruit underrepresented cultural groups.

# Ethical Principles in Psychotherapy

**5.5-13** What ethical principles guide psychotherapy?

**Therapy for all** Therapy was once available only for the wealthy and well-connected. Teletherapy, low-cost and no-cost community programs, and mental health apps have put help just a few clicks away.

Psychotherapists use different approaches to help reduce their clients' suffering. But before psychotherapists begin their treatment, they must follow their country's ethical principles and code of conduct (APA, 2017).

According to the American Psychological Association, your therapist should follow these principles:

- *Beneficence and nonmaleficence* Seek to benefit you (*beneficence*) and do you no harm (*nonmaleficence*).
- *Fidelity and responsibility* Establish a feeling of trust and a defined role as your therapist, uphold a professional standard of conduct, and be of service to the therapeutic community.
- *Integrity* Be honest, truthful, and accurate.
- *Justice* Be fair and promote justice for you and others, helping everyone to have access to the benefits of therapy.
- *Respect for people's rights and dignity* Respect the dignity and worth of you and others, recognizing the right to privacy, confidentiality, and self-determination.

AP® Science Practice

## Check Your Understanding

**Examine the Concept**

▶ Describe the ethical principles for therapists set forth by the American Psychological Association.

**Apply the Concept**

▶ How might your culture and values influence the sort of therapy you would welcome — or your willingness to seek therapy at all?

*Answers to the Examine the Concept questions can be found in Appendix C at the end of the book.*

## Module 5.5c REVIEW

### 5.5-8 Does psychotherapy work? How can we know?

- Clients' and therapists' positive testimonials cannot prove that therapy is effective, and the placebo effect and *confirmation bias* makes it difficult to judge whether improvement occurred because of the treatment.

- Using *meta-analyses* to statistically combine the results of hundreds of randomized psychotherapy outcome studies, researchers have found that individuals with disorders who do not receive treatment often improve, but those who undergo psychotherapy are more likely to improve — and to improve more quickly and with less risk of relapse.

### 5.5-9 Are some psychotherapies more effective than others for specific disorders?

- No one type of psychotherapy is generally superior to all others. Therapy is most effective for individuals with clear-cut, specific problems.

- Some therapies are more effective for specific disorders. Cognitive and cognitive-behavioral therapies have been effective in helping clients cope with anxiety, posttraumatic stress disorder, insomnia, and depression; behavioral conditioning therapies in treating behavior problems such as bed-wetting, specific phobias, compulsions, and sexual dysfunctions; psychodynamic therapy for clients with depression and anxiety; and nondirective (person-centered) counseling for clients with mild to moderate depression.

- Abnormal states tend to return to normal on their own, and the placebo effect can create the impression that a treatment has been effective.

- *Evidence-based practice* integrates the best available research with clinicians' expertise and clients' unique circumstances.

### 5.5-10 What three elements are shared by all forms of psychotherapy?

- All psychotherapies offer new hope for discouraged people; a fresh perspective; and (if the therapist is effective) an empathic, trusting, and caring relationship.

- The emotional bond of trust and understanding between therapist and client—the *therapeutic alliance*—is an important element in effective therapy.

### 5.5-11 What personal factors influence the therapist-client relationship?

- Therapists differ both from one another and from their clients in culture, values, and personal identity. These differences—in cultural background, religiosity, or attitudes toward LGBTQ people, for example—may create a mismatch between therapists' and clients' goals and priorities. By building their cultural competence, therapists can better serve diverse clients.

### 5.5-12 When should a person seek therapy, and what should people look for when selecting a therapist?

- People should seek professional help if they experience feelings of hopelessness, deep and lasting depression, self-destructive behavior, disruptive fears, sudden mood shifts, suicidal thoughts, compulsive rituals, or hearing or seeing things that others don't.

- High school counseling offices are generally good starting points for counseling options, and they may offer some free services. Many people also find therapists, and may meet with a therapist, online or via a mental health app.

- A person seeking therapy may want to ask about the therapist's treatment approach, values, credentials, and fees. An important consideration is whether the therapy seeker feels comfortable and able to establish a bond with the therapist.

- Recognizing the importance of a strong therapeutic alliance, the American Psychological Association accredits programs that provide training in cultural sensitivity and that recruit underrepresented cultural groups.

### 5.5-13 What ethical principles guide psychotherapy?

- Psychotherapists must follow their country's ethical principles and code of conduct.

- According to the APA, therapists should aim to uphold certain principles, including to benefit others and do no harm (*beneficence* and *nonmaleficence*); to be honest, truthful, and accurate (*fidelity* and *responsibility*); to establish trust (*integrity*); to be fair and promote justice for their clients and others (*justice*); and to respect clients' dignity, including their rights to privacy, confidentiality, and self-determination (*respect for people's rights and dignity*).

## AP® Practice Multiple Choice Questions

1. Greta recently participated in a study of people with major depressive disorder. After spending two weeks on a 100-person waitlist for therapy, she and 49 others were randomly assigned to receive therapy. The remaining 50 people received no therapy. Later, all participants were evaluated and their symptoms assessed by a team of psychologists who did not know who had or had not received treatment. In what type of study did Greta participate?
   a. Meta-analysis
   b. Normal distribution
   c. Randomized clinical trial
   d. Evidence-based practice

2. Having recently become a therapist, Waylan feels motivated to tell his friends about the research on the effectiveness of psychotherapy. Which of the following would be the most accurate statement Waylan could say to his friends?
   a. The average client who receives therapy sees greater improvement than 80 percent of untreated individuals.
   b. Psychotherapy causes improvement in 80 percent of individuals who have sought therapy.
   c. Clients who receive psychotherapy are no more likely to improve than individuals who have not sought therapy.
   d. The average client who receives psychotherapy is 90 percent satisfied with their experience in therapy.

3. Dr. Omesh is conducting an experiment investigating the relationship between the therapist-client bond and the extent to which clients are able to overcome their difficulties. Which of the following is most likely Dr. Omesh's independent variable?
   a. Therapeutic alliance
   b. Hope
   c. New perspective
   d. Fidelity

4. Knowing that you have taken AP® Psychology, a friend asks your opinion about which type of psychotherapy she should consider to help her overcome anxiety. What would be your advice?
   a. Psychodynamic therapy is best for anxiety.
   b. Behavioral therapy has achieved the best outcomes when treating different types of anxiety.
   c. Cognitive and cognitive-behavioral therapies have demonstrated effectiveness for treating anxiety.
   d. It does not matter what type of psychotherapy she chooses, because anxiety can only be treated with medication.

5. When choosing the most effective therapy for each of her clients, Dr. Anthony considers psychological research, her own clinical experience, and clients' unique treatment preferences. What approach does Dr. Anthony likely use?
   a. Conversion therapy
   b. Evidence-based practice
   c. Person-centered therapy
   d. Meta-analysis

6. Which of the following scenarios illustrates the confirmation bias in the context of therapy?
   a. Dr. Seinfeld focuses on negative aspects of his client's life, reinforcing the client's self-doubt and insecurities.
   b. Dr. Austin selectively seeks evidence and remembers information that supports her preexisting beliefs about a client's condition.
   c. Dr. King's clients tend to overlook positive changes and improvements in their mental health, leading to a distorted perception of their progress.
   d. Dr. Redd tends to disregard evidence-based treatment approaches and rely solely on his personal experiences and intuition.

**7.** Andy is in therapy for depression. He experiences positive outcomes solely due to the power of his belief in the therapy's effectiveness. Which of the following concepts is Andy demonstrating?

a. Confirmation bias
b. Effort justification
c. Placebo effect
d. Sudden gains

**8.** Dr. Chambers has recently received his license to provide therapy to clients. He is aware that he is obligated to benefit his clients and do no harm to them. Which ethical guidelines does this represent?

a. Fidelity and responsibility
b. Beneficence and nonmaleficence
c. Respect for people's rights and dignity
d. Integrity and justice

# Module 5.5d Treatment of Psychological Disorders: The Biomedical Therapies and Preventing Psychological Disorders

## LEARNING TARGETS

**5.5-14** Describe the drug therapies, and explain how double-blind studies help researchers evaluate a drug's effectiveness.

**5.5-15** Describe how brain stimulation and psychosurgery are used to treat specific disorders.

**5.5-16** Describe why therapeutic lifestyle change and hypnosis are considered effective biomedical therapies, and describe how they work.

**5.5-17** Describe what may help prevent psychological disorders, and evaluate the importance of developing resilience.

## The Biomedical Therapies

Psychotherapy is one way to treat psychological disorders. The other is *biomedical therapy*—treatments derived from the *biological perspective*. Biomedical treatments can change the brain's chemistry with drugs; affect its circuitry with electrical stimulation, magnetic impulses, or psychosurgery; or influence its responses with lifestyle changes or hypnosis. Unlike talk therapies, biomedical therapies can have significant side effects.

# Drug Therapies

**5.5-14** What are the drug therapies? How do double-blind studies help researchers evaluate a drug's effectiveness?

By far the most widely used biomedical treatments today are the drug therapies, which interact with the nervous system to treat disorders. Most drugs for anxiety and depression are prescribed by primary care providers, followed by psychiatrists and, in some U.S. states, psychologists. Psychoactive drugs may interact with specific neurotransmitters in the central nervous system to address possible biochemical causes of psychological disorders.

Since the 1950s, discoveries in **psychopharmacology** have revolutionized the treatment of people with severe disorders, liberating hundreds of thousands from hospital confinement. Thanks to drug therapies and community mental health programs, today's resident population of psychiatric hospitals has dropped to a small fraction of what it once was. For some who are unable to care for themselves, however, *deinstitutionalization* has meant homelessness, not liberation.

Almost any new treatment, including drug therapy, is greeted by an initial wave of enthusiasm as many people apparently improve. But that enthusiasm often diminishes on closer examination. To evaluate any new drug's effectiveness, researchers also need to know the following:

- How many people recover *without* treatment, and how quickly?
- Is recovery due to the drug or to the placebo effect? When patients or mental health workers expect positive results, they may see what they expect, not what really happens. Even mere exposure to advertising about a drug's supposed effectiveness can increase its effect (Kamenica et al., 2013).

To control for these influences, drug researchers give half the patients the drug, and the other half a similar-appearing placebo. Because neither the staff nor the patients know who gets which, this is called a *double-blind procedure*. The good news: In double-blind studies, several types of drugs effectively treat psychological disorders.

## Antipsychotic Drugs

An accidental discovery launched a treatment revolution for people with *psychosis*. The discovery: Certain drugs, used for other medical purposes, calmed the hallucinations or delusions that are part of these patients' split from reality. First-generation **antipsychotic drugs**, such as chlorpromazine (sold as Thorazine), dampened responsiveness to irrelevant stimuli. Thus, they provided the most help to patients experiencing positive (actively inappropriate) symptoms of schizophrenia, such as auditory hallucinations and paranoia (Leucht et al., 2018). (Antipsychotic drugs are less effective in changing negative symptoms, such as apathy and withdrawal.)

The molecules of most conventional antipsychotic drugs are similar enough to molecules of the neurotransmitter dopamine to occupy its receptor sites and block its activity. This finding reinforces the idea that an overactive dopamine system contributes to schizophrenia. (Perhaps you can guess an occasional side effect of the dopamine-increasing drug often given to patients with Parkinson's disease: occasional hallucinations.)

Antipsychotics also have powerful side effects. Some produce sluggishness, tremors, and twitches similar to those seen with Parkinson's disease (Kaplan & Saddock, 1989). Long-term use can cause *tardive dyskinesia*—a movement disorder related to the regulation of dopamine in the nervous system—which produces involuntary movements of the facial muscles, tongue, and limbs. Many of the newer-generation antipsychotics, such as risperidone (Risperdal) and olanzapine (Zyprexa), have fewer of these effects (Furukawa et al.,

Edward Koren The New Yorker Collection/The Cartoon Bank

*"Our psychopharmacologist is a genius."*

### AP® Science Practice

**Research**

Just thinking you are getting a treatment can relieve your symptoms. This placebo effect is well documented in psychology. Double-blind studies allow researchers to check a treatment's actual effects apart from the participants' and the staff's belief in its healing powers. Module 0.4 provides a nice discussion of the double-blind procedure.

### AP® Exam Tip

The discussion of drug therapies is a great opportunity for you to review information about neurotransmitters and brain function. See Modules 1.3 and 1.4 if you need to brush up on these topics.

**psychopharmacology** the study of the effects of drugs on mind and behavior.

**antipsychotic drugs** drugs used to treat schizophrenia and other forms of severe thought disorders.

2015). These drugs may, however, increase the risk of obesity and diabetes (Buchanan et al., 2010; Tiihonen et al., 2009). To identify doses that reduce symptoms with fewer side effects, researchers have combed through data for more than 20 antipsychotic medications (Leucht et al., 2020).

Antipsychotics, combined with life-skills programs and family support, have given new hope to many people with schizophrenia (Goff et al., 2017; Guo, 2010). Computer programs now help clinicians identify which people with schizophrenia will benefit from specific antipsychotic medications (Lee et al., 2018; Yu et al., 2018b). Hundreds of thousands of patients have returned to work and to near-normal lives (Leucht et al., 2003). Elyn Saks (2007), a University of Southern California law professor, knows what it means to live with schizophrenia. Thanks to her treatment, which combines an antipsychotic drug and psychotherapy, she noted, "Now I'm mostly well. I'm mostly thinking clearly. I do have episodes, but it's not like I'm struggling all of the time to stay on the right side of the line."

## Antianxiety Drugs

Like alcohol, **antianxiety drugs**, such as Xanax and Ativan, depress central nervous system activity (and so should not be used in combination with alcohol). Some antianxiety drugs have been successfully used in combination with psychological therapy to enhance exposure therapy's extinction of learned fears and to help relieve the symptoms of posttraumatic stress disorder and obsessive-compulsive disorder (Davis, 2005; Kushner et al., 2007).

Some critics fear that antianxiety drugs may reduce symptoms without resolving the underlying problems, especially when used as an ongoing treatment. "Popping a Xanax" at the first sign of tension can create a learned response: The immediate relief reinforces a person's tendency to take drugs when anxious. Antianxiety drugs can also be addictive. Regular users who stop taking these drugs may experience increased anxiety, insomnia, and other withdrawal symptoms.

## Antidepressant Drugs

The **antidepressant drugs** were named for their ability to lift people up from a state of depression, and this was their main use until recently. These drugs are now also increasingly used to treat anxiety disorders, obsessive-compulsive and related disorders, and posttraumatic stress disorder (Beaulieu et al., 2019; Merz et al., 2019; Slee et al., 2019). Many work by increasing the availability of neurotransmitters, such as norepinephrine or serotonin, which elevate arousal and mood and are scarce when a person experiences feelings of depression or anxiety. The most commonly prescribed drugs in this group, including Prozac and its cousins Zoloft and Paxil, work by blocking the normal reuptake process. Given their use in treating disorders other than depressive ones—from anxiety to strokes—these drugs are most often called *selective serotonin reuptake inhibitors (SSRIs)* rather than antidepressants (Kramer, 2011).

Some of the older antidepressant drugs work by blocking the reabsorption or breakdown of both norepinephrine and serotonin. Though effective, these dual-action drugs have potential side effects, such as dry mouth, weight gain, hypertension, and dizzy spells (Anderson, 2000; Mulrow, 1999). Administering them by means of a patch, which bypasses the intestines and liver, helps reduce such side effects (Bodkin & Amsterdam, 2002).

But be advised: Patients with depression who begin taking antidepressants do not wake up the next morning singing "It's a beautiful day!" SSRIs begin to influence neurotransmission within hours, but their full psychological effect may take four weeks (and may involve a side effect of diminished sexual desire). One possible reason for the delay is that increased serotonin promotes new synapses plus *neurogenesis*—the birth of new brain cells—perhaps reversing stress-induced loss of neurons (Launay et al., 2011).

**antianxiety drugs** drugs used to control anxiety and agitation.

**antidepressant drugs** drugs used to treat depressive disorders, anxiety disorders, obsessive-compulsive and related disorders, and posttraumatic stress disorder. (Several widely used antidepressant drugs are *selective serotonin reuptake inhibitors—SSRIs.*)

For those at risk of suicide, researchers are also exploring the possibility of quicker-acting antidepressants. One is ketamine—an anesthetic that is also sometimes used as a risky, psychedelic party drug—which blocks hyperactive receptors for glutamate, a neurotransmitter. Ketamine can provide relief from depression in as little as an hour (McIntyre et al., 2021). But the relief often dissipates in a week, which raises questions about the risks of repeated use (Schatzberg, 2019; Zimmermann et al., 2020). Given that ketamine acts as an opioid, one skeptic wonders if ketamine clinics are "nothing more than modern opium dens" (George, 2018). But others note that ketamine stimulates new synapses, aiding long-lasting change (Beyeler, 2019). Some drug companies are hoping to develop ketamine-like, fast-acting drugs with fewer side effects (Kirby, 2015). Researchers are also exploring therapeutic benefits of microdosing psychedelic drugs such as psilocybin (Reiff et al., 2020; Vollenweider & Preller, 2020).

Cognitive therapy, by helping people reverse their habitual negative thinking style, can boost drug-aided relief from depression and reduce posttreatment relapses (Amick et al., 2015). Some clinicians attack depression from both below and above. They use antidepressant drugs to work, bottom-up, on the emotion-related limbic system. And they use cognitive-behavioral therapy to work, top-down, to change frontal lobe activity and thinking (Guidi & Fava, 2021).

*"If this doesn't help you don't worry, it's a placebo."*

Researchers generally agree that people with depression often improve after a month on antidepressant drugs. But after allowing for natural recovery and the placebo effect, how big is the drug effect? The effect is consistent but, critics argue, not very big (Cipriani et al., 2018; Kirsch, 2010). In double-blind clinical trials, placebos produced improvement comparable to about 75 percent of the active drug's effect. For patients with severe depression, there is less of a placebo effect and the added drug benefit is somewhat greater (Fournier et al., 2010; Kirsch et al., 2008; Olfson & Marcus, 2009). Given the negative side effects of antidepressant drugs, some clinicians advise beginning with psychotherapy before introducing antidepressants (Strayhorn, 2019; Svaldi et al., 2019). "If [drugs] are to be used at all," notes Irving Kirsch (2016), "it should be as a last resort." *The point to remember:* If you're concerned about your mental health, consult with a mental health professional to determine the best treatment for you.

## Mood-Stabilizing Medications

In addition to antipsychotic, antianxiety, and antidepressant drugs, psychiatrists have *mood-stabilizing drugs* in their arsenal. One of them, Depakote, was originally used to treat epilepsy. It was also found to be effective in controlling the manic episodes associated with bipolar disorders. Another drug, the simple salt *lithium*, effectively levels the emotional highs and lows of bipolar disorders.

In the 1940s, Australian physician John Cade discovered that lithium calmed guinea pigs. Wondering if it might do the same for humans, he first tried it himself (to confirm its safety), and then on 10 people with mania—all of whom improved dramatically (Brown, 2019). About 7 in 10 people with bipolar disorders benefit from a long-term daily dose of this cheap salt, which helps prevent or ease manic episodes and, to a lesser extent, lifts depression (Solomon et al., 1995). Kay Redfield Jamison (1995) described the effect:

> Lithium prevents my seductive but disastrous highs, diminishes my depressions, clears out the wool and webbing from my disordered thinking, slows me down, gentles me out, keeps me from ruining my career and relationships, keeps me out of a hospital, alive, and makes psychotherapy possible. (pp. 88–89)

Taking lithium also correlates with a lower risk of suicide among people with bipolar disorders—about one-sixth the risk of those not taking lithium (Oquendo et al., 2011).

Naturally occurring lithium in drinking water has also been correlated with lower suicide rates (across 18 Japanese cities and towns) and lower crime rates (across 27 Texas counties) (Ohgami et al., 2009; Schrauzer & Shrestha, 1990, 2010; Terao et al., 2010). Lithium works.

---

**AP® Science Practice**

## Check Your Understanding

### Examine the Concept

▶ Explain what is meant by this statement: "Some clinicians attack depression from both below and above."

▶ Describe the difference between antipsychotic drugs and antidepressant drugs in terms of how they work.

*Answers to the Examine the Concept questions can be found in Appendix C at the end of the book.*

### Apply the Concept

▶ If a friend experiencing depression asked, how would you summarize the available drug therapies?

---

# Brain Stimulation

> **5.5-15** How are brain stimulation and psychosurgery used in treating specific disorders?

## Electroconvulsive Therapy

Another biomedical treatment, **electroconvulsive therapy (ECT)**, manipulates the brain by shocking it. When ECT was first introduced in 1938, the wide-awake person was strapped to a table and jolted with electricity to the brain. This procedure, which produced convulsions and brief unconsciousness, gained a barbaric image. Although that image lingers, today's ECT is much kinder and gentler, and no longer "convulsive." The person receives a general anesthetic and a muscle relaxant (to prevent bodily convulsions). A psychiatrist then delivers a brief electrical pulse, sometimes only to the brain's right side, which triggers a 30- to 60-second brain seizure (McCall et al., 2017). Within 30 minutes, the person awakens and remembers nothing of the treatment or of the preceding hours.

Study after study confirms that ECT can effectively treat severe depression in "treatment-resistant" patients who have not responded to drug therapy (Fink, 2009; Giacobbe et al., 2018; Ross et al., 2018). After three such sessions each week for two to four weeks, 70 percent or more of patients receiving today's ECT improve markedly, without discernible brain damage or increased dementia risk (Osler et al., 2018). ECT also reduces suicidal thoughts and has been credited with saving many people from suicide (Rhee et al., 2021). A *Journal of the American Medical Association* editorial concluded that "the results of ECT in treating severe depression are among the most positive treatment effects in all of medicine" (Glass, 2001).

How does ECT relieve severe depression—and, in other studies, mania (Elias et al., 2021)? After more than 70 years, no one knows for sure. One patient likened ECT to the smallpox vaccine, which was saving lives before we knew how it worked. Perhaps the brief electric current calms neural centers where overactivity produces depression. Some research indicates that ECT stimulates neurogenesis (new neurons) and new synaptic connections (Joshi et al., 2016; Rotheneichner et al., 2014; Wang et al., 2017b).

No matter how impressive the results, the idea of electrically shocking a person's brain still strikes many as barbaric, especially given our ignorance about why ECT works. Moreover, the mood boost may not last long. Many ECT-treated patients eventually relapse back

**electroconvulsive therapy (ECT)** a biomedical therapy for severe depression in which a brief electric current is sent through the brain of an anesthetized person.

into depression, although relapses are somewhat fewer for those who also receive antidepressant drugs or who do aerobic exercise (Rosenquist et al., 2016; Salehi et al., 2016). *The bottom line:* In the minds of many psychiatrists and patients, ECT is a lesser evil than severe depression's anguish and risk of suicide. After ECT, psychiatrist Rebecca Barchas (2021) reported "regaining my joie de vivre, my high level of motivation, and my ability to make decisions."

## Alternative Neurostimulation Therapies

Three other neural stimulation techniques—mild cranial electrical stimulation, magnetic stimulation, and deep brain stimulation—also aim to treat the depressed brain (**Figure 5.5-6**).

**Transcranial Electrical Stimulation** In contrast to ECT, which produces a brain seizure with about 800 milliamps of electricity, *transcranial direct current stimulation (tDCS)* administers a weak one- to two-milliamp current to the scalp. Skeptics argue that such a current is too weak to penetrate the brain (Underwood, 2016). But research suggests that tDCS is a modestly effective treatment for depression (Razza et al., 2020).

**transcranial magnetic stimulation (TMS)** the application of repeated pulses of magnetic energy to the brain; used to stimulate or suppress brain activity.

**Magnetic Stimulation** Depressed moods also sometimes improve when a painless procedure called **transcranial magnetic stimulation (TMS)** is performed on wide-awake patients in sessions over several weeks. Repeated pulses surging through a magnetic coil held close to the skull can stimulate or suppress activity in areas of the cortex. Like tDCS (and unlike ECT), the TMS procedure produces no memory loss or other serious side effects, aside from possible headaches.

Results with this therapy are mixed. Some studies have found that, for 30 to 40 percent of people with depression, TMS works, although it is less effective than ECT (Carmi et al., 2019; Mutz et al., 2019). TMS also reduces some schizophrenia symptoms, such as social apathy and memory loss (Osoegawa et al., 2018; Xiu et al., 2020). How it works is unclear. One possible explanation is that the stimulation energizes the brain's left frontal lobe, which is relatively inactive during depression (Helmuth, 2001). Repeated stimulation may cause nerve cells to form new functioning circuits through the process of *long-term potentiation* (see Module 2.3 for more details on LTP). Another possible explanation is a placebo effect: People benefit when, after being given a credible explanation, they believe TMS will work (Geers et al., 2019; Yesavage et al., 2018).

## Figure 5.5-6
### A stimulating experience

Today's neurostimulation therapies apply strong or mild electricity, or magnetic energy, either to the skull's surface or directly to brain neurons.

**Deep Brain Stimulation** Other patients whose depression has resisted both drugs and ECT have benefited from an experimental treatment pinpointing a neural hub that bridges the thinking frontal lobes to the limbic system (Becker et al., 2016; Brunoni et al., 2017;

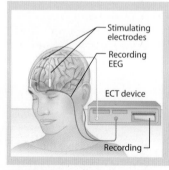

**Electroconvulsive therapy (ECT)**
Psychiatrist administers a strong current, which triggers a brain seizure in the anesthetized patient.

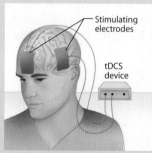

**Transcranial direct current stimulation (tDCS)**
Psychiatrist applies a weak current to the scalp.

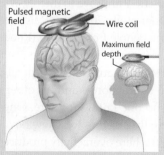

**Transcranial magnetic stimulation (TMS)**
Psychiatrist sends a painless magnetic field through the skull to the surface of the cortex to alter brain activity.

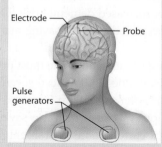

**Deep brain stimulation (DBS)**
Psychiatrist stimulates electrodes implanted in "sadness centers" to calm those areas.

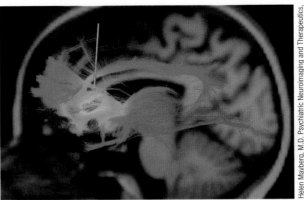

A depression switch? By comparing the brains of patients with and without depression, researcher Helen Mayberg identified a brain area (highlighted in red) that appears active in people who are depressed or sad, and whose activity may be calmed by deep brain stimulation.

Ryder & Holtzheimer, 2016). This area, which is overactive in the brain of a depressed or temporarily sad person, typically calms when treated by ECT or antidepressants. To experimentally activate neurons that inhibit this negative activity, neuroscientist Helen Mayberg drew upon *deep brain stimulation (DBS)* technology, sometimes used to treat Parkinson's tremors. Since 2003, she and her colleagues have used DBS to treat some 200 depressed patients with implanted electrodes in a brain area that functions as the neural "sadness center" (Lozano & Mayberg, 2015). For some patients, DBS produces large and enduring reductions in depression (Crowell et al., 2019; Kisely et al., 2018). "The bottom line," notes Mayberg, "is that if you get better, you stay better" (Carey, 2019).

## Psychosurgery

Because its effects are irreversible, **psychosurgery** is the most drastic and least-used biomedical intervention for changing behavior. In the 1930s, Portuguese physician Egas Moniz developed what would become the best-known psychosurgical operation: the **lobotomy**. Moniz found that cutting the nerves connecting the frontal lobes with the inner brain's emotion-controlling centers calmed uncontrollably emotional and violent patients. In what would later become, in others' hands, a crude but quick and easy procedure, a neurosurgeon would shock the patient into a coma, hammer an icepick-like instrument through the top of each eye socket into the brain, and then wiggle it to sever connections running up to the frontal lobes. Between 1936 and 1954, tens of thousands of people with mental illness were "lobotomized" (Valenstein, 1986).

Although the intention was simply to disconnect emotion from thought, the effect was often more drastic. A lobotomy usually decreased misery or tension, but it also produced a permanently lethargic, immature, uncreative person. During the 1950s, after some 35,000 people had been lobotomized in the United States alone, calming drugs became available and psychosurgery became scorned.

Today, lobotomies are history. More precise, micro-scale psychosurgery is sometimes used in extreme cases. For example, if a patient suffers uncontrollable seizures, surgeons can deactivate the specific nerve clusters that cause or transmit the convulsions. MRI-guided precision surgery is also occasionally done to cut the circuits or to lesion brain tissue involved in severe major depressive disorder and obsessive-compulsive disorder (Carey, 2011; Coenen et al., 2020; Kim et al., 2018). Because these procedures are irreversible, neurosurgeons perform them only as a last resort.

**AP® Science Practice**

### Research

Because APA ethical guidelines do not allow for random assignment to psychosurgery, there are no experimental psychosurgery data. Instead, researchers rely on individual case studies, a nonexperimental method.

**psychosurgery** surgery that removes or destroys brain tissue to change behavior.

**lobotomy** a psychosurgical procedure once used to calm uncontrollably emotional or violent patients. The procedure cut the nerves connecting the frontal lobes to the emotion-controlling centers of the inner brain.

**Failed lobotomy** This 1940 photo shows Rosemary Kennedy (center) at age 22 with brother (and future U.S. president) John and sister Jean. A year later, her father approved a lobotomy that doctors suggested would control her reportedly violent mood swings. The procedure left Rosemary confined to a hospital with an infantile mentality for the next 63 years, until her death in 2005.

**Examine the Concept**

▶ Describe the neurostimulation therapies in terms of how they are administered.

**Apply the Concept**

▶ What were your impressions of biomedical therapies before reading this section? Are any of your views different now? Why or why not?

*Answers to the Examine the Concept questions can be found in Appendix C at the end of the book.*

## Therapeutic Lifestyle Change and Hypnosis

> **5.5-16** Why are therapeutic lifestyle change and hypnosis considered effective biomedical therapies, and how do they work?

### Therapeutic Lifestyle Change

We find it convenient to talk of separate psychological and biological influences, but everything psychological is also biological. Thus, our lifestyle—exercise, nutrition, relationships, recreation, relaxation, religious or spiritual engagement, and service to others—affects our mental health (Bennie et al., 2020; Walsh, 2011). (See Developing Arguments: Therapeutic Lifestyle Change.)

Every thought and feeling depends on the functioning brain. Every creative idea, every moment of joy or anger, every experience of depression emerges from the electrochemical activity of the living brain. Anxiety disorders, obsessive-compulsive and related disorders, posttraumatic stress disorder, depressive disorders, bipolar disorders, and schizophrenia are all biological events. Some psychologists consider even psychotherapy to be a biological treatment, because changing the way we think and behave is a brain-changing experience (Kandel, 2013). When psychotherapy relieves behaviors associated with obsessive-compulsive disorder or schizophrenia, PET scans reveal a calmer brain (Habel et al., 2010; Schwartz et al., 1996). As we have seen over and over, *a human being is an integrated biopsychosocial system.*

### Hypnosis

Even words can temporarily change your brain activity. **Hypnosis** can reduce both pain and anxiety (though research does not support its use in other contexts, such as recovering supposedly repressed memories or regressing in age). Imagine you are about to be hypnotized. The hypnotist invites you to sit back, fix your gaze on a spot high on the wall, and relax. You hear a quiet, low voice suggest, "Your eyes are growing tired. . . . Your eyelids are becoming heavy . . . now heavier and heavier. . . . They are beginning to close. . . . You are becoming more deeply relaxed. . . . Your breathing is now deep and regular. . . . Your muscles are becoming more and more relaxed. . . . Your whole body is beginning to feel like lead." After a few minutes of this *hypnotic induction,* you may experience hypnosis.

Hypnotists have no magical mind-control power; they merely focus people's attention on certain images or behaviors. To some extent, we are all open to suggestion. But highly hypnotizable people—such as the 20 percent who can carry out a suggestion not to react to an open bottle of smelly ammonia—are especially suggestible and imaginative (Barnier & McConkey, 2004; Silva & Kirsch, 1992). Their brain also displays altered activity when under hypnosis in regions associated with pain, such as the prefrontal cortex (Wolf et al., 2022).

Can hypnosis relieve pain? *Yes.* When unhypnotized people put their arm in an ice bath, they felt intense pain within 25 seconds (Elkins et al., 2012; Jensen, 2008). When hypnotized

**hypnosis** a social interaction in which one person (the hypnotist) suggests to another (the subject) that certain perceptions, feelings, thoughts, or behaviors will spontaneously occur; in a therapeutic context, the hypnotist attempts to use suggestion to reduce unpleasant physical sensations or emotions.

 **AP® Science Practice** ## Developing Arguments

### Therapeutic Lifestyle Change

**LIFESTYLE**
(exercise, nutrition, relationships, recreation, service to others, relaxation, and religious or spiritual engagement) → influences our **BRAIN AND BODY** → affects our **MENTAL HEALTH**[1]

## APPLICATION TO THERAPY

**Our shared history has prepared us to be physically active and socially engaged.**

Our ancestors hunted, gathered, and built in groups.

Modern researchers have found that outdoor activity in a natural environment reduces stress and promotes health.[2]

Training seminars promote therapeutic lifestyle change.[3] Small groups of people with depression undergo a 12-week training program with the following goals:

**Aerobic exercise,** 30 minutes a day, at least three times weekly (increases fitness and vitality, stimulates endorphins)

Regular aerobic exercise rivals the healing power of antidepressant drugs.[4]

**Light exposure,** 15 to 30 minutes each morning with a light box (amplifies arousal, influences hormones)

**Reducing rumination,** by identifying and redirecting negative thoughts (enhances positive thinking)

**Adequate sleep,** with a goal of 7 to 8 hours per night.

A complete night's sleep boosts immunity and increases energy, alertness, and mood.[5]

ZZZZZZZZZZZZZZZZZZZZZZZZZZ

**Social connection,** with less alone time and at least two meaningful social engagements weekly (helps satisfy the human need to belong)

**Nutritional supplements,** including a daily supplement with omega-3 fatty acids (reduces aggressive behavior)[6]

### Initial small study (74 participants)[7]

 77% of those who completed the program experienced relief from depressive symptoms.

 Only 19% of those assigned to a treatment-as-usual control group showed similar results.

Future research will try to identify which parts of the treatment produce the therapeutic effect.

**The biomedical therapies assume that mind and body are a unit:**

**Affect one and you will affect the other.**

## Developing Arguments Questions

- Identify the reasoning behind the claim that our lifestyle affects our mental health.

- Using scientifically derived evidence, explain how adequate sleep impacts mental health.

- Suppose you have a friend who is mildly depressed. Using scientifically derived evidence, what advice would you give them about aerobic exercise and outdoor activity?

1. Sánchez-Villegas et al., 2015; Walsh, 2011. 2. MacKerron & Mourato, 2013; NEEF, 2015; Phillips, 2011. 3. Ilardi, 2009. 4. Babyak et al., 2000; Salmon, 2001; Schuch et al., 2016. 5. Gregory et al., 2009; Walker & van der Helm, 2009. 6. Bègue et al., 2017; Raine et al., 2018. 7. Ilardi, 2009, 2016.

**Dissociation or social influence?**
This hypnotized woman being tested by researcher Ernest Hilgard showed no pain when her arm was placed in an ice bath. She said the water felt cold, but not painful. But asked to press a key if some part of her felt the pain, she did so. To Hilgard (1986, 1992), this was evidence of divided consciousness, or "dissociation" from the pain. The social influence perspective, however, maintains that people responding this way are caught up in playing the role of "good subject."

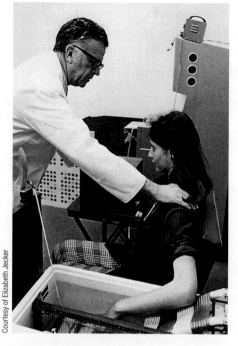

Courtesy of Elizabeth Jecker

people did the same after being given suggestions to feel no pain, they indeed reported feeling little pain. Hypnosis can also reduce some forms of chronic and disability-related pain (Adachi et al., 2014; Bowker & Dorstyn, 2016).

In surgical experiments, hypnotized patients have required less medication, recovered sooner, and left the hospital earlier than unhypnotized patients in a control group (Askay & Patterson, 2007; Hammond, 2008; Spiegel, 2007). Nearly 10 percent of us can become so deeply hypnotized that even major surgery can be performed without anesthesia. Half of us can gain at least some pain relief from hypnosis. The surgical use of hypnosis has flourished in Europe, where one Belgian medical team has performed more than 5000 surgeries with a combination of hypnosis, local anesthesia, and a mild sedative (Facco, 2016; Song, 2006).

Hypnosis can also reduce anxiety. In experiments, participants treated with hypnosis have experienced more anxiety reduction than those in control conditions (Valentine et al., 2019). Moreover, the anxiety reduction persisted. Hypnosis has similarly reduced anxiety in patients with cancer (Chen et al., 2017).

Psychologists have proposed two explanations for how hypnosis works:

- **Social influence theory** contends that hypnosis is a by-product of normal social and mental processes (Lynn et al., 1990, 2015; Spanos & Coe, 1992). In this view, hypnotized people, like actors caught up in a role, begin to feel and behave in ways appropriate for "good hypnotic subjects." They may allow the hypnotist to direct their attention away from pain.

**dissociation** a split in consciousness, which allows some thoughts and behaviors to occur simultaneously with others.

**posthypnotic suggestion** a suggestion, made during a hypnosis session, to be carried out after the subject is no longer hypnotized; used by some clinicians to help control undesired symptoms and behaviors.

- **Dissociation theory** proposes that hypnosis is a special dual-processing state of **dissociation**—a split between different levels of consciousness. Dissociation theory seeks to explain why, when no one is watching, previously hypnotized people may later carry out **posthypnotic suggestions** (Perugini et al., 1998). It also offers an explanation for why people hypnotized for pain relief may show activity in areas of the brain that receive sensory information, but not in areas that normally process pain-related information (Rainville et al., 1997).

*Selective attention* (see Module 2.1) may also play a role in hypnotic pain and anxiety relief. Brain scans show that hypnosis increases activity in frontal lobe attention systems (Oakley & Halligan, 2013). So, while hypnosis does not block sensory input itself, it may redirect our attention to other stimuli.

---

**AP® Science Practice**  **Check Your Understanding**

**Examine the Concept**

▶ Describe some examples of lifestyle changes people can make to enhance their mental health.

▶ Describe two theories explaining how hypnosis works.

*Answers to the Examine the Concept questions can be found in Appendix C at the end of the book.*

**Apply the Concept**

▶ In what ways do you think *your* lifestyle is affecting your mental health?

## Exploring Research Methods & Design

The text describes the findings from a surgical experiment in which hypnotized patients required less medication, recovered sooner, and left the hospital earlier than unhypnotized patients in a control group.

- Explain why this is an experiment (as opposed to a correlational study).

- Identify the independent and dependent variables.

- What conclusions can (or can't) the researchers draw at the end of this experiment?

- Describe one ethical guideline researchers must follow in this experiment.

\* \* \*

Table 5.5-4 summarizes some aspects of the biomedical therapies we've discussed.

| TABLE 5.5-4 Comparing Biomedical Therapies | | | |
|---|---|---|---|
| **Therapy** | **Presumed Problem** | **Therapy Aim** | **Therapy Technique** |
| *Drug therapies* | Neurotransmitter malfunction | Control symptoms of psychological disorders. | Alter brain chemistry through drugs. |
| *Brain stimulation* | Depressive disorders (ECT is used only for severe, treatment-resistant depressive disorders.) | Alleviate depression, especially when it is unresponsive to drugs or other forms of therapy. | Stimulate the brain through electroconvulsive shock, mild electrical stimulation, magnetic impulses, or deep brain stimulation. |
| *Psychosurgery* | Brain malfunction | Relieve severe disorders. | Remove or destroy brain tissue. |
| *Therapeutic lifestyle change* | Stress, anxiety, and depression | Restore healthy biological state. | Alter lifestyle through adequate exercise, sleep, nutrition, and other changes. |
| *Hypnosis* | Pain and anxiety | Alleviate pain and reduce anxiety. | Alter brain activity through hypnotic induction. |

# Preventing Psychological Disorders and Building Resilience

**5.5-17** What may help prevent psychological disorders, and why is it important to develop resilience?

Psychotherapies and biomedical therapies tend to locate the cause of psychological disorders within the person. We infer that people who act cruelly must be cruel and that people who act "crazy" must be "sick." We attach labels to such people, thereby distinguishing them from "normal" folks. It follows, then, that we try to treat "abnormal" people by giving them insight into their problems, by changing their thinking, by helping them gain control with drugs.

There is an alternative viewpoint: We could interpret many psychological disorders as understandable responses to a disturbing and stressful world. According to this view, it is not just the person who needs treatment. Rather, as the soaring mental health problems during the Covid pandemic illustrated, it's also the person's social context. Although today's psychotherapies and biomedical therapies have helped many individuals, rates of depression, suicide, and addiction have worsened (Insel, 2022). While vaccinations and antibiotics have added years to the average life, mental health services have not added comparable joy to the average life. Unhealthy situations can make for unhappy people. Thus, it is better to prevent problems by reforming an unhealthy situation and developing people's coping competencies than to wait for and then treat problems.

## Preventive Mental Health

A story about the rescue of a drowning person from a rushing river illustrates this viewpoint: Having successfully administered first aid to the victim, the rescuer spots another struggling person and pulls that person out, too. After a half-dozen repetitions, the rescuer suddenly turns and starts running away while the river sweeps yet another floundering person into view. "Aren't you going to rescue that person?" asks a bystander. "No way," the rescuer replies. "I'm going upstream to find out what's pushing all these people in."

*Preventive mental health* is upstream work. It seeks to prevent psychological casualties by identifying and alleviating the conditions that cause them. As George Albee (1986, 2006) pointed out, there is abundant evidence that poverty, lack of meaningful work, constant criticism, unemployment, and discrimination undermine people's sense of competence, personal control, and self-esteem. Such stresses increase their risk of depression, alcohol use disorder, and suicide. To prevent psychological casualties, we should, Albee contended, support programs that work to improve these demoralizing situations.

Preventing psychological problems means empowering those who have learned an attitude of helplessness, and changing environments that breed loneliness, suicidal thinking, and excessive alcohol and drug use. It means teaching children how to manage their emotions, get along with others, and keep up with academic demands (Godwin, 2020). It means harnessing positive psychology interventions to enhance human flourishing. One intervention taught adolescents that personality isn't fixed—people can change—and reduced their chances of future depression by 40 percent (Miu & Yeager, 2015). This result is no fluke: Preventive therapies have consistently reduced the risk for depression (Breedvelt et al., 2018).

In short, "everything aimed at improving the human condition, at making life more fulfilling and meaningful, may be considered part of primary prevention of mental or emotional disturbance" (Kessler & Albee, 1975, p. 557). Prevention can sometimes provide a double payoff. People with a strong sense of life's meaning are more engaging socially (Stillman et al., 2011). By strengthening people's sense of meaning in life, we may also lessen their loneliness as they become more engaging companions.

Among the upstream prevention workers are *community psychologists*. Mindful of how people interact with their environment, they focus on creating environments that support psychological health. Through their research and social action, community psychologists aim to empower people and to enhance their competence, health, and well-being.

## Building Resilience

Preventive mental health includes efforts to build individuals' *resilience*. Faced with extreme suffering or trauma, some people experience lasting harm, some experience stable resilience, and some actually experience growth (Myers, 2019). In the aftermath of the 9/11 terror attacks, many New Yorkers exhibited resilience. This was especially true for those who enjoyed supportive close relationships and who had not recently experienced other stressful events (Bonanno et al., 2007). More than 9 in 10 New Yorkers, although stunned and grief-stricken by 9/11, did *not* have a dysfunctional stress reaction. Among those who did, the stress

**Disability and resilience**
"Sometimes it takes dealing with a disability — the trauma, the relearning, the months of rehabilitation therapy — to uncover our true abilities and how we can put them to work for us in ways we may have never imagined." — U.S. Senator and Retired Lieutenant Colonel Tammy Duckworth, who lost both legs as an Army helicopter pilot in the Iraq War.

Chip Somodevilla/Getty Images

symptoms were mostly gone by the following January (Person et al., 2006). Even most combat-stressed veterans, most political rebels who have survived torture, and most people with spinal cord injuries do not later exhibit posttraumatic stress disorder (Bonanno et al., 2012; Mineka & Zinbarg, 1996).

Struggling with challenging crises can lead to **posttraumatic growth**. Many survivors of cancer have reported a greater appreciation for life, more meaningful relationships, increased personal strength, changed priorities, and a richer spiritual life (Tedeschi & Calhoun, 2004). Out of even our worst experiences, some good can come, especially when we can imagine new possibilities (Mangelsdorf et al., 2019; Roepke, 2015). As with positive experiences, suffering can beget new sensitivity and strength.

 **AP® Science Practice**

## Exploring Research Methods & Design

Imagine you are a researcher who wants to test the following hypothesis:

*The more supportive one's family relationships are, the more resilient one is during times of stress.*

Design a study to test this hypothesis, then address the following questions.

- Is the study you designed to test this research question correlational or experimental? Why?

- Identify your variables. What is your operational definition of each?

- Identify the statistical measure you would use to assess the relationship between your variables.

- What ethical guidelines, if any, would prevent you from using random assignment when studying this topic?

*Remember, you can always revisit Unit 0 to review information related to psychological research.*

**AP® Science Practice**

## Check Your Understanding

**Examine the Concept**

▶ What is the difference between preventive mental health and the biomedical therapies?

▶ Describe posttraumatic growth.

**Apply the Concept**

▶ Can you think of a specific way that improving the environment in your own community might prevent some psychological disorders among its residents?

*Answers to the Examine the Concept questions can be found in Appendix C at the end of the book.*

* * *

If you just finished reading this book, your AP® course introduction to psychological science is nearly complete. Our tour of psychological science has taught us much—and you, too?—about our moods and memories, about the reach of our unconscious, about how we flourish and struggle, about how we perceive our physical and social worlds, and about how our biology and culture shape us. We've also learned how psychological research arrives at these conclusions. As your guides on this tour, we hope that you have shared our fascination, grown in your understanding and compassion, and sharpened your critical thinking. And we hope you enjoyed the ride.

With every good wish for your future endeavors (including on the AP® exam!),

David G. Myers
davidmyers.org
@DavidGMyers

Nathan DeWall
@cndewall

Elizabeth Yost Hammer
@eyhammer

**posttraumatic growth** positive psychological changes following a struggle with extremely challenging circumstances and life crises.

**5.5-14** What are the drug therapies? How do double-blind studies help researchers evaluate a drug's effectiveness?

- *Psychopharmacology* has helped make drug therapy the most widely used biomedical therapy.

- *Antipsychotic drugs* are used in treating schizophrenia; some block dopamine activity. Side effects may include tardive dyskinesia (involuntary movements of facial muscles, tongue, and limbs) or increased risk of obesity and diabetes.

- *Antianxiety drugs*, which depress central nervous system activity, are used to treat anxiety disorders, obsessive-compulsive disorder, and posttraumatic stress disorder, and can be addictive.

- *Antidepressant drugs*, which often increase the availability of serotonin and norepinephrine, are used to treat depression, anxiety disorders, obsessive-compulsive and related disorders, and posttraumatic stress disorder. Given their use in treating disorders other than depressive ones (from anxiety to strokes), these drugs are most often called selective serotonin reuptake inhibitors (SSRIs). Quicker-acting antidepressants may include ketamine and microdoses of psychedelic drugs such as psilocybin.

- Lithium and Depakote are mood stabilizers prescribed for individuals with a bipolar disorder.

- Studies may use a double-blind procedure to avoid the placebo effect and researchers' bias.

**5.5-15** How are brain stimulation and psychosurgery used in treating specific disorders?

- *Electroconvulsive therapy (ECT)*, in which a brief electric current is sent through the brain of an anesthetized patient, is an effective treatment for severe depression in people who have not responded to other therapy.

- Newer alternative neurostimulation treatments for depression include transcranial direct current stimulation (tDCS), *transcranial magnetic stimulation (TMS)*, and deep brain stimulation (DBS; may calm an overactive brain region linked with negative emotions in some patients).

- *Psychosurgery* removes or destroys brain tissue in hopes of modifying behavior.
  - Radical psychosurgical procedures such as the *lobotomy* are no longer performed.

- Today's microscale psychosurgery, MRI-guided precision brain surgery, and brain tissue lesioning are rare, last-resort treatments because the effects are irreversible.

**5.5-16** Why are therapeutic lifestyle change and hypnosis considered effective biomedical therapies, and how do they work?

- Therapeutic lifestyle change and hypnosis are considered biomedical therapies because they influence the way the brain responds. Mind and body are a unit; affect one and you will affect the other.

- Our exercise, nutrition, relationships, recreation, service to others, relaxation, and religious or spiritual engagement affect our mental health. People who undergo a program of aerobic exercise, adequate sleep, light exposure, social engagement, rumination reduction, and better nutrition have gained relief from depressive symptoms.

- *Hypnosis* can reduce pain and anxiety. Social influence theory (which contends that hypnosis is a by-product of normal social and mental processes), dissociation theory (which proposes that hypnosis is a state of *dissociation*, which explains *posthypnotic suggestion*), and selective attention are proposed explanations for hypnotic pain and anxiety relief.

**5.5-17** What may help prevent psychological disorders, and why is it important to develop resilience?

- Preventive mental health programs are based on the idea that many psychological disorders could be prevented by identifying and alleviating the conditions that cause them, such as poverty, lack of meaningful work, constant criticism, unemployment, and discrimination.

- Community psychologists work to prevent psychological disorders by turning destructive environments into ones that support psychological health. This includes efforts to build individuals' *resilience*, helping people cope with and recover from stress.

- Struggling with challenges can lead to *posttraumatic growth*.

# AP® Practice Multiple Choice Questions

1. Horatio treats psychological disorders with medical and surgical procedures. Which perspective does he apply?

   a. Behavioral
   b. Biological
   c. Cognitive
   d. Psychodynamic

2. Dr. McQueen, a psychiatrist, often prescribes antidepressants to his patients. Dr. McQueen always talks with patients about the possible unwanted effects they may experience while taking these medications. Which of the following does Dr. McQueen discuss?

   a. Side effects
   b. Placebo effect
   c. Hypnosis
   d. Withdrawal effects

3. Penelope sees a therapist who uses suggestion to change her thoughts, behaviors, feelings, and perceptions. Her therapist uses

   a. electroconvulsive therapy.
   b. deep brain stimulation.
   c. ketamine.
   d. hypnosis.

4. Dana was prescribed an antipsychotic medication to treat symptoms associated with schizophrenia. Which neurotransmitter is most likely to be affected by this medication?

   a. Epinephrine
   b. Dopamine
   c. Norepinephrine
   d. Serotonin

5. Zeke was diagnosed with a bipolar disorder. Which medication is his psychiatrist most likely to prescribe to treat this disorder?

   a. Lithium
   b. Xanax
   c. Zoloft
   d. Ativan

**Use the following scenario to answer questions 6 and 7:**

Dr. Etchiverie conducted a study on the effectiveness of antidepressants. She found that, after two months of taking an antidepressant drug, 80 percent of the study participants reported a reduction in their depressive symptoms.

6. Which of the following is the most likely confounding variable in Dr. Etchiverie's study?

   a. Comorbid anxiety
   b. Withdrawal effect
   c. Placebo effect
   d. Exercise

7. What methods could be implemented to reduce the influence of this confounding variable on the study results?

   a. Dr. Etchiverie could conduct a longitudinal study.
   b. Dr. Etchiverie could conduct an experiment with a double-blind procedure.
   c. Dr. Etchiverie could conduct a survey.
   d. Dr. Etchiverie could conduct a naturalistic observation in the patients' typical environments.

# UNIT 5 Review

## KEY TERMS AND CONTRIBUTORS TO REMEMBER

health psychology, p. 638

psychoneuroimmunology, p. 638

stress, p. 639

approach and avoidance motives, p. 643

Kurt Lewin, p. 643

Hans Selye, p. 643

general adaptation syndrome (GAS), p. 644

tend-and-befriend response, p. 644

coronary heart disease, p. 648

Type A, p. 648

Type B, p. 648

catharsis, p. 650

coping, p. 654

problem-focused coping, p. 654

emotion-focused coping, p. 654

personal control, p. 654

learned helplessness, p. 655

external locus of control, p. 656

internal locus of control, p. 656

self-control, p. 657

Martin Seligman, p. 663

positive psychology, p. 663

subjective well-being, p. 663

feel-good, do-good phenomenon, p. 664

adaptation-level phenomenon, p. 667

relative deprivation, p. 667

broaden-and-build theory, p. 669

character strengths and virtues, p. 670

resilience, p. 673

aerobic exercise, p. 673

mindfulness meditation, p. 677

gratitude, p. 678

psychological disorder, p. 685

medical model, p. 686

diathesis-stress model, p. 686

epigenetics, p. 686

DSM-5-TR, p. 688

anxiety disorders, p. 699

social anxiety disorder, p. 699

generalized anxiety disorder, p. 700

panic disorder, p. 700

agoraphobia, p. 700

specific phobia, p. 701

obsessive-compulsive disorder, (OCD), p. 702

hoarding disorder, p. 703

posttraumatic stress disorder (PTSD), p. 703

trauma- and stressor-related disorders, p. 703

depressive disorders, p. 711

bipolar disorders, p. 711

major depressive disorder, p. 712

persistent depressive disorder, p. 712

bipolar I disorder, p. 713

mania, p. 713

bipolar II disorder, p. 713

rumination, p. 718

schizophrenia spectrum disorders, p. 722

psychotic disorders, p. 722

delusion, p. 723

chronic schizophrenia, p. 724

acute schizophrenia, p. 724

dissociative disorders, p. 730

dissociative identity disorder (DID), p. 730

dissociative amnesia, p. 731

personality disorders, p. 732

antisocial personality disorder, p. 732

feeding and eating disorders, p. 735

anorexia nervosa, p. 735

bulimia nervosa, p. 735

neurodevelopmental disorders, p. 737

autism spectrum disorder (ASD), p. 738

attention-deficit/hyperactivity disorder (ADHD), p. 740

Dorothea Dix, p. 746

deinstitutionalization, p. 746

psychotherapy, p. 746

biomedical therapy, p. 746

eclectic approach, p. 747

Sigmund Freud, p. 747

psychoanalysis, p. 747

resistance, p. 747

interpretation, p. 747

transference, p. 747

psychodynamic therapy, p. 748

insight therapies, p. 748

person-centered therapy, p. 749

Carl Rogers, p. 749

active listening, p. 749

unconditional positive regard, p. 750

behavior therapy, p. 753

counterconditioning, p. 754

Mary Cover Jones, p. 754

Joseph Wolpe, p. 754

exposure therapies, p. 754

systematic desensitization, p. 754

virtual reality exposure therapy, p. 755

aversive conditioning, p. 755

B. F. Skinner, p. 756

token economy, p. 756

cognitive therapy, p. 757

Albert Ellis, p. 758

rational-emotive behavior therapy (REBT), p. 758

Aaron Beck, p. 758

cognitive-behavioral therapy (CBT), p. 760

group therapy, p. 762

family therapy, p. 762

confirmation bias, p. 767

meta-analysis, p. 768

evidence-based practice, p. 770

therapeutic alliance, p. 771

psychopharmacology, p. 778

antipsychotic drugs, p. 778

antianxiety drugs, p. 779

antidepressant drugs, p. 779

electroconvulsive therapy (ECT), p. 781

transcranial magnetic stimulation (TMS), p. 782

psychosurgery, p. 783

lobotomy, p. 783

hypnosis, p. 784

Ernest Hilgard, p. 786

dissociation, p. 786

posthypnotic suggestion, p. 786

posttraumatic growth, p. 789

# Unit 5 AP® Practice Multiple Choice Questions

**1.** After a fire alarm, Liam's temperature, blood pressure, and respiration remained high, and he also had an outpouring of hormones. Which phase of the general adaptation syndrome was Liam most likely in?

a. Exhaustion
b. Resistance
c. Alarm
d. Collapse

**2.** Dr. Garriott tries to impact stress among his patients because he knows that

a. surgical wounds heal more slowly in stressed people.
b. stress has no effect on people who are exposed to cold viruses.
c. there is no correlation between stress and longevity.
d. stress makes us more resistant to infection and heart disease.

**3.** Kaiser blames his failures on himself but blames his successes on luck. This example illustrates

a. emotional memory.
b. social-cognitive perspective.
c. explanatory style.
d. dissociative reasoning.

**4.** The Evers' new neighbors make more money and drive nicer cars than the Evers. The Evers used to be content with what they had, but they are now jealous of the status of their new neighbors. The best explanation for this change is

a. the feel-good, do-good phenomenon.
b. the tend-and-befriend response.
c. relative deprivation.
d. the adaptation-level phenomenon.

**5.** Cairo's psychological symptoms interfere with his relationships, which is considered

a. catatonic.
b. dysfunctional.
c. positive.
d. dissociative.

**6.** Selena believes that all behavior comes from the interaction between biology and environment. Which best aligns with her belief?

a. Genetics and physiology
b. Children and parents
c. Experience and wisdom
d. Nature and nurture

**7.** Who is showing symptoms of generalized anxiety disorder?

a. Shelia, who has unexplainable and continual tension
b. Tim, who experiences sudden episodes of intense dread
c. Denny, who has irrational and intense fear of a specific object or situation
d. Arlene, who has repetitive thoughts or actions

**8.** People with obsessive-compulsive disorder may report feeling less anxious after they clean, which causes them to want to clean again the next time they feel anxious. This demonstrates the principle of

a. stimulus generalization.
b. stimulus discrimination.
c. spontaneous recovery.
d. reinforcement.

**9.** Nolan experiences compulsions. What is he most likely to demonstrate?

   a. Worry about exposure to germs or toxins
   b. Fear that something terrible is about to happen
   c. Anxiety when objects are not lined up in an exact pattern
   d. Checking repeatedly to see if doors are locked

**10.** Kayla fought in an overseas war zone. After returning home, she finds it difficult to sleep and has a feeling of near-constant anxiety. She is most likely experiencing

   a. posttraumatic stress disorder.
   b. panic disorder.
   c. a bipolar disorder.
   d. a depressive disorder.

**11.** Shelley seeks therapy for help with the same diagnosis as most people who seek therapy. What is Shelley most likely to be diagnosed with?

   a. Depression
   b. Bipolar disorders
   c. Posttraumatic stress disorder
   d. Dissociative identity disorder

**12.** Anna Jo's risk of a bipolar disorder dramatically increases if she

   a. has suffered a debilitating injury.
   b. has an adoptive parent who has the disorder.
   c. has a biological parent with the disorder.
   d. has above-average intelligence.

**13.** Harper is exhibiting a split from reality that shows itself in disorganized speech, disturbed perceptions, and diminished or inappropriate emotional expression. These symptoms are associated with which psychological disorder(s)?

   a. Schizophrenia
   b. Depressive disorders
   c. Bipolar disorder
   d. Anxiety disorders

**14.** Yvette's identical twin was diagnosed with schizophrenia. Which statement is most accurate?

   a. Yvette likely has been diagnosed with an anxiety disorder.
   b. Yvette likely has been diagnosed with a depressive disorder.
   c. Yvette likely lives with someone diagnosed with schizophrenia.
   d. Yvette likely suffers from schizophrenia.

**15.** Amanda has been diagnosed with schizophrenia. Her main symptom is hearing voices that are not there, which is known as a

   a. delusion.
   b. paranoid thought.
   c. rumination.
   d. hallucination.

**16.** Bert feels no regret after violating others' rights and is quite clever at manipulating those around him. These are characteristics of

   a. antisocial personality disorder.
   b. avoidant personality disorder.
   c. histrionic personality disorder.
   d. narcissistic personality disorder.

**17.** Lu diets excessively and spends at least three hours a day in the gym after school. Lu has become underweight, and her parents are concerned that she may be developing

   a. narcissistic personality disorder.
   b. binge-eating disorder.
   c. bulimia nervosa.
   d. anorexia nervosa.

**18.** In which kind of therapy would the therapist be most likely to note the following during a session: "Blocks in the flow of free associations indicate resistance"?

   a. Cognitive therapy
   b. Psychoanalysis
   c. Person-centered therapy
   d. Behavioral therapy

**19.** Gladys cannot choose between humanistic therapy and psychoanalytic therapy, accurately stating they are similar because

   a. both approaches focus on the present more than on the past.
   b. both approaches are more concerned with conscious feelings than with unconscious feelings.
   c. both approaches focus on taking immediate responsibility for one's feelings.
   d. both approaches are generally considered insight therapies.

**20.** Dr. Trinity echoes, restates, and seeks clarification when she is working with her therapy clients, using techniques that are collectively called

   a. active listening.
   b. virtual reality exposure therapy.
   c. systematic desensitization.
   d. family therapy.

**21.** In an effort to help a child overcome a fear of cats, a therapist pairs a trigger stimulus (something associated with cats) with a new stimulus (for example, an appealing snack or toy) that causes an emotional response that is incompatible with fear. Which clinical orientation is this therapist using?

a. Psychodynamic
b. Behavioral
c. Biomedical
d. Humanistic

**22.** Lea, a client with depression, has been visiting a therapist for several months. During each session, she is challenged on her irrational thinking. The therapist is likely using Albert Ellis' version of

a. rational-emotive behavioral therapy.
b. aversive conditioning.
c. insight therapy.
d. person-centered therapy.

**23.** Dr. Leibowitz encourages his clients to change their thoughts and actions through

a. psychodynamic therapy.
b. person-centered therapy.
c. family therapy.
d. cognitive-behavioral therapy.

**24.** When she shared about her anxiety in a social counseling setting, Jessica discovered that others also feel anxious during tests. In what type of therapy is she engaging?

a. Psychodynamic therapy
b. Humanistic therapy
c. Cognitive therapy
d. Group therapy

**25.** Colten visits a therapist for his depression. In addition to talking to Colten about his problems, the therapist also prescribes medication. This therapist is most likely to be a

a. psychiatrist.
b. social worker.
c. clinical social worker.
d. counselor.

**26.** What should Henly say to convince her brother of the benefits of regular exercise?

a. Aerobic exercise alleviates depression only when antidepressant drugs are also taken.
b. Aerobic exercise has no impact on mental health.
c. Aerobic exercise provides relief for depressive symptoms.
d. Aerobic exercise is most effective for treating schizophrenia.

**27.** Auden no longer experiences hallucinations associated with his diagnosis of schizophrenia since he began anti-psychotic medication. What neurotransmitter was likely impacted?

a. Adrenaline
b. Epinephrine
c. Serotonin
d. Dopamine

**28.** Carlos has been prescribed an SSRI to treat his illness. This type of drug is classified as a(n)

a. antidepressant.
b. antipsychotic.
c. antianxiety.
d. mood-stabilizer.

**29.** Eloise continues to experience depressive symptoms despite taking numerous antidepressant medications. What treatment might her doctor recommend?

a. Electroconvulsive therapy
b. Lobotomy
c. Antipsychotic drugs
d. Antianxiety drugs

**30.** After overcoming severe anxiety and dealing with some physical health issues, Grace finds herself having a greater appreciation for life and a sense of increased personal strength. Her psychotherapist identifies this as

a. transference.
b. posttraumatic growth.
c. humanism.
d. behavior modification.

**31.** Alicia uses psychological science to enhance individual and community health, improve health care systems, and advocate for wellness-promoting public policies. She is most likely in which field of psychology?

a. Health
b. Positive
c. Clinical
d. Counseling

**Use the following scenario to answer questions 32 and 33:**

Dr. Ruscher is interested in stress and public speaking. She randomly selects 20 college students and 20 nonstudents to be in her study. The college student participants give a 10-minute presentation on the French Revolution, and the nonstudent participants read a book about the French Revolution for 10 minutes. Dr. Ruscher then measures all participants' cortisol levels and finds that the presentation group has a higher average cortisol level than the control group. Dr. Ruscher concludes that public speaking causes stress.

**32.** What is the operational definition of the dependent variable in this study?

a. The French Revolution
b. College student versus nonstudent status
c. Cortisol levels
d. The 10-minute time frame

**33.** Which of the following statements is true of Dr. Ruscher's conclusion?

a. Her conclusion is accurate, because she used random selection.
b. Her conclusion is inaccurate, because she has a confounding variable.
c. Her conclusion is accurate, because this is a correlational study.
d. Her conclusion is inaccurate, because cortisol is a poor indicator of stress.

**34.** Who is experiencing an approach-approach conflict?

a. Amy, who is angry at her peers for not completing their part of a group assignment
b. Magnus, who lashed out at his little brother because he is mad at his teacher
c. Owen, who is trying to decide if he will accept a lucrative summer job even though he doesn't want to put in the hours
d. Tati, who is trying to decide which of her favorite colleges to attend now that she has been accepted to both

**Use the following graph to answer questions 35 and 36:**

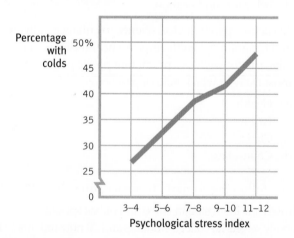

Psychological stress index

**35.** What statistical concept is illustrated in this graph?

a. A positive correlation
b. A histogram
c. A bimodal distribution
d. Regression toward the mean

**36.** What conclusion can you appropriately draw from this graph?

a. Stress causes people to catch a cold.
b. People with the highest stress scores were most vulnerable to the cold virus.
c. Catching a cold causes an increase in stress.
d. People with the lowest stress scores were most vulnerable to the cold virus.

**37.** Yeva wants to start her paper with a true statement about the relationship between money and happiness. What should she write?

a. Personal income has no relationship to happiness.
b. Over time, a rising economic tide has resulted in increased happiness and decreased depression.
c. People in countries where most people have a secure livelihood tend to be happier than those in poor countries.
d. Economic growth has been accompanied by rising inequality, which increases general happiness.

**38.** Who is engaging in problem-focused coping?

a. Christy, who watches funny videos to cheer herself up when her best friend moves away
b. Sadie, who goes on a run when she is angry at her mother
c. Nico, who eats a pint of ice cream when he is lonely
d. Dave, who goes to see a tutor after failing a chemistry exam

**39.** Although depression runs in Willow's family, Willow did not experience these symptoms until after she had a major car accident and lost her job. This example illustrates

a. the medical model.
b. the diathesis-stress model.
c. epigenetics.
d. heritability.

**40.** Thelma is applying to medical school. Even though her grades are lower than she would like, she believes in her abilities and feels that her success is in her own hands. Thelma is displaying which of the following characteristics?

a. Internal locus of control
b. Resilience
c. Learned helplessness
d. External locus of control

**41.** Anvil has taken an antipsychotic drug for decades. What movement disorder might he experience?

a. Tardive dyskinesia
b. Dissociation
c. Compulsion
d. Autism spectrum disorder

**42.** Karlina wants to reduce adverse childhood experiences because research shows that

a. they lead to PTSD for most children.
b. they are unrelated to stress in adulthood.
c. they can influence long-term stress responses and negatively impact health.
d. they keep children in the alarm stage of the general adaptation syndrome.

**43.** Marney is experiencing a negative symptom of schizophrenia. What might she be experiencing?

a. Delusions
b. Disorganized speech
c. Flat affect
d. Hallucinations

**44.** Frank is competitive, hard-driving, impatient, verbally aggressive, and anger-prone. A therapist would most likely describe him as

a. manic.
b. Type A.
c. resilient.
d. Type B.

Go to Appendix D to complete the **AP® Practice** Evidence-Based Question and Article Analysis Question for this unit.

# Enrichment Modules

# Module EM.1 Influences on Drug Use

## LEARNING TARGET

**EM.1-1** Explain why some people become regular users of consciousness-altering drugs.

**EM.1-1** Why do some people become regular users of consciousness-altering drugs?

Drug use by North American youth increased during the 1970s. Then, with increased drug education and a more realistic and deglamorized media depiction of taking drugs, drug use declined sharply (except for a small rise in the mid-1980s). After the early 1990s, the cultural antidrug voices softened, and some drugs for a time were again glamorized in music and films.

Consider, for example, historical trends in the use of marijuana:

- In the University of Michigan's annual survey of 15,000 U.S. high school seniors, the proportion who said there is "great risk" in regular marijuana use rose from 35 percent in 1978 to 79 percent in 1991, then retreated to 30 percent in 2018 (Miech et al., 2019).

- After peaking in 1978, marijuana use by U.S. high school seniors declined through 1992, then rose and held steady until beginning to trend back up in 2017 (**Figure EM.1-1**). Canadian use among 15- to 24-year-olds has been similarly trending upward since 2012, and by late 2018 this rate was 15 percent among all Canadians age 15 and older (CCSA, 2017; Statistics Canada, 2019). European teen drug use has been lower, but with trends mirroring those in North America: rising marijuana and declining cigarette use (Wadley & Lee, 2016).

**AP® Science Practice**

### Research

The historical trends in marijuana use represent non-experimental research. Researchers used surveys to obtain self-reported drug use from a representative sample.

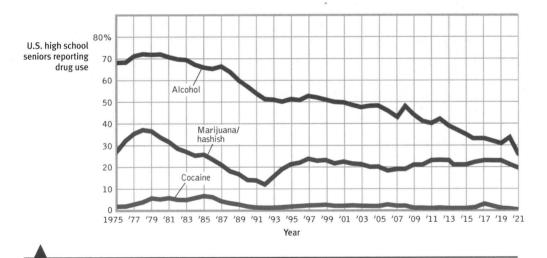

**Figure EM.1-1**

**Trends in drug use**

The percentage of U.S. twelfth graders who said they had used alcohol or marijuana during the past 30 days largely declined from the late 1970s to the 1990s, when it partially rebounded for a few years. Reported cocaine use has declined since the mid-1980s. (Data from Johnston et al., 2022.) Outside the United States, teens' drug use has also declined. In Europe, 15-year-olds' weekly alcohol use has plummeted — dropping from 26 percent to 13 percent between 2002 and 2014; in Britain it dropped from 46 percent to 10 percent (WHO, 2018b). (Data from Johnston et al., 2017; Miech et al., 2016; Johnston, L. D., Miech, R. A., O'Malley, P. M., Bachman, J. G., Schulenberg, J. E., & Patrick, M. E. (2022). *Monitoring the Future national survey results on drug use 1975-2021: Overview, key findings on adolescent drug use.* Ann Arbor: Institute for Social Research, University of Michigan.)

sutiporn/iStock/Getty Images

Warning signs of alcohol use disorder:

- Drinking binges
- Craving alcohol
- Use results in unfulfilled work, school, or home tasks
- Failing to honor a resolve to drink less
- Continued use even when aware of risks involved
- Avoiding family or friends when drinking

For some adolescents, occasional drug use represents thrill seeking. Yet why do some adolescents, but not others, become regular drug users? In search of answers, researchers have engaged biological, psychological, and social-cultural levels of analysis.

## Biological Influences

Some people may be biologically vulnerable to particular drugs. For example, an accumulating body of evidence shows that heredity influences some aspects of substance use problems, especially those appearing by early adulthood (Crabbe, 2002):

- *Genetics*. Researchers have identified genes associated with alcohol use disorder, and they are seeking genes that contribute to tobacco addiction (Stacey et al., 2012). These culprit genes seemingly produce deficiencies in the brain's natural dopamine reward system: While triggering temporary dopamine-produced pleasure, the addictive drugs disrupt normal dopamine balance. Studies of how drugs reprogram the brain's reward systems raise hopes for anti-addiction drugs that might block or blunt the effects of alcohol and other drugs (Volkow & Boyle, 2018).

- *Twin studies*. If an identical rather than a fraternal twin is diagnosed with alcohol use disorder, the other twin is at increased risk for alcohol problems (Kendler et al., 2002). In marijuana use, too, identical twins more closely resemble each other than do fraternal twins.

- *Adoption studies*. One study tracked 18,115 Swedish adoptees. Those with drug-abusing biological parents were at doubled risk of drug abuse, indicating a genetic influence — a finding confirmed in another Swedish study of 14,000+ twins and 1.3 million other siblings. But then those with drug-abusing adoptive siblings also had a doubled risk of drug abuse, indicating an environmental influence (Kendler et al., 2012; Maes et al., 2016). So, what might those environmental influences be?

## Psychological and Social-Cultural Influences

Throughout this text, you have seen that biological, psychological, and social-cultural factors interact to produce behavior. So, too, with problematic drug use (**Figure EM.1-2**). Those individuals without close, secure attachments to family and friends are more likely to turn to substance use (Fairbairn et al., 2018). One psychological factor that has appeared in studies of youth and young adults is the feeling that life is meaningless and directionless (Newcomb &

**Figure EM.1-2**

**Levels of analysis for disordered drug use**

The biopsychosocial approach enables researchers to investigate disordered drug use from complementary perspectives.

**Biological influences:**
- genetic predispositions
- variations in neurotransmitter systems

**Psychological influences:**
- lacking sense of purpose
- significant stress
- psychological disorders, such as depression

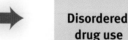

**Disordered drug use**

**Social-cultural influences:**
- difficult environment
- cultural acceptance of drug use
- negative peer influences

Harlow, 1986). This feeling is common among school dropouts who subsist without job skills, without privilege, and with little hope.

Sometimes the psychological influence is obvious. Many heavy users of alcohol, marijuana, and cocaine have experienced significant stress or failure and are depressed. Girls with a history of depression, eating disorders, or sexual or physical abuse are at increased risk for problematic substance use. So are youth undergoing school or neighborhood transitions (CASA, 2003; Logan et al., 2002). By temporarily dulling their psychological pain, psychoactive drugs may offer them a way to avoid coping with depression, anger, anxiety, or insomnia. (As Unit 3 explained, behavior is often controlled more by its immediate consequences than by its later ones.)

Smoking and vaping usually begin during early adolescence. (If cigarette manufacturers haven't made you their devoted customer by the time you reach college or university, they almost surely never will.) Adolescents, self-conscious and often thinking the world is watching their every move, are especially vulnerable to smoking's allure. They may first light up to imitate glamorous celebrities, to project a mature image, to handle stress, or to get the social reward of acceptance by other users (Cin et al., 2007; DeWall & Pond, 2011; Tickle et al., 2006). Mindful of these tendencies, tobacco product companies have effectively modeled smoking with themes that appeal to youths: attractiveness, independence, adventurousness, and social approval (Surgeon General, 2012).

Rates of drug use also vary across cultural and ethnic groups. One survey of European teens found that lifetime marijuana use ranged from 5 percent in Norway to more than eight times higher in the Czech Republic (Romelsjö et al., 2014). Alcohol and other drug addiction rates have also been low among actively religious people, with extremely low rates observed among Orthodox Jews, Mormons, Mennonites, and the Amish (DeWall et al., 2014; Salas-Wright et al., 2012).

Typically, teens who start smoking also have friends who smoke, who suggest its pleasures and offer them cigarettes (Rose et al., 1999). Among teens whose parents and best friends are nonsmokers, the smoking rate is close to zero (Moss et al., 1992; also see **Figure EM.1-3**). Similarly, if teens' friends use drugs, the odds are double that they will, too (Liu et al., 2017). Peers throw the parties and provide (or don't provide) the drugs. Teens who come from happy families, who do not begin drinking before age 15, and who do well in school tend not to use drugs, largely because they rarely associate with teens who do (Bachman et al., 2007; Hingson et al., 2006; Odgers et al., 2008).

Adolescents' expectations—what they *believe* friends are doing and favoring—also influence their behavior (Vitória et al., 2009). One study surveyed sixth graders in 22 U.S. states. How many believed their friends had smoked marijuana? About 14 percent. How many of those friends acknowledged doing so? Only 4 percent (Wren, 1999). Likewise, university students are not immune to such misperceptions: Drinking dominates social occasions partly because students overestimate their peers' enthusiasm for alcohol and underestimate their views of its risks (Prentice & Miller, 1993; Self, 1994) (**Table EM.1-1**).

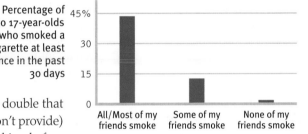

**Figure EM.1-3**
**Peer influence**

Kids seldom smoke if their friends don't (Philip Morris, 2003). A correlation-causation question: Does the close link between teen smoking and friends' smoking reflect peer influence? Teens seeking similar friends? Or both?

---

**TABLE EM.1-1  Facts About "Higher" Education**

- College and university students drink more alcohol than their nonstudent peers and exhibit 2.5 times the general population's rate of substance abuse. After college, most adults "mature out" of problem alcohol use (Lee et al., 2018).

- Fraternity and sorority members report nearly twice the binge-drinking rate of nonmembers.

- Since 1993, campus smoking rates have declined, alcohol use has been steady, and abuse of prescription opioids, stimulants, tranquilizers, and sedatives has increased, as has marijuana use.

Information from NCASA, 2007

**Nic-a-teen** Few people start smoking or vaping past the vulnerable teen and early-adult years. Eager to hook customers whose addiction will give them business for years to come, tobacco product companies focus on a young target market. Seeing celebrities, such as singer Lily Allen, smoking or vaping may tempt young people to imitate them. In 2017, more than one-third of youth-rated (G, PG, PG-13) American movies showed smoking (CDC, 2018b).

**FYI**

The percentage of adults drinking weekly or more varies by country:

| | |
|---|---|
| United States | 30% |
| Canada | 40% |
| Britain | 58% |

(Gallup Poll, data from Moore, 2006)

**❝** Substance use disorders don't discriminate; they affect the rich and the poor; they affect all ethnic groups. This is a public health crisis, but we do have solutions. **❞**

*— U.S. Surgeon General Vivek Murthy, 2016*

When students' overestimates of peer drinking are corrected, alcohol use often subsides (Moreira et al., 2009).

People whose beginning use of drugs was influenced by their peers are more likely to stop using when their friends stop or their social network changes (Chassin & MacKinnon, 2015). One study that followed 12,000 adults over 32 years found that smokers tend to quit in clusters (Christakis & Fowler, 2008). Within a social network, the odds of a person quitting increased when a spouse, friend, or co-worker stopped smoking. Similarly, most soldiers who engaged in problematic drug use while in Vietnam ceased their drug use after returning home (Robins et al., 1974).

As always with correlations, the traffic between friends' drug use and our own may be two-way: Our friends influence us. Social networks matter. But we also select as friends those people who share our likes and dislikes.

What do the findings on drug use suggest for drug prevention and treatment programs? Three channels of influence seem possible:

- Educate young people about the long-term costs of a drug's temporary pleasures.
- Help young people find other ways to boost their self-esteem and discover their purpose in life.
- Attempt to modify peer associations or to "inoculate" youth against peer pressures by training them in refusal skills.

People rarely abuse drugs if they understand the physical and psychological costs, feel good about themselves and the direction their lives are taking, and have a peer group that disapproves of using drugs. These educational, psychological, and social-cultural factors may help explain why 26 percent of U.S. high school dropouts, but only 6 percent of those with a postgraduate education, report smoking (CDC, 2011).

SNAPSHOTS at jasonlove.com

Once upon a time, peer pressure caused Bob to start smoking.

Twenty years later, it forces him to quit.

© Jason Love

## Check Your Understanding

### Examine the Concept

▶ Explain why tobacco companies try so hard to get customers hooked as teens.

▶ Studies have found that people who begin drinking in their early teens are much more likely to develop alcohol use disorder than those who begin at age 21 or older. What possible explanations might there be for this finding?

*Answers to the Examine the Concept questions can be found in Appendix C at the end of the book.*

### Apply the Concept

▶ Drinking dominates parties when students overestimate other students' enthusiasm for alcohol. What sorts of misperceptions exist at your high school?

## Module EM.1 REVIEW

**EM.1-1 Why do some people become regular users of consciousness-altering drugs?**

- Some people may be biologically vulnerable to particular drugs, such as alcohol.

- Psychological factors (such as stress or depression) and social factors (such as peer pressure) combine to lead

many people to experiment with drugs. Cultural and ethnic groups have differing rates of drug use.

- Each type of influence—biological, psychological, and social-cultural—offers a possible path for drug prevention and treatment programs.

## Multiple Choice

1. Dr. Kesler studies biological influences on drug use. Which might be a variable she studies?

   a. Variations in neurotransmitter systems
   b. The type of urban environment
   c. Peer influence
   d. The degree to which one feels a sense of purpose

2. Otto is a high school student. Based on results from studies that examine perceived rates of alcohol use, Otto will likely

   a. overestimate the percentage of fellow students who drink.
   b. accurately estimate the percentage of fellow students who drink.
   c. slightly underestimate the percentage of fellow students who drink.
   d. greatly underestimate the percentage of fellow students who drink.

# Module EM.2 Psychology at Work

For many people, to live is to work. Work supports us, enabling us to obtain food, water, and shelter. Work connects us, meeting our social needs. Work helps define us. Meeting someone for the first time and wondering about their identity, we may ask, "So, what do you do?"

We vary in our job satisfaction. On the day we leave the workforce, some of us will sadly bid our former employer farewell; others will gladly tell our former employer good riddance.

Few of us will look back and say we have followed a predictable career path. We will have changed jobs, with some of us doing so quite often. The trigger for those changes may have been shifting needs in the economy. Rapid technological change has made some jobs disappear, with new ones taking their place—and not always smoothly. In other cases, the changes may reflect a desire for better pay, happier on-the-job relationships, or more fulfilling work.

You might view your job as a necessary chore or a meaningful calling. You might also approach your job as an opportunity to do the bare minimum *or* to maximize your potential. And you may find your job to be an experience of either tedious boredom or of absorbing *flow*. Let's take a look at how psychologists can help explain why some jobs are more rewarding than others.

## Flow

### EM.2-1 What is *flow*?

Individuals across various occupations vary in their attitudes toward their work. Some view their work as a *job*, an unfulfilling but necessary way to make money. Others view their work as a *career*, an opportunity to advance from one position to a better position. The rest—those who view their work as a *calling*, a fulfilling and socially useful activity—report the highest satisfaction with their work and with their lives (Dik & Duffy, 2012; Wrzesniewski & Dutton, 2001).

These findings would not surprise Mihaly Csikszentmihalyi [chick-SENT-me-hi] (1990, 1999). He observed that our quality of life increases when we are purposefully engaged.

**Life disrupted** Playing and socializing online are ever-present sources of distraction. It takes energy to resist checking our phones, and time to refocus mental concentration after each disruption. Such frequent interruptions disrupt flow, so it's a good idea to instead schedule regular breaks for checking our handheld devices.

Between the anxiety of being overwhelmed and stressed, and the apathy of being underwhelmed and bored, lies a zone in which we experience **flow**. When was the last time you experienced flow? Perhaps you can recall being in a zoned-out flow state while online. If so, then perhaps you can sympathize with the two Northwest Airlines pilots who in 2009 were so focused on their laptops that they missed their control tower's messages. The pilots flew 150 miles past their Minneapolis destination—and lost their jobs.

Csikszentmihalyi formulated the flow concept after studying artists who spent hour after hour painting or sculpting with focused concentration. Immersed in a project, they worked as if nothing else mattered, and then, when finished, they promptly moved on. The artists seemed driven less by external rewards—money, praise, and promotion—than by the intrinsic rewards of creating their art. Nearly 200 other studies have confirmed that *intrinsic motivation* enhances performance (Cerasoli et al., 2014).

Csikszentmihalyi studied dancers, chess players, surgeons, writers, parents, mountain climbers, sailors, and farmers. His research included Australians, North Americans, Koreans, Japanese, and Italians. Participants ranged in age from the teen years to the golden years. A clear principle emerged: It's exhilarating to flow with an activity that fully engages our skills (Fong et al., 2015). Flow experiences boost our sense of self-esteem, competence, and well-being. One research team studied 10,000 Swedish twins and found that frequent flow experiences reduced their risk of depression and burnout (Mosing et al., 2018). A focused mind is a happy mind.

Idleness may sound like bliss. You may dream of a future filled with streaming movies, sleeping in, and no responsibilities. In reality, purposeful work enriches our lives. People who leave the workforce tend to become unhappy, but rejoining the workforce rapidly improves their mood (Zhou et al., 2019). Busy people are often happy people (Hsee et al., 2010; Robinson & Martin, 2008).

## Finding Your Own Flow, and Matching Interests to Work

Want to identify your own path to flow? You can start by pinpointing your strengths and the types of work that may prove satisfying and successful. Marcus Buckingham and Donald Clifton (2001) suggested asking yourself four questions:

1. Which activities give me pleasure? Bringing order out of chaos? Playing host? Helping others? Challenging sloppy thinking?

2. Which activities leave me wondering "When can I do this again?" rather than "When will this be over?"

3. Which sorts of challenges do I relish? And which do I dread?

4. Which sorts of tasks do I learn easily? And which do I struggle with?

### AP® Science Practice

#### Research

Correlations reveal the extent to which two variables (such as flow experiences and depression) relate. However, correlational research cannot explain what causes them to relate. Perhaps flow experiences reduce depression. Or perhaps depression leads to reduced flow experiences (the directionality problem). Or perhaps some third variable, such as stress, reduces flow and increases depression.

#### FYI

Have you ever noticed that when you are immersed in an activity, time flies? Conversely, when you are watching the clock, it seems to move more slowly? French researchers have confirmed that the more we attend to an event's duration, the longer it seems to last (Couli et al., 2004).

**flow** a completely involved, focused state, with diminished awareness of self and time; results from full engagement of our skills.

*"Let's face it: you and this organization have never been a good fit."*

You may find your skills engaged and time flying when you're teaching or selling or writing or cleaning or consoling or creating or repairing. If an activity feels good, if it comes easily, if you look forward to it, then look deeper. You'll see your strengths at work (Buckingham, 2007). For a free (requires registration) assessment of your own strengths, take the "Brief Strengths Test" at AuthenticHappiness.sas.upenn.edu.

The U.S. Department of Labor also offers a career interest questionnaire through its Occupational Information Network (O*NET). At MyNextMove.org/explore/ip, you will need about 10 minutes to respond to 60 items, indicating how much you would like or dislike activities ranging from building kitchen cabinets to playing a musical instrument. You will then receive feedback on how strongly your responses reflect six interest types (Holland, 1996):

- *Realistic* (hands-on doers)
- *Investigative* (thinkers)
- *Artistic* (creators)
- *Social* (helpers, teachers)
- *Enterprising* (persuaders, deciders)
- *Conventional* (organizers)

Finally, depending on how much training you are willing to complete, you will be shown occupations that fit your interest pattern (selected from a national database of 900+ occupations).

Do what you love and you will love what you do. Career counseling science aims, first, to assess people's differing values, personalities, and, especially, *interests*, which are remarkably stable and predictive of future life choices and outcomes (Dik & Rottinghaus, 2013). (Your job may change, but your interests today will likely still be your interests in 10 years.) Second, it aims to alert people to well-matched vocations—vocations with a good *person-environment fit*. It pays to have a job that fits your personality. People who are highly open earn more if they hold jobs that demand openness (actors); people who are highly conscientious earn more if they work in jobs that require conscientiousness (financial managers) (Denissen et al., 2018).

One study assessed 400,000 high school students' interests and then followed them over time. The take-home finding: "Interests uniquely predict academic and career success over and above cognitive ability and personality" (Rounds & Su, 2014). Sixty other studies have confirmed this point both for students in school and workers on the job: Interests

**AP® Science Practice**

## Research

A research design that follows people over time (such as the study of 400,000 high school students) is longitudinal. This is in contrast to cross-sectional research that compares people of different ages at one point in time.

predict both performance and persistence (Nye et al., 2012). Lack of job fit can fuel frustration, resulting in unproductive and even hostile work behavior (Harold et al., 2016). One fee-based online service, jobzology.com, was developed by *industrial-organizational psychologists* to put career counseling science into action. First, it assesses people's interests, values, personalities, and workplace culture preferences. It then suggests occupations and connects them to job listings.

# Industrial-Organizational Psychology

**EM.2-2** What are three key areas of study related to industrial-organizational psychology?

In developed nations, work has expanded from farming to manufacturing to *knowledge work*. More and more work is *outsourced* to temporary employees and consultants or to workers telecommuting from off-site workplaces (Gallup, 2020). (This book and its teaching package are developed and produced by a team of people in a dozen cities, from Alberta to Florida.)

**Industrial-organizational (I/O) psychologists** study how people perform in the modern workplace. How can psychologists help organizations make work more satisfying and productive? How can organizations, and individual workers, manage work in a way that maximizes productivity while avoiding **burnout**? What can be done to improve relationships between people working together? These are among the questions that fascinate I/O psychologists as they apply psychology's principles to the workplace and help organizations develop best practices (**Table EM.2-1**).

**industrial-organizational (I/O) psychology** the application of psychological concepts and methods to optimizing human behavior in workplaces.

**burnout** physical, emotional, or mental exhaustion, brought on by an overburdening workload, which may negatively impact motivation, performance, and attitude.

### TABLE EM.2-1 I/O Psychology and Human Factors Psychology at Work

As scientists, consultants, and management professionals, industrial-organizational (I/O) psychologists may be found helping organizations to resolve work-family conflicts, build employee retention, address organizational climate, or promote team work. Human factors psychologists contribute to safety and improved designs.

| Personnel Psychology: Maximizing Human Potential | Organizational Psychology: Building Better Organizations |
|---|---|
| **Developing training programs to increase job seekers' success** <br> **Selecting and placing employees** <br> • Developing and testing assessment tools for selecting, placing, and promoting workers <br> • Analyzing job content <br> • Optimizing worker placement | **Developing organizations** <br> • Analyzing organizational structures <br> • Maximizing worker satisfaction and productivity <br> • Facilitating organizational change |
| **Training and developing employees** <br> • Identifying needs <br> • Designing training programs <br> • Evaluating training programs | **Enhancing quality of work life** <br> • Expanding individual productivity <br> • Identifying elements of satisfaction <br> • Redesigning jobs <br> • Balancing work and nonwork life in an era of social media, smart phones, and other technologies |
| **Appraising performance** <br> • Developing guidelines <br> • Measuring individual performance <br> • Measuring organizational performance | **Human Factors Psychology** <br> • Designing optimal work environments <br> • Optimizing person-machine interactions <br> • Developing systems technologies |

Information from the Society of Industrial and Organizational Psychology. For more information about I/O psychology and related job opportunities, visit siop.org.

**The modern workforce** The editorial and production team that guides the development of this book and its resources works from far-flung places. From West to East: Ann Heath in Oregon, Trish Morgan in Alberta, Canada, Christine Brune in Colorado, Carlise Stembridge in Minnesota, Kathryn Brownson in Michigan, Betty Probert in Florida, Lauren Samuelson in Pennsylvania, Heidi Bamatter, Won McIntosh, and Ann Kirby-Payne in New York, Talia Green and Karen Misler in New Jersey, and Danielle Slevens in Massachusetts.

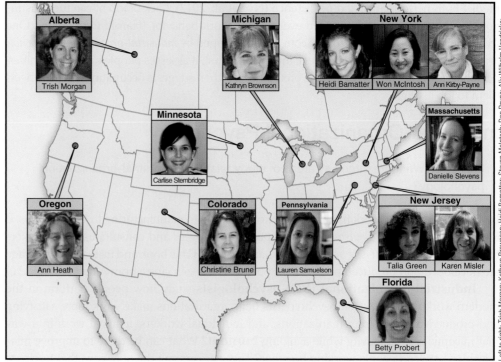

- The I/O psychology subfield of **personnel psychology** applies psychology's methods and principles to selecting, placing, training, and evaluating workers. Personnel psychologists match people with jobs, by identifying and placing well-suited candidates. The I/O psychology subfield of **organizational psychology** considers how work environments and management styles influence worker motivation, satisfaction, and productivity. It focuses on modifying jobs and supervision in ways that boost morale and productivity.

- **Human factors psychology**, now a distinct field allied with I/O psychology, explores how machines and environments can be optimally designed to fit human abilities. Human factors psychologists study people's natural perceptions and inclinations to create user-friendly machines and work settings.

## Personnel Psychology

**EM.2-3** How do personnel psychologists facilitate job seeking, employee selection, work placement, and performance appraisal?

Psychologists assist organizations at various stages of selecting and assessing employees. They may help identify needed job skills, develop effective selection methods, recruit and evaluate diverse applicants, introduce and train new employees, appraise performance, and facilitate team building among people with different cultural backgrounds. They also seek to enhance the well-being and productivity of "neurodiverse" workers—those on the autism spectrum, or those challenged by attention-deficit/hyperactivity disorder (ADHD), a learning disorder, or brain injury (Weinberg & Doyle, 2017).

Personnel psychologists also help job seekers. Across four dozen studies, training programs (which teach job-search skills, improve self-presentation, boost self-confidence, promote goal setting, and enlist support) have nearly tripled job seekers' success (Liu et al., 2014).

**personnel psychology** an I/O psychology subfield that helps with job seeking, and with employee recruitment, selection, placement, training, appraisal, and development.

**organizational psychology** an I/O psychology subfield that examines organizational influences on worker satisfaction and productivity and facilitates organizational change.

**human factors psychology** a field of psychology allied with I/O psychology that explores how people and machines interact and how machines and physical environments can be made safe and easy to use.

## Using Strengths for Successful Selection

As a new AT&T human resources executive, psychologist Mary Tenopyr (1997) was assigned to solve a problem: Customer-service representatives were failing at their jobs at a high rate. After concluding that many of the hires were ill matched to the demands of their new positions, Tenopyr developed a new selection instrument:

1. She asked new applicants to respond to various test questions (without as yet making any use of their responses).

2. She followed up later to assess which of the applicants excelled on the job.

3. She identified the earlier test questions that best predicted success.

The happy result of her data-driven work was a new test that enabled AT&T to identify likely-to-succeed representatives. Personnel selection techniques such as this one aim to recruit people with the kind of strengths that will enable them and their organization to flourish. Marry the strengths of people with the tasks of organizations and the result is often prosperity and profit.

## Do Interviews Predict Performance?

Employee selection usually includes an interview. Indeed, many interviewers feel confident of their ability to predict long-term job performance from a get-acquainted (*unstructured*) interview. What's therefore shocking is how error-prone interviewers' predictions may be when predicting job or graduate school success. General mental ability has been a better predictor, especially for complex jobs—for which it indicates people's ability to learn new skills (Schmidt & Hunter, 2004). Informal interviews are less informative than aptitude tests, work samples, job knowledge tests, and past job performance. After examining thousands of informal interviews and later job success, a Google study found "zero relationship. It's a complete random mess" (Bock, 2013).

### Unstructured Interviews and the Interviewer Illusion

Traditional, *unstructured interviews* can provide a sense of someone's personality—their expressiveness, warmth, and verbal ability, for example. But these informal interviews also give interviewees considerable power to control the impression they are making in the interview situation (Barrick et al., 2009). Why, then, do many interviewers have such faith in their ability to discern interviewees' fitness for a job? "I have excellent interviewing skills," I/O psychology consultants often hear, "so I don't need reference checking as much as someone who doesn't have my ability to read people." Overrating one's ability to predict people's futures is called the *interviewer illusion* (Dana et al., 2013; Nisbett, 1987). Five factors explain interviewers' overconfidence:

- **Interviewers presume that people are what they seem to be in the interview situation.** An unstructured interview may create a false impression of a person's behavior toward others in different situations. Some interviewees may feign desired attitudes, others may be nervous. As personality psychologists explain—and as Module 4.1 explored—when meeting others, we discount the enormous influence of varying situations and mistakenly presume that what we see is what we will get. But research on everything from chattiness to conscientiousness reveals that how we behave reflects not only our enduring traits but also the details of the particular situation (such as wanting to impress in a job interview).

- **Interviewers' preconceptions and moods color how they perceive interviewees' responses** (Cable & Gilovich, 1998; Macan & Dipboye, 1994). If interviewers instantly like a person who perhaps is similar to themselves, they may interpret the person's assertiveness as indicating "confidence" rather than "arrogance." If told certain applicants have been prescreened, interviewers are disposed to judge them more favorably. Such interviewers are showing *confirmation bias*, which we learned about in Module 5.5: They search for information that supports their preconceptions about a job candidate and ignore or distort contradictory evidence (Skov & Sherman, 1986).

- **Interviewers judge people relative to those interviewed just before and after them** (Simonsohn & Gino, 2013). If you are being interviewed for business or medical school, hope for a time when the other interviewees have been weak.

- **Interviewers more often follow the successful careers of the people they have hired than the successful careers of those they have rejected.** This missing feedback prevents interviewers from getting a reality check on their hiring ability.

- **Interviews disclose the interviewee's good intentions, which are less revealing than habitual behaviors** (Ouellette & Wood, 1998). Intentions matter. People can change. But the best predictor of the person we will be is the person we have been. Compared with work-avoiding university students, those who engage in their tasks are more likely, a decade and more later, to be engaged workers (Salmela-Aro et al., 2009). In one 40-year study, responsible, high-performing 12-year-old students tended to grow up to become successful, high-earning adult workers (Spengler et al., 2015). Wherever we go, we take ourselves along.

Hoping to improve prediction and selection, personnel psychologists have put people in simulated work situations, sought information on past performance, aggregated evaluations from multiple interviews, administered tests, and developed job-specific interviews.

## Structured Interviews

Unlike casual conversation aimed at getting a feel for someone, **structured interviews** offer a disciplined method of collecting information. A personnel psychologist may analyze a job, script questions, and train interviewers. The interviewers then ask all applicants the same questions, in the same order, and rate each applicant on established scales.

In an unstructured interview, someone might ask, "How organized are you?" "How well do you get along with people?" or "How do you handle stress?" Street-smart applicants know how to score high: "Although I sometimes drive myself too hard, I handle stress by prioritizing and delegating, and leaving time for sleep and exercise."

By contrast, structured interviews pinpoint strengths (attitudes, behaviors, knowledge, and skills) that distinguish high performers in a particular line of work. The process includes outlining job-specific situations and asking candidates to explain how they would handle them, and how they handled similar situations in their prior employment. "Tell me about a time when you were caught between conflicting demands, without time to accomplish both. How did you handle that?" In its interviews, Google has asked, "Give me an example of a time when you solved an analytically difficult problem" (Bock, 2013).

To reduce memory distortions and bias, the interviewer takes notes and makes ratings as the interview proceeds and avoids irrelevant and follow-up questions. The structured interview therefore feels less warm, but that can be explained to the applicant: "This conversation won't typify how we relate to each other in this organization."

A review of 150 findings revealed that structured interviews had double the predictive accuracy of unstructured interviews (Schmidt & Hunter, 1998; Wiesner & Cronshaw, 1988). Structured interviews also reduce bias, such as against overweight applicants (Kutcher & Bragger, 2004).

If, instead, we let our intuitions bias the hiring process, noted Malcolm Gladwell (2000, p. 86), then "all we will have done is replace the old-boy network, where you hired your nephew, with the new-boy network, where you hire whoever impressed you most when you shook his hand. Social progress, unless we're careful, can merely be the means by which we replace the obviously arbitrary with the not so obviously arbitrary."

**AP® Science Practice**

### Research

Structured interviews typically indicate qualitative research. This is in contrast to quantitative research which relies on numerical data.

**structured interview** an interview process that asks the same job-relevant questions of all applicants, each of whom is rated on established scales.

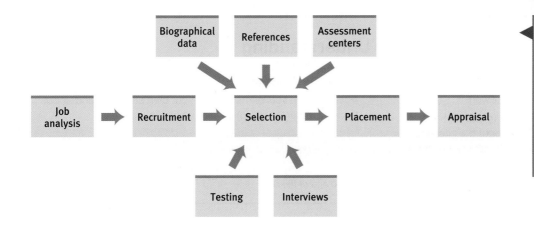

**Figure EM.2-1**
**Personnel psychologists at work**

Personnel psychologists consult in human resources activities, from job definition to recruitment to employee appraisal. The assessment center approach may be used to evaluate potential and existing employees.

To recap, personnel psychologists help train job seekers, and they assist organizations in analyzing jobs, recruiting well-suited applicants, and selecting and placing employees. They also appraise employees' performance (**Figure EM.2-1**)—our next topic.

## Appraising Performance

Performance appraisal serves organizational purposes: It helps decide who to keep on staff, how to appropriately reward and pay people, and how to better harness employee strengths, sometimes through job shifts or promotions. Performance appraisal also serves individual purposes: Feedback affirms workers' strengths and helps motivate needed improvements.

Performance appraisal methods include:

- *Checklists* on which supervisors simply check specific behaviors that describe the worker ("always attends to customers' needs," "takes long breaks").

- *Graphic rating scales* on which a supervisor checks, perhaps on a five-point scale, how often a worker is dependable, productive, and so forth.

- *Behavior rating scales* on which a supervisor checks scaled behaviors that describe a worker's performance. If rating the extent to which a worker "follows procedures," the supervisor might mark the employee somewhere between "often takes shortcuts" and "always follows established procedures" (Levy, 2003).

In some organizations, performance feedback comes not only from supervisors but also from all organizational levels. If you join an organization that practices *360-degree feedback* (**Figure EM.2-2**), you will rate yourself, your manager, and your other colleagues, and you will be rated by your manager, other colleagues, and customers (Green, 2002). The net result is often more open communication and more complete appraisal.

Performance appraisal, like other social judgments, is vulnerable to bias (Murphy & Cleveland, 1995). *Halo errors* occur when someone's overall evaluation of an employee, or of a personal trait such as their friendliness, biases ratings of their specific work-related behaviors, such as their reliability. *Leniency* and *severity errors* reflect evaluators' tendencies to be either too easy or too harsh on everyone. *Recency errors* occur when raters focus only on easily remembered recent behavior. By using multiple raters and developing objective, job-relevant performance measures, personnel psychologists seek to support their organizations while also helping employees perceive the appraisal process as fair.

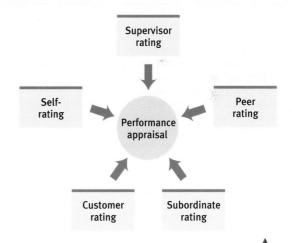

**Figure EM.2-2**
**360-degree feedback**

With multisource 360-degree feedback, our knowledge, skills, and behaviors are rated by ourselves and those around us. Professors, for example, may be rated by their department chairs, their students, and their colleagues. After receiving all these ratings, professors discuss the 360-degree feedback with their department chair.

## Check Your Understanding

**An engaged employee** Mohamed Mamow, left, was joined by his employer in saying the Pledge of Allegiance as he became a U.S. citizen. Mamow and his wife met in a Somali refugee camp. Since then, he has supported his family by working as a machine operator. Mindful of his responsibility — "I don't like to lose my job. I have a responsibility for my children and my family" — he would arrive for work a half hour early and tend to every detail on his shift. "He is an extremely hard-working employee," noted his employer, and "a reminder to all of us that we are really blessed" (Roelofs, 2010).

# Organizational Psychology

> **EM.2-4** What is the role of organizational psychologists?

Recruiting, hiring, training, and appraising capable and diverse workers matters, but so does employee motivation and morale. Organizational psychologists assist with efforts to motivate and engage employees, and they also explore effective leadership.

## Satisfaction and Engagement at Work

I/O psychologists have found that satisfaction with work, and with work-life balance, feeds overall satisfaction with life (Bowling et al., 2010). Lower job stress (sometimes supported by telecommuting) feeds better health (Allen et al., 2015).

Satisfied employees also contribute to successful organizations. Positive moods at work enhance creativity, persistence, and helpfulness (Ford et al., 2011; Jeffrey et al., 2014; Shockley et al., 2012). Are engaged, happy workers also less often absent? Less likely to quit? Less prone to theft? More punctual? More productive? Statistical digests of prior research have found a modest positive correlation between individual job satisfaction and performance (Judge et al., 2001; Ng et al., 2009). In one analysis of 4500 employees at 42 British manufacturing companies, the most productive workers were those who found their work environment satisfying (Patterson et al., 2004).

Some organizations seem to have a knack for cultivating more engaged and productive employees. In the United States, *Fortune*'s "100 Best Companies to Work For" have also produced markedly higher-than-average returns for their investors (Yoshimoto & Frauenheim, 2018). And consider a study of more than 198,000 employees in nearly 8000 business units of 36 large companies (including some 1100 bank branches, 1200 stores, and 4200 teams or departments). James Harter, Frank Schmidt, and Theodore Hayes (2002) explored correlations between various measures of organizational success and *employee engagement*—the extent of workers' involvement, enthusiasm, and identification with their organizations (**Table EM.2-2**).

| TABLE EM.2-2 **Three Types of Employees** |
|---|
| *Engaged*: working with passion and feeling a profound connection to their company or organization. |
| *Not engaged*: putting in the time but investing little passion or energy in their work. |
| *Actively disengaged*: unhappy workers undermining what their colleagues accomplish. |
| Information from Gallup via Crabtree, 2005. |

Courtesy of New Lanark Trust

**Doing well while doing good: "The Great Experiment"** At the end of the 1700s, the New Lanark, Scotland, cotton mill had more than 1000 workers. Many were children drawn from Glasgow's poorhouses. They worked 13-hour days and lived in grim conditions.

On a visit to Glasgow, Welsh-born Robert Owen — an idealistic young cotton-mill manager — chanced to meet and marry the mill owner's daughter. Owen and some partners purchased the mill and on the first day of the 1800s began what he said was "the most important experiment for the happiness of the human race that had yet been instituted at any time in any part of the world" (Owen, 1814). The exploitation of child and adult labor was, he observed, producing unhappy and inefficient workers. Owen showed *transformational leadership* when he undertook numerous innovations: a nursery for preschool children, education for older children (with encouragement rather than corporal punishment), Sundays off, health care, paid sick days, unemployment pay for days when the mill could not operate, and a company store selling goods at reduced prices. He also innovated a goals- and worker-assessment program that included detailed records of daily productivity and costs but with "no beating, no abusive language."

The ensuing commercial success fueled a humanitarian reform movement. By 1816, with decades of profitability still ahead, Owen believed he had demonstrated "that society may be formed so as to exist without crime, without poverty, with health greatly improved, with little if any misery, and with intelligence and happiness increased a hundredfold." Although his utopian vision has not been fulfilled, Owen's great experiment laid the groundwork for employment practices that have today become accepted in much of the world.

They found that engaged workers (compared with disengaged workers who are just putting in their time) knew what was expected of them, had what they needed to do their work, felt fulfilled in their work, had regular opportunities to do what they do best, perceived that they were part of something significant, and had opportunities to learn and develop. They also found that business units with engaged employees had more loyal customers, lower turnover rates, higher productivity, and greater profits.

What percentage of employees are engaged? One massive study of 6.4 million people in 159 countries showed that only about 15 percent of workers reported being engaged (Gallup, 2017, 2020). Engagement—feeling involved in and enthusiastic about one's work—is highest among people who have knowledge-based jobs, flexible hours, and freedom to work remotely. More organizations now offer such benefits in the hopes of increasing employee engagement (Eisenberger et al., 2019).

But what causal arrows explain this correlation between business success and employee morale and engagement? Does success boost morale, or does high morale boost success? In a follow-up longitudinal study of 142,000 workers, researchers found that, over time, employee attitudes predicted future business success (more than the other way around) (Harter et al., 2010). Many other studies confirm that happy workers tend to be good workers (Ford et al., 2011; Seibert et al., 2011; Shockley et al., 2012). One analysis compared companies with top-quartile versus below-average employee engagement levels. Over a three-year period, earnings grew 2.6 times faster for the companies with highly engaged workers (Ott, 2007). It pays to have employees engaged.

## Effective Leadership

**EM.2-5** How can leaders be most effective?

Engaged employees don't just happen. Most have effective **leaders**—people who motivate and influence them to enable their group's success, and who engage their interests and loyalty (Royal, 2019). Great managers support employees' well-being, articulate goals clearly, and lead in ways that suit the situation and consider the cultural context.

**leadership** an individual's ability to motivate and influence others to contribute to their group's success.

**Task significance** People find their work meaningful and engaging when it has task significance — when they view their work as benefiting others (Allan, 2017).

## Setting Specific, Challenging Goals

Measurable objectives, such as "finish gathering the history paper information by Friday," focus our attention and stimulate us to persist and to be creative. Goals motivate achievement, especially when combined with progress reports (Harkin et al., 2016). For many people, a landmark in time — a special birthday, the new year or new school term, graduation, a new job — spurs personal goal setting (Dai et al., 2014). Action plans that break large goals into smaller steps (subgoals) and that specify *implementation intentions* — when, where, and how to achieve those steps — increase the chances of completing a project on time (Fishbach et al., 2006; Gollwitzer & Sheeran, 2006). Through a task's ups and downs, we best sustain our mood and motivation when we focus on immediate goals (such as daily study) rather than distant goals (such as a class grade). Better to have our nose to the grindstone than our eye on the ultimate prize (Houser-Marko & Sheldon, 2008).

Thus, before beginning each new edition of this book, our author-editor-staff team *manages by objectives* — we agree on target dates for the completion of each draft. If we focus on achieving each of these short-term goals, the prize — an on-time book — takes care of itself. So, to motivate high productivity, effective leaders work with people to define explicit goals, subgoals, and implementation plans, and then provide feedback on progress. Such goals are SMART goals — *s*pecific, *m*easurable, *a*ctionable, *r*ealistic, and *t*ime-bound (SIOP, 2018).

## Choosing an Appropriate Leadership Style

Effective leaders of laboratory groups, work teams, and large corporations often exude *charisma* — an ability to influence others while making them comfortable (Goethals & Allison, 2014; Tskhay et al., 2018). Charismatic people have the ability to inspire others' loyalty and to focus their enthusiasm (Grabo & van Vugt, 2016).

Charisma can bolster leadership, especially when combined with practical managerial skills (Vergauwe et al., 2018). What other qualities help? Leadership styles vary, depending on both the qualities of the leader and the demands of the situation (Badura et al., 2019). In some situations (think of a commander leading troops into battle), a directive style may be needed (Fiedler, 1981). In other situations — developing a comedy show, for example — a leader might get better results by using a democratic style that welcomes team member creativity.

Leaders differ in the personal qualities they bring to the job. Some excel at **task leadership** — by setting standards, organizing work, and focusing attention on goals.

**❝** *Good leaders don't ask more than their constituents can give, but they often ask — and get — more than their constituents intended to give or thought it was possible to give.* **❞**

— *John W. Gardner,* Excellence, *1984*

**task leadership** goal-oriented leadership that sets standards, organizes work, and focuses attention on goals.

To keep the group centered on its mission, task leaders typically use a directive style, which can work well if the leader gives good directions (Fiedler, 1987).

Other managers excel at **social leadership**. They explain decisions, help group members solve their conflicts, and build teams that work well together (Evans & Dion, 1991; Pfaff et al., 2013). Social leaders, many of whom are women, often have a democratic style. They share authority and welcome team members' opinions. Social leadership and team-building increases morale and productivity (Shuffler et al., 2011, 2013). We usually feel more satisfied and motivated, and perform better, when we can participate in decision making (Cawley et al., 1998; Pereira & Osburn, 2007). Moreover, when members are sensitive to one another and participate equally, groups solve problems with greater "collective intelligence" (Woolley et al., 2010).

In one study of 50 Dutch companies, the firms with the highest morale had chief executives who most inspired their colleagues "to transcend their own self-interests for the sake of the collective" (de Hoogh et al., 2004). *Transformational leadership* of this kind motivates others to identify with and commit themselves to the group's mission.

> **social leadership** group-oriented leadership that builds teamwork, mediates conflict, and offers support.

Transformational leaders, many of whom are natural extraverts, articulate high standards, inspire people to share their vision, and offer personal attention (Bono & Judge, 2004). The frequent result is more engaged, trusting, and effective workers (Turner et al., 2002). Women, more than men, tend to exhibit transformational leadership qualities (Wang et al., 2018).

Studies in India, Taiwan, and Iran suggest that effective managers—whether in coal mines, banks, or government offices—often exhibit a high degree of *both* task and social leadership (Smith & Tayeb, 1989). As achievement-minded people, effective managers care about how well work is done, yet they are sensitive to their subordinates' needs. Workers in family-friendly organizations that offer flexible working hours report feeling greater job satisfaction and loyalty to their employers (Butts et al., 2013; Roehling et al., 2001). Over time, U.S. senators who practice common virtues (humility, wisdom, and courage) become more influential in leadership roles than do those who practice manipulation and intimidation (ten Brinke et al., 2016). Social virtues work.

**The power of positive coaching** Football coach Pete Carroll, who led the University of Southern California to two national championships and the Seattle Seahawks to a Super Bowl championship, has combined positive enthusiasm and fun workouts with "a commitment to a nurturing environment that allows people to be themselves while still being accountable to the team" (Trotter, 2014). "It shows you can win with positivity," noted former Seahawks defensive star Richard Sherman. "It's literally all positive reinforcement," said teammate Jimmy Graham (Belson, 2015).

**Positive Reinforcement** Effective leadership often builds on a basic principle of *operant conditioning*: To teach a behavior, catch a person doing something right and reinforce it. It sounds simple, but many managers are like parents who, when a child brings home a near-perfect school report card, focus on the one low grade in a troublesome biology class and ignore the rest. "Sixty-five percent of Americans received NO praise or recognition in the workplace last year," reported the Gallup Organization (2004).

**Fulfilling the Need to Belong** A work environment that satisfies employees' need to belong is energizing. Employees who enjoy high-quality colleague relationships engage with their work with more vigor (Carmeli et al., 2009). In one study, Gallup researchers asked more than 15 million employees worldwide if they have a "best friend at work." The 30 percent who do "are *seven times* as likely to be engaged in their jobs" as those who don't, report Tom Rath and James Harter (2010). And, as we noted earlier, positive, engaged employees are a hallmark of thriving organizations.

**Participative Management** Employee participation in decision making is common in Sweden, Japan, the United States, and elsewhere (Cawley et al., 1998; Sundstrom et al., 1990). Workers given a chance to voice their opinion and be part of the decision-making process have responded more positively to the final decision (van den Bos & Spruijt, 2002). They also feel more empowered and are likely, therefore, to be more creative and committed (Hennessey & Amabile, 2010; Seibert et al., 2011).

The ultimate in employee participation is the employee-owned company, of which there are said to be some 2000 in the United States—including Publix Supermarkets with its nearly 200,000 employees (Lapp, 2019). One such company in my [DM's] town is the Fleetwood Group—a thriving 165-employee manufacturer of educational furniture and wireless communication. Every employee owns part of the company, and as a group they own 100 percent. The more years employees work, the more they own, yet no one owns more than 5 percent. Like every corporate president, Fleetwood's president works for his stockholders—who also just happen to be his employees.

As a company that endorses faith-inspired "respect and care for each team member-owner," Fleetwood is free to place people above profits. Thus, when orders lagged during a recession, the employee-owners decided that job security meant more to them than profits. So the company paid otherwise idle workers to do community service, such as answering phones at nonprofit agencies and building Habitat for Humanity houses. Employee ownership attracts and retains talented people, which for Fleetwood has meant company success.

## Cultural Influences on Leadership Styles

> **EM.2-6** What cultural influences need to be considered when choosing an effective leadership style?

I/O psychology sprang from North American roots. So, how well do its leadership principles apply to cultures worldwide?

One worldwide investigation, Project GLOBE (Global Leadership and Organizational Behavior Effectiveness), has studied cultural variations in leadership expectations (House et al., 2001). Some cultures, for example, encourage collective sharing of resources and rewards; others are more individualist. Some cultures minimize traditional gender roles; others accentuate them. Some cultures prioritize being friendly, caring, and kind; others encourage a "me first" attitude. The program's first research phase studied 17,300 leaders of 950 organizations in 61 countries (Brodbeck et al., 2008; Dorfman et al., 2012). One finding: Leaders who fulfill expectations, such as by being directive in some cultures or participative in others, tend to be successful. Cultures shape leadership and what makes for leadership success.

Nevertheless, some leader behaviors are universally effective. From its massive study of nearly 50,000 business units in 45 countries, the Gallup Organization observed that thriving companies tend to focus on identifying and enhancing employee *strengths* (rather than punishing their deficiencies). Doing so predicts increased employee engagement, customer satisfaction, and profitability (Rigoni & Asplund, 2016a,b). *Strengths-based* leadership pays dividends, supporting happier, more creative, and more productive employees in workplaces with less absenteeism and turnover (Amabile & Kramer, 2011; De Neve et al., 2013).

Moreover, the same principles affect college student satisfaction, retention, and future success (Larkin et al., 2013; Ray & Kafka, 2014). Students who feel supported by caring friends and mentors, and engaged in their campus life, tend to persist and ultimately succeed during school and after graduation.

\* \* \*

So far, we have considered *personnel psychology*, the I/O psychology subfield that focuses on training job seekers and assisting with employee selection, placement, appraisal, and development. We have also considered *organizational psychology*, the I/O psychology subfield that focuses on worker satisfaction and productivity, and on organizational change. Next, we turn to *human factors psychology*, which explores the human-machine interface.

---

**AP® Science Practice**

## Check Your Understanding

**Examine the Concept**

▶ Describe the two basic types of leadership. How do the most effective managers employ these leadership strategies?

▶ What characteristics are important for transformational leaders?

**Apply the Concept**

▶ How might you use what you've learned about effective goal-setting to achieve more in your own life?

*Answers to the Apply the Concept questions can be found in Appendix C at the end of the book.*

---

# Human Factors Psychology

**EM.2-7** How do human factors psychologists work to create user-friendly machines and work settings?

Designs sometimes neglect the human factor. Cognitive scientist Donald Norman (2001) bemoaned the complexity of assembling his new HDTV, related components, and seven remotes into a usable home theater system: "I was VP of Advanced Technology at Apple. I can program dozens of computers in dozens of languages. I understand television, really, I do. . . . It doesn't matter: I am overwhelmed."

*Human factors psychologists* work with designers and engineers to tailor appliances, machines, and work settings to our natural perceptions and inclinations. Bank ATM machines are internally more complex than remote controls ever were, yet thanks to human factors engineering, ATMs are easier to operate. Digital recorders have solved the TV recording problem with a simple select-and-click menu system ("record that one"). Apple similarly engineered easy usability into the iPhone and iPad. Handheld and wearable technologies are increasingly making use of *haptic* (touch-based) feedback — opening a phone with a thumbprint, sharing your heartbeat via a smartwatch, or having GPS directional instructions ("turn left" arrow) "drawn" on your skin with other wrist-worn devices.

Norman hosts a website (jnd.org) that illustrates good designs that fit people (**Figure EM.2-3**). Human factors psychologists also help design efficient environments. An ideal kitchen layout, researchers have found, puts needed items close to their usage point and near eye level. It locates work areas to enable doing tasks in order, such as

**Figure EM.2-3**

**Designing products that fit people**

Human factors expert Donald Norman offers these and other examples of effectively designed products. The Ride On Carry On foldable chair attachment, "designed by a flight attendant mom," enables a small suitcase to double as a stroller. The Oxo measuring cup allows the user to see the quantity from above.

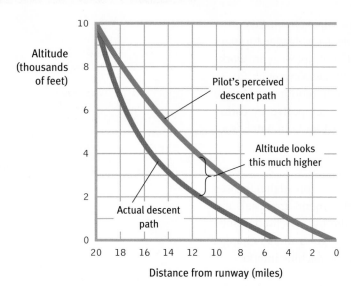

**Figure EM.2-4**

**The human factor in accidents**

Lacking distance cues when approaching a runway from over a dark surface, pilots simulating a night landing tended to fly too low. (Data from Kraft, 1978.)

*Altitude (thousands of feet)*

Pilot's perceived descent path

Altitude looks this much higher

Actual descent path

*Distance from runway (miles)*

placing the refrigerator, stove, and sink in a triangle. It creates counters that enable hands to work at or slightly below elbow height (Boehm-Davis, 2005).

Understanding human factors can help prevent accidents. By studying the human factors in driving accidents, psychologists seek to devise ways to reduce the distractions, fatigue, and inattention that contribute to 1.25 million annual worldwide traffic fatalities (WHO, 2016). At least two-thirds of all commercial air accidents have been caused by human error (Shappell et al., 2007). After beginning commercial flights in the 1960s, the Boeing 727 was involved in several landing accidents caused by pilot error. Psychologist Conrad Kraft (1978) noted a common setting for these accidents: All took place at night, and all involved landing short of the runway after crossing a dark stretch of water or unilluminated ground. Kraft reasoned that, on rising terrain, city lights beyond the runway would project a larger retinal image, making the ground seem farther away than it was. By re-creating these conditions in flight simulations, Kraft discovered that pilots were deceived into thinking they were flying higher than their actual altitudes (**Figure EM.2-4**). Aided by Kraft's finding, the airlines began requiring the co-pilot to monitor the altimeter—calling out altitudes during the descent—and the accidents diminished.

Human factors psychologists can also help us to function in other settings. Consider the available *assistive listening* technologies in various theaters, auditoriums, and places of worship. One technology, commonly available in the United States, requires a headset attached to a pocket-sized receiver. The well-meaning people who provide these systems correctly understand that the technology puts sound directly into the user's ears. Alas, few people with hearing loss elect the hassle and embarrassment of locating, requesting, wearing, and returning a conspicuous headset. Most such units therefore sit in closets. As an alternative, Britain, the Scandinavian countries, Australia, and now many parts of the United States have installed *loop systems* (see hearingloop.org) that broadcast customized sound directly through a person's own hearing aid. When suitably equipped, a hearing aid can be transformed by a discreet touch of a switch into a customized in-the-ear speaker. When offered convenient, inconspicuous, personalized sound, many more people elect to use assistive listening.

Designs that enable safe, easy, and effective interactions between people and technology often seem obvious after the fact. Why, then, aren't they more common? Technology developers, like all of us, sometimes mistakenly assume that others share their expertise—that what's clear to them will similarly be clear to others (Camerer et al., 1989; Nickerson, 1999). When people rap their knuckles on a table to convey a familiar tune (try this with a friend), they often expect their listener to recognize it. But for the listener, this is a near-impossible task (Newton, 1991). When you know a thing, it's hard to mentally simulate what it's like not to know—a phenomenon called the *curse of knowledge*.

*The point to remember*: Everyone benefits when designers and engineers tailor machines, technologies, and environments to fit human abilities and behaviors, when they user-test their work before production and distribution, and when they remain mindful of the curse of knowledge.

❝ *The better you know something, the less you remember about how hard it was to learn.* ❞

— *Psychologist Steven Pinker,* The Sense of Style, *2014*

**The human factor in safe landings** Advanced cockpit design and rehearsed emergency procedures aided pilot Chesley "Sully" Sullenberger, a U.S. Air Force Academy graduate who earned a master's degree in industrial psychology. In 2009, Sullenberger's instantaneous decisions safely guided his disabled airplane onto New York City's Hudson River, where all 155 of the passengers and crew were safely evacuated.

Steven Day/AP Photo

---

**AP® Science Practice**

## Check Your Understanding

### Examine the Concept

▶ Explain what is meant by the *curse of knowledge*. What does it have to do with the work of human factors psychologists?

### Apply the Concept

▶ What situations have you experienced (using new technology, visiting new or remodeled building spaces, taking various modes of transportation) where the design did not work well? What situations have you experienced in which planners did a particularly good job matching machines and physical environments to our abilities and expectations?

*Answers to the Examine the Concept questions can be found in Appendix C at the end of the book.*

---

# Module EM.2 REVIEW

**EM.2-1** What is *flow*?

● *Flow* is a completely involved, focused state of consciousness with diminished awareness of self and time. It results from fully engaging one's skills.

**EM.2-2** What are three key areas of study related to industrial-organizational psychology?

● I/O psychology's three subfields are *personnel, organizational,* and *human factors* psychology.

**EM.2-3** How do personnel psychologists facilitate job seeking, employee selection, work placement, and performance appraisal?

● Personnel psychologists work with job seekers to improve their searching and self-presentation skills, and with organizations to devise selection methods for new employees, recruit and evaluate applicants, design and evaluate training programs, identify people's strengths, analyze job content, and appraise individual and organizational performance.

● Unstructured interviews foster the interviewer illusion; *structured interviews* pinpoint job-relevant strengths and are better predictors of performance.

● Checklists, graphic rating scales, and behavior rating scales are useful performance appraisal methods.

**EM.2-4** What is the role of organizational psychologists?

● Organizational psychologists examine influences on worker satisfaction and productivity and facilitate organizational change. Employee satisfaction and engagement tend to correlate with organizational success.

**EM.2-5** How can leaders be most effective?

● Effective leaders set specific challenging goals and choose an appropriate leadership style. Leadership style may be goal-oriented (*task leadership*), group-oriented (*social leadership*), or some combination of the two.

**EM.2-6** What cultural influences need to be considered when choosing an effective leadership style?

- Leaders who fulfill their culture's expectations—by promoting individualism or collectivism, showing kindness or aggressiveness, or accentuating or downplaying of gender roles—tend to be successful.

- Other leader behaviors—such as supporting employees by focusing on their strengths—are universally effective.

**EM.2-7** How do human factors psychologists work to create user-friendly machines and work settings?

- Human factors psychologists contribute to human safety and improved design by encouraging developers and designers to consider human perceptual abilities, to avoid the curse of knowledge, and to test users to reveal perception-based problems.

---

## Multiple Choice

1. Carla is reading a gripping novel and loses track of time, making her late for practice. Carla may have been experiencing
   a. flow.
   b. I/O psychology.
   c. self-efficacy.
   d. performance appraisal.

2. Job seekers at a technology company are screened by different interviewers, but each is asked the same questions. The company is making use of
   a. structured interviews.
   b. employee engagement.
   c. unstructured interviews.
   d. human factors psychology.

3. Mr. Sears is seeking 360-degree feedback from his employees. He is most likely engaging in
   a. interviews.
   b. performance appraisal.
   c. employee selection.
   d. transformational leadership.

4. Dr. V.K. uses structured interviews in his research. Which is most likely true about Dr. V.K.'s research?
   a. He does qualitative research.
   b. He does experimental research.
   c. He cannot do non-experimental research.
   d. He only does quantitative research.

5. Dr. Millis is an industrial-organizational psychologist. Which of the following questions is her research most likely to address?
   a. How can machines be optimally designed to fit human abilities?
   b. What makes a structured interview valid?
   c. What makes people perform well in the workplace?
   d. Do experiences of flow increase over the lifespan?

# Module EM.3 Animal Thinking and Language

## Do Other Species Share Our Cognitive Skills?

**EM.3-1** What do we know about thinking in other species?

Other animals are surprisingly smart (de Waal, 2016) (**Figure EM.3-1**). In her 1908 book *The Animal Mind*, pioneering psychologist Margaret Floy Washburn argued that animals' consciousness and intelligence can be inferred from their behavior. In 2012, neuroscientists convening at the University of Cambridge added that animal consciousness can also be inferred from their brains: "Nonhuman animals, including all mammals and birds," possess the neural networks "that generate consciousness" (Low, 2012). Consider, then, what animal brains can do. Module 2.2b described animals displaying insight, but here are some other animal tricks.

### Using Concepts and Numbers

By touching screens in quest of a food reward, black bears have learned to sort pictures into animal and nonanimal categories, or concepts (Vonk et al., 2012). Chimpanzees, gorillas, and monkeys also form concepts, such as *cat* and *dog*. After monkeys have learned these concepts, certain frontal lobe neurons in their brain fire in response to new "cat-like" images, others to new "dog-like" images (Freedman et al., 2001). Even pigeons—mere birdbrains—can sort objects (pictures of cars, cats, chairs, and flowers) into categories. Shown a picture of a never-before-seen chair, pigeons will reliably peck a key that represents *chairs* (Wasserman, 1995).

### Transmitting Culture

Like humans, other species invent behaviors and transmit cultural patterns to their observing peers and offspring (Boesch-Achermann & Boesch, 1993). Forest-dwelling chimpanzees select different tools for different purposes—a heavy stick for making holes, a light, flexible stick for fishing for termites, a pointed stick for roasting marshmallows. (Just kidding: They don't roast marshmallows, but they have surprised us with their sophisticated tool use [Sanz et al., 2004]). Researchers have found at least 39 local customs related to chimpanzee tool use, grooming, and courtship (Claidière & Whiten, 2012; Whiten & Boesch, 2001). One group may slurp termites directly from a stick; another group may pluck them off individually. One group may break nuts with a stone hammer, while their neighbors use a wooden hammer. One chimpanzee discovered that tree moss could absorb water for drinking from a waterhole, and within six days seven other observant chimpanzees began doing the same (Hobaiter et al., 2014). These transmitted behaviors,

(a)

(b)

**Figure EM.3-1**
**Animal talents**

(a) One male chimpanzee in Sweden's Furuvik Zoo was observed every morning collecting stones into a neat little pile, which later in the day he used as ammunition to pelt visitors (Osvath & Karvonen, 2012). (b) Crows studied by Christopher Bird and Nathan Emery (2009) quickly learned to raise the water level in a tube and nab a floating worm by dropping in stones. Other crows have used twigs to probe for insects, and bent strips of metal to reach food.

**AP® Science Practice**

**Research**

Recall from Module 0.5 that animal researchers must follow ethical guidelines, as do researchers who work with human participants.

**Animal cognition in action** Until his death in 2007, Alex, an African Grey parrot, categorized and named objects (Pepperberg, 2009, 2012, 2013). Among his jaw-dropping numerical skills was the ability to comprehend numbers up to 8. He could speak the number of objects. He could add two small clusters of objects and announce the sum. He could indicate which of two numbers was greater. And he gave correct answers when shown various groups of objects. Asked, for example, "What color four?" (meaning "What's the color of the objects of which there are four?"), he could speak the answer.

along with differing communication and hunting styles, are the chimpanzee version of cultural diversity.

Several studies have brought chimpanzee and baboon cultural transmission into the laboratory (Claidière et al., 2014; Horner et al., 2006). If Chimpanzee A obtains food either by sliding or by lifting a door, Chimpanzee B will then typically do the same to get food. And so will Chimpanzee C after observing Chimpanzee B. Across a chain of six animals, chimpanzees see, and chimpanzees do.

## Other Cognitive Skills

A baboon in an 80-member troop can distinguish every other member's voice (Jolly, 2007). Great apes, dolphins, and elephants recognize themselves in a mirror, demonstrating self-awareness. Dolphins form coalitions, cooperatively hunt, and learn tool use from one another (Bearzi & Stanford, 2010). In Shark Bay, Western Australia, a small group of dolphins learned to use marine sponges as protective nose guards when probing the sea floor for fish (Krützen et al., 2005). Elephants also display their abilities to learn, remember, discriminate smells, empathize, cooperate, teach, and spontaneously use tools (Byrne et al., 2009). Chimpanzees show altruism, cooperation, and group aggression. Like humans, they will purposefully kill their neighbor to gain land, and they grieve over dead relatives (Anderson et al., 2010; Biro et al., 2010; Mitani et al., 2010).

\* \* \*

There is no question that other species display many remarkable cognitive skills. But one big question remains: Do they, like humans, exhibit language?

## Do Other Species Have Language?

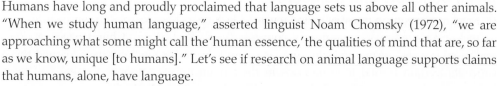

**EM.3-2** What do we know about other species' capacity for language?

Humans have long and proudly proclaimed that language sets us above all other animals. "When we study human language," asserted linguist Noam Chomsky (1972), "we are approaching what some might call the 'human essence,' the qualities of mind that are, so far as we know, unique [to humans]." Let's see if research on animal language supports claims that humans, alone, have language.

Some animals display basic language processing. Pigeons can learn the difference between words and nonwords, but they could never read this book (Scarf et al., 2016). Other animals show impressive comprehension and communication. Various monkey species sound different alarm cries for different predators, such as a barking call for a leopard, a cough for an eagle, and a chuttering for a snake. Hearing the leopard alarm, vervets climb the nearest tree. Hearing the eagle alarm, they rush into the bushes. Hearing the snake chutter, they stand up and scan the ground (Byrne, 1991; Clarke et al., 2015; Coye et al., 2015). To indicate such things as a type of threat—an eagle, a leopard, a falling tree, a neighboring group—monkeys will combine 6 different calls into a 25-call sequence (Balter, 2010). But are such communications language?

Psychologists Allen Gardner and Beatrix Gardner (1969) aroused enormous scientific and public interest with their work with Washoe, a young chimpanzee. Building on chimpanzees' natural tendencies for gestured communication, they taught Washoe sign language. After four years, Washoe could use 132 signs; by her life's end in 2007, she was using 250 signs (Metzler, 2011; Sanz et al., 1998).

During the 1970s, more and more reports came in. Some chimpanzees were stringing signs together to form sentences. Washoe, for example, signed "You me go out, please." Some word combinations seemed creative—saying *water bird* for "swan" or *apple-which-is-orange* for "orange" (Patterson, 1978; Rumbaugh, 1977).

**Talking hands** Human language appears to have evolved from gestured communications (Corballis, 2002, 2003; Pollick & de Waal, 2007). Even today, gestures are naturally associated with spontaneous speech, and similarly so for blind and sighted speakers of a given language (Özçaliskan et al., 2016). Both gesture and speech communicate, and when they convey the same rather than different information (as they do in baseball's sign language), we humans understand faster and more accurately (Hostetter, 2011; Kelly et al., 2010). Outfielder William Hoy, the first deaf player to join the major leagues (1892), reportedly helped invent hand signals for "Strike!", "Safe!" (shown here), and "Yerr out!" (Pollard, 1992). Referees in all sports now use invented signs, and fans are fluent in sports sign language.

But by the late 1970s, other psychologists were growing skeptical. Were the chimps language champs or were the researchers chumps? Consider, said the skeptics:

- Ape vocabularies and sentences are simple, rather like those of a 2-year-old child. And apes gain their limited vocabularies only with great difficulty (Wynne, 2004, 2008). Speaking or signing children can easily soak up dozens of new words each week, and 60,000 by adulthood.

- Chimpanzees can make signs or push buttons in sequence to get a reward. But pigeons, too, can peck a sequence of keys to get grain (Straub et al., 1979). The apes' signing might be nothing more than aping their trainers' signs and learning that certain arm movements produce rewards (Terrace, 1979).

- When information is unclear, we are prone to *perceptual set*—a tendency to see what we want or expect to see (Module 2.1a). Interpreting chimpanzee signs as language may have been little more than the trainers' wishful thinking (Terrace, 1979). When Washoe signed *water bird*, she may have been separately naming *water* and *bird*.

- "Give orange me give eat orange me eat orange . . ." is a far cry from the exquisite syntax of a 3-year-old (Anderson, 2004; Pinker, 1995). Rules of syntax in human language govern the order of words in sentences, so to a child, "You tickle" and "Tickle you" communicate different ideas. A chimpanzee, lacking these rules of syntax, might use the same sequence of signs for both phrases.

Controversy can stimulate progress, and in this case, it triggered more evidence of chimpanzees' abilities to think and communicate. One surprising finding was that Washoe trained her adopted son Loulis to use the signs she had learned. After her second infant died, Washoe became withdrawn when told, "Baby dead, baby gone, baby finished." Two weeks later, researcher-caretaker Roger Fouts (1992, 1997) signed better news: "I have baby for you." Washoe reacted with instant excitement. Hair on end, she swaggered and panted while signing over and again, "Baby, my baby." It took several hours for the foster mom and infant to warm to each other, but then Washoe broke the ice by signing, "Come baby" and cuddling Loulis. Without human assistance, Loulis eventually picked up 68 signs, simply by observing Washoe and three other language-trained chimps signing together.

Even more stunning was a later report: Kanzi, a bonobo with a reported 384-word vocabulary, could understand syntax in spoken English (Savage-Rumbaugh et al., 1993, 2009). Kanzi, who appears to have the receptive language ability of a human 2-year-old, has responded appropriately when asked, "Can you show me the light?" and "Can you bring me the [flash]light?" and "Can you turn the light on?" Given stuffed animals and asked—for the first time—to "make the dog bite the snake," he put the snake to the dog's mouth.

So, how should we interpret such studies? Are humans the only language-using species? If by *language* we mean an ability to communicate through a meaningful sequence of symbols, then apes are indeed capable of language. But if we mean a verbal or signed expression of complex grammar, most psychologists would now agree that humans alone possess language. Moreover, 2½-year-old children display some cognitive abilities, such as following an actor's gaze to a target, that are unmatched even by chimpanzees (Herrmann et al., 2010). Humans, alone, also have a version of a gene (*FOXP2*) that helps enable the lip, tongue, and vocal cord movements of human speech (Lieberman, 2013). Humans with a mutated form of this gene have difficulty speaking words.

One thing is certain: Studies of animal language and thinking have moved psychologists toward a greater appreciation of other species' remarkable abilities (Friend, 2004; Rumbaugh & Washburn, 2003; Wilson et al., 2015). In the past, many psychologists doubted that other species could plan, form concepts, count, use tools, or show compassion (Thorpe, 1974). Today, thanks to animal researchers, we know better. Other species exhibit insight, show family loyalty, communicate with and care for one another, and transmit cultural patterns across generations. Working out what this means for the moral rights of other animals is an unfinished task.

*Susanne Baus/AFP/Newscom*

**Comprehending canine** Border collie Rico had a vocabulary of 200 human words. If asked to retrieve a toy with a name he had never heard, Rico would pick out a new toy from a group of familiar items (Kaminski et al., 2004). Hearing that name for the second time four weeks later, Rico more often than not would retrieve the same toy. Another border collie, Chaser, has set an animal record by learning more than 1000 object names (Pilley, 2013). Like a 3-year-old child, she can also categorize them by function and shape. She can "fetch a ball" or "fetch a doll."

*Paul Fusco/Magnum Photos*

**But is this language?** Chimpanzees' ability to express themselves in American Sign Language (ASL) raises questions about the very nature of language. Here, the trainer is asking, "What is this?" The sign in response is "Baby." Does the response constitute language?

## Check Your Understanding

**Examine the Concept**

▶ If your dog barks at a stranger at the door, does this qualify as language? What if the dog yips in a telltale way to let you know she needs to go out?

**Apply the Concept**

▶ Can you think of a time when you felt an animal was communicating with you? How might you put such intuition to a test?

*Answers to the Examine the Concept questions can be found in Appendix C at the end of the book.*

# Module EM.3 REVIEW

**EM.3-1 What do we know about thinking in other species?**

- Researchers make inferences about other species' consciousness and intelligence based on behavior. The main focus of such research has been the great apes, but other species have also been studied.

- Evidence to date shows that other species can use concepts, numbers, and tools, and they can transmit learning from one generation to the next (cultural transmission). They also show insight, self-awareness, altruism, cooperation, and grief.

**EM.3-2 What do we know about other species' capacity for language?**

- A number of great apes (mostly chimpanzees) have learned to communicate with humans by signing or by pushing buttons, have developed vocabularies of nearly 400 words, have communicated by stringing these words together, have taught their skills to younger animals, and have shown some understanding of syntax.

- While only humans communicate in complex sentences, primates' and other animals' impressive abilities to think and communicate challenge humans to consider what this means about the moral rights of other species.

## Multiple Choice

**1.** Which of the following is an example of an animal using concepts?

a. A parrot identifies the number and color of objects.
b. A dog identifies the scent of its owner.
c. A parrot learns to say phrases.
d. A dog fetches a thrown stick.

**2.** Dr. Valentine found that apes share certain customs, such as ways of using tools. Her discovery is an example of

a. self-awareness.
b. cultural transmission.
c. insight.
d. language use.

# Enrichment Modules Review

## KEY TERMS AND CONTRIBUTORS TO REMEMBER

flow, p. 805

industrial-organizational (I/O)
    psychology, p. 807

burnout, p. 807

personnel psychology, p. 808

organizational psychology, p. 808

human factors psychology, p. 808

structured interview, p. 810

leadership, p. 813

task leadership, p. 814

social leadership, p. 815

# Appendix A PRACTICE AP®-STYLE EXAM

## Section I
## MULTIPLE CHOICE

**1.** A job advertisement for a salesperson position stated that the company was looking for extraverted, conscientious, agreeable employees who are open to trying new things and who can manage their emotional reactions well. What personality theory does this job advertisement illustrate?

   a. Trait theories
   b. Psychodynamic theories
   c. Psychoanalytic theories
   d. Humanistic theories

**2.** Warren has a bacterial infection that has affected the ability of the rods in his eyes to function correctly. This issue should have the greatest impact on which of the following?

   a. Visual clarity
   b. Peripheral vision
   c. Color vision
   d. Shape constancy

**3.** Ethan believes in recycling. He often reads books about the benefits of recycling; however, he found himself skipping over a magazine article about the problems associated with recycling. In this example, Ethan demonstrated

   a. a heuristic.
   b. overconfidence.
   c. a mental set.
   d. confirmation bias.

**4.** Joe is taking a new job on the night shift next week. His supervisors have informed him that he may have some problems with his level of alertness and his memory as he adjusts to his new overnight work schedule. Joe's supervisors are sharing with Joe their knowledge of

   a. circadian rhythms.
   b. REM sleep.
   c. sleep spindles.
   d. NREM sleep.

**5.** A researcher who is trying to determine how sociocultural changes might be correlated with the incidence of bipolar disorder would be most interested in which of the following?

   a. The brain changes in a person with bipolar disorder as measured by a PET scan
   b. The association between rates of poverty and cases of bipolar disorder
   c. Neurotransmitter levels in patients diagnosed with bipolar disorder
   d. The number of close biological relatives who also suffer from bipolar disorder

**6.** Zeina cocked her head to the side immediately when she heard the fire truck's siren. Turning her head enabled each ear to detect a slightly different intensity of sound, thereby enabling her to determine the siren's

   a. pitch.
   b. frequency.
   c. location.
   d. tone.

**7.** How many phonemes are in the word charity?

   a. Four
   b. Three
   c. Two
   d. One

**8.** People diagnosed with obsessive-compulsive disorder experience compulsions. Which of the following is a compulsion?

   a. Eric frequently worries that there may be germs on his hands.
   b. Brianna has an ongoing fear that she might have left the oven on at home.
   c. Stefan often feels great anxiety if things are not in exact order in his room.
   d. Tyrik flips the light switch seven times every evening when he gets home.

**9.** Darla's family has a pet dog. When Darla sees a cat for the first time, she points and says "dog." Darla is demonstrating

   a. accommodation.
   b. fixation.
   c. assimilation.
   d. dual processing.

**10.** Persephone wants to borrow her friend's car for the weekend. She starts by asking her friend if she can borrow the car for an entire month. Her friend declines, stating it would be too long. Persephone then follows up by asking if she can borrow the car for just the weekend. In this scenario, Persephone's initial request for borrowing the car for a month is an example of which persuasion technique?

   a. Central route
   b. Peripheral route
   c. Foot-in-the-door
   d. Door-in-the-face

**11.** A rat jumps each time it sees a green light flash because the green light has always appeared just before an electric shock. In classical conditioning, the initial learning of the connection between the light and the shock is referred to as

   a. spontaneous recovery.
   b. extinction.
   c. generalization.
   d. acquisition.

**12.** Which of the following examples is the best illustration of cognitive dissonance?

   a. The cult member who admires the leader of his group and follows the leader without doubt
   b. The teacher who reprimands a student because she feels the student could do much better academically despite past poor performance
   c. The librarian who dreams of returning to graduate school to become a professor and who begins to submit applications
   d. The student who loves math but after failing a calculus test says he doesn't like calculus that much anyway

**13.** At his doctor's appointment, Phil shared that the sleeping pill the doctor previously prescribed no longer worked at the original dosage. To his doctor's dismay, Phil confided that he had been taking more than the recommended amount of the drug to get the same effect. Phil's increasing intake of the drug reflects

a. withdrawal.
b. tolerance.
c. catharsis.
d. REM rebound.

**14.** Dr. Talisman wanted to conduct a study on positive symptoms of schizophrenia. Which of the following would be an appropriate operational definition in his study?

a. Auditory hallucination frequency
b. Amount of time demonstrating flat affect
c. Number of friends
d. Variability in vocal patterns during a brief phone call

**15.** What psychological concept was likely examined in the study that this photo depicts?

Mark Parisi/offthemark.com

a. Cognitive development
b. Modeling
c. Attachment
d. Prenatal development

**16.** A principal wants to avoid the vandalism and inappropriate behavior that occurred at last year's Halloween dance. This year, she decides to increase the lighting in the parking lots, ban students from wearing face paint, and increase the number of video cameras near the gym. These ideas are most closely linked to the principle of

a. group polarization.
b. social facilitation.
c. superordinate goals.
d. deindividuation.

**17.** When she was a baby, Lucey's parents described her as easy-going and laid back. Now at 10 years old, she continues to demonstrate these characteristics. What concept is captured in this example?

a. Schema
b. Reflexes
c. Temperament
d. Fixation

**18.** Dr. Barnard measured the duration that babies looked at a stuffed dog toy before looking away. He found that babies tended to look away more quickly after they had seen the stuffed dog toy a few times. What concept is illustrated in this example?

a. Sensory adaptation
b. Infantile amnesia
c. Perceptual constancy
d. Habituation

**19.** While playing lacrosse, Tanner sustained an injury that led to the loss of binocular vision. This injury would have the greatest impact on Tanner's

a. visual acuity.
b. color vision.
c. accommodation.
d. depth perception.

**20.** Which of the following best describes the trends depicted in the graph?

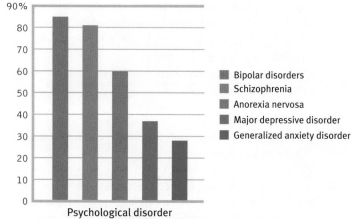

Heritability estimates (percentage of variation due to genetic influence)

Bipolar disorders
Schizophrenia
Anorexia nervosa
Major depressive disorder
Generalized anxiety disorder

Psychological disorder

a. Approximately 35 percent of a person's likelihood of developing major depressive disorder is due to genetic factors.

b. Most people have a moderate risk of developing anorexia nervosa over the course of their lifetimes.

c. People are more likely to be diagnosed with bipolar disorder than they are to be diagnosed with generalized anxiety disorder.

d. We can attribute approximately 35 percent of the variation among individuals diagnosed with major depressive disorder to genetic factors.

**21.** Fatima fell while skateboarding and sustained a traumatic brain injury that made it difficult for her to differentiate between hot and cold. Which brain area was most likely impacted in Fatima's fall?

a. Motor cortex
b. Somatosensory cortex
c. Frontal lobe
d. Occipital lobe

**22.** Dr. Valdez found a strong negative correlation between amount of sleep and student grades. Which coefficient could represent his result?

a. 0.42
b. −0.31
c. 0.74
d. −0.88

**23.** Dr. Villar studies unlearned and complex patterns of behavior, such as the human tendency to sleep when we are tired. Which motivation theory does she examine?

a. Arousal theory
b. Achievement motivation theory
c. Instinct theory
d. The hierarchy of needs

**24.** What form of speech is depicted in this cartoon?

*"Got idea. Talk better. Combine words. Make sentences."*

PR INC/Science Source

a. Babbling
b. Telegraphic
c. One-word
d. Universal grammar

**25.** Dr. Stow wants to administer a projective test to his client. What test should he give?

a. A test designed to reveal a person's ability to do a task they have not tried before
b. A test that shows a person's preferences based on responses to multiple-choice questions
c. A test that measures blood flow to various brain regions
d. A test that prompts a person to reveal hidden conflicts by responding to ambiguous stimuli

**26.** Mr. Winters is a trainer who encourages his clients to exercise more frequently. Instead of simply rewarding them after they exercise, he rewards them for each step they take toward getting more exercise—each time they put on their running shoes, each time they climb stairs at work, each time they walk instead of drive. Reinforcing each time his clients get closer to the desired exercising behavior is known as

a. conforming.
b. extinguishing.
c. social loafing.
d. shaping.

**27.** Often restaurants will require groups of eight or more to pay a tip of 18 percent. This is based on the belief that in larger parties, individuals will often leave a smaller tip because "someone else will pay more." These restaurant owners are likely aware of the impact of

a. the fundamental attribution error.
b. hindsight bias.
c. confirmation bias.
d. diffusion of responsibility.

**28.** In a research study, Dr. Regalis has participants listen to different kinds of music while she uses a brain scan to examine their brain functioning. Dr. Regalis is most likely studying which part of the brain?

a. Temporal lobe
b. Occipital lobe
c. Broca's area
d. Motor cortex

**29.** As Dmitri experiences an anxiety attack, he may experience a series of changes that are coordinated by the sympathetic nervous system. Which one of the following would Dmitri likely experience?

a. Increased heart rate
b. Slower breathing
c. Decreased salivation
d. Increased rate of digestion

**30.** Joanna's grandmother told her, "When we were little, we couldn't afford new clothes, so our mother made us clothing out of potato sacks." Joanna's great-grandmother's ability to envision how a potato sack could be used as material for clothing suggests that she was able to overcome

a. confirmation bias.
b. fixation.
c. algorithms.
d. overconfidence.

31. Which of the following is an example of variable-ratio reinforcement?

   a. College acceptance letters arrive around the date of April 1.
   b. Percy sometimes gives his dog a cookie when his dog walks by strangers without barking.
   c. Esmerelda discovered a shark's tooth after several hours of searching for one on the beach.
   d. When Stu had been working on his homework for one hour, his mother allowed him to go outside and play.

32. Although she was interested in learning about Freud's psychoanalysis and Skinner's behaviorism, Jane most enjoyed the focus on optimism and healthy personal growth associated with

   a. biological psychology.
   b. humanistic psychology.
   c. cognitive psychology.
   d. social-cultural psychology.

33. Dr. MacGavin wanted to conduct a study on the effect of a new drug on the part of the brain that is most involved in maintaining homeostasis in body temperature. What would be an appropriate dependent variable in this study?

   a. Activity in the somatosensory cortex
   b. The drug
   c. Activity in the thalamus
   d. Activity in the hypothalamus

34. Dr. Du uses aversive conditioning to treat a child's bed-wetting problem. Dr. Du is using which of the following approaches?

   a. Cognitive
   b. Biological
   c. Behavioral
   d. Evolutionary

35. What psychological disorder is represented in this graph?

   a. Social anxiety disorder
   b. Specific phobia
   c. Agoraphobia
   d. Generalized anxiety disorder

36. Dr. Dagon wants to follow the American Psychological Association's ethical principles for psychotherapy. What should he do?

   a. He should strive to do no harm to his clients.
   b. He should provide free therapy to most of his clients.
   c. He should keep his fees hidden from clients and other professionals.
   d. He should debrief his participants when therapy is finished.

37. Which of the following statements is most typical of the approach of a cognitive therapist?

   a. "Let's go back to your statement about your happiness as a child."
   b. "When you say, 'No one likes me,' that's illogical because you do have close friends."
   c. "What I hear you saying is you are angry, and I can hear the frustration in your voice."
   d. "I'm going to start teaching you to relax, and then we'll slowly deal with your phobia."

38. Dr. Alscott has examined two sets of data from his research. In the first set, the standard deviation was very small, while in the second set there was a much larger standard deviation. Based on this information, what conclusion can be drawn from these two sets?

   a. The median was greater than the mean in the second set.
   b. There was a statistically significant effect in the second data set but not the first data set.
   c. The standard deviation in both sets revealed a positive correlation between the data.
   d. Most data points were closer to the mean in the first set than in the second data set.

**39.** Beatrix studies how people's bodies produce a similar reaction to all kinds of stress, noting that people become more exhausted with prolonged stress. What does Beatrix most likely study?

a. The opponent-process theory
b. Systematic desensitization
c. The general adaptation syndrome
d. The global assessment of functioning

**40.** To stop having seizures, Kyrolo had surgery to cut his corpus callosum, which resulted in his left hand and right hand sometimes engaging in conflicting actions. What is Kyrolo experiencing?

a. Parallel processing
b. Neurogenesis
c. Split brain
d. Kinesthis

**41.** Which of the following psychological concepts is depicted in this figure?

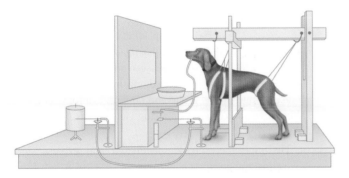

a. Epigenetics
b. Classical conditioning
c. Cognitive dissonance
d. Schizophrenia

**42.** By seeing if infants would crawl over what appeared to be a sharp ledge, Dr. Sullivan attempted to measure which psychological concept?

a. Color vision
b. Sound localization
c. Depth perception
d. Creativity

**43.** Dr. Mbabazi uses systematic desensitization in her work with clients. Dr. Mbabazi is likely an expert in treating which psychological disorder?

a. Specific phobia
b. Schizophrenia
c. Bipolar disorder
d. Major depressive disorder

**44.** A manager at an ice cream store wants to increase sales, so he creates a program to rank his employees' sales. His goal is to give a cash prize each week to the employee who has sold the highest number of ice cream cones. His strategy is based on the idea of

a. internal locus of control.     c. sensation seeking.
b. extrinsic motivation.          d. self-efficacy.

**45.** The fire alarm has malfunctioned and sounded so many times in their school that Susannah and Tia no longer even flinch when they hear it. They even remained in the school library during a fire drill because they assumed it was another malfunction. Their failure to respond as they once did to the fire alarm shows the process of

a. acquisition.        c. accommodation.
b. discrimination.     d. extinction.

**46.** Dr. Anders wants to investigate how people of different ages communicate via the internet, so she does an experiment with three groups of three different ages: 18- to 21-year-olds, 47- to 50-year-olds, and 75- to 78-year-olds. Which of the following accurately identifies the design element in this research study?

a. Dr. Anders conducted a case study on autonomy.
b. Dr. Anders conducted a longitudinal study on competence.
c. Dr. Anders conducted a cross-sectional study on relatedness.
d. Dr. Anders conducted an experiment on obedience.

**47.** Dr. Weber conducted a study in which she told one group of women that women typically do poorly on a specific test. She determined that this group performed more poorly on the test compared to another group of women who were not given such information about performance. This example illustrates

a. stereotype threat.
b. hindsight bias.
c. the mere exposure effect.
d. social facilitation.

**48.** During a dental procedure, Xavier is injected with a drug that is designed to greatly reduce his pain by interfering with the sending of pain signals. What is a logical conclusion about how the drug operates at the neural level?

a. The drug is preventing action potentials from being transmitted.
b. The drug is preventing neurotransmitters from being reabsorbed by neurons.
c. The drug is preventing optimal functioning of the occipital lobes.
d. The drug is preventing the myelin sheath from protecting the axon.

**49.** While waiting for his doctor, Raylan looked at a picture that has an image hidden among the dots. Because each of his eyes has a slightly different image projected on the retina, he can perceive depth and see the hidden image. Which term best describes this process?

a. Relative motion        c. Retinal disparity
b. Convergence            d. Relative height

**50.** A therapist tells a CEO that he yells and screams at his staff due to behavior he learned as a child. When he was a child, he threw temper tantrums to get his way. What is the term for this defense mechanism?

a. Regression

b. Reaction formation

c. Projection

d. Rationalization

**51.** Which of the following accurately describes the trends depicted in the data presented?

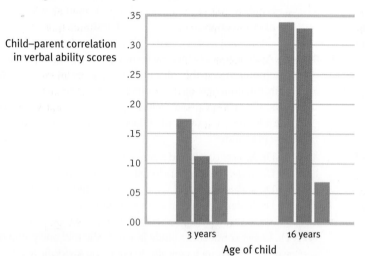

Child–parent correlation in verbal ability scores

Non-adopted children and their biological parents

Adopted children and their biological parents

Adopted children and their adoptive parents

Age of child

a. As the years went by in their adoptive families, children's verbal ability scores became more like their biological parents' scores.

b. As the years went by in their adoptive families, children's verbal ability scores became more like their adoptive parents' scores.

c. As the years went by in their adoptive families, children's verbal ability scores became more like their adoptive siblings' scores.

d. As the years went by in their adoptive families, children's verbal ability scores became more like non-adopted children's scores.

**52.** A babysitter cuts a sandwich into three equal pieces, then keeps two and gives one to the child she is caring for. The child is upset that this is unfair, so the babysitter divides the child's piece into two. Since each of them now has two pieces, the child is content. According to Jean Piaget, this is because the child lacks

a. accommodation.

b. assimilation.

c. object permanence.

d. conservation.

**53.** Seven-year-old Daniel was able to see that the dot-to-dot puzzle was going to form a picture of a tiger even before he started drawing on the puzzle. Which Gestalt principle helped Daniel perceive the tiger from all the unconnected dots?

a. Proximity

b. Figure-ground

c. Texture gradient

d. Closure

**54.** Dr. Kombo conducted an experiment in which he randomly assigned participants to interact with either encouraging people or abrasive people. He monitored participants' physiological arousal levels during the interaction. Participants then labeled their arousal as joyous or irritable. Although arousal levels were similar across the two groups, participants' ratings depended on their environments, which illustrates support for which theory of emotions?

a. Psychodynamic

b. Humanistic

c. Behavioral

d. Cognitive

**55.** Ascribing to the behavioral perspective, Mrs. Johansen accurately told her students that she punishes them to

a. make them feel sorry for a behavior.

b. associate a positive consequence with a negative consequence.

c. make a behavior less likely to happen again.

d. allow the behavior to only occur again during a spontaneous recovery.

**56.** When Eli initially joined an online group that was working against increased government spending, he had only mild views on the topic. If he continues in the group and rarely gets information from alternative sources with opposing views, what might be the outcome?

a. He might become deindividuated and express views against the group's beliefs.

b. He might use social facilitation to spread the group's views more widely online.

c. He might use confirmation bias to seek out sources that challenge his beliefs.

d. His views and the group members' views might become more intensely felt over time.

**57.** When seeking to hire a new creative director for an advertising agency, Amina decided that she wanted to find a person who could devise numerous ways to solve problems. A person talented in this area would most likely be good at

a. divergent thinking.

b. convergent thinking.

c. belief perseverance.

d. executive functioning.

**58.** Dr. Truckee wanted to conduct a study on how personality traits are impacted by trying a variety of foods over time. Which of the following would be an appropriate dependent variable for Dr. Truckee's study?

a. Personality inventory

b. Intelligence test

c. Projective personality test

d. Various foods

**59.** Jason saw a car speeding down the highway. "They are speeding, so they must be bad," said Jason to his father without considering situational factors that might lead to the driver speeding. Jason's statement is an example of

a. the availability heuristic.
b. the representativeness heuristic.
c. stereotype threat.
d. the fundamental attribution error.

**60.** Maria, an 11-month-old baby, was happily playing with her stuffed dogs when her mother left to get groceries. When left with the babysitter, Maria became distressed, but when her mother returned, she smiled and reached for her mother. Which of the following is likely true for Maria?

a. Maria exhibits anxious attachment.
b. Maria exhibits secure attachment.
c. Maria exhibits avoidant attachment.
d. Maria exhibits permissive attachment.

**61.** A researcher finds a difference between an experimental group and a control group that is less likely due to chance and more likely due to the manipulation of the independent variable. This finding then is most likely to be

a. a replication.
b. statistically significant.
c. a confidence interval.
d. reliable but not valid.

**62.** Anastasia watched her mother mow the lawn and wash the car with a washcloth. Anastasia then used her toy lawn mower to mow the lawn and used a rag to clean her toy car. Which concept is described in this example?

a. Observational learning
b. Classical conditioning
c. Operant conditioning
d. Latent learning

**63.** Which of the following is an example of a self-fulfilling prophecy?

a. Ivy does not think her teacher has treated her fairly, so she complains to her principal, who sets up a meeting with Ivy, her parents, and the teacher to discuss the issues in class.
b. Samuel's teacher puts him in a group with struggling students, and Samuel, normally a good student, responds by doing very poor work, getting placed in the same group the next week.
c. Rachel writes a letter to the editor about her concerns with the city council, and as a result her social studies teacher praises her in class for her civic engagement.
d. Nyah's father takes her out of an advanced class because she is struggling at first, but she responds by working even harder and making better grades in all of her classes.

**64.** At the paint store, Paul was unable to correctly identify the right shade of blue to match the walls of his living room, so he purchased various hues and brought them home. Which of the following concepts best applies to this scenario?

a. Sensory adaptation
b. Absolute threshold
c. Just-noticeable difference
d. Transduction

**65.** Teachers at York High School were dismayed at a new test they would be required to take to demonstrate their ability as educators. Rather than being a test of content knowledge or of teaching techniques, the new test would measure their reaction time to a series of rapidly flashed abstract images—not a skill they normally need in the classroom. Despite the assurances of the test's creator, the teachers argued that a test like this would have low

a. validity.
b. reliability.
c. statistical significance.
d. replicability.

**66.** What psychological concept is depicted in this graph?

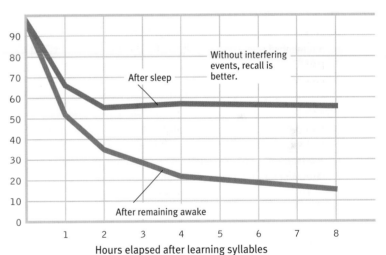

a. Misinformation effect
b. Retroactive interference
c. Proactive interference
d. Sensitive period

**67.** LeAnne accurately demonstrated that Vygotsky's theory differed from Piaget's theory by stating that Vygotsky

a. emphasized the role of the social environment.
b. thought that Piaget ignored the psychosexual development of children.
c. questioned Piaget's focus on adult development.
d. focused more on moral development.

**68.** Dr. Kateryna, a psychologist, found evidence that someone's depression decreased after taking an antidepressant. Which of the following variables provides biological evidence for this finding?

   a. Their beliefs about their own abilities and attitudes improved.

   b. The number of contacts with their friends and families increased.

   c. Their ability to establish and work toward long-term goals increased.

   d. Serotonin levels in their blood increased.

**69.** Instead of methodically poring through the atlas to find the correct map, Ivan just flipped to the section of the book where he thought it might be. Using a strategy based on a hunch rather than examining each page carefully involves the use of

   a. an algorithm.      c. confirmation bias.

   b. a heuristic.        d. fixation.

**70.** On the very first day of class, Mr. Boyarsky gave his students a test. When some students complained, he responded that he wanted to know what their talents were, so he was giving them a test to predict what kind of skills they might learn best. Mr. Boyarsky's test was a(n)

   a. aptitude test.

   b. intelligence test.

   c. achievement test.

   d. personality test.

**71.** When a basketball star graduated from college with a degree in geography, he made $2 million in his first position in a professional basketball league, after which the average salary for a geography major soared. In a situation like this, where one unusual bit of data greatly inflates the average, it is best to use which measure of central tendency?

   a. Mean

   b. Median

   c. Standard deviation

   d. Mode

**72.** What form of psychotherapy is represented in this figure?

   a. Behavioral      c. Humanistic

   b. Psychodynamic   d. Cognitive

**73.** Zara was recently diagnosed with multiple sclerosis. Her doctor told her that her neurons experienced deterioration in such a way that led to slower and incomplete neural transmission along the axon. What part of the neuron experienced deterioration?

   a. Cell body

   b. Neurotransmitter

   c. Dendrite

   d. Myelin sheath

*Use the following scenario to answer questions 74 and 75:*

Dr. Warren is testing whether there is a relationship between the consumption of caffeine and memory. She randomly divides 300 participants into three groups and gives each participant an energy drink to consume. Some of the drinks have high levels of caffeine, some have medium levels, and some have none at all—but they all taste the same. About 30 minutes later, Dr. Warren has the participants play a memory game on the computer where they have to match faces and names together. At the end of the game, the computer thanks them for playing, and their scores are sent to Dr. Warren's lab.

**74.** The dependent variable in the experiment is

   a. the energy drinks.

   b. the participants' scores from the memory game.

   c. the amount of caffeine they consumed.

   d. their explanations about how they played the game.

**75.** The independent variable in the experiment described is

   a. how quickly the participants matched the names and faces.

   b. the participants' scores from the memory game.

   c. the amount of caffeine they consumed.

   d. their explanations about how they played the game.

## Section II
## EVIDENCE-BASED QUESTION

**INSTRUCTIONS**: Answer the following question using the 3 sources provided. Your response to the question should be provided in three distinct parts: A, B, and C. Use appropriate psychological terminology in your response.

For both Part B and Part C, each piece of evidence must be cited using the "Source [Number]" designation in parentheses following the cited material or embedded in the sentence. For example,

- Parenthetical citation: (Source 1).
- Embedded citation: According to Source 1, . . .

1. Using the provided sources, develop and justify an argument about the effectiveness of group work for class projects.

   **(A)** Propose a specific and defensible claim based in psychological science that responds to the question.

   **(B.i)** Support your claim using at least one piece of specific and relevant evidence from one of the sources provided.

   **(B.ii)** Use a psychological perspective, theory, concept, or research finding learned in AP® Psychology to explain how your evidence supports your claim.

   **(C.i)** Using a different source than the one you used in Part (B.i), support your claim using at least one piece of specific and relevant evidence.

   **(C.ii)** Use a psychological perspective, theory, concept, or research finding learned in AP® Psychology—different than the one you used in Part (B.ii)—to explain how your evidence in Part (C.i) supports your claim.

## Source 1:

| Introduction |
|---|
| The utilization of group work as an educational tool is widely utilized by teachers. Numerous scientific studies have supported the advantages of students learning in groups. However, the present study examines the dynamics within groups during group work that influence students' learning. Why is group work successful sometimes while unsuccessful other times? |
| **Participants** |
| The participants included 210 students (172 female and 38 male) from two universities in Sweden. |
| **Method** |
| To measure experiences with and conceptions of group work, participants completed questionnaires containing multiple-choice and open-ended questions. |
| **Results and Discussion** |
| The results indicate that the majority of students reported positive experiences of group work in terms of academic learning. They also reported that group work served a social function, providing opportunities to interact with classmates. However, this had a downside when the group climate or group process was negative, which participants reported actually hampered learning. These results have implications for teachers who assign group work in their courses. |

Information from: Hammar Chiriac, E. (2014). Group work as an incentive for learning - students' experiences of group work. *Frontiers in psychology, 5*, 558. https://doi.org/10.3389/fpsyg.2014.00558

## Source 2:

| Introduction |
|---|
| How individuals perform in groups is an important area of research with implications for everything from school projects to the workplace. Sometimes working in groups enhances performance and other times it can hurt it. The present study investigated how working alone or with a partner influences performance. |
| **Participants** |
| The participants were 48 pairs of college students. |
| **Method** |
| Participants were instructed to make noise by cheering while blindfolded and wearing earphones. Determined by random assignment, half the participants were told they were alone for this task while the other half were told they were working with a partner. |
| **Results and Discussion** |
| Participants made more noise when they thought they were alone compared to when they thought they were working with a partner. However, in follow-up studies, when participants were informed that their individual performance would be measured, even in pairs, this difference disappeared. |

Information from: Hardy, C., & Latané, B. (1986). Social loafing on a cheering task. *Social Science, 71*(2-3), 165–172.

## Source 3:

| Introduction |
|---|
| Students can learn valuable skills from group work including critical thinking and communication. Group work can also foster teamwork and expose students to a variety of ways to solve problems. This study attempted to address the question, could group exams be an effective type of group work? The researchers hypothesized that the benefits of group midterm exams will lead to significantly higher final exam scores. |
| **Participants** |
| One hundred sixty-one business school students enrolled in an income tax class taught by the same instructor who participated in this study. |
| **Method** |
| Participants were administered a midterm exam. Students in the control group took it individually, while the experimental group took it in groups of three. After each group exam, students evaluated their group members. Finally, an individual, comprehensive final exam was administered individually to all students. |
| **Results and Discussion** |
| The researchers found that students in the experimental group (group exams) earned significantly higher grades on the final exam than the control group. |

Information from: Hite, P. A. (1996). An experimental study of the effectiveness of group exams in an individual income tax class. *Issues in Accounting Education, 11*(1), 61. https://www.proquest.com/scholarly-journals /experimental-study-effectiveness-group-exams/docview/210937720/se-2

# ARTICLE ANALYSIS QUESTION

**INSTRUCTIONS**: Answer the following question using the source provided. Your response to the question should be provided in six distinct parts: A, B, C, D, E, and F. Use appropriate psychological terminology in your response.

2. Using the source provided, respond to the following questions.

   (A) Identify the research method used in the study.

   (B) Identify the operational definition of the independent variable.

   (C) Describe the meaning of the differences in the means between the nature soundscape and urban soundscape groups.

   (D) Identify at least one ethical guideline applied by the researchers.

   (E) Explain the extent to which the research findings may or may not be generalizable using specific and relevant evidence from the study.

   (F) Explain how at least one of the research findings supports or refutes the advice that algebra teachers should play nature sounds in their classrooms while students are working on difficult problems.

## Source:

| Introduction |
|---|
| Past research has demonstrated the benefits of time in nature on overall well-being. Additionally, there is evidence that it can have cognitive benefits by restoring the ability to pay attention and lowering stress levels. The present study extends this research by exploring the cognitive benefits of nature sounds versus urban sounds on cognitive performance. |
| **Participants** |
| Sixty-three college students participated in the study. |
| **Method** |
| Soundscape (natural versus urban) was randomly assigned. The natural soundscapes contained sounds of birdsong, rainfall, etc. The urban soundscapes included the sounds of traffic and machinery. Each soundscape was presented for the same amount of time and at the same volume. After providing written consent, participants were exposed to either the natural or urban soundscape. They then engaged in a demanding cognitive task where they were required to remember a sequence of numbers backwards over a series of trials. |

*(Continued)*

### Results and Discussion

The researchers found the results in the following graph. These results were statistically significant. Exposure to nature sounds improved cognitive performance in comparison to urban soundscapes. Cognitive improvement was not related to how pleasant participants found each soundscape.

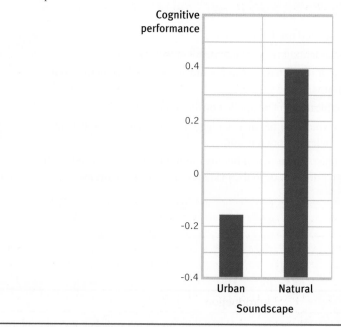

Information from: Van Hedger, S. C., Nusbaum, H. C., Clohisy, L., Jaeggi, S. M., Buschkuehl, M., & Berman, M. G. (2019). Of cricket chirps and car horns: The effect of nature sounds on cognitive performance. *Psychonomic Bulletin & Review, 26*(2), 522–530. https://doi.org/10.3758/s13423-018-1539-1

# Appendix B PREPARING FOR FURTHER PSYCHOLOGY STUDIES

*This appendix was written by Jennifer Zwolinski, University of San Diego.*

In Module EM.2, you learned about the work that different types of psychologists do and where they do it. Here you will find answers to important questions about pursuing the study of psychology: Will psychology be the right college major for you? What are the various levels of psychology education, and what kinds of jobs are available at those levels? What are some ways you can improve your chances for college success, and for admission to graduate school?

## The Psychology Major

### What Could You Do With a Degree in Psychology?

Lots! As a psychology major, you would graduate with a scientific mindset and an awareness of basic principles of human behavior (biological, developmental, mental disorder–related, social). This background would prepare you for success in many areas, including business, health services, marketing, law, sales, teaching, and the helping professions (a broad category of jobs–from paramedic to police officer–that involves direct outreach to individuals). You could even go on to graduate school for specialized training to become a psychology professional. Here, you'll find the answers to important questions about pursuing the study of psychology: Is psychology the right major for you? What are the various levels of psychology education, and what kinds of jobs are available at those levels? What are psychology's specialized subfields? What are some ways you can improve your chances of admission to graduate school?

### How Do You Know If Psychology Is the Right Major for You?

To see if you would be well matched with a major in psychology, start by considering the questions below.

Do you:

- enjoy learning about the ways we think and behave, and why?
- appreciate the value of applying the scientific method to answer questions?
- have an interest in a career that requires interpersonal skills?
- want to learn critical thinking and analytical skills?
- want to learn communication and presentation skills?
- want to gain research methodology skills such as assessment and statistical analysis?
- want to work in human or animal services?
- have a desire to apply psychological principles to understand or solve personal, social, organizational, or environmental problems?

If you answered "yes" to most or all of these questions, then psychology may be the right major for you.

## How Popular Is the Psychology Major?

Psychology, the fourth most popular major, tied with engineering and biological/biomedical sciences in the 2019–2020 academic year. More than 119,000 people graduated with a bachelor's degree in psychology, representing nearly 6 percent of all degrees conferred from U.S. colleges and universities. Business (19 percent), health professions and related programs (13 percent), and social science and history (8 percent) occupied the top three spots (National Center for Education Statistics [NCES], 2022a).

This number of conferred undergraduate degrees in psychology has increased a whopping 915 percent from 1950 to 2020 (NCES, 2022b), and it is likely that psychology will remain a very popular major among undergraduate students. This popularity is observed at the graduate level as well. From 2010 to 2020, the number of graduate degrees in psychology increased by approximately 15 percent at both the master's level and the doctoral level (NCES, 2022b) (**Figure B.1**).

## Who Is Studying Psychology at the Undergraduate and Graduate Levels?

In 2019–2020, a full 79 percent of the graduating psychology majors with bachelor's degrees were women (NCES, 2022b). In that same time period, approximately 80 percent of psychology master's degree recipients and 75 percent of doctorate recipients were women (NCES, 2022b). Approximately 64 percent of all psychology doctorate recipients in 2021 were White, a decline of more than 15 percent from 2011 (APA, 2021a). In this same ten-year span, the racial and ethnic diversity of doctorate recipients grew, with a 37 percent increase among Black/African Americans, a 40 percent increase among Hispanic Americans, and a 20 percent increase among Asians (APA, 2021a).

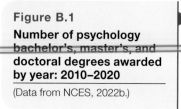

**Figure B.1**

**Number of psychology bachelor's, master's, and doctoral degrees awarded by year: 2010–2020**

(Data from NCES, 2022b.)

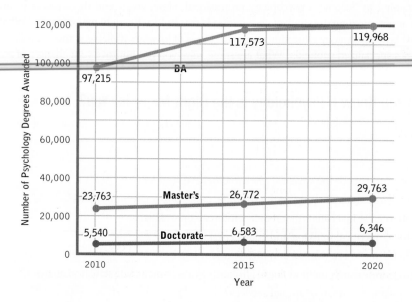

## What Are the Main Reasons That Undergraduate Students Choose to Study Psychology?

Among the reasons students cite for choosing a psychology major are that it provides the ability to help others, incorporates interesting subject matter, produces a better understanding of self and others, includes good career or salary potential, and offers the ability to conduct research (Mulvey & Grus, 2010). An earlier study also found that a positive experience in students' Introduction to Psychology class played a key role in their decisions to major (Marrs, Barb, & Ruggiero, 2007).

# What Types of Skills Would You Learn as a Psychology Major?

Across all occupations, employers value skills in leadership and management, social perceptiveness, critical thinking and analysis, speaking and active listening, and flexibility with new systems (Landrum & McCarthy, 2018; Naufel et al., 2018). These skills align with the American Psychological Association's (APA) learning goals and outcomes (**Table B.1** and **Table B.2**) for psychology majors. In addition to exceptional interpersonal and communication skills, psychology majors develop a number of methodological skills that result from the focus on the scientific study of human and animal behavior. The study of statistics and research methodology contributes to a scientific mindset that emphasizes exploring and managing uncertainty, critical thinking and analytical skills, and logical thinking abilities. The ability to analyze data using statistics, conduct database searches, and integrate multiple sources of information are helpful in a number of professional settings. Prospective employers appreciate the excellent written and verbal communication skills among students who present their research projects at conferences and become proficient in APA style. By meeting APA's learning goals, psychology majors will be well prepared for numerous professional opportunities and a range of graduate training options.

| **TABLE B.1   APA (2023) Guidelines for the Undergraduate Psychology Major 3.0: Learning Goals and Outcomes** |
|---|
| **Goal 1: Content Knowledge and Applications** |
| 1.1 Describe key concepts, principles, and theories in psychological science. <br> 1.2 Develop a working knowledge of psychology's major subfields. <br> 1.3 Represent significant aspects of the history of psychological science. <br> 1.4 Apply psychological content to solve practical problems. <br> 1.5 Relate examples of psychology's integrative themes (See **Table B.2**). |
| **Goal 2: Scientific Inquiry and Critical Thinking** |
| 2.1 Exercise scientific reasoning to investigate psychological phenomena. <br> 2.2 Interpret, design, and evaluate basic psychological research. <br> 2.3 Incorporate sociocultural factors in scientific research practices. <br> 2.4 Use statistics to evaluate quantitative research findings. |
| **Goal 3: Values in Psychological Science** |
| 3.1 Employ ethical standards in research, practice, and academic contexts. <br> 3.2 Develop and practice interpersonal and intercultural responsiveness. <br> 3.3 Apply psychological principles to strengthen community and improve quality of life. |
| **Goal 4: Communication, Psychological Literacy, and Technology Skills** |
| 4.1 Interact effectively with others. <br> 4.2 Write and present effectively for different purposes. <br> 4.3 Provide evidence of psychological literacy. <br> 4.4 Exhibit appropriate technological skills to improve communication. |
| **Goal 5: Personal and Professional Development** |
| 5.1 Exhibit effective self-regulation. <br> 5.2 Refine project management skills. <br> 5.3 Display effective judgment in professional interactions. <br> 5.4 Cultivate workforce collaboration skills. <br> 5.5 Demonstrate appropriate workforce technological skills. <br> 5.6 Develop direction for life after graduation. |

(Information from APA, 2023. )

**TABLE B.2  Psychology's Integrative Themes**

| |
|---|
| A. Psychological science relies on empirical evidence and adapts as new data develop. |
| B. Psychological science explains general principles that govern behavior while recognizing individual differences. |
| C. Psychological, biological, social, and cultural factors influence behavior and mental processes. |
| D. Psychological science values diversity, promotes equity, and fosters inclusion in pursuit of a more just society. |
| E. Our perceptions and biases filter our experiences of the world through an imperfect personal lens. |
| F. Applying psychological principles can change our lives, organizations, and communities in positive ways. |
| G. Ethical principles guide psychological science research and practice. |

But you don't have to major in psychology to acquire lasting benefits. When undergraduate seniors who had taken Introduction to Psychology years earlier were asked about their experiences in the course, both majors and non-majors indicated that the class offered important study skills and other foundational skills they applied to different courses, as well as a perspective that changed their social understanding and interactions with others (Hard, Lovett, & Brady, 2019). These are remarkable outcomes for the estimated 1.2 to 1.6 million students who enroll in an introductory psychology course each year (Gurung et al., 2016).

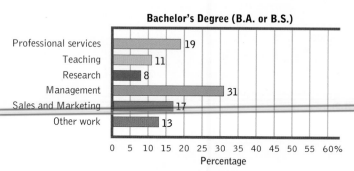

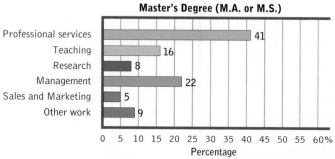

# Career Options With a Degree in Psychology

## What Could You Do With a Bachelor's Degree in Psychology?

In 2019, over 3.7 million individuals held a bachelor's degree in psychology (APA, 2021b). For 57 percent of these graduates, the bachelor's degree in psychology was their highest degree (APA, 2021b). The other 43 percent chose to pursue graduate school, either in psychology (14 percent) or in another field such as law, business, education, or medicine (28 percent) (APA, 2021b).

Drew Appleby (n.d.) provides a list of 300 careers that would be of interest to psychology majors—including those pursuing advanced degrees. The list includes links for more information about professional responsibilities, salaries, and job outlook for each career. (See https://teachpsych.org/resources/Documents/otrp/resources/appleby/Poster%20Careers.pdf.)

According to 2019 data from the National Science Foundation (APA, 2021c), career paths differ depending on the type of psychology degree that individuals received (**Figure B.2**). For example, about half of individuals with graduate degrees in psychology worked in professional services, which includes positions in health care, financial and legal services, and counseling (Stamm & Fowler, 2019). In comparison, whereas some individuals with a bachelor's degree in psychology worked in professional services, many of them worked in management, sales and marketing, and teaching (Stamm & Fowler, 2019).

U.S. Census data from 2020 showed that individuals with any form of psychology degree were most likely to be employed by elementary and secondary schools; colleges, universities, and

**Figure B.2**

**Where do people work with varying psychology degrees?**

professional schools; general medical and surgical hospitals; and specialty (except psychiatric and substance abuse) hospitals (DataUSA, n.d.).

The extent to which employees report that their jobs are related to their degree in psychology depends on their level of advanced training in psychology. For example, in 2019, 62 percent of U.S. respondents whose highest degree was a bachelor's degree said that their jobs were directly related to their psychology training. This increased to 89 percent for master's degree recipients and 96 percent for doctoral recipients (APA, 2021c).

## How Could a Psychology Degree Help You to Get a Job After Graduating?

A psychology major will prepare you for many possible career paths. It has a "workforce advantage" that helps to distinguish psychology majors from other majors in the liberal arts (Halonen & Dunn, 2017). Undergraduate psychology majors have a good understanding of the knowledge, skills, and abilities (KSAs) that potential employers are looking for, such as listening, problem solving, and having the desire and ability to learn (Miller & Carducci, 2015). By matching employers' desired KSAs with the ones that you will develop in the psychology major, you will be able to tailor your résumé to the job and increase your chances of finding employment that matches your skills.

One of the first steps to getting a job with a bachelor's degree in psychology is articulating your skills to potential employers. Some skills that are distinctive to the psychology major include data management and analysis (e.g., evaluating data and graphs), behavioral interpretation (e.g., describing and predicting behavioral claims), and interpersonal competencies (e.g., managing difficult situations and working effectively in teams) (Halonen & Dunn, 2017). Other steps that will help you to secure a job after graduation include knowing the options for a degree in psychology (see Figure B.2), participating in diverse applied learning opportunities such as hands-on research and internships, and marketing your skills and talents (including having an "elevator pitch" to communicate how your skills align with employer needs, a professional résumé, and professional references) (Appleby, Hettich & Spencer, n.d.; Appleby et al., 2019). Making use of the resource books listed at the end of this appendix, as well as building relationships with mentors, advisors, and networking groups, can help you find the job that best suits your interests.

## What Type of Salary Could You Expect With a Degree in Psychology? Would a Graduate Degree Increase Your Income Potential?

Within six months of graduation from college in 2021, the mean starting salary among psychology bachelor's degree recipients was $40,043, compared to $58,862 for all majors (NACE, 2022). The mean starting salary for master's recipients was $56,617, compared to $72,105 for all master's recipients (NACE, 2022). In 2021, median full-time salaries for social and related scientists were $71,000 for a bachelor's degree recipient, $72,000 for a master's degree recipient, and $91,000 for a doctoral recipient (National Center for Science and Engineering Statistics [NCSES], 2022a). In 2017, psychologists in management positions earned nearly twice as much as psychologists in teaching positions (APA, 2018a). Clearly, earnings tend to increase with education, and higher levels of education will almost always yield greater financial rewards over the course of a career (Carnevale, 2016).

Of course, earning potential is not the only reason to choose a major. In one recent study of college graduates across all majors, 61 percent reported that they would change their major if they could. The number one reason they provided was the chance to pursue their passion, which ranked higher than better job opportunities and better compensation (Johnson, 2020). Use what you are learning in this course to decide whether your passion aligns with a major in psychology.

## What Kind of Job Satisfaction Could You Expect If You Work in a Psychology Field?

For individuals with a bachelor's, master's, or doctoral degree in psychology, overall job satisfaction is high—85, 89, and 96 percent, respectively (APA, 2021b). For psychologists with doctoral degrees, satisfaction levels varied by primary work activity; those in professional services reported the highest levels, followed by teaching, management, research, and other service sectors (Lin, Christidis, & Conroy, 2019).

# Postgraduate Degrees

## Why Should You Consider Attending Graduate School in Psychology?

Whether you hold a bachelor's, master's, or doctoral degree in psychology, approximately 75% of all degree type recipients had full-time employment in 2019 (APA, 2021c). If you choose to earn a graduate degree in psychology, you will be in good company. Approximately 43 percent of those with a bachelor's degree in psychology go on to pursue some form of graduate education (APA, 2021b). In addition to a higher salary and strong job satisfaction, a graduate degree in psychology will give you proficiency in an area of psychological specialization and increased opportunities to work in diverse areas of psychology.

Job prospects in the field of psychology are much better for individuals with graduate degrees. Employment for psychologists is expected to grow 6 percent from 2021 to 2031, about as fast as the average 5 percent for all occupations (U.S. Bureau of Labor Statistics [BLS], 2022). Opportunities will increase for clinical, counseling, and school psychologists in particular, because of increased demand for psychological services in schools, hospitals, social service agencies, and mental health centers (BLS, 2022). The APA expects a 30 percent increase in the number of psychologist positions from 2015 to 2030, with the greatest demand in health practitioner offices, elementary schools, and hospitals, respectively (APA, 2018a). The APA further anticipates that between 2015 and 2030, there will not be enough licensed doctoral psychologists to meet the need for therapy in certain populations, such as older adults and Hispanic populations (Bailey, 2020). If you are interested in the clinical track, there will be plenty of opportunities to play an important role in supporting these projected clinical needs. But first, you will need a graduate degree.

## What's the Difference Between a Master's Degree and a Doctorate Degree in Psychology?

Both degrees would prepare you for more specialized training in psychology and increase your job opportunities in the field of psychology beyond the bachelor's degree.

A master's degree in psychology requires at least two years of full-time graduate study in a specific subfield of psychology. In addition to specialized course work in psychology, requirements usually include practical experience in an applied setting or a master's thesis reporting on an original research project. You might acquire a master's degree to do specialized work in psychology. As a graduate with a master's degree, you might handle research and data collection and analysis in a university, government, or private industry setting. You might work under the supervision of a psychologist with a doctorate, providing some clinical service such as therapy or testing. Or you might find a job in the health, government, industry, or education fields. You might also acquire a master's degree as a stepping stone for more advanced study in a doctoral program in psychology, which would expand the number of employment opportunities available to you.

It takes more time to complete a doctoral degree in psychology, relative to a master's degree. Among graduates who earned a research doctorate (Ph.D.) in psychology in 2021, the average time to degree completion was 6.9 years after starting graduate school, or 8.6 years after finishing their bachelor's degree (National Center for Science and Engineering Statistics [NCSES], 2022b). The doctoral degree you choose to pursue would depend on your career goals. You may choose to earn a doctor of philosophy (Ph.D.) in psychology if your career goals are geared toward conducting research, or a doctor of psychology (Psy.D.) if you are more interested in becoming a practicing clinician. Training for the Ph.D. culminates in a dissertation (an extensive research paper you will be required to defend orally) based on original research. Courses in quantitative research methods, which include the use of computer-based analysis, are an important part of graduate study and are necessary to complete the dissertation. Psy.D. training may be based on clinical (therapeutic) work and examinations rather than a dissertation. Many psychologists who earn a Ph.D. in clinical or counseling psychology conduct research and practice as psychotherapists. If you pursue clinical and counseling psychology programs, you should expect at least a one-year internship in addition to the regular course work, clinical practice, and research. It is important to note, however, that psychologists with Psy.D. degrees are not the only ones who work as psychotherapists; some types of counselors and therapists may practice with only master's degrees.

Figure **B.3** lists by subfield the Ph.D.s earned in the United States in 2021, the most recent year for which these data are available (APA, 2021a). Among the doctorates awarded in 2021, the most popular subfield was clinical psychology (34%), followed by general psychology (24%). Of these doctorates, 54 percent were classified as health service, and the remainder were classified as research (APA, 2021a). As previously noted, both master's and doctoral degrees in psychology increased approximately 30% over the last decade (NCES, 2022b).

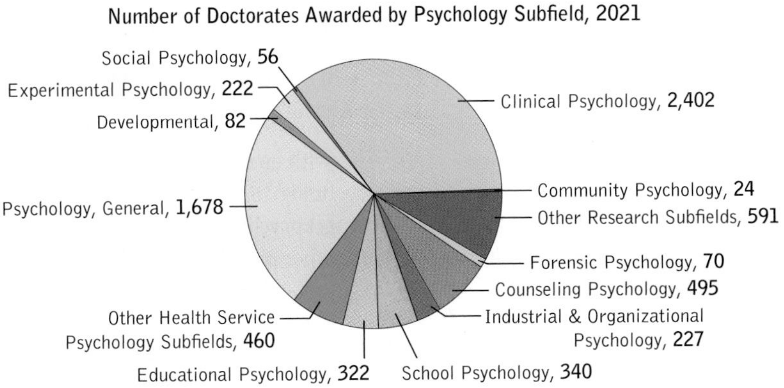

**Number of Doctorates Awarded by Psychology Subfield, 2021**

Social Psychology, 56
Experimental Psychology, 222
Developmental, 82
Psychology, General, 1,678
Clinical Psychology, 2,402
Community Psychology, 24
Other Research Subfields, 591
Forensic Psychology, 70
Counseling Psychology, 495
Industrial & Organizational Psychology, 227
Other Health Service Psychology Subfields, 460
Educational Psychology, 322
School Psychology, 340

▲

**Figure B.3**
**Psychology degrees awarded by subfield, 2021**

(Data from National Center for Education Statistics, Integrated Postsecondary Education Data System [IPEDS], 2021 Completion Survey.)

# Preparing Early for Graduate Study in Psychology

Competition for openings in advanced degree programs in psychology is keen. If you plan to go to graduate school after college, there are a number of things you can do in advance to maximize your chances of gaining admission to the school of your choice.

The first step is to take full advantage of your opportunities in high school. By enrolling in challenging elective courses and working hard to develop an academic skill set, you will have paved the way for success in college. Successful students also take the time to learn effective study skills and to establish disciplined study habits. Involve yourself in extracurricular activities, gain some experience in the world of work by taking on a part-time job, and look for opportunities to volunteer in your school and community. In addition to helping you grow as a person, becoming a well-rounded student with high standards helps you to earn scholarships and increases your chances of being accepted by the colleges and universities of particular interest to you.

During your first year at college, continue to maximize opportunities and obtain the experience needed to gain admission to a competitive program. Kristy Arnold and Kelly Horrigan (2002) offer a number of suggestions to facilitate this process:

1. **Network.** Get to know faculty members and the psychology department by attending activities and meetings. This will be especially helpful when you apply to graduate school or for a job, because many applications require two to three letters of reference. Become involved in psychology clubs and in Psi Chi, the national honor society in psychology. These meetings will help you connect with other students who have similar interests and expose you to a broader study of the field.

2. **Become actively involved in research as early as possible.** Start by doing simple tasks such as data entry and data collection, and over time you will be prepared to conduct your own research project under the supervision of a research mentor. Consider applying for summer research positions through your university or from other organizations such as the American Psychological Association Summer Science Fellowship program or the National Science Foundation Research Experiences for Undergraduates (REU) program, which will test your interest in academic careers and build your skills for future study in psychology.

3. **Volunteer or get a job in a psychology-related field.** Getting involved in this way will demonstrate your willingness to apply psychological concepts to real-world settings. Further, it will showcase your ability to juggle a number of tasks successfully, such as those required for work and school—an important skill for graduate school success.

4. **Maintain good grades.** Demonstrate your ability to do well in graduate school by successfully completing challenging courses, especially those related to your interests. (See Module 2.7 for tips on how to do well in this course and other courses, and how to improve your retention of the information you are learning.) In your junior year of college, you can start to review admissions requirements for graduate programs. If you need to complete the Graduate Record Exam (GRE), the standardized test for applicants to graduate school, you can begin studying for the test. If you start preparing early and maintain high grades, you will be ready for success in your graduate school application and study.

# For More Information

## How Can You Learn More About the Psychology Major and the Field of Psychology?

1. Talk with as many people as possible who have experience in the discipline of psychology. Your psychology teacher or school counselor may have some tips. Try to learn about opportunities to contact psychology majors, graduate students in psychology, psychology instructors and advisors, and other professionals who trained in psychology or who work in the field.

2. Read books, such as those listed at the end of this appendix.

3. Take advantage of online resources, which can help you to determine whether you would be well matched for a major and a career in psychology.

   - Watch online videos showcasing different careers in psychology, such as those found at drkit.org/psychology or https://www.apa.org/applied-psychology/career-videos.
   - Play the Career Interest Game (career.missouri.edu/career-interest-game).
   - Get more information about specific jobs in psychology from the Bureau of Labor Statistics Occupational Outlook Handbook (OOH) or the Occupational Information Network (O*NET).
   - Visit the websites of the American Psychological Association (apa.org) and Association for Psychological Science (psychologicalscience.org). The APA has a lot to offer high school students who are interested in learning more about psychology. To learn more about membership at the high school level (which includes subscriptions to APA journals and mobile apps), visit apa.org/membership/hs-student/index.aspx. You can also become a member of the Psychology Student Network (apa.org/ed/precollege/psn/index.aspx).
   - Learn more about the national honor societies in psychology, Psi Chi and Psi Beta.

## What Are Some Books That Can Help You to Learn More About the Major, Careers, and Graduate School in Psychology?

American Psychological Association (n.d.). *Graduate study in psychology.* https://gradstudy.apa.org.

Geher, G. (2019). *Own your psychology major!: A guide to student success.* Washington, DC: American Psychological Association.

Hettich, P. (2020). *An eye on the workplace: Achieving a career with a bachelor's in psychology!* E-book published by Psi Chi, International Honor Society in Psychology.

Kuther, T. (2019). *The psychology major's handbook* (5th ed.). Thousand Oaks, CA: Sage.

Landrum, E., & Davis, S. (2020). *The psychology major: Career options and strategies for success* (6th ed.). Upper Saddle River, NJ: Pearson.

Morgan, B. L., Korschgen, A. J., & Basten, B. (2022). *Majoring in Psyc? Career options for psychology undergraduates* (6th ed.). Long Grove, IL: Waveland Press, Inc.

Silvia, P. J., Delaney, P. F., & Marcovitch, S. (2017). *What psychology majors could (and should) be doing: A guide to research experience, professional skills, and your options after college.* Washington, DC: American Psychological Association.

Sternberg, R. (2017). *Career paths in Psychology: Where your degree path can take you* (3rd ed). Washington, DC: American Psychological Association.

## Unit 0

### An Introduction to Psychological Science Practices: Research Methods and Data Interpretation

### Module 0.1 The Scientific Attitude, Critical Thinking, and Developing Arguments

**Page 0-6**

**Explain what's involved in critical thinking.**

**Answer:** Examining assumptions, appraising the source, discerning hidden biases, evaluating evidence, and assessing conclusions are essential parts of critical thinking.

### Module 0.2 The Need for Psychological Science

**Page 0-12**

**Explain the difference between hindsight bias and overconfidence.**

**Answer:** Hindsight bias is the tendency to believe, after learning about an outcome, that we would have foreseen it. Overconfidence is our belief that we are correct despite a lack of proof.

### Module 0.3 The Scientific Method

**Page 0-16**

**Explain the role of peer review in the scientific process.**

**Answer:** Peer reviewers are scientific experts who evaluate a research article's theory, originality, and accuracy to determine if it should be published.

**Explain why replication is important.**

**Answer:** By repeating the essence of a research study, usually with different participants, researchers can see whether the basic finding can be reproduced. If they get similar results, confidence in the finding's reliability grows.

**Page 0-20**

**Explain why we cannot assume that case studies always reveal general principles that apply to all of us.**

**Answer:** Because case studies rely on a single person or group, we cannot generalize the findings to others.

**Explain how the wording can change the results of a survey.**

**Answer:** Changes in wording can lead to bias or confusion, which can change how people answer the questions.

**Explain the differences among case studies, naturalistic observation, and surveys.**

**Answer:** Case studies examine one individual or group in depth, while surveys look at many cases. Naturalistic observation records behavior in naturally occurring situations, as opposed to the self-report nature of surveys.

### Module 0.4 Correlation and Experimentation

**Page 0-26**

**How would you interpret a *correlation coefficient* of –0.87?**

**Answer:** A correlation coefficient is a statistical index of the relationship between two variables. A correlation coefficient of –0.87 means the variables relate inversely (as one goes up the other goes down), and this relationship is strong.

**Describe a scatterplot.**

**Answer:** A scatterplot is a graphed cluster of dots, each of which represents the values of two variables. The slope of the points suggests the direction of the relationship between the two variables. The amount of scatter suggests the strength of the relationship (little scatter indicates a higher correlation).

**Page 0-29**

**By using *random assignment*, researchers are able to control for _____ _____, which are other factors besides the independent variable(s) that may influence research results.**

**Answer:** confounding variables

**Match the term on the left (i through iii) with the description on the right (a through c).**

| | |
|---|---|
| i. Double-blind procedure | a. In an experiment, the outcome that is measured; the variable that may change when the independent variable is manipulated |
| ii. Dependent variable | b. Helps minimize preexisting differences between experimental and control groups |
| iii. Random assignment | c. Controls for the placebo effect; neither researchers nor participants know who receives the real treatment |

**Answer:** i, c; ii, a; iii, b

**Explain the difference between random assignment and random sampling.**

**Answer:** Random assignment ensures that participants are placed in the experimental and control groups by chance, thus minimizing preexisting differences between the groups. Random sampling creates a representative sample because everyone in the population has an equal chance of being included in the sample.

### Module 0.5 Research Design and Ethics in Psychology

**Page 0-37**

**Explain the difference between quantitative and qualitative research methods.**

**Answer:** Quantitative research methods use numerical data to represent degrees of a variable, such as scores on a survey. Qualitative research methods rely on in-depth, narrative data, such as data obtained through structured interviews.

**Describe informed consent and debriefing, and explain their importance to research.**

Answer: Informed consent gives potential participants enough information about a study to enable them to choose whether they wish to participate. Debriefing is the postexperimental explanation of a study, including its purpose and any deceptions, to its participants.

## Module 0.6  Statistical Reasoning in Everyday Life

**Page 0-43**

**Explain what is meant by mean, mode, median, and percentile rank.**

Answer: The mean is the arithmetic average of a distribution, obtained by adding the scores and then dividing by the number of scores. The mode is the most frequently occurring score(s) in a distribution. The median is the middle score in a distribution; half the scores are above it and half are below it. Percentile rank is determined by calculating the percentage of scores that are lower than a given score.

**We determine how much scores vary around the average in a way that includes information about the _____ of scores (difference between highest and lowest) by using the _____ _____ formula.**

Answer: range; standard deviation

**Page 0-46**

**_____ statistics summarize data, while _____ statistics determine whether data can be generalized to other populations.**

Answer: Descriptive; inferential

**Explain the three principles we should keep in mind when deciding if it is safe to infer a population difference from a sample difference.**

Answer: Representative samples are better than biased (unrepresentative) samples. Bigger samples are better than smaller ones. More estimates are better than fewer estimates.

# Unit 1
## Biological Bases of Behavior

### Module 1.1  Interaction of Heredity and Environment

**Page 6**

**Explain contemporary psychology's position on the nature–nurture issue.**

Answer: Psychological events stem from the interaction of nature and nurture, rather than from either of them acting alone.

**Page 8**

**Explain the principle of natural selection.**

Answer: Natural selection is the process by which nature selects from chance variations those traits that best enable an organism to survive and reproduce in a particular environment.

**Page 11**

**Explain the difference between heredity and environment.**

Answer: Heredity refers to the genetic transfer of characteristics from parents to offspring, while environment includes every non-genetic influence.

**Explain some effects of small genetic variations within and between species.**

Answer: Slight person-to-person genetic variations make us unique, influencing traits such as intelligence, happiness, and height. In other species, they cause differences in behaviors such as aggression and gender differences.

**Page 15**

**Explain how researchers use twin and adoption studies to learn about psychological principles.**

Answer: Researchers use twin and adoption studies to understand how much variation among individuals is due to genetic makeup and how much is due to environmental factors. Some studies compare the traits and behaviors of identical twins (same genes) and fraternal twins (different genes, as in any two siblings). They also compare adopted children with their adoptive and biological parents. Some studies compare traits and behaviors of twins raised together or separately.

**Page 18**

**Match the following terms (i–iii) to the correct definition (a–c).**

| | |
|---|---|
| i. Epigenetics | a. Study of the relative effects of our genes and our environment on our behavior. |
| ii. Heredity | b. The genetic transfer of characteristics from parents to offspring. |
| iii. Behavior genetics | c. Study of environmental factors that affect how our genes are *expressed*. |

Answer: i, c; ii, b; iii, a

### Module 1.2  Overview of the Nervous System

**Page 24**

**Match the type of neuron (i–iii) to its description (a–c).**

| | |
|---|---|
| i. Motor neurons | a. Carry incoming messages from sensory receptors to the CNS. |
| ii. Sensory neurons | b. Communicate within the CNS and process information between incoming and outgoing messages. |
| iii. Interneurons | c. Carry outgoing messages from the CNS to muscles and glands. |

Answer: i, c; ii, a; iii, b

**Explain how the ANS was involved in Hawaiians' terrified responses, and in calming their bodies once they realized it was a false alarm.**

Answer: When these individuals became terrified, the sympathetic division of the ANS aroused them, pumping out the stress hormones epinephrine and norepinephrine to prepare them for fight or flight. Then the parasympathetic division of the ANS took over when the crisis passed, restoring their bodies to a calm physiological and emotional state.

## Module 1.3a The Neuron and Neural Firing: Neural Communication and the Endocrine System

### Page 30

**Explain the functions of the dendrites, the axon, and the cell body.**

**Answer:** Dendrites receive and integrate messages, conducting impulses toward the cell body. The axon is the segmented neuron extension that passes messages through its branches to other neurons or to muscles or glands. The cell body contains the nucleus, which is the cell's life-support center.

**Explain the *refractory period*.**

**Answer:** In neural processing, the refractory period is a brief resting pause that occurs after a neuron has fired; subsequent action potentials cannot occur until the axon returns to its resting state.

### Page 32

**Explain *reuptake*. What two other things can happen to excess neurotransmitters after a neuron reacts?**

**Answer:** Reuptake occurs when excess neurotransmitters are reabsorbed by the sending neuron. They can also drift away or be broken down by enzymes.

**Explain what happens in the synaptic gap.**

**Answer:** Neurons send neurotransmitters (chemical messengers) across this tiny space between one neuron's terminal branch and the next neuron's dendrite or cell body.

### Page 35

**Serotonin, dopamine, and endorphins are all chemical messengers called _____.**

**Answer:** neurotransmitters

### Page 37

**Explain the relationship between the nervous and endocrine systems.**

**Answer:** Both of these communication systems produce chemical molecules that act on the body's receptors to influence our behavior and emotions. The endocrine system, which secretes hormones into the bloodstream, delivers its messages much more slowly than the speedy nervous system, and the effects of the endocrine system's messages tend to linger much longer than those of the nervous system.

## Module 1.3b The Neuron and Neural Firing: Substance Use Disorders and Psychoactive Drugs

### Page 41

**Explain *substance use disorder*. What determines whether someone has a substance use disorder?**

**Answer:** Substance use disorder is characterized by continued substance use despite resulting life disruption. It might be diagnosed as a disorder when substance use continues despite significant life disruptions.

### Page 45

**Which category of psychoactive drugs is known to calm neural activity and slow body functions?**

**Answer:** Depressants

### Page 48

**Explain how a *stimulant* affects behavior.**

**Answer:** Stimulants are drugs that excite neural activity and speed up body functions, making people feel more alert.

**Explain the physiological effects of nicotine.**

**Answer:** A rush of nicotine signals the central nervous system to release a flood of epinephrine and norepinephrine, which diminish appetite and boost alertness and mental efficiency. Dopamine and opioids temporarily calm anxiety and reduce sensitivity to pain.

**Explain the withdrawal symptoms someone should expect when quitting smoking.**

**Answer:** Nicotine-withdrawal symptoms include strong cravings, insomnia, anxiety, irritability, distractibility, and difficulty concentrating. However, if one sticks with it, the craving and withdrawal symptoms will gradually dissipate over about six months.

### Page 53

**How would you explain each category of psychoactive drugs to a classmate?**

**Answer:** Depressants dampen neural activity and slow body functions, whereas stimulants excite neural activity and speed up body functions. Hallucinogens distort perceptions and evoke sensory images in the absence of sensory input.

## Module 1.4a The Brain: Neuroplasticity and Tools of Discovery

### Page 57

**Explain *neuroplasticity*.**

**Answer:** Neuroplasticity is the brain's ability to change, especially during childhood, by reorganizing after damage or by building new pathways based on experience.

**Explain how learning a new skill affects the structure of our brain.**

**Answer:** It will produce learning-related changes in your brain.

### Page 61

**Match the scanning technique (i-iii) with the correct description (a–c).**

| | |
|---|---|
| i. fMRI scan | a. Tracks radioactive glucose to reveal brain *activity*. |
| ii. PET scan | b. Tracks successive images of brain tissue to show brain *function*. |
| iii. MRI scan | c. Uses magnetic fields and radio waves to show brain *anatomy*. |

**Answer:** i, b; ii, a; iii, c

## Module 1.4b The Brain: Brain Regions and Structures

**Page 66**

**Explain some brain functions that happen without any conscious effort.**

**Answer:** Because our brain processes information outside of our awareness, activities such as breathing, sleeping, coordination, motor movement, and balance happen without any conscious effort.

**The _____ is a crossover point where nerves from the left side of the brain are mostly linked to the right side of the body, and vice versa.**

**Answer:** brainstem

**Page 70**

**Explain the functions of the key structures of the limbic system.**

**Answer:** The *amygdala* is involved in aggression and fear responses. The *hypothalamus* is involved in bodily maintenance, pleasurable rewards, and control of the hormonal systems. The *hippocampus* processes memory of facts and events. The *thalamus* relays messages between lower brain centers and the cerebral cortex. The *pituitary gland* is the master endocrine gland.

**Page 77**

**Which part of the human brain distinguishes us most from other animals?**

**Answer:** Cerebral cortex

**Explain the differences among the brain's four lobes in terms of their location and function.**

**Answer:** The frontal lobes lie just behind your forehead; they are involved in speaking and muscle movements and in making plans and judgments. The parietal lobes are the portion of the cerebral cortex lying at the top of the head and toward the rear; they receive sensory input for touch and body position. The occipital lobes are the portion of the cerebral cortex lying at the back of the head; they receive information from the visual fields. The temporal lobes are the portion of the cerebral cortex lying roughly above the ears; they receive auditory information.

## Module 1.4c The Brain: Damage Responses and Brain Hemispheres

**Page 84**

**Explain what is meant by *split brain*.**

**Answer:** Split brain is a condition resulting from surgery that separates the brain's two hemispheres by cutting the fibers (mainly those of the corpus callosum) connecting them.

**Explain the classic split-brain studies.**

**Answer:** Researchers asked split-brain patients to stare at a dot as they flashed words like HE and ART on a screen. HE appeared in the patients' left visual field (which transmits information to the right hemisphere) and ART in their right field (which transmits information to the left hemisphere). When the researchers asked patients to *say* what they had seen, they said ART. But when asked to *point* with their left hand to what they had seen, they pointed to HE. Given an opportunity to express itself, each hemisphere indicated what it had seen.

## Module 1.5a Sleep: Consciousness

**Page 88**

**Explain *consciousness*.**

**Answer:** Consciousness is our subjective awareness of ourselves and our environment.

**Page 89**

**Explain what a cognitive neuroscientist does.**

**Answer:** A cognitive neuroscientist studies brain activity linked with cognition (thinking, knowing, remembering, and communicating).

**Page 91**

**What is *dual processing*?**

**Answer:** Dual processing is the principle that information is often simultaneously processed on separate conscious and unconscious tracks. In vision, for example, the visual action track normally guides our conscious visual processing, while the visual perception track normally operates unconsciously, enabling our quick recognition of objects.

**Explain blindsight.**

**Answer:** Blindsight is a condition in which a person can respond to a visual stimulus without consciously experiencing it.

## Module 1.5b Sleep: Sleep Stages and Theories

**Page 99**

**Explain the differences among the stages of sleep.**

**Answer:** In Stage 1, we relax and slip into sleep, and we may experience hypnagogic sensation. In Stage 2, we relax more deeply and experience periodic bursts of rapid, rhythmic brain-wave activity (sleep spindles). In Stage 3, we are in deep sleep and our brain emits large, slow delta waves. In REM, we have waking-like brain activity, yet the body is asleep and externally calm. REM sleep is associated with dreaming.

**Explain the role of the suprachiasmatic nucleus in sleep.**

**Answer:** The suprachiasmatic nucleus helps monitor the brain's release of melatonin, which affects our circadian rhythm.

**Explain how REM sleep relates to dreaming.**

**Answer:** During REM sleep, your heart rate rises, your breathing becomes rapid and irregular, and every half-minute or so your eyes dart around in momentary bursts of activity behind closed lids. It is during this time that people report dreaming.

**Page 100**

**Explain how sleep aids in memory consolidation.**

**Answer:** Our memories are consolidated during slow-wave deep sleep, by replaying recent learning and strengthening neural connections. Sleep reactivates recent experiences stored in the hippocampus and moves them to permanent storage elsewhere in the cortex.

## Module 1.5c Sleep: Sleep Loss, Sleep Disorders, and Dreams

**Page 107**

**A well-rested person would be more likely to have _____ (trouble concentrating/quick reaction times) and a sleep-deprived person would be more likely to _____ (gain weight/fight off a cold).**

**Answer:** quick reaction times; gain weight

**Page 108**

**Explain each of the sleep disorders presented in Table 1.5-3.**

**Answer:** Insomnia is marked by ongoing difficulty falling or staying asleep. Narcolepsy is characterized by sudden attacks of overwhelming sleepiness. People with sleep apnea stop breathing repeatedly while sleeping. Sleep walking is characterized by repeated episodes of complex behavior, such as walking, while asleep.

**Page 113**

**Explain the theories that propose explanations for why we dream.**

**Answer:** The theories are (1) information-processing (dreams sort the day's events and consolidate memories); (2) physiological function (dreams pave neural pathways); (3) activation-synthesis (REM sleep triggers random neural activity that the mind weaves into stories); and (4) cognitive development (dreams reflect the dreamer's developmental stage).

## Module 1.6a Sensation: Basic Concepts

**Page 120**

**Explain the difference between bottom-up and top-down processing.**

**Answer:** In bottom-up processing, information processing begins with the sensory receptors and works up to the brain's integration of sensory information. In contrast, in top-down processing, information processing is guided by higher-level mental processes, as when we construct perceptions by drawing on our experience and expectations.

**Explain the basic steps of transduction.**

**Answer:** Transduction is the conversion of one form of energy into another. In sensation, it is the transformation of physical energy, such as sights, sounds, and smells, into neural impulses that the brain can interpret.

**Page 122**

**Explain sensory adaptation.**

**Answer:** Sensory adaptation refers to our diminished sensitivity to routinely encountered odors, sights, sounds, and touches. It allows us to focus our attention on informative changes in our environment.

## Module 1.6b Sensation: Vision

**Page 133**

**Some nocturnal animals, such as toads, mice, rats, and bats, have impressive night vision thanks to having many more _____ (rods/cones) than _____ (rods/cones) in their retinas. These creatures probably have very poor _____ (color/black-and-white) vision.**

**Answer:** rods; cones; color

**Cats are able to open their _____ much wider than we can, which allows more light into their eyes so they can see better at night.**

**Answer:** pupils

**Explain the difference between the two key theories of color vision. Are they contradictory or complementary? Explain.**

**Answer:** The *Young-Helmholtz trichromatic theory* states that the retina contains color receptors for red, green, and blue. The *opponent-process theory* states that we have opponent-process cells in the retina and thalamus for red-green, blue-yellow, and white-black. These theories are complementary and outline the two stages of color vision: (1) The retina's receptors for red, green, and blue respond to different color stimuli. (2) The receptors' signals are then processed by the opponent-process cells on their way to the visual cortex in the brain.

## Module 1.6c Sensation: Hearing

**Page 141**

**The amplitude of a sound wave determines our perception of _____ (loudness/pitch).**

**Answer:** loudness

**The longer the sound waves are, the _____ (lower/higher) their frequency and the _____ (higher/lower) their pitch.**

**Answer:** lower; lower

## Module 1.6d Sensation: Skin, Chemical, and Body Senses and Sensory Interaction

**Page 148**

**Explain the gate-control theory of pain.**

**Answer:** This theory posits that the spinal cord contains a neurological "gate" that either blocks pain signals or allows them to pass on to the brain. The "gate" is opened by the activity of pain signals traveling up small nerve fibers, and is closed by activity in larger fibers or by information coming from the brain.

**Explain the differences among the biological, psychological, and social-cultural influences on pain.**

**Answer:** Biological influences include activity in the spinal cord's large and small fibers, genetic differences in endorphin production, and the brain's interpretation of the central nervous system activity. Psychological influences refer to our attention to pain, learning based on experience, and expectations. Social-cultural influences include the presence of others, our empathy for others' pain, and cultural expectations.

**Page 155**

**Explain the difference between our systems for sensing smell, touch, and taste.**

**Answer:** Olfactory receptor cells send messages to the brain's olfactory bulb, and then onward to the temporal lobe's primary smell cortex. We have receptors in the skin, which detect pressure, warmth, cold, and pain. Our tongues have taste buds, each containing a pore that catches food chemicals and then releases them. Some receptors respond mostly to sweet-tasting molecules, others to salty-, sour-, umami-, or bitter-tasting ones.

**Where are the kinesthetic receptors and the vestibular sense receptors located?**

**Answer:** Kinesthetic receptors are located in our joints, tendons, and muscles. Vestibular sense receptors are located in our inner ear.

# Unit 2
## Cognition

### Module 2.1a Perception: Influences on Perception

**Page 169**

**Explain an attentional principle that magicians may use to fool us.**

**Answer:** Our *selective attention* allows us to focus on only a limited portion of our surroundings. *Inattentional blindness* explains why we don't perceive some things when we are distracted. And *change blindness* happens when we fail to notice a relatively unimportant change in our environment. All of these principles help magicians fool us, as they direct our attention elsewhere while performing their tricks.

**Page 170**

**Explain bottom-up and top-down processing. Which of these does perceptual set involve?**

**Answer:** Information processing occurs both from the bottom up (beginning with the sensory receptors, and working up to the brain's integration of sensory information) and from the top down (as we draw from our experience and expectations when constructing perceptions). Perceptual set involves top-down processing, because it draws on our experiences, assumptions, and expectations when interpreting stimuli.

**Page 173**

**Explain how emotions can influence our perceptions. Provide a piece of evidence to support your point.**

**Answer:** Emotions can nudge our perceptions in one direction or another. For example, hearing sad music can predispose people to perceive a sad meaning in spoken homophonic words—*mourning* rather than *morning, die* rather than *dye, pain* rather than *pane.*

### Module 2.1b Perception: Perceptual Organization and Interpretation

**Page 179**

**What do we mean when we say that, in perception, "the whole may exceed the sum of its parts"?**

**Answer:** Gestalt psychologists used this saying to describe our perceptual tendency to organize clusters of sensations into meaningful forms or coherent groups.

**Explain how convergence and retinal disparity relate to depth perception.**

**Answer:** Convergence is a binocular cue to nearby objects' distance, enabled by the inward angle of the eyes. Retinal disparity is also a binocular cue for perceiving depth. By comparing retinal images from the two eyes, the brain computes distance—the greater the disparity (difference) between the two images, the closer the object.

**Page 184**

**Explain perceptual adaptation.**

**Answer:** Perceptual adaptation is the ability to adjust to changed sensory input, including an artificially displaced or even inverted visual field.

### Module 2.2a Thinking, Problem Solving, Judgments, and Decision Making: Concepts and Creativity

**Page 189**

**Describe *prototypes* and explain how they might feed discrimination.**

**Answer:** A prototype is a mental image or best example of a category that provides a quick and easy method for sorting items into categories. When we categorize people, we mentally shift them toward our category prototypes or our stereotypes.

**Explain cognition and metacognition.**

**Answer:** Cognition includes all the mental activities associated with thinking, knowing, remembering, and communicating. Metacognition is cognition about our cognition; it includes keeping track of and evaluating our mental processes.

**Page 191**

**Explain convergent and divergent thinking. When might each be most helpful?**

**Answer:** Convergent thinking is narrowing of the available problem solutions to determine the single best solution. Divergent thinking is expanding the number of possible problem solutions; it is most useful when creativity is desired.

**Explain the five components of creativity identified by Robert Sternberg.**

**Answer:** (1) *Expertise*—well-developed knowledge—furnishes the ideas, images, and phrases we use as mental building blocks. (2) *Imaginative thinking skills* provide the ability to see things in novel ways, to recognize patterns, and to make connections. (3) A *venturesome personality* seeks new experiences, tolerates ambiguity and risk, and perseveres in overcoming obstacles. (4) *Intrinsic motivation* is the quality of being driven more by interest, satisfaction, and challenge than by external pressures. (5) A *creative environment* sparks, supports, and refines creative ideas.

### Module 2.2b Thinking, Problem Solving, Judgments, and Decision Making: Solving Problems and Making Decisions

**Page 195**

**Explain the difference between algorithms and heuristics.**

**Answer:** An algorithm is a methodical, logical rule or procedure that guarantees solving a particular problem. It contrasts with the usually speedier—but also more error-prone—use of heuristics. A heuristic is a mental shortcut that often allows us to make judgments and solve problems efficiently.

**Explain *fixation*. Provide a specific example.**

**Answer:** Fixation in cognition is the inability to see a problem from a new perspective, creating an obstacle to problem solving. For example, someone might fail to see that dental floss can be used as string to tie something together.

## Page 198

**Explain the difference between the representativeness heuristic and the availability heuristic.**

**Answer:** The representativeness heuristic includes judging the likelihood of events in terms of how well they seem to represent, or match, particular prototypes. This may lead us to ignore other relevant information. The availability heuristic includes judging the likelihood of events based on their availability in memory. If instances come readily to mind (perhaps because of their vividness), we presume such events are common.

## Page 203

**Match each process or strategy (i-x) with its description (a–j).**

| | | | |
|---|---|---|---|
| i. | Algorithm | a. | Inability to view problems from a new angle; focuses thinking but hinders creative problem solving |
| ii. | Intuition | b. | Methodological rule or procedure that guarantees a solution but requires time and effort |
| iii. | Insight | c. | Your fast, automatic, effortless feelings and thoughts based on your experience; huge and adaptive but can lead you to overfeel and underthink |
| iv. | Heuristic | d. | Simple thinking shortcut that lets you act quickly and efficiently but puts you at risk for errors |
| v. | Fixation | e. | Sudden Aha! reaction that instantly reveals the solution |
| vi. | Confirmation bias | f. | Tendency to search for support for your own views and to ignore contradictory evidence |
| vii. | Overconfidence | g. | Holding on to your beliefs even after they are proven wrong; closing your mind to new ideas |
| viii. | Creativity | h. | Overestimating the accuracy of your beliefs and judgments; allows you to be happier and to make decisions more easily, but puts you at risk for errors |
| ix. | Framing | i. | Wording a question or statement so that it evokes a desired response; can mislead people and influence their decisions |
| x. | Belief perseverance | j. | The ability to produce novel and valuable ideas |

**Answer:** i, b; ii, c; iii, e; iv, d; v, a; vi, f; vii, h; viii, j; ix, i; x, g

## Module 2.3 Introduction to Memory

### Page 209

**Explain each of the three retention measures. Provide examples of each.**

**Answer:** Recall is retrieving information that is not currently in your conscious awareness but that was learned at an earlier time.

A fill-in-the-blank question tests your recall. Recognition includes identifying items previously learned. A multiple-choice question tests your recognition. Relearning is learning something more quickly when you learn it a second or later time. When you review the first weeks of course work to prepare for your final exam, it will be easier to relearn the material than it was to learn it initially.

### Page 210

**Explain how the *working memory* concept updated the classic Atkinson-Shiffrin three-stage multi-store model.**

**Answer:** The newer idea of *working memory* emphasizes the active processing that we now know takes place in Atkinson-Shiffrin's short-term memory stage. While the Atkinson-Shiffrin model viewed short-term memory as a temporary holding space, working memory plays a key role in processing new information and connecting it to previously stored information.

**Explain the two basic functions of working memory.**

**Answer:** The two functions of working memory are (1) active processing of incoming visual and auditory information, and (2) focusing our spotlight of attention.

### Page 212

**Explain *long-term potentiation*.**

**Answer:** Long-term potentiation (LTP) is an increase in a nerve cell's firing potential after brief, rapid stimulation. It's the neural basis for learning and memory.

## Module 2.4 Encoding Memories

### Page 218

**Explain the difference between *automatic* and *effortful* processing, and offer some examples of each.**

**Answer:** *Automatic* processing occurs unconsciously (automatically) for such things as the sequence and frequency of a day's events, and reading and comprehending words in our own language(s). *Effortful* processing requires attention and awareness. It happens, for example, when we work hard to learn new material in class or new lines for a play.

**At which of Atkinson-Shiffrin's three memory stages would *iconic* and *echoic* memory occur?**

**Answer:** Sensory memory

### Page 223

**Explain the difference between shallow and deep processing.**

**Answer:** Shallow processing is encoding on a basic level, based on the structure or appearance of words. In contrast, deep processing is encoding semantically, based on the meaning of the words, and tends to yield the best retention.

**Explain the self-reference effect.**

**Answer:** The self-reference effect is the tendency to remember self-relevant information.

## Module 2.5 Storing Memories

### Page 230

**Which parts of the brain are important for *implicit* memory processing, and which parts play a key role in *explicit* memory processing?**

**Answer:** The cerebellum and basal ganglia are important for *implicit* memory processing, and the frontal lobes and hippocampus are key to *explicit* memory processing.

**Which brain area responds to stress hormones by helping to create stronger memories?**

**Answer:** Amygdala

## Module 2.6  Retrieving Memories

**Page 235**

**Explain *priming*.**

**Answer:** Priming is the activation (often without our awareness) of associations. It is often an implicit memory, without conscious awareness.

**When we are tested immediately after viewing a list of words, we tend to recall the first and last items best, which is known as the _____ _____ effect.**

**Answer:** serial position

**Explain the benefits of interleaving.**

**Answer:** Interleaving improves retention. Mixing your study of psychology with your study of other subjects boosts long-term retention and protects against overconfidence.

## Module 2.7  Forgetting and Other Memory Challenges

**Page 244**

**Explain what is meant by encoding failure.**

**Answer:** Encoding failure occurs when unattended information never enters our memory system. What we fail to encode, we will never remember.

**Explain the difference between proactive and retroactive interference, providing an example of each.**

**Answer:** Proactive interference is the forward-acting disruptive effect of older learning on the recall of new information. For example, your elementary school Spanish class is interfering with your current Italian class. Retroactive (backward-acting) interference occurs when new learning disrupts your recall of old information. For example, you can't recall your old phone number now that you have learned your new one.

**Freud believed that we _____ unacceptable memories to minimize anxiety.**

**Answer:** repress

**Page 249**

**Explain the *misinformation effect*.**

**Answer:** The misinformation effect occurs when a memory has been corrupted by misleading information.

**Explain how source amnesia relates to false memories.**

**Answer:** Source amnesia is a faulty memory for how, when, or where information was learned or imagined (as when misattributing information to a wrong source). Source amnesia, along with the misinformation effect, is at the heart of many false memories.

**Page 251**

**Explain how memory researchers' findings can benefit education.**

**Answer:** They can boost your performance in class and on tests if you follow some research-based suggestions that can help you remember information when you need it.

## Module 2.8a  Intelligence and Achievement: Theories of Intelligence

**Page 260**

**Explain how the existence of savant syndrome supports Gardner's theory of multiple intelligences. What supports the concept of *g*?**

**Answer:** People with savant syndrome have limited mental ability overall but possess one or more exceptional skills. According to Howard Gardner, this suggests that our abilities come in separate packages rather than being fully expressed by one general intelligence that encompasses all our talents. General intelligence (*g*) is supported by the fact that those who score high in one area, such as verbal intelligence, typically score higher than average in other areas, such as spatial or reasoning ability.

**Explain how the Cattell-Horn-Carroll theory describes intelligence.**

**Answer:** This theory states that our intelligence is based on a general ability factor as well as other specific abilities, bridged by crystallized and fluid intelligence.

**Describe the four components of emotional intelligence.**

**Answer:** Emotional intelligence is characterized by (1) perceiving emotions, such as recognizing them in faces, music, and stories, and identifying our own emotions; (2) understanding emotions by predicting them and how they may change and blend; (3) managing emotions, such as knowing how to express them in varied situations, and how to handle others' emotions; and (4) using emotions to facilitate adaptive or creative thinking.

## Module 2.8b  Intelligence and Achievement: Assessing Intelligence

**Page 265**

**Explain what Binet hoped to achieve by establishing a child's mental age.**

**Answer:** Binet hoped that determining the child's mental age (the age that typically corresponds to a certain level of performance) would help identify appropriate school placements.

**What is the IQ score of a 4-year-old with a mental age of 5?**

**Answer:** 125 ($5 \div 4 \times 100 = 125$)

**Page 268**

**Explain the three criteria that a psychological test must meet to be widely accepted.**

**Answer:** A psychological test must be *standardized* (pretested on a representative sample of people), *reliable* (yielding consistent results), and *valid* (measuring and predicting what it is supposed to).

**Compare and contrast content validity and predictive validity.**

**Answer:** Content validity is the extent to which a test samples the behavior that is of interest. Predictive validity is the extent to which a test predicts the behavior it is designed to predict. It is assessed by computing the correlation between test scores and the criterion behavior (also called criterion-related validity).

## Module 2.8c Intelligence and Achievement: Stability of, and Influences on, Intelligence

### Page 274

**Explain the changes in crystallized and fluid intelligence over the lifespan.**

**Answer:** Crystallized intelligence (Gc) is our accumulated knowledge, as reflected in vocabulary and analogies tests, which increases up to old age. Fluid intelligence (Gf) is our ability to reason speedily and abstractly, as when solving novel logic problems. It may decline as we age.

### Page 279

**If environments become more equal, the heritability of intelligence will**

a. increase.

b. decrease.

c. be unchanged.

**Answer:** a. (Heritability—variation explained by genetic influences—will increase as environmental variation decreases.)

**The heritability of intelligence scores will be greater in a society of equal opportunity than in a society of extreme economic inequality. Explain why.**

**Answer:** In the former case, genes alone—as opposed to access to good schools, for example—would account for the differences in the scores.

## Module 2.8d Intelligence and Achievement: Group Differences and the Question of Bias

### Page 286

**Explain the difference between a test that is culturally biased and a test that is scientifically biased.**

**Answer:** The scientific meaning of bias hinges solely on whether a test predicts future behavior for all groups of test-takers, not just for some. That is, does the test predict what it is supposed to predict? A test is culturally biased if it is unfair—if test scores will be influenced by the test-takers' developed abilities, which reflect, in part, their education and cultural experiences.

**Describe the psychological principle that may help explain why women tend to score higher on math tests when none of their fellow test-takers are men.**

**Answer:** This difference might be due to stereotype threat, a self-confirming concern that one will be evaluated based on a negative stereotype. With no men present, the stereotype that women don't do well in math is not activated.

# Unit 3
## Development and Learning

## Module 3.1 Themes and Methods in Developmental Psychology

### Page 299

**Explain the difference between longitudinal and cross-sectional studies.**

**Answer:** Cross-sectional research compares people of different ages at the same point in time, while longitudinal research follows and retests the same people over time.

**Developmental researchers who emphasize learning and experience are supporting _____; those who emphasize biological maturation are supporting _____.**

**Answer:** continuity; stages

## Module 3.2a Physical Development Across the Lifespan: Prenatal Development, Infancy, and Childhood

### Page 306

**Explain what is meant by, "a pregnant woman never smokes, vapes, or drinks alone."**

**Answer:** Teratogens, such as nicotine and alcohol, can damage an embryo or a fetus by entering the bloodstream of the fetus.

**Explain the effect of teratogens on prenatal development.**

**Answer:** Teratogens are agents, such as chemicals and viruses, that can reach the embryo or fetus during prenatal development and cause harm.

### Page 309

**Explain *maturation*.**

**Answer:** Maturation is the biological growth processes that enable orderly changes in behavior, relatively uninfluenced by experience.

**Explain what is meant by *critical* or *sensitive period*.**

**Answer:** A critical period is an optimal period early in the life of an organism when exposure to certain stimuli or experiences produces normal development.

## Module 3.2b Physical Development Across the Lifespan: Adolescence and Adulthood

### Page 318

**Explain what is meant by *adolescence*.**

**Answer:** Adolescence is the transition period from childhood to adulthood, extending from puberty to independence.

**Explain the physical changes in the brain during adolescence.**

**Answer:** As teens mature, their prefrontal cortex continues to develop. The continuing growth of myelin, the fatty tissue that forms around axons and speeds neurotransmission, enables better communication with other brain regions.

## Module 3.3a Gender and Sexual Orientation: Gender Development

### Page 325

**Explain what is meant by *gender*.**

**Answer:** In psychology, gender refers to the attitudes, feelings, and behaviors that a given culture associates with a person's biological sex.

**Explain physical and relational aggression in terms of gender differences.**

**Answers:** Physical aggression is any physical or verbal behavior intended to harm someone physically or emotionally and is more common in males. Relational aggression is an act of aggression (physical or verbal) intended to harm a person's relationship or social standing and is slightly more common in females.

### Page 327

**Describe the two major sex hormones.**

**Answer:** The primary male sex hormone is testosterone. The primary female sex hormone is estrogen.

**Explain what is meant by *puberty*.**

**Answer:** Puberty is the period of sexual maturation, when a person usually becomes capable of reproducing.

### Page 331

**Explain what is meant by *gender roles*. What do their variations tell us about our human capacity for learning and adaptation?**

**Answer:** Gender roles are social rules or norms for accepted and expected female and male behaviors. The norms associated with various roles, including gender roles, vary widely in different cultural contexts, which demonstrates that we are able to learn and adapt to the social demands of different environments.

**_____ is our personal sense of being male, female, neither, or some combination of male and female, regardless of whether this identity matches our sex assigned at birth.**

**Answer:** Gender identity

## Module 3.3b Gender and Sexual Orientation: The Biology and Psychology of Sex

### Page 337

**Explain the factors that influence sexual motivation.**

**Answer:** Biological influences include sexual maturity and sex hormones. Psychological factors include exposure to stimulating conditions and sexual fantasies. Social-cultural influences include family and society values, religious and personal values, cultural expectations, and media.

**Describe four factors that contribute to sexual restraint among teens.**

**Answer:** Intelligence, religious engagement, father presence, and participating in service learning are associated with an increase in sexual restraint.

### Page 339

**Explain some ways in which gender roles are changing.**

**Answer:** The gap in roles is shrinking in some cases. For example, brute strength has become less important for power and status,
women are the majority of medical students, and there is a shrinking gender gap in housework and other unpaid work, such as child care.

**What is meant by the statement, "We are both creatures and creators of our worlds"?**

**Answer:** Many things about us are the products of our genes and environments, and our decisions today design our environments tomorrow. Our hopes, goals, and expectations influence our destiny—and that is what enables cultures to vary and to change.

## Module 3.3c Gender and Sexual Orientation: Sexual Orientation

### Page 347

**Explain what is meant by *sexual orientation*.**

**Answer:** Sexual orientation is a person's sexual and emotional attraction to another person and the behavior and/or social affiliation that may result from this attraction.

**Explain two ways prenatal hormone exposure influences sexual orientation.**

**Answer:** (1) Exposure to the hormone levels typically experienced by female fetuses during a critical period in the second trimester may predispose females later to become attracted to males. (2) Male fetuses may stimulate the mother's immune system to produce antibodies. After each pregnancy with a male fetus, the maternal antibodies may become stronger and may prevent a subsequent male fetus' brain from developing in a male-typical pattern.

## Module 3.4 Cognitive Development Across the Lifespan

### Page 353

**Explain mental operations.**

**Answer:** Mental operations include imagining an action and mentally reversing it.

**Explain what is meant by *egocentrism*.**

**Answer:** Egocentrism refers to the preoperational child's difficulty in taking another's point of view.

### Page 358

**Use Piaget's first three stages of cognitive development to explain why children are not just miniature adults in the way they think.**

**Answer:** Infants in the sensorimotor stage tend to be focused only on their own perceptions of the world and may, for example, be unaware that objects continue to exist when unseen. A preoperational child is still egocentric and incapable of appreciating simple logic, such as the reversibility of operations. A preteen in the concrete operational stage is beginning to think logically about concrete events but not about abstract concepts.

**Explain the theory of mind.**

**Answer:** Theory of mind focuses on our ability to understand our own and others' mental states.

**Page 360**

**Explain the evidence on brain-exercise programs for older adults.**

**Answer:** Although our brain remains plastic throughout life, brain-exercise programs improve performance only on closely related tasks, not on unrelated tasks.

## Module 3.5 Communication and Language Development

**Page 367**

**Explain Noam Chomsky's view of language development.**

**Answer:** Linguist Noam Chomsky proposed that language is an unlearned human trait, separate from other parts of human cognition. He theorized that we are born with a built-in predisposition to learn a language's set of rules that enable people to communicate, called universal grammar (UG).

**Explain the difference between *receptive* language and *productive* language. Give an example to illustrate each.**

**Answer:** Infants normally start developing *receptive language* skills (ability to understand what is said to and about them) around four months of age. They understand when they are told "no." Then, starting with babbling at four months and beyond, infants normally start building *productive language* skills (the ability to produce sounds and eventually words). They can eventually say "no."

**Identify three pieces of evidence to support the claim that it is difficult to learn a new language in adulthood.**

**Answer:** (1) There seems to be a critical (or sensitive) period for mastering certain aspects of language before the language-learning window gradually closes. (2) Children exposed to low-quality language often display less language skill. (3) Those who learned their second language early learned it best.

**Page 369**

**_____ _____ is one part of the brain that, if damaged, might impair your ability to speak words. Damage to _____ _____ might impair your ability to understand language.**

**Answer:** Broca's area; Wernicke's area

**Page 371**

**Explain the theory of linguistic determinism.**

**Answer:** This theory refers to Whorf's extreme hypothesis that language determines the way we think, and that we can't think about things for which we have no words.

**Explain what is meant by *linguistic relativism*.**

**Answer:** Linguistic relativism refers to the idea that language influences (but doesn't necessarily determine) the way we think.

## Module 3.6a Social-Emotional Development Across the Lifespan: Infancy and Childhood

**Page 379**

**Explain the difference between imprinting and attachment.**

**Answer:** Attachment is the normal process by which we form emotional ties with important others. Imprinting occurs only in certain animals that have a critical period very early in their development during which they must form their attachments, and they do so in an inflexible manner.

**Page 384**

**Explain what is meant by *self-concept*.**

**Answer:** Self-concept is our understanding and assessment of who we are.

**Explain the differences among the four parenting styles.**

**Answer:** (1) *Authoritarian* parents are coercive; they impose rules and expect obedience. (2) *Permissive* parents are unrestraining; they make few demands, set few limits, and use little punishment. (3) *Neglectful* parents are uninvolved; they are neither demanding nor responsive. They are careless, inattentive, and do not seek a close relationship with their children. (4) *Authoritative* parents are both demanding and responsive. They exert control by setting rules, but, especially with older children, they encourage open discussion and allow exceptions.

## Module 3.6b Social-Emotional Development Across the Lifespan: Adolescence, Emerging Adulthood, and Adulthood

**Page 390**

**Match the psychosocial development stage (i-viii) with the issue that Erikson believed we wrestle with at that stage (a–h).**

| | |
|---|---|
| i. Infancy | a. Generativity and stagnation |
| ii. Toddlerhood | b. Integrity and despair |
| iii. Preschool | c. Initiative and guilt |
| iv. Elementary school | d. Intimacy and isolation |
| v. Adolescence | e. Identity and role confusion |
| vi. Young adulthood | f. Competence and inferiority |
| vii. Middle adulthood | g. Trust and mistrust |
| viii. Late adulthood | h. Autonomy and shame and doubt |

**Answer:** i, g; ii, h; iii, c; iv, f; v, e; vi, d; vii, a; viii, b

**Page 397**

**Explain what is meant by *emerging adulthood*. How does culture/geographic region impact this?**

**Answer:** Emerging adulthood is a period from about age 18 to the mid-twenties, when many persons in prosperous Western cultures are no longer adolescents but have not yet achieved full independence as adults.

**Explain the relationship between cohabitation and divorce.**

**Answer:** Research has shown that living together before marriage predicts an increased likelihood of future divorce. There are several possible explanations for this correlation. First, those who choose to live together are often less committed to the enduring marriage ideal. Second, they may become even less supportive of this ideal while cohabiting. Third, people may be more reluctant to break up with a cohabiting partner than a dating partner, despite suspecting that the relationship is unsustainable.

## Module 3.7a  Classical Conditioning: Basic Concepts

**Page 402**

**What is learning?**

**Answer:** Learning is the process of acquiring through experience new and relatively enduring information or behaviors.

**Explain the difference between associative and cognitive learning. Provide an example to illustrate the differences.**

**Answer:** Associative learning is learning that certain events occur together. The events may be two stimuli (as in classical conditioning) or a response and its consequence (as in operant conditioning). An example of associative learning would be doing your chores because you associate that with getting an allowance. Cognitive learning is the acquisition of mental information, whether by observing events, by watching others, or through language. An example of cognitive learning would be learning how to fix your hair by watching your older sibling.

**Page 408**

**The first step of classical conditioning, when an NS becomes a CS, is called _____. When the UCS no longer follows the CS, and the CR becomes weakened, this is called _____.**

**Answer:** acquisition; extinction

**Explain the difference between discrimination and generalization.**

**Answer:** Generalization is the tendency to respond to stimuli that are similar to a CS. Discrimination is the learned ability to distinguish between a CS and other irrelevant stimuli.

**Page 409**

**Explain two important contributions of Pavlov's research.**

**Answer:** (1) Many other responses to many other stimuli can be classically conditioned in many other organisms. (2) Pavlov showed us how a process such as learning can be studied objectively.

## Module 3.7b  Classical Conditioning: Applications and Biological Limits

**Page 415**

**Explain how therapists might use conditioning to reduce their clients' fears.**

**Answer:** By having clients confront their fears often or for an extended period, extinction will occur and the fear response will diminish.

**Explain what is meant by *biological preparedness*. Give an example to illustrate the concept.**

**Answer:** Biological preparedness refers to a biological predisposition to learn associations, such as between taste and nausea, that have survival value.

## Module 3.8a  Operant Conditioning: Basic Concepts

**Page 420**

**With classical conditioning, we learn associations between events we _____ (do/do not) control. With operant conditioning, we learn associations between our behavior and _____ (resulting/random) events.**

**Answer:** do not; resulting

**Explain the process of shaping.**

**Answer:** Shaping is an operant conditioning procedure in which reinforcers guide behavior toward closer and closer approximations of the desired behavior.

**Page 424**

**Explain the difference between primary and conditioned reinforcers.**

**Answer:** A primary reinforcer is an innately reinforcing stimulus, such as one that satisfies a biological need. A conditioned reinforcer (also known as a secondary reinforcer) is a stimulus that gains its reinforcing power through its association with a primary reinforcer.

**Page 426**

**Explain the difference between positive and negative punishment.**

**Answer:** Both types of punishment reduce the likelihood of a response. In positive punishment, one administers an aversive stimulus. In negative punishment, one withdraws a rewarding stimulus.

**Explain five arguments against physical punishment. Identify reasoning that supports each argument.**

**Answer:** (1) Punished behavior is suppressed, not forgotten. This temporary state may (negatively) reinforce parents' punishing behavior. (2) Physical punishment does not replace the unwanted behavior. It does not provide direction for appropriate behavior, so children might stop one unwanted behavior but continue others. (3) Punishment teaches discrimination among situations. Children will learn to avoid the unwanted behavior only in certain situations, such as around the parents. (4) Punishment teaches fear. Children will associate punishment with a parent or teacher and learn to fear and avoid them. (5) Physical punishment may increase aggression by modeling violence as a way to cope with problems. Spanked children are at increased risk for aggression.

## Module 3.8b  Operant Conditioning: Applications, Biological Limits, and Contrasts With Classical Conditioning

**Page 432**

**Explain how artificial intelligence uses reinforcement principles to mimic human learning.**

**Answer:** Artificial intelligence programs perform actions faster than humans do, enabling the programs to quickly learn to repeat reinforced actions (what leads to winning) and avoid punished responses (what leads to losing).

**Salivating in response to a tone paired with food is a(n) _____ (involuntary/voluntary) behavior; pressing a bar to obtain food is a(n) _____ (involuntary/voluntary) behavior.**

**Answer:** involuntary; voluntary

## Module 3.9  Social, Cognitive, and Neurological Factors in Learning

**Page 437**

**Explain *latent learning*. Provide an example.**

**Answer:** Latent learning is learning that occurs but is not apparent until there is an incentive to demonstrate it. By exploring a maze with no reinforcement, for example, rats can learn it and complete it quickly once a reinforcement is present.

**Explain insight learning.**

**Answer:** Insight learning is the sudden realization of a problem's solution. It contrasts with strategy-based solutions.

**Page 444**

**Explain how both observation and imitation are important in modeling.**

**Answer:** Modeling is the process of observing and imitating a specific behavior.

**What are mirror neurons? Explain how they relate to imitation and empathy.**

**Answer:** Mirror neurons are believed to fire when we perform certain actions or observe another doing so. The brain's mirroring of another's action may enable imitation and empathy.

# Unit 4
## Social and Personality

## Module 4.1 Attribution Theory and Person Perception
**Page 456**

**Explain the *fundamental attribution error*.**

**Answer:** This is the tendency for observers, when analyzing others' behavior, to underestimate the impact of the situation and to overestimate the impact of personal disposition.

**Page 457**

**How can social comparison both help and harm us?**

**Answer:** By comparing ourselves to others, we judge whether we're succeeding or failing. When we succeed, our self-esteem rises. But when we come up short, our self-esteem can plummet.

**Page 465**

**Explain the differences among stereotyping, prejudice, and discrimination.**

**Answer:** Prejudice is an unjustifiable and usually negative attitude toward a group and its members, while unjustifiable negative behavior is discrimination. Stereotypes refer to our beliefs about groups.

**Explain scapegoat theory.**

**Answer:** This belief arises when prejudiced judgment causes us to blame an undeserving person or group for a problem.

## Module 4.2 Attitude Formation and Attitude Change
**Page 470**

**Explain the *foot-in-the-door phenomenon*.**

**Answer:** This refers to the tendency for people who have first agreed to a small request to comply later with a larger request.

**Explain how cognitive dissonance can lead to attitude change.**

**Answer:** Cognitive dissonance theory proposes that we act to reduce the discomfort (dissonance) we feel when two of our thoughts

(cognitions) are inconsistent. For example, when we become aware that our attitudes and our actions clash, we can reduce the resulting dissonance by changing our attitudes.

**Page 473**

**Under what circumstances would peripheral route persuasion be most effective? What about central route persuasion?**

**Answer:** Peripheral route persuasion occurs when people are influenced by incidental cues, such as a speaker's attractiveness. It is more effective with speedy, emotion-based judgments. Central route persuasion occurs when interested people's thinking is influenced by considering evidence and arguments. It is more effective for carefully considered judgments.

## Module 4.3a Psychology of Social Situations: Conformity and Obedience
**Page 478**

**Which of the following strengthens conformity to a group?**

a. Finding the group attractive
b. Feeling secure
c. Coming from an individualist culture
d. Having made a prior commitment

**Answer:** a

**Page 484**

**Explain the difference between conformity and obedience.**

**Answer:** Conformity refers to adjusting our behavior or thinking to coincide with a group standard, whereas obedience is following orders.

**Which situations have researchers found to be most likely to encourage obedience in participants?**

**Answer:** People are more likely to obey when the person giving the orders is close at hand and is perceived to be a legitimate authority figure; when a powerful or prestigious institution supports the authority figure; when the victim is depersonalized or at a distance; and when there are no role models for defiance.

## Module 4.3b Psychology of Social Situations: Group Behavior
**Page 488**

**What is *social facilitation*, and why does it improve performance with a well-learned task?**

**Answer:** This improved performance in the presence of others is most likely to occur with a well-learned task because the added arousal caused by an audience tends to strengthen the most likely response.

**Explain social loafing, and identify one way it has been operationally defined.**

**Answer:** Social loafing is when people tend to exert less effort when working with a group than they would alone. It has been operationally defined as the amount of effort in rope-pulling.

**Page 493**

**Explain groupthink.**

**Answer:** Groupthink is the mode of thinking that occurs when the desire for harmony in a decision-making group overrides a realistic appraisal of alternatives.

**What is *culture*, and why do humans need it more than other social animals do?**

**Answer:** Culture refers to the enduring behaviors, ideas, attitudes, values, and traditions shared by a group of people and transmitted from one generation to the next. In humans, social living, imitation, division of labor, and language have ensured the preservation of innovation.

## Module 4.3c Psychology of Social Situations: Aggression

**Page 502**

**Explain the frustration-aggression principle.**

**Answer:** This is the principle that frustration—the blocking of an attempt to achieve some goal—creates anger, which can generate aggression.

**What biological, psychological, and social-cultural influences interact to produce aggressive behaviors?**

**Answer:** Our biology (our genes, neural systems, and biochemistry—including testosterone and alcohol levels) influences our aggressive tendencies. Psychological factors (such as frustration, previous rewards for aggressive acts, and observation of others' aggression) can trigger any aggressive tendencies we may have. Social-cultural influences (such as exposure to violent media or whether we've grown up in a "culture of honor") can also affect our aggressive responses.

## Module 4.3d Psychology of Social Situations: Attraction

**Page 509**

**Explain how proximity relates to attraction.**

**Answer:** Proximity (geographic nearness) increases liking, in part because of the mere exposure effect—exposure to novel stimuli increases liking of those stimuli.

**How does being physically attractive influence others' perceptions?**

**Answer:** Being physically attractive tends to elicit positive first impressions. People tend to assume that attractive people are healthier, happier, and more socially skilled than others are.

**Page 511**

**Explain the difference between passionate and companionate love.**

**Answer:** Passionate love is an aroused state of intense positive absorption in another person, which is usually present at the beginning of a romantic relationship. Companionate love is the deep affectionate attachment we feel for those with whom our lives are intertwined.

**Describe self-disclosure.**

**Answer:** Self-disclosure is the act of revealing intimate aspects of ourselves to others.

## Module 4.3e Psychology of Social Situations: Altruism, Conflict, and Peacemaking

**Page 516**

**Explain the social psychology principle the Kitty Genovese incident illustrates.**

**Answer:** The Kitty Genovese case demonstrated the bystander effect, as each witness assumed many others were also aware of the event. In the presence of others, an individual is less likely to notice a situation, correctly interpret it as an emergency, and take responsibility for offering help.

**Page 522**

**Explain the *self-fulfilling prophecy*.**

**Answer:** A self-fulfilling prophecy is when a belief leads to its own fulfillment.

**Describe four ways to reconcile conflicts and promote peace.**

**Answer:** Peacemakers should encourage (1) equal-status contact, (2) cooperation to achieve *superordinate goals* (shared goals that override differences), (3) understanding through communication, and (4) reciprocated conciliatory gestures (each side gives a little).

## Module 4.4 Introduction to Personality

**Page 526**

**Explain what is meant by *personality*.**

**Answer:** Personality refers to an individual's characteristic patterns of thinking, feeling, and acting.

**Differentiate among the five theoretical perspectives of personality.**

**Answer:** (1) Freud's psychoanalytic theory proposed that childhood sexuality and unconscious motivations influence personality. (2) The humanistic theories focused on our inner capacities for growth and self-fulfillment. (3) Trait theories examine characteristic patterns of behavior (traits). (4) Social-cognitive theories explore the interaction between people's traits (including their thinking) and their social context. (5) Modern psychodynamic theories of personality view human behavior as a dynamic interaction between the conscious mind and the unconscious mind, including associated motives and conflicts.

## Module 4.5a Psychoanalytic and Humanistic Theories of Personality: Psychoanalytic and Psychodynamic Theories

**Page 533**

**How does Freud define the unconscious?**

**Answer:** The unconscious, according to Freud, is a reservoir of mostly unacceptable thoughts, wishes, feelings, and memories. This view is in contrast to that held by contemporary psychologists, who define the unconscious as information processing of which we are unaware.

**Explain the purpose of defense mechanisms.**

**Answer:** Defense mechanisms in psychoanalytic theory are the ego's protective methods of reducing anxiety by unconsciously distorting reality.

## Page 538

### What do critics see as the most serious problem with Freud's theory?

**Answer:** Freud's theory has been criticized as not scientifically testable and offering after-the-fact explanations, focusing too much on sexual conflicts in childhood, and being based on the idea of repression, which has not been supported by modern research.

### Describe how modern-day research psychologists think of the unconscious.

**Answer:** Contemporary psychologists describe the unconscious as information processing of which we are unaware. This processing includes schemas that control our perceptions, priming, implicit memories of learned skills, instantly activated emotions, and the implicit prejudice and stereotypes that filter our information processing of others' traits and characteristics.

## Module 4.5b Psychoanalytic and Humanistic Theories of Personality: Humanistic Theories

### Page 546

### Explain how the humanistic theories provided a fresh perspective.

**Answer:** The humanistic theories sought to turn psychology's attention away from drives and conflicts and toward our growth potential. This movement's focus on the way people strive for self-determination and self-realization was in contrast to Freudian theory and strict behaviorism.

### Explain the difference between self-actualization and self-transcendence.

**Answer:** Maslow proposed that *self-actualization* is the motivation to fulfill one's potential, and one of the ultimate psychological needs. The other is self-transcendence, which is the striving for identity, meaning, and purpose beyond the self.

## Module 4.6a Social-Cognitive and Trait Theories of Personality: Trait Theories

### Page 556

### Explain what is meant by *trait*.

**Answer:** A trait is a characteristic pattern of behavior or a disposition to feel and act in certain ways, as assessed by self-report inventories and peer reports.

### Describe the Big Five personality factors. Why are they scientifically useful?

**Answer:** The Big Five personality factors are *o*penness (imaginative, prefers variety, independent), *c*onscientiousness (organized, careful, disciplined), *e*xtraversion (sociable, fun-loving, affectionate), *a*greeableness (soft-hearted, trusting, helpful), and *n*euroticism (emotional stability versus instability; anxious, insecure, self-pitying): OCEAN. These factors may be objectively measured, they are relatively stable over the lifespan, and they apply to all cultures in which they have been studied.

## Page 558

### Explain some ways that personality test scores predict our behavior.

**Answer:** Our scores on personality tests predict our *average* behavior across many situations much better than they predict our specific behavior in any given situation. For example, conscientiousness predicts better school performance and workplace success.

## Module 4.6b Social-Cognitive and Trait Theories of Personality: Social-Cognitive Theories

### Page 563

### Explain the social-cognitive perspective, including reciprocal determinism.

**Answer:** The social-cognitive perspective views behavior as being influenced by the interaction between people's traits and their social context. This includes reciprocal determinism, which is the interacting influences of behavior, internal cognition, and environment.

### Page 566

### Explain three specific ways in which individuals and environments interact.

**Answer:** (1) Different people choose different environments. (2) Our personality shapes how we interpret and react to events. (3) Our personality helps create situations to which we react.

## Module 4.6c Social-Cognitive and Trait Theories of Personality: Exploring the Self

### Page 573

### Explain two negative effects of high self-esteem.

**Answer:** Inflated self-esteem can lead to blindness to one's own incompetence and self-serving bias.

### Explain what is meant by *self-serving bias*.

**Answer:** Self-serving bias is a readiness to perceive ourselves favorably.

### Page 576

### Explain the difference between individualist and collectivist cultures.

**Answer:** Individualists give priority to personal goals over group goals and tend to define their identity in terms of their own personal attributes. Collectivists give priority to group goals over individual goals and tend to define their identity in terms of group identifications.

## Module 4.7a Motivation: Motivational Concepts

### Page 582

### Explain what is meant by *motivation*.

**Answer:** Motivation is defined as a need or desire that energizes and directs behavior.

### Explain the Yerkes-Dodson law.

**Answer:** The Yerkes-Dodson law states that performance increases with arousal only up to a point, beyond which performance decreases.

## Page 584

**Explain the differences among the big ideas of the classic motivation theories.**

**Answer:** (1) Instincts and evolutionary theory: There is a genetic basis for unlearned, species-typical behavior (such as birds building nests or infants rooting for a nipple). (2) Drive-reduction theory: Physiological needs (such as hunger and thirst) create an aroused state that drives us to reduce the need (for example, by eating or drinking). (3) Arousal theory: Our need to maintain an optimal level of arousal motivates behaviors that meet no physiological need (such as our yearning for stimulation and our hunger for information). (4) Maslow's hierarchy of needs: We prioritize survival-based needs and then social needs more than the needs for esteem and meaning.

## Module 4.7b Motivation: Affiliation and Achievement

### Page 590

**Describe our affiliation need.**

**Answer:** Affiliation need is the need to build and maintain relationships and to feel part of a group.

**Describe the three needs we are motivated to satisfy, according to self-determination theory.**

**Answer:** According to self-determination theory, we strive to satisfy three needs: competence, autonomy (a sense of personal control), and relatedness.

### Page 593

**Explain how social media use is associated with teen mental health.**

**Answer:** Results from studies vary, but overall, there is a small positive correlation between adolescents' social media time and their risk of depression, anxiety, and self-harm.

### Page 596

**Explain what is meant by *achievement motivation*.**

**Answer:** Achievement motivation is a desire for significant accomplishment, for mastery of skills or ideas, for control, and for attaining a high standard.

## Module 4.7c Motivation: Hunger Motivation

### Page 602

**Explain the body's set point and how it relates to hunger.**

**Answer:** The set point is the point at which the "weight thermostat" may be set. When the body falls below this weight, increased hunger and a lowered metabolic rate may combine to restore lost weight.

**Explain how ghrelin levels relate to hunger.**

**Answer:** Ghrelin is the hormone secreted by an empty stomach that sends "I'm hungry" signals to the brain.

### Page 604

**Explain some ways in which culture influences taste preferences.**

**Answer:** Culture affects what we like to eat. Conditioning can intensify or alter taste preferences.

## Page 606

**Why can two people of the same height, age, and activity level maintain the same weight, even if one of them eats much less than the other does?**

**Answer:** Genetically influenced set/settling points, metabolism, and other factors influence the way our bodies burn calories. Sleep deprivation, which makes us more vulnerable to weight gain, may also factor in.

## Module 4.8a Emotion: Theories and Physiology of Emotion

### Page 613

**Emotion researchers have disagreed about whether emotional responses occur in the absence of cognitive processing. How would you characterize the approach of each of the following researchers: Zajonc, LeDoux, and Lazarus?**

**Answer:** Zajonc and LeDoux suggested that we experience some emotions without any conscious, cognitive appraisal. Lazarus emphasized the importance of appraisal and cognitive labeling in our experience of emotion.

### Page 617

**What roles do the two divisions of the autonomic nervous system play in our emotional responses?**

**Answer:** The *sympathetic division* of the ANS arouses us for more intense experiences of emotion, pumping out the stress hormones epinephrine and norepinephrine to prepare our body for fight or flight. The *parasympathetic division* of the ANS takes over when a crisis passes, restoring our body to a calm physiological and emotional state.

## Module 4.8b Emotion: Expressing and Experiencing Emotion

### Page 627

**Describe some gender differences in nonverbal behavior.**

**Answer:** Women report experiencing emotions more deeply, and they tend to be more adept at reading nonverbal behavior than men are.

**Explain the difference between the facial feedback effect and the behavioral feedback effect.**

**Answer:** The facial feedback effect is the tendency of facial muscle states to trigger corresponding feelings such as fear, anger, or happiness. The behavior feedback effect is the tendency of behavior to influence our own and others' thoughts, feelings, and actions.

# Unit 5
## Mental and Physical Health

## Module 5.1a Introduction to Health Psychology: Stress and Illness

### Page 645

**The field of _____ studies mind-body interactions, including the effects of psychological, neural, and endocrine functioning on the immune system and overall health.**

**Answer:** psychoneuroimmunology

**Explain the stages in Selye's general adaptation syndrome (GAS).**

**Answer:** In Phase 1 (alarm), you have an alarm reaction, as your sympathetic nervous system is suddenly activated. With your resources mobilized, you are now ready to fight back. During Phase 2 (resistance), your temperature, blood pressure, and respiration remain high. Your endocrine system pumps epinephrine and norepinephrine into your bloodstream. As time passes, with no relief from stress, your body's reserves dwindle and you enter Phase 3 (exhaustion). With exhaustion, you become more vulnerable to illness.

### Page 647

**Explain three effects of stress on our immune system.**

**Answer:** (1) Surgical wounds heal more slowly in stressed people. (2) Stressed people are more vulnerable to colds. (3) Stress can hasten the course of disease.

### Page 651

**Which component of the Type A personality has been linked most closely to coronary heart disease?**

**Answer:** Feeling angry and negative much of the time

**Which one of the following is an effective strategy for reducing angry feelings?**

a. **Retaliate verbally or physically.**

b. **Wait or "simmer down."**

c. **Express anger in action or fantasy.**

d. **Review the grievance silently.**

**Answer:** b

## Module 5.1b  Introduction to Health Psychology: Coping With Stress

### Page 656

**Explain the difference between emotion-focused coping and problem-focused coping.**

**Answer:** Problem-focused coping is attempting to alleviate stress directly—by changing the stressor or the way we interact with that stressor. In contrast, emotion-focused coping is attempting to alleviate stress by avoiding or ignoring a stressor and attending to emotional needs related to our stress reaction.

### Page 660

**Explain some ways that social support enhances health.**

**Answer:** Social support calms us, improves our sleep, and reduces blood pressure.

## Module 5.2a  Positive Psychology: Positive Emotions and Positive Traits

### Page 669

**Does personal income predict happiness?**

**Answer:** Personal income predicts happiness, but only up to a satiation point. After that point, it does not.

**Explain the adaptation-level phenomenon.**

**Answer:** The adaptation-level phenomenon refers to our tendency to form judgments (of sounds, of lights, of income) relative to a neutral level defined by our prior experience.

### Page 670

**Explain the broaden-and-build theory.**

**Answer:** This theory proposes that positive emotions broaden our awareness and motivate us to build novel and meaningful skills and resilience that improve well-being.

## Module 5.2b  Positive Psychology: Enhancing Well-Being

### Page 682

**Explain the relationship between aerobic exercise and psychological health.**

**Answer:** Sustained exercise that increases heart and lung fitness helps alleviate depression and anxiety.

## Module 5.3  Explaining and Classifying Psychological Disorders

### Page 689

**Describe ways that psychological disorders are both universal and culture-specific.**

**Answer:** Some psychological disorders are culture-specific. For example, anorexia nervosa occurs mostly in Western cultures, and *taijin-kyofusho* appears largely in Japan. Other disorders, such as schizophrenia, are universal—they occur in all cultures.

**Explain the biopsychosocial approach. Why is it important in our understanding of psychological disorders?**

**Answer:** Biological, psychological, and social-cultural influences combine to produce psychological disorders. This approach helps us understand that our well-being is affected by our genes, brain functioning, and inner thoughts and feelings, as well as the influences of our social and cultural environments.

**Explain the value and the dangers of labeling individuals with disorders.**

**Answer:** Therapists and others apply disorder labels to communicate with one another using a common language, and to share concepts during research. Clients may benefit from knowing that they are not the only ones with these symptoms. The dangers of labeling people are that (1) people may begin to act as they have been labeled and (2) the labels can trigger assumptions that will change people's behavior toward those labeled.

### Page 696

**Explain the relationship between poverty and psychological disorders.**

**Answer:** Poverty-related stresses can help trigger disorders, but disabling disorders can also contribute to poverty. Thus, poverty and disorder are often a chicken-and-egg situation; it's hard to know which came first.

## Module 5.4a  Selection of Categories of Psychological Disorders: Anxiety Disorders, Obsessive-Compulsive and Related Disorders, and Trauma- and Stressor-Related Disorders

### Page 701

**Describe the symptoms of generalized anxiety disorder.**

**Answer:** Generalized anxiety disorder is an anxiety disorder in which a person is continually tense, apprehensive, and in a state of autonomic nervous system arousal.

### Describe the difference between generalized anxiety disorder and a specific phobia.

**Answer:** Generalized anxiety disorder is marked by excessive and uncontrollable worry, in which a person is continually tense. A specific phobia is an anxiety disorder marked by a persistent, irrational fear and avoidance of a *specific* object, activity, or situation.

### Page 705

### Describe the symptoms of posttraumatic stress disorder.

**Answer:** Posttraumatic stress disorder (PTSD) is a disorder characterized by haunting memories, nightmares, hypervigilance, avoidance of trauma-related stimuli, social withdrawal, jumpy anxiety, numbness of feeling, and/or insomnia after a traumatic experience.

### Page 708

### Researchers believe that conditioning and cognitive processes are aspects of learning that contribute to anxiety disorders. Explain some *biological* factors that also contribute to these disorders.

**Answer:** Biological factors include inherited temperament differences and other gene variations; experience-altered brain pathways; and inherited responses that had survival value for our distant ancestors.

## Module 5.4b Selection of Categories of Psychological Disorders: Depressive Disorders and Bipolar Disorders

### Page 720

### Describe the relationship between explanatory style and depression.

**Answer:** A negative explanatory style (blaming yourself, thinking the worst, etc.) feeds depression.

### Describe the vicious cycle of depressed thinking.

**Answer:** (1) Stressful experiences interpreted through (2) a brooding, negative explanatory style create (3) a hopeless, depressed state that (4) hampers the way the person thinks and acts. These thoughts and actions, in turn, fuel (1) further stressful experiences such as rejection.

## Module 5.4c Selection of Categories of Psychological Disorders: Schizophrenia Spectrum Disorders

### Page 727

### Describe the positive and negative symptoms of schizophrenia.

**Answer:** People with schizophrenia may display symptoms that are positive (inappropriate behaviors are present) or negative (appropriate behaviors are absent). Those with positive symptoms may experience disturbed perceptions, talk in disorganized and deluded ways, or exhibit inappropriate laughter, tears, or rage. Those with negative symptoms may exhibit an absence of emotion in their voices, expressionless faces, or mute and rigid bodies.

### Describe the factors that contribute to the onset and development of schizophrenia.

**Answer:** Biological factors include abnormalities in brain structure and function and a genetic predisposition to the disorder. Environmental factors such as nutritional deprivation, exposure to viruses, and maternal stress contribute by activating the genes that increase risk. Exposure to many environmental triggers can increase the odds of developing schizophrenia.

## Module 5.4d Selection of Categories of Psychological Disorders: Dissociative Disorders, Personality Disorders, Feeding and Eating Disorders, and Neurodevelopmental Disorders

### Page 732

### Explain the difference between the psychodynamic and learning perspectives on dissociative identity disorder symptoms as a way of dealing with anxiety.

**Answer:** The psychodynamic explanation of DID symptoms is that they are defenses against anxiety generated by unacceptable urges. The learning perspective attempts to explain these symptoms as behaviors that have been reinforced by relieving anxiety.

### Page 735

### Describe the differences among the behavioral patterns in Cluster A, Cluster B, and Cluster C personality disorders.

**Answer:** In Cluster A, people appear eccentric or odd, as in the suspiciousness of paranoid personality disorder; the social detachment of schizoid personality disorder; or the magical thinking of schizotypal personality disorder. In Cluster B, people appear dramatic, emotional, or erratic, as in the unstable, attention-getting borderline personality disorder; the self-focused and self-inflating narcissistic personality disorder; the excessively emotional histrionic personality disorder; and the callous, and often dangerous, antisocial personality disorder. In Cluster C, people appear anxious or fearful, as in the fearful sensitivity to rejection that predisposes individuals to the withdrawn avoidant personality disorder; the clinging behavior of dependent personality disorder; and the preoccupation with orderliness, perfectionism, and control that characterizes obsessive-compulsive personality disorder.

### Explain how biological and psychological factors contribute to antisocial personality disorder.

**Answer:** Twin and adoption studies show that biological relatives of people with this disorder are at increased risk for antisocial behavior. Researchers have also observed differences in brain activity and structure in antisocial criminals. Negative environmental factors, such as poverty or childhood abuse, may channel genetic traits such as fearlessness in more dangerous directions—toward aggression and away from social responsibility.

### Page 737

### Describe anorexia nervosa, bulimia nervosa, and binge-eating disorders.

**Answer:** Anorexia nervosa is an eating disorder in which a person maintains a starvation diet despite being significantly underweight, and has an inaccurate self-perception. It is sometimes accompanied by excessive exercise. Bulimia nervosa is an eating disorder in which a person's binge eating (usually of high-calorie foods) is followed by inappropriate weight-loss–promoting behavior, such as vomiting, laxative use, fasting, or excessive exercise. Binge-eating disorder is marked by significant binge-eating episodes, followed by distress, disgust, or guilt, but without the compensatory behavior that marks bulimia nervosa.

## Page 742

### Describe the symptoms of ASD.

**Answer:** Autism spectrum disorder is marked by limitations in communication and social interaction, and by rigidly fixated interests and repetitive behaviors.

## Module 5.5a Treatment of Psychological Disorders: Introduction to Therapy, and Psychodynamic and Humanistic Therapies

### Page 750

### Why do relatively few North American therapists now offer traditional psychoanalysis?

**Answer:** Much of its underlying theory is not supported by scientific research, in that analysts' interpretations cannot be proven or disproven. In addition, psychoanalysis takes considerable time and money, often involving years of several expensive sessions per week.

### Describe the eclectic approach to therapy.

**Answer:** This approach to psychotherapy uses techniques from multiple forms of therapy.

### Describe the difference between psychodynamic therapy and person-centered therapy.

**Answer:** Psychodynamic therapy derives from the psychoanalytic tradition and views individuals as responding to unconscious forces and childhood experiences. Person-centered therapy derives from the humanistic perspective. The therapist uses techniques such as active listening within an accepting, genuine, empathic environment to facilitate clients' growth.

## Module 5.5b Treatment of Psychological Disorders: Behavioral, Cognitive, and Group Therapies

### Page 757

### Describe the difference between behavior therapies and insight therapies.

**Answer:** The insight therapies assume that self-awareness leads to well-being. Behavior therapists, influenced by the behavioral perspective, assume that problem behaviors are the problem. They offer clients strategies for reducing unwanted behaviors.

### Exposure therapies and aversive conditioning are applications of _____ conditioning. Token economies are an application of _____ conditioning.

**Answer:** classical; operant

### Page 764

### Describe how person-centered and cognitive therapies differ.

**Answer:** Person-centered therapies focus on barriers to self-understanding and self-acceptance. They view growth as coming from unconditional positive regard, acceptance, genuineness, and empathy. Therapists listen actively and reflect clients' feelings. Cognitive therapies focus on negative, self-defeating thinking, and try to promote healthier thinking and self-talk by training people to dispute their negative thoughts and attributions.

### Describe *cognitive-behavioral therapy*. What sorts of problems does this therapy best address?

**Answer:** Cognitive-behavioral therapy (CBT) combines cognitive therapy (changing self-defeating thinking) with behavior therapy (changing behavior). CBT effectively treats disorders that are marked by unhealthy emotion regulation, such as depression.

### Describe some benefits of group therapy.

**Answer:** Group therapy saves therapists' time and clients' money. It offers a space for exploring social behaviors and developing social skills. It enables people to see that others share their problems. It provides feedback as clients try out new ways of behaving.

## Module 5.5c Treatment of Psychological Disorders: Evaluating Psychotherapies

### Page 772

### Describe how the *placebo effect* can bias clients' and clinicians' appraisals of the effectiveness of psychotherapies.

**Answer:** The *placebo effect* is the healing power of *belief* in a treatment. Patients and therapists who expect a treatment to be effective may believe it was.

### What is *evidence-based practice*?

**Answer:** Using this approach, therapists make decisions about treatment based on research evidence, clinical expertise, and knowledge of the client.

### Describe the three elements that are shared by all forms of psychotherapy.

**Answer:** All psychotherapies offer (1) new hope for discouraged people, (2) a fresh perspective, and (3) an empathic, trusting, and caring relationship.

### Page 775

### Describe the ethical principles for therapists set forth by the American Psychological Association.

**Answer:** *Beneficence and nonmaleficence*: Seek to benefit you (beneficence) and do you no harm (nonmaleficence). *Fidelity and responsibility*: Establish a feeling of trust and a defined role as your therapist, uphold a professional standard of conduct, and be of service to the therapeutic community. *Integrity*: Be honest, truthful, and accurate. *Justice*: Be fair and promote justice for you and others, helping everyone to have access to the benefits of therapy. *Respect for people's rights and dignity*: Respect the dignity and worth of you and others, recognizing the right to privacy, confidentiality, and self-determination.

## Module 5.5d Treatment of Psychological Disorders: The Biomedical Therapies and Preventing Psychological Disorders

### Page 781

### Explain what is meant by this statement: "Some clinicians attack depression from both below and above."

**Answer:** Some clinicians use antidepressant drugs to work, bottom-up, on the emotion-related limbic system. In addition, they use cognitive-behavioral therapy to work, top-down, on frontal lobe activity and thinking.

### Describe the difference between antipsychotic drugs and antidepressant drugs in terms of how they work.

**Answer:** The molecules of most conventional antipsychotic drugs are similar enough to molecules of the neurotransmitter dopamine to occupy its receptor sites and block its activity. Many antidepressant drugs used to treat depressive disorders work by increasing the availability of neurotransmitters, such as norepinephrine or serotonin, which elevate arousal and mood and are scarce when a person experiences feelings of depression or anxiety.

### Page 784

### Describe the neurostimulation therapies in terms of how they are administered.

**Answer:** Electroconvulsive therapy (ECT) manipulates the brain by shocking it with a brief electric current that is sent through the brain of an anesthetized person. In contrast to ECT, transcranial direct current stimulation (tDCS) administers a weak electrical current to the scalp. Transcranial magnetic stimulation (TMS) is the application of repeated pulses of magnetic energy to the brain in an effort to stimulate or suppress brain activity in areas of the cortex. Finally, in deep brain stimulation (DBS), electrodes are implanted in a brain area.

### Page 786

### Describe some examples of lifestyle changes people can make to enhance their mental health.

**Answer:** Many lifestyle factors—including exercise, nutrition, relationships, recreation, relaxation, religious or spiritual engagement, and service to others—affect our mental health.

### Describe two theories explaining how hypnosis works.

**Answer:** Social influence theory contends that hypnosis is a by-product of normal social and mental processes. Dissociation theory proposes that hypnosis is a special dual-processing state of dissociation—a split between different levels of consciousness.

### Page 789

### What is the difference between preventive mental health and the biomedical therapies?

**Answer:** Biomedical therapies treat disorders. Instead of treating them, preventive mental health seeks to avoid disorders by identifying and alleviating the conditions that cause them.

### Describe posttraumatic growth.

**Answer:** Posttraumatic growth refers to positive psychological changes following a struggle with extremely challenging circumstances and life crises.

## Enrichment Modules

## Module EM.1 Influences on Drug Use

### Page 803

### Explain why tobacco companies try so hard to get customers hooked as teens.

**Answer:** Nicotine is powerfully addictive, and individuals who start paving the neural pathways it affects when young may find it very hard to stop using it. As a result, tobacco companies may have life-long customers. Moreover, evidence suggests that if cigarette manufacturers haven't hooked customers by early adulthood, they most likely won't.

### Studies have found that people who begin drinking in their early teens are much more likely to develop alcohol use disorder than those who begin at age 21 or after. What possible explanations might there be for this finding?

**Answer:** Possible explanations include (1) biological factors (a person could have a biological predisposition to both early use and later abuse, or alcohol use could modify a person's neural pathways); (2) psychological factors (early use could establish taste preferences for alcohol); and (3) social-cultural factors (early use could influence enduring habits, attitudes, activities, or peer relationships that could foster alcohol use disorder).

## Module EM.2 Psychology at Work

### Page 812

### What is the value of finding flow in our work?

**Answer:** We become more likely to view our work as fulfilling and socially useful, and we experience higher self-esteem, competence, and overall well-being.

### A human resources director explains to you that "I don't bother with tests or references. It's all about the interview." Based on I/O psychology research, what concerns does this raise?

**Answer:** (1) Interviewers may presume people are what they seem to be in interviews. (2) Interviewers' preconceptions and moods color how they perceive interviewees' responses. (3) Interviewers judge people relative to other recent interviewees. (4) Interviewers tend to track the successful careers of the people they hire, not the successful careers of the people they reject. (5) Interviews tend to disclose prospective workers' good intentions, not their habitual behaviors.

### Page 817

### Describe the two basic types of leadership. How do the most effective managers employ these leadership strategies?

**Answer:** Task leadership is goal-oriented. Managers using this style set standards, organize work, and focus attention on goals. Social leadership is group-oriented. Managers using this style build teamwork, mediate conflict, and offer support. Research indicates that effective managers exhibit both task and social leadership, depending on the situation and the person.

### What characteristics are important for transformational leaders?

**Answer:** Transformational leaders are able to inspire others to share a vision and commit themselves to a group's mission. They tend to be naturally extraverted and set high standards.

**Page 819**

**Explain what is meant by the *curse of knowledge*. What does it have to do with the work of human factors psychologists?**

**Answer:** To develop safer machines and work environments, human factors psychologists stay mindful of the curse of knowledge—the tendency for experts to mistakenly assume that others share their knowledge.

## Module EM.3 Animal Thinking and Language

**Page 824**

**If your dog barks at a stranger at the door, does this qualify as language? What if the dog yips in a telltale way to let you know she needs to go out?**

**Answer:** These are definitely communications. But if language consists of words and the grammatical rules we use to combine them to communicate meaning, few scientists would label a dog's barking and yipping as language.

## Unit 1 Biological Bases of Behavior

### EVIDENCE-BASED QUESTION

**INSTRUCTIONS:** Answer the following question using the 3 sources provided. Your response to the question should be provided in three distinct parts: A, B, and C. Use appropriate psychological terminology in your response.

For both Part B and Part C, each piece of evidence must be cited using the "Source [Number]" designation in parentheses following the cited material or embedded in the sentence. For example,

- Parenthetical citation: (Source 1).
- Embedded citation: According to Source 1, . . .

1. Using the provided sources, develop and justify an argument about the extent to which sleep promotes memory consolidation.

   **(A)** Propose a specific and defensible claim based in psychological science that responds to the question.

   **(B.i)** Support your claim using at least one piece of specific and relevant evidence from one of the sources provided.

   **(B.ii)** Use a psychological perspective, theory, concept, or research finding learned in AP® Psychology to explain how your evidence supports your claim.

   **(C.i)** Using a different source than the one you used in Part (B.i), support your claim using at least one piece of specific and relevant evidence.

   **(C.ii)** Use a psychological perspective, theory, concept, or research finding learned in AP® Psychology—different than the one you used in part (B.ii)—to explain how your evidence in Part (C.i) supports your claim.

## Source 1:

| Introduction |
|---|
| Sleep improves memory consolidation, but little research has been conducted on the role of sleep in helping children learn different types of words. Much of the past research has focused on how sleep improves the learning of nouns, but few studies have investigated how sleep improves children's learning of verbs, which tend to be more complex. |
| **Participants** |
| The participants consisted of 42 two-year-olds. All children were developing typically and only spoke English. |
| **Method** |
| Two-year-olds were presented with new verbs, and researchers tested their knowledge of the words immediately after presentation. Then, some children were randomly assigned to stay awake for 4 hours, while other children were randomly assigned to take a 4-hour nap. After this 4-hour period, the children's memory of the verbs was retested. |
| **Results and Discussion** |
| The children who had napped demonstrated greater retention of the verbs than the children who stayed awake. This study allowed research to conclude that sleep directly affects children's language development. |

Information from: He, A. X., Huang, S., Waxman, S., & Arunachalam, S. (2020). Two-year-olds consolidate verb meanings during a nap. *Cognition, 198.* https://doi.org/10.1016/j.cognition.2020.104205

## Source 2:

| Introduction |
|---|
| Because learning complex, coordinated motor skills such as juggling 3 balls involves explicit memory, researchers wondered whether learning such a motor skill would be improved with sleep. |

| Participants |
|---|
| Sixteen female college students participated in the study. |

| Method |
|---|
| Researchers had participants practice juggling in the morning and tested their skill by measuring how many balls they caught. The researchers then randomly assigned 8 of the participants to take a 2-hour nap after practice (the nap group), while the other 8 stayed awake (the control group). They retested juggling skill after that 2-hour period. |

| Results and Discussion |
|---|
| The results are presented in the graph that follows. |

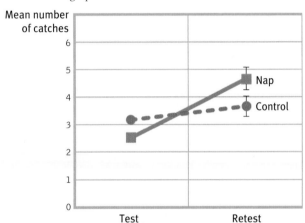

Data from: Morita, Y., Ogawa, K., & Uchida, S. (2012). The effect of a daytime 2-hour nap on complex motor skill learning. *Sleep and Biological Rhythms, 10*(4), 302–309. https://doi.org/10.1111/j.1479-8425.2012.00576.x

## Source 3:

| Literature Review |
|---|
| The authors reviewed the decades of scientific evidence related to rapid-eye-movement (REM) sleep. REM sleep is associated with dreaming and with "wake-like" brain activity. People tend to experience more REM sleep after they have engaged in procedural memory tasks and declarative memory tasks that involve complex or emotional information. When people go without REM sleep, they tend to have difficulty with recall. There may be some connection with REM sleep and memory problems associated with aging and Alzheimer's disease. |

Information from: Boyce, R., & Adamantidis, A. (2017). REM sleep on it! *Neuropsychopharmacology, 42*(1), 375–376. https://doi.org/10.1038/npp.2016.2

# ARTICLE ANALYSIS QUESTION

**INSTRUCTIONS**: Answer the following question using the source provided. Your response to the question should be provided in six distinct parts: A, B, C, D, E, and F. Use appropriate psychological terminology in your response.

2. Using the source provided, respond to the following questions:

   **(A)** Identify the research method used in the study.

   **(B)** State one way the dependent variable was operationally defined.

   **(C)** Describe the meaning of statistical significance in the context of this study.

   **(D)** Identify at least one ethical guideline applied by the researchers.

   **(E)** Explain the extent to which the research findings may or may not be generalizable using specific and relevant evidence from the study.

   **(F)** Explain how at least one of the research findings supports or refutes the claim that LY2216684 is effective in treating MDD.

## Source:

| Introduction |
| --- |
| A new norepinephrine reuptake inhibitor LY2216684 is being developed to treat major depressive disorder (MDD). LY2216684's efficacy and safety will be compared to a placebo in patients with MDD. Escitalopram, a selective serotonin reuptake inhibitor (SSRI), was used as a comparison. |

| Participants |
| --- |
| Four hundred and sixty-nine adults who resided in India, Mexico, Romania, and the United States and who were outpatients diagnosed with MDD as defined by the *Diagnostic and Statistical Manual of Mental Disorders-Fourth Edition-Text Revision* (DSM-IV-TR) participated in this study. |

| Method |
| --- |
| Institutional review boards approved the study, and participants consented to the study in writing. Participants were randomly assigned to receive LY2216684, escitalopram, or a placebo pill for eight weeks, and patients and research staff were unaware of which treatment participants were assigned to. Participants completed the clinician-administered Hamilton Depression Rating Scale and the Self-Rated Quick Inventory of Depressive Symptomatology to measure the extent to which these substances impact the experience of MDD. |

| Results and Discussion |
| --- |
| The group who took LY2216684 did not show statistically significant reduction in depressive symptoms compared to the placebo group when measured by the Hamilton Depression Rating Scale. However, both the group who took LY2216684 and the group who took escitalopram showed statistically significant reduction in depressive symptoms as measured by the Self-Rated Quick Inventory of Depressive Symptomatology. |

Information from: Dubé, S., Dellva, M. A., Jones, M., Kielbasa, W., Padich, R., Saha, A., & Rao, P. (2010). A study of the effects of LY2216684, a selective norepinephrine reuptake inhibitor, in the treatment of major depression. *Journal of Psychiatric Research, 44*(6), 356–263. https://www.doi.org/10.1016/j.jpsychires.2009.09.013

# Unit 2 Cognition

## EVIDENCE-BASED QUESTION

**INSTRUCTIONS:** Answer the following question using the 3 sources provided. Your response to the question should be provided in three distinct parts: A, B, and C. Use appropriate psychological terminology in your response.

For both Part B and Part C, each piece of evidence must be cited using the "Source [Number]" designation in parentheses following the cited material or embedded in the sentence. For example,

- Parenthetical citation: (Source 1).
- Embedded citation: According to Source 1, . . .

1. Using the provided sources, develop and justify an argument about the effectiveness of eyewitness testimony in legal cases.

   **(A)** Propose a specific and defensible claim based in psychological science that responds to the question.

   **(B.i)** Support your claim using at least one piece of specific and relevant evidence from one of the sources provided.

   **(B.ii)** Use a psychological perspective, theory, concept, or research finding learned in AP® Psychology to explain how your evidence supports your claim.

   **(C.i)** Using a different source than the one you used in Part (B.i), support your claim using at least one piece of specific and relevant evidence.

   **(C.ii)** Use a psychological perspective, theory, concept, or research finding learned in AP® Psychology—different than the one you used in part (B.ii)—to explain how your evidence in Part (C.i) supports your claim.

## Source 1:

| Introduction |
| --- |
| The researchers studied the influence of eyewitness testimony on jurors. Specifically, they were interested in how learning about the unreliability of eyewitness accounts affected juror deliberations and verdicts. |
| **Participants** |
| Two hundred forty university students who were registered to vote participated in the study. |
| **Method** |
| Participants served as hypothetical jurors in groups of six for a fabricated case involving a violent crime. The major piece of evidence against the defendant in this hypothetical case was eyewitness testimony. Prior to deliberating, half of the groups read about the unreliability of eyewitness testimony, while the other half did not. |
| **Results and Discussion** |
| Those who read about the unreliability of eyewitness testimony spent significantly more time discussing the eyewitness testimony itself while deliberating and handed down fewer convictions than did groups who had not read the information. |

Information from: Loftus, E. F. (1980). Impact of expert psychological testimony on the unreliability of eyewitness identification. *Journal of Applied Psychology, 65*(1), 9–15. https://doi.org/10.1037/0021-9010.65.1.9

| Introduction |
|---|
| Of the initial 200+ cases in which individuals were erroneously convicted in the United States, a notable 77% were based on inaccuracies in eyewitness identifications. However, forensic evidence, such as DNA, is not foolproof either. Therefore, researchers explored the impact of different forms of evidence on decision-making of jurors. |
| **Participants** |
| Four hundred and eighty participants were randomly selected from jury-eligible adults in the state of Delaware. |
| **Method** |
| Participants were exposed to a video of a mock trial about an armed robbery. The mock trial video included opening statements from attorneys, eyewitness testimony, expert testimony on DNA evidence, and closing arguments. After watching the video, participants formed mock juries and were told to render a verdict. Participants also completed questionnaires measuring how both eyewitness and forensic evidence related to their verdicts. |
| **Results and Discussion** |
| While the results showed the importance of forensic evidence, the researchers found that eyewitness testimony played a substantial role in jurors' decisions. The jurors' perceptions of the credibility of the eyewitness during the trial played a stronger role in their verdicts than other types of evidence. The relationship between the perception of eyewitness credibility and a guilty verdict was statistically significant ($p < .001$). |

Information from: O'Neill Shermer, L., Rose, K. C., & Hoffman, A. (2011). Perceptions and credibility: Understanding the nuances of eyewitness testimony. *Journal of Contemporary Criminal Justice, 27*(2), 183–203.

## Source 3:

| Literature Review |
|---|
| The authors reviewed the existing scientific evidence related to eyewitness memory. Eyewitness memory is widely believed to be unreliable because eyewitness misidentifications play a role in the majority of DNA exonerations of wrongfully convicted people. In addition, researchers know that memory can be unreliable, even when individuals feel highly confident in their memories. As a result, many researchers argue that eyewitness testimony should be disregarded, or at least used with caution in criminal trials. But what about eyewitnesses' testimony closer to the time of the crime where there is less time for memory distortions, such as identifying someone in a lineup? Does confidence equate to accuracy at that time? Scientifically derived evidence suggests that, in line with what researchers know about recognition memory, feeling highly confident in one's memory *at that time* is related to accuracy. |

Information from: Wixted, J. T., Mickes, L., Clark, S. E., Gronlund, S. D., & Roediger, H. L. III. (2015). Initial eyewitness confidence reliably predicts eyewitness identification accuracy. *American Psychologist, 70*(6), 515–526. https://doi.org/10.1037/a0039510

## ARTICLE ANALYSIS QUESTION

**INSTRUCTIONS**: Answer the following question using the source provided. Your response to the question should be provided in six distinct parts: A, B, C, D, E, and F. Use appropriate psychological terminology in your response.

2. Using the source provided, respond to the following questions:

    **(A)** Identify the research method used in the study.

    **(B)** Identify the operational definition of the independent variable.

**(C)** Describe the meaning of the differences in the means between the draw and write groups.

**(D)** Describe one ethical guideline the researchers would have been required to follow in this study.

**(E)** Explain the extent to which the research findings may or may not be generalizable using specific and relevant evidence from the study.

**(F)** Explain how at least one of the research findings supports or refutes the authors' claim that drawing a word causes better recall of that word.

## Source:

| Introduction |
|---|
| Past research has shown that when encoding information we process it at different levels, and that depth of processing affects our long-term retention. The present study was designed to investigate the effect of drawing versus writing on free recall memory performance. Because drawing the object a word represents takes deeper, more effortful processing than simply writing a word, the researchers speculated that those who draw words will have better recall than those who write words. |

| Participants |
|---|
| Forty-seven undergraduate college students participated in this study. |

| Method |
|---|
| Participants were randomly assigned to one of two conditions: drawing or writing. Each participant, individually in a testing room, was presented with a list of words and was asked to either draw the word or write the word on a screen. After a brief distractor task, participants were then asked to freely recall as many words as possible from the original list. |

| Results and Discussion |
|---|
| The researchers collected data on the number of words correctly recalled for each condition and analyzed the results using both descriptive statistics and inferential statistics. The results, presented in the following graph, were statistically significant. Those in the draw condition recalled significantly more words than those in the write condition. |

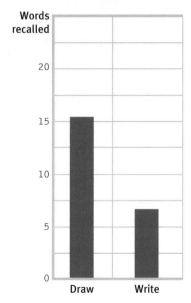

Information from: Wammes, J. D., Meade, M. E., & Fernandes, M. A. (2016). The drawing effect: Evidence for reliable and robust memory benefits in free recall. *The Quarterly Journal of Experimental Psychology, 69*(9), 1752–1776.

# Unit 3 Development and Learning

## EVIDENCE-BASED QUESTION

**INSTRUCTIONS:** Answer the following question using the 3 sources provided. Your response to the question should be provided in three distinct parts: A, B, and C. Use appropriate psychological terminology in your response.

For both Part B and Part C, each piece of evidence must be cited using the "Source [Number]" designation in parentheses following the cited material or embedded in the sentence. For example,

- Parenthetical citation: (Source 1).
- Embedded citation: According to Source 1, . . .

1. Using the provided sources, develop and justify an argument about the impact of teratogens on the development of children.

   **(A)** Propose a specific and defensible claim based in psychological science that responds to the question.

   **(B.i)** Support your claim using at least one piece of specific and relevant evidence from one of the sources provided.

   **(B.ii)** Use a psychological perspective, theory, concept, or research finding learned in AP® Psychology to explain how your evidence supports your claim.

   **(C.i)** Using a different source than the one you used in Part (B.1), support your claim using at least one piece of specific and relevant evidence.

   **(C.ii)** Use a psychological perspective, theory, concept, or research finding learned in AP® Psychology—different than the one you used in part (B.ii)—to explain how your evidence in Part (C.i) supports your claim.

## Source 1:

| Introduction |
|---|
| Researchers are concerned about the effects of teratogens such as alcohol, caffeine, and tobacco on the development of children. This study specifically focused on the effects of teratogens on motor development. |
| **Participants** |
| Participants were 449 4-year-old children. Mothers were predominantly married and middle class. |
| **Method** |
| After being exposed prenatally to alcohol, caffeine, and tobacco, children completed motor movement tasks using the Wisconsin Fine Motor Steadiness Battery and the Gross Motor Scale. |
| **Results and Discussion** |
| The link between prenatal maternal alcohol consumption and motor delays was linear with alcohol exposure being positively correlated with motor difficulties. Additionally, maternal alcohol consumption was negatively correlated with IQ scores. |

Information from: Barr, H. M., Streissguth, A. P., Darby, B. L., & Sampson, P. D. (1990). Prenatal exposure to alcohol, caffeine, tobacco, and aspirin: Effect on fine and gross motor performance in 4-year-old children. *Developmental Psychology, 26*(3), 339–348. https://psycnet.apa.org/doi/10.1037/0012-1649.26.3.339

## Source 2:

| Introduction |
|---|
| There is considerable concern about the impact of substance use during pregnancy. The present study examined how prenatal exposure to marijuana relates to children's long-term developmental outcomes. |

| Participants |
|---|
| The participants consisted of 829 pregnant women; most were single, while half were white and half were African-American. |

| Method |
|---|
| The researchers tracked participants over time by conducting interviews with women at the fourth and seventh months of pregnancy. Both mothers and children were assessed at delivery, as well as at 8, 18, and 36 months after birth. At each stage of the study, mothers were asked about their lifestyle, living situation, and current substance use, while children were assessed on their physical and cognitive development. |

| Results and Discussion |
|---|
| The findings showed a statistically significant negative relationship between prenatal marijuana exposure and the cognitive performance of 3-year-old children ($p < .05$). These effects were particularly linked to exposure during the first and second trimesters of pregnancy. |

Information from: Day, N. L., Richardson, G. A., Goldschmidt, L., Robles, N., Taylor, P. M., Stoffer, D. S., Cornelius, M. D., & Geva, D. (1994). Effect of prenatal marijuana exposure on the cognitive development of off-spring at age three. *Neurotoxicology and teratology, 16*(2), 169–175. https://doi.org/10.1016/0892-0362(94)90114-7

## Source 3:

| Literature Review |
|---|
| The authors reviewed the past research on prenatal exposure to phenytoin, an anticonvulsant medication. Phenytoin is considered a teratogen in animal samples, and it is associated with behavioral changes among human samples who have experienced prenatal exposure to the substance, including sensory issues, increased hyperactivity, and problems with learning and memory. Future researchers should more systematically examine behavioral changes after phenytoin exposure in animals and humans to draw additional conclusions about the neurotoxicity effects of this substance. |

Information from: Adams, J., Vorhees, C. V., & Middaugh, L. D. (1990). Developmental neurotoxicity of anticonvulsants: Human and animal evidence on phenytoin. *Neurotoxicity and Teratology, 12*(3), 203–214. https://doi.org/10.1016/0892-0362(90)90092-Q

## ARTICLE ANALYSIS QUESTION

**INSTRUCTIONS**: Answer the following question using the source provided. Your response to the question should be provided in six distinct parts: A, B, C, D, E, and F. Use appropriate psychological terminology in your response.

2. Using the source provided, respond to the following questions:

   **(A)** Identify the research method used in the study.

   **(B)** Identify the operational definition of one variable in the study.

   **(C)** Describe the meaning of the correlation coefficient in this study.

   **(D)** Identify at least one ethical guideline applied by the researchers.

   **(E)** Explain the extent to which the research findings may or may not be generalizable using specific and relevant evidence from the study.

   **(F)** Explain how at least one of the research findings supports or refutes the idea that adolescents' endorsement of the personal fable is related to risk-taking behaviors.

## Source:

| Introduction |
|---|
| Two related characteristics define adolescent egocentrism: the imaginary audience and the personal fable. The current researchers investigated the extent to which adolescents' endorsement of the personal fable related to risk-taking behaviors, predicting a positive correlation between these two variables. |
| **Participants** |
| A sample of 119 students from a middle school was recruited to participate in the study. |
| **Method** |
| The students delivered informational packets to their parents for consideration, and the students who obtained parental permission were allowed to participate in the study. The participants then completed the 12-item Personal Fable Scale. The participants rated their answers on a 5-point Likert scale based on the extent to which they believed each of the personal fable items related to them. They also completed the 10-item Risk-Taking Scale, where they indicated the way that they would respond to hypothetical risky situations. The Risk-Taking Scale's item scoring ranged from 1 (would refrain from risk) to 3 (would take risk). |
| **Results and Discussion** |
| The correlation coefficient between personal fable endorsement and risk-taking was .365, and the significance level was $p < .01$. |

Information from: Alberts, A., Elkind, D., & Ginsberg, S. (2007). The personal fable and risk-taking in early adolescence. *Journal of Youth and Adolescence, 36*(1), 71–76. https://www.doi.org/10.1007/s10964-006-9144-4

# Unit 4 Social Psychology and Personality

## EVIDENCE-BASED QUESTION

**INSTRUCTIONS:** Answer the following question using the 3 sources provided. Your response to the question should be provided in three distinct parts: A, B, and C. Use appropriate psychological terminology in your response.

For both Part B and Part C, each piece of evidence must be cited using the "Source [Number]" designation in parentheses following the cited material or embedded in the sentence. For example,

- Parenthetical citation: (Source 1).
- Embedded citation: According to Source 1, . . .

1. Using the provided sources, develop and justify an argument about the impact of social media on teens' well-being.

   **(A)** Propose a specific and defensible claim based in psychological science that responds to the question.

   **(B.i)** Support your claim using at least one piece of specific and relevant evidence from one of the sources provided.

   **(B.ii)** Use a psychological perspective, theory, concept, or research finding learned in AP® Psychology to explain how your evidence supports your claim.

   **(C.i)** Using a different source than the one you used in Part (B.i), support your claim using at least one piece of specific and relevant evidence.

   **(C.ii)** Use a psychological perspective, theory, concept, or research finding learned in AP® Psychology—different than the one you used in part (B.ii)—to explain how your evidence in Part (C.i) supports your claim.

## Source 1:

| Introduction |
|---|
| The relationship between social media use and well-being in youth is a concern for parents, educators, and researchers alike. This study examined the relationships between social media use and well-being in young girls. |
| **Participants** |
| Recruited through *Discovery Girls* magazine, 3,461 North American girls ages 8 to 12 participated in the study. |
| **Method** |
| Participants completed an online survey study that measured media use (including video games, posting on social media sites, and texting) as well as face-to-face communication. |
| **Results and Discission** |
| Statistical analyses indicated that social well-being was negatively related to social media use, especially when use centered on interpersonal interaction. Media multitasking was also negatively associated with social well-being. However, face-to-face communication was positively associated with social well-being. Cell phone ownership in general was not associated with children's socioemotional well-being. |

Information from: Pea, R., Nass, C., Meheula, L., Rance, M., Kumar, A., Bamford, H., Nass, M., Simha, A., Stillerman, B., Yang, S., & Zhou, M. (2012). Media use, face-to-face communication, media multitasking, and social well-being among 8- to 12-year-old girls. *Developmental Psychology, 48*(2), 327–336. https://doi.org/10.1037/a0027030

## Source 2:

| Introduction |
|---|
| Earlier studies reveal that smartphone usage has a two-way connection with loneliness. On one hand, the internet accessed through smartphones can enhance relationships and reduce loneliness, but on the other hand, it can replace meaningful time spent in face-to-face interactions, leading to an increase in loneliness. This current study specifically investigated the link between loneliness and smartphone use. |
| **Participants** |
| The participants were 302 undergraduate students at a large Canadian University who had at least one week of smartphone screen use data. The mean age was 18.85 years. |
| **Method** |
| After providing consent, participants completed an online survey that included self-report measures of loneliness and usage data on their smartphones. |
| **Results and Discussion** |
| The correlations showed a positive association between loneliness and longer screen time ($r = .18$, $p < .05$). However, no statistically significant relationships were observed between loneliness and other smartphone activities such as picking up the phone or using communication apps. |

Information from: MacDonald, K. B., & Schermer, J. A. (2021). Loneliness unlocked: Associations with smartphone use and personality. *Acta psychologica, 221*, 103454. https://doi.org/10.1016/j.actpsy.2021.103454

## Source 3:

| Introduction |
|---|
| Social media use in personal and professional contexts is common, and it can be both addictive and distracting. The present study investigated the effects of social media distractions on academic tasks, as well as individuals' levels of stress related to technology and happiness. |
| **Participants** |
| Participants consisted of 209 undergraduate college students enrolled in an information systems course at a university in the Western United States. They were given course credit for participating. |
| **Method** |
| To measure task performance, researchers created a classroom academic task. They also assessed participants' self-reported social media usage, stress, and happiness levels. |
| **Results and Discussion** |
| The findings revealed that higher levels of personal social media usage were associated with lower task performance, increased stress, and decreased happiness. |

Information from: Brooks, S. (2015). Does personal social media usage affect efficiency and well-being? *Computers in Human Behavior, 46*, 26–37. https://doi.org/10.1016/j.chb.2014.12.053

# ARTICLE ANALYSIS QUESTION

**INSTRUCTIONS**: Answer the following question using the source provided. Your response to the question should be provided in six distinct parts: A, B, C, D, E, and F. Use appropriate psychological terminology in your response. Use complete sentences in your response; outlines or bulleted lists alone are not acceptable.

2. Using the source provided, respond to the following questions:

   **(A)** Identify the research method used in the study.

   **(B)** Identify the operational definition of horror film enjoyment.

   **(C)** Describe the meaning of statistical significance as it relates to the findings of the study.

   **(D)** Identify at least one ethical guideline applied by the researchers.

   **(E)** Explain the extent to which the research findings may or may not be generalizable using specific and relevant evidence from the study.

   **(F)** Explain how at least one of the research findings supports or refutes the researchers' hypothesis.

## Source:

| Introduction |
| --- |
| Some people would never willingly go see a horror film, while others find horror films very enjoyable. The present study examines the factors that influence people's horror film attendance and enjoyment. The researchers surveyed audience members of a mainstream, popular horror film to identify predictors of why individuals are drawn to these films. They hypothesized that age would be negatively correlated to horror film appeal. |
| **Participants** |
| One hundred fifty-five male and female movie-goers were interviewed leaving a theater after viewing a popular horror film. Participants ranged from 15 to 45 years old. Seventy percent of participants were between the ages of 18 and 21. |
| **Method** |
| Trained interviewers approached individuals as they were leaving the theater. After individuals verbally agreed to participate, the interviewer asked a series of questions about how much they enjoyed horror films and how frequently they attended horror films. Both variables were measured on a scale of 1 to 5 with higher numbers indicating more enjoyment and frequency. They also asked for age and gender. When the interviews were completed, the researchers explained the purpose of the study and addressed any questions the participants had. |
| **Results and Discussion** |
| The researchers found that younger participants viewed horror films more often than older participants. These results were statistically significant. This relationship seems to be explained by younger peoples' higher level of sensation-seeking. |

Information from: Tamborini, R., & Stiff, J. (1987). Predictors of horror film attendance and appeal: An analysis of the audience for frightening films. *Communication Research, 14*(4), 415–436. https://doi.org/10.1177/009365087014004003

# Unit 5 Mental and Physical Health

## EVIDENCE-BASED QUESTION

**INSTRUCTIONS:** Answer the following question using the 3 sources provided. Your response to the question should be provided in three distinct parts: A, B, and C. Use appropriate psychological terminology in your response.

For both Part B and Part C, each piece of evidence must be cited using the "Source [Number]" designation in parentheses following the cited material or embedded in the sentence. For example,

- Parenthetical citation: (Source 1).
- Embedded citation: According to Source 1, . . .

1. Using the provided sources, develop and justify an argument about the extent to which gratitude impacts subjective well-being.

   **(A)** Propose a specific and defensible claim based in psychological science that responds to the question.

   **(B.i)** Support your claim using at least one piece of specific and relevant evidence from one of the sources provided.

   **(B.ii)** Use a psychological perspective, theory, concept, or research finding learned in AP® Psychology to explain how your evidence supports your claim.

   **(C.i)** Using a different source than the one you used in Part (B.i), support your claim using at least one piece of specific and relevant evidence.

   **(C.ii)** Use a psychological perspective, theory, concept, or research finding learned in AP® Psychology—different than the one you used in part (B.ii)—to explain how your evidence in Part (C.i) supports your claim.

## Source 1:

| Introduction |
| --- |
| While there are many ways to increase gratitude and subjective well-being, this study focused on the role of counting blessings. The researchers were specifically interested in whether gratitude could be a useful intervention for individuals in prison. |
| **Participants** |
| The participants consisted of 124 prisoners in China. All participants were male. |
| **Method** |
| Determined by random assignment, participants either wrote about things they were grateful for, or they wrote about a neutral, control topic. Researchers then assessed self-reported gratitude levels and subjective well-being. |
| **Results and Discussion** |
| The prisoners who wrote about grateful things demonstrated higher levels of gratitude and higher levels of subjective well-being than the prisoners who wrote about neutral topics. The researchers concluded that counting one's blessings can be beneficial in prison settings. |

Information from: Peng, J., Xiao, Y., Zhang, J., Sun, H., Huang, Q., & Shao, Y. (2022). Benefits of counting blessings in basic psychological needs satisfaction and subjective well-being of prisoners. *Psychology, Crime & Law, 28*(2), 198–213. https://doi.org/10.1080/1068316X.2021.1905814

## Source 2:

| Introduction |
|---|
| Successful aging encompasses both physical and mental well-being. The present study examined the benefits of gratitude on mental well-being in older adults. |
| **Participants** |
| All participants were from southern Spain. They included 124 adults between the ages of 60 and 89, 50 women and 74 men. |
| **Method** |
| Determined by random assignment, half the participants completed a gratitude intervention in which they were trained on expressing gratitude (the experimental group). The other half had no such training (control group). Depression and positive affect scores were obtained via surveys for all participants three times: one week before the gratitude intervention, one week after the gratitude intervention, and a month after completion of the gratitude intervention. |
| **Results and Discussion** |
| Those trained in gratitude had higher positive affect levels than the control group. However, the gratitude training did not decrease depression. The results are represented in the graphs that follow. |

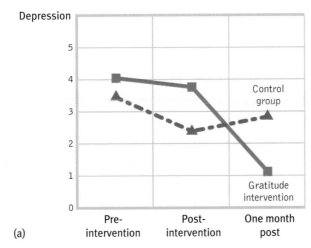

(a)

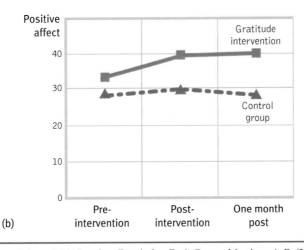

(b)

Information from: Salces-Cubero, I. M., Ramírez-Fernández, E., & Ortega-Martínez, A. R. (2019). Strengths in older adults: Differential effect of savoring, gratitude, and optimism on well-being. *Aging & Mental Health, 23*(8), 1017-1024. https://doi.org/10.1080/13607863.2018.1471585

| Introduction |
| --- |
| Social media allows people to witness other individuals' mental processes when observing what is posted on others' walls or feeds. Based on social learning theory and emotional contagion, this pilot study examined the extent to which viewing other people's gratefulness as posted on social media impacted their subjective well-being. |

| Participants |
| --- |
| Participants consisted of forty-nine male and female Italian young adults. The mean age was 26.63 years. |

| Method |
| --- |
| Participants were randomly exposed to grateful messages on social media for two weeks. The control group had no such exposure. Researchers then measured subsequent subjective well-being. |

| Results and Discussion |
| --- |
| After being exposed to other people's grateful messages, the participants' subjective well-being was enhanced, and they reported more satisfaction with life. Researchers concluded that social media can serve the purpose of disseminating gratitude and its effect on subjective well-being. |

Information from: Sciara, S., Villani, D., Di Natale, A. F., & Regalia, C. (2021). Gratitude and social media: A pilot experiment on the benefits of exposure to others' grateful interactions on Facebook. *Frontiers in Psychology, 12.* https://doi.org/10.3389/fpsyg.2021.667052

## ARTICLE ANALYSIS QUESTION

**INSTRUCTIONS**: Answer the following question using the source provided. Your response to the question should be provided in six distinct parts: A, B, C, D, E, and F. Use appropriate psychological terminology in your response. Use complete sentences in your response; outlines or bulleted lists alone are not acceptable.

2. Using the source provided, respond to the following questions:

    **(A)** Identify the research method used in the study.

    **(B)** Identify the operational definition of stress.

    **(C)** Describe the meaning of the correlation coefficient of .531 between stress and head pain level for the chronic headache group.

    **(D)** Identify at least one ethical guideline applied by the researchers.

    **(E)** Explain the extent to which the research findings may or may not be generalizable using specific and relevant evidence from the study.

    **(F)** Explain how at least one of the research findings supports or refutes the claim that the relationship between stress and headache pain is stronger the more headaches one experiences.

## Source:

| Introduction |
|---|
| Headaches are common in adolescence, with approximately one-third of all adolescents experiencing headaches. Past research has linked headaches and stress in some populations; however, the purpose of this study was to investigate the relationship between in-the-moment stress levels and the level of pain associated with headaches among adolescent girls. The researchers assessed whether the correlation between stress and head pain differs based on headache frequency. Are girls who have frequent headaches more likely to report a relationship between stress levels and level of head pain? |

| Participants |
|---|
| This study used convenience sampling to recruit teenage girls, ranging in age from 14 to 18 years, to participate in the study. Data were collected at an urban, Pacific Northwest high school, and 31 teen girls finished all study materials. |

| Method |
|---|
| Before data collection, the study was approved by an Institutional Review Board. Participants completed an electronic diary questionnaire seven times randomly each day across a 21-day period. In this questionnaire, they rated their head pain at each time on a 0 (no head pain) to 100 (severe head pain) scale. They also rated the amount of stress they were experiencing at that time on a 0 (no stress) to 100 (extreme stress) scale. Based on how often the participants experienced headaches, they were put in one of three groups: low headache group (experiencing headaches 0 to 15 percent of the time), moderate headache group (experiencing headaches 21 to 39 percent of the time), and chronic headache group (experiencing headaches 51 to 79 percent of the time). |

| Results and Discussion |
|---|
| The correlation between stress and head pain level for the chronic headache group was .531. The correlation between stress and head pain level for the moderate headache group was .086. The correlation between stress and head pain level for the low headache group was .077. |
| The researchers argue that this topic deserves more research attention, given that headaches are so common. |

Information from: Björling, E. A. (2009). The momentary relationship between stress and headache in adolescent girls. *Headache: The Journal of Head and Face Pain, 49*(8), 1186–1197. https://doi.org/10.1111/j.1526-4610.2009.01406.x

# Glossary / Glosario

## English

## Español

**24 character strengths and virtues** a classification system to identify positive traits; organized into categories of wisdom, courage, humanity, justice, temperance, and transcendence. (p. 670)

**24 fortalezas y virtudes del carácter** sistema de clasificación para identificar rasgos positivos; se organizan en categorías de sabiduría, coraje, humanidad, justicia, templanza y trascendencia. (p. 670)

## A

**absolute threshold** the minimum stimulus energy needed to detect a particular stimulus 50 percent of the time. (p. 117)

**umbral absoluto** el mínimo de energía que requiere un estímulo para tener 50 por ciento de probabilidades de ser detectado. (p. 117)

**accommodation** (1) in sensation and perception, the process by which the eye's lens changes shape to focus images of near or far objects on the retina. (2) in developmental psychology, adapting our current schemas (understandings) to incorporate new information. (pp. 126, 189, 349)

**acomodación** (1) en sensación y percepción, proceso por el cual la lente del ojo cambia de forma para enfocar imágenes de objetos cercanos o lejanos en la retina. (2) en psicología del desarrollo, adaptar nuestros esquemas (entendimientos) actuales para incorporar información nueva. (pp. 126, 189, 349)

**achievement motivation** a desire for significant accomplishment, for mastery of skills or ideas, for control, and for attaining a high standard. (p. 594)

**motivación del logro** deseo de conseguir un logro significativo, de dominar habilidades o ideas, de control, y de alcanzar un estándar elevado. (p. 594)

**achievement test** a test designed to assess what a person has learned. (p. 262)

**prueba de rendimiento** prueba diseñada para evaluar los aprendizajes de una persona. (p. 262)

**acquisition** in classical conditioning, the initial stage, when one links a neutral stimulus and an unconditioned stimulus so that the neutral stimulus begins triggering the conditioned response. In operant conditioning, the strengthening of a reinforced response. (p. 405)

**adquisición** etapa inicial, en el condicionamiento clásico, donde uno relaciona un estímulo neutral con un estímulo no condicionado de tal manera que el estímulo neutral provoca una respuesta condicionada. En el condicionamiento operante, es el fortalecimiento de una respuesta reforzada. (p. 405)

**action potential** a neural impulse; a brief electrical charge that travels down an axon. (p. 29)

**acción potencial** un impulso neural; una breve carga eléctrica que viaja por un axón. (p. 29)

**active listening** empathic listening in which the listener echoes, restates, and seeks clarification. A feature of Rogers' person-centered therapy. (p. 749)

**escucha activa** forma de escuchar con empatía en la cual, la persona que escucha resuena, reafirma y busca clarificar las palabras de la otra persona. Es un rasgo de la terapia centrada en la persona de Carl Rogers. (p. 749)

**actor-observer bias** the tendency for those acting in a situation to attribute their behavior to external causes, but for observers to attribute others' behavior to internal causes. This contributes to the *fundamental attribution error* (which focuses on our explanations for others' behavior). (p. 455)

**sesgo actor-observador** tendencia de aquellos que actúan en una situación a atribuir su comportamiento a causas externas, mientras los observadores atribuyen el comportamiento de otros a causas internas. Esto contribuye al *error fundamental de atribución* (que se centra en nuestras explicaciones sobre el comportamiento de los demás). (p. 455)

**acute schizophrenia** (also called *reactive schizophrenia*) a form of schizophrenia that can begin at any age; frequently occurs in response to a traumatic event, and from which recovery is much more likely. (p. 724)

**esquizofrenia aguda** (también conocida como *esquizofrenia reactiva*) tipo de esquizofrenia que puede comenzar a cualquier edad; con frecuencia ocurre como respuesta a un evento traumático del cuál es más probable que uno se recupere. (p. 724)

**adaptation-level phenomenon** our tendency to form judgments (of sounds, of lights, of income) relative to a neutral level defined by our prior experience. (p. 667)

**fenómeno del nivel de adaptación** nuestra tendencia a formar juicios (de sonidos, de luces, de ingresos) en relación con un nivel neutral definido por nuestra experiencia previa. (p. 667)

**addiction** an everyday term for compulsive substance use (and sometimes for dysfunctional behavior patterns, such as out-of-control gambling) that continue despite harmful consequences. (See also **substance use disorder**.) (p. 43)

**adicción** término de uso común para describir el uso compulsivo de sustancias (y a veces para patrones de comportamiento disfuncional, como apostar sin control) que es continuo a pesar de sus consecuencias dañinas. (Ver también **trastorno de uso de sustancias**). (p. 43)

**adolescence** the transition period from childhood to adulthood, extending from puberty to independence. (p. 312)

**adolescencia** el periodo de transición de la infancia hacia la edad adulta, que se extiende desde la pubertad hasta la independencia. (p. 312)

**aerobic exercise** sustained exercise that increases heart and lung fitness; also helps alleviate anxiety. (p. 673)

**ejercicio aeróbico** ejercicio continuo que mejora la condición pulmonar y cardiovascular; también ayuda a aliviar la ansiedad. (p. 673)

**affiliation need** the need to build and maintain relationships and to feel part of a group. (p. 586)

**necesidad de afiliación** la necesidad de construir y mantener relaciones y sentirse parte de un grupo. (p. 586)

| | |
|---|---|
| **aggression** any physical or verbal behavior intended to harm someone physically or emotionally. (pp. 321, 496) | **agresión** cualquier comportamiento físico o verbal que tiene la intención de lastimar, ya sea emocionalmente o físicamente, a otra persona. (pp. 321, 496) |
| **agonist** a molecule that increases a neurotransmitter's action. (p. 34) | **agonista** molécula que incrementa la acción de un neurotransmisor. (p. 34) |
| **agoraphobia** fear or avoidance of situations, such as crowds or wide open places, where one may experience a loss of control and panic. (p. 700) | **agorafobia** miedo o tendencia a evitar situaciones, como multitudes o espacios abiertos, donde uno puede experimentar una pérdida de control y pánico. (p. 700) |
| **algorithm** a methodical, logical rule or procedure that guarantees solving a particular problem. Contrasts with the usually speedier—but also more error-prone—use of *heuristics*. (p. 193) | **algoritmo** regla o procedimiento metódico y lógico que garantiza la resolución de un problema particular. Contrasta con el uso de la *heurística* que es más veloz pero también más propensa a los errores. (p. 193) |
| **all-or-none response** a neuron's reaction of either firing (with a full-strength response) or not firing. (p. 30) | **respuesta de todo o nada** la reacción de una neurona que dispara (con una respuesta total) o no dispara. (p. 30) |
| **alpha waves** the relatively slow brain waves of a relaxed, awake state. (p. 95) | **ondas alfa** las ondas cerebrales relativamente lentas del estado despierto y relajado. (p. 95) |
| **altruism** unselfish regard for the welfare of others. (p. 514) | **altruismo** consideración generosa por el bienestar de otros. (p. 514) |
| **amygdala** [uh-MIG-duh-la] two lima-bean-sized neural clusters in the limbic system; linked to emotion. (p. 66) | **amígdalas** dos cúmulos neurales del tamaño de una haba que forman parte del sistema límbico; están vinculadas a las emociones. (p. 66) |
| **androgyny** displaying traditionally masculine and traditionally feminine psychological characteristics. (p. 329) | **androginia** cuando una persona muestra rasgos psicológicos tradicionalmente masculinos y tradicionalmente femeninos. (p. 329) |
| **anorexia nervosa** an eating disorder in which a person (usually an adolescent female) maintains a starvation diet despite being significantly underweight, and has an inaccurate self-perception; sometimes accompanied by excessive exercise. (p. 735) | **anorexia nerviosa** trastorno alimenticio en el cual una persona (normalmente mujer adolescente) mantiene una dieta de hambre a pesar de tener el peso significativamente por debajo de lo normal, y tiene una percepción imprecisa de sí misma; a veces también conlleva ejercicio en exceso. (p. 735) |
| **antagonist** a molecule that inhibits or blocks a neurotransmitter's action. (p. 34) | **antagonista** molécula que inhibe la acción de un neurotransmisor. (p. 34) |
| **anterograde amnesia** an inability to form new memories. (p. 239) | **amnesia anterógrada** la incapacidad de formar nuevas memorias. (p. 239) |
| **antianxiety drugs** drugs used to control anxiety and agitation. (p. 779) | **ansiolíticos** medicamentos para controlar la ansiedad y la agitación. (p. 779) |
| **antidepressant drugs** drugs used to treat depressive disorders, anxiety disorders, obsessive-compulsive and related disorders, and post-traumatic stress disorder. (Several widely used antidepressant drugs are *selective serotonin reuptake inhibitors—SSRIs*.) (p. 779) | **antidepresivos** medicamentos para tratar trastornos depresivos, trastornos de ansiedad, trastornos obsesivo-compulsivos y trastornos relacionados, y el trastorno por estrés postraumático. (Varios de los antidepresivos comunes son *inhibidores selectivos de la recaptación de serotonina—ISRS*.) (p. 779) |
| **antipsychotic drugs** drugs used to treat schizophrenia and other forms of severe thought disorders. (p. 778) | **medicamentos antipsicóticos** medicamentos que se usan para tratar la esquizofrenia y otros tipos de trastornos severos del pensamiento. (p. 778) |
| **antisocial behavior** negative, destructive, harmful behavior. The opposite of prosocial behavior. (p. 442) | **comportamiento antisocial** comportamiento destructivo, negativo, dañino. Lo opuesto al comportamiento prosocial. (p. 442) |
| **antisocial personality disorder** a personality disorder in which a person (usually a man) exhibits a lack of conscience for wrongdoing, even toward friends and family members; may be aggressive and ruthless or a clever con artist. (p. 732) | **trastorno de la personalidad antisocial** trastorno de la personalidad en el cual una persona (normalmente hombre) no está consciente de haber causado un mal, incluso hacia amigos o familiares puede ser agresivo, despiadado o incluso puede llegar a ser un astuto estafador. (p. 732) |
| **anxiety disorders** a group of disorders characterized by excessive fear and anxiety and related maladaptive behaviors. (p. 699) | **trastornos de ansiedad** grupo de trastornos caracterizados por un miedo y ansiedad excesivos y comportamientos maladaptativos relacionados. (p. 699) |
| **aphasia** impairment of language, usually caused by left hemisphere damage either to Broca's area (impairing speaking) or to Wernicke's area (impairing understanding). (p. 368) | **afasia** discapacidad del lenguaje, generalmente provocado por daños en el hemisferio izquierdo del cerebro, ya sea en el área de Broca (que afecta al habla) o al área de Wernicke (que afecta la comprensión). (p. 368) |
| **approach and avoidance motives** the drive to move toward (approach) or away from (avoid) a stimulus. (p. 643) | **motivos de acercamiento y evitación** impulso de acercarse (acercamiento) o alejarse (evitar) un estímulo. (p. 643) |
| **aptitude test** a test designed to predict a person's future performance; *aptitude* is the capacity to learn. (p. 262) | **prueba de aptitud** prueba diseñada para predecir el desempeño futuro de una persona; *aptitud* es la capacidad para aprender. (p. 262) |
| **asexual** having no sexual attraction toward others. (p. 333) | **asexual** que no siente atracción sexual hacia otros. (p. 333) |

**assimilation** interpreting our new experiences in terms of our existing schemas. (p. 189, 349)

**asimilación** interpretar nuestras nuevas experiencias según nuestros esquemas existentes (p. 189, 349)

**association areas** areas of the cerebral cortex that are not involved in primary motor or sensory functions; rather, they are involved in higher mental functions such as learning, remembering, thinking, and speaking. (p. 75)

**áreas de asociación** áreas de la corteza cerebral que no se involucran en las funciones primarias motrices o sensoriales; en vez de eso, se involucran en funciones mentales superiores como el aprender, recordar, pensar y hablar. (p. 75).

**associative learning** learning that certain events occur together. The events may be two stimuli (as in classical conditioning) or a response and its consequence (as in operant conditioning). (p. 401)

**aprendizaje asociativo** aprender que ciertos sucesos ocurren juntos. Los sucesos pueden ser dos estímulos (como en el condicionamiento clásico) o una respuesta y su consecuencia (como en el condicionamiento operativo). (p. 401)

**attachment** an emotional tie with others; shown in young children by their seeking closeness to caregivers and showing distress on separation. (p. 374)

**apego** conexión emocional con otras personas; la muestran los niños pequeños al buscar cercanía con sus cuidadores y aflicción al separarse de ellos. (p. 374)

**attention-deficit/hyperactivity disorder (ADHD)** a psychological disorder marked by extreme inattention and/or hyperactivity and impulsivity. (p. 740)

**trastorno por déficit de atención con hiperactividad (TDAH)** trastorno psicológico marcado por una falta de atención extrema y/o hiperactividad e impulsividad. (p. 740)

**attitudes** feelings, often influenced by our beliefs, that predispose us to respond in a particular way to objects, people, and events. (p. 468)

**actitudes** sentimientos, muchas veces influenciados por nuestras creencias, que nos predisponen a responder de una manera especial a los objetos, la gente y los sucesos. (p. 468)

**attribution theory** the theory that we explain someone's behavior by crediting either the situation (a *situational attribution*) or the person's stable, enduring traits (a *dispositional attribution*). (p. 454)

**teoría de atribución** teoría según la cual el comportamiento de alguien se atribuye a una situación (*atribución situacional*) o a los rasgos estables y duraderos (una *atribución de disposición*) de aquella persona. (p. 454)

**audition** the sense or act of hearing. (p. 135)

**audición** sentido o acto de oír. (p. 135)

**autism spectrum disorder (ASD)** a disorder that appears in childhood and is marked by limitations in communication and social interaction, and by rigidly fixated interests and repetitive behaviors. (p. 738)

**trastorno del espectro autista (ASD, en inglés)** trastorno que aparece en la infancia, marcado por limitaciones de comunicación e interacción social, y por una fijación rígida en sus intereses y comportamientos repetitivos. (p. 738)

**autokinetic effect** the illusory movement of a still spot of light in a dark room. (p. 179)

**efecto autocinético** movimiento ilusorio de un punto fijo en una habitación oscura. (p. 179)

**automatic processing** unconscious encoding of incidental information, such as space, time, and frequency, and of familiar or well-learned information, such as sounds, smells, and word meanings. (p. 215)

**procesamiento automático** codificación inconsciente de información incidental, como espacio, tiempo y frecuencia, y de información familiar bien aprendida, como sonidos, olores y los significados de palabras. (p. 215)

**autonomic** [aw-tuh-NAHM-ik] **nervous system (ANS)** the part of the peripheral nervous system that controls the glands and the muscles of the internal organs (such as the heart). Its sympathetic division arouses; its parasympathetic division calms. (p. 23)

**sistema nervioso autónomo (ANS, en inglés)** la parte del sistema nervioso periférico que controla los músculos y las glándulas de los órganos internos (por ejemplo, el corazón). Su división simpática estimula; su división parasimpática tranquiliza. (p. 23)

**availability heuristic** judging the likelihood of events based on their availability in memory; if instances come readily to mind (perhaps because of their vividness), we presume such events are common. (p. 196)

**heurística de la disponibilidad** juzgar la probabilidad de un evento a partir de la disponibilidad de eventos similares en la memoria; si hay instancias que vienen rápidamente a la mente (quizás por su intensidad), suponemos que tales eventos son comunes. (p. 196)

**aversive conditioning** associates an unpleasant state (such as nausea) with an unwanted behavior (such as drinking alcohol). (p. 755)

**condicionamiento aversivo** asocia estados desagradables (como la náusea) con un comportamiento no deseado (como beber alcohol). (p. 755)

**axon** the segmented neuron extension that passes messages through its branches to other neurons or to muscles or glands. (p. 29)

**axón** extensión segmentada de las neuronas que transmite mensajes a través de sus terminales a otras neuronas o a músculos o glándulas. (p. 29)

# B

**babbling stage** the stage in speech development, beginning around 4 months, during which an infant spontaneously utters various sounds that are not all related to the household language. (p. 365)

**etapa de balbuceo** etapa en el desarrollo del habla, que comienza alrededor de los 4 meses, durante la cual un bebé emite espontáneamente sonidos que no están relacionados con el lenguaje del hogar. (p. 365)

**barbiturates** drugs that depress central nervous system activity, reducing anxiety but impairing memory and judgment. (p. 44)

**barbitúricos** medicamentos que deprimen la actividad del sistema nervioso central, de tal manera que reducen la ansiedad pero afectan la memoria y el juicio. (p. 44)

| | |
|---|---|
| **basal metabolic rate** the body's resting rate of energy output. (p. 602) | **tasa metabólica basal** tasa de producción de energía del cuerpo en reposo. (p. 602) |
| **basic trust** according to Erik Erikson, a sense that the world is predictable and trustworthy; said to be formed during infancy by appropriate experiences with responsive caregivers. (p. 378) | **confianza básica** de acuerdo con Erik Erikson, la sensación según la cual el mundo es un lugar predecible y digno de confianza; se dice que se forma durante la infancia por medio de experiencias apropiadas con cuidadores responsivos. (p. 378) |
| **behavior feedback effect** the tendency of behavior to influence our own and others' thoughts, feelings, and actions. (p. 626) | **efecto de retroalimentación del comportamiento** tendencia del comportamiento de influir en los pensamientos, sentimientos y acciones propias y ajenas. (p. 626) |
| **behavior genetics** the study of the relative power and limits of genetic and environmental influences on behavior. (p. 5) | **genética conductual** el estudio del poder relativo y las limitaciones de las influencias genéticas y ambientales sobre el comportamiento. (p. 5) |
| **behavior therapy** therapy that uses learning principles to reduce unwanted behaviors. (p. 753) | **terapia del comportamiento** terapia que usa principios de aprendizaje para reducir comportamientos no deseados. (p. 753) |
| **behavioral approach** focuses on the effects of learning on our personality development. (p. 561) | **enfoque conductual** se enfoca en los efectos del aprendizaje en el desarrollo de nuestra personalidad. (p. 561) |
| **behaviorism** the view that psychology (1) should be an objective science that (2) studies behavior without reference to mental processes. Most research psychologists today agree with (1) but not with (2). (p. 403) | **conductismo** perspectiva según la cual la psicología (1) debe ser una ciencia objetiva que should be an objective que (2) estudia el comportamiento sin referencia a los procesos mentales. La mayoría de los psicólogos investigadores est[an de acuerdo con (1) pero no con (2). (p. 403) |
| **belief perseverance** the persistence of one's initial conceptions even after the basis on which they were formed has been discredited. (p. 199) | **perseverancia de las creencias** la persistencia de nuestras concepciones iniciales aún cuando las bases que las sostienen han sido desacreditadas. (p. 199) |
| **Big Five factors** five traits—*openness, conscientiousness, extraversion, agreeableness,* and *neuroticism*—that describe personality. (Also called the *five-factor model*.) (p. 552) | **los cinco grandes factores** cinco grandes rasgos (*apertura, escrupulosidad, extroversión, amabilidad y neuroticismo*) que describen a la personalidad. (También conocido como *modelo de los cinco factores*). (p. 552) |
| **binocular cue** a depth cue, such as retinal disparity, that depends on the use of two eyes. (p. 177) | **pista binocular** pista de profundidad, como la disparidad retiniana, que depende del uso de ambos ojos. (p. 177) |
| **biological psychology** the scientific study of the links between biological (genetic, neural, hormonal) and psychological processes. (Some biological psychologists call themselves *behavioral neuroscientists, neuropsychologists, behavior geneticists, physiological psychologists,* or *biopsychologists*.) (p. 55) | **psicología biológica** el estudio científico de la relación entre los procesos biológicos (genéticos, neurales, hormonales) y psicológicos. (Algunos psicólogos biológicos se hacen llamar *neurocientíficos del comportamiento, neuropsicólogos, genetistas conductuales, psicólogos de la fisiología,* o *biopsicólogos*). (p. 55) |
| **biomedical therapy** prescribed medications or procedures that act directly on the person's physiology. (p. 746) | **terapia biomédica** medicamentos recetados o procedimientos que actúan directamente sobre la psicología de una persona. (p. 746) |
| **biopsychosocial approach** an integrated approach that incorporates biological, psychological, and social-cultural levels of analysis. (p. 56) | **enfoque biopsicológico** enfoque integrado que incorpora niveles de análisis biológicos, psicológicos y socioculturales. (p. 56) |
| **bipolar disorders** a group of disorders in which a person alternates between the hopelessness and lethargy of depression and the overexcited state of mania. (Formerly called *manic-depressive disorder*.) (p. 711) | **trastorno bipolar** grupo de trastornos en los cuales una persona alterna entre el letargo y la desesperación de la depresión y la sobreexcitación del estado maníaco. (Anteriormente se conocía como *trastorno maníaco-depresivo*). (p. 711) |
| **bipolar I disorder** the most severe form, in which people experience a euphoric, talkative, highly energetic, and overly ambitious state that lasts a week or longer. (p. 713) | **trastorno bipolar I** forma más severa, en la cual las personas experimentan un estado eufórico, hablador, energético y excesivamente ambicioso que dura una semana o más. (p. 713) |
| **bipolar II disorder** a less severe form of bipolar in which people move between depression and a milder hypomania. (p. 713) | **trastorno bipolar II** forma del trastorno menos severa en la cual se transita entre la depresión y una forma de hipomanía más moderada. (p. 713) |
| **blind spot** the point at which the optic nerve leaves the eye, creating a "blind" spot because no receptor cells are located there. (p. 126) | **punto ciego** el punto donde el nervio óptico sale del ojo, y crea así un punto "ciego" por la ausencia de células receptoras en este sitio. (p. 126) |
| **blindsight** a condition in which a person can respond to a visual stimulus without consciously experiencing it. (p. 90) | **visión ciega** condición en la cual una persona puede responder a un estímulo visual sin experimentarlo de manera consciente. (p. 90) |
| **bottom-up processing** information processing that begins with the sensory receptors and works up to the brain's integration of sensory information. (p. 116) | **procesamiento abajo-arriba** procesamiento de información que comienza en los receptores sensoriales y avanza hacia la integración de información sensorial en el cerebro. (p. 116) |

| | |
|---------|---------|
| **brainstem** the central core of the brain, beginning where the spinal cord swells as it enters the skull; the brainstem is responsible for automatic survival functions. (p. 65) | **tronco cerebral** el núcleo central del cerebro, que comienza donde la médula se ensancha y entra en el cráneo; el tronco cerebral es responsable de las funciones automáticas de supervivencia . (p. 65) |
| **broaden-and-build theory** proposes that positive emotions broaden our awareness, which over time helps us build novel and meaningful skills and resilience that improve well-being. (p. 669) | **teoría de ampliación y construcción** propone que las emociones positivas amplían nuestros pensamientos que, con el tiempo, nos ayuda a construir destrezas significantes y resiliencia para lograr mayor bienestar. (p. 669) |
| **Broca's area** a frontal lobe brain area, usually in the left hemisphere, that helps control language expression by directing the muscle movements involved in speech. (p. 368) | **área de Broca** área del lóbulo frontal del cerebro, generalmente en el hemisferio izquierdo, que ayuda a controlar la expresión del lenguaje al dirigir los movimientos musculares involucrados en el habla. (p. 368) |
| **bulimia nervosa** an eating disorder in which a person's binge eating (usually of high-calorie foods) is followed by inappropriate weight-loss-promoting behavior, such as vomiting, laxative use, fasting, or excessive exercise. (p. 735) | **bulimia nerviosa** trastorno alimenticio en el cual una persona ingiere compulsivamente alimentos (generalmente altos en calorías) seguido por un comportamiento inadecuado que promueve la pérdida de peso, como el vómito, el uso de laxantes, el ayuno o el ejercicio excesivo. (p. 735) |
| **burnout** physical, emotional, or mental exhaustion, brought on by an overburdening workload, which may negatively impact motivation, performance, and attitude. (p. 807) | **síndrome de desgaste profesional** agotamiento físico, emocional o mental provocado por una carga excesiva de trabajo que puede impactar negativamente nuestra motivación, desempeño y actitud. (p. 807) |
| **bystander effect** the tendency for any given bystander to be less likely to give aid if other bystanders are present. (p. 515) | **efecto del espectador** tendencia que tienen las personas a no brindar ayuda si hay otras personas presentes. (p. 515) |

## C

| | |
|---------|---------|
| **case study** a non-experimental technique in which one individual or group is studied in depth in the hope of revealing universal principles. (p. 0–16) | **estudio de caso** técnica de observación no experimental en la cual se estudia a un individuo o grupo a profundidad con la esperanza de revelar principios universales. (p. 0–16) |
| **catharsis** in psychology, the idea that "releasing" aggressive energy (through action or fantasy) relieves aggressive urges. (p. 650) | **catarsis** en la psicología, la idea según la cual "liberar" energía agresiva (por medio de la acción o fantasía) ayuda a reducir impulsos agresivos en las personas. (p. 650) |
| **Cattell-Horn-Carroll (CHC) theory** the theory that our intelligence is based on *g* as well as specific abilities, bridged by *Gf* and *Gc*. (p. 255) | **teoría de Catell-Horn-Carroll (CHC)** teoría según la cual nuestra inteligencia se basa en *g* así como en capacidades específicas conectadas por *Gf* y *Gc*. (p. 255) |
| **cell body** the part of a neuron that contains the nucleus; the cell's life-support center. (p. 28) | **cuerpo celular** la parte de una neurona que contiene el núcleo; soporte vital de la célula. (p. 28) |
| **central executive** a memory component that coordinates the activities of the *phonological loop* and *visuospatial sketchpad*. (p. 210) | **ejecutivo central** componente de memoria que coordina las actividades del *bucle fonológico* y el *boceto visoespacial*. (p. 210) |
| **central nervous system (CNS)** the brain and spinal cord. (p. 22) | **sistema nervioso central (SNC)** el cerebro y la médula espinal. (p. 22) |
| **central route persuasion** occurs when interested people's thinking is influenced by considering evidence and arguments. (p. 471) | **ruta central de persuasión central** se produce cuando el pensamiento de las personas se ve influenciado al considerar evidencia y argumentos. (p. 471) |
| **cerebellum** [sehr-uh-BELL-um] the hindbrain's "little brain" at the rear of the brainstem; its functions include processing sensory input, coordinating movement output and balance, and enabling nonverbal learning and memory. (p. 65) | **cerebelo** el "pequeño cerebro" del rombencéfalo ubicado en la parte posterior del tronco encefálico; sus funciones incluyen el procesamiento de información sensorial, la coordinación de los movimientos y el equilibrio y la habilitación del lenguaje no verbal y la memoria. (p. 65) |
| **cerebral** [seh-REE-bruhl] **cortex** the intricate fabric of interconnected neural cells covering the forebrain's cerebral hemispheres; the body's ultimate control and information-processing center. (p. 70) | **corteza cerebral** capa delgada de neuronas conectadas entre sí, que forman los hemisferios cerebrales del prosencéfalo; es el principal centro de control y procesamiento de información del organismo. (p. 70) |
| **change blindness** failing to notice changes in the environment; a form of *inattentional blindness*. (p. 168) | **ceguera al cambio** no darse cuenta de cambios en el entorno. Una forma de *ceguera por falta de atención*. (p. 168) |
| **character strengths and virtues** a classification system to identify positive traits; organized into categories of wisdom, courage, humanity, justice, temperance, and transcendence. (p. 670) | **fortalezas y virtudes del carácter** sistema de clasificación que identifica rasgos positivos; se organiza en las categorías de sabiduría, coraje, humanidad, justicia, templanza y trascendencia. (p. 670) |
| **chronic schizophrenia** (also called *process schizophrenia*) a form of schizophrenia in which symptoms usually appear by late adolescence or early adulthood. As people age, psychotic episodes last longer and recovery periods shorten. (p. 724) | **esquizofrenia crónica** (también se le dice *esquizofrenia procesal*) tipo de esquizofrenia en la que los síntomas aparecen generalmente en la adolescencia tardía o adultez temprana. A medida que las personas envejecen, los episodios psicóticos se vuelven más largos y los períodos de recuperación se vuelven más cortos. (p. 724) |

**chunking** organizing items into familiar, manageable units; often occurs automatically. (p. 218)

**agrupamiento** organizar artículos en unidades conocidas y manejables; a menudo ocurre automáticamente. (p. 218)

**circadian** [ser-KAY-dee-an] **rhythm** our biological clock; regular bodily rhythms (for example, of temperature and wakefulness) that occur on a 24-hour cycle. (p. 94)

**ritmo circadiano** reloj biológico; ritmos periódicos del organismo (por ejemplo, el de temperatura y estado de vigilia) que ocurren en ciclos de 24 horas. (p. 94)

**classical conditioning** a type of learning in which we link two or more stimuli; as a result, to illustrate with Pavlov's classic experiment, the first stimulus (a tone) comes to elicit behavior (drooling) in anticipation of the second stimulus (food). (p. 403)

**condicionamiento clásico** tipo de aprendizaje en el cual aprendemos a relacionar dos o más estímulos; como resultado, con el experimento clásico de Pavlov como ejemplo, el primer estímulo (un timbre) provoca un comportamiento (salivación) en anticipación del segundo estímulo (comida). (p. 403)

**cochlea** [KOHK-lee-uh] a coiled, bony, fluid-filled tube in the inner ear; sound waves traveling through the cochlear fluid trigger nerve impulses. (p. 137)

**cóclea** estructura tubular en forma de espiral, ósea y rellena de líquido que se halla en el oído interno; las ondas sonoras que pasan por el líquido coclear desencadenan impulsos nerviosos. (p. 137)

**cochlear implant** a device for converting sounds into electrical signals and stimulating the auditory nerve through electrodes threaded into the cochlea. (p. 138)

**implante coclear** dispositivo que convierte sonidos en señales eléctricas que estimulan el nervio auditivo mediante electrodos enhebrados en la cóclea. (p. 138)

**cognition** all the mental activities associated with thinking, knowing, remembering, and communicating. (pp. 187, 349)

**cognición** todas las actividades mentales asociadas con pensar, saber, recordar y comunicar. (pp. 187, 349)

**cognitive dissonance theory** the theory that we act to reduce the discomfort (dissonance) we feel when two of our thoughts (cognitions) are inconsistent. For example, when we become aware that our attitudes and our actions clash, we can reduce the resulting dissonance by changing our attitudes. (p. 470)

**teoría de la disonancia cognitiva** teoría según la cual actuamos para reducir la incomodidad (disonancia) cuando sentimos que dos de nuestros pensamientos (cogniciones) son disonantes. Por ejemplo, cuando nos damos cuenta que hay un choque entre nuestras actitudes y nuestras acciones, podemos reducir la disonancia resultante con cambios de actitud. (p. 470)

**cognitive learning** the acquisition of mental information, whether by observing events, by watching others, or through language. (p. 402)

**aprendizaje cognitivo** adquisición de información mental, ya sea a partir de la observación de acontecimientos, la observación de otras personas o a través del lenguaje. (p. 402)

**cognitive map** a mental representation of the layout of one's environment. For example, after exploring a maze, rats act as if they have learned a cognitive map of it. (p. 436)

**mapa cognitivo** imagen mental del trazado de nuestro entorno. Por ejemplo, después de recorrer un laberinto, las ratas actúan como si se hubieran aprendido un mapa del laberinto. (p. 436)

**cognitive neuroscience** the interdisciplinary study of the brain activity linked with cognition. (p.88)

**neurociencia cognitiva** estudio interdisciplinario de la actividad cerebral relacionada con la cognición. (p.88)

**cognitive therapy** therapy that teaches people new, more adaptive ways of thinking; based on the assumption that thoughts intervene between events and our emotional reactions. (p. 757)

**terapia cognitiva** enfoque terapéutico en que se les enseña a los pacientes nuevas formas de pensar de un modo más adaptativo. se basa en el supuesto de que los pensamientos intervienen entre los eventos y nuestras reacciones emocionales. (p. 757)

**cognitive-behavioral therapy (CBT)** a popular integrative therapy that combines cognitive therapy (changing self-defeating thinking) with behavior therapy (changing behavior). (p. 760)

**terapia congnitivo-conductual (CBT, en inglés)** tipo común de terapia integradora que combina la terapia cognitiva (cambia el pensamiento contraproducente) con terapia conductual (cambiar el comportamiento). (p. 760)

**cohort** a group of people sharing a common characteristic, such as from a given time period. (p. 272)

**cohorte** grupo de personas que comparten cierta característica, por ejemplo, un periodo en el tiempo. (p. 272)

**collective unconscious** Carl Jung's concept of a shared, inherited reservoir of memory traces from our species' history. (p. 534)

**inconsciente colectivo** concepto propuesto por Carl Jung en relación a un conjunto compartido de recuerdos heredados de la historia de nuestra especie. (p. 534)

**collectivism** a cultural pattern that prioritizes the goals of important groups (often one's extended family or work group). (p. 574)

**colectivismo** patrón cultural que da prioridad a las metas de grupos importantes (puede ser la familia extendida o el grupo laboral). (p. 574)

**color constancy** perceiving familiar objects as having consistent color, even if changing illumination alters the wavelengths reflected by the object. (p. 180)

**constancia del color** percibir objetos familiares como si tuvieran un color constante, incluso cuando cambios en la iluminación alteran las longitudes de onda que refleja el objeto. (p. 180)

**companionate love** the deep affectionate attachment we feel for those with whom our lives are intertwined. (p. 510)

**amor compañero** apego afectuoso profundo que sentimos por aquellos con quienes nuestras vidas se entrelazan. (p. 510)

**concept** a mental grouping of similar objects, events, ideas, or people. (p. 187)

**concepto** agrupamiento mental de objetos, eventos, ideas y personas similares. (p. 187)

**concrete operational stage** in Piaget's theory, the stage of cognitive development (from about 7 to 11 years of age) at which children can perform the mental operations that enable them to think logically about concrete (actual, physical) events. (p. 352)

**etapa del pensamiento lógico-concreto** en la teoría de Piaget, la fase del desarrollo cognitivo (aproximadamente desde los 7 hasta los 11 años de edad) en la cual los niños pueden llevar a cabo las operaciones mentales que les permiten pensar lógicamente sobre eventos concretos (reales y físicos). (p. 352)

**conditioned reinforcer** a stimulus that gains its reinforcing power through its association with a primary reinforcer; also known as a *secondary reinforcer*. (p. 421)

**reforzador condicionado** estímulo que obtiene sus poderes de reforzamiento a través de una asociación con un reforzador primario; también denominado *reforzador secundario*. (p. 421)

**conditioned response (CR)** in classical conditioning, a learned response to a previously neutral (but now conditioned) stimulus (CS). (p. 405)

**respuesta condicionada (rc)** en el condicionamiento clásico, la respuesta aprendida a un estímulo previamente neutral (pero ahora condicionado). (p. 405)

**conditioned stimulus (CS)** in classical conditioning, an originally neutral stimulus that, after association with an unconditioned stimulus (UCS), comes to trigger a conditioned response (CR). (p. 405)

**estímulo condicionado (ec)** en el condicionamiento clásico, un estímulo originalmente intrascendente que, después de verse asociado con un estímulo incondicionado (ei) produce una respuesta condicionada. (p. 405)

**conduction hearing loss** a less common form of hearing loss, caused by damage to the mechanical system that conducts sound waves to the cochlea. (p. 138)

**pérdida de la audición por conducción** tipo menos común de sordera atribuible a daños en el sistema mecánico que conduce ondas sonoras a la cóclea. (p. 138)

**cones** retinal receptors that are concentrated near the center of the retina and that function in daylight or in well-lit conditions. Cones detect fine detail and give rise to color sensations. (p. 126)

**conos** receptores que se concentran cerca del centro de la retina; con la luz del día o en lugares bien iluminados, los conos detectan detalles finos y producen la sensación del color. (p. 126)

**confirmation bias** a tendency to search for information that supports our preconceptions and to ignore or distort contradictory evidence. (pp. 194, 767)

**sesgo confirmatorio** tendencia a buscar información que confirme nuestras ideas preconcebidas y de hacer caso omiso o de distorsionar las pruebas que las contradigan. (pp. 194, 767)

**conflict** a perceived incompatibility of actions, goals, or ideas. (p. 518)

**conflicto** incompatibilidad percibida de acciones, metas o ideas. (p. 518)

**conformity** adjusting our behavior or thinking to coincide with a group standard. (p. 476)

**conformidad** tendencia a ajustar el comportamiento o la forma de pensar hasta hacerlos coincidir con las normas de un grupo. (p. 476)

**confounding variable** in an experiment, a factor other than the factor being studied that might influence a study's results. (p. 0–28)

**variable de confusión** en un experimento, un factor distinto del factor que se está estudiando que podría afectar los resultados de un estudio. (p. 0–28)

**consciousness** our subjective awareness of ourselves and our environment. (p. 87)

**consciencia** percepción de nosotros mismos y de nuestro entorno. (p. 87)

**conservation** the principle (which Piaget believed to be a part of concrete operational reasoning) that properties such as mass, volume, and number remain the same despite changes in the forms of objects. (p. 351)

**conservación** principio (que para Piaget forma parte del razonamiento operacional concreto) según el cual ciertas propiedades (ej., masa, volumen y número) no varían pese a modificaciones en la forma de los objetos. (p. 351)

**construct validity** how much a test measures a concept or trait. (p. 267)

**validez del constructo** qué tanto mide una prueba un concepto o rasgo. (p. 267)

**content validity** the extent to which a test samples the behavior that is of interest. (p. 267)

**validez del contenido** grado en que las muestras prueban el comportamiento que es de interés. (p. 267)

**continuous reinforcement schedule** reinforcing the desired response every time it occurs. (p. 422)

**reforzamiento continuo** reforzar la respuesta deseada cada vez que ocurre. (p. 422)

**control group** in an experiment, the group *not* exposed to the treatment; contrasts with the experimental group and serves as a comparison for evaluating the effect of the treatment. (p. 0–27)

**grupo control** en un experimento, el grupo de participantes que *no* se expone al tratamiento; el grupo de control sirve de comparación para evaluar el efecto del tratamiento en el grupo sometido al tratamiento. (p. 0–27)

**convergence** a cue to nearby objects' distance, enabled by the brain combining retinal images. (p. 177)

**convergencia** señal de la distancia de los objetos cercanos, habilitada por el cerebro que combina imágenes retinianas. (p. 177)

**convergent thinking** narrowing the available problem solutions to determine the single best solution. (p. 189)

**razonamiento convergente** reducción de las soluciones disponibles con el fin de determinar cuál es la mejor solución a un problema. (p. 189)

**coping** alleviating stress using emotional, cognitive, or behavioral methods. (p. 654)

**afrontamiento** aliviar estrés por medio de métodos emocionales, cognitivos o de comportamiento. (p. 654)

**cornea** the eye's clear, protective outer layer, covering the pupil and iris. (p. 124)

**córnea** capa protectora transparente exterior del ojo, que cubre la pupila y el iris. (p. 124)

**coronary heart disease** the clogging of the vessels that nourish the heart muscle; the leading cause of death in many developed countries. (p. 648)

**corpus callosum** [KOR-pus kah-LOW-sum] the large band of neural fibers connecting the two brain hemispheres and carrying messages between them. (p. 81)

**correlation** a measure of the extent to which two factors vary together, and thus of how well either factor predicts the other. (p. 0–22)

**correlation coefficient** a statistical index of the relationship between two things (from −1.00 to +1.00). (p. 0–22)

**counterconditioning** behavior therapy procedures that use classical conditioning to evoke new responses to stimuli that are triggering unwanted behaviors; include *exposure therapies* and *aversive conditioning*. (p. 754)

**creativity** the ability to produce new and valuable ideas. (p. 189)

**critical period** an optimal period early in the life of an organism when exposure to certain stimuli or experiences produces normal development. (p. 307)

**critical thinking** thinking that does not automatically accept arguments and conclusions. Rather, it examines assumptions, appraises the source, discerns hidden biases, evaluates evidence, and assesses conclusions. (p. 0–6)

**cross-sectional study** research that compares people of different ages at the same point in time. (pp. 271, 297)

**crystallized intelligence (*Gc*)** our accumulated knowledge and verbal skills; tends to increase with age. (p. 255)

**CT (computed tomography) scan** a series of X-ray photographs taken from different angles and combined by computer into a composite representation of a slice of the brain's structure. (p. 59)

**culture** the enduring behaviors, ideas, attitudes, values, and traditions shared by a group of people and transmitted from one generation to the next. (p. 491)

**enfermedad coronaria** obstrucción de los vasos que nutren el músculo cardíaco; causa principal de muerte en los Estados Unidos y muchos otros países. (p. 648)

**cuerpo calloso** banda grande de fibras neuronales que conecta los dos hemisferios del cerebro y transmite mensajes entre ellos. (p. 81)

**correlación** medida del grado en que dos factores varían juntos y por ende, si uno puede predecir al otro. (p. 0–22)

**coeficiente de correlación** índice estadístico de la relación entre dos cosas (del −1.00 al +1.00). (p. 0–22)

**contracondicionamiento** técnicas de terapia conductual que se valen del condicionamiento clásico para provocar respuestas alternativas a estímulos que producen comportamientos no deseados; incluye las *terapias de exposición* y el *condicionamiento aversivo*. (p. 754)

**creatividad** capacidad para generar ideas novedosas y valiosas. (p. 189)

**período crítico** etapa inicial de la vida de los organismos, en la cual son necesarios ciertos estímulos o experiencias para permitir su desarrollo normal. (p. 307)

**pensamiento crítico** forma de pensar que no admite razones ni conclusiones automáticamente. En cambio, se evalúan las fuentes, se buscan los sesgos ocultos, se analiza la evidencia y se estudian las conclusiones. (p. 0–6)

**estudio de corte transversal** estudio en el que personas de diferentes edades se comparan unas con otras en un mismo punto en el tiempo. (pp. 271, 297)

**inteligencia cristalizada (*Gc*)** todos los conocimientos y capacidades verbales que acumulamos; tiende a aumentar con la edad. (p. 255)

**TC (tomografía computarizada)** serie de imágenes de rayos-X tomadas desde ángulos distintos y combinadas por computadora para formar una representación compuesta de un corte de la estructura cerebral. (p. 59)

**cultura** ideas, actitudes, valores y tradiciones preponderantes compartidas por un grupo de personas y que se transmiten de generación en generación. (p. 491)

# D

**debriefing** the postexperimental explanation of a study, including its purpose and any deceptions, to its participants. (p. 0–35)

**deep processing** encoding semantically, based on the meaning of the words; tends to yield the best retention. (p. 222)

**defense mechanisms** in psychoanalytic theory, the ego's protective methods of reducing anxiety by unconsciously distorting reality. (p. 532)

**deindividuation** the loss of self-awareness and self-restraint occurring in group situations that foster arousal and anonymity. (p. 487)

**deinstitutionalization** the process, begun in the late twentieth century, of moving people with psychological disorders out of institutional facilities. (p. 746)

**déjà vu** that eerie sense that "I've experienced this before." Cues from the current situation may unconsciously trigger retrieval of an earlier experience. (p. 246)

**delta waves** the large, slow brain waves associated with deep sleep. (p. 96)

**rendición de informes** explicación que se les da a los participantes de un estudio sobre sus fines y los posibles engaños que los investigadores pudieron haber utilizado. (p. 0–35)

**procesamiento profundo** codificación semántica basada en el significado de las palabras; suele ser ideal para la retención. (p. 222)

**mecanismos de defensa** en la teoría del psicoanálisis, los métodos de protección del ego para reducir la ansiedad mediante la distorsión inconsciente de la realidad. (p. 532)

**desindividualización** pérdida de la identidad personal y del autocontrol en situaciones de grupo que fomentan la excitación y el anonimato. (p. 487)

**desinstitucionalización** proceso, iniciado a finales del siglo veinte, de sacar a las personas con trastornos psicológicos de centros institucionales. (p. 746)

**déjà vu** sensación extraña de haber vivido antes una experiencia específica. Ciertas pistas del presente inmediato pueden evocar una vivencia previa. (p. 246)

**ondas delta** ondas cerebrales grandes y lentas asociadas con sueño profundo. (p. 96)

**delusion** a false belief, often of persecution or grandeur, that may accompany psychotic disorders. (p. 723)

**delirio** creencias falsas, a menudo de persecución o de grandeza que pueden acompañar a trastornos psicóticos. (p. 723)

**dendrites** a neuron's often bushy, branching extensions that receive and integrate messages, conducting impulses toward the cell body. (p. 28)

**dendritas** prolongaciones de las neuronas que reciben mensajes y envían impulsos hacia el cuerpo neuronal. (p. 28)

**dependent variable** in an experiment, the outcome that is measured; the variable that may change when the independent variable is manipulated. (p. 0–28)

**variable dependiente** el valor que se mide en un experimento;. es la variable que puede cambiar cuando se manipula la variable independiente. (p. 0–28)

**depressants** drugs that reduce neural activity and slow body functions. (p. 41)

**depresivos** agentes químicos que reducen (deprimen) la actividad neuronal y disminuyen las funciones del organismo. (p. 41)

**depressive disorders** a group of disorders characterized by an enduring sad, empty, or irritable mood, along with physical and cognitive changes that affect a person's ability to function. (p. 711)

**trastornos depresivos** grupo de trastornos caracterizados por la persistencia de estados de ánimo tristes, vacíos o irritables, junto con cambios físicos y cognitivos que afectan la capacidad de funcionamiento de las personas. (p. 711)

**depth perception** the ability to see objects in three dimensions although the images that strike the retina are two-dimensional; allows us to judge distance. (p. 176)

**percepción de la profundidad** capacidad de ver objetos en tres dimensiones aún cuando las imágenes percibidas por la retina son bidimensionales. Nos permite juzgar la distancia. (p. 176)

**descriptive statistics** numerical data used to measure and describe characteristics of groups; include measures of central tendency and measures of variation. (p. 0–41)

**estadística descriptiva** datos numéricos que se usan para medir y describir características de grupos; incluye medidas de tendencia central y medidas de variación. (p. 0–41)

**developmental psychology** a branch of psychology that studies physical, cognitive, and social change throughout the lifespan. (p. 297)

**psicología del desarrollo** rama de la psicología que estudia los cambios físicos, cognitivos y sociales que ocurren a lo largo de la vida. (p. 297)

**diathesis-stress model** the concept that genetic predispositions (diathesis) combine with environmental stressors (stress) to influence psychological disorder. (p. 687)

**modelo de diátesis-estrés** concepto según el cual predisposiciones genéticas (diátesis) se combinan con factores estresantes ambientales para influir en un trastorno psicológico. (p. 687)

**difference threshold** the minimum difference between two stimuli required for detection 50 percent of the time. We experience the difference threshold as a *just noticeable difference* (or jnd). (p. 120)

**umbral de diferencia** la diferencia mínima entre dos estímulos que una persona puede detectar el 50 por ciento de las veces. El umbral diferencial se experimenta como una *diferencia apenas perceptible* (o jnd, en inglés). (p. 120)

**discrimination** (1) in classical conditioning, the learned ability to distinguish between a conditioned stimulus and other stimuli that have not been associated with a conditioned stimulus. (In operant conditioning, the ability to distinguish responses that are reinforced from similar responses that are not reinforced.) (2) in social psychology, unjustifiable negative behavior toward a group or its members. (pp. 408, 457)

**discriminación** (1) según el condicionamiento clásico, es la capacidad aprendida de distinguir entre un estímulo condicionado y otros estímulos que no han sido asociados con un estímulo condicionado. (En el condicionamiento operante, la capacidad de distinguir las respuestas que son reforzadas de las que no lo son.) (2) en psicología social, comportamiento negativo injustificado contra un grupo o sus miembros. (pp. 408, 457)

**discriminative stimulus** in operant conditioning, a stimulus that elicits a response after association with reinforcement (in contrast to related stimuli not associated with reinforcement). (p. 419)

**estímulo discriminativo** en el condicionamiento operante, un estímulo que genera una respuesta después de ser asociado con un reforzamiento (en contraste con estímulos relacionados que no están asociados con un reforzamiento). (p. 419)

**dissociation** a split in consciousness, which allows some thoughts and behaviors to occur simultaneously with others. (p. 786)

**disociación** una apertura en el conocimiento consciente que permite que algunos pensamientos y comportamientos ocurran en forma simultánea con otros. (p. 786)

**dissociative amnesia** a disorder in which people with intact brains reportedly experience memory gaps; people with dissociative amnesia may report not remembering trauma-related specific events, people, places, or aspects of their identity and life history. (p. 731)

**amnesia disociativa** trastorno en el que las personas con cerebros intactos dicen experimentar vacíos memorísticos; las personas con amnesia disociativa pueden decir que no recuerdan eventos, personas, lugares o aspectos específicos relacionados con el trauma de su identidad e historia de vida. (p. 731)

**dissociative disorders** a controversial, rare group of disorders characterized by a disruption of or discontinuity in the normal integration of consciousness, memory, identity, emotion, perception, body representation, motor control, and behavior. (p. 730)

**trastornos disociativos** grupo controvertido y raro de trastornos caracterizados por una interrupción o discontinuidad en la integración normal de la conciencia, la memoria, la identidad, la emoción, la percepción, la representación corporal, el control motor y el comportamiento. (p. 730)

**dissociative identity disorder (DID)** a rare dissociative disorder in which a person exhibits two or more distinct and alternating personalities. (Formerly called *multiple personality disorder*.) (p. 730)

**trastorno disociativo de identidad (TDI)** trastorno disociativo poco común, en el cual una persona exhibe dos o más personalidades claramente definidas que se alternan entre sí. (También se denomina trastorno de *personalidad múltiple*). (p. 730)

**divergent thinking** expanding the number of possible problem solutions; creative thinking that diverges in different directions. (p. 189)

**razonamiento divergente** expansión del número de soluciones a un problema. Pensamiento creativo que se ramifica en múltiples direcciones. (p. 189)

**double-blind procedure** an experimental procedure in which both the research participants and the research staff are ignorant (blind) about whether the research participants have received the treatment or a placebo. Commonly used in drug-evaluation studies. (p. 0–28)

**procedimiento doble ciego** en un experimento, procedimiento en el cual tanto los participantes como el personal de investigación ignoran (van a ciegas) quién ha recibido el tratamiento y quién el placebo. (p. 0–28)

**dream** a sequence of images, emotions, and thoughts passing through a sleeping person's mind. (p. 109)

**sueño** secuencia de imágenes, emociones y pensamientos que fluyen en la mente de una persona dormida. (p. 109)

**drive-reduction theory** the idea that a physiological need creates an aroused state (a drive) that motivates an organism to satisfy the need. (p. 580)

**teoría de la reducción del impulso** concepto según el cual una necesidad fisiológica crea un estado de excitación (un impulso) que motiva al organismo a satisfacer tal necesidad. (p. 580)

**DSM-5-TR** the American Psychiatric Association's *Diagnostic and Statistical Manual of Mental Disorders*, Fifth Edition, Text Revision; a widely used system for classifying psychological disorders. (p. 688)

**DSM-5-TR** *Manual diagnóstico y estadístico de los trastornos mentales*, quinta edición, texto revisado; un sistema reconocido para clasificar trastornos psicológicos. (p. 688)

**dual processing** the principle that information is often simultaneously processed on separate conscious and unconscious tracks. (p. 90)

**procesamiento dual** principio que sostiene que la información se procesa simultáneamente en vías separadas conscientes e inconscientes. (p. 90)

## E

**echoic memory** a momentary sensory memory of auditory stimuli; if attention is elsewhere, sounds and words can still be recalled within 3 or 4 seconds. (p. 216)

**memoria ecoica** memoria sensorial momentánea de estímulos auditivos; aún cuando uno no presta atención, es posible recordar palabras por 3 o 4 segundos. (p. 216)

**eclectic approach** an approach to psychotherapy that uses techniques from various forms of therapy. (p. 747)

**enfoque ecléctico** enfoque de psicoterapia que emplea técnicas de varias formas de terapia. (p. 747)

**ecological systems theory** a theory of the social environment's influence on human development, using five nested systems (microsystem; mesosystem; exosystem; macrosystem; chronosystem) ranging from direct to indirect influences. (p. 374)

**teoría ecológica de los sistemas** teoría del entorno social y su influencia en el desarrollo humano, que utiliza cinco sistemas anidados (microsistema, mesosistema, exosistema, macrosistema, cronosistema) que van desde influencias directas a indirectas. (p. 374)

**EEG (electroencephalogram)** an amplified recording of the waves of electrical activity sweeping across the brain's surface. These waves are measured by electrodes placed on the scalp. (p. 58)

**EEG (electroencefalograma)** el registro de las ondas de actividad eléctrica que circulan por la superficie del cerebro. Las ondas se miden a través de electrodos colocados sobre el cuero cabelludo. (p. 58)

**effect** experimental results caused by expectations alone; any effect on behavior caused by the administration of an inert substance or condition, which the recipient assumes is an active agent. (p. 0–28)

**efecto** resultados experimentales causados únicamente por expectativas; cualquier efecto en el comportamiento causado por la administración de una sustancia inerte o una condición, que el receptor asume como un agente activo. (p. 0–28)

**effect size** the strength of the relationship between two variables. The larger the effect size, the more one variable can be explained by the other. (p. 0–45)

**tamaño del efecto** magnitud de la relación entre dos variables. Entre mayor sea el tamaño del efecto, más sirve una variable para explicar la otra. (p. 0–45)

**effortful processing** encoding that requires attention and conscious effort. (p. 215)

**procesamiento con esfuerzo** codificación que requiere de atención y esfuerzo conscientes. (p. 215)

**ego** the partly conscious, "executive" part of personality that, according to Freud, mediates among the demands of the id, the superego, and reality. The ego operates on the *reality principle*, satisfying the id's desires in ways that will realistically bring pleasure rather than pain. (p. 530)

**ego** la parte parcialmente consciente y "ejecutiva" de la personalidad que, según Freud, media entre las demandas del ello, el superego y la realidad. El ego opera según el *principio de realidad*, para satisfacer los deseos del id en formas que de manera realista le brindarían placer en lugar de dolor. (p. 530)

**egocentrism** in Piaget's theory, the preoperational child's difficulty taking another's point of view. (p. 351)

**egocentrismo** según la teoría de Piaget, la dificultad de los niños en la etapa preoperacional para aceptar un punto de vista ajeno. (p. 351)

**electroconvulsive therapy (ECT)** a biomedical therapy for severe depression in which a brief electric current is sent through the brain of an anesthetized person. (p. 781)

**terapia electroconvulsiva (TEC)** terapia biomédica para pacientes con depresión severa en la que se envía una corriente eléctrica de corta duración a través del cerebro de una persona anestesiada. (p. 781)

**embodied cognition** the influence of bodily sensations, gestures, and other states on cognitive preferences and judgments. (p. 155)

**cognición incorporada** la influencia de sensaciones del organismo, y otros estados sobre las preferencias y juicios cognitivos. (p. 155)

**emerging adulthood** a period from about age 18 to the mid-twenties, when many persons in Western cultures are no longer adolescents but have not yet achieved full independence as adults. (p. 391)

**madurez emergente** etapa que se extiende desde los 18 hasta alrededor de los 25 años, durante la cual muchas personas en los países occidentales ya no son adolescentes pero aún no han alcanzado la independencia plena de un adulto. (p. 391)

**emotion** a response of the whole organism, involving (1) physiological arousal, (2) expressive behaviors, and, most importantly, (3) conscious experience resulting from one's interpretations. (p. 609)

**emoción** reacción que involucra a todo el organismo e incluye (1) excitación fisiológica, (2) comportamientos expresivos y, sobre todo, (3) la experiencia consciente que resulta de nuestras interpretaciones. (p. 609)

**emotion-focused coping** attempting to alleviate stress by avoiding or ignoring a stressor and attending to emotional needs related to our stress reaction. (p. 654)

**superación con enfoque en las emociones** medidas para sobrellevar las tensiones enfocándose en aliviar o hacer caso omiso de una situación estresante y atender las necesidades emocionales relacionadas con nuestra reacción al estrés. (p. 654)

**emotional intelligence** the ability to perceive, understand, manage, and use emotions. (p. 258)

**inteligencia emocional** capacidad de percibir, entender, administrar y hacer uso de las emociones. (p. 258)

**empirically derived test** a test (such as the MMPI) created by selecting from a pool of items those that discriminate between groups. (p. 552)

**prueba empírica** una prueba (por ejemplo, la MMPI) creada al seleccionar, de un conjunto de elementos, a aquellos que discriminan entre grupos. (p. 552)

**encoding** the process of getting information into the memory system—for example, by extracting meaning. (p. 209)

**codificación** el proceso de ingresar información al sistema de memoria; por ejemplo, mediante la extracción de significado. (p. 209)

**encoding specificity principle** the idea that cues and contexts specific to a particular memory will be most effective in helping us recall it. (p. 233)

**principio de especificidad de codificación** idea según la cual las pistas y los contextos específicos de un recuerdo particular serán las más efectivas para ayudarnos a recordarlo. (p. 233)

**endocrine** [EN-duh-krin] **system** the body's "slow" chemical communication system; a set of glands and fat tissue that secrete hormones into the bloodstream. (p. 35)

**sistema endócrino** sistema "lento" de comunicación química del cuerpo; conjunto de glándulas y tejido graso que secretan hormonas al torrente sanguíneo. (p. 35)

**endorphins** [en-DOR-fins] "morphine within"—natural, opioid-like neurotransmitters linked to pain control and to pleasure. (p. 34)

**endorfinas** "morfina interna"; neurotransmisores naturales similares a los opioides que están asociados con el control del dolor y con el placer. (p. 34)

**environment** every nongenetic influence, from prenatal nutrition to our experiences of the people and things around us. (p. 9)

**entorno** toda influencia externa, desde la alimentación prenatal hasta nuestras experiencias del apoyo social que se recibe más adelante en la vida. (p. 9)

**epigenetics** "above" or "in addition to" (*epi*) genetics; the study of the molecular mechanisms by which environments can influence genetic expression (without a DNA change). (pp. 16, 687)

**epigenética** "encima de" o "además de" (*epi*) genética; estudio de los mecanismos moleculares por los cuales el entorno influye en la expresión genética (sin un cambio en el ADN). (pp. 16, 687)

**episodic memory** explicit memory of personally experienced events; one of our two conscious memory systems (the other is *semantic memory*). (p. 227)

**memoria episódica** memoria explícita de eventos experimentados personalmente. Uno de los dos sistemas de memoria conscientes (el otro es la *memoria semántica*). (p. 227)

**equity** a condition in which people receive from a relationship in proportion to what they give to it. (p. 510)

**equidad** condición en la cual la persona recibe de manera proporcional lo que aporta a una relación. (p. 510)

**estrogens** sex hormones, such as estradiol, that contribute to female sex characteristics and are secreted in greater amounts by females than by males. (p. 325)

**estrógenos** hormonas sexuales, como el estradiol, secretadas en mayor cantidad en la mujer que en el hombre. (p. 325)

**evidence-based practice** clinical decision making that integrates the best available research with clinical expertise and patient characteristics and preferences. (p. 770)

**práctica basada en la evidencia** toma de decisiones clínicas que integra lo mejor de las investigaciones disponibles con la especialización clínica y las características y preferencias del paciente. (p. 770)

**evolutionary psychology** the study of the evolution of behavior and the mind, using principles of natural selection. (p. 5)

**psicología evolutiva** estudio de la evolución del comportamiento y la mente, que emplea los principios de la selección natural. (p. 5)

**executive functions** cognitive skills that work together, enabling us to generate, organize, plan, and implement goal-directed behavior. (p. 193)

**función ejecutiva** habilidades cognitivas que, en conjunto, nos permiten generar, organizar, planificar e implementar comportamientos dirigidos hacia objetivos. (p. 193)

**experiment** a research method in which an investigator manipulates one or more factors (independent variables) to observe the effect on some behavior or mental process (the dependent variable). By *random assignment* of participants, the experimenter aims to control other relevant factors. (p. 0–27)

**experimento** método de investigación en el cual el investigador manipula uno o más factores (variables independientes) para observar su efecto en un comportamiento o proceso mental (variable dependiente). Al ser los participantes *asignados de manera aleatoria*, los investigadores procuran controlar otros factores relevantes. (p. 0–27)

**experimental group** in an experiment, the group exposed to the treatment, that is, to one version of the independent variable. (p. 0–27)

**grupo experimental** sujetos de un experimento que están expuestos al tratamiento, o sea, a una versión de la variable independiente. (p. 0–27)

**experimenter bias** bias caused when researchers may unintentionally influence results to confirm their own beliefs. (p. 0–28)

**sesgo del experimentador** variable de confusión en la investigación que se produce cuando los investigadores pueden influir involuntariamente en los resultados para confirmar sus propias creencias. (p. 0–28)

**explicit memory** retention of facts and experiences that we can consciously know and "declare." (Also called *declarative memory*.) (p. 215)

**memoria explícita** retención de hechos y vivencias personales que tenemos la capacidad de reconocer y "expresar" conscientemente. También se le dice *memoria declarativa*. (p. 215)

**exposure therapies** behavioral techniques, such as *systematic desensitization* and *virtual reality exposure therapy*, that treat anxieties by exposing people (in imaginary or actual situations) to the things they fear and avoid. (p. 754)

**terapias de exposición** técnicas conductuales, como la *desensibilización sistemática* y la *terapia de exposición a una realidad virtual* para tratar la ansiedad exponiendo a la persona (en situaciones imaginarias o reales) a las cosas que teme y evita. (p. 754)

**external locus of control** the perception that outside forces beyond our personal control determine our fate. (p. 656)

**centro de control externo** impresión de que nuestro destino está determinado por fuerzas que están más allá de nuestro control. (p. 656)

**extinction** in classical conditioning, the diminishing of a conditioned response when an unconditioned stimulus does not follow a conditioned stimulus. (In operant conditioning, when a response is no longer reinforced.) (p. 406)

**extinción** en el condicionamiento clásico, la disminución de una respuesta condicionada cuando un estímulo incondicionado no sigue a un estímulo condicionado. (En el condicionamiento operante, cuando una respuesta ya no se refuerza). (p. 406)

**extrinsic motivation** the desire to perform a behavior to receive promised rewards or avoid threatened punishment. (p. 587)

**motivación extrínseca** deseo de llevar a cabo un comportamiento para obtener una recompensa o evitar el castigo. (p. 587)

# F

**facial feedback effect** the tendency of facial muscle states to trigger corresponding feelings such as fear, anger, or happiness. (p. 626)

**efecto de reacción facial** tendencia de los músculos faciales a provocar sentimientos correspondientes como el miedo, el enojo o la felicidad. (p. 626)

**factor analysis** a statistical procedure that identifies clusters of related items (called factors) on a test; used to identify different dimensions of performance that underlie a person's total score. (p. 255)

**análisis de factores** procedimiento estadístico que identifica conjuntos de artículos relacionados (conocidos como factores) en una prueba; se usa para identificar distintas dimensiones del desempeño que subyace el puntaje total de una persona. (p. 255)

**falsifiable** the possibility that an idea, hypothesis, or theory can be disproven by observation or experiment. (p. 0–14)

**falsificable** posibilidad de que una idea, hipótesis o teoría pueda ser refutada mediante la observación o experimentación. (p. 0–14)

**family therapy** therapy that treats people in the context of their family system. Views an individual's unwanted behaviors as influenced by, or directed at, other family members. (p. 762)

**terapia de familia** tipo de terapia que trata a las personas en el contexto de su sistema familiar. Esta terapia considera que los comportamientos no deseados de una persona son influenciados por otros miembros de la familia o están dirigidos hacia ellos. (p. 762)

**feature detectors** nerve cells in the brain's visual cortex that respond to specific features of the stimulus, such as shape, angle, or movement. (p. 130)

**detectores específicos** células nerviosas del cerebro que responden a características específicas de un estímulo, como las formas, los ángulos y el movimiento. (p. 130)

**feeding and eating disorders** a group of disorders characterized by altered consumption or absorption of food that impairs health or psychological functioning. (Feeding disorders typically occur in infants and young children, whereas eating disorders affect people who self-feed.) (p. 735)

**trastornos alimenticios** grupo de trastornos caracterizados por el consumo o absorción alterados de alimentos que afecta la salud o el funcionamiento psicológico. (Ciertos trastornos ocurren en infantes y niños pequeños que reciben alimentación, mientras que otros afectan a personas que se alimentan a sí mismas). (p. 735)

**feel-good, do-good phenomenon** people's tendency to be helpful when in a good mood. (p. 664)

**fenómeno de sentirse bien y hacer el bien** tendencia a ayudar a los demás cuando estamos de buen humor. (p. 664)

**fetal alcohol syndrome (FAS)** physical and cognitive function deficits in children caused by their birth mother's heavy drinking during pregnancy. In severe cases, symptoms include a small, out-of-proportion head and distinct facial features. (p. 304)

**síndrome de alcoholismo fetal (SAF)** déficits funcionales físicos y cognitivos en los niños causadas por la intensa ingestión de alcohol de la madre biológica durante el embarazo. En casos agudos, los síntomas incluyen desproporciones en el tamaño de la cabeza, que puede ser demasiado pequeña y rasgos faciales distintivos. (p. 304)

**figure-ground** the organization of the visual field into objects (the *figures*) that stand out from their surroundings (the *ground*). (p. 175)

**figura-trasfondo** organización del campo visual en objetos (*las figuras*) que se distinguen de sus entornos (*los trasfondos*). (p. 175)

**fixation** in cognition, the inability to see a problem from a new perspective; an obstacle to problem solving. (p. 195)

**fijación** en términos cognitivos la incapacidad de ver un problema desde una perspectiva nueva; un impedimento para resolver problemas. (p. 195)

**fixed mindset** the view that intelligence, abilities, and talents are unchangeable, even with effort. (p. 278)

**mentalidad fija** la creencia de que la inteligencia, las habilidades y los talentos no cambian, incluso con esfuerzo. (p. 278)

**fixed-interval schedule** in operant conditioning, a reinforcement schedule that reinforces a response only after a specified time has elapsed. (p. 423)

**cronograma de intervalo fijo** según el condicionamiento operante, cronograma de reforzamiento que refuerza la respuesta solo después de haber transcurrido un tiempo específico. (p. 423)

**fixed-ratio schedule** in operant conditioning, a reinforcement schedule that reinforces a response only after a specified number of responses. (p. 422)

**flashbulb memory** a clear memory of an emotionally significant moment or event. (p. 229)

**flow** a completely involved, focused state, with diminished awareness of self and time; results from full engagement of our skills. (p. 805)

**fluid intelligence** *(Gf)* our ability to reason speedily and abstractly; tends to decrease with age, especially during late adulthood. (p. 255)

**Flynn effect** the rise in intelligence test performance over time and across cultures. (p. 266)

**fMRI (functional MRI)** a technique for revealing blood flow and, therefore, brain activity by comparing successive MRI scans. fMRI scans show brain function as well as structure. (p. 59)

**foot-in-the-door phenomenon** the tendency for people who have first agreed to a small request to comply later with a larger request. (p. 469)

**forebrain** consists of the cerebral cortex, thalamus, and hypothalamus; manages complex cognitive activities, sensory and associative functions, and voluntary motor activities. (p. 65)

**formal operational stage** in Piaget's theory, the stage of cognitive development (normally beginning about age 12) at which people begin to think logically about abstract concepts. (p. 352)

**fovea** the central focal point in the retina, around which the eye's cones cluster. (p. 127)

**framing** the way an issue is posed; how an issue is framed can significantly affect decisions and judgments. (p. 200)

**fraternal (dizygotic) twins** individuals who developed from separate fertilized eggs. They are genetically no closer than ordinary siblings, but they share a prenatal environment. (p. 12)

**free association** in psychoanalysis, a method of exploring the unconscious in which the person relaxes and says whatever comes to mind, no matter how trivial or embarrassing. (p. 529)

**frequency** the number of complete wavelengths that pass a point in a given time (for example, per second). (p. 136)

**frequency theory** in hearing, the theory that the rate of nerve impulses traveling up the auditory nerve matches the frequency of a tone, thus enabling us to sense its pitch. (Also called *temporal coding.*) (p. 140)

**frontal lobes** the portion of the cerebral cortex lying just behind the forehead. They enable linguistic processing, muscle movements, higher-order thinking, and executive functioning (such as making plans and judgments). (p. 71)

**frustration-aggression principle** the principle that frustration—the blocking of an attempt to achieve some goal—creates anger, which can generate aggression. (p. 498)

**fundamental attribution error** the tendency for observers, when analyzing others' behavior, to underestimate the impact of the situation and to overestimate the impact of personal disposition. (p. 454)

**cronograma de proporción fija** según el condicionamiento operante, cronograma de reforzamiento que refuerza la respuesta solo después de darse un número específico de respuestas. (p. 422)

**memoria de flash** memoria clara de un momento o evento emocionalmente significativo. (p. 229)

**flujo** estado pleno de concentración con reducción de percepción de uno mismo y del tiempo; es el resultado de emplear plenamente nuestras habilidades. (p. 805)

**inteligencia fluida** *(Gf)* nuestra capacidad para razonar de manera rápida y abstracta; tiende a disminuir con la edad, especialmente en la vejez. (p. 255)

**efecto Flynn** aumento de rendimiento en pruebas de inteligencia a lo largo del tiempo y entre culturas. (p. 266)

**IRMf (imagen de resonancia magnética funcional)** técnica para observar la circulación de la sangre y, por lo tanto, la actividad cerebral mediante la comparación de imágenes de resonancia magnética sucesivas. Las imágenes de resonancia magnética funcional muestran el funcionamiento del cerebro. (p. 59)

**fenómeno del pie en la puerta** tendencia de la gente a acceder primero a una solicitud menor para después acceder a una solicitud más significativa. (p. 469)

**prosencéfalo** consiste en la corteza cerebral, el tálamo y el hipotálamo; controla actividades cognitivas complejas, funciones sensoriales y asociativas y actividades voluntarias motrices. (p. 65)

**período operacional formal** en la teoría de Piaget, el período en el desarrollo cognitivo (normalmente empieza a los 12 años) en el que la persona empieza a pensar lógicamente sobre conceptos abstractos. (p. 352)

**fovea** el punto central de enfoque en la retina, alrededor del cuál se agrupan los conos del ojo. (p. 127)

**encuadre** forma en que se presenta un asunto; el encuadre puede influir considerablemente en las decisiones y las opiniones. (p. 200)

**gemelos fraternos (dizigóticos)** individuos que se desarrollaron de dos óvulos fecundados. Genéticamente no son más cercanos que hermanos comunes, pero comparten un entorno prenatal. (p. 12)

**asociación libre** en psicoanálisis, método de explorar el inconsciente en el que la persona se relaja y dice lo primero que le viene a la mente, sin importar si es poco importante o incómodo. (p. 529)

**frecuencia** número de ondas completas que pasan un punto en un tiempo dado (por ejemplo, por segundo). (p. 136)

**teoría de frecuencia** en la audición, teoría según la cual la velocidad de los impulsos que viajan por el nervio auditivo coincide con la frecuencia de un tono, lo cual nos permite percibir su altura. (También conocida como *codificación temporal*). (p. 140)

**lóbulos frontales** porción de la corteza cerebral que se halla inmediatamente detrás de la frente. Permiten el procesamiento lingüístico, los movimientos musculares, el pensamiento de orden superior y el funcionamiento ejecutivo (como hacer planes y formar juicios). (p. 71)

**principio de frustración-agresión** principio según el cual la frustración—el bloqueo de un intento para lograr alguna meta—crea ira, y por consecuencia puede generar agresión. (p. 498)

**error de atribución fundamental** tendencia de los observadores, cuando analizan el comportamiento ajeno, a sobrestimar el impacto de la situación y sobreestimar el impacto de la disposición personal. (p. 454)

**gate-control theory** the theory that the spinal cord contains a neurological "gate" that blocks pain signals or allows them to pass on to the brain. The "gate" is opened by the activity of pain signals traveling up small nerve fibers and is closed by activity in larger fibers or by information coming from the brain. (p. 145)

**gender** in psychology, the attitudes, feelings, and behaviors that a given culture associates with a person's biological sex. (*See also gender identity.*) (p. 320)

**gender identity** our personal sense of being male, female, neither, or some combination of male and female, regardless of whether this identity matches our sex assigned at birth, and the social affiliation that may result from this identity. (p. 329)

**gender role** a set of expected behaviors, attitudes, and traits for men and for women. (p. 328)

**gender typing** the acquisition of a traditional masculine or feminine role. (p. 329)

**general adaptation syndrome (GAS)** Selye's concept of the body's adaptive response to stress in three phases—alarm, resistance, exhaustion. (p. 645)

**general intelligence (g)** according to Spearman and others, underlies all mental abilities and is therefore measured by every task on an intelligence test. (p. 255)

**generalization** (also called *stimulus generalization*) in classical conditioning, the tendency, once a response has been conditioned, for stimuli similar to the conditioned stimulus to elicit similar responses. (In operant conditioning, when responses learned in one situation occur in other, similar situations.) (p. 407)

**generalized anxiety disorder** an anxiety disorder in which a person is continually tense, apprehensive, and in a state of autonomic nervous system arousal. (p. 700)

**genes** the biochemical units of heredity. (p. 9)

**genome** the complete instructions for making an organism. (p. 9)

**gestalt** an organized whole. Gestalt psychologists emphasized our tendency to integrate pieces of information into meaningful wholes. (p. 174)

**glial cells (glia)** cells in the nervous system that support, nourish, and protect neurons; they may also play a role in learning, thinking, and memory. (p. 29)

**glucose** the form of sugar that circulates in the blood and provides the major source of energy for body tissues. When its level is low, we feel hunger. (p. 600)

**grammar** in a language, a system of rules that enables us to communicate with and understand others. Semantics is the language's set of rules for deriving meaning from sounds, and syntax is its set of rules for combining words into grammatically sensible sentences. (p. 364)

**gratitude** an appreciative emotion people often experience when they benefit from other's actions or recognize their own good fortune. (p. 678)

**grit** in psychology, passion and perseverance in the pursuit of long-term goals. (pp. 258, 294)

**teoría de la compuerta** teoría según la cual la médula espinal contiene una "compuerta neurológica" que bloquea señales de dolor o permite que lleguen al cerebro. La "compuerta" se abre con la actividad de señales de dolor que viajan por fibras nerviosas pequeñas y se cierra con la actividad de fibras más grandes o con información que llega del cerebro. (p. 145)

**género** en psicología, las actitudes, sentimientos y comportamientos que una determinada cultura asocia con el sexo biológico de una persona. (Ver también *identidad de género*). (p. 320)

**identidad de género** nuestro sentido personal de ser hombre, mujer, ninguno/a o alguna combinación de masculino y femenino, independientemente de si esta identidad coincide con nuestro sexo asignado al nacer, y la afiliación social que puede resultar de esta identidad. (p. 329)

**papel de género** conjunto de expectativas, actitudes y rasgos de cómo las mujeres y los hombres deben ser o comportarse. (p. 328)

**tipificación de género** adquisición de un papel tradicional masculino o femenino. (p. 329)

**síndrome de adaptación general** término usado por Selye para referirse a la respuesta adaptativa del cuerpo ante estrés, que se da en tres etapas: alarma, resistencia y agotamiento. (p. 645)

**factor g de inteligencia general** según Spearman y otros, subyace todas las habilidades mentales específicas y es, por tanto, cuantificado por cada función en una prueba de inteligencia. (p. 255)

**generalización** (también conocida como generalización de estímulos) según el condicionamiento clásico, tendencia posterior al condicionamiento, de responder de manera similar a los estímulos que se parecen al estímulo condicionado. (En el condicionamiento operante, cuando se refuerzan también las respuestas a estímulos similares.) (p. 407)

**trastorno de ansiedad general** trastorno de ansiedad en el cual una persona está constantemente tensa, asustada y con el sistema nervioso autónomo activado. (p. 700)

**genes** unidades bioquímicas de la herencia. (p. 9)

**genoma** instrucciones completas para crear un organismo. (p. 9)

**Gestalt** un todo organizado. Los psicólogos de la Gestalt enfatizan nuestra tendencia a integrar segmentos de información en organismos únicos significativos. (p. 174)

**células gliales** células del sistema nervioso que apoyan, alimentan y protegen a las neuronas; también pueden desempeñar un papel en el aprendizaje, el razonamiento y la memoria. (p. 29)

**glucosa** forma de azúcar que circula en la sangre y es la mayor fuente de energía para los tejidos del cuerpo. Cuando baja su nivel, sentimos hambre. (p. 600)

**grammar** en un lenguaje, un sistema de reglas que nos permite comunicarnos y entender a los demás. La semántica es el conjunto de reglas del lenguaje para derivar el significado a partir de los sonidos, y la sintaxis es su conjunto de reglas para combinar palabras en frases gramaticalmente correctas. (p. 364)

**gratitud** emoción apreciativa que las personas experimentan cuando se benefician de las acciones de otros o reconocen su buena fortuna. (p. 678)

**determinación** en la psicología, "determinación" se refiere a la pasión y perseverancia en la búsqueda de metas a largo plazo. (pp. 258, 294)

**GRIT** Graduated and Reciprocated Initiatives in Tension-Reduction—a strategy designed to decrease international tensions. (p. 521)

**GRIT** (Iniciativas Graduadas y Recíprocas en Reducción de Tensión)— estrategia diseñada para reducir tensiones internacionales. (p. 521)

**group polarization** the enhancement of a group's prevailing inclinations through discussion within the group. (p. 489)

**efecto de polarización de grupo** solidificación y fortalecimiento de las posiciones imperantes en un grupo mediante diálogos en el grupo. (p. 489)

**group therapy** therapy conducted with groups rather than individuals, providing benefits from group interaction. (p. 762)

**terapia de grupo** tratamiento que se realiza con grupos en lugar de con personas individuales, y que genera beneficios de la interacción del grupo. (p. 762)

**grouping** the perceptual tendency to organize stimuli into coherent groups. (p. 175)

**agrupamiento** tendencia de percepción que clasifica los estímulos en grupos que tienen sentido. (p. 175)

**groupthink** the mode of thinking that occurs when the desire for harmony in a decision-making group overrides a realistic appraisal of alternatives. (p. 491)

**pensamiento colectivo** modo de pensar que ocurre cuando el deseo de armonía en un grupo que toma de decisiones colectivas anula la evaluación objetiva de las alternativas. (p. 491)

**growth mindset** a focus on learning and growing rather than viewing abilities as fixed. (p. 278)

**mentalidad de crecimiento** enfoque que se basa en aprender y crecer en lugar de considerar que las habilidades son algo fijo. (p. 278)

**gustation** our sense of taste. (p. 148)

**gustación** nuestro sentido del gusto. (p. 148)

# H

**habituation** decreasing responsiveness with repeated stimulation. As infants gain familiarity with repeated exposure to a stimulus, their interest wanes and they look away sooner. (pp. 305, 401)

**aclimatación** reducir el nivel de respuesta ante estimulación repetitiva. A medida que los bebés se familiarizan con la exposición repetida a un estímulo, su interés disminuye y desvían la mirada más rápidamente. (pp. 305, 401)

**hallucinations** false sensory experiences, such as seeing something in the absence of an external visual stimulus. (p. 96)

**alucinaciones** vivencia sensorial falsa, por ejemplo, cuando una persona ve algo sin haber ningún estímulo visual externo. (p. 96)

**hallucinogens** psychedelic ("mind-manifesting") drugs that distort perceptions and evoke sensory images in the absence of sensory input. (p. 50)

**alucinógenos** fármacos psicodélicos ("que se manifiestan en la mente") que distorsionan las percepciones y desencadenan imágenes sensoriales sin la intervención de estímulos sensoriales. (p. 50)

**health psychology** a subfield of psychology that explores the impact of psychological, behavioral, and cultural factors on health and wellness. (p. 638)

**psicología de la salud** área de la psicología que explora el impacto de los factores psicológicos, conductuales y culturales en la salud y el bienestar. (p. 638)

**heredity** the genetic transfer of characteristics from parents to offspring. (p. 9)

**herencia** transferencia genética de rasgos de padres a descendientes. (p. 9)

**heuristic** a simple thinking strategy—a mental shortcut—that often allows us to make judgments and solve problems efficiently; usually speedier but also more error-prone than an *algorithm*. (p. 193)

**heurística** estrategia de pensamiento sencilla—(un atajo mental)—que a menudo nos permite formar juicios y resolver problemas de manera eficiente; en general es más expedita que utilizar *algoritmos*, pero también hay mayor propensión a errores. (p. 193)

**hierarchy of needs** Maslow's levels of human needs, beginning at the base with physiological need. Often visualized as a pyramid, with needs nearer the base taking priority until they are satisfied. (p. 542)

**jerarquía de necesidades** los niveles de Maslow de las necesidades humanas comienza con las necesidades fisiológicas. Frecuentemente representada como una pirámide, donde las necesidades más próximas a la base son prioridad hasta ser satisfechas. (p. 542)

**higher-order conditioning** a procedure in which the conditioned stimulus in one conditioning experience is paired with a new neutral stimulus, creating a second (often weaker) conditioned stimulus. For example, an animal that has learned that a tone predicts food might then learn that a light predicts the tone and begin responding to the light alone. (Also called *second-order conditioning*.) (p. 406)

**condicionamiento de orden superior** procedimiento donde se junta un estímulo condicionado de una experiencia de condicionamiento con un estímulo neutral, que crea un segundo estímulo condicionado (en general menos fuerte). Por ejemplo, un animal que ha aprendido que cierto timbre predice la llegada de comida, podría aprender también que hay una luz que predice el tono y entonces responder nada más a la luz. (También conocido como *condicionamiento de segundo orden*). (p. 406)

**hindbrain** consists of the medulla, pons, and cerebellum; directs essential survival functions, such as breathing, sleeping, and wakefulness, as well as coordination and balance. (p. 63)

**rombencéfalo** consiste en la médula, la protuberancia y el cerebelo; dirige funciones esenciales de supervivencia como la respiración, el sueño y la vigilia, además de la coordinación y el equilibrio. (p. 63)

**hindsight bias** the tendency to believe, after learning an outcome, that one would have foreseen it. (Also known as the *I-knew-it-all-along phenomenon*.) (p. 0–10)

**distorsión retrospectiva** tendencia a creer, al enterarse de un resultado, que uno lo pudo haber previsto. (También conocido como el fenómeno de *yo ya lo sabía*). (p. 0–10)

**hippocampus** a neural center located in the limbic system; helps process explicit (conscious) memories—of facts and events—for storage. (pp. 68, 227)

**hipocampo** centro neuronal ubicado en el sistema límbico; ayuda a procesar recuerdos explícitos (conscientes) de hechos y eventos para almacenarlos de manera accesible. (pp. 68, 227)

**histogram** a bar graph depicting a frequency distribution. (p. 0–41)

**histograma** gráfica de barras que muestra una distribución de frecuencias. (p. 0–41)

**hoarding disorder** a persistent difficulty parting with possessions, regardless of their value. (p. 703)

**síndrome de acumulación compulsiva** dificultad continua para deshacerse de cosas que se tienen, sin que importe su valor. (p. 703)

**homeostasis** a tendency to maintain a balanced or constant internal state; the regulation of any aspect of body chemistry, such as blood glucose, around a particular level. (p. 580)

**homeostasis** tendencia a mantener un estado interno constante o equilibrado; la regulación de todos los aspectos de la química del organismo, tal como los niveles de glucosa, alrededor de un nivel particular. (p. 580)

**hormones** chemical messengers that are manufactured by the endocrine glands, travel through the bloodstream, and affect other tissues. (p. 36)

**hormonas** mensajeros químicos producidos por las glándulas endocrinas, que circulan por la sangre y tienen efecto en los tejidos del cuerpo. (p. 36)

**hue** the dimension of color that is determined by the wavelength of light; what we know as the color names *blue, green*, and so forth. (p. 124)

**tono** dimensión del color determinada por la longitud de la onda de luz; lo que conocemos como los nombres de los colores: *azul, verde*, etc. (p. 124)

**human factors psychology** a field of psychology allied with I/O psychology that explores how people and machines interact and how machines and physical environments can be made safe and easy to use. (p. 808)

**psicología de factores humanos** división de la psicología relacionada con la psicología I/O que explora la interacción entre las personas y las máquinas, y las maneras de hacer que las máquinas y los entornos físicos sean más seguros y fáciles de utilizar. (p. 808)

**humanistic theories** theories that view personality with a focus on the potential for healthy personal growth. (p. 542)

**teorías humanistas** teorías que perciben a la personalidad con un enfoque sobre el potencial para un crecimiento personal saludable. (p. 542)

**hypnagogic sensations** bizarre experiences, such as jerking or a feeling of falling or floating weightlessly, while transitioning to sleep. (Also called *hypnic sensations*.) (p. 96)

**sensaciones hipnagógicas** experiencias extrañas, como sacudirse o una sensación de caer o flotar de manera ligera, mientras uno transita hacia el sueño. (También conocidas como *sensaciones hípnicas*). (p. 96)

**hypnosis** a social interaction in which one person (the hypnotist) suggests to another (the subject) that certain perceptions, feelings, thoughts, or behaviors will spontaneously occur; in a therapeutic context, the hypnotist attempts to use suggestion to reduce unpleasant physical sensations or emotions. (p. 784)

**hipnosis** interacción social en la cual una persona (el hipnotizador) le sugiere a otra persona (el sujeto) que ciertas percepciones, sentimientos, pensamientos o comportamientos se producirán espontáneamente; en un contexto terapéutico, el hipnotista prueba la sugestión para reducir sensaciones físicas desagradables o emociones. (p. 784)

**hypothalamus** [hi-po-THAL-uh-muss] a limbic system neural structure lying below (*hypo*) the thalamus; it directs several maintenance activities (eating, drinking, body temperature), helps govern the endocrine system, and is linked to emotion and reward. (p. 67)

**hipotálamo** estructura neuronal del sistema límbico localizada debajo (*hipo*) del tálamo; regula actividades como comer, beber, y la temperatura del cuerpo; dirige varias actividades de mantenimiento (comer, beber, temperatura corporal); ayuda a dirigir el sistema endocrino, y está conectado a las emociones y las recompensas. (p. 67)

**hypothesis** a testable prediction, often implied by a theory. (p. 0–14)

**hipótesis** predicción comprobable, a menudo implicada por una teoría. (p. 0–14)

# I

**iconic memory** a momentary sensory memory of visual stimuli; a photographic or picture-image memory lasting no more than a few tenths of a second. (p. 216)

**memoria icónica** recuerdo sensorial momentáneo de un estímulo visual; una memoria fotográfica o un recuerdo parecido a una fotografía que dura no más de algunas décimas de segundo. (p. 216)

**id** a reservoir of unconscious psychic energy that, according to Freud, strives to satisfy basic sexual and aggressive drives. The id operates on the *pleasure principle*, demanding immediate gratification. (p. 530)

**id** depósito de energía psíquica inconsciente que, según Freud, busca satisfacer los impulsos sexuales y agresivos esenciales. El id funciona de acuerdo al *principio del placer*, exigiendo satisfacción inmediata. (p. 530)

**identical (monozygotic) twins** individuals who developed from a single fertilized egg that split in two, creating two genetically identical organisms. (p. 11)

**gemelos idénticos (monozigóticos)** individuos que se desarrollaron de un solo óvulo fertilizado que se subdivide en dos para así crear dos organismos genéticamente idénticos. (p. 11)

**identity** our sense of self; according to Erikson, the adolescent's task is to solidify a sense of self by testing and integrating various roles. (p. 386)

**identidad** sentido de autorreconocimiento; según Erikson, la tarea del adolescente consiste en solidificar su sentido de sí mismo probando e integrando una variedad de papeles. (p. 386)

**illusory correlation** perceiving a relationship where none exists, or perceiving a stronger-than-actual relationship. (p. 0–26)

**correlación ilusoria** percibir una relación donde no la hay, o percibir una relación más fuerte de la que sí existe. (p. 0–26)

**implicit memory** retention of learned skills or classically conditioned associations independent of conscious recollection. (Also called *nondeclarative memory*.) (p. 215)

**memoria implícita** retención de habilidades aprendidas o asociaciones condicionadas clásicas, sin tener consciencia del aprendizaje. (También se le dice *memoria no declarativa*). (p. 215)

**imprinting** the process by which certain animals form strong attachments during early life. (p. 375)

**inattentional blindness** failing to see visible objects when our attention is directed elsewhere. (p. 167)

**incentive** a positive or negative environmental stimulus that motivates behavior. (p. 581)

**independent variable** in an experiment, the factor that is manipulated; the variable whose effect is being studied. (p. 0–28)

**individualism** a cultural pattern that emphasizes people's own goals over group goals and defines identity mainly in terms of unique personal attributes. (p. 573)

**industrial-organizational (I/O) psychology** the application of psychological concepts and methods to optimizing human behavior in workplaces. (p. 807)

**inferential statistics** numerical data that allow one to generalize—to infer from sample data the probability of something being true of a population. (p. 0–44)

**informational social influence** influence resulting from a person's willingness to accept others' opinions about reality. (p. 478)

**informed consent** giving potential participants enough information about a study to enable them to choose whether they wish to participate. (p. 0–35)

**ingroup** "us"—people with whom we share a common identity. (p. 462)

**ingroup bias** the tendency to favor our own group. (p. 462)

**inner ear** the innermost part of the ear, containing the cochlea, semicircular canals, and vestibular sacs. (p. 137)

**insecure attachment** demonstrated by infants who display either a clinging, *anxious attachment* or an *avoidant attachment* that resists closeness. (p. 376)

**insight** a sudden realization of a problem's solution; contrasts with strategy-based solutions. (p. 194)

**insight learning** solving problems through sudden insight; contrasts with strategy-based solutions. (p. 436)

**insight therapies** therapies that aim to improve psychological functioning by increasing a person's awareness of underlying motives and defenses. (p. 748)

**insomnia** recurring problems in falling or staying asleep. (p. 107)

**instinct** a complex behavior that is rigidly patterned throughout a species and is unlearned. (p. 580)

**instinctive drift** the tendency of learned behavior to gradually revert to biologically predisposed patterns. (p. 431)

**intelligence** the ability to learn from experience, solve problems, and use knowledge to adapt to new situations. (p. 254)

**impronta** proceso mediante el cual ciertos animales forman lazos fuertes desde el inicio de sus vidas. (p. 375)

**ceguera por falta de atención** incapacidad para ver objetos visibles cuando nuestra atención se dirige a otra parte. (p. 167)

**incentivo** estímulo positivo o negativo del entorno que motiva el comportamiento. (p. 581)

**variable independiente** factor que se manipula en un experimento; la variable cuyo efecto es el objeto de estudio. (p. 0–28)

**individualismo** patrón cultural que destaca las metas personales sobre las metas del grupo, y patrón cultural que destaca la identidad propia principalmente a través de cualidades personales únicas. (p. 573)

**psicología industrial y organizacional (I/O)** aplicación de conceptos y métodos psicológicos al comportamiento humano en el entorno laboral. (p. 807)

**estadística inferencial** datos numéricos que permiten generalizar—o inferir a partir de los datos de una muestra—la probabilidad de que algo sea verdadero dentro de una población. (p. 0–44)

**influencia social informativa** influencia resultante de la disposición de una persona a aceptar las opiniones de otros acerca de la realidad. (p. 478)

**consentimiento informado** dar a las personas información suficiente sobre un estudio para permitirles decidir si desean o no participar. (p. 0–35)

**endogrupo** "nosotros"; personas con quienes uno comparte una identidad común. (p. 462)

**estereotipo de grupo propio** tendencia a favorecer al grupo al que se pertenece. (p. 462)

**oído interno** parte más interna del oído; contiene la cóclea, los canales semicirculares y los sacos vestibulares. (p. 137)

**apego inseguro** comportamiento de infantes muestran un *apego ansioso* aferrado o un *apego evasivo* que evita la cercanía. (p. 376)

**agudeza** entendimiento repentino de cómo se resuelve un problema; contrasta con las soluciones basadas en estrategias. (p. 194)

**aprendizaje perspicaz** resolver problemas a partir de una percepción repentina; contrasta con las soluciones basadas en estrategias. (p. 436)

**tratamientos con agudeza** terapias que aspiran a mejorar el funcionamiento psicológico mediante el aumento en la conciencia de la persona de los motivos y las defensas subyacentes. (p. 748)

**insomnio** dificultades recurrentes para quedarse dormido o conciliar el sueño. (p. 107)

**instinto** comportamiento complejo rígidamente arraigado a una especie y que no es aprendido. (p. 580)

**deriva instintiva** tendencia de los aprendizajes aprendidos a revertirse gradualmente a patrones biológicos predispuestos. (p. 431)

**inteligencia** capacidad de aprender de las experiencias, de resolver problemas y de utilizar el conocimiento para adaptarse a situaciones nuevas. (p. 254)

| | |
|---|---|
| **intelligence quotient (IQ)** defined originally as the ratio of mental age (*ma*) to chronological age (*ca*) multiplied by 100 (thus, IQ = *ma/ca* × 100). On contemporary intelligence tests, the average performance for a given age is assigned a score of 100. (p. 264) | **coeficiente intelectual (CI)** cifra definida originalmente como la edad mental (*em*) dividida entre la edad cronológica (*ec*) y el resultado multiplicado por 100 (por lo tanto, CI = *em/ec* × 100). En las pruebas actuales de inteligencia, al desempeño promedio en una prueba de inteligencia se le asigna un puntaje de 100. (p. 264) |
| **intelligence test** a method for assessing an individual's mental aptitudes and comparing them with those of others, using numerical scores. (p. 262) | **prueba de inteligencia** método para evaluar las aptitudes mentales de los individuos y compararlas con las de otros a través de puntajes numéricos. (p. 262) |
| **intensity** the amount of energy in a light wave or sound wave, which influences what we perceive as brightness or loudness. Intensity is determined by the wave's amplitude (height). (p. 124) | **intensidad** cantidad de energía en una onda de luz o en una onda sonora que percibimos como brillo o volumen. La intensidad la determina la amplitud (altura) de la onda. (p. 124) |
| **interaction** the interplay that occurs when the effect of one factor (such as environment) depends on another factor (such as heredity). (p. 15) | **interacción** la situación que se produce cuando el efecto de un factor (por ejemplo, el entorno) depende de otro factor (por ejemplo, la herencia). (p. 15) |
| **interleaving** a retrieval practice strategy that involves mixing the study of different topics. (p. 235) | **intercalar** estrategia de práctica de recuperación que consiste en mezclar el estudio de diferentes temas. (p. 235) |
| **internal locus of control** the perception that we control our own fate. (p. 656) | **foco de control interno** impresión de que controlamos nuestro propio destino. (p. 656) |
| **interneurons** neurons within the brain and spinal cord; they communicate internally and process information between the sensory inputs and motor outputs. (p. 22) | **interneuronas** neuronas ubicadas dentro del cerebro y la médula espinal. Se comunican internamente y procesan la información entre los estímulos sensoriales y las respuestas motoras. (p. 22) |
| **interpretation** in psychoanalysis, the analyst's noting of supposed dream meanings, resistances, and other significant behaviors and events in order to promote insight. (p. 747) | **interpretación** en psicoanálisis, las observaciones del analista con relación al significado de los sueños, las resistencias, y otras conductas y eventos significativos, a fin de promover la sagacidad. (p. 747) |
| **intersex** possessing male and female biological sexual characteristics at birth. (p. 321) | **intersexo** poseer características biológicas sexuales masculinas y femeninas al nacer. (p. 321) |
| **intimacy** in Erikson's theory, the ability to form close, loving relationships; a primary developmental task in young adulthood. (p. 388) | **intimidad** según la teoría de Erikson, la capacidad de formar relaciones amorosas cercanas; una de las principales funciones de desarrollo en la adultez temprana. (p. 388) |
| **intrinsic motivation** the desire to perform a behavior effectively for its own sake. (p. 587) | **motivación intrínseca** deseo de realizar una conducta de manera adecuada simplemente por la mera satisfacción de hacerlo bien. (p. 587) |
| **intuition** an effortless, immediate, automatic feeling or thought, as contrasted with explicit, conscious reasoning. (p. 195) | **intuición** sentimiento o pensamiento automático e inmediato, que no precisa esfuerzo alguno, que se contrasta con el razonamiento explícito y consciente. (p. 195) |
| **iris** a ring of muscle tissue that forms the colored portion of the eye around the pupil and controls the size of the pupil opening. (p. 124) | **iris** tejido musculoso en forma de aro que forma la sección colorida de los ojos alrededor de la pupila y controla el tamaño de la apertura de la pupila. (p. 124) |

## J

| | |
|---|---|
| **just-world phenomenon** the tendency for people to believe the world is just and that people therefore get what they deserve and deserve what they get. (p. 461) | **fenómeno del "mundo justo"** tendencia a creer que el mundo es justo y que por tanto, las personas obtienen lo que se merecen y se merecen lo que obtienen. (p. 461) |

## K

| | |
|---|---|
| **kinesthesis** [kin-ehs-THEE-sis] our movement sense—our system for sensing the position and movement of individual body parts. (p. 152) | **cinestesia** nuestro sentido del movimiento; nuestro sistema para sentir la posición y movimiento de partes individuales del cuerpo. (p. 152) |

## L

| | |
|---|---|
| **language** our agreed-upon systems of spoken, written, or signed words and the ways we combine them to communicate meaning. (p. 363) | **lenguaje** palabras habladas, escritas o en señas y las maneras acordadas que se combinan para comunicar significado. (p. 363) |
| **latent learning** learning that occurs but is not apparent until there is an incentive to demonstrate it. (p. 436) | **aprendizaje latente** aprendizaje que no es aparente sino hasta que hay un incentivo para demostrarlo. (p. 436) |

**law of effect** Thorndike's principle that behaviors followed by favorable (or *reinforcing*) consequences become more likely, and that behaviors followed by unfavorable (or *punishing*) consequences become less likely. (p. 417)

**leadership** an individual's ability to motivate and influence others to contribute to their group's success. (p. 813)

**learned helplessness** the hopelessness and passive resignation humans and other animals learn when unable to avoid repeated aversive events. (p. 655)

**learning** the process of acquiring through experience new and relatively enduring information or behaviors. (p. 400)

**lens** the transparent structure behind the pupil that changes shape to help focus images on the retina. (p. 125)

**lesion** [LEE-zhuhn] tissue destruction. Brain lesions may occur naturally (from disease or trauma), during surgery, or experimentally (using electrodes to destroy brain cells). (p. 58)

**levels of analysis** the differing complementary views, from biological to psychological to social-cultural, for analyzing any given phenomenon. (p. 56)

**limbic system** neural system located mostly in the forebrain—below the cerebral hemispheres—that includes the *amygdala, hypothalamus, hippocampus, thalamus,* and *pituitary gland;* associated with emotions and drives. (p. 66)

**linguistic determinism** Whorf's hypothesis that language determines the way we think. (p. 369)

**linguistic relativism** the idea that language influences the way we think. (p. 369)

**lobotomy** a psychosurgical procedure once used to calm uncontrollably emotional or violent patients. The procedure cut the nerves connecting the frontal lobes to the emotion-controlling centers of the inner brain. (p. 783)

**long-term memory** the relatively permanent and limitless archive of the memory system. Includes knowledge, skills, and experiences. (p. 209)

**long-term potentiation (LTP)** an increase in a nerve cell's firing potential after brief, rapid stimulation; a neural basis for learning and memory. (p. 211)

**longitudinal study** research that follows and retests the same people over time. (pp. 271, 297)

**loose culture** a place with flexible and informal norms. (p. 492)

# M

**major depressive disorder** a disorder in which a person experiences five or more symptoms lasting two or more weeks, in the absence of drug use or a medical condition, at least one of which must be either (1) depressed mood or (2) loss of interest or pleasure. (p. 712)

**mania** a hyperactive, wildly optimistic state in which dangerously poor judgment is common. (p. 713)

---

**ley de efecto** principio propuesto por Thorndike en el que se propone que las conductas seguidas por consecuencias favorables (o *de refuerzo*) se vuelven más comunes, mientras que las conductas seguidas por consecuencias desfavorables (o *de castigo*) se repiten con menor frecuencia. (p. 417)

**liderazgo** capacidad de un individuo de motivar e influir a otros para que contribuyan al éxito del grupo. (p. 813)

**indefensión aprendida** desesperación y resignación pasiva que los humanos y otros animales desarrollan cuando son incapaces de evitar eventos repetidos que generan aversión. (p. 655)

**aprendizaje** proceso de adquirir, mediante la experiencia información o conductas nuevas y relativamente permanentes. (p. 400)

**lente** estructura transparente ubicada detrás de la pupila que cambia de forma para ayudar a enfocar imágenes en la retina. (p. 125)

**lesión** destrucción de tejido. Las lesiones cerebrales pueden ocurrir naturalmente (por enfermedad o trauma), durante cirugía, o de manera experimental (usando electrodos para destruir células cerebrales). (p. 58)

**niveles de análisis** distintas perspectivas que se complementan, desde perspectivas biológicas hasta psicológicas y socioculturales, que se emplean para analizar cualquier fenómeno. (p. 56)

**sistema límbico** sistema de neuronas ubicado principalmente en el prosencéfalo, debajo del cerebro hemisferios: incluye la *amígdala*, el *hipotálamo, hipocampo, tálamo* y *glándula pituitaria;* asociado con emociones e impulsos. (p. 66)

**determinismo lingüístico** hipótesis de Whorf que sostiene que el lenguaje determina la forma en que pensamos. (p. 369)

**relativismo lingüístico** idea según la cual el lenguaje influye en cómo pensamos. (p. 369)

**lobotomía** procedimiento psicoquirúrgico que otrora se usó para calmar a pacientes emocionalmente incontrolables o violentos. En el procedimiento se cortaban los nervios entre los lóbulos frontales y los centros en el interior del cerebro que controlan las emociones. (p. 783)

**memoria de largo plazo** el archivo relativamente permanente e ilimitado del sistema de memoria. Incluye conocimientos, habilidades y experiencias. (p. 209)

**potenciación a largo plazo (PLP)** aumento en la eficacia de una célula nerviosa para transmitir impulsos sinápticos. Se considera la base neuronal del aprendizaje y la memoria. (p. 211)

**estudio longitudinal** investigación en la que las mismas personas se estudian una y otra vez durante un lapso de tiempo prolongado. (pp. 271, 297)

**cultura abierta** lugar con normas flexibles e informales. (p. 492)

**trastorno depresivo mayor** trastorno en el cual una persona experimenta cinco o más síntomas que duran dos o más semanas, en ausencia de consumo de drogas o una condición médica, de los cuales al menos uno tiene que ser ya sea (1) un estado de ánimo deprimido o (2) la pérdida de interés o placer. (p. 712)

**manía** estado de ánimo marcado por un estado de hiperactividad y optimismo desenfrenado, caracterizado por la falta de juicio. (p. 713)

**maturation** biological growth processes that enable orderly changes in behavior, relatively uninfluenced by experience. (p. 306)

**maduración** procesos de crecimiento biológico que casi siempre conducen a cambios ordenados en el comportamiento y son independientes de la experiencia. (p. 306)

**mean** the arithmetic average of a distribution, obtained by adding the scores and then dividing by the number of scores. (p. 0–42)

**promedio** media aritmética de una distribución que se obtiene sumando las puntuaciones y luego dividiendo el total entre el número de puntuaciones. (p. 0–42)

**median** the middle score in a distribution; half the scores are above it and half are below it. (p. 0–42)

**media** puntuación central de una distribución; la mitad de las puntuaciones se encuentran por encima y la mitad se encuentran por debajo de la media. (p. 0–42)

**medical model** the concept that diseases, in this case psychological disorders, have physical causes that can be *diagnosed, treated,* and, in most cases, *cured,* often through treatment in a *hospital.* (p. 686)

**modelo médico** concepto que afirma que las enfermedades, en este caso los trastornos psicológicos, tienen causas físicas que se pueden *diagnosticar, tratar* y, en la mayoría de los casos, *curar,* generalmente por medio de tratamientos que se llevan a cabo en un *hospital.* (p. 686)

**medulla** [muh-DUL-uh] the hindbrain structure that is the brainstem's base; controls heartbeat and breathing. (p. 65)

**médula** estructura del rombencéfalo que forma la base del tronco encefálico; controla la frecuencia cardíaca y la respiración. (p. 65)

**MEG (magnetoencephalography)** a brain-imaging technique that measures magnetic fields from the brain's natural electrical activity. (p. 58)

**MEG (magnetoencefalografía)** técnica para tomar imágenes del cerebro que mide los campos magnéticos de la actividad eléctrica natural del cerebro. (p. 58)

**memory** the persistence of learning over time through the encoding, storage, and retrieval of information. (p. 206)

**memoria** aprender de manera persistente a través del tiempo usando la codificación, el almacenaje y la recuperación de la información. (p. 206)

**memory consolidation** the neural storage of a long-term memory. (p. 227)

**consolidación de la memoria** almacenaje neural de la memoria a largo plazo. (p. 227)

**menarche** [meh-NAR-key] the first menstrual period. (p. 326)

**menarquía** primer periodo menstrual. (p. 326)

**menopause** the time of natural cessation of menstruation; also refers to the biological changes a woman experiences as her ability to reproduce declines. (p. 314)

**menopausia** el momento del cese natural de la menstruación; también se refiere a los cambios biológicos que experimentan las mujeres cuando disminuye su capacidad reproductiva. (p. 314)

**mental age** a measure of intelligence test performance devised by Binet; the level of performance typically associated with children of a certain chronological age. Thus, a child who does as well as an average 8-year-old is said to have a mental age of 8. (p. 263)

**edad mental** medida de desempeño en la prueba de inteligencia diseñada por Binet. La edad cronológica del niño que corresponde característicamente a un nivel dado de desempeño. Por ende, se dice que un niño que se desempeña como una persona normal de 8 años, tiene una edad mental de 8 años. (p. 263)

**mental set** a tendency to approach a problem in one particular way, often a way that has been successful in the past. (p. 195)

**mentalidad** tendencia a abordar los problemas de una manera particular, con frecuencia, una manera que ha funcionado anteriormente. (p. 195)

**mere exposure effect** the tendency for repeated exposure to novel stimuli to increase our liking of them. (p. 504)

**efecto de la mera exposición** tendencia de la exposición repetida a estímulos novedosos a aumentar la atracción a tales estímulos. (p. 504)

**meta-analysis** a statistical procedure for analyzing the results of multiple studies to reach an overall conclusion. (pp. 0–44, 768)

**meta-análisis** método no experimental; este procedimiento se utiliza para analizar los resultados de procedimiento estadístico para analizar los resultados de múltiples estudios y llegar a una conclusión general. (pp. 0–44, 768)

**metacognition** cognition about our cognition; keeping track of and evaluating our mental processes. (p. 187)

**metacognición** cognición sobre nuestra cognición; seguir y evaluar nuestros procesos mentales. (p. 187)

**midbrain** found atop the brainstem; connects the hindbrain with the forebrain, controls some motor movement, and transmits auditory and visual information. (p. 63)

**mesencéfalo** se ubica en la parte superior del tronco del encéfalo; conecta al rombencéfalo con el prosencéfalo, controla algunos movimientos motrices y transmite información auditiva y visual. (p. 63)

**middle ear** the chamber between the eardrum and cochlea containing three tiny bones that concentrate the vibrations of the eardrum on the cochlea's oval window. (p. 137)

**oído medio** cámara ubicada entre el tímpano y la cóclea; contiene tres huesos pequeños que concentran las vibraciones del tímpano y de la ventana oval de la cóclea. (p. 137)

**mindfulness meditation** a reflective practice in which people attend to current experiences in a nonjudgmental and accepting manner. (p. 677)

**meditación a conciencia plena** práctica reflexiva en la que las personas atienden a las vivencias del momento de una manera tolerante y no condenatoria. (p. 677)

**Minnesota Multiphasic Personality Inventory (MMPI)** the most widely researched and clinically used of all personality tests. Originally developed to identify emotional disorders (still considered its most appropriate use), this test is now used for many other screening purposes. (p. 552)

**Inventario de Personalidad Polifacética de Minnesota (IPPM)** prueba de personalidad más ampliamente investigada y utilizada de todas las pruebas. Creada originalmente para identificar trastornos emocionales (y todavía se la utiliza con tal fin), esta prueba se utiliza en la actualidad para muchas actividades de preselección. (p. 552)

**mirror neurons** neurons that some scientists believe fire when we perform certain actions or observe another doing so. The brain's mirroring of another's action may enable imitation and empathy. (p. 439)

**neuronas espejo** neuronas que, según algunos científicos, se disparan cuando llevamos a cabo ciertas acciones o cuando vemos que las hace alguien más. Esta forma del cerebro de reflejar las acciones de otros posiblemente habilite la imitación y la empatía. (p. 439)

**mirror-image perceptions** mutual views often held by conflicting parties, as when each side sees itself as ethical and peaceful and views the other side as evil and aggressive. (p. 519)

**percepciones idénticas** opiniones mutuas que generalmente sostienen las partes que discrepan o experimentan conflictos entre sí, como cuando cada parte se ve a sí misma como ética y pacifica, y a la otra parte la ve como malvada y agresiva. (p. 519)

**misinformation effect** occurs when a memory has been corrupted by misleading information. (p. 245)

**efecto de información errónea** ocurre cuando un recuerdo se corrompe al recibir información engañosa. (p. 245)

**mnemonics** [nih-MON-iks] memory aids, especially those techniques that use vivid imagery and organizational devices. (p. 219)

**nemotecnia** apoyos memorísticos, sobre todo técnicas que utilizan imágenes brillantes y dispositivos organizacionales. (p. 219)

**mode** the most frequently occurring score(s) in a distribution. (p. 0–42)

**moda** puntuación o puntuaciones que ocurren con mayor frecuencia en una distribución. (p. 0–42)

**modeling** the process of observing and imitating a specific behavior. (p. 437)

**modelar** proceso de observar e imitar un comportamiento en particular. (p. 437)

**monocular cue** a depth cue, such as interposition or linear perspective, available to either eye alone. (p. 179)

**indicación monocular** señal de profundidad como la interposición y la perspectiva lineal, que se puede percibir con un ojo a la vez. (p. 179)

**mood-congruent memory** the tendency to recall experiences that are consistent with one's current good or bad mood. (p. 233)

**memoria congruente con el estado de ánimo** tendencia a recordar experiencias que concuerdan con el buen o mal estado de ánimo que estamos viviendo. (p. 233)

**motivation** a need or desire that energizes and directs behavior. (p. 579)

**motivación** necesidad o deseo que promueve y dirige el comportamiento. (p. 579)

**morpheme** in a language, the smallest unit that carries meaning; may be a word or a part of a word (such as a prefix). (p. 364)

**morfema** en un lenguaje, la unidad más pequeña que lleva significado; puede ser una palabra o una parte de una palabra (como un prefijo). (p. 364)

**motor (efferent) neurons** neurons that carry outgoing information from the brain and spinal cord to the muscles and glands. (p. 22)

**neurona motriz (eferente)** neurona que lleva la información desde el cerebro y la médula espinal hacia los músculos y las glándulas. (p. 22)

**motor cortex** a cerebral cortex area at the rear of the frontal lobes that controls voluntary movements. (p. 72)

**corteza motora** área de la corteza cerebral en la parte posterior de los lóbulos frontales. Controla los movimientos voluntarios. (p. 72)

**MRI (magnetic resonance imaging)** a technique that uses magnetic fields and radio waves to produce computer-generated images of soft tissue. MRI scans show brain anatomy. (p. 59)

**imagen de resonancia magnética (IRM)** técnica que emplea campos magnéticos y ondas de radio para producir imágenes computarizadas de tejidos blandos. Las imágenes de IRM nos permiten visualizar la anatomía del cerebro. (p. 59)

**mutation** a random error in gene replication that leads to a change. (p. 7)

**mutación** error aleatorio en la replicación de los genes que provoca a un cambio. (p. 7)

**myelin** [MY-uh-lin] **sheath** a fatty tissue layer segmentally encasing the axons of some neurons; it enables vastly greater transmission speed as neural impulses hop from one node to the next. (p. 29)

**funda de mielina** tejido adiposo que cubre los axones de algunas neuronas; habilita velocidades de transmisión más alta para enviar impulsos neurales de un nodo al siguiente. (p. 29)

# N

**narcissism** excessive self-love and self-absorption. (p. 571)

**narcisismo** amor propio y ensimismamiento excesivos. (p. 571)

**narcolepsy** a sleep disorder characterized by uncontrollable sleep attacks. The affected person may lapse directly into REM sleep, often at inopportune times. (p. 107)

**narcolepsia** trastorno caracterizado por ataques incontrolables de sueño. La personas afectada por la narcolepsia caen directamente en el sueño MOR incluso en momentos inoportunos. (p. 107)

**natural selection** the principle that the inherited traits enabling an organism to survive and reproduce in a particular environment will (in competition with other trait variations) most likely be passed on to succeeding generations. (p. 5)

**selección natural** principio según el cual los rasgos heredados permiten a un organismo a sobrevivir en cierto entorno, serán (en competencia con otras variaciones) las que más probablemente se transmitan a las generaciones futuras. (p. 5)

**naturalistic observation** a non-experimental technique of observing and recording behavior in naturally occurring situations without trying to manipulate and control the situation. (p. 0–17)

**observación naturalista** técnica no experimental para observar y registrar la conducta en situaciones reales sin tratar de manipular y controlar la situación. (p. 0–17)

**nature–nurture issue** the longstanding controversy over the relative contributions that genes and experience make to the development of psychological traits and behaviors. Today's science views traits and behaviors as arising from the interaction of nature and nurture. (p. 4)

**near-death experience** an altered state of consciousness reported after a close brush with death (such as cardiac arrest); often similar to drug-induced hallucinations. (p. 50)

**negative reinforcement** increasing behaviors by stopping or reducing an aversive stimulus. A negative reinforcer is any stimulus that, when *removed* after a response, strengthens the response. (*Note*: Negative reinforcement is not punishment.) (p. 420)

**nerves** bundled axons that form neural cables connecting the central nervous system with muscles, glands, and sensory organs. (p. 22)

**nervous system** the body's speedy, electrochemical communication network, consisting of all the nerve cells of the peripheral and central nervous systems. (p. 22)

**neurodevelopmental disorders** central nervous system abnormalities (usually in the brain) that start in childhood and alter thinking and behavior (as in intellectual limitations or a psychological disorder). (p. 737)

**neurogenesis** the formation of new neurons. (pp. 81, 211)

**neuron** a nerve cell; the basic building block of the nervous system. (p. 28)

**neuroplasticity** the brain's ability to change, especially during childhood, by reorganizing after damage or by building new pathways based on experience. (p. 57)

**neurotransmitters** chemical messengers that cross the synaptic gaps between neurons. When released by the sending neuron, neurotransmitters travel across the synapse and bind to receptor sites on the receiving neuron, thereby influencing whether that neuron will generate a neural impulse. (p. 31)

**neutral stimulus (NS)** in classical conditioning, a stimulus that elicits no response before conditioning. (p. 405)

**normal curve** a symmetrical, bell-shaped curve that describes the distribution of many types of data; most scores fall near the mean (about 68 percent fall within one standard deviation of it) and fewer and fewer scores lie near the extremes. (Also called a *normal distribution*.) (pp. 0–43, 266)

**normative social influence** influence resulting from a person's desire to gain approval or avoid disapproval. (p. 478)

**norms** a society's understood rules for accepted and expected behavior. Norms prescribe "proper" behavior in individual and social situations. (p. 475)

**NREM sleep** non-rapid eye movement sleep; encompasses all sleep stages except for REM sleep. (p. 95)

**nudge** framing choices in a way that encourages people to make beneficial decisions. (p. 200)

**debate de naturaleza–crianza** controversia de antaño acerca del aporte relativo que ejercen los genes y las vivencias en el desarrollo de los rasgos y comportamientos psicológicos. En la ciencia psicológica actual se opina que los rasgos y comportamientos tienen origen en la interrelación entre la naturaleza y la crianza. (p. 4)

**experiencia al borde de la muerte** estado de alteración de la consciencia experimentado por personas que tienen un encuentro cercano con la muerte (por ejemplo, cuando se sufre un paro cardíaco). A menudo es similar a las alucinaciones inducidas por los estupefacientes. (p. 50)

**reforzamiento negativo** aumento en la expresión de comportamientos mediante la interrupción o reducción de un estímulo negativo. Un reforzamiento negativo es todo aquello que, cuando se *elimina* después de una reacción, refuerza la reacción. (*Nota*: el reforzamiento negativo no significa castigo). (p. 420)

**nervios** axones agrupados que forman cables neurales y que conectan el sistema nervioso central con músculos, glándulas y órganos sensoriales. (p. 22)

**sistema nervioso** veloz red electroquímica de comunicación del cuerpo que consta de todas las células nerviosas del sistema nervioso central y periférico. (p. 22)

**trastornos del desarrollo neurológico** anomalías en el sistema nervioso central (generalmente en el cerebro) que surgen en la infancia temprana y alteran el pensamiento y el comportamiento (como en limitaciones intelectuales o en trastornos psicológicos). (p. 737)

**neurogénesis** formación de neuronas nuevas. (pp. 81, 211)

**neurona** célula nerviosa; componente básico del sistema nervioso. (p. 28)

**neuroplasticidad** capacidad de cambio del cerebro, particularmente en la infancia, al reordenarse después de daños o construyendo nuevas vías a través de la experiencia. (p. 57)

**neurotransmisores** mensajeros químicos que cruzan las sinapsis entre neuronas. Al ser liberados por la neurona, los neurotransmisores cruzan la sinapsis y se adhieren al sitio receptor de la neurona que los recibe y con ello influyen en si esa neurona generará un impulso neural. (p. 31)

**estímulos neutrales (EN)** según el condicionamiento clásico, un estímulo que no produce respuesta antes del condicionamiento. (p. 405)

**curva normal** curva asimétrica en forma de campana que describe la distribución de muchos tipos de datos; la mayoría de los puntajes caen cerca de la media (cerca del 68 por ciento caen dentro de una desviación estándar de uno de la media) y hay cada vez menos puntajes cerca de los extremos. (También conocida como *distribución normal*). (pp. 0–43, 266)

**influencia social normativa** influencia resultante del deseo de una persona de obtener la aprobación o evitar la desaprobación de los demás. (p. 478)

**normas** reglas de una sociedad sobre el comportamiento aceptado y esperado. Las normas describen el comportamiento "apropiado" en situaciones individuales y sociales. (p. 475)

**sueño NMOR** sueño sin movimiento ocular rápido; incluye todas las fases del sueño excepto el sueño MOR. (p. 95)

**empujoncito** presentar opciones de manera que animan a la gente a tomar decisiones benéficas. (p. 200)

# O

**obedience** complying with an order or a command. (p. 478)

**obediencia** cumplir con una orden o mandato. (p. 478)

**obesity** defined as a body mass index (BMI) measurement of 30 or higher, which is calculated from our weight-to-height ratio. (Individuals who are overweight have a BMI of 25 or higher.) (p. 604)

**obesidad** se define como una medida de índice de masa corporal, (IMC) de 30 o más, que se calcula a partir de nuestra relación peso-altura. (Los individuos con soprepeso tienen medidas de 25 o más). (p. 604)

**object permanence** the awareness that things continue to exist even when not perceived. (p. 350)

**permanencia de los objetos** reconocimiento de que las cosas siguen existiendo aunque no las veamos. (p. 350)

**observational learning** learning by observing others. (Also called *social learning*.) (p. 437)

**aprendizaje observacional** aprender observando a los demás. (También conocido como *aprendizaje social*.) (p. 437)

**obsessive-compulsive disorder (OCD)** a disorder characterized by unwanted repetitive thoughts (obsessions), actions (compulsions), or both. (p. 702)

**trastorno obsesivo-compulsivo (TOC)** trastorno que se caracteriza por pensamientos (obsesiones) y/o acciones (compulsiones) repetitivos y no deseados o ambos. (p. 702)

**occipital** [ahk-SIP-uh-tuhl] **lobes** the portion of the cerebral cortex lying at the back of the head; it includes areas that receive information from the visual fields. (p. 71)

**lóbulos occipitales** sección de la corteza cerebral ubicada en la parte posterior de la cabeza; incluye las áreas que reciben información de los campos visuales. (p. 71)

**olfaction** our sense of smell. (p. 149)

**olfato** nuestro sentido del olor. (p. 149)

**one-word stage** the stage in speech development, from about age 1 to 2, during which a child speaks mostly in single words. (p. 365)

**etapa holofrástica** etapa en el desarrollo del habla, entre el primer y segundo año en la que el niño se expresa principalmente con palabras aisladas. (p. 365)

**operant behavior** behavior that operates on the environment, producing a consequence. (p. 402)

**comportamiento operante** comportamiento que opera en el entorno, produciendo una consecuencia. (p. 402)

**operant chamber** in operant conditioning research, a chamber (also known as a *Skinner box*) containing a bar or key that an animal can manipulate to obtain a food or water reinforcer; attached devices record the animal's rate of bar pressing or key pecking. (p. 418)

**cámara operante** Caja (también conocida como *cámara de Skinner*) que contiene una barra o tecla que un animal puede manipular para obtener un reforzamiento de comida o agua; con una serie de dispositivos conectados se graba la cantidad de veces que el animal presiona la barra. (p. 418)

**operant conditioning** a type of learning in which a behavior becomes more likely to recur if followed by a reinforcer or less likely to recur if followed by a punisher. (p. 417)

**condicionamiento operante** aprendizaje en el que el comportamiento se torna más probable si es seguido por un reforzamiento o se atenúa si es seguido por un castigo. (p. 417)

**operational definition** a carefully worded statement of the exact procedures (operations) used in a research study. For example, *human intelligence* may be operationally defined as what an intelligence test measures. (Also known as *operationalization*.) (p. 0–15)

**definición operacional** declaración redactada con gran cuidado en la que se detallan los procedimientos (operaciones) exactos que se usan en un estudio de investigación. Por ejemplo, la *inteligencia humana* puede ser operacionalmente definida como lo que se mide en una prueba de inteligencia. (También conocido como *operacionalización*.) (p. 0–15)

**opioids** opium and its derivatives; they depress neural activity, temporarily lessening pain and anxiety. (p. 44)

**opioides** del opio y sus derivados; deprimen la actividad neural, con lo cual reducen el dolor y la ansiedad. (p. 44)

**opponent-process theory** the theory that opposing retinal processes (red-green, blue-yellow, white-black) enable color vision. For example, some cells are stimulated by green and inhibited by red; others are stimulated by red and inhibited by green. (p. 130)

**teoría de proceso de oponentes** Teoría que manifiesta que los procesos opuestos de la retina (rojo-verde, amarillo-azul, blanco-negro) posibilitan la visualización de los colores. Por ejemplo, algunas células se estimulan con el verde y se inhiben con el rojo; otras se estimulan con el rojo y se inhiben con el verde. (p. 130)

**optic nerve** the nerve that carries neural impulses from the eye to the brain. (p. 126)

**nervio óptico** nervio que transporta los impulsos neuronales del ojo al cerebro. (p. 126)

**organizational psychology** an I/O psychology subfield that examines organizational influences on worker satisfaction and productivity and facilitates organizational change. (p. 808)

**psicología organizacional** subdisciplina de la psicología I/O que examina las influencias organizacionales en la satisfacción y productividad de los trabajadores, y facilita el cambio organizacional. (p. 808)

**ostracism** deliberate social exclusion of individuals or groups. (p. 589)

**ostracismo** exclusión social deliberada de individuos o grupos. (p. 589)

**other-race effect** the tendency to recall faces of one's own race more accurately than faces of other races. Also called the *cross-race effect* and the *own-race bias*. (p. 463)

**efecto de otras razas** tendencia a recordar caras de la raza de uno mismo con mayor precisión que las caras de otras razas. También se conoce como *efecto de raza cruzada* o *sesgo de rasa propia*. (p. 463)

**outgroup** "them"—those perceived as different or apart from our ingroup. (p. 462)

**grupo ajeno** "ellos", o, las personas a las que percibimos como distintas o separadas, que no forman parte de nuestro grupo. (p. 462)

**overconfidence** the tendency to be more confident than correct—to overestimate the accuracy of our beliefs and judgments. (p. 198)

**exceso de confianza** tendencia a ser más confiado que acertado, o sea, a sobreestimar las creencias y las opiniones propias. (p. 198)

**panic disorder** an anxiety disorder marked by unpredictable, minutes-long episodes of intense dread in which a person may experience terror and accompanying chest pain, choking, or other frightening sensations; often followed by worry over a possible next attack. (p. 700)

**trastorno de pánico** trastorno de ansiedad marcado por el inicio repentino y recurrente de episodios impredecibles de aprehensión intensa o terror que pueden durar varios minutos, en los cuales la persona puede sentir dolor de pecho, sofocamiento, y otras sensaciones atemorizantes; a menudo la preocupación es por la posibilidad de un posible nuevo ataque. (p. 700)

**parallel processing** processing multiple aspects of a stimulus or problem simultaneously. (pp. 91, 132, 209)

**procesamiento en paralelo** procesamiento simultáneo de múltiples aspectos de un estímulo o problema. (pp. 91, 132, 209)

**parasympathetic nervous system** the division of the autonomic nervous system that calms the body, conserving its energy. (p. 23)

**sistema nervioso autonómico parasimpático** subdivisión del sistema nervioso autonómico que calma el cuerpo y conserva su energía. (p. 23)

**parietal** [puh-RYE-uh-tuhl] **lobes** the portion of the cerebral cortex lying at the top of the head and toward the rear; it receives sensory input for touch and body position. (p. 71)

**lóbulos parietales** región de la corteza cerebral en la parte superior y hacia la parte posterior de la cabeza; recibe entradas sensoriales del tacto y la posición del cuerpo. (p. 71)

**partial (intermittent) reinforcement schedule** reinforcing a response only part of the time; results in slower acquisition of a response but much greater resistance to extinction than does continuous reinforcement. (p. 422)

**calendario de reforzamiento parcial (intermitente)** reforzamiento de una respuesta tan solo una parte del tiempo; tiene como resultado la adquisición más lenta de una respuesta pero mucho más resistente a la extinción que el reforzamiento continuo. (p. 422)

**passionate love** an aroused state of intense positive absorption in another, usually present at the beginning of a romantic relationship. (p. 509)

**amor apasionado** estado excitado de intensa y positiva absorción en otro ser. Por lo general se observa al comienzo de una relación de amor romántica. (p. 509)

**peer reviewers** scientific experts who evaluate a research article's theory, originality, and accuracy. (p. 0–14)

**revisores** expertos científicos que evalúan la teoría, originalidad y precisión de un artículo de investigación. (p. 0–14)

**percentile rank** the percentage of scores that are lower than a given score. (p. 0-42)

**rango percentil** porcentaje de puntuaciones que son inferiores a una puntuación determinada. (p. 0-42)

**perception** the process by which our brain organizes and interprets sensory information, enabling us to recognize objects and events as meaningful. (p. 116)

**percepción** proceso mediante el cual el cerebro organiza e interpreta la información sensorial transformándola en objetos y sucesos que tienen sentido. (p. 116)

**perceptual adaptation** the ability to adjust to changed sensory input, including an artificially displaced or even inverted visual field. (p. 183)

**adaptación perceptiva** capacidad de ajustarnos a un estímulo sensorial cambiado, como por ejemplo un campo visual artificialmente desplazado o incluso invertido. (p. 183)

**perceptual constancy** perceiving objects as unchanging (having consistent color, brightness, shape, and size) even as illumination and retinal images change. (p. 180)

**constancia perceptual** percepción de que los objetos no cambian (que su color, brillo, forma y tamaño son consistentes) incluso cuando la iluminación y las imágenes de la retina cambian. (p. 180)

**perceptual set** a mental predisposition to perceive one thing and not another. (p. 169)

**predisposición perceptiva** predisposición mental para percibir una cosa y no otra. (p. 169)

**peripheral nervous system (PNS)** the sensory and motor neurons that connect the central nervous system (CNS) to the rest of the body. (p. 22)

**sistema nervioso periférico (SNP)** neuronas motoras y sensoriales que conectan el sistema nervioso central (SNC) con el resto del cuerpo. (p. 22)

**peripheral route persuasion** occurs when people are influenced by incidental cues, such as a speaker's attractiveness. (p. 471)

**ruta de persuasión periférica** se produce cuando las personas se ven influenciadas por señales triviales, como el atractivo del orador. (p. 471)

**persistent depressive disorder** a disorder in which people experience a depressed mood on more days than not for at least 2 years (formerly called dysthymia.) (p. 712)

**trastorno depresivo persistente** trastorno en el que se experimenta un estado de ánimo decaído durante la mayor parte de los días a lo largo de dos años (antes conocido como como distimia). (p. 712)

**person perception** how we form impressions of ourselves and others, including attributions of behavior. (p. 454)

**percepción de la persona** la manera en que formamos impresiones de nosotros mismos, incluyendo las atribuciones del comportamiento. (p. 454)

**person-centered therapy** a humanistic therapy, developed by Carl Rogers, in which the therapist uses techniques such as *active listening* within an accepting, genuine, empathic environment to facilitate clients' growth. (Also called *client-centered therapy*.) (p. 749)

**terapia centrada en la persona** terapia humanista, desarrollada por Carl Rogers, donde el terapeuta usa técnicas como *escuchar activamente* dentro de un entorno genuino y empático de aceptación para facilitar el crecimiento del cliente. (También conocida como *terapia centrada en el cliente*). (p. 749)

**personal control** our sense of controlling our environment rather than feeling helpless. (p. 654)

**control personal** nuestro sentido de control del entorno en lugar de sentirnos impotentes. (p. 654)

**personality** an individual's characteristic pattern of thinking, feeling, and acting. (p. 526)

**personalidad** forma característica de pensar, sentir y actuar de una persona. (p. 526)

**personality disorders** a group of disorders characterized by enduring inner experiences or behavior patterns that differ from someone's cultural norms and expectations, are pervasive and inflexible, begin in adolescence or early adulthood, are stable over time, and cause distress or impairment. (p. 732)

**trastornos de la personalidad** grupo de trastornos caracterizados por experiencias internas duraderas o patrones de comportamiento que difieren de las normas culturales y expectativas de alguien, son persistentes e inflexibles, comienzan en la adolescencia o edad adulta temprana, son estables a lo largo del tiempo y causan angustia o deterioro. (p. 732)

**personality inventory** a questionnaire (often with *true-false* or *agree-disagree* items) on which people respond to items designed to gauge a wide range of feelings and behaviors; used to assess selected personality traits. (p. 552)

**inventario de personalidad** cuestionario (a menudo de preguntas de *falso o verdadero* o de *desacuerdo/acuerdo*) en el que las personas responden a consultas diseñadas para medir una amplia gama de sentimientos y conductas; se usa para evaluar ciertos rasgos de la personalidad. (p. 552)

**personality psychology** the scientific study of personality and its development, structure, traits, processes, variations, and disordered forms (personality disorders). (p. 453)

**psicología de la personalidad** estudio científico de la personalidad y su desarrollo, estructura, rasgos, procesos, variaciones y formas desordenadas (trastornos de la personalidad). (p. 453)

**personnel psychology** an I/O psychology subfield that helps with job seeking, and with employee recruitment, selection, placement, training, appraisal, and development. (p. 808)

**psicología del personal** área de la psicología industrial/organizacional que ayuda con la búsqueda de empleo, el reclutamiento de empleados, la selección, la colocación, el entrenamiento, la evaluación y el desarrollo. (p. 808)

**persuasion** changing people's attitudes, potentially influencing their actions. (p. 471)

**persuasión** cambiar las actitudes de la gente, potencialmente influyendo en sus acciones. (p. 471)

**PET (positron emission tomography) scan** technique for detecting brain activity that displays where a radioactive form of glucose goes while the brain performs a given task. (p. 59)

**TEP (tomografía por emisión de positrones)** técnica para detectar la actividad cerebral que muestra hacia dónde se dirige un tipo de glucosa radiactiva en el momento en que el cerebro realiza una función particular. (p. 59)

**phi phenomenon** an illusion of movement created when two or more adjacent lights blink on and off in quick succession. (p. 179)

**fenómeno phi** ilusión de movimiento creada por dos o más luces adyacentes que parpadean en sucesión rápida. (p. 179)

**phoneme** in a language, the smallest distinctive sound unit. (p. 364)

**fonema** en un lenguaje, la unidad de sonido más pequeña y distintiva. (p. 364)

**phonological loop** a memory component that briefly holds auditory information. (p. 210)

**bucle fonológico** componente de la memoria que retiene brevemente información auditiva. (p. 210)

**physiological need** a basic bodily requirement. (p. 580)

**necesidad fisiológica** exigencia básica del cuerpo. (p. 580)

**pitch** a tone's experienced highness or lowness; depends on frequency. (p. 136)

**tono** propiedad de los sonidos que los caracteriza como agudos o graves; depende de la frecuencia. (p. 136)

**place theory** in hearing, the theory that links the pitch we hear with the place where the cochlea's membrane is stimulated. (Also called *place coding.*) (p. 140)

**teoría del lugar** en la audición, la teoría que relaciona el tono que escuchamos con el sitio donde se estimula la membrana de la cóclea. (También se conoce como *codificación de lugar.*) (p. 140)

**placebo** [pluh-SEE-bo; Latin for "I shall please"] **effect** experimental results caused by expectations alone; any effect on behavior caused by the administration of an inert substance or condition, which the recipient assumes is an active agent. (p. 0–28)

**efecto placebo** resultados producidos únicamente por las expectativas; cualquier efecto sobre el comportamiento causado por el suministro de una sustancia o condición inerte, que el receptor supone que es un agente activo. (p. 0–28)

**polygraph** a machine used in attempts to detect lies; measures emotion-linked changes in perspiration, heart rate, and breathing. (p. 616)

**polígrafo** máquina, utilizada comúnmente con la intención de detectar mentiras; mide cambios vinculados a las emociones en la transpiración, la frecuencia cardíaca y la respiración. (p. 616)

**population** all those in a group being studied, from which samples may be drawn. (*Note:* Except for national studies, this does not refer to a country's whole population.) (p. 0–19)

**población** todos aquellos que constituyen el grupo que se está estudiando, a partir del cual se pueden tomar muestras. (*Nota:* salvo en estudios de alcance nacional, no se refiere a la totalidad de la población de un país). (p. 0–19)

**positive psychology** the scientific study of human flourishing, with the goals of promoting strengths and virtues that foster well-being, resilience, and positive emotions, and that help individuals and communities to thrive. (p. 663)

**psicología positiva** estudio científico del funcionamiento humano, que tiene las metas de promover fortalezas y virtudes que fomentan el bienestar, la resiliencia y las emociones positivas, y que ayudan a los individuos y comunidades a prosperar. (p. 663)

**positive reinforcement** increasing behaviors by presenting a pleasurable stimulus. A positive reinforcer is any stimulus that, when *presented* after a response, strengthens the response. (p. 420)

**reforzamiento positivo** aumento en la expresión de comportamientos mediante la presentación de estímulos placenteros, por ejemplo, un alimento. Un reforzamiento positivo es cualquier cosa que, *presentada* después de una respuesta, refuerza esa respuesta. (p. 420)

**posthypnotic suggestion** a suggestion, made during a hypnosis session, to be carried out after the subject is no longer hypnotized; used by some clinicians to help control undesired symptoms and behaviors. (p. 786)

**sugerencia poshipnótica** sugerencia que se hace durante una sesión de hipnotismo, que el sujeto debe realizar cuando ya no está hipnotizado; la usan algunos practicantes para ayudar a controlar síntomas y conductas no deseadas. (p. 786)

**posttraumatic growth** positive psychological changes following a struggle with extremely challenging circumstances and life crises. (p. 789)

**crecimiento postraumático** cambios psicológicos positivos después de luchar contra circunstancias extremadamente difíciles y crisis de la vida. (p. 789)

**posttraumatic stress disorder (PTSD)** a disorder characterized by haunting memories, nightmares, hypervigilance, avoidance of trauma-related stimuli, social withdrawal, jumpy anxiety, numbness of feeling, and/or insomnia that lingers for four weeks or more after a traumatic experience. (p. 703)

**trastorno por estrés postraumático (TEPT)** trastorno de ansiedad caracterizado por recuerdos inquietantes, pesadillas, hipervigilancia, evitación de estímulos relacionados con el trauma, aislamiento social, ansiedad asustadiza, y/o insomnio que perdura por cuatro semanas o más después de una experiencia traumática. (p. 703)

**predictive validity** the success with which a test predicts the behavior it is designed to predict; it is assessed by computing the correlation between test scores and the criterion behavior. (Also called *criterion-related validity*.) (p. 267)

**validez predictiva** nivel de éxito con el que una prueba predice el comportamiento para el que ha sido diseñada para predecir. Se evalúa mediante la medición de la correlación de los resultados de las pruebas y el comportamiento de criterio. (También se conoce como *validez relacionada con el criterio*). (p. 267)

**prejudice** an unjustifiable and usually negative attitude toward a group and its members. Prejudice generally involves negative emotions, stereotyped beliefs, and a predisposition to discriminatory action. (p. 457)

**prejuicio** actitud injustificable y normalmente negativa hacia un grupo y sus integrantes. Los prejuicios generalmente implican emociones negativas, creencias estereotipadas, y una predisposición a la acción discriminatoria. (p. 457)

**preoperational stage** in Piaget's theory, the stage (from about 2 to 6 or 7 years of age) at which a child learns to use language but does not yet comprehend the mental operations of concrete logic. (p. 351)

**etapa preoperacional** en la teoría de Piaget, la etapa (desde alrededor de los 2 hasta los 6 o 7 años de edad) en la que el niño aprende a utilizar el lenguaje; pero todavía no comprende las operaciones mentales de la lógica concreta. (p. 351)

**preparedness** a biological predisposition to learn associations, such as between taste and nausea, that have survival value. (p. 413)

**estado de preparación** predisposición biológica a aprender asociaciones, por ejemplo entre cierto sabor y la sensación de náusea, que tienen valor para la supervivencia. (p. 413)

**primary reinforcer** an innately reinforcing stimulus, such as one that satisfies a biological need. (p. 421)

**reforzador primario** suceso que es inherentemente reforzador y a menudo satisface una necesidad biológica. (p. 421)

**primary sex characteristics** the body structures (ovaries, testes, and external genitalia) that make sexual reproduction possible. (p. 326)

**características primarias del sexo** estructuras del organismo (ovarios, testículos y aparatos genitales externos) que posibilitan la reproducción sexual. (p. 326)

**priming** the activation, often unconsciously, of certain associations, thus predisposing one's perception, memory, or response. (pp. 119, 233)

**preparación** activación de asociaciones en nuestra memoria, a menudo de manera inconsciente, que nos dispone a percibir o recordar objetos o sucesos de una manera determinada. (pp. 119, 233)

**proactive interference** the forward-acting disruptive effect of older learning on the recall of *new* information. (p. 242)

**interferencia proactiva** efecto interruptor del aprendizaje anterior sobre la manera de recordar información *nueva*. (p. 242)

**problem-focused coping** attempting to alleviate stress directly—by changing the stressor or the way we interact with that stressor. (p. 654)

**superación con enfoque en los problemas** intento de sobrellevar el estrés de manera directa cambiando ya sea lo que produce la tensión o la forma en que nos relacionamos con dicho factor de estrés. (p. 654)

**projective test** a personality test, such as the TAT or Rorschach, that provides ambiguous images designed to trigger projection of one's inner dynamics and explore the preconscious and unconscious mind. (p. 538)

**prueba de proyección** tipo de prueba de la personalidad, como la prueba TAT o de Rorschach, que muestra imágenes ambiguas a los sujetos para provocar una proyección de sus dinámicas internas y explora la mente preconsciente e inconsciente. (p. 538)

**prosocial behavior** positive, constructive, helpful behavior. The opposite of antisocial behavior. (p. 441)

**comportamiento prosocial** comportamiento positivo, constructivo, útil. Lo contrario del comportamiento antisocial. (p. 441)

**prototype** a mental image or best example of a category. Matching new items to a prototype provides a quick and easy method for sorting items into categories (as when comparing feathered creatures to a prototypical bird, such as a crow). (p. 187)

**prototipo** imagen mental o mejor ejemplo de una categoría. Al cotejar artículos nuevos con un prototipo se trabaja con un método rápido y sencillo para clasificar artículos en categorías (tal como cuando se comparan animales de plumas con un ave prototípico, como un cuervo). (p. 187)

**psychoactive drug** a chemical substance that alters the brain, causing changes in perceptions and moods. (p. 40)

**fármaco psicoactivo** sustancia química que altera el cerebro y provoca cambios en las percepciones y el estado de ánimo. (p. 40)

**psychoanalysis** (1) Freud's theory of personality that attributes thoughts and actions to unconscious motives and conflicts; the techniques used in treating psychological disorders by seeking to expose and interpret unconscious tensions. (2) Sigmund Freud's therapeutic technique. Freud believed the patient's free associations, resistances, dreams, and transferences—and the analyst's interpretations of them—released previously repressed feelings, allowing the patient to gain self-insight. (pp. 528, 747)

**psicoanálisis** (1) teoría de Freud sobre la personalidad que atribuye los pensamientos y las acciones a motivos y conflictos inconscientes; las técnicas utilizadas en el tratamiento de trastornos psicológicos al buscar exponer e interpretar las tensiones inconscientes. (2) El método terapéutico de Freud. Freud creía que las asociaciones libres, las resistencias, los sueños y las transferencias del paciente (así como la interpretación de ellas por parte del analista) liberaban sentimientos antes reprimidos, permitiendo que el paciente adquiriera agudeza introspectiva. (pp. 528, 747)

**psychodynamic theories** theories that view personality with a focus on the unconscious mind and the importance of childhood experiences. (p. 528)

**teorías psicodinámicas** visión de la personalidad con una concentración en el subconsciente de la mente y en la importancia de las vivencias en la niñez. (p. 528)

**psychodynamic therapy** therapy deriving from the psychoanalytic tradition; views individuals as responding to unconscious forces and childhood experiences, and seeks to enhance self-insight. (p. 748)

**terapia psicodinámica** enfoque terapéutico que se deriva de la tradición psicoanalítica; se observa a los individuos como si respondieran a fuerzas inconscientes y experiencias de la niñez, y se busca agudizar la introspección. (p. 748)

**psychological disorder** a disturbance in people's thoughts, emotions, or behaviors that causes distress or suffering and impairs their daily lives. (p. 685)

**trastorno psicológico** trastorno en los pensamientos, emociones o comportamientos de las personas que causa angustia o sufrimiento, y que afecta negativamente su vida diaria. (p. 685)

**psychology** the science of behavior and mental processes. (p. 3)

**psicología** ciencia del comportamiento y procesos mentales. (p. 3)

**psychometrics** the scientific study of the measurement of human abilities, attitudes, and traits. (p. 265)

**psicometría** estudio científico de medición de las habilidades, actitudes y rasgos humanos. (p. 265)

**psychoneuroimmunology** the study of how psychological, neural, and endocrine processes together affect our immune system and resulting health. (p. 638)

**psiconeuroimunología** estudio de cómo los procesos psicológicos, neuronales y endocrinos se combinan en nuestro organismo para influenciar nuestro sistema inmunológico y la salud en general. (p. 638)

**psychopharmacology** the study of the effects of drugs on mind and behavior. (p. 778)

**psicofarmacología** estudio de los efectos de los medicamentos sobre la mente y el comportamiento. (p. 778)

**psychophysics** the study of relationships between the physical characteristics of stimuli, such as their intensity, and our psychological experience of them. (p. 117)

**psicofísica** el estudio de las relaciones entre las características físicas de los estímulos, por ejemplo su intensidad, y nuestra experiencia psicológica de esos estímulos. (p. 117)

**psychosurgery** surgery that removes or destroys brain tissue in an effort to change behavior. (p. 783)

**psicocirugía** cirugía que extrae o destruye tejido cerebral para cambiar el comportamiento. (p. 783)

**psychotherapy** treatment involving psychological techniques; consists of interactions between a trained therapist and someone seeking to overcome psychological difficulties or achieve personal growth. (p. 746)

**psicoterapia** tratamiento que incluye técnicas psicológicas; consiste en interacciones entre un terapeuta cualificado y una persona que desea superar dificultades psicológicas o lograr un crecimiento personal. (p. 746)

**psychotic disorders** a group of disorders marked by irrational ideas, distorted perceptions, and a loss of contact with reality. (p. 722)

**trastornos psicóticos** conjunto de trastornos caracterizados por ideas irracionales, percepciones distorsionadas y pérdida de contacto con la realidad. (p. 722)

**puberty** the period of sexual maturation, during which a person usually becomes capable of reproducing. (p. 312)

**pubertad** período de maduración sexual durante el cual la persona normalmente adquiere la capacidad de reproducirse. (p. 312)

**punishment** an event that tends to *decrease* the behavior that it follows. (p. 424)

**castigo** evento que *disminuye* el comportamiento que le precede. (p. 424)

**pupil** the adjustable opening in the center of the eye through which light enters. (p. 124)

**pupila** la apertura ajustable del centro del ojo que permite el acceso de la luz. (p. 124)

## Q

**qualitative research** a research method that relies on in-depth, narrative data that are not translated into numbers. (p. 0–33)

**investigación cualitativa** método de investigación que depende de datos narrativos profundos que no se traducen en números. (p. 0–33)

**quantitative research** a research method that relies on quantifiable, numerical data. (p. 0–33)

**investigación cuantitativa** método de investigación que se basa en datos numéricos cuantificables. (p. 0–33)

**random assignment** assigning participants to experimental and control groups by chance, thus minimizing preexisting differences between the different groups. (p. 0–27)

**asignación aleatoria** asignación de participantes al grupo experimental o al de control. Se realiza al azar para minimizar las diferencias preexistentes que pudiese haber entre los grupos asignados. (p. 0–27)

**random sample** a sample that fairly represents a population because each member has an equal chance of inclusion. (p. 0–19)

**muestra aleatoria** muestra que representa justamente la población, gracias a que cada elemento de la población tiene igual oportunidad de ser seleccionado. (p. 0–19)

**range** the difference between the highest and lowest scores in a distribution. (p. 0–43)

**rango** diferencia entre las puntuaciones más alta y más baja en una distribución. (p. 0–43)

**rational-emotive behavior therapy (REBT)** a confrontational cognitive therapy, developed by Albert Ellis, that vigorously challenges people's illogical, self-defeating attitudes and assumptions. (p. 758)

**terapia racional emotiva conductual (TREC)** terapia cognitiva de confrontación desarrollada por Albert Ellis, que cuestiona vigorosamente las actitudes y suposiciones ilógicas y derrotistas de las personas. (p. 758)

**recall** a measure of memory in which the person must retrieve information learned earlier, as on a fill-in-the-blank test. (p. 207)

**recordación** memoria que se demuestra recuperando información aprendida anteriormente, tal como en las pruebas que consisten en rellenar espacios en blanco. (p. 207)

**reciprocal determinism** the interacting influences of behavior, internal cognition, and environment. (p. 561)

**determinismo recíproco** la interacción de las influencias del comportamiento, cognición interna y el entorno. (p. 561)

**reciprocity norm** an expectation that people will help, not hurt, those who have helped them. (p. 517)

**norma de reciprocidad** expectativa de que las personas ayudarán, y no harán daño, a aquellos que las han ayudado. (p. 517)

**recognition** a measure of memory in which the person identifies items previously learned, as on a multiple-choice test. (p. 208)

**reconocimiento** memoria que se demuestra identificando cosas que se aprendieron anteriormente, tal como en las pruebas de opción múltiple. (p. 208)

**reconsolidation** a process in which previously stored memories, when retrieved, are potentially altered before being stored again. (p. 244)

**reconsolidación** proceso en el que los recuerdos almacenados, al ser recuperados, son potencialmente alterados antes de ser almacenados nuevamente. (p. 244)

**reflex** a simple, automatic response to a sensory stimulus, such as the knee-jerk response. (p. 25)

**reflejo** respuesta simple y automática a un estímulo sensorial, por ejemplo el reflejo rotular (mover la pierna para evitar un peligro repentino). (p. 25)

**refractory period** in neural processing, a brief resting pause that occurs after a neuron has fired; subsequent action potentials cannot occur until the axon returns to its resting state. (p. 30)

**período refractario** en el procesamiento neuronal, una breve fase de descanso que se produce después de que una neurona ha disparado. No se pueden producir potenciales subsiguientes de acción hasta que el axón vuelva a su estado de reposo. (p. 30)

**regression toward the mean** the tendency for extreme or unusual scores or events to fall back (regress) toward the average. (p. 0–26)

**regresión hacia la media** tendencia hacia las puntuaciones o eventos extremos o poco comunes para así retornar (regresar) hacia el promedio. (p. 0–26)

**reinforcement** in operant conditioning, any event that *strengthens* the behavior it follows. (p. 418)

**reforzamiento** según el condicionamiento operante, todo suceso que *fortalezca* el comportamiento al que sigue. (p. 418)

**reinforcement schedule** a pattern that defines how often a desired response will be reinforced. (p. 422)

**plan de reforzamiento** patrón que define la frecuencia con que se reforzará una respuesta deseada. (p. 422)

**relational aggression** an act of aggression (physical or verbal) intended to harm a person's relationship or social standing. (p. 322)

**regresión relacional** acto de agresión (sea física o verbal) que tiene por intención hacerle daño a las relaciones de la persona o a su estatus social. (p. 322)

**relative deprivation** the perception that we are worse off relative to those with whom we compare ourselves. (p. 667)

**privación relativa** impresión de que estamos en peor situación que aquellos con quienes nos comparamos. (p. 667)

**relearning** a measure of memory that assesses the amount of time saved when learning material again. (p. 208)

**reaprendizaje** medida de memoria que evalúa el tiempo que se ahorra cuando se aprende algo por segunda vez. (p. 208)

**reliability** the extent to which a test yields consistent results, as assessed by the consistency of scores on two halves of the test, on alternative forms of the test, or on retesting. (p. 267)

**fiabilidad** grado de coherencia de los resultados de una prueba, que se comprueba por la uniformidad de las puntuaciones en las dos mitades de la prueba, en formas distintas de la prueba, o al repetir la prueba. (p. 267)

**REM rebound** the tendency for REM sleep to increase following REM sleep deprivation. (p. 112)

**rebote de MOR** tendencia al aumento del sueño MOR como consecuencia de la privación del sueño MOR. (p. 112)

**REM sleep** rapid eye movement sleep; a recurring sleep stage during which vivid dreams commonly occur. Also known as *paradoxical sleep*, because the muscles are relaxed (except for minor twitches) but other body systems are active. (Sometimes called *R sleep*.) (p. 94)

**sueño MOR** sueño de movimiento ocular rápido; etapa recurrente del sueño durante la cual generalmente ocurren sueños gráficos. También se conoce como *sueño paradójico*, porque los músculos están relajados (salvo unos espasmos mínimos) pero los demás sistemas del cuerpo están activos. (p. 94)

**REM sleep behavior disorder** a sleep disorder in which normal REM paralysis does not occur; instead, twitching, talking, or even kicking or punching may occur, often acting out one's dream. (p. 107)

**trastorno del comportamiento del sueño MOR** trastorno del sueño en el que no se produce la parálisis normal del sueño MOR; en cambio, se producen espasmos, se habla o se dan patadas o puñetazos que pueden representar el sueño de la persona en cuestión. (p. 107)

**replication** repeating the essence of a research study, usually with different participants in different situations, to see whether the basic finding can be reproduced. (p. 0–15)

**replicación** repetir la esencia de un estudio de investigación, por lo general con participantes diferentes y en situaciones diferentes, para ver si las conclusiones básicas se pueden reproducir. (p. 0–15)

**representativeness heuristic** judging the likelihood of events in terms of how well they seem to represent, or match, particular prototypes; may lead us to ignore other relevant information. (p. 196)

**heurística de la representatividad** juzga la probabilidad de cierto evento en función de qué tan bien representan o corresponden a prototipos particulares; posiblemente nos lleve a ignorar otra información relevante. (p. 196)

**repression** in psychoanalytic theory, the basic defense mechanism that banishes from consciousness anxiety-arousing thoughts, feelings, and memories. (pp. 243, 532)

**represión** en la teoría del psicoanálisis, el mecanismo básico de defensa por medio del cual el sujeto elimina de su consciente aquellos pensamientos, emociones o recuerdos que le producen ansiedad. (pp. 243, 532)

**resilience** the personal strength that helps people cope with stress and recover from adversity and even trauma. (p. 673)

**resiliencia** fuerza personal que ayuda a las personas a asumir con flexibilidad situaciones de estrés y recuperarse de la adversidad e incluso de un trauma. (p. 673)

**resistance** in psychoanalysis, the blocking from consciousness of anxiety-laden material. (p. 747)

**resistencia** en el psicoanálisis, bloquear del consciente aquello que está cargado de ansiedad. (p. 747)

**respondent behavior** behavior that occurs as an automatic response to some stimulus. (p. 402)

**comportamiento de respuesta** comportamiento que ocurre como respuesta automática a un estímulo. (p. 402)

**reticular formation** a nerve network that travels through the brainstem into the thalamus; it filters information and plays an important role in controlling arousal. (p. 65)

**formación reticular** red de nervios que atraviesa el tronco encefálico e ingresa en el tálamo; filtra información y desempeña un papel importante en el control de la excitación. (p. 65)

**retina** the light-sensitive back inner surface of the eye, containing the receptor rods and cones plus layers of neurons that begin the processing of visual information. (p. 125)

**retina** superficie en la parte interior trasera del ojo que es sensible a la luz y que contiene los receptores de luz llamados bastoncillos y conos, además de capas de neuronas que inician el procesamiento de la información visual. (p. 125)

**retinal disparity** a binocular cue for perceiving depth. By comparing retinal images from the two eyes, the brain computes distance—the greater the disparity (difference) between the two images, the closer the object. (p. 177)

**disparidad retiniana** clave binocular para la percepción de la profundidad. Mediante la comparación de las imágenes que provienen de ambos ojos, el cerebro calcula la distancia. Cuanto mayor sea la disparidad (diferencia) entre dos imágenes, más cerca estará el objeto. (p. 177)

**retrieval** the process of getting information out of memory storage. (p. 209)

**recuperación** proceso de extraer la información que está almacenada en la memoria. (p. 209)

**retroactive interference** the backward-acting disruptive effect of newer learning on the recall of *old* information. (p. 242)

**interferencia retroactiva** efecto interruptor de algo nuevo que se ha aprendido en la capacidad de recordar información *vieja*. (p. 242)

**retrograde amnesia** an inability to remember information from one's past. (p. 239)

**amnesia retrógrada** incapacidad de una persona para recordar información de su pasado. (p. 239)

**reuptake** a neurotransmitter's reabsorption by the sending neuron. (p. 32)

**recaptación** reabsorción de un neurotransmisor por la neurona emisora. (p. 32)

**rods** retinal receptors that detect black, white, and gray, and are sensitive to movement; necessary for peripheral and twilight vision, when cones don't respond. (p. 126)

**bastoncillos** receptores de la retina que detectan el negro, el blanco y el gris, y que son sensibles al movimiento; necesarios para la visión periférica y en la penumbra cuando los conos no responden. (p. 126)

**role** a set of expectations (*norms*) about a social position, defining how those in the position ought to behave. (pp. 328, 469)

**rol** conjunto de expectativas (*normas*) acerca de una posición social, que definen la forma en que deben comportarse las personas que ocupan esa posición. (pp. 328, 469)

**Rorschach inkblot test** a projective test designed by Hermann Rorschach; seeks to identify people's inner feelings by analyzing how they interpret 10 inkblots. (p. 538)

**prueba de Rorschach** prueba proyectiva diseñado por Hermann Rorschach; busca identificar los sentimientos internos de las personas mediante el análisis de cómo interpretan un conjunto de 10 manchas de tinta. (p. 538)

**rumination** compulsive fretting; *overthinking* our problems and their causes. (p. 718)

**ruminación** preocupación compulsiva; *pensar excesivamente* en nuestros problemas y sus causas. (p. 718)

## S

**sampling bias** a flawed sampling process that produces an unrepresentative sample. (p. 0–19)

**sesgo de muestreo** proceso de muestreo fallido que produce una muestra no representativa. (p. 0–19)

**savant syndrome** a condition in which a person otherwise limited in mental ability has an exceptional specific skill, such as in computation or drawing. (p. 256)

**síndrome de savant** condición según la cual una persona de capacidad mental limitada, cuenta con una destreza excepcional en un campo como la computación o el dibujo. (p. 256)

**scaffold** in Vygotsky's theory, a framework that offers children temporary support as they develop higher levels of thinking. (p. 354)

**andamiaje** en la teoría de Vygotsky, estructura que ofrece apoyo provisional a los niños mientras desarrollan un orden más alto de pensamiento. (p. 354)

**scapegoat theory** the theory that prejudice offers an outlet for anger by providing someone to blame. (p. 463)

**teoría del chivo expiatorio** teoría que expone que el prejuicio ofrece un escape para el enojo porque nos brinda a alguien a quien culpar. (p. 463)

**scatterplot** a graphed cluster of dots, each of which represents the values of two variables. The slope of the points suggests the direction of the relationship between the two variables. The amount of scatter suggests the strength of the correlation (little scatter indicates high correlation). (p. 0–22)

**gráfico de aspersión** conjunto de datos graficados, cada uno de los cuales representa los valores de dos variables. La pendiente de los puntos sugiere el sentido de la relación entre las dos variables. El nivel de aspersión sugiere la fuerza de la correlación (un bajo nivel de aspersión indica alta correlación). (p. 0–22)

**schema** a concept or framework that organizes and interprets information. (pp. 188, 349)

**esquema** concepto o marco referencial que organiza e interpreta la información. (pp. 188, 349)

**schizophrenia spectrum disorders** a group of disorders characterized by delusions, hallucinations, disorganized thinking or speech, disorganized or unusual motor behavior, and negative symptoms (such as diminished emotional expression); includes *schizophrenia* and *schizotypal personality disorder*. (p. 722)

**trastornos del espectro de la esquizofrenia** conjunto de trastornos caracterizados por delirios, alucinaciones, pensamiento o discurso desorganizado, comportamiento motor desorganizado o inusual, y síntomas negativos (como expresión emocional disminuida); incluye la *esquizofrenia* y el *trastorno de personalidad esquizotípico*. (p. 722)

**secondary sex characteristics** nonreproductive sexual traits, such as female breasts and hips, male voice quality, and body hair. (p. 326)

**características secundarias del sexo** rasgos sexuales no relacionados con la reproducción, tales como los senos y las caderas de las mujeres, la calidad de la voz del varón, y el vello corporal. (p. 326)

**secure attachment** demonstrated by infants who comfortably explore environments in the presence of their caregiver, show only temporary distress when the caregiver leaves, and find comfort in the caregiver's return. (p. 376)

**apego seguro** exhibido por infantes que exploran su entorno cómodamente en la presencia de su cuidador, sólo muestran angustia temporal en ausencia del cuidador, y se consuelan con el retorno del cuidador. (p. 376)

**selective attention** focusing conscious awareness on a particular stimulus. (p. 166)

**atención selectiva** enfocar la consciencia en un estímulo en particular. (p. 166)

**self** in modern psychology, assumed to be the center of personality, the organizer of our thoughts, feelings, and actions. (p. 568)

**yo** en la psicología moderna, se asume que es el centro de la personalidad, el organizador de nuestros pensamientos, sentimientos y acciones. (p. 568)

**self-actualization** according to Maslow, one of the ultimate psychological needs that arises after basic physical and psychological needs are met and self-esteem is achieved; the motivation to fulfill one's potential. (p. 542)

**autorrealización** según Maslow, necesidad psicológica que surge después de satisfacer las necesidades físicas y psicológicas y de lograr la autoestima; motivación para realizar nuestro potencial pleno. (p. 542)

**self-concept** all our thoughts and feelings about ourselves in answer to the question, "Who am I?" (pp. 381, 545)

**concepto de uno mismo** todo lo que pensamos y sentimos acerca de nosotros mismos cuando respondemos a la pregunta: "¿Quién soy?". (pp. 381, 545)

**self-control** the ability to control impulses and delay short-term gratification for greater long-term rewards. (p. 657)

**autocontrol** capacidad de controlar los impulsos y demorar la gratificación a corto plazo con el fin de obtener mayores recompensas a largo plazo. (p. 657)

**self-determination theory** the theory that we feel motivated to satisfy our needs for competence, autonomy, and relatedness. (p. 587)

**teoría de la autodeterminación** teoría que establece que sentimos motivación por satisfacer nuestras necesidades de competencia, autonomía y relación. (p. 587)

**self-disclosure** the act of revealing intimate aspects of ourselves to others. (p. 511)

**revelación personal** revelación a los demás de cosas íntimas de nuestro ser. (p. 511)

**self-efficacy** our sense of competence and effectiveness. (p. 569)

**autoeficacia** nuestros sentimientos de competencia y eficacia. (p. 569)

**self-esteem** our feelings of high or low self-worth. (p. 569)

**self-fulfilling prophecy** a belief that leads to its own fulfillment. (p. 519)

**self-report bias** bias when people report their behavior inaccurately. (p. 0–19)

**self-serving bias** a readiness to perceive ourselves favorably. (p. 570)

**self-transcendence** according to Maslow, the striving for identity, meaning, and purpose beyond the self. (p. 542)

**semantic memory** explicit memory of facts and general knowledge; one of our two conscious memory systems (the other is *episodic memory*). (p. 227)

**sensation** the process by which our sensory receptors and nervous system receive and represent stimulus energies from our environment. (p. 116)

**sensorimotor stage** in Piaget's theory, the stage (from birth to nearly 2 years of age) at which infants know the world mostly in terms of their sensory impressions and motor activities. (p. 350)

**sensorineural hearing loss** the most common form of hearing loss, caused by damage to the cochlea's receptor cells or to the auditory nerve; also called *nerve deafness*. (p. 138)

**sensory (afferent) neurons** neurons that carry incoming information from the body's tissues and sensory receptors to the brain and spinal cord. (p. 22)

**sensory adaptation** diminished sensitivity as a consequence of constant stimulation. (p. 120)

**sensory interaction** the principle that one sense may influence another, as when the smell of food influences its taste. (p. 154)

**sensory memory** the immediate, very brief recording of sensory information in the memory system. (p. 209)

**sensory receptors** sensory nerve endings that respond to stimuli. (p. 116)

**sequential processing** processing one aspect of a stimulus or problem at a time; generally used to process new information or to solve difficult problems. (p. 91)

**serial position effect** our tendency to recall best the last items in a list initially (a *recency effect*) and the first items in a list after a delay (a *primacy effect*). (p. 234)

**set point** the point at which the "weight thermostat" may be set. When the body falls below this weight, increased hunger and a lowered metabolic rate may combine to restore lost weight. (p. 601)

**sex** in psychology, the biologically influenced characteristics by which people define *male*, and *female*, and *intersex*. (p. 320)

**sexual aggression** any physical or verbal behavior of a sexual nature that is unwanted or intended to harm someone physically or emotionally. Can be expressed as either *sexual harassment* or *sexual assault*. (p. 329)

**autoestima** nuestros sentimientos de alto o bajo valor. (p. 569)

**profecía autorrealizada** creencia que conduce a su propia realización. (p. 519)

**sesgo de autorreporte** sesgo que se produce cuando las personas informan su comportamiento de manera inexacta. (p. 0-19)

**sesgo autocomplaciente** disposición para percibirnos a nosotros mismos de manera favorable. (p. 570)

**autotrascendencia** según Maslow, esfuerzo por alcanzar una identidad, un sentido y un propósito que vaya más allá de uno mismo. (p. 542)

**memoria semántica** memoria explícita de hechos y conocimientos generales. Uno de los dos sistemas de memoria consciente (el otro es la *memoria episódica*). (p. 227)

**sensación** proceso mediante el cual los receptores sensoriales y el sistema nervioso reciben las energías de los estímulos provenientes de nuestro entorno. (p. 116)

**etapa sensoriomotriz** en la teoría de Piaget, la etapa (de los 0 a los 2 años de edad) en la cual los bebés conocen el mundo principalmente en términos de sus impresiones sensoriales y actividades motoras. (p. 350)

**pérdida de la audición sensorineuronal** la forma más común de sordera, causada por daños a las células receptoras de la cóclea o el nervio de la audición; también se le dice *sordera nerviosa*. (p. 138)

**neurona sensorial (aferente)** neurona que conduce la información que le llega desde los tejidos del cuerpo y los receptores sensoriales al cerebro y la médula espinal. (p. 22)

**adaptación sensorial** disminución en la sensibilidad como respuesta a la estimulación constante. (p. 120)

**interacción sensorial** principio según el cual un sentido puede influir en otro, como cuando el olor de la comida influye en su sabor. (p. 154)

**memoria sensorial** registro breve e inmediato de la información sensorial en el sistema de la memoria. (p. 209)

**receptores sensoriales** terminales nerviosas sensoriales que responden a estímulos. (p. 116)

**procesamiento secuencial** procesamiento de un aspecto de un estímulo o problema a la vez; se utiliza cuando centramos la atención en tareas nuevas o complejas. (p. 91)

**efecto de posición serial** tendencia a recordar con mayor facilidad los últimos elementos de una lista en un principio (*efecto de recencia*) y los primeros elementos de la lista con el paso del tiempo (*efecto de primacía*). (p. 234)

**punto fijo** punto de supuesto equilibrio en el "termostato del peso" de una persona. Cuando el cuerpo alcanza un peso por debajo de este punto, se produce un aumento en el hambre y una disminución en el índice metabólico, los cuales pueden actuar para restablecer el peso perdido. (p. 601)

**sexo** en psicología, las características biológicas por las cuales la sociedad define al *hombre*, la *mujer*, y a las personas *intersexo*. (p. 320)

**agresión sexual** cualquier comportamiento físico o verbal de naturaleza sexual no deseado o que tiene la intención de causar daños físicos o emocionales. Se puede llamar también *acoso sexual* o *asalto sexual*. (p. 329)

**sexual orientation** according to the APA (2015), "a person's sexual and emotional attraction to another person and the behavior and/or social affiliation that may result from this attraction." (p. 341)

**orientación sexual** según la APA (2015), "la atracción sexual y emocional de una persona hacia otra persona y el comportamiento y/o afiliación social que puede resultar de esta atracción." (p. 341)

**sexuality** our thoughts, feelings, and actions related to our physical attraction to another. (p. 333)

**sexualidad** nuestros pensamientos, sentimientos y acciones relacionadas con la atracción física hacia alguien más. (p. 333)

**shallow processing** encoding on a basic level, based on the structure or appearance of words. (p. 222)

**procesamiento superficial** codificación en un nivel básico, según la estructura o la apariencia de las palabras. (p. 222)

**shaping** an operant conditioning procedure in which reinforcers guide behavior toward closer and closer approximations of the desired behavior. (p. 418)

**modelamiento** procedimiento del condicionamiento operante en el cual los reforzadores conducen una acción con aproximaciones sucesivas hasta lograr el comportamiento deseado. (p. 418)

**short-term memory** briefly activated memory of a few items (such as digits of a phone number while calling) that is later stored or forgotten. (p. 209)

**memoria de corto plazo** memoria que se activa brevemente con algunos elementos (como los dígitos de un número de teléfono durante una llamada) que luego se almacena u olvida. (p. 209)

**signal detection theory** a theory predicting how and when we detect the presence of a faint stimulus (*signal*) amid background stimulation (*noise*). Assumes there is no single absolute threshold and that detection depends partly on a person's experience, expectations, motivation, and alertness. (p. 117)

**teoría de la detección de señales** teoría que predice cómo y cuando detectamos la presencia de un estímulo débil (*señal*) cuando hay estímulos de fondo (*ruido*). Supone que no hay un umbral absoluto y que la detección depende en parte en las experiencias, expectativas, motivaciones y estado de alerta de la persona. (p. 117)

**single-blind procedure** an experimental procedure in which the research participants are ignorant (blind) about whether they have received the treatment or a placebo. (p. 0–28)

**procedimiento simple ciego** procedimiento experimental en el cual los participantes de la investigación desconocen (están a ciegas) si han recibido el tratamiento o un placebo. (p. 0–28)

**skewed distribution** a representation of scores that lack symmetry around their average value. (p. 0–42)

**sesgo de distribución** representación de puntajes que carece de simetría alrededor de su valor promedio. (p. 0–42)

**sleep** a periodic, natural loss of consciousness—as distinct from unconsciousness resulting from a coma, general anesthesia, or hibernation. (Adapted from Dement, 1999.) (p. 93)

**sueño** pérdida del conocimiento periódica y natural; a diferencia de la inconsciencia que puede resultar del estado de coma, de la anestesia general o de la hibernación. (Adaptado de Dement, 1999.) (p. 93)

**sleep apnea** a sleep disorder characterized by temporary cessations of breathing during sleep and repeated momentary awakenings. (p. 107)

**apnea del sueño** trastorno del sueño en el que se interrumpe repetidamente la respiración hasta que el nivel de oxígeno en la sangre disminuye tanto que la persona tiene que despertarse para respirar. (p. 107)

**social anxiety disorder** intense fear and avoidance of social situations. (p. 699)

**trastorno de ansiedad social** miedo intenso y evasión de situaciones sociales. (p. 699)

**social clock** the culturally preferred timing of social events such as marriage, parenthood, and retirement. (p. 392)

**reloj social** manera que la sociedad prefiere para marcar el tiempo adecuado de los eventos sociales, tales como el matrimonio, la paternidad y la jubilación. (p. 392)

**social desirability bias** bias from people's responding in ways they presume a researcher expects or wishes. (p. 0–19)

**sesgo de deseabilidad social** sesgo de respuesta de acuerdo a las expectativas o deseos percibidos del investigador. (p. 0–19)

**social exchange theory** the theory that our social behavior is an exchange process, the aim of which is to maximize benefits and minimize costs. (p. 517)

**teoría de intercambio social** teoría según la cual nuestro comportamiento se encuentra en un estado de intercambio, cuyo fin es maximizar los beneficios y minimizar los costos. (p. 517)

**social facilitation** in the presence of others, improved performance on simple or well-learned tasks, and worsened performance on difficult tasks. (p. 486)

**facilitación social** en la presencia de terceros, mejoramiento del desempeño en funciones sencillas o bien aprendidas y el empeoramiento del desempeño en funciones difíciles. (p. 486)

**social identity** the "we" aspect of our self-concept; the part of our answer to "Who am I?" that comes from our group memberships. (pp. 387, 462)

**identidad social** aspecto de "nosotros" dentro de nuestro concepto de nosotros mismos; parte de nuestra respuesta a "¿Quién soy?" que proviene de nuestra pertenencia a grupos. (pp. 387, 462)

**social leadership** group-oriented leadership that builds teamwork, mediates conflict, and offers support. (p. 815)

**liderazgo social** liderazgo orientado al grupo que crea trabajo en equipo, media el conflicto y ofrece apoyo. (p. 815)

**social learning theory** the theory that we learn social behavior by observing and imitating and by being rewarded or punished. (p. 329)

**teoría del aprendizaje social** teoría según la cual aprendemos comportamientos sociales a través de la observación e imitación y por medio de recompensas y castigos. (p. 329)

**social loafing** the tendency for people in a group to exert less effort when pooling their efforts toward attaining a common goal than when individually accountable. (p. 487)

**holgazanería social** tendencia de las personas en un grupo de realizar menos esfuerzo cuando juntan sus esfuerzos para lograr una meta común que cuando son responsables individualmente. (p. 487)

**social psychology** the scientific study of how we think about, influence, and relate to one another. (p. 453)

**psicología social** estudio científico de cómo nos relacionamos con los demás y cómo influimos y pensamos en ellos. (p. 453)

**social script** a culturally modeled guide for how to act in various situations. (pp. 336, 499)

**guión social** guía modelada culturalmente acerca de cómo actuar en diversas situaciones. (pp. 336, 499)

**social trap** a situation in which two parties, by each pursuing their self-interest rather than the good of the group, become caught in mutually destructive behavior. (p. 518)

**trampa social** situación en la cual dos partes, al perseguir cada uno su interés propio y no el del grupo, caen en comportamientos mutuamente destructivos. (p. 518)

**social-cognitive perspective** a view of behavior as influenced by the interaction between people's traits (including their thinking) and their social context. (p. 561)

**perspectiva sociocognitiva** contempla al comportamiento como susceptible a la influencia de la interacción entre los rasgos de las personas (que incluye su pensamiento) y su contexto social. (p. 561)

**social-responsibility norm** an expectation that people will help those needing their help. (p. 517)

**norma de responsabilidad social** expectativa según la cual las personas ayudarán a aquellos que necesitan ayuda. (p. 517)

**somatic nervous system** the division of the peripheral nervous system that controls the body's skeletal muscles. Also called the *skeletal nervous system*. (p. 23)

**sistema nervioso somático** división del sistema nervioso periférico que controla los músculos esqueléticos del cuerpo. También llamado *sistema nervioso esquelético*. (p. 23)

**somatosensory cortex** a cerebral cortex area at the front of the parietal lobes that registers and processes body touch and movement sensations. (p. 74)

**corteza somatosensorial** región de la corteza cerebral en la parte delantera de los lóbulos parietales. Registra y procesa el tacto y las sensaciones de movimiento. (p. 74)

**source amnesia** faulty memory for how, when, or where information was learned or imagined (as when *misattributing information to a wrong source*). Source amnesia, along with the misinformation effect, is at the heart of many false memories. (p. 246)

**amnesia de la fuente** recuerdo errado de cómo, cuándo o dónde se aprendió o se imaginó la información (como cuando se atribuye información errónea a una fuente equivocada). La amnesia de la fuente, junto con el efecto de información errónea, son la razón de muchos recuerdos falsos. (p. 246)

**spacing effect** the tendency for *distributed* study or practice to yield better long-term retention than is achieved through *massed* study or practice. (p. 220)

**efecto de memoria espaciada** tendencia en la que el estudio o la práctica *distribuida* rinde mejor retención a largo plazo que el estudio o práctica *en masa*. (p. 220)

**specific phobia** an anxiety disorder marked by a persistent, irrational fear and avoidance of a specific object, activity, or situation. (p. 700)

**fobia específica** trastorno de ansiedad marcada por un temor persistente e irracional y la evitación de un objeto, actividad o situación específico. (p. 700)

**spermarche** [sper-MAR-key] the first ejaculation. (p. 326)

**espermarca** primera eyaculación. (p. 326)

**split brain** a condition resulting from surgery that isolates the brain's two hemispheres by cutting the fibers (mainly those of the corpus callosum) connecting them. (p. 82)

**cerebro dividido** condición en la que los dos hemisferios cerebrales se privan de la comunicación mediante el corte quirúrgico de las fibras que los conectan (principalmente las del cuerpo calloso). (p. 82)

**spontaneous recovery** the reappearance, after a pause, of a weakened conditioned response. (p. 406)

**recuperación espontánea** reaparición, después de una pausa, de una respuesta condicionada debilitada. (p. 406)

**spotlight effect** overestimating others' noticing and evaluating our appearance, performance, and blunders (as if we presume a spotlight shines on us). (p. 568)

**efecto de foco** sobrestimar la atención y evaluación de nuestra apariencia, desempeño y errores por parte de los demás (como si asumiéramos que un foco o luz de escenario brilla sobre nosotros). (p. 568)

**standard deviation** a computed measure of how much scores vary around the mean score. (p. 0–43)

**desviación estándar** medición computada de cuánto varía cierta puntuación con respecto a la puntuación media. (p. 0–43)

**standardization** defining uniform testing procedures and meaningful scores by comparison with the performance of a pretested group. (p. 265)

**estandarización** definir procedimientos de medición uniformes y puntuaciones significativos mediante la comparación del desempeño de un grupo examinado con anterioridad. (p. 265)

**Stanford-Binet** the widely used American revision (by Terman at Stanford University) of Binet's original intelligence test. (p. 264)

**Stanford-Binet** revisión norteamericana (por Terman en la Universidad de Stanford) de la prueba original de inteligencia de Binet. Esta prueba es de uso extenso. (p. 264)

**statistical significance** a statistical statement of how likely it is that a result (such as a difference between samples) occurred by chance, assuming there is no difference between the populations being studied. (p. 0–45)

**significancia estadística** declaración estadística de la probabilidad de que un resultado (como una diferencia entre muestras) ocurrió por casualidad, bajo la suposición de que no hay diferencia entre las poblaciones que se están estudiando. (p. 0–45)

| | |
|---|---|
| **stereotype** a generalized (sometimes accurate but often overgeneralized) belief about a group of people. (p. 457) | **estereotipo** creencia (a veces acertada, pero frecuentemente demasiado generalizada) sobre las características de un grupo. (p. 457) |
| **stereotype threat** a self-confirming concern that one will be evaluated based on a negative stereotype. (p. 285) | **amenaza de estereotipos** preocupación autoconfirmada de que nos evaluarán con base en un estereotipo negativo. (p. 285) |
| **stimulants** drugs that excite neural activity and speed up body functions. (p. 45) | **estimulantes** fármacos que excitan la actividad neuronal y aceleran las funciones corporales. (p. 45) |
| **stimulus** any event or situation that evokes a response. (p. 401) | **estímulo** todo suceso o situación que provoca una respuesta. (p. 401) |
| **storage** the process of retaining encoded information over time. (p. 209) | **almacenamiento** retención a través del tiempo de información codificada. (p. 209) |
| **strange situation** a procedure for studying child-caregiver attachment; a child is placed in an unfamiliar environment while their caregiver leaves and then returns, and the child's reactions are observed. (p. 376) | **situación desconocida** procedimiento para estudiar el apego entre niño y cuidador; se coloca al niño en un entorno desconocido mientras su cuidador se va y regresa. Entretanto se observan las reacciones del niño. (p. 376) |
| **stranger anxiety** the fear of strangers that infants commonly display, beginning by about 8 months of age. (p. 374) | **miedo a los extraños** miedo a los extraños que manifiestan los bebés normalmente a partir de alrededor de los 8 meses de edad. (p. 374) |
| **stress** the process by which we perceive and respond to certain events, called *stressors*, that we appraise as threatening or challenging. (p. 639) | **estrés** proceso mediante el cual percibimos y respondemos a ciertos eventos llamados *estresores*, los cuales evaluamos como amenazantes o desafiantes. (p. 639) |
| **stroboscopic movement** an illusion of continuous movement (as in a motion picture) experienced when viewing a rapid series of slightly varying still images. (p. 179) | **movimiento estroboscópico** ilusión de movimiento continuo (como en una película) que se experimenta al ver una serie rápida de imágenes fijas que varían mínimamente. (p. 179) |
| **structured interview** an interview process that asks the same job-relevant questions of all applicants, each of whom is rated on established scales. (p. 810) | **entrevista estructurada** proceso de entrevista en el que se hacen las mismas preguntas laborales a todos los solicitantes, los cuales son calificados sobre escalas establecidas. (p. 810) |
| **subjective well-being** self-perceived happiness or satisfaction with life. Used along with measures of objective well-being (for example, physical and economic indicators) to evaluate people's quality of life. (p. 663) | **bienestar subjetivo** felicidad o satisfacción con la vida de uno mismo. Se emplea junto con medidas de bienestar objetivas (por ejemplo, con indicadores físicos y económicos) para evaluar nuestra calidad de vida. (p. 663) |
| **subliminal** below one's absolute threshold for conscious awareness. (p. 118) | **subliminal** aquello que ocurre por debajo de nuestro umbral absoluto de la consciencia. (p. 118) |
| **substance use disorder** a disorder characterized by continued substance use despite significant life disruption. (p. 40) | **trastornos causados por el uso de estupefacientes** trastorno caracterizado por uso prolongado de una sustancia a pesar de los efectos negativos en la vida de quienes abusan de las sustancias. (p. 40) |
| **superego** the partly conscious part of personality that, according to Freud, represents internalized ideals and provides standards for judgment (the conscience) and for future aspirations. (p. 530) | **supergo** en el psicoanálisis freudiano, componente parcialmente consciente de la personalidad que representa ideales internalizados y proporciona parámetros de juicio (la consciencia) y para fijarse metas futuras. (p. 530) |
| **superordinate goals** shared goals that override differences among people and require their cooperation. (p. 520) | **metas comunes** metas compartidas que hacen caso omiso de las diferencias entre las personas y que requieren su cooperación. (p. 520) |
| **suprachiasmatic nucleus (SCN)** a pair of cell clusters in the hypothalamus that controls circadian rhythm. In response to light, the SCN adjusts melatonin production, thus modifying our feelings of sleepiness. (p. 98) | **núcleo supraquiasmático (NSQ)** par de grupos de células en el hipotálamo que controlan el ritmo circadiano. Como respuesta a la luz, el núcleo supraquiasmático ajusta la producción de melatonina, modificando de esta manera los niveles de somnolencia. (p. 98) |
| **survey** a non-experimental technique for obtaining the self-reported attitudes or behaviors of a particular group, usually by questioning a representative, *random sample* of the group. (p. 0–18) | **encuesta** técnica no experimental para obtener actitudes o conductas del grupo autoinformadas por las personas; generalmente mediante preguntas que se le plantean a una *muestra aleatoria* y representativa de dicho grupo. (p. 0–18) |
| **sympathetic nervous system** the division of the autonomic nervous system that arouses the body, mobilizing its energy. (p. 23) | **sistema nervioso simpático** subdivisión del sistema nervioso autonómico que en despierta al cuerpo y moviliza su energía. (p. 23) |
| **synapse** [SIN-aps] the junction between the axon tip of the sending neuron and the dendrite or cell body of the receiving neuron. The tiny gap at this junction is called the *synaptic gap* or *synaptic cleft*. (p. 31) | **sinapsis** intersección entre el extremo del axón de una neurona que envía un mensaje y la dendrita o cuerpo celular de la neurona receptora. El pequeño espacio entre estos puntos de contacto se denomina *brecha sináptica* o *hendidura sináptica*. (p. 31) |

**systematic desensitization** a type of exposure therapy that associates a pleasant relaxed state with gradually increasing anxiety-triggering stimuli. Commonly used to treat specific phobias. (p. 754)

**desensibilización sistemática** tipo de terapia de exposición en la cual se asocia un estado tranquilo y agradable con estímulos que van aumentando paulatinamente y que provocan ansiedad. De uso común para tratar fobias específicas. (p. 754)

## T

**task leadership** goal-oriented leadership that sets standards, organizes work, and focuses attention on goals. (p. 814)

**liderazgo orientado a la tarea** liderazgo orientado a objetivos que establece estándares, organiza el trabajo y enfoca la atención sobre metas. (p. 814)

**telegraphic speech** the early speech stage in which a child speaks like a telegram—"go car"—using mostly nouns and verbs. (p. 365)

**habla telegráfica** la etapa temprana del habla en la cuál los niños hablan como telegrama—"va carro"—mediante sustantivos y verbos principalmente. (p. 365)

**temperament** a person's characteristic emotional reactivity and intensity. (p. 376)

**temperamento** reactividad e intensidad emocionales características de una persona. (p. 376)

**temporal lobes** the portion of the cerebral cortex lying roughly above the ears; it includes the auditory areas, each of which receives information primarily from the opposite ear. They also enable language processing. (p. 71)

**lóbulos temporales** región de la corteza cerebral ubicada aproximadamente encima de las orejas; incluye las áreas auditivas, cada una de las cuales recibe información principalmente del oído opuesto. También permiten el procesamiento del lenguaje. (p. 71)

**tend-and-befriend response** under stress, people (especially women) may nurture themselves and others (*tend*) and bond with and seek support from others (*befriend*). (p. 645)

**respuesta de cuidarse y amigarse** en situaciones de estrés, las personas (sobre todo las mujeres) pueden ver por sí mismos y por otros (*se cuidan*), a la vez que forman vínculos y buscan apoyo de otros (*amigarse*). (p. 645)

**teratogens** agents, such as chemicals and viruses, that can reach the embryo or fetus during prenatal development and cause harm. (p. 304)

**teratógeno** agentes, químicos o virales, que pueden afectar al embrión o al feto durante el desarrollo prenatal, produciéndole daño. (p. 304)

**terror-management theory** a theory of death-related anxiety; explores people's emotional and behavioral responses to reminders of their impending death. (p. 537)

**teoría del manejo del terror** teoría de la ansiedad relacionada con la muerte; explora las respuestas emotivas y conductuales de las personas ante recordatorios de su muerte inevitable. (p. 537)

**testing effect** enhanced memory after retrieving, rather than simply rereading, information. Also referred to as a *retrieval practice effect* or *test-enhanced learning*. (p. 221)

**efecto de prueba** recuerdo aumentado luego de recuperar la información, en lugar de simplemente volver a leerla. También conocido como *efecto de práctica de recuperación* o *aprendizaje intensificado por pruebas*. (p. 221)

**testosterone** the most important male sex hormone. Males and females have it, but the additional testosterone in males stimulates the growth of the male sex organs during the fetal period and the development of male sex characteristics during puberty. (p. 325)

**testosterona** la hormona sexual masculina más importante. La tienen tanto los varones como las mujeres pero la cantidad adicional en los varones estimula el crecimiento de los órganos sexuales masculinos durante el período fetal y el desarrollo de las características sexuales masculinas secundarias en la pubertad. (p. 325)

**thalamus** [THAL-uh-muss] the forebrain's sensory control center, located on top of the brainstem; it directs messages to the sensory receiving areas in the cortex and transmits replies to the cerebellum and medulla. (p. 65)

**tálamo** centro sensorial de control del prosencéfalo ubicado encima del tronco encefálico; dirige mensajes sensoriales a la corteza cerebral y transmite respuestas al cerebelo y la médula. (p. 65)

**Thematic Apperception Test (TAT)** a projective test in which people express their inner feelings and interests through the stories they make up about ambiguous scenes. (p. 538)

**prueba de apercepción temática (PAT)** prueba proyectiva en la que el individuo expresa sus sentimientos e intereses internos mediante historias que inventa en torno a escenas ambiguas. (p. 538)

**theory** an explanation using an integrated set of principles that organizes observations and predicts behaviors or events. (p. 0–14)

**teoría** explicación que emplea principios que organizan observaciones y predicen comportamientos o sucesos. (p. 0–14)

**theory of mind** people's ideas about their own and others' mental states—about their feelings, perceptions, and thoughts, and the behaviors these might predict. (p. 355)

**teoría de la mente** conceptos que tienen las personas acerca de sus propios procesos mentales y de los de los demás; es decir, de sus sentimientos, percepciones y pensamiento y de los comportamientos que estos podrían predecir. (p. 355)

**therapeutic alliance** a bond of trust and mutual understanding between a therapist and client, who work together constructively to overcome the client's problem. (p. 771)

**alianza terapéutica** vínculo de confianza y comprensión mutua que se establece entre el terapeuta y el cliente, que trabajan juntos de manera constructiva para superar el problema del cliente. (p. 771)

**threshold** the level of stimulation required to trigger a neural impulse. (p. 30)

**umbral** nivel de estimulación requerido para desencadenar una respuesta neural. (p. 30)

**tight culture** a place with clearly defined and reliably imposed norms. (p. 492)

**cultura cerrada** lugar con normas claramente definidas y normas impuestas de manera confiable. (p. 492)

**token economy** an operant conditioning procedure in which people earn a token for exhibiting a desired behavior and can later exchange tokens for privileges or treats. (p. 756)

**economía de fichas** procedimiento del condicionamiento operante en el que las personas se ganan una ficha cuando exhiben un comportamiento deseado y luego pueden intercambiar las fichas ganadas por privilegios o para darse algún gusto. (p. 756)

**tolerance** the diminishing effect with regular use of the same dose of a drug, requiring the user to take larger and larger doses before experiencing the drug's effect. (p. 43)

**tolerancia** disminución del efecto con el uso regular de la misma dosis de un fármaco, lo que requiere que el usuario tome dosis cada vez mayores para poder experimentar el efecto del fármaco. (p. 43)

**top-down processing** information processing guided by higher-level mental processes, as when we construct perceptions drawing on our experience and expectations. (p. 116)

**procesamiento de arriba hacia abajo** procesamiento de la información orientado por procesos mentales de alto nivel, como cuando construimos percepciones basándonos en nuestras vivencias y expectativas. (p. 116)

**trait** a characteristic pattern of behavior or a disposition to feel and act in certain ways, as assessed by self-report inventories and peer reports. (p. 549)

**rasgo** patrón de comportamiento característico o disposición a sentirse y actuar de cierta forma, según se evalúa en los inventarios de autoinformes e informes de pares. (p. 549)

**transcranial magnetic stimulation (TMS)** the application of repeated pulses of magnetic energy to the brain; used to stimulate or suppress brain activity. (p. 782)

**estimulación magnética transcraneal (TMS)** la aplicación de pulsos repetidos de energía magnética al cerebro; se usa para estimular o suprimir la actividad cerebral. (p. 782)

**transduction** conversion of one form of energy into another. In sensation, the transforming of physical energy, such as sights, sounds, and smells, into neural impulses the brain can interpret. (p. 117)

**transducción** transformación de un tipo de energía en otro. En las sensaciones, transformación de la energía física, tales como las imágenes, los sonidos y los olores, en impulsos neuronales que el cerebro tiene la capacidad de interpretar. (p. 117)

**transference** in psychoanalysis, the patient's transfer to the analyst of emotions linked with other relationships (such as love or hatred for a parent). (p. 747)

**transferencia** en el psicoanálisis, la transferencia de emociones ligadas a otras relaciones, del paciente al analista (tales como el amor o el odio hacia el padre o la madre). (p. 747)

**trauma- and- stressor- related disorders** a group of disorders in which exposure to a traumatic or stressful event is followed by psychological distress. (p. 703)

**trastornos relacionados con traumas y factores de estrés** grupo de trastornos en los cuales un suceso traumático o estresante es seguido de angustia psicológica. (p. 703)

**two-word stage** beginning about age 2, the stage in speech development during which a child speaks mostly in two-word statements. (p. 365)

**etapa de dos palabras** a partir de los 2 años de edad, etapa del desarrollo del lenguaje durante la cual el niño emite mayormente frases de dos palabras. (p. 365)

**Type A** Friedman and Rosenman's term for competitive, hard-driving, impatient, verbally aggressive, and anger-prone people. (p. 648)

**Tipo A** término de Friedman y Rosenman para referirse a las personas competitivas, compulsivas, impacientes, verbalmente agresivas y con tendencia a enojarse. (p. 648)

**Type B** Friedman and Rosenman's term for easygoing, relaxed people. (p. 648)

**Tipo B** término de Friedman y Rosenman para referirse a las personas tolerantes, relajadas y tranquilas. (p. 648)

## U

**unconditional positive regard** a caring, accepting, nonjudgmental attitude, which Carl Rogers believed would help clients develop self-awareness and self-acceptance. (Also known as *unconditional regard*.) (pp. 544, 750)

**consideración positiva incondicional** actitud de cuidado, aceptación y parcialidad. Según Rogers, así los clientes desarrollarían consciencia y aceptación de sí mismos. (También se conoce como *consideración incondicional*). (pp. 544, 750)

**unconditioned response (UCR)** in classical conditioning, an unlearned, naturally occurring response (such as salivation) to an unconditioned stimulus (UCS) (such as food in the mouth). (p. 405)

**respuesta incondicionada (RI)** en el condicionamiento clásico, la respuesta no aprendida e innata que es producida por un estímulo incondicionado (EI) (como la salivación cuando la comida está en la boca). (p. 405)

**unconditioned stimulus (UCS)** in classical conditioning, a stimulus that unconditionally—naturally and automatically—triggers an unconditioned response UCR). (p. 405)

**estímulo incondicionado (EI)** en el condicionamiento clásico, estímulo que provoca una respuesta incondicionalmente (RI) y de manera natural y automática. (p. 405)

**unconscious** according to Freud, a reservoir of mostly unacceptable thoughts, wishes, feelings, and memories. According to contemporary psychologists, information processing of which we are unaware. (p. 529)

**inconsciente** según Freud, un depósito de pensamientos, deseos, sentimientos y recuerdos, en su mayoría inaceptables. Según los psicólogos contemporáneos, el procesamiento de información del cual no tenemos consciencia. (p. 529)

**universal grammar** humans' innate predisposition to understand the principles and rules that govern grammar in all languages. (p. 364)

**gramática universal** predisposición innata de los humanos para entender los principios y reglas que gobiernan la gramática en todas las lenguas. (p. 364)

## V

**validity** the extent to which a test or experiment measures or predicts what it is supposed to. (See also *predictive validity*.) (pp. 0–29, 267)

**validez** grado en que una prueba mide o predice lo que se supone debe medir o predecir. (Ver también *validez predictiva*.) (pp. 0–29, 267)

**variable** anything that can vary and is feasible and ethical to measure. (p. 0–22)

**variable** todo aquello que varía y que es viable y ético para ser medido. (p. 0–22)

**variable-interval schedule** in operant conditioning, a reinforcement schedule that reinforces a response at unpredictable time intervals. (p. 423)

**calendario de intervalo variable** según el condicionamiento operante, calendario de reforzamientos que refuerza una respuesta en intervalos de tiempo impredecibles. (p. 423)

**variable-ratio schedule** in operant conditioning, a reinforcement schedule that reinforces a response after an unpredictable number of responses. (p. 422)

**plan de proporción variable** en el condicionamiento operante, plan de reforzamientos que refuerza una respuesta después de un número impredecible de respuestas. (p. 422)

**vestibular sense** our balance sense; our sense of body movement and position that enables our sense of balance. (p. 152)

**sentido vestibular** nuestro sentido de equilibrio; sentido de movimiento y posición del cuerpo que habilita nuestro sentido de equilibrio. (p. 152)

**virtual reality exposure therapy** a counterconditioning technique that treats anxiety through creative electronic simulations in which people can safely face specific fears, such as flying, spiders, or public speaking. (p. 755)

**terapia de exposición a una realidad virtual** técnica del contracondicionamiento que trata la ansiedad mediante estimulaciones electrónicas creativas en las cuales las personas enfrentan a sus temores específicos, como volar, ver una araña o hablar en público. (p. 755)

**visuospatial sketchpad** a memory component that briefly holds information about objects' appearance and location in space. (p. 210)

**boceto visoespacial** componente de la memoria que retiene brevemente información sobre el aspecto y ubicación de los objetos en el espacio. (p. 210)

**visual cliff** a laboratory device for testing depth perception in infants and young animals. (p. 176)

**precipicio visual** dispositivo del laboratorio con el que se examina la percepción de profundidad en los bebés y en animales de corta edad. (p. 176)

## W

**wavelength** the distance from the peak of one light or sound wave to the peak of the next. Electromagnetic wavelengths vary from the short gamma waves to the long pulses of radio transmission. (p. 124)

**longitud de onda** distancia entre la cresta de una onda de luz o de sonido y la cresta de la siguiente onda. La longitud de las ondas electromagnéticas varían desde las ondas gamma cortas hasta los largos pulsos de transmisión de radio. (p. 124)

**Weber's law** the principle that, to be perceived as different, two stimuli must differ by a constant minimum percentage (rather than a constant amount). (p. 120)

**ley de Weber** principio que sostiene que para que dos estímulos se perciban como distintos, estos deben diferir por un porcentaje mínimo constante (en vez de por una cantidad constante). (p. 120)

**Wechsler Adult Intelligence Scale (WAIS)** the WAIS and its companion versions for children are the most widely used intelligence tests; they contain verbal and performance (nonverbal) subtests. (p. 265)

**escala de la Inteligencia de Wechsler para adultos (EIWA)** la prueba EIWA y su versión adaptada para niños son las pruebas de inteligencia más ampliamente utilizadas. Incluyen subpruebas verbales y de desempeño (no verbales). (p. 265)

**Wernicke's area** a brain area, usually in the left temporal lobe, involved in language comprehension and expression. (p. 368)

**área de Wernicke** área del cerebro, generalmente en el lóbulo temporal izquierdo, involucrada en la comprensión y expresión del lenguaje. (p. 368)

**withdrawal** the discomfort and distress that follow discontinuing an addictive drug or behavior. (p. 43)

**síndrome de abstinencia** la incomodidad y angustia que resulta cuando se deja de utilizar un estupefaciente adictivo o se suspende una conducta. (p. 43)

**working memory** a newer understanding of short-term memory; conscious, active processing of both (1) incoming sensory information, and (2) information retrieved from long-term memory. (p. 210)

**memoria operativa** entendimiento más reciente de la memoria a corto plazo; el procesamiento consciente y activo de tanto (1) información sensorial, y (2) información recuperada de la memoria a largo plazo. (p. 210)

## X

**X chromosome** the sex chromosome found in females and males. Females typically have two X chromosomes; males typically have one. An X chromosome from each parent produces a female child. (p. 325)

**cromosoma X** cromosoma del sexo que se encuentra en el varón y en la hembra. Las mujeres por lo general tienen dos cromosomas X; los hombres por lo general tienen un cromosoma X. Con un cromosoma X del padre y otro de la madre, se produce una mujer. (p. 325)

**Y chromosome** the sex chromosome typically found only in males. When paired with an X chromosome from the mother, it produces a male child. (p. 325)

**cromosoma Y** cromosoma del sexo que solamente se halla en los hombres. Cuando se aparea con un cromosoma X de la madre, produce un varón. (p. 325)

**Yerkes-Dodson law** the principle that performance increases with arousal only up to a point, beyond which performance decreases. (p. 582)

**Ley de Yerkes-Dodson** principio que establece que el rendimiento aumenta con la excitación solamente hasta un punto; más allá de este punto el rendimiento disminuye. (p. 582)

**Young-Helmholtz trichromatic (three-color) theory** the theory that the retina contains three different types of color receptors—one most sensitive to red, one to green, one to blue—which, when stimulated in combination, can produce the perception of any color. (p. 129)

**teoría tricromática de Young-Helmholtz** teoría de que la retina contiene tres tipos distintos de receptores de color: uno más sensible al rojo, otro al verde y otro al azul. Al estimularse en conjunto, estos receptores son capaces de producir la percepción de cualquier color. (p. 129)

# Index

Keel, P. K., 735
Keesey, R. E., 601
Keiser, H. N., 283
Keith, S. W., 605
Keitner, D., 613
Keller, C., 657
Keller, H., 665
Keller, P. S., 104
Kellerman, J., 620
Kelling, S. T., 149
Kelly, A. E., 758
Kelly, D. J., 504
Kelly, M., 15
Kelly, S., 15
Kelly, S. D., 366, 822
Kelly, T. A., 772
Kelly, Y., 0:24
Kemeny, M. E., 642, 654
Kempe, C. C., 380
Kempe, R. S., 380
Kempermann, G., 81
Kendall-Tackett, K. A., 248
Kendler, K. S., 12, 14, 15, 43, 47, 276, 382,
    691, 716, 734, 800
Kendrick, K. M., 207
Kennedy, J. F., 491, 522
Kennedy, R., 783
Kenrick, D. T., 307, 583
Kensinger, E. A., 228
Kent, N., 338
Kent de Grey, R. G., 659
Keough, K. A., 530
Keramati, M., 49
Keresztes, A., 227
Kern, M. L., 557
Kernis, M. H., 572
Kerns, J. C., 604
Kerr, N. L., 487
Kessler, M., 788
Kessler, R. C., 294, 693, 694, 695, 702,
    715
Ketamine, 780
Ketchum, K., 109
Keyes, K. M., 103
Keynes, M., 714
Keys, A., 599–600
Khanna, S., 50
Khazanchi, S., 190
Khodagholy, D., 228
Kiatpongsan, S., 667
Kiecolt-Glaser, J. K., 638, 645
Kiehl, K. A., 734
Kiesow, H., 324
Kihlstrom, J., 201, 732
Kihlstrom, J. F., 258
Kikuchi, H., 731
Kiley, J., 489
Kilgore, A., 69
Kille, D. R., 155
Kilmann, P. R., 336
Kilpatrick, L. A., 678
Kilpeläinen, T. O., 674
Kim, B. S. K., 772
Kim, E. S., 368, 658
Kim, H., 555, 574
Kim, J., 641
Kim, M., 783
Kim, S. H., 191, 551
Kimble, G., 413
Kinesthesia, 152, 153
King, D. W., 704
King, L. A., 583, 660
King, M. L., Jr., 441
King, S., 725

Kinnier, R. T., 394
Kin selection, sexual orientation and,
    345
Kinsey, A., 333–334
Kipnis, J., 638
Kirby, D., 337
Kirby, T., 780
Kirby-Payne, A., 808
Kirkpatrick, L., 724
Kirsch, I., 0:28, 780, 784
Kisely, M. A., 783
Kish, D., 57
Kisilevsky, B. S., 304
Kisley, M. A., 395
Kitahara, C. M., 605
Kitaoka, A., 128
Kitayama, S., 369, 395, 455, 575, 576, 648,
    650, 668, 772
Kivimaki, M., 655
Kivipelto, B. E., 317
Kivisto, A. J., 496
Kivlighan, D. M., 769
Klahr, A. M., 382
Klayman, J., 194
Kleck, R. E., 660
Klein, C., 579
Klein, D. N., 715
Kleinke, C. L., 620
Kleinmuntz, B., 616
Kleitman, N., 94
Klemm, W. R., 64
Klentz, B., 508
Klimstra, T. A., 386, 388, 554
Kline, D., 316
Kline, N. S., 719
Klinefelter syndrome, 327
Klinke, N. S., 139
Kluemper, D. H., 551
Knapp, S., 248
Knee-jerk reflex, 25
Knickmeyer, E., 736
Knight, R. T., 154
Knightley, K., 737
Knoblich, G., 194
Knolle, F., 207
Knowles, E. D., 622
Knuts, I. J. E., 701
Knutsen, J., 739
Knutsson, A., 98
Ko, A., 586
Kobayashi, Y., 625
Kocevar, G., 255
Koch, C., 105, 131
Kocsis, J. H., 773
Koelling, R., 413–414
Koenig, A., 262
Koenig, H. G., 680
Koenig, L. B., 680
Koenig, O., 25
Koerner, B., 623
Koerting, J., 346, 347
Kofler, M. F., 741
Koh, A. W. L., 250
Kohlberg's moral development
    theory, 298
Kohler, I., 183
Köhler, W., 194, 436–437
Kok, B. E., 669
Kokkalis, J., 50
Kolassa, I.-T., 707
Kolb, B., 307
Kondoh, K., 151
Königs, M., 60
Konkle, T., 207

Kontula, O., 315
Koole, S. L., 537
Kopp, S. J., 229
Koppel, L., 571
Kornell, N., 235
Kosslyn, S., 25
Kotchick, B. A., 336
Kotkin, M., 767
Kotov, R., 715
Kotzur, P. F., 519
Kounios, J., 194
Kovelman, I., 368
Kowalski, R. M., 488
Koyanagi, A., 380
Kozak, M. J., 754
Kposowa, A., 691
Kraft, C., 818
Kraft, T., 626
Krahé, B., 626
Kramer, A., 664–665, 779
Kramer, A. D. I., 627
Kramer, A. F., 317, 674
Kramer, S. J., 817
Kranz, F., 330, 344
Kraus, M. W., 622
Krech, D., 307
Kret, M. E., 125
Kretch, K. S., 177
Kring, A. M., 622, 623, 723
Kringelbach, M. L., 68
Krishnan, A., 740
Krizan, Z., 104
Kroneisen, M., 219
Kroonenberg, P. M., 376
Krosnick, J. A., 119, 299
Kross, E., 355, 570, 589, 608, 651
Krueger, J. M., 105
Krueger, R. F., 295
Krueze, L. J., 760
Kruger, J., 352, 570, 621
Krumhansl, C. L., 207
Krützen, M., 822
Krynen, R. C., 154
Ksir, C., 48
Kteily, N. S., 462
Kubzansky, L. D., 649, 657
Kuchynka, S. L., 328
Kuehn, B., 304
Kuehner, C., 715
Kuhl, P. K., 364, 365
Kulik, J., 229
Kumar, A., 681
Kumar, M. B., 690
Kuncel, N. R., 257, 267, 278
Kunst-Wilson, W. R., 611
Kunzmann, U., 392
Kupfer, D. J., 740
Kupper, S., 676
Kurtycz, L. M., 0:35
Kurtz, J. E., 555
Kushlev, K., 582, 589, 664
Kushner, M. G., 779
Kutcher, E. J., 810
Kuttler, A. F., 324
Kuzawa, C. W., 16, 306
Kwauk, C., 266
Kwong, A. S. F., 388
Kyaga, S., 714
Kypri, K., 498

LaBar, K. S., 621
Labeling, diagnostic, 688–689

Lacasse, K., 625
Lacey, M., 517
Lachman, M. E., 392
Ladd, G. T., 87
Laeng, B., 125
LaFrance, M., 321, 621, 622
LaFreniere, L. S., 706
Lai, C. K., 91, 459
Laird, J. D., 625
Lakin, J., 441
Lakin, J. L., 476
Laland, K. N., 16
Lally, P., 401
La Londe, K. B., 419
Lam, C. B., 329
Lam, M., 727
Lamarche, V. M., 572
Lambert, N. M., 500
Lambert, W. E., 370
Lamberton, C., 323
Lambird, K. H., 572
Lammers, J., 472
Lampert, M., 0:18
Landale, N. S., 304
Landau, E., 347
Landau, M. J., 568
Landberg, J., 498
Landmesser, A., 483
Landor, A. M., 458
Landrum, E., B:8
Landry, M. J., 50
Lang, C., 609
Lange, N., 740
Lange, E. J., 656, 689
Lange, S., 304
Langer, E. J., 656, 689
Langlois, J. H., 507, 508
Långström, N. H., 345
Language, 363–373. See also Speech
    in animals, 822–823
    bilingualism and, 368, 369, 370–371
    brain areas for, 81, 82–83, 84–85, 368
    in cognitive development, 354–355
    cultural aspects of, 369–370
    definition of, 363
    lateralization and, 82–83
    productive, 365–366
    receptive, 364–365
    structural components of, 364
    thinking and, 369–371
    universal grammar and, 364
Language acquisition device, 364
Language development, 363–367
    babbling stage of, 365
    in hearing impaired, 366, 367
    one-word stage of, 365
    of productive language,
        365–366
    of receptive language, 364–365
    stages of, 365
    two-word stage of, 365
Language learning
    in animals, 822–823
    critical periods for, 366
    in infants, 309
    prenatal, 304
Language processing, subfunctions
    in, 368
Lansdall-Welfare, T., 713
Lantos, D., 571
Lanzetta, J. T., 626
Lapp, D., 815
Larkin, J. E., 817
Larkin, K., 344
Larkina, M., 309